한 권으로 끝내는

해커스
토익
900+plus

LC + RC + VOCA

해커스 어학연구소

실시간 토익시험 정답확인&해설강의
Hackers.co.kr

한 권으로 끝내는
해커스 토익
900+ plus

LC + RC + VOCA

시험장에도 들고 가는 토익 기출 VOCA 학습법

1. **매일 하루 분량의 단어를 암기합니다.**
   본인이 선택한 학습 플랜(본책 p.10~11)에 따라 10일 또는 5일 완성을 목표로 합니다.
2. **무료 단어암기 mp3와 함께 이동할 때나 자투리 시간을 활용하여 단어를 암기합니다.**
   단어암기 mp3는 www.HackersIngang.com에서 무료로 다운 받거나, DAY별 QR코드를 활용하세요.

| 목차 |

DAY 01	**PART 1**	기출 어휘
DAY 02	**PART 2**	기출 어휘
DAY 03	**PART 3**	기출 어휘
DAY 04	**PART 4**	기출 어휘
DAY 05	**PART 5&6**	기출 어휘
DAY 06	**PART 5&6**	기출 어휘
DAY 07	**PART 5&6**	기출 어휘
DAY 08	**PART 5&6**	기출 어휘
DAY 09	**PART 7**	기출 어휘
DAY 10	**PART 7**	기출 어휘

저작권자 ⓒ 2025, 해커스 어학연구소 이 책 및 음성파일의 모든 내용, 이미지, 디자인, 편집 형태에 대한 저작권은 저자에게 있습니다.
서면에 의한 저자와 출판사의 허락 없이 내용의 일부 혹은 전부를 인용, 발췌하거나 복제, 배포할 수 없습니다.

DAY 01 PART 1 기출 어휘

☑ PART 1에 반드시 나오는 최신 기출 어휘들이므로, 확실히 암기해 둡니다. 🎧 VOCA_D01.mp3

001	**merchandise**	n 상품, 물품
002	**stack**	n 더미, 쌓아올린 것 v 쌓다, 쌓이다
003	**rack**	n 선반, 받침대 v 선반에 놓다
004	**dock**	n 부두, 선창 n (배를) 부두에 대다
005	**pour**	v 붓다, 쏟다
006	**potted**	adj 화분에 심은
007	**stock**	n 재고, 저장품 v 비축하다, 축적하다
008	**column**	n 기둥, 열
009	**dispenser**	n 기계, 용기
010	**stroll**	v 거닐다, 산책하다 n 산책
011	**railing**	n 난간, 울타리
012	**lamppost**	n 가로등
013	**strap**	n 끈, 띠 v 묶다
014	**occupied**	adj 점유된, 사용 중인
015	**bush**	n 덤불, 관목
016	**flyer**	n 전단, 광고지
017	**shoreline**	n 해안가, 물가
018	**doorway**	n 출입구, 현관
019	**overhead**	adj 머리 위의, 상공의 adv 머리 위에
020	**bin**	n 통, 용기

021	**carton**	n 판지 상자, 골판지 상자
022	**pole**	n 기둥, 장대, 막대기
023	**onlooker**	n 구경꾼, 관찰자
024	**tow**	v 끌다, 견인하다 n 끌기, 견인
025	**waterfront**	n 수변, 해안가
026	**dip**	v 담그다, 적시다 n 살짝 담금
027	**paved**	adj 포장된, 매끄러운
028	**stepstool**	n 발판, 디딤대
029	**clipboard**	n 클립보드, 서류 끼우개
030	**spill**	v 흘리다, 쏟다 n 유출물
031	**rinse**	v 헹구다, 씻다
032	**lid**	n 뚜껑, 덮개
033	**sidewalk**	n 보도, 인도
034	**scrub**	v 문지르다, 문질러 씻다
035	**hillside**	n 언덕 경사면
036	**grasp**	v 움켜잡다, 이해하다 n 움켜짐, 이해
037	**detach**	v 분리하다, 떼어내다
038	**cupboard**	n 찬장, 식기장
039	**knob**	n 손잡이
040	**saw**	v 자르다, 켜다 n 톱

DAY 01   PART 1 기출 어휘

041	**shoelace**	[n] 신발끈, 구두끈
042	**porch**	[n] 현관
043	**arched**	[adj] 아치형의, 굽은
044	**dustpan**	[n] 쓰레받기
045	**rake**	[v] 갈퀴로 긁다 [n] 갈퀴
046	**chimney**	[n] 굴뚝, 굴뚝 모양의 것
047	**sip**	[v] 홀짝이다, 조금씩 마시다 [n] 한 모금
048	**broom**	[n] 빗자루, 비
049	**ceramic**	[n] 도자기 [adj] 도자기의
050	**stool**	[n] 의자, 걸상
051	**coil**	[n] 코일, 감은 것 [v] 감다, 말다
052	**grip**	[n] 손잡이 [v] 꽉 쥐다
053	**workbench**	[n] 작업대
054	**side by side**	나란히, 서로 옆에
055	**cash register**	금전 등록기
056	**take apart**	분해하다, 해체하다
057	**lane marking**	차선 표시, 도로 표시
058	**lay out**	펼치다, 배치하다, 제시하다
059	**luggage rack**	(열차·버스 등의) 선반
060	**kneel down**	무릎을 꿇다

만점 완성 어휘

061	**patio**	n 안뜰, 파티오
062	**crate**	n 상자, 나무 상자
063	**suspend**	v 매달다, 걸어두다
064	**ramp**	n 경사로, 진입로
065	**shovel**	n 삽 v 삽으로 파다
066	**shed**	n 헛간, 창고
067	**corridor**	n 복도, 통로
068	**crouch**	v 쪼그리다, 웅크리다
069	**canopy**	n 차양, 덮개, 천막
070	**podium**	n 연단, 단상
071	**wheelbarrow**	n 손수레, 외바퀴 수레
072	**platter**	n 큰 접시
073	**windowpane**	n 창문 유리
074	**windowsill**	n 창턱, 창 아랫부분
075	**irrigate**	v 관개하다, 물을 대다
076	**ornate**	adj 장식이 화려한, 정교한
077	**loading dock**	짐을 싣거나 내리는 곳
078	**sort through**	훑어보다, 분류하다
079	**light fixture**	조명 기구
080	**shelving unit**	선반, 수납장

DAY 02 — PART 2 기출 어휘

☑ PART 2에 반드시 나오는 최신 기출 어휘들이므로, 확실히 암기해 둡니다.　　🎧 VOCA_D02.mp3

081	**agenda**	n 의제, 안건
082	**postpone**	v 연기하다, 미루다
083	**reception**	n 접수, 수신
084	**vacant**	adj 비어 있는, 공석인
085	**destination**	n 목적지, 행선지
086	**mechanic**	n 정비공, 기계공
087	**cancellation**	n 취소, 해약
088	**inspection**	n 검사, 점검
089	**assign**	v 맡기다, 배정하다
090	**manufacture**	n 제조, 생산 v 제조하다
091	**depart**	v 출발하다, 떠나다
092	**leftover**	n 남은 음식, 잔여물 adj 남은, 잔여의
093	**reference**	n 추천서, 참고
094	**injury**	n 부상, 상해
095	**launching**	n 출시, 발사
096	**courtyard**	n 안뜰, 안마당
097	**replacement**	n 교체, 대체품
098	**persuasive**	adj 설득력 있는, 납득시키는
099	**administrator**	n 관리자, 행정관
100	**laboratory**	n 실험실, 연구소

101	**chronological**	[adj] 연대순의, 시간적인
102	**breakroom**	[n] 휴게실
103	**recognize**	[v] 인식하다, 알아보다, 인정하다
104	**compile**	[v] 편집하다, 수집하다
105	**satellite**	[n] 위성, 인공위성
106	**sweetener**	[n] 감미료, 단맛을 내는 물질
107	**electrician**	[n] 전기 기술자
108	**well-attended**	[adj] 많은 사람이 참석한, 참석률이 높은
109	**qualification**	[n] 자격, 능력
110	**brand-new**	[adj] 아주 새로운, 신품의
111	**assist**	[v] 돕다, 조력하다
112	**paperless**	[adj] 종이를 쓰지 않는, 전자화된
113	**combination**	[n] 결합, 조합
114	**premiere**	[n] 초연, 첫 공개 [v] 첫 선을 보이다
115	**aggressive**	[adj] 공격적인, 적극적인
116	**unlocked**	[adj] 잠기지 않은, 열린
117	**break down**	고장나다, 분해하다
118	**conference call**	전화 회의
119	**sales representative**	영업 사원
120	**in charge of**	~을 담당하는, ~을 맡고 있는

DAY 02 — PART 2 기출 어휘

121	be ahead of	~보다 앞서다, ~보다 우위에 있다
122	security measures	보안 조치, 안전 대책
123	executive summary	개요서
124	processing fee	처리 수수료
125	real estate	부동산, 대지
126	florist shop	꽃집
127	shipping fee	배송료
128	look over	검토하다, 살펴보다
129	in place	제자리에, 적절한 위치에
130	traffic congestion	교통 혼잡
131	technical support	기술 지원
132	sales figures	판매 수치, 매출액
133	take off	이륙하다, (옷 등을) 벗다
134	office supply	사무용품
135	out of order	고장난
136	come up with	~을 생각해내다, ~을 제안하다
137	intend for	~을 위해 의도하다, ~을 위해 만들다
138	baggage claim	수하물 찾는 곳
139	taxi stand	택시 정류장
140	hiring initiative	채용 계획

만점 완성 어휘

141	**compressor**	n 압축기, 압축 장치
142	**acquisition**	n 인수, 획득
143	**transfer**	v 이동하다, 전근하다
144	**competent**	adj 유능한, 적임인
145	**portrait**	n 초상화, 인물 사진
146	**exposition**	n 전시회, 박람회
147	**résumé**	n 이력서
148	**province**	n 지방, 도, 영역, 분야
149	**stiff**	adj 뻣뻣한, 딱딱한
150	**mop**	n 대걸레, 마포 v 대걸레질하다
151	**halt**	n 정지, 중단 v 멈추다
152	**engrave**	v 새기다, 조각하다
153	**payroll**	n (기업의) 급여 대상자 명단, 급여 지불 총액
154	**conductor**	n 지휘자, 안내원
155	**short-staffed**	adj 인력이 부족한
156	**sales pitch**	판매 권유, 영업 제안, 판촉 설명
157	**budget surplus**	예산 잉여금
158	**security clearance**	비밀 정보 사용 허가
159	**savings account**	저축 계좌, 예금 통장
160	**on hand**	재고로 있는, 보유 중인, 사용 가능한

DAY 03 — PART 3 기출 어휘

☑ PART 3에 반드시 나오는 최신 기출 어휘들이므로, 확실히 암기해 둡니다.   🎧 VOCA_D03.mp3

161	**sustainable**	[adj] 지속 가능한, 유지 가능한
162	**plumber**	[n] 배관공, 수도 설비공
163	**prescription**	[n] 처방, 처방전
164	**detergent**	[n] 세제, 합성 세제
165	**dimension**	[n] 치수, 크기
166	**archive**	[n] 기록 보관소 [v] 기록소에 보관하다
167	**alternate**	[adj] 번갈아 하는, 대체의 [v] 번갈아 나오게 만들다
168	**botanical**	[adj] 식물의, 식물학의
169	**harbor**	[n] 항구, 항만
170	**lodging**	[n] 임시 숙소, 하숙
171	**rebate**	[n] 환불금, 할인
172	**culinary**	[adj] 요리의, 부엌의
173	**thermostat**	[n] 온도 조절 장치
174	**inadequate**	[adj] 부적절한, 불충분한
175	**archeologist**	[n] 고고학자
176	**excursion**	[n] 짧은 여행, 유람
177	**sustainability**	[n] 지속 가능성
178	**duration**	[n] 지속, 기간
179	**reimbursement**	[n] 상환, 환불
180	**layover**	[n] 도중 하차

181 ☐	**consistency**	[n] 일관성, 농도
182 ☐	**landlord**	[n] 집주인, 건물주
183 ☐	**ordinance**	[n] 법령, 조례
184 ☐	**misconception**	[n] 오해, 잘못된 생각
185 ☐	**pharmacist**	[n] 약사, 조제사
186 ☐	**nursery**	[n] 탁아소, 묘목장
187 ☐	**pharmaceuticals**	[n] 제약 회사
188 ☐	**distraction**	[n] 주의산만, 오락거리
189 ☐	**intuitive**	[adj] 직관적인, 본능적인
190 ☐	**oddly**	[adv] 이상하게, 특이하게
191 ☐	**stunning**	[adj] 멋진, 훌륭한
192 ☐	**prehistoric**	[adj] 선사 시대의, 아주 옛날의
193 ☐	**tangle**	[n] 얽힘, 엉킴 [v] 얽히다
194 ☐	**lawnmower**	[n] 잔디 깎는 기계
195 ☐	**pier**	[n] 부두, 기둥
196 ☐	**deck**	[n] 갑판, 데크 [v] 장식하다
197 ☐	**excluded**	[adj] 제외된, 배제된
198 ☐	**punctuality**	[n] 시간 엄수
199 ☐	**rash**	[n] 발진, 충동 [adj] 성급한, 경솔한
200 ☐	**composition**	[n] 구성, 작문

DAY 03 — PART 3 기출 어휘

201	hectic	[adj] 바쁜, 혼란스러운
202	freight	[n] 화물, 운임 [v] 운송하다
203	ventilation	[n] 환기, 통풍
204	vendor	[n] 판매 회사, 노점상
205	poetry	[n] 시, 운문
206	municipal	[adj] 지방 자치의, 시립의
207	ornament	[n] 장식품, 장신구 [v] 장식하다
208	rigorously	[adv] 엄격하게, 철저하게
209	crucial	[adj] 중요한, 결정적인
210	resolve	[v] 해결하다, 결심하다
211	janitor	[n] 관리인, 잡역부
212	reinforcement	[n] 보강, 강화
213	turnout	[n] 참가자의 수, 투표율
214	focus group	표적 집단, 포커스 그룹
215	cost estimate	비용 견적
216	around the clock	24시간 내내
217	take inventory	재고를 조사하다
218	excavation site	발굴 현장
219	marine biologist	해양 생물학자
220	pull over	차를 대다, 길 한쪽으로 빠지다

만점 완성 어휘

221	**furnace**	n 용광로
222	**retrieve**	v 회수하다, 되찾다
223	**mural**	n 벽화
224	**raffle**	n 경품 추첨, 복권
225	**apprentice**	n 견습생, 수습생
226	**pavilion**	n 부속 건물, 별관
227	**cluttered**	adj 어수선한, 어질러진
228	**permeable**	adj 침투성 있는, 투과성의
229	**reconfiguration**	n 재구성, 재배치
230	**carousel**	n (공항의) 회전식 원형 컨베이어
231	**deteriorate**	v 악화되다, 나빠지다
232	**disinfectant**	n 소독제, 살균제
233	**swamp**	n 늪, 습지 v 쇄도하다
234	**brass**	n 놋쇠, 황동
235	**gimmick**	n 요령, 속임수
236	**deplane**	v 비행기에서 내리다
237	**drenched**	adj 흠뻑 젖은
238	**overhaul**	n 점검 v 점검하다
239	**glitch**	n 사소한 결함, 오류
240	**shingle**	n 조약돌, 작은 간판

DAY 04 — PART 4 기출 어휘

☑ PART 4에 반드시 나오는 최신 기출 어휘들이므로, 확실히 암기해 둡니다.   🔊 VOCA_D04.mp3

241	inventory	n 재고, 목록
242	reassurance	n 확신, 안심시키기
243	retreat	n 휴양지, 퇴각 v 물러나다
244	compliment	n 칭찬, 찬사 v 칭찬하다
245	sculpture	n 조각상, 조각품
246	aviation	n 항공, 비행
247	itinerary	n 여행 일정표
248	repave	v 다시 포장하다
249	plumbing	n 배관, 수도 설비
250	referral	n 추천, 소개
251	restoration	n 복원, 회복
252	disrupt	v 방해하다, 붕괴시키다
253	attire	n 복장, 의상
254	purify	v 정화하다, 순화하다
255	pharmaceutical	adj 제약의 n 의약품
256	sculptor	n 조각가
257	facilitate	v 촉진하다, 용이하게 하다
258	insulated	adj 단열된, 격리된
259	drain	n 배수구 v 배수하다
260	patent	n 특허, 전매특허 adj 특허의

261	**enthusiast**	n 열광적인 사람, 애호가
262	**binoculars**	n 쌍안경
263	**hesitant**	adj 망설이는, 주저하는
264	**margin**	n 여백, 가장자리
265	**arena**	n 경기장, 활동 무대
266	**hydrate**	v 수분을 공급하다
267	**integrity**	n 정직, 성실
268	**telecommute**	v 원격 근무하다
269	**exclude**	v 제외하다, 배제하다
270	**auditor**	n 회계 감사관, 청강생
271	**surge**	n 급증, 큰 파도
272	**feasible**	adj 실행 가능한, 가능한
273	**artifact**	n 인공물, 인공 유물
274	**confidentiality**	n 기밀성, 비밀 유지
275	**festivity**	n 축제 행사
276	**gourmet**	n 미식가 adj 미식가의
277	**astronomy**	n 천문학, 우주론
278	**prescribe**	v 처방하다, 지시하다
279	**assessment**	n 평가, 사정
280	**congestion**	n 혼잡, 정체

DAY 04 — PART 4 기출 어휘

281	**statistics**	n 통계, 통계학
282	**manufacturing**	n 제조업
283	**mechanical**	adj 기계의, 기계적인
284	**align**	v 정렬하다, 조정하다
285	**petition**	n 청원, 탄원서 v 청원하다
286	**governor**	n 주지사, 통치자
287	**weed**	n 잡초
288	**power outage**	정전
289	**bulk order**	대량 주문
290	**price quote**	견적서
291	**have in common**	공통점이 있다
292	**figure out**	알아내다, 이해하다
293	**on foot**	도보로
294	**close a deal**	거래를 성사시키다
295	**on track**	제대로 진행되고 있는
296	**city dweller**	도시 거주자
297	**benefits package**	복리 후생 제도
298	**help oneself to**	~을 자유롭게 먹다
299	**phase out**	단계적으로 폐지하다
300	**buy one get one free**	하나 사면 하나 무료

만점 완성 어휘

301	**compliance**	n 준수, 따름
302	**orchard**	n 과수원, 과일 농장
303	**deem**	v 여기다, 생각하다
304	**discretionary**	adj 재량의, 임의의
305	**dim**	adj 어두운, 희미한
306	**superintendent**	n 관리자, 감독관
307	**observatory**	n 천문대, 관측소
308	**textile**	n 직물, 옷감
309	**disrepair**	n 황폐, 파손 상태
310	**waiver**	n 면제, 포기
311	**seeder**	n 씨 뿌리는 기계, 파종기
312	**weaver**	n 방직공, 직조공
313	**welding**	n 용접
314	**commemorative**	adj 기념의, 기념하는
315	**lumber**	n 목재, 목자재 v 느릿느릿 움직이다
316	**clog**	v 막히다, 막다
317	**asymmetrical**	adj 비대칭의
318	**endorse**	v 지지하다, 보증하다
319	**consent form**	동의서
320	**probationary period**	시험채용 기간, 수습 기간

DAY 05 — PART 5&6 기출 어휘

☑ PART 5&6에 반드시 나오는 최신 기출 어휘들이므로, 확실히 암기해 둡니다. 🎧 VOCA_D05.mp3

321	**distribute**	v 분배하다, 배포하다
322	**donate**	v 기부하다, 기증하다
323	**implement**	v 실행하다, 이행하다
324	**absorb**	v 흡수하다, 빨아들이다
325	**undergo**	v 겪다, 경험하다
326	**nominate**	v 지명하다, 추천하다
327	**grant**	v 수여하다, 허가하다
328	**streamline**	v 간소화하다, 능률적으로 하다
329	**analyze**	v 분석하다, 검토하다
330	**compensate**	v 보상하다, 배상하다
331	**boost**	v 북돋우다, 증진시키다
332	**accumulate**	v 축적하다, 모으다
333	**engage**	v 관여하다, 참여하다
334	**showcase**	v 전시하다 n 전시
335	**merge**	v 합병하다, 통합하다
336	**combine**	v 결합하다, 합치다
337	**exceed**	v 초과하다, 능가하다
338	**compete**	v 경쟁하다, 겨루다
339	**stimulate**	v 자극하다, 격려하다
340	**prioritize**	v 우선시하다, 중요시하다

341	**neglect**	v 소홀히 하다, 무시하다
342	**omit**	v 생략하다, 하지 않다
343	**proceed**	v 진행하다, 나아가다
344	**surround**	v 둘러싸다, 에워싸다
345	**brighten**	v 밝게 하다, 환하게 하다
346	**originate**	v 기원하다, 유래하다
347	**simplify**	v 단순화하다, 간략하게 하다
348	**assume**	v 가정하다, 추정하다
349	**comprehend**	v 이해하다, 파악하다
350	**arise**	v 발생하다, 생겨나다
351	**misplace**	v 잘못 놓다, 놓고 잊어버리다
352	**broaden**	v 넓히다, 확장하다
353	**withdraw**	v 철회하다, 물러나다, 인출하다
354	**patronize**	v 후원하다, 애용하다
355	**dedicate**	v 헌신하다, 바치다
356	**administer**	v 관리하다, 집행하다
357	**commend**	v 칭찬하다, 추천하다
358	**perceive**	v 인식하다, 지각하다
359	**applaud**	v 박수갈채하다, 칭찬하다
360	**distinguish**	v 구별하다, 식별하다

DAY 05 — PART 5&6 기출 어휘

361	overturn	v 뒤집다, 전복시키다
362	overwhelm	v 압도하다, 당혹스럽게 하다
363	diagnose	v 진단하다, 판단하다
364	proclaim	v 선언하다, 공표하다
365	interpret	v 해석하다, 통역하다
366	resign	v 사임하다, 퇴직하다
367	obstruct	v 방해하다, 차단하다
368	inflate	v 부풀리다, 팽창시키다
369	forbid	v 금지하다, 허락하지 않다
370	chase	v 추격하다, 쫓다
371	execute	v 실행하다, 집행하다
372	admit	v 인정하다, 시인하다
373	confess	v 고백하다, 자백하다
374	inhabit	v 거주하다, 살다
375	urge	v 촉구하다, 재촉하다
376	formulate	v 공식화하다, 만들다
377	externalize	v 외재화하다, 외부로 표출하다
378	domesticate	v 길들이다, 가축화하다
379	reinforce	v 강화하다, 보강하다
380	publicize	v 공표하다, 홍보하다

만점 완성 어휘

381	**retain**	v 보유하다, 유지하다
382	**sustain**	v 지속하다, 유지하다
383	**commence**	v 시작하다, 개시하다
384	**entitle**	v 자격을 주다, 권리를 부여하다
385	**designate**	v 지정하다, 임명하다
386	**uphold**	v 지지하다, 받들다
387	**fling**	v 던지다, 내던지다
388	**affiliate**	v 제휴하다, 연합하다
389	**consolidate**	v 통합하다, 공고히 하다
390	**enlist**	v 요청하다, 입대시키다
391	**revoke**	v 취소하다, 철회하다
392	**convene**	v 소집하다, 회합하다
393	**dispose**	v 처분하다, 배치하다
394	**impose**	v 부과하다, 강요하다
395	**refrain**	v 삼가다, 자제하다
396	**authenticate**	v 인증하다, 확인하다
397	**suffice**	v 충분하다
398	**hinder**	v 방해하다, 저해하다
399	**deduct**	v 공제하다, 빼다
400	**constitute**	v 구성하다, 이루다

DAY 06 — PART 5&6 기출 어휘

PART 5&6에 반드시 나오는 최신 기출 어휘들이므로, 확실히 암기해 둡니다. 🔊 VOCA_D06.mp3

401	initiative	n 주도권, 주도 adj 주도적인
402	expertise	n 전문 지식, 기술
403	durability	n 내구성, 지속성
404	submission	n 제출, 항복, 복종
405	statement	n 진술, 성명서
406	priority	n 우선순위, 우선권
407	distribution	n 분배, 유통, 배포
408	tenant	n 세입자, 거주자
409	specification	n 명세서, 설명서
410	authority	n 권위, 권한
411	formula	n 공식, 제조법
412	authorization	n 승인, 허가
413	milestone	n 이정표, 중요한 단계
414	reliability	n 신뢰성, 믿음직함
415	coordinator	n 조정자, 코디네이터
416	assurance	n 확신, 보증
417	correspondence	n 서신, 일치
418	consumption	n 소비, 사용량
419	inspiration	n 영감, 창의적 자극
420	motivation	n 동기, 의욕

421	circumstance	n 상황, 환경
422	acceptance	n 수용, 승낙
423	presence	n 존재, 출석
424	diversity	n 다양성, 상이
425	protocol	n 외교 의례, (조약의) 초안
426	excellence	n 우수성, 탁월함
427	impression	n 인상, 감명
428	alignment	n 정렬, 일치
429	complication	n 합병증, 복잡함
430	enrollment	n 등록, 입학
431	declaration	n 선언, 공표
432	scope	n 범위, 영역
433	disturbance	n 방해, 동요
434	companion	n 동반자, 친구, 동료
435	provision	n 조항, 규정
436	involvement	n 관여, 참여
437	obligation	n 의무, 책임
438	deduction	n 공제, 차감
439	entirety	n 전체, 총체
440	transparency	n 투명성, 명료함

DAY 06 — PART 5&6 기출 어휘

441	accessibility	n 접근성, 이용 가능성
442	relevance	n 관련성, 적절성
443	accordance	n 일치, 조화
444	fossil	n 화석, 유물 adj 화석의
445	compound	n 화합물, 합성물 adj 복합적인
446	contraction	n 수축, 축소
447	speculation	n 추측, 투기
448	persistence	n 지속성, 고집
449	opposition	n 반대, 저항
450	surveyor	n 측량사, 조사관
451	inclusion	n 포함, 수용
452	longevity	n 장수, 장기 지속
453	tide	n 흐름, 물결
454	resignation	n 사임, 사직
455	proximity	n 근접, 접근
456	enlargement	n 확대, 확장
457	readership	n 독자층, 독자
458	boundary	n 경계, 한계
459	generosity	n 관대함, 너그러움
460	plaque	n 명판, 현판

만점 완성 어휘

461	**consent**	n 동의, 승낙 v 동의하다
462	**affiliation**	n 제휴, 관계
463	**clutter**	n 잡동사니, 무질서 v 어지르다
464	**transit**	n 수송, 통과
465	**practitioner**	n 실무자, 개업 의사
466	**loop**	n 고리, 순환 v 순환하다
467	**lubrication**	n 미끄럽게 함, 윤활
468	**commendation**	n 표창, 칭찬, 추천
469	**sealant**	n 밀폐제
470	**stipend**	n 봉급, 급료
471	**pledge**	n 서약, 맹세 v 서약하다
472	**constraint**	n 제약, 구속
473	**correspondent**	n 특파원, 통신원
474	**batter**	n 반죽, 타자 v 치다, 때리다
475	**receptacle**	n 용기, 수용기
476	**vigor**	n 활력, 정력
477	**elimination**	n 제거, 배제
478	**expedition**	n 원정, 탐험대
479	**refurbishment**	n 개조, 수리
480	**compatibility**	n 호환성, 양립성

DAY 07 PART 5&6 기출 어휘

☑ PART 5&6에 반드시 나오는 최신 기출 어휘들이므로, 확실히 암기해 둡니다. 🎧 VOCA_D07.mp3

481	**innovative**	adj 혁신적인, 창의적인
482	**fragile**	adj 약한, 부서지기 쉬운
483	**eligible**	adj 자격이 있는, 적격의
484	**exclusive**	adj 배타적인, 독점적인
485	**prompt**	adj 신속한, 즉각적인 v 자극하다 n 촉구
486	**considerable**	adj 상당한, 중요한
487	**disruptive**	adj 파괴적인, 방해하는
488	**considerate**	adj 사려 깊은, 배려하는
489	**compelling**	adj 강제적인, 설득력 있는
490	**knowledgeable**	adj 지식이 풍부한, 박식한
491	**costly**	adj 비용이 많이 드는, 값비싼
492	**decisive**	adj 결정적인, 확고한
493	**noticeable**	adj 눈에 띄는, 현저한
494	**confidential**	adj 기밀의, 비밀의
495	**approximate**	adj 대략적인, 근사치의
496	**probable**	adj 있음직한, 개연성이 높은
497	**prolonged**	adj 연장된, 지속된
498	**timely**	adj 시기적절한, 때맞춘
499	**promising**	adj 유망한, 촉망되는
500	**genuine**	adj 진짜의, 진정한

501	prohibitive	adj 금지하는, 비싸서 엄두가 안 나는
502	congested	adj 혼잡한, 붐비는
503	obedient	adj 순종하는, 복종하는
504	vulnerable	adj 취약한, 약한
505	obligated	adj 의무가 있는, 강요된
506	reputable	adj 평판이 좋은
507	prevalent	adj 널리 퍼진, 일반적인
508	constructive	adj 건설적인, 유익한
509	plentiful	adj 풍부한, 넉넉한
510	steep	adj 가파른, 급격한
511	assorted	adj 여러 가지의, 각양각색의
512	diagnostic	adj 진단의, 진단용의
513	diagnosable	adj 진단 가능한
514	mutual	adj 상호간의, 공동의
515	notable	adj 주목할 만한, 현저한
516	invalid	adj 무효의, 병약한
517	inconsiderate	adj 사려 깊지 못한
518	indefinite	adj 불명확한, 무기한의
519	repetitious	adj 반복적인, 되풀이하는
520	oval	adj 타원형의 n 타원

DAY 07 — PART 5&6 기출 어휘

521	**appreciative**	adj 감사하는, 고마워하는
522	**humble**	adj 겸손한, 소박한
523	**periodic**	adj 주기적인, 정기적인
524	**scenic**	adj 경치가 좋은, 아름다운
525	**acquainted**	adj 익숙한, 알고 있는
526	**reluctant**	adj 꺼리는, 마지못해 하는
527	**absorbing**	adj 흡수하는, 몰두시키는
528	**prestigious**	adj 명망 있는, 일류의
529	**regulatory**	adj 규제하는, 통제하는
530	**captivating**	adj 사로잡는, 매혹적인
531	**massive**	adj 거대한, 대규모의
532	**contemporary**	adj 동시대의, 현대의 n 동시대인
533	**exhausted**	adj 지친, 소모된
534	**hospitable**	adj 환대하는, 친절한
535	**recurring**	adj 반복되는, 되풀이되는
536	**deliberate**	adj 고의적인, 신중한
537	**favorable**	adj 호의적인, 유리한
538	**versatile**	adj 다용도의, 다재다능한
539	**cost-effective**	adj 비용 효율적인, 경제적인
540	**on duty**	근무 중인, 일하고 있는

만점 완성 어휘

541	tentative	adj	임시의, 시험적인
542	liable	adj	책임이 있는, 쉽게 ~하는
543	collaborative	adj	협력적인, 협조적인
544	glamorous	adj	매력적인, 화려한
545	robust	adj	강건한, 튼튼한
546	chronic	adj	만성적인, 오래 지속되는
547	perceptive	adj	통찰력 있는, 지각력이 예민한
548	exquisite	adj	정교한, 섬세한
549	indigenous	adj	토착의, 원주민의
550	rigorous	adj	엄격한, 철저한
551	secluded	adj	외딴, 격리된
552	lingering	adj	오래 지속되는, 남아있는
553	impartial	adj	공정한, 치우치지 않는
554	concise	adj	간결한, 짧은
555	substantial	adj	상당한, 실질적인
556	exploratory	adj	탐구적인, 탐험적인
557	lenient	adj	관대한, 너그러운
558	sequential	adj	순차적인, 연속적인
559	succinct	adj	간결한, 요점만 말하는
560	amicable	adj	우호적인, 친선의

DAY 08 — PART 5&6 기출 어휘

☑ PART 5&6에 반드시 나오는 최신 기출 어휘들이므로, 확실히 암기해 둡니다. ○ VOCA_D08.mp3

561	**automatically**	adv 자동으로, 저절로
562	**enthusiastically**	adv 열정적으로, 열렬히
563	**occasionally**	adv 때때로, 가끔
564	**randomly**	adv 무작위로, 임의로
565	**spaciously**	adv 넓게, 널찍하게
566	**roughly**	adv 대략, 거칠게
567	**lately**	adv 최근에, 요즘
568	**precisely**	adv 정확히, 정밀하게
569	**halfway**	adv 중간에, 부분적으로
570	**exceptionally**	adv 예외적으로, 특별히
571	**intentionally**	adv 의도적으로, 고의로
572	**permanently**	adv 영구적으로, 영원히
573	**neatly**	adv 깔끔하게, 단정하게
574	**surprisingly**	adv 놀랍게도, 뜻밖에
575	**mistakenly**	adv 잘못하여, 착각으로
576	**loosely**	adv 느슨하게, 헐겁게
577	**firmly**	adv 단단히, 확고하게
578	**legally**	adv 합법적으로, 법적으로
579	**reliably**	adv 신뢰할 수 있게, 믿음직하게
580	**enormously**	adv 엄청나게, 막대하게

581	brightly	adv 밝게, 환하게
582	quite	adv 꽤, 상당히
583	potentially	adv 잠재적으로, 가능성 있게
584	barely	adv 간신히, 겨우
585	kindly	adv 친절하게
586	possibly	adv 아마도, 혹시
587	somewhere	adv 어딘가에
588	collectively	adv 집합적으로, 공동으로
589	variably	adv 변하기 쉽게, 다양하게
590	comparably	adv 비교할 만하게, 필적하게
591	vaguely	adv 모호하게, 애매하게
592	reasonably	adv 합리적으로, 적당히
593	competitively	adv 경쟁적으로, 경쟁력 있게
594	elsewhere	adv 다른 곳에, 딴 데서
595	personably	adv 인간적으로, 호감 있게
596	regretfully	adv 유감스럽게도, 애석하게
597	cautiously	adv 조심스럽게, 신중하게
598	resistantly	adv 저항하며, 반항적으로
599	noticeably	adv 눈에 띄게, 현저하게
600	irresponsibly	adv 무책임하게, 책임감 없이

DAY 08 — PART 5&6 기출 어휘

601	**objectively**	adv 객관적으로, 공정하게
602	**productively**	adv 생산적으로, 효율적으로
603	**durably**	adv 내구성 있게, 오래가게
604	**reluctantly**	adv 마지못해, 꺼려하며
605	**domestically**	adv 국내에서, 가정적으로
606	**routinely**	adv 일상적으로, 정기적으로
607	**momentarily**	adv 순간적으로, 잠깐
608	**collaboratively**	adv 협력적으로, 공동으로
609	**deliberately**	adv 고의로, 신중하게
610	**repeatedly**	adv 반복해서, 되풀이하여
611	**factually**	adv 실제로, 사실상
612	**thoughtfully**	adv 사려 깊게, 배려하여
613	**reportedly**	adv 보도에 따르면, 전해진 바에 의하면
614	**profitably**	adv 수익성 있게, 이익이 나게
615	**carelessly**	adv 부주의하게, 조심성 없이
616	**professionally**	adv 전문적으로, 직업적으로
617	**comprehensively**	adv 포괄적으로, 종합적으로
618	**pleasantly**	adv 즐겁게, 기분 좋게
619	**remarkably**	adv 현저하게, 두드러지게
620	**approximately**	adv 대략, 근사치로

만점 완성 어휘

621	seamlessly	adv	매끄럽게, 원활하게
622	keenly	adv	날카롭게, 예민하게
623	immensely	adv	막대하게, 대단히
624	consequently	adv	결과적으로, 따라서
625	respectively	adv	각각, 개별적으로
626	spontaneously	adv	자발적으로, 즉흥적으로
627	intermittently	adv	간헐적으로, 때때로
628	deceptively	adv	현혹적으로, 기만적으로
629	infinitely	adv	무한히, 끝없이
630	briskly	adv	활발하게, 경쾌하게
631	compliantly	adv	순응하여, 준수하며
632	abundantly	adv	풍부하게, 많이
633	impulsively	adv	충동적으로, 즉흥적으로
634	respectfully	adv	공손하게, 경의를 표하며
635	swiftly	adv	신속하게, 재빨리
636	cordially	adv	정중하게, 친절하게
637	deservedly	adv	당연히, 마땅히
638	vigorously	adv	활기차게, 정력적으로
639	consecutively	adv	연속하여
640	predominantly	adv	주로, 대체로

DAY 09 — PART 7 기출 어휘

☑ PART 7에 반드시 나오는 최신 기출 어휘들이므로, 확실히 암기해 둡니다. 🎧 VOCA_D09.mp3

641	**supervisor**	[n] 감독관, 관리자
642	**procedure**	[n] 절차, 과정
643	**tailor**	[v] 맞추다, 조정하다 [n] 재단사
644	**substitution**	[n] 대체, 교체
645	**accommodation**	[n] 숙박 시설, 편의 시설
646	**souvenir**	[n] 기념품, 선물
647	**flexibility**	[n] 유연성, 융통성
648	**institution**	[n] 기관, 단체
649	**reverse**	[v] 뒤집다, 반대로 하다 [adj] 반대의, 역의
650	**connectivity**	[n] 연결성, 접속성
651	**prospective**	[adj] 장래의, 예상되는
652	**subsidiary**	[adj] 부수적인, 보조적인 [n] 자회사
653	**assembled**	[adj] 모인, 집합된
654	**faucet**	[n] 수도꼭지, 밸브
655	**complex**	[adj] 복잡한, 다양한 [n] 복합 건물
656	**bulky**	[adj] 부피가 큰, 거대한
657	**navigate**	[v] 항해하다, 길을 찾다
658	**transcript**	[n] 글로 옮긴 기록
659	**preservation**	[n] 보존, 보전
660	**postdoctoral**	[adj] 박사 (학위 취득) 후의

661	**liability**	[n] 책임, 의무
662	**construction**	[n] 공사
663	**straightforward**	[adj] 간단한, 솔직한
664	**uninhabited**	[adj] 사람이 살지 않는, 비어있는
665	**bustling**	[adj] 붐비는, 활기찬
666	**refresher**	[n] 복습, 재교육
667	**fusion**	[n] 융합, 결합
668	**logbook**	[n] 업무 일지
669	**detector**	[n] 탐지기, 감지기
670	**agronomy**	[n] 농업 경제학
671	**puppet**	[n] 인형, 꼭두각시
672	**nontoxic**	[adj] 독성이 없는, 무해한
673	**saturated**	[adj] 포화된, 가득 찬
674	**pram**	[n] 유모차, 영아용 수레
675	**modest**	[adj] 겸손한, 검소한
676	**furnish**	[v] 제공하다, 공급하다
677	**dimmable**	[adj] 흐릿하게 할 수 있는
678	**literary**	[adj] 문학의, 문학적인
679	**insulation**	[n] 절연, 단열재
680	**tidal**	[adj] 조수의, 간만이 있는

DAY 09 — PART 7 기출 어휘

681	**rig**	n 장비, 장치 v 장착하다
682	**unwind**	v 긴장을 풀다
683	**irregularity**	n 불규칙성, 변칙
684	**seam**	n 이음매, 이은 자국
685	**delegation**	n 대표단, 위임
686	**backorder**	n 주문 적체
687	**outlying**	adj 외곽의, 벽지의
688	**administrate**	v 관리하다, 행정을 맡다
689	**well-established**	adj 잘 확립된, 명성이 있는
690	**eager to**	~을 열망하는, ~을 갈망하는
691	**keynote speech**	기조 연설
692	**wear and tear**	낡음, 마모
693	**follow up on**	~에 대해 후속 조치를 취하다
694	**catch up**	~을 따라잡다, 추격하다
695	**on the spur of the moment**	즉흥적으로, 충동적으로
696	**intend to**	~할 의향이 있다, ~하려고 하다
697	**balance due**	미지불 잔액
698	**cater to**	~에 맞춰 제공하다, ~을 충족시키다
699	**out of business**	폐업한, 영업을 중단한
700	**make the most of**	~을 최대한으로 활용하다

만점 완성 어휘

701	**refurbish**	v 개조하다, 수리하다
702	**hastily**	adv 서둘러, 급히
703	**expedite**	v 촉진하다, 가속화하다
704	**preliminary**	adj 예비적인, 사전의
705	**receptive**	adj 수용적인, 받아들이기 쉬운
706	**reinstate**	v 복직시키다, 원상 복구하다
707	**stub**	n 짧은 남은 부분
708	**petal**	n 꽃잎
709	**word-of-mouth**	adj 구전의, 말로 전하는
710	**liaison**	n 연락, 연락 담당자
711	**concoct**	v 고안하다, 꾸미다
712	**biometric**	adj 생체 인식의
713	**disembark**	v 하선하다, (배나 비행기에서) 내리다
714	**relic**	n 유물, 유적
715	**demolition**	n 철거, 파괴
716	**cutlery**	n 식탁용 칼붙이, 수저류
717	**embroider**	v 수를 놓다, 장식하다
718	**addendum**	n 추가 항목, 보충 서류
719	**sneak peek**	예고편
720	**sabbatical leave**	안식휴가

DAY 10 — PART 7 기출 어휘

☑ PART 7에 반드시 나오는 최신 기출 어휘들이므로, 확실히 암기해 둡니다.   ◯ VOCA_D10.mp3

721	**additional**	adj 추가의, 부가적인
722	**component**	n 구성 요소, 부품
723	**verify**	v 확인하다, 검증하다
724	**reputation**	n 명성, 평판
725	**discontinue**	v 중단하다
726	**waive**	v 포기하다, 면제하다
727	**independently**	adv 독립적으로, 자립적으로
728	**bookkeeping**	n 부기, 장부 기록
729	**eliminate**	v 제거하다, 없애다
730	**loyalty**	n 충성, 충실
731	**prolong**	v 연장하다, 지연시키다
732	**patron**	n 후원자, 고객
733	**canal**	n 운하, 수로
734	**lodge**	v 묵다, 투숙하다 n 오두막
735	**diploma**	n 졸업장, 수료증
736	**institute**	v 설립하다, 제정하다 n 연구소
737	**apprenticeship**	n 견습 기간, 수습 기간
738	**thread**	n 실, 섬유 v 꿰다
739	**decent**	adj 괜찮은, 적당한
740	**incomplete**	adj 불완전한, 미완성의

741	sanitation	n 위생, 청결
742	minimally	adv 최소한으로, 아주 조금
743	comparatively	adv 비교적, 상대적으로
744	mingle	v 섞다, 어울리다
745	recertification	n 재인증, 갱신
746	capture	v 포착하다, 붙잡다 n 포획
747	privilege	n 특권, 권리
748	longstanding	adj 오래된, 장기적인
749	equivalent	adj 동등한, 상당하는 n 상응물
750	visualization	n 시각화, 영상화
751	distinguished	adj 저명한, 탁월한
752	edible	adj 식용의, 먹을 수 있는
753	confer	v 협의하다, 수여하다
754	temper	v 완화하다, 조절하다 n 기질
755	underlying	adj 근본적인, 기저의
756	germinate	v 발아하다, 싹트다
757	sadden	v 슬프게 하다
758	solemn	adj 엄숙한, 장엄한
759	fleet	n 함대 adj 빠른, 쾌속의
760	bear	v 견디다, 참다

DAY 10 — PART 7 기출 어휘

761	**liner**	[n] 내장재, 안감
762	**fiberglass**	[n] 유리 섬유
763	**encrypted**	[adj] 암호화된
764	**groundbreaking**	[adj] 획기적인, 혁신적인
765	**knit**	[v] 뜨개질하다, 짜다
766	**concierge**	[n] 안내원, 수위
767	**flavorful**	[adj] 풍미 있는, 맛좋은
768	**numeracy**	[n] 수리 능력, 계산 능력
769	**shrub**	[n] 관목, 덤불
770	**expedited**	[adj] 신속히 처리된, 촉진된
771	**non-refundable**	[adj] 환불 불가능한
772	**top-notch**	[adj] 최고의
773	**release form**	양도 계약서
774	**at no cost**	무료로, 비용 없이
775	**make sense**	이치에 맞다, 의미가 통하다
776	**be willing to**	기꺼이 ~하다
777	**comparative analysis**	비교 분석
778	**take advantage of**	~을 이용하다
779	**run an errand**	심부름하다
780	**set apart**	구별하다, 분리하다

만점 완성 어휘

781	**solicit**	v 요청하다, 간청하다
782	**biodegradable**	adj 생분해성의, 자연 분해되는
783	**gutter**	n 홈통, 배수로
784	**morale**	n 사기, 의욕
785	**inauguration**	n 취임식, 개회식
786	**solidify**	v 굳히다, 강화하다
787	**upholstery**	n 덮개 천, 내장재
788	**redeem**	v 보완하다, 만회하다
789	**earthenware**	adj 도기의
790	**defray**	v 상쇄하다, 충당하다
791	**custodian**	n 관리인
792	**appraise**	v 평가하다, 감정하다
793	**reconfigure**	v 재구성하다, 다시 배열하다
794	**replenish**	v 보충하다, 다시 채우다
795	**grapple**	v 붙잡고 싸우다, 고심하다
796	**precipitation**	n 강수량, 침전
797	**ergonomic**	adj 인체공학적인
798	**concession stand**	매점, 판매 부스
799	**brick and mortar**	소매 거래
800	**off-peak**	비수기의, 한가한 시간대의

MEMO

MEMO

MEMO

한 권으로 끝내는 해커스 토익 900+ LC+RC+VOCA

토익,
한 권으로
고득점 달성하세요.

취업, 졸업, 공무원 시험, 승진…

여러분의 멋진 꿈을 향해 가는 길에 토익 점수가 걸림돌이 되어서는 안 되겠죠?
《해커스 토익 900+》는 여러분이 다른 중요한 일들에 더 집중할 수 있도록,
꼭 필요한 내용만으로 토익 목표 점수를 빠르게 달성할 수 있게 구성되었습니다.

CONTENTS

책의 특징과 구성   6
토익 소개   8
900+ 정복 학습 플랜   10

LC

PART 1

DAY 01   사람 중심 사진   14
- 빈출 문제 집중 훈련
- 고난도 문제 완전 정복

DAY 02   사물/풍경 중심 사진   18
- 빈출 문제 집중 훈련
- 고난도 문제 완전 정복

PART 2

DAY 03   의문사 의문문   24
- 빈출 문제 집중 훈련
- 고난도 문제 완전 정복

DAY 04   일반/기타 의문문 및 평서문   26
- 빈출 문제 집중 훈련
- 고난도 문제 완전 정복

PART 3

DAY 05   회사 업무 및 사무기기   30
- 빈출 문제 집중 훈련
- 고난도 문제 완전 정복

DAY 06   일상 생활 및 여행/여가   33
- 빈출 문제 집중 훈련
- 고난도 문제 완전 정복

DAY 07   마케팅/판매 및 재무   36
- 빈출 문제 집중 훈련
- 고난도 문제 완전 정복

PART 4

DAY 08   음성 메시지 및 회의 발췌   40
- 빈출 문제 집중 훈련
- 고난도 문제 완전 정복

DAY 09   안내, 방송, 광고   43
- 빈출 문제 집중 훈련
- 고난도 문제 완전 정복

DAY 10   연설 및 소개   46
- 빈출 문제 집중 훈련
- 고난도 문제 완전 정복

RC

PART 5&6

DAY 01 명사와 대명사 — 50
- 빈출 문제 집중 훈련
- 고난도 문제 완전 정복

DAY 02 형용사와 부사 — 54
- 빈출 문제 집중 훈련
- 고난도 문제 완전 정복

DAY 03 동사 — 58
- 빈출 문제 집중 훈련
- 고난도 문제 완전 정복

DAY 04 to 부정사, 동명사, 분사 — 62
- 빈출 문제 집중 훈련
- 고난도 문제 완전 정복

DAY 05 전치사, 접속사, 관계사 — 66
- 빈출 문제 집중 훈련
- 고난도 문제 완전 정복

DAY 06 어휘와 어구 — 70
- 빈출 문제 집중 훈련
- 고난도 문제 완전 정복

PART 7

DAY 07 이메일/편지, 메시지 대화문, 광고 — 76
- 빈출 문제 집중 훈련
- 고난도 문제 완전 정복

DAY 08 기사, 양식, 공고 — 82
- 빈출 문제 집중 훈련
- 고난도 문제 완전 정복

DAY 09 이중 지문 — 88
- 빈출 문제 집중 훈련
- 고난도 문제 완전 정복

DAY 10 삼중 지문 — 94
- 빈출 문제 집중 훈련
- 고난도 문제 완전 정복

시험장에도 들고 가는 토익 기출 VOCA 별책

DAY 01 PART 1 기출 어휘	**DAY 06** PART 5&6 기출 어휘
DAY 02 PART 2 기출 어휘	**DAY 07** PART 5&6 기출 어휘
DAY 03 PART 3 기출 어휘	**DAY 08** PART 5&6 기출 어휘
DAY 04 PART 4 기출 어휘	**DAY 09** PART 7 기출 어휘
DAY 05 PART 5&6 기출 어휘	**DAY 10** PART 7 기출 어휘

실전모의고사

실전모의고사 1	101
실전모의고사 2	143
실전모의고사 3	185
온라인 실전모의고사	Hackers.co.kr

해설집 책 속의 책

책의 특징과 구성

LC, RC, VOCA를 한 권으로 목표 달성

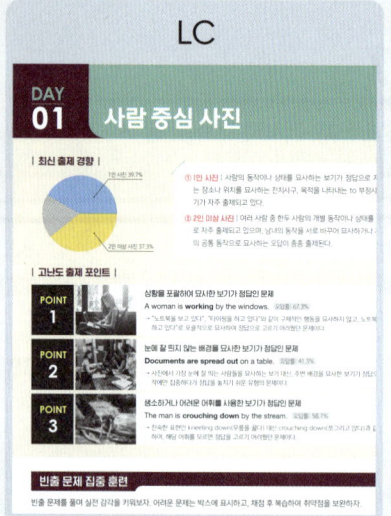

최신 경향이 반영된 빈출 문제와 고난도 문제 집중 공략

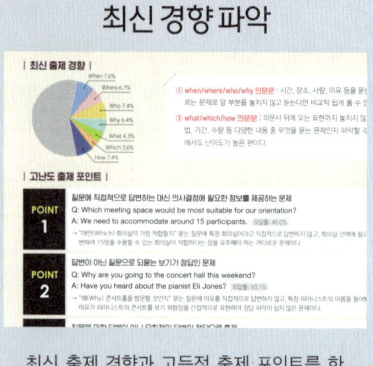

최신 출제 경향과 고득점 출제 포인트를 한 눈에 파악할 수 있습니다.

토익에 반드시 나오는 빈출 문제를 실수없이 완벽히 해결할 수 있도록 집중 훈련할 수 있습니다.

900+ 고득점을 위해 필요한 고난도 문제를 철저히 분석하고 완벽히 대비할 수 있습니다.

실전모의고사 4회분으로 실전에 철저히 대비

실전모의고사

실제 시험과 동일한 최신 출제 경향을 반영한 실전모의고사 3회분으로 실전에 철저히 대비할 수 있습니다.

온라인 실전모의고사

온라인 모의고사를 추가로 풀어보며 목표 점수를 위한 최종 점검과 실전 감각을 강화할 수 있습니다.

Answer Sheet

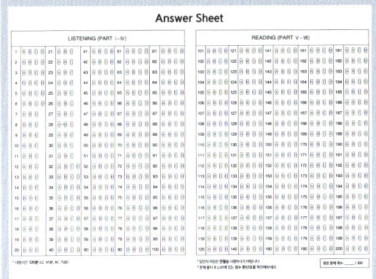

실제 시험과 동일한 Answer Sheet를 사용하여 답안 마킹과 시간 관리를 연습하면, 실전 감각을 극대화할 수 있습니다.

 ## 다양한 부가 학습자료로 고득점 완성

단어암기장

핵심 어휘를 정리한 단어암기장과 MP3로, 이동할 때나 자투리 시간에 효율적으로 단어를 암기할 수 있습니다.

고득점 핵심 노트

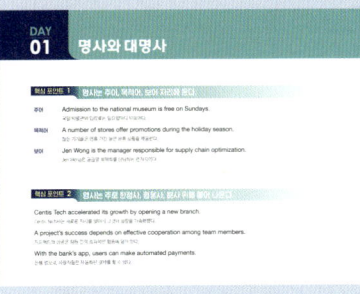

PART 5&6에서 반드시 알아야 하는 고득점 핵심 문법 포인트를 학습하여 고난도 문제에도 철저히 대비할 수 있습니다.

해설집

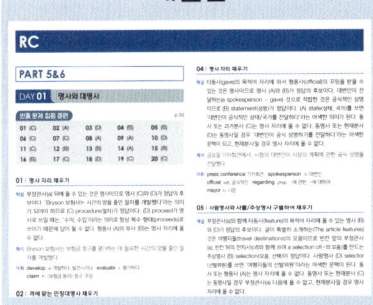

정확한 해석과 해설로 문제를 확실하게 이해할 수 있습니다. 상세한 오답 설명을 통해 틀린 문제의 원인을 파악하고 보완할 수 있습니다.

토익 소개

토익이란 무엇인가?

TOEIC은 Test Of English for International Communication의 약자로 영어가 모국어가 아닌 사람들을 대상으로 언어 본래의 기능인 '커뮤니케이션' 능력에 중점을 두고 일상생활 또는 국제 업무 등에 필요한 실용영어 능력을 평가하는 시험입니다. 토익은 일상생활 및 비즈니스 현장에서 필요로 하는 내용을 평가하기 위해 개발되었으며, 다음과 같은 실용적인 주제들을 주로 다루고 있습니다.

- **협력 개발**: 연구, 제품 개발
- **재무 회계**: 대출, 투자, 세금, 회계, 은행 업무
- **일반 업무**: 계약, 협상, 마케팅, 판매
- **기술 영역**: 전기, 공업 기술, 컴퓨터, 실험실
- **사무 영역**: 회의, 서류 업무
- **물품 구입**: 쇼핑, 물건 주문, 대금 지불
- **식사**: 레스토랑, 회식, 만찬
- **문화**: 극장, 스포츠, 피크닉
- **건강**: 의료 보험, 병원 진료, 치과
- **제조**: 생산 조립 라인, 공장 경영
- **직원**: 채용, 은퇴, 급여, 진급, 고용 기회
- **주택**: 부동산, 이사, 기업 부지

토익 시험의 구성

구성	내용	문항 수	시간	배점
Listening Test	PART 1 │ 사진 묘사 PART 2 │ 질의 응답 PART 3 │ 짧은 대화 PART 4 │ 짧은 담화	6문항 (1번-6번) 25문항 (7번-31번) 39문항, 13지문 (32번-70번) 30문항, 10지문 (71번-100번)	45분	495점
Reading Test	PART 5 │ 단문 빈칸 채우기 [문법/어휘] PART 6 │ 장문 빈칸 채우기 [문법/어휘/문장 고르기] PART 7 │ 지문 읽고 문제 풀기 [독해] 　- 단일 지문 (Single Passage) 　- 이중 지문 (Double Passages) 　- 삼중 지문 (Triple Passages)	30문항 (101번-130번) 16문항, 4지문 (131번-146번) 54문항, 15지문 (147번-200번) - 29문항, 10지문 (147번-175번) - 10문항, 2세트 (176번-185번) - 15문항, 3세트 (186번-200번)	75분	495점
Total	7 PARTS	200문항	120분	990점

토익, 접수부터 성적 확인까지!

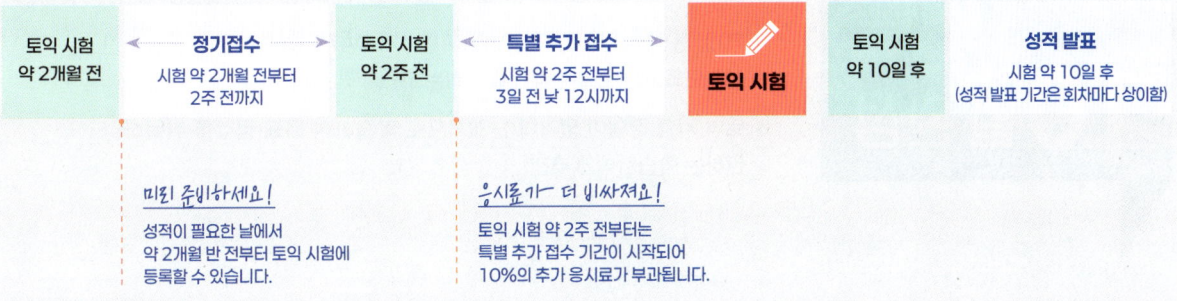

1. 토익 접수
- 인터넷 접수 기간을 TOEIC위원회 인터넷 사이트(www.toeic.co.kr) 혹은 공식 애플리케이션에서 확인하세요. 정기 토익은 시험 약 2개월 전부터 접수가 가능하며, 특별 추가 접수 기간에는 정기접수 기간 응시료에서 10%가 추가된 응시료로 접수할 수 있습니다.
- 추가 토익 시험은 2월과 8월에 있으며 이외에도 연중 상시로 시행되니 인터넷으로 확인하고 접수해야 합니다.
- 접수 시, jpg 형식의 사진 파일이 필요하므로 미리 준비해야 합니다.

2. 토익 응시
- 토익 응시일 이전에 시험 장소 및 수험번호를 미리 확인합니다.
- 시험 당일 신분증이 없으면 시험에 응시할 수 없으므로, 반드시 ETS에서 요구하는 신분증(주민등록증, 운전면허증, 공무원증 등)을 지참해야 합니다. ETS에서 인정하는 신분증 종류는 TOEIC위원회 인터넷 사이트(www.toeic.co.kr)에서 확인 가능합니다.

3. 성적 확인

성적 발표일	시험일로부터 약 10일 이후 (성적 발표 기간은 회차마다 상이함)
성적 확인 방법	TOEIC위원회 인터넷 사이트(www.toeic.co.kr) 혹은 공식 애플리케이션
성적표 수령 방법	우편 수령 또는 온라인 출력 (시험 접수 시 선택) *온라인 출력은 성적 발표 즉시 발급 가능하나, 우편 수령은 약 7일가량의 발송 기간이 소요될 수 있음

900+ 정복 학습 플랜

정석모드
10일 완성

- 10일 동안 매일 LC, RC, VOCA를 1개 DAY씩 학습하면서 중간중간 실전모의고사로 실전 감각을 익히는 코스
- 토익 시험 경험이 없거나 단계적으로 학습하여 목표 점수를 취득하길 원하는 학습자에게 추천

1일차	2일차	3일차	4일차	5일차
☐ LC DAY 01	☐ LC DAY 02	☐ LC DAY 03	☐ LC DAY 04	☐ LC DAY 05
☐ RC DAY 01	☐ RC DAY 02	☐ RC DAY 03	☐ RC DAY 04	☐ RC DAY 05
☐ VOCA DAY 01	☐ VOCA DAY 02	☐ VOCA DAY 03	☐ VOCA DAY 04	☐ VOCA DAY 05
		☐ 실전모의고사 1		

6일차	7일차	8일차	9일차	10일차
☐ LC DAY 06	☐ LC DAY 07	☐ LC DAY 08	☐ LC DAY 09	☐ LC DAY 10
☐ RC DAY 06	☐ RC DAY 07	☐ RC DAY 08	☐ RC DAY 09	☐ RC DAY 10
☐ VOCA DAY 06	☐ VOCA DAY 07	☐ VOCA DAY 08	☐ VOCA DAY 09	☐ VOCA DAY 10
☐ 실전모의고사 2				☐ 실전모의고사 3

*학습이 완료된 DAY에 체크(√) 표시를 하세요.

스피드 모드
5일 완성

- 5일 동안 매일 LC, RC, VOCA를 2개 DAY씩 학습하면서, 이틀마다 실전 모의고사를 1회씩 풀어보는 코스
- 짧은 기간에 집중하여 목표 점수를 취득하길 원하는 학습자에게 추천

1일차	2일차	3일차	4일차	5일차
☐ LC DAY 01-02	☐ LC DAY 03-04	☐ LC DAY 05-06	☐ LC DAY 07-08	☐ LC DAY 09-10
☐ RC DAY 01-02	☐ RC DAY 03-04	☐ RC DAY 05-06	☐ RC DAY 07-08	☐ RC DAY 09-10
☐ VOCA DAY 01-02	☐ VOCA DAY 03-04	☐ VOCA DAY 05-06	☐ VOCA DAY 07-08	☐ VOCA DAY 09-10
☐ 실전모의고사 1		☐ 실전모의고사 2		☐ 실전모의고사 3

*학습이 완료된 DAY에 체크(√) 표시를 하세요.

실전 모드
5일 완성

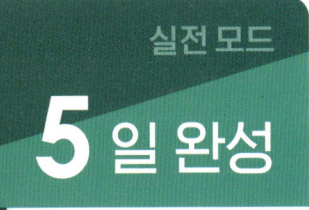

- 2일 동안 LC, RC, VOCA를 집중 학습 후, 3일 동안 모의고사 3회분을 실제 시험처럼 풀어 실전 감각을 끌어올리는 코스
- 토익 시험을 기본적으로 알고 있고 모의고사 위주로 빠르게 고득점을 취득하길 원하는 학습자에게 추천

1일차	2일차	3일차	4일차	5일차
☐ LC DAY 01-05	☐ LC DAY 06-10	☐ 실전모의고사 1	☐ 실전모의고사 2	☐ 실전모의고사 3
☐ RC DAY 01-05	☐ RC DAY 06-10			
☐ VOCA DAY 01-05	☐ VOCA DAY 06-10			

*학습을 완료한 DAY에 체크(√) 표시를 하세요.
*하루 학습 시간이 부족하다면, LC/RC에서는 '고난도 문제 완전 정복'만 학습하여 빠르게 준비할 수 있습니다.

PART 1

DAY 01 　사람 중심 사진
DAY 02 　사물/풍경 중심 사진

PART 1 | 알아보기

PART 1은 1번부터 6번까지 총 6문제로, 사진을 보고 4개의 보기를 들은 후, 사진을 가장 잘 묘사한 것을 선택하는 파트이다. 문제지에는 사진만 제시되고, 보기는 음성으로만 들려준다.

시험이 시작되면 리스닝 영역이 총 4개의 파트로 구성되어 있고, 약 45분간 진행된다는 디렉션이 나온 후, PART 1 진행 방식을 알려주는 디렉션이 이어서 나온다.

고득점 전략
이 디렉션은 읽거나 들을 필요가 없다. 디렉션이 나오는 1분 40초~2분 동안 PART 5 문제를 최소 4~6 문제 정도 미리 풀어놓는 것이 좋다.

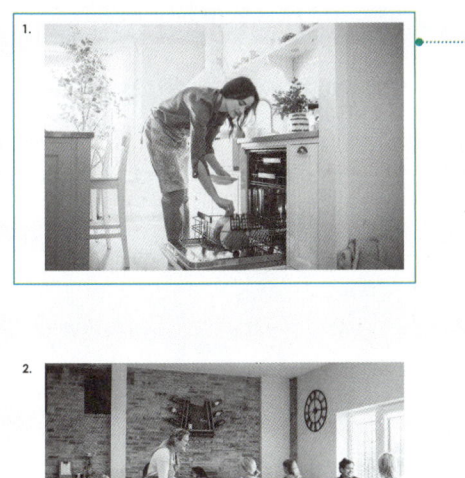

각 문제의 보기를 다음과 같이 들려준다.

Number 1.
Look at the picture marked number 1 in your test book.
(A) The woman is wiping a counter.
(B) The woman is putting a plate in the sink.
(C) The woman is bending over an appliance.
(D) The woman is sitting on a chair.

고득점 전략
보기는 한 번만 들려준다. 듣는 동안 O, X, △ 표시를 하면, 불확실한 보기를 구분하고 명확한 오답을 배제하는 데 도움이 된다.

DAY 01 사람 중심 사진

최신 출제 경향

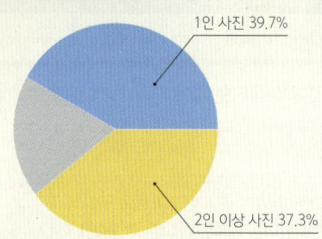

1인 사진 39.7%
2인 이상 사진 37.3%

① **1인 사진** | 사람의 동작이나 상태를 묘사하는 보기가 정답으로 자주 출제되는데, 최근에는 장소나 위치를 묘사하는 전치사구, 목적을 나타내는 to 부정사구가 붙어 길이가 긴 보기가 자주 출제되고 있다.

② **2인 이상 사진** | 여러 사람 중 한두 사람의 개별 동작이나 상태를 묘사하는 보기가 정답으로 자주 출제되고 있으며, 남녀의 동작을 서로 바꾸어 묘사하거나 개별 동작을 모든 사람들의 공통 동작으로 묘사하는 오답이 종종 출제된다.

고난도 출제 포인트

POINT 1

상황을 포괄하여 묘사한 보기가 정답인 문제
A woman is **working** by the windows. 오답률: 67.3%

→ "노트북을 보고 있다", "타이핑을 하고 있다"와 같이 구체적인 행동을 묘사하지 않고, 노트북으로 작업하는 상황을 "일을 하고 있다"로 포괄적으로 묘사하여 정답으로 고르기 어려웠던 문제이다.

POINT 2

눈에 잘 띄지 않는 배경을 묘사한 보기가 정답인 문제
Documents are spread out on a table. 오답률: 41.3%

→ 사진에서 가장 눈에 잘 띄는 사람들을 묘사하는 보기 대신, 주변 배경을 묘사한 보기가 정답으로 출제되었다. 사람들의 동작에만 집중하다가 정답을 놓치기 쉬운 유형의 문제이다.

POINT 3

생소하거나 어려운 어휘를 사용한 보기가 정답인 문제
The man is **crouching down** by the stream. 오답률: 58.7%

→ 친숙한 표현인 kneeling down(무릎을 꿇다) 대신 crouching down(쪼그리고 앉다)과 같은 다소 생소한 어휘를 사용하여, 해당 어휘를 모르면 정답을 고르기 어려웠던 문제이다.

빈출 문제 집중 훈련

🎧 D01_빈출

빈출 문제를 풀며 실전 감각을 키워보자. 어려운 문제는 박스에 표시하고, 채점 후 복습하여 취약점을 보완하자.

01

(A) (B) (C) (D)

02

(A) (B) (C) (D)

03

(A)   (B)   (C)   (D)

04

(A)   (B)   (C)   (D)

05

(A)   (B)   (C)   (D)

06

(A)   (B)   (C)   (D)

07

(A)   (B)   (C)   (D)

08

(A)   (B)   (C)   (D)

09

(A)   (B)   (C)   (D)

10

(A)   (B)   (C)   (D)

고난도 문제 완전 정복

🎧 D01_고난도

고난도 문제를 풀며, 완벽하게 실전을 대비하자. 어려운 문제는 박스에 표시하고, 채점 후 복습하여 완전히 내 것으로 만들자.

☐
01

(A)   (B)   (C)   (D)

☐
02

(A)   (B)   (C)   (D)

☐
03

(A)   (B)   (C)   (D)

☐
04

(A)   (B)   (C)   (D)

정답·해석·해설 p.4

DAY 02 사물/풍경 중심 사진

mp3 바로 듣기

| 최신 출제 경향 |

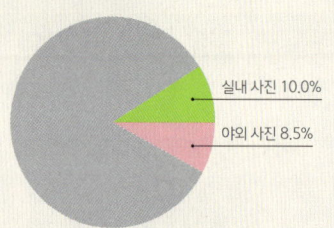
실내 사진 10.0%
야외 사진 8.5%

① **실내 사진** | 집, 사무실, 식당, 상점 등의 실내 공간에서 가구, 책, 전등과 같은 사물의 상태나 위치를 묘사하는 보기가 정답으로 자주 출제된다. 사람이 없는 사진에서 사람의 동작을 묘사하는 동사가 포함된 보기도 오답으로 종종 출제된다.

② **야외 사진** | 강, 공원, 도로, 주차장, 공사장 등 야외 공간에서 건물이나 교통수단의 상태나 위치를 묘사하는 보기가 정답으로 자주 출제된다.

| 고난도 출제 포인트 |

눈에 잘 띄지 않는 배경을 묘사한 보기가 정답인 문제
The building contains multiple levels. 오답률: 74.0%
→ 사진에서 가장 눈에 잘 띄는 트럭이 아니라 주변 배경에 있는 건물을 묘사한 보기가 정답으로 출제되어, 눈에 잘 띄는 사물(truck)에만 집중하다가 정답을 놓치기 쉬운 유형의 문제이다.

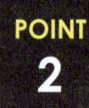

수동 진행형(be being p.p.)으로 상태를 묘사한 보기가 정답인 문제
Some potted plants are being displayed. 오답률: 20.9%
→ 사람이 없는 사물 사진에서 수동 진행형(be being p.p.)이 정답으로 출제된 문제이다. 수동 진행형은 일반적으로 사람의 동작을 나타내지만, be being displayed(진열되어 있다)는 사물의 배치 상태도 나타낼 수 있어서 주의해야 한다.

생소하거나 어려운 어휘를 사용한 보기가 정답인 문제
Telephone lines are suspended above the street. 오답률: 57.6%
→ 친숙한 표현인 hang(걸려 있다) 대신 suspend(매달다)라는 다소 생소한 어휘를 사용하여, 해당 어휘를 모르면 정답을 고르기 어려웠던 문제이다.

| 빈출 문제 집중 훈련 |

🎧 D02_빈출

빈출 문제를 풀며 실전 감각을 키워보자. 어려운 문제는 박스에 표시하고, 채점 후 복습하여 취약점을 보완하자.

☐ 01

(A) (B) (C) (D)

☐ 02

(A) (B) (C) (D)

03

(A)　　(B)　　(C)　　(D)

04

(A)　　(B)　　(C)　　(D)

05

(A)　　(B)　　(C)　　(D)

06

(A)　　(B)　　(C)　　(D)

07

(A) (B) (C) (D)

08

(A) (B) (C) (D)

09

(A) (B) (C) (D)

10

(A) (B) (C) (D)

고난도 문제 완전 정복

고난도 문제를 풀며, 완벽하게 실전을 대비하자. 어려운 문제는 박스에 표시하고, 채점 후 복습하여 완전히 내 것으로 만들자.

☐
01

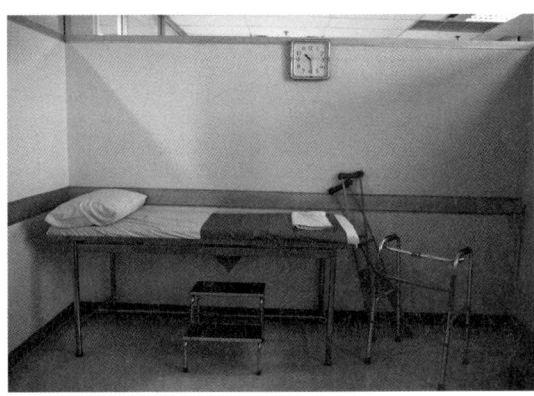

(A)   (B)   (C)   (D)

☐
02

(A)   (B)   (C)   (D)

☐
03

(A)   (B)   (C)   (D)

☐
04

(A)   (B)   (C)   (D)

PART 2

DAY 03 　의문사 의문문
DAY 04 　일반/기타 의문문 및 평서문

PART 2 | 알아보기

PART 2는 7번부터 31번까지 총 25문제로, 하나의 질문 또는 문장과 그에 대한 3개의 응답을 듣고 가장 적절하게 응답한 보기를 선택하는 파트이다. 문제지에는 번호와 디렉션만 제시되고, 질문과 보기는 음성으로만 들려준다.

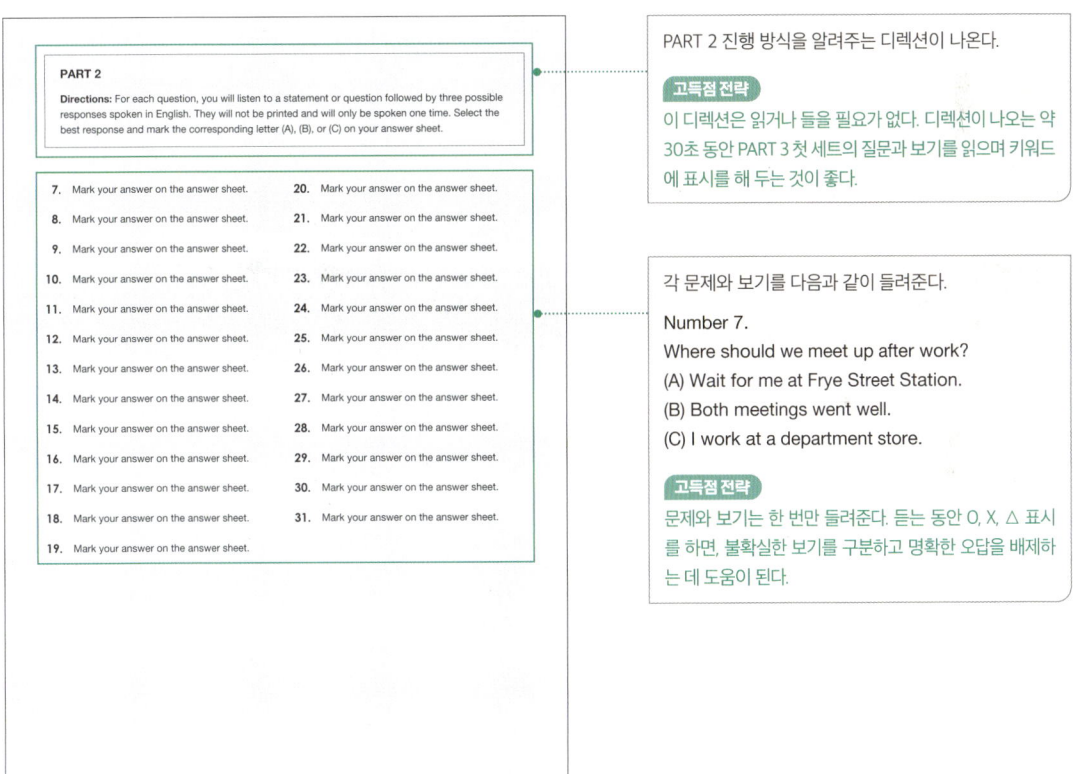

PART 2 진행 방식을 알려주는 디렉션이 나온다.

고득점 전략

이 디렉션은 읽거나 들을 필요가 없다. 디렉션이 나오는 약 30초 동안 PART 3 첫 세트의 질문과 보기를 읽으며 키워드에 표시를 해 두는 것이 좋다.

각 문제와 보기를 다음과 같이 들려준다.

Number 7.
Where should we meet up after work?
(A) Wait for me at Frye Street Station.
(B) Both meetings went well.
(C) I work at a department store.

고득점 전략

문제와 보기는 한 번만 들려준다. 듣는 동안 O, X, △ 표시를 하면, 불확실한 보기를 구분하고 명확한 오답을 배제하는 데 도움이 된다.

DAY 03 의문사 의문문

최신 출제 경향

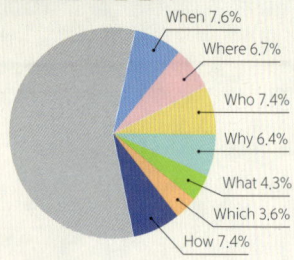

When 7.6%
Where 6.7%
Who 7.4%
Why 6.4%
What 4.3%
Which 3.6%
How 7.4%

① **when/where/who/why 의문문** | 시간, 장소, 사람, 이유 등을 묻는 질문을 듣고 정보를 고르는 문제로 앞 부분을 놓치지 않고 듣는다면 비교적 쉽게 풀 수 있는 편이다.

② **what/which/how 의문문** | 의문사 뒤에 오는 표현까지 놓치지 않고 들어야 의견, 종류, 방법, 기간, 수량 등 다양한 내용 중 무엇을 묻는 문제인지 파악할 수 있어 의문사 의문문 중에서도 난이도가 높은 편이다.

고난도 출제 포인트

POINT 1 질문에 직접적으로 답변하는 대신 의사결정에 필요한 정보를 제공하는 문제
Q: Which meeting space would be most suitable for our orientation?
A: We need to accommodate around 15 participants. 오답률: 40.0%
→ "어떤(Which) 회의실이 가장 적합할지" 묻는 질문에 특정 회의실이라고 직접적으로 답변하지 않고, 회의실 선택에 필요한 정보인 참석 인원 수로 답변하여 15명을 수용할 수 있는 회의실이 적합하다는 점을 유추해야 하는 까다로운 문제이다.

POINT 2 답변이 아닌 질문으로 되묻는 보기가 정답인 문제
Q: Why are you going to the concert hall this weekend?
A: Have you heard about the pianist Eli Jones? 오답률: 60.1%
→ "왜(Why) 콘서트홀을 방문할 것인지" 묻는 질문에 이유를 직접적으로 답변하지 않고, 특정 피아니스트의 이름을 들어봤는지 되묻는 방식으로, 방문 이유가 피아니스트의 콘서트를 보기 위함임을 간접적으로 표현하여 정답 파악이 쉽지 않은 문제이다.

POINT 3 질문에 대한 답변이 아닌 우회적인 답변이 정답으로 출제
Q: How often should the cooling system be checked?
A: Refer to your guide. 오답률: 32.7%
→ "냉각 시스템을 얼마나 자주(How often) 점검해야 하는지" 묻는 질문에 직접적으로 주기를 언급하지 않고, 안내서를 참고하라는 우회적인 답변을 제시해 직관적으로 정답을 선택하기 어려운 문제이다.

빈출 문제 집중 훈련

🎧 D03_빈출

빈출 문제를 풀며 실전 감각을 키워보자. 어려운 문제는 박스에 표시하고, 채점 후 복습하여 취약점을 보완하자.

☐ 01 Mark your answer. (A) (B) (C)
☐ 02 Mark your answer. (A) (B) (C)
☐ 03 Mark your answer. (A) (B) (C)
☐ 04 Mark your answer. (A) (B) (C)
☐ 05 Mark your answer. (A) (B) (C)
☐ 06 Mark your answer. (A) (B) (C)
☐ 07 Mark your answer. (A) (B) (C)
☐ 08 Mark your answer. (A) (B) (C)
☐ 09 Mark your answer. (A) (B) (C)
☐ 10 Mark your answer. (A) (B) (C)

11 Mark your answer. (A) (B) (C)
12 Mark your answer. (A) (B) (C)
13 Mark your answer. (A) (B) (C)
14 Mark your answer. (A) (B) (C)
15 Mark your answer. (A) (B) (C)

16 Mark your answer. (A) (B) (C)
17 Mark your answer. (A) (B) (C)
18 Mark your answer. (A) (B) (C)
19 Mark your answer. (A) (B) (C)
20 Mark your answer. (A) (B) (C)

정답 · 해석 · 해설 p.8

고난도 문제 완전 정복

🎧 D03_고난도

고난도 문제를 풀며, 완벽하게 실전을 대비하자. 어려운 문제는 박스에 표시하고, 채점 후 복습하여 완전히 내 것으로 만들자.

01 Mark your answer. (A) (B) (C)
02 Mark your answer. (A) (B) (C)
03 Mark your answer. (A) (B) (C)
04 Mark your answer. (A) (B) (C)
05 Mark your answer. (A) (B) (C)
06 Mark your answer. (A) (B) (C)
07 Mark your answer. (A) (B) (C)
08 Mark your answer. (A) (B) (C)
09 Mark your answer. (A) (B) (C)
10 Mark your answer. (A) (B) (C)

11 Mark your answer. (A) (B) (C)
12 Mark your answer. (A) (B) (C)
13 Mark your answer. (A) (B) (C)
14 Mark your answer. (A) (B) (C)
15 Mark your answer. (A) (B) (C)
16 Mark your answer. (A) (B) (C)
17 Mark your answer. (A) (B) (C)
18 Mark your answer. (A) (B) (C)
19 Mark your answer. (A) (B) (C)
20 Mark your answer. (A) (B) (C)

정답 · 해석 · 해설 p.11

DAY 04 일반/기타 의문문 및 평서문

mp3 바로 듣기

최신 출제 경향

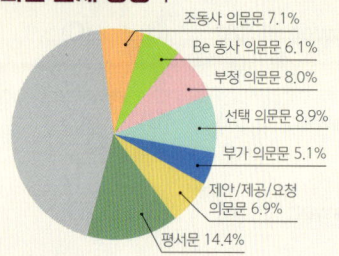

- 조동사 의문문 7.1%
- Be 동사 의문문 6.1%
- 부정 의문문 8.0%
- 선택 의문문 8.9%
- 부가 의문문 5.1%
- 제안/제공/요청 의문문 6.9%
- 평서문 14.4%

① **일반 의문문** | 조동사 의문문, Be 동사 의문문, 부정 의문문 등이 출제되며, 과거와 달리 Yes/No로 응답하는 정답 보기가 점차 줄어드는 추세이다.

② **기타 의문문** | 선택 의문문, 부가 의문문, 제안/제공/요청 의문문 등이 출제되며, 이 중 선택 의문문이 가장 많이 나온다.

③ **평서문** | 평서문은 일정한 응답 패턴이 없어서 난이도가 높은 편인데, 최근 들어 출제 비율이 꾸준히 증가하고 있다.

고난도 출제 포인트

POINT 1 문제 상황을 진술하는 평서문에 대안을 제시하는 답변이 정답인 문제
Q: The store is totally out of strawberries.
A: Raspberries would also work for that dessert. 오답률: 48.9%
→ 딸기가 없다는 문제 상황을 진술할 평서문에 그 디저트를 만들 때는 라즈베리도 괜찮을 것이라는 답변이 정답인 문제로, 디저트 재료에 관해 대화하고 있다는 맥락을 파악하여 실질적인 대안을 제시하는 응답을 골라야 하는 어려운 문제이다.

POINT 2 선택 의문문에서 제시된 선택지를 둘 다 고르지 않는 답변이 정답인 문제
Q: Should I take our guests to the hotel, or will you?
A: Let's just arrange for a shuttle bus. 오답률: 52.1%
→ 자신과 상대방 중 누가 고객을 데려다줄지 고르라는 선택 의문문에서, 두 선택지를 모두 고르지 않고 셔틀버스를 준비하자며 제3의 대안으로 답변한 보기가 정답인 문제로, 제시된 선택지 중 하나를 고르는 데 집중했다면 정답을 놓치기 쉬운 문제이다.

POINT 3 특정 인물에 관한 조동사 의문문에 제3자가 언급된 답변이 정답인 문제
Q: Has Mr. Rodriguez visited the new headquarters?
A: Jonathan gave him a tour. 오답률: 34.6%
→ Mr. Rodriguez에 관한 질문에 Jonathan이라는 다른 인물이 언급된 답변이 정답인 문제로, him이 질문의 Mr. Rodriguez를 가리키는 것을 파악하지 못하면 관련 없는 응답으로 오해하기 쉬운 어려운 문제이다.

빈출 문제 집중 훈련

🎧 D04_빈출

빈출 문제를 풀며 실전 감각을 키워보자. 어려운 문제는 박스에 표시하고, 채점 후 복습하여 취약점을 보완하자.

☐ 01 Mark your answer. (A) (B) (C)
☐ 02 Mark your answer. (A) (B) (C)
☐ 03 Mark your answer. (A) (B) (C)
☐ 04 Mark your answer. (A) (B) (C)
☐ 05 Mark your answer. (A) (B) (C)
☐ 06 Mark your answer. (A) (B) (C)
☐ 07 Mark your answer. (A) (B) (C)
☐ 08 Mark your answer. (A) (B) (C)
☐ 09 Mark your answer. (A) (B) (C)
☐ 10 Mark your answer. (A) (B) (C)

11 Mark your answer. (A) (B) (C)	16 Mark your answer. (A) (B) (C)
12 Mark your answer. (A) (B) (C)	17 Mark your answer. (A) (B) (C)
13 Mark your answer. (A) (B) (C)	18 Mark your answer. (A) (B) (C)
14 Mark your answer. (A) (B) (C)	19 Mark your answer. (A) (B) (C)
15 Mark your answer. (A) (B) (C)	20 Mark your answer. (A) (B) (C)

정답 · 해석 · 해설 p.15

고난도 문제 완전 정복

🎧 D04_고난도

고난도 문제를 풀며, 완벽하게 실전을 대비하자. 어려운 문제는 박스에 표시하고, 채점 후 복습하여 완전히 내 것으로 만들자.

01 Mark your answer. (A) (B) (C)	11 Mark your answer. (A) (B) (C)
02 Mark your answer. (A) (B) (C)	12 Mark your answer. (A) (B) (C)
03 Mark your answer. (A) (B) (C)	13 Mark your answer. (A) (B) (C)
04 Mark your answer. (A) (B) (C)	14 Mark your answer. (A) (B) (C)
05 Mark your answer. (A) (B) (C)	15 Mark your answer. (A) (B) (C)
06 Mark your answer. (A) (B) (C)	16 Mark your answer. (A) (B) (C)
07 Mark your answer. (A) (B) (C)	17 Mark your answer. (A) (B) (C)
08 Mark your answer. (A) (B) (C)	18 Mark your answer. (A) (B) (C)
09 Mark your answer. (A) (B) (C)	19 Mark your answer. (A) (B) (C)
10 Mark your answer. (A) (B) (C)	20 Mark your answer. (A) (B) (C)

정답 · 해석 · 해설 p.18

PART 3

DAY 05 회사 업무 및 사무기기
DAY 06 일상 생활 및 여행/여가
DAY 07 마케팅/판매 및 재무

PART 3 | 알아보기

PART 3는 32번부터 70번까지 총 39문제로, 회사 생활 또는 일상생활에서 일어나는 2~3명의 대화를 듣고 그와 관련된 3개의 문제를 푸는 유형이다. 문제지에는 각 문제의 질문과 4개의 보기가 제시되고, 대화와 질문을 음성으로 들려준다.

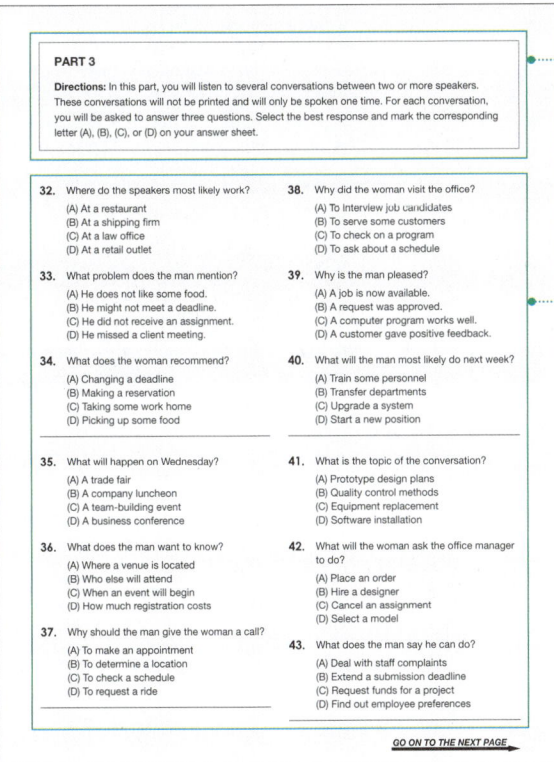

PART 3 진행 방식을 알려주는 디렉션이 나온다.

고득점 전략

이 디렉션은 읽거나 들을 필요가 없다. 디렉션이 나오는 약 30초 동안 PART 3의 질문과 보기를 읽으며 키워드에 표시를 해 두는 것이 좋다.

대화와 각 문제의 질문을 다음과 같이 들려준다.

Questions 32 through 34 refer to the following conversation.

W: Are you still working on that agreement for Harper Express? Let's go grab lunch. It's almost noon, and I heard there's a new food truck just down the block.

M: You can go without me. I'm working on a legal document for another client I was assigned to.

……

Number 32.
Where do the speakers most likely work?
Number 33.
What problem does the man mention?
Number 34.
What does the woman recommend?

고득점 전략

대화를 모두 듣고 나서 문제를 풀려고 하면 내용이 기억나지 않을 수 있으니 대화를 듣는 동안 바로 문제를 푸는 것이 좋다. 즉, 대화가 끝났을 때 정답도 선택되어 있어야 한다. 또한, 대화가 끝난 후 질문을 들려주는 시간에는 다음 세트의 질문과 보기를 미리 확인하면서 주요 키워드에 표시를 해 두면, 다음 세트를 푸는 데 도움이 된다.

DAY 05 회사 업무 및 사무기기

mp3 바로 듣기

| 최신 출제 경향 |

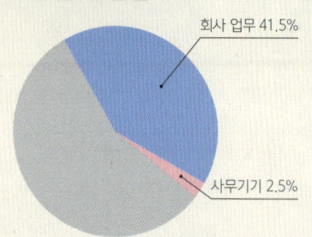
회사 업무 41.5%
사무기기 2.5%

① **회사 업무** | 안건 논의, 업무 지원 요청, 직원 교육 등 다양한 업무 관련 내용이 출제된다. 특히, 업무 과중 상황에 대한 해결책 모색이나 일정 조율 등이 지속적으로 출제되고 있다.

② **사무기기** | 컴퓨터, 소프트웨어, 복사기와 같은 일반적인 사무기기를 소재로 한 내용이 주로 출제되며, 최근에는 최신 AI 기술과 관련된 내용도 등장한다.

| 고난도 출제 포인트 |

POINT 1

단서가 직접적으로 언급되지 않는 화자 문제

W: Now, I've finished explaining how our frozen meals are made.
M: I'm curious about the ingredients used to prepare them.
W: Sure, I'll explain that as we start the factory tour.

Q What industry does the woman work in?
(A) Food manufacturing (o)
(B) Kitchenware production (x)

→ 여자가 냉동식품 생산 과정을 설명한 뒤 공장 견학을 시작하겠다고 한 내용을 통해, 여자가 식품 제조업에서 일하고 있음을 추론해야 하는 까다로운 문제이다. 오답률 45.0%

POINT 2

회사 업무 및 사무기기 주제에 등장하는 고난도 어휘

authorization 승인	reinforcement 보강	quote 견적	clarification 설명	ventilation 환기
reimbursement 상환	retrieve 회수하다	reconfiguration 재구성	distract 방해하다	credential 자격증
transaction 거래	durable 내구성이 있는	criteria 기준	overhaul 점검	glitch 사소한 결함

빈출 문제 집중 훈련

🎧 D05_빈출

빈출 문제를 풀며 실전 감각을 키워보자. 어려운 문제는 박스에 표시하고, 채점 후 복습하여 취약점을 보완하자.

☐ **01** What problem does the man mention?

(A) A database is incomplete.
(B) A client is dissatisfied.
(C) A workspace is locked.
(D) An account is inaccessible.

☐ **02** Why will the man contact Ms. Sheppard?

(A) To change a password
(B) To identify a problem
(C) To confirm a decision
(D) To discuss an assignment

☐ **03** What will the woman probably do next?

(A) Locate some files
(B) Install an application
(C) Schedule a meeting
(D) Print some copies

☐ **04** What type of event is the man preparing for?

(A) A shareholders' meeting
(B) A training session
(C) A company banquet
(D) A trade fair

☐ **05** What does the woman agree to do?

(A) Take a survey
(B) Assist a colleague
(C) Prepare some charts
(D) Give a presentation

☐ **06** What will the man do tomorrow morning?

(A) Read a report
(B) Conduct some research
(C) Submit an assignment
(D) Send an e-mail

07 Why have customers made complaints?

(A) A sale period was cut short.
(B) A machine error occurred.
(C) A process takes too long.
(D) A parking lot is too small.

08 What does the woman say about the machines?

(A) They are used at other locations.
(B) They will cut down on expenses.
(C) They were discussed in a meeting.
(D) They have been fully repaired.

09 What does Adam suggest?

(A) Rescheduling an afternoon gathering
(B) Hiring an additional agent
(C) Mentioning an idea to a supervisor
(D) Offering discounts to customers

10 What is the conversation mainly about?

(A) Touring a property
(B) Promoting a sale
(C) Managing an account
(D) Hiring a financial consultant

11 Why does the man want to meet with Debbie Meyers?

(A) To obtain some information
(B) To make an investment
(C) To pass on some documents
(D) To request a transfer

12 What does the woman say about Debbie Meyers?

(A) She retired from the company.
(B) She was given a higher position.
(C) She asked for some assistance.
(D) She supervises an entire division.

13 What are the speakers mainly discussing?

(A) Vacancies for an event
(B) Products to put on display
(C) Services offered at a fair
(D) Renovations to a facility

14 What does the woman say about the booth near the entrance?

(A) It is more expensive than others.
(B) It has already been reserved.
(C) It does not offer much space.
(D) It has a stand for posters.

15 What will the woman most likely do next?

(A) Contact a convention center
(B) Set up a booth
(C) Cancel a reservation
(D) Hang some banners

16 What problem does the man describe?

(A) Some quotes have not been received.
(B) A construction project has been delayed.
(C) Some price estimates are too high.
(D) A building lease has expired.

17 What does the woman say about the building materials supplier?

(A) It cannot deliver some supplies.
(B) It has not received a payment.
(C) It has yet to contact her.
(D) It has sent out a price list.

18 What will the woman probably do next?

(A) Request a deadline extension
(B) Wait for authorization
(C) Retrieve a budget proposal
(D) Ask for price estimates

고난도 문제 완전 정복

고난도 문제를 풀며, 완벽하게 실전을 대비하자. 어려운 문제는 박스에 표시하고, 채점 후 복습하여 완전히 내 것으로 만들자.

☐
01 Where does the conversation most likely take place?
(A) At a real estate agency
(B) At an advertising firm
(C) At a software company
(D) At a financial institution

☐
02 What does the woman say about the evaluations?
(A) They were introduced recently.
(B) They will increase in frequency.
(C) They include updated criteria.
(D) They are conducted annually.

☐
03 Why does the man say, "All employees qualify?"
(A) To address a complaint
(B) To criticize a decision
(C) To confirm a point
(D) To express concern

☐
04 What are the speakers mainly discussing?
(A) Some product advertisements
(B) A department store display
(C) A successful product line
(D) Some market research

☐
05 What problem do the speakers discuss?
(A) A marketing meeting was postponed.
(B) Promotional materials were not received.
(C) A project schedule was not updated.
(D) Team members were unavailable.

☐
06 What will the woman most likely do next?
(A) Outline a draft for an article
(B) Meet a team leader
(C) Attend a presentation
(D) Approve a campaign

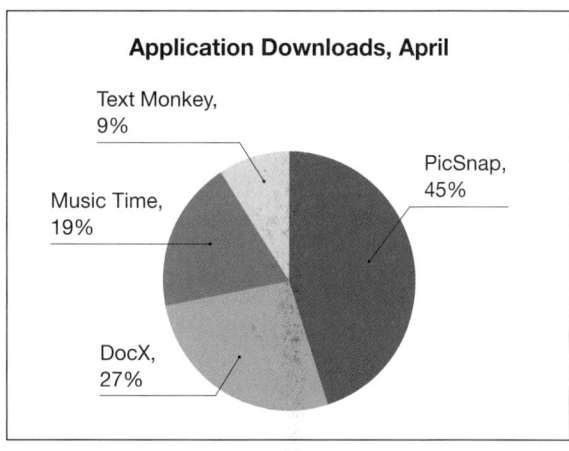

☐
07 What is the conversation mainly about?
(A) A departmental downsizing
(B) An upcoming product launch
(C) A change in leadership
(D) A request for overtime hours

☐
08 What is the man planning to do?
(A) Postpone a regular staff meeting
(B) Announce a decision to personnel
(C) Download a competitor's programs
(D) Consider taking on a different role

☐
09 Look at the graphic. Which application will be improved?
(A) PicSnap
(B) DocX
(C) Music Time
(D) Text Monkey

DAY 06 일상 생활 및 여행/여가

mp3 바로 듣기

| 최신 출제 경향 |

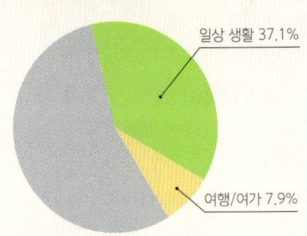
일상 생활 37.1%
여행/여가 7.9%

① **일상 생활** | 제품 주문·반품·교환, 주거시설 관리, 미용 및 의료 서비스 이용 관련 내용이 자주 출제된다. 최근에는 디지털 기술을 활용한 서비스와 관련된 대화가 증가하고 있다.

② **여행/여가** | 항공편 예약, 여행 일정 관리, 여행 중 겪는 문제 상황, 공연·전시 관람 관련 내용이 자주 출제된다.

| 고난도 출제 포인트 |

POINT 1 의도 파악 문제의 단서가 인용어구 앞에 있는 문제

W: I checked the catalog and really liked the tile design.
M: The installer already wrapped up their work.
W: Can't you do something about it? I really love the tile design.

Q What does the woman mean when she says, "I really love the tile design"?
(A) She is asking for additional work. (o)
(B) She is complimenting the design choice. (x)

→ 일반적으로 의도 파악 문제의 단서는 인용어구 뒤에 제시되는데, 대화의 마지막에 인용어구가 제시되어서 앞부분의 대화를 제대로 파악하지 못한다면 정답을 고르기 어려운 문제이다. 오답률: 37.2%

POINT 2 일상 생활 및 여행/여가 주제에 등장하는 고난도 어휘

measurement 면적	lawnmower 잔디 깎는 기계	plumber 배관공	punctuality 시간 엄수	observatory 천문대
recurring 반복해서 발생하는	ornament 장식품	malfunction 오작동	hospitality 환대, 접대	expedition 탐험, 여행
itinerary 여행 일정	complaint 불만	inconvenience 불편	expire 만료되다	pottery 도자기

빈출 문제 집중 훈련

 D06_빈출

빈출 문제를 풀며 실전 감각을 키워보자. 어려운 문제는 박스에 표시하고, 채점 후 복습하여 취약점을 보완하자.

□ **01** Where are the speakers?
(A) At a bookstore
(B) At a fitness center
(C) At a public library
(D) At a shopping complex

□ **02** What is the man impressed with?
(A) The knowledgeable staff
(B) The comfortable furniture
(C) The large selection of books
(D) The number of workstations

□ **03** What will the man most likely do next?
(A) Apply for a membership
(B) Walk to his apartment
(C) Buy some materials
(D) Return to his desk

□ **04** What is the purpose of the man's call?
(A) To request overnight shipping
(B) To inquire about a delay
(C) To discuss an order
(D) To ask about a price

□ **05** What does the woman offer to do?
(A) Send a new product
(B) Check a shipping date
(C) Notify a store manager
(D) Repair a damaged item

□ **06** Why does the man decline the woman's offer?
(A) He does not have a warranty.
(B) He no longer requires the merchandise.
(C) He is worried about postage costs.
(D) He already purchased another item.

07 Why is the man calling?

(A) His service has to be renewed.
(B) His laptop needs to be replaced.
(C) His wireless router will not turn on.
(D) His Internet is not working properly.

08 What is mentioned about the man's computer?

(A) It was purchased recently.
(B) It was sent to a shop.
(C) It will be repaired for free.
(D) It will arrive this week.

09 What does the woman recommend the man do?

(A) Contact a professional technician
(B) Pay a service fee online
(C) Install a program again
(D) Connect to another device

10 How did the woman learn about a promotion?

(A) By speaking to a friend
(B) By accessing a Web Site
(C) By reading a newsletter
(D) By listening to the radio

11 Why does the man suggest testing a bicycle?

(A) To determine whether it functions properly
(B) To examine whether it is durable
(C) To confirm that it is the right size
(D) To make sure that it has a safety feature

12 What does the man ask the woman to do?

(A) Fill out a form
(B) Check some price tags
(C) Wait in a line
(D) Present a credit card

13 Who most likely is the man?

(A) A property manager
(B) A business owner
(C) A maintenance worker
(D) A building tenant

14 What problem does the man mention?

(A) An appliance is not working.
(B) A light bulb needs to be replaced.
(C) A technician has not arrived.
(D) A gathering has been postponed.

15 What does the man plan to do tonight?

(A) Attend a class
(B) Visit a relative
(C) Prepare a meal
(D) Call a worker

16 Who most likely is the woman?

(A) An architect
(B) A real estate agent
(C) A financial consultant
(D) A home decorator

17 What does the man say about the house?

(A) It is not within his budget.
(B) It is currently being remodeled.
(C) It is situated near a river.
(D) It is in the downtown area.

18 Why will the woman contact Mr. Voss?

(A) To make an offer
(B) To negotiate a loan
(C) To request additional time
(D) To set up a showing

고난도 문제 완전 정복

D06_고난도

고난도 문제를 풀며, 완벽하게 실전을 대비하자. 어려운 문제는 박스에 표시하고, 채점 후 복습하여 완전히 내 것으로 만들자.

01 Where do the speakers most likely work?

(A) At a theater
(B) At a coffee shop
(C) At a concert hall
(D) At a supermarket

02 What does the man say about *Winter Wind*?

(A) It has a strong cast.
(B) It received praise from critics.
(C) It is not very long.
(D) It only had three performances.

03 What will the women probably do this weekend?

(A) Publish a review
(B) Watch a show
(C) Go to a rehearsal
(D) Audition for a play

04 According to the woman, what is the problem?

(A) An order was not delivered.
(B) A service is not reliable.
(C) An item was not installed.
(D) A product is not in stock.

05 Where did the man put the curtains he bought?

(A) In a hallway
(B) In a living room
(C) In a kitchen
(D) In a dining room

06 What does the woman imply when she says, "it's not all bad news"?

(A) A room measurement is accurate.
(B) An option is available.
(C) An order can be placed online.
(D) A refund can be provided.

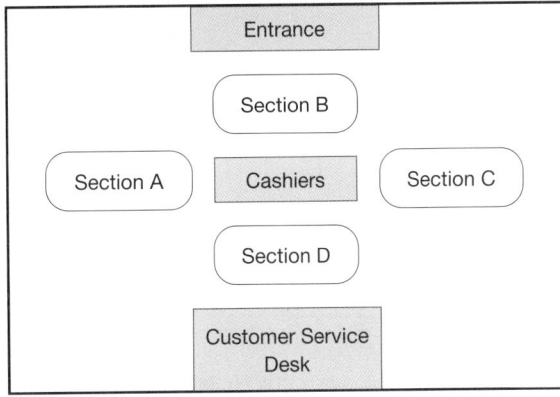

07 Look at the graphic. Where are the hair dryers located?

(A) Section A
(B) Section B
(C) Section C
(D) Section D

08 What problem does the woman mention about the Kenwick Turbo Dryer?

(A) It is not eligible for a discount.
(B) It consumes too much energy.
(C) It breaks too easily.
(D) It is not the size she needs.

09 What will the woman most likely do next?

(A) Follow an employee
(B) Pay for a purchase
(C) Test out a product
(D) Exchange a device

DAY 07 마케팅/판매 및 재무

| 최신 출제 경향 |

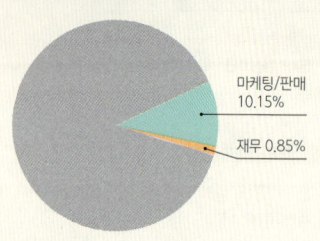

마케팅/판매 10.15%
재무 0.85%

① **마케팅/판매** | 할인 이벤트, 프로모션 등 고객 유치 및 홍보 전략에 대해 논의하거나 제품의 문제점에 대한 대안을 제시하는 내용이 자주 출제된다. 최근에는 SNS, 뉴스레터와 같은 마케팅 수단을 언급하는 대화가 증가하는 추세이다.

② **재무** | 매출, 고객 수, 이용률과 같은 성과 지표를 검토하며 실적을 분석하거나 대출이나 투자, 예산 분배 등 자금 관련 논의를 하는 대화가 주로 출제된다.

| 고난도 출제 포인트 |

POINT 1 대화 흐름 속에서 바뀐 정보를 묻는 문제

M: Can you pick me up in front of the bookstore?
W: I got it. I'll be there in 30 minutes.
M: Oh, actually, in front of the mall would be better.

Q Where will the man wait?
(A) In front of the shopping mall (o)
(B) In front of the bookstore (x)

→ 남자가 처음에는 자신을 서점 앞으로 데리러 와 달라고 했다가 이후에 장소를 쇼핑몰 앞으로 변경한 대화 내용을 듣고, 남자가 기다릴 장소를 고르는 문제이다. 나중에 언급된 쇼핑몰 앞을 놓치면 초기에 언급된 서점 앞을 정답으로 고르기 쉽다. 오답률: 47.4%

POINT 2 마케팅/판매 및 재무 주제에 자주 등장하는 고난도 어휘

inventory 재고	identical 동일한	intuitive 직관적인	eligible for ~의 대상이다	bulk order 대량 주문
referral 소개	verification 검증	warranty 보증서	interactive 상호적인	portable 휴대 가능한
contractor 도급업자	reliable 신뢰할 수 있는	realtor 부동산 업자	collaborate 협력하다	gimmick 수법

빈출 문제 집중 훈련

 D07_빈출

빈출 문제를 풀며 실전 감각을 키워보자. 어려운 문제는 박스에 표시하고, 채점 후 복습하여 취약점을 보완하자.

☐ **01** Where do the speakers most likely work?

(A) At a financial institution
(B) At a manufacturing plant
(C) At a retail outlet
(D) At an engineering firm

☐ **02** What is mentioned about A-13?

(A) It will be recalled.
(B) It will be discontinued.
(C) It will be discounted.
(D) It will be restocked.

☐ **03** What did the man place on the woman's desk?

(A) An installation invoice
(B) A store catalog
(C) An instructional manual
(D) A fiscal document

☐ **04** Why is the man calling?

(A) To negotiate a contract
(B) To share a meeting result
(C) To change a travel itinerary
(D) To set up an appointment

☐ **05** What does the woman want to discuss?

(A) Recruiting additional staff
(B) Extending a deadline
(C) Assigning a task
(D) Pursuing a business deal

☐ **06** What does the man agree to do when he returns?

(A) Organize a gathering
(B) Stop by the woman's office
(C) Appoint a team leader
(D) Reschedule a future trip

07 What problem do the speakers discuss?

(A) Some goods are out of stock.
(B) A proposal was not accepted.
(C) Product sales are low.
(D) A device is malfunctioning.

08 According to the man, what are consumers dissatisfied with?

(A) The selection of games
(B) The price of a console
(C) The cost of equipment
(D) The terms of a warranty

09 Why does the woman want to hold a meeting with other employees?

(A) To develop a survey
(B) To brainstorm ideas
(C) To prepare a budget
(D) To plan a launch

10 What does the man want to do?

(A) Proofread a manuscript
(B) Report some errors
(C) Review some data
(D) Contact a consultant

11 Where will the man go next?

(A) To a copy room
(B) To a print shop
(C) To a client's office
(D) To a reception area

12 What will Corinne most likely do next?

(A) Check a financial forecast
(B) Print out a document
(C) Calculate costs for a project
(D) Send some requested data

고난도 문제 완전 정복

D07_고난도

고난도 문제를 풀며, 완벽하게 실전을 대비하자. 어려운 문제는 박스에 표시하고, 채점 후 복습하여 완전히 내 것으로 만들자.

01 What problem does the woman mention?

(A) A complaint has been made.
(B) A component is unavailable.
(C) An event has been canceled.
(D) A product is defective.

02 What does the man mean when he says, "We'd better play it safe"?

(A) He would like to inform a director.
(B) He plans to announce a recall.
(C) He wants to delay a release date.
(D) He is going to conduct some tests.

03 What does the woman suggest?

(A) Prioritizing a task
(B) Canceling a presentation
(C) Advertising a product
(D) Forming a partnership

04 What does the man request?

(A) Some contact information
(B) A list of materials
(C) A legal document
(D) Some blueprints

05 What has the woman already done?

(A) Met with a contractor
(B) Toured a construction site
(C) Changed an agenda
(D) Corrected some mistakes

06 Why does the man need to leave?

(A) A colleague must be picked up.
(B) He has to send a package.
(C) A supervisor asked for help.
(D) He has a business appointment.

PART 4

DAY 08 음성 메시지 및 회의 발췌
DAY 09 안내, 방송, 광고
DAY 10 연설 및 소개

PART 4 | 알아보기

PART 4는 71번부터 100번까지 총 30문제로, 한 사람이 이야기하는 음성 메시지나 공지, 연설, 방송 등의 담화를 듣고 그와 관련된 3개의 문제를 푸는 파트이다. 문제지에는 각 문제의 질문과 4개의 보기가 제시되고, 담화와 질문을 음성으로 들려준다.

PART 4

Directions: In this part, you will listen to several short talks by a single speaker. These talks will not be printed and will only be spoken one time. For each talk, you will be asked to answer three questions. Select the best response and mark the corresponding letter (A), (B), (C), or (D) on your answer sheet.

---

71. Who most likely is the speaker?
    (A) A bank employee
    (B) A travel agent
    (C) A personal accountant
    (D) A project manager

72. What problem does the speaker mention?
    (A) A credit card has expired.
    (B) A bill has not been paid.
    (C) An application was suspended.
    (D) An account cannot be accessed.

73. What does the speaker say the listener should do?
    (A) Apply for a program
    (B) Submit a document
    (C) Have some photos taken
    (D) Contact a homeowner

74. What is being advertised?
    (A) A delivery company
    (B) A ride service
    (C) A luggage retailer
    (D) A car manufacturer

75. What is offered for free?
    (A) Drinks
    (B) A travel pouch
    (C) A drop-off service
    (D) Headphones

76. According to the speaker, how can the listeners receive a discount?
    (A) By using a mobile application
    (B) By entering a promotional code
    (C) By giving feedback online
    (D) By picking up a brochure

77. Where do the listeners most likely work?
    (A) At a service center
    (B) At a jewelry store
    (C) At a modeling agency
    (D) At a wedding venue

78. What will Mr. Foley do?
    (A) Meet with some customers
    (B) Inspect some goods
    (C) Discuss some products
    (D) Process an online order

79. Why does the speaker say, "Most of you in the sales department are new"?
    (A) To explain the purpose of a policy change
    (B) To stress the importance of a meeting
    (C) To reschedule a training session
    (D) To suggest some improvements

80. What is the announcement mainly about?
    (A) Monthly festivals
    (B) Remodeled bus stops
    (C) Route changes
    (D) Weather updates

81. What can the listeners find on a Web site?
    (A) A company's reviews
    (B) A sign-in sheet
    (C) An event timetable
    (D) A revised schedule

82. What are the listeners encouraged to do?
    (A) Reserve seats ahead of time
    (B) Plan to spend more time than usual
    (C) Drive instead of taking a bus
    (D) Register on a Web site

GO ON TO THE NEXT PAGE

PART 4 진행 방식을 알려주는 디렉션이 나온다.

고득점 전략
이 디렉션은 읽거나 들을 필요가 없다. 디렉션은 약 30초 로, PART 4의 질문과 보기를 읽으며 키워드에 표시를 해 두는 것이 좋다.

담화와 각 문제의 질문을 다음과 같이 들려준다.

Questions 71 through 73 refer to the following telephone message.

Good morning. This message is for Gary Boris. I'm contacting you on behalf of Hart Federal Bank. Unfortunately, your application for a home loan has been put on hold.
......

Number 71.
Who most likely is the speaker?
Number 72.
What problem does the speaker mention?
Number 73.
What does the speaker say the listener should do?

고득점 전략
담화를 모두 듣고 나서 문제를 풀려고 하면 내용이 기억나 지 않을 수 있으니 담화를 듣는 동안 바로 문제를 푸는 것이 좋다. 즉, 담화가 끝났을 때 정답도 선택되어 있어야 한다. 또한, 담화가 끝난 후 질문을 들려주는 시간에는 다음 세트 의 질문과 보기를 미리 확인하면서 주요 키워드에 표시를 해 두면, 다음 문제를 푸는 데 도움이 된다.

DAY 08 음성 메시지 및 회의 발췌

mp3 바로 듣기

| 최신 출제 경향 |

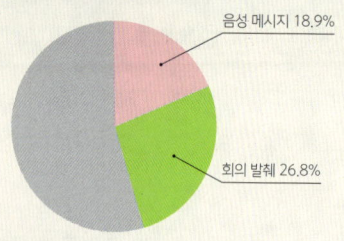
음성 메시지 18.9%
회의 발췌 26.8%

① **음성 메시지** | 제품 주문이나 배송 상태 확인, 투어나 행사장 예약 및 일정 조정, 시설 유지 보수를 위한 논의, 회의 및 발표 준비 등에 대한 내용이 자주 출제된다.

② **회의 발췌** | 판매 실적 분석, 정책 변경, 행사 준비 등에 대한 주요 안건이나 결정 사항을 중심으로 한 내용이 자주 출제된다. 최근에는 디지털 전환과 관련된 업무 방식 변화와 관련된 내용도 증가하는 추세이다.

| 고난도 출제 포인트 |

POINT 1 주요 단서가 담화 초반에만 등장해서 놓치기 쉬운 문제

W: Attention, staff! Our med clinic is testing a new app. Please use it and share your feedback! Your opinion matters because many colleagues will be using the app.

Q Who most likely is the listener?
(A) Doctors (o)
(B) Application developers (x)

→ 초반에 "우리 병원(Our med clinic)"에서 새 어플리케이션을 테스트할 것이라고 짧게 언급된 후, 이어서 어플리케이션에 대한 피드백을 요청하는 내용이 담화의 대부분을 차지하기 때문에 청자들의 직업을 '어플리케이션 개발자'로 착각할 수 있는 문제이다. 오답률: 43.0%

POINT 2 음성 메시지 및 회의 발췌에 자주 등장하는 고난도 어휘

questionnaire 설문지	cover (내용을) 다루다	grant 승인하다	file 제출하다	registration 등록
modify 수정하다	prototype 시제품	preliminary 예비의	shortage 부족	appropriate 적절한
publicize 홍보하다	spokesperson 대변인	retailer 소매점	commit 약속하다	assign 배정하다

빈출 문제 집중 훈련

🎧 D08_빈출

빈출 문제를 풀며 실전 감각을 키워보자. 어려운 문제는 박스에 표시하고, 채점 후 복습하여 취약점을 보완하자.

01 What was introduced a week ago?
(A) A government regulation
(B) Safety procedures
(C) A dress code
(D) Phone scripts

02 What does the speaker ask the listeners to do?
(A) Contact some customers
(B) Fill out a brief survey
(C) Print out some documents
(D) Read over an agreement

03 How will the speaker notify the listeners about future alterations?
(A) By posting on a Web site
(B) By distributing a document
(C) By sending them a message
(D) By holding an office meeting

04 Who is the speaker?
(A) A gardener
(B) A business owner
(C) An assistant
(D) An event coordinator

05 What does the speaker suggest the listener do?
(A) Send an invitation
(B) Tour a facility
(C) Reserve a different date
(D) Attend a party

06 What can Paris Gardens arrange for an extra charge?
(A) A musical performance
(B) Event decorations
(C) A larger space
(D) A catering service

07 Why is the firm organizing a special event for next week?

(A) To attract customers to sign up for a service
(B) To provide information on a new electronic device
(C) To show gratitude for its employees' hard work
(D) To launch an application for tablets

08 According to the speaker, who will be asked to attend the demonstration?

(A) A corporate executive
(B) Local residents
(C) A company spokesperson
(D) Media representatives

09 What are the listeners asked to do?

(A) Print out brochures
(B) Test a prototype
(C) Work at an event
(D) Show up early

10 Who most likely is the speaker calling?

(A) A construction supervisor
(B) A property owner
(C) An office manager
(D) A government official

11 What must the listener do before work begins?

(A) Evaluate a recent project
(B) Get approval from a supervisor
(C) Sign a legal agreement
(D) Conduct a preliminary inspection

12 According to the speaker, what is Gabriel Hernandez responsible for?

(A) Returning some building materials
(B) Filing some documentation
(C) Reviewing a permit application
(D) Overseeing some renovations

13 What type of business does the speaker work for?

(A) An electronics retailer
(B) A telecommunications firm
(C) A power company
(D) A consulting agency

14 What caused the problem?

(A) Scheduled maintenance
(B) Flood damage
(C) Supply shortages
(D) Circuit malfunctions

15 What should the listeners do if a problem is not resolved?

(A) File a complaint
(B) Call a hotline
(C) Talk to a technician
(D) Return a device

16 Where does the speaker work?

(A) At a rental agency
(B) At a service center
(C) At a parking facility
(D) At a supply store

17 What did the speaker do this morning?

(A) Met with a customer
(B) Assisted a colleague
(C) Processed a payment
(D) Inspected a facility

18 Why did Ms. Yoon receive a free service?

(A) A vehicle is under warranty.
(B) She was charged a certain amount.
(C) A coupon was used.
(D) She is a loyal customer.

고난도 문제 완전 정복

고난도 문제를 풀며, 완벽하게 실전을 대비하자. 어려운 문제는 박스에 표시하고, 채점 후 복습하여 완전히 내 것으로 만들자.

☐
01 Why did the speaker arrange the meeting?

(A) To ask for assistance
(B) To provide an update
(C) To describe a problem
(D) To announce a decision

☐
02 What did the speaker do last weekend?

(A) He donated to a charity.
(B) He visited a construction site.
(C) He helped to restore a local park.
(D) He cleaned garbage from waterways.

☐
03 What does the speaker say Rebecca will do?

(A) Show photos from an event
(B) Give a financial report
(C) Explain a registration process
(D) Discuss upcoming plans

☐
04 What is the message mainly about?

(A) A problem with a draft
(B) A revision to a contract
(C) A subscription for a publication
(D) A process for a payment

☐
05 What will most likely happen on August 20?

(A) A writer will provide a manuscript.
(B) A novel will be revised.
(C) A book will be published.
(D) An editor will approve a change.

☐
06 What does the speaker imply when she says, "This shouldn't be a problem for you"?

(A) She has reviewed a revised text.
(B) She thinks a deadline is reasonable.
(C) She intends to reassign a task.
(D) She has responded to an inquiry.

Queen Spa
2456 Brentwood Avenue, Chicago

Buy One Service, Get One Free

This coupon is valid from June 1 to June 30.

☐
07 Why is the speaker calling?

(A) To announce a cancellation
(B) To change an appointment
(C) To ask for a payment
(D) To clarify a request

☐
08 Look at the graphic. What service is the coupon valid for in June?

(A) Skin treatment
(B) Thai massage
(C) Foot massage
(D) Aromatherapy massage

☐
09 Why does the speaker need the man's decision quickly?

(A) To place an order
(B) To cancel a reservation
(C) To calculate a discount
(D) To assign an employee

DAY 09 안내, 방송, 광고

mp3 바로 듣기

최신 출제 경향

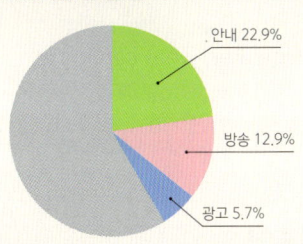
안내 22.9%
방송 12.9%
광고 5.7%

① **안내** | 공공장소나 사무실, 대중 교통 등에서 이루어지는 행사 일정 공지, 운영 시간 안내, 교통 시설 이용 안내가 주로 다뤄진다.

② **방송** | 뉴스 요약, 라디오 방송, 팟캐스트 등의 형태로 출제되고, 지역 축제 소개나 문화 행사 홍보와 같은 일상 생활 주제뿐만 아니라 긴급 상황 발생에 대한 대처 방안도 자주 등장한다.

③ **광고** | 다양한 상품 및 서비스 소개 또는 할인 혜택 홍보 등, 비즈니스 주제뿐만 아니라 일상 생활과 밀접한 광고가 출제된다.

고난도 출제 포인트

POINT 1
생소한 소재와 어려운 어휘가 등장하는 문제

M: Are you looking for sustainable options for your landscaping projects? Our biodegradable plant pots enrich the soil as they decompose. They've been popular among professionals in the field.	Q Who most likely are the listeners? (A) Landscape designers (o) (B) Environment experts (x)

→ 생소한 소재인 천연 재료로 만든 화분에 대한 담화에서 biodegradable(생분해되는), decompose(분해하다)와 같은 어려운 어휘들이 사용되어 담화의 내용을 파악하기 까다롭다. **오답률: 54.3%**

POINT 2
안내, 방송, 광고에 자주 등장하는 고난도 어휘

assortment 여러 가지 모음   complimentary 무료의   compartment 칸   reclaim 되찾다   component 부품
cosponsor 공동 후원하다   conventional 기존의   venue 행사장   traction 접지력   precaution 예방 조치
estimate 견적   fermentation 발효   boost 신장시키다   furnishing 가구   pharmaceutical 제약의

빈출 문제 집중 훈련

 D09_빈출

빈출 문제를 풀며 실전 감각을 키워보자. 어려운 문제는 박스에 표시하고, 채점 후 복습하여 취약점을 보완하자.

☐ **01** What products does the business sell?
(A) Home furnishings
(B) Office supplies
(C) Factory equipment
(D) Electronic components

☐ **02** What is mentioned about the business?
(A) It offers a wide range of goods.
(B) It is larger than other outlets.
(C) It is located in the downtown area.
(D) It provides fast delivery.

☐ **03** What is being offered to the listeners?
(A) Sample products
(B) Store memberships
(C) Price reductions
(D) Complimentary services

☐ **04** What event is being announced?
(A) A singing competition
(B) A gallery opening
(C) A community fair
(D) A music festival

☐ **05** What does the speaker say about the event?
(A) It will be downsized.
(B) It was extended by a day.
(C) It will last a weekend.
(D) It has free admission.

☐ **06** What is included with a ticket purchase?
(A) Beverage vouchers
(B) A parking pass
(C) Clothing items
(D) A phone accessory

07 Who is Juan Lopez?

(A) A radio host
(B) An event planner
(C) A movie actor
(D) A news anchor

08 Why does the speaker want to talk about *Low Tides*?

(A) It is very popular.
(B) It is being released soon.
(C) It just started filming.
(D) It won an award.

09 According to the speaker, what does Mr. Lopez do every year?

(A) Give out an award
(B) Direct a production
(C) Sponsor an art festival
(D) Organize an event

10 What impact does the speaker say the park will have?

(A) It will lead to new regulations.
(B) It will contribute to economic growth.
(C) It will help increase population.
(D) It will boost Danko Fairs' profits.

11 What is mentioned about Danko Fairs?

(A) It delayed the start of a construction project.
(B) It expanded into another country recently.
(C) It received funding from the government.
(D) It operates facilities in different communities.

12 What will most likely happen in June?

(A) Plans will be made public.
(B) Tickets will be put on sale.
(C) A schedule will be announced.
(D) Cost estimates will be determined.

13 What type of business is being advertised?

(A) A sporting goods retailer
(B) An athletic complex
(C) A community center
(D) A movie theater

14 According to the speaker, what service is available?

(A) Equipment rentals
(B) Facility tours
(C) Training sessions
(D) Advance bookings

15 Why would the listeners visit the business's Web site?

(A) To check a schedule
(B) To place an order
(C) To view images
(D) To confirm a reservation

16 Where is the announcement being made?

(A) In an airport
(B) On a train platform
(C) At a baggage claim
(D) At a bus station

17 What should the listeners do with large suitcases?

(A) Put them in an overhead compartment
(B) Send them separately
(C) Put them in a storage space
(D) Place them on a cart

18 What does the speaker say about the luggage tickets?

(A) They should be printed in advance.
(B) They will be required at a later time.
(C) They have been handed out.
(D) They must be turned in at a counter.

고난도 문제 완전 정복

🎧 D09_고난도

고난도 문제를 풀며, 완벽하게 실전을 대비하자. 어려운 문제는 박스에 표시하고, 채점 후 복습하여 완전히 내 것으로 만들자.

01 What is the podcast mainly about?

(A) Tips for driving in winter
(B) New transportation regulations
(C) Forecasted weather conditions
(D) Changes to insurance policies

02 What does the speaker recommend for travelers in mountainous areas?

(A) Downloading a map
(B) Bringing equipment
(C) Inspecting a vehicle
(D) Conserving fuel

03 What is a feature of the application?

(A) It provides alternate routes for drivers.
(B) It warns of unsafe road conditions.
(C) It transmits a vehicle's location.
(D) It shows when emergency personnel will arrive.

04 What type of business is being advertised?

(A) A heating system manufacturer
(B) A window installation company
(C) An auto repair shop
(D) A research laboratory

05 What does the speaker mean when she says, "Why not get the best of both worlds?"

(A) A new service is being introduced.
(B) Many options are currently available.
(C) An item for sale has multiple benefits.
(D) Special discounts are being offered.

06 What can the listeners do on the Web site?

(A) Check prices
(B) Purchase items
(C) Submit questions
(D) Download a catalog

Charlottesville Chocolates Tour Schedule	
Time	Area
8:00 A.M.	Fermentation room
9:00 A.M.	Drying racks
10:00 A.M.	Roasting area
11:00 A.M.	Packaging area

07 What does the speaker say about Charlottesville Chocolates?

(A) It is owned by a local farmer.
(B) It is a major regional producer.
(C) It purchases processed cocoa.
(D) It developed a new flavor of candy.

08 What distinguishes Charlottesville Chocolates from its competitors?

(A) Its production methods
(B) Its marketing techniques
(C) Its high profitability
(D) Its distribution network

09 Look at the graphic. When will the seed harvesting room be visited?

(A) At 8:00 A.M.
(B) At 9:00 A.M.
(C) At 10:00 A.M.
(D) At 11:00 A.M.

DAY 10 연설 및 소개

| 최신 출제 경향 |

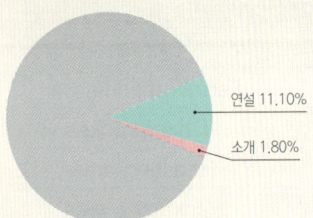

연설 11.10%
소개 1.80%

① **연설** | 모임이나 행사장에서 하는 인사말, 오리엔테이션 설명, 사내 정책 변경 등에 대한 내용이 주로 나온다.

② **소개** | 시상식 수상자, 기조연설자 등 인물을 소개하는 내용이 주로 나오고, 신제품, 서비스, 기관 등을 소개하는 내용도 출제된다.

| 고난도 출제 포인트 |

POINT 1
화자의 말에 함축된 의도를 추론해야 하는 문제

W: Hi, I'm going to write some design principles on the board. If you're familiar with them, please raise your hand. I have been a graphic designer for a decade, and I will be teaching the class today.

Q Why should listeners raise their hands?
(A) To offer an explanation (○)
(B) To ask about a design (×)

→ 담화에서 화자가 'If you're familiar ~ raise your hand'라고 말한 의도가 청자에게 디자인 원리에 관한 설명을 요청하고 있다는 것임을 추론해서 정답을 골라야 하는 어려운 문제이다. 오답률: 43.6%

POINT 2
연설 및 소개에 자주 등장하는 고난도 어휘

launch 출시(하다)	physician 의사	inquiry 문의	terminate 끝내다	applause 박수
undergo 겪다	achievement 공로	commission 의뢰하다	personnel 직원	emerging 떠오르는
procedure 절차	distribute 분배하다	entrepreneur 기업가	discontinue 중단하다	association 협회

빈출 문제 집중 훈련

🎧 D10_빈출

빈출 문제를 풀며 실전 감각을 키워보자. 어려운 문제는 박스에 표시하고, 채점 후 복습하여 취약점을 보완하자.

☐ 01 What is the purpose of the talk?
(A) To inform a patient
(B) To explain a procedure
(C) To announce a closure
(D) To ask for suggestions

☐ 02 What are new patients required to do?
(A) Talk to a physician
(B) Set up an appointment
(C) Wait in a reception area
(D) Fill out a document

☐ 03 What will the speaker distribute?
(A) Application forms
(B) User passwords
(C) Informational handouts
(D) Employee ID cards

☐ 04 Where most likely are the listeners?
(A) At a retirement celebration
(B) At a graduation party
(C) At a business opening
(D) At an awards ceremony

☐ 05 What most likely is the speaker's job?
(A) Store clerk
(B) Chef
(C) Waiter
(D) Food critic

☐ 06 What does the speaker say about Mali Kaya?
(A) She has accepted a new position.
(B) She will open a restaurant.
(C) She leads an organization.
(D) She relocated to Chicago recently.

07 What is taking place?

(A) A business seminar
(B) A product launch
(C) A board meeting
(D) An employee gathering

08 Why does *The Wabash Herald* want to change its business model?

(A) To reduce unnecessary spending
(B) To access foreign markets
(C) To target a specific demographic
(D) To expand its printing operations

09 What does the speaker encourage the listeners to do?

(A) Gather feedback
(B) Sign up subscribers
(C) Update a plan
(D) Verify data

10 What will the listeners receive?

(A) Customer surveys
(B) Employee timecards
(C) Sign-in sheets
(D) Personnel handbooks

11 What does the speaker ask the listeners to do?

(A) Take a short break
(B) Return to work
(C) Review some guidelines
(D) Propose some solutions

12 What does the speaker offer to do?

(A) Make an outline
(B) Organize training sessions
(C) Demonstrate a device
(D) Answer questions

고난도 문제 완전 정복

고난도 문제를 풀며, 완벽하게 실전을 대비하자. 어려운 문제는 박스에 표시하고, 채점 후 복습하여 완전히 내 것으로 만들자.

01 What is the purpose of the convention?

(A) To showcase new medical equipment
(B) To provide details on industry trends
(C) To promote emerging companies
(D) To attract potential investors

02 What does the speaker encourage the listeners to do?

(A) Check a schedule
(B) Visit some booths
(C) Prepare some questions
(D) Read a publication

03 What does the speaker imply when he says, "The party will be held in the Greenfield Ballroom"?

(A) An event will begin in a few minutes.
(B) An attendee is in the wrong room.
(C) A venue was changed.
(D) A space is too small for an activity.

04 What was Capital Group hired to do?

(A) Promote a board game
(B) Conduct market research
(C) Distribute goods
(D) Analyze a budget

05 According to the speaker, what is the problem?

(A) A company cannot fulfill an order.
(B) An employee filed a complaint.
(C) A product got negative feedback.
(D) A factory has to close down.

06 What has the speaker decided to do?

(A) Arrange a focus group
(B) Respond to questions
(C) Request more funding
(D) Discontinue a product

PART 5&6

DAY 01   명사와 대명사
DAY 02   형용사와 부사
DAY 03   동사
DAY 04   to 부정사, 동명사, 분사
DAY 05   전치사, 접속사, 관계사
DAY 06   어휘와 어구

PART 5&6 | 알아보기

PART 5는 101번부터 130번까지 총 30문제로, 한 문장의 빈칸에 알맞은 문법 사항이나 어휘를 4개의 보기 중에서 골라 채우는 파트이다. PART 6은 131번부터 146번까지 총 16문제로, 한 지문 내의 4개 빈칸에 알맞은 문법 사항, 어휘, 그리고 문장을 4개의 보기 중에서 골라 채우는 파트이다.

PART 5

리딩 영역은 총 3개의 파트로 구성되어 있고, 약 75분간 진행된다는 디렉션이 나온다. 그 아래에 PART 5 진행 방식을 알려주는 디렉션이 이어서 온다.

고득점 전략
이 디렉션은 읽을 필요가 없다. 리딩은 PART 7을 풀 시간을 충분히 확보하는 것이 중요하므로, PART5의 30문제는 11분 안에 푸는 것을 목표로 하는 것이 좋다.

PART 5는 문법과 어휘를 묻는 문제가 출제되는데, 30문제 중 약 20문제가 문법을 묻고, 약 10문제가 어휘를 묻는다.

고득점 전략
문법 문제는 문장 전체를 해석하려 하지 말고, 빈칸 앞뒤를 보고 문장 구조를 파악하여 시간을 절약하는 것이 좋다. 어휘 문제는 전체 문장의 흐름을 파악한 후 빈칸 주변 단어와의 호응 관계를 주목하여 푸는 것이 좋다.

PART 6

PART 6 진행 방식을 알려주는 디렉션이 나온다.

고득점 전략
이 디렉션도 읽을 필요가 없으므로 바로 문제를 풀기 시작한다. PART 6의 16문제는 8분 안에 푸는 것을 목표로 하는 것이 좋다.

PART 6는 문법 문제가 평균 7~8문제, 어휘 문제가 평균 4~5문제, 문장 고르기 문제가 4문제 출제된다.

고득점 전략
먼저 문법과 어휘 문제를 빈칸 앞뒤 위주로 보며 빠르게 풀고 난 뒤, 문장 문제를 가장 마지막에 풀면 시간을 절약할 수 있다.

DAY 01 명사와 대명사

| 최신 출제 경향 |

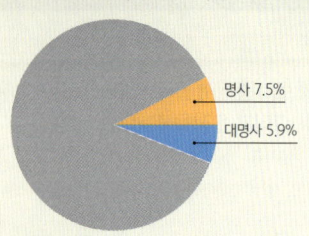

명사 7.5%
대명사 5.9%

① **명사** | 빈칸 앞뒤만 보고 명사 자리임을 파악하면 바로 정답을 고를 수 있는 쉬운 문제가 주로 출제되지만, 최근에는 형태가 비슷한 명사들 중 문맥에 맞는 것을 골라야 하는 고난도 문제가 증가하고 있다.

② **대명사** | 쉽게 풀 수 있는 인칭대명사가 가장 많이 출제되고, 그다음으로 부정대명사가 많이 출제된다. 최근에는 부정대명사 중 anyone, one, neither가 가장 많이 출제되고 있다.

| 고난도 출제 포인트 |

POINT 1 형태가 비슷한 명사의 의미 차이를 구별하는 문제
Efforts to reduce household plastic (**use** / using) include promoting reusable items. 오답률: 56.0%
→ plastic과 함께 '플라스틱 사용'이라는 의미의 복합 명사 plastic use를 만드는 명사 use가 정답이다. 타동사 use의 동명사 using은 뒤에 목적어가 있어야 한다.

POINT 2 전치사 뒤에 소유대명사가 나오는 문제
This strategic approach represents the most innovative business model of (him / **his**). 오답률: 71.8%
→ 전치사 of의 목적어 자리이고, '그의 사업 모델 중 가장 혁신적인 것'이라는 의미여야 하므로 소유대명사 his가 정답이다. him은 '그를 나타내는 사업 모델'이라는 어색한 의미가 된다.

POINT 3 셀 수 있을 때와 셀 수 없을 때 의미가 달라지는 명사를 구별하는 문제
The shelving system will require some (**assembly** / assemblies) before installation in the office. 오답률: 64.8%
→ assembly가 '조립'의 의미로 쓰일 때 셀 수 없는 명사이기 때문에 단수형 assembly가 정답이다. 참고로, assembly가 셀 수 있는 명사로 쓰일 때는 '의회, 집회'의 의미이다.

빈출 문제 집중 훈련

빈출 문제를 풀며 실전 감각을 키워보자. 어려운 문제는 박스에 표시하고, 채점 후 복습하여 취약점을 보완하자.

PART 5

01 Bryson Insurance developed a ------- that reduced the amount of time needed to evaluate a claim.

(A) procedural (B) procedurally
(C) procedure (D) proceed

02 Ms. Tang's work will be passed on to another member of her team, as ------- will be taking a leave of absence.

(A) she (B) her
(C) hers (D) herself

03 Michael Anderson finds ------- too overwhelmed by the volume of paperwork to deal with and needs some assistance.

(A) he (B) his
(C) him (D) himself

04 At Friday's press conference, a spokesperson from City Hall gave an official ------- regarding the mayor's plans.

(A) state (B) statement
(C) stated (D) stating

05 The article features a ------- of the best travel destinations in Europe with detailed descriptions and helpful tips.
(A) select
(B) selection
(C) selecting
(D) selector

06 BVG Home Furnishings has been consistent in showing ------- in its merchandise displays, which are attractive and appealing to buyers.
(A) create
(B) creatively
(C) creativity
(D) creative

07 CleanMaster has tested every competing laundry detergent and claims that ------- is the most effective against tough stains and odors.
(A) they
(B) their
(C) theirs
(D) themselves

08 Recent reports demonstrate that Southeast Asian countries have decreased their ------- on fossil fuels by using alternative energy sources.
(A) reliance
(B) relies
(C) reliable
(D) reliability

09 The Namath Research Center is expanding its data ------- capabilities to support advanced scientific investigations.
(A) analysis
(B) analyze
(C) analyzed
(D) analyzes

10 The most visited ------- in Smithfield National Park is the Busch Waterfall, which is the tallest in the country.
(A) attract
(B) attracted
(C) attracts
(D) attraction

11 Upon checking in at the car rental service at the airport, Mr. McBride learned that he had to pay an unexpected fuel -------.
(A) surcharging
(B) surcharges
(C) surcharge
(D) surcharged

12 Customers can order larger beverages at ------- extra cost by presenting their Coffee Tree loyalty cards.
(A) none
(B) no
(C) not
(D) nor

13 Both candidates were highly skilled and showed great potential during the final evaluation, but ------- received the offer.
(A) himself
(B) neither
(C) anybody
(D) whoever

14 Government grants are available to ------- who are developing green energy solutions.
(A) those
(B) them
(C) someone
(D) anyone

15 As the artist's work has so many -------, the gallery has reserved a bigger room for the exhibition of the paintings.
(A) admired
(B) admirers
(C) admires
(D) admirable

16 Owell Mining's management team will take the necessary steps to ensure that ------- remain competitive in the global market.
(A) their
(B) they
(C) them
(D) theirs

Questions 17-20 refer to the following e-mail.

To: Rob Whitlock <robwhitlock@mail.co.uk>
From: Sandy Jenson <sandy@divinefoods.com>
Subject: Service request
Date: November 15

Dear Mr. Whitlock,

I am contacting you regarding the recent inquiry you made with our ------- company. The request we received indicates that you need our services for a corporate dinner taking place on December 23. According to your e-mail, there will be roughly 100 people attending the -------, and you would like both meat and vegetarian menu options.

-------. In order to proceed, we will require a consultation session to select the menu and discuss further event details. To schedule an appointment at ------- earliest convenience, please call me at 555-0294. I will need to know in advance when you are coming, so I can make the necessary preparations.

All the best,
Sandy Jenson
Client coordinator
Divine Foods

17 (A) landscape
   (B) design
   (C) catering
   (D) accounting

18 (A) gatherer
   (B) gathered
   (C) gather
   (D) gathering

19 (A) We made sure to reserve a larger table for the group.
   (B) Please indicate which dish you liked best on the form.
   (C) I am happy to say that we are available on that date.
   (D) The item you selected is unfortunately sold out.

20 (A) you
   (B) yours
   (C) your
   (D) yourself

고난도 문제 완전 정복

고난도 문제를 풀며, 완벽하게 실전을 대비하자. 어려운 문제는 박스에 표시하고, 채점 후 복습하여 완전히 내 것으로 만들자.

01 Ms. Carter's development of the innovative marketing strategy was an achievement of ------- that caught the attention of senior management.

(A) she (B) her
(C) hers (D) herself

02 The committee found several potential flaws in the ------- presented by the research department.

(A) suggesting (B) suggestions
(C) suggestive (D) suggested

03 The transportation authority announced that it will impose a $25 fine on ------- driver caught in violation of the parking policy.

(A) any (B) other
(C) few (D) whole

04 The Immigration Service usually grants ------- on tourist visas provided they have not expired yet at the time of application.

(A) extend (B) extending
(C) extents (D) extensions

05 Although some members of the executives attended the conference, ------- were unable to participate due to scheduling conflicts.

(A) those (B) another
(C) others (D) either

06 The key to the company's recent success was the ------- of cutting-edge software development tools.

(A) acquisition (B) acquired
(C) acquires (D) acquire

07 The electric scooter produced by Mobility Tech is much more expensive than ------- of its major competitor.

(A) what (B) such
(C) that (D) all

08 At the online retailer's warehouse, the ------- of items for delivery is done swiftly using automated machinery.

(A) pack (B) packer
(C) packed (D) packing

09 The National Science Institute's evaluation committee found that ------- of the submitted proposals met all of the required criteria.

(A) none (B) nothing
(C) nobody (D) anything

10 The digital marketing industry has seen significant growth as ------- shift their focus toward online channels.

(A) advertisements (B) advertising
(C) advertisers (D) advertises

11 Premium account holders can make unlimited ------- between their checking and savings accounts without additional fees.

(A) transferable (B) transferring
(C) transfers (D) transferred

12 Since Dr. Mbeki and Dr. Gupta are experts in renewable energy, ------- would be an excellent keynote speaker for the environmental symposium.

(A) neither (B) which
(C) either (D) whoever

DAY 02 형용사와 부사

고득점 핵심 노트

| 최신 출제 경향 |

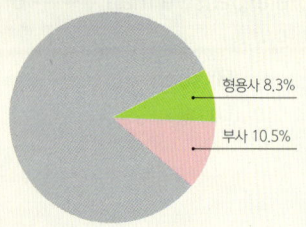
형용사 8.3%
부사 10.5%

① **형용사** | 빈칸 앞뒤만 보고 형용사 자리임을 파악하면 바로 정답을 고를 수 있는 쉬운 문제가 많이 출제되지만, 최근에는 형태가 비슷한 형용사들 중 문맥에 맞는 것을 골라야 하는 고난도 문제가 증가하고 있다.

② **부사** | 빈도 부사 문제가 꾸준히 출제된다. 특히 PART 6에서는 앞뒤 문장의 의미 관계를 정확히 이해해야 정답을 고를 수 있는 까다로운 접속부사 문제가 출제된다.

| 고난도 출제 포인트 |

POINT 1 형태가 비슷한 형용사 구별하여 채우는 문제
The clinic requires a $60 (diagnosable / **diagnostic**) fee for a comprehensive health examination. 오답률: 67.0%
→ 명사 fee를 수식하면서 '진단 비용'이라는 의미여야 하므로 '진단의'라는 의미의 형용사 diagnostic이 정답이다. 참고로, diagnosable은 '진단할 수 있는'이라는 의미이다.

POINT 2 보어 자리에 오면서 특정 전치사와 함께 쓰이는 형용사
The corporate logo designed by top branding experts is (**symbolic** / symbolized) of the company's innovative spirit. 오답률: 62.6%
→ be 동사(is) 뒤의 보어 자리에 오면서 of와 함께 '~을 상징하는'이라는 의미를 만드는 형용사 symbolic이 정답이다.

POINT 3 be 동사 뒤에 오면서 문장 전체를 수식하는 부사와 주격 보어 형용사를 구별하는 문제
The significant drop in sales was (possible / **possibly**) a reflection of consumer trends. 오답률: 62.6%
→ 문장 전체를 수식하면서 '아마도 ~였을 것이다'라는 의미를 만드는 부사 possibly가 정답이다.

빈출 문제 집중 훈련

빈출 문제를 풀며 실전 감각을 키워보자. 어려운 문제는 박스에 표시하고, 채점 후 복습하여 취약점을 보완하자.

PART 5

01 The personnel manager screened dozens of applicants until a ------- candidate was found for the position.

(A) suit (B) suitable
(C) suitably (D) suiting

02 The newly built Masterson Convention Center won several architectural awards for its ------- concept and design.

(A) innovation (B) innovative
(C) innovatively (D) innovate

03 Last week, the CEO ------- authorized a raise in pay for all full-time staff working at the factory in Jakarta.

(A) officiate (B) officially
(C) officials (D) official

04 The moving company apologized for damaging the furniture and said the client would be compensated -------.

(A) accorded (B) according
(C) accords (D) accordingly

05 The success of the Greenway fundraiser was attributed to ------- individual donations by the organization's members.
(A) many
(B) much
(C) very
(D) rather

06 On most days, the customer service line is busy and must be ------- dialed before a representative becomes available.
(A) repetitive
(B) repetition
(C) repeatedly
(D) repeated

07 Darwood Manufacturing frequently sends promising young employees to leadership seminars as they will likely become ------- staff someday.
(A) manage
(B) managerial
(C) manages
(D) managed

08 Although ------- errors are to be expected when analyzing large amounts of data, researchers must convey accurate information overall.
(A) less
(B) some
(C) both
(D) every

09 ------- with its recent decline in sales revenue, Morton Electronics is still a highly profitable company.
(A) Even
(B) Early
(C) Ever since
(D) So that

10 The newly appointed head of accounting approaches challenges more ------- than the previous manager did.
(A) system
(B) systemic
(C) systematic
(D) systemically

11 Scientists at the Center for Agriculture are working on crop varieties that are highly ------- to common plant diseases.
(A) resist
(B) resistance
(C) resistant
(D) resistantly

12 Job applications for the sales position should be handed in ------- to Capita's human resources department.
(A) direct
(B) directed
(C) directs
(D) directly

13 Established 20 years -------, CyberPulse Dynamics continues to challenge traditional approaches in cybersecurity.
(A) previous
(B) ago
(C) later
(D) yet

14 The feedback from clients regarding our customer service has been ------- positive since the implementation of the new response protocol.
(A) noticeably
(B) notices
(C) noticeable
(D) noticing

15 ------- any space remained in the auditorium for the real estate agents who arrived at the conference late.
(A) Never
(B) Unlikely
(C) Slightly
(D) Hardly

16 The manufacturing processes employed at all Virgo Star factories are ------- with environmental sustainability guidelines.
(A) compliant
(B) compliantly
(C) compliance
(D) complied

PART 6

Questions 17-20 refer to the following e-mail.

To: Hunter Leitch <hunterleitch@shag.com>
From: Marvin Goodly <marvingoodly@shag.com>
Date: January 20
Subject: Sales report

I appreciate your preparing the sales report for last year. Overall, it is quite thorough, and the layout is easy to follow. -------, the chart is logical and straightforward to interpret.
              17

However, I would like to request a few minor modifications. -------. First, there should be some more
                                                                18
details on which region accounted for the ------- number of purchases of Armin area rugs, since
                                            19
that is the only product we presently offer internationally. Because we are considering expanding our overseas market, this information could be helpful. Also, I would like to know more about the change in the way Dudley rugs were marketed. The report should ------- indicate if the new strategy
                                                                                          20
had any significant impact on the number sold. If you have any questions, please do not hesitate to ask.

Best wishes,
Marvin Goodly

17. (A) Granted
    (B) Either way
    (C) In particular
    (D) In reality

18. (A) You were highly recommended for the position.
    (B) We found a number of typographical errors.
    (C) I hope they won't take too much time.
    (D) Let me know if I understood your requests correctly.

19. (A) great
    (B) greater
    (C) greatly
    (D) greatest

20. (A) clarity
    (B) clear
    (C) clearly
    (D) clearance

고난도 문제 완전 정복

고난도 문제를 풀며, 완벽하게 실전을 대비하자. 어려운 문제는 박스에 표시하고, 채점 후 복습하여 완전히 내 것으로 만들자.

01 After listening to proposals from the two marketing teams, Mr. Kowalski determined that ------- option seemed appropriate.

(A) several (B) most
(C) neither (D) none

02 Researchers found no ------- differences of statistical significance in patients' responses to the new treatment.

(A) observation (B) observable
(C) observing (D) observant

03 The production schedule has been running -------, so the supervisor has no choice but to add another shift.

(A) lateness (B) late
(C) lately (D) latest

04 The business development team is currently in the ------- phase of its overseas expansion project.

(A) explore (B) exploratory
(C) explorations (D) explored

05 ------- party in the lawsuit can submit additional evidence during the trial as long as all procedural rules are observed.

(A) Indeed (B) Still
(C) Inside (D) Either

06 Investors will visit the manufacturing plant ------- this year to assess its production capabilities before making a decision.

(A) later (B) almost
(C) immediately (D) soon

07 The online education startup Forsante as of now has ------- two small offices in the San Jose metropolitan area.

(A) else (B) only
(C) including (D) beyond

08 Sterkis Tech is constantly looking for ------- experienced engineers to lead its product development teams.

(A) highly (B) high
(C) higher (D) highest

09 Our new platform is incredibly responsive and, -------, users have experienced seamless interactions.

(A) first of all (B) on the contrary
(C) as an alternative (D) more importantly

10 Ostia Wellness Center charges an affordable ------- fee for a screening to detect early indicators of poor health.

(A) diagnose (B) diagnosable
(C) diagnostic (D) diagnosed

11 Sales representatives ------- travel to remote locations except when critical client presentations are required.

(A) little (B) seldom
(C) far (D) almost

12 Scientists at the Halston Institute have been investigating the ------- factors contributing to climate change for over three decades.

(A) determine (B) determinable
(C) determining (D) determination

정답 · 해석 · 해설 p.62

DAY 03 동사

| 최신 출제 경향 |

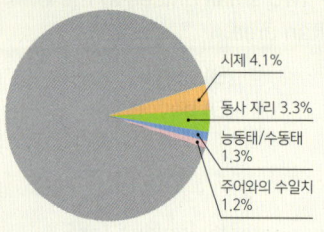

시제 4.1%
동사 자리 3.3%
능동태/수동태 1.3%
주어와의 수일치 1.2%

① **시제** | 최근에는 현재완료진행 시제 문제가 까다롭게 출제되고 있다.
② **동사 자리** | 조동사 뒤의 빈칸에 동사원형을 고르는 문제가 가장 많이 출제된다.
③ **능동태/수동태** | 4형식이나 5형식 동사의 수동태를 고르는 어려운 문제들이 출제된다.
④ **주어와의 수일치** | 주어와 동사 사이에 긴 수식어가 있어 까다로운 수일치 문제가 꾸준히 출제된다.

| 고난도 출제 포인트 |

POINT 1 시간을 나타내는 종속절에 알맞은 시제를 채우는 문제
The software will not be released until it (will be tested / **has been tested**) thoroughly. 오답률: 63.0%
→ until이 이끄는 절이 '테스트가 완료되기 전까지는 출시되지 않을 것'이라는 의미이므로 완료 시제 has been tested가 정답이다.

POINT 2 자동사의 올바른 분사 형태를 채우는 문제
In the tech industry, operational expenses have been (**rising** / risen) gradually for years. 오답률: 62.0%
→ rise는 자동사로 수동태를 만들 수 없으므로 현재분사 rising이 정답이다.

POINT 3 긴 주어로 인해 동사 자리를 찾기 어려운 문제
Customer service response times (variable / **vary**) depending on support team workload. 오답률: 53.2%
→ 문장에 동사가 없으므로 동사 vary가 정답이다. 주어가 Customer service response times로 길기 때문에 문장 구조 파악이 어렵다.

빈출 문제 집중 훈련

빈출 문제를 풀며 실전 감각을 키워보자. 어려운 문제는 박스에 표시하고, 채점 후 복습하여 취약점을 보완하자.

PART 5

01 Mr. Mendoza ------- a designer to handle the interior decoration of his new home last month.
(A) hired (B) has hired
(C) is hiring (D) will hire

02 A National Medical Association committee composed of nine officials ------- one member each year to represent the group at professional gatherings.
(A) choose (B) chooses
(C) choosing (D) chosen

03 Bridgeport's annual craft fair is ------- in the main auditorium of the Oak Bay Community Center.
(A) holding (B) hold
(C) holds (D) held

04 The city government should ------- problems commonly faced by small business owners, like high taxes and complex regulations.
(A) addressing (B) addressed
(C) addresses (D) address

05 Mr. Didier ------- from his business trip to London next Wednesday, just in time for an important client meeting.

(A) return
(B) will return
(C) returned
(D) returning

06 Mai-Thai Resort in Phuket ------- right beside the beach and is just a 10-minute drive from the airport.

(A) situates
(B) has situated
(C) is situated
(D) situating

07 While Ms. Khalil was making final revisions on her analysis of the marketing data, she realized she ------- out some key information.

(A) leave
(B) leaving
(C) is left
(D) had left

08 All orders made through Bergdorf Clothing's online store ------- within two days of purchase to the buyer's home address.

(A) sent
(B) will send
(C) are sent
(D) were sending

09 In the coming weeks, the accounting team ------- the quarterly financial reports for the board meeting.

(A) prepare
(B) preparing
(C) was preparing
(D) will be preparing

10 Two members of the administrative department ------- a report once all of the information has been collected.

(A) have submitted
(B) are submitted
(C) will submit
(D) to submit

11 The building of the new hospital in Bendersville was completely ------- by federal and state government grants.

(A) funding
(B) funds
(C) funded
(D) fund

12 The branch manager requested that employees ------- at least two hours of their time each quarter to professional development.

(A) dedicate
(B) dedicates
(C) have dedicated
(D) are dedicating

13 ------- up the interior of your home with colorful patterned wallpaper from Desmond Design.

(A) Bright
(B) Brighten
(C) Brightens
(D) Brightening

14 The season premiere of the TV show *Tucker Grant* ------- by a record audience of 15.8 million.

(A) was enjoying
(B) was enjoyed
(C) will enjoy
(D) enjoys

15 Because Wilson Construction ------- the budget for the new sports stadium, it could not modify the design.

(A) to finalize
(B) is finalized
(C) had finalized
(D) has been finalized

16 All those who ------- at the community center's fundraising event will receive a certificate.

(A) assists
(B) assisted
(C) assisting
(D) to assist

PART 6

Questions 17-20 refer to the following letter.

March 15
Anthony Christie
121 Washington Avenue
Jackson, MS 39211

Dear Mr. Christie,

As discussed at our last meeting, we are willing to hire you as a senior research scientist. Please review the enclosed contract to learn the conditions of your -------. If you choose to accept the offer, we propose a start date of Monday, April 4.
                                                                                              17

At a minimum, your job responsibilities ------- conducting research on various chemical applications. Other tasks may be assigned as the need arises. -------.
                                                      18   19

Your starting salary will be $7,000 a month. Other benefits ------- in the enclosed contract. If everything looks satisfactory, please inform me of your decision by replying to this letter before March 25.
                                                                                20

Yours Truly,
Jennifer Williams
Apex Chemicals

17 (A) assistance
    (B) employment
    (C) settlement
    (D) membership

18 (A) included
    (B) have included
    (C) will include
    (D) were included

19 (A) You will have to justify your department's activities to management.
    (B) Just in case, we have given these assignments to another staff member.
    (C) Of course, these will be limited to your areas of expertise.
    (D) We believe that everyone can benefit from occasional training.

20 (A) detail
    (B) are detailing
    (C) will detail
    (D) are detailed

고난도 문제 완전 정복

고난도 문제를 풀며, 완벽하게 실전을 대비하자. 어려운 문제는 박스에 표시하고, 채점 후 복습하여 완전히 내 것으로 만들자.

01 Mr. Nussbaum ------- to a three-year contract with Decker Engineering after his company made 3D printing technology feasible.

(A) agrees (B) agreeing
(C) agreed (D) has been agreed

02 A number of systemic vulnerabilities with the software ------- avoided if the company had conducted more comprehensive testing.

(A) were being (B) will be
(C) will have been (D) could have been

03 Museum employees have blocked off a section to prevent visitors from wandering into the area where a painting -------.

(A) is restoring (B) having been restored
(C) had restored (D) is being restored

04 Consumers are ------- to be significantly influenced by online reviews when choosing which model of smartphone to purchase.

(A) thinking (B) thoughts
(C) thinks (D) thought

05 Ms. Rodriguez ------- European banking regulations and then report her findings to the board of directors.

(A) was researching (B) has researched
(C) will research (D) is researching

06 CyberDyne was forced to scale back its efforts in developing artificial intelligence models because costs had been steadily -------.

(A) rise (B) rose
(C) rising (D) risen

07 The manager has recommended that the team ------- the project timeline to accommodate potential delays.

(A) revise (B) has revised
(C) is revising (D) will revise

08 According to the Harford Transportation Department's records, not all parking tickets issued last year ------- paid yet.

(A) were being (B) have been
(C) to be (D) to have been

09 Reese Technologies developed a software application that ------- financial analysts to accurately track market fluctuations.

(A) allow (B) allows
(C) to allow (D) allowing

10 Mr. Reynolds must postpone advertising the position until the list of job requirements ------- by the human resources manager.

(A) approves (B) is approving
(C) has been approved (D) will be approved

11 The remarkable generosity of donors ------- the foundation to provide scholarships to hundreds of deserving students.

(A) enable (B) enabling
(C) has enabled (D) have been enabled

12 The IT support team was glad to ------- a cost-effective solution without having to replace the entire system.

(A) be found (B) have found
(C) finds (D) found

정답·해석·해설 p.65

DAY 04 to 부정사, 동명사, 분사

고득점 핵심 노트

최신 출제 경향

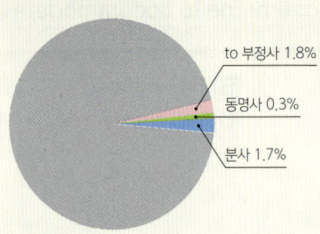
to 부정사 1.8%
동명사 0.3%
분사 1.7%

① **to 부정사** | 사역동사의 목적격 보어 자리에 오는 원형부정사를 골라야 하는 고난도 문제가 출제된다.

② **동명사** | 전치사 to 뒤에 동명사를 채우는 문제가 많이 출제된다.

③ **분사** | 분사와 분사가 수식하는 명사 간의 능동 및 수동 관계를 파악하여 현재분사나 과거분사를 선택하는 문제가 꾸준히 출제된다.

고난도 출제 포인트

POINT 1 전치사 뒤에서 명사를 수식하는 현재분사를 채우는 문제
Due to (worsen / **worsening**) economic conditions, profits declined substantially. 오답률: 51.9%
→ 전치사(Due to) 뒤에 오는 명사구(economic conditions)를 수식할 수 있는 현재분사 worsening이 정답이다. 앞의 to를 to 부정사로 혼동하여 동사원형을 고르지 않도록 주의한다.

POINT 2 준사역동사 뒤에 원형 부정사를 채우는 문제
Regular feedback helps (encouraging / **encourage**) team members to improve their performance. 오답률: 51.8%
→ 준사역동사 help는 원형 부정사나 to 부정사를 목적어로 취할 수 있으므로 원형 부정사 encourage가 정답이다.

POINT 3 전치사 뒤에서 명사구를 목적어로 취하는 동명사를 채우는 문제
The guide suggests ways of (**appreciating** / appreciative) nature photography. 오답률: 65.8%
→ 전치사(of) 뒤에 오면서 명사구(nature photography)를 목적어로 취할 수 있는 동명사 appreciating이 정답이다.

빈출 문제 집중 훈련

빈출 문제를 풀며 실전 감각을 키워보자. 어려운 문제는 박스에 표시하고, 채점 후 복습하여 취약점을 보완하자.

PART 5

01 Instead of donating money to help the flood victims, Mercer Energy Inc. has decided ------- needed services and goods.

(A) contribution (B) contributed
(C) to contribute (D) will contribute

02 The consultant suggested ------- on the healthy aspects of Chordolla Chips' product to differentiate it from competing brands.

(A) focus (B) focused
(C) focuses (D) focusing

03 Widely ------- as a leading figure in the solar industry, Mr. Baker delivered an insightful presentation at the energy convention.

(A) recognized (B) recognizing
(C) recognize (D) to recognize

04 ------- the free trial from CrossArts Media, users have to download and register on the company's mobile app.

(A) Claim (B) Claims
(C) To claim (D) Claiming

05 Wentworth TV Studios is preparing a content development schedule for its recently ------- documentary film division.
(A) creating
(B) create
(C) creates
(D) created

06 Since ------- Anil Kahn as CEO of Electa, Ms. Harris has announced a large-scale restructuring initiative for the organization.
(A) replacing
(B) replaced
(C) replace
(D) replacement

07 Using various advanced ------- devices, meteorologists can predict some weather changes several days ahead.
(A) measure
(B) will measure
(C) measuring
(D) to measure

08 Let the experts at Mentoria Professional Education ------- a tailored training program for your employees.
(A) design
(B) designs
(C) to design
(D) designing

09 HR departments seeking ------- workplace diversity should establish inclusive recruitment strategies.
(A) foster
(B) fosters
(C) fostered
(D) to foster

10 The modern office environment appears significantly less ------- than traditional cubicle arrangements.
(A) clutter
(B) clutters
(C) cluttered
(D) cluttering

11 Subscribe to our digital newsletter ------- informed about the latest industry trends.
(A) stay
(B) staying
(C) to stay
(D) to be stayed

12 The innovative insulation material helps maintain temperature stability by ------- thermal energy.
(A) absorbs
(B) absorbed
(C) absorption
(D) absorbing

13 ------- the yearly marketing plan has been the responsibility of Ms. Hurley and her team at Keener Apparel's headquarters in Miami.
(A) Produce
(B) Produced
(C) Producing
(D) Production

14 Rachel competed in the Professional Coding Tournament, ------- her skills with exceptional precision.
(A) displays
(B) displaying
(C) to display
(D) had displayed

15 To improve efficiency and ------- simplified frameworks, TechCore Solutions implemented a comprehensive workflow optimization strategy.
(A) introduce
(B) introduces
(C) introducing
(D) introduced

16 The ------- board of NovaMed Healthcare approved the CEO's decision to open a new location in Minneapolis.
(A) governed
(B) governing
(C) govern
(D) governs

PART 6

Questions 17-20 refer to the following article.

Strong Opposition to the Proposed Landfill

May 15—Citizens in Alta, Wyoming, were outraged when the mayor revealed a plan to construct a landfill site near ------- residential areas. At a town hall meeting last Wednesday, local business owners and prominent community figures combined forces ------- their strong concerns over the proposal.
                                                                                    17   18

Jacob Gormand, a small farm operator, made his opposition to the project clear when given a chance to speak at the meeting. "A landfill like this could lead to ------- of the groundwater in the area, which would result in toxic pollution entering Alta's drinking water supply," he argued.
                                                                                                                                           19

Experts further warn that there could be other adverse environmental effects. In spite of these concerns, government officials have indicated that they will not alter the construction plan. -------.
   20

17 (A) populated
(B) population
(C) populating
(D) populate

18 (A) express
(B) expressed
(C) expression
(D) to express

19 (A) evaporation
(B) utilization
(C) contamination
(D) precipitation

20 (A) Residents can expect to move into the completed structure soon.
(B) The approval process normally takes three to six months.
(C) Work on the site is currently scheduled to commence on June 17.
(D) Urgent concerns are handled by the city's emergency services department.

고난도 문제 완전 정복

고난도 문제를 풀며, 완벽하게 실전을 대비하자. 어려운 문제는 박스에 표시하고, 채점 후 복습하여 완전히 내 것으로 만들자.

01 Due to ------- trade disputes, major exporters are expected to report significant declines in revenues next quarter.

(A) intensifying (B) intensity
(C) intensify (D) intension

02 After analyzing multiple software options, the IT manager considered which platform ------- for the company's network.

(A) implementing (B) had implemented
(C) implement (D) to implement

03 Dr. Akira Nakamura will be tasked with ------- complex data analysis for the international project.

(A) conducting (B) conducted
(C) conducts (D) conduct

04 ------- avoid fines from the state government, manufacturers must take steps to ensure compliance with all environmental regulations.

(A) With (B) As long as
(C) In order to (D) Owing to

05 The new AirBlock filtration system by Wintex Solutions prevents dust from ------- in sensitive electronic components.

(A) accumulate (B) accumulation
(C) accumulated (D) accumulating

06 Findings from the study may help administrators ------- better educational strategies.

(A) identify (B) identifying
(C) identified (D) identifies

07 Public health guidelines were created to inform the public that ------- improperly prepared seafood can lead to serious illness.

(A) consumer (B) consumption
(C) consumes (D) consuming

08 Dyson Tek emerged as a leader in bioengineering as a result of its ------- approach to developing new technologies.

(A) determiner (B) determined
(C) determinedly (D) determination

09 ------- from the products of its competitors, Bowman's latest smartwatch includes a number of innovative features.

(A) Different (B) Difference
(C) Differently (D) Differentiate

10 Visitors to the Haeda Gallery's exhibit on Inna Endo will discover a new way of ------- the artist's photography.

(A) appreciate (B) appreciation
(C) appreciative (D) appreciating

11 The project manager encouraged her team members ------- their reporting methods for more efficient communication.

(A) streamlining (B) streamlined
(C) to streamline (D) streamlines

12 The museum has created an informative brochure ------- all exhibitions and their corresponding locations within the building.

(A) lists (B) listed
(C) listing (D) to be listed

DAY 05 전치사, 접속사, 관계사

| 최신 출제 경향 |

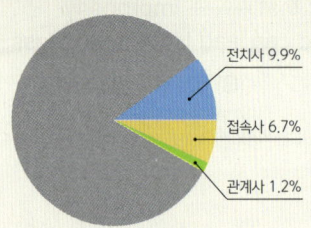

전치사 9.9%
접속사 6.7%
관계사 1.2%

① **전치사** | 시점/기간, 양보, 이유와 관련된 전치사 문제가 많이 출제된다.
② **접속사** | 시간, 조건, 양보와 관련된 부사절 접속사 문제가 많이 출제된다.
③ **관계사** | 주격/목적격/소유격을 구별하여 올바른 관계대명사를 채우는 문제가 많이 출제된다.

| 고난도 출제 포인트 |

POINT 1 미묘한 의미 차이를 구별하여 문맥에 맞는 전치사를 채우는 문제
(**In light of** / According to) the weather forecast, outdoor events were postponed. 오답률: 81.2%
→ '일기 예보를 고려하여 야외 행사가 연기되었다'라는 의미이므로, In light of(~을 고려하여)가 정답이다. According to(~에 따르면)는 뒤에 정보의 출처가 올 때 사용되므로 문맥상 적합하지 않다.

POINT 2 명사절 접속사 what과 that 구별하는 문제
The new law sparked (that / **what**) critics call controversy. 오답률: 44.9%
→ 뒤에 목적어가 생략된 불완전한 절이 왔으므로 명사절 접속사 what이 정답이다. that은 뒤에 완전한 절이 와야 한다.

POINT 3 격에 맞는 관계대명사를 채우는 문제
Taro Yoshida, (who / **whose**) design approach challenged tradition, reshaped engineering. 오답률: 49.7%
→ 관계절 내에서 design approach가 누구의 것인지 나타내므로 소유격 관계대명사 whose가 정답이다. design을 동사로 혼동하여 주격 관계대명사 who를 정답으로 고르지 않도록 주의한다.

| 빈출 문제 집중 훈련 |

빈출 문제를 풀며 실전 감각을 키워보자. 어려운 문제는 박스에 표시하고, 채점 후 복습하여 취약점을 보완하자.

PART 5

☐ **01** The movie sequel *Eight Dragons* earned higher profits ------- received poorer reviews than the previous film.
(A) nor   (B) but
(C) so   (D) still

☐ **02** Mr. Shimojo's chain of restaurants in Osaka has expanded to 10 locations ------- the beginning of this year.
(A) by   (B) until
(C) since   (D) within

☐ **03** Edmonton Enterprises planned to relocate its headquarters to 112th Avenue ------- to 97th Street.
(A) like   (B) or
(C) at   (D) either

☐ **04** The district has several foreign language academic institutions, some ------- have yet to obtain official accreditation for their curriculum.
(A) whose   (B) which
(C) for that   (D) of which

05 The consultant was hired full-time ------- the successful launch of the computer system he was advising Allman Electronics on.

(A) following (B) under
(C) according to (D) on behalf of

06 ------- safety reasons, the manager of the parking garage urges customers not to keep valuable items in their vehicles.

(A) Around (B) Upon
(C) Since (D) For

07 The firm will be unable to repay its loan ------- it can secure $1.1 million in funding.

(A) as if (B) furthermore
(C) unless (D) hence

08 ------- the region's economic problems, employment figures have steadily improved in sectors such as healthcare and technology.

(A) Including (B) Except
(C) Despite (D) While

09 ------- the auto mechanic completes repairs on the first delivery truck, the second one will be sent in.

(A) Thanks to (B) In order to
(C) As well as (D) As soon as

10 A transit employee announced that the Blue Line was running ------- schedule due to overcrowding on platforms.

(A) toward (B) ahead
(C) beyond (D) behind

11 ------- defective ground traffic equipment, the international airport canceled all inbound flights on Friday.

(A) Because of (B) Subsequently
(C) Apart from (D) Therefore

12 Sales of the frozen food product have been slow ------- it has been promoted heavily in stores for months.

(A) even though (B) so that
(C) whereas (D) until then

13 *Mystery at Dawn* was such a popular movie ------- it was sold out at theaters every weekend for two months.

(A) soon (B) that
(C) right (D) yet

14 Because fixing the software problems was ------- the ability of anyone in the department, external technical support was requested.

(A) except (B) beyond
(C) without (D) opposite

15 The marketing team has been asked to look ------- customer complaints registered on the company's Web site.

(A) within (B) amid
(C) into (D) onto

16 Sempercom already has numerous telephone and Internet subscribers ------- Europe and is planning to branch out into streaming services.

(A) along (B) above
(C) without (D) throughout

Questions 17-20 refer to the following advertisement.

Cook Like a Pro with Cook Art's Home Pro

Cook Art's all-new Home Pro stainless steel cookware set makes an ideal gift for the holiday season. -------(17). Offering users a superior cooking experience, the pots and pans in this package are designed by professional chef Eric Warner.

Warner says, "I tried to create a set -------(18) would allow users to produce restaurant-quality meals from home. -------(19) all 10 pieces being made from high-grade steel for even heat distribution, they are easy to clean, dishwasher-safe, and stylish in appearance."

For the next two weeks, the Home Pro set is -------(20) sale for the reduced price of $129.99—an incredible savings of $50 off the regular price! To take advantage of this deal, visit www.cookart.com today.

17
(A) Pick one up for a loved one or even for yourself.
(B) Your free sample should arrive within the next two weeks.
(C) Try it free for 30 days and cancel at any time.
(D) Gift cards are accepted as payment in our stores.

18
(A) all
(B) who
(C) what
(D) that

19
(A) Regardless of
(B) As a result of
(C) In addition to
(D) With regard to

20
(A) on
(B) in
(C) onto
(D) within

고난도 문제 완전 정복

고난도 문제를 풀며, 완벽하게 실전을 대비하자. 어려운 문제는 박스에 표시하고, 채점 후 복습하여 완전히 내 것으로 만들자.

01 Measuring the firm's sales and revenues ------- those of its competitors shows how well it has performed.

(A) except (B) throughout
(C) between (D) against

02 The maintenance crew starts working at 7 A.M. to ensure that the office is clean ------- employees arrive.

(A) despite (B) from
(C) before (D) within

03 ------- weather conditions were not optimal for the marathon, most participants believed the event was a great success.

(A) Though (B) Why
(C) However (D) After

04 Questions ------- the company's ongoing negotiations with the Price Corporation will not be addressed during Thursday's press conference.

(A) on account of (B) inside
(C) across   (D) pertaining to

05 Dr. Sophia Sanchez will give this morning's talk on renewable resources ------- the original speaker.

(A) in light of (B) as of
(C) in place of (D) except for

06 Page markers indicate ------- it is necessary for each of the parties to the agreement to affix their signatures.

(A) where (B) what
(C) whose (D) which

07 ------- the city's high speed rail facility, many of the company's staff would take much longer to commute to work.

(A) Given that (B) With all
(C) But for   (D) Whereas

08 Ms. Gluck will be leaving the firm at the end of the month ------- management does not find a replacement.

(A) excepting (B) as though
(C) even if   (D) provided that

09 Artists have established exhibit spaces in ------- was formerly an industrial park used to manufacture steel.

(A) where (B) why
(C) what (D) whom

10 A subway line runs ------- the full length of Ogden Avenue, and three stops are located along the street.

(A) toward (B) beneath
(C) after (D) behind

11 ------- is responsible for the equipment malfunction should report it immediately to the maintenance department.

(A) Whatever (B) Whoever
(C) Someone (D) Whose

12 The business conference will address current industry trends ------- future market projections for the next decade.

(A) as well as (B) only if
(C) regardless (D) as a result

DAY 06 어휘와 어구

| 최신 출제 경향 |

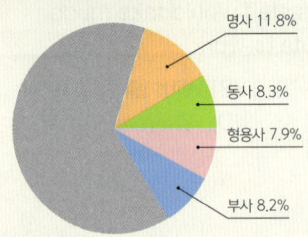

- 명사 11.8%
- 동사 8.3%
- 형용사 7.9%
- 부사 8.2%

① **명사, 동사** | 최근에는 문맥이나 쓰임에 따라 의미가 다른 다의어가 종종 출제된다.

② **형용사, 부사** | 문법적으로 가능해 보이거나 해석상 정답으로 착각할 수 있는 어휘가 오답 보기로 제시되는 고난도 문제가 최근 자주 출제되고 있다.

| 고난도 출제 포인트 |

POINT 1 익숙하지 않은 표현을 완성하는 형용사 어휘 채우는 문제

Supplier contracts are (**subject** / required) to periodic performance assessments. 오답률: 81.3%

→ to 다음에 명사구(periodic performance assessments)가 나왔기 때문에 'be subject to + 명사(~의 대상이 되다)'를 완성하는 형용사 subject가 정답이다. 'be required to + 동사(~하도록 요구되다)' 표현이 익숙하여 혼동하기 쉬우므로 주의해야 한다.

POINT 2 미묘한 의미 차이를 구별하여 부사 어휘를 채우는 문제

The hospital's generator will (**seamlessly** / durably) provide electricity during power outages. 오답률: 74.3%

→ '끊김 없이 전기를 공급하다'라는 의미를 완성하는 seamlessly(끊김 없이)가 정답이다. 발전기의 특성과 관련있다고 생각하기 쉬운 durably(튼튼하게)와 혼동하지 않도록 주의해야 한다.

POINT 3 고난도 동사 어휘를 채우는 문제

The mayor has (perceived / **pledged**) to improve public transportation services for commuters. 오답률: 69.1%

→ '대중교통 서비스를 개선하기로 약속했다'는 의미가 되어야 하므로 pledged(약속하다)가 정답이다.

| 빈출 문제 집중 훈련 |

빈출 문제를 풀며 실전 감각을 키워보자. 어려운 문제는 박스에 표시하고, 채점 후 복습하여 취약점을 보완하자.

PART 5

01 Provided that prices remain ------- throughout the year, the central bank sees no justification to adjust interest rates.

(A) stable (B) credible
(C) feasible (D) adaptable

02 Community members seeking to participate in the volunteer program are encouraged to ------- their time or skills.

(A) import (B) benefit
(C) devote (D) delegate

03 ------- in its history, Edelman's Supermarket started as a single store but has since expanded to 50 locations.

(A) Early (B) Away
(C) Even (D) Instead

04 Students may gain ------- to the university's online database of academic journals using their assigned identification numbers.

(A) report (B) perspective
(C) confidence (D) access

05 The judges will convene and reach their final decisions before the winners of the music competition are ------- to the audience.
(A) voted
(B) monitored
(C) announced
(D) entered

06 The managing editor reviewed Ms. Oakley's article and said that it will require substantial ------- before it can be published.
(A) revision
(B) notification
(C) negotiation
(D) correlation

07 Shareholders are allowed to ------- no more than three people to represent them on the board of directors.
(A) nominate
(B) evaluate
(C) commit
(D) attach

08 The firm secured ------- contracts worth billions of dollars in total, following business trips to Kyrgyzstan, India, and South Africa.
(A) variable
(B) lucrative
(C) moderate
(D) knowledgeable

09 A brand-new Simtek phone ------- sells for about $400 in stores but can be bought online for just $325.
(A) rarely
(B) before
(C) almost
(D) ordinarily

10 By the time she was 40, Ms. Henry achieved every career goal she had set out to ------- as a young journalism graduate.
(A) believe
(B) determine
(C) challenge
(D) accomplish

11 Sandona Retail's share price dropped after it failed to meet the ------- it had made at the beginning of the year.
(A) impressions
(B) outcomes
(C) conclusions
(D) projections

12 To make it easy for customers to install the equipment, Peninsula Networks provides user manuals ------- with color pictures.
(A) illustrated
(B) subscribed
(C) complimented
(D) abbreviated

13 A government grant along with ------- made by local business owners helped pay for the hospital wing's renovations.
(A) admissions
(B) propositions
(C) evaluations
(D) contributions

14 Despite ------- attempts to arrive at an agreement, the two firms continue to differ on some conditions in the proposed contract.
(A) successful
(B) numerous
(C) executive
(D) premature

15 Ms. Haryadi did exceptional work on the development project and ------- was given a promotion and a modest pay raise.
(A) considerably
(B) receptively
(C) consequently
(D) alternatively

16 Hundreds of residents signed a petition to save the historic building, but unfortunately the structure was demolished -------.
(A) apart
(B) enough
(C) however
(D) anyway

PART 6

Questions 17-20 refer to the following letter.

Dear Stockholders,

I am pleased to announce that Gravura Development has completed all of the necessary requirements to obtain its investment from Lydia Capital Ventures. We are now ------- to proceed
                                                                                              17
with constructing our first copper wire factory in Lusaka, Zambia. As you know, the facility will be located near multiple copper mines. ------- Over the coming months, I will personally be visiting the
                                                                 18
area to check on the ------- of construction there. To receive periodic updates on the project, please
                       19
go to our Web site at www.gravura.com and join our mailing list. In closing, I'd like to thank all of you once again for your support as we ------- on this exciting new enterprise.
                                                               20

Thank you,
Peter Merck
CEO, Gravura Development

17 (A) easy
    (B) able
    (C) right
    (D) useful

18 (A) The region is known for its incredible plant and animal life.
    (B) Copper is in demand because of its many practical uses.
    (C) Please indicate your willingness to place an investment.
    (D) Thus, we will have several good sources for our raw materials.

19 (A) span
    (B) deposit
    (C) progress
    (D) subsidy

20 (A) embark
    (B) remain
    (C) appear
    (D) reflect

고난도 문제 완전 정복

고난도 문제를 풀며, 완벽하게 실전을 대비하자. 어려운 문제는 박스에 표시하고, 채점 후 복습하여 완전히 내 것으로 만들자.

01 Those who wish to ------- the Aylesbury Spring Festival this May must purchase tickets at the town hall.

(A) engage (B) attend
(C) participate (D) perform

02 Analysts are concerned about the ------- at which the domestic currency has rapidly lost its value.

(A) point (B) rate
(C) time (D) account

03 Randall University has ------- out a job announcement seeking a faculty administrator for its newly opened robotics engineering department.

(A) put (B) reached
(C) carried (D) figured

04 Because of the ------- schedule for the month of October, the company is planning to hire temporary staff.

(A) standard (B) permanent
(C) continual (D) demanding

05 The manager always takes time to plan every project -------, which ensures their precise implementation.

(A) comparatively (B) symmetrically
(C) equitably (D) meticulously

06 The contractor hired a different company to handle the ------- of debris from the building's construction site.

(A) shortage (B) removal
(C) sacrifice (D) renewal

07 Management tries to create an ------- work environment by involving employees in decisions about company policies.

(A) enriched (B) inclusive
(C) orderly (D) exotic

08 It is the ------- of the compensation committee that Emblem Corporation should not award bonuses until profitability improves.

(A) setting (B) capacity
(C) position (D) admission

09 The committee examined ------- validated research findings before approving the policy amendments.

(A) assuredly (B) inherently
(C) comprehensively (D) leniently

10 By purchasing products that are ------- with its existing machinery, Horizon Textiles can reduce its equipment upgrade expenses.

(A) collective (B) cooperative
(C) compatible (D) cordial

11 Industry experts recommend that traditional banks ------- their investment strategy to adapt to financial technology innovations.

(A) deliver (B) overhaul
(C) embrace (D) prohibit

12 The new software update integrates ------- with existing systems, requiring no additional configuration from users.

(A) seamlessly (B) sporadically
(C) graciously (D) durably

정답 · 해석 · 해설 p.76

PART 7

DAY 07 이메일/편지, 메시지 대화문, 광고
DAY 08 기사, 양식, 공고
DAY 09 이중 지문
DAY 10 삼중 지문

PART 7 | 알아보기

PART 7은 147번부터 200번까지 총 54문제로, 지문을 읽고 그와 관련된 2~5개의 질문에 답하는 파트이다. 단일 지문 10개, 이중 지문 2 세트, 삼중 지문 3 세트가 나온다.

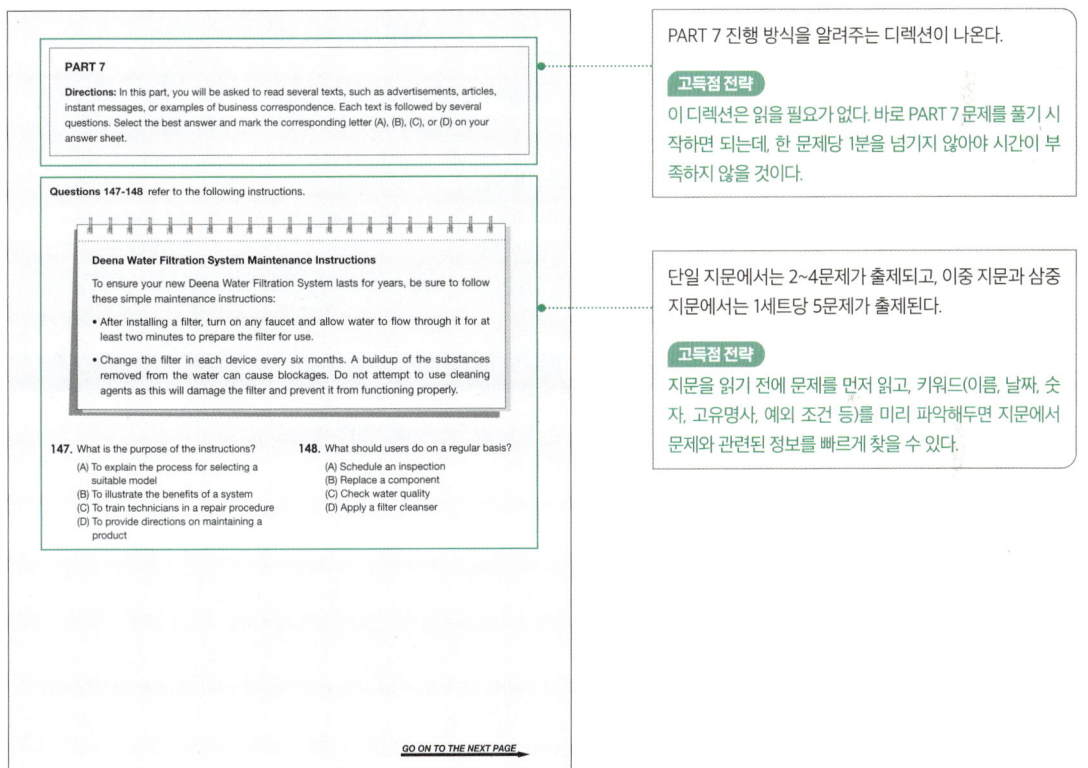

PART 7 진행 방식을 알려주는 디렉션이 나온다.

고득점 전략
이 디렉션은 읽을 필요가 없다. 바로 PART 7 문제를 풀기 시작하면 되는데, 한 문제당 1분을 넘기지 않아야 시간이 부족하지 않을 것이다.

단일 지문에서는 2~4문제가 출제되고, 이중 지문과 삼중 지문에서는 1세트당 5문제가 출제된다.

고득점 전략
지문을 읽기 전에 문제를 먼저 읽고, 키워드(이름, 날짜, 숫자, 고유명사, 예외 조건 등)를 미리 파악해두면 지문에서 문제와 관련된 정보를 빠르게 찾을 수 있다.

DAY 07 이메일/편지, 메시지 대화문, 광고

최신 출제 경향

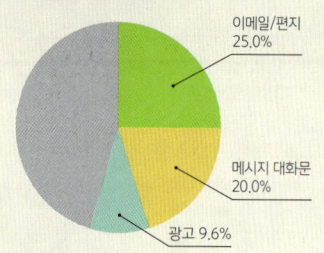

- 이메일/편지 25.0%
- 메시지 대화문 20.0%
- 광고 9.6%

① **이메일/편지** | 주로 회사 내 공지, 고객 응대 등 비즈니스 관련 내용이 많이 출제된다.

② **메시지 대화문** | 두 명 이상의 인물이 의견을 주고받으며 업무에 관한 협의를 하는 내용이 자주 나온다.

③ **광고** | 상품이나 서비스를 홍보하는 지문으로, 다른 유형의 지문에 비해 길이가 짧은 문장들이 많아 어렵지 않은 편이다.

고난도 출제 포인트

POINT 1
정답의 단서가 어려운 단어로 패러프레이징된 문제

We provide spaces tailored to your events.
· Room A: Accommodates up to 50 people and its layout can be quickly changed.
· Room B: Fits up to 30 people and includes a terrace.

Q What is true about Room A?
(A) It can be easily reconfigured. (o)
(B) It features an outdoor area. (×)

→ 지문에 나온 'its layout can be quickly changed(배치가 빠르게 변경될 수 있다)'가 'can be easily reconfigured(쉽게 재배치될 수 있다)'로 패러프레이징된 정답을 골라야 하는데, reconfigure(재배치하다)라는 단어를 모르면 정답을 고르기 어려운 문제이다. 오답률: 53.0%

POINT 2
이메일/편지, 메시지 대화문, 광고에 자주 등장하는 고난도 어휘

| consent 동의하다 | substitution 대체, 교체 | reinstate 복직시키다 | allocate 할당하다 | patronage 이용, 애용 |
| solicit 요청하다, 간청하다 | moderator 조정자 | competitive 경쟁력 있는 | merge 합병하다 | expedite 더 신속히 처리하다 |

빈출 문제 집중 훈련

빈출 문제를 풀며 실전 감각을 키워보자. 어려운 문제는 박스에 표시하고, 채점 후 복습하여 취약점을 보완하자.

Questions 01-02 refer to the following e-mail.

To: Lenny Stewart <lstewart@bigmail.com>
From: Michelle Andrews <m_andrews@tiletown.com>
Date: November 14

I am currently away from the office on vacation and will not be returning until December 6. During this time, I will have limited access to my e-mail and will not be available to answer my phone. If you have an urgent request requiring immediate attention, please contact my assistant Theodore Larson at 555-2309. Otherwise, please expect a response on or after the 6th of December. Thank you.

Michelle Andrews
Account representative
Tile Town

01 What is the purpose of the e-mail?
(A) To notify management of a problem
(B) To request access to an account
(C) To inform the recipient of an absence
(D) To provide a customer's contact details

02 What is suggested about Theodore Larson?
(A) He is an employee at Tile Town.
(B) He is away on holiday until December 6.
(C) He is Ms. Andrews' supervisor.
(D) He is a technical representative.

Questions 03-05 refer to the following advertisement.

Web Space Helps You Get Noticed Online!
120 Laramie Avenue, Chicago, IL 60644
555-9002 | www.webspace.com

In today's world, the success of your business or organization often depends on the content, quality, and design of your Web site. — [1] —. A Web site should load quickly and have a clean and readable layout even on a smartphone. — [2] —. If it's overly technical, unattractive, outdated, and difficult to use, your customers may take their business elsewhere. — [3] —. Put Web Space in charge, and we can help you create a Web site that is visually appealing, accessible to all users, and easy to navigate.

Web Space has been serving various communities for two decades. — [4] —. We have grown right along with the quickly-developing world of the Internet and are up-to-date with online functions, trends, and layouts. Today, we offer the following services in Web site design and creation:

- Content editing
- Calendars
- Search engine optimization
- Registration forms
- Multimedia content
- Web site security

You can take a look at many of the wonderful sites we have designed for companies and organizations by browsing www.webspace.com. Contact us by e-mailing info@webspace.com.

03 What is being advertised?

(A) A computer equipment retailer
(B) A Web site development company
(C) An Internet research firm
(D) An online payment service

04 What is mentioned about Web Space?

(A) It is conducting a consumer survey.
(B) It sells many of its products online.
(C) It has been in business for 10 years.
(D) It can create an assortment of online content.

05 In which of the positions marked [1], [2], [3], and [4] does the following sentence best belong?

"Don't allow your competitors to leave you behind."

(A) [1]
(B) [2]
(C) [3]
(D) [4]

Questions 06-09 refer to the following text-message chain.

Hilda Jacobsen [9:37 A.M.]
Larry, how's your schedule looking for the week? Anything major going on?

Larry Boyd [9:39 A.M.]
Not really. I was planning to spend most of my time working on the Hanifan project, but there's no rush. They don't need my designs for their office interior for another two weeks.

Larry Boyd [9:40 A.M.]
Something I can help you with?

Hilda Jacobsen [9:42 A.M.]
I was wondering if you were available to join me on Wednesday to meet with some representatives from Digitek. I'll be pitching a lobby renovation idea to them. I really want their company as a client, so I think it would be great if you could help direct the conversation to my proposal's selling points.

Larry Boyd [9:42 A.M.]
I hear you. What time is this meeting?

Hilda Jacobsen [9:43 A.M.]
It's at 10:30 A.M. We can take my car from here. I'll buy you lunch when we're done.

Larry Boyd [9:44 A.M.]
It's a deal. I'll see you on Wednesday. We'll be coming back to the office, right?

Hilda Jacobsen [9:45 A.M.]
Yes. I will e-mail you more details about the project in a moment. Thanks!

06 What is suggested about Mr. Boyd?

(A) He needs to reschedule a client meeting.
(B) He asked for an extension on a deadline.
(C) He is working on plans for an interior.
(D) He will be reassigned to a new project.

07 What is true about Ms. Jacobsen?

(A) She has finalized details on an office interior design.
(B) She plans to meet with a Hanifan representative.
(C) Her schedule was changed at the last minute.
(D) She hopes to acquire Digitek as a new client.

08 At 9:44 A.M., what does Mr. Boyd mean when he writes, "It's a deal"?

(A) He is satisfied with the outcome of a business negotiation.
(B) He is confident about a proposal's chances of success.
(C) He consents to accompanying his colleague to a meeting.
(D) He is willing to do some work in exchange for assistance with a task.

09 What will Mr. Boyd do after lunch on Wednesday?

(A) Direct a meeting with staff members
(B) Send an e-mail with project details
(C) Return to his workplace
(D) Suggest changes to a lobby

Questions 10-13 refer to the following online chat discussion.

Adriana Scorsese [10:10 A.M.] As I mentioned in the e-mail I sent to both of you on May 14, my department will begin looking for applicants next month. I'd like to confirm the hiring requirements for each of your departments. Kathy, the accounting team needs two new members, right?

Kathy Chiu [10:14 A.M.] Actually, the situation has changed since we last spoke. Jack Wallace informed me of his decision to leave us on May 31. Regarding this issue, may I get back to you later?

Adriana Scorsese [10:14 A.M.] Got it. Charles, what about you? Do you still require six new employees for marketing?

Charles Jones [10:15 A.M.] That's right. We are planning several campaigns to boost sales of the company's newest product, so we'll need a lot of staff. And they should have experience with social media promotions. Maybe this could be specified in the job advertisement.

Adriana Scorsese [10:18 A.M.] My assistant, Judith Harper, is in charge of writing the advertisements, and I'll make sure she includes that requirement. I'll send the advertisements to each of you on May 18 to review.

Kathy Chiu [10:19 A.M.] I'm going to be attending a seminar in Chicago that day. Would it be alright if I provide you with my feedback on May 20?

Adriana Scorsese [10:19 A.M.] No problem. There's one more thing. I'd like to review your training plans in advance. I've already received Kathy's, but I am still waiting for yours, Charles.

Charles Jones [10:21 A.M.] Sorry about that. I can e-mail it to you on Friday afternoon. Will that work for you?

Adriana Scorsese [10:22 A.M.] Perfect. Thanks.

---

10 In which department does Ms. Scorsese most likely work?

(A) Accounting
(B) Marketing
(C) Human resources
(D) Sales

11 At 10:14 A.M., what does Ms. Chiu mean when she writes "Regarding this issue, may I get back to you later?"

(A) She will be busy on an upcoming date.
(B) She has to respond to an urgent e-mail.
(C) She needs to update her requirements.
(D) She is planning to transfer departments.

12 On which date will Ms. Chiu be absent from the office?

(A) May 14
(B) May 18
(C) May 20
(D) May 31

13 What does Mr. Jones say he will do?

(A) Organize a training seminar for staff
(B) Review a post on a social media platform
(C) Provide some information to a colleague
(D) Update some data in the company records

고난도 문제 완전 정복

고난도 문제를 풀며, 완벽하게 실전을 대비하자. 어려운 문제는 박스에 표시하고, 채점 후 복습하여 완전히 내 것으로 만들자.

Questions 01-03 refer to the following e-mail.

TO: Steven Joyce <sjoyce@fastmail.com>
FROM: Fast Track Records <information@fasttrackrecords.com>
DATE: May 20
SUBJECT: Information

Dear Mr. Joyce,

Every year on the third Saturday of May, we celebrate Record Store Day as a way to honor the independent spirit of record stores. This year, Fast Track Records will once again be partnering with all the other major stores in the city for a day of music celebration. As you are a member of our Music Fans Club, we are forwarding you the planned highlights of the day:

11 A.M.—12 P.M.	John Kher, Sarah Feinstein, Ernest Yates, and other local music critics will be reading selections from their work at Gold Sounds Records.
12 P.M.—5 P.M.	Marshalltown Records will be offering a special discount on all jazz and blues records. Stop by the store, and receive up to 50 percent off on your favorite albums.
1 P.M.—5 P.M.	Duke Records will stage a raffle for a variety of merchandise, including vinyl cases, T-shirts, and other items.
2:30 P.M.—3:30 P.M.	Local rock band The Chimney Sweeps will be performing an in-store concert at Desert Island Records.
4 P.M.—5 P.M.	Gold Sounds Records will be holding a music-themed trivia contest. Winners will receive special prizes including autographed records and posters.
5 P.M.—8 P.M.	A party will be held at Marshalltown Records.

If you have questions about the events and activities, call Fast Track Records at 555-3009 or reply to this e-mail. A detailed schedule with further festivities can be found at www.fasttrackrecords.com/recordstoreday.

01 What is the purpose of the e-mail?
(A) To announce a record store's grand opening
(B) To list music-related events for the summer months
(C) To provide a schedule for a special celebration
(D) To keep members informed of local concerts

02 What is NOT mentioned as an activity planned for Record Store Day?
(A) A store-sponsored contest
(B) A musical performance
(C) A speech by a musician
(D) A reading from local reviewers

03 What is stated about Marshalltown Records?
(A) It specializes in jazz and blues records.
(B) It has two branches in the city.
(C) It is giving away a selection of merchandise.
(D) It will be the venue for the final event.

Questions 04-07 refer to the following letter.

October 15

Jeremiah Nam
3049 Oak Way
Sunnydale, WI 84774

Dear Mr. Nam,

As you may have heard or read in the news, Sunny-Link Internet Services will be merging with Cranston Connect under the name of SC Media. By combining Sunny-Link's passion for serving customers with Cranston Connect's technological capabilities, SC Media will be able to offer a wider range of high-speed broadband packages at competitive prices. We are excited about this new prospect as it will also allow our customers to gain access to exciting new products being planned, including a streaming service for video-on-demand, TV subscriptions, and phone plans.

Rest assured, clients who are on existing or ongoing contracts will continue to enjoy uninterrupted service with no change in fees. Billing will be conducted under the new name of SC Media, and banks and other financial firms have already been notified of the change. However, customers submitting payment online will have to register on the new Web site at www.scmedia.com. Once you have done so, you will be sent a confirmation e-mail containing a link back to our Web site. After you click on the link, your online account will be accessible, and you will be able to make payments by credit card or direct deposit from an online payment site.

Thank you for your continued patronage.

Miriam Steinberg
Miriam Steinberg
Director of customer relations

04 Why was the letter written?

(A) To provide details on fee changes
(B) To announce a new Internet service
(C) To solicit payment of a bill
(D) To inform a client of corporate changes

05 According to the letter, what benefit might customers get?

(A) A reduction in monthly fees
(B) A better selection of products
(C) A trial offer on new packages
(D) A higher level of customer service

06 The word "prospect" in paragraph 1, line 5, is closest in meaning to

(A) opportunity
(B) forecast
(C) search
(D) proposal

07 What is indicated about SC Media?

(A) It will notify banks of the change.
(B) It is in the process of updating its Web site.
(C) It accepts different methods of payment.
(D) It was purchased by another company.

DAY 08 기사, 양식, 공고

최신 출제 경향

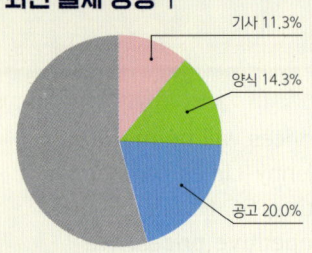

기사 11.3%
양식 14.3%
공고 20.0%

① **기사** | 신문이나 잡지에 기재되는 정보성 내용으로, 최근에는 정보량이 많고 문장이 긴 난이도가 높은 기사가 자주 출제된다.

② **양식** | 구매내역서, 영수증, 일정표, 신청서 등 실생활에서 접할 수 있는 다양한 양식이 출제된다.

③ **공고** | 조직 또는 단체가 구성원에게 전달하는 공지 사항이 자주 출제된다.

고난도 출제 포인트

POINT 1 함정에 빠지기 쉬운 오답 보기가 제시된 문제

| EcoRevive is celebrating its 30th anniversary this year. Its achievements in the past 10 years are particularly noteworthy. | Q When was EcoRevive established?
(A) 10 years ago (○)
(B) 30 years ago (×) |

→ 지문의 '30주년(30th anniversary)'이라는 단서를 보고 30 years ago를 맞춰야 하지만, '지난 10년(past 10 years)'이라는 표현 때문에 10 years ago를 잘못 고를 수 있는 문제이다. 오답률: 32.5%

POINT 2 기사, 양식, 공고에 자주 등장하는 고난도 어휘

| appraise 평가하다 | defray 돌려주다 | parcel 소포, 택배 | insure 보험에 들다 | recipient 수혜자, 수령인 |
| underserved 소외된 | illustrious 저명한 | exclusive 독점의 | garment 의류 | ergonomic 인체공학적인 |

빈출 문제 집중 훈련

빈출 문제를 풀며 실전 감각을 키워보자. 어려운 문제는 박스에 표시하고, 채점 후 복습하여 취약점을 보완하자.

Questions 01-02 refer to the following brochure.

Jeju Sea and Surfing Activities

Welcome to Jeju, Korea's largest island. Jeju provides plenty of activities for adventurous travelers who don't mind getting wet! Some of the many activities you can try are listed below.

- Take a two-hour cruise from the northern port of Jeju City and marvel at the ancient rock formations around the island.
- Go scuba diving in the sea around the town of Hallim and see hundreds of colorful marine species.
- The waves on the island's southern side are excellent for experienced surfers, but beginners should stick to the calmer water in the west.

Please enjoy your time exploring the marine activities around Jeju Island, but avoid going into the water alone. In addition, please do not dive from the cliffs around the island. There may be rocks just below the surface of the water which can be very dangerous.

01 What is mentioned about Jeju Island?

(A) It has calmer waves on the west side.
(B) It often has high levels of rainfall.
(C) It has rock climbing facilities for tourists.
(D) It usually is busiest in the summer.

02 According to the brochure, why should visitors avoid jumping from the cliffs?

(A) Climbing cliffs is very slippery.
(B) Sea creatures could be harmed.
(C) Dangerous rocks are in the water.
(D) The areas are closed to the public.

Questions 03-05 refer to the following article.

Chic Life Magazine

Marilyn DuBois's Spring Farewell

(20 December)—Next month, famed designer Marilyn DuBois will put on a show for her spring collection, which will be the last line of clothing she will ever produce. The fashion world was shocked in November when Ms. DuBois made the unexpected announcement about her plans to retire next February. Although only 45 years old, Ms. DuBois has had an illustrious career in the apparel design industry, opening nearly 200 boutiques worldwide.

In an exclusive interview with our magazine, Ms. DuBois provided us with some details about her retirement. "I've had a wonderful career designing clothes," she said, "but the constant expectation from the public for me to create innovative work has been stressful." Ms. DuBois further explained that her sister Janelle will take over as CEO of DuBois Corporation beginning in February. "She is eager to start and has my full confidence in the role," Ms. DuBois said.

With Ms. DuBois at a high point in her career, fashion professionals are sad to see her move on. At the same time, they excitedly anticipate what the future might bring for DuBois Corporation under her sister's leadership.

03 According to the article, what will happen next year?

(A) A garment designer will come to the end of her career.
(B) An announcement about an industry event will be made.
(C) A photo shoot for a magazine will take place.
(D) A fashion show will be held at a boutique.

04 What has been a cause of concern for Marilyn DuBois?

(A) Reduced sales in her stores
(B) A declining passion for her work
(C) Pressure to be creative
(D) A change in public opinion

05 What can be inferred about Janelle DuBois?

(A) She has plans for hiring new fashion models.
(B) Her promotion to CEO has been well received.
(C) She majored in fashion design in college.
(D) Her designs have attracted more attention than her sister's.

Questions 06-09 refer to the following Web page.

MyPost.com

Home | Business | Products and Services | About us | Help | Register | Log in

You are here: MyPost > Help

What is MyPost and how does it work?
MyPost provides a US-based delivery address for customers living overseas. Since not all online retailers in the US will ship internationally, MyPost allows you to use its physical address located in the US as a shipment transfer point to temporarily store ordered items. — [1] —. So, the next time you shop with an online US retailer, simply enter your MyPost address on the shipping form, and we will take care of the rest. MyPost uses an advanced tracking system and can also provide additional services, such as temporary storage and item repacking. Currently, we ship to over 64 countries around the world.

How do I register with MyPost?
To use MyPost, register for an online account by clicking here. There are no registration or subscription fees. — [2] —.

How much does it cost to ship an item?
Cost is based on the weight and dimensions of your parcel. You can estimate the cost of a shipment at any time by using the shipping calculator on our home page. — [3] —.

Are there weight and size restrictions for items sent through MyPost?
The minimum chargeable weight is 500 grams. The maximum parcel weight is 30 kilograms. Maximum parcel dimensions are 3 meters (length x width).

How long will it take to receive my shipment?
Once your parcel has been shipped from our overseas warehouse, we estimate it should take approximately 7-10 working days for delivery to the address you specify. — [4] —.

06 Who would most likely be interested in MyPost's services?

(A) Companies relocating abroad
(B) Business owners needing domestic delivery
(C) Customers ordering items from US Web sites
(D) Clients wishing to cut their shipping costs

07 What is indicated about MyPost?

(A) It has storage facilities in the US.
(B) It has special arrangements with trucking companies.
(C) It does not insure items under 500 grams.
(D) It charges extra for parcels over three meters in length.

08 What is stated about the services?

(A) They are discounted for repeat customers.
(B) They are priced according to weight and size.
(C) They include sales of packing supplies.
(D) They cost less than other companies.

09 In which of the positions marked [1], [2], [3], and [4] does the following sentence best belong?

"Pay only for the services you need."

(A) [1]
(B) [2]
(C) [3]
(D) [4]

Questions 10-13 refer to the following article.

Building Towards a Brighter Future

(July 17)—For Antonio, a young boy growing up in the city of Jamane, life is a series of challenges. But thanks to EduAid's Fund-A-School project, he will have access to an education. Antonio is one of hundreds of recipients involved in EduAid's educational assistance programs, which construct school buildings in underserved areas around the world.

EduAid's Fund-A-School project is mainly supported by contributions from businesses. In exchange for donations starting from $1,000 and proceeding upwards, companies can use EduAid's logo on their products to demonstrate their commitment to education. In addition, they may deduct the amounts of such donations from their tax obligations. One such firm, England's Goodman Industries, promised to donate enough money to construct five schools over the next 12 months.

Apart from building schools, EduAid hopes to benefit local economies by providing the inhabitants of certain areas with fair wages. Residents in these areas are offered positions at EduAid as construction workers and teachers. The teachers develop their own lesson plans based on their familiarity with local needs and customs. But they also receive expert assistance from qualified volunteers who oversee teacher training and conduct other administrative work.

Individuals or businesses interested in being EduAid supporters, either through financial donation or volunteering, can visit their site online at www.eduAid.org for further details.

10 What does the article mention about Antonio?

(A) He is a part-time volunteer for EduAid.
(B) He recently moved to the city of Jamane.
(C) He is getting support from the Fund-A-School project.
(D) He receives a daily allowance for food.

11 The word "obligations" in paragraph 2, line 4 is closest in meaning to

(A) engagements
(B) dedications
(C) necessities
(D) responsibilities

12 What is NOT stated about the Fund-A-School project?

(A) Companies can display a logo to prove they have made a large donation.
(B) The highest amount it has received so far is $1,000.
(C) A firm is helping it to build five more schoolhouses.
(D) Its activities benefit the local economy as well.

13 According to the article, what do some volunteers do?

(A) Raise money from overseas
(B) Construct the school buildings
(C) Perform some administrative work
(D) Carry supplies from the nearest city

Questions 01-03 refer to the following announcement.

Cultural Invasion

Following the success of last year's event, the city of Singapore will be holding a second Cultural Invasion from Friday, April 20 to Sunday, April 22. Open to the public, this unique celebration of the arts gathers creative talent from all over the world to participate in a three-day cultural exchange. In addition to special exhibits, lectures, and workshops curated by the Singapore Art Museum, the event will feature:

- A launch party, where Dubai-based multimedia specialist Tima Khan will project her colorful images onto a giant outdoor screen. The event is free and open to the public.

- A collaborative art fair co-hosted by famed jewelry designer Palma Quinn and Singapore's own Vicki Vong at the Marina Bay Public Gardens. The event is free, but reservations are required.

- An interactive light-and-mirror installation along Smith Street in Chinatown, which will be narrated by Hong Kong performance artist Xia Ben. The event is free and open to the public.

- Guided cultural excursions of Singapore's historic districts, which will be decorated with designs by noted Hungarian street artist Koborlo. Tours are available to the public at a cost of $20 (Singapore) per person and include a meet-and-greet with the artist. Groups leave from the Orchard Road Bus Terminal.

Please visit www.culturalinvasion.sg for more information and to see the full lineup of planned activities. Download area maps and promotional vouchers for food and entertainment options sponsored by participating establishments.

01 What is stated about Cultural Invasion?

(A) It aims to promote tourism in Singapore.
(B) It usually takes place in mid-April.
(C) It is funded by the Singapore Art Museum.
(D) It was held once the year before.

02 Which of the featured events will be hosted by two people?

(A) The launch party
(B) The interactive exhibit
(C) The garden art fair
(D) The cultural excursion

03 What is indicated about the planned activities?

(A) They mostly take place in one area.
(B) They will all feature professional artists.
(C) They all require advance registration.
(D) They may be subject to change.

Questions 04-07 refer to the following information.

Wyndham Studio

At Wyndham Studio, we believe that fine art makes a worthy investment. But as with any investment, proper care must be taken to ensure that its value is protected. To help you enjoy your fine art purchase for many years to come, we offer the following helpful tips.

- When handling paintings, make sure your hands are clean and avoid touching the artwork's surface directly. Though not always necessary, wearing disposable vinyl gloves is a good idea.
- If you plan on displaying your artwork, have it professionally framed. Improper framing could substantially diminish the artwork's quality. Contact us for a list of framers that we work with.
- No matter what you intend to do with your artwork, always safeguard against extreme temperature, water damage, and sunlight. Keep it away from bright windows, fireplaces, and indoor air vents. Beware of light bulbs that emit strong heat as they could distort delicate artwork. If you live in a humid climate, consider a dehumidifier. It helps remove moisture from the air. You can also store the artwork in a climate-controlled room.
- Last but not least, protect your artwork from airborne pollutants. Uncovered art is especially susceptible to dust and must be lightly brushed to remove collected particles. Never use chemical cleaners of any kind.

For additional information, or to purchase some of the aforementioned items from our product catalog, go to www.wyndhamstudio.com. Those spending more than $500 on any artwork are eligible for a 25 percent discount on items listed on our site.

04 What is the information mainly about?

(A) Appraising the value of an artwork
(B) Buying fine art as an investment
(C) Preserving and maintaining art
(D) Finding a reputable art dealer

05 What is NOT indicated about Wyndham Studio?

(A) It sells fine works of art.
(B) It provides in-house framing.
(C) It maintains an online store.
(D) It offers discounts on some purchases.

06 What is recommended for humid conditions?

(A) Storing art in an airtight container
(B) Displaying art in a sunny room
(C) Putting artwork in a plastic case
(D) Using a device that reduces moisture

07 What are art owners told to avoid when handling works of art?

(A) Wearing vinyl gloves
(B) Hanging artwork
(C) Using cleaning solutions
(D) Covering with certain fabrics

DAY 09 이중 지문

최신 출제 경향

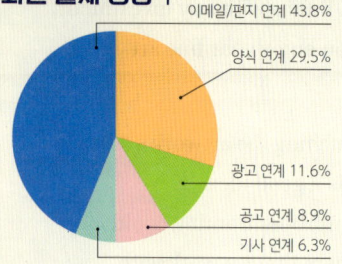

이메일/편지 연계 43.8%
양식 연계 29.5%
광고 연계 11.6%
공고 연계 8.9%
기사 연계 6.3%

① **이메일/편지 연계** | 이메일과 그에 대해 회신하는 또 다른 이메일 지문이 출제되는 경우가 가장 많다.

② **양식 연계** | 책자, 일정표, 영수증 등의 다양한 양식과 그 양식에서 언급된 내용에 대해 문의하는 이메일/편지 지문이 자주 출제된다.

③ **광고/공고/기사 연계** | 주로 첫 번째 지문에서 언급된 특정 정보에 대해 두 번째 지문에서 추가 설명하거나 문의하는 형식으로 나온다.

고난도 출제 포인트

POINT 1
여러 곳에 흩어진 단서를 연결해야 하는 복합적인 연계 문제

지문 1: 이메일
> We need to recruit a manager for the restaurant. It is important to find someone to replace Mr. Louis. Currently, our candidates are Emily Johnson, Raj Patel, and Sohee Kwon.

지문 2: 이메일
> I have been working for two weeks now, and although there is still some time left until the opening, everything is progressing very well.
> Emily Johnson

Q: What is suggested about Ms. Johnson? A: She was taken on as Mr. Louis's successor. 오답률: 37.7%

→ 첫 번째 이메일에서 Mr. Louis의 대체 인력 채용이 필요하다고 하며 Emily Johnson이 후보 중 하나라는 내용이 나오고, 두 번째 이메일에서 Emily Johnson이 일을 한지 2주가 되었다고 한 내용을 종합하여 '그녀는 Mr. Louis의 후임자로 채용되었다'는 것을 추론해야 하는 까다로운 연계 문제이다.

POINT 2
이중 지문에 자주 등장하는 고난도 어휘

patron 고객	grateful 감사하는	subscription 구독	attraction 명소	fill in 작성하다
inattentive 부주의한	replacement 교환품	strategy 전략	coordinate 편성하다	drill 훈련
overview 개요	deposit 예금하다	visibility 눈에 띔	refurbish 새로 꾸미다	summarize 요약하다

빈출 문제 집중 훈련

빈출 문제를 풀며 실전 감각을 키워보자. 어려운 문제는 박스에 표시하고, 채점 후 복습하여 취약점을 보완하자.

Questions 01-05 refer to the following invoice and e-mail.

INVOICE: MR-3848589	Drapers Window Coverings
DATE: September 1	(702) 555-4523, www.draperswindow.com

CLIENT	Marilyn Ravenwood	
ADDRESS	738 Grover Avenue, Madison, WI 53532	
ORDERS and SERVICES	QUANTITY	COST
Red silk curtains	1	$488.00
Bamboo blinds	1	$238.00
Delivery and installation services		$160.00
	Subtotal	$886.00
	Tax	$88.60
	Amount payable	$974.60

Payments by cash, bank transfer, or credit card are accepted. Payment must be made in full within one week of the invoice date. Receipts will be mailed to the indicated address. Should you have any questions about the invoice, send an e-mail to scottforester@drapers.com.

TO	Scott Forester <scottforester@drapers.com>
FROM	Marilyn Ravenwood <mraven@tomail.com>
DATE	September 6
SUBJECT	Invoice question

Dear Mr. Forester,

Your staff member delivered the curtains and blinds yesterday, and I am very pleased with how they turned out. The products look almost exactly as they did on the Web site. In addition, the installation services provided saved a lot of time and trouble. I sent you a payment via bank transfer yesterday. Please let me know when you receive it, and send the receipt to my company at: Ferndale Interiors, 83 Larch Drive, Madison, WI 53534. The address indicated in the invoice is my client's.

Also, I have another client that has hired me to redecorate his dining room. For his project, he would like the same items I ordered for Grover Avenue. I will need the exact same number of curtains but double that of the blinds. Could you inform me how much you would charge? Let me know if you need additional details.

Thanks so much!

Marilyn Ravenwood

---

01 What is indicated about Drapers Window Coverings?

(A) It is located on Grover Avenue.
(B) It has several outlets around the country.
(C) It provides delivery services.
(D) It does not accept credit card payments.

02 According to the invoice, when must full payment be made?

(A) At the time of purchase
(B) Upon receipt of the order
(C) Within 48 hours of delivery
(D) Within the seven days of the invoice date

03 What is mentioned about Ms. Ravenwood?

(A) She lives on Larch Drive in Madison.
(B) She wants to make change to an ongoing order.
(C) She runs an interior decorating business.
(D) She may have sent the wrong amount of payment.

04 What most likely is true about Ms. Ravenwood's new client?

(A) He wants to purchase two sets of blinds.
(B) He is redecorating several rooms.
(C) He has shopped with Drapers before.
(D) He is moving into a new home.

05 What has Mr. Forester been asked to do?

(A) Send some replacements
(B) Recommend other products
(C) Visit an apartment
(D) Provide a cost estimate

Questions 06-10 refer to the following e-mail and form.

To	Warren Dawson <w.dawson@wamail.com>
From	Amber Sulaporn <amsula@redrubyresort.com>
Date	July 24
Subject	A small request

Dear Mr. Dawson,

We hope you enjoyed your stay at the Red Ruby Resort here in Phuket, Thailand, on July 16-18. It was a pleasure having you.

To keep our level of service high, we kindly ask our guests to complete a survey concerning their visit. The questionnaire can be found on our Web site. We would be grateful if you could complete the form and submit it.

Upon completion of the survey, you will be provided with a coupon number for a 20 percent discount on any future stay. Simply provide the number when making a reservation, and the amount will be deducted from your bill.

Sincerely,

Amber Sulaporn
Guest relations supervisor, Red Ruby Resort

Red Ruby Resort **Customer Survey Form**

Thank you for your feedback. The responses you provide will allow us to improve our facilities and services.

Name	Warren Dawson	Age	42
Number of Guests	Four	Citizenship	American

1. How did you hear about Red Ruby Resort?
   It was recommended by a coworker.

2. What did you think of our rooms and facilities?
   The facilities were clean, the swimming pool was amazing, and beach access was satisfactory. However, we stayed in one of the beachfront cottages, and it felt outdated. The décor looked old-fashioned, and the old air conditioner was loud.

3. What did you think of our services and dining options?
   My family and I enjoyed all the food, especially the assortment of local fruit at the buffet breakfast. Your staff was attentive and friendly.

4. Would you stay at Red Ruby Resort again?
   Yes. We enjoyed the visit, particularly the island excursions on the second day of our visit! I also felt that your prices were reasonable.

5. Would you like to be on Red Ruby Resort's monthly e-mail list?
   Yes.

If you do not receive the newsletter within a month, contact Amber Sulaporn.

06 What does Ms. Sulaporn ask Mr. Dawson to do?

(A) Send a gift certificate
(B) Provide feedback
(C) Submit a payment
(D) Confirm travel dates

07 In the e-mail, the word "deducted" in paragraph 3, line 2, is closest in meaning to

(A) detached
(B) shortened
(C) subtracted
(D) decreased

08 What is NOT indicated about Mr. Dawson?

(A) He traveled with a group.
(B) He was satisfied with the dining options.
(C) He changed rooms during his stay.
(D) He thinks some facilities need to be updated.

09 What does Mr. Dawson suggest about the Red Ruby Resort?

(A) It has discounts for groups.
(B) Some of its staff were inattentive.
(C) It employs local tour guides.
(D) It offers short trips for guests.

10 What should guests do if the newsletter does not arrive?

(A) Call a resort representative
(B) Reach out to the guest relations supervisor
(C) Fill in another subscription form
(D) Check their online account information

Questions 01-05 refer to the following advertisement and e-mail.

Crystalline Hotel
Make your next special event even MORE special!

Whether you are holding a wedding or anniversary party, or hosting a business event, Chile's Crystalline Hotel can orchestrate all the arrangements for you at one of four locations in Santiago, Concepcion, Valparaiso, and La Serena! Simply relax and let us take care of everything.

Spacious event halls can seat groups of up to 250 people. They can be decorated to your requirements, and floral arrangements are also available. Each hall comes with a state-of-the-art sound and light system, with projectors and screens included for your use. Although we do not provide entertainment, we can give you a list of agencies that do.

Choose from a wide variety of buffet or table-service menus with dishes to suit every taste. Our expert chefs can prepare European, Asian, and American foods and cook for those with special dietary preferences.

And take advantage of our advance booking offer! Make a reservation at least three months in advance to receive complimentary table settings prepared by our in-house florist! Contact us at events@crystalline.com to book your next event at the Crystalline Hotel!

Service in Spanish, English, and Portuguese is available. The hotel offers free valet parking for guests.

TO   Celia Perez <celiap@crystalline.com>
FROM   Mindy Johnson <mjohnson@fastemail.com>
SUBJECT October 22 wedding
DATE   January 2

Dear Ms. Perez,

Thank you so much for responding to my message and confirming that you do have a vacant event hall for my wedding reception on October 22. My fiancé and I have heard excellent reviews about your hotel's wedding services from a friend of his, who seemed particularly impressed by the elegance of your location. So, we would like to book the hall for that day, with a full bar and buffet dinner for 250 guests.

Also, as I am originally from Australia, I will have around 20 relatives flying in for the wedding, and some of them will require rooms. Could you let me know if you have any available for October 21-22?

Once again, we are so pleased that you will be hosting our reception.

Regards,
Mindy Johnson

01 For whom is the advertisement most likely intended?

(A) Tourists seeking unique Chilean attractions
(B) People planning special occasions
(C) Trainees learning about hotel services
(D) Business travelers requiring meeting venues

02 What is NOT a service offered by Crystalline Hotel?

(A) Multilingual assistance
(B) Valet parking
(C) Food catering
(D) Musical entertainment

03 What does Ms. Johnson mention about her fiancé?

(A) He wrote a review of the hotel.
(B) He knows someone who was married at the hotel.
(C) He has relatives arriving from abroad.
(D) He booked rooms for his guests.

04 What does Ms. Johnson inquire about?

(A) Availability of special menus
(B) Accommodation vacancies
(C) Costs of services
(D) Airport transportation

05 What can be concluded about Ms. Johnson's event?

(A) It will take place by the hotel pool.
(B) It qualifies for a special offer on flowers.
(C) It will require an audiovisual system.
(D) It has not yet been confirmed.

DAY 10 삼중 지문

최신 출제 경향

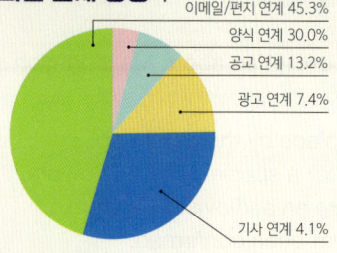

- 이메일/편지 연계 45.3%
- 양식 연계 30.0%
- 공고 연계 13.2%
- 광고 연계 7.4%
- 기사 연계 4.1%

① **이메일/편지 연계** | 이메일과 그에 대해 회신하는 또 다른 이메일, 그리고 관련 영수증 등의 양식이 연계되는 경우가 많다.

② **양식 연계** | 제품 및 서비스에 대한 브로슈어, 고객의 이용 후기, 후기를 작성한 고객에게 직원이 보낸 이메일과 같은 다양한 조합으로 출제된다.

③ **공고/광고/기사 연계** | 주로 첫 번째 지문에서 언급된 특정 정보에 대해 두 번째 지문에서 추가로 설명하거나 문의를 하고, 세 번째 지문에 그 이후 진행된 내용이 정리되어 나온다.

고난도 출제 포인트

POINT 1
간접적으로 제시된 단서로 정답을 추론해야 하는 연계 문제

지문 1: 웹페이지
At Oslo's Health Innovation Conference, Sam Ruth won an award for his Wellness Companion app. The event was recorded and available online.

지문 2: 이메일
Dear Mr. Ruth
Please stay one more day after the conference to visit our hospital. We will meet with our hospital staff that day.

지문 3: 후기
★★★★★ Evelyn Thatcher
As an individual researcher who has evaluated many health apps, I find this app exceptionally effective.

Q: What is true about the LM Hospital? A: It is located in Oslo. 오답률: 44.8%

→ 첫 번째 지문에서는 Oslo의 Health Innovation 컨퍼런스에서 Sam Ruth가 수상했다는 정보가 제시되고, 두 번째 지문에서 "visit our hospital"이라는 표현으로 병원 관계자가 Mr. Ruth에게 병원 방문을 위해 컨퍼런스가 끝난 후 하루 더 머물러 달라고 요청하는 내용이 나온다. 이 두 정보를 연결하여 해당 병원이 컨퍼런스와 같은 도시인 Oslo에 위치한다는 것을 추론해야 하는 까다로운 연계 문제이다.

POINT 2
삼중 지문에 자주 등장하는 고난도 어휘

initiate 시작하다	augment 늘리다	tailor 맞추다	defray 돌려주다	allocate 할당하다
diploma 졸업장	vigorous 격렬한	tentative 임시의	oversee 감독하다	in advance 미리
robust 굳건한	furnishing 가구	verify 입증하다	feasibility 실행 가능성	distinguished 유명한

빈출 문제 집중 훈련

빈출 문제를 풀며 실전 감각을 키워보자. 어려운 문제는 박스에 표시하고, 채점 후 복습하여 취약점을 보완하자.

Questions 01-05 refer to the following article, e-mail, and schedule.

Skyliner Extends Its Reach

MIAMI (January 2)—Skyliner has announced it will be launching new routes out of Miami this year. Starting next month, the airline will initiate daily nonstop services to Las Vegas. In addition, there will be twice-weekly nonstop flights to the Caribbean cities of Kingston, Nassau, and Port of Spain.

"We are pleased to offer our customers a wider selection by adding these destinations," CEO Jeff Prince said in a statement. "By the end of June, Skyliner will be flying to 30 different locations from Miami, the site of both its main hub and corporate headquarters. This number will go up as we augment our reach to include more destinations in South America."

Skyliner has grown robustly in recent years thanks to its low-cost positioning and vigorous customer focus. Its expansion has also helped to satisfy rising market demand following the closure of competing carrier Midway.

Details of the new routes will be publicized on the company's Web site at a later date. For more information, visit www.skylinerairlines.com.

To: Linda Ferry <l.ferry@skylinerairlines.com>
From: Paul Adams <p.adams@skylinerairlines.com>
Subject: Training
Date: January 19
Attachment: schedule

Linda,

We have tentatively scheduled training dates for the staff at Skyliner's newest destinations. However, there has been one minor alteration in that we've decided to delay the launch of service to one of the cities. The training schedule for this delayed launch will be announced later.

So, from February 16 to 20, we have you in charge of the one-week orientation for all new staff at our headquarters, followed by on-site instruction in Las Vegas after that. Ms. Warren will handle the two remaining cities but has indicated that she can also assist with the orientation. If you have any scheduling conflicts, please let me know. Once the schedule has been finalized, I will take care of all the travel arrangements.

Paul

Skyliner Training Schedule

Date	Event
February 16-20 (Miami)	Orientation training for all new staff working at new destinations and on new routes
February 23-27 (Las Vegas)	Training for ticketing agents and administrative staff
March 1-5 (Kingston)	Training for ticketing agents and administrative staff
March 8-12 (Port of Spain)	Training for ticketing agents and administrative staff

01 What is predicted to happen at Skyliner?
(A) It will overtake its closest competitors.
(B) It will move its main hub to Miami.
(C) It will add more South American routes.
(D) It will begin offering an online check-in service.

02 What does the article suggest about Skyliner?
(A) It raised its fares over the past year.
(B) It has benefited from Midway's closure.
(C) It may offer discounts on new routes.
(D) It conducted a survey of its customers.

03 What will Ms. Ferry probably do on February 18?
(A) Oversee an orientation in Miami
(B) Travel to a new airline destination
(C) Join Ms. Warren in Kingston
(D) Receive service training

04 What has Ms. Warren volunteered to do?
(A) Write some more detailed training material
(B) Take care of some travel arrangements
(C) Help familiarize staff with company operations
(D) Provide an updated schedule to a colleague

05 Which route has Skyliner decided to delay?
(A) Port of Spain
(B) Las Vegas
(C) Nassau
(D) Kingston

Questions 06-10 refer to the following Web page, flyer, and e-mail.

www.applewoodInt.com

| Home | About | News | Contact Us |

Applewood Interiors

Celebrate the arrival of spring with Applewood Interiors! Browse our collection of products for your living room, kitchen, dining room, and office from April 1 to April 15 and enjoy discounts of up to 50 percent on items from last year's inventory. This offer is limited to items purchased in-store. Shop now at your nearest Applewood Interiors location. For inquiries or assistance, please call our hotline at 555-8999 or e-mail cs2@applewoodint.com.

Applewood Interiors Spring Sale
April 1 to 15

DINING ROOM
Paulina cherry table, seats 8, $970
Richardson walnut table, seats 6, $649
Onyx oak table, seats 6, $629
Remington cherry table, seats 8, $779

KITCHEN & OUTDOORS
Enthuse pine kitchen counter, $299
Montaigne oak outdoor bench, $239

BEDROOM
Komfort King pine bed frame, $379
Clover oak night table, $319
Ambassador cherry dresser, $229

OFFICE
Scrito desk with double drawer, $399
Buchtal walnut bookcase, $278
Doozie filing cabinet, $244

* All prices shown are inclusive of 50% discounts. Free shipping is included for purchases over $990. Products come with a limited three-year warranty.

To: Customer Service <cs2@applewoodint.com>
From: Ida Shermer <ida_shermer@mountainmail.com>
Subject: Inquiry
Date: April 2

Hello,

I recently bought a new home in Hastings, and I am furnishing my home. In my dining room, I have a cabinet and buffet table made of cherry wood and would like a dining table made of the same material. Due to my tight budget, I cannot spend more than $900 on a dining table. Could you let me know what options you have?

I'm also interested in purchasing a dresser of the same material to match my new home's décor.

I would be grateful if you could verify the feasibility of having these furnishings arrive at my new residence no later than the 25th.

Thank you,
Ida Shermer

06 According to the Web page, what is suggested about Applewood Interiors?

(A) It is celebrating a store anniversary.
(B) It manufactures its own products.
(C) It operates multiple locations.
(D) It is launching a designer collection.

07 What is indicated about the items on the flyer?

(A) They can also be bought online.
(B) They come with an additional discount.
(C) They consist of old merchandise.
(D) They come with free shipping.

08 In the e-mail, the word "tight" in paragraph 1, line 3 is closest in meaning to

(A) cramped
(B) withdrawn
(C) restricted
(D) attached

09 Which product line would Applewood Interiors most likely recommend to Ms. Shermer?

(A) Onyx
(B) Paulina
(C) Richardson
(D) Remington

10 Why does Ms. Shermer mention the 25th of the month in her e-mail?

(A) To ensure her home renovation is completed by that deadline
(B) To confirm that her furniture will be delivered by that date
(C) To accommodate guests arriving after that date
(D) To finalize her budget planning for additional purchases

고난도 문제 완전 정복

고난도 문제를 풀며, 완벽하게 실전을 대비하자. 어려운 문제는 박스에 표시하고, 채점 후 복습하여 완전히 내 것으로 만들자.

Questions 01-05 refer to the following form, e-mail, and receipt.

GEORGIAN CRUISE LINES
ITINERARY AND RESERVATION CONFIRMATION

Name	Antonia Blaine	E-mail	anblaine@itmail.com
Passport Number	PV948344	Phone	(507) 555-4995
Reservation Number	AB-4995	Address	1233 Minton Street, Spokane, WA 99485

Mediterranean Cruise Package: August 3-August 12

Departure	August 3, 10:30 A.M.
Arrival	August 12, 4 P.M.
Number of Travelers	2
Names of Travelers	Antonia Blaine, Rosalind Purefoy
Cabin	303
Type	Executive suite
Ports of Call	Naples, Sardinia, Barcelona, Mallorca

Please check that all the information listed above is correct, and notify Georgian Cruise Lines at reservations@georgiancruiselines.com if there are any errors. Reservations canceled within one month of departure are nonrefundable. All other change requests will be charged a fee of €150 per passenger.

TO	<reservations@georgiancruiselines.com>
FROM	Antonia Blaine <anblaine@itmail.com>
DATE	June 12
SUBJECT	Reservation AB-4995

Dear Madam or Sir,

I booked a cruise with your company for my sister and myself from August 3 through August 12. Unfortunately, I need to cancel the booking for my sister. She has an unexpected commitment at the bank where she works during those dates. I will still be going on the cruise as scheduled, though.

I would also like to request a cabin with a better view. I am currently in one on the third level, but I would prefer to be on the eighth level or higher. I paid for our trip by credit card, so would it be possible to use that to pay the penalty fee for the change to my booking? You should have the number in your records, but you may call me at 555-4995 if you require confirmation. For security reasons, I'd rather not supply my card information over e-mail.

Sincerely yours,
Antonia Blaine

Georgian Cruise Lines

Cruise Package Receipt

Reservation: AB-4995   Dates of Travel: August 3 to 12

Issue date: August 12
Passenger name: Antonia Blaine
Cabin Type: Deluxe
Deck Level: 9

Description	Price
Room Charges (free meals included)	€450.00
Food & Beverage (additional)	€84.00
Entertainment (additional)	€59.00
Other:	
Package Tour Sardinia	€60.00
Package Tour Barcelona	€125.00
Total:	€778.00

Charge to: Worldpass Credit Card
Name on the credit card: Antonia Blaine

01 What information is provided on the form?

(A) The cost of a cruise ticket
(B) Ms. Purefoy's contact details
(C) Accepted payment methods
(D) A list of destinations

02 What is suggested about Ms. Blaine?

(A) She paid with her sister's card.
(B) She had to sign a document.
(C) She qualified for a refund.
(D) She canceled the booking for herself.

03 What is mentioned about Ms. Blaine's sister?

(A) She was overcharged for a cruise booking.
(B) She is employed at a financial institution.
(C) She has changed her time of departure.
(D) She will reschedule a work-related event.

04 What does Ms. Blaine have a question about?

(A) Onboard activities for adults
(B) Her scheduled departure date
(C) A penalty payment method
(D) A request for technical assistance

05 What can be concluded about Georgian Cruise Lines?

(A) It made some changes to its reservation policy.
(B) It offers free package tours to long-term customers.
(C) It requested Ms. Blaine's payment details by e-mail.
(D) It moved Ms. Blaine into a different room.

실시간 토익시험 정답확인&해설강의
Hackers.co.kr

한 권으로 끝내는 해커스 토익 900+ LC+RC+VOCA

실전모의고사

1

잠깐! 테스트 전 아래 사항을 꼭 확인하세요.

1. Answer Sheet(p.227), 연필, 지우개, 시계를 준비하셨나요? ☐
2. Listening mp3를 들을 준비가 되셨나요? ☐

모든 준비가 완료되었으면 목표 점수를 떠올린 후 테스트를 시작합니다.
시험 시간 120분내에 문제 풀이와 답안지 마킹까지 모두 완료해야 합니다.

🎧 TEST1.mp3

실전용·복습용 문제풀이 mp3 무료 다운로드 및 스트리밍 바로듣기 (HackersIngang.com)

* 실제 시험장의 소음까지 재현해 낸 고사장 소음/매미 버전, 영국식·호주식 발음 집중 버전, 고속 버전까지 구매하면 실전에 더욱 완벽히 대비할 수 있습니다.

무료 mp3 바로듣기

LISTENING TEST

In this section, you must demonstrate your ability to understand spoken English. This section is divided into four parts and will take approximately 45 minutes to complete. Do not mark the answers in your test book. Use the answer sheet that is provided separately.

PART 1

Directions: For each question, you will listen to four short statements about a picture in your test book. These statements will not be printed and will only be spoken one time. Select the statement that best describes what is happening in the picture and mark the corresponding letter (A), (B), (C), or (D) on the answer sheet.

Sample Answer

The statement that best describes the picture is (B), "The man is sitting at the desk." So, you should mark letter (B) on the answer sheet.

1.

2.

3.

4.

5.

6.

PART 2

Directions: For each question, you will listen to a statement or question followed by three possible responses spoken in English. They will not be printed and will only be spoken one time. Select the best response and mark the corresponding letter (A), (B), or (C) on your answer sheet.

7. Mark your answer on the answer sheet.
8. Mark your answer on the answer sheet.
9. Mark your answer on the answer sheet.
10. Mark your answer on the answer sheet.
11. Mark your answer on the answer sheet.
12. Mark your answer on the answer sheet.
13. Mark your answer on the answer sheet.
14. Mark your answer on the answer sheet.
15. Mark your answer on the answer sheet.
16. Mark your answer on the answer sheet.
17. Mark your answer on the answer sheet.
18. Mark your answer on the answer sheet.
19. Mark your answer on the answer sheet.
20. Mark your answer on the answer sheet.
21. Mark your answer on the answer sheet.
22. Mark your answer on the answer sheet.
23. Mark your answer on the answer sheet.
24. Mark your answer on the answer sheet.
25. Mark your answer on the answer sheet.
26. Mark your answer on the answer sheet.
27. Mark your answer on the answer sheet.
28. Mark your answer on the answer sheet.
29. Mark your answer on the answer sheet.
30. Mark your answer on the answer sheet.
31. Mark your answer on the answer sheet.

PART 3

Directions: In this part, you will listen to several conversations between two or more speakers. These conversations will not be printed and will only be spoken one time. For each conversation, you will be asked to answer three questions. Select the best response and mark the corresponding letter (A), (B), (C), or (D) on your answer sheet.

32. Where do the speakers most likely work?
    (A) At a restaurant
    (B) At a shipping firm
    (C) At a law office
    (D) At a retail outlet

33. What problem does the man mention?
    (A) He does not like some food.
    (B) He might not meet a deadline.
    (C) He did not receive an assignment.
    (D) He missed a client meeting.

34. What does the woman recommend?
    (A) Changing a deadline
    (B) Making a reservation
    (C) Taking some work home
    (D) Picking up some food

35. What will happen on Wednesday?
    (A) A trade fair
    (B) A company luncheon
    (C) A team-building event
    (D) A business conference

36. What does the man want to know?
    (A) Where a venue is located
    (B) Who else will attend
    (C) When an event will begin
    (D) How much registration costs

37. Why should the man give the woman a call?
    (A) To make an appointment
    (B) To determine a location
    (C) To check a schedule
    (D) To request a ride

38. Why did the woman visit the office?
    (A) To interview job candidates
    (B) To serve some customers
    (C) To check on a program
    (D) To ask about a schedule

39. Why is the man pleased?
    (A) A job is now available.
    (B) A request was approved.
    (C) A computer program works well.
    (D) A customer gave positive feedback.

40. What will the man most likely do next week?
    (A) Train some personnel
    (B) Transfer departments
    (C) Upgrade a system
    (D) Start a new position

41. What is the topic of the conversation?
    (A) Prototype design plans
    (B) Quality control methods
    (C) Equipment replacement
    (D) Software installation

42. What will the woman ask the office manager to do?
    (A) Place an order
    (B) Hire a designer
    (C) Cancel an assignment
    (D) Select a model

43. What does the man say he can do?
    (A) Deal with staff complaints
    (B) Extend a submission deadline
    (C) Request funds for a project
    (D) Find out employee preferences

GO ON TO THE NEXT PAGE

44. What problem does the woman mention?

(A) A device has been damaged.
(B) A promotion has ended.
(C) A part is missing.
(D) A coupon is invalid.

45. What does the woman mean when she says, "I bought it over two years ago"?

(A) A model is not available.
(B) A repair should be made.
(C) An item has lasted a long time.
(D) A guarantee has expired.

46. What does the woman want to do?

(A) Examine a product
(B) Compare some prices
(C) Sign up for a service
(D) Contact another branch

47. Where most likely do the speakers work?

(A) At a financial institution
(B) At a cell phone store
(C) At an IT consulting firm
(D) At a software company

48. What is suggested about the mobile application?

(A) It was designed by Robert Nolan.
(B) It is missing an important feature.
(C) It was affected by a database problem.
(D) It is not yet available to the public.

49. What is the woman asked to do?

(A) Attend a launch party
(B) Call a mobile phone number
(C) Provide a status update
(D) Check an Internet connection

50. Who is the woman?

(A) A radio host
(B) An author
(C) A show producer
(D) A journalist

51. Why does the woman say, "I'll be traveling for the next few weeks"?

(A) To reject a request
(B) To schedule some interviews
(C) To answer survey questions
(D) To suggest a topic of discussion

52. What will the man probably do next?

(A) Begin an interview
(B) Organize a trip
(C) Supply a list
(D) Transfer a call

53. What are the speakers mainly discussing?

(A) Office renovations
(B) Student enrollment
(C) Registration fees
(D) Teaching availability

54. Why does the man congratulate Jasmine?

(A) She completed a course.
(B) She found new employment.
(C) She received a pay raise at work.
(D) She expanded her class schedule.

55. Who most likely is Sheila?

(A) An office manager
(B) A salesperson
(C) A yoga instructor
(D) A football coach

56. What industry do the speakers most likely work in?

(A) Marketing
(B) Film
(C) Fashion design
(D) Construction

57. What does the man like about a new product line?

(A) Its colors
(B) Its patterns
(C) Its price
(D) Its fit

58. What will the speakers do next?

(A) Move a product display
(B) Create some patterns
(C) Present some drawings
(D) Analyze sales data

59. What event are the speakers most likely planning?

(A) A facility tour
(B) An art exhibition
(C) A gallery relocation
(D) A photo shoot

60. What does the woman agree to do?

(A) Meet with an artist
(B) Reject some submissions
(C) Draft an agreement
(D) Check an address

61. What does the woman ask for?

(A) The location of a meeting
(B) The use of a vehicle
(C) The name of an artist
(D) The floor plan of a gallery

Palace Theater

Film	Showtime
Out of Town	6:30 P.M.
Tonight	7:00 P.M.
With Peter	7:30 P.M.
When We Go	8:00 P.M.

62. What did the woman do this afternoon?

(A) She visited a theater.
(B) She read an article.
(C) She listened to a voice message.
(D) She purchased some tickets.

63. Look at the graphic. Which movie will the speakers watch?

(A) *Out of Town*
(B) *Tonight*
(C) *With Peter*
(D) *When We Go*

64. What does the man suggest?

(A) Taking a bus
(B) Going by car
(C) Getting some snacks
(D) Watching some trailers

GO ON TO THE NEXT PAGE

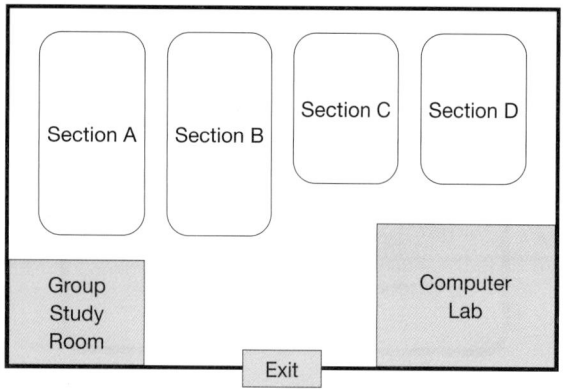
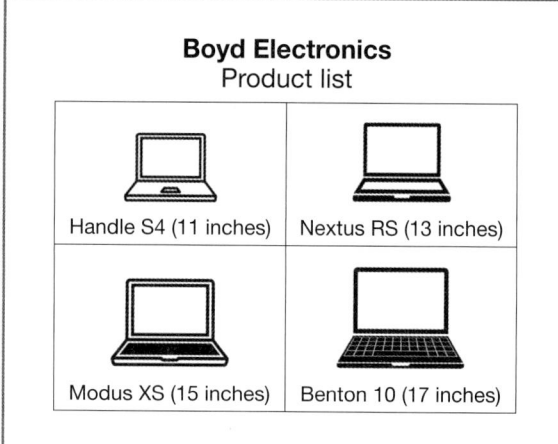

65. What does the woman ask the man to do?

(A) Put some items on hold
(B) Renew a subscription
(C) Update a library membership
(D) Make a recommendation

66. Look at the graphic. Which section will the woman search in?

(A) Section A
(B) Section B
(C) Section C
(D) Section D

67. According to the man, what is available on a Web site?

(A) Reviews from members
(B) Coupons for shoppers
(C) Details about audiobooks
(D) Information about policies

68. Look at the graphic. Which item is currently not in stock?

(A) Handle S4
(B) Nextus RS
(C) Modus XS
(D) Benton 10

69. What did the woman recently do?

(A) Delivered some products
(B) Arranged inventory
(C) Checked a schedule
(D) Spoke with a supplier

70. What is mentioned about a shipment?

(A) It is going to be delivered soon.
(B) It was smaller than expected.
(C) It had to be returned to a seller.
(D) It was mailed out two days ago.

PART 4

Directions: In this part, you will listen to several short talks by a single speaker. These talks will not be printed and will only be spoken one time. For each talk, you will be asked to answer three questions. Select the best response and mark the corresponding letter (A), (B), (C), or (D) on your answer sheet.

71. Who most likely is the speaker?

    (A) A bank employee
    (B) A travel agent
    (C) A personal accountant
    (D) A project manager

72. What problem does the speaker mention?

    (A) A credit card has expired.
    (B) A bill has not been paid.
    (C) An application was suspended.
    (D) An account cannot be accessed.

73. What does the speaker say the listener should do?

    (A) Apply for a program
    (B) Submit a document
    (C) Have some photos taken
    (D) Contact a homeowner

74. What is being advertised?

    (A) A delivery company
    (B) A ride service
    (C) A luggage retailer
    (D) A car manufacturer

75. What is offered for free?

    (A) Drinks
    (B) A travel pouch
    (C) A drop-off service
    (D) Headphones

76. According to the speaker, how can the listeners receive a discount?

    (A) By using a mobile application
    (B) By entering a promotional code
    (C) By giving feedback online
    (D) By picking up a brochure

77. Where do the listeners most likely work?

    (A) At a service center
    (B) At a jewelry store
    (C) At a modeling agency
    (D) At a wedding venue

78. What will Mr. Foley do?

    (A) Meet with some customers
    (B) Inspect some goods
    (C) Discuss some products
    (D) Process an online order

79. Why does the speaker say, "Most of you in the sales department are new"?

    (A) To explain the purpose of a policy change
    (B) To stress the importance of a meeting
    (C) To reschedule a training session
    (D) To suggest some improvements

80. What is the announcement mainly about?

    (A) Monthly festivals
    (B) Remodeled bus stops
    (C) Route changes
    (D) Weather updates

81. What can the listeners find on a Web site?

    (A) A company's reviews
    (B) A sign-in sheet
    (C) An event timetable
    (D) A revised schedule

82. What are the listeners encouraged to do?

    (A) Reserve seats ahead of time
    (B) Plan to spend more time than usual
    (C) Drive instead of taking a bus
    (D) Register on a Web site

GO ON TO THE NEXT PAGE

83. Where are the listeners?

(A) At a town hall
(B) At an art fair
(C) At a shopping mall
(D) At a historical museum

84. What is featured in the special exhibit?

(A) Photographs
(B) Films
(C) Artifacts
(D) Garments

85. What does the speaker mean when she says, "there are no group tours scheduled today"?

(A) Tickets for a popular attraction have sold out.
(B) The listeners will be unable to attend an exhibit.
(C) The listeners don't have to worry about a crowd.
(D) A building will be closing earlier than scheduled.

86. Where most likely does the listener work?

(A) At a post office
(B) At a bookstore
(C) At a hotel
(D) At a repair center

87. What problem does the speaker mention?

(A) A product has been lost.
(B) An item has been damaged.
(C) A service has not restarted.
(D) A vacation plan was canceled.

88. What does the speaker say she has already done?

(A) She signed a receipt.
(B) She mailed a letter.
(C) She visited an office.
(D) She made an online inquiry.

89. What is the announcement mainly about?

(A) The date of a screening
(B) The duration of a project
(C) Advice from executives
(D) Feedback from a test audience

90. What are the listeners asked to do?

(A) Silence mobile phones
(B) Select a preference
(C) Develop new ideas
(D) Meet with a group of people

91. Why does the speaker say, "I'll be meeting the producer again next Tuesday"?

(A) To indicate a deadline
(B) To change a schedule
(C) To correct an error
(D) To make a complaint

92. What is mentioned about Mr. Naresh?

(A) He transferred to a new department.
(B) He recently retired from work.
(C) He ordered more equipment.
(D) He was given a promotion.

93. According to the speaker, why will Mr. Naresh visit local stations?

(A) To give informational talks
(B) To deliver office supplies
(C) To carry out inspections
(D) To train some workers

94. What will the listeners do after a speech?

(A) Watch a demonstration
(B) Register for an event
(C) Fill out a survey
(D) Attend a gathering

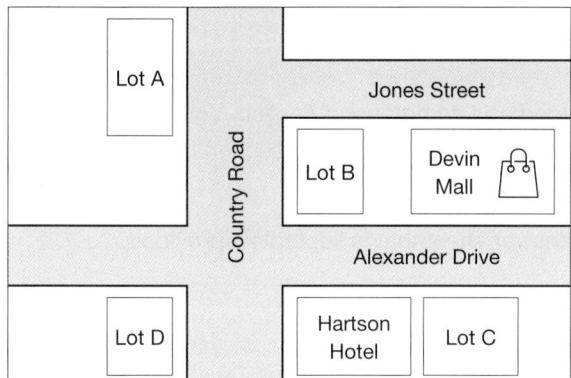
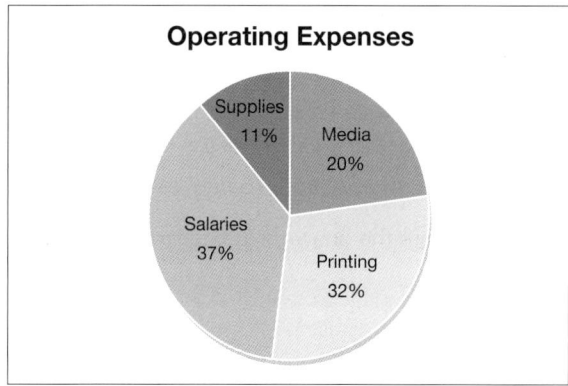

95. Who most likely are the listeners?

(A) Shoppers
(B) Festival planners
(C) News reporters
(D) Sales personnel

96. Look at the graphic. Which lot will be used for an event?

(A) Lot A
(B) Lot B
(C) Lot C
(D) Lot D

97. What are the listeners reminded to do?

(A) Take public transportation
(B) Purchase a ticket
(C) Display a parking pass
(D) Try a new menu item

98. Who most likely are the listeners?

(A) Financial advisors
(B) Marketing professionals
(C) Accounting staff
(D) Company shareholders

99. Look at the graphic. Which expense will most likely be reduced?

(A) Media
(B) Printing
(C) Salaries
(D) Supplies

100. What will happen next?

(A) A report will be handed out.
(B) A presentation will be given.
(C) A task will be explained.
(D) A decision will be announced.

This is the end of the Listening test. Turn to PART 5 in your test book.

GO ON TO THE NEXT PAGE

READING TEST

In this section, you must demonstrate your ability to read and comprehend English. You will be given a variety of texts and asked to answer questions about these texts. This section is divided into three parts and will take 75 minutes to complete.

Do not mark the answers in your test book. Use the answer sheet that is separately provided.

PART 5

Directions: In each question, you will be asked to review a statement that is missing a word or phrase. Four answer choices will be provided for each statement. Select the best answer and mark the corresponding letter (A), (B), (C), or (D) on the answer sheet.

---

101. There are no vacancies at the Starlight Hotel, ------- several rooms are available at the Pinehill Inn.

(A) but
(B) as
(C) neither
(D) nor

102. The project director submitted ------- marketing proposal yesterday for immediate implementation.

(A) he
(B) him
(C) his
(D) himself

103. Brinity Electronics' latest refrigerator shows a significant ------- in energy use compared to its predecessor.

(A) reduction
(B) reduced
(C) reduce
(D) reducing

104. During delivery, packages that contain delicate items must be handled -------.

(A) caution
(B) cautious
(C) cautions
(D) cautiously

105. Mr. Sawaya asked all department managers to cut expenses, ------- to the company's financial difficulties.

(A) pointing
(B) points
(C) pointed
(D) point

106. The service centers of Terta Corporation ------- specialized software to track customer complaints.

(A) employ
(B) employs
(C) employing
(D) has employed

107. Board members hope to decrease labor costs by ------- manufacturing to regions with lower average wages.

(A) inverting
(B) substituting
(C) shifting
(D) transforming

108. -------, the staff at Godsal Appliances attend company-sponsored training seminars on new technologies in the market.

(A) Potentially
(B) Similarly
(C) Occasionally
(D) Unanimously

109. Customers signing up for a one-year ------- to Emerald Mobile will receive a month of free service.

(A) subscribe
(B) subscriber
(C) subscription
(D) subscribes

110. ------- push the device's reset button whenever the Internet disconnects, and the problem will be fixed immediately.

(A) Simple
(B) Simply
(C) Simpler
(D) Simplify

111. If the noise from the air purifier is disturbing your sleep, you can activate night mode ------- the fan speed.

(A) lowers
(B) to lower
(C) lower
(D) lowered

112. HynaCorp's newest chemical plant will be fully ------- by the end of the quarter.

(A) function
(B) functional
(C) functionally
(D) functions

113. Burnside Travel's customers can easily customize their tour packages by selecting ------- activities.

(A) admitted
(B) optional
(C) affluent
(D) reliable

114. The café located ------- the lobby of the Harborview Condominium offers discounts to all tenants.

(A) among
(B) at
(C) to
(D) in

115. Once the committee had thoroughly reviewed Mr. Souko's business proposal, it ------- him a considerable grant.

(A) charged
(B) awarded
(C) accessed
(D) donated

116. At the beginning of last month, Hightower Bank's West Covina branch ------- to El Monte Street.

(A) moves
(B) moved
(C) has moved
(D) will move

117. The Kerner Foundation expects to receive most of its funding this year ------- corporate sponsorships.

(A) over
(B) along
(C) through
(D) across

118. Although Hamada's SUV has a higher safety rating than Sunza's, ------- vehicles have received high scores for performance.

(A) and
(B) both
(C) either
(D) several

119. Bolson Limited announced that it would stop producing ------- plastic containers in order to protect the environment.

(A) capable
(B) decisive
(C) effective
(D) disposable

120. Mr. Kim's ------- performance as a project leader led to him being offered a senior management position at Hartek Insurance.

(A) noting
(B) notability
(C) notable
(D) notably

GO ON TO THE NEXT PAGE

121. Please check the article before ------- it on the Web site to prevent the publication of content with factual errors.

    (A) upload
    (B) uploaded
    (C) uploading
    (D) to upload

122. ------- the charity auction, participants will attend a free concert at Brighton Hall featuring several local bands.

    (A) Toward
    (B) Upon
    (C) Whereas
    (D) Following

123. Even though airline miles usually expire after a given period, ------- offered by Leisure Air do not.

    (A) they
    (B) them
    (C) those
    (D) there

124. Employees may refer to the ------- on the intranet for the different project deadlines.

    (A) catalog
    (B) category
    (C) formation
    (D) timetable

125. The ------- growth in the retail sector has led to unusually high profits for the Coleman Department Store chain.

    (A) except
    (B) exception
    (C) exceptional
    (D) exceptionally

126. The factory workers at Quartman Enterprises were hoping for sizable pay raises as well as a better ------- package.

    (A) benefited
    (B) benefits
    (C) benefiter
    (D) benefiting

127. The candidate for the sales position made ------- a positive impression during the interview that he was hired immediately.

    (A) so
    (B) too
    (C) very
    (D) such

128. Venus Fashion was unsuccessful with its television campaign and turned to social media to ------- its products.

    (A) generate
    (B) exchange
    (C) market
    (D) contribute

129. The hundreds of customers attending the opening of Beppo Computers' newest store were lined up in an ------- manner.

    (A) order
    (B) orders
    (C) orderly
    (D) ordering

130. A meeting will be held for everyone who agreed ------- at next weekend's event.

    (A) volunteer
    (B) to volunteer
    (C) volunteering
    (D) will volunteer

PART 6

Directions: In this part, you will be asked to read four English texts. Each text is missing a word, phrase, or sentence. Select the answer choice that correctly completes the text and mark the corresponding letter (A), (B), (C), or (D) on the answer sheet.

Questions 131-134 refer to the following flyer.

Introducing the Forge

Lodz Technological Institute (LTI) proudly introduces the Forge. The Forge is a ------- (131.) run by a community of creators, where amateur inventors can develop their projects. ------- (132.) your interest lies in electronics, carpentry, or metalworking, the Forge can help you realize your creative vision. It offers ------- (133.) access to a range of equipment, such as 3D printers, laser cutters, and more. All LTI students are welcome to use the equipment on their own during regular university hours. Machinery may be used for free, and materials are provided at a low cost when required. ------- (134.). Stop by the Kaminski Building, or visit www.lodz.edu/forge for more information.

---

131. (A) group
(B) course
(C) workspace
(D) conference

132. (A) Whether
(B) Unless
(C) Although
(D) Whereas

133. (A) paid
(B) shared
(C) supervised
(D) finished

134. (A) We will notify you when enrollment is open.
(B) Donated items may be dropped off at the office.
(C) We can even help you order whatever you may need.
(D) Membership fees must be paid in advance each month.

GO ON TO THE NEXT PAGE

Questions 135-138 refer to the following e-mail.

TO: Joe Hamlin <joe.ham@homeready.com>
FROM: Caroline Quigley <car.qui@homeready.com>
DATE: August 9
SUBJECT: Sales manager

Dear Mr. Hamlin,

I'm writing to let you know that Deborah Watson, one of our sales managers, will be ------- our manufacturing facility on August 16. Ms. Watson is new to our company. -------, it is important for her to have a tour of the entire factory and learn how our appliances are made.

As the supervisor of the factory, you are the most qualified to give Ms. Watson the tour. Please ------- her around the manufacturing facility so that she can become familiar with how we produce our merchandise. -------. Also, encourage her to ask questions and talk to some of our workers.

Sincerely,

Caroline Quigley
Regional Manager, Home Ready Appliances

135. (A) evaluating
(B) leaving
(C) visiting
(D) suspending

136. (A) For example
(B) In contrast
(C) Unusually
(D) Accordingly

137. (A) promote
(B) accompany
(C) recruit
(D) demonstrate

138. (A) Let me know if you think she should be hired after the visit.
(B) It may be possible to eliminate this defect before production.
(C) All of your expenses during the trip will be reimbursed by August.
(D) Give special attention to the assembly line area.

Questions 139-142 refer to the following article.

Stelly's Latest Work Sells Out

NEW ORLEANS (April 24)—Local writer Maria Stelly took almost a decade ------- her novel *Mystery Street*. But when the book was finally ------- to 17 bookstores across New Orleans on Monday, it sold out in just two days.
139. **140.**

"Even though my first publication was moderately successful, I'm surprised by the popularity of *Mystery Street*, and I'm thankful for all my fans," said Stelly. She believes that an innovative marketing strategy is partially responsible for the book's popularity. -------. Additional copies of Stelly's new book ------- available by April 30.
141.
142.

139. (A) wrote
(B) had written
(C) to write
(D) writer

140. (A) distributed
(B) reported
(C) connected
(D) compared

141. (A) This involves targeting readers who are active on social media.
(B) New Orleans has never hosted the ceremony before.
(C) Stelly only began writing fiction a year ago.
(D) Stelly's first novel was about a young girl who grew up on a farm.

142. (A) became
(B) have become
(C) were becoming
(D) will become

Questions 143-146 refer to the following e-mail.

To: Rajesh Singh <rajesh.singh@indiaclothing.in>
From: Faria Deveraj <f.deveraj@mumbai.gov.in>
Date: October 12
Subject: Scheduled Inspection

Dear Mr. Singh,

On October 17, your clothing factory will undergo its yearly government inspection. This annual ------- will verify that all labor laws are being followed. Your factory passed the ------- evaluation with no major problems, so our inspectors hope to see a similar level of compliance this time around.

You are ------- obliged to provide access to any part of the factory that the inspectors wish to see. Failure to comply in this regard may result in fines and further investigation. Also, the inspectors need to confirm that workers are being properly compensated. -------.

Thank you for your attention to this matter.

Faria Deveraj
Inspection Team Leader
City Government of Mumbai

143. (A) meeting
(B) investment
(C) summary
(D) assessment

144. (A) decided
(B) forthcoming
(C) previous
(D) ultimate

145. (A) legally
(B) legality
(C) legal
(D) legitimate

146. (A) A copy of the receipt for your recent payment has been sent to you in the mail.
(B) The human resources department will need to prepare the relevant documents.
(C) Consequently, the company wishes to avoid paying any such penalties.
(D) We are interested in hearing about certain products that were recalled.

PART 7

Directions: In this part, you will be asked to read several texts, such as advertisements, articles, instant messages, or examples of business correspondence. Each text is followed by several questions. Select the best answer and mark the corresponding letter (A), (B), (C), or (D) on your answer sheet.

Questions 147-148 refer to the following instructions.

Deena Water Filtration System Maintenance Instructions

To ensure your new Deena Water Filtration System lasts for years, be sure to follow these simple maintenance instructions:

- After installing a filter, turn on any faucet and allow water to flow through it for at least two minutes to prepare the filter for use.

- Change the filter in each device every six months. A buildup of the substances removed from the water can cause blockages. Do not attempt to use cleaning agents as this will damage the filter and prevent it from functioning properly.

147. What is the purpose of the instructions?

(A) To explain the process for selecting a suitable model
(B) To illustrate the benefits of a system
(C) To train technicians in a repair procedure
(D) To provide directions on maintaining a product

148. What should users do on a regular basis?

(A) Schedule an inspection
(B) Replace a component
(C) Check water quality
(D) Apply a filter cleanser

GO ON TO THE NEXT PAGE

Questions 149-150 refer to the following e-mail.

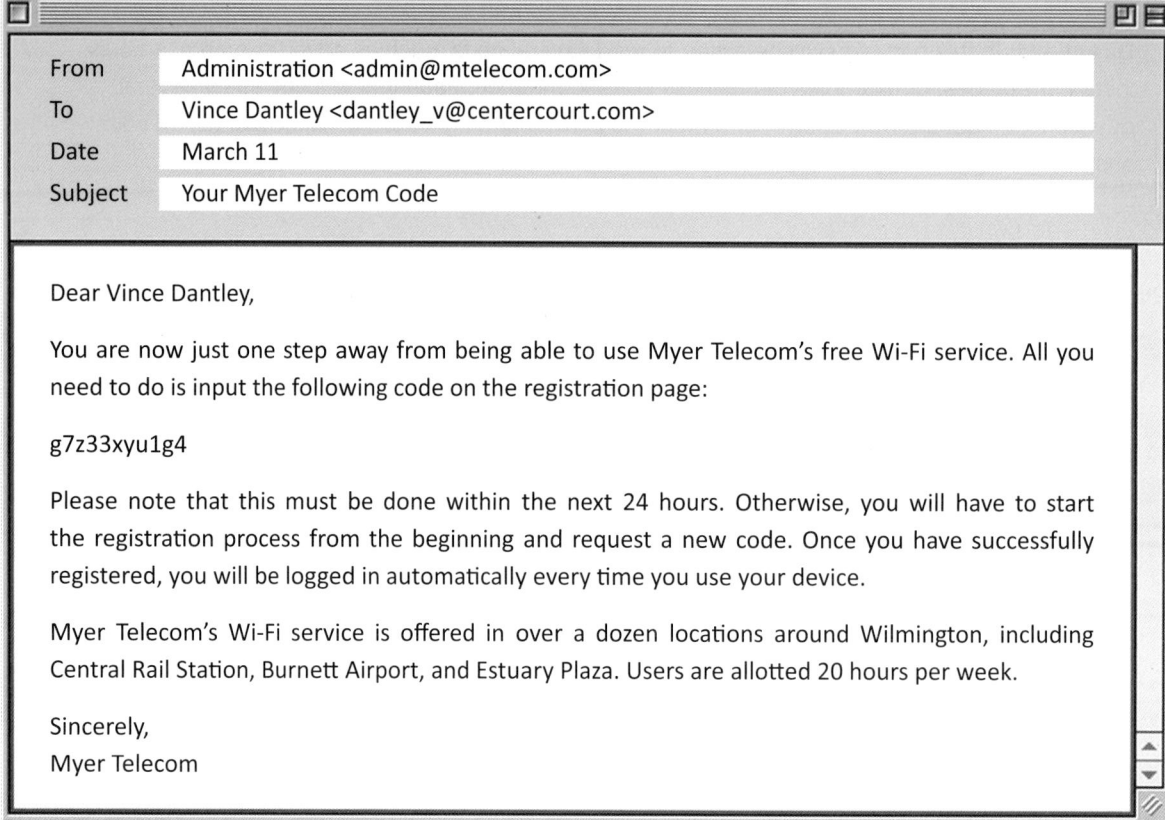

From	Administration <admin@mtelecom.com>
To	Vince Dantley <dantley_v@centercourt.com>
Date	March 11
Subject	Your Myer Telecom Code

Dear Vince Dantley,

You are now just one step away from being able to use Myer Telecom's free Wi-Fi service. All you need to do is input the following code on the registration page:

g7z33xyu1g4

Please note that this must be done within the next 24 hours. Otherwise, you will have to start the registration process from the beginning and request a new code. Once you have successfully registered, you will be logged in automatically every time you use your device.

Myer Telecom's Wi-Fi service is offered in over a dozen locations around Wilmington, including Central Rail Station, Burnett Airport, and Estuary Plaza. Users are allotted 20 hours per week.

Sincerely,
Myer Telecom

149. What can be inferred about Mr. Dantley?

(A) He has not completed a registration process.
(B) He was not able to remember a code.
(C) He paid for a mobile phone application.
(D) He relocated to Wilmington recently.

150. What is NOT indicated about Myer Telecom's Wi-Fi service?

(A) It connects automatically for registered users.
(B) It is available in some transportation facilities.
(C) It was launched less than a year ago.
(D) It can be used for a limited amount of time.

Questions 151-153 refer to the following article.

Renovations Completed at Faber Medical and Dental

June 24—Wallberg Health Group will be reopening its newly renovated third floor at Faber Medical and Dental in Doeville tomorrow. The inclusion of 14 additional examination rooms is expected to help reduce patient waiting periods while allowing medical staff to spend more time on consultations.

According to Wallberg Health Group representative Joan Bronson, visits to Faber Medical and Dental rose nearly 22 percent last year alone. "The residents of Doeville are getting older, which has resulted in more patients needing to see a doctor. Until now, Faber Medical and Dental has lacked the resources to give these patients the attention they deserve."

To keep up with the growing demand, Faber Medical and Dental has also hired nine additional registered nurses and two doctors. Part of the third floor will continue to function as an administrative office. The 25 staff members that formerly occupied the entire floor will return there to resume their duties. They were sent to Wallberg Health Group's Sharaton and McCollough locations when the six-month, nearly $1.4 million renovation project began.

151. What is the purpose of the article?

(A) To announce a management change at a clinic
(B) To complain about the lack of available medical staff
(C) To report that a facility will soon be accessible
(D) To describe a process for hiring doctors

152. What caused the demand to increase at Faber Medical and Dental?

(A) Improved services
(B) A hospital closure
(C) An aging population
(D) Free consultations

153. What is indicated about the administrative staff?

(A) They will receive training for their new positions.
(B) They were temporarily reassigned to other locations.
(C) They were asked to take a short-term leave of absence.
(D) They were relocated to a newly constructed building.

GO ON TO THE NEXT PAGE

Questions 154-155 refer to the following text-message chain.

Dan Hummel (8:19 P.M.)
I've got some bad news about Natalia Manco's European tour. We're going to have to postpone the rest of her concerts until further notice.

Phoebe Fiscella (8:21 P.M.)
Are you serious? We've already sold a lot of tickets for those shows.

Dan Hummel (8:24 P.M.)
I know, but she is very ill, so there is no chance that she will be able to sing anytime soon. I will start working on a statement for the media. We also need to let the halls where she is scheduled to perform know about the situation. Could you do that right now?

Phoebe Fiscella (8:25 P.M.)
Possibly. But it's pretty late now. If some of the managers have left for home already, I'll have to contact them when they return to their offices tomorrow.

154. Why has part of the tour been delayed?

(A) Shows have not received good reviews.
(B) A performer has a schedule conflict.
(C) A singer has a health issue.
(D) Tickets have not been selling well.

155. At 8:25 P.M., what does Ms. Fiscella mean when she writes, "Possibly"?

(A) She cannot confirm that Ms. Manco's concerts will sell out.
(B) She might meet with a representative of the media tomorrow.
(C) She will likely provide refunds to people who purchased tickets.
(D) She may not be able to fulfill Mr. Hummel's request immediately.

Questions 156-157 refer to the following announcement.

Annenberg County Community Job Fair

Tuesday, June 15, 1:00 P.M. to 5:00 P.M.
At Annenberg Convention Center — Seaview Ballroom, 2nd Floor

Need a job?
Come meet representatives of various local companies including:
- Wender Hotel Services
- Porter Medical Center
- Gelec Inc.
- Renew Manufacturing
- Annenberg Transportation
- Oarfield Technical

The event is free to attend, but participants must register in advance at www.annenbergcounty.com/events. The deadline for registration is June 5. On the day of the job fair, dress professionally, bring copies of your résumé and cover letter to hand out, and be prepared for on-the-spot interviews. Annenberg Convention Center is a two-minute walk from Exit 6 of Gibbs Station, and parking is available at a cost of $10 per hour.

156. What must those interested in attending the job fair do by June 5?

(A) Make a payment online
(B) Visit a registration booth
(C) Sign up on a Web page
(D) Complete an application form

157. What is indicated about the Annenberg Convention Center?

(A) It is accessible by public transportation.
(B) It has a small number of parking spaces.
(C) It is closed on weekday mornings.
(D) It is adjacent to a well-known hotel.

Questions 158-161 refer to the following online chat discussion.

Neil Webb [4:20 P.M.]
Hi, everyone. I met with our department manager, Mr. Tate, this morning, and he asked me to organize a team to make a commercial for the national supermarket chain Vatusi Foods. Elsa, are you available?

Elsa Moss [4:23 P.M.]
I'd like to help out, but I am currently working on the Dresden Apparel campaign. I won't be able to do both projects at the same time.

Neil Webb [4:23 P.M.]
I forgot about that. Courtney, you're the team leader for that campaign. Could you spare Elsa for a few weeks? She worked on the Vatusi Foods advertisement we produced last year, so she should be involved in this one.

Courtney McGuire [4:24 P.M.]
If it's absolutely necessary, I can transfer her to your team. But that's going to make it difficult to meet my deadline.

Neil Webb [4:25 P.M.]
Why don't I ask Mr. Tate to assign two of the junior marketing staff to your project to make up for the loss of Elsa?

Courtney McGuire [4:26 P.M.]
I'd appreciate that. Otherwise, I might have to ask Dresden Apparel for an extension. Elsa, you can start on the Vatusi Foods campaign at the end of the week.

Elsa Moss [4:27 P.M.]
Got it. Neil, do you know when the team will get together to discuss this project?

Neil Webb [4:30 P.M.]
Friday morning. We will meet in the conference room on the second floor at 10 A.M. I'll send you an e-mail with the agenda.

158. What did Mr. Tate do this morning?

(A) Introduced a new team member
(B) Assigned a task to a subordinate
(C) Talked to a department head
(D) Provided feedback on an advertisement

159. What is indicated about Vatusi Foods?

(A) It hired additional staff recently.
(B) It is a locally owned company.
(C) It disliked a commercial idea.
(D) It has worked with Ms. Moss before.

160. At 4:26 P.M., what does Ms. McGuire most likely mean when she writes, "I'd appreciate that"?

(A) She feels that a worker should not be reassigned.
(B) She needs an extension of a project deadline.
(C) She thinks that a campaign should not be released.
(D) She wants some employees added to her team.

161. What will Ms. Moss most likely do on Friday?

(A) Evaluate the performance of some employees
(B) Participate in a meeting with members of a new team
(C) Send an e-mail to a former client of the company
(D) Give a presentation about Dresden Apparel

GO ON TO THE NEXT PAGE

Questions 162-164 refer to the following advertisement.

QUEENSBORO PIZZA

We deliver free to all neighborhoods in Hartford!*

From now until June 30, you can order a Queen's Combo at a discounted price of $19.99. Choose any three of the following items:

1 medium cheese pizza
1 spaghetti with meat sauce
1 Caesar salad with grilled chicken
6 buttered breadsticks
10 spicy chicken wings

Plus, all summer long, buy any large pizza with premium toppings and receive a large cheese pizza absolutely free!

Premium toppings include:
Feta cheese
Sun-dried tomatoes
Roasted red peppers

Ordering is quick and easy using our new smartphone application! Download the application and register your personal details and payment information to get started. Enter the promotional code 4SUMR at checkout to get 20 percent off on your first order.

*For areas outside Hartford city limits, there is a delivery charge of $5.

---

162. What is NOT true about Queensboro Pizza?

(A) It charges a fee for all deliveries.
(B) It serves other items besides pizza.
(C) It makes pizzas in at least two sizes.
(D) It accepts orders through a mobile application.

163. What is indicated about the Queen's Combo?

(A) It includes a complimentary side salad.
(B) It is limited to delivery orders only.
(C) Its items can be changed.
(D) Its price is available for a limited time only.

164. How can customers receive a free pizza?

(A) By using a credit card to pay
(B) By entering a summer prize draw
(C) By ordering an item with special ingredients
(D) By presenting a voucher at a restaurant

Questions 165-167 refer to the following memo.

MEMO

TO: All staff
FROM: Patricia Diaz, CEO, BestSnack Inc.
DATE: March 18
SUBJECT: Exciting news

I'm delighted to announce to everyone that our BestSnack Vending Machine will be launched in 1,000 test locations nationwide starting next Monday. As you all know, the BestSnack is our vending machine with the latest advancements in touch-screen technology. — [1] —. It allows users to choose beverages and snacks tailored to their nutritional needs by selecting items based on categories. There are zero-calorie, low-carbohydrate, and sugar-free options. — [2] —. The marketing team is currently in the process of creating press releases informing national news outlets about the BestSnack. — [3] —. As employees, you are invited to participate in the testing process by trying items from these machines. — [4] —. Details about machine locations and item prices will be provided to you this week.

165. What is one purpose of the memo?

(A) To announce a company policy change
(B) To describe plans to launch a product trial
(C) To report an addition to the company cafeteria
(D) To introduce a new benefit available to employees

166. What does Ms. Diaz say that the marketing staff is doing?

(A) Conducting a survey on people's eating habits
(B) Developing official statements for media companies
(C) Arranging a meeting with the company's suppliers
(D) Planning a campaign event for the near future

167. In which of the positions marked [1], [2], [3], and [4] does the following sentence best belong?

"We will also be posting a public message on our Web site."

(A) [1]
(B) [2]
(C) [3]
(D) [4]

GO ON TO THE NEXT PAGE

Questions 168-171 refer to the following advertisement.

Freewater Lavender Farm

Looking for a unique experience? Visit the Freewater Lavender Farm at 821 Corkscrew Road just outside of Lewiston City! The farm's picturesque location and beautiful surroundings make it the ideal place to relax.

Stroll among our fields of fragrant lavender and sample homemade delights such as lemonade, teas, cakes, and cookies—all perfectly flavored with the farm's finest lavender—at the Freewater Café! Stop by our gift shop for products containing lavender, including soaps, lotions, and oils. We also carry handicrafts from local artisans and jams, pickles, and cheeses from local farmers.

The café features an outdoor sitting area with views of the river and mountains. Freewater Lavender Farm also has a beautiful outdoor dining area with tables and benches and an area for groups to picnic.

And naturally, a trip to the farm wouldn't be complete without a purchase of beautiful and fragrant lavender blossoms! Drop by our harvest booth and pick up a bunch of dried or fresh lavender for only $12. For further details on our operations and services, visit www.freewaterlavender.com today!

168. What is the advertisement mainly about?

(A) Attractions at an agricultural facility
(B) New products at a local farm
(C) The health benefits of natural foods
(D) A regional crafts fair for artisans

169. The word "finest" in paragraph 2, line 2, is closest in meaning to

(A) best
(B) smoothest
(C) most
(D) largest

170. What is NOT a feature of Freewater Lavender Farm?

(A) A dining establishment serving homemade goods
(B) An area for having outdoor meals
(C) A store selling a variety of local items
(D) A gallery featuring the work of regional artists

171. What can visitors do at the farm's booth?

(A) Register to host a special function
(B) Buy some flowers
(C) Try samples of products
(D) Purchase admission tickets

Questions 172-175 refer to the following Web page.

https://www.clearyfoods.com

Cleary Foods

Home | Shop | Locations | Rewards Program | News | Contact Us

Dear Shoppers:

Cleary Foods has a lot more to offer than just high-quality grocery products and household necessities.

1. The butchers in our fresh meat section are happy to cut your meat into pieces and trim away fat. They will also sharpen your cooking knives for you. — (1) —. If they are busy taking orders, just drop your knives off at the designated knife station and retrieve them when you're done shopping.

2. When the weather is warm, remember to ask our staff to package frozen items with dry ice so they don't melt on the way home. — (2) —. Also, try our brand-new rapid beverage chiller if you're purchasing unrefrigerated drinks.

3. We can place special orders for products that we do not have in stock, provided that our vendors offer them. Just fill out a request form at the customer service desk and give it to the employee working there. — (3) —.

Make sure to take advantage of these services on your next visit to Cleary Foods. — (4) —. Click here for a complete list of participating stores.

---

172. What is suggested about the butchers at Cleary Foods?

(A) They are glad to flavor purchases with special seasonings.
(B) They provide customers with tips on meat preparation.
(C) They offer daily discounts on a variety of products.
(D) They may be unable to perform a service right away.

173. What is mentioned about Cleary Foods' new piece of equipment?

(A) It is located near the checkout aisles.
(B) It cools beverages quickly.
(C) It requires payment of a fee to use.
(D) It produces dry ice for grocery bags.

174. What is true about special orders?

(A) They are only available to members of a program.
(B) Customers are required to make payment in advance.
(C) They may be delivered to a home address for an extra charge.
(D) Requests may be placed at the customer service area.

175. In which of the positions marked [1], [2], [3], and [4] does the following sentence best belong?

"They are currently available at select locations around the country."

(A) [1]
(B) [2]
(C) [3]
(D) [4]

GO ON TO THE NEXT PAGE

Questions 176-180 refer to the following advertisement and e-mail.

Join the Littleton Library Community Learning Series

The Littleton Library Community Learning Series is back by popular demand. Book a 30-minute consultation with an expert and get advice on matters related to business registration, accounting, sales, and more. Be sure to book this soon, as this program has always been popular. Adamant Consulting will offer assistance to current and prospective small-business owners during scheduled hours at the library. Adamant Consulting operates a business center for entrepreneurs. Further details about Adamant Consulting are available at www.adamant.com.

Consultations are free for residents and will take place from 10:00 A.M. to 1:00 P.M. on the dates shown below. To register for an appointment, call the library at 555-7184 or e-mail info@littletonlib.net. Proof of residence will be required to confirm your place.

Consultation dates:
- Tuesday, July 18
- Wednesday, August 2
- Thursday, August 17
- Saturday, September 2
- Tuesday, September 12

Please note that dates are subject to change. In the event of cancellation or delay, a notice will be posted on www.littletonlib.net.

To	Littleton Library <info@littletonlib.net>
From	Mary Voss <m.voss@mtnmail.com>
Subject	Inquiry
Date	July 21

To Whom It May Concern:

I heard from a friend that your library is offering free business consultations. This would be perfect for me because I am planning to open my own company. I meet the requirement for a complimentary consultation, but I am unavailable during the week due to some work obligations. Do you have any slots open on a weekend? If so, I'd like to make an appointment. Please let me know as soon as possible. Thank you!

Sincerely,
Mary Voss

176. What is suggested about the Littleton Library?

(A) It opens at 10 o'clock in the morning.
(B) It has hosted consultations in the past.
(C) It recently introduced some business courses.
(D) It has a center for entrepreneurs.

177. According to the advertisement, what will be posted on a Web site?

(A) Profiles of course instructors
(B) Details regarding discussion topics
(C) Announcements about schedule changes
(D) Directions to a venue

178. What is true about Ms. Voss?

(A) She recently moved to Littleton.
(B) Her friend is a consultant.
(C) She intends to start a company.
(D) Her library membership expired.

179. Which date is Ms. Voss available to attend a consultation?

(A) August 2
(B) August 17
(C) September 2
(D) September 12

180. In the e-mail, the word "meet" in paragraph 1, line 2, is closest in meaning to

(A) encounter
(B) join
(C) contact
(D) fulfill

GO ON TO THE NEXT PAGE

Questions 181-185 refer to the following press release and e-mail.

February 14—Larcorn Development is pleased to announce the opening of two new residential properties in the Portland area. City View Apartments will be completed on May 10 of this year and will include 200 units. Its convenient location in the business district is sure to make it popular among young professionals. The building will also feature amenities such as a fitness center and an entertainment lounge that can be used without charge by residents. Larcorn is also constructing Star Condominiums on Park Drive, which will include 100 luxury apartments and an assortment of high-end shops and restaurants in a 20-story building. The completion date for this project is July 28. For more information about both of these properties, visit www.larcorn.com.

To	Sheila Bridges <s.bridges@mailranger.com>
From	Victor Marino <v.marino@topspeedmovers.com>
Date	July 22
Subject	Confirmation
Attachment	Invoice

Dear Ms. Bridges,

I just wanted to confirm the schedule for next week. Our movers will arrive at your current residence on August 1 at 7:30 A.M. We estimate that it will take approximately three hours to pack your belongings and load them onto the truck, which means that we should arrive at City View Apartments by 11:30 A.M. Please remind the building manager to grant us access to the unit at that time.

I also wanted to let you know that there is an error in the invoice you received on July 14. You were mistakenly charged $980 when you should have been billed $882. The coupon you presented qualifies you for a 10 percent price deduction, but this was not included. I have attached a corrected invoice to this e-mail. I apologize for any inconvenience our mistake may have caused.

Sincerely,

Victor Marino
Assistant Manager, Topspeed Movers

181. What is true about Larcorn Development?

(A) It won a competitive bid to construct an office tower.
(B) It has a celebration planned for a specific date.
(C) It plans to complete two projects in the same year.
(D) It has model units available for buyers to see.

182. What is mentioned about Star Condominiums?

(A) It will be finished on May 10.
(B) It will include commercial spaces.
(C) It will be located in a business area.
(D) It will overlook a city park.

183. What is suggested about Ms. Bridges?

(A) She will pay a monthly maintenance fee.
(B) She will have free access to a gym.
(C) She will receive a discount coupon.
(D) She will visit the moving company's office.

184. What is Ms. Bridges asked to do?

(A) Confirm the quantity of an order
(B) Contact a building manager
(C) Submit an additional payment
(D) Reply to a previous e-mail

185. What problem does Mr. Marino mention?

(A) An invoice was not sent.
(B) An apartment cannot be accessed.
(C) An appointment cannot be changed.
(D) A discount was not applied.

GO ON TO THE NEXT PAGE

Questions 186-190 refer to the following e-mails and schedule.

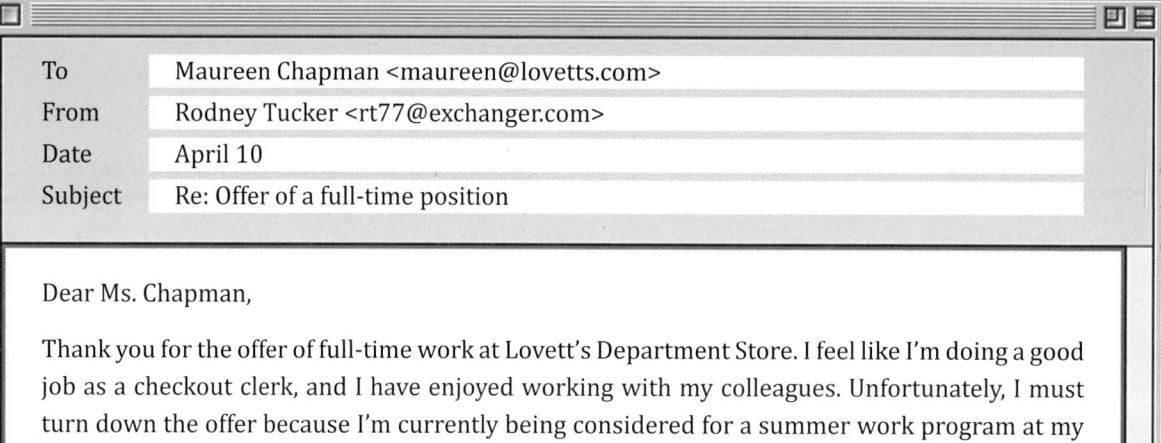

To	Maureen Chapman <maureen@lovetts.com>
From	Rodney Tucker <rt77@exchanger.com>
Date	April 10
Subject	Re: Offer of a full-time position

Dear Ms. Chapman,

Thank you for the offer of full-time work at Lovett's Department Store. I feel like I'm doing a good job as a checkout clerk, and I have enjoyed working with my colleagues. Unfortunately, I must turn down the offer because I'm currently being considered for a summer work program at my school's Department of Computing that would allow me to earn course credits while employed at a software company. The program runs from June through August. If I'm admitted into the program, I will not even have time for a part-time position. Otherwise, I would be happy to keep working for Lovett's Department Store until I graduate in December of this year. After that, I plan to work at the insurance firm my uncle owns.

Thanks,
Rodney Tucker

Electronics Section, Lovett's Department Store

Weekday Schedule for the second week of June

	June 9	June 10	June 11	June 12	June 13
Morning	• Hazel Gates • Annie Montrose	• Dion Kirk • Hazel Gates	• Annie Montrose • Chico Benavidez	• Hazel Gates • Rodney Tucker	• Chico Benavidez • Rodney Tucker
Lunchtime	• Annie Montrose	• Hazel Gates	• Chico Benavidez	• Rodney Tucker	• Dion Kirk
Afternoon	• Rodney Tucker	• Chico Benavidez • Rodney Tucker	• Chico Benavidez • Rodney Tucker	• Chico Benavidez	• Annie Montrose • Dion Kirk

Full-time staff: Chico Benavidez (35 hours), Rodney Tucker (35 hours)
Part-time staff: Hazel Gates (12 hours), Dion Kirk (11 hours), Annie Montrose (15 hours)
*Weekends throughout the month will be covered by Chico Benavidez and Rodney Tucker.

To	All Staff <staff@lovetts.com>
From	Maureen Chapman <maureen@lovetts.com>
Date	December 3
Subject	Employee Resignation

Dear Staff,

I would like to inform everyone that Rodney Tucker, one of our most valued workers, will be leaving Lovett's Department Store. Mr. Tucker has been an important member of our organization. He began as a part-time employee and was later promoted to the position of section manager. A farewell party will be held for him in the staff room from 8 to 9 P.M. on December 5. Employees working in the Appliance Section, which Mr. Tucker has managed over the last six months, are obviously expected to attend. I hope to see everyone there.

Sincerely,

Maureen Chapman
Human Resources Manager, Lovett's Department Store

---

186. What is suggested about Mr. Tucker?

(A) He did not get the summer job that he wanted.
(B) He designed a computer program for a retail store.
(C) He usually travels during the summer holidays.
(D) He was not given an opportunity to earn overtime pay.

187. When did some part-timers work together in the afternoon?

(A) June 8
(B) June 10
(C) June 12
(D) June 13

188. What can be inferred about Lovett's Department Store?

(A) Its branches all have the same hours of operation.
(B) Its part-time employees only work on weekdays in June.
(C) It runs a management training program for staff.
(D) It only recently began to sell computers.

189. Why is Mr. Tucker most likely leaving Lovett's Department Store?

(A) He failed to satisfy some requirements.
(B) He plans to expand his family's business.
(C) He is preparing to relocate to a different city.
(D) He will take a position at a relative's company.

190. According to the second e-mail, who is expected to attend the goodbye party?

(A) Members of a rewards program
(B) Contributors to an organization's fundraiser
(C) Suppliers for the appliance section
(D) Staff stationed in a certain area

GO ON TO THE NEXT PAGE

Questions 191-195 refer to the following floor plan and e-mails.

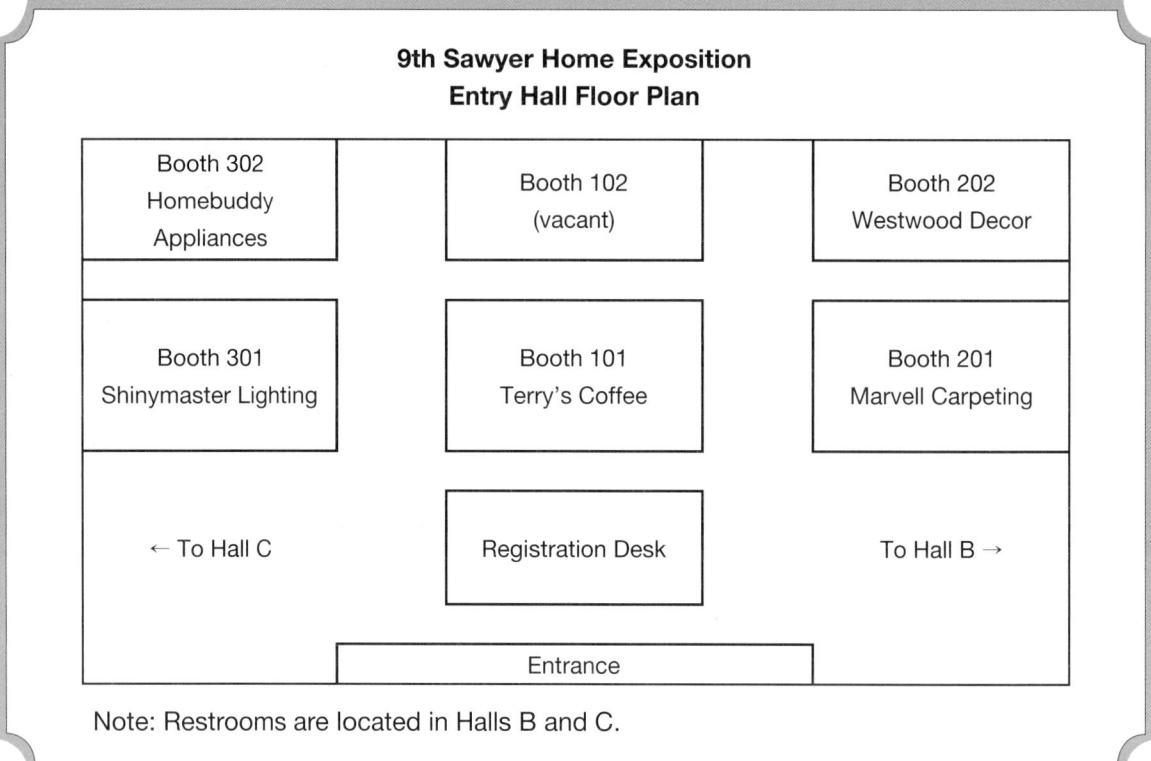

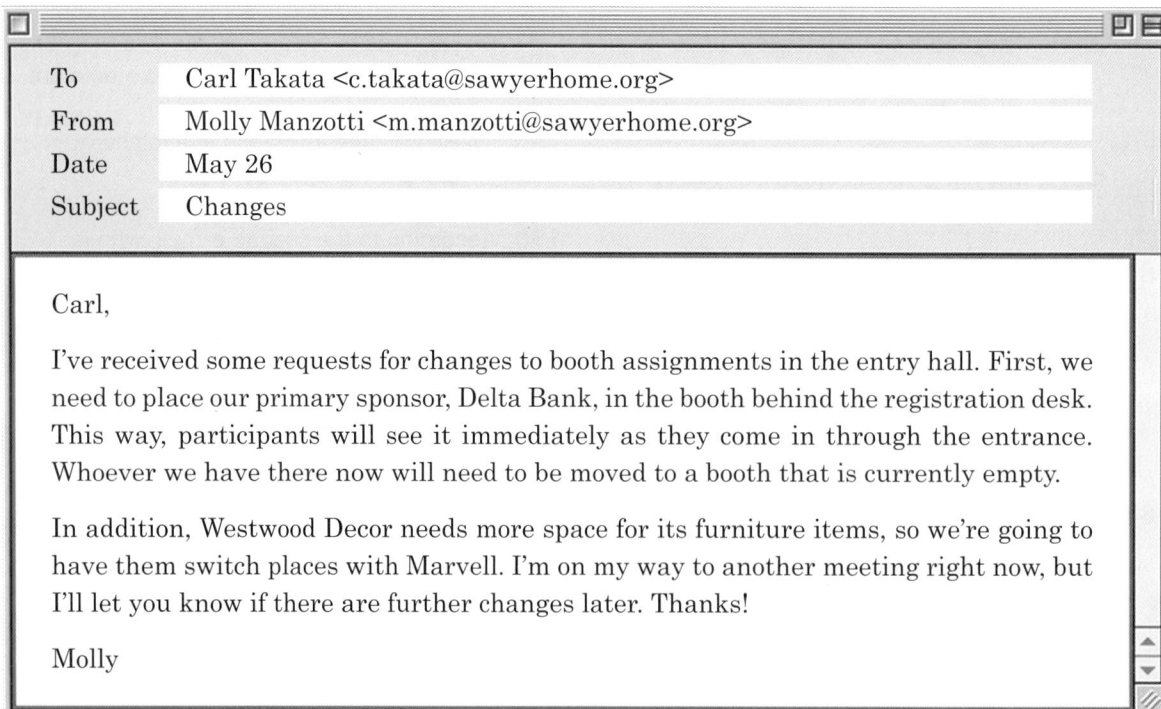

To: Carl Takata <c.takata@sawyerhome.org>
From: Molly Manzotti <m.manzotti@sawyerhome.org>
Date: May 26
Subject: Update

Hi Carl,

So sorry I couldn't get back to you sooner. I've been busy negotiating with clients about prices and booth assignments, and there's been an additional change since this morning. The planning committee wants to keep companies that sell similar items located as close to each other as possible. That means we'll be moving the occupant of Booth 302 into Hall C. I still have a long list of vendors in need of booth assignments. I'll bring it tomorrow when I stop by the venue at around 9 A.M. Let me know if I can pick anything up for you along the way. See you!

Molly

---

191. Where might customers find light fixtures?

(A) Booth 101
(B) Booth 201
(C) Booth 301
(D) Booth 302

192. Whose booth is Delta Bank replacing?

(A) Terry's Coffee
(B) Marvell Carpeting
(C) Westwood Decor
(D) Shinymaster Lighting

193. What is indicated about Westwood Decor?

(A) It is a primary event sponsor.
(B) It is being moved into a different hall.
(C) It needs more space for its merchandise.
(D) It requested a booth behind Marvell Carpeting.

194. What can be inferred about Hall C?

(A) It has lower-priced booths.
(B) It does not have any restrooms.
(C) It will hold all of the appliance sellers.
(D) It was added to accommodate more vendors.

195. What does Ms. Manzotti say she is going to bring to Mr. Takata?

(A) A floor plan
(B) A food order
(C) An event calendar
(D) A list of vendors

GO ON TO THE NEXT PAGE

Questions 196-200 refer to the following announcement, Web page, and e-mail.

Arizona Medical Professionals Association (AMPA)
We are pleased to announce the release of our Spring Events Calendar for this year.

April 16 – NEW MEMBERS WELCOME
Welcome reception for new members at the Desert Hotel in Phoenix from 4:00 to 6:00 P.M. Snacks and beverages will be provided.

April 19 – PRESENTATION
The country's most popular medical journal, *Modern Journal of Medicine*, will be hosting a special presentation from 6:00 to 7:00 P.M. at the AMPA Conference Center in Phoenix.

April 23 – LECTURE AND BOOK SIGNING
AMPA will be hosting a lecture and book-signing event with esteemed medical author and leading expert on health-care issues Dr. Katherine Bradley from 9:00 to 11:00 A.M. at the Book Stop bookstore in Glendale, Arizona.

May 2 to 4 – ANNUAL CONFERENCE
The 51st Annual AMPA Conference will be held in Las Vegas, Nevada, this year.

All events are exclusively for registered AMPA members. To join, please visit www.ampa.org.

---

www.ampa.org

Arizona Medical Professionals Association (AMPA)

| Login | Resources | Events | **Membership** | Contact | About |

How to register

1. Sign up for an account on the Web site and complete the membership application form.
2. Upload a scanned copy of your medical license.
3. Where applicable, include the name of the person or organization that referred you.

Benefits

- Connect with other professionals.
- Advance your education with online seminars.
- Get access to professional resources.
- Receive complimentary subscriptions to all leading medical journals.
- NEW! To help with maintenance costs, we have recently introduced banner advertising on our Web site, for which members may obtain discounts. For more information, please contact the support team.

[Join Today]

To: Salvador Lopez <s.lopez@ampa.org>
From: Amy Sharpe <a.sharpe@healthwide.com>
Subject: Advertising
Date: February 18

Dear Mr. Lopez,

I represent the company that is publishing Dr. Katherine Bradley's latest book, *New Age of Healing*. In anticipation of the book's release at the AMPA event in April, we would like to advertise the book on your Web site. In connection with this, I was wondering whether Dr. Bradley's membership benefits could be extended to us. If so, we would like to enter her membership number on the application form for advertisers on your Web site. Please let me know at your earliest convenience.

Sincerely,
Amy Sharpe
Marketing Associate, Healthwide Publications

---

196. What is true about the event to greet newly registered AMPA members?

(A) It will take place at a conference center.
(B) It will begin at six o'clock in the evening.
(C) It will feature a speech by an organizer.
(D) It will include refreshments for attendees.

197. What is implied about AMPA members?

(A) They completed their medical training at the same institution.
(B) They can subscribe for free to *Modern Journal of Medicine*.
(C) They are encouraged to volunteer their services.
(D) They form the country's largest professional association.

198. What are prospective members asked to provide?

(A) A payment for an annual fee
(B) Details about their place of employment
(C) An electronic copy of a certificate
(D) Preferences for communications

199. What has the AMPA recently done?

(A) Changed the date of an annual event
(B) Increased a fee for members
(C) Established a partner organization
(D) Added advertising to its Web site

200. Who most likely is Mr. Lopez?

(A) A marketing consultant
(B) A commercial director
(C) An event planner
(D) A support administrator

This is the end of the test. You may review Parts 5, 6, and 7 if you finish the test early.

실시간 토익시험 정답확인&해설강의

Hackers.co.kr

한 권으로 끝내는 해커스 토익 900+ LC+RC+VOCA

실전모의고사

2

잠깐! 테스트 전 아래 사항을 꼭 확인하세요.

1. Answer Sheet(p.229), 연필, 지우개, 시계를 준비하셨나요? ☐
2. Listening mp3를 들을 준비가 되셨나요? ☐

모든 준비가 완료되었으면 목표 점수를 떠올린 후 테스트를 시작합니다.
시험 시간 120분내에 문제 풀이와 답안지 마킹까지 모두 완료해야 합니다.

🎧 TEST2.mp3
실전용·복습용 문제풀이 mp3 무료 다운로드 및 스트리밍 바로듣기 (HackersIngang.com)
* 실제 시험장의 소음까지 재현해 낸 고사장 소음/매미 버전, 영국식·호주식 발음 집중 버전, 고속 버전까지
 구매하면 실전에 더욱 완벽히 대비할 수 있습니다.

무료 mp3 바로듣기

LISTENING TEST

In this section, you must demonstrate your ability to understand spoken English. This section is divided into four parts and will take approximately 45 minutes to complete. Do not mark the answers in your test book. Use the answer sheet that is provided separately.

PART 1

Directions: For each question, you will listen to four short statements about a picture in your test book. These statements will not be printed and will only be spoken one time. Select the statement that best describes what is happening in the picture and mark the corresponding letter (A), (B), (C), or (D) on the answer sheet.

Sample Answer

The statement that best describes the picture is (B), "The man is sitting at the desk." So, you should mark letter (B) on the answer sheet.

1.

2.

GO ON TO THE NEXT PAGE

3.

4.

5.

6.

GO ON TO THE NEXT PAGE

PART 2

Directions: For each question, you will listen to a statement or question followed by three possible responses spoken in English. They will not be printed and will only be spoken one time. Select the best response and mark the corresponding letter (A), (B), or (C) on your answer sheet.

7. Mark your answer on the answer sheet.
8. Mark your answer on the answer sheet.
9. Mark your answer on the answer sheet.
10. Mark your answer on the answer sheet.
11. Mark your answer on the answer sheet.
12. Mark your answer on the answer sheet.
13. Mark your answer on the answer sheet.
14. Mark your answer on the answer sheet.
15. Mark your answer on the answer sheet.
16. Mark your answer on the answer sheet.
17. Mark your answer on the answer sheet.
18. Mark your answer on the answer sheet.
19. Mark your answer on the answer sheet.
20. Mark your answer on the answer sheet.
21. Mark your answer on the answer sheet.
22. Mark your answer on the answer sheet.
23. Mark your answer on the answer sheet.
24. Mark your answer on the answer sheet.
25. Mark your answer on the answer sheet.
26. Mark your answer on the answer sheet.
27. Mark your answer on the answer sheet.
28. Mark your answer on the answer sheet.
29. Mark your answer on the answer sheet.
30. Mark your answer on the answer sheet.
31. Mark your answer on the answer sheet.

PART 3

Directions: In this part, you will listen to several conversations between two or more speakers. These conversations will not be printed and will only be spoken one time. For each conversation, you will be asked to answer three questions. Select the best response and mark the corresponding letter (A), (B), (C), or (D) on your answer sheet.

32. According to the man, what did customers complain about?

    (A) The size of a space
    (B) The taste of a dish
    (C) The menu options
    (D) The operating hours

33. What took place last month?

    (A) An industry fair
    (B) A training session
    (C) A sales presentation
    (D) A culinary class

34. Who will the woman e-mail?

    (A) An owner
    (B) A cook
    (C) A critic
    (D) A consultant

35. Who most likely is the man?

    (A) A bicycle repairperson
    (B) A public transport driver
    (C) A city official
    (D) A bus passenger

36. What problem does the man mention?

    (A) An engine has malfunctioned.
    (B) Some instructions are unclear.
    (C) A lock cannot be fastened.
    (D) There is no more room for passengers.

37. What does the woman inquire about?

    (A) When another bus will arrive
    (B) How much a service will cost
    (C) Why a ride will take so long
    (D) Whether someone else can help

38. What is the conversation mainly about?

    (A) A recent order
    (B) A client's project
    (C) A new workspace
    (D) A work assignment

39. Why does the woman need help?

    (A) A task may be time-consuming.
    (B) A space needs to be cleaned.
    (C) Some files have gone missing.
    (D) A deadline is approaching.

40. What does the man offer to do?

    (A) Call a client
    (B) Take over a project
    (C) Postpone an appointment
    (D) Contact a department

41. What did the woman do last week?

    (A) She traveled abroad.
    (B) She reviewed a report.
    (C) She conducted surveys.
    (D) She sent applications.

42. What does the man request?

    (A) Extending a deadline
    (B) Prioritizing a task
    (C) Sending an e-mail
    (D) Updating a Web site

43. What will the woman probably do next?

    (A) Request an office form
    (B) Meet with a supervisor
    (C) Contact a delivery person
    (D) Take a short break

GO ON TO THE NEXT PAGE

44. What are the speakers mainly discussing?

    (A) A grand opening
    (B) A job interview
    (C) A safety inspection
    (D) An investor gathering

45. What is mentioned about a factory?

    (A) It is almost ready for operation.
    (B) It requires more employees.
    (C) It must be relocated.
    (D) It has new equipment.

46. What does the woman imply when she says, "You were at the facility recently"?

    (A) She wants the man to speak at an event.
    (B) She plans to inspect a manufacturing plant.
    (C) She needs the man to adjust a work schedule.
    (D) She hopes to find out the cause of a delay.

47. Where is the conversation taking place?

    (A) At an auto repair shop
    (B) At a parking lot
    (C) At a real estate office
    (D) At an apartment building

48. What is Ms. Willets concerned about?

    (A) A street has no parking.
    (B) A home is under construction.
    (C) An area is difficult to access.
    (D) A location might be noisy.

49. What does the man recommend?

    (A) Taking a different route
    (B) Reviewing details about a listing
    (C) Delaying a visit to a property
    (D) Submitting an inquiry in person

50. What was recently e-mailed to staff?

    (A) A questionnaire
    (B) A benefits update
    (C) A training schedule
    (D) A meeting reminder

51. What is mentioned about the employees?

    (A) They must sign an agreement.
    (B) They will get more time off.
    (C) They must complete a survey.
    (D) They will have to work overtime.

52. What task does the woman need to complete?

    (A) A budget proposal
    (B) A staffing schedule
    (C) A supply chain analysis
    (D) A survey form

53. What type of business do the men most likely work for?

    (A) A clothing shop
    (B) A furniture store
    (C) An interior design firm
    (D) A moving company

54. What does the woman want to do?

    (A) Make an exchange
    (B) Compare some prices
    (C) Test out some merchandise
    (D) Utilize a discount code

55. What is mentioned about the woman's product?

    (A) It was purchased online.
    (B) It will arrive soon.
    (C) It is not damaged.
    (D) It is not available.

56. What is the purpose of the call?

(A) To discuss a client meeting
(B) To ask about delivery status
(C) To review marketing materials
(D) To assign project roles

57. What will take place next Friday?

(A) A contract negotiation
(B) A staff training
(C) A product presentation
(D) A partnership meeting

58. What does Aiko say she will do?

(A) Speak with another team
(B) Prepare technical specifications
(C) Update financial projections
(D) Revise the company Web site

59. Why was the man out of the office last week?

(A) He examined clinical trial data.
(B) He tested laboratory equipment.
(C) He visited a medical clinic.
(D) He met with a company executive.

60. Why does the man say, "We'll be expanding soon"?

(A) To indicate that an employee will be promoted
(B) To explain that a legal agreement must be revised
(C) To suggest that some advertisements should be created
(D) To imply that additional funds may be necessary

61. What does the woman ask the man to do?

(A) Give a presentation
(B) Reschedule an appointment
(C) Take part in a meeting
(D) Talk to a branch manager

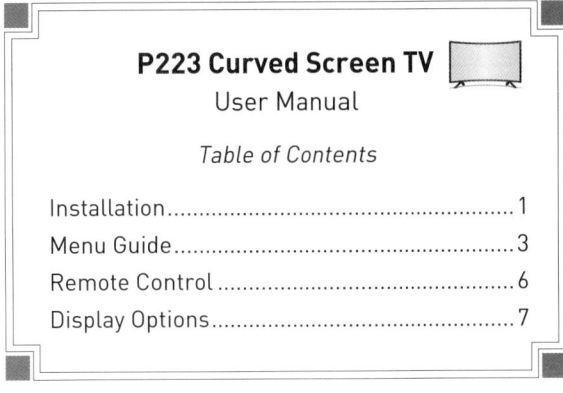

62. Why did a manager buy a television?

(A) A conference room was renovated.
(B) A previous device was malfunctioning.
(C) A store was having a promotion.
(D) A product received a positive review.

63. What does the woman say she already did?

(A) She adjusted some settings.
(B) She installed additional speakers.
(C) She recycled packaging materials.
(D) She read through a user manual.

64. Look at the graphic. Which page will the man probably read?

(A) Page 1
(B) Page 3
(C) Page 6
(D) Page 7

GO ON TO THE NEXT PAGE

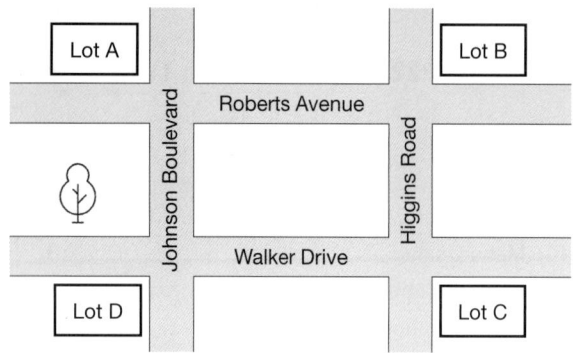
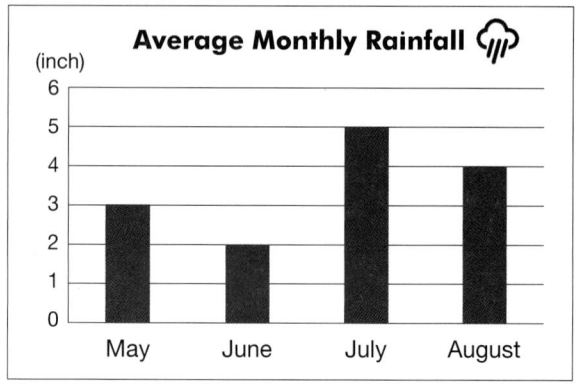

65. What problem does the man mention?
(A) He went to the wrong address.
(B) He does not have a ride.
(C) He is unhappy with a doctor.
(D) He missed an appointment.

66. What does the woman ask the man to do?
(A) Take public transportation
(B) Write down a phone number
(C) Arrive early
(D) Call a physician

67. Look at the graphic. Where will the man most likely park?
(A) Lot A
(B) Lot B
(C) Lot C
(D) Lot D

68. Who most likely is the woman?
(A) A university professor
(B) A financial consultant
(C) A corporate researcher
(D) A market analyst

69. Look at the graphic. Which month is the woman concerned about?
(A) May
(B) June
(C) July
(D) August

70. What does the man want to do on Friday?
(A) Meet with a colleague
(B) Release a report
(C) Speak to a customer
(D) Tour a farm

PART 4

Directions: In this part, you will listen to several short talks by a single speaker. These talks will not be printed and will only be spoken one time. For each talk, you will be asked to answer three questions. Select the best response and mark the corresponding letter (A), (B), (C), or (D) on your answer sheet.

71. Where are the listeners?

    (A) At a library
    (B) At a factory
    (C) At a furniture store
    (D) At an automobile dealership

72. What is mentioned about the ElectraDesk?

    (A) It requires further assembly.
    (B) It is currently being painted.
    (C) It contains a special feature.
    (D) It is a best-selling item.

73. What are the listeners asked to do?

    (A) Return safety equipment
    (B) Take the lead
    (C) Save questions for later
    (D) Be careful of vehicles

74. Who most likely is the speaker?

    (A) A magazine editor
    (B) A sports photographer
    (C) A soccer player
    (D) A fund-raiser organizer

75. What does the speaker ask the listener to do?

    (A) Interview an athlete
    (B) Add a few photographs
    (C) Revise a document
    (D) Do some volunteer work

76. What will probably take place tomorrow morning?

    (A) A staff meeting
    (B) A charity event
    (C) A sporting competition
    (D) A product launch

77. What is the purpose of the talk?

    (A) To sell publications
    (B) To encourage exercise
    (C) To introduce a program
    (D) To announce awards

78. What does the speaker mean when he says, "I can't see a single empty seat"?

    (A) The listeners must register quickly.
    (B) The listeners should stand up.
    (C) A presentation is starting soon.
    (D) A new program is popular.

79. Who is Carolyn Woods?

    (A) A film producer
    (B) A textbook publisher
    (C) A school instructor
    (D) An event organizer

80. Why is the business holding a sale?

    (A) To mark an opening
    (B) To recognize a holiday
    (C) To thank some customers
    (D) To promote some new products

81. What will be provided with some purchases?

    (A) A floor rug
    (B) A lighting fixture
    (C) A cleaning appliance
    (D) A clothing accessory

82. According to the speaker, what can the listeners find on a Web site?

    (A) Updated prices
    (B) Product images
    (C) Store addresses
    (D) Order forms

GO ON TO THE NEXT PAGE

83. What is the speaker mainly discussing?

(A) A project deadline
(B) Marketing techniques
(C) A new policy
(D) Software development

84. Why does the speaker say, "He has managed similar issues for us in the past"?

(A) To show someone's suitability
(B) To ask for more help
(C) To express concern
(D) To complain about a decision

85. What will Keith Thompson do next week?

(A) Meet a client
(B) Present a plan
(C) Upgrade a program
(D) Hire a designer

86. What is the report mainly about?

(A) A construction proposal
(B) An upcoming election
(C) A road closure
(D) A tax increase

87. According to the speaker, what must a new council head do?

(A) Appoint a member
(B) Reduce a budget
(C) Attend a conference
(D) Create a development plan

88. Why does the speaker say a task will not be easy?

(A) There is public opposition.
(B) There are damaged facilities.
(C) There is limited funding.
(D) There are too many regulations.

89. Who most likely is the listener?

(A) A truck driver
(B) A travel agent
(C) A security guard
(D) A maintenance worker

90. What does the speaker mean when she says, "they will move into the apartment sooner than I thought"?

(A) A plan should be changed.
(B) A task was completed early.
(C) A problem has been solved.
(D) A delivery must be postponed.

91. What does the speaker ask the listener to do?

(A) Call a resident
(B) Speak with an assistant
(C) Provide some samples
(D) Cancel a meeting

92. Where most likely are the listeners?

(A) At an art museum
(B) At a convention center
(C) At a guitar shop
(D) At a music academy

93. What has been placed on the table?

(A) Some music sheets
(B) Some instruments
(C) A photo album
(D) A class schedule

94. What will the listeners probably do next?

(A) Discuss a piece of music
(B) Enjoy some refreshments
(C) Watch a performance
(D) Gather in groups

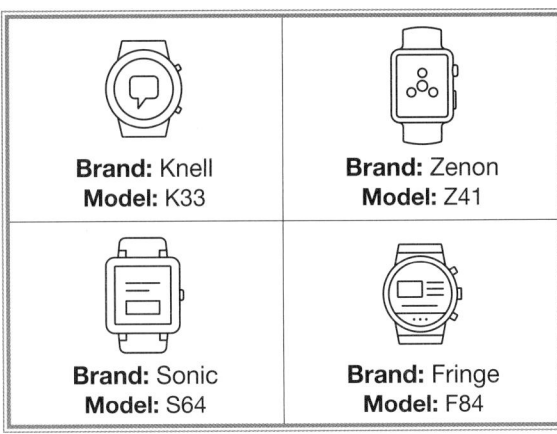

Order Form	
Items	Quantity
Wall mounts	12
Tables	5
Lights	18
Glass cases	7

95. What is the speaker mainly discussing?

(A) A customer complaint
(B) Employee schedules
(C) Advertising materials
(D) A sales event

96. Look at the graphic. Which brand's model is out of stock?

(A) Knell
(B) Zenon
(C) Sonic
(D) Fringe

97. What does the speaker recommend doing?

(A) Reducing prices
(B) Redirecting shoppers
(C) Promoting a warranty
(D) Extending an event

98. What will probably happen next week?

(A) A gallery will host a special guest.
(B) A business meeting will be held.
(C) An artist will present some works.
(D) A space will be reorganized.

99. Look at the graphic. Which number is incorrect?

(A) 12
(B) 5
(C) 18
(D) 7

100. What does the speaker suggest?

(A) Reserving a display area
(B) Requesting expedited shipping
(C) Forwarding an e-mail
(D) Exchanging items

This is the end of the Listening test. Turn to PART 5 in your test book.

GO ON TO THE NEXT PAGE

READING TEST

In this section, you must demonstrate your ability to read and comprehend English. You will be given a variety of texts and asked to answer questions about these texts. This section is divided into three parts and will take 75 minutes to complete.

Do not mark the answers in your test book. Use the answer sheet that is separately provided.

PART 5

Directions: In each question, you will be asked to review a statement that is missing a word or phrase. Four answer choices will be provided for each statement. Select the best answer and mark the corresponding letter (A), (B), (C), or (D) on the answer sheet.

101. Vintron Labs employees have been working ------- to ensure the final product is perfect.

    (A) tireless
    (B) more tireless
    (C) tirelessly
    (D) tirelessness

102. The machines ------- the Nova Parking Garage accept some forms of mobile payment as well as all major credit cards.

    (A) among
    (B) to
    (C) in
    (D) onto

103. Should the outstanding bill be paid ------- the next 15 days, Hampton Electric will not apply a penalty.

    (A) upon
    (B) within
    (C) behind
    (D) toward

104. Western Financial plans to hire ------- to handle Ms. Kovac's duties during her leave of absence.

    (A) other
    (B) whom
    (C) anyone
    (D) someone

105. Mr. Walker contacted Nevris Software's customer support team ------- to recover the accidentally deleted files.

    (A) thoroughly
    (B) enthusiastically
    (C) nearly
    (D) immediately

106. Coach Agarwal is ------- that his team will make it all the way to the finals of the Youth Soccer League this year.

    (A) attentive
    (B) sharp
    (C) certain
    (D) diligent

107. This washing machine produced by Sauber Appliances has functioned for 20 years without requiring much -------.

    (A) convenience
    (B) maintenance
    (C) protection
    (D) resistance

108. LightTrek's video-editing software did not sell well ------- having a number of impressive features.

    (A) yet
    (B) despite
    (C) than
    (D) since

109. Mara Media has made it a policy to never give ------- for other companies to use its copyrighted images.

(A) certification
(B) declaration
(C) discipline
(D) consent

110. If you are interested in working at a particular branch of Cooper Fitness, please ------- your preference on the job application form.

(A) recognize
(B) initiate
(C) state
(D) tolerate

111. Mr. Ebbets has been responsible for ------- Stonefrost Holdings' legal department for over a decade.

(A) manager
(B) manage
(C) managing
(D) managed

112. Ms. Olsen ------- a temporary workspace over the next few days because of the water leak in her office.

(A) was using
(B) using
(C) has used
(D) will be using

113. After successfully completing the Green Valley housing project, Goldfield Properties aims to become one of Asia's ------- land developers.

(A) led
(B) leads
(C) leading
(D) leaders

114. Several news reports ------- that Braxco Chemical and Haskill Industries are considering a merger in the coming year.

(A) implement
(B) respond
(C) acquire
(D) indicate

115. During the Donald's Doughnuts anniversary event, ------- took advantage of the promotion to get a free sandwich with a coffee purchase.

(A) many
(B) either
(C) little
(D) another

116. Red Pail Hardware has a greater variety of products, but the goods at Jerry's Home Supplies are more -------.

(A) afforded
(B) affords
(C) affording
(D) affordable

117. Seaward Insurance's president called a meeting ------- a replacement for Anita Wilson, who is resigning in three months.

(A) appointment
(B) appoint
(C) appointed
(D) to appoint

118. Following the strategy session, Mr. Hoffman appeared ------- in his team's ability to meet the deadline.

(A) confidence
(B) confidently
(C) confiding
(D) confident

119. Each employee will be expected to participate in the workshop ------- his or her position at the company.

(A) regardless of
(B) other than
(C) such as
(D) except for

120. Perkins Healthcare's Web site included some ------- information concerning the job application process.

(A) contradictor
(B) contradiction
(C) contradictory
(D) contradict

GO ON TO THE NEXT PAGE

121. Although customs forms can be obtained at the airport of arrival, some airlines distribute them to passengers ------- on the plane.

(A) overhead
(B) beforehand
(C) indoors
(D) elsewhere

122. Mr. Turner's ------- creations have earned him a reputation as an innovative fashion designer.

(A) cooperative
(B) ingenious
(C) appreciative
(D) conducive

123. Being partnered with an experienced staff member for two weeks would be of ------- help to newly hired staff.

(A) customary
(B) extravagant
(C) intelligent
(D) immense

124. By participating in physical therapy sessions and stretching frequently, Ms. Lee ------- recovered from her injury.

(A) progressive
(B) progress
(C) progressively
(D) progression

125. Chloe Newman showed her athletic ------- by qualifying for the prestigious Valley River Running Competition.

(A) potential
(B) authority
(C) property
(D) acquisition

126. Wassco Engineering's stockholders were pleased with the ------- profitable government contract that the company secured.

(A) extremely
(B) heavily
(C) vividly
(D) promptly

127. The salary paid to the top ------- at CK Logistics is one of the highest in the industry.

(A) execute
(B) execution
(C) executive
(D) executing

128. Evertech's newest blender was removed from store shelves ------- reports that it includes defective components.

(A) instead of
(B) because of
(C) whenever
(D) provided

129. A purchase request form must be signed by a supervisor, ------- it will not be approved.

(A) or
(B) nevertheless
(C) and
(D) also

130. Lyon Broadcasting's staff will be awarded annual bonuses that are ------- to revenue growth.

(A) complimentary
(B) budgetary
(C) enough
(D) proportional

PART 6

Directions: In this part, you will be asked to read four English texts. Each text is missing a word, phrase, or sentence. Select the answer choice that correctly completes the text and mark the corresponding letter (A), (B), (C), or (D) on the answer sheet.

Questions 131-134 refer to the following announcement.

Help Us Preserve Landmark Park!

May 15 | 10 A.M. to 4 P.M.

Join the Dothan City Youth League's annual cleanup event. Activities include picking up litter as well as washing walls and footpaths. Volunteers will be provided ------- equipment for all tasks. However, since supplies may be limited, we encourage you to bring your own gear.
131.

Participants ------- into groups and assigned specific areas to clean. A supervisor will determine your assignments on the morning of the event. Remember to dress -------.
132. **133.**

If you are considering providing aid to the Dothan City Youth League, your contributions will be used for this and future events. -------. Your support is crucial to our success. Register for the cleanup event at www.dothanyouth.org.
134.

131. (A) with
 (B) of
 (C) for
 (D) to

132. (A) separated
 (B) were separated
 (C) have been separated
 (D) will be separated

133. (A) appropriate
 (B) appropriateness
 (C) more appropriate
 (D) appropriately

134. (A) We will announce our fall cleanup dates in August.
 (B) We look forward to your involvement.
 (C) Attendance was higher than anticipated.
 (D) The park may be rented for private events.

GO ON TO THE NEXT PAGE

Questions 135-138 refer to the following e-mail.

To: Angela Thornberry <athornberry@fastmail.com>
From: Vincent Nakamura <vnakamura@traxcomputers.com>
Subject: Your laptop
Date: June 18

Dear Ms. Thornberry,

I am writing about the Trax 2700 laptop you dropped off at our store on June 15 because of problems with its screen. After sending it to our ------- for examination, we discovered that it contained a faulty component. At present, your laptop is being -------. As requested, we are also thoroughly testing the device to see if there are any other issues.

Because this problem appears to have been entirely our fault, we'd like to offer you a $50 voucher for use at our retail store. -------, an e-coupon of the same value for use on our Web site is also available. Just let us know which you'd prefer.

-------. Please call customer service if there is a delay.

Best wishes,

Vincent Nakamura
Customer Satisfaction Department

---

135. (A) technicality
(B) technical
(C) technicians
(D) technology

136. (A) replaced
(B) repaired
(C) shipped
(D) recalled

137. (A) Regrettably
(B) Subsequently
(C) Approximately
(D) Alternatively

138. (A) The model you inquired about is no longer available at this location.
(B) We will send the computer back to you within three days.
(C) You are not covered under the warranty as it has expired.
(D) We have been receiving a number of complaints about our service.

Questions 139-142 refer to the following notice.

Dear customers,

Banerjee Roof Tiles will be upgrading the computer system. This is expected to affect how we manage order submissions, handle e-mails, and deliver customer support. Our online ordering system will be disabled between May 20 and May 31. -------139.-------. Our personnel will be glad to assist you. Provided everything -------140.------- smoothly, normal operations should resume by June 1.

During the last week of May, we will also focus on staff training, -------141.------- familiarizing employees with the new system. Consequently, we will be unable to offer our -------142.------- service and support.

We apologize for the inconvenience and thank you for your patience.

139. (A) Directions for alternative routes are available on our Web site.
(B) If you'd like to place an order, please call during business hours.
(C) Therefore, some items will not be in stock for the duration of this issue.
(D) We will accept product returns under our terms and conditions.

140. (A) will be proceeded
(B) proceeds
(C) proceed
(D) has been proceeded

141. (A) otherwise
(B) in case
(C) thereby
(D) as a result of

142. (A) public
(B) approved
(C) usual
(D) selective

GO ON TO THE NEXT PAGE

Questions 143-146 refer to the following e-mail.

To: Alison Jackson <ajackson@champleather.com>
From: Victoria Green <vgreen@champleather.com>
Subject: New policy
Date: June 15

Hi, Alison.

Please share the following information with our staff. I want to make sure ------- in the company are aware of our new policy. Effective November 1, the company will require periodic medical checks of certain groups of employees. -------. Specifically, the policy covers personnel who ------- to hazardous conditions at work, such as workers who handle chemicals. The policy also affects employees whose health is crucial to the safe performance of their jobs. -------, our delivery truck drivers must undergo health checks to make sure that they are fit to operate heavy vehicles. We will discuss this in more detail over the coming days.

Sincerely,
Victoria Green
Champ Leather

143. (A) all
(B) them
(C) every
(D) these

144. (A) A detailed proposal has been left on your desk.
(B) The rising cost of labor is expected to be a challenge.
(C) The commission approved the measure last week.
(D) Management has changed how it classifies some employees.

145. (A) have been exposing
(B) expose
(C) have exposed
(D) are exposed

146. (A) Conversely
(B) Rather than
(C) In particular
(D) Continuously

PART 7

Directions: In this part, you will be asked to read several texts, such as advertisements, articles, instant messages, or examples of business correspondence. Each text is followed by several questions. Select the best answer and mark the corresponding letter (A), (B), (C), or (D) on your answer sheet.

Questions 147-148 refer to the following advertisement.

Spaces for Rent

Located at 57 Buckwold Drive, this recently renovated commercial property is in the heart of Renuville and is within walking distance of many cafés and shops. It is also just two blocks from Renfrew Park. Each of its 11 floors includes 10,500 square feet of office space. There is also a large underground garage. Tenants and their visitors may leave their vehicles there at no charge. All floors in the building are ready for immediate occupancy. Call 555-9982 for more information or to request a viewing.

147. What is a feature of 57 Buckwold Drive?

(A) It contains residential units.
(B) It is centrally located.
(C) It has a view of a park.
(D) It includes furnished offices.

148. What are tenants able to do?

(A) Obtain a discount on large offices
(B) Request regular cleaning services
(C) Use a parking facility for free
(D) Delay payment on the initial rent

GO ON TO THE NEXT PAGE

Questions 149-150 refer to the following e-mail.

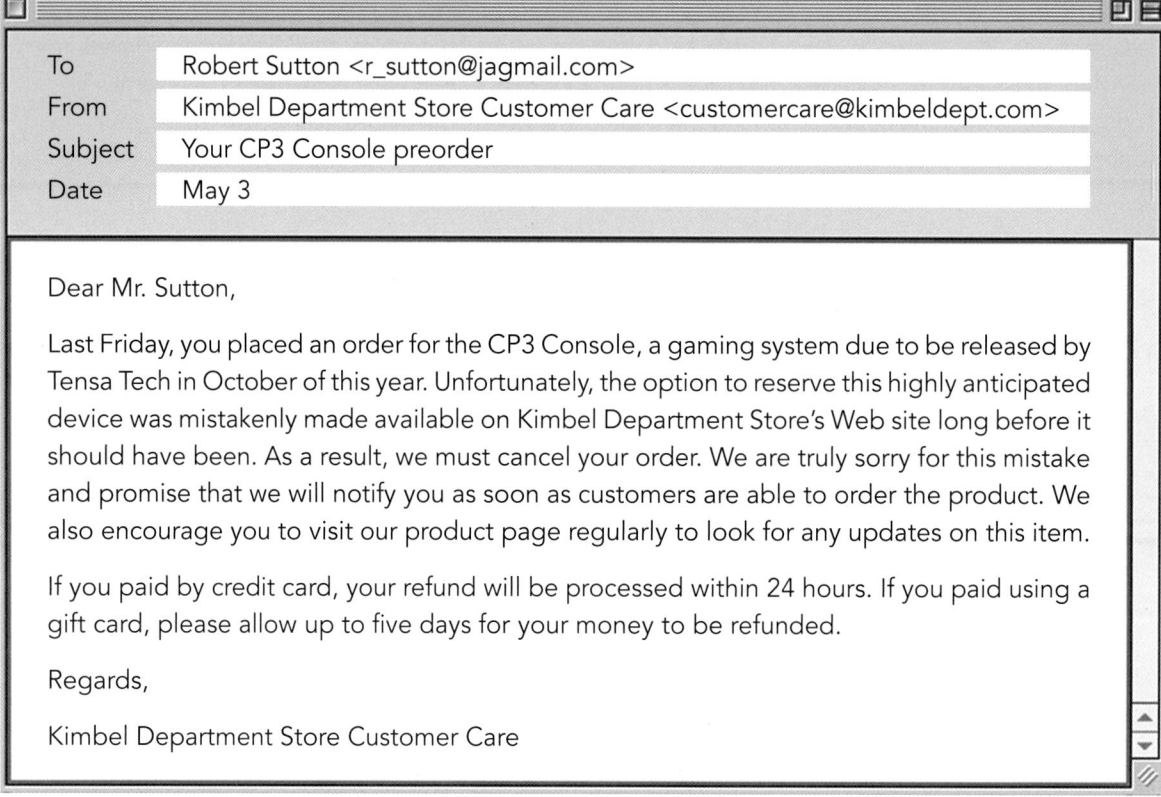

To: Robert Sutton <r_sutton@jagmail.com>
From: Kimbel Department Store Customer Care <customercare@kimbeldept.com>
Subject: Your CP3 Console preorder
Date: May 3

Dear Mr. Sutton,

Last Friday, you placed an order for the CP3 Console, a gaming system due to be released by Tensa Tech in October of this year. Unfortunately, the option to reserve this highly anticipated device was mistakenly made available on Kimbel Department Store's Web site long before it should have been. As a result, we must cancel your order. We are truly sorry for this mistake and promise that we will notify you as soon as customers are able to order the product. We also encourage you to visit our product page regularly to look for any updates on this item.

If you paid by credit card, your refund will be processed within 24 hours. If you paid using a gift card, please allow up to five days for your money to be refunded.

Regards,

Kimbel Department Store Customer Care

149. What is suggested about Mr. Sutton?

(A) He purchased a defective item.
(B) He canceled an order due to a mistake.
(C) He paid for an item with a gift card.
(D) He submitted a payment online last Friday.

150. When will Kimbel Department Store contact Mr. Sutton again?

(A) After a refund request has been approved
(B) When a device is available for purchase
(C) After a store's inventory has been restocked
(D) When the location of a product launch is revealed

Questions 151-152 refer to the following article.

Talk of the Town   *Hamilton Enquirer*

Hamilton Native Wins Award
By Troy Cheung

January 6—Vino Kiwi CEO Gloria Wilson received the Company of the Year award from the National Business Forum (NBF) last week. Her company, which offers holiday packages in New Zealand's wine country, beat several competitors in the tourism category.

Each year, a wide range of professional organizations nominate companies for consideration. The NBF then evaluates these firms on diverse criteria such as service standards and customer satisfaction to determine the best company in each field. During this process, Vino Kiwi received 4.5 points out of a possible 5.

When asked to comment, Ms. Wilson said, "This is a great honor that validates years of hard work." She thanked family, friends, and coworkers for their support and invited the public to try her services. Further information about Vino Kiwi may be found at www.vinokiwi.com.

151. What does the article mainly discuss?

(A) The government regulations for a local industry
(B) A business group's charitable contributions
(C) The criteria for membership in an organization
(D) A business's recent accomplishment

152. According to the article, what is one of the tasks of the National Business Forum?

(A) Promoting businesses in international markets
(B) Managing a fund that supports local companies
(C) Assessing recommendations from other organizations
(D) Selecting entrepreneurs to represent the country

GO ON TO THE NEXT PAGE

Questions 153-155 refer to the following memo.

MEMO

TO: All staff
FROM: Curtis Henderson, Manager
DATE: August 29
SUBJECT: Weekly progress reports

It has come to my attention that the weekly progress reports being submitted by the staff are not only inconsistent and incomplete but are also turned in late on many occasions. These reports play a major role in assessing your progress at Mayfield Incorporated; hence, the content and manner in which you submit them will definitely affect your quarterly evaluations.

To assist you in submitting your reports in a timely fashion and to ensure that the content is uniform across departments, we have designed a new form which you will begin using this week. The form will be distributed to you by your supervisors, who will explain how to fill it in and what information is required. These instructions should be followed precisely. If information is missing or unclear, the report will be returned to you for revision.

You are expected to submit these reports every Friday at 5:30 P.M. Only those on vacation or on sick leave are not required to meet this deadline. Failure to submit reports on time will be reflected in your evaluations. It may also ultimately affect your chances of being promoted or getting a salary increase. I hope that you will fully cooperate in getting your properly written weekly progress reports to your supervisors on time.

Thank you.

---

153. What problem does Mr. Henderson mention?

(A) Staff are not fulfilling a requirement properly.
(B) Financial reports have not been completed.
(C) Employees received low evaluation scores.
(D) Clients have complained about work quality.

154. What will supervisors do this week?

(A) Assess an employee's suitability for a promotion
(B) Demonstrate a new method of reporting
(C) Collect vacation request forms
(D) Revise documents needed for a presentation

155. What does Mr. Henderson suggest about missing the deadline?

(A) It will affect the supervisor-worker relationship.
(B) It is acceptable only for specified reasons.
(C) It will reflect poorly on the department's manager.
(D) It must be supported by an explanation.

Questions 156-157 refer to the following text-message chain.

Frank Danes (10:40 A.M.)
Sorry to bother you, but I was wondering whether I could get off early on Friday. I'm going to Denver for the weekend and was hoping to catch a 4 P.M. flight. Would it be OK to leave work after lunch?

Maria Faubert (10:42 A.M.)
I don't expect the office will be too busy, but are you sure nothing urgent needs to be done?

Frank Danes (10:43 A.M.)
Nothing is pending.

Maria Faubert (10:45 A.M.)
It should be fine, then. Just send me a reminder on Friday morning.

Frank Danes (10:48 A.M.)
Great! Oh, don't I need to fill out a leave request form for this?

Maria Faubert (10:50 A.M.)
No, because it isn't a full day.

Frank Danes (10:51 A.M.)
Understood. Thanks.

156. At 10:43 A.M., what does Mr. Danes most likely mean when he writes, "Nothing is pending"?

(A) He did not receive a special request.
(B) He is uncertain whether a flight is available.
(C) He has no tasks demanding immediate attention.
(D) He was able to move the deadline for a project.

157. What is suggested about the company?

(A) It requires staff to complete forms for full-day absences.
(B) It usually closes at four in the afternoon.
(C) It organizes weekly staff training sessions.
(D) It makes travel arrangements for business trips.

GO ON TO THE NEXT PAGE

Questions 158-160 refer to the following memo.

Peele, Knowles, and Associates

TO: Secretarial Staff
FROM: Marjorie Dodds, Office Manager

I am pleased to inform the law firm's secretarial staff that office policies regarding the lunch break have been updated. After receiving feedback from you during our meeting last week, management has decided to implement the following changes:

The lunch break will be extended by 30 minutes on Fridays, so it will last from 12:00 P.M. to 1:30 P.M. During this time, the offices will be closed, so make sure to switch your telephones to our answering service. Be sure to notify our regular clients of this change as well. The administrative staff will take care of recording a new message for the machine.

Secretarial staff may now turn down requests from superiors to work through the lunch break. Of course, if they do work overtime, they will receive double their usual pay.

Those with questions regarding these changes may speak with me directly or send me an e-mail at marjdodds@peeleknowlesassoc.com.

---

158. The word "implement" in paragraph 1, line 3, is closest in meaning to

(A) account for
(B) carry out
(C) dispose of
(D) attend to

159. What are the administrative staff probably going to do?

(A) Monitor the number of breaks taken by staff
(B) Gather comments and suggestions about policies
(C) Create a recorded message for incoming calls
(D) Take over the reception desk during breaks

160. What is mentioned about secretarial staff?

(A) They will receive extra pay for working during their lunch break.
(B) They must get permission from supervisors to do overtime.
(C) They are obligated to work through the lunch break if requested.
(D) They need to e-mail their break schedules to a manager.

Questions 161-163 refer to the following article.

Why You Should Join a Business Association

By Jan de Vries

Joining a business association provides many benefits to business owners, such as visibility, networking opportunities, and training. These and other advantages could be just the things your business needs to grow and thrive. — [1] —.

For instance, when Martha Yancey first opened her graphic design company a decade ago, finding customers was difficult because she was not well-known in the local community. By joining a business association, she was able to introduce herself to potential customers and receive multiple client referrals. — [2] —. "Additionally," she said, "my interactions led me to other business owners who could provide essential services, like my current electrician and accountant."

Similarly, when Lucas Smitt was starting out, he knew plenty about furniture repair but almost nothing about operating a business. "Through my membership in a business association, I was able to get access to free and discounted seminars, workshops, and online classes. — [3] —. From these, I learned how to run a company properly." This November, Smitt Restoration will be celebrating its 10th successful year.

Naturally, the benefits like those mentioned do not always come free. Most associations charge an annual membership fee and expect regular participation in official functions and events. — [4] —.

161. What is suggested about Ms. Yancey?

(A) She joined a group at first to meet new friends.
(B) Her company was in a difficult location to access.
(C) She got her product idea from another member.
(D) She met her accountant through a business association.

162. What can be inferred about Mr. Smitt?

(A) He was still in school when he started his firm.
(B) He was referred to a business association by Ms. Yancey.
(C) He opened a company at about the same time as Ms. Yancey.
(D) He teaches other young entrepreneurs how to run their businesses.

163. In which of the positions marked [1], [2], [3], and [4] does the following sentence best belong?

"However, the cost is small compared to the value offered in return."

(A) [1]
(B) [2]
(C) [3]
(D) [4]

GO ON TO THE NEXT PAGE

Questions 164-167 refer to the following online chat discussion.

Travis Coleman	[12:00 P.M.]	Someone named James Vine called to ask whether the hotel will be purchasing any new equipment.
Sheila Leblanc	[12:03 P.M.]	Right. I talked to him last week and asked him to send us a catalog. I left it with you at the front desk, Travis.
Gabby Ross	[12:04 P.M.]	If possible, I think we should get larger buffet tables for the dining area now that it's been expanded. By the way, how are the other renovations going?
Sheila Leblanc	[12:04 P.M.]	They've been a challenge. The contractors we hired say the pool won't be ready in time. We may have to delay reopening the hotel for two weeks.
Sheila Leblanc	[12:04 P.M.]	As for the buffet tables, I agree. I bookmarked two in the catalog. Travis, can you find them and describe them for Gabby?
Travis Coleman	[12:07 P.M.]	No problem. The first one is black and has a glass sneeze guard and under-the-counter refrigeration. The second is maple and has heat lamps above the food pans and trays for ice. Which one do you prefer?
Gabby Ross	[12:10 P.M.]	The first one sounds better. It's not easy to keep food cool just with ice. But I'll need a bit of time to think about it before making a final decision.
Sheila Leblanc	[12:11 P.M.]	OK, let me know. I'm finishing up the recreation room today, so I'll be down in the basement if you need me.

164. Who did Mr. Coleman speak to recently?

(A) A hotel manager
(B) An event organizer
(C) A real estate agent
(D) An equipment salesperson

165. At 12:04 P.M., what does Ms. Leblanc mean when she writes, "They've been a challenge"?

(A) Progress is slow on a remodeling project.
(B) Some product descriptions are difficult to understand.
(C) A task cannot be completed by service providers.
(D) Some appliances did not come with instructions.

166. What buffet table feature will most likely influence Ms. Ross's decision?

(A) The hanging heating elements
(B) The hardwood exterior
(C) The built-in refrigerators
(D) The glass sneeze guard

167. Where does Ms. Leblanc plan to go shortly?

(A) The swimming pool
(B) The front desk
(C) The dining area
(D) The recreation room

Questions 168-171 refer to the following e-mail.

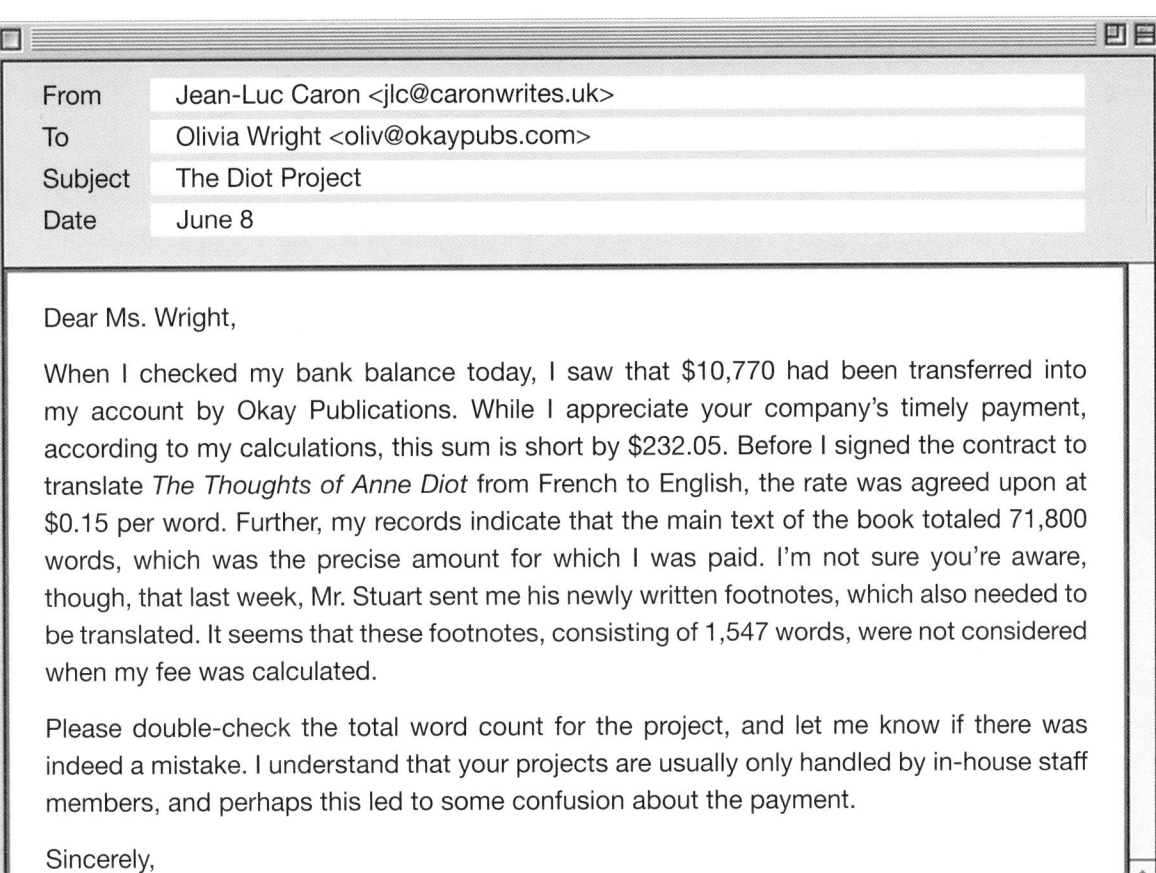

From: Jean-Luc Caron <jlc@caronwrites.uk>
To: Olivia Wright <oliv@okaypubs.com>
Subject: The Diot Project
Date: June 8

Dear Ms. Wright,

When I checked my bank balance today, I saw that $10,770 had been transferred into my account by Okay Publications. While I appreciate your company's timely payment, according to my calculations, this sum is short by $232.05. Before I signed the contract to translate *The Thoughts of Anne Diot* from French to English, the rate was agreed upon at $0.15 per word. Further, my records indicate that the main text of the book totaled 71,800 words, which was the precise amount for which I was paid. I'm not sure you're aware, though, that last week, Mr. Stuart sent me his newly written footnotes, which also needed to be translated. It seems that these footnotes, consisting of 1,547 words, were not considered when my fee was calculated.

Please double-check the total word count for the project, and let me know if there was indeed a mistake. I understand that your projects are usually only handled by in-house staff members, and perhaps this led to some confusion about the payment.

Sincerely,
Jean-Luc Caron

168. Why did Mr. Caron write the e-mail?

(A) To point out a billing error
(B) To clarify some writing instructions
(C) To suggest corrections to a manuscript
(D) To follow up on overdue work

169. The word "precise" in paragraph 1, line 6, is closest in meaning to

(A) strict
(B) close
(C) true
(D) exact

170. Who most likely is Mr. Stuart?

(A) An author
(B) A publishing manager
(C) A document translator
(D) A magazine editor

171. What is indicated about Ms. Wright?

(A) She rarely works with outside contractors.
(B) She did not check the current exchange rate.
(C) She is the director of a finance department.
(D) She will have to revise a contract.

Questions 172-175 refer to the following form.

OAKPORT COMPUTING
Job Training Program

Oakport Computing regularly offers employees the opportunity to enhance their skills and knowledge through its job training program. — [1] —.

The list of courses below is based on an online survey completed by all employees. Except where indicated, each course has been designed to be completed in half a day. Nevertheless, due to budget restrictions, we can only offer three at a time. — [2] —. Using the attached form, please select the three courses you are most interested in attending and submit it by June 3. The company will present a final selection of courses based on everyone's choices and announce the course dates on June 6. — [3] —.

Please choose the three courses that you are most interested in attending:

Employee Name: Kevin Montoya   **Date:** June 1

- General Job Skills
    ___ Time Management
    ___ Presentation Skills
    ___ Problem Solving*
    ✓ Working with Teams

- Technical Skills
    ___ Advanced Programming*
    ✓ Big Data Analysis*
    ✓ Network Security*
    ___ User Interface Design

* One-day course

To find out which courses will be offered, go to www.oakport.com/training on June 6. There will also be information on how to register. Employees are responsible for securing permission from their supervisors to participate. — [4] —.

172. What is one purpose of the form?

(A) To invite volunteers to join an activity
(B) To reduce a list of options
(C) To gather feedback on a course
(D) To announce classes for new employees

173. Which course can be completed in half a day?

(A) Problem Solving
(B) Working with Teams
(C) Advanced Programming
(D) Network Security

174. What is suggested about Mr. Montoya?

(A) He submitted his application form late.
(B) His supervisor will not approve a request.
(C) He may not take all the courses he chose.
(D) His main job involves giving presentations.

175. In which of the positions marked [1], [2], [3], and [4] does the following sentence best belong?

"This must be done at least two weeks prior to the start of the courses."

(A) [1]
(B) [2]
(C) [3]
(D) [4]

GO ON TO THE NEXT PAGE

Questions 176-180 refer to the following notice and memo.

Charity Car Auction

The 21st Annual Charity Car Auction will be held on June 25 at Metropolitan Park. This yearly activity is sponsored by several major automobile manufacturers and raises money for children's charities around the state.

The park will open to the public at 10 A.M. The auction starts at 1 P.M. and ends at 6 P.M., and you will find great deals on cars and trucks, including commercial vehicles. Bring the family and enjoy a fun day outside. In addition to the auction, there will be a vintage car exhibit, food booths, play areas, and vendors selling various car-related products. Tickets for this event are $5 per person.

For inquiries, call 555-3403, and visit www.charitycarauction.org to get a preview of the cars for sale.

MEMO

June 15
To: All Metropolitan Park staff
From: Joel Gage, Park Services Director
Subject: Event preparations

In preparation for the 21st Annual Charity Car Auction, I'd like to give everyone some reminders. One day before the event, we will be receiving deliveries of vehicles for the auction and the planned display. The cars for sale will stay in our secure parking lot while the vintage ones will be brought inside through the north entrance.

On the day of the event, the south entrance will be opened to pedestrians, the east entrance will be reserved for park and event staff, and the west entrance will be designated for emergency personnel. Assistance with traffic and crowd management will be provided by the city's police department.

If you have any questions, do not hesitate to call or stop by my office on the park grounds. Note that I will be unavailable next week as I will be traveling to Chicago to attend a conference. I will see all of you on the day of the deliveries.

176. What is the notice mainly about?

(A) A product launch
(B) An outdoor concert
(C) A fundraising activity
(D) A sports event

177. Why should readers visit a Web site?

(A) To make a booth reservation
(B) To submit proposals for future events
(C) To see some offerings in advance
(D) To purchase tickets for a group

178. What is mentioned about the vintage cars?

(A) They will be offered as prizes in a draw.
(B) They will be sold on the last day of the event.
(C) They will be transported through the north gate.
(D) They will be parked in a secure parking lot.

179. What can be inferred about Mr. Gage?

(A) He will return from a business trip before June 25.
(B) He is seeking volunteer workers to assist emergency crews.
(C) He will move to a new office at the end of the month.
(D) He is planning to take a vacation in Chicago next week.

180. In the memo, the word "management" in paragraph 2, line 3, is closest in meaning to

(A) control
(B) authority
(C) executive
(D) operation

GO ON TO THE NEXT PAGE

Questions 181-185 refer to the following Web page and e-mail.

www.atgf.com

Atlantic Toys and Games Fair

Congratulations! You have successfully registered for the Atlantic Toys and Games Fair. This year's event takes place on April 4 at the Noguiera Convention Hall in Funchal, Portugal.

Please take a moment to carefully review your registration details.

Registrant Name: Kenneth Fruman	
E-mail Address: kenfrum@burgudeco.com	
Registration Date: January 15	
Entry Category: all-access pass	* includes admittance to display hall containing 60 booths and 20 exhibits, speaker sessions by guest experts, and industry insider meet-ups
T-shirt Size: large	* gift to be included in event package
Chosen Payment Method: bank transfer **Fee Due:** €35 **OUR BANKING DETAILS** Bank Name: Avantage Bank Account Holder: ATGF Account Number: 7334-8921-5960-66	* payment must be submitted on or prior to January 23 * confirmation e-mail will be sent after receipt of payment

[Edit] [Return to Home]

To	Kenneth Fruman <kenfrum@burgudeco.com>
From	Patricia Laroux <assistant@atgf.com>
Subject	Registration
Date	January 17

Dear Mr. Fruman,

Thank you for registering for the Atlantic Toys and Games Fair. We have received your bank transfer payment of €70 and will mail your event package to you on January 20. The package will include two all-access passes. Unfortunately, we cannot send you the package gift that was originally advertised as we have run out. Consequently, we'll be providing you with desk calendars instead.

If you haven't booked accommodations yet, I'd recommend doing so as soon as possible since there are only three hotels near the Noguiera Convention Hall. For information on Funchal hotels, check www.visitfunchal.com/placestostay.

Respectfully yours,
Patricia Laroux, Planning assistant
Atlantic Toys and Games Fair

181. What is one purpose of the Web page?

(A) To inform association members about an event
(B) To confirm a reservation for a booth
(C) To provide instructions for sending money
(D) To register a participant in a workshop

182. What is NOT mentioned as being accessible by all-access pass holders?

(A) Talks by specialists
(B) Product demonstrations
(C) Display spaces
(D) Networking sessions

183. What is indicated about Mr. Fruman?

(A) He was sent an event package on January 17.
(B) He received a confirmation e-mail with an attached receipt.
(C) He also purchased a pass for another person.
(D) He is renting an exhibition space in the display hall.

184. What can be inferred about the Atlantic Toys and Games Fair?

(A) It raised the registration fee this year.
(B) It takes place in a different country each time.
(C) It provides ticket refunds only until January 23.
(D) It no longer has T-shirts to offer attendees.

185. What is mentioned about Noguiera Convention Hall?

(A) It is adjacent to the city's airport.
(B) It has been the venue for the fair in the past.
(C) It is holding two events at the same time.
(D) It is located close to accommodation facilities.

GO ON TO THE NEXT PAGE

Questions 186-190 refer to the following advertisement, invoice, and e-mail.

Dyna Flooring
Clearance Sale

Throughout this August, Dyna Flooring will be holding a clearance sale to make way for new inventory. Enjoy great deals on a variety of merchandise for home and office use, including products by top-rated brands like Disena, Molik, Maitland, and more.

✓ 10 percent general discount on every product
✓ 20 percent off merchandise increasing in price next month
✓ 30 percent off bulk purchases of discontinued products

The sale extends to items sold online and in stores across the Midwest. An additional special discount of 10 percent applies to customers who purchase items at a store, and Dyna Club rewards program members receive an additional 20 percent off.

Free delivery on all orders of $500 or more!
For additional information, go to www.dynaflooring.com or visit your nearest Dyna Flooring location.

Dyna Flooring
www.dynaflooring.com

Sold to: Danielle Welch
Company: Westwood Accounting
Payment method: Verifian credit card

Transaction date: August 29
Dyna Club member? Yes

Product code	Item	Quantity	Price
MKT1431Y	Molik ceramic kitchen tile (10% off)	24	$388.80
CTJN9091G	Johnson grey carpet tile (10% off)	16	$264.00
CTLS3816B	Laster blue carpet tile (30% off)	58	$740.95
FTIN643RW	Intone wood-finish floor tile (20% off)	12	$787.20
Terms: Refunds will only be issued in the form of store credit. Purchased items may be exchanged for ones of equal or lesser value for as long as supplies last.		Subtotal	$2,180.95
		Less 10%	($218.10)
		Tax	$130.86
		Shipping	$0.00
		TOTAL	$2,093.71

Thank you for your business!

To: Customer service <cs@dynaflooring.com>
From: Danielle Welch <c.welch@westwoodaccts.com>
Date: September 2
Subject: Recent order

To Whom It May Concern:

I recently purchased some items during your sale in August. Unfortunately, one of the items turned out to be the wrong color for our newly redesigned office kitchen, so I want to exchange it for a similar product. If no suitable items are available, I would like a refund instead. I also noticed that I should have received an additional special discount of 20 percent as a Dyna Club member. Please credit my account for this additional discount or advise me on further actions that need to be taken. Thank you.

Sincerely,
Danielle Welch
Purchasing manager
Westwood Accounting

---

186. What is the purpose of the advertisement?

(A) To promote the launch of an online shopping service
(B) To encourage customers to join a membership program
(C) To introduce a monthlong cost-saving opportunity
(D) To advertise a product made out of new materials

187. What is mentioned about Dyna Flooring?

(A) It is the exclusive distributor of Disena products.
(B) It has opened stores in multiple countries.
(C) It only carries items suitable for office use.
(D) It offers free shipping for qualifying orders.

188. What is indicated on the invoice?

(A) Ms. Welch attended the final day of a sale.
(B) Some items are currently out of stock.
(C) Johnson's tiles were delivered ahead of schedule.
(D) Intone's tiles will increase in price next month.

189. What is suggested about Ms. Welch?

(A) She paid for her items in person.
(B) She is eligible for store credit of around $200.
(C) She was in charge of redesigning an office.
(D) She used rewards points to pay for a purchase.

190. What does Ms. Welch want Dyna Flooring to do?

(A) Sign her up for a membership program
(B) Refund the cost of shipping
(C) Send her installation instructions
(D) Apply an additional price reduction

GO ON TO THE NEXT PAGE

Questions 191-195 refer to the following information and forms.

Elfman Home Cooling
Warranty Claims

Elfman is committed to serving the needs of its customers. All equipment we sell comes with a six-month parts and labor warranty. If you experience problems during the warranty period, a technician will visit your home or business and perform all necessary repairs free of charge. In addition, if your unit malfunctions within one month of purchase, we will replace it at our expense.

To submit a warranty claim, go to www.elfmanequip.com/customers. You will be asked to enter your username and password. Then, click the CLAIMS button at the bottom of the screen to access the online form. To ensure timely processing, fill out the claim form completely.

Elfman Home Cooling Claim Form

Claim number: EC1081626
Date: August 3
Customer name: Larry Regan
Address: 219 Duncan Street, Forsyth, GA 31029
Tel.: 555-4086
E-mail: l.regan@pellstone.com
Product: Elfman central air conditioner
Model: AU-0951   **Serial number:** P118946QJ

Problem Description:
The unit is fine for the first 30 minutes after it starts, but then it begins to make a strange noise that becomes progressively louder. It is very difficult for the staff in my office to work. This is the first problem I have had since I purchased the unit about seven months ago.

Elfman Home Cooling Claim Form

Claim number: EK0194114
Date: August 15
Customer name: Michelle Bowman
Address: 176 King Boulevard, High Springs, FL 32643
Tel.: 555-7182
E-mail: m.bowman@springmail.com
Product: Elfman ventilation system
Model: PK-4317   **Serial number:** T27386HX

Problem Description:
This morning, I noticed that very little air was coming out of the vents. I turned the unit off to check for any blockages but did not see anything out of the ordinary. Given that it was installed less than two weeks ago, this is unacceptable.

---

191. How can customers submit a warranty claim?

(A) By visiting a service center
(B) By mailing a written request
(C) By accessing an online account
(D) By installing a mobile application

192. What is suggested about Mr. Regan?

(A) He will have to wait several days for a technician to visit.
(B) He contacted a company representative by e-mail.
(C) He requested a discount on an air conditioner.
(D) He will have to pay for the cost of repairs.

193. What is mentioned in the form completed by Mr. Regan?

(A) He ordered the latest model of an appliance.
(B) His office will be closed until repairs are performed.
(C) His unit functions properly when first turned on.
(D) He purchased an Elfman product on August 3.

194. What can be inferred about Ms. Bowman?

(A) She failed to fill out a form completely.
(B) She will receive a replacement product.
(C) She installed some equipment incorrectly.
(D) She ordered extra parts for a ventilation system.

195. What is indicated on the form completed by Ms. Bowman?

(A) She was visited by a technician.
(B) She did not register on a company Web site.
(C) She tried to determine the cause of a problem.
(D) She does not know the serial number of a device.

GO ON TO THE NEXT PAGE

Questions 196-200 refer to the following letter, brochure, and information.

September 20

Arapali Express
Nichi Building, Lalmati
Jabalpur, Madhya Pradesh 482002

To Whom It May Concern,

I wish to tell you about my experience as a passenger on Arapali Express Flight AE010 on September 7. Overall, it was satisfactory. I appreciated being able to board before some of the other passengers and that the Wi-Fi was not very costly to use. However, I almost immediately had trouble with my video monitor and, despite the flight crew's assistance, never got it to work. Thankfully, the flight wasn't too long, or I would have become extremely frustrated. I hope you will take steps to ensure that all on-board devices are working properly in the future.

Yours truly,
Sandra Bulsara

Arapali Express Cabin Classes and Amenities

First Class
- Increased baggage allowance
- Priority check-in and boarding
- Complimentary Wi-Fi
- Gourmet meal service with free premium snacks and drinks
- Extra-large seat monitor with handheld device
- Complimentary luxury skin-care kit

Business Class
- Increased baggage allowance
- Priority check-in and boarding
- Complimentary Wi-Fi
- Scheduled meal service with free premium snacks and drinks
- Large seat monitor with touch-screen access

Premium Economy Class (international flights only)
- Increased baggage allowance
- Priority boarding
- Paid Wi-Fi access
- Scheduled meal service
- Regular seat monitor

Economy Class
- Paid Wi-Fi access
- Scheduled meal service
- Regular seat monitor

Arapali Express In-Flight Magazine

New movies this month:
To watch a movie, switch on your video monitor and use the available controls to navigate the screen. Headphones are provided free of charge. For assistance, please call the attention of an in-flight crew member.

Route	Movie	Genre	Length
Within India	Mr. Matchbox	documentary	83 minutes
India to Africa	Tabla in Heaven	drama	112 minutes
India to Southeast Asia	Boman Verma's Fantastic Adventures	comedy	98 minutes
India to the Middle East	Bride from Nagpur	romance	121 minutes
India to Europe	Tiger that Roams the City	thriller	105 minutes

Notes:
1. Only P360 and P380 aircraft are equipped with touch screens and handheld devices.
2. Wi-Fi is available on all aircraft except P110s and P120s.

196. Why was the letter written?
(A) To apply for compensation
(B) To change a flight itinerary
(C) To report a policy violation
(D) To convey some feedback

197. In which class was Ms. Bulsara probably seated?
(A) First Class
(B) Business Class
(C) Premium Economy Class
(D) Economy Class

198. What is available exclusively to passengers in first class?
(A) Bonus airline miles
(B) Larger baggage allowance
(C) Free Wi-fi
(D) Skin-care products

199. What is suggested about the movie, *Mr. Matchbox*?
(A) It is the only one provided free of charge to all classes.
(B) It cannot be viewed by Premium Economy passengers.
(C) It is the latest movie to be added to the airline's selections.
(D) It will not be played on aircraft with touch-screen monitors.

200. What is indicated about the handheld video controls?
(A) They are not provided on international flights.
(B) They must be specifically requested ahead of time.
(C) They are not installed on some models of airplanes.
(D) They cost a small additional charge to use.

This is the end of the test. You may review Parts 5, 6, and 7 if you finish the test early.

실시간 토익시험 정답확인&해설강의
Hackers.co.kr

한 권으로 끝내는 해커스 토익 900+ LC+RC+VOCA

실전모의고사

3

잠깐! 테스트 전 아래 사항을 꼭 확인하세요.

1. Answer Sheet(p.231), 연필, 지우개, 시계를 준비하셨나요? ☐
2. Listening mp3를 들을 준비가 되셨나요? ☐

모든 준비가 완료되었으면 목표 점수를 떠올린 후 테스트를 시작합니다.
시험 시간 120분내에 문제 풀이와 답안지 마킹까지 모두 완료해야 합니다.

🎧 TEST3.mp3
실전용·복습용 문제풀이 mp3 무료 다운로드 및 스트리밍 바로듣기 (HackersIngang.com)
* 실제 시험장의 소음까지 재현해 낸 고사장 소음/매미 버전, 영국식·호주식 발음 집중 버전, 고속 버전까지
  구매하면 실전에 더욱 완벽히 대비할 수 있습니다.

무료 mp3 바로듣기

LISTENING TEST

In this section, you must demonstrate your ability to understand spoken English. This section is divided into four parts and will take approximately 45 minutes to complete. Do not mark the answers in your test book. Use the answer sheet that is provided separately.

PART 1

Directions: For each question, you will listen to four short statements about a picture in your test book. These statements will not be printed and will only be spoken one time. Select the statement that best describes what is happening in the picture and mark the corresponding letter (A), (B), (C), or (D) on the answer sheet.

Sample Answer

The statement that best describes the picture is (B), "The man is sitting at the desk." So, you should mark letter (B) on the answer sheet.

1.

2.

GO ON TO THE NEXT PAGE

3.

4.

5.

6.

PART 2

Directions: For each question, you will listen to a statement or question followed by three possible responses spoken in English. They will not be printed and will only be spoken one time. Select the best response and mark the corresponding letter (A), (B), or (C) on your answer sheet.

7. Mark your answer on the answer sheet.
8. Mark your answer on the answer sheet.
9. Mark your answer on the answer sheet.
10. Mark your answer on the answer sheet.
11. Mark your answer on the answer sheet.
12. Mark your answer on the answer sheet.
13. Mark your answer on the answer sheet.
14. Mark your answer on the answer sheet.
15. Mark your answer on the answer sheet.
16. Mark your answer on the answer sheet.
17. Mark your answer on the answer sheet.
18. Mark your answer on the answer sheet.
19. Mark your answer on the answer sheet.
20. Mark your answer on the answer sheet.
21. Mark your answer on the answer sheet.
22. Mark your answer on the answer sheet.
23. Mark your answer on the answer sheet.
24. Mark your answer on the answer sheet.
25. Mark your answer on the answer sheet.
26. Mark your answer on the answer sheet.
27. Mark your answer on the answer sheet.
28. Mark your answer on the answer sheet.
29. Mark your answer on the answer sheet.
30. Mark your answer on the answer sheet.
31. Mark your answer on the answer sheet.

PART 3

Directions: In this part, you will listen to several conversations between two or more speakers. These conversations will not be printed and will only be spoken one time. For each conversation, you will be asked to answer three questions. Select the best response and mark the corresponding letter (A), (B), (C), or (D) on your answer sheet.

32. What event is taking place?
    (A) A business seminar
    (B) An awards ceremony
    (C) A charity fund-raiser
    (D) A shareholders' meeting

33. What does the man request?
    (A) A company name
    (B) A work address
    (C) A seat number
    (D) A confirmation code

34. What will the man most likely do next?
    (A) Bring out a beverage
    (B) Escort a guest
    (C) Check a list
    (D) Explain an agenda

35. What are the speakers mainly discussing?
    (A) A client contract
    (B) A project deadline
    (C) A flight booking
    (D) A company regulation

36. What does the woman say about her last business trip?
    (A) It was not very long.
    (B) It included a whole team.
    (C) It did not cost a lot.
    (D) It was not fully reimbursed.

37. Which department do the men most likely work in?
    (A) Human resources
    (B) Accounting
    (C) Technology
    (D) Sales

38. Where most likely does the woman work?
    (A) At a public relations firm
    (B) At a newspaper company
    (C) At a management firm
    (D) At a government office

39. What does the man want to learn more about?
    (A) An upcoming set of articles
    (B) A potential amount of readership
    (C) A special subscription offer
    (D) An early enrollment period

40. What will most likely happen on Tuesday?
    (A) Some journalists will meet.
    (B) Residents will gather for an event.
    (C) An interview will be conducted.
    (D) A story will be released.

41. What problem does the woman mention?
    (A) She forgot about some plans.
    (B) She cannot go to an event.
    (C) Her car needs to be fixed.
    (D) Her conference materials are lost.

42. What does the man suggest?
    (A) Replacing some components
    (B) Taking public transportation
    (C) Riding with someone else
    (D) Contacting a customer

43. What does the woman inquire about?
    (A) Whether she can be picked up
    (B) If she must change her schedule
    (C) How far away a location is
    (D) Where a colleague wants to go

GO ON TO THE NEXT PAGE

44. Where do the speakers most likely work?

(A) At a recruitment agency
(B) At an architectural firm
(C) At a financial institution
(D) At a law office

45. What will happen during the meeting next week?

(A) A contract will be finalized.
(B) A schedule will be discussed.
(C) A demonstration will be given.
(D) A design will be revealed.

46. Why does the woman say, "This is going to be her first time in a management role"?

(A) To stress the importance of a project
(B) To indicate that a colleague was promoted
(C) To encourage the man to support an initiative
(D) To express doubt about a person's ability

47. Who most likely are the men?

(A) Repair specialists
(B) Sales associates
(C) Research participants
(D) Conference attendees

48. What is mentioned about the computer manual?

(A) It has been recently updated.
(B) It uses a small font size.
(C) It is printed in multiple languages.
(D) It lacks clarity in a certain part.

49. What do the men suggest?

(A) Using more images
(B) Printing some copies
(C) Shortening a handbook
(D) Adding an introduction

50. Where most likely are the speakers?

(A) At a clothing boutique
(B) At a retail outlet
(C) At a department store
(D) At a beauty salon

51. What does the woman want to do?

(A) Get a haircut
(B) Make a purchase
(C) Arrange an appointment
(D) Speak to a manager

52. What does the man say about Nature's Touch brand?

(A) It is used by some of the stylists.
(B) It is made with organic ingredients.
(C) It is completely sold out.
(D) It is on sale until the end of the week.

53. What did the woman recently do?

(A) Gave a presentation
(B) Visited a store
(C) Joined a team
(D) Reviewed a document

54. What problem does the woman mention?

(A) A financial report was inaccurate.
(B) A new service failed to launch.
(C) A company's sales have decreased.
(D) A competitor offers larger discounts.

55. Why does the man say, "our customers have to visit our shops in person"?

(A) To explain a process
(B) To reject a suggestion
(C) To confirm a decision
(D) To indicate a problem

56. What does the man plan to do on Friday evening?

(A) Stop by a trade show
(B) Attend a photography class
(C) Go to an exhibit
(D) Participate in a workshop

57. What does the woman say about the budget report?

(A) It contains financial errors.
(B) Its deadline was extended.
(C) It requires additional data.
(D) It was already submitted.

58. What does the man suggest?

(A) Exploring a museum
(B) Meeting a relative
(C) Contacting a colleague
(D) Having a meal

59. Where most likely does the man work?

(A) At a laboratory
(B) At a shipping company
(C) At an electronics retailer
(D) At a warehouse

60. Why does the man want to get an item soon?

(A) He needs to test its accuracy.
(B) He will conduct a product analysis.
(C) He has to replace a broken machine.
(D) He requires it for his upcoming work.

61. What does the man ask about?

(A) The installation of some equipment
(B) The deadline for a project
(C) The date of a delivery
(D) The progress of some research

Park		Building A	Building B
Johnson Street			
Building C	Subway Station	Elm Avenue	Post Office	Building D

62. Why is the dinner being held?

(A) To announce a manager's promotion
(B) To commemorate a company's founding
(C) To celebrate a branch opening
(D) To welcome a potential client

63. Look at the graphic. Which building will the man visit in the afternoon?

(A) Building A
(B) Building B
(C) Building C
(D) Building D

64. What did the man do this morning?

(A) Met with a manager
(B) Greeted a visiting CEO
(C) Paid a deposit
(D) Spoke with an assistant

GO ON TO THE NEXT PAGE

Stonewall Café

Side Options

House salad
Lemon kale salad
Roasted potatoes
Pan-fried green beans

65. Why does the man apologize to the woman?

(A) He did not provide timely service.
(B) He made a minor mistake.
(C) An entrée is no longer available.
(D) A line was longer than expected.

66. Look at the graphic. Which side dish does the woman select?

(A) House salad
(B) Lemon kale salad
(C) Roasted potatoes
(D) Pan-fried green beans

67. What does the man offer to do?

(A) Modify an existing order
(B) Bring another menu
(C) Speak with a restaurant manager
(D) Inquire about a beverage

SkyJet Airlines

Dallas, TX → Denver, CO
June 6

Time	Flight
8:00 A.M.	247
10:30 A.M.	451
1:15 P.M.	663
3:45 P.M.	819

68. Why are the speakers traveling to Denver?

(A) To give a presentation
(B) To launch a campaign
(C) To promote a new regional branch
(D) To consider an investment opportunity

69. What was the man informed of?

(A) An award nomination
(B) A client meeting
(C) A project deadline
(D) A reimbursement plan

70. Look at the graphic. Which flight will the speakers most likely take?

(A) Flight 247
(B) Flight 451
(C) Flight 663
(D) Flight 819

PART 4

Directions: In this part, you will listen to several short talks by a single speaker. These talks will not be printed and will only be spoken one time. For each talk, you will be asked to answer three questions. Select the best response and mark the corresponding letter (A), (B), (C), or (D) on your answer sheet.

71. Why is the speaker calling?
    (A) To request a refund
    (B) To report an issue
    (C) To confirm an order
    (D) To reschedule a meeting

72. According to the speaker, what is a benefit of the Weyden Platinum?
    (A) It has a powerful motor.
    (B) It has multiple settings.
    (C) It is easy to move around.
    (D) It is available in various sizes.

73. What does the speaker recommend?
    (A) Seeing a device in person
    (B) Getting an extended warranty
    (C) Participating in a contest
    (D) Returning an item to a shop

74. What is the speaker mainly discussing?
    (A) A news conference
    (B) A product launch
    (C) A potential contract
    (D) A corporate merger

75. What does the speaker mention about Hanaway and Glarris Incorporated?
    (A) It is developing a consumer product.
    (B) It offers consulting services.
    (C) It operates in Europe.
    (D) It is relocating its main office.

76. According to the speaker, what will happen over the next two months?
    (A) Employees will be transferred.
    (B) Communications will be improved.
    (C) Customer surveys will be conducted.
    (D) Promotional materials will be prepared.

77. What kind of product is being advertised?
    (A) An energy bar
    (B) A breakfast cereal
    (C) A sports beverage
    (D) A fitness tracker

78. What does the speaker mention about Power Source?
    (A) It has been recommended by a celebrity.
    (B) It was developed by athletes.
    (C) It has received positive reviews.
    (D) It includes several kinds of vitamins.

79. What does the speaker mean when he says, "This won't last for long"?
    (A) A product is not available.
    (B) A promotion is expected to be popular.
    (C) A new product line will be launched.
    (D) A sale will expire soon.

80. What is the broadcast mainly about?
    (A) A local celebration
    (B) A sports competition
    (C) A new park attraction
    (D) A city music institute

81. What does the speaker say parents will enjoy?
    (A) Some prizes
    (B) Some performances
    (C) Some rides
    (D) Some contests

82. What will happen at 8 P.M.?
    (A) A festival commercial will be aired.
    (B) A government official will be interviewed.
    (C) A food booth will be set up.
    (D) A musical event will take place.

GO ON TO THE NEXT PAGE

83. What does the speaker say the listeners will do?

(A) Observe a professional chef
(B) Sample some appetizers
(C) Put on some aprons
(D) Cook multiple dishes

84. What has the speaker placed on the counters for the listeners?

(A) Registration forms
(B) Recipe printouts
(C) Baking ingredients
(D) Kitchen utensils

85. Why do the listeners need a partner?

(A) They are doing teambuilding exercises.
(B) They have to brainstorm ideas.
(C) There are limited cooking implements.
(D) There is a shortage of ingredients.

86. Who most likely is the listener?

(A) A curator
(B) A real estate agent
(C) An artist
(D) A gallery manager

87. What does the speaker imply when she says, "Electric Space has tall ceilings and a large back entrance"?

(A) A potential venue is ideal.
(B) A building was recently renovated.
(C) A location was accurately advertised.
(D) A rental facility is fairly priced.

88. What does the speaker instruct the listener to do?

(A) Review the terms of a lease
(B) Inform her of a decision
(C) Stop by a gallery in person
(D) Submit a portfolio of work

89. Who does the speaker say is coming to visit?

(A) The head of a research facility
(B) An insurance agent
(C) The director of a major company
(D) A government inspector

90. Where will the meeting take place?

(A) In the main lobby
(B) In a break room
(C) In a conference room
(D) In an office

91. According to the speaker, what will be discussed during the meeting?

(A) Details of an upcoming visit
(B) Upgrades to safety equipment
(C) New duties for company personnel
(D) Revised goals for the factory

92. What is the main topic of the news report?

(A) A social media service
(B) A new software program
(C) A technological update
(D) A corporate acquisition

93. What does the speaker imply when she says, "This isn't significant by itself"?

(A) A search engine does not function properly.
(B) A piece of equipment received a minor update.
(C) A service is not popular with some users.
(D) A development could have other benefits.

94. Who is Briana Clinton?

(A) An investment manager
(B) A software developer
(C) A company executive
(D) A media representative

Larkville Interiors Invoice		
Item	Quantity	Cost
Wallpaper	10	$380
Glue	11	$175
Roller	2	$50
Labor	5	$200
	Total:	$805

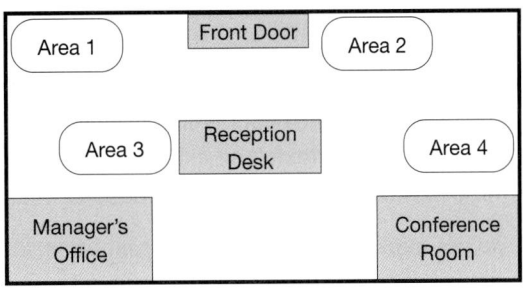

95. Why is the speaker calling?

(A) To check the status of a project
(B) To suggest a schedule change
(C) To confirm an office location
(D) To cancel an appointment

96. What does the speaker ask the listener to do?

(A) Contact his secretary
(B) Make a payment
(C) Approve a plan
(D) Order some supplies

97. Look at the graphic. Which quantity on the invoice needs to be updated?

(A) 10
(B) 11
(C) 2
(D) 5

98. According to the speaker, what will happen tomorrow?

(A) Some equipment will be set up.
(B) A desk will be removed.
(C) A guest list will be printed.
(D) Some devices will be demonstrated.

99. Look at the graphic. Where is Printer 102 situated?

(A) Area 1
(B) Area 2
(C) Area 3
(D) Area 4

100. What does the speaker suggest the listeners do?

(A) Contact a technician
(B) Refer to some instructions
(C) Visit a reception desk
(D) Send an e-mail

This is the end of the Listening test. Turn to PART 5 in your test book.

GO ON TO THE NEXT PAGE

READING TEST

In this section, you must demonstrate your ability to read and comprehend English. You will be given a variety of texts and asked to answer questions about these texts. This section is divided into three parts and will take 75 minutes to complete.

Do not mark the answers in your test book. Use the answer sheet that is separately provided.

PART 5

Directions: In each question, you will be asked to review a statement that is missing a word or phrase. Four answer choices will be provided for each statement. Select the best answer and mark the corresponding letter (A), (B), (C), or (D) on the answer sheet.

101. Emily helped ------- to the complimentary snacks and beverages at the store's grand opening event.

(A) she
(B) herself
(C) hers
(D) her

102. ------- to the e-mail from Mr. Yates as soon as possible, and ask questions if anything is unclear.

(A) Response
(B) Responding
(C) Respond
(D) Responds

103. ------- the city council has voted in favor of funding the new community center, its construction should begin soon.

(A) Now that
(B) If only
(C) Rather than
(D) In spite of

104. The wildlife preserve was created by the Florida Nature Commission to ------- the state's endangered species.

(A) protect
(B) protection
(C) protective
(D) protecting

105. Delvium Automotive's new policy aims to address the issue of employees who are ------- late for work.

(A) adequately
(B) formerly
(C) routinely
(D) friendly

106. The Lexington Building's new tenant ------- in the next couple of days, so the owner is getting everything ready.

(A) to arrive
(B) has arrived
(C) is arriving
(D) arrival

107. The banquet hall was ------- decorated for the Langhorne Foundation's fundraising gala on June 11.

(A) attractive
(B) attractively
(C) attraction
(D) attracting

108. The Whitby Town Council recently prepared a brochure specifying ways that residents can play an ------- role in the community.

(A) activate
(B) active
(C) action
(D) activity

109. Please ------- yourselves with the new office policies by consulting the updated employee manual.

(A) relieve
(B) converse
(C) arrange
(D) familiarize

110. The advertising team is ------- pressure to complete its campaign proposal in time for the business planning session.

(A) within
(B) through
(C) under
(D) among

111. BelTrax has ------- ranked as one of the top providers of marketing research since its foundation seven years ago.

(A) conveniently
(B) temporarily
(C) consistently
(D) wishfully

112. Mansfield Chemical is considering building an extension that ------- additional space for the newly purchased machinery.

(A) will have provided
(B) would provide
(C) had provided
(D) to provide

113. Other than a few ------- complaints that were easily addressed, the feedback on ShieldX's antivirus program has been generally positive.

(A) defensive
(B) current
(C) minor
(D) complex

114. ------- who return a vehicle to Speedy Auto Rental after the designated time will be required to pay a $45 late fee.

(A) Everybody
(B) Those
(C) This
(D) Which

115. About 15 minutes before the keynote speaker was scheduled to take the stage, ------- seat in the auditorium was occupied.

(A) plenty
(B) all
(C) every
(D) most

116. Limerick Books has managed to stay competitive by developing ------- ways to attract new customers.

(A) invent
(B) invention
(C) inventive
(D) invented

117. Ms. Waddill provided a few members of her department with an ------- covering the key points of the CEO's speech.

(A) objection
(B) expansion
(C) overview
(D) experience

118. ------- extensive safety training, Desmond Construction has significantly reduced the number of accidents at its worksites.

(A) Prior to
(B) On behalf of
(C) Owing to
(D) According to

119. ------- at the Latipa Film Festival increased by nearly 30 percent this year, yet the organizers still lost money.

(A) Attend
(B) Attendee
(C) Attendant
(D) Attendance

120. During the summer, the popular Marigold Hotel is always fully booked ------- the large number of rooms in the facility.

(A) thereby
(B) even though
(C) aside from
(D) notwithstanding

GO ON TO THE NEXT PAGE

121. The Madison Music Concert administrators received an official ------- from the city government to hold the event.

(A) permit
(B) permissive
(C) permits
(D) permissively

122. A small section of Glegg Park has been set aside ------- for pets and their owners.

(A) relatively
(B) intensely
(C) immeasurably
(D) exclusively

123. Coast College's library is open late for students looking for a ------- place to study than their dormitories.

(A) quiet
(B) quietly
(C) quieter
(D) quietest

124. Ms. Nissim, the founder of Hartwell Industries, will ------- a talk on effective sales strategies at the Global Commerce Convention.

(A) deliver
(B) register
(C) showcase
(D) imply

125. Items needing ------- discussion will be added to next Monday's meeting agenda.

(A) quite
(B) rather
(C) further
(D) throughout

126. When ------- with suppliers, Mr. Sinclair focuses primarily on payment terms and delivery times.

(A) adopting
(B) appearing
(C) negotiating
(D) finishing

127. Tenor Michael Amato gained widespread ------- for his superb performances at the Frankfurt Opera.

(A) criticism
(B) persuasion
(C) deliberation
(D) recognition

128. ------- having television stations across the state, Nicholson Media owns several magazines and newspapers.

(A) Besides
(B) Rather
(C) Among
(D) Along

129. Representatives from the most internationally ------- financial services firms will be speaking at next week's summit.

(A) respectfully
(B) respect
(C) respected
(D) respective

130. TNP Tech's software may be downloaded for free until May 1 but will cost $19.99 -------.

(A) since
(B) thereafter
(C) consequently
(D) now

PART 6

Directions: In this part, you will be asked to read four English texts. Each text is missing a word, phrase, or sentence. Select the answer choice that correctly completes the text and mark the corresponding letter (A), (B), (C), or (D) on the answer sheet.

Questions 131-134 refer to the following notice.

ATTENTION ALL TENANTS

Wimberley Group is ------- its billing system to an electronic one. Effective February 1, cash and
                         131.

personal checks will no longer be accepted. -------.
                                             132.

Every tenant needs to create a user profile at www.wimberleygroup.com. After logging in, you will

be able to ------- a payment. You can do this by selecting the unpaid bill and then clicking "Pay" at
           133.

the bottom of the screen. ------- you hit the button, the amount you designate will be deducted from
                          134.

your registered credit card or bank account. If you wish to arrange automatic payments, click the

button labeled "Pay Every Month."

If you have any questions, send an e-mail to help@wimberleygroup.com. Thank you for your

cooperation.

---

131. (A) inducing
(B) fluctuating
(C) converting
(D) recovering

132. (A) Tenants had found the system easy to use.
(B) This means that all tenants must pay their rent online.
(C) Use of the new system will be completely optional.
(D) Only certain Wimberley Group occupants will be affected.

133. (A) afford
(B) receive
(C) demand
(D) make

134. (A) Even if
(B) During
(C) Although
(D) As soon as

GO ON TO THE NEXT PAGE

Questions 135-138 refer to the following memo.

To: All Staff of Brentwood Corp.
From: Dale Rosen, Human Resources Chief
Date: February 26
Subject: Mobile phone usage

Over the past month, several department managers have expressed concerns about the use of mobile phones in the workplace. In particular, the ------- of training sessions has decreased significantly. Thus, Brentwood Corp. ------- to launch a new policy. From now on, employees' mobile phones must be turned off during a session. This is to prevent -------. It is our hope that staff will be able to better concentrate on the topics being discussed. -------. If an urgent call or message is expected, please notify your supervisor beforehand, and you may keep your phone on in silent mode.

135. (A) duration
 (B) attendance
 (C) productivity
 (D) number

136. (A) deciding
 (B) was deciding
 (C) decides
 (D) has decided

137. (A) errors
 (B) charges
 (C) regulations
 (D) interruptions

138. (A) Personal devices will be provided by the company.
 (B) You can access the Internet on your phone as needed.
 (C) The audiovisual system must be reserved in advance.
 (D) We will allow one exception to this office rule.

Questions 139-142 refer to the following announcement.

Notice for All Staff

The shopping mall where our store is located will be closed from December 24 to 26. -------, some of you will be coming in on December 24 to set up for our post-holiday sale. The guard who usually opens the mall doors in the morning will be off duty during this time. -------. Daniel Monahan is the most senior staff member, so I will give it to him, and he will let everyone inside.

It is vital that you ------- Daniel at the entrance at exactly 10 A.M. We don't want to waste time making him go back and forth to open the doors, so please be considerate and arrive -------.

Thank you for your understanding.

Alison Culpepper
Store manager

139. (A) Besides
(B) Otherwise
(C) Accordingly
(D) However

140. (A) Making sure we answer customer inquiries in a timely manner is our priority.
(B) You should be able to use your employee pass to access the mall.
(C) A security code will therefore be required to enter the building.
(D) You will need to handle unfinished work caused by his absence.

141. (A) are meeting
(B) meet
(C) had met
(D) met

142. (A) punctually
(B) regularly
(C) politely
(D) impressively

Questions 143-146 refer to the following letter.

Eric Frears
6633 7th Street
Sacramento, CA 95673

Dear Mr. Frears,

Thank you for considering The Aldrich at Shasta Lake. ------- providing a high quality of life has always been our priority, it is no surprise that we have hundreds of satisfied residents.

As a member of our community, you will have ------- to around-the-clock medical care and assistance with cooking and cleaning. There are also frequent get-togethers and volunteering opportunities at local events. We hope to make every day as ------- as it can be.

Come for a visit, take a look around, and experience retirement living in The Aldrich at Shasta Lake. -------. I look forward to welcoming you!

Mona Sorenstein
Executive Director
The Aldrich Retirement Community

143. (A) Whether
     (B) Especially
     (C) Although
     (D) Given that

144. (A) access
     (B) accessed
     (C) accessing
     (D) accessible

145. (A) obvious
     (B) fulfilling
     (C) influential
     (D) fortunate

146. (A) Call before our peak season begins.
     (B) We treat our employees here like they are family.
     (C) We are confident you will find it worthy of calling home.
     (D) Your room has been prepared as you requested.

PART 7

Directions: In this part, you will be asked to read several texts, such as advertisements, articles, instant messages, or examples of business correspondence. Each text is followed by several questions. Select the best answer and mark the corresponding letter (A), (B), (C), or (D) on your answer sheet.

Questions 147-148 refer to the following advertisement.

Job Vacancy

The Fentonville Board of Planning and Zoning is seeking an office clerk to take meeting notes and file records. The newly hired clerk will only have to perform their duties from 9:00 A.M. to 5:00 P.M. on Mondays and Wednesdays. The ideal candidate will have excellent typing skills, pay close attention to detail, and be comfortable working independently. Clerical experience is preferred but not necessary. The pay is $25 per hour. Résumés should be e-mailed to recruitment@fentonville.gov by March 4.

147. What information is included in the advertisement?

(A) Job duties
(B) Overtime rate
(C) Start date
(D) Insurance benefits

148. What can be inferred about the position?

(A) It involves intensive team work.
(B) It requires record keeping experience.
(C) It involves a lot of travel.
(D) It is on a part-time basis.

GO ON TO THE NEXT PAGE

Questions 149-150 refer to the following ticket.

WALLACE TRANSPORTATION: TICKET

PLEASE PRINT THIS OUT

PASSENGER: William Singer
PHONE NUMBER: 555-3201
HOME ADDRESS: 21 West 74th St., New York, NY 10023

TICKET NUMBER: 41249101ABKOA
CLASS: Regular
FARE: $52.00

DATE OF DEPARTURE: August 11

ITINERARY:

Depart: New York City	5:10 A.M.
Arrive: Pittsburgh	12:12 P.M.
Depart: Pittsburgh	1:20 P.M.
Arrive: Columbus	4:50 P.M.
Depart: Columbus	5:30 P.M.
Arrive: Chicago	10:05 P.M.

Your bus will leave the Park Avenue Coach Terminal in New York City at 5:10 A.M. Please have your ticket ready to present to the driver when you board. Passengers are permitted to bring two pieces of luggage on board. No refunds will be provided to passengers who miss their departure. To cancel your ticket, please call 555-8843.

---

149. What is indicated about Mr. Singer?

(A) He bought a return ticket.
(B) He was charged a reduced fare.
(C) He plans on staying the night in Columbus.
(D) He is a resident of New York.

150. What information is NOT included on the ticket?

(A) The company's refund policy
(B) The arrival time in Pittsburgh
(C) The baggage allowance
(D) The operating hours of a bus terminal

Questions 151-152 refer to the following letter.

August 12

Nisa Miskin
Inman Pharmaceuticals
92450 Interstate 164
Boise, ID 83714

Dear Ms. Miskin,

I am a representative of Well Time Insurance, and we would be very interested in meeting with you to discuss what we can offer your firm. Our employee insurance packages are popular among many businesses and organizations.

Well Time Insurance offers a variety of packages covering every type of insurance need, such as medical, mental health, dental, life, and more. Popular packages include Health Plus and the complete Choice Care. You can customize the Health Plus package to suit your organization's needs. Disability and parental leave are included with the Choice Care package.

I will contact your office within the next two weeks to find out if you'd like to set up an appointment. If you would like to speak with me sooner, please call 555-4433.

Sincerely,

Lucas Moreland
Well Time Insurance Client Services

---

151. What is the purpose of the letter?

(A) To introduce an employee training program
(B) To propose a business meeting
(C) To extend an invitation to a seminar
(D) To compare a variety of insurance packages

152. What is an advantage of the Health Plus package?

(A) It includes every type of insurance.
(B) It can be adjusted to meet requirements.
(C) It is the most affordable plan.
(D) It covers extended leave for new parents.

GO ON TO THE NEXT PAGE

Questions 153-154 refer to the following text-message chain.

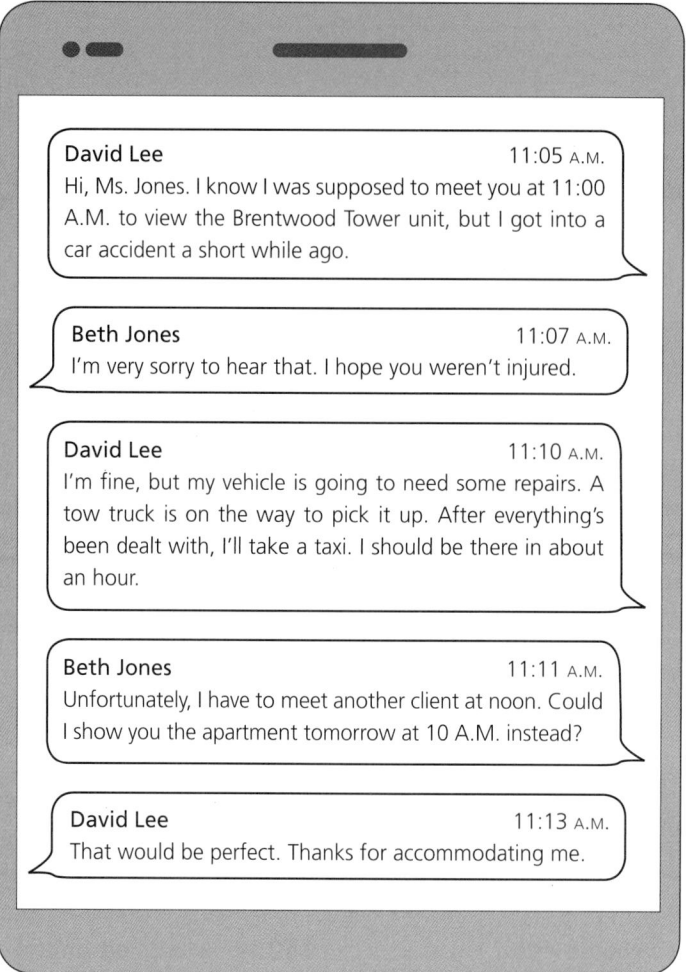

David Lee — 11:05 A.M.
Hi, Ms. Jones. I know I was supposed to meet you at 11:00 A.M. to view the Brentwood Tower unit, but I got into a car accident a short while ago.

Beth Jones — 11:07 A.M.
I'm very sorry to hear that. I hope you weren't injured.

David Lee — 11:10 A.M.
I'm fine, but my vehicle is going to need some repairs. A tow truck is on the way to pick it up. After everything's been dealt with, I'll take a taxi. I should be there in about an hour.

Beth Jones — 11:11 A.M.
Unfortunately, I have to meet another client at noon. Could I show you the apartment tomorrow at 10 A.M. instead?

David Lee — 11:13 A.M.
That would be perfect. Thanks for accommodating me.

153. Why did Mr. Lee miss his appointment?

(A) He selected a route that was congested.
(B) He was involved in a traffic accident.
(C) He went to the wrong apartment unit.
(D) He met with another realtor in the morning.

154. At 11:13 A.M., what does Mr. Lee mean when he writes, "That would be perfect"?

(A) He is familiar with a location.
(B) He is satisfied with an apartment.
(C) He is available the following day.
(D) He is prepared to meet at noon.

Questions 155-157 refer to the following e-mail.

To: Peter Leopold <peterleopold@netmail.com>
From: Susan Wright <susanw@greatwebwork.com>
Subject: Apology
Date: August 15

Dear Mr. Leopold,

I am sorry that you were not satisfied with our firm's services and regret any inconvenience you may have experienced. I appreciate that you took the time to communicate why you felt our design work on your Web site did not meet your expectations. Your feedback was constructive and fair. Your customers should not struggle to find the information they need, and the fact that incorrect images were used on some pages is completely unacceptable.

I believe that there must have been some miscommunication during our initial meeting, and I would like to discuss the problems and come up with some acceptable solutions for you.

You have expressed satisfaction with our work in the past, and I feel that we've generally maintained a certain level of quality in all the projects we have completed for you. You are a valued client, and I hope that your recent experience does not negatively affect our working relationship in the future.

I hope to hear from you soon.

Sincerely,

Susan Wright
Great Web Work

155. According to Ms. Wright, what did Mr. Leopold recently do?

(A) Designed a corporate Web site
(B) Recommended a designer
(C) Provided some feedback
(D) Filled out a form

156. According to Ms. Wright, what might have caused some problems?

(A) A presentation was inconveniently rescheduled.
(B) Important team members were absent from a meeting.
(C) Some requests were interpreted incorrectly.
(D) Mr. Leopold had insufficient time to explain his requirements.

157. What is suggested about Ms. Wright?

(A) She has worked with Mr. Leopold before.
(B) She has agreed to a partial refund.
(C) She disagrees with some comments.
(D) She canceled a service contract.

Questions 158-161 refer to the following announcement.

Eagle Canyon City Park

Over the past month, there has been a sharp increase in reported sightings of raccoons in the open spaces of the park. The park rangers suspect the creatures are attracted by food scraps that are left—whether on purpose or accidentally—by visitors to the park. — [1] —. The city's public health department does not want to encourage the raccoons to leave the wooded areas of the park as they can be carriers of disease and pose a risk to visitors and their pets. — [2] —. With that in mind:

- Please do not leave any garbage in the park—either take it with you when you leave, or place it in the closed garbage bins that are located throughout the park.
- If you see raccoons, do not approach them or give them food as they are wild animals with sharp claws and can be dangerous when they feel frightened.

— [3] —. To eliminate any refuse in the park that might attract these animals, we will be holding a volunteer park cleanup on Saturday, June 27. Anyone interested in taking part should report to the visitor center near the park's main entrance to register. — [4] —. All participants will be provided with protective gloves and vests, water, and a light lunch.

158. Why was the announcement written?

(A) To declare a public meeting
(B) To announce the opening of a wildlife park
(C) To provide directions to a visitor center
(D) To alert visitors of a problem

159. What is stated about Eagle Canyon City Park?

(A) It was inspected by the health department.
(B) It closes for maintenance on Saturdays.
(C) It has some trash receptacles set up.
(D) It will include more picnic areas soon.

160. What will volunteers be given?

(A) A map of the park
(B) Some food to distribute to animals
(C) A certificate of accomplishment
(D) Some protective gear

161. In which of the positions marked [1], [2], [3], and [4] does the following sentence best belong?

"We are hoping that at least 15 people will sign up for this event."

(A) [1]
(B) [2]
(C) [3]
(D) [4]

Questions 162-165 refer to the following online chat discussion.

Ana Muller	4:55 P.M.	My manager just told me that our company will be introducing a new bonus system. I'm really excited about it.
Dennis Judd	4:57 P.M.	I heard the same thing. Employees who receive a score of 4.5 or higher on their evaluations will qualify for a bonus. It will be the equivalent of 10 percent of their total annual salary.
Ana Muller	4:58 P.M.	That's right. The bonus will be awarded one month after the evaluation has been completed.
Carrie Novak	4:59 P.M.	When will this system take effect?
Dennis Judd	5:00 P.M.	In about a month, I believe. There will be an official announcement later this week.
Carrie Novak	5:02 P.M.	I had my annual evaluation three months ago, around the time I extended my contract. It doesn't seem fair that other employees will receive the bonus before I do.
Carrie Novak	5:03 P.M.	Maybe I should arrange a meeting about this matter.
Ana Muller	5:04 P.M.	I would wait until you have more information. I don't think the company will roll out the system in a way that puts some employees at a disadvantage.
Carrie Novak	5:06 P.M.	Maybe you're right. I hope that we get some more details soon, though.
Dennis Judd	5:08 P.M.	The human resources team will likely provide everyone with an updated employee manual when the announcement is made next week. Apparently, they are working on it now.

162. What is the company planning to do?

(A) Provide incentives to employees
(B) Increase the annual salaries of all workers
(C) Change some evaluation criteria
(D) Advertise a management position

163. What is Ms. Novak concerned about?

(A) A project schedule has not been updated.
(B) A supervisor expressed dissatisfaction with her work.
(C) An incentive was not distributed to some staff members.
(D) A performance review has already concluded.

164. At 5:06 P.M., what does Ms. Novak mean when she writes, "Maybe you're right"?

(A) A policy will likely be implemented fairly.
(B) A request will probably not be approved.
(C) An opportunity may not be available.
(D) A meeting might be organized shortly.

165. What is mentioned about the human resources team?

(A) It has decided to reassign several employees.
(B) It is in the process of revising some guidelines.
(C) It will hold an information session next week.
(D) It requested staff feedback on a benefit.

Questions 166-168 refer to the following information.

Hanlan's Coffee Company — Ethical Purchasing Policy

At Hanlan's, we know that our customers like to drink only the finest coffee from around the world. We also recognize that they want to be sure that the people who grow that coffee are treated fairly. Many coffee producers create poor working conditions and provide their workers with low pay, which are practices that Hanlan's does not support. — [1] —.

Coffee companies that buy their stock on the open market never know exactly where it comes from. But at Hanlan's, we take a different approach. We have exclusive contracts with farms in Guatemala, Ethiopia, and Vietnam. — [2] —. Because of this, we know exactly who is producing our coffee and the conditions under which it is being grown. We appreciate all the hard work of our farmers and ensure that they have acceptable working conditions. But our commitment doesn't end there. — [3] —. Hanlan's pays them an additional 10 percent above current market prices as our way of saying thanks.

Furthermore, to give even more back to these communities, we have started the Hanlan's Development Foundation. Each year through this organization, we put 5 percent of our total corporate profits into building and improving schools in the villages near where our coffee is grown. The main goal is to make certain that all our farmers' children have the opportunity to receive a full education and pursue their dreams. — [4] —.

Find out more about Hanlan's development projects, our coffee producers, and what you can do to support our cause at www.hanlancoffee.com/foundation.

166. What is indicated about Hanlan's Coffee Company's partner farms?

(A) They sell their products on the open market.
(B) They are subsidized by local governments.
(C) They grow a number of different crops.
(D) They are situated in several countries.

167. Who does the Hanlan's Development Foundation mostly benefit?

(A) International agriculture researchers
(B) Coffee farmers' children
(C) Employees working abroad
(D) Members of a coffee growers' association

168. In which of the positions marked [1], [2], [3], and [4] does the following sentence best belong?

"We also make certain that they receive adequate compensation for their efforts."

(A) [1]
(B) [2]
(C) [3]
(D) [4]

Questions 169-171 refer to the following article.

Ping's Head Honored as Tech Woman of the Year

By Carmen Morris

Rebecca Curtis, CEO of software company Ping, has been named the most successful woman in the tech world by *Gadget Lover* magazine. Ms. Curtis, who took over the company five years ago and transformed it into a thriving multi-platform enterprise, has accepted an invitation to deliver a speech at the *Gadget Lover* annual conference on December 2.

Ms. Curtis's achievements as CEO have been widely celebrated. When she replaced the previous CEO, Mark Spalding, Ping was mainly known for its word processing software. Due to the influx of new word processing products, Ping's software was not selling as well as it once had. Ms. Curtis quickly reversed that situation by developing a wide range of high-quality software including photo editing and spreadsheet programs. Now the name Ping is notable for its cutting-edge, dependable technology.

Over the next several years, Ms. Curtis says Ping will create a membership plan for its customers. Those who sign up will be able to download new Ping products at a reduced rate. Ms. Curtis says the company also plans to redevelop its Web site. With all these plans ahead, Ping is expected to grow even more. Most experts agree that Ms. Curtis has been the primary reason behind the company's success.

169. What is stated about Ping?

(A) It recently hired new programmers.
(B) It was founded five years ago.
(C) It regularly sponsors a technology event.
(D) It was associated with a particular software type.

170. What is NOT mentioned about Rebecca Curtis?

(A) She agreed to speak at a conference.
(B) She was Ping's first female CEO.
(C) She was recognized by a magazine.
(D) She helped Ping expand its product line.

171. According to the article, what is Ping expected to do?

(A) It will develop a new hardware product.
(B) It will close down its Web site permanently.
(C) It will offer programs at lower prices.
(D) It will merge with another company.

GO ON TO THE NEXT PAGE

Questions 172-175 refer to the following report.

City Trends Report—Valencia

Tourism numbers in Valencia have been increasing for three years running as people are beginning to discover this often-underrated city on the eastern coast of Spain. At the beginning of the survey period, the city received just under one million visitors a year, but the latest figure has jumped to over 1.4 million.

There are a number of factors that can account for this change. The new Sanchez Museum of Iberian Art and its nearby conference facilities have proven to be a big draw since opening last year. Also, upgrades to rail services from Valencia to Madrid and Barcelona have reduced travel time significantly. With a major airport expansion due to be completed before the end of the year, things are expected to get even better for Valencia.

In addition, the city government's launch of an international advertising campaign two years ago has also proved beneficial. The city was marketed in television, print, and social media advertisements as a tourism destination. Reactions to the campaign continue to be positive.

Finally, in addition to being praised as a destination for tourists and business travelers, Valencia is increasingly being recognized as an excellent place to live. The consultancy Apollo and Company recently put the city in third place in a report measuring the quality of life in small European cities. They cited its lovely waterfront location, low housing costs, and modern infrastructure as reasons for its high ranking.

172. What is the report mainly about?

(A) Campaigns to make a city more livable
(B) Upgrades to an international conference facility
(C) Changes to a government's building codes
(D) Improvements to a city's tourism industry

173. What is NOT mentioned as a reason for the figure increase?

(A) A new museum facility
(B) An updated tax policy
(C) A marketing campaign
(D) An improved transportation system

174. What is indicated about Madrid?

(A) It was selected by a consultancy as having a high quality of life.
(B) It was less popular with tourists than Barcelona for three years.
(C) Its rail connection to Valencia has been enhanced.
(D) Its city council hired a firm to develop a marketing strategy.

175. What is one reason Valencia was ranked third among small European cities?

(A) It is popular with business travelers.
(B) It recently updated its waterfront.
(C) It offers residents affordable homes.
(D) It hosts a lot of international events.

GO ON TO THE NEXT PAGE

Questions 176-180 refer to the following letter and e-mail.

Maxfield Financial Group

May 10

Bethany Aldridge
18 Juniper Road
Westport, CT 06880

Dear Ms. Aldridge,

This letter is in response to your request to sign up for paperless statements. Your statements will now be sent via e-mail on the 25th of each month. These statements will also be accessible from your online account, and you will be able to print them at your convenience. They will contain all of the same information that is included in your paper statements. In order to protect your account details, please ensure that the device you use to download and save your paperless statements is secure.

If you would like a paper statement mailed to your primary address in addition to the paperless one, log on to your account and check the "Mail My Statement" box under "Delivery Preferences." Keep in mind that Maxfield Financial Group does charge an annual fee of $24 to clients who choose to receive paper statements.

Best regards,

Customer Service
Maxfield Financial Group

To: Bethany Aldridge <bethanyal22@totalmail.net>
From: Customer Service <cs@maxfieldfin.com>
Date: May 25
Subject: Your May Statement
Attachment: May_Statement

Dear Ms. Aldridge,

Please find attached your Maxfield Financial Group electronic account statement for the month of May. As this is the first electronic statement that has been sent to you, please review it carefully and contact our service center if you have any questions or concerns. We have received your payment, and the hard copy of your statement will arrive via mail within the next five to seven days.

To ensure that you receive monthly statements, make sure to keep your current e-mail and postal address on file with us. If you are planning to change them, simply update them in the "Personal Information" section of our Web site.

Sincerely,
Customer Service
Maxfield Financial Group

176. What is the purpose of the letter?

(A) To explain how to change a password
(B) To inform a customer of a change
(C) To request payment of a charge
(D) To answer an inquiry about a policy

177. What is stated about paperless statements in the letter?

(A) They must be retained by recipients for tax purposes.
(B) They require an assigned password to open.
(C) They can be accessed from an online account.
(D) They contain more detail than the paper documents that are mailed.

178. According to the letter, how can printed copies of statements be requested?

(A) By e-mailing the service center
(B) By calling the accounts department
(C) By selecting an option online
(D) By sending a request form

179. Why has Ms. Aldridge been asked to review her digital statement?

(A) It includes an important notification.
(B) It has the incorrect contact information.
(C) It shows some additional charges for services.
(D) It is the first one she has received.

180. What can be inferred about Ms. Aldridge?

(A) She notified a financial provider of an address change.
(B) She must submit a complete payment within seven days.
(C) She reported an error found on a monthly statement.
(D) She paid a yearly charge to Maxfield Financial Group.

GO ON TO THE NEXT PAGE

Questions 181-185 refer to the following invitation and online post.

Invitation to Special Event

Pakori is opening its third store in Luton, and you are invited to learn about the goods and services we offer before it officially opens for business!

WHEN
Sunday, April 6, at 12:00 P.M.

WHERE
Shop A209, Ayleswood Mall
1452 Crestwood Road

WHAT
This is an exclusive event for select artists, bloggers, and media representatives. It will include a discussion of Pakori's business practices, services, and products. Refreshments and gifts will be provided.

Please confirm your attendance by calling us at 555-9922 before April 1. Otherwise, your name will be removed from our guest list.

Pakori is a luxury jewelry store selling one-of-a-kind, handmade items. For more information, visit www.pakori.com.

---

www.blogaboutit.com/juliescharms

Julie's Charms—A Fine Jewelry Blog

Pakori at Ayleswood Mall — Posted: April 9

The new Pakori store in Ayleswood Mall boasts a gorgeous collection of wedding rings. According to manager Arlene Pitts, these are this location's specialty. Having blogged about Pakori's flagship store in London six months ago, I was asked to attend a special viewing of the new store shortly before it officially opened. It is everything you'd expect it to be — luxurious, spacious, and well lit. The other guests and I admired the handcrafted charms in our gift bags as we listened to Ms. Pitts describe how Pakori operates. While I was already somewhat familiar with its eco-friendly practices and commitment to quality, I was really impressed to learn that Pakori has partnered with a mine in Madagascar. Unlike other jewelry makers who may not be aware of where their gems come from, Pakori is directly involved in the process.

Read More >

ABOUT ME
I'm Julie Mendel, the blogger behind Julie's Charms. I started this blog a decade ago to share my passion for jewelry. I am a certified gemologist with six years of experience at a Luton jewelry boutique and contribute regularly to other publications.

181. What is the invitation for?

(A) An art workshop
(B) A product launch party
(C) An information session
(D) An art exhibit

182. What is mentioned about Pakori?

(A) It has more than one location.
(B) It sells many popular brands.
(C) It is based in the city of Luton.
(D) It creates custom items for clients.

183. Why was Ms. Mendel invited to the event?

(A) She purchased a wedding ring.
(B) She wrote about a store online.
(C) She has expressed interest in buying a franchise.
(D) She works as a journalist in Luton.

184. What is indicated about Ms. Mendel?

(A) She contacted Pakori before April 1.
(B) She owns her own jewelry store.
(C) She brought a guest with her to an event.
(D) She only writes about eco-friendly businesses.

185. According to the online post, why does Pakori stand out from other jewelry stores?

(A) It has opened stores in Madagascar.
(B) It is affiliated with a supplier of raw materials.
(C) It creates jewelry using only rare gems.
(D) It focuses primarily on wedding rings.

GO ON TO THE NEXT PAGE

Questions 186-190 refer to the following article, Web page, and e-mail.

Gunton City Council to Consider Blandfolk Superstore Proposal

At a Gunton City Council meeting on May 2, members listened to a presentation by representatives of Blandfolk Superstore about building a branch locally. The retail giant proposed erecting an outlet just within city limits on Medford Avenue. However, the chosen land has not yet been authorized for commercial establishments, so Blandfolk has requested that the property be rezoned. Gunton mayor Claire O'Rourke told representatives that the council would discuss the proposition this month. A spokesperson for Blandfolk said the corporation hopes the proposal will pass, emphasizing that the development would provide employment for up to 190 local residents.

Gunton Herald
www.guntonherald.com

Home | News | Sports | Business | Entertainment | Lifestyle | **Opinion** | Contact Us

Readers' Comments

Ronald Pinero posted on May 7:

I am writing in regard to an article printed in your newspaper's May 3 edition about the construction proposal from Blandfolk Superstore. As a long-time business owner in Gunton, I am concerned. I manage Ballas Closet, a clothing store in the downtown area. Large corporate retailers have forced many smaller stores out of business where they have opened. I'm not sure most businesses like mine will be able to compete without significantly dropping prices and, by extension, the quality of our goods. For now, Gunton is a very vibrant and diverse city, and I hope the mayor and council members will reject the proposal in order to keep it that way.

TO	Ronald Pinero <rpinero@dailymaily.com>
FROM	Adeline Morris <amorris@guntoncoc.org>
DATE	May 8
SUBJECT	Request from Gunton COC

Dear Mr. Pinero,

I came across your comment on the *Gunton Herald* Web site. Your concern is something that the board of the Gunton Chamber of Commerce has been discussing, and we agree that something must be done to protect stores in the downtown area, like yours. On June 3, the city council will be holding a public meeting that some of us will be attending. It would be helpful if you joined us at the event. You could give a short talk describing the concerns you mentioned in your comment. Please let me know if you would like to participate.

Sincerely yours,

Adeline Morris
Secretary, Gunton Chamber of Commerce

186. What is the article mainly about?

(A) A mayor's recent proposal
(B) A corporation's request for rezoning
(C) A city's thriving downtown scene
(D) A council's efforts to reduce unemployment

187. What does Mr. Pinero want Ms. O'Rourke to do?

(A) Turn down a proposition from Blandfolk Superstore
(B) Meet with executives from Ballas Closet
(C) Rezone some property to allow for construction
(D) Defer funding for private business owners

188. In the article, the word "limits" in paragraph 1, line 4, is closest in meaning to

(A) regulations
(B) borders
(C) levels
(D) obstacles

189. What will take place on June 3?

(A) Those on the Gunton City Council will vote on a plan.
(B) Some Chamber of Commerce members will attend a public hearing.
(C) Construction of a large retail outlet will get underway.
(D) Ms. Morris will voice some concerns at a press conference.

190. What is indicated about Ms. Morris?

(A) She is in charge of relocation for the city council.
(B) She runs a store that sells items at bargain prices.
(C) She thinks that Ballas Closet should be supported.
(D) She signed a petition sponsored by Gunton City Council.

GO ON TO THE NEXT PAGE

Questions 191-195 refer to the following invoice, e-mail, and newsletter.

Invoice Date: October 4

From: Oresund Graphics and Design
   49 Rozenstraat, Arnhem, Netherlands
To: Kaiser Investment Services
   1 Kornmarkt, Floor 4, Frankfurt, Germany

Services	Charges
Design, Layout, and Photography of Annual Shareholders Report	€745
Design and Layout of *Investing with Kaiser* Brochure	€545
Design and Layout of Terms and Conditions Booklet	€300
Total Due	€1,590

Payment is due in 15 days. Requests for additional changes will incur a €100 surcharge per document. For rush printing, add €250. Please note that we no longer accept checks.

To	Alexander Svensson <alex.svensson@oresund.nl>
From	Christine Kaufmann <ckaufmann@kaiserinvestment.de>
Date	October 7
Subject	Changes to publications

Dear Mr. Svensson,

We received your invoice yesterday along with the proofs. Thank you for your excellent work. I showed the final drafts to our managing director and, overall, he was pleased. However, he has requested that we change the photograph used on the front cover. He thinks it failed to convey the mood we were going for. We have commissioned a photographer to take a new picture, and I will send it to you by Friday. Unfortunately, we cannot move our original due date as the brochures have to be shipped in time for a campaign launch event we have planned for November.

If our request presents a problem, please let me know right away. You can reach me by phone at 555-2309, extension #42. Thank you!

Christine Kaufmann
Publications Manager
Kaiser Investment Services

Kaiser Investment Services Company Newsletter

Year-End Message from Our CEO

As we come to the end of another year, I want to take this opportunity to thank everyone for their commitment and hard work. Once again, Kaiser Investment Services has outperformed analysts' expectations and generated substantial profits for its clients and shareholders. Not only that, but we also continue to top customer satisfaction surveys on financial services companies in Germany. As we reflect on these successes, let us continue to look forward with optimism. In this December issue of the newsletter, learn more about our ongoing expansion into North America and see photos from last month's launch of our marketing campaign in the United States, which was well attended by several potential clients. I will see you all at our annual holiday party!

Sincerely,
Matthias Furst

---

191. What is true about Oresund Graphics and Design?

(A) It accepts checks in the mail as payment.
(B) It did not take pictures for a booklet.
(C) It has its own finance department.
(D) It is located on the fourth floor of a building.

192. What is suggested about Kaiser Investment Services?

(A) It is planning to hire a full-time photographer.
(B) It did not receive all of the promised documents.
(C) It may be charged for paying an invoice late.
(D) It will have to pay a fee of €100 for a revision.

193. Why would Ms. Kaufmann be contacted?

(A) To confirm an appointment
(B) To request a deadline extension
(C) To verify payment details
(D) To address a concern

194. What is one purpose of the newsletter?

(A) To recognize a firm's top employees
(B) To present a company's achievements
(C) To announce the results of a sale
(D) To report a recent company merger

195. What most likely did Kaiser Investment Services do recently?

(A) It held a retirement party for staff members.
(B) It conducted a survey among employees.
(C) It launched a series of new products in Germany.
(D) It distributed brochures to potential US clients.

GO ON TO THE NEXT PAGE

Questions 196-200 refer to the following e-mail, schedule, and form.

TO: El Paso Center for the Digital Arts <questions@elpasodigital.com>
FROM: Raymond Hardy <rayhardy@goodmail.com>
DATE: April 30
SUBJECT: Classes

To Whom It May Concern:

As the head of an amateur photography club here in El Paso, I was very excited to hear that your organization will be offering a group discount on photography classes this summer. Four of us are interested in taking the landscape photography class. Three other members plan to register for the one on wedding photography. Could you send me some more information?

Please include details about where these classes are going to take place and how much they'll cost, and I will pass the information on.

Best regards,

Raymond Hardy
President
Homestead Photo Club

El Paso Center for the Digital Arts - *Upcoming One-Day Classes, May 8-12*

Date	May 8 (Mon)	May 9 (Tues)	May 10 (Wed)	May 11 (Thurs)	May 12 (Fri)
Time	7:30 P.M.	8:00 P.M.	8:00 P.M.	8:30 P.M.	7:00 P.M.
Class	Professional Photography Software	Marketing Your Photos	Fashion Photography	Landscape Photography	Wedding Photography
Instructor	Lindsay Arias	Carrie Felix	Ben Greenwood	Sue Adler	Finley Kolwalski
Cost	$50	$48	$52	$54	$47

El Paso Center for the Digital Arts - *Class Registration Form*

Please fill in the following details:

Name	Raymond Hardy	Address	2094 Firebird Drive, El Paso, TX 79901
Phone	555-3004	E-mail	rayhardy@goodmail.com

Do you have any professional photography experience?   Yes ☐   No ■

Course	Landscape Photography
Payment method	Cash

The El Paso Center for the Digital Arts is a nonprofit organization established to advance people's knowledge of film, photography, and graphic design. Please note that the center does not provide any cameras or accessories, so participants must supply their own. Those who sign up as a group of three or more will receive a special group rate of $30 each. We will confirm your registration within 24 hours of receiving payment. Tuition fees are nonrefundable and must be paid one week prior to the start of a course.

196. What is the purpose of the e-mail?

(A) To recruit people to a photography club
(B) To request information on some courses
(C) To register for an upcoming contest
(D) To give feedback on a recent lecture

197. What is true about the Homestead Photo Club?

(A) All of its members work as professional photographers.
(B) Most of its members have taken classes before.
(C) Some of its members want to take a class that is held on a Friday.
(D) A few of its members want to sign up for three or more classes.

198. In the form, the phrase "established" in paragraph 1, line 1, is closest in meaning to

(A) supported
(B) founded
(C) verified
(D) determined

199. How much will Mr. Hardy probably have to pay for his class?

(A) $30
(B) $47
(C) $52
(D) $54

200. What will Mr. Hardy be required to do?

(A) Speak with an instructor prior to the start of a course
(B) Bring his own photography equipment
(C) Provide a piece of identification
(D) Submit proof of previous experience

This is the end of the test. You may review Parts 5, 6, and 7 if you finish the test early.

점수 환산표

아래는 실전모의고사를 위한 점수 환산표입니다. 문제 풀이 후, 정답 개수를 세어 자신의 토익 리스닝/리딩 점수를 예상해봅니다.

정답 수	리스닝 점수	리딩 점수	정답 수	리스닝 점수	리딩 점수	정답 수	리스닝 점수	리딩 점수
100	495	495	66	305	305	32	135	125
99	495	495	65	300	300	31	130	120
98	495	495	64	295	295	30	125	115
97	495	485	63	290	290	29	120	110
96	490	480	62	285	280	28	115	105
95	485	475	61	280	275	27	110	100
94	480	470	60	275	270	26	105	95
93	475	465	59	270	265	25	100	90
92	470	460	58	265	260	24	95	85
91	465	450	57	260	255	23	90	80
90	460	445	56	255	250	22	85	75
89	455	440	55	250	245	21	80	70
88	450	435	54	245	240	20	75	70
87	445	430	53	240	235	19	70	65
86	435	420	52	235	230	18	65	60
85	430	415	51	230	220	17	60	60
84	425	410	50	225	215	16	55	55
83	415	405	49	220	210	15	50	50
82	410	400	48	215	205	14	45	45
81	400	390	47	210	200	13	40	40
80	395	385	46	205	195	12	35	35
79	390	380	45	200	190	11	30	30
78	385	375	44	195	185	10	25	30
77	375	370	43	190	180	9	20	25
76	370	360	42	185	175	8	15	20
75	365	355	41	180	170	7	10	20
74	355	350	40	175	165	6	5	15
73	350	345	39	170	160	5	5	15
72	340	340	38	165	155	4	5	10
71	335	335	37	160	150	3	5	5
70	330	330	36	155	145	2	5	5
69	325	320	35	150	140	1	5	5
68	315	315	34	145	135	0	5	5
67	310	310	33	140	130			

※ 점수 환산표는 해커스토익 사이트 유저 데이터를 근거로 제작되었으며, 주기적으로 업데이트되고 있습니다. 해커스토익 사이트(Hackers.co.kr)에서 최신 경향을 반영하여 업데이트된 점수환산기를 이용하실 수 있습니다. (토익 > 토익게시판 > 토익점수환산기)

Answer Sheet

LISTENING (PART I~IV)

#	A	B	C	D
1	Ⓐ	Ⓑ	Ⓒ	Ⓓ
2	Ⓐ	Ⓑ	Ⓒ	Ⓓ
3	Ⓐ	Ⓑ	Ⓒ	Ⓓ
4	Ⓐ	Ⓑ	Ⓒ	Ⓓ
5	Ⓐ	Ⓑ	Ⓒ	Ⓓ
6	Ⓐ	Ⓑ	Ⓒ	Ⓓ
7	Ⓐ	Ⓑ	Ⓒ	
8	Ⓐ	Ⓑ	Ⓒ	
9	Ⓐ	Ⓑ	Ⓒ	
10	Ⓐ	Ⓑ	Ⓒ	
11	Ⓐ	Ⓑ	Ⓒ	
12	Ⓐ	Ⓑ	Ⓒ	
13	Ⓐ	Ⓑ	Ⓒ	
14	Ⓐ	Ⓑ	Ⓒ	
15	Ⓐ	Ⓑ	Ⓒ	
16	Ⓐ	Ⓑ	Ⓒ	
17	Ⓐ	Ⓑ	Ⓒ	
18	Ⓐ	Ⓑ	Ⓒ	
19	Ⓐ	Ⓑ	Ⓒ	
20	Ⓐ	Ⓑ	Ⓒ	

Items 21–40, 41–60, 61–80, 81–100 each have options Ⓐ Ⓑ Ⓒ Ⓓ.

READING (PART V~VII)

Items 101–120, 121–140, 141–160, 161–180, 181–200 each have options Ⓐ Ⓑ Ⓒ Ⓓ.

맞은 문제 개수: _____ / 200

* 시험시간: **120분** (LC 45분, RC 75분)
* 단안지 마킹은 **연필**을 사용하시기 바랍니다.
* 문제 풀이 후 p.226에 있는 점수 **환산표**를 확인해보세요.

한 권으로 끝내는 해커스 토익 900+

LC + RC + VOCA

초판 2쇄 발행 2025년 8월 11일
초판 1쇄 발행 2025년 6월 13일

지은이	해커스 어학연구소
펴낸곳	㈜해커스 어학연구소
펴낸이	해커스 어학연구소 출판팀
주소	서울특별시 서초구 강남대로61길 23 ㈜해커스 어학연구소
고객센터	02-537-5000
교재 관련 문의	publishing@hackers.com
동영상강의	HackersIngang.com
ISBN	978-89-6542-776-6 (13740)
Serial Number	01-02-01

저작권자 ⓒ 2025, 해커스 어학연구소
이 책 및 음성파일의 모든 내용, 이미지, 디자인, 편집 형태에 대한 저작권은 저자에게 있습니다.
서면에 의한 저자와 출판사의 허락 없이 내용의 일부 혹은 전부를 인용, 발췌하거나 복제, 배포할 수 없습니다.

외국어인강 1위, 해커스인강
HackersIngang.com
해커스인강

- 해커스 토익 스타강사의 **본 교재 인강**
- 효과적인 LC 학습을 돕는 **무료 교재 MP3**
- 전략적인 단어 암기를 돕는 **단어암기장**

영어 전문 포털, 해커스토익
Hackers.co.kr
해커스토익

- 최신 출제경향이 반영된 **온라인 실전모의고사**
- 매월 적중예상특강 및 실시간 토익시험 정답확인/해설강의
- 매일 실전 LC/RC 문제, 정기토익 기출단어, 토익 단어시험지 자동생성기 등 다양한 무료 학습 콘텐츠

헤럴드 선정 2018 대학생 선호브랜드 대상 '대학생이 선정한 외국어인강' 부문 1위

5천 개가 넘는
해커스토익 무료 자료!

대한민국에서 공짜로 토익 공부하고 싶으면 　해커스토익 Hackers.co.kr 　검색

토익 강의 　무료

베스트셀러 1위 토익 강의 150강 무료 서비스,
누적 시청 1,900만 돌파!

토익 실전 문제 　무료
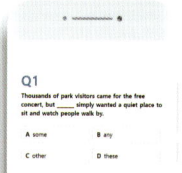

토익 RC/LC 풀기, 모의토익 등
실전토익 대비 문제 제공!

최신 특강 　무료

2,400만뷰 스타강사의
압도적 적중예상특강 매달 업데이트!

고득점 달성 비법 　무료

토익 고득점 달성팁, 파트별 비법,
점수대별 공부법 무료 확인

가장 빠른 정답까지!

615만이 선택한 해커스 토익 정답!
시험 직후 가장 빠른 정답 확인

[5천여 개] 해커스토익(Hackers.co.kr) 제공 총 무료 콘텐츠 수 (~2017.08.30)
[베스트셀러 1위] 교보문고 종합 베스트셀러 토익/토플 분야 토익 RC 기준 1위(2005~2023년 연간 베스트셀러)
[1,900만] 해커스토익 리딩 무료강의 및 해커스토익 스타트 리딩 무료강의 누적 조회수(중복 포함, 2008.01.01~2018.03.09 기준)
[2,400만] 해커스토익 최신경향 토익적중예상특강 누적 조회수(2013~2021, 중복 포함)
[615만] 해커스영어 해커스토익 정답 실시간 확인서비스 PC/MO 방문자 수 총합/누적, 중복 포함(2016.05.01~2023.02.22)

더 많은
토익무료자료 보기 ▶

한 권으로 끝내는
해커스 토익 900+
LC + RC + VOCA

정답·해석·해설
해설집

해커스 어학연구소

저작권자 ⓒ 2025, 해커스 어학연구소 이 책 및 음성파일의 모든 내용, 이미지, 디자인, 편집 형태에 대한 저작권은 저자에게 있습니다.
서면에 의한 저자와 출판사의 허락 없이 내용의 일부 혹은 전부를 인용, 발췌하거나 복제, 배포할 수 없습니다.

LC

PART 1

DAY 01 사람 중심 사진

빈출 문제 집중 훈련   p.14

| 01 (D) | 02 (A) | 03 (D) | 04 (C) | 05 (B) |
| 06 (D) | 07 (B) | 08 (A) | 09 (C) | 10 (A) |

01 | 1인 사진 🎧 미국

(A) She's installing a shelf in a store.
(B) She's taking out a book.
(C) She's watering a potted plant.
(D) She's grasping an item with both hands.

install v. 설치하다 take out 꺼내다 water v. (식물에) 물을 주다
potted adj. 화분에 심은 grasp v. (움켜)잡다, 꽉 쥐다

해석 (A) 그녀는 상점에서 선반을 설치하고 있다.
(B) 그녀는 책을 꺼내고 있다.
(C) 그녀는 화분에 심은 식물에 물을 주고 있다.
(D) 그녀는 두 손으로 물건을 잡고 있다.

해설 (A) [x] installing a shelf(선반을 설치하고 있다)는 여자의 동작과 무관하므로 오답이다. 사진에 있는 선반(shelf)을 사용하여 혼동을 주었다.
(B) [x] 사진에 책(book)이 없으므로 오답이다. She's taking out (그녀는 꺼내고 있다)까지만 듣고 정답으로 선택하지 않도록 주의한다.
(C) [x] watering a potted plant(화분에 심은 식물에 물을 주고 있다)는 여자의 동작과 무관하므로 오답이다. 사진에 있는 화분에 심은 식물(potted plant)을 사용하여 혼동을 주었다.
(D) [o] 여자가 두 손으로 물건을 잡고 있는 모습을 가장 잘 묘사한 정답이다.

02 | 2인 이상 사진 🎧 캐나다

(A) Some people are examining a map in the tall grass.
(B) One of the people is taking off a backpack.
(C) Some people are standing in a shaded area.
(D) One of the people is pointing in one direction.

examine v. 살펴보다 take off ~을 벗다 backpack n. 배낭
shaded adj. 그늘진 point v. 가리키다 direction n. 방향

해석 (A) 몇몇 사람들이 높은 풀밭에서 지도를 살펴보고 있다.
(B) 사람들 중 한 명이 배낭을 벗고 있다.
(C) 몇몇 사람들이 그늘진 곳에 서 있다.
(D) 사람들 중 한 명이 한 방향을 가리키고 있다.

해설 (A) [o] 사람들이 높은 풀밭에서 지도를 살펴보고 있는 모습을 가장 잘 묘사한 정답이다.

(B) [x] 사진에서 배낭(backpack)은 보이지만, 배낭을 벗고 있는(taking off a backpack) 사람은 없으므로 오답이다.
(C) [x] 사진에 그늘진 곳(shaded area)이 없으므로 오답이다.
(D) [x] 사진에 한 방향을 가리키고 있는(pointing in one direction) 사람이 없으므로 오답이다.

03 | 1인 사진 🎧 영국

(A) He's emptying out a garbage can.
(B) He's repairing cracks in the pavement.
(C) He's cutting the grass along a sidewalk.
(D) He's using a broom to sweep up leaves.

empty v. 비우다 crack n. 균열, 틈 pavement n. 보도, 인도
sidewalk n. 인도 broom n. 빗자루 sweep up ~을 쓸다

해석 (A) 그는 쓰레기통을 비우고 있다.
(B) 그는 보도의 균열을 수리하고 있다.
(C) 그는 인도를 따라 잔디를 깎고 있다.
(D) 그는 나뭇잎을 쓸기 위해 빗자루를 사용하고 있다.

해설 (A) [x] 사진에 쓰레기통(garbage can)이 없으므로 오답이다.
(B) [x] repairing cracks(균열을 수리하고 있다)는 남자의 동작과 무관하므로 오답이다.
(C) [x] cutting the grass along a sidewalk(인도를 따라 잔디를 깎고 있다)는 남자의 동작과 무관하므로 오답이다. 사진에 있는 인도(sidewalk)를 사용하여 혼동을 주었다.
(D) [o] 남자가 나뭇잎을 쓸기 위해 빗자루를 사용하고 있는 모습을 가장 잘 묘사한 정답이다.

04 | 1인 사진 🎧 영국

(A) She's taking a sip from a mug.
(B) A table is being cleared off.
(C) A lamp has been switched on.
(D) She's adjusting some curtains.

sip n. 한 모금 clear off ~을 치우다 switch on ~을 켜다 adjust v. 조절하다

해석 (A) 그녀는 머그잔에서 한 모금을 마시고 있다.
(B) 테이블이 치워지고 있다.
(C) 램프가 켜져 있다.
(D) 그녀는 커튼을 조절하고 있다.

해설 (A) [x] taking a sip from a mug(머그잔에서 한 모금을 마시고 있다)는 여자의 동작과 무관하므로 오답이다. 사진에 있는 머그잔(mug)을 사용하여 혼동을 주었다.
(B) [x] 사진에서 테이블(table)은 보이지만, 치워지고 있는(being cleared off) 모습은 아니므로 오답이다.
(C) [o] 램프가 켜져 있는 모습을 가장 잘 묘사한 정답이다.
(D) [x] adjusting some curtains(커튼을 조절하고 있다)는 여자의 동작과 무관하므로 오답이다. 사진에 있는 커튼(curtains)을 사용하여 혼동을 주었다.

05 | 2인 이상 사진　🎧 캐나다

(A) Some cups have been set on a table.
(B) **Some of the chairs are unoccupied.**
(C) A pattern has been painted on a wall.
(D) One of the people is leaning over a couch.

set v. 놓다, 설치하다　unoccupied adj. 비어 있는　pattern n. 무늬
lean over ~ 너머로 몸을 구부리다

해석　(A) 몇몇 컵들이 테이블 위에 놓여 있다.
　　(B) 몇몇 의자들이 비어 있다.
　　(C) 벽에 무늬가 그려져 있다.
　　(D) 사람들 중 한 명이 소파 너머로 몸을 구부리고 있다.

해설　(A) [x] 사진에 컵들이(cups)이 없으므로 오답이다.
　　(B) [o] 몇몇 의자들이 비어 있는 모습을 가장 잘 묘사한 정답이다.
　　(C) [x] 사진에 무늬(pattern)가 없으므로 오답이다.
　　(D) [x] 사진에 소파 너머로 몸을 구부리고 있는(leaning over a couch) 사람이 없으므로 오답이다.

06 | 1인 사진　🎧 미국

(A) He's doing up the buttons on his coat.
(B) He's removing ice from a vehicle.
(C) He's parking his car near a building.
(D) **He's shoveling snow on the ground.**

do up ~의 단추를 채우다, 잠그다　remove v. 치우다　vehicle n. 차량
shovel v. 삽으로 퍼내다, 삽질하다; n. 삽

해석　(A) 그는 그의 코트의 단추를 채우고 있다.
　　(B) 그는 차량에서 얼음을 치우고 있다.
　　(C) 그는 건물 근처에 그의 차를 주차하고 있다.
　　(D) 그는 바닥의 눈을 삽으로 퍼내고 있다.

해설　(A) [x] doing up the buttons on his coat(그의 코트의 단추를 채우고 있다)는 남자의 동작과 무관하므로 오답이다.
　　(B) [x] removing ice from a vehicle(차량에서 얼음을 치우고 있다)는 남자의 동작과 무관하므로 오답이다. He's removing ice (그는 얼음을 치우고 있다)까지만 듣고 정답으로 선택하지 않도록 주의한다.
　　(C) [x] parking his car(그의 차를 주차하고 있다)는 남자의 동작과 무관하므로 오답이다.
　　(D) [o] 남자가 바닥의 눈을 삽으로 퍼내고 있는 모습을 가장 잘 묘사한 정답이다.

07 | 2인 이상 사진　🎧 캐나다

(A) Dishes have been piled in a sink.
(B) **A basket has been filled with fruits.**
(C) A woman is putting food in a container.
(D) They're pulling bread out of an oven.

pile v. 쌓다　fill with ~으로 채우다　container n. 그릇, 용기　pull out 꺼내다

해석　(A) 접시들이 싱크대 안에 쌓여 있다.
　　(B) 바구니가 과일들로 채워져 있다.
　　(C) 여자가 음식을 그릇에 놓고 있다.
　　(D) 그들이 오븐에서 빵을 꺼내고 있다.

해설　(A) [x] 접시들이(Dishes)이 싱크대 안에 쌓여 있는(piled in a sink) 모습이 아니므로 오답이다.
　　(B) [o] 바구니가 과일들로 채워져 있는 모습을 가장 잘 묘사한 정답이다.
　　(C) [x] 사진에 음식을 그릇에 놓고 있는(putting food in a container) 여자가 없으므로 오답이다.
　　(D) [x] 사진에 빵을 꺼내고 있는(pulling bread out) 사람들이 없으므로 오답이다.

08 | 2인 이상 사진　🎧 호주

(A) **The man is reaching for his luggage.**
(B) The woman is opening a suitcase.
(C) The man is putting on his jacket.
(D) The woman is typing at a computer.

reach for ~을 향해 손을 뻗다　luggage n. 수하물, 짐　type v. 타자 치다

해석　(A) 남자가 자신의 수하물을 향해 손을 뻗고 있다.
　　(B) 여자가 여행 가방을 열고 있다.
　　(C) 남자가 자신의 재킷을 입고 있다.
　　(D) 여자가 컴퓨터에 타자를 치고 있다.

해설　(A) [o] 남자가 자신의 수하물을 향해 손을 뻗고 있는 모습을 가장 잘 묘사한 정답이다.
　　(B) [x] opening a suitcase(여행 가방을 열고 있다)는 여자의 동작과 무관하므로 오답이다. 사진에 있는 여행 가방(suitcase)을 사용하여 혼동을 주었다.
　　(C) [x] putting on(입고 있다)은 남자의 동작과 무관하므로 오답이다. 옷·모자·구두 등을 이미 착용한 상태를 나타내는 wearing과 입고 있는 중인 동작을 나타내는 putting on을 혼동하지 않도록 주의한다.
　　(D) [x] 사진에 컴퓨터(computer)가 없으므로 오답이다.

09 | 1인 사진　🎧 미국

(A) Bottles are arranged on a tray in a café.
(B) The man is preparing a beverage.
(C) **Machines are lined up on a counter.**
(D) The man is folding up some napkins.

arrange v. 정리하다, 배열하다　beverage n. 음료　line up 정렬하다
counter n. 조리대, 카운터　fold up ~을 접다

해석　(A) 병들이 카페의 쟁반 위에 정리되어 있다.
　　(B) 남자가 음료를 준비하고 있다.
　　(C) 기계들이 조리대 위에 정렬되어 있다.
　　(D) 남자가 냅킨을 접고 있다.

해설　(A) [x] 사진에서 병들(Bottles)은 보이지만, 쟁반 위에 정리되어 있는(arranged on a tray) 모습은 아니므로 오답이다.
　　(B) [x] preparing a beverage(음료를 준비하고 있다)는 남자의 동작과 무관하므로 오답이다.
　　(C) [o] 기계들이 조리대 위에 정렬되어 있는 모습을 가장 잘 묘사한 정답이다.
　　(D) [x] folding up some napkins(냅킨을 접고 있다)는 남자의 동작과 무관하므로 오답이다.

10 | 2인 이상 사진 🔊 캐나다

(A) **One of the women is handing over an item.**
(B) Some products are being weighed on a scale.
(C) Some goods are being wrapped in paper.
(D) One of the women is looking through her purse.

hand over 건네주다   weigh v. 무게를 재다   scale n. 저울   wrap v. 포장하다
look through 살펴보다   purse n. 지갑

해석 (A) 여자들 중 한 명이 물건을 건네주고 있다.
(B) 몇몇 제품들이 저울에서 무게가 재어지고 있다.
(C) 몇몇 물건들이 종이에 포장되고 있다.
(D) 여자들 중 한 명이 지갑을 살펴보고 있다.

해설 (A) [o] 여자들 중 한 명이 물건을 건네주고 있는 모습을 가장 잘 묘사한 정답이다.
(B) [x] 사진에 제품들(products)이 보이지만 무게가 재어지고 있는(being weighed) 모습은 아니므로 오답이다.
(C) [x] 사진에 물건들(goods)이 보이지만 포장되고 있는(being wrapped) 모습은 아니므로 오답이다.
(D) [x] 사진에 지갑을 살펴보고 있는(looking through her purse) 여자가 없으므로 오답이다. 사진에 있는 지갑(purse)을 사용하여 혼동을 주었다.

고난도 문제 완전 정복
p.17

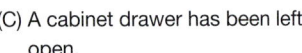

01 (B)   02 (C)   03 (A)   04 (C)

01 | 1인 사진 🔊 호주

(A) The man is tightening the straps on a bag.
(B) **A lamp has been set up against a wall.**
(C) A cabinet drawer has been left open.
(D) The man is drinking from a water bottle.

tighten v. 조이다, 단단히 하다   strap n. 끈, 띠   lamp n. 램프, 등
set up ~을 놓다, 세우다   against prep. ~ 가까이, ~에 기대어
cabinet n. 수납장   drawer n. 서랍

해석 (A) 남자가 가방의 끈을 조이고 있다.
(B) 램프가 벽 가까이 놓여 있다.
(C) 수납장 서랍이 열려 있다.
(D) 남자가 물병으로 물을 마시고 있다.

해설 (A) [x] tightening the straps(끈을 조이고 있다)는 남자의 동작과 무관하므로 오답이다. 사진에 있는 가방(bag)을 사용하여 혼동을 주었다.
(B) [o] 램프가 벽 가까이 놓여 있는 모습을 가장 잘 묘사한 정답이다.
(C) [x] 사진에서 수납장 서랍(cabinet drawer)은 보이지만, 열려 있는(has been left open) 모습은 아니므로 오답이다.
(D) [x] drinking from a water bottle(물병으로 물을 마시고 있다)은 남자의 동작과 무관하므로 오답이다. 사진에 있는 물병(water bottle)을 사용하여 혼동을 주었다.

02 | 2인 이상 사진 🔊 영국

(A) One of the men is carrying some tiles.
(B) One of the men is climbing down a ladder.
(C) **Some workers are attaching panels to a roof.**
(D) Some lights are being installed on a building.

carry v. 나르다   climb down 내려가다   ladder n. 사다리
attach v. 부착하다   install v. 설치하다

해석 (A) 남자들 중 한 명이 타일들을 나르고 있다.
(B) 남자들 중 한 명이 사다리를 내려가고 있다.
(C) 몇몇 작업자들이 지붕에 판들을 부착하고 있다.
(D) 몇몇 조명들이 건물에 설치되고 있다.

해설 (A) [x] 사진에 타일들을 나르고 있는(carrying some tiles) 남자가 없으므로 오답이다.
(B) [x] 사진에 사다리를 내려가고 있는(climbing down a ladder) 남자가 없으므로 오답이다.
(C) [o] 작업자들이 지붕에 판들을 부착하고 있는 모습을 가장 잘 묘사한 정답이다.
(D) [x] 사진에 조명들(lights)이 없으므로 오답이다.

03 | 1인 사진 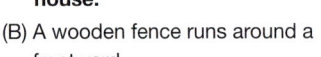  🔊 호주

(A) **A path leads to the entrance of a house.**
(B) A wooden fence runs around a front yard.
(C) The man is trimming some bushes with a saw.
(D) The man is plugging equipment into an outlet.

path n. 길   lead to ~으로 이어지다   entrance n. 출입구, 문
wooden adj. 나무로 된   fence n. 울타리   trim v. 다듬다   bush n. 덤불
saw n. 톱   plug v. 플러그를 꽂다   equipment n. 장비   outlet n. 콘센트

해석 (A) 길이 집의 출입구로 이어진다.
(B) 나무로 된 울타리가 앞마당을 둘러싸고 있다.
(C) 남자가 톱으로 덤불을 다듬고 있다.
(D) 남자가 장비의 플러그를 콘센트에 꽂고 있다.

해설 (A) [o] 길이 집의 출입구로 이어지는 모습을 가장 잘 묘사한 정답이다.
(B) [x] 사진에 나무로 된 울타리(wooden fence)가 없으므로 오답이다.
(C) [x] trimming some bushes(덤불을 다듬고 있다)는 남자의 동작과 무관하므로 오답이다.
(D) [x] plugging equipment into an outlet(장비의 플러그를 콘센트에 꽂고 있다)은 남자의 동작과 무관하므로 오답이다.

04 | 2인 이상 사진 🔊 영국

(A) Some cars are exiting a parking garage.
(B) Some people are fixing a traffic light.
(C) **A pedestrian is crossing at an intersection.**
(D) A cyclist is removing a bicycle from a rack.

exit v. 나가다　parking garage 주차장 빌딩　fix v. 수리하다
traffic light 신호등　pedestrian n. 보행자　intersection n. 교차로
cyclist n. 자전거 타는 사람　remove v. 치우다, 제거하다　rack n. 거치대

해석　(A) 몇몇 차들이 주차장 빌딩에서 나가고 있다.
　　　(B) 몇몇 사람들이 신호등을 수리하고 있다.
　　　(C) 보행자가 교차로를 건너고 있다.
　　　(D) 자전거 타는 사람이 거치대에서 자전거를 치우고 있다.

해설　(A) [×] 사진에서 차들(cars)은 보이지만, 주차장 빌딩에서 나가고 있는 (exiting a parking garage) 모습은 아니므로 오답이다.
　　　(B) [×] 사진에 신호등을 수리하고 있는(fixing a traffic light) 사람들이 없으므로 오답이다.
　　　(C) [○] 보행자가 교차로를 건너고 있는 모습을 가장 잘 묘사한 정답이다.
　　　(D) [×] 사진에 거치대에서 자전거를 치우고 있는(removing a bicycle from a rack) 사람이 없으므로 오답이다. 사진에 있는 cyclist (자전거 타는 사람)를 사용하여 혼동을 주었다.

DAY 02　사물/풍경 중심 사진

빈출 문제 집중 훈련　　　　　　　　　　　　p.18

01 (D)　02 (B)　03 (B)　04 (B)　05 (C)
06 (C)　07 (R)　08 (B)　09 (R)　10 (D)

01 | 야외 사진　　　　　　　　　　　🎧 미국

(A) Some merchandise has been left in a basket.
(B) Some shop windows are being cleaned.
(C) A bicycle is on display inside a store.
(D) A bicycle is propped against a wall.

merchandise n. 물품, 상품　display n. 진열, 전시
prop against ~에 기대어 놓다, 받쳐 놓다

해석　(A) 몇몇 물품들이 바구니에 남겨져 있다.
　　　(B) 몇몇 상점 창문들이 청소되고 있다.
　　　(C) 자전거 한 대가 상점 내부에 진열되어 있다.
　　　(D) 자전거 한 대가 벽에 기대어 놓여 있다.

해설　(A) [×] 사진에 바구니에 남겨진(left in a basket) 물품들이 없으므로 오답이다. 사진에 있는 바구니(basket)를 사용하여 혼동을 주었다.
　　　(B) [×] 사진에서 창문들(windows)은 보이지만, 청소되고 있는(being cleaned) 모습은 아니므로 오답이다.
　　　(C) [×] 사진이 상점 내부(inside a store)가 아니므로 오답이다. A bicycle is on display(자전거 한 대가 진열되어 있다)까지만 듣고 정답으로 선택하지 않도록 주의한다.
　　　(D) [○] 자전거 한 대가 벽에 기대어 놓여 있는 모습을 가장 잘 묘사한 정답이다.

02 | 실내 사진　　　　　　　　　　　🎧 호주

(A) A rug is spread out under a kitchen table.
(B) There are some flowers arranged in a vase.
(C) A lamp is positioned between two paintings.

(D) Some books are scattered on the floor.

rug n. 깔개　spread out 펼치다　arrange v. 정리하다, 정렬하다
vase n. 꽃병　position v. 배치하다, 두다　scatter v. 흩어지게 하다

해석　(A) 깔개가 주방 테이블 아래에 펼쳐져 있다.
　　　(B) 꽃병에 정리되어 있는 몇몇 꽃들이 있다.
　　　(C) 램프가 두 그림 사이에 배치되어 있다.
　　　(D) 몇몇 책들이 바닥에 흩어져 있다.

해설　(A) [×] 사진에 깔개(rug)는 보이지만, 주방 테이블 아래에 펼쳐져 있는 (spread out under a kitchen table) 모습은 아니므로 오답이다.
　　　(B) [○] 꽃병에 정리되어 있는 몇몇 꽃들이 있는 모습을 가장 잘 묘사한 정답이다.
　　　(C) [×] 사진에 램프(lamp)는 보이지만, 두 그림 사이에 배치되어 있는 (positioned between two paintings) 모습은 아니므로 오답이다.
　　　(D) [×] 사진에 책들(books)은 보이지만, 바닥에 흩어져 있는(scattered on the floor) 모습은 아니므로 오답이다.

03 | 야외 사진　　　　　　　　　　　🎧 호주

(A) Signs are posted on the side of an empty street.
(B) Lane markings have been painted on a road.
(C) Some buildings are visible in the distance.
(D) A tent has been set up next to a roadway.

sign n. 표지판　post v. 게시하다　side n. 측면　lane marking 차선 표시
visible adj. 보이는, 눈에 띄는　in the distance 먼 곳에　set up 설치하다
roadway n. 도로

해석　(A) 표지판들이 비어있는 거리의 측면에 게시되어 있다.
　　　(B) 차선 표시들이 도로에 그려져 있다.
　　　(C) 몇몇 건물들이 먼 곳에 보인다.
　　　(D) 텐트가 도로 옆에 설치되어 있다.

해설　(A) [×] 사진에 표지판들(Signs)이 없으므로 오답이다.
　　　(B) [○] 차선 표시들이 도로에 그려져 있는 모습을 가장 잘 묘사한 정답이다.
　　　(C) [×] 사진에 건물들(buildings)이 없으므로 오답이다.
　　　(D) [×] 사진에 텐트(tent)가 없으므로 오답이다.

04 | 실내 사진　　　　　　　　　　　🎧 미국

(A) Some floor tiles are being replaced by workers.
(B) Some light fixtures are suspended from the ceiling.
(C) A doorway opens out onto a balcony.
(D) There are some screens hanging from the wall.

replace v. 교체하다　light fixture 조명 기구　suspend v. 매달다
ceiling n. 천장　doorway n. 출입구　hang v. 걸다

해석　(A) 몇몇 바닥 타일이 작업자들에 의해 교체되고 있다.
　　　(B) 몇몇 조명 기구들이 천장에 매달려 있다.
　　　(C) 출입구가 발코니로 열려 있다.
　　　(D) 벽에 걸려 있는 몇몇 스크린들이 있다.

해설　(A) [×] 사진에 작업자들(workers)이 없으므로 오답이다.

(B) [○] 몇몇 조명 기구들이 천장에 매달려 있는 모습을 가장 잘 묘사한 정답이다.
(C) [×] 사진에 출입구(doorway)가 없으므로 오답이다.
(D) [×] 사진에 스크린들(screens)이 없으므로 오답이다.

05 | 실내 사진 캐나다

(A) There are some posters on a wall beside a shelf.
(B) Some drawers are filled up with office supplies.
(C) **There are some photos pinned to a bulletin board.**
(D) Some plants are being placed into empty pots.

drawer n. 서랍 fill up 채우다 office supply 사무용품
pin v. (핀 등으로) 고정시키다 bulletin board 게시판 pot n. 화분

해석 (A) 선반 옆의 벽에 몇몇 포스터들이 있다.
(B) 몇몇 서랍들이 사무용품으로 채워져 있다.
(C) 몇몇 사진들이 게시판에 고정되어 있다.
(D) 몇몇 식물들이 빈 화분들 속에 놓여지고 있다.

해설 (A) [×] 사진에 포스터들(posters)이 없으므로 오답이다.
(B) [×] 사진에 서랍들(drawers)이 없으므로 오답이다.
(C) [○] 몇몇 사진들이 게시판에 고정되어 있는 모습을 가장 잘 묘사한 정답이다.
(D) [×] 사진에 식물들(plants)은 보이지만, 빈 화분들 속에 놓여지고 있는(being placed into empty pots) 모습은 아니므로 오답이다.

06 | 야외 사진 영국

(A) There's some water pooled on a path.
(B) Some lampposts are lighting up a path.
(C) **Some poles have fallen over onto the road.**
(D) Some cones have been stacked in a corner.

pool v. 고이다 path n. 길, 통로 lamppost n. 가로등 light up 밝히다
pole n. 기둥 fall over 넘어지다 cone n. 원뿔형 교통 표지 stack v. 쌓다

해석 (A) 길에 물이 고여 있다.
(B) 몇몇 가로등들이 길을 밝히고 있다.
(C) 몇몇 기둥들이 도로 위로 넘어져 있다.
(D) 몇몇 원뿔형 교통 표지들이 구석에 쌓여 있다.

해설 (A) [×] 사진에 물(water)이 없으므로 오답이다.
(B) [×] 사진에 가로등들(lampposts)이 없으므로 오답이다.
(C) [○] 몇몇 기둥들이 도로 위로 넘어져 있는 모습을 가장 잘 묘사한 정답이다.
(D) [×] 사진에서 원뿔형 교통 표지들(cones)은 보이지만, 구석에 쌓여 있는(stacked in a corner) 모습은 아니므로 오답이다.

07 | 야외 사진 미국

(A) Some food has been laid out in a campground.
(B) Some baskets are arranged on a park bench.
(C) **Picnic tables are set up in a grassy area.**
(D) Canopies cover an outdoor dining area.

lay out 펼치다 campground n. 캠핑장 arrange v. 정렬하다
grassy adj. 풀로 덮인 canopy n. 차양, 덮개

해석 (A) 몇몇 음식이 캠핑장에 펼쳐져 있다.
(B) 몇몇 바구니들이 공원 벤치 위에 정렬되어 있다.
(C) 피크닉 테이블들이 풀로 덮인 구역에 설치되어 있다.
(D) 차양이 야외 식사 공간을 덮고 있다.

해설 (A) [×] 사진에 음식(food)이 없으므로 오답이다.
(B) [×] 사진에 바구니들(baskets)이 없으므로 오답이다.
(C) [○] 피크닉 테이블들이 풀로 덮인 구역에 설치되어 있는 모습을 가장 잘 묘사한 정답이다.
(D) [×] 사진에 차양(Canopies)이 없으므로 오답이다.

08 | 실내 사진 캐나다

(A) A screen has been switched on.
(B) **Some chairs are facing each other across a table.**
(C) An outdoor table is being wiped down.
(D) Some windows are being opened in a meeting room.

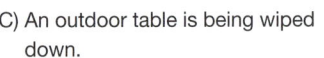

face v. 마주보다 outdoor adj. 야외의 wipe down 닦다

해석 (A) 스크린이 켜져 있다.
(B) 몇몇 의자들이 테이블을 가로질러 서로 마주보고 있다.
(C) 야외 테이블이 닦이고 있다.
(D) 몇몇 창문들이 회의실에서 열리고 있다.

해설 (A) [×] 사진에서 스크린(screen)은 보이지만, 켜져 있는(has been switched on) 모습은 아니므로 오답이다.
(B) [○] 몇몇 의자들이 테이블을 가로질러 서로 마주보고 있는 모습을 가장 잘 묘사한 정답이다.
(C) [×] 사진에 야외 테이블(outdoor table)이 없으므로 오답이다.
(D) [×] 사진에서 창문들(windows)은 보이지만, 열리고 있는(being opened) 모습은 아니므로 오답이다.

09 | 실내 사진 영국

(A) A rug has been rolled up in front of a sofa.
(B) A plant has been hung from the ceiling.
(C) **A blanket has been left on a couch.**
(D) A chair has been positioned under a window.

rug n. 깔개 hang v. 매달다, 걸다 blanket n. 담요 couch n. 소파
position v. 배치하다, 두다

해석 (A) 깔개가 소파 앞에 말려져 있다.
(B) 식물이 천장에 매달려 있다.
(C) 담요가 소파에 놓여 있다.
(D) 의자가 창문 아래에 배치되어 있다.

해설 (A) [×] 사진에 깔개(rug)는 보이지만, 말려 있는(rolled up) 모습은 아니므로 오답이다.
(B) [×] 사진에 식물(plant)은 보이지만, 천장에 매달려 있는(has been hung from the ceiling) 모습은 아니므로 오답이다.
(C) [○] 담요가 소파에 놓여 있는 모습을 가장 잘 묘사한 정답이다.
(D) [×] 사진에서 의자(chair)는 보이지만, 창문 아래에 배치되어 있는

(has been positioned under a window) 모습은 아니므로 오답이다.

10 | 실내 사진 호주

(A) Some carts are being pushed down an aisle.
(B) Several ladders have been leaned against a shelf.
(C) Some objects have been stored under some desks.
(D) There are some tables arranged in a row.

aisle n. 통로 ladder n. 사다리 lean against ~에 기대다 object n. 물건
store v. 보관하다 arrange v. 배치하다, 배열하다 in a row 일렬로

해석 (A) 몇몇 카트들이 통로를 따라 밀려가고 있다.
(B) 몇몇 사다리들이 선반에 기대어져 있다.
(C) 몇몇 물건들이 책상 아래에 보관되어 있다.
(D) 일렬로 배치된 몇몇 테이블들이 있다.

해설 (A) [×] 사진에 카트들(carts)이 없으므로 오답이다.
(B) [×] 사진에 사다리들(ladders)이 없으므로 오답이다.
(C) [×] 사진에 책상 아래에 보관된(have been stored under some desks) 물건들이 없으므로 오답이다.
(D) [○] 몇몇 테이블들이 일렬로 배치되어 있는 모습을 가장 잘 묘사한 정답이다.

고난도 문제 완전 정복   p.21

| 01 (C) | 02 (D) | 03 (B) | 04 (A) |

01 | 실내 사진 호주

(A) Some coats are folded up on a bed.
(B) A pillow is being placed on a bed.
(C) A clock has been mounted on a wall.
(D) A step stool is being assembled.

pillow n. 베개 mount v. 고정하다, 설치하다 step stool 계단식 의자
assemble v. 조립하다

해석 (A) 몇몇 코트들이 침대 위에 접혀 있다.
(B) 베개가 침대에 놓이고 있다.
(C) 시계가 벽에 고정되어 있다.
(D) 계단식 의자가 조립되고 있다.

해설 (A) [×] 사진에 코트들(coats)이 없으므로 오답이다.
(B) [×] 사진에서 베개(pillow)는 보이지만, 놓이고 있는(being placed) 모습은 아니므로 오답이다.
(C) [○] 시계가 벽에 고정되어 있는 모습을 가장 잘 묘사한 정답이다.
(D) [×] 사진에서 계단식 의자(step stool)는 보이지만, 조립되고 있는 (being assembled) 모습은 아니므로 오답이다.

02 | 야외 사진 영국

(A) A structure is being constructed in a park.
(B) Some leaves have been raked into a pile.

(C) Some lumber has been gathered on the grass.
(D) A sculpture is being displayed in a landscaped area.

structure n. 구조물 construct v. 세우다, 건설하다 rake v. 갈퀴로 모으다
pile n. 더미 lumber n. 목재 gather v. 모으다 sculpture n. 조각상
landscape v. 조경을 하다; n. 조경

해석 (A) 공원에서 구조물이 세워지고 있다.
(B) 몇몇 나뭇잎이 갈퀴로 모아져 더미를 이루고 있다.
(C) 몇몇 목재가 잔디 위에 모아져 있다.
(D) 조각상이 조경된 구역에 전시되어 있다.

해설 (A) [×] 사진에 세워지고 있는(being constructed) 구조물이 없으므로 오답이다.
(B) [×] 사진에서 나뭇잎(leaves)은 보이지만, 갈퀴로 모아져 있는(have been raked) 모습은 아니므로 오답이다.
(C) [×] 사진에 목재(lumber)가 없으므로 오답이다.
(D) [○] 조각상이 조경된 구역에 전시되어 있는 모습을 가장 잘 묘사한 정답이다.

03 | 야외 사진 미국

(A) Some tablecloths are being removed.
(B) There are some tables under an awning.
(C) A railing has been erected around a patio.
(D) Chairs have been placed in a circle inside a restaurant.

tablecloth n. 식탁보 remove v. 치우다, 제거하다 awning n. 차양
railing n. 난간, 철책 erect v. 세우다, 건립하다 patio n. 테라스, 베란다
in a circle 원을 이루어

해석 (A) 몇몇 식탁보가 치워지고 있다.
(B) 차양 아래에 몇몇 테이블이 있다.
(C) 난간이 테라스 주위에 세워져 있다.
(D) 의자들이 식당 내부에 원을 이루어 배치되어 있다.

해설 (A) [×] 사진에서 식탁보(tablecloths)는 보이지만, 치워지고 있는(being removed) 모습은 아니므로 오답이다.
(B) [○] 차양 아래에 몇몇 테이블이 있는 모습을 가장 잘 묘사한 정답이다.
(C) [×] 사진에 난간(railing)이 없으므로 오답이다.
(D) [×] 사진에서 의자들(Chairs)은 보이지만, 식당 내부에 원을 이루어 배치되어 있는(have been placed in a circle inside a restaurant) 모습은 아니므로 오답이다.

04 | 야외 사진 캐나다

(A) A balcony extends above a building's entryway.
(B) Some windows are covered with sale signs.
(C) Some tourists are waiting in line to enter a building.
(D) A banner has been hung on the wall of a structure.

extend v. 뻗다 entryway n. 입구

해석 (A) 발코니가 건물 입구 위로 뻗어 있다.
(B) 몇몇 창문들이 판매 표지판으로 덮여 있다.
(C) 몇몇 관광객들이 건물에 들어가기 위해 줄을 서 있다.

(D) 현수막이 건물의 벽에 걸려 있다.

해설 (A) [o] 발코니가 건물 입구 위로 뻗어 있는 모습을 가장 잘 묘사한 정답이다.
(B) [x] 사진에서 창문들(windows)은 보이지만, 판매 표지판으로 덮여 있는(covered with sale signs) 모습은 아니므로 오답이다.
(C) [x] 사진에 관광객들(tourists)이 없으므로 오답이다.
(D) [x] 사진에 현수막(banner)이 없으므로 오답이다.

PART 2

DAY 03 의문사 의문문

빈출 문제 집중 훈련 p.24

01 (C)	02 (C)	03 (B)	04 (C)	05 (A)
06 (C)	07 (B)	08 (C)	09 (A)	10 (C)
11 (B)	12 (B)	13 (C)	14 (A)	15 (B)
16 (A)	17 (C)	18 (B)	19 (B)	20 (A)

01 | How 의문문   미국 → 영국

How long is the conference going to last?
(A) The firm is growing very quickly.
(B) It's mandatory for staff.
(C) Two days in total.

conference n. 회의   last v. 지속되다   firm n. 회사   mandatory adj. 의무의

해석 회의가 얼마나 오래 지속될 예정인가요?
(A) 회사가 매우 빠르게 성장하고 있어요.
(B) 그것은 직원들에게 의무예요.
(C) 총 이틀이요.

해설 (A) [x] going - growing의 유사 발음 어휘를 사용하여 혼동을 준 오답이다.
(B) [x] 회의가 얼마나 오래 지속될 예정인지를 물었는데, 이와 관련이 없는 그것은 직원들에게 의무라는 말로 응답했으므로 오답이다. 질문의 conference(회의)를 나타낼 수 있는 It을 사용하여 혼동을 주었다.
(C) [o] 총 이틀이라는 말로, 회의가 지속될 기간을 언급했으므로 정답이다.

02 | When 의문문   영국 → 캐나다

When will the assistant director return?
(A) Let me know if you need assistance.
(B) She supervises our team.
(C) Either this week or next week.

assistant director 조감독   assistance n. 도움, 지원   supervise v. 감독하다

해석 조감독이 언제 돌아오나요?
(A) 도움이 필요하시면 저에게 알려주세요.
(B) 그녀는 우리 팀을 감독해요.
(C) 이번 주나 다음 주요.

해설 (A) [x] assistant - assistance의 유사 발음 어휘를 사용하여 혼동을 준 오답이다.
(B) [x] 질문의 assistant director(조감독)에서 연상할 수 있는 supervise(감독하다)를 사용하여 혼동을 준 오답이다.
(C) [o] 이번 주나 다음 주라는 말로, 조감독이 돌아올 시기를 언급했으므로 정답이다.

03 | Where 의문문   캐나다 → 미국

Where is the new shopping complex being built?
(A) We completed it quickly.
(B) Probably near the financial district.
(C) To buy some new shoes.

shopping complex 쇼핑 단지   complete v. 완성하다   district n. 지구, 지역

해석 새로운 쇼핑 단지가 어디에 건설되고 있나요?
(A) 우리는 그것을 빠르게 완성했어요.
(B) 아마도 금융 지구 근처요.
(C) 새로운 신발을 사기 위해서요.

해설 (A) [x] 새로운 쇼핑 단지가 어디에 건설되고 있는지를 물었는데, 이와 관련이 없는 그것을 빠르게 완성했다는 말로 응답했으므로 오답이다. 질문의 new shopping complex(새로운 쇼핑 단지)를 나타낼 수 있는 it을 사용하여 혼동을 주었다.
(B) [o] 아마도 금융 지구 근처라는 말로, 새로운 쇼핑 단지가 건설되고 있는 장소를 언급했으므로 정답이다.
(C) [x] 질문의 shopping complex(쇼핑 단지)와 관련 있는 buy(사다)를 사용하여 혼동을 준 오답이다.

04 | When 의문문   호주 → 미국

When was the board meeting?
(A) I thought it was really boring.
(B) OK, we can go then.
(C) Didn't Mr. Walker tell you?

board n. 이사회, 위원회   boring adj. 지루한

해석 이사회 회의는 언제였나요?
(A) 저는 그것이 정말 지루했다고 생각했어요.
(B) 좋아요, 우리는 그때 갈 수 있어요.
(C) Mr. Walker가 당신에게 말하지 않았나요?

해설 (A) [x] board - boring의 유사 발음 어휘를 사용하여 혼동을 준 오답이다.
(B) [x] 이사회 회의가 언제였는지를 물었는데, 이와 관련이 없는 그때 갈 수 있다는 말로 응답했으므로 오답이다.
(C) [o] Mr. Walker가 당신에게 말하지 않았냐고 되물어, Mr. Walker가 이사회 회의가 언제였는지 알 것이라는 답변을 간접적으로 전달했으므로 정답이다.

05 | How 의문문   호주 → 영국

How far away is the cinema from here?
(A) About four blocks.
(B) Tickets are sold out.
(C) What movies are showing?

cinema n. 영화관   sold out 매진된

해석 영화관이 여기서 얼마나 떨어져 있나요?
(A) 약 네 블록이요.
(B) 티켓이 매진됐어요.
(C) 어떤 영화가 상영 중인가요?

해설 (A) [o] 약 네 블록이라는 말로, 영화관이 떨어져 있는 거리를 언급했으므로 정답이다.

(B) [×] 질문의 cinema(영화관)와 관련 있는 tickets(티켓)를 사용하여 혼동을 준 오답이다.
(C) [×] 질문의 cinema(영화관)와 관련 있는 movies(영화)를 사용하여 혼동을 준 오답이다.

06 | Which 의문문
영국 → 호주

Which supermarket did you visit yesterday?
(A) We ran out of groceries.
(B) Because they offer a wide selection.
(C) The one on Belmont Street.

groceries n. 식료품

해석 어제 어느 슈퍼마켓을 방문했나요?
(A) 우리는 식료품이 다 떨어졌어요.
(B) 그들이 다양한 상품을 제공하기 때문이에요.
(C) Belmont가에 있는 거요.

해설 (A) [×] 질문의 supermarket(슈퍼마켓)과 관련 있는 groceries(식료품)를 사용하여 혼동을 준 오답이다.
(B) [×] 어제 어느 슈퍼마켓을 방문했는지를 물었는데, 이와 관련이 없는 그들이 다양한 상품을 제공하기 때문이라는 말로 응답했으므로 오답이다.
(C) [○] Belmont가에 있는 것에 갔다는 말로, 방문한 슈퍼마켓을 언급했으므로 정답이다.

07 | Who 의문문
미국 → 캐나다

Who contacted Dr. Nelson's patient?
(A) It has been rescheduled.
(B) The head receptionist.
(C) We appreciate your patience.

contact v. 연락하다 patient n. 환자 reschedule v. 일정을 변경하다
head n. 장, 우두머리, 수석 receptionist n. 접수원 appreciate v. 감사하다
patience n. 인내

해석 누가 Dr. Nelson의 환자에게 연락했나요?
(A) 그것은 일정이 변경되었어요.
(B) 접수팀장이요.
(C) 당신의 인내에 감사드립니다.

해설 (A) [×] 누가 Dr. Nelson의 환자에게 연락했는지를 물었는데, 이와 관련이 없는 그것은 일정이 변경되었다는 말로 응답했으므로 오답이다.
(B) [○] 접수팀장이라는 말로, Dr. Nelson의 환자에게 연락한 사람을 언급했으므로 정답이다.
(C) [×] patient - patience의 유사 발음 어휘를 사용하여 혼동을 준 오답이다.

08 | How 의문문
호주 → 미국

How do I switch off the conveyor belt?
(A) Productivity has increased at the plant.
(B) Once we pitch the idea to our team.
(C) Press the red button on that panel.

switch off 끄다 conveyor belt 컨베이어 벨트 productivity n. 생산성
plant n. 공장 pitch v. 제안하다

해석 컨베이어 벨트를 어떻게 끄나요?
(A) 공장의 생산성이 증가했어요.
(B) 일단 우리가 우리 팀에 아이디어를 제안하면요.
(C) 저 패널에 있는 빨간색 버튼을 누르세요.

해설 (A) [×] 질문의 conveyor belt(컨베이어 벨트)에서 연상할 수 있는 장소와 관련된 plant(공장)를 사용하여 혼동을 준 오답이다.
(B) [×] 컨베이어 벨트를 어떻게 끄는지를 물었는데, 이와 관련이 없는 우리 팀에 아이디어를 제안하면이라는 말로 응답했으므로 오답이다.
(C) [○] 저 패널에 있는 빨간색 버튼을 누르라는 말로, 컨베이어 벨트를 끄는 방법을 언급했으므로 정답이다.

09 | Why 의문문
호주 → 영국

Why didn't Susan attend the fundraiser?
(A) There was a scheduling conflict.
(B) Only for an hour.
(C) At the Westmont Hotel.

attend v. 참석하다 fundraiser n. 기금 모금 행사
scheduling conflict 겹치는 일정

해석 Susan은 왜 기금 모금 행사에 참석하지 않았나요?
(A) 겹치는 일정이 있었어요.
(B) 단지 1시간 동안이요.
(C) Westmont 호텔에서요.

해설 (A) [○] 겹치는 일정이 있었다는 말로, Susan이 기금 모금 행사에 참석하지 않은 이유를 언급했으므로 정답이다.
(B) [×] Susan이 기금 모금 행사에 참석하지 않은 이유를 물었는데, 이와 관련이 없는 단지 1시간 동안이라는 말로 응답했으므로 오답이다.
(C) [×] 질문의 fundraiser(기금 모금 행사)에서 연상할 수 있는 장소와 관련된 Hotel(호텔)을 사용하여 혼동을 준 오답이다.

10 | When 의문문
영국 → 호주

When did we receive the bill from the Internet provider?
(A) Yes, it's been slow lately.
(B) You can make an online payment.
(C) Let me review our financial records.

receive v. 받다 bill n. 청구서 provider n. 제공업체
financial record 재무 기록

해석 우리는 언제 인터넷 제공업체로부터 청구서를 받았나요?
(A) 네, 최근에 느려졌어요.
(B) 온라인으로 결제하실 수 있어요.
(C) 우리 재무 기록을 확인해 볼게요.

해설 (A) [×] 의문사 의문문에 Yes로 응답했으므로 오답이다. 질문의 Internet(인터넷)에서 연상할 수 있는 속도와 관련된 slow(느린)를 사용하여 혼동을 주었다.
(B) [×] 언제 인터넷 제공업체로부터 청구서를 받았는지를 물었는데, 이와 관련이 없는 온라인으로 결제하실 수 있다는 말로 응답했으므로 오답이다. 질문의 bill(청구서)과 관련된 payment(결제)를 사용하여 혼동을 주었다.
(C) [○] 재무 기록을 확인해 보겠다는 말로, 청구서를 언제 받았는지를 모른다는 것을 간접적으로 전달했으므로 정답이다.

11 | Where 의문문
호주 → 영국

Where did Janet get these quarterly sales figures?
(A) The figures look promising.
(B) Our boss passed out a report.
(C) After the promotion ends.

quarterly adj. 분기별의   sales figure 매출 수치
promising adj. 전망이 좋은, 유망한   pass out 나눠 주다
promotion n. 판촉 행사

해석 Janet은 이 분기별 매출 수치를 어디에서 구했나요?
(A) 그 수치들은 전망이 좋아요.
(B) 우리 상사가 보고서를 나눠 주었어요.
(C) 판촉 행사가 끝나고요.

해설 (A) [x] 질문의 figures를 반복 사용하여 혼동을 준 오답이다.
(B) [o] 우리 상사가 보고서를 나눠 주었다는 말로, Janet이 분기별 매출 수치를 얻은 출처를 언급했으므로 정답이다.
(C) [x] Janet이 분기별 매출 수치를 얻은 장소를 물었는데, 시점으로 응답했으므로 오답이다. 질문의 Where를 When으로 혼동하여 이를 정답으로 선택하지 않도록 주의한다.

12 | Who 의문문
영국 → 캐나다

Who plans to contact a carpenter for a price quote?
(A) They paid a fair price.
(B) It might be best if I handle that myself.
(C) No, not since Monday.

contact v. 연락하다   carpenter n. 목수   quote n. 견적   fair adj. 타당한
handle v. 처리하다

해석 누가 가격 견적을 위해 목수에게 연락할 계획인가요?
(A) 그들은 타당한 가격을 지불했어요.
(B) 제가 직접 처리하는 게 최선일 것 같아요.
(C) 아니요, 월요일 이후로는 안 했어요.

해설 (A) [x] 질문의 price를 반복 사용하여 혼동을 준 오답이다.
(B) [o] 자신이 직접 처리하는 게 최선일 것 같다는 말로, 자신이 목수에게 연락할 계획임을 언급했으므로 정답이다.
(C) [x] 의문사 의문문에 No로 응답했으므로 오답이다.

13 | When 의문문
캐나다 → 호주

When should we leave for the airport?
(A) This airplane is very fuel-efficient.
(B) During a flight to Beijing.
(C) Noon at the very latest.

fuel-efficient adj. 연료 효율적인   at the very latest 늦어도

해석 우리는 언제 공항으로 출발해야 하나요?
(A) 이 비행기는 매우 연료 효율적이에요.
(B) 베이징으로 가는 비행 중에요.
(C) 늦어도 정오예요.

해설 (A) [x] 질문의 airport(공항)과 관련 있는 airplane(비행기)을 사용하여 혼동을 준 오답이다.
(B) [x] 질문의 airport(공항)과 관련 있는 flight(비행)를 사용하여 혼동을 준 오답이다.
(C) [o] 늦어도 정오라는 말로, 공항으로 출발해야 하는 시간을 언급했으므로 정답이다.

14 | How 의문문
미국 → 캐나다

How did you like traveling in Southeast Asia?
(A) I really want to visit again.
(B) On a seven-day tour.
(C) Sure, for your next reservation.

Southeast Asia 동남아시아   tour n. 여행, 관광

해석 동남아시아 여행이 어땠나요?
(A) 정말 다시 방문하고 싶어요.
(B) 7일 여행으로요.
(C) 물론이죠, 당신의 다음 예약을 위해서요.

해설 (A) [o] 정말 다시 방문하고 싶다는 말로, 동남아시아 여행이 좋았음을 간접적으로 전달했으므로 정답이다.
(B) [x] traveling(여행)과 같은 의미인 tour를 사용하여 혼동을 준 오답이다.
(C) [x] 동남아시아 여행이 어땠는지를 물었는데, 이와 관련이 없는 당신의 다음 예약을 위해서라는 말로 응답했으므로 오답이다.

15 | What 의문문
캐나다 → 미국

What are you planning to order for the office party?
(A) I'm checking with the team first.
(B) They have excellent service.
(C) I already ate, thanks.

order v. 주문하다

해석 사무실 파티를 위해 무엇을 주문할 계획인가요?
(A) 저는 먼저 팀과 확인하고 있어요.
(B) 그들은 훌륭한 서비스를 제공해요.
(C) 저는 이미 먹었어요, 고마워요.

해설 (A) [o] 먼저 팀과 확인 중이라는 말로, 사무실 파티를 위해 무엇을 주문할지 모른다는 것을 간접적으로 전달했으므로 정답이다.
(B) [x] 질문의 order(주문하다)에서 연상할 수 있는 service(서비스)를 사용하여 혼동을 준 오답이다.
(C) [x] 사무실 파티를 위해 무엇을 주문할 계획인지를 물었는데, 이와 관련이 없는 자신은 이미 먹었다는 말로 응답했으므로 오답이다.

16 | Where 의문문
영국 → 호주

Where is Ms. Suzuki's office?
(A) Didn't the sales team move downstairs?
(B) My office is being redecorated.
(C) No, she's taking leave next week.

redecorate v. 다시 꾸미다, 새로 장식하다   leave n. 휴가

해석 Ms. Suzuki의 사무실은 어디에 있나요?
(A) 영업팀이 아래층으로 이동하지 않았나요?
(B) 제 사무실은 다시 꾸며지고 있어요.
(C) 아니요, 그녀는 다음 주에 휴가를 가요.

해설 (A) [o] 영업팀이 아래층으로 이동하지 않았냐고 되물어, 영업팀에 속한 Ms. Suzuki의 사무실이 아래층에 있을 거라는 답변을 간접적으로 전달했으므로 정답이다.
(B) [x] 질문의 office(사무실)를 반복 사용하여 혼동을 준 오답이다.
(C) [x] 의문사 의문문에 No로 응답했으므로 오답이다. 질문의 Ms. Suzuki를 나타낼 수 있는 she를 사용하여 혼동을 주었다.

17 | Who 의문문

호주 → 영국

Who requested the changes to the contract?
(A) The final agreement.
(B) Mr. Beloit was charged twice.
(C) I haven't heard anything about that.

contract n. 계약   agreement n. 계약, 동의   charge v. 청구하다

해석 누가 계약 변경을 요청했나요?
(A) 최종 계약이요.
(B) Mr. Beloit가 두 번 청구를 받았어요.
(C) 저는 그것에 대해 아무것도 듣지 못했어요.

해설 (A) [×] contract(계약)와 같은 의미인 agreement를 사용하여 혼동을 준 오답이다.
(B) [×] 질문의 contract(계약)와 관련 있는 charged(청구를 받다)를 사용하여 혼동을 준 오답이다. Mr. Beloit까지만 듣고 정답으로 고르지 않도록 주의한다.
(C) [○] 그것에 대해 아무것도 듣지 못했다는 말로, 누가 계약 변경을 요청했는지 모른다는 것을 간접적으로 전달했으므로 정답이다.

18 | Why 의문문

미국 → 캐나다

Why aren't the telephones working?
(A) My office is on the third floor.
(B) You should ask someone in maintenance.
(C) OK, I'll connect your call.

maintenance n. 유지 보수   connect v. 연결하다

해석 왜 전화기들이 작동하지 않나요?
(A) 제 사무실은 3층에 있어요.
(B) 유지 보수 담당자에게 물어보는 게 좋겠어요.
(C) 네, 전화를 연결해 드릴게요.

해설 (A) [×] 왜 전화기들이 작동하지 않는지를 물었는데, 이와 관련이 없는 사무실은 3층에 있다는 말로 응답했으므로 오답이다.
(B) [○] 유지 보수 담당자에게 물어보는 게 좋겠다는 말로, 왜 전화기들이 작동하지 않는지 모른다는 것을 간접적으로 전달했으므로 정답이다.
(C) [×] 질문의 telephones(전화기들)와 관련 있는 call(전화)을 사용하여 혼동을 준 오답이다.

19 | Who 의문문

호주 → 미국

Who drove you home yesterday?
(A) After we left the expo.
(B) Actually, I rode the bus.
(C) No, thanks. I don't need it.

expo n. 박람회

해석 어제 누가 당신을 집에 태워다 주었나요?
(A) 우리가 박람회를 떠난 후에요.
(B) 사실, 저는 버스를 탔어요.
(C) 고맙지만, 괜찮아요. 전 필요 없어요.

해설 (A) [×] 누가 집에 태워다 주었는지를 물었는데, 이와 관련이 없는 박람회를 떠난 후라는 말로 응답했으므로 오답이다.
(B) [○] 사실 버스를 탔다는 말로, 자신을 집에 태워다 준 사람이 없음을 간접적으로 전달했으므로 정답이다.
(C) [×] 누가 집에 태워다 주었는지를 물었는데, 이와 관련이 없는 거절의 말로 응답했으므로 오답이다.

20 | What 의문문

호주 → 영국

What did the contractor say about the project?
(A) The building permit was approved.
(B) At a construction conference.
(C) In order to build the structure.

contractor n. 계약자   permit n. 허가   construction n. 건설
conference n. 회의   structure n. 구조물

해석 계약업자가 프로젝트에 대해 뭐라고 말했나요?
(A) 건축 허가가 승인되었어요.
(B) 건설 회의에서요.
(C) 구조물을 짓기 위해서요.

해설 (A) [○] 건축 허가가 승인되었다는 말로, 계약업자가 프로젝트에 대해 말한 내용을 언급했으므로 정답이다.
(B) [×] contractor - construction의 유사 발음 어휘를 사용하여 혼동을 준 오답이다.
(C) [×] 계약업자가 프로젝트에 대해 뭐라고 말했는지를 물었는데, 이와 관련이 없는 구조물을 짓기 위해서라는 말로 응답했으므로 오답이다.

고난도 문제 완전 정복

p.25

01 (C)	02 (C)	03 (C)	04 (A)	05 (B)
06 (A)	07 (B)	08 (C)	09 (B)	10 (B)
11 (A)	12 (B)	13 (A)	14 (B)	15 (C)
16 (A)	17 (B)	18 (B)	19 (A)	20 (A)

01 | Where 의문문

미국 → 영국

Where should I leave these packages?
(A) We will start packing this evening.
(B) From the moving company.
(C) Please ask my secretary.

package n. 소포   pack v. 짐을 싸다   moving company 이사 업체
secretary n. 비서

해석 이 소포들을 어디에 두어야 하나요?
(A) 우리는 오늘 저녁에 짐을 싸기 시작할 거예요.
(B) 이사 업체에서요.
(C) 제 비서에게 물어보세요.

해설 (A) [×] packages - packing의 유사 발음 어휘를 사용하여 혼동을 준 오답이다.
(B) [×] 소포들을 어디에 두어야 하는지를 물었는데, 이와 관련이 없는 이사 회사에서라는 말로 응답했으므로 오답이다.
(C) [○] 비서에게 물어보라는 말로, 소포들을 어디에 두어야 하는지 모른다는 것을 간접적으로 전달했으므로 정답이다.

02 | Who 의문문

캐나다 → 미국

Who is leading the seminar on Friday?
(A) An event venue was reserved.
(B) To discuss industry changes.
(C) Didn't you hear that it was canceled?

venue n. 장소   reserve v. 예약하다   discuss v. 논의하다   industry n. 산업

해석 금요일에 세미나는 누가 이끌 예정인가요?

(A) 행사 장소가 예약되었어요.
(B) 산업 변화를 논의하기 위해서요.
(C) 그것이 취소된 것을 못 들으셨나요?

해설 (A) [×] 질문의 seminar(세미나)와 관련 있는 event(행사)를 사용하여 혼동을 준 오답이다.
(B) [×] 질문의 seminar(세미나)에서 연상할 수 있는 discuss(논의하다)를 사용하여 혼동을 준 오답이다.
(C) [o] 그것이 취소된 것을 못 들었냐고 되물어, 금요일 세미나가 취소되어 이끌 사람이 필요 없다는 것을 간접적으로 전달했으므로 정답이다.

03 | How 의문문
영국 → 캐나다

How quickly can your team revise this marketing report?
(A) Your timing was perfect.
(B) It was reported yesterday.
(C) We're busy with another project.

revise v. 수정하다

해설 당신의 팀은 얼마나 빨리 이 마케팅 보고서를 수정할 수 있나요?
(A) 당신의 타이밍은 완벽했어요.
(B) 그것은 어제 보고되었어요.
(C) 우리는 다른 프로젝트로 바빠요.

해설 (A) [×] 얼마나 빨리 마케팅 보고서를 수정할 수 있는지를 물었는데, 이와 관련이 없는 타이밍이 완벽했다는 말로 응답했으므로 오답이다.
(B) [×] report - reported의 유사 발음 어휘를 사용하여 혼동을 준 오답이다.
(C) [o] 다른 프로젝트로 바쁘다는 말로, 마케팅 보고서를 빨리 수정하기 어렵다는 것을 간접적으로 전달했으므로 정답이다.

04 | Where 의문문
호주 → 미국

Where can I pick up an application form?
(A) I'm wondering the same thing.
(B) For the customer service position.
(C) By the end of the week.

pick up 받다, 가져가다   application form 지원서   wonder v. 궁금해하다

해설 어디에서 지원서를 받을 수 있나요?
(A) 저도 같은 것을 궁금해하고 있어요.
(B) 고객 서비스 직책을 위한 거예요.
(C) 이번 주 말까지요.

해설 (A) [o] 자신도 같은 것을 궁금해하고 있다는 말로, 어디에서 지원서를 받을 수 있는지 모른다는 것을 간접적으로 전달했으므로 정답이다.
(B) [×] 질문의 application form(지원서)과 관련 있는 position(직책)을 사용하여 혼동을 준 오답이다.
(C) [×] 어디에서 지원서를 받을 수 있는지를 물었는데, 시점으로 응답했으므로 오답이다. 질문의 Where를 When으로 혼동하여 이를 정답으로 선택하지 않도록 주의한다.

05 | When 의문문
캐나다 → 미국

When should Brendon and I stop by your office?
(A) His office is across the hall.
(B) I'll be out of town this week.
(C) At the corporate headquarters.

stop by 들르다   corporate n. 회사   headquarters n. 본사

해설 Brendon과 제가 언제 당신의 사무실에 들러야 할까요?
(A) 그의 사무실은 복도 건너편에 있어요.
(B) 저는 이번 주에 시외로 나가 있을 거예요.
(C) 회사 본사에서요.

해설 (A) [×] 질문의 office를 반복 사용하여 혼동을 준 오답이다.
(B) [o] 자신이 이번 주에 시외로 나가 있을 것이라는 말로, 당장은 사무실에 들를 수 없음을 간접적으로 전달했으므로 정답이다.
(C) [×] 언제 사무실에 들러야 할지를 물었는데, 장소로 응답했으므로 오답이다. 질문의 When을 Where로 혼동하여 이를 정답으로 선택하지 않도록 주의한다.

06 | Who 의문문
미국 → 영국

Who do you think we should hire for the project?
(A) The final decision will be made by the director.
(B) I expected it to be higher than that.
(C) It was a detailed study on artificial intelligence.

hire v. 고용하다   expect v. 예상하다   artificial intelligence 인공 지능

해설 프로젝트를 위해 우리가 누구를 고용해야 한다고 생각하시나요?
(A) 최종 결정은 관리자가 내릴 거예요.
(B) 저는 그것보다 더 높을 것으로 예상했어요.
(C) 그것은 인공 지능에 대한 상세한 연구였어요.

해설 (A) [o] 최종 결정은 관리자가 내릴 것이라는 말로, 누구를 고용해야 하는지 모른다는 것을 간접적으로 전달했으므로 정답이다.
(B) [×] hire - higher의 유사 발음 어휘를 사용하여 혼동을 준 오답이다.
(C) [×] 프로젝트를 위해 누구를 고용해야 한다고 생각하는지를 물었는데, 이와 관련이 없는 그것은 인공 지능에 대한 상세한 연구였다는 말로 응답했으므로 오답이다. 질문의 project(프로젝트)를 나타낼 수 있는 It을 사용하여 혼동을 주었다.

07 | When 의문문
영국 → 캐나다

When can we discuss our travel expenses?
(A) No, that's too expensive.
(B) I'm on a tight schedule today.
(C) From Boston to New York City.

discuss v. 논의하다   travel expense 출장비

해설 우리가 언제 출장비에 대해 논의할 수 있나요?
(A) 아니요, 그것은 너무 비싸요.
(B) 저는 오늘 일정이 빡빡해요.
(C) 보스턴에서 뉴욕시까지요.

해설 (A) [×] 의문사 의문문에 No로 응답했으므로 오답이다. expenses - expensive의 유사 발음 어휘를 사용하여 혼동을 주었다.
(B) [o] 오늘 일정이 빡빡하다는 말로, 오늘은 어렵다는 것을 간접적으로 전달했으므로 정답이다.
(C) [×] 질문의 travel(출장)에서 연상할 수 있는 여행 경로 관련 표현인 from Boston to New York City(보스턴에서 뉴욕시까지)를 사용하여 혼동을 준 오답이다.

08 | Where 의문문
영국 → 미국

Where do you intend to open a new branch of your café?
(A) To buy a coffee and a muffin.
(B) Go to the Collingwood branch, please.
(C) I'm still conducting market research.

intend v. ~할 생각이다, 의도하다 branch n. 지점 conduct v. 하다, 수행하다
market research 시장 조사

해석 당신은 카페의 새 지점을 어디에 열 생각인가요?
(A) 커피와 머핀을 사기 위해서요.
(B) Collingwood 지점으로 가 주세요.
(C) 저는 아직 시장 조사를 하는 중이에요.

해설 (A) [×] 질문의 café(카페)와 관련 있는 coffee and muffin(커피와 머핀)을 사용하여 혼동을 준 오답이다.
(B) [×] 질문의 branch를 반복 사용하여 혼동을 준 오답이다.
(C) [o] 아직 시장 조사를 하는 중이라는 말로, 카페의 새 지점을 열 장소를 결정하지 못했음을 간접적으로 전달했으므로 정답이다.

09 | How 의문문
호주 → 영국

How did Mr. Paulson's speech go?
(A) Are you going home?
(B) Everyone seemed to enjoy it.
(C) To the beach, I think.

speech n. 연설

해석 Mr. Paulson의 연설은 어땠나요?
(A) 집에 가시나요?
(B) 모두가 그것을 즐긴 것 같아요.
(C) 제 생각에는 해변으로요.

해설 (A) [×] go - going의 유사 발음 어휘를 사용하여 혼동을 준 오답이다.
(B) [o] 모두가 그것을 즐긴 것 같다는 말로, Mr. Paulson의 연설이 성공적이었음을 간접적으로 전달했으므로 정답이다.
(C) [×] speech - beach의 유사 발음 어휘를 사용하여 혼동을 준 오답이다.

10 | Which 의문문
미국 → 캐나다

Which hotel should we stay at during our next trip?
(A) I'll cancel our room reservation.
(B) A more affordable one than last time.
(C) One of the best travel guidebooks I bought.

reservation n. 예약 affordable adj. 가격이 적당한

해석 우리의 다음 여행 중에 어느 호텔에 묵어야 할까요?
(A) 제가 우리의 객실 예약을 취소할게요.
(B) 지난번보다 더 가격이 적당한 곳이요.
(C) 제가 산 최고의 여행 안내서 중 하나예요.

해설 (A) [×] 질문의 hotel(호텔)과 관련 있는 room reservation(객실 예약)을 사용하여 혼동을 준 오답이다.
(B) [o] 지난번보다 더 가격이 적당한 곳이라는 말로, 묵어야 할 호텔에 대한 의견을 제시했으므로 정답이다.
(C) [×] 질문의 trip(여행)에서 연상할 수 있는 travel guidebooks(여행 안내서)를 사용하여 혼동을 준 오답이다.

11 | How 의문문
호주 → 캐나다

How many people have joined the aerobics class?
(A) Not as many as I was hoping.
(B) Courses are offered at the gym.
(C) I've tried it many times before.

aerobics n. 에어로빅 offer v. 제공하다

해석 에어로빅 강좌에 몇 명이나 등록했나요?
(A) 제가 바랐던 것만큼 많지는 않아요.
(B) 강좌들은 체육관에서 제공돼요.
(C) 저는 그것을 이전에 여러 번 시도해 봤어요.

해설 (A) [o] 자신이 바랐던 것만큼 많지는 않다는 말로, 에어로빅 강좌에 등록한 사람 수가 적다는 것을 간접적으로 전달했으므로 정답이다.
(B) [×] class(강좌)와 같은 의미인 courses를 사용하여 혼동을 준 오답이다.
(C) [×] 에어로빅 강좌에 몇 명이나 등록했는지를 물었는데, 이와 관련이 없는 자신이 그것을 이전에 여러 번 시도해 봤다는 말로 응답했으므로 오답이다. 질문의 aerobics class(에어로빅 강좌)를 나타낼 수 있는 it을 사용하여 혼동을 주었다.

12 | When 의문문
영국 → 호주

When will you begin the consumer research?
(A) The performance is starting in 10 minutes.
(B) That depends on my schedule.
(C) Oh, the research laboratory.

consumer research 소비자 조사 research laboratory 연구소

해석 언제 소비자 조사를 시작할 건가요?
(A) 공연은 10분 후에 시작해요.
(B) 그건 제 일정에 달려 있어요.
(C) 아, 연구소요.

해설 (A) [×] begin(시작하다)과 같은 의미인 start를 사용하여 혼동을 준 오답이다.
(B) [o] 그것은 자신의 일정에 달려 있다는 말로, 언제 소비자 조사를 시작할지 모른다는 것을 간접적으로 전달했으므로 정답이다.
(C) [×] 질문의 research를 반복 사용하여 혼동을 준 오답이다.

13 | Why 의문문
캐나다 → 미국

Why isn't the year-end banquet being held at a hotel?
(A) Who told you that?
(B) Regarding our annual spending.
(C) It begins early this evening.

year-end adj. 연말의 banquet n. 연회 regarding prep. ~에 관하여 spending n. 지출

해석 왜 연말 연회가 호텔에서 개최되지 않나요?
(A) 누가 당신에게 그것을 말했나요?
(B) 우리의 연간 지출에 관해서요.
(C) 그것은 오늘 저녁 일찍 시작해요.

해설 (A) [o] 누가 그것을 말했는지를 되물어, 연말 연회가 호텔에서 개최되지 않는 것을 몰랐다는 것을 간접적으로 전달했으므로 정답이다.
(B) [×] 질문의 year-end banquet(연말 연회)에서 연상할 수 있는 주제와 관련된 annual spending(연간 지출)을 사용하여 혼동을 준 오답이다.
(C) [×] 질문의 year-end banquet(연말 연회)에서 연상할 수 있는 행사 일정과 관련된 early this evening(오늘 저녁 일찍)을 사용하여 혼동을 준 오답이다.

14 | What 의문문
캐나다 → 영국

What type of show is taking place at the performance hall?
(A) This software is performing very well.
(B) Look on the Web site.

(C) The building was recently renovated.

performance hall 공연장 perform v. 작동하다, 수행하다

해석 공연장에서 어떤 종류의 공연이 열리나요?
(A) 이 소프트웨어는 아주 잘 작동하고 있어요.
(B) 웹사이트에서 확인해 보세요.
(C) 그 건물은 최근에 개조되었어요.
해설 (A) [×] performance - performing의 유사 발음 어휘를 사용하여 혼동을 준 오답이다.
(B) [○] 웹사이트에서 확인해 보라는 말로, 공연장에서 어떤 종류의 공연이 열리는지 모른다는 것을 간접적으로 전달했으므로 정답이다.
(C) [×] 질문의 performance hall(공연장)과 관련 있는 building(건물)을 사용하여 혼동을 준 오답이다.

15 | When 의문문
🎧 호주 → 캐나다

When should I sign up for the information session?
(A) I signed up online.
(B) Very informative, actually.
(C) Registration ends in a week.

sign up 등록하다 information session 설명회 informative adj. 유익한
registration n. 등록

해석 제가 언제 설명회에 등록해야 하나요?
(A) 저는 온라인으로 등록했어요.
(B) 사실, 매우 유익했어요.
(C) 등록은 일주일 후에 마감돼요.
해설 (A) [×] 질문의 sign up을 signed up으로 반복 사용하여 혼동을 준 오답이다.
(B) [×] information - informative의 유사 발음 어휘를 사용하여 혼동을 준 오답이다.
(C) [○] 등록이 일주일 후에 마감된다는 말로, 설명회에 등록해야 하는 마감 시점을 전달했으므로 정답이다.

16 | Who 의문문
🎧 미국 → 호주

Who was selected to oversee the Marlow project?
(A) That has yet to be announced.
(B) They're excited for the opportunity.
(C) The president finally chose a venue.

select v. 선택하다 oversee v. 감독하다 announce v. 발표하다
opportunity n. 기회 venue n. 장소

해석 누가 Marlow 프로젝트를 감독하도록 선택되었나요?
(A) 그것은 아직 발표되지 않았어요.
(B) 그들은 그 기회에 기뻐하고 있어요.
(C) 사장이 마침내 장소를 선택했어요.
해설 (A) [○] 그것은 아직 발표되지 않았다는 말로, 누가 Marlow 프로젝트를 감독하도록 선택되었는지 모른다는 것을 간접적으로 전달했으므로 정답이다.
(B) [×] 누가 Marlow 프로젝트를 감독하도록 선택되었는지를 물었는데, 이와 관련이 없는 그들은 그 기회에 기뻐하고 있다는 말로 응답했으므로 오답이다. 질문의 Marlow project(Marlow 프로젝트)를 나타낼 수 있는 opportunity(기회)를 사용하여 혼동을 주었다.
(C) [×] selected(선택했다)와 같은 의미인 chose를 사용하여 혼동을 준 오답이다.

17 | How 의문문
🎧 캐나다 → 영국

How much did you spend organizing the appreciation dinner?
(A) Could you send it to me?
(B) Lewis is in charge of that.
(C) The dining area was not large enough.

spend v. 지출하다 organize v. 준비하다, 조직하다
appreciation dinner 감사 만찬 in charge of ~을 담당하는

해석 감사 만찬을 준비하는 데 얼마를 지출했나요?
(A) 그것을 저에게 보내주시겠어요?
(B) Lewis가 그것을 담당하고 있어요.
(C) 식사 공간이 충분히 크지 않았어요.
해설 (A) [×] spend - send의 유사 발음 어휘를 사용하여 혼동을 준 오답이다.
(B) [○] Lewis가 그것을 담당하고 있다는 말로, 감사 만찬을 준비하는 데 얼마를 지출했는지 모른다는 것을 간접적으로 전달했으므로 정답이다.
(C) [×] 질문의 appreciation dinner(감사 만찬)에서 연상할 수 있는 dining area(식사 공간)를 사용하여 혼동을 준 오답이다.

18 | Why 의문문
🎧 호주 → 미국

Why has the director chosen not to extend the project deadline?
(A) In order to get an extension.
(B) He's explaining his decision today.
(C) Don't forget about our project.

director n. 관리자 extend v. 연장하다 decision n. 결정

해석 관리자는 왜 프로젝트 마감일을 연장하지 않기로 결정했나요?
(A) 연장을 받기 위해서요.
(B) 그는 오늘 그의 결정을 설명할 거예요.
(C) 우리의 프로젝트를 잊지 마세요.
해설 (A) [×] extend - extension의 유사 발음 어휘를 사용하여 혼동을 준 오답이다. In order to까지만 듣고 정답으로 고르지 않도록 주의한다.
(B) [○] 그는 오늘 그의 결정을 설명할 것이라는 말로, 관리자가 왜 프로젝트 마감일을 연장하지 않기로 결정했는지 모른다는 것을 간접적으로 전달했으므로 정답이다.
(C) [×] 질문의 project를 반복 사용하여 혼동을 준 오답이다.

19 | Who 의문문
🎧 호주 → 캐나다

Who can make this deposit at the bank for me?
(A) Do you need that done today?
(B) Into the company account.
(C) Another teller needs to be hired.

deposit n. 입금(액); v. 입금하다 account n. 계좌 teller n. 은행원

해석 누가 저를 대신하여 이 입금액을 은행에 넣어 줄 수 있나요?
(A) 그것이 오늘 처리되어야 하나요?
(B) 회사 계좌로요.
(C) 다른 은행원이 고용되어야 해요.
해설 (A) [○] 그것이 오늘 처리되어야 하는지를 되물어, 은행에 입금하는 것에 대한 추가 정보를 요구했으므로 정답이다.
(B) [×] 질문의 deposit(입금액)과 관련 있는 account(계좌)를 사용하여 혼동을 준 오답이다.

(C) [×] 질문의 bank(은행)와 관련 있는 teller(은행원)를 사용하여 혼동을 준 오답이다.

20 | What 의문문
캐나다 → 미국

What seems to be wrong with the Internet connection?
(A) It's working on my computer.
(B) There isn't a connecting flight.
(C) I posted mine on the Web site.

connection n. 연결 connecting flight 연결 항공편 post v. 게시하다

해석 인터넷 연결에 무슨 문제가 있는 것 같나요?
(A) 제 컴퓨터에서는 작동하고 있어요.
(B) 연결 항공편이 없어요.
(C) 저는 제 것을 웹사이트에 게시했어요.

해설 (A) [○] 자신의 컴퓨터에서는 작동하고 있다는 말로, 인터넷 연결 문제가 상대방의 컴퓨터에만 있을 가능성을 간접적으로 전달했으므로 정답이다.
(B) [×] connection - connecting의 유사 발음 어휘를 사용하여 혼동을 준 오답이다.
(C) [×] 질문의 Internet(인터넷)과 관련 있는 Web site(웹사이트)를 사용하여 혼동을 준 오답이다.

DAY 04   일반/기타 의문문 및 평서문

빈출 문제 집중 훈련   p.26

01 (B)	02 (A)	03 (B)	04 (A)	05 (C)
06 (C)	07 (B)	08 (A)	09 (C)	10 (B)
11 (A)	12 (A)	13 (A)	14 (A)	15 (B)
16 (A)	17 (C)	18 (B)	19 (A)	20 (A)

01 | 조동사 의문문
캐나다 → 영국

Will you join us for the team dinner tonight?
(A) The restaurant is located on Main Street.
(B) Yes. I'll be there at 7 P.M.
(C) What were you cooking?

locate v. 위치하다

해석 오늘 밤 팀 저녁 회식에 우리와 함께 하실 건가요?
(A) 그 식당은 Main가에 위치해 있어요.
(B) 네. 저녁 7시에 거기에 갈게요.
(C) 당신은 무엇을 요리하고 있었나요?

해설 (A) [×] 질문의 team dinner(팀 저녁 회식)에서 연상할 수 있는 restaurant(식당)을 사용하여 혼동을 준 오답이다.
(B) [○] Yes로 저녁 회식에 함께 하겠다고 전달한 후, 저녁 7시에 가겠다고 부연 설명을 했으므로 정답이다.
(C) [×] 질문의 team dinner(팀 저녁 회식)에서 연상할 수 있는 cooking(요리하다)을 사용하여 혼동을 준 오답이다.

02 | 부정 의문문
호주 → 미국

Aren't there enough handouts for everyone?
(A) No. We ran out.
(B) A handout for this program.
(C) Everyone is finally here.

handout n. 유인물, 배포 자료 run out 소진되다, 다 떨어지다

해석 모든 사람들을 위해 충분한 유인물이 있지 않나요?
(A) 아니요. 소진되었어요.
(B) 이 프로그램을 위한 유인물이요.
(C) 모든 사람들이 마침내 여기 모였어요.

해설 (A) [○] No로 유인물이 없음을 전달한 후, 소진되었다는 부연 설명을 했으므로 정답이다.
(B) [×] 질문의 handouts를 handout으로 반복 사용하여 혼동을 준 오답이다.
(C) [×] 질문의 everyone을 반복 사용하여 혼동을 준 오답이다.

03 | 선택 의문문
미국 → 영국

Should we use the paper or the cloth napkins for the event?
(A) I'm afraid they only sell clothing.
(B) The cloth ones seem more attractive.
(C) For the tables in the main dining area.

attractive adj. 매력적인

해석 행사를 위해 종이 냅킨을 써야 할까요, 아니면 천 냅킨을 써야 할까요?
(A) 유감이지만 그들은 의류만 판매하는 것 같아요.
(B) 천으로 된 것들이 더 매력적으로 보여요.
(C) 주요 식사 공간에 있는 테이블들을 위해서요.

해설 (A) [×] cloth - clothing의 유사 발음 어휘를 사용하여 혼동을 준 오답이다.
(B) [○] 천으로 된 것들이 더 매력적으로 보인다는 말로, 천 냅킨을 선택했으므로 정답이다.
(C) [×] 질문의 napkins(냅킨)에서 연상할 수 있는 식사와 관련된 dining area(식사 공간)를 사용하여 혼동을 준 오답이다.

04 | 부가 의문문
미국 → 호주

The chef is still preparing the food, isn't he?
(A) Yes. It should be ready soon.
(B) No, the entrée wasn't very good.
(C) A well-known French cook.

chef n. 요리사 entrée n. 주요리 well-known adj. 유명한

해석 요리사가 아직 음식을 준비하고 있어요, 그렇지 않나요?
(A) 네. 그것은 곧 준비될 거예요.
(B) 아니요, 주요리가 매우 좋지는 않았어요.
(C) 유명한 프랑스 요리사요.

해설 (A) [○] Yes로 요리사가 아직 음식을 준비하고 있다고 전달한 후, 곧 준비될 것이라는 부연 설명을 했으므로 정답이다.
(B) [×] 질문의 food(음식)와 관련 있는 entrée(주요리)를 사용하여 혼동을 준 오답이다.
(C) [×] chef(요리사)와 같은 의미인 cook을 사용하여 혼동을 준 오답이다.

05 | 조동사 의문문
캐나다 → 영국

Did you discuss the production goals with Mr. Chan last Monday?
(A) The factory tour has begun.
(B) I already have a prior engagement.

(C) Yes. He seemed quite pleased with them.

production n. 생산 goal n. 목표 prior adj. 우선하는, 전의 engagement n. 약속 be pleased with ~에 만족하다

해석 지난 월요일에 Mr. Chan과 생산 목표에 대해 논의했나요?
(A) 공장 견학이 시작되었어요.
(B) 저는 이미 선약이 있어요.
(C) 네. 그는 그것들에 꽤 만족한 것으로 보였어요.

해설 (A) [x] 질문의 production(생산)에서 연상할 수 있는 장소와 관련된 factory(공장)를 사용하여 혼동을 준 오답이다.
(B) [x] 지난 월요일에 Mr. Chan과 생산 목표에 대해 논의했는지를 물었는데, 이와 관련이 없는 이미 선약이 있다는 말로 응답했으므로 오답이다.
(C) [o] Yes로 지난 월요일에 Mr. Chan과 생산 목표에 대해 논의했음을 전달한 후, 그는 그것들에 꽤 만족한 것으로 보였다는 부연 설명을 했으므로 정답이다.

06 | 평서문   영국 → 캐나다

I'd like to learn more about the services offered by your firm.
(A) We learned a lot in the workshop.
(B) Which firm does she represent?
(C) Read through this brochure.

firm n. 회사 represent v. 대표하다 brochure n. 안내 책자

해석 저는 당신의 회사에서 제공되는 서비스에 대해 더 알고 싶습니다.
(A) 우리는 워크숍에서 많은 것을 배웠어요.
(B) 그녀는 어느 회사를 대표하나요?
(C) 이 안내 책자를 읽어보세요.

해설 (A) [x] learn - learned의 유사 발음 어휘를 사용하여 혼동을 준 오답이다.
(B) [x] 질문의 firm을 반복 사용하여 혼동을 준 오답이다.
(C) [o] 이 안내 책자를 읽어보라는 말로, 회사에서 제공하는 서비스에 대한 정보를 얻을 수 있는 방법을 제시했으므로 정답이다.

07 | 조동사 의문문   미국 → 호주

Did you enjoy visiting the museum?
(A) We have some visitors.
(B) It exceeded my expectations.
(C) To arrange an exhibit.

exceed v. 넘어서다, 초과하다 expectation n. 기대 arrange v. 준비하다 exhibit n. 전시회, 전시품

해석 당신은 박물관 방문을 즐겼나요?
(A) 우리는 몇몇 방문객들이 있어요.
(B) 그것은 제 기대를 넘어섰어요.
(C) 전시회를 준비하기 위해서요.

해설 (A) [x] visiting - visitors의 유사 발음 어휘를 사용하여 혼동을 준 오답이다.
(B) [o] 그것은 자신의 기대를 넘어섰다는 말로, 박물관 방문을 즐겼다는 것을 간접적으로 전달했으므로 정답이다.
(C) [x] 질문의 museum(박물관)과 관련 있는 exhibit(전시회)을 사용하여 혼동을 준 오답이다.

08 | 선택 의문문   캐나다 → 영국

Would you rather go to a Chinese restaurant or order in some pizza?
(A) I can finish the rest for you.
(B) It doesn't really matter to me.
(C) No, I'll pay the delivery person.

rest n. 나머지 delivery person 배달원

해석 중국 음식점에 가고 싶나요, 아니면 피자를 주문하고 싶나요?
(A) 제가 당신을 위해 나머지를 끝낼 수 있어요.
(B) 저는 정말 상관없어요.
(C) 아니요, 제가 배달원에게 지불할 거예요.

해설 (A) [x] restaurant - rest의 유사 발음 어휘를 사용하여 혼동을 준 오답이다.
(B) [o] 자신은 정말 상관없다는 말로, 중국 음식점에 가는 것과 피자를 주문하는 것 둘 다 간접적으로 선택하지 않은 정답이다.
(C) [x] 질문의 order(주문하다)에서 연상할 수 있는 직업과 관련된 delivery person(배달원)을 사용하여 혼동을 준 오답이다.

09 | 평서문   영국 → 캐나다

Let's meet at the station at 2 P.M.
(A) Yes, it was a long trip.
(B) No, we took the bus.
(C) I'll wait by the main entrance.

station n. 역 main entrance 정문

해석 우리 오후 2시에 역에서 만나요.
(A) 네, 그것은 긴 여행이었어요.
(B) 아니요, 우리는 버스를 탔어요.
(C) 정문에서 기다릴게요.

해설 (A) [x] 질문의 station(역)에서 연상할 수 있는 활동과 관련된 trip(여행)을 사용하여 혼동을 준 오답이다.
(B) [x] 질문의 station(역)에서 연상할 수 있는 교통 수단과 관련된 bus(버스)를 사용하여 혼동을 준 오답이다.
(C) [o] 정문에서 기다리겠다는 말로, 구체적인 장소를 제안하고 있으므로 정답이다.

10 | Be동사 의문문   영국 → 호주

Are you going to a corporate retreat for the weekend?
(A) Have a nice time!
(B) That's right. I'm leaving on Friday.
(C) Yes, ship it by Sunday.

corporate n. 기업 retreat n. 연수 ship v. 배송하다

해석 주말에 기업 연수에 가시나요?
(A) 즐거운 시간 보내세요!
(B) 맞아요. 저는 금요일에 떠나요.
(C) 네, 일요일까지 그것을 배송해주세요.

해설 (A) [x] 주말에 기업 연수에 가는지를 물었는데, 이와 관련이 없는 즐거운 시간을 보내라는 내용으로 응답했으므로 오답이다.
(B) [o] That's right으로 주말에 기업 연수에 간다는 것을 전달한 후, 금요일에 떠난다는 부연 설명을 했으므로 정답이다.
(C) [x] 질문의 weekend(주말)와 관련 있는 Sunday(일요일)를 사용하여 혼동을 준 오답이다. Yes까지만 듣고 정답으로 고르지 않도록 주의한다.

11 | 평서문
영국 → 호주

I noticed that this vase was damaged after I bought it.
(A) You can exchange it or get a refund.
(B) After the convention begins.
(C) I love it, thank you.

vase n. 꽃병 damage v. 손상시키다 exchange v. 교환하다
convention n. 회의, 대회

해석 이 꽃병을 산 후에 이것이 손상되었다는 것을 알아챘어요.
   (A) 교환하시거나 환불을 받으실 수 있습니다.
   (B) 회의가 시작된 후에요.
   (C) 그것이 마음에 들어요, 감사합니다.

해설 (A) [o] 교환하거나 환불을 받을 수 있다는 말로, 문제점에 대한 해결책을 제시했으므로 정답이다.
   (B) [x] 질문의 after를 반복 사용하여 혼동을 준 오답이다.
   (C) [x] 꽃병을 산 후에 손상되었다는 것을 알아챘다고 했는데, 이와 관련이 없는 그것이 마음에 든다며 감사하다는 말로 응답했으므로 오답이다. 질문의 vase(꽃병)를 나타낼 수 있는 it을 사용하여 혼동을 주었다.

12 | 요청 의문문
미국 → 캐나다

Could you tell me where we keep the printer paper?
(A) There's some in that cabinet.
(B) I will tell them about it.
(C) It needs a new cartridge.

cartridge n. 카트리지, 잉크심

해석 프린터 용지를 어디에 보관하는지 알려주실 수 있나요?
   (A) 저 캐비닛에 조금 있어요.
   (B) 그들에게 그것에 관해 알려줄게요.
   (C) 새 카트리지가 필요해요.

해설 (A) [o] 저 캐비닛에 (프린터 용지가) 조금 있다는 말로, 프린터 용지를 보관하는 장소를 언급했으므로 정답이다.
   (B) [x] 질문의 tell을 반복 사용하여 혼동을 준 오답이다.
   (C) [x] 질문의 printer(프린터)와 관련 있는 cartridge(카트리지)를 사용하여 혼동을 준 오답이다.

13 | 조동사 의문문
호주 → 영국

Did anyone send the schedule to the guests?
(A) That was Gary's responsibility.
(B) I guess I'll join.
(C) Oh, that's my calendar.

responsibility n. 할 일, 책임 calendar n. 달력

해석 누군가 손님들에게 일정표를 보냈나요?
   (A) 그것은 Gary가 할 일이었어요.
   (B) 제가 참여할게요.
   (C) 아, 저것은 제 달력이에요.

해설 (A) [o] 그것은 Gary가 할 일이었다는 말로, Gary가 손님들에게 일정표를 보냈을 것임을 간접적으로 전달했으므로 정답이다.
   (B) [x] guests - guess의 유사 발음 어휘를 사용하여 혼동을 준 오답이다.
   (C) [x] 질문의 schedule(일정표)에서 연상할 수 있는 calendar(달력)를 사용하여 혼동을 준 오답이다.

14 | 평서문
호주 → 영국

A few of our executives will visit our branch next month.
(A) I'll notify all of the staff.
(B) The president has approved the changes.
(C) Yes, the workshop ended in April.

executive n. 임원 branch n. 지사 notify v. 알리다, 통지하다
approve v. 승인하다

해석 우리의 몇몇 임원들이 다음 달에 우리 지사를 방문할 예정이에요.
   (A) 제가 모든 직원들에게 알릴게요.
   (B) 사장이 변경 사항들을 승인했어요.
   (C) 네, 워크숍은 4월에 끝났어요.

해설 (A) [o] 모든 직원들에게 알리겠다는 말로, 임원들의 지사 방문 소식과 관련하여 자신이 할 일을 전달하고 있으므로 정답이다.
   (B) [x] 질문의 executives(임원들)에서 연상할 수 있는 president(사장)를 사용하여 혼동을 준 오답이다.
   (C) [x] 질문의 month(달)와 관련 있는 April(4월)을 사용하여 혼동을 준 오답이다.

15 | 부가 의문문
캐나다 → 미국

The promotional offer is available until this Friday, right?
(A) The customer didn't qualify for a discount.
(B) That's what the flyer says.
(C) This workstation is available for use.

promotional adj. 판촉(용)의 offer n. 할인 available adj. 유효한
qualify for ~의 자격이 되다 discount n. 할인 flyer n. 전단지
workstation n. 작업대

해석 판촉 할인이 이번 주 금요일까지 유효하죠, 그렇죠?
   (A) 그 고객은 할인 자격이 되지 않았어요.
   (B) 전단지에 그렇게 쓰여 있어요.
   (C) 이 작업대는 사용 가능해요.

해설 (A) [x] offer(할인)와 같은 의미인 discount를 사용하여 혼동을 준 오답이다.
   (B) [o] 전단지에 그렇게 쓰여 있다는 말로, 판촉 할인이 이번 주 금요일까지 유효함을 간접적으로 전달했으므로 정답이다.
   (C) [x] 질문의 available을 반복 사용하여 혼동을 준 오답이다.

16 | 평서문
미국 → 호주

The workers hired to renovate our hotel will start working on Monday.
(A) They'll be remodeling the lobby, right?
(B) The film will start at 8 P.M.
(C) I'll confirm our room reservations.

hire v. 고용하다 renovate v. 개조하다 remodel v. 개조하다
confirm v. 확정하다, 확인하다 reservation n. 예약

해석 우리 호텔을 개조하기 위해 고용된 근로자들이 월요일에 작업을 시작할 거예요.
   (A) 그들이 로비를 개조할 거죠, 그렇죠?
   (B) 영화는 오후 8시에 시작할 거예요.
   (C) 저희 객실 예약을 확정할게요.

해설 (A) [o] 그들이 로비를 개조할 것인지를 되물어, 호텔 개조에 대한 추가 정보를 요구한 정답이다.
   (B) [x] 질문의 start를 반복 사용하여 혼동을 준 오답이다.

(C) [x] 질문의 hotel(호텔)과 관련 있는 room reservations(객실 예약)를 사용하여 혼동을 준 오답이다.

17 | 제안 의문문
🎧 캐나다 → 호주

Why don't you share your research findings next week?
(A) I studied economics in college.
(B) To assess consumer opinions.
(C) The data won't be ready by then.

research n. 연구 finding n. 결과 assess v. 평가하다
consumer n. 소비자 opinion n. 의견

해석 다음 주에 당신의 연구 결과를 공유하는 게 어때요?
(A) 저는 대학에서 경제학을 공부했어요.
(B) 소비자 의견을 평가하기 위해서요.
(C) 그때까지 데이터가 준비되지 않을 거예요.

해설 (A) [x] 질문의 research(연구)와 관련 있는 studied(공부했다)를 사용하여 혼동을 준 오답이다.
(B) [x] 질문의 research findings(연구 결과)에서 연상할 수 있는 consumer opinions(소비자 의견)을 사용하여 혼동을 준 오답이다.
(C) [o] 그때까지 데이터가 준비되지 않을 것이라는 말로, 다음 주에 연구 결과를 공유하자는 제안을 간접적으로 거절했으므로 정답이다.

18 | 부정 의문문
🎧 캐나다 → 미국

Wasn't there an announcement about our work schedule the other day?
(A) Should we order another one?
(B) I don't remember anything being said about that.
(C) Well, it was his first day there.

announcement n. 공지 order v. 주문하다

해석 며칠 전에 우리 업무 일정에 관한 공지가 있지 않았나요?
(A) 다른 것을 주문해야 할까요?
(B) 그것에 대해 아무 말도 들은 기억이 없어요.
(C) 글쎄요, 그곳에서 그의 첫 날이었어요.

해설 (A) [x] other - another의 유사 발음 어휘를 사용하여 혼동을 준 오답이다.
(B) [o] 그것에 대해 아무 말도 들은 기억이 없다는 말로, 며칠 전에 업무 일정에 관한 공지가 있었는지 모른다는 것을 간접적으로 전달했으므로 정답이다.
(C) [x] 질문의 day를 반복 사용하여 혼동을 준 오답이다.

19 | 선택 의문문
🎧 영국 → 호주

Do you want to interview Ms. Brady first on Monday or start with Ms. Collins?
(A) There are better-qualified candidates.
(B) In the second-floor meeting room.
(C) She accepted our job offer.

interview v. 면접을 보다 better-qualified adj. 더 나은 자격을 갖춘
candidate n. 지원자 job offer 일자리 제의

해석 월요일에 Ms. Brady를 먼저 면접 보고 싶으신가요, 아니면 Ms. Collins부터 시작하고 싶으신가요?
(A) 더 나은 자격을 갖춘 지원자들이 있어요.
(B) 2층 회의실에서요.
(C) 그녀는 저희의 일자리 제의를 받아들였어요.

해설 (A) [o] 더 나은 자격을 갖춘 지원자들이 있다는 말로, Ms. Brady와 Ms. Collins 둘 다 간접적으로 선택하지 않은 정답이다.
(B) [x] 질문의 interview(면접을 보다)에서 연상할 수 있는 장소와 관련된 meeting room(회의실)을 사용하여 혼동을 준 오답이다.
(C) [x] 질문의 interview(면접을 보다)에서 연상할 수 있는 job offer(일자리 제의)를 사용하여 혼동을 준 오답이다. 질문의 Ms. Brady 또는 Ms. Collins를 나타낼 수 있는 She를 사용하여 혼동을 주었다.

20 | Be동사 의문문
🎧 호주 → 미국

Am I supposed to lock up the building before I leave?
(A) The janitor takes care of that.
(B) We can look for it later.
(C) It's on the left side of the building.

lock up 문단속을 하다 janitor n. 관리인 look for ~을 찾다

해석 떠나기 전에 제가 건물 문단속을 해야 하나요?
(A) 관리인이 그것을 담당해요.
(B) 우리는 나중에 그것을 찾아볼 수 있어요.
(C) 그것은 건물의 왼쪽에 있어요.

해설 (A) [o] 관리인이 그것을 담당한다는 말로, 상대방이 건물 문단속을 할 필요가 없음을 간접적으로 전달했으므로 정답이다.
(B) [x] 떠나기 전에 건물 문단속을 해야 하는지를 물었는데, 이와 관련이 없는 나중에 그것을 찾아볼 수 있다는 말로 응답했으므로 오답이다.
(C) [x] 질문의 building을 반복 사용하여 혼동을 준 오답이다.

고난도 문제 완전 정복
p.27

01 (B)	02 (C)	03 (A)	04 (C)	05 (A)
06 (C)	07 (A)	08 (B)	09 (B)	10 (A)
11 (A)	12 (B)	13 (C)	14 (A)	15 (B)
16 (A)	17 (B)	18 (C)	19 (A)	20 (C)

01 | 부정 의문문
🎧 미국 → 캐나다

Shouldn't we reserve a table at the restaurant in advance?
(A) No, the coffee table.
(B) Could you handle that?
(C) I often eat at that restaurant.

reserve v. 예약하다 in advance 미리 handle v. 처리하다

해석 우리가 식당에 테이블을 미리 예약해야 하지 않을까요?
(A) 아니요, 커피 테이블이요.
(B) 당신이 그것을 처리해 주실 수 있나요?
(C) 저는 종종 그 식당에서 식사해요.

해설 (A) [x] 질문의 table을 반복 사용하여 혼동을 준 오답이다. No까지만 듣고 정답으로 고르지 않도록 주의한다.
(B) [o] 그것을 처리해 줄 수 있는지 되물어, 상대방에게 식당에 테이블을 미리 예약해 달라고 요청했으므로 정답이다.
(C) [x] 질문의 restaurant을 반복 사용하여 혼동을 준 오답이다.

02 | Be동사 의문문
캐나다 → 영국

Is Ms. Klein waiting in the reception area?
(A) The area is spacious enough.
(B) The receptionist is taking a break.
(C) I haven't checked.

reception n. 접수 spacious adj. 넓은 receptionist n. 접수원
break n. 휴식

해석 Ms. Klein이 접수 구역에서 기다리고 있나요?
(A) 그 구역은 충분히 넓어요.
(B) 접수원이 휴식을 취하고 있어요.
(C) 확인해보지 않았어요.

해설 (A) [x] 질문의 area를 반복 사용하여 혼동을 준 오답이다.
(B) [x] reception - receptionist의 유사 발음 어휘를 사용하여 혼동을 준 오답이다.
(C) [o] 확인해보지 않았다는 말로, Ms. Klein이 접수 구역에서 기다리고 있는지 모른다는 것을 간접적으로 전달했으므로 정답이다.

03 | 평서문
미국 → 호주

The keynote speaker will be arriving at the venue late.
(A) I'll have Ms. Calloway present first then.
(B) Yes, the microphone isn't working.
(C) The CEO sent it on time.

keynote speaker 기조 연설자 venue n. 장소 present v. 발표하다
microphone n. 마이크

해석 기조 연설자가 장소에 늦게 도착할 예정이에요.
(A) 그럼 Ms. Calloway가 먼저 발표하도록 할게요.
(B) 네, 마이크가 작동하지 않아요.
(C) 대표이사가 그것을 제시간에 보냈어요.

해설 (A) [o] 그럼 Ms. Calloway가 먼저 발표하도록 하겠다는 말로, 문제점에 대한 해결책을 제시했으므로 정답이다.
(B) [x] 질문의 keynote speaker(기조 연설자)에서 연상할 수 있는 사물과 관련된 microphone(마이크)을 사용하여 혼동을 준 오답이다.
(C) [x] 질문의 late(늦게)와 반대 의미인 on time(제시간에)을 사용하여 혼동을 준 오답이다.

04 | 선택 의문문
영국 → 미국

Do you want to hold the video conference now or this afternoon?
(A) To discuss financial projections.
(B) Yes, if I have enough time.
(C) Let's do it within an hour.

video conference 화상 회의 financial projection 재무 계획
within prep. ~이내에

해석 화상 회의를 지금 열고 싶나요, 아니면 오늘 오후에 열고 싶나요?
(A) 재무 계획에 대해 논의하기 위해서요.
(B) 네, 제가 충분한 시간이 있다면요.
(C) 한 시간 이내에 합시다.

해설 (A) [x] 질문의 video conference(화상 회의)에서 연상할 수 있는 discuss(논의하다)를 사용하여 혼동을 준 오답이다.
(B) [x] 선택 의문문에 Yes로 응답했으므로 오답이다. now or this afternoon(지금 아니면 오늘 오후)에서 연상할 수 있는 time(시간)을 사용하여 혼동을 주었다.
(C) [o] 한 시간 이내에 하자는 말로, 지금과 오늘 오후 둘 다 간접적으로 선택하지 않은 정답이다.

05 | 제공 의문문
호주 → 캐나다

Do you want me to help you prepare for the orientation?
(A) Please bring these materials to the conference room.
(B) I don't mind helping you set up the room beforehand.
(C) It was held downstairs on the first floor.

set up 준비하다, 설치하다 beforehand adv. 미리

해석 오리엔테이션을 준비하시는 걸 도와드릴까요?
(A) 이 자료들을 회의실로 가져다주세요.
(B) 저는 당신이 미리 방을 준비하는 것을 기꺼이 도와드릴 수 있어요.
(C) 그것은 아래층 1층에서 개최되었어요.

해설 (A) [o] 이 자료들을 회의실로 가져다 달라는 말로, 오리엔테이션을 준비하는 걸 도와주겠다는 제공을 간접적으로 수락했으므로 정답이다.
(B) [x] help you prepare(준비를 돕다)와 같은 의미인 helping you set up을 사용하여 혼동을 준 오답이다.
(C) [x] 오리엔테이션 준비를 도와줄지를 물었는데, 이와 관련이 없는 그것은 아래층 1층에서 개최되었다는 말로 응답했으므로 오답이다. 질문의 orientation(오리엔테이션)을 나타낼 수 있는 It을 사용하여 혼동을 주었다.

06 | 평서문
캐나다 → 영국

We need to replace all of our outdated equipment.
(A) We visited many places so far.
(B) Put some paper in the printer.
(C) That will be expensive.

replace v. 교체하다 outdated adj. 구식의, 낡은 equipment n. 장비
expensive adj. 비싼

해석 우리는 우리의 모든 구식 장비를 교체해야 해요.
(A) 우리는 지금까지 많은 장소를 방문했어요.
(B) 프린터에 종이를 넣으세요.
(C) 그것은 비쌀 거예요.

해설 (A) [x] replace - places의 유사 발음 어휘를 사용하여 혼동을 준 오답이다.
(B) [x] 질문의 equipment(장비)에서 연상할 수 있는 회사 장비와 관련된 printer(프린터)를 사용하여 혼동을 준 오답이다.
(C) [o] 그것은 비쌀 것이라는 말로, 모든 구식 장비를 교체하는 것을 간접적으로 거절했으므로 정답이다.

07 | 부정 의문문
호주 → 미국

Doesn't Mr. Miyazaki want to transfer to another department?
(A) Yes, but I'm not sure which one.
(B) He transferred the funds today.
(C) Another closure was announced.

transfer v. 이동하다, 넘겨주다 department n. 부서 fund n. 자금
closure n. 폐쇄 announce v. 발표하다

해석 Mr. Miyazaki는 다른 부서로 이동하고 싶어 하지 않나요?
(A) 네, 하지만 어느 부서인지 전 잘 몰라요.

(B) 그는 오늘 자정을 넘겼어요.
(C) 또 다른 폐쇄가 발표되었어요.

해설 (A) [o] Yes로 Mr. Miyazaki가 다른 부서로 이동하고 싶어 한다고 전달한 후, 어느 부서인지 자신은 잘 모른다는 부연 설명을 했으므로 정답이다.
(B) [x] transfer - transferred의 유사 발음 어휘를 사용하여 혼동을 준 오답이다.
(C) [x] 질문의 another를 반복 사용하여 혼동을 준 오답이다.

08 | 평서문
미국 → 호주

It's not the best time for employees to go on holiday.
(A) Yes, an orientation for employees.
(B) We're really busy these days.
(C) I spent it with my family.

employee n. 직원 holiday n. 휴가

해석 지금은 직원들이 휴가를 가기에 최적의 시기가 아니에요.
(A) 네, 직원들을 위한 오리엔테이션이요.
(B) 우리는 요즘 정말 바빠요.
(C) 저는 가족과 함께 보냈어요.

해설 (A) [x] 질문의 employees를 반복 사용하여 혼동을 주었다.
(B) [o] 우리는 요즘 정말 바쁘다는 말로, 지금은 직원들이 휴가를 가기에 최적의 시기가 아니라는 의견에 동의했으므로 정답이다.
(C) [x] 질문의 holiday(휴가)를 나타낼 수 있는 it을 사용하여 혼동을 준 오답이다.

09 | 부가 의문문
영국 → 호주

You're stopping by my studio on Friday, aren't you?
(A) Yes, I left it in your studio.
(B) I won't be able to make it.
(C) It's on the next street.

stop by 들르다 make it ~할 수 있다, ~에 참석하다

해석 당신은 금요일에 제 스튜디오에 들를 거죠, 그렇지 않나요?
(A) 네, 저는 그것을 당신의 스튜디오에 두고 왔어요.
(B) 저는 그러지 못할 것 같아요.
(C) 그것은 다음 거리에 있어요.

해설 (A) [x] 질문의 studio를 반복 사용하여 혼동을 준 오답이다. Yes까지만 듣고 정답으로 고르지 않도록 주의한다.
(B) [o] 자신은 그러지 못할 것 같다는 말로, 금요일에 상대방의 스튜디오에 들르지 못한다는 것을 전달했으므로 정답이다.
(C) [x] 질문의 studio(스튜디오)를 나타낼 수 있는 It을 사용하여 혼동을 준 오답이다.

10 | 평서문
영국 → 캐나다

I suggest putting new brakes on your vehicle.
(A) Please make the repairs.
(B) They're open to suggestions.
(C) Yes, I purchased a new car.

vehicle n. 차량 repair n. 수리 suggestion n. 제안
purchase v. 구매하다

해석 당신의 차량에 새 브레이크를 장착하는 것을 제안드립니다.
(A) 수리해 주세요.
(B) 그들은 제안에 열려 있습니다.
(C) 네, 저는 새 차를 구매했어요.

해설 (A) [o] 수리해 달라는 말로, 새 브레이크를 장착하라는 제안을 수락했으므로 정답이다.
(B) [x] suggest - suggestions의 유사 발음 어휘를 사용하여 혼동을 준 오답이다.
(C) [x] 질문의 new를 반복 사용하고, vehicle(차량)과 관련 있는 car(차)를 사용하여 혼동을 준 오답이다.

11 | 조동사 의문문
미국 → 캐나다

Does the overhead compartment have enough room for my bag?
(A) Please place it under your seat.
(B) It is a very nice suitcase.
(C) We'll be landing very soon.

overhead adj. 머리 위의 compartment n. 칸 room n. 공간
place v. 놓다 suitcase n. 여행 가방 land v. 착륙하다

해석 머리 위의 칸에 제 가방을 넣을 충분한 공간이 있나요?
(A) 당신의 좌석 아래에 놓아주세요.
(B) 그것은 아주 멋진 여행 가방이에요.
(C) 우리는 곧 착륙할 거예요.

해설 (A) [o] 당신의 좌석 아래에 놓으라는 말로, 머리 위의 칸에 가방을 넣을 충분한 공간이 없음을 간접적으로 전달했으므로 정답이다.
(B) [x] 질문의 bag(가방)과 관련 있는 suitcase(여행 가방)를 사용하여 혼동을 준 오답이다.
(C) [x] 머리 위의 칸에 가방을 넣을 충분한 공간이 있는지를 물었는데, 이와 관련이 없는 우리는 곧 착륙할 것이라는 말로 응답했으므로 오답이다.

12 | 평서문
영국 → 호주

I've invited another interior designer to my house tomorrow.
(A) Really? I prefer the first apartment.
(B) I hope the consultation goes well.
(C) The exterior is being painted.

consultation n. 상담 exterior n. 외관, 외부

해석 저는 내일 또 다른 인테리어 디자이너를 제 집에 초대했어요.
(A) 정말요? 저는 첫 번째 아파트를 더 선호해요.
(B) 상담이 잘 진행되기를 바라요.
(C) 외관이 칠해지는 중이에요.

해설 (A) [x] 질문의 house(집)에서 연상할 수 있는 주거 공간과 관련된 apartment(아파트)를 사용하여 혼동을 준 오답이다.
(B) [o] 상담이 잘 진행되기를 바란다는 말로, 인테리어 디자이너를 초대한 것에 대한 응원의 메시지를 전달했으므로 정답이다.
(C) [x] 질문의 interior(인테리어, 내부)와 반대 의미인 exterior(외관, 외부)를 사용하여 혼동을 준 오답이다.

13 | 부가 의문문
영국 → 미국

You've visited this city in the past, right?
(A) My friend will be here in June.
(B) It's past the library.
(C) On several occasions, actually.

past n. 과거; adv. 지나서 occasion n. 차례, 시기, 경우

해석 당신은 과거에 이 도시를 방문한 적이 있어요, 그렇죠?

(A) 제 친구가 6월에 이곳에 올 거예요.
(B) 그것은 도서관을 지나서 있어요.
(C) 사실, 여러 차례요.

해설 (A) [×] 질문의 this city(이 도시)를 나타낼 수 있는 here를 사용하여 혼동을 준 오답이다.
(B) [×] 질문의 past(과거)를 '지나서'라는 의미의 부사로 반복 사용하여 혼동을 준 오답이다.
(C) [○] 사실 여러 차례라는 말로, 과거에 이 도시를 방문한 적이 있음을 간접적으로 전달했으므로 정답이다.

14 | 부정 의문문   미국 → 캐나다

Didn't you go on an excursion during your vacation?
(A) There wasn't enough time.
(B) Well, what would you like to do?
(C) The hotel staff will book one for us.

excursion n. 여행, 여행 일정 vacation n. 휴가 book v. 예약하다

해설 휴가 중에 여행을 가지 않았나요?
(A) 시간이 충분하지 않았어요.
(B) 음, 당신은 무엇을 하고 싶은가요?
(C) 호텔 직원이 우리를 위해 하나 예약해 줄 거예요.

해설 (A) [○] 시간이 충분하지 않았다는 말로, 휴가 중에 여행을 가지 않았음을 간접적으로 전달했으므로 정답이다.
(B) [×] 휴가 중에 여행을 가지 않았는지를 물었는데, 이와 관련이 없는 당신은 무엇을 하고 싶은지 되물었으므로 오답이다.
(C) [×] 질문의 excursion(여행)에서 연상할 수 있는 hotel(호텔)을 사용하여 혼동을 준 오답이다.

15 | 조동사 의문문   캐나다 → 영국

Should we edit the pictures before printing them?
(A) Everyone met the photographer.
(B) They could be a little brighter.
(C) It is my new camera.

edit v. 편집하다 bright adj. 밝은

해설 사진들을 출력하기 전에 편집해야 할까요?
(A) 모두가 사진작가를 만났어요.
(B) 그것들이 조금 더 밝아도 좋아요.
(C) 그것은 저의 새 카메라예요.

해설 (A) [×] 질문의 pictures(사진들)와 관련 있는 photographer(사진작가)를 사용하여 혼동을 준 오답이다.
(B) [○] 그것들이 조금 더 밝아도 좋다는 말로, 사진들을 출력하기 전에 편집하는 것을 간접적으로 제안했으므로 정답이다.
(C) [×] 질문의 pictures(사진들)와 관련 있는 camera(카메라)를 사용하여 혼동을 준 오답이다.

16 | Be동사 의문문   미국 → 캐나다

Is the S12 sedan going to be launched in October?
(A) Not until next year.
(B) A sports utility vehicle.
(C) September was unusually cool.

launch v. 출시하다 sports utility vehicle (SUV) 스포츠 유틸리티 차량
unusually adv. 이례적으로

해설 S12 세단이 10월에 출시될 예정인가요?
(A) 다음 해까지는 아니에요.
(B) 스포츠 유틸리티 차량이요.
(C) 9월은 이례적으로 시원했어요.

해설 (A) [○] 다음 해까지는 아니라는 말로, S12 세단이 10월에 출시될 예정이 아님을 간접적으로 전달했으므로 정답이다.
(B) [×] 질문의 sedan(세단)에서 연상할 수 있는 차종과 관련된 sports utility vehicle(스포츠 유틸리티 차량)을 사용하여 혼동을 준 오답이다.
(C) [×] 질문의 October(10월)에서 연상할 수 있는 달과 관련된 September(9월)를 사용하여 혼동을 준 오답이다.

17 | 선택 의문문   캐나다 → 미국

Should I post the job advertisement now, or will you review it first?
(A) There were many applicants.
(B) Can you print it out for me?
(C) Let's watch a preview first.

post v. 게시하다 advertisement n. 광고 applicant n. 지원자
preview n. 예고편

해설 제가 채용 광고를 지금 게시할까요, 아니면 당신이 먼저 검토하실 건가요?
(A) 지원자가 많았어요.
(B) 그것을 인쇄해 주실 수 있나요?
(C) 먼저 예고편을 봅시다.

해설 (A) [×] 질문의 job advertisement(채용 광고)와 관련 있는 applicants(지원자)를 사용하여 혼동을 준 오답이다.
(B) [○] 그것을 인쇄해 줄 수 있는지 되물어, 먼저 검토하는 것을 간접적으로 선택했으므로 정답이다.
(C) [×] review - preview의 유사 발음 어휘를 사용하여 혼동을 준 오답이다.

18 | 제안 의문문   호주 → 캐나다

Would you like to upgrade your seat for the flight?
(A) The most recent update.
(B) Please find your seat.
(C) That depends on the cost.

upgrade v. 등급을 올리다 flight n. 항공편 recent adj. 최근의
depend v. ~에 달려 있다 cost n. 비용

해설 항공편 좌석 등급을 올리시고 싶으신가요?
(A) 가장 최근의 업데이트예요.
(B) 당신의 좌석을 찾으세요.
(C) 그것은 비용에 달려 있어요.

해설 (A) [×] upgrade - update의 유사 발음 어휘를 사용하여 혼동을 준 오답이다.
(B) [×] 질문의 seat을 반복 사용하여 혼동을 준 오답이다.
(C) [○] 그것은 비용에 달려 있다는 말로, 항공편 좌석 등급을 올리고 싶을지 모른다는 것을 전달했으므로 정답이다.

19 | 조동사 의문문   미국 → 호주

Does the daily lunch special come with French fries?
(A) All side dishes cost extra.
(B) I'll check on your order.
(C) We specialized in that.

lunch special 점심 특선 메뉴 extra adv. 추가로
specialize v. 전문적으로 하다

해석 일일 점심 특선 메뉴에 감자튀김이 함께 나오나요?
(A) 모든 곁들임 요리는 추가 비용이 듭니다.
(B) 제가 당신의 주문을 확인해 볼게요.
(C) 저희는 그것을 전문적으로 했어요.

해설 (A) [o] 모든 곁들임 요리는 추가 비용이 든다는 말로, 일일 점심 특선 메뉴에 감자튀김이 함께 나오지 않는다는 것을 간접적으로 전달했으므로 정답이다.
(B) [x] 질문의 lunch special(점심 특선 메뉴)과 관련 있는 order(주문)를 사용하여 혼동을 준 오답이다.
(C) [x] special - specialized의 유사 발음 어휘를 사용하여 혼동을 준 오답이다.

20 | 선택 의문문
호주 → 영국

Do you want me to send the package by express or regular mail?
(A) The express bus is leaving.
(B) To ship some goods overseas.
(C) There's no need to rush.

package n. 소포 express adj. 속달의, 급행의 regular adj. 일반적인
overseas adv. 해외로 rush n. 서두름, 급함

해석 제가 소포를 속달 우편으로 보내기를 원하시나요, 아니면 일반 우편으로 보내기를 원하시나요?
(A) 급행 버스가 떠나고 있어요.
(B) 해외로 물건을 배송하기 위해서요.
(C) 서두를 필요가 없어요.

해설 (A) [x] 질문의 express를 반복 사용하여 혼동을 준 오답이다.
(B) [x] 질문의 mail(우편)과 관련 있는 ship(배송하다)을 사용하여 혼동을 준 오답이다.
(C) [o] 서두를 필요가 없다는 말로, 일반 우편으로 보내는 것을 간접적으로 선택했으므로 정답이다.

PART 3

DAY 05 회사 업무 및 사무기기

빈출 문제 집중 훈련
p.30

01 (D)	02 (B)	03 (A)	04 (A)	05 (B)
06 (A)	07 (C)	08 (B)	09 (C)	10 (C)
11 (A)	12 (B)	13 (A)	14 (C)	15 (A)
16 (A)	17 (C)	18 (D)		

[01-03]
호주 → 미국

Questions 01-03 refer to the following conversation.

M: Bethany, have you been able to log in to our company's online records database today? I'm trying to locate some client files, but [01]whenever I enter my ID and password, I get an error message saying that my account is locked.

W: That's strange. Hold on a minute... Yeah, I was just able to sign in like usual.

M: Hmm... [02]I'd better call Ms. Sheppard in the IT department to ask what is going on.

W: Good idea. In the meantime, why don't you write down the names of the files you are trying to retrieve? [03]I'm not busy right now, so I can find them in the database for you.

locate v. 찾아내다 account n. 계정 in the meantime 그 사이에
retrieve v. 검색하다, 되찾아오다

해석
01-03번은 다음 대화에 관한 문제입니다.
남: Bethany, 오늘 우리 회사의 온라인 기록 데이터베이스에 로그인할 수 있었나요? 저는 몇몇 고객 파일을 찾아내려고 하는데, [01]ID와 비밀번호를 입력할 때마다 제 계정이 잠겨 있다는 오류 메시지가 떠요.
여: 이상하네요. 잠시만요... 네, 저는 방금 평소처럼 로그인할 수 있었어요.
남: 흠... [02]IT 부서의 Ms. Sheppard에게 전화해서 무슨 일이 일어나고 있는지 물어보는 게 좋겠어요.
여: 좋은 생각이에요. 그 사이에, 검색하려고 하는 파일들의 이름을 적어두는 게 어떠세요? [03]저는 지금 바쁘지 않아서, 당신을 위해 데이터베이스에서 그것들을 찾아볼 수 있어요.

01 | 문제점 문제

해석 남자는 무슨 문제를 언급하는가?
(A) 데이터베이스가 불완전하다.
(B) 고객이 불만족했다.
(C) 작업 공간이 잠겨 있다.
(D) 계정에 접근할 수 없다.

해설 남자의 말에서 부정적인 표현이 언급된 주변을 주의 깊게 듣는다. 남자가 "whenever I enter my ID and password, I get an error message saying that my account is locked"라며 ID와 비밀번호를 입력할 때마다 계정이 잠겨 있다는 오류 메시지가 뜬다고 하였다. 따라서 (D)가 정답이다.

어휘 incomplete adj. 불완전한 dissatisfied adj. 불만족한
workspace n. 작업 공간 inaccessible adj. 접근할 수 없는

02 | 이유 문제

해석 남자는 왜 Ms. Sheppard에게 연락할 것인가?
(A) 비밀번호를 변경하기 위해
(B) 문제를 파악하기 위해
(C) 결정을 확인하기 위해
(D) 과제에 대해 논의하기 위해

해설 남자의 말에서 질문의 핵심 어구(Ms. Sheppard)가 언급된 주변을 주의 깊게 듣는다. 남자가 "I'd better call Ms. Sheppard in the IT department to ask what is going on."이라며 IT 부서의 Ms. Sheppard에게 전화해서 무슨 일이 일어나고 있는지 물어보는 게 좋겠다고 하였다. 따라서 (B)가 정답이다.

어휘 identify v. 파악하다 confirm v. 확인하다 decision n. 결정
assignment n. 과제, 임무

03 | 다음에 할 일 문제

해석 여자는 다음에 무엇을 할 것 같은가?
(A) 파일들을 찾는다.
(B) 애플리케이션을 설치한다.
(C) 회의 일정을 잡는다.

(D) 복사본을 인쇄한다.

해설 대화의 마지막 부분을 주의 깊게 듣는다. 여자가 "I'm not busy right now, so I can find them in the database for you."라며 지금 바쁘지 않아서, 남자를 위해 데이터베이스에서 그것들(파일들)을 찾아볼 수 있다고 하였다. 따라서 (A)가 정답이다.

어휘 install v. 설치하다

[04-06]

호주 → 미국

Questions 04-06 refer to the following conversation.

M: Patricia, ⁰⁵can you help me? I'm supposed to analyze the data from our recent market research, but ⁰⁴I'm preparing a presentation for a meeting with the company's shareholders. I don't have enough time to do both tasks, so I would really appreciate some assistance.

W: ⁰⁵Sure, I can help. I'll go over the figures and create a report summarizing all of the relevant information. I can begin right away.

M: Thank you! Please give me the report before you go home today, and ⁰⁶I'll read your research results early tomorrow morning. That should give me enough time to complete my presentation.

W: No problem. And let me know if you need me to do anything else.

analyze v. 분석하다   shareholder n. 주주   appreciate v. 감사하다
assistance n. 도움   go over 검토하다   figure n. 수치
summarize v. 요약하다   relevant adj. 관련된

해설

04-06번은 다음 대화에 관한 문제입니다.

남: Patricia, ⁰⁵저를 도와주실 수 있나요? 저는 최근 시장 조사의 데이터를 분석하기로 되어있는데, ⁰⁴회사 주주들과의 회의를 위한 발표를 준비하고 있어요. 두 업무를 모두 할 시간이 충분하지 않아서, 도움을 주신다면 정말 감사하겠습니다.

여: ⁰⁵물론이죠, 도와드릴게요. 제가 수치들을 검토하고 모든 관련 정보를 요약한 보고서를 작성할게요. 바로 시작할 수 있어요.

남: 감사합니다! 오늘 퇴근하기 전에 보고서를 주시면, ⁰⁶내일 아침 일찍 당신의 조사 결과를 읽을게요. 그러면 제 발표를 완성할 시간이 충분할 것 같네요.

여: 문제없어요. 그리고 제가 다른 일을 해야 한다면 알려주세요.

04 | 특정 세부 사항 문제

해석 남자는 어떤 유형의 행사를 준비하고 있는가?
(A) 주주 회의
(B) 교육 세션
(C) 회사 연회
(D) 무역 박람회

해설 대화에서 질문의 핵심 어구(preparing)가 언급된 주변을 주의 깊게 듣는다. 남자가 "I'm preparing a presentation for a meeting with the company's shareholders"라며 회사 주주들과의 회의를 위한 발표를 준비하고 있다고 하였다. 따라서 (A)가 정답이다.

어휘 banquet n. 연회   trade fair 무역 박람회

05 | 특정 세부 사항 문제

해석 여자는 무엇을 하는 데 동의하는가?
(A) 설문조사를 한다.
(B) 동료를 돕는다.
(C) 차트를 준비한다.
(D) 발표를 한다.

해설 여자의 말에서 질문의 핵심 어구(agree to do)와 관련된 내용을 주의 깊게 듣는다. 남자가 "can you help me?"라고 여자에게 도움을 청하자, 여자가 "Sure, I can help. I'll go over the figures and create a report summarizing all of the relevant information."이라며 도와주겠다면서 수치들을 검토하고 모든 관련 정보를 요약한 보고서를 작성하겠다고 하였다. 따라서 (B)가 정답이다.

어휘 survey n. 설문조사

06 | 다음에 할 일 문제

해석 남자는 내일 아침에 무엇을 할 것인가?
(A) 보고서를 읽는다.
(B) 조사를 수행한다.
(C) 과제를 제출한다.
(D) 이메일을 보낸다.

해설 질문의 핵심 어구(tomorrow morning)가 언급된 주변을 주의 깊게 듣는다. 남자가 "I'll read your research results early tomorrow morning"이라며 내일 아침 일찍 조사 결과를 읽겠다고 하였다. 따라서 (A)가 정답이다.

어휘 conduct v. 수행하다   submit v. 제출하다   assignment n. 과제

Paraphrasing

research results 조사 결과 → a report 보고서

[07-09]

캐나다 → 미국 → 호주

Questions 07-09 refer to the following conversation with three speakers.

M1: Natalie and Brad, do you think we should install automated payment machines in our shopping mall's parking lot?

W: Definitely. ⁰⁷I've heard many complaints from visitors about having to wait in line to pay our parking attendant.

M2: I agree. The system's very inefficient. Cars get backed up when there are many shoppers trying to exit the parking lot at the same time.

W: ⁰⁸Using automated machines in the lot will likely save us more money in the long run, since we wouldn't have to pay the wages of the parking attendants. ⁰⁹What do you think, Adam?

M1: Good point. ⁰⁹Let's bring this up to our manager at the staff meeting this afternoon.

automated adj. 자동의   complaint n. 불만   parking attendant 주차 요원
inefficient adj. 비효율적인   back up (교통, 일 등이) 밀리다
exit v. 나가다, 퇴장하다   lot n. 주차장, 부지   in the long run 결국에는
wage n. 임금   bring up 제기하다

해설

07-09번은 다음 세 명의 대화에 관한 문제입니다.

남1: Natalie 그리고 Brad, 우리 쇼핑몰의 주차장에 자동 결제 기계를 설치해야 한다고 생각하나요?

여: 물론이죠. ⁰⁷방문객들로부터 주차 요원에게 돈을 지불하기 위해 줄을 서서 기다려야 하는 것에 대한 불만을 많이 들었어요.

남2: 동의해요. 그 시스템은 매우 비효율적이에요. 많은 쇼핑객들이 동시에 주차장을 나가려고 할 때 차들이 밀려요.

여: ⁰⁸주차장에서 자동 기계를 사용하면 주차 요원들의 임금을 지불할 필요가

없기 때문에 결국에는 우리가 더 많은 돈을 절약할 수 있을 거예요. ⁰⁹어떻게 생각해요, Adam?
남1: 좋은 지적이네요. ⁰⁹오늘 오후 직원 회의에서 관리자에게 이 문제를 제기해 보죠.

07 | 이유 문제

해석 고객들이 왜 불만을 제기했는가?
(A) 세일 기간이 단축되었다.
(B) 기계 오류가 발생했다.
(C) 과정이 너무 오래 걸린다.
(D) 주차장이 너무 작다.

해설 질문의 핵심 어구(complaints)가 언급된 주변을 주의 깊게 듣는다. 여자가 "I've heard many complaints from visitors about having to wait in line to pay our parking attendant."라고 말하며 방문객들로부터 주차 요원에게 돈을 지불하기 위해 줄을 서서 기다려야 하는 것에 대한 불만을 많이 들었다고 했다. 따라서 (C)가 정답이다.

어휘 period n. 기간 occur v. 발생하다

08 | 언급 문제

해석 여자는 기계에 대해 무엇이라 말하는가?
(A) 다른 장소들에서 사용된다.
(B) 비용을 절감할 것이다.
(C) 회의에서 논의되었다.
(D) 완전히 수리되었다.

해설 여자의 말에서 질문의 핵심 어구(machines)가 언급된 주변을 주의 깊게 듣는다. 여자가 "Using automated machines in the lot will likely save us more money in the long run, since we wouldn't have to pay the wages of the parking attendants."라고 말하며 주차장에서 자동 기계를 사용하면 주차 요원들의 임금을 지불할 필요가 없기 때문에 결국에는 더 많은 돈을 절약할 수 있을 것이라고 했다. 따라서 (B)가 정답이다.

어휘 cut down 절감하다 expense n. 비용

Paraphrasing
save ~ more money 더 많은 돈을 절약하다 → cut down on expenses 비용을 절감하다

09 | 제안 문제

해석 Adam은 무엇을 제안하는가?
(A) 오후 모임 일정 변경하기
(B) 추가 직원 고용하기
(C) 관리자에게 아이디어 언급하기
(D) 고객들에게 할인 제공하기

해설 Adam의 말에서 제안과 관련된 표현이 언급된 다음을 주의 깊게 듣는다. 여자가 "What do you think, Adam?"이라며 Adam에게 어떻게 생각하는지 묻자, 남자1[Adam]이 "Let's bring this up to our manager at the staff meeting this afternoon."이라고 말하며 오후 직원 회의에서 관리자에게 이 문제를 제기해 보자고 하였다. 따라서 (C)가 정답이다.

어휘 gathering n. 모임 agent n. 직원 supervisor n. 관리자

Paraphrasing
bring this up to ~ manager 관리자에게 이 문제를 제기하다 → Mentioning an idea to a supervisor 관리자에게 아이디어 언급하기

[10-12]
Questions 10-12 refer to the following conversation.

영국 → 캐나다

W: Clyde, ¹⁰you've been assigned to the Henderson account. You'll be overseeing all of Mr. Henderson's assets and future investments. This will include his real estate sale that is scheduled to take place this Saturday.
M: OK. Debbie Meyers was previously in charge of that account, wasn't she? ¹¹I'd like to meet with her in order to be briefed on the status of that transaction.
W: Yes. ¹²She was in charge of it until her promotion last week. Seeing as how she handled the account for several years, it's a good idea for you two to communicate.

oversee v. 관리하다, 감독하다 asset n. 자산 investment n. 투자
real estate 부동산 be in charge of ~을 담당하다
brief v. 간단히 설명하다; adj. 간단한 status n. 현황 transaction n. 거래
promotion n. 승진

해석 10-12번은 다음 대화에 관한 문제입니다.
여: Clyde, ¹⁰당신은 Henderson 계좌를 담당하게 되었어요. Mr. Henderson의 모든 자산과 향후 투자를 관리하게 될 거예요. 이것은 이번 토요일에 진행될 예정인 그의 부동산 매각도 포함할 것이에요.
남: 알겠습니다. 이전에는 Debbie Meyers가 그 계좌를 담당했었죠, 그렇지 않나요? ¹¹저는 그 거래의 현황에 대해 간단히 설명을 받기 위해 그녀와 만나고 싶어요.
여: 네. ¹²그녀는 지난주 승진하기 전까지 그것을 담당했어요. 그녀가 수년간 그 계좌를 다룬 것을 감안하면, 두 분이 소통하는 것은 좋은 생각이에요.

10 | 주제 문제

해석 대화는 주로 무엇에 관한 것인가?
(A) 건물 견학
(B) 판매 촉진
(C) 계좌 관리
(D) 재정 상담가 고용

해설 대화의 주제를 묻는 문제이므로, 대화의 초반을 반드시 듣는다. 여자가 "you've been assigned to the Henderson account. You'll be overseeing all of Mr. Henderson's assets and future investments."라며 Clyde가 Henderson 계좌를 담당하게 되었다고 하고, Mr. Henderson의 모든 자산과 향후 투자를 관리하게 될 것이라고 한 후, 계좌 관리에 대한 내용으로 대화가 이어지고 있다. 따라서 (C)가 정답이다.

어휘 tour v. 견학하다, 둘러보다 promote v. 촉진하다 consultant n. 상담가

11 | 이유 문제

해석 남자는 왜 Debbie Meyers와 만나고 싶어 하는가?
(A) 정보를 얻기 위해
(B) 투자를 하기 위해
(C) 문서를 전달하기 위해
(D) 전근을 요청하기 위해

해설 질문의 핵심 어구(meet with Debbie Meyers)와 관련된 내용을 주의 깊게 듣는다. 남자가 "I'd like to meet with her[Debbie Meyers] in order to be briefed on the status of that transaction."이라며 거래의 현황에 대해 간단히 설명을 받기 위해 Debbie Meyers와 만나고 싶다고 하였다. 따라서 (A)가 정답이다.

어휘 obtain v. 얻다 pass on 전달하다 transfer n. 전근, 이동

12 | 언급 문제

해석 여자는 Debbie Meyers에 대해 무엇을 말하는가?
(A) 회사에서 은퇴했다.
(B) 더 높은 직위를 받았다.
(C) 도움을 요청했다.
(D) 부서 전체를 감독한다.

해설 여자의 말에서 질문의 핵심 어구(Debbie Meyers)와 관련된 내용을 주의 깊게 듣는다. 여자가 "She[Debbie Meyers] was in charge of it until her promotion last week."이라며 Debbie Meyers가 지난주 승진하기 전까지 그것을 담당했다고 한 것을 통해, 그녀가 더 높은 직위를 받았음을 알 수 있다. 따라서 (B)가 정답이다.

어휘 retire v. 은퇴하다 position n. 직위 assistance n. 도움
supervise v. 감독하다 division n. 부서

Paraphrasing

promotion 승진 → was given a higher position 더 높은 직위를 받았다

[13-15]

🎧 미국 → 캐나다

Questions 13-15 refer to the following conversation.

W: Mr. Jones, ¹³**we need to book a space for the upcoming business services fair**. The convention center has only two booths left. One is by the front doors and the other is close to the stage.
M: Thanks for reminding me. Let's reserve the spot near the entrance. Our booth should get a lot of attention from passing visitors.
W: ¹⁴**The organizer told me the reason that space isn't booked yet is because it's the smallest one.** It's only three meters wide. Do you think that's large enough?
M: Yes. We can create smaller banners and posters than we had originally planned. ¹⁵**Could you complete the booking right away?**

book v. 예약하다 upcoming adj. 다가오는 reserve v. 예약하다
spot n. 자리, 장소 entrance n. 입구 attention n. 관심
passing adj. 지나가는 organizer n. 기획자, 주최자 originally adv. 원래
complete v. 완료하다

해석
13-15번은 다음 대화에 관한 문제입니다.

여: Mr. Jones, ¹³우리는 다가오는 사업 서비스 박람회를 위한 공간을 예약해야 해요. 컨벤션 센터에는 두 개의 부스만 남아 있어요. 하나는 정문 근처에 있고 다른 하나는 무대 근처에 있어요.
남: 상기시켜줘서 고마워요. 입구 근처의 자리를 예약합시다. 우리 부스는 지나가는 방문객들로부터 많은 관심을 받을 거예요.
여: ¹⁴기획자가 저에게 말하길, 그 공간이 아직 예약되지 않은 이유는 가장 작은 공간이기 때문이라고 해요. 너비가 3미터밖에 되지 않는대요. 그것이 충분히 크다고 생각하시나요?
남: 네. 우리가 원래 계획했던 것보다 더 작은 배너와 포스터를 만들면 돼요. ¹⁵지금 바로 예약을 완료해 주시겠어요?

13 | 주제 문제

해석 화자들은 주로 무엇에 대해 논의하고 있는가?
(A) 행사를 위한 빈자리
(B) 전시할 제품들

(C) 박람회에서 제공되는 서비스
(D) 시설 보수

해설 대화의 주제를 묻는 문제이므로, 대화의 초반을 반드시 듣는다. 여자가 "we need to book a space for the upcoming business services fair"라며 다가오는 사업 서비스 박람회를 위한 공간을 예약해야 한다고 말한 뒤, 행사를 위한 빈자리에 대한 내용으로 대화가 이어지고 있다. 따라서 (A)가 정답이다.

어휘 vacancy n. 빈자리, 공석 display n. 전시, 진열 facility n. 시설

14 | 언급 문제

해석 여자는 입구 근처 부스에 대해 무엇을 말하는가?
(A) 다른 것들보다 더 비싸다.
(B) 이미 예약되었다.
(C) 넓은 공간을 제공하지 않는다.
(D) 포스터를 위한 받침대가 있다.

해설 여자의 말에서 질문의 핵심 어구(the booth near the entrance)와 관련된 내용을 주의 깊게 듣는다. 여자가 "The organizer told me the reason that space isn't booked yet is because it's the smallest one."이라며 기획자가 그녀에게 말하길, 그 공간이 아직 예약되지 않은 이유는 가장 작은 공간이기 때문이라고 한 것을 통해, 입구 근처 부스가 넓은 공간을 제공하지 않는다는 것을 알 수 있다. 따라서 (C)가 정답이다.

15 | 다음에 할 일 문제

해석 여자는 다음에 무엇을 할 것 같은가?
(A) 컨벤션 센터에 연락한다.
(B) 부스를 설치한다.
(C) 예약을 취소한다.
(D) 배너를 건다.

해설 대화의 마지막 부분을 주의 깊게 듣는다. 남자가 여자에게 "Could you complete the booking right away?"라며 지금 바로 예약을 완료해 주겠냐고 물었다. 따라서 (A)가 정답이다.

어휘 contact v. 연락하다 set up 설치하다 hang v. 걸다

[16-18]

🎧 캐나다 → 영국

Questions 16-18 refer to the following conversation.

M: Excuse me, Tanya. I'm working on the budget analysis for our project. I need to calculate the expected expenses for construction materials, permits, and blueprints. But ¹⁶**I haven't received any price estimates from you yet**.
W: I apologize. ¹⁷**I'm still waiting to hear back from the company that supplies our materials.** However, I do have the other estimates you require at my desk. I can get those for you right now.
M: Honestly, I'm most concerned about the material costs. Would you mind reaching out to the vendor this morning? The budget proposal is due tomorrow, and it's vital that I don't miss the deadline.
W: Got it. ¹⁸**I'll contact the supplier immediately and request those estimates for you.**

budget n. 예산 calculate v. 계산하다 construction n. 건설
permit n. 허가증 blueprint n. 설계도, 청사진 price estimate 가격 견적
reach out 연락하다 vendor n. 공급업체 proposal n. 제안서
vital adj. 매우 중요한, 필수적인 supplier n. 공급업체
immediately adv. 즉시

해석
16-18번은 다음 대화에 관한 문제입니다.

남: 실례합니다, Tanya. 저는 우리 프로젝트의 예산 분석을 작업하는 중이에요. 건설 자재, 허가증, 그리고 설계도에 대한 예상 비용을 계산해야 합니다. 하지만 ¹⁶아직 당신에게서 어떤 가격 견적도 받지 못했어요.
여: 죄송합니다. ¹⁷저는 아직 우리 자재를 공급하는 회사로부터 답변을 기다리고 있어요. 하지만, 당신이 요청하신 다른 견적들은 제 책상에 있어요. 지금 바로 가져다 드릴 수 있습니다.
남: 솔직히, 저는 자재 비용에 가장 관심이 있어요. 오늘 오전에 공급업체에 연락해 주실 수 있을까요? 예산 제안서를 내일까지 제출해야 하고, 마감일을 놓치지 않는 것이 매우 중요해요.
여: 알겠습니다. ¹⁸즉시 공급업체에 연락해서 견적을 요청할게요.

16 | 문제점 문제

해석 남자는 어떤 문제점을 말하는가?
(A) 견적을 받지 못했다.
(B) 건설 프로젝트가 지연되었다.
(C) 가격 견적이 너무 높다.
(D) 건물 임대차 계약이 만료되었다.

해설 남자의 말에서 부정적인 표현이 언급된 주변을 주의 깊게 듣는다. 남자가 "I haven't received any price estimates from you yet"이라며 어떤 가격 견적도 받지 못했다고 하였다. 따라서 (A)가 정답이다.

어휘 quote n. 견적 lease n. 임대차 계약 expire v. 만료되다

17 | 언급 문제

해석 여자는 건물 자재 공급업체에 대해 무엇을 말하는가?
(A) 공급품을 배달할 수 없다.
(B) 대금을 받지 못했다.
(C) 아직 그녀에게 연락하지 않았다.
(D) 가격 목록을 보냈다.

해설 여자의 말에서 질문의 핵심 어구(building materials supplier)와 관련된 내용을 주의 깊게 듣는다. 여자가 "I'm still waiting to hear back from the company that supplies our materials."라며 자재를 공급하는 회사로부터 답변을 기다리고 있다고 했으므로 건물 자재 공급업체는 아직 그녀에게 연락하지 않았음을 알 수 있다. 따라서 (C)가 정답이다.

어휘 deliver v. 배달하다 supply n. 공급품, 공급 payment n. 대금, 지불 price list 가격 목록

18 | 다음에 할 일 문제

해석 여자는 다음에 무엇을 할 것 같은가?
(A) 마감일 연장을 요청한다.
(B) 승인을 기다린다.
(C) 예산 제안서를 회수한다.
(D) 가격 견적을 요청한다.

해설 대화의 마지막 부분을 주의 깊게 듣는다. 여자가 "I'll contact the supplier immediately and request those estimates for you."라며 즉시 공급업체에 연락해서 견적을 요청하겠다고 한 것을 통해 여자가 가격 견적을 요청할 것임을 알 수 있다. 따라서 (D)가 정답이다.

어휘 extension n. 연장 authorization n. 승인 retrieve v. 회수하다, 되찾다

Paraphrasing
request ~ estimates 견적을 요청하다 → Ask for price estimates 가격 견적을 요청하다

고난도 문제 완전 정복   p.32

| 01 (B) | 02 (D) | 03 (C) | 04 (A) | 05 (B) |
| 06 (B) | 07 (C) | 08 (B) | 09 (C) | |

[01-03]
영국 → 호주

Questions 01-03 refer to the following conversation.

W: ⁰¹**Thank you for coming in to be interviewed for the graphic designer position at our advertising agency**, David. Now that the interview is over, do you have any questions?
M: Yes, I do. The job posting mentioned that you provide bonuses based on performance. Could you explain how this system works?
W: Of course. ⁰²**Evaluations are done every June**, and a high enough score will result in a bonus payment. ⁰³**All employees qualify for this incentive program.**
M: All employees qualify? ⁰³So that includes new staff as well.
W: Exactly. We think it is important that every worker has a chance to be rewarded.
M: That's good to hear. It seems like a great way to keep everyone motivated.

advertising agency 광고 대행사 job posting 구인 공고 bonus n. 상여금
performance n. 성과 evaluation n. 평가 incentive n. 장려금
reward v. 보상하다 motivate v. 동기를 부여하다

해석
01-03번은 다음 대화에 관한 문제입니다.

여: ⁰¹저희 광고 대행사의 그래픽 디자이너 직책에 대한 면접을 보러 와주셔서 감사합니다, David. 이제 면접이 끝났는데, 혹시 질문이 있으신가요?
남: 네, 있습니다. 구인 공고에는 성과에 따른 상여금을 제공한다고 언급되어 있었는데요. 이 시스템이 어떻게 운영되는지 설명해 주실 수 있나요?
여: 물론이죠. ⁰²평가는 매년 6월에 이루어지고, 충분히 높은 점수를 받으면 상여금이 지급됩니다. ⁰³모든 직원들이 이 장려금 프로그램의 대상이 됩니다.
남: 모든 직원이 대상이 돼요? ⁰³그럼 신입 직원들도 포함되는군요.
여: 정확해요. 저희는 모든 직원이 보상받을 기회를 갖는 것이 중요하다고 생각합니다.
남: 그것 좋네요. 모두가 동기 부여되도록 유지하는 좋은 방법인 것 같습니다.

01 | 장소 문제

해석 대화는 어디에서 일어나는 것 같은가?
(A) 부동산 중개소에서
(B) 광고 회사에서
(C) 소프트웨어 회사에서
(D) 금융 기관에서

해설 대화에서 장소와 관련된 표현을 놓치지 않고 듣는다. 여자가 "Thank you for coming in to be interviewed for the graphic designer position at our advertising agency"라며 광고 대행사의 그래픽 디자이너 직책에 대한 면접을 보러 와줘서 감사하다고 하였다. 따라서 (B)가 정답이다.

어휘 real estate 부동산 institution n. 기관

Paraphrasing
advertising agency 광고 대행사 → advertising firm 광고 회사

02 | 언급 문제

해석 여자는 평가에 대해 무엇이라 말하는가?
(A) 최근에 도입되었다.
(B) 빈도가 증가할 것이다.
(C) 갱신된 기준을 포함한다.
(D) 매년 실시된다.

해설 여자의 말에서 질문의 핵심 어구(evaluations)가 언급된 주변을 주의 깊게 듣는다. 여자가 "Evaluations are done every June"이라며 평가는 매월 6월에 이루어진다고 하였다. 따라서 (D)가 정답이다.

어휘 recently adv. 최근에 frequency n. 빈도 criteria n. 기준
annually adv. 매년

03 | 의도 파악 문제

해석 남자는 왜 "모든 직원이 대상이 돼요?"라고 말하는가?
(A) 불만을 제기하기 위해
(B) 결정을 비판하기 위해
(C) 요점을 확인하기 위해
(D) 우려를 표하기 위해

해설 질문의 인용어구(All employees qualify?)가 언급된 주변을 주의 깊게 듣는다. 여자가 "All employees qualify for this incentive program."이라며 모든 직원들이 장려금 프로그램의 대상이 된다고 하자, 남자가 "So that includes new staff as well."이라며 그럼 신입 직원들도 포함된다고 한 것을 통해 남자가 요점을 확인하고 있음을 알 수 있다. 따라서 (C)가 정답이다.

어휘 address v. 제기하다, 다루다 criticize v. 비판하다 concern n. 우려

[04-06]
캐나다 → 호주 → 영국

Questions 04-06 refer to the following conversation with three speakers.

M1: Leon, ⁰⁴do you have the advertisement drafts made by the marketing team? They're designing some billboards for our latest shampoo line, and ⁰⁵I still haven't been provided with the drafts.

M2: No, I don't, Mr. Kelly. The team leader was supposed to send them to me this morning, but she never did.

M1: Katie, could you call her and find out when we can expect them?

W: Actually, I was planning to drop something off at the marketing department in a few minutes. ⁰⁶I'll ask the head of that team about the drafts when I get there.

M1: Leon and I will need the drafts before our presentation about the campaign to the corporate executives tomorrow morning.

draft n. 초안 billboard n. 광고판 corporate adj. 기업의
executive n. 임원

해석
04-06번은 다음 세 명의 대화에 관한 문제입니다.
남1: Leon, 마케팅팀에서 만든 광고 초안이 있나요? 그들은 우리의 최신 샴푸 라인을 위한 광고판을 디자인하고 있는데, ⁰⁵저는 아직 초안을 받지 못했어요.
남2: 아니요, 없습니다, Mr. Kelly. 팀장이 오늘 아침에 그것들을 저에게 보내기로 되어 있었지만, 보내지 않았어요.
남1: Katie, 그녀에게 전화해서 그것들을 언제 받을 수 있는지 알아봐 줄래요?
여: 사실, 저는 몇 분 후에 마케팅 부서에 뭔가를 전달하러 갈 예정이었어요. ⁰⁶제가 그곳에 가면 그 팀의 책임자에게 초안에 대해 물어볼게요.
남1: Leon과 저는 내일 아침 기업 임원들에게 할 캠페인에 관한 발표 전에 초안이 필요할 거예요.

04 | 주제 문제

해석 화자들이 주로 논의하고 있는 것은 무엇인가?
(A) 제품 광고
(B) 백화점 전시
(C) 성공적인 제품 라인
(D) 시장 조사

해설 대화의 주제를 묻는 문제이므로, 대화의 초반을 반드시 듣는다. 남자1이 "do you have the advertisement drafts made by the marketing team?"이라며 마케팅팀에서 만든 광고 초안이 있냐고 물은 후, 제품 광고에 대한 내용으로 대화가 이어지고 있다. 따라서 (A)가 정답이다.

어휘 department store 백화점

05 | 문제점 문제

해석 화자들은 무슨 문제를 언급하는가?
(A) 마케팅 회의가 연기되었다.
(B) 홍보 자료를 받지 못했다.
(C) 프로젝트 일정이 업데이트되지 않았다.
(D) 팀원들이 부재중이었다.

해설 대화에서 부정적인 표현이 언급된 주변을 주의 깊게 듣는다. 남자1이 "I still haven't been provided with the drafts"라며 아직 초안을 받지 못했다고 하였다. 따라서 (B)가 정답이다.

어휘 postpone v. 연기하다 promotional adj. 홍보의
unavailable adj. 부재중인, 이용할 수 없는

06 | 다음에 할 일 문제

해석 여자는 다음에 무엇을 할 것 같은가?
(A) 기사 초안 개요를 작성한다.
(B) 팀장을 만난다.
(C) 발표에 참석한다.
(D) 캠페인을 승인한다.

해설 대화의 마지막 부분을 주의 깊게 듣는다. 여자가 "I'll ask the head of that team about the drafts when I get there[marketing department]."라며 마케팅 부서에 가면 팀의 책임자에게 초안에 대해 물어보겠다고 하였다. 따라서 (B)가 정답이다.

어휘 outline v. 개요를 작성하다 approve v. 승인하다

[07-09]
호주 → 영국

Questions 07-09 refer to the following conversation and pie chart.

M: Hey, Hadley. ⁰⁷I'd like you to lead the software development team when Raoul retires in two weeks. ⁰⁸If you accept the position, I'll tell our developers at the meeting this afternoon.

W: Really? I'm honored that you selected me for the position. I'd love to take on that role. Do you know what my first assignment will be?

M: Yes. You'll be overseeing a project updating one of our applications.

W: Are you referring to Text Monkey? I know it was downloaded the least in April.

M: No. That application has already been dealt with. Actually, ⁰⁹I'm talking about the one with the second fewest downloads that month. It must be improved.

lead v. 이끌다   retire v. 은퇴하다   honored adj. 영광인
position n. 자리, 위치   oversee v. 감독하다   refer to ~을 말하다, 언급하다
least adv. 가장 적게   improve v. 개선하다

해석
07-09번은 다음 대화와 원 그래프에 관한 문제입니다.

남: 안녕하세요, Hadley. ⁰⁷2주 후에 Raoul이 은퇴하면 당신이 소프트웨어 개발팀을 이끌어주었으면 합니다. ⁰⁸만약 당신이 그 자리를 수락한다면, 오늘 오후 회의에서 우리 개발자들에게 알리겠습니다.
여: 정말요? 저를 그 자리에 선택해 주셔서 영광입니다. 그 역할을 맡고 싶어요. 제 첫 번째 임무가 무엇이 될지 아시나요?
남: 네. 당신은 우리 애플리케이션 중 하나를 업데이트하는 프로젝트를 감독하게 될 거예요.
여: Text Monkey를 말씀하시는 건가요? 4월에 가장 적게 다운로드되었던 것으로 알고 있어요.
남: 아니요. 그 애플리케이션은 이미 처리되었어요. 사실, ⁰⁹저는 그 달에 다운로드가 두 번째로 적었던 애플리케이션을 말하는 겁니다. 그것은 꼭 개선되어야 해요.

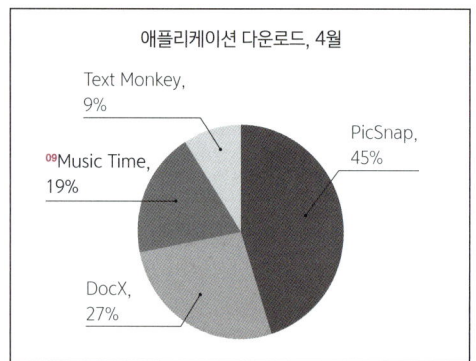

07 | 주제 문제

해석 대화는 주로 무엇에 관한 것인가?
(A) 부서 축소
(B) 다가오는 제품 출시
(C) 리더십 변경
(D) 초과 근무 요청

해설 대화의 주제를 묻는 문제이므로, 대화의 초반을 반드시 듣는다. 남자가 "I'd like you to lead the software development team when Raoul retires in two weeks."라며 2주 후에 Raoul이 은퇴하면 소프트웨어 개발팀을 이끌어주었으면 한다고 하며, 리더십 변경에 대한 내용으로 대화가 이어지고 있다. 따라서 (C)가 정답이다.

어휘 downsizing n. 축소   upcoming adj. 다가오는   launch n. 출시
overtime n. 초과 근무

08 | 특정 세부 사항 문제

해석 남자는 무엇을 계획하고 있는가?
(A) 정기 직원 회의를 연기한다.
(B) 직원들에게 결정을 알린다.
(C) 경쟁사의 프로그램을 다운로드 한다.
(D) 다른 역할을 맡는 것을 고려한다.

해설 질문의 핵심 어구(planning to do)와 관련된 내용을 주의 깊게 듣는다. 남자가 "If you accept the position, I'll tell our developers at the meeting this afternoon."이라며 여자가 그 자리를 수락한다면 오후 회의에서 개발자들에게 알리겠다고 하였다. 따라서 (B)가 정답이다.

어휘 postpone v. 연기하다   personnel n. 직원   competitor n. 경쟁사
take on ~을 맡다

09 | 시각 자료 문제

해석 시각 자료를 보아라. 어떤 애플리케이션이 개선될 것인가?
(A) PicSnap
(B) DocX
(C) Music Time
(D) Text Monkey

해설 제시된 원 그래프의 정보를 확인한 후 질문의 핵심 어구(be improved)와 관련된 내용을 주의 깊게 듣는다. 남자가 "I'm talking about the one with the second fewest downloads that month[April]. It must be improved."라며 그 달[4월]에 다운로드가 두 번째로 적었던 애플리케이션이 꼭 개선되어야 한다고 했고, 4월에 다운로드가 두 번째로 적은 것은 Music Time임을 원 그래프에서 알 수 있다. 따라서 (C)가 정답이다.

DAY 06 일상 생활 및 여행/여가

빈출 문제 집중 훈련   p.33

01 (C)	02 (D)	03 (A)	04 (C)	05 (A)
06 (B)	07 (D)	08 (A)	09 (C)	10 (B)
11 (C)	12 (A)	13 (D)	14 (A)	15 (C)
16 (B)	17 (C)	18 (A)		

[01-03]   캐나다 → 미국

Questions 01-03 refer to the following conversation.

M: ⁰¹I really like this new public library. It's more spacious and modern than I had anticipated. And ⁰²I'm impressed with how many computer stations are available for use.
W: I agree. I plan on coming here more often. Actually, I signed up for a library card last week and already checked out a couple of books. ⁰³You should get a card at the front desk.
M: ⁰³I think I'll do that. My apartment is only two blocks from here, so it would be easy for me to stop by in the evenings.

public library 공립 도서관   spacious adj. 넓은, 공간이 넓은
anticipate v. 예상하다, 기대하다   impressed adj. 인상적인, 감명을 받은
available adj. 이용 가능한   check out (도서관에서) 대출하다
front desk 안내 데스크   stop by 들르다

해석
01-03번은 다음 대화에 관한 문제입니다.

남: ⁰¹전 이 새로운 공립 도서관이 정말 마음에 들어요. 제가 예상했던 것보다 더 넓고 현대적이에요. 그리고 ⁰²이용 가능한 컴퓨터가 얼마나 많은지 인상적이네요.
여: 동의해요. 저는 여기에 더 자주 올 계획이에요. 사실, 저는 지난주에 도서관 카드를 신청했고 이미 책 몇 권을 대출받았어요. ⁰³안내 데스크에서 카드를 만드세요.
남: ⁰³그렇게 할 생각이에요. 제 아파트가 여기서 두 블록밖에 안 떨어져 있으니까, 저녁에 들르기 쉬울 것 같아요.

01 | 장소 문제

해석 화자들은 어디에 있는가?
(A) 서점에
(B) 피트니스 센터에

(C) 공립 도서관에
(D) 쇼핑 단지에

해설 대화에서 장소와 관련된 표현을 놓치지 않고 듣는다. 남자가 "I really like this new public library."라며 이 새로운 공립 도서관이 정말 마음에 든다고 한 것을 통해 화자들은 공립 도서관에 있음을 알 수 있다. 따라서 (C)가 정답이다.

어휘 complex n. (건물) 단지

02 | 특정 세부 사항 문제

해석 남자는 무엇에 감명을 받았는가?
(A) 아는 것이 많은 직원
(B) 편안한 가구
(C) 넓은 선택 범위의 책들
(D) 작업 공간의 수

해설 질문의 핵심 어구(impressed with)가 언급된 주변을 주의 깊게 듣는다. 남자가 "I'm impressed with how many computer stations are available for use."라며 이용 가능한 컴퓨터가 얼마나 많은지 인상적이라고 하였다. 따라서 (D)가 정답이다.

어휘 knowledgeable adj. 아는 것이 많은 comfortable adj. 편안한
workstation n. 작업 공간, 일하는 자리

03 | 다음에 할 일 문제

해석 남자는 다음에 무엇을 할 것 같은가?
(A) 회원권을 신청한다.
(B) 그의 아파트로 걸어간다.
(C) 자료를 구매한다.
(D) 그의 책상으로 돌아간다.

해설 대화의 마지막 부분을 주의 깊게 듣는다. 여자가 "You should get a (library) card at the front desk."라며 안내 데스크에서 (도서관) 카드를 만들라고 하자, 남자가 "I think I'll do that."이라며 그렇게 할 생각이라고 한 것을 통해 남자가 회원권을 신청할 것임을 알 수 있다. 따라서 (A)가 정답이다.

어휘 apply v. 신청하다 material n. 자료

[04-06]

Questions 04-06 refer to the following conversation. 호주 → 미국

M: Hi. My name is Ryan Moyer, and ⁰⁴I recently ordered some sneakers on your Web site. They arrived today, but I was sent the wrong color. I received a black pair, but I had ordered the same item in white.

W: I apologize for the error, Mr. Moyer. ⁰⁵We will be happy to send you another pair. Please send the shoes back to us, and we will replace them for you. Again, sorry about the inconvenience.

M: Actually, I had intended to take the shoes on a trip tomorrow. ⁰⁶Since they won't get here before I leave, I don't need them anymore. I'd rather just receive a refund.

W: I understand. I'll process your request now.

sneakers n. 운동화 apologize v. 사과하다 replace v. 교체하다
inconvenience n. 불편 refund n. 환불 process v. 처리하다

해석
04-06번은 다음 대화에 관한 문제입니다.
남: 안녕하세요. 제 이름은 Ryan Moyer이고, ⁰⁴최근에 귀사 웹사이트에서 운동화를 주문했습니다. 그것들이 오늘 도착했는데, 잘못된 색상이 배송되었어요. 검정색 한 켤레를 받았는데, 저는 같은 제품을 흰색으로 주문했었어요.
여: 실수에 대해 사과드립니다, Mr. Moyer. ⁰⁵다른 한 켤레를 기꺼이 보내드리겠습니다. 신발을 저희에게 반송해 주시면, 교환해 드리겠습니다. 다시 한 번 불편을 드려 죄송합니다.
남: 사실, 저는 내일 여행에 그 신발을 가져가려고 했었어요. ⁰⁶제가 떠나기 전에 이곳에 도착하지 않을 것이니 이제 그것들이 더 이상 필요하지 않아요. 차라리 그냥 환불을 받고 싶습니다.
여: 알겠습니다. 지금 귀하의 요청을 처리해드리겠습니다.

04 | 목적 문제

해석 남자의 전화의 목적은 무엇인가?
(A) 익일 배송을 요청하기 위해
(B) 지연에 관해 문의하기 위해
(C) 주문에 대해 논의하기 위해
(D) 가격에 관해 물어보기 위해

해설 전화의 목적을 묻는 문제이므로, 대화의 초반을 반드시 듣는다. 남자가 "I recently ordered some sneakers on your Web site. They arrived today, but I was sent the wrong color."라며 웹사이트에서 운동화를 주문했는데 잘못된 색상이 배송되었다고 한 것을 통해 주문에 대해 논의하기 위해 전화하고 있음을 알 수 있다. 따라서 (C)가 정답이다.

어휘 overnight shipping 익일 배송 inquire v. 문의하다

05 | 제안 문제

해석 여자는 무엇을 해주겠다고 제안하는가?
(A) 새 제품을 보내준다.
(B) 배송 날짜를 확인한다.
(C) 상점 관리자에게 알린다.
(D) 손상된 물품을 수리한다.

해설 여자의 말에서 제안과 관련된 표현이 언급된 주변을 주의 깊게 듣는다. 여자가 남자에게 "We will be happy to send you another pair."라며 기꺼이 다른 한 켤레를 보내주겠다고 하였다. 따라서 (A)가 정답이다.

어휘 notify v. 알리다

06 | 이유 문제

해석 남자는 왜 여자의 제안을 거절하는가?
(A) 보증서를 가지고 있지 않다.
(B) 더 이상 그 상품이 필요하지 않다.
(C) 우편 비용이 걱정된다.
(D) 이미 다른 상품을 구매했다.

해설 질문의 핵심 어구(decline the woman's offer)와 관련된 내용을 주의 깊게 듣는다. 남자가 "Since they won't get here before I leave, I don't need them anymore."라며 자신이 떠나기 전에 이곳에 도착하지 않을 것이니 이제 그것들이 더 이상 필요하지 않다고 하였다. 따라서 (B)가 정답이다.

어휘 warranty n. 보증서 require v. 필요하다 merchandise n. 상품
postage cost 우편 비용 purchase v. 구매하다

Paraphrasing

don't need ~ anymore 더 이상 필요하지 않다 → no longer requires 더 이상 필요하지 않다

[07-09]

Questions 07-09 refer to the following conversation.   호주 → 영국

M: Hello. ⁰⁷I'm experiencing recurring problems with my wireless Internet connection. I found this telephone number for assistance on my bill and was hoping you could help me solve the issue.
W: Certainly. What seems to be wrong with your service?
M: ⁰⁸I just bought a new laptop a few days ago, and it keeps dropping the wireless signal. Sometimes it's able to connect, but it won't remain connected for very long. I find it very frustrating because I use the Internet quite often.
W: ⁰⁹I strongly suggest reinstalling your router software. If you want, I can direct you through that process over the phone. It should only take about 10 minutes to complete.

recurring adj. 반복해서 발생하는   wireless adj. 무선의   connection n. 연결
assistance n. 도움   drop v. 끊다, 그만두다   signal n. 신호
frustrating adj. 답답한   strongly adv. 강력하게   reinstall v. 재설치하다
direct v. 안내하다

해석
07-09번은 다음 대화에 관한 문제입니다.

남: 안녕하세요. ⁰⁷저 무선 인터넷 연결에 반복해서 발생하는 문제를 겪고 있어요. 요금 청구서에서 도움을 위한 이 전화번호를 찾았고, 제가 문제를 해결할 수 있도록 도와주시면 좋겠어요.
여: 물론이죠. 서비스에 어떤 문제가 있는 것 같으세요?
남: ⁰⁸저는 바로 며칠 전에 새 노트북을 구입했는데, 무선 신호가 계속 끊겨요. 가끔 연결이 되긴 하지만, 아주 오래 연결 상태가 유지되지 않아요. 저는 인터넷을 꽤 자주 사용하기 때문에 매우 답답해요.
여: ⁰⁹라우터 소프트웨어를 재설치하시는 것을 강력히 권장드려요. 원하신다면, 전화로 그 과정을 안내해 드릴 수 있어요. 완료하는 데 약 10분 정도만 걸릴 거예요.

07 | 목적 문제

해석 남자가 왜 전화를 하고 있는가?
(A) 서비스를 갱신해야 한다.
(B) 노트북을 교체해야 한다.
(C) 무선 라우터가 켜지지 않는다.
(D) 인터넷이 제대로 작동하지 않는다.

해설 전화의 목적을 묻는 문제이므로, 대화의 초반을 반드시 듣는다. 남자가 "I'm experiencing recurring problems with my wireless Internet connection."이라며 무선 인터넷 연결에 반복해서 발생하는 문제를 겪고 있다고 한 것을 통해 인터넷이 제대로 작동하지 않음을 알 수 있다. 따라서 (D)가 정답이다.

어휘 renew v. 갱신하다   replace v. 교체하다   properly adv. 제대로

08 | 언급 문제

해석 남자의 컴퓨터에 대해 무엇이 언급되는가?
(A) 최근에 구입되었다.
(B) 가게에 보내졌다.
(C) 무료로 수리될 것이다.
(D) 이번 주에 도착할 것이다.

해설 질문의 핵심 어구(man's computer)와 관련된 내용을 주의 깊게 듣는다. 남자가 "I just bought a new laptop a few days ago"라며 바로 며칠 전에 새 노트북을 구입했다고 하였다. 따라서 (A)가 정답이다.

어휘 purchase v. 구입하다   recently adv. 최근에   repair v. 수리하다

09 | 제안 문제

해석 여자는 남자에게 무엇을 하라고 제안하는가?
(A) 전문 기술자에게 연락한다.
(B) 온라인으로 서비스 요금을 지불한다.
(C) 프로그램을 다시 설치한다.
(D) 다른 장치에 연결한다.

해설 여자의 말에서 제안과 관련된 표현이 언급된 주변을 주의 깊게 듣는다. 여자가 "I strongly suggest reinstalling your router software."라며 라우터 소프트웨어를 재설치하는 것을 강력히 권장한다고 하였다. 따라서 (C)가 정답이다.

어휘 professional adj. 전문적인   device n. 장치, 기기

Paraphrasing

reinstalling ~ router software 라우터 소프트웨어를 재설치하는 것 → Install a program again 프로그램을 다시 설치하다

[10-12]

Questions 10-12 refer to the following conversation.   미국 → 캐나다

W: Excuse me. ¹⁰I read on your Web site that your store is holding a promotion on used bikes this weekend. I'm wondering if you can show me your options.
M: Yes, absolutely. All of our used products are 20 percent off both today and tomorrow. However, before you make a choice, ¹¹I suggest taking the bike you are interested in for a test ride to make sure it is the correct size for you.
W: OK. I think I'd like to ride the red one.
M: Sure. But first, ¹²I need you to quickly complete this form. It indicates that our store isn't responsible if you get injured while using the bike.

promotion n. 할인 행사   used adj. 중고의   indicate v. 명시하다, 나타내다
responsible adj. 책임이 있는   injure v. 부상을 입다

해석
10-12번은 다음 대화에 관한 문제입니다.

여: 실례합니다. ¹⁰저는 귀사의 웹사이트에서 귀사가 이번 주말에 중고 자전거 할인 행사를 진행한다는 것을 읽었어요. 저에게 옵션들을 보여주실 수 있을지 궁금합니다.
남: 네, 물론이죠. 저희의 모든 중고 제품은 오늘과 내일 20퍼센트 할인입니다. 하지만, 선택하시기 전에, ¹¹관심 있으신 자전거를 시운전해 보시고 그것이 당신에게 맞는 크기인지 확인하시길 제안드려요.
여: 좋아요. 저는 빨간색 자전거를 타보고 싶네요.
남: 물론입니다. 하지만 먼저, ¹²이 양식을 빠르게 작성해 주셔야 해요. 이것은 자전거 사용 중 부상을 입으셔도 저희 매장은 책임이 없다는 내용을 명시합니다.

10 | 방법 문제

해석 여자는 어떻게 할인 행사에 대해 알게 되었는가?
(A) 친구와 대화함으로써
(B) 웹사이트에 접속함으로써
(C) 소식지를 읽음으로써
(D) 라디오를 들음으로써

해설 여자의 말에서 질문의 핵심 어구(learn about a promotion)와 관련된 내용을 주의 깊게 듣는다. 여자가 "I read on your Web site that your store is holding a promotion on used bikes this weekend."라며 웹사이트에서 이번 주말에 중고 자전거 할인 행사를 진행한다는 것을 읽었다고 하였다. 따라서 (B)가 정답이다.

어휘 newsletter n. 소식지

11 | 이유 문제

해석 남자는 왜 자전거를 시험해 보는 것을 제안하는가?
(A) 제대로 작동하는지 알아내기 위해
(B) 내구성이 있는지 검사하기 위해
(C) 적절한 크기인지 확인하기 위해
(D) 안전 장치가 있는지 확인하기 위해

해설 질문의 핵심 어구(suggest testing a vehicle)와 관련된 내용을 주의 깊게 듣는다. 남자가 "I suggest taking the bike you are interested in for a test ride to make sure it is the correct size for you"라며 관심 있는 자전거를 시운전해 보고 그것이 여자에게 맞는 크기인지 확인하길 제안한다고 하였다. 따라서 (C)가 정답이다.

어휘 determine v. 알아내다 function v. 작동하다 properly adv. 제대로
examine v. 검사하다 durable adj. 내구성이 있는

12 | 요청 문제

해석 남자는 여자에게 무엇을 하라고 요청하는가?
(A) 양식을 작성한다.
(B) 가격표를 확인한다.
(C) 줄을 서서 기다린다.
(D) 신용 카드를 제시한다.

해설 남자의 말에서 요청과 관련된 표현이 포함된 문장을 주의 깊게 듣는다. 남자가 여자에게 "I need you to quickly complete this form"이라며 양식을 빠르게 작성해 줘야 한다고 하였다. 따라서 (A)가 정답이다.

어휘 fill out 작성하다 price tag 가격표 present v. 제시하다

Paraphrasing
complete ~ form 양식을 작성하다 → Fill out a form 양식을 작성하다

[13-15]
🎧 캐나다 → 영국

Questions 13-15 refer to the following conversation.

M: Good morning. My name is Andy Conrad, and [13]**I moved into Unit 401 a week ago**. There's a gas stove in the kitchen, but [14]**I'm unable to get the burners to light**. I think there's something wrong with it.

W: Are you sure you're trying to light it properly? The dial has to be pushed in for a couple of seconds before the burner ignites.

M: I tried that, but it didn't work. Could you send a maintenance worker to look at it this afternoon? [15]**I want to cook dinner for some friends tonight**, so I need the stove to be repaired soon.

stove n. 가스레인지, 난로 light v. 불을 붙이다 ignite v. 점화하다
maintenance worker 정비공

해석
13-15번은 다음 대화에 관한 문제입니다.

남: 안녕하세요. 제 이름은 Andy Conrad이고, [13]일주일 전에 401호로 이사 왔습니다. 주방에 가스레인지가 있는데, [14]버너에 불이 붙지 않네요. 뭔가 문제가 있는 것 같습니다.

여: 제대로 불을 붙이려고 한 게 확실한가요? 버너가 점화되기 전에 다이얼이 몇 초 동안 눌러야 합니다.

남: 그렇게 해봤는데, 작동하지 않았어요. 그것을 점검하기 위해 오늘 오후에 정비공을 보내주실 수 있을까요? [15]오늘 밤에 친구들을 위해 저녁을 요리할 예정이라서, 가스레인지가 빨리 수리되어야 합니다.

13 | 화자 문제

해석 남자는 누구인 것 같은가?
(A) 부동산 관리자
(B) 사업체 소유주
(C) 정비공
(D) 건물 주민

해설 대화에서 신분 및 직업과 관련된 표현을 놓치지 않고 듣는다. 남자가 "I moved into Unit 401 a week ago"라며 일주일 전에 401호로 이사 왔다고 했으므로 남자는 건물 주민임을 알 수 있다. 따라서 (D)가 정답이다.

어휘 property n. 부동산 tenant n. 주민, 세입자

14 | 문제점 문제

해석 남자가 어떤 문제점을 말하는가?
(A) 가전제품이 작동하지 않는다.
(B) 전구가 교체되어야 한다.
(C) 기술자가 도착하지 않았다.
(D) 모임이 연기되었다.

해설 남자의 말에서 부정적인 표현이 언급된 주변을 주의 깊게 듣는다. 남자가 "I'm unable to get the burners to light"이라며 버너에 불이 붙지 않는다고 하였다. 따라서 (A)가 정답이다.

어휘 appliance n. 가전제품 light bulb 전구 gathering n. 모임
postpone v. 연기하다

Paraphrasing
burners 버너 → appliance 가전제품

15 | 다음에 할 일 문제

해석 남자는 오늘 밤에 무엇을 할 계획인가?
(A) 수업에 참석한다.
(B) 친척을 방문한다.
(C) 식사를 준비한다.
(D) 작업자에게 전화한다.

해설 남자의 말에서 질문의 핵심 어구(tonight)가 언급된 주변을 주의 깊게 듣는다. 남자가 "I want to cook dinner for some friends tonight"이라며 오늘 밤에 친구들을 위해 저녁을 요리할 예정이라고 하였다. 따라서 (C)가 정답이다.

어휘 attend v. 참석하다 relative n. 친척

Paraphrasing
cook dinner 저녁을 요리하다 → Prepare a meal 식사를 준비하다

[16-18]
🎧 미국 → 캐나다

Questions 16-18 refer to the following conversation.

W: Hello, [16]**this is Julia Monroe from Decker Realty**. I'm checking in to see if you've reached a decision about the house I showed you last week. I hope you've had enough time to consider it.

M: I've decided to purchase the house. Though it's not very spacious, my family was impressed with its location. ¹⁷**We're really excited to live near the river.**
W: Congratulations! ¹⁸**It's important that we move quickly and submit an offer before other potential buyers do. I'll connect with Mr. Voss, the seller, right away.** Are you still comfortable with the price we discussed earlier?
M: Yes, I am. Please call me back as soon as possible to let me know how everything goes.

realty n. 부동산   spacious adj. 넓은   location n. 위치   submit v. 제출하다
offer n. 제안   potential adj. 잠재적인

해석
16-18번은 다음 대화에 관한 문제입니다.
여: 안녕하세요. ¹⁶Decker 부동산의 Julia Monroe입니다. 지난주에 제가 보여드린 집에 대해 결정을 내리셨는지 확인하려고 전화드려요. 고려하실 시간은 충분히 가지셨길 바랍니다.
남: 저는 그 집을 구매하기로 결정했어요. 그리 넓지는 않지만, 제 가족은 그 위치에 감명을 받았어요. ¹⁷우리는 강 근처에 살게 될 것을 정말 기대하고 있어요.
여: 축하드려요! ¹⁸다른 잠재적 구매자들보다 먼저 신속하게 움직여서 제안을 제출하는 것이 중요합니다. 저는 즉시 판매자인 Mr. Voss에게 연락하겠습니다. 이전에 논의했던 가격에 여전히 만족하시나요?
남: 네, 그렇습니다. 모든 것이 어떻게 진행되는지 알려주기 위해 가능한 한 빨리 다시 전화해 주세요.

16 | 화자 문제

해석 여자는 누구인 것 같은가?
(A) 건축가
(B) 부동산 중개인
(C) 재정 상담가
(D) 실내 장식자

해설 대화에서 신분 및 직업과 관련된 표현을 놓치지 않고 듣는다. 여자가 "this is Julia Monroe from Decker Realty"라며 Decker 부동산의 Julia Monroe라고 한 것을 통해 여자가 부동산 중개인이라는 것을 알 수 있다. 따라서 (B)가 정답이다.

어휘 architect n. 건축가   real estate agent 부동산 중개인   decorator n. 장식가, 도배업자

17 | 언급 문제

해석 남자는 집에 대해 무엇을 말하는가?
(A) 그의 예산 내에 있지 않다.
(B) 현재 리모델링되는 중이다.
(C) 강 근처에 위치해 있다.
(D) 도심 지역에 있다.

해설 남자의 말에서 질문의 핵심 어구(the house)가 언급된 주변을 주의 깊게 듣는다. 남자가 "We're really excited to live near the river."라며 강 근처에 살게 될 것을 정말 기대하고 있다고 하였다. 따라서 (C)가 정답이다.

어휘 budget n. 예산   situate v. 위치시키다

18 | 이유 문제

해석 여자는 왜 Mr. Voss에게 연락할 것인가?
(A) 제안을 하기 위해
(B) 대출을 협상하기 위해
(C) 추가 시간을 요청하기 위해
(D) 집 구경을 준비하기 위해

해설 질문의 핵심 어구(contact Mr. Voss)와 관련된 내용을 주의 깊게 듣는다. 여자가 "It's important that we move quickly and submit an offer before other potential buyers do. I'll connect with Mr. Voss, the seller, right away."라며 다른 잠재적 구매자들보다 먼저 신속하게 움직여서 제안을 제출하는 것이 중요하다고 한 후, 즉시 판매자인 Mr. Voss에게 연락하겠다고 하였다. 따라서 (A)가 정답이다.

어휘 negotiate v. 협상하다   loan n. 대출   additional adj. 추가적인   set up 준비하다   showing n. 집 구경

Paraphrasing

submit an offer 제안을 제출하다 → make an offer 제안을 하다

고난도 문제 완전 정복   p.35

| 01 (B) | 02 (A) | 03 (B) | 04 (D) | 05 (B) |
| 06 (B) | 07 (D) | 08 (D) | 09 (A) | |

[01-03]   미국 → 호주 → 영국

Questions 01-03 refer to the following conversation with three speakers.

W1: ⁰¹**Before we open the café, there is something I want to ask.** Have either of you seen the play *Winter Wind*? The Rutherford Theater has extended it for another three performances because the first one sold out so quickly.
M: I attended the opening with a friend, and we were both very impressed. ⁰²**It's an amazing show that features some incredible performers.**
W2: I wanted to see *Winter Wind* when it opened, but I was so busy at work that I didn't have any time to catch the performance. ⁰³**Now that more shows have been added, I think I'll go on Sunday.**
W1: ⁰³**Let's go together. I've been hoping to check it out myself.**

play n. 연극   extend v. 연장하다   performance n. 공연
attend v. 참석하다   feature v. 출연시키다   incredible adj. 대단한
performer n. 배우, 공연자

해석
01-03번은 다음 세 명의 대화에 관한 문제입니다.
여1: ⁰¹카페를 열기 전에 물어보고 싶은 게 있어요. 여러분 중에 *Winter Wind*라는 연극을 본 적이 있나요? Rutherford 극장이 첫 공연이 너무 빨리 매진되어서 세 번 더 연장했대요.
남: 저는 친구와 함께 초연에 참석했었고, 둘 다 매우 감명받았어요. ⁰²대단한 배우들이 출연하는 정말 멋진 공연이에요.
여2: *Winter Wind*가 시작했을 때 보고 싶었는데, 일 때문에 너무 바빠서 공연을 볼 시간이 전혀 없었어요. ⁰³이제 더 많은 공연이 추가되어서, 저는 일요일에 가볼 생각이에요.
여1: ⁰³같이 가요. 저도 그것을 꼭 직접 보고 싶었거든요.

01 | 화자 문제

해석 화자들은 어디에서 일하는 것 같은가?
(A) 극장에서
(B) 커피숍에서
(C) 콘서트홀에서

(D) 슈퍼마켓에서

해설 대화에서 신분 및 직업과 관련된 표현을 놓치지 않고 듣는다. 여자1이 "Before we open the café, there is something I want to ask."라며 카페를 열기 전에 물어보고 싶은 게 있다고 한 것을 통해 화자들이 커피숍에서 일하고 있음을 알 수 있다. 따라서 (B)가 정답이다.

Paraphrasing

café 카페 → coffee shop 커피숍

02 | 언급 문제

해설 남자는 Winter Wind에 대해 무엇을 말하는가?
(A) 실력 있는 출연진이 있다.
(B) 비평가들로부터 찬사를 받았다.
(C) 길이가 그리 길지 않다.
(D) 공연이 단 3회뿐이었다.

해설 남자의 말에서 질문의 핵심 어구(Winter Wind)와 관련된 내용을 주의 깊게 듣는다. 남자가 "It's an amazing show that features some incredible performers."라며 Winter Wind는 대단한 배우들이 출연하는 정말 멋진 공연이라고 하였다. 따라서 (A)가 정답이다.

어휘 strong adj. 실력 있는 cast n. 출연진 praise n. 찬사 critic n. 비평가

Paraphrasing

features ~ incredible performers 대단한 배우들이 출연하다 → has ~ strong cast 실력 있는 출연진이 있다

03 | 다음에 할 일 문제

해설 여자들은 이번 주말에 무엇을 할 것 같은가?
(A) 논평을 발행한다.
(B) 공연을 관람한다.
(C) 리허설에 간다.
(D) 연극 오디션을 본다.

해설 질문의 핵심 어구(women ~ do this weekend)와 관련된 내용을 주의 깊게 듣는다. 여자2가 "Now that more shows have been added, I think I'll go on Sunday."라며 이제 더 많은 공연이 추가되어서 일요일에 가볼 생각이라고 하자, 여자1이 "Let's go together. I've been hoping to check it out myself."라며 같이 가자고 한 후, 자신도 그것을 꼭 직접 보고 싶었다고 한 것을 통해 여자들은 주말에 Winter Wind 공연을 함께 관람할 것임을 알 수 있다. 따라서 (B)가 정답이다.

어휘 publish v. 발행하다 review n. 논평 audition v. 오디션을 보다; n. 오디션

[04-06]

캐나다 → 영국

Questions 04-06 refer to the following conversation.

M: Excuse me. 04I know you sell green-and-white curtains made by Pearlman, but I can't see them anywhere.

W: 04I'm sorry, but we sold out a couple of days ago. And because Pearlman will release a new product line next month, we won't be ordering any more.

M: Oh, no. 05I purchased a set for my living room when they were on sale three weeks ago. But now I'd like matching sets for my kitchen and dining room.

W: Well, it's not all bad news. 06If you'll follow me this way, this is what other customers like you picked. It's made of a similar material and has an identical pattern.

sold out 다 팔린 release v. 출시하다 dining room 식사실
material n. 천, 재료 identical adj. 동일한

해석 04-06번은 다음 대화에 관한 문제입니다.

남: 실례합니다. 04저는 이곳이 Pearlman에서 만든 녹색과 흰색 커튼을 판매한다는 것을 알고 있는데, 그것들을 어디에서도 찾을 수가 없네요.

여: 04죄송하지만, 며칠 전에 다 팔렸어요. 그리고 Pearlman이 다음 달에 새 제품 라인을 출시할 예정이라서, 더 이상 주문하지 않을 거예요.

남: 오, 이런. 05저는 3주 전 세일할 때 거실용으로 한 세트를 구매했거든요. 하지만 지금은 주방과 식사실에도 어울리는 세트를 구하고 싶어요.

여: 음, 나쁜 소식만 있는 건 아니에요. 06이쪽으로 저를 따라오시면, 이것이 당신과 같은 다른 고객들이 선택한 제품이에요. 비슷한 천으로 만들어졌고 동일한 패턴을 가지고 있어요.

04 | 문제점 문제

해설 여자에 따르면, 무엇이 문제인가?
(A) 주문이 배달되지 않았다.
(B) 서비스가 신뢰할 수 없다.
(C) 물품이 설치되지 않았다.
(D) 제품이 재고가 없다.

해설 대화에서 부정적인 표현이 언급된 주변을 주의 깊게 듣는다. 남자가 "I know you sell green-and-white curtains made by Pearlman, but I can't see them anywhere."라며 이곳이 Pearlman에서 만든 녹색과 흰색 커튼을 판매한다는 것을 알고 있지만, 그것들을 어디에서도 찾을 수 없다고 하자, 여자가 "I'm sorry, but we sold out a couple of days ago."라며 죄송하지만 며칠 전에 다 팔렸다고 하였다. 따라서 (D)가 정답이다.

어휘 reliable adj. 신뢰할 수 있는 in stock 재고가 있는

Paraphrasing

sold out 다 팔린 → not in stock 재고가 없는

05 | 특정 세부 사항 문제

해설 남자는 구매한 커튼을 어디에 두었는가?
(A) 복도에
(B) 거실에
(C) 주방에
(D) 식사실에

해설 질문의 핵심 어구(curtains he bought)와 관련된 내용을 주의 깊게 듣는다. 남자가 "I purchased a set for my living room when they were on sale three weeks ago."라며 3주 전 세일할 때 거실용으로 한 세트를 구매했다고 하였다. 따라서 (B)가 정답이다.

어휘 hallway n. 복도

06 | 의도 파악 문제

해설 여자가 "나쁜 소식만 있는 건 아니에요"라고 말할 때 무엇을 의도하는가?
(A) 방 측정 치수가 정확하다.
(B) 한 옵션이 이용 가능하다.
(C) 주문을 온라인으로 할 수 있다.
(D) 환불이 제공될 수 있다.

해설 질문의 인용어구(it's not all bad news)가 언급된 주변을 주의 깊게 듣는다. 여자가 "If you'll follow me this way, this is what other customers like you picked. It's made of a similar material and has an identical pattern."이라며 남자와 같은 다른 고객들이 선택한 제품을 보여주며, 비슷한 천으로 만들어졌고 동일한 패턴을 가지고 있다

고 한 것을 통해 한 옵션이 이용 가능함을 알 수 있다. 따라서 (B)가 정답이다.

어휘 measurement n. 측정 치수, 측정 값 accurate adj. 정확한

[07-09]

영국 → 호주

Questions 07-09 refer to the following conversation and floor plan.

> W: Excuse me, where are your hair dryers located?
> M: ⁰⁷They're in the section farthest from the main entrance, right between the cashiers and the customer service desk. Are you looking for a specific item? ⁰⁸You may be interested in knowing there's a sale on the Kenwick Turbo Dryer. It's quite powerful, and it's 40 percent off this week.
> W: ⁰⁸I'm looking for one that is compact and portable. The Kenwick Turbo Dryer is too big to take with me when I travel.
> M: I see. We do have several travel hair dryers in stock. ⁰⁹Just follow me, and I'll show you our different models.
>
> locate v. 위치시키다 specific adj. 특정한, 구체적인 compact adj. 소형인
> portable adj. 휴대 가능한

해석
07-09번은 다음 대화와 평면도에 관한 문제입니다.

여: 실례합니다, 헤어 드라이어는 어디에 위치해있나요?
남: ⁰⁷헤어 드라이어는 정문에서 가장 먼 구역에 있습니다, 계산대와 고객 서비스 데스크 바로 사이에요. 특정 제품을 찾고 계신가요? ⁰⁸Kenwick Turbo 드라이어가 할인 중이라는 걸 아시면 관심있으실 지도 모르겠네요. 꽤 강력한 제품이고, 이번 주에 40퍼센트 할인 중이에요.
여: ⁰⁸저는 소형이고 휴대 가능한 것을 찾고 있어요. Kenwick Turbo 드라이어는 제가 여행할 때 가지고 다니기에 너무 커요.
남: 알겠습니다. 저희는 여러 개의 여행용 헤어 드라이어를 재고로 가지고 있습니다. ⁰⁹저를 따라오시면 다양한 모델을 보여드릴게요.

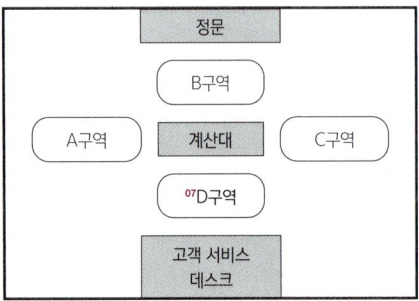

07 | 시각 자료 문제

해석 시각 자료를 보아라. 헤어 드라이어는 어디에 있는가?
(A) A구역
(B) B구역
(C) C구역
(D) D구역

해설 제시된 평면도의 정보를 확인한 후 질문의 핵심 어구(hair dryers)와 관련된 내용을 주의 깊게 듣는다. 남자가 "They're in the section farthest from the main entrance, right between the cashiers and the customer service desk."라며 헤어 드라이어는 정문에서 가장 먼 구역에 있고, 계산대와 고객 서비스 데스크 바로 사이라고 했으므로, 이 조건에 맞는 구역은 D구역임을 평면도에서 알 수 있다. 따라서 (D)가 정답이다.

08 | 문제점 문제

해석 여자는 Kenwick Turbo 드라이어에 대해 무슨 문제를 언급하는가?
(A) 할인 대상이 아니다.
(B) 너무 많은 에너지를 소비한다.
(C) 너무 쉽게 고장난다.
(D) 여자가 필요한 크기가 아니다.

해설 여자의 말에서 질문의 핵심 어구(Kenwick Turbo Dryer)와 관련된 내용을 주의 깊게 듣는다. 남자가 "You may be interested in knowing there's a sale on the Kenwick Turbo Dryer."라며 Kenwick Turbo 드라이어가 할인 중이라고 하자, 여자는 "I'm looking for one that is compact and portable. The Kenwick Turbo Dryer is too big to take with me when I travel."이라며 자신은 소형이고 휴대 가능한 것을 찾고 있다고 한 후, Kenwick Turbo 드라이어는 여행할 때 가지고 다니기에 너무 크다고 했다. 따라서 (D)가 정답이다.

어휘 eligible for ~의 대상인, ~을 받을 자격이 있는 consume v. 소비하다

09 | 다음에 할 일 문제

해석 여자는 다음에 무엇을 할 것 같은가?
(A) 직원을 따라간다.
(B) 구매 대금을 지불한다.
(C) 제품을 시험해 본다.
(D) 기기를 교환한다.

해설 대화의 마지막 부분을 주의 깊게 듣는다. 남자가 "Just follow me, and I'll show you our different models."라며 자신을 따라오면 다양한 모델을 보여주겠다고 한 것을 통해 여자가 직원을 따라갈 것임을 알 수 있다. 따라서 (A)가 정답이다.

어휘 exchange v. 교환하다

DAY 07 마케팅/판매 및 재무

빈출 문제 집중 훈련   p.36

01 (C)	02 (C)	03 (D)	04 (B)	05 (C)
06 (A)	07 (C)	08 (A)	09 (B)	10 (C)
11 (A)	12 (D)			

[01-03]

미국 → 호주

Questions 01-03 refer to the following conversation.

> W: Kento, ⁰¹do you have the figures for the dishwasher units our store sold over the last three months? ⁰²I intend to reduce the price of any that have not been performing well.
> M: ⁰²The A-13 Economy Washer from Durbin Incorporated is our worst seller at the moment. It has had low sales figures for the last two months. However, ⁰³didn't you read the financial report that I left on your desk earlier? It includes all those details.
> W: No. I haven't been able to get back to my office, as I had several meetings with suppliers this morning. Thanks for leaving me a copy. I'll take a look at it when I get a chance.
>
> figure n. 수치, 숫자 dishwasher n. 식기 세척기 intend to ~하려고 생각하다
> perform v. 성과를 내다, 수행하다 seller n. 판매 제품, 판매자
> sales figure 판매 실적 financial report 재정 보고서

해석

01-03번은 다음 대화에 관한 문제입니다.

여: Kento, ⁰¹지난 3개월 동안 우리 매장에서 판매한 식기 세척기 장치의 수치가 있나요? ⁰²성과를 잘 내지 못하는 것들의 가격을 모두 내리려고 생각해요.

남: ⁰²Durbin사의 A-13 Economy Washer가 현재 우리의 최악의 판매 제품이에요. 지난 두 달 동안 판매 실적이 저조했어요. 그런데, ⁰³제가 오늘 아침 당신의 책상에 올려둔 재정 보고서를 읽지 않으셨나요? 그것은 모든 세부 정보를 포함하고 있어요.

여: 아니요. 오늘 아침에 공급 업체들과 몇몇 회의가 있어서 제 사무실로 돌아갈 수 없었어요. 복사본을 남겨주셔서 감사해요. 기회가 될 때 살펴볼게요.

01 | 화자 문제

해석 화자들은 어디에서 일하는 것 같은가?
(A) 금융 기관에서
(B) 제조 공장에서
(C) 소매점에서
(D) 엔지니어링 회사에서

해설 대화에서 신분 및 직업과 관련된 표현을 놓치지 않고 듣는다. 여자가 "do you have the figures for the dishwasher units our store sold over the last three months?"라며 지난 3개월 동안 우리 매장에서 판매한 식기 세척기 장치의 수치가 있냐고 물은 것을 통해 화자들이 소매점에서 일하고 있음을 알 수 있다. 따라서 (C)가 정답이다.

어휘 institution n. 기관 manufacturing plant 제조 공장 retail outlet 소매점 firm n. 회사

Paraphrasing

store 매장 → retail outlet 소매점

02 | 언급 문제

해석 A-13에 대해 무엇이 언급되는가?
(A) 회수될 것이다.
(B) 생산이 중단될 것이다.
(C) 할인될 것이다.
(D) 재입고될 것이다.

해설 질문의 핵심 어구(A-13)가 언급된 주변을 주의 깊게 듣는다. 여자가 남자에게 "I intend to reduce the price of any that have not been performing well."이라며 성과를 잘 내지 못하는 것들의 가격을 모두 내리려고 생각한다고 하자, 남자가 "The A-13 Economy Washer from Durbin Incorporated is our worst seller at the moment."라며 Durbin사의 A-13 Economy Washer가 현재 최악의 판매 제품이라고 한 것을 통해, A-13은 할인될 것임을 알 수 있다. 따라서 (C)가 정답이다.

어휘 recall v. 회수하다 discontinue v. (생산을) 중단하다 discount v. 할인하다 restock v. 재입고하다

03 | 특정 세부 사항 문제

해석 남자는 여자의 책상에 무엇을 놓았는가?
(A) 설치 송장
(B) 매장 카탈로그
(C) 사용 설명서
(D) 재정 문서

해설 대화에서 남자의 말을 주의 깊게 듣는다. 남자가 "didn't you read the financial report that I left on your desk earlier?"라며 오늘 아침 책상에 올려둔 재정 보고서를 읽지 않았는지 묻고 있다. 따라서 (D)가 정답이다.

어휘 installation n. 설치 invoice n. 송장 fiscal adj. 재정의

Paraphrasing

financial report 재정 보고서 → fiscal document 재정 문서

[04-06]

캐나다 → 미국

Questions 04-06 refer to the following conversation.

M: Rita, it's Dean calling from Los Angeles. ⁰⁴I'm contacting you to discuss my meeting with the CEO of Bower Industries. We've agreed to sign a contract.
W: So we're going to distribute Bower Industries' merchandise along the East Coast?
M: Yes. Beginning in May.
W: That's great news! Seeing as an agreement has now been reached, ⁰⁵we should talk about which staff member will be put in charge of managing relations with the client.
M: ⁰⁶I'll arrange a meeting with our team about the matter as soon as I get back.

contact v. 연락하다 distribute v. 유통하다, 배포하다 merchandise n. 상품 agreement n. 합의

해석

04-06번은 다음 대화에 관한 문제입니다.

남: Rita, 저는 Dean이고, 로스앤젤레스에서 전화드리고 있습니다. ⁰⁴Bower 산업 대표이사와의 회의에 대해 논의하려고 연락드렸어요. 우리는 계약에 서명하기로 합의했어요.

여: 그럼 우리가 Bower 산업의 상품을 동부 해안을 따라 유통하게 되는 건가요?

남: 네. 5월부터요.

여: 정말 좋은 소식이네요! 이제 합의가 이루어진 것으로 보아, ⁰⁵어떤 직원이 고객과의 관계 관리를 담당하게 될지에 대해 이야기해야 할 것 같네요.

남: ⁰⁶제가 돌아가자마자 이 문제에 대해 우리 팀과 회의를 준비할게요.

04 | 목적 문제

해석 남자가 왜 전화하는가?
(A) 계약을 협상하기 위해
(B) 회의 결과를 공유하기 위해
(C) 여행 일정을 변경하기 위해
(D) 약속을 잡기 위해

해설 전화의 목적을 묻는 문제이므로, 대화의 초반을 반드시 듣는다. 남자가 "I'm contacting you to discuss my meeting with the CEO of Bower Industries. We've agreed to sign a contract."라며 Bower 산업 대표이사와의 회의에 대해 논의하려고 연락했다고 한 후, 계약에 서명하기로 합의했다고 한 것을 통해 회의 결과를 공유하기 위해 전화하고 있음을 알 수 있다. 따라서 (B)가 정답이다.

어휘 negotiate v. 협상하다 itinerary n. 여행 일정 appointment n. 약속

05 | 특정 세부 사항 문제

해석 여자는 무엇을 논의하고 싶은가?
(A) 추가 직원 모집
(B) 마감 기한 연장
(C) 업무 배정
(D) 사업 거래 추진

해설 질문의 핵심 어구(discuss)와 관련된 내용을 주의 깊게 듣는다. 여자가

"we should talk about which staff member will be put in charge of managing relations with the client"라며 어떤 직원이 고객과의 관계 관리를 담당하게 될지에 대해 이야기해야 할 것 같다고 했다. 따라서 (C)가 정답이다.

어휘 recruit v. 모집하다   extend v. 연장하다   assign v. 배정하다, 할당하다
pursue v. 추진하다

Paraphrasing

put in charge 담당하게 하다 → Assigning a task 업무 배정

06 | 특정 세부 사항 문제

해석 남자는 돌아왔을 때 무엇을 하기로 동의하는가?
(A) 모임을 조직한다.
(B) 여자의 사무실에 들른다.
(C) 팀장을 임명한다.
(D) 향후 여행 일정을 재조정한다.

해설 질문의 핵심 어구(agree to do when he returns)와 관련된 내용을 주의 깊게 듣는다. 남자가 "I'll arrange a meeting with our team about the matter as soon as I get back."이라며 돌아가자마자 이 문제에 대해 팀과 회의를 준비하겠다고 했다. 따라서 (A)가 정답이다.

어휘 organize v. 조직하다   appoint v. 임명하다
reschedule v. 일정을 재조정하다

Paraphrasing

arrange a meeting 회의를 준비하다 → Organize a gathering 모임을 조직하다

[07-09]

Questions 07-09 refer to the following conversation. 호주 → 영국

M: The corporate office just released our business's quarterly financial report. It looks like the TruePlay video game console is not selling very well. ⁰⁷We sold 20 percent fewer devices than expected in the first three months of the year.

W: Yes, I saw the report too. Why do you think the device is performing so poorly?

M: Well, I just finished surveying some consumers. ⁰⁸Many of the people said that there are not enough games available for the system. That seems to be the primary concern.

W: I see. ⁰⁹We should hold a meeting with some other staff members to come up with ways of addressing the issue.

release v. 발표하다   quarterly adj. 분기별의   primary adj. 주요한, 주된
come up with (해답 등을) 찾아내다   address v. 해결하다

해석
07-09번은 다음 대화에 관한 문제입니다.

남: 본사에서 방금 우리 사업의 분기별 재무 보고서를 발표했어요. TruePlay 비디오게임 콘솔이 그리 잘 팔리지 않는 것 같아요. ⁰⁷우리는 올해 첫 3개월 동안 예상보다 20퍼센트 더 적은 기기를 판매했어요.

여: 네, 저도 그 보고서를 봤어요. 왜 그 기기가 그렇게 저조한 성과를 내고 있다고 생각하세요?

남: 음, 방금 몇몇 소비자들을 대상으로 설문조사를 마쳤어요. ⁰⁸많은 사람들이 그 시스템에 이용 가능한 게임이 충분하지 않다고 말했어요. 그것이 주요 문제인 것 같아요.

여: 알겠어요. ⁰⁹우리는 다른 직원들과 회의를 열어 그 문제를 해결할 방법을 찾아내야 할 것 같아요.

07 | 문제점 문제

해석 화자들은 무슨 문제에 대해 논의하는가?
(A) 일부 상품이 품절되었다.
(B) 제안이 받아들여지지 않았다.
(C) 제품 판매량이 저조하다.
(D) 기기가 오작동하고 있다.

해설 대화에서 부정적인 표현이 언급된 주변을 주의 깊게 듣는다. 남자가 "We sold 20 percent fewer devices than expected in the first three months of the year."라며 올해 첫 3개월 동안 예상보다 20퍼센트 더 적은 기기를 판매했다고 하였다. 따라서 (C)가 정답이다.

어휘 out of stock 품절된   proposal n. 제안   malfunction v. 오작동하다

Paraphrasing

sold ~ fewer devices 더 적은 기기를 판매했다 → Product sales are low 제품 판매량이 저조하다

08 | 특정 세부 사항 문제

해석 남자에 따르면, 소비자들은 무엇을 불만스러워하는가?
(A) 선택 가능한 게임들
(B) 콘솔의 가격
(C) 장비 비용
(D) 보증 조건

해설 질문의 핵심 어구(consumers dissatisfied with)와 관련된 내용을 주의 깊게 듣는다. 남자가 "Many of the people said that there are not enough games available for the system."이라며 많은 사람들이 시스템에 이용 가능한 게임이 충분하지 않다고 말했다고 했다. 따라서 (A)가 정답이다.

어휘 selection n. 선택 가능한 것들   terms n. 조건   warranty n. 보증

09 | 이유 문제

해석 여자는 왜 다른 직원들과 회의를 열고 싶어 하는가?
(A) 설문조사를 개발하기 위해
(B) 아이디어를 브레인스토밍하기 위해
(C) 예산을 준비하기 위해
(D) 출시를 계획하기 위해

해설 질문의 핵심 어구(hold a meeting)가 언급된 주변을 주의 깊게 듣는다. 여자가 "We should hold a meeting with some other staff members to come up with ways of addressing the issue."라며 다른 직원들과 회의를 열어 그 문제를 해결할 방법을 찾아내야 할 것 같다고 했다. 따라서 (B)가 정답이다.

어휘 budget n. 예산   launch n. 출시

Paraphrasing

come up with ways 방법을 찾아내다 → brainstorm ideas 아이디어를 브레인스토밍하다

[10-12]

Questions 10-12 refer to the following conversation with three speakers. 캐나다 → 미국 → 영국

M: Corinne, have you made the necessary adjustments to the financial forecast for next quarter? ¹⁰I'd like to review the data before my conference call this afternoon.

W1: Actually, I asked Sarah to revise the report. Sarah, are you done with that report?

W2: Yes, I just finished updating the charts with the projected revenues and expenses. I asked one of the interns to print it out. **[11]He should be in the room on the second floor with all the photocopiers.**

M: Oh, OK. [11]**I'll head over there right now.** While I'm doing that, [12]**Corinne, would you please e-mail me our most updated sales figures?** Thanks.

adjustment n. 수정, 조정   forecast n. 전망, 예측   revise v. 수정하다
figure n. 수치

해석
10-12번은 다음 세 명의 대화에 관한 문제입니다.
남: Corinne, 다음 분기의 재무 전망에 필요한 수정을 했나요? 오늘 오후에 있을 전화 회의 전에 [10]그 데이터를 검토하고 싶어요.
여1: 사실, 저는 Sarah에게 보고서를 수정해 달라고 부탁했어요. Sarah, 그 보고서 완료했나요?
여2: 네, 방금 전에 예상 수익과 비용 차트 업데이트를 마쳤어요. 인턴 중 한 명에게 그것을 출력해 달라고 부탁했어요. [11]그는 모든 복사기가 있는 2층 방에 있을 거예요.
남: 아, 알겠어요. [11]지금 바로 그곳으로 갈게요. 제가 그것을 하는 동안, [12]Corinne, 가장 최신 판매 수치를 이메일로 보내주겠어요? 고마워요.

10 | 특정 세부 사항 문제

해석 남자는 무엇을 하길 원하는가?
(A) 원고를 교정한다.
(B) 오류를 보고한다.
(C) 데이터를 검토한다.
(D) 상담가에게 연락한다.

해설 대화에서 남자의 말을 주의 깊게 듣는다. 남자가 "I'd like to review the data"라고 말하며 데이터를 검토하고 싶다고 했다. 따라서 (C)가 정답이다.

어휘 proofread v. 교정하다   manuscript n. 원고   consultant n. 상담가

11 | 특정 세부 사항 문제

해석 남자는 다음에 어디로 갈 것인가?
(A) 복사실로
(B) 인쇄소로
(C) 고객의 사무실로
(D) 접수 구역으로

해설 질문의 핵심 어구(go next)와 관련된 내용을 주의 깊게 듣는다. 여자2가 "He[one of the interns] should be in the room on the second floor with all the photocopiers."라며 인턴 중 한 명이 모든 복사기가 있는 2층 방에 있을 것이라고 하자, 남자가 "I'll head over there right now."라며 지금 바로 그곳으로 가겠다고 했다. 따라서 (A)가 정답이다.

어휘 reception n. 접수

12 | 다음에 할 일 문제

해석 Corinne은 다음에 무엇을 할 것 같은가?
(A) 재무 전망을 확인한다.
(B) 문서를 출력한다.
(C) 프로젝트 비용을 계산한다.
(D) 요청된 데이터를 보낸다.

해설 대화의 마지막 부분을 주의 깊게 듣는다. 남자가 "Corinne, would you please e-mail me our most updated sales figures?"라며 가장 최신 판매 수치를 이메일로 보내달라고 요청했다. 따라서 (D)가 정답이다.

어휘 calculate v. 계산하다

Paraphrasing

e-mail ~ sales figures 판매 수치를 이메일로 보내다 → Send some requested data 요청된 데이터를 보내다

고난도 문제 완전 정복   p.37

| 01 (D) | 02 (C) | 03 (A) | 04 (C) | 05 (D) |
| 06 (D) |

[01-03]   영국 → 캐나다

Questions 01-03 refer to the following conversation.

W: [01]**A problem has been discovered with the coffeemaker we are about to release. Apparently, it overheats when it's left on for more than an hour**, which is a safety hazard.

M: Hmm . . . [02]**That's definitely a problem. We'd better play it safe.** [02]**Our partner retailers will have to be notified that the product will ship later than originally scheduled.**

W: Got it. And [03]**our engineers should focus on figuring out the cause of this problem. It is more important than anything else they are working on.**

M: I agree. We need this issue to be resolved quickly.

release v. 출시하다   apparently adv. 보아하니   overheat v. 과열되다
hazard n. 위험요소   play it safe 위험을 피하다   retailer n. 소매업체
notify v. 알리다   figure out 알아내다   resolve v. 해결하다

해석
01-03번은 다음 대화에 관한 문제입니다.
여: [01]우리가 출시하려는 커피 메이커에서 문제가 발견되었어요. 보아하니, 1시간 이상 켜두면 과열되는데, 이것은 안전 위험요소예요.
남: 흠... [02]확실히 문제네요. 위험을 피하는 게 좋겠어요. [02]우리 제휴 소매업체들에 상품이 기존에 예정되었던 것보다 더 늦게 배송될 거라고 알려야겠어요.
여: 알겠어요. 그리고 [03]우리 엔지니어들이 이 문제의 원인을 알아내는 것에 집중해야 해요. 이것은 그들이 작업 중인 어떤 것보다도 더 중요해요.
남: 동의해요. 우린 이 문제를 빨리 해결해야 해요.

01 | 문제점 문제

해석 여자는 어떤 문제점을 말하는가?
(A) 불만이 제기되었다.
(B) 부품이 이용 불가능하다.
(C) 행사가 취소되었다.
(D) 제품에 결함이 있다.

해설 여자의 말에서 부정적인 표현이 언급된 주변을 주의 깊게 듣는다. 여자가 "A problem has been discovered with the coffeemaker we are about to release. Apparently, it overheats when it's left on for more than an hour"라며 출시하려는 커피 메이커에서 문제가 발견되었고, 1시간 이상 켜두면 과열된다고 말한 것을 통해 제품에 결함이 있음을 알 수 있다. 따라서 (D)가 정답이다.

어휘 component n. 부품   defective adj. 결함이 있는

02 | 의도 파악 문제

해석 남자는 "위험을 피하는 게 좋겠어요"라고 말할 때 무엇을 의도하는가?
(A) 책임자에게 알리고 싶어한다.
(B) 회수를 발표할 계획이다.
(C) 출시 날짜를 연기하고 싶어한다.
(D) 몇몇 테스트를 수행할 것이다.

해설 질문의 인용어구(We'd better play it safe)가 언급된 주변을 주의 깊게 듣는다. 남자가 "That's definitely a problem."이라며 확실히 문제라고 한 후, "Our partner retailers will have to be notified that the product will ship later than originally scheduled."라며 제휴 소매업체들에 상품이 기존에 예정되었던 것보다 더 늦게 배송될 거라고 알려야겠다고 한 것을 통해 남자가 출시 날짜를 연기하고 싶어함을 알 수 있다. 따라서 (C)가 정답이다.

어휘 announce v. 발표하다 recall n. 회수 release n. 출시

03 | 제안 문제

해석 여자는 무엇을 제안하는가?
(A) 업무를 우선시하기
(B) 발표 취소하기
(C) 상품 광고하기
(D) 제휴 관계 형성하기

해설 여자의 말에서 제안과 관련된 표현이 언급된 내용을 주의 깊게 듣는다. 여자가 남자에게 "our engineers should focus on figuring out the cause of this problem. It is more important than anything else they are working on."이라며 자신들의 엔지니어들은 이 문제의 원인을 알아내는 것에 집중해야 하고, 이것이 그들이 작업 중인 어떤 것보다도 더 중요하다고 하였다. 따라서 (A)가 정답이다.

어휘 prioritize v. 우선시하다 partnership n. 제휴

[04-06]
🎧 호주 → 미국

Questions 04-06 refer to the following conversation.

M: Marianne, ⁰⁴can you get me a copy of our contract with Bold Corporation before the end of the day? I was informed about a potential error in it regarding some of the estimated material costs for our building project. If so, we need to make the revisions before sending the agreement out to be signed.

W: ⁰⁵Some incorrect prices were accidentally included, but I've already fixed the errors. Do you still want me to give you a copy of the agreement to look over?

M: Yes, but ⁰⁶I have to leave now because one of our clients asked to meet with me. Just place it on my desk, and I'll check it later.

W: Got it. Let me know if you want to discuss it later.

potential adj. 잠재적인 regarding prep. ~에 관하여
estimated adj. 견적의 agreement n. 계약서
accidentally adv. 실수로, 우연히 look over 검토하다 place v. 두다, 놓다

해석
04-06번은 다음 대화에 관한 문제입니다.

남: Marianne, ⁰⁴Bold사와의 계약서 사본을 오늘 중으로 제게 가져다 주시겠어요? 우리 건축 프로젝트를 위한 자재 견적 비용에 관해서 잠재적인 오류가 있다는 통보를 받았어요. 만약 그렇다면, 계약서가 서명되도록 발송하기 전에 수정을 해야 해요.

여: ⁰⁵잘못된 가격이 몇 개 실수로 포함됐지만, 제가 이미 그 오류들을 바로잡았어요. 그래도 검토하실 수 있게 계약서 한 부를 가져다 드릴까요?

남: 네, 그런데 ⁰⁶고객 중 한 분이 저를 만나길 요청했기 때문에 지금 나가봐야 해요. 그걸 제 책상 위에 두시면 나중에 확인할게요.

여: 알겠어요. 나중에 그것에 관해 논의하고 싶으시면 말해주세요.

04 | 요청 문제

해석 남자는 무엇을 요청하는가?
(A) 연락처
(B) 자재 목록
(C) 법적 서류
(D) 청사진

해설 남자의 말에서 요청과 관련된 표현이 언급된 주변을 주의 깊게 듣는다. 남자가 "can you get me a copy of our contract with Bold Corporation ~?"이라며 Bold사와의 계약서 사본을 가져다 달라고 요청하였다. 따라서 (C)가 정답이다.

어휘 contact information 연락처 legal adj. 법적인, 법률의
blueprint n. 청사진, 상세한 계획

> **Paraphrasing**
> a copy of ~ contract 계약서 사본 → A legal document 법적 서류

05 | 특정 세부 사항 문제

해석 여자는 이미 무엇을 했는가?
(A) 계약자를 만났다.
(B) 공사 현장을 둘러보았다.
(C) 의제를 변경했다.
(D) 실수를 정정했다.

해설 질문의 핵심 어구(already)가 언급된 주변을 주의 깊게 듣는다. 여자가 "Some incorrect prices were accidentally included, but I've already fixed the errors."라며 잘못된 가격이 몇 개 실수로 포함됐지만, 이미 그 오류들을 바로잡았다고 하였다. 따라서 (D)가 정답이다.

어휘 contractor n. 계약자, 도급업자 tour v. 둘러보다, 견학하다
construction n. 공사 site n. 현장, 부지 agenda n. 의제, 협의 사항
correct v. 정정하다

> **Paraphrasing**
> fixed the errors 오류들을 바로잡았다 → Corrected some mistakes 실수를 정정했다

06 | 이유 문제

해석 남자는 왜 나가야 하는가?
(A) 동료를 마중 나가야 한다.
(B) 소포를 보내야 한다.
(C) 관리자가 도움을 요청했다.
(D) 비즈니스 약속이 있다.

해설 남자의 말에서 질문의 핵심 어구(leave)가 언급된 주변을 주의 깊게 듣는다. 남자가 "I have to leave now because one of our clients asked to meet with me"라며 고객 중 한 명이 만나길 요청했기 때문에 나가봐야 한다고 하였다. 따라서 (D)가 정답이다.

어휘 pick up 마중 나가다 supervisor n. 관리자

PART 4

DAY 08 음성 메시지 및 회의 발췌

빈출 문제 집중 훈련
p.40

01 (D)	02 (B)	03 (C)	04 (D)	05 (C)
06 (A)	07 (B)	08 (D)	09 (C)	10 (B)
11 (C)	12 (D)	13 (C)	14 (B)	15 (B)
16 (B)	17 (A)	18 (B)		

[01-03]
[영국]

Questions 01-03 refer to the following excerpt from a meeting.

> **01As we have now been using our new telemarketing scripts for a week, I would like to get your opinions on them.** Specifically, I want to know if you feel the scripts are helpful for dealing with customers. However, rather than hold an open discussion, **02I'm going to pass out simple questionnaires for everyone to fill out. Please answer all of the questions and feel free to add comments at the end. 03Once I've collected the forms and read over the responses, I'll decide whether the scripts should be modified. I'll inform you all about my decision next Monday via e-mail**, at which point I'll distribute new scripts if necessary.

telemarketing n. 전화 판매 **script** n. 대본 **specifically** adv. 구체적으로
open discussion 공개 논의 **pass out** 나눠주다 **questionnaire** n. 설문지
fill out 작성하다 **modify** v. 수정하다 **distribute** v. 배포하다

해석
01-03번은 다음 회의 발췌에 관한 문제입니다.

01우리가 이제 새로운 전화 판매 대본을 일주일 동안 사용해 왔으니, 그것에 대한 여러분의 의견을 듣고 싶습니다. 구체적으로, 저는 여러분이 고객을 대하는 데 그 대본이 도움이 된다고 느끼는지 알고 싶습니다. 하지만, 공개 논의를 하기보다는, 02모두가 작성할 간단한 설문지를 나눠드리겠습니다. 모든 질문에 답변해 주시고 마지막에 의견을 자유롭게 추가해 주세요. 03제가 양식을 수거하고 응답을 검토한 후에, 대본이 수정되어야 할지 결정하겠습니다. 다음 주 월요일에 이메일을 통해 제 결정에 대해 여러분 모두에게 알려드리겠으며, 필요한 경우 이때 새로운 대본을 배포하겠습니다.

01 | 특정 세부 사항 문제

해석 무엇이 일주일 전에 도입되었는가?
(A) 정부 규정
(B) 안전 절차
(C) 복장 규정
(D) 전화 대본

해설 질문의 핵심 어구(introduced a week ago)와 관련된 내용을 주의 깊게 듣는다. "As we have now been using our new telemarketing scripts for a week, I would like to get your opinions on them."이라며 이제 새로운 전화 판매 대본을 일주일 동안 사용해 왔으니 의견을 듣고 싶다고 하였다. 따라서 (D)가 정답이다.

어휘 **introduce** v. 도입하다, 소개하다 **regulation** n. 규정 **procedure** n. 절차
dress code 복장 규정

Paraphrasing

telemarketing scripts 전화 판매 대본 → Phone scripts 전화 대본

02 | 요청 문제

해석 화자는 청자들에게 무엇을 하라고 요청하는가?
(A) 고객들에게 연락한다.
(B) 간단한 설문조사를 작성한다.
(C) 서류를 출력한다.
(D) 계약서를 검토한다.

해설 지문의 중후반에서 요청과 관련된 표현이 포함된 부분을 주의 깊게 듣는다. "I'm going to pass out simple questionnaires for everyone to fill out. Please answer all of the questions and feel free to add comments at the end."라며 모두가 작성할 간단한 설문지를 나눠주겠다고 한 후, 모든 질문에 답변하고 마지막에 의견을 자유롭게 추가해 달라고 하였다. 따라서 (B)가 정답이다.

어휘 **contact** v. 연락하다 **brief** adj. 간단한 **agreement** n. 계약서

Paraphrasing

simple questionnaires 간단한 설문지 → brief survey 간단한 설문조사

03 | 방법 문제

해석 화자는 향후 변경 사항에 대해 청자들에게 어떻게 알릴 것인가?
(A) 웹사이트에 게시함으로써
(B) 문서를 배포함으로써
(C) 메시지를 보냄으로써
(D) 사무실 회의를 개최함으로써

해설 질문의 핵심 어구(notify ~ about future alterations)와 관련된 내용을 주의 깊게 듣는다. 지문에서 "Once I've collected the forms and read over the responses, I'll decide whether the scripts should be modified. I'll inform you all about my decision next Monday via e-mail"이라며 양식을 수거하고 응답을 검토한 후에 대본이 수정되어야 할지 결정하겠다고 하고, 다음 주 월요일에 이메일을 통해 결정에 대해 청자들에게 알려주겠다고 하였다. 따라서 (C)가 정답이다.

어휘 **alteration** n. 변경 사항 **post** v. 게시하다

Paraphrasing

inform ~ via e-mail 이메일을 통해 알리다 → sending ~ a message 메시지를 보내다

[04-06]
[미국]

Questions 04-06 refer to the following telephone message.

> **04This is Camille Bordeaux, the event planner at Paris Gardens.** I received your message about holding a gathering at our banquet hall. I'm sorry to inform you that another person has already reserved the space for the day you requested, July 9. However, **05we can accommodate your group on either July 8 or 10. If either of these dates is suitable, I encourage you to book one before anyone else does.** And **06regarding your inquiry about music, we can arrange a live band for an additional fee.** This service is very popular among our customers, so it is definitely worth the extra expense. Feel free to contact me if you have any questions.

receive v. 받다 **gathering** n. 모임 **banquet** n. 연회 **reserve** v. 예약하다
accommodate v. 수용하다 **suitable** adj. 적합한 **encourage** v. 권하다
book v. 예약하다 **inquiry** n. 문의 **additional fee** 추가 요금
definitely adv. 확실히 **worth** adj. 가치가 있는 **expense** n. 비용

해석

04-06번은 다음 전화 메시지에 관한 문제입니다.

⁰⁴Paris Gardens의 행사 기획자 Camille Bordeaux입니다. 저희 연회장에서 모임을 개최하고자 하는 귀하의 메시지를 받았습니다. 유감스럽게도 귀하께서 요청하신 7월 9일에는 이미 다른 분이 그 공간을 예약하셨습니다. 하지만, ⁰⁵저희는 7월 8일이나 10일에 귀하의 그룹을 수용할 수 있습니다. 이 날짜들 중 하나가 적합하시다면, 다른 분이 예약하시기 전에 빨리 예약하시길 권해드립니다. 그리고 ⁰⁶음악에 관한 귀하의 문의에 대해 말씀드리자면, 저희는 추가 요금으로 라이브 밴드를 준비해 드릴 수 있습니다. 이 서비스는 저희 고객들 사이에서 매우 인기가 있어서, 추가 비용을 지불할 만한 가치가 확실히 있습니다. 질문이 있으시다면 자유롭게 연락해 주십시오.

04 | 화자 문제

해석 화자는 누구인가?
(A) 정원사
(B) 사업주
(C) 조수
(D) 행사 책임자

해설 지문에서 신분 및 직업과 관련된 표현을 놓치지 않고 듣는다. "This is Camille Bordeaux, the event planner at Paris Gardens."라며 Paris Gardens의 행사 기획자 Camille Bordeaux라고 했으므로 화자는 행사 책임자임을 알 수 있다. 따라서 (D)가 정답이다.

어휘 gardener n. 정원사   assistant n. 조수   coordinator n. 책임자

05 | 제안 문제

해석 화자는 청자에게 무엇을 하라고 제안하는가?
(A) 초대장을 보낸다.
(B) 시설을 둘러본다.
(C) 다른 날짜를 예약한다.
(D) 파티에 참석한다.

해설 지문에서 제안과 관련된 표현이 포함된 문장을 주의 깊게 듣는다. "we can accommodate your group on either July 8 or 10. If either of these dates is suitable, I encourage you to book one before anyone else does."라며 7월 8일이나 10일에 청자의 그룹을 수용할 수 있으며, 이 날짜들 중 하나가 적합하다면 다른 사람이 예약하기 전에 빨리 예약하기를 권한다고 하였다. 따라서 (C)가 정답이다.

어휘 invitation n. 초대장   facility n. 시설   attend v. 참석하다

Paraphrasing
book 예약하다 → Reserve 예약하다

06 | 특정 세부 사항 문제

해석 Paris Gardens는 추가 비용으로 무엇을 준비할 수 있는가?
(A) 음악 공연
(B) 행사 장식
(C) 더 넓은 공간
(D) 출장 연회 서비스

해설 질문의 핵심 어구(extra charge)와 관련된 내용을 주의 깊게 듣는다. "regarding your inquiry about music, we can arrange a live band for an additional fee"라며 음악에 관한 문의에 대해 추가 요금으로 라이브 밴드를 준비할 수 있다고 했으므로 음악 공연을 준비할 수 있음을 알 수 있다. 따라서 (A)가 정답이다.

어휘 performance n. 공연   decoration n. 장식   catering n. 출장 연회

Paraphrasing
additional fee 추가 요금 → extra charge 추가 비용
a live band 라이브 밴드 → A musical performance 음악 공연

[07-09]
Questions 07-09 refer to the following excerpt from a meeting.

On September 19, our firm's much-anticipated tablet, the Glide II, is going to be released. ⁰⁷In order to publicize the device prior to its launch, I want a product demonstration to be held in Manhattan next week. The demonstration will highlight the product's features and how easy it is to use. Moreover, ⁰⁸I intend to invite people from the press to cover the event. I'm hoping this will give us an opportunity to gain some free publicity and further promote our company. Now, ⁰⁹I'd like to know if anyone is willing to take part in the demonstration. At least five employees will need to participate.

firm n. 회사   publicize v. 홍보하다   demonstration n. 시연회
highlight v. 강조하다, 부각시키다   feature n. 특징   press n. 언론
cover v. 취재하다   publicity n. 홍보   participate v. 참여하다

해석
07-09번은 다음 회의 발췌에 관한 문제입니다.

9월 19일에 우리 회사의 많은 기대를 모으는 태블릿, Glide II가 출시될 예정입니다. ⁰⁷출시 전에 기기를 홍보하기 위해서, 저는 다음 주에 맨해튼에서 제품 시연회를 개최하고 싶습니다. 이 시연회는 제품의 특징과 얼마나 사용하기 쉬운지를 강조할 것입니다. 또한, ⁰⁸저는 행사를 취재할 언론인들을 초대하려고 합니다. 이것이 무료 홍보 기회를 얻고 우리 회사를 더욱 알리길 바랍니다. 이제, ⁰⁹시연회에 참여할 의향이 있는 분이 있는지 알고 싶습니다. 최소 다섯 명의 직원들이 참여해야 합니다.

07 | 이유 문제

해석 회사는 왜 다음 주에 특별 행사를 조직하는가?
(A) 고객들이 서비스에 등록하도록 끌어들이기 위해
(B) 새로운 전자기기에 관한 정보를 제공하기 위해
(C) 직원들이 열심히 일한 것에 감사를 표하기 위해
(D) 태블릿용 애플리케이션을 출시하기 위해

해설 질문의 핵심 어구(organizing a special event)와 관련된 내용을 주의 깊게 듣는다. "In order to publicize the device prior to its launch, I want a product demonstration to be held in Manhattan next week."이라며 출시 전에 기기를 홍보하기 위해서 다음 주에 맨해튼에서 제품 시연회를 개최하고 싶다고 한 후, "The demonstration will highlight the product's features and how easy it is to use."라며 이 시연회는 제품의 특징과 얼마나 사용하기 쉬운지를 강조할 것이라고 하였다. 따라서 (B)가 정답이다.

어휘 attract v. 끌어들이다   electronic device 전자기기   gratitude n. 감사

08 | 특정 세부 사항 문제

해석 화자에 따르면, 누가 시연회에 참석하도록 요청받을 것인가?
(A) 기업 임원
(B) 지역 주민
(C) 회사 대변인
(D) 언론 관계자

해설 질문의 핵심 어구(asked to attend the demonstration)와 관련된 내용을 주의 깊게 듣는다. "I intend to invite people from the press to cover the event"라며 행사를 취재할 언론인들을 초대하려고 한다고 하

였다. 따라서 (D)가 정답이다.

어휘 corporate adj. 기업의 executive n. 임원 resident n. 주민
spokesperson n. 대변인 representative n. 관계자

Paraphrasing
people from the press 언론인들 → Media representatives 언론 관계자

09 | 요청 문제

해설 청자들은 무엇을 하도록 요청받는가?
(A) 책자를 인쇄한다.
(B) 시제품을 테스트한다.
(C) 행사에서 일한다.
(D) 일찍 도착한다.

해설 지문의 중후반에서 요청과 관련된 표현이 포함된 부분을 주의 깊게 듣는다. "I'd like to know if anyone is willing to take part in the demonstration. At least five employees will need to participate."이라며 시연회에 참여할 의향이 있는 사람이 있는지 알고 싶다고 한 후, 최소 다섯 명의 직원들이 참여해야 한다고 하였다. 따라서 (C)가 정답이다.

어휘 brochure n. 책자 prototype n. 시제품

Paraphrasing
take part in the demonstration 시연회에 참여하다 → Work at an event 행사에서 일하다

[10-12]
Questions 10-12 refer to the following telephone message. 🎧 캐나다

Hello, Mr. Bardem. This is Jorge Cruz, and ¹⁰**I'm calling to inform you that a construction permit has been granted for the building you own**. Now that we have the permit, we can start remodeling as early as next Monday. As discussed at our previous meeting, however, ¹¹**before any work begins, a formal contract needs to be signed**. Could you stop by our office this week to fill out the necessary paperwork? Once the contract has been signed, ¹²**the project manager, Gabriel Hernandez, will take care of arranging the demolition work and planned renovations**. I look forward to hearing from you soon and getting everything underway.

construction permit 건축 허가 grant v. 승인하다 remodeling n. 개조
formal adj. 정식의 sign v. 서명하다 demolition n. 철거
renovation n. 보수 공사 get underway v. 시작하다

해설
10-12번은 다음 전화 메시지에 관한 문제입니다.
안녕하세요, Mr. Bardem. 저는 Jorge Cruz이고, ¹⁰귀하가 소유하신 건물에 대한 건축 허가가 승인되었음을 알려드리기 위해 전화드립니다. 이제 허가를 받았으니, 빠르면 다음 주 월요일부터 개조를 시작할 수 있습니다. 하지만 저희의 이전 회의에서 논의했듯이, ¹¹어떤 작업이든 시작되기 전에 정식 계약서가 서명되어야 합니다. 이번 주 중에 저희 사무실에 들러서 필요한 서류를 작성해 주시겠습니까? 계약서에 서명이 완료되면, ¹²프로젝트 관리자인 Gabriel Hernandez가 철거 작업과 계획된 보수 공사 준비를 담당할 것입니다. 곧 연락 주시고 모든 것을 시작할 수 있기를 기대합니다.

10 | 청자 문제

해설 화자는 누구에게 전화하고 있는가?
(A) 건설 감독관
(B) 부동산 소유자
(C) 사무실 관리자
(D) 정부 공무원

해설 지문에서 신분 및 직업과 관련된 표현을 놓치지 않고 듣는다. "I'm calling to inform you that a construction permit has been granted for the building you own"이라며 Mr. Bardem이 소유한 건물에 대한 건축 허가가 승인되었음을 알리기 위해 전화하고 있다고 했으므로 청자가 부동산 소유자임을 알 수 있다. 따라서 (B)가 정답이다.

어휘 supervisor n. 감독관 property n. 부동산, 재산 official n. 공무원

Paraphrasing
building 건물 → property 부동산

11 | 특정 세부 사항 문제

해설 청자는 일이 시작되기 전에 무엇을 해야 하는가?
(A) 최근 프로젝트를 평가한다.
(B) 감독관으로부터 승인을 받는다.
(C) 법적 계약서에 서명한다.
(D) 예비 검사를 실시한다.

해설 질문의 핵심 어구(must ~ do before work begins)와 관련된 내용을 주의 깊게 듣는다. "before any work begins, a formal contract needs to be signed"라며 어떤 작업이든 시작되기 전에 정식 계약서가 서명되어야 한다고 하였다. 따라서 (C)가 정답이다.

어휘 evaluate v. 평가하다 recent adj. 최근의 approval n. 승인
agreement n. 계약서 conduct v. 실시하다 preliminary adj. 예비의
inspection n. 검사

Paraphrasing
formal contract 정식 계약서 → legal agreement 법적 계약서

12 | 특정 세부 사항 문제

해설 화자에 따르면, Gabriel Hernandez는 무엇을 담당하는가?
(A) 건축 자재 반납하기
(B) 서류 제출하기
(C) 허가 신청서 검토하기
(D) 보수 공사 감독하기

해설 질문의 핵심 어구(Gabriel Hernandez)가 언급된 주변을 주의 깊게 듣는다. "the project manager, Gabriel Hernandez, will take care of arranging the demolition work and planned renovations"라며 프로젝트 관리자인 Gabriel Hernandez가 철거 작업과 계획된 보수 공사 준비를 담당할 것이라고 하였다. 따라서 (D)가 정답이다.

어휘 return v. 반납하다 file v. 제출하다 documentation n. 서류
review v. 검토하다 application n. 신청서 oversee v. 감독하다

Paraphrasing
take care of arranging ~ planned renovations 계획된 보수 공사 준비를 담당하다 → Overseeing some renovations 보수 공사 감독하기

[13-15]
Questions 13-15 refer to the following recorded message. 🎧 호주

¹³**You have reached the Pearson Electric Company.** ¹⁴**Due to significant damage from last night's flood, the downtown area of Pearson City is currently experiencing a power outage.** However, electricity is expected to be fully restored by 11 A.M. ¹⁵If you still

don't have power in your area by then, please call our emergency hotline at 555-1259 to report your problem. For other concerns, please stay on the line, and a representative will be with you shortly.

significant adj. 심각한 flood n. 홍수 power outage 정전
fully adv. 완전히 restore v. 복구하다 emergency n. 비상
hotline n. 서비스 전화, 직통 전화 report v. 신고하다 representative n. 직원
shortly adv. 곧, 금세

해석
13-15번은 다음 녹음 메시지에 관한 문제입니다.
¹³귀하는 Pearson 전력 회사에 연락하셨습니다. ¹⁴어젯밤 홍수로 인해 발생한 심각한 손상으로 인해, Pearson시의 시내 지역은 현재 정전을 겪고 있습니다. 하지만, 전기는 오전 11시까지 완전히 복구될 것으로 예상됩니다. ¹⁵그때까지 귀하의 지역에 여전히 전기가 들어오지 않는다면, 비상 서비스 전화 555-1259로 전화하셔서 문제를 신고해 주시기 바랍니다. 다른 문의사항이 있으시면, 통화를 계속 유지해 주시면 직원이 곧 응대해 드리겠습니다.

13 | 화자 문제

해석 화자는 어떤 종류의 업체에서 일하는가?
(A) 전자제품 소매점
(B) 통신 회사
(C) 전력 회사
(D) 자문 기관

해설 지문에서 신분 및 직업과 관련된 표현을 놓치지 않고 듣는다. "You have reached the Pearson Electric Company."라며 청자가 Pearson 전력 회사에 연락했다고 한 뒤, 정전 관련 안내를 하였다. 이를 통해 화자는 전력 회사에서 일하고 있음을 알 수 있다. 따라서 (C)가 정답이다.

어휘 retailer n. 소매점 telecommunications n. 통신 power n. 전력
consulting n. 자문, 상담

14 | 특정 세부 사항 문제

해석 무엇이 문제를 야기했는가?
(A) 예정된 정비
(B) 홍수 피해
(C) 공급 부족
(D) 회로 오작동

해설 질문의 핵심 어구(caused the problem)와 관련된 내용을 주의 깊게 듣는다. "Due to significant damage from last night's flood, the downtown area of Pearson City is currently experiencing a power outage."라며 어젯밤 홍수로 인해 발생한 심각한 손상으로 인해, Pearson시의 시내 지역은 현재 정전을 겪고 있다고 하였다. 따라서 (B)가 정답이다.

어휘 supply n. 공급 shortage n. 부족 circuit n. 회로
malfunction n. 오작동

15 | 특정 세부 사항 문제

해석 청자들은 문제가 해결되지 않는다면 무엇을 해야 하는가?
(A) 불만을 제기한다.
(B) 서비스 전화에 전화한다.
(C) 기술자에게 말한다.
(D) 기기를 반납한다.

해설 질문의 핵심 어구(problem is not resolved)와 관련된 내용을 주의 깊게 듣는다. "If you still don't have power in your area by then, please call our emergency hotline at 555-1259 to report your problem."이라며 그때까지 여전히 전기가 들어오지 않는다면 비상 서비스 전화로 전화하여 문제를 신고하라고 하였다. 따라서 (B)가 정답이다.

어휘 file v. 제기하다 complaint n. 불만 technician n. 기술자

[16-18] 호주
Questions 16-18 refer to the following telephone message.

Ms. Yoon, ¹⁶**this is Harry Dunn from Ultimate Auto.** I just want to let you know that your vehicle has been fixed. ¹⁷**As we discussed when we met this morning, your back brakes were worn down.** I changed them, so they should work much better from now on. Also, ¹⁸**since your bill exceeded $300, you received a free oil change.** You can pick up your vehicle whenever it's convenient for you. Our shop closes at 8 P.M. every day.

vehicle n. 차량 wear down 마모시키다 exceed v. 초과하다
convenient adj. 편리한

해석
16-18번은 다음 전화 메시지에 관한 문제입니다.
Ms. Yoon, ¹⁶저는 Ultimate Auto의 Harry Dunn입니다. 귀하의 차량이 수리되었음을 알려드리고자 합니다. ¹⁷오늘 아침 저희가 만났을 때 논의했던 대로, 귀하의 뒤 브레이크가 마모되어 있었습니다. 제가 그것들을 교체했으니, 이제부터는 훨씬 더 잘 작동할 겁니다. 또한, ¹⁸귀하의 요금이 300달러를 초과했기 때문에, 무료 오일 교환을 받으셨습니다. 귀하께서 편리하신 아무 때나 차량을 가져가실 수 있습니다. 저희 정비소는 매일 오후 8시에 문을 닫습니다.

16 | 화자 문제

해석 화자는 어디에서 일하는가?
(A) 대여점에서
(B) 정비소에서
(C) 주차 시설에서
(D) 물품 창고에서

해설 지문에서 신분 및 직업과 관련된 표현을 놓치지 않고 듣는다. "this is Harry Dunn from Ultimate Auto"라며 Ultimate Auto의 Harry Dunn이라고 한 후, "I just want to let you know that your vehicle has been fixed."라며 차량이 수리되었음을 알려주고자 한다는 것을 통해 화자가 정비소에서 일한다는 것을 알 수 있다. 따라서 (B)가 정답이다.

어휘 rental n. 대여 service center 정비소 facility n. 시설
supply store 물품 창고

17 | 특정 세부 사항 문제

해석 화자는 오늘 아침에 무엇을 했는가?
(A) 고객과 만났다.
(B) 동료를 도왔다.
(C) 결제를 처리했다.
(D) 시설을 점검했다.

해설 질문의 핵심 어구(this morning)가 언급된 주변을 주의 깊게 듣는다. "As we discussed when we met this morning, your back brakes were worn down."이라며 오늘 아침 화자가 청자를 만났을 때 논의했던 대로 뒤 브레이크가 마모되어 있었다고 한 것을 통해 화자는 오늘 아침에 고객과 만났음을 알 수 있다. 따라서 (A)가 정답이다.

어휘 assist v. 돕다 colleague n. 동료 process v. 처리하다

18 | 이유 문제

해석 Ms. Yoon은 왜 무료 서비스를 받았는가?
(A) 차량이 보증 기간 내에 있다.
(B) 일정 금액이 청구되었다.

(C) 쿠폰이 사용되었다.
(D) 단골 고객이다.

해설 질문의 핵심 어구(free service)와 관련된 내용을 주의 깊게 듣는다. "since your bill exceeded $300, you received a free oil change"라며 요금이 300달러를 초과했기 때문에 무료 오일 교환을 받았다고 하였다. 따라서 (B)가 정답이다.

어휘 under warranty 보증 기간 내에 있는 loyal customer 단골 고객

Paraphrasing

bill exceeded $300 요금이 300달러를 초과했다 → was charged a certain amount 일정 금액이 청구되었다

고난도 문제 완전 정복
p.42

| 01 (B) | 02 (D) | 03 (D) | 04 (A) | 05 (C) |
| 06 (B) | 07 (D) | 08 (C) | 09 (D) | |

[01-03]

Questions 01-03 refer to the following excerpt from a meeting. 🎧 캐나다

⁰¹/⁰²**I asked you all here today to share the results of the Clean Water Alliance event that we held last Saturday. ⁰²We removed over three tons of trash from Oak River.** It took a lot of work, but we had lots of help from local volunteers, so the event was quite successful. In fact, sponsors I spoke to at the event have already committed to help us with our next project. We hope to raise $100,000 by October to reduce pollution caused by boats. ⁰³**Rebecca will now provide you with an overview of our planned campaign.**

alliance n. 연합, 동맹 remove v. 제거하다 volunteer n. 자원봉사자
sponsor n. 후원자 commit v. 약속하다 raise v. 모금하다, 모으다
pollution n. 오염

해석
01-03번은 다음 회의 발췌에 관한 문제입니다.
⁰¹/⁰²저는 지난 토요일에 개최한 Clean Water 연합 행사의 결과를 공유하기 위해 오늘 여러분 모두를 이곳에 오라고 요청드렸습니다. ⁰²우리는 Oak강에서 3톤이 넘는 쓰레기를 제거했습니다. 많은 작업이 필요했지만, 지역 자원봉사자들의 많은 도움이 있어서 행사는 꽤 성공적이었습니다. 사실, 제가 행사에서 이야기를 나눈 후원자들은 이미 우리의 다음 프로젝트를 도울 것을 약속했습니다. 우리는 10월까지 보트로 인한 오염을 줄이기 위한 10만 달러를 모금하기를 희망합니다. ⁰³Rebecca가 이제 우리의 계획된 캠페인의 개요를 제공할 것입니다.

01 | 이유 문제

해석 화자는 왜 회의를 준비했는가?
(A) 도움을 요청하기 위해
(B) 업데이트를 제공하기 위해
(C) 문제를 설명하기 위해
(D) 결정을 발표하기 위해

해설 질문의 핵심 어구(arranged the meeting)와 관련된 내용을 주의 깊게 듣는다. "I asked you all here today to share the results of the Clean Water Alliance event that we held last Saturday."라며 지난 토요일에 개최한 Clean Water 연합 행사의 결과를 공유하기 위해 모두를 불렀다고 하였다. 따라서 (B)가 정답이다.

어휘 assistance n. 도움

Paraphrasing

share the results 결과를 공유하다 → provide an update 업데이트를 제공하다

02 | 특정 세부 사항 문제

해석 화자는 지난 주말에 무엇을 했는가?
(A) 자선단체에 기부했다.
(B) 건설 현장을 방문했다.
(C) 지역 공원을 복원하는 것을 도왔다.
(D) 수로에서 쓰레기를 청소했다.

해설 질문의 핵심 어구(last weekend)와 관련된 내용을 주의 깊게 듣는다. "I asked you all here today to share the results of the Clean Water Alliance event that we held last Saturday. We removed over three tons of trash from Oak River."라며 지난 토요일에 개최한 Clean Water 연합 행사의 결과를 공유하기 위해 모두를 불렀다고 한 후, 자신들이 Oak강에서 3톤이 넘는 쓰레기를 제거했다고 하였다. 따라서 (D)가 정답이다.

어휘 donate v. 기부하다 charity n. 자선단체 construction n. 건설
restore v. 복원하다 garbage n. 쓰레기 waterway n. 수로

Paraphrasing

removed ~ trash from ~ River ~강에서 쓰레기를 제거했다 → cleaned garbage from waterways 수로에서 쓰레기를 청소했다

03 | 다음에 할 일 문제

해석 화자는 Rebecca가 무엇을 할 것이라고 말하는가?
(A) 행사의 사진들을 보여준다.
(B) 재정 보고서를 제공한다.
(C) 등록 절차를 설명한다.
(D) 다가오는 계획에 대해 논의한다.

해설 질문의 핵심 어구(Rebecca)가 언급된 주변을 주의 깊게 듣는다. "Rebecca will now provide you with an overview of our planned campaign."이라며 Rebecca가 이제 계획된 캠페인의 개요를 제공할 것이라고 하였다. 따라서 (D)가 정답이다.

어휘 registration n. 등록 upcoming adj. 다가오는

Paraphrasing

planned campaign 계획된 캠페인 → upcoming plans 다가오는 계획

[04-06]

Questions 04-06 refer to the following telephone message. 미국

Hello, Mr. Silva. This is Sharma Priya, the new editor for your manuscript at Lilith Publications. ⁰⁴**I read over your latest submission this morning and noticed an error.** In Chapter 1, your main character states that she was raised on a farm, but she later mentions her childhood apartment. The apartment reference also appears in other sections of the book. As you know, ⁰⁵**the publication date is August 20.** ⁰⁶**Therefore, I need you to revise the manuscript and send it to me by next Wednesday at the latest. This shouldn't be a problem for you.** ⁰⁶**There are only a few changes to be made.** Let me know if you have any questions.

editor n. 편집자 manuscript n. 원고 read over 끝까지 다 읽다
submission n. 제출본 childhood n. 어린 시절 reference n. 언급

해석
04-06번은 다음 전화 메시지에 관한 문제입니다.

안녕하세요, Mr. Silva. 저는 Lilith 출판사에서 귀하의 원고를 담당하는 새 편집자 Sharma Priya입니다. ⁰⁴오늘 아침 귀하의 최근 제출본을 끝까지 다 읽어보았는데 오류를 발견했습니다. 1장에서 귀하의 주인공은 농장에서 자랐다고 언급하지만, 나중에는 그녀의 어린 시절 아파트에 대해 언급합니다. 이 아파트에 대한 언급은 책의 다른 부분에서도 등장합니다. 아시다시피, ⁰⁵출판일은 8월 20일입니다. ⁰⁶따라서, 늦어도 다음 주 수요일까지 원고를 수정하셔서 저에게 보내 주셔야 합니다. 이것이 귀하께 문제가 되지 않을 것입니다. ⁰⁶단지 몇 가지 사항만 변경되면 됩니다. 질문이 있으시다면 저에게 알려주세요.

04 | 주제 문제
해석 메시지는 주로 무엇에 대한 것인가?
(A) 초안의 문제
(B) 계약서 수정
(C) 출판물 구독
(D) 지불 절차

해설 메시지의 주제를 묻고 있으므로 지문의 초반을 반드시 듣는다. "I read over your latest submission this morning and noticed an error."라며 최근 제출본을 끝까지 다 읽어보았는데 오류를 발견했다고 한 후, 초안의 문제에 대한 내용으로 지문이 이어지고 있다. 따라서 (A)가 정답이다.

어휘 draft n. 초안 revision n. 수정 subscription n. 구독

05 | 다음에 할 일 문제
해석 8월 20일에 무슨 일이 일어날 것인가?
(A) 작가가 원고를 제공할 것이다.
(B) 소설이 수정될 것이다.
(C) 책이 출판될 것이다.
(D) 편집자가 변경을 승인할 것이다.

해설 질문의 핵심 어구(August 20)가 언급된 주변을 주의 깊게 듣는다. "the publication date is August 20"라며 출판일은 8월 20일이라고 하였다. 따라서 (C)가 정답이다.

어휘 novel n. 소설 approve v. 승인하다

06 | 의도 파악 문제
해석 화자는 "이것은 귀하께 문제가 되지 않을 것입니다"라고 말할 때 무엇을 의도하는가?
(A) 수정된 글을 검토했다.
(B) 마감일이 합리적이라고 생각한다.
(C) 업무를 다시 맡기려고 생각한다.
(D) 문의에 답변했다.

해설 질문의 인용어구(This shouldn't be a problem for you)가 언급된 주변을 주의 깊게 듣는다. "Therefore, I need you to revise the manuscript and send it to me by next Wednesday at the latest."라며 늦어도 다음 주 수요일까지 원고를 수정해서 자신에게 보내 줘야 한다고 한 후, 이것은 청자에게 문제가 되지 않을 것이라고 했다. "There are only a few changes to be made."라며 단지 몇 가지 사항만 변경되면 된다고 한 것을 통해 마감일이 합리적이라고 생각함을 알 수 있다. 따라서 (B)가 정답이다.

어휘 reasonable adj. 합리적인, 타당한 reassign v. 다시 맡기다
respond v. 답변하다 inquiry n. 문의

[07-09] 영국
Questions 07-09 refer to the following telephone message and coupon.

> Hello, Mr. Hall. ⁰⁷**This is Bianca from Queen Spa calling about the appointment you made for Saturday at 2 P.M.** Unfortunately, ⁰⁷**you didn't mention which service you want in your message.** We offer over 30 different massage and skin treatments. For a full description of them, visit our Web site. While you're there, feel free to download one of our monthly special coupons. ⁰⁸In June, we're offering half off Thai massages, buy-one-get-one-free couple's foot massages, and a free candle with aromatherapy massages. ⁰⁹After you decide which service you want, let us know as soon as possible. That way I can schedule the appropriate therapist for that day. Thank you.

skin n. 피부 treatment n. 관리 description n. 설명
buy-one-get-one-free adj. 하나를 구매하면 하나는 무료인
aromatherapy n. 향기 요법 appropriate adj. 적절한 therapist n. 치료사

해석
07-09번은 다음 전화 메시지와 쿠폰에 관한 문제입니다.

안녕하세요, Mr. Hall. ⁰⁷저는 Queen 스파의 Bianca이며 고객님께서 토요일 오후 2시에 잡으신 예약에 대해 연락드립니다. 안타깝게도, ⁰⁷고객님께서는 메시지에 어떤 서비스를 원하시는지 언급하지 않으셨습니다. 저희는 30가지가 넘는 다양한 마사지와 피부 관리를 제공합니다. 그것들에 대한 자세한 설명은 저희 웹사이트를 방문해 주세요. 웹사이트에 방문하실 때, 저희 월별 특별 쿠폰들 중 하나를 자유롭게 다운로드받으십시오. ⁰⁸6월에는 태국 마사지 반값 할인, 하나를 구매하면 하나는 무료인 커플 발 마사지, 그리고 무료 향초가 포함된 향기 요법 마사지를 제공하고 있습니다. ⁰⁹어떤 서비스를 원하시는지 결정하신 후, 가능한 한 빨리 알려주십시오. 그래야 해당 날짜에 적절한 치료사의 일정을 잡을 수 있습니다. 감사합니다.

> Queen 스파
> 시카고, Brentwood가 2456번지
>
> ⁰⁸서비스 하나 구매 시 하나는 무료
>
> 이 쿠폰은 6월 1일부터 6월 30일까지 유효합니다.

07 | 목적 문제
해석 화자는 왜 전화하고 있는가?
(A) 취소를 알리기 위해
(B) 약속을 변경하기 위해
(C) 지불을 요청하기 위해
(D) 요청을 명확히 하기 위해

해설 전화 메시지의 목적을 묻는 문제이므로, 지문의 초반을 주의 깊게 듣는다. "This is Bianca from Queen Spa calling about the appointment you made for Saturday at 2 P.M."이라며 자신을 Queen 스파의 Bianca라고 소개하고, 청자가 토요일 오후 2시에 잡은 예약에 대해 연락한다고 한 후, "you didn't mention which service you want in your message"라며 청자가 메시지에 어떤 서비스를 원하는지 언급하지 않았다고 하였다. 따라서 (D)가 정답이다.

어휘 cancellation n. 취소 clarify v. 명확히 하다

08 | 시각 자료 문제

해석 시각 자료를 보아라. 6월의 어떤 서비스에 쿠폰이 유효한가?
(A) 피부 관리
(B) 태국 마사지
(C) 발 마사지
(D) 향기 요법 마사지

해설 제시된 쿠폰의 정보를 확인한 후 질문의 핵심 어구(valid for in June)와 관련된 내용을 주의 깊게 듣는다. "In June, we're offering half off Thai massages, buy-one-get-one-free couple's foot massages, and a free candle with aromatherapy massages."라며 6월에는 태국 마사지 반값 할인, 하나를 구매하면 하나는 무료인 커플 발 마사지, 그리고 무료 향초가 포함된 향기 요법 마사지를 제공한다고 하였다. 쿠폰에서 서비스 하나 구매 시, 하나는 무료라고 하였으므로 쿠폰이 발 마사지에 유효함을 알 수 있다. 따라서 (C)가 정답이다.

어휘 valid adj. 유효한

09 | 이유 문제

해석 화자는 왜 남자의 결정이 빨리 필요한가?
(A) 주문을 하기 위해
(B) 예약을 취소하기 위해
(C) 할인을 계산하기 위해
(D) 직원을 배정하기 위해

해설 질문의 핵심 어구(need the man's decision quickly)와 관련된 내용을 주의 깊게 듣는다. "After you decide which service you want, let us know as soon as possible. That way I can schedule the appropriate therapist for that day."라며 어떤 서비스를 원하는지 결정한 후, 가능한 한 빨리 알려주면 해당 날짜에 적절한 치료사의 일정을 잡을 수 있다고 하였다. 따라서 (D)가 정답이다.

어휘 calculate v. 계산하다 assign v. 배정하다

Paraphrasing
schedule ~ therapist 치료사의 일정을 잡다 → assign an employee 직원을 배정하다

DAY 09 안내, 방송, 광고

빈출 문제 집중 훈련
p.43

01 (B)	02 (A)	03 (C)	04 (D)	05 (C)
06 (A)	07 (C)	08 (B)	09 (D)	10 (B)
11 (D)	12 (A)	13 (B)	14 (D)	15 (A)
16 (D)	17 (C)	18 (B)		

[01-03] 미국

Questions 01-03 refer to the following advertisement.

Scissors Office Needs is pleased to announce the grand opening of its Milwaukee store! Our newest branch launches this Saturday at 67th Avenue. ⁰¹Check out our amazing selection of stationery, ink cartridges, and office equipment. And ⁰²unlike other office supply stores in the area, Scissors also carries a vast assortment of desks, chairs, and conference tables. ⁰³Join us this week from 10 A.M. to 8 P.M. daily for great promotional offers and a 15 percent discount off your first purchase! These are great deals that you will not want to miss out on. We look forward to serving you soon!

stationery n. 문구류 equipment n. 용품, 장비
promotional adj. 판촉의, 홍보의 offer n. (짧은 기간 동안의) 할인

해석
01-03번은 다음 광고에 관한 문제입니다.
Scissors Office Needs사는 밀워키 매장의 개점을 알리게 되어 기쁩니다! 저희의 최신 지점이 이번 주 토요일에 67번가에서 문을 엽니다. ⁰¹저희의 놀라운 문구류, 잉크 카트리지, 그리고 사무용품들을 확인해 보세요. 그리고 ⁰²이 지역의 다른 사무용품 매장과는 달리, Scissors사는 다양한 종류의 책상, 의자, 회의용 테이블도 구비하고 있습니다. ⁰³이번 주 매일 오전 10시부터 오후 8시까지 저희와 함께하셔서 훌륭한 판촉 할인과 첫 구매 시 15퍼센트 할인을 받으세요! 이것들은 놓치고 싶지 않을 좋은 혜택입니다. 곧 여러분을 모실 수 있기를 기대합니다!

01 | 특정 세부 사항 문제

해석 회사는 어떤 제품을 판매하는가?
(A) 가정용 가구
(B) 사무용품
(C) 공장 장비
(D) 전자 부품

해설 질문의 핵심 어구(products ~ sell)와 관련된 내용을 주의 깊게 듣는다. "Check out our amazing selection of stationery, ink cartridges, and office equipment."라며 놀라운 문구류, 잉크 카트리지, 그리고 사무용품들을 확인해 보라고 하였다. 따라서 (B)가 정답이다.

어휘 furnishing n. 가구 component n. 부품

02 | 언급 문제

해석 회사에 대해 무엇이 언급되는가?
(A) 다양한 상품을 제공한다.
(B) 다른 할인점보다 더 크다.
(C) 시내 지역에 위치해 있다.
(D) 빠른 배송을 제공한다.

해설 질문의 핵심 어구(business)와 관련된 내용을 주의 깊게 듣는다. "unlike other office supply stores in the area, Scissors also carries a vast assortment of desks, chairs, and conference tables"라며 이 지역의 다른 사무용품 매장과는 달리, Scissors는 다양한 종류의 책상, 의자, 회의용 테이블도 구비하고 있다고 하였다. 따라서 (A)가 정답이다.

어휘 outlet n. 할인점 downtown adj. 시내의, 도심지의 delivery n. 배송

03 | 특정 세부 사항 문제

해석 청자들에게 무엇이 제공되는가?
(A) 샘플 제품
(B) 매장 멤버십
(C) 가격 할인
(D) 무료 서비스

해설 질문의 핵심 어구(offered to listeners)와 관련된 내용을 주의 깊게 듣는다. "Join us this week from 10 A.M. to 8 P.M. daily for great promotional offers and a 15 percent discount off your first purchase!"라며 이번 주 매일 오전 10시부터 오후 8시까지 판촉 할인과 첫 구매 시 15퍼센트 할인을 받으라고 하였다. 따라서 (C)가 정답이다.

어휘 reduction n. 할인, 인하 complimentary adj. 무료의

Paraphrasing
15 percent discount 15퍼센트 할인 → Price reductions 가격 할인

[04-06]
Questions 04-06 refer to the following advertisement. 영국

This June, **⁰⁴the Zion Rock Festival will be returning once again to Ohio**! Cosponsored by Stanly Records and Radio Today, this year's festival is expected to be the largest one yet. In addition to some of the country's most popular rock bands, ⁰⁵**this weekend-long event will feature numerous groups from Ohio and the surrounding area**. The tickets are only $45 per person if you purchase them in advance! ⁰⁶**That price includes two complimentary drink coupons as well as the entrance fee.** To preorder your tickets, visit www.zionrockfest.com.

cosponsor v. 공동 후원하다   weekend-long adj. 주말 내내의
surrounding adj. 주변의   in advance 미리   complimentary adj. 무료의
entrance fee 입장료   preorder v. 미리 주문하다

해석
04-06번은 다음 광고에 관한 문제입니다.

이번 6월, ⁰⁴Zion 록 페스티벌이 오하이오에 다시 돌아옵니다! Stanly Records와 Radio Today의 공동 후원을 받으며, 올해의 페스티벌은 지금까지 가장 큰 규모가 될 것으로 예상됩니다. 나라의 가장 인기 있는 록 밴드들뿐만 아니라, ⁰⁵주말 내내 열리는 이 행사는 오하이오와 그 주변 지역의 수많은 그룹들을 선보일 것입니다. 티켓은 미리 구매하시면 1인당 단 45달러입니다! ⁰⁶그 가격에는 입장료뿐만 아니라 두 개의 무료 음료 쿠폰도 포함되어 있습니다. 티켓을 미리 주문하시려면 www.zionrockfest.com을 방문하세요.

04 | 주제 문제
해석 어떤 행사가 공지되고 있는가?
(A) 노래 경연 대회
(B) 갤러리 개장
(C) 지역 박람회
(D) 음악 축제

해설 광고의 주제를 묻는 문제이므로, 지문의 초반을 반드시 듣는다. "the Zion Rock Festival will be returning once again to Ohio"라며 Zion 록 페스티벌이 오하이오에 다시 돌아온다고 하였다. 따라서 (D)가 정답이다.

어휘 competition n. 경연 대회   fair n. 박람회

Paraphrasing
Rock Festival 록 페스티벌 → music festival 음악 축제

05 | 언급 문제
해석 화자는 행사에 대해 무엇을 말하는가?
(A) 규모가 축소될 것이다.
(B) 하루 더 연장되었다.
(C) 주말 내내 지속될 것이다.
(D) 무료 입장이다.

해설 질문의 핵심 어구(event)가 언급된 주변을 주의 깊게 듣는다. "this weekend-long event will feature numerous groups from Ohio and the surrounding area"라며 주말 내내 열리는 이 행사는 오하이오와 그 주변 지역의 수많은 그룹들을 선보일 것이라고 하였다. 따라서 (C)가 정답이다.

어휘 downsize v. 규모를 축소하다   extend v. 연장하다   last v. 지속되다
admission n. 입장

Paraphrasing
weekend-long event 주말 내내 열리는 행사 → last a weekend 주말 내내 지속되다

06 | 특정 세부 사항 문제
해석 티켓 구매에 무엇이 포함되어 있는가?
(A) 음료 쿠폰
(B) 주차권
(C) 의류 상품
(D) 휴대폰 액세서리

해설 질문의 핵심 어구(included with a ticket purchase)와 관련된 내용을 주의 깊게 듣는다. "That price includes two complimentary drink coupons as well as the entrance fee."라며 그 가격에는 입장료뿐만 아니라 두 개의 무료 음료 쿠폰도 포함되어 있다고 하였다. 따라서 (A)가 정답이다.

어휘 beverage n. 음료   voucher n. 쿠폰   clothing n. 의류

Paraphrasing
complimentary drink coupons 무료 음료 쿠폰 → Beverage vouchers 음료 쿠폰

[07-09]
Questions 07-09 refer to the following radio broadcast. 캐나다

You're listening to *The Culture Show* with John Dewey on Radio KQSR. We have a very special episode for you this morning, as ⁰⁷**I'll be interviewing the award-winning actor Juan Lopez**. ⁰⁸**Because Mr. Lopez's most recent film, *Low Tides*, is being released this weekend**, we're going to discuss the movie and his role in it. Following that, I'll ask Mr. Lopez about plans to make his directorial debut sometime next year. Finally, ⁰⁹**we'll end the show by talking about an upcoming film festival that Mr. Lopez organizes every year in New York City**. You'll hear all about that and more after a brief break, so stay tuned!

release v. 개봉하다, 출시하다   directorial adj. 감독의   debut n. 데뷔
upcoming adj. 다가오는   organize v. 개최하다, 조직하다

해석
07-09번은 다음 라디오 방송에 관한 문제입니다.

여러분은 KQSR 라디오의 John Dewey와 함께하는 *The Culture Show*를 듣고 계십니다. 오늘 아침에는 아주 특별한 에피소드가 있는데요, ⁰⁷제가 상을 받은 배우 Juan Lopez를 인터뷰할 예정입니다. ⁰⁸Mr. Lopez의 가장 최신 영화인 *Low Tides*가 이번 주말에 개봉되기 때문에, 우리는 그 영화와 그의 역할에 대해 논의할 것입니다. 이어서, 저는 Mr. Lopez에게 내년에 감독으로 데뷔할 계획에 대해 물어볼 것입니다. 마지막으로, ⁰⁹우리는 Mr. Lopez가 매년 뉴욕시에서 개최하는 다가올 영화제에 관해 이야기하며 쇼를 마무리할 것입니다. 짧은 휴식 후에 이 모든 것과 더 많은 이야기를 들으실 수 있으니, 채널 고정하세요!

07 | 특정 세부 사항 문제
해석 Juan Lopez는 누구인가?
(A) 라디오 진행자
(B) 행사 기획자
(C) 영화 배우
(D) 뉴스 앵커

해설 질문의 핵심 어구(Juan Lopez)가 언급된 주변을 주의 깊게 듣는다. "I'll be interviewing the award-winning actor Juan Lopez"라며 상을 받은 배우 Juan Lopez를 인터뷰할 예정이라고 하였다. 따라서 (C)가 정답이다.

어휘 host n. 진행자

08 | 이유 문제

해설 화자는 왜 *Low Tides*에 관해 이야기하길 원하는가?
(A) 매우 인기가 있다.
(B) 곧 개봉된다.
(C) 막 촬영을 시작했다.
(D) 상을 받았다.

해설 질문의 핵심 어구(*Low Tides*)가 언급된 주변을 주의 깊게 듣는다. "Because Mr. Lopez's most recent film, *Low Tides*, is being released this weekend"라며 Mr. Lopez의 최신 영화인 *Low Tides*가 이번 주말에 개봉된다고 하였다. 따라서 (B)가 정답이다.

09 | 특정 세부 사항 문제

해설 화자에 따르면, Mr. Lopez는 매년 무엇을 하는가?
(A) 상을 수여한다.
(B) 작품을 감독한다.
(C) 예술 축제를 후원한다.
(D) 행사를 개최한다.

해설 질문의 핵심 어구(Mr. Lopez do every year)와 관련된 내용을 주의 깊게 듣는다. "we'll end the show by talking about an upcoming film festival that Mr. Lopez organizes every year in New York City"라며 Mr. Lopez가 매년 뉴욕시에서 개최하는 다가올 영화제에 관해 이야기하며 쇼를 마무리할 것이라고 하였다. 따라서 (D)가 정답이다.

어휘 production n. 작품   sponsor v. 후원하다

Paraphrasing

film festival 영화제 → event 행사

[10-12]

Questions 10-12 refer to the following news report. 영국

The state government has accepted a proposal to build an amusement park near Pine Bay. **¹⁰Officials believe that the park will boost the local economy by providing jobs and attracting tourists during the summer. ¹¹The park will be constructed by Danko Fairs, which runs nine similar theme parks in cities around the country.** The project is set to begin on July 10 and will take 12 months to complete. **¹²Danko Fairs intends to release a detailed blueprint of the park to the public on June 11.**

amusement park 놀이공원   boost v. 신장시키다, 경기를 부양하다
attract v. 유치하다, 끌어당기다   construct v. 건설하다   run v. 운영하다
blueprint n. 청사진, 계획

해설
10-12번은 다음 뉴스 보도에 관한 문제입니다.

주 정부가 Pine Bay 근처에 놀이공원을 건설하자는 제안을 수락했습니다. ¹⁰관계자들은 이 공원이 일자리를 제공하고 여름철에 관광객을 유치함으로써 지역 경제를 신장시킬 것이라고 믿습니다. ¹¹공원은 Danko Fairs사에 의해 건설될 것인데, Danko Fairs사는 전국 도시에서 9개의 유사한 테마파크를 운영합니다. 이 프로젝트는 7월 10일에 시작되어 완료까지 12개월이 소요될 예정입니다. ¹²Danko Fairs사는 6월 11일에 공원의 상세한 청사진을 대

중에게 공개할 예정입니다.

10 | 특정 세부 사항 문제

해설 화자는 공원이 어떤 영향을 미칠 것이라고 말하는가?
(A) 새로운 규제로 이어질 것이다.
(B) 경제 성장에 기여할 것이다.
(C) 인구 증가에 도움이 될 것이다.
(D) Danko Fairs사의 수익을 증대시킬 것이다.

해설 질문의 핵심 어구(impact)와 관련된 내용을 주의 깊게 듣는다. "Officials believe that the park will boost the local economy by providing jobs and attracting tourists during the summer."라며 관계자들은 공원이 일자리를 제공하고 여름철에 관광객을 유치함으로써 지역 경제를 신장시킬 것이라고 믿는다고 하였다. 따라서 (B)가 정답이다.

어휘 regulation n. 규제, 규정   contribute to ~에 기여하다   population n. 인구
profit n. 수익

Paraphrasing

boost the local economy 지역 경제를 신장시키다 → contribute to economic growth 경제 성장에 기여하다

11 | 언급 문제

해설 Danko Fairs사에 대해 무엇이 언급되는가?
(A) 건설 프로젝트의 시작을 연기했다.
(B) 최근에 다른 국가로 확장했다.
(C) 정부의 재정 지원을 받았다.
(D) 다양한 지역 사회에서 시설들을 운영한다.

해설 질문의 핵심 어구(Danko Fairs)가 언급된 주변을 주의 깊게 듣는다. "The park will be constructed by Danko Fairs, which runs nine similar theme parks in cities around the country."라며 공원은 Danko Fairs사에 의해 건설될 것인데, Danko Fairs사는 전국 도시에서 9개의 유사한 테마파크를 운영한다고 하였다. 따라서 (D)가 정답이다.

어휘 expand v. 확장하다   operate v. 운영하다   facility n. 시설

Paraphrasing

runs ~ theme parks 테마파크를 운영하다 → operates facilities 시설들을 운영하다

12 | 다음에 할 일 문제

해설 6월에 무슨 일이 일어날 것인가?
(A) 계획이 공개될 것이다.
(B) 티켓이 판매될 것이다.
(C) 일정이 발표될 것이다.
(D) 비용 견적이 결정될 것이다.

해설 질문의 핵심 어구(in June)와 관련된 내용을 주의 깊게 듣는다. "Danko Fairs intends to release a detailed blueprint of the park to the public on June 11."이라며 Danko Fairs사는 6월 11일에 공원의 상세한 청사진을 대중에게 공개할 예정이라고 하였다. 따라서 (A)가 정답이다.

어휘 make public 공개하다   put on sale 판매하다   estimate n. 견적

Paraphrasing

release a detailed blueprint ~ to the public 상세한 청사진을 대중에게 공개하다 → Plans will be made public 계획이 공개될 것이다

[13-15]

Questions 13-15 refer to the following advertisement. 🎧 호주

¹³**The Fridley Sports Center is finally open to the public! Our complex was recently renovated, so we now have over 25,000 square meters of sports venues and space for you to enjoy.** With 10 tennis courts, an Olympic-size pool, and an outdoor soccer field, there are enough activities for everyone! ¹⁴**All of the facilities at our complex can be reserved in advance for organized sporting events and recreational outings.** Otherwise, individuals are welcome to use them on a first-come, first-served basis. ¹⁵**To learn more about what the Fridley Sports Center has to offer or view our rates and schedule, visit us at www.fridleysports.com.**

complex n. 단지, 시설   renovate v. 개조하다   venue n. 장소
Olympic-size adj. 올림픽 규격의   reserve v. 예약하다
in advance 미리, 사전에   organized adj. 계획된
recreational adj. 레크리에이션용의   outing n. 야유회
first-come, first-served 선착순   rate n. 요금, 가격

해석
13-15번은 다음 광고에 관한 문제입니다.
¹³Fridley 스포츠 센터가 마침내 개방되었습니다! 저희 단지는 최근에 개조되어, 여러분이 즐길 수 있는 25,000 제곱미터가 넘는 스포츠 장소와 공간을 보유하게 되었습니다. 10개의 테니스 코트, 올림픽 규격의 수영장, 야외 축구장이 있어 모든 사람을 위한 충분한 활동 공간이 있습니다! ¹⁴저희 단지의 모든 시설은 계획된 스포츠 행사와 레크리에이션용 야유회를 위해 미리 예약될 수 있습니다. 그렇지 않으면, 개인들은 선착순으로 그것들을 이용할 수 있습니다. ¹⁵Fridley 스포츠 센터가 제공하는 것에 대해 더 알아보거나 요금과 일정을 확인하려면, www.fridleysports.com을 방문하세요.

13 | 주제 문제

해석 어떤 종류의 사업이 광고되고 있는가?
(A) 스포츠 용품 소매점
(B) 체육 시설
(C) 커뮤니티 센터
(D) 영화관

해설 광고의 주제를 묻는 문제이므로, 지문의 초반을 반드시 듣는다. "The Fridley Sports Center is finally open to the public! Our complex was recently renovated, so we now have over 25,000 square meters of sports venues and space for you to enjoy."라며 Fridley 스포츠 센터가 마침내 개방되었다고 한 후, 단지가 최근에 개조되어 25,000 제곱미터가 넘는 스포츠 시설과 공간을 보유하게 되었다고 한 것을 통해 체육 시설이 광고되고 있음을 알 수 있다. 따라서 (B)가 정답이다.

어휘 retailer n. 소매점   athletic adj. 체육의

14 | 특정 세부 사항 문제

해석 화자에 따르면, 어떤 서비스가 이용 가능한가?
(A) 장비 대여
(B) 시설 투어
(C) 훈련 세션
(D) 사전 예약

해설 질문의 핵심 어구(service is available)와 관련된 내용을 주의 깊게 듣는다. 지문에서 "All of the facilities at our complex can be reserved in advance for organized sporting events and recreational outings."라며 모든 시설은 계획된 스포츠 행사와 레크리에이션용 야유회를 위해 미리 예약될 수 있다고 하였다. 따라서 (D)가 정답이다.

어휘 rental n. 대여   advance adj. 사전의; n. 전진

Paraphrasing

be reserved in advance 미리 예약되다 → Advance bookings 사전 예약

15 | 이유 문제

해석 청자들은 왜 사업체의 웹사이트를 방문할 것인가?
(A) 일정을 확인하기 위해
(B) 주문을 하기 위해
(C) 이미지를 보기 위해
(D) 예약을 확인하기 위해

해설 질문의 핵심 어구(visit the business's Web site)와 관련된 내용을 주의 깊게 듣는다. 지문에서 "To learn more about what the Fridley Sports Center has to offer or view our rates and schedule, visit us at www.fridleysports.com."이라며 Fridley 스포츠 센터가 제공하는 것에 대해 더 알아보거나 요금과 일정을 확인하려면, www.fridleysports.com을 방문하라고 하였다. 따라서 (A)가 정답이다.

어휘 confirm v. 확인하다   reservation n. 예약

[16-18]

Questions 16-18 refer to the following announcement. 🎧 미국

¹⁶**Attention, passengers of Bus 21. Your bus will be departing in five minutes.** As a reminder, ¹⁷**suitcases that are too large to fit in the overhead compartments must be placed in the cargo area underneath the vehicle.** ¹⁸**The bus driver will provide a luggage ticket to anyone who has to store his or her baggage. Note that passengers will need these vouchers to reclaim their baggage after the trip.** So if you receive a ticket, make sure not to lose it. Once again, thank you for choosing Express Bus.

depart v. 출발하다   overhead adj. 머리 위의   compartment n. 칸, 칸막이
cargo n. 화물   underneath prep. 아래에   luggage n. 수하물
baggage n. 짐, 수하물   voucher n. 증표, 상품권   reclaim v. 되찾다

해석
16-18번은 다음 공고에 관한 문제입니다.
¹⁶주목해 주세요, 21번 버스 승객 여러분. 여러분의 버스는 5분 후에 출발할 예정입니다. 안내 말씀드리자면, ¹⁷머리 위 칸에 들어가기에 너무 큰 여행 가방은 차량 아래의 화물칸에 두셔야 합니다. ¹⁸버스 기사가 짐을 보관해야 하는 분들에게 수하물 표를 제공할 것입니다. 승객들은 여행 후 짐을 되찾기 위해 이 증표들이 필요하다는 점을 유의하세요. 따라서 만약 표를 받으시면, 잃어버리지 않도록 하십시오. 다시 한 번, Express Bus를 선택해 주셔서 감사합니다.

16 | 장소 문제

해석 공고는 어디에서 일어나고 있는가?
(A) 공항에서
(B) 기차 승강장에서
(C) 수하물 찾는 곳에서
(D) 버스 터미널에서

해설 공고가 이루어지는 장소를 묻는 문제이므로, 장소와 관련된 표현을 놓치지 않고 듣는다. "Attention, passengers of Bus 21. Your bus will be departing in five minutes."라며 21번 버스 승객들에게 주목해 달라고 한 후, 승객들의 버스는 5분 후에 출발할 예정이라고 한 것을 통해 공고가 버스 터미널에서 일어나고 있음을 알 수 있다. 따라서 (D)가 정답이다.

어휘 platform n. 승강장   baggage claim 수하물 찾는 곳

17 | 특정 세부 사항 문제

해석 청자들은 큰 여행 가방에 대하여 무엇을 해야 하는가?
(A) 머리 위 칸에 넣는다.
(B) 별도로 보낸다.
(C) 보관 공간에 넣는다.
(D) 카트에 올려놓는다.

해설 질문의 핵심 어구(large suitcases)와 관련된 내용을 주의 깊게 듣는다. "suitcases that are too large to fit in the overhead compartments must be placed in the cargo area underneath the vehicle"이라며 머리 위 칸에 들어가기에 너무 큰 여행 가방은 차량 아래의 화물칸에 둬야 한다고 하였다. 따라서 (C)가 정답이다.

어휘 separately adv. 별도로 storage n. 보관

Paraphrasing

be placed in the cargo area underneath the vehicle 차량 아래의 화물칸에 두다 → Put them in a storage space 보관 공간에 넣다

18 | 언급 문제

해석 화자는 수하물 표에 대해 무엇을 말하는가?
(A) 미리 출력되어야 한다.
(B) 나중에 필요할 것이다.
(C) 이미 배부되었다.
(D) 카운터에 제출되어야 한다.

해설 질문의 핵심 어구(luggage tickets)와 관련된 내용을 주의 깊게 듣는다. "The bus driver will provide a luggage ticket to anyone who has to store his or her baggage."라며 버스 기사가 짐을 보관해야 하는 승객들에게 수하물 표를 제공할 것이라고 한 후, "Note that passengers will need these vouchers to reclaim their baggage after the trip."이라며 승객들은 여행 후 짐을 되찾기 위해 이 증표들이 필요하다는 점을 유의하라고 하였다. 따라서 (B)가 정답이다.

어휘 hand out 배부하다 turn in 제출하다

고난도 문제 완전 정복   p.45

| 01 (A) | 02 (B) | 03 (C) | 04 (B) | 05 (C) |
| 06 (A) | 07 (B) | 08 (A) | 09 (A) | |

[01-03]   영국

Questions 01-03 refer to the following podcast.

Welcome back to the podcast. ⁰¹Today, we're discussing the safety precautions you should take if you drive in hazardous winter conditions. To protect yourself, follow these recommendations. First, invest in winter tires designed for maximum traction on snow and ice. ⁰²When traveling through mountainous regions, always carry tire chains as a precautionary measure in case of poor road conditions. We also recommend downloading the National Weather Bureau's mobile application, which uses GPS technology to provide real-time weather warnings. ⁰³An innovative feature of this app is that it will automatically alert emergency services if you are involved in an accident, and provide your precise location. For more winter driving tips, visit www.thecarpeople.com.

precaution n. 예방 조치 hazardous adj. 위험한 traction n. 접지력 mountainous adj. 산악의 real-time adj. 실시간의 innovative adj. 혁신적인 alert v. 알리다 precise adj. 정확한

해석 01-03번은 다음 팟캐스트에 관한 문제입니다.

팟캐스트에 다시 오신 것을 환영합니다. ⁰¹오늘은 위험한 겨울 날씨에 운전할 때 취해야 할 안전 예방 조치에 대해 논의하겠습니다. 당신 스스로를 보호하기 위해, 다음 권장 사항들을 따르세요. 첫째, 눈과 얼음에서 최대 접지력을 발휘하도록 설계된 겨울용 타이어에 투자하세요. ⁰²산악 지역을 여행할 때는 열악한 도로 상황에 대비하여 항상 타이어 체인을 예방책으로 휴대하세요. 우리는 GPS 기술을 사용하여 실시간 기상 경보를 제공하는 국립기상국의 모바일 애플리케이션을 다운로드하는 것 또한 권장합니다. ⁰³이 앱의 혁신적인 기능은 당신이 사고를 당했을 경우 자동으로 긴급 구조대에 알리고 당신의 정확한 위치를 제공한다는 것입니다. 더 많은 겨울 운전 팁을 위해서, www.thecarpeople.com을 방문하세요.

01 | 주제 문제

해석 팟캐스트는 주로 무엇에 관한 것인가?
(A) 겨울철 운전을 위한 조언들
(B) 새로운 교통 규정
(C) 예보된 기상 상황
(D) 보험 정책의 변화

해설 팟캐스트의 주제를 묻는 문제이므로, 지문의 초반을 반드시 듣는다. "Today, we're discussing the safety precautions you should take if you drive in hazardous winter conditions."라며 위험한 겨울 날씨에 운전할 때 취해야 할 안전 예방 조치에 대해 논의하겠다고 하였다. 따라서 (A)가 정답이다.

어휘 forecast v. 예보하다 insurance n. 보험

02 | 제안 문제

해석 화자는 산악 지역을 여행하는 사람들에게 무엇을 제안하는가?
(A) 지도 다운로드하기
(B) 장비 가져오기
(C) 차량 점검하기
(D) 연료 절약하기

해설 질문의 핵심 어구(mountainous areas)와 관련된 내용을 주의 깊게 듣는다. "When traveling through mountainous regions, always carry tire chains as a precautionary measure in case of poor road conditions."라며 산악 지역을 여행할 때는 열악한 도로 상황에 대비하여 항상 타이어 체인을 예방책으로 휴대하라고 하였다. 따라서 (B)가 정답이다.

어휘 inspect v. 점검하다 conserve v. 절약하다

Paraphrasing

tire chains 타이어 체인 → equipment 장비

03 | 특정 세부 사항 문제

해석 애플리케이션의 기능은 무엇인가?
(A) 운전자에게 대체 경로를 제공한다.
(B) 안전하지 않은 도로 상황을 경고한다.
(C) 차량의 위치를 전송한다.
(D) 응급 요원이 언제 도착할지 보여준다.

해설 질문의 핵심 어구(feature of the application)와 관련된 내용을 주의 깊게 듣는다. "An innovative feature of this app is that it will automatically alert emergency services if you are involved in an accident, and provide your precise location."이라며 이 앱의 혁신

적인 기능은 사고를 당했을 경우 자동으로 긴급 구조대에 알리고 정확한 위치를 제공하는 것이라고 하였다. 따라서 (C)가 정답이다.

어휘 alternate adj. 대체의 transmit v. 전송하다
emergency personnel 응급 요원

Paraphrasing

provide ~ precise location 정확한 위치를 제공하다 → transmit ~ location 위치를 전송한다

[04-06]

영국

Questions 04-06 refer to the following advertisement.

Are you tired of watching your heating costs soar during the harsh winter months? Looking to maximize your home's energy efficiency while minimizing your utility expenses? Patterson and Cooper has the solution you've been seeking. [04]We specialize in the installation of double-glazed windows. [05]Our thermal-barrier technology prevents 95 percent of the heat from escaping—nearly twice the efficiency of conventional windows. As a result, our satisfied clients consistently report reductions of up to 30 percent in their annual heating expenditures while still enjoying a warm, comfortable indoor environment. Why not get the best of both worlds? [06]Visit our Web site to explore our competitive pricing options and schedule a consultation.

soar v. 치솟다, 급등하다 maximize v. 극대화하다 minimize v. 최소화하다
utility expense 공과금 installation n. 설치
double-glazed window 이중 유리창
thermal-barrier technology 단열 기술 conventional adj. 기존의, 전통적인
expenditure n. 지출, 비용 competitive adj. 경쟁력 있는

해석
04-06번은 다음 광고에 관한 문제입니다.

혹독한 겨울철에 난방비가 치솟는 것을 지켜보는 데 지치셨나요? 공과금을 최소화하면서 집의 에너지 효율을 극대화하고 싶으신가요? Patterson and Cooper사가 귀하가 찾고 계셨던 해결책을 가지고 있습니다. [04]저희는 이중 유리창 설치를 전문으로 합니다. [05]저희의 단열 기술은 열의 95퍼센트가 빠져나가는 것을 방지하는데, 이는 기존 창문 효율의 거의 두 배에 달합니다. 그 결과, 저희의 만족한 고객들은 따뜻하고 편안한 실내 환경을 계속해서 누리면서 연간 난방 지출에서 최대 30퍼센트까지의 절감을 꾸준히 보고하고 있습니다. 왜 두 가지 장점을 모두 잡지 않으시나요? [06]저희 웹사이트를 방문하셔서 경쟁력 있는 가격 옵션들을 살펴보시고 상담을 예약하세요.

04 | 주제 문제

해석 어떤 종류의 사업이 광고되고 있는가?
(A) 난방 시스템 제조업체
(B) 창문 설치 회사
(C) 자동차 정비소
(D) 연구소

해설 광고의 주제를 묻는 문제이므로, 지문의 초반을 반드시 듣는다. "We specialize in the installation of double-glazed windows."라며 이중 유리창 설치를 전문으로 한다고 하였다. 따라서 (B)가 정답이다.

어휘 manufacturer n. 제조업체 auto repair shop 자동차 정비소
research laboratory 연구소

05 | 의도 파악 문제

해석 화자는 "왜 두 가지 장점을 모두 잡지 않으시나요?"라고 말할 때 무엇을 의도하는가?
(A) 새로운 서비스가 소개되고 있다.
(B) 현재 많은 옵션이 이용 가능하다.
(C) 판매 중인 품목이 많은 장점을 가지고 있다.
(D) 특별 할인이 제공되고 있다.

해설 질문의 인용어구(Why not get the best of both worlds?)가 언급된 주변을 주의 깊게 듣는다. "Our thermal-barrier technology prevents 95 percent of the heat from escaping—nearly twice the efficiency of conventional windows."라며 단열 기술이 열의 95퍼센트가 빠져나가는 것을 방지하는데, 이는 기존 창문 효율의 거의 두 배에 달한다고 한 후, "As a result, our satisfied clients consistently report reductions of up to 30 percent in their annual heating expenditures while still enjoying a warm, comfortable indoor environment."라며 만족한 고객들은 따뜻하고 편안한 실내 환경을 계속해서 누리면서 연간 난방 지출에서 최대 30퍼센트까지의 절감을 꾸준히 보고하고 있다고 한 것을 통해 판매 중인 품목이 많은 장점을 가지고 있음을 알 수 있다. 따라서 (C)가 정답이다.

어휘 available adj. 이용 가능한

06 | 특정 세부 사항 문제

해석 청자들은 웹사이트에서 무엇을 할 수 있는가?
(A) 요금을 확인한다.
(B) 물품을 구매한다.
(C) 질문을 제출한다.
(D) 카탈로그를 다운로드한다.

해설 질문의 핵심 어구(Web site)가 언급된 주변을 주의 깊게 듣는다. "Visit our Web site to explore our competitive pricing options and schedule a consultation."이라며 웹사이트를 방문하여 경쟁력 있는 가격 옵션들을 살펴보고 상담을 예약하라고 하였다. 따라서 (A)가 정답이다.

어휘 submit v. 제출하다

Paraphrasing

explore ~ competitive pricing options 경쟁력 있는 가격 옵션들을 살펴보다 → Check prices 요금을 확인하다

[07-09]

호주

Questions 07-09 refer to the following talk and schedule.

[07]Welcome to Charlottesville Chocolates, one of the largest chocolate producers in West Africa. [08]Unlike most of our competitors, we do not simply take processed cocoa and turn it into chocolate candy. We use a unique production process that begins with our experts working closely with local farmers to select the highest-quality cacao pods. We then roast the seeds in-house and use them to make our renowned chocolate bars that are sold all over the world. [09]You'll see most of this process today aside from the portion that takes place in the fermentation room, which is undergoing repairs. Instead, we'll visit the seed harvesting area at that allotted time. Now, if everyone's ready, we'll begin.

producer n. 제조업체 competitor n. 경쟁사 processed adj. 가공한
unique adj. 독특한 pod n. (콩 따위의) 깍지, 꼬투리 renowned adj. 유명한
aside from ~을 제외하고 portion n. 부분 fermentation n. 발효
harvesting n. 수확 allotted adj. 할당된

해석
07-09번은 다음 담화와 일정표에 관한 문제입니다.

⁰⁷서아프리카에서 가장 큰 초콜릿 제조업체 중 하나인 Charlottesville Chocolates에 오신 것을 환영합니다. ⁰⁸대부분의 경쟁사들과 달리, 저희는 단순히 가공한 코코아를 받아서 그것을 초콜릿 사탕류로 만들지 않습니다. 저희는 최고 품질의 카카오 깍지를 선별하기 위해 전문가들이 현지 농부들과 긴밀하게 협력하는 것으로 시작하는 독특한 생산 과정을 이용합니다. 그런 다음 저희는 사내에서 씨앗을 볶고 전 세계에 판매되는 저희의 유명한 초콜릿 바를 만들기 위해 그것들을 사용합니다. ⁰⁹오늘 여러분은 수리 중인 발효실에서 진행되는 부분을 제외하고 이 과정의 대부분을 보게 될 것입니다. 대신, 그 할당된 시간에는 씨앗 수확 구역을 방문할 예정입니다. 이제, 모두 준비되었다면, 시작하겠습니다.

Charlottesville Chocolates 견학 일정	
시간	장소
⁰⁹오전 8시	발효실
오전 9시	건조대
오전 10시	볶는 구역
오전 11시	포장 구역

07 | 언급 문제

해석 화자는 Charlottesville Chocolates에 대해 무엇을 말하는가?
(A) 현지 농부가 소유하고 있다.
(B) 주요한 지역 제조업체이다.
(C) 가공된 코코아를 구매한다.
(D) 새로운 맛의 사탕류를 개발했다.

해설 질문의 핵심 어구(Charlottesville Chocolates)가 언급된 주변을 주의 깊게 듣는다. "Welcome to Charlottesville Chocolates, one of the largest chocolate producers in West Africa."라며 서아프리카에서 가장 큰 초콜릿 제조업체 중 하나인 Charlottesville Chocolates에 오신 것을 환영한다고 하였다. 따라서 (B)가 정답이다.

어휘 regional adj. 지역의 flavor n. 맛

08 | 특정 세부 사항 문제

해석 Charlottesville Chocolates를 경쟁사와 구별하는 것은 무엇인가?
(A) 생산 방법
(B) 마케팅 기법
(C) 높은 수익성
(D) 유통망

해설 질문의 핵심 어구(competitors)가 언급된 주변을 주의 깊게 듣는다. "Unlike most of our competitors, we do not simply take processed cocoa and turn it into chocolate candy. We use a unique production process that begins with our experts working closely with local farmers to select the highest-quality cacao pods."라며 대부분의 경쟁사들과 달리, Charlottesville Chocolates는 단순히 가공된 코코아를 받아서 그것을 초콜릿 사탕류로 만들지 않고, 최고 품질의 카카오 깍지를 선별하기 위해 전문가들이 현지 농부들과 긴밀하게 협력하는 것으로 시작하는 독특한 생산 과정을 이용한다고 하였다. 따라서 (A)가 정답이다.

어휘 technique n. 기법 profitability n. 수익성 distribution network 유통망

Paraphrasing
production process 생산 과정 → production methods 생산 방법

09 | 시각 자료 문제

해석 시각 자료를 보아라. 씨앗 수확 구역은 언제 방문되는가?
(A) 오전 8시에
(B) 오전 9시에
(C) 오전 10시에
(D) 오전 11시에

해설 제시된 일정표의 정보를 확인한 후 질문의 핵심 어구(seed harvesting room)와 관련된 내용을 주의 깊게 듣는다. "You'll see most of this process today aside from the portion that takes place in the fermentation room, which is undergoing repairs. Instead, we'll visit the seed harvesting area at that allotted time."이라며 수리 중인 발효실에서 진행되는 부분을 제외하고 이 과정의 대부분을 보게 될 것이고, 대신 그 할당된 시간에 씨앗 수확 구역을 방문할 예정이라고 하였다. 일정표에서 발효실에 할당된 시간은 오전 8시이므로 그 시간에 씨앗 수확 구역을 방문하게 될 것임을 알 수 있다. 따라서 (A)가 정답이다.

DAY 10 연설 및 소개

빈출 문제 집중 훈련   p.46

01 (B)	02 (D)	03 (C)	04 (D)	05 (B)
06 (C)	07 (D)	08 (C)	09 (A)	10 (D)
11 (C)	12 (D)			

[01-03] 호주

Questions 01-03 refer to the following instructions.

⁰¹I want to begin today by briefly explaining how to process new patients here at the clinic. As receptionists, ⁰²you'll ask every new patient to fill out a form. It is necessary for them to do this, as it allows our doctors to better understand patients' medical histories. Once the document has been properly completed, create a digital copy of the document by scanning it on this machine. Then, file the original version of the form in the main filing cabinet. Next, ⁰³I'm going to hand out copies of our guidelines for dealing with insurance companies.

process v. 처리하다 patient n. 환자 receptionist n. 접수원
fill out 작성하다 medical history 병력 properly adv. 제대로, 적절히
deal with ~를 (상)대하다

해석
01-03번은 다음 설명에 관한 문제입니다.

⁰¹오늘은 이 병원에서 새로운 환자들을 처리하는 방법에 대해 간략히 설명하며 시작하고 싶습니다. 접수원으로서, ⁰²여러분은 모든 새로운 환자에게 양식을 작성하도록 요청할 것입니다. 이는 의사들이 환자들의 병력을 더 잘 이해할 수 있게 해주기 때문에, 그들이 이것을 하는 것은 필수적입니다. 서류가 제대로 완료되면, 이 기계로 스캔하여 서류의 디지털 사본을 만드세요. 그런 다음, 양식의 원본 버전을 메인 서류 캐비닛에 보관하세요. 다음으로, ⁰³저는 보험 회사들을 상대하기 위한 지침들의 사본을 나눠드리겠습니다.

01 | 목적 문제

해석 담화의 목적은 무엇인가?
(A) 환자에게 알리기 위해
(B) 절차를 설명하기 위해
(C) 폐쇄를 발표하기 위해

(D) 제안을 요청하기 위해

해설 담화의 목적을 묻는 문제이므로, 지문의 초반을 반드시 듣는다. "I want to begin today by briefly explaining how to process new patients here at the clinic."이라며 병원에서 새로운 환자들을 처리하는 방법에 대해 간략히 설명하고 싶다고 한 후, 새로운 환자를 처리하는 절차에 대한 내용으로 지문이 이어지고 있다. 따라서 (B)가 정답이다.

어휘 procedure n. 절차

Paraphrasing

explaining how to process 처리하는 방법을 설명하기 → explain a procedure 절차를 설명하다

02 | 요청 문제

해설 새로운 환자들은 무엇을 하라고 요청받는가?
(A) 의사에게 말한다.
(B) 예약을 잡는다.
(C) 접수 구역에서 기다린다.
(D) 서류를 작성한다.

해설 질문의 핵심 어구(new patients)와 관련된 내용을 주의 깊게 듣는다. "you'll ask every new patient to fill out a form"이라며 모든 새로운 환자에게 양식을 작성하도록 요청할 것이라고 하였다. 따라서 (D)가 정답이다.

어휘 physician n. 의사 appointment n. 예약 reception area 접수 구역
document n. 서류, 문서

Paraphrasing

fill out a form 양식을 작성하다 → Fill out a document 서류를 작성하다

03 | 특정 세부 사항 문제

해설 화자는 무엇을 배포할 것인가?
(A) 신청 양식
(B) 사용자 비밀번호
(C) 정보를 제공하는 유인물
(D) 직원 사원증

해설 질문의 핵심 어구(distribute)와 관련된 내용을 주의 깊게 듣는다. "I'm going to hand out copies of our guidelines for dealing with insurance companies."라며 보험 회사들을 상대하기 위한 지침들의 사본을 나눠주겠다고 하였다. 따라서 (C)가 정답이다.

어휘 distribute v. 배포하다, 나눠주다 application form 신청 양식
handout n. 유인물

Paraphrasing

copies of ~ guidelines for dealing with insurance companies 보험 회사들을 상대하기 위한 지침들의 사본 → Informational handouts 정보를 제공하는 유인물

[04-06]

Questions 04-06 refer to the following introduction. 🇨🇦 캐나다

04I am honored to present Darin Kurt with the Lifetime Achievement Award this evening. I have known him for over 15 years—05my first job cooking was at one of his restaurants, and I still use the skills he taught me today. Throughout his career, Mr. Kurt has operated some of the finest dining establishments in the city, winning praise from diners and professional food critics alike. 06And his influence in our industry will likely be even greater when he replaces Mali Kaya as the head of the Chicago Restaurant Association next month. I would now like to ask Mr. Kurt to come up on the stage.

honored adj. 영광스러운 present v. (상을) 수여하다 achievement n. 공로
dining establishment 식당 praise n. 찬사 critic n. 평론가
replace v. 대신하다 head n. 회장, 책임자 association n. 협회

해석 04-06번은 다음 소개에 관한 문제입니다.
04오늘 저녁 Darin Kurt에게 평생 공로상을 수여하게 되어 영광입니다. 저는 그를 15년 넘게 알아왔는데, 05제가 처음 요리 일을 시작한 곳이 그의 식당 중 한 곳이었고, 저는 그가 저에게 가르쳐 준 기술들을 오늘날까지도 여전히 사용하고 있습니다. 그의 경력 내내, Mr. Kurt는 도시에서 가장 훌륭한 몇몇 식당들을 운영해왔으며, 식당 손님들과 전문 음식 평론가들 모두에게서 찬사를 받았습니다. 06그리고 그가 다음 달에 Mali Kaya를 대신하여 시카고 레스토랑 협회장이 되면, 우리 업계에서의 그의 영향력은 아마 훨씬 더 커질 것입니다. 이제 Mr. Kurt를 무대 위로 모시겠습니다.

04 | 장소 문제

해설 청자들은 어디에 있는 것 같은가?
(A) 은퇴 기념식에
(B) 졸업 파티에
(C) 사업 개업식에
(D) 시상식에

해설 지문에서 장소와 관련된 표현을 놓치지 않고 듣는다. "I am honored to present Darin Kurt with the Lifetime Achievement Award this evening."이라며 Darin Kurt에게 평생 공로상을 수여하게 되어 영광이라고 한 것을 통해 청자들이 시상식에 있는 것을 알 수 있다. 따라서 (D)가 정답이다.

어휘 retirement n. 은퇴 celebration n. 기념식 graduation n. 졸업

05 | 화자 문제

해설 화자의 직업은 무엇인 것 같은가?
(A) 가게 점원
(B) 요리사
(C) 웨이터
(D) 음식 평론가

해설 지문에서 신분 및 직업과 관련된 표현을 놓치지 않고 듣는다. "my first job cooking was at one of his restaurants, and I still use the skills he taught me today"라며 처음 요리 일을 시작한 곳이 그의 식당 중 한 곳이라고 한 후, 그가 자신에게 가르쳐 준 기술들을 오늘날까지도 여전히 사용하고 있다고 했으므로 화자는 요리사임을 알 수 있다. 따라서 (B)가 정답이다.

어휘 clerk n. 점원, 직원

06 | 언급 문제

해설 화자는 Mali Kaya에 대해 무엇을 말하는가?
(A) 새로운 직책을 수락했다.
(B) 식당을 열 것이다.
(C) 한 조직을 이끈다.
(D) 최근에 시카고로 이사했다.

해설 질문의 핵심 어구(Mali Kaya)가 언급된 주변을 주의 깊게 듣는다. "And his influence in our industry will likely be even greater when he replaces Mali Kaya as the head of the Chicago Restaurant Association next month."라며 Darin Kurt가 다음 달에 Mali Kaya를 대신하여 시카고 레스토랑 협회장이 되면, 업계에서의 그의 영향력은 아

마 훨씬 더 커질 것이라고 했으므로 Mali Kaya가 현재 시카고 레스토랑 협회를 이끌고 있음을 알 수 있다. 따라서 (C)가 정답이다.

어휘 relocate v. 이사하다, 이주하다

[07-09]

Questions 07-09 refer to the following talk. 미국

⁰⁷**We are holding this staff gathering to announce that *The Wabash Herald* plans to discontinue its print publications.** ⁰⁸**In order to appeal to younger consumers, we have decided to change our business model and turn the newspaper into a purely online publication.** Over the next two years, we will slowly reduce the number of newspapers that we print and eventually cease altogether. At the end of this transition, all of our content will be on our Web site. Although we feel this change is necessary, we hope the decision will not upset our long-time readers. ⁰⁹**I urge you to reach out to our current subscribers and find out any concerns they might have with our plan so we can address these issues.**

discontinue v. 중단하다   appeal to ~의 관심을 끌다
purely adv. 전적으로   cease v. 중단하다   transition n. 전환
urge v. 권장하다, 촉구하다   subscriber n. 구독자

해석
07-09번은 다음 담화에 관한 문제입니다.
⁰⁷저희는 The Wabash Herald지가 인쇄물 발행을 중단할 계획임을 발표하기 위해 이 직원 모임을 열고 있습니다. ⁰⁸더 젊은 소비자들의 관심을 끌기 위해, 저희는 비즈니스 모델을 변경하여 신문을 전적으로 온라인 출판물로 전환하기로 결정했습니다. 향후 2년 동안, 저희는 인쇄하는 신문의 수를 서서히 줄이고 결국에는 완전히 중단할 것입니다. 이 전환의 끝 무렵에, 저희의 모든 콘텐츠는 웹사이트에 게재될 것입니다. 저희는 이 변화가 필요하다고 생각하지만, 이 결정이 오랜 독자들을 실망시키지 않기를 바랍니다. ⁰⁹현재 저희의 구독자들에게 연락하여 우리 계획에 대해 그들이 가질 수 있는 우려사항을 파악하고, 이러한 문제들을 해결할 수 있도록 할 것을 권장합니다.

07 | 특정 세부 사항 문제

해석 무슨 일이 일어나고 있는가?
(A) 사업 세미나
(B) 제품 출시
(C) 이사회 회의
(D) 직원 모임

해설 질문의 핵심 어구(taking place)와 관련된 내용을 주의 깊게 듣는다. "We are holding this staff gathering to announce that The Wabash Herald plans to discontinue its print publications."라며 The Wabash Herald지가 인쇄물 발행을 중단할 계획임을 발표하기 위해 직원 모임을 열고 있다고 하였다. 따라서 (D)가 정답이다.

어휘 launch n. 출시   board n. 이사회

Paraphrasing

staff 직원 → employee 직원

08 | 이유 문제

해석 The Wabash Herald지는 왜 비즈니스 모델을 변경하고 싶어 하는가?
(A) 불필요한 지출을 줄이기 위해
(B) 해외 시장에 접근하기 위해
(C) 특정 인구 집단을 대상으로 삼기 위해
(D) 인쇄 작업을 확장하기 위해

해설 질문의 핵심 어구(change ~ business model)가 언급된 주변을 주의 깊게 듣는다. "In order to appeal to younger consumers, we have decided to change our business model and turn the newspaper into a purely online publication."이라며 더 젊은 소비자들의 관심을 끌기 위해 비즈니스 모델을 변경하여 신문을 전적으로 온라인 출판물로 전환하기로 결정했다고 하였다. 따라서 (C)가 정답이다.

어휘 reduce v. 줄이다   spending n. 지출   access v. 접근하다
specific adj. 특정한   demographic n. 인구 집단, 인구 통계
expand v. 확장하다   operation n. 작업

Paraphrasing

appeal to younger consumers 더 젊은 소비자들의 관심을 끌다
→ target a specific demographic 특정 인구 집단을 대상으로 삼다

09 | 제안 문제

해석 화자는 청자들이 무엇을 하도록 권장하는가?
(A) 의견을 모은다.
(B) 구독자들을 가입시킨다.
(C) 계획을 업데이트한다.
(D) 데이터를 검증한다.

해설 지문에서 제안과 관련된 표현이 포함된 문장을 주의 깊게 듣는다. "I urge you to reach out to our current subscribers and find out any concerns they might have with our plan so we can address these issues."라며 현재 구독자들에게 연락하여 계획에 대해 그들이 가질 수 있는 우려사항을 파악하고, 이러한 문제들을 해결할 수 있도록 할 것을 권장한다고 하였다. 따라서 (A)가 정답이다.

어휘 gather v. 모으다   verify v. 검증하다

Paraphrasing

find out ~ concerns 우려사항을 파악하다 → Gather feedback 의견을 모으다

[10-12]

Questions 10-12 refer to the following talk. 미국

Since this is your first day at Star Enterprises, you will all spend the morning undergoing a basic orientation. ¹⁰**I'm going to begin by passing around copies of our employee manual.** It contains crucial information about the company's various regulations. Moreover, the manual explains what we expect from staff, so ¹¹**I want everyone to spend about an hour reading through the rules and instructions in the materials**. After you are finished, ¹²**I will assist you with any inquiries you may have**. Then we'll use the rest of the morning to walk around the company facilities, at which point I'll introduce you to your colleagues.

undergo v. 받다, 겪다   pass around 나눠주다, ~을 돌리다
crucial adj. 중요한, 결정적인   read through 꼼꼼히 읽다
inquiry n. 문의, 질문

해석
10-12번은 다음 담화에 관한 문제입니다.
오늘은 Star Enterprises사에서 여러분의 첫날이기 때문에, 모두 기본 오리엔테이션을 받으며 오전을 보낼 것입니다. ¹⁰제가 직원 안내서 사본을 나눠주는 것으로 시작하겠습니다. 여기에는 회사의 다양한 규정에 관한 중요한 정보들이 들어 있습니다. 또한, 이 안내서는 우리가 직원들에게 무엇을 기대하는지를 설명하고 있으므로, ¹¹여러분 모두 한 시간 정도를 들여 이 자료에 있는 규

정과 지침들을 꼼꼼히 읽어 보시길 바랍니다. 이를 마친 뒤에, ¹²여러분이 가질 수 있는 모든 문의에 대해 도와드리겠습니다. 그런 뒤 남은 오전 시간은 회사 시설을 둘러보는 데 사용할 것이며, 그때 여러분을 여러분의 동료들에게 소개해 드리겠습니다.

10 | 특정 세부 사항 문제

해석 청자들은 무엇을 받을 것인가?
(A) 고객 설문 조사
(B) 직원 근무 시간 기록표
(C) 참가 신청서
(D) 직원 안내 책자

해설 질문의 핵심 어구(receive)와 관련된 내용을 주의 깊게 듣는다. "I'm going to begin by passing around copies of our employee manual."이라며 청자들에게 직원 안내서 사본을 나눠주겠다고 하였다. 따라서 (D)가 정답이다.

어휘 timecard n. 근무 시간 기록표 personnel n. 직원, 사람들
handbook n. 안내 책자

Paraphrasing
employee manual 직원 안내서 → Personnel handbooks 직원 안내 책자

11 | 요청 문제

해석 화자는 청자들에게 무엇을 하라고 요청하는가?
(A) 잠깐 휴식한다.
(B) 업무에 복귀한다.
(C) 지침을 확인한다.
(D) 해결책을 제안한다.

해설 지문의 중후반에서 요청과 관련된 표현이 언급된 주변을 주의 깊게 듣는다. "I want everyone to spend about an hour reading through the rules and instructions in the materials"라며 청자들에게 한 시간 정도를 들여 자료에 있는 규정과 지침들을 꼼꼼히 읽어 보라고 요청하였다. 따라서 (C)가 정답이다.

어휘 propose v. 제안하다 solution n. 해결책, 해법

Paraphrasing
read through 꼼꼼히 읽다 → Review 확인하다

12 | 제안 문제

해석 화자는 무엇을 해주겠다고 제안하는가?
(A) 초안을 작성한다.
(B) 교육 활동을 준비한다.
(C) 장비를 시연한다.
(D) 질문에 대답한다.

해설 지문의 중후반에서 제안과 관련된 표현이 언급된 주변을 주의 깊게 듣는다. "I will assist you with any inquiries you may have"라며 청자들이 가질 수 있는 모든 문의에 대해 도와주겠다고 하였다. 따라서 (D)가 정답이다.

어휘 outline n. 초안 demonstrate v. 시연하다

Paraphrasing
assist ~ with any inquiries 모든 문의에 대해 돕다 → Answer questions 질문에 대답하다

고난도 문제 완전 정복   p.47

01 (B)   02 (D)   03 (C)   04 (B)   05 (C)
06 (D)

[01-03]   호주

Questions 01-03 refer to the following introduction.

⁰¹Welcome to the Fifth Annual Seattle Medical Convention. This is an opportunity to learn about current developments in the field of medicine. In a few minutes, I'll bring out our keynote speaker, Kathie Yang. ⁰²She's the author of a best-selling book titled *The Future of Healthcare* . . . I strongly encourage all of you to check it out. Before we welcome Ms. Yang, I have a quick announcement about the party planned for attendees after today's talks. The party will be held in the Greenfield Ballroom. ⁰³The second-floor auditorium where the party was originally supposed to take place has a water leak. Now, let's give a warm round of applause for Ms. Yang.

field n. 분야 keynote speaker 기조 연설자 attendee n. 참석자
auditorium n. 강당 water leak 누수, 물 새는 것 applause n. 박수

해석
01-03번은 다음 소개에 관한 문제입니다.

⁰¹제5회 연례 시애틀 의료 컨벤션에 오신 것을 환영합니다. 이것은 의학 분야의 최신 발전에 대해 배울 수 있는 기회입니다. 잠시 후, 저는 우리의 기조 연설자인 Kathie Yang을 모시겠습니다. ⁰²그녀는 *The Future of Healthcare*라는 제목의 가장 잘 팔리는 책의 저자입니다... 저는 여러분 모두가 그 책을 확인해 보시기를 강력히 권합니다. Ms. Yang을 맞이하기 전에, 오늘 강연 후 참석자들을 위해 계획된 파티에 관한 간단한 공지가 있습니다. 파티는 Greenfield Ballroom에서 열릴 것입니다. ⁰³파티가 원래 열릴 예정이었던 2층 강당에 누수가 있습니다. 자, 이제 Ms. Yang에게 따뜻한 박수를 보내 주시기 바랍니다.

01 | 특정 세부 사항 문제

해석 컨벤션의 목적은 무엇인가?
(A) 새로운 의료 장비를 공개하기 위해
(B) 업계 동향에 대한 세부 사항을 제공하기 위해
(C) 신흥 기업을 홍보하기 위해
(D) 잠재적인 투자자들을 유치하기 위해

해설 질문의 핵심 어구(convention)가 언급된 주변을 주의 깊게 듣는다. "Welcome to the Fifth Annual Seattle Medical Convention."이라며 제5회 연례 시애틀 의료 컨벤션에 온 것을 환영한다고 한 후, "This is an opportunity to learn about current developments in the field of medicine."이라며 이것은 의학 분야의 최신 발전에 대해 배울 수 있는 기회라고 하였다. 따라서 (B)가 정답이다.

어휘 showcase v. 공개하다 trend n. 동향, 추세
emerging adj. 신흥의, 떠오르는 potential adj. 잠재적인

Paraphrasing
current developments in the field of medicine 의학 분야의 최신 발전 → industry trends 업계 동향

02 | 제안 문제

해석 화자는 청자들에게 무엇을 하도록 제안하는가?
(A) 일정표를 확인한다.
(B) 부스들을 방문한다.

(C) 질문들을 준비한다.
(D) 출판물을 읽는다.

해설 지문에서 제안과 관련된 표현이 포함된 문장을 주의 깊게 듣는다. "She's the author of a best-selling book titled *The Future of Healthcare* . . . I strongly encourage all of you to check it out."이라며 그녀는 *The Future of Healthcare*라는 제목의 가장 잘 팔리는 책의 저자이고, 청자들 모두가 그 책을 확인해 보기를 강력히 권한다고 하였다. 따라서 (D)가 정답이다.

어휘 publication n. 출판물

Paraphrasing
check it out 그것을 확인해 보다 → Read a publication 출판물을 읽다

03 | 의도 파악 문제

해설 화자는 "파티는 Greenfield Ballroom에서 열릴 것입니다"라고 말할 때 무엇을 의도하는가?
(A) 행사가 몇 분 안에 시작될 것이다.
(B) 참석자가 잘못된 방에 있다.
(C) 장소가 변경되었다.
(D) 공간이 활동하기에 너무 작다.

해설 질문의 인용어구(The party will be held in the Greenfield Ballroom)가 언급된 주변을 주의 깊게 듣는다. "The second-floor auditorium where the party was originally supposed to take place has a water leak."이라며 파티가 원래 열릴 예정이었던 2층 강당에 누수가 있다고 한 것을 통해 파티 장소가 변경되었음을 알 수 있다. 따라서 (C)가 정답이다.

어휘 venue n. 장소

[04-06]

Questions 04-06 refer to the following talk. 캐나다

I would like to take a few minutes to get everyone up to date on our latest project. As was discussed earlier this quarter, ⁰⁴**I commissioned Capital Group to conduct a market analysis on behalf of our company**. Well, ⁰⁵**the results have come back, and they are not promising**. As it turns out, our newest board game, Tagline, did not test well with its target consumer group. ⁰⁵**Most users thought the instructions were too complicated.** Moreover, many people found Tagline to be too similar to other games that are already on the market. Given the response from consumers, ⁰⁶**I have chosen to stop producing Tagline and channel our resources elsewhere**.

latest adj. 최근의 commission v. 의뢰하다; n. 위원회 analysis n. 분석
on behalf of ~을 대신하여 promising adj. 전망이 좋은, 유망한
complicated adj. 복잡한 channel v. 쏟다, 돌리다

해석
04-06번은 다음 담화에 관한 문제입니다.
잠시 시간을 내어 모든 분들께 우리의 최근 프로젝트에 대한 최신 정보를 알려 드리고 싶습니다. 이번 분기 초에 논의되었듯이, ⁰⁴저는 우리 회사를 대신해 시장 분석을 실시하도록 Capital Group사에 의뢰했습니다. 음, ⁰⁵결과가 돌아왔고, 그것들은 전망이 좋지 않습니다. 드러난 바와 같이, 우리의 최신 보드게임인 Tagline은 표적 소비자 집단을 대상으로 좋은 평가를 얻지 못했습니다. ⁰⁵대부분의 사용자들은 설명이 너무 복잡하다고 생각했습니다. 더불어, 많은 사람들은 Tagline이 이미 시장에 있는 다른 게임들과 너무 유사하다고 생각했습니다. 소비자들의 반응을 고려할 때, ⁰⁶저는 Tagline의 생산을 중단하고 우리의 자원을 다른 곳에 쏟기로 결정했습니다.

04 | 특정 세부 사항 문제

해석 Capital Group사는 무엇을 하도록 고용되었는가?
(A) 보드게임을 홍보한다.
(B) 시장 조사를 실시한다.
(C) 상품을 분배한다.
(D) 예산을 분석한다.

해설 질문의 핵심 어구(Capital Group)가 언급된 주변을 주의 깊게 듣는다. "I commissioned Capital Group to conduct a market analysis on behalf of our company."라며 화자의 회사를 대신해 시장 분석을 실시하도록 Capital Group사에 의뢰했다고 하였다. 따라서 (B)가 정답이다.

어휘 promote v. 홍보하다 conduct v. 실시하다 distribute v. 분배하다
budget n. 예산

05 | 특정 세부 사항 문제

해석 화자에 따르면, 무엇이 문제인가?
(A) 회사가 주문품을 조달할 수 없다.
(B) 직원이 항의를 제기했다.
(C) 제품이 부정적인 의견을 받았다.
(D) 공장이 문을 닫아야 한다.

해설 질문의 핵심 어구(problem)와 관련된 내용을 주의 깊게 듣는다. "the results have come back, and they are not promising"이라며 Capital Group사의 시장 분석 결과가 돌아왔는데 전망이 좋지 않다고 한 후, "Most users thought the instructions were too complicated."라며 대부분의 사용자들은 설명이 너무 복잡하다고 생각했다고 하였다. 따라서 (C)가 정답이다.

어휘 fulfill an order 주문품을 조달하다 file a complaint 항의를 제기하다

06 | 특정 세부 사항 문제

해석 화자는 무엇을 하기로 결정했는가?
(A) 소비자 집단을 정한다.
(B) 질문들에 응답한다.
(C) 더 많은 자금을 요청한다.
(D) 상품 생산을 중단한다.

해설 질문의 핵심 어구(decided to do)와 관련된 내용을 주의 깊게 듣는다. "I have chosen to stop producing Tagline and channel our resources elsewhere"라며 Tagline의 생산을 중단하고 자원을 다른 곳에 쏟기로 결정했다고 하였다. 따라서 (D)가 정답이다.

어휘 discontinue v. (생산을) 중단하다

Paraphrasing
stop producing 생산을 중단하다 → Discontinue 생산을 중단하다

RC

PART 5&6

DAY 01 명사와 대명사

빈출 문제 집중 훈련 p.50

01 (C)	02 (A)	03 (D)	04 (B)	05 (B)
06 (C)	07 (C)	08 (A)	09 (A)	10 (D)
11 (C)	12 (B)	13 (B)	14 (A)	15 (B)
16 (B)	17 (C)	18 (D)	19 (C)	20 (C)

01 | 명사 자리 채우기

해설 부정관사(a) 뒤에 올 수 있는 것은 명사이므로 명사 (C)와 (D)가 정답의 후보이다. 'Bryson 보험사는 시간의 양을 줄인 절차를 개발했다'라는 의미가 되어야 하므로 (C) procedure(절차)가 정답이다. (D) proceed가 명사로 쓰일 때는, '수익, 수입'이라는 의미로 항상 복수 형태(proceeds)로 쓰이기 때문에 답이 될 수 없다. 형용사 (A)와 부사 (B)는 명사 자리에 올 수 없다.

해석 Bryson 보험사는 보험금 청구를 평가하는 데 필요한 시간의 양을 줄인 절차를 개발했다.

어휘 develop v. 개발하다, 발전시키다   evaluate v. 평가하다
claim n. (보험금 등의) 청구, 주장

02 | 격에 맞는 인칭대명사 채우기

해설 as가 이끄는 절의 동사(will be taking) 앞 빈칸에는 주어가 와야 하므로 주어 역할을 할 수 있는 주격 인칭대명사 (A)와 소유대명사 (C)가 정답의 후보이다. 휴가를 가는(will be taking a leave of absence) 주체는 Ms. Tang이므로 주격 인칭대명사 (A) she가 정답이다. (C) hers를 쓰면 '그녀의 것이 휴가를 가다'라는 어색한 의미가 된다. 목적격 또는 소유격 인칭대명사 (B)와 재귀대명사 (D)는 주어 자리에 올 수 없다. 참고로, 재귀대명사는 주어와 목적어가 동일한 대상을 가리킬 때 목적어 자리에 쓰이거나, 강조하고자 하는 주어나 목적어 바로 뒤에 온다는 것을 알아둔다.

해석 Ms. Tang의 업무는 그녀의 팀의 다른 구성원에게 넘겨질 것인데, 그녀가 휴가를 갈 것이기 때문이다.

어휘 pass on 넘기다, 전달하다   leave of absence 휴가, 결근

03 | 재귀대명사 채우기

해설 타동사(finds)의 목적어 자리에 올 수 있는 소유대명사 (B), 목적격 인칭대명사 (C), 재귀대명사 (D)가 정답의 후보이다. 약간의 도움을 필요로 한다(needs some assistance)고 했으므로, '그 자신이 압도당해 있다고 느끼다'라는 의미가 되어야 한다. 따라서, 주어와 목적어가 동일한 대상을 가리킬 때 목적어 자리에 올 수 있는 재귀대명사 (D) himself가 정답이다. (B)나 (C)를 쓰면 '그의 것이 너무 압도당해 있다', '그(다른 누군가)가 너무 압도당해 있다'라는 어색한 문맥이 된다. 주격 인칭대명사 (A)는 목적어 자리에 올 수 없다.

해석 Michael Anderson은 처리해야 할 서류의 양에 그 자신이 너무 압도당해 있다고 느끼고 약간의 도움을 필요로 한다.

어휘 overwhelmed adj. 압도당한   volume n. 양, 부피
paperwork n. 서류, 서류 작업   assistance n. 도움, 지원

04 | 명사 자리 채우기

해설 타동사(gave)의 목적어 자리에 와서 형용사(official)의 꾸밈을 받을 수 있는 것은 명사이므로 명사 (A)와 (B)가 정답의 후보이다. 대변인이 전달하는(a spokesperson ~ gave) 것으로 적합한 것은 공식적인 성명이므로 (B) statement(성명)이 정답이다. (A) state(상태, 국가)를 쓰면 '대변인이 공식적인 상태/국가를 전달하다'라는 어색한 의미가 된다. 동사 또는 과거분사 (C)는 명사 자리에 올 수 없다. 동명사 또는 현재분사 (D)는 동명사일 경우 '대변인이 공식 성명하기를 전달하다'라는 어색한 문맥이 되고, 현재분사일 경우 명사 자리에 올 수 없다.

해석 금요일 기자회견에서, 시청의 대변인이 시장의 계획에 관한 공식 성명을 전달했다.

어휘 press conference 기자회견   spokesperson n. 대변인
official adj. 공식적인   regarding prep. ~에 관한, ~에 대하여
mayor n. 시장

05 | 사람명사와 사물/추상명사 구별하여 채우기

해설 부정관사(a)와 함께 타동사(feature)의 목적어 자리에 올 수 있는 명사 (B)와 (D)가 정답의 후보이다. 글이 특별히 소개하는(The article features) 것은 여행지들(travel destinations)의 모음이므로 빈칸 앞의 부정관사 (a), 빈칸 뒤의 전치사(of)와 함께 쓰여 a selection of(~의 모음)를 만드는 추상명사 (B) selection(모음, 선택)이 정답이다. 사람명사 (D) selector (선발위원)를 쓰면 '여행지들의 선발위원'이라는 어색한 문맥이 된다. 동사 또는 형용사 (A)는 명사 자리에 올 수 없다. 동명사 또는 현재분사 (C)는 동명사일 경우 부정관사(a) 다음에 올 수 없고, 현재분사일 경우 명사 자리에 올 수 없다.

해석 그 글은 유럽 최고의 여행지들 모음을 자세한 설명 및 유용한 팁과 함께 특별히 소개하고 있다.

어휘 feature v. 특별히 소개하다   destination n. 목적지   description n. 설명

06 | 명사 자리 채우기

해설 타동사(showing) 뒤에 와서 목적어로 쓰일 수 있는 것은 명사이므로 명사 (C) creativity(독창성, 창조력)가 정답이다. 참고로, showing은 전치사(in) 뒤에 와서 동명사로 쓰였지만, 여전히 동사의 성질을 가지고 있기 때문에 목적어가 필요하다는 것을 알아둔다. 동사 (A), 부사 (B), 형용사 (D)는 명사 자리에 올 수 없다.

해석 BVG Home Furnishings사는 상품 진열에 있어서 독창성을 보여주는 데 한결같고, 이 진열은 매력적이고 구매자들의 마음을 이끈다.

어휘 consistent adj. 한결같은   merchandise n. 상품   display n. 진열, 전시
appealing adj. 마음을 이끄는

07 | 격에 맞는 인칭대명사 채우기

해설 빈칸은 명사절의 주어 자리이므로 주어 자리에 들어갈 수 있는 주격 인칭대명사 (A)와 소유대명사 (C)가 정답의 후보이다. '그들의 것이 심한 얼룩과 냄새에 가장 효과적이라고 주장한다'라는 의미가 되어야 하므로 (C) theirs가 정답이다. 주격 인칭대명사 (A) they는 '그들이 심한 얼룩과 냄새에 가장 효과적이라고 주장한다'라는 어색한 문맥을 만들기 때문에 답이 될 수 없다. 소유격 인칭대명사 (B)와 재귀대명사 (D)는 주어 자리에 올 수 없다.

해석 CleanMaster사는 모든 경쟁 세탁용 세제를 시험해보았고 그들의 것이 심한 얼룩과 냄새에 가장 효과적이라고 주장한다.

어휘 compete v. 경쟁하다   detergent n. 세제   claim v. 주장하다
effective adj. 효과적인   tough adj. 심한   stain n. 얼룩   odor n. 냄새

08 | 명사 자리 채우기

해설 타동사(have decreased)의 목적어 자리에 올 수 있으면서 소유격 인칭대명사(their)의 꾸밈을 받을 수 있는 것은 명사이므로 명사 (A)와 (D)가 정답의 후보이다. '대체 에너지 자원을 사용함으로써 화석 연료에 대한 의존을 줄여왔다'라는 문맥이므로 (A) reliance(의존)가 정답이다. (D) reliability(신뢰도)를 쓰면 '대체 에너지 자원을 사용함으로써 화석 연료에 대한 신뢰도를 줄여왔다'라는 어색한 문맥이 된다. 동사 (B)와 형용사 (C)는 명사 자리에 올 수 없다.

해석 최근 보고서는 동남아시아 국가들이 대체 에너지 자원을 사용함으로써 화석 연료에 대한 의존을 줄여왔다는 것을 보여준다.

어휘 demonstrate v. 보여주다, 설명하다 fossil fuel 화석 연료
alternative energy 대체 에너지 source n. 자원, 원천
rely v. 의존하다, 믿다 reliable adj. 믿을 수 있는

09 | 다른 명사를 수식하는 명사 채우기

해설 빈칸은 빈칸 앞 명사 data와 빈칸 뒤 명사 capabilities와 함께 복합 명사를 이루는 자리이므로 명사를 수식할 수 있는 명사 (A)와 과거분사 (C)가 정답의 후보이다. '그것의 데이터 분석 능력'이라는 의미가 되어야 하므로 '데이터 분석'이라는 의미의 복합 명사 data analysis를 만드는 명사 (A) analysis(분석)가 정답이다. 과거분사 (C)를 쓸 경우 '데이터가 분석된 능력을 확장하다'라는 어색한 문맥이 되므로 답이 될 수 없다. 동사 (B)와 (D)는 명사를 꾸밀 수 없다.

해석 Namath 연구 센터는 첨단 과학 연구를 지원하기 위해 그것의 데이터 분석 능력을 확장하고 있다.

어휘 capability n. 능력, 역량 support v. 지원하다
advanced adj. 첨단의, 고급의 investigation n. 연구, 조사

10 | 명사 자리 채우기

해설 형용사 역할을 하는 과거분사(visited)의 꾸밈을 받을 수 있는 것은 명사이므로 명사 (D) attraction(명소)가 정답이다. 동사 (A)와 (C), 동사 또는 과거분사 (B)는 명사 자리에 올 수 없다.

해석 Smithfield 국립 공원에서 가장 많이 방문되는 명소는 Busch 폭포인데, 이것은 전국에서 가장 높다.

어휘 waterfall n. 폭포, 폭포수 attract v. (주의·흥미 등을) 끌다

11 | 다른 명사를 수식하는 명사 채우기

해설 빈칸은 타동사(pay)의 목적어 자리이므로 빈칸 앞 명사 fuel을 뒤에서 수식할 수 있는 현재분사 (A)와 과거분사 (D), 명사 fuel과 함께 복합 명사를 이루는 명사 (B)와 (C) 모두가 정답의 후보이다. '유류할증료를 지불하다'라는 의미가 되어야 하므로 '유류할증료'라는 의미의 복합 명사 fuel surcharge를 만들면서 앞의 부정관사(an)와 함께 쓸 수 있는 단수 명사 (C) surcharge(할증료)가 정답이다. 현재분사 (A) surcharging과 과거분사 (D) surcharged는 각각 '할증료를 부과하는/할증료가 부과되는 유류'라는 의미로 어색한 문맥을 만들기 때문에 답이 될 수 없다. (B)는 동사일 경우 명사를 꾸밀 수 없다.

해석 공항에서 렌터카 서비스에 체크인을 한 후 Mr. McBride는 예상치 못한 유류할증료를 지불해야 한다는 사실을 알게 되었다.

어휘 unexpected adj. 예상치 못한

12 | 부정형용사 채우기

해설 빈칸 뒤의 명사구(extra cost)를 꾸미기 위해서는 형용사가 와야 하므로 부정형용사 (B) no(하나의 ~도 없는)가 정답이다. 대명사 (A) none은 '아무도 ~ 않다'라는 의미로, 단독으로 명사 자리에 온다. 부사 (C) not은 '~이 아니다, ~하지 않다'라는 의미로, 명사 앞에 올 수는 있지만 '(뒤에 나오는 명사)가 아니다'라는 문맥을 만드는 것이고, 명사를 꾸밀 수는 없다.

접속사 (D) nor은 주로 neither와 함께 쓰여 상관접속사 neither A nor B(A도 B도 아니다)를 만든다.

해석 고객들은 Coffee Tree사 고객 카드를 제시함으로써 추가 비용 없이 더 큰 음료를 주문할 수 있다.

어휘 beverage n. 음료 cost n. 비용, 경비 present v. 제시하다; adj. 현재의
loyalty card 고객 카드

13 | 부정대명사 채우기

해설 빈칸은 등위접속사로 연결된 절의 주어 자리이므로, 주어 역할을 할 수 있는 부정대명사 (B)와 (C), 복합관계대명사 (D)가 정답의 후보이다. '둘 다 제안을 받지 못했다'라는 의미가 되어야 하므로, 이미 언급한 두 개의 대상이 모두 아닌 경우를 나타내는 (B) neither(둘 중 누구도 아닌)가 정답이다. (C) anybody는 불특정한 다수의 사람들을 대신할 때 쓰이고, (D) whoever는 '누구든 제안을 받은 사람'이라는 의미로 어색한 문맥을 만들기 때문에 답이 될 수 없다. 재귀대명사 (A)는 주어 자리에 올 수 없다.

해석 두 지원자 모두 매우 숙련되었고 최종 평가에서 큰 잠재력을 보였지만, 둘 중 누구도 제안을 받지 못했다.

어휘 candidate n. 지원자 highly adv. 매우 potential n. 잠재력
evaluation n. 평가 offer n. 제안; v. 제안하다

14 | 지시대명사 those 채우기

해설 빈칸은 관계절(who are developing ~)의 꾸밈을 받는 명사 자리이므로 지시대명사 (A)와 부정대명사 (C), (D)가 정답의 후보이다. 뒤에 나온 관계절의 동사 are가 복수 동사이므로 복수 동사와 짝을 이루는 (A) those(~하는 사람들)가 정답이다. (C) someone과 (D) anyone은 단수 취급하므로 답이 될 수 없다. 목적격 인칭대명사 (B) them은 관계절의 선행사가 될 수 없다.

해석 정부 지원금은 친환경 에너지 해결책을 개발하고 있는 사람들이 이용할 수 있다.

어휘 grant n. 지원금, 보조금 green energy 친환경 에너지 solution n. 해결책

15 | 명사 자리 채우기

해설 빈칸은 타동사(has)의 목적어 자리에 오면서 형용사(many)의 꾸밈을 받는 명사 자리이므로, (B) admirers(팬, 찬미하는 사람)가 정답이다. 동사 또는 과거분사 (A), 동사 (C), 형용사 (D)는 명사 자리에 올 수 없다.

해석 그 화가의 작품은 팬이 너무 많아서, 미술관은 그림 전시를 위한 더 큰 공간을 따로 잡아 두었다.

어휘 reserve v. 따로 잡아 두다, 예약하다 exhibition n. 전시

16 | 격에 맞는 인칭대명사 채우기

해설 빈칸은 명사절 접속사(that)가 이끄는 절의 주어 자리이므로, 주어 역할을 할 수 있는 주격 인칭대명사 (B)와 소유대명사 (D)가 정답의 후보이다. team은 집합명사로 복수 취급할 수 있으므로 복수를 가리키는 인칭대명사 (B) they가 정답이다. 소유대명사 (D)를 쓸 경우 '그들의 것이 글로벌 시장에서 경쟁력을 유지하는 것을 보장하다'라는 어색한 의미를 만들기 때문에 답이 될 수 없다. 소유격 인칭대명사 (A)와 목적격 인칭대명사 (C)는 주어 자리에 올 수 없다.

해석 Owell Mining사의 관리팀은 그들이 글로벌 시장에서 경쟁력을 유지하는 것을 보장하기 위해 필요한 조치를 취할 것이다.

어휘 take steps 조치를 취하다 ensure v. 보장하다 remain v. 유지하다
competitive adj. 경쟁력 있는

17-20번은 다음 이메일에 관한 문제입니다.

수신: Rob Whitlock <robwhitlock@mail.co.uk>
발신: Sandy Jenson <sandy@divinefoods.com>
제목: 서비스 요청
날짜: 11월 15일

Mr. Whitlock께,

17귀하께서 저희 출장 음식 회사에 하신 최근 문의에 대해 연락드립니다. 저희가 받은 요청은 귀하께서 12월 23일에 있을 회사 저녁 만찬에 저희 서비스가 필요하다는 것을 명시합니다. 18귀하의 이메일에 따르면, 대략 100명이 그 모임에 참석할 것이고, 고기와 채식 메뉴 옵션 둘 다를 원하고 계십니다.

19저희가 그 날짜에 가능하다는 것을 알려드리게 되어 기쁩니다. 진행하기 위해서, 메뉴를 선택하고 추가적인 행사 세부 사항을 논의하기 위한 상담 세션이 필요할 것입니다. 20가급적 빨리 약속을 잡으시려면, 555-0294로 저에게 전화 주십시오. 귀하께서 언제 오시는지 미리 알고 있어야 필요한 준비를 할 수 있습니다.

Sandy Jenson
고객 담당자
Divine Foods사

inquiry n. 문의 request n. 요청 corporate adj. 회사의, 법인의
roughly adv. 대략 vegetarian adj. 채식의; n. 채식주의(자)
in advance 미리 preparation n. 준비

17 | 명사 어휘 고르기 주변 문맥 파악

해설 '____ 회사에 하신 문의에 대해 연락한다'라는 문맥이므로 빈칸 뒤의 명사(company)와 복합 명사를 만들 수 있는 모든 보기가 정답의 후보이다. 빈칸이 있는 문장만으로 정답을 고를 수 없으므로 주변 문맥이나 전체 문맥을 파악한다. 뒤 문장에서 '회사 저녁 만찬에 서비스가 필요하다(need ~ services for a corporate dinner)'고 했으므로 이 회사는 음식 서비스를 제공하는 회사임을 알 수 있다. 따라서 (C) catering (출장 음식)이 정답이다. (A) landscape은 '조경', (B) design은 '설계, 디자인', (D) accounting은 '회계'라는 의미이다.

18 | 사람명사와 사물/추상명사 구별하여 채우기

해설 정관사(the) 뒤에 올 수 있는 것은 명사이므로 명사 (A)와 (D)가 정답의 후보이다. 100명이 참석하는(100 people attending) 것은 행사이므로 행사를 나타내는 추상명사 (D) gathering(모임)이 정답이다. 사람명사 (A) gatherer(수집하는 사람)는 '100명이 수집하는 사람에 참석하다'라는 어색한 문맥을 만든다. 동사 또는 과거분사 (B)와 동사 (C)는 명사 자리에 올 수 없다.

19 | 알맞은 문장 고르기

해석 (A) 저희는 그룹을 위해 더 큰 테이블을 예약하는 것을 확실히 했습니다.
(B) 어떤 요리가 가장 마음에 드셨는지 양식에 표시해 주세요.
(C) 저희가 그 날짜에 가능하다는 것을 알려드리게 되어 기쁩니다.
(D) 귀하가 선택하신 항목은 유감스럽게도 품절되었습니다.

해설 뒤 문장 'In order to proceed, we will require a consultation session to select the menu and discuss further event details.'에서 진행하기 위해서는 메뉴를 선택하고 추가적인 행사 세부 사항을 논의하기 위한 상담 세션이 필요할 것이라고 하고 있으므로, 빈칸에는 진행하는 것과 관련된 내용이 들어가야 함을 알 수 있다. 따라서 (C)가 정답이다.

어휘 reserve v. 예약하다 sold out 품절된

20 | 격에 맞는 인칭대명사 채우기

해설 명사구(earliest convenience) 앞에서 형용사처럼 명사를 꾸밀 수 있는 인칭대명사는 소유격이므로 (C) your가 정답이다. 주격 인칭대명사 (A), 소유대명사 (B), 재귀대명사 (D)는 명사를 꾸밀 수 없다.

고난도 문제 완전 정복 p.53

01 (C)	02 (B)	03 (A)	04 (D)	05 (C)
06 (A)	07 (C)	08 (D)	09 (A)	10 (C)
11 (C)	12 (C)			

01 | 격에 맞는 인칭대명사 채우기

해설 전치사(of)의 목적어 자리에 올 수 있는 목적격 인칭대명사 또는 소유격 인칭대명사 (B), 소유대명사 (C), 재귀대명사 (D)가 정답의 후보이다. 'Ms. Carter의 혁신적인 마케팅 전략의 개발은 고위 경영진의 주목을 끈 그녀의 성과였다'라는 의미가 되어야 하므로 of와 함께 '그녀의'라는 의미로 쓰이는 소유대명사 (C) hers가 정답이다. 참고로 'of + 소유대명사'는 소유격을 나타냄을 알아둔다. (B)는 목적격 인칭대명사일 경우 that절의 꾸밈을 받을 수 없고, 소유격 인칭대명사일 경우 뒤에 명사가 와야 하므로 답이 될 수 없다. 재귀대명사 (D)는 주어와 목적어가 동일한 대상을 가리킬 때 목적어 자리에 올 수 있지만, 동일한 대상을 가리키는 주어가 없으므로 답이 될 수 없다. 주격 인칭대명사 (A)는 목적어 자리에 올 수 없다.

해석 Ms. Carter의 혁신적인 마케팅 전략의 개발은 고위 경영진의 주목을 끈 그녀의 성과였다.

어휘 development n. 개발 innovative adj. 혁신적인 strategy n. 전략 achievement n. 성과, 업적 catch the attention 주목을 끌다 senior adj. 고위의

02 | 명사 자리 채우기

해설 정관사(the) 다음에 올 수 있고 빈칸 뒤의 과거분사구(presented by ~)의 꾸밈을 받을 수 있는 것은 명사이므로 명사 (B) suggestions(제안들)가 정답이다. 동명사 또는 현재분사 (A)는 동명사일 경우 '연구 부서가 제출한 제안하기'라는 어색한 문맥이 되고, 현재분사일 경우 명사 자리에 올 수 없다. 형용사 (C)와 동사 또는 과거분사 (D)는 명사 자리에 올 수 없다.

해석 위원회는 연구 부서가 제출한 제안들에서 몇 가지 잠재적인 결점들을 발견했다.

어휘 committee n. 위원회 potential adj. 잠재적인 flaw n. 결점, 결함

03 | 부정형용사 채우기

해설 단수 명사(driver)와 함께 쓰일 수 있는 부정형용사 (A)와 형용사 (D)가 정답의 후보이다. '적발된 어떤 운전자에게라도 벌금을 부과할 것이다'라는 의미이므로 (A) any(어떤 ~라도)가 정답이다. 부정형용사 (B) other(다른)와 수량 형용사 (C) few(거의 없는)는 복수 가산 명사와 함께 쓰인다.

해석 교통 당국은 주차 규정을 위반하여 적발된 어떤 운전자에게라도 25달러의 벌금을 부과할 것이라고 발표했다.

어휘 authority n. 당국, 권한 impose v. 부과하다, 도입하다 fine n. 벌금 in violation of ~을 위반하여 policy n. 규정, 정책

04 | 명사 자리 채우기

해설 타동사(grants)의 목적어 자리에 올 수 있는 것은 명사이므로 명사 (C)와 (D)가 정답의 후보이다. '여행 비자 연장을 승인한다'라는 의미가 되어야 하므로 (D) extensions(연장)가 정답이다. (C) extents(정도)를 쓰면 '여행 비자 정도를 승인한다'라는 어색한 의미가 되므로 답이 될 수 없다. 동사 (A)는 명사 자리에 올 수 없다. 동명사 또는 현재분사 (B)는 동명사

일 경우 연장하는 행위 자체를 강조하며 동사 grants와 함께 쓸 수 없고, 현재분사일 경우 명사 자리에 올 수 없다.

해석 출입국 관리소는 신청 시에 여행 비자가 아직 만료되지 않았다면 일반적으로 여행 비자 연장을 승인한다.

어휘 Immigration Service 출입국 관리소 grant v. 승인하다
provided conj. ~이라면 expire v. 만료되다 application n. 신청

05 | 부정대명사 채우기

해설 빈칸은 주절의 주어 자리로 명사가 와야 하므로 대명사인 모든 보기가 정답의 후보이다. '일부 구성원들은 참석했지만 다른 이들은 참여할 수 없었다'라는 의미가 되어야 하므로 부정대명사 (C) others(다른 이들)가 정답이다. (A) those는 'those + 수식어(관계절, 분사구, 전치사구)'의 형태로 '~한 사람들'이라는 의미로 쓰이거나, 앞에 언급된 복수 명사를 대신하는 지시대명사로 쓰이므로 답이 될 수 없다. those가 지시형용사로 쓰일 경우 뒤에 복수 명사가 온다. 부정대명사 (B) another(또 다른 하나)와 대명사 (D) either(어느 하나)는 복수 동사(were)와 쓰일 수 없다.

해석 경영진의 일부 구성원들은 회의에 참석했지만, 다른 이들은 일정 충돌로 인해 참여할 수 없었다.

어휘 attend v. 참석하다 conference n. 회의 participate v. 참여하다
due to ~으로 인해 scheduling conflict 일정 충돌

06 | 명사 자리 채우기

해설 정관사(the)와 전치사(of) 사이에 올 수 있는 것은 명사이므로 명사 (A) acquisition(획득, 인수)이 정답이다. 동사 또는 과거분사 (B), 동사 (C)와 (D)는 명사 자리에 올 수 없다.

해석 회사의 최근 성공의 핵심은 최첨단 소프트웨어 개발 도구의 획득이었다.

어휘 key n. 핵심, 열쇠 cutting-edge adj. 최첨단의

07 | 지시대명사 채우기

해설 전치사(than)의 목적어 역할을 하면서 전치사구(of ~ competitor)의 꾸밈을 받는 명사 자리이므로 대명사 (B)와 (D), 지시대명사 (C)가 정답의 후보이다. '주요 경쟁사의 전동 스쿠터보다 비싸다'라는 의미가 되어야 하므로 앞에 나온 단수 명사(electric scooter)를 대신하는 지시대명사 (C) that이 정답이다. (B)나 (D)를 쓰면 '주요 경쟁사의 그러한 것', '주요 경쟁사의 모든 것'이라는 어색한 문맥이 된다. 의문사 또는 관계대명사 (A) what은 전치사구의 꾸밈을 받을 수 없다.

해석 Mobility Tech사에서 생산하는 전동 스쿠터는 주요 경쟁사의 것보다 훨씬 비싸다.

어휘 competitor n. 경쟁 상대

08 | 명사 자리 채우기

해설 정관사(the)와 전치사(of) 사이에 올 수 있는 것은 명사이므로 명사 (A)와 (B), 명사 역할을 하는 동명사 (D)가 정답의 후보이다. '자동화된 기계를 사용해 포장하는 것이 신속하게 처리된다'라는 문맥이므로 동사 pack(포장하다)의 동명사형 (D) packing이 정답이다. 명사 (A)도 해석상 그럴듯해 보이지만 '꾸러미'라는 의미로 포장된 물건 자체를 의미하므로 답이 될 수 없다. (B)를 쓰면 '배송을 위한 상품의 포장 업자가 신속하게 처리된다'라는 어색한 문맥이 된다. 동사 또는 과거분사 (C)는 명사 자리에 올 수 없다.

해석 온라인 소매업체의 창고에서는 자동화된 기계를 사용해 배송을 위한 상품을 포장하는 것이 신속하게 처리된다.

어휘 retailer n. 소매업체 warehouse n. 창고 swiftly adv. 신속하게, 빨리
automated adj. 자동화된 machinery n. 기계

09 | 부정대명사 채우기

해설 빈칸은 명사절 접속사(that)가 이끄는 절의 주어 자리이므로 주어 자리에 올 수 있는 부정대명사 모두가 정답의 후보이다. '아무것도 필요한 모든 기준을 충족시키지 않았다'라는 의미가 되어야 하므로 (A) none(아무것도 ~ 않다)이 정답이다. (B) nothing(아무것도 ~ 아니다)은 전치사 of와 쓰일 때 뒤에 추상명사 또는 불가산 명사가 와야 하고, (C) nobody(아무도 ~ 않는)는 뒤에 나온 명사(proposals)와 동일한 사물을 지칭하지 않으므로 정답이 될 수 없다. (D) anything(아무 것)을 부정적인 의미로 사용하려면 부정어(not)와 함께 쓰여야 한다.

해석 국립과학연구소의 평가 위원회는 제출된 제안서 중 아무것도 필요한 모든 기준을 충족시키지 않았다는 것을 발견했다.

어휘 evaluation n. 평가 committee n. 위원회 submit v. 제출하다
proposal n. 제안서 criteria n. 기준

10 | 사람명사와 사물/추상명사 구별하여 채우기

해설 빈칸은 부사절 접속사(as)가 이끄는 절의 주어 자리이므로, 명사 (A), (B), (C)가 정답의 후보이다. '광고주들이 온라인 채널로 초점을 옮기다'라는 의미가 되어야 하므로 사람명사 (C) advertisers(광고주들)가 정답이다. (A)를 쓰면 '광고들이 온라인 채널로 초점을 옮기다'라는 어색한 문맥이 되고, 단수 명사 (B)는 복수 동사(shift)와 쓰일 수 없을 뿐만 아니라 '광고(업)이 온라인 채널로 초점을 옮기다'라는 어색한 문맥이 된다. 동사 (D)는 명사 자리에 올 수 없다.

해석 디지털 마케팅 산업은 광고주들이 온라인 채널로 초점을 옮기면서 상당한 성장을 보여줬다.

어휘 significant adj. 상당한 shift v. 옮기다 focus n. 초점

11 | 명사 자리 채우기

해설 형용사(unlimited)의 꾸밈을 받을 수 있는 것은 명사이므로 명사 역할을 하는 동명사 (B)와 명사 (C)가 정답의 후보이다. '무제한 이체를 할 수 있다'라는 의미가 되어야 하므로, 명사 (C) transfers(이체, 이동)가 정답이다. 참고로, make transfers는 '이체하다'라는 의미의 관용 표현으로 쓰인다. 동명사 (B)도 해석상 그럴듯해 보이지만, 이체하는 행위 자체를 강조하며, 동사 make와 함께 쓸 수 없다. 형용사 (A)와 동사 또는 과거분사 (D)는 명사 자리에 올 수 없다.

해석 프리미엄 계좌 보유자들은 추가 수수료 없이 그들의 예금 계좌와 저축 계좌 간에 무제한 이체를 할 수 있다.

어휘 holder n. 보유자 unlimited adj. 무제한의 additional adj. 추가의
transferable adj. 이동이 가능한

12 | 부정대명사 채우기

해설 빈칸은 주절의 주어 자리이므로, 주어 자리에 올 수 있는 모든 보기가 정답의 후보이다. '둘 중 누구 하나든 기조 연설자로 훌륭하다'라는 의미가 되어야 하므로 부정대명사 (C) either(둘 중 어느 하나)가 정답이다. (A) neither는 '둘 다 아닌 것'이라는 의미이므로 답이 될 수 없다. 명사절 접속사 또는 관계대명사 (B) which와 복합관계대명사 (D) whoever는 뒤에 또 다른 절이 와야 하므로 답이 될 수 없다.

해석 Dr. Mbeki와 Dr. Gupta는 재생 에너지 전문가이기 때문에, 둘 중 누구 하나든 환경 학술 토론회의 기조 연설자로 훌륭할 것이다.

어휘 expert n. 전문가 renewable energy 재생 에너지
keynote speaker 기조 연설자 symposium n. 학술 토론회

DAY 02 형용사와 부사

빈출 문제 집중 훈련
p.54

01 (B)	02 (B)	03 (B)	04 (D)	05 (A)
06 (C)	07 (B)	08 (B)	09 (A)	10 (D)
11 (C)	12 (D)	13 (B)	14 (A)	15 (D)
16 (A)	17 (C)	18 (C)	19 (D)	20 (C)

01 | 형용사 자리 채우기

해설 빈칸 뒤의 명사(candidate)를 꾸밀 수 있는 것은 형용사이므로 형용사 (B)와 형용사 역할을 하는 현재분사 (D)가 정답의 후보이다. '적합한 후보가 찾아질 때까지 많은 지원자들을 검토했다'라는 의미가 되어야 하므로 형용사 (B) suitable(적합한)이 정답이다. 현재분사 (D)는 '적합하게 하는 후보'라는 어색한 문맥을 만들기 때문에 답이 될 수 없다. 명사 또는 동사 (A)는 명사일 경우 candidate(후보)과 복합 명사를 이룰 수 없고, 동사일 경우 명사를 꾸밀 수 없다. 부사 (C)는 명사를 꾸밀 수 없다.

해석 인사부장은 그 자리에 적합한 후보가 찾아질 때까지 많은 지원자들을 검토했다.

어휘 screen v. 검토하다, 가려내다   dozens of 많은   applicant n. 지원자
candidate n. 후보   position n. 자리, 위치
suit n. 정장; v. ~에게 맞다, 어울리다

02 | 형용사 자리 채우기

해설 빈칸 뒤의 명사(concept)를 꾸밀 수 있는 것은 형용사이므로 형용사 (B) innovative(혁신적인)가 정답이다. 명사 (A) innovation(혁신)은 concept(컨셉)와 복합 명사를 이룰 수 없고, 부사 (C)와 동사 (D)는 명사를 꾸밀 수 없다.

해석 새로 지어진 Masterson 컨벤션 센터는 혁신적인 컨셉과 디자인으로 여러 건축상을 받았다.

어휘 architectural adj. 건축의   innovate v. 혁신하다, 쇄신하다

03 | 부사 자리 채우기

해설 빈칸 뒤의 동사(authorized)를 꾸밀 수 있는 것은 부사이므로 부사 (B) officially(공식적으로)가 정답이다. 동사 (A), 명사 (C), 명사 또는 형용사 (D)는 동사를 꾸밀 수 없다.

해석 지난주에 최고 경영자는 자카르타에 있는 공장에서 근무하는 모든 정규직 직원들을 위한 급여 인상을 공식적으로 승인했다.

어휘 authorize v. 승인하다, 허가하다   raise n. 인상; v. 올리다
full-time adj. 정규직의   officiate v. 공무를 수행하다
official n. 공무원, 임원; adj. 공식적인

04 | 부사 자리 채우기

해설 동사(would be compensated)를 꾸밀 수 있는 것은 부사이므로 부사 (B)와 (D)가 정답의 후보이다. '고객이 그에 맞게 보상받을 것이다'라는 의미가 되어야 하므로 (D) accordingly(그에 맞게)가 정답이다. (B) according은 주로 'according to + 명사'(~에 따르면)의 형태로 쓰인다. 동사 또는 과거분사 (A), 명사 또는 동사 (C)는 부사 자리에 올 수 없다.

해석 이삿짐 운송 회사는 가구를 손상시킨 것에 대해 사과했고 고객이 그에 맞게 보상받을 것이라고 말했다.

어휘 moving company 이삿짐 운송 회사   apologize v. 사과하다
damage v. 손상시키다; n. 손상   compensate v. 보상하다
accord v. 일치시키다, (권한·지위 등을) 부여하다; n. 합의

05 | 수량 표현 채우기

해설 빈칸 뒤에 복수 가산 명사(donations)가 있으므로 복수 가산 명사 앞에 오는 수량 표현 (A) many(많은)가 정답이다. (B) much(많은)는 불가산 명사 앞에 온다. (C) very는 주로 '매우, 몹시'라는 의미의 부사로 쓰이지만, 형용사로 쓰일 경우 주로 the, 소유격 인칭대명사 등과 함께 쓰며 '바로 그'라는 의미를 나타낸다. 부사 (D) rather(오히려, 차라리)는 명사를 꾸밀 수 없다.

해석 Greenway 모금 행사의 성공은 그 단체의 회원들의 많은 개인 기부 덕분으로 여겨졌다.

어휘 fundraiser n. 모금 행사   be attributed to ~의 덕분으로 여겨지다
individual adj. 개인의   donation n. 기부   organization n. 단체

06 | 부사 자리 채우기

해설 동사(must be ~ dialed)를 꾸밀 수 있는 것은 부사이므로 부사 (C) repeatedly(반복적으로)가 정답이다. 형용사 (A), 명사 (B), 동사 또는 과거분사 (D)는 동사를 꾸밀 수 없다.

해석 거의 매일, 고객 서비스 번호는 통화 중이어서 직원이 응대할 수 있게 되기 전까지 반복적으로 전화를 걸어야 한다.

어휘 busy adj. 통화 중인   dial v. 전화를 걸다   representative n. 직원, 대표자
available adj. ~할 수 있는, 이용할 수 있는

07 | 형용사 자리 채우기

해설 빈칸 뒤의 명사(staff)를 꾸밀 수 있는 형용사 (B)와 형용사 역할을 하는 과거분사 (D)가 정답의 후보이다. '언젠간 관리 직원이 될 가능성이 높다'라는 의미가 되어야 하므로 형용사 (B) managerial(관리의, 운영의)가 정답이다. 과거분사 (D) managed를 쓸 경우, '언젠간 관리되는 직원이 될 가능성이 높다'라는 어색한 문맥이 된다. 동사 (A)와 (C)는 명사를 꾸밀 수 없다.

해석 Darwood 제조사는 유망한 젊은 직원들이 언젠간 관리 직원이 될 가능성이 높기 때문에 종종 그들을 리더십 세미나로 보낸다.

어휘 promising adj. 유망한, 장래성 있는

08 | 수량 표현 채우기

해설 복수 가산 명사(errors) 앞에 쓸 수 있는 수량 표현 (B)와 (C)가 정답의 후보이다. '많은 양의 자료를 분석할 때 약간의 오류는 예상되지만'이라는 의미가 되어야 하므로 (B) some(약간의)이 정답이다. (C) both(둘 다의)를 쓰면 '많은 양의 자료를 분석할 때 둘 다의 오류는 예상되지만'이라는 어색한 문맥이 된다. (A) less(~보다 적은)는 불가산 명사 앞에 쓰이고, (D) every(모든)는 단수 가산 명사 앞에 쓰인다.

해석 비록 많은 양의 자료를 분석할 때 약간의 오류는 예상되지만, 연구원들은 전체적으로 정확한 정보를 전달해야 한다.

어휘 analyze v. 분석하다, 검토하다   convey v. 전달하다, 운반하다
accurate adj. 정확한   overall adv. 전체적으로

09 | 강조 부사 채우기

해설 전치사구(with ~ revenues) 전체를 수식할 수 있는 것은 부사이므로 부사 (A)와 (B)가 정답의 후보이다. '심지어 최근 판매 수익 감소에도 여전히 수익성이 높은 회사이다'라는 의미가 되어야 하므로 단어나 구를 앞에서 강조하는 강조 부사 (A) Even(심지어 ~도)이 정답이다. (B) Early(일찍)를 쓰면 '최근 판매 수익 감소가 일찍 있는 채로, 여전히 수익성이 높은 회사이다'라는 어색한 문맥이 된다. 참고로, Early가 전치사구를 수식할 때는 Early in the morning(아침 일찍), Early in life(인생 초반에)와 같이 특정 시점을 나타낼 때 주로 사용된다. (C) Ever since(~이후로 줄곧)와 (D) So that(~하기 위해)은 완전한 절과 함께 쓰인다.

해석 심지어 최근 판매 수익 감소에도, Morton Electronics사는 여전히 수익성이 높은 회사이다.
어휘 revenue n. 수익 profitable adj. 수익성이 높은

10 | 부사 자리 채우기

해설 동사(approaches)를 꾸밀 수 있는 것은 부사이므로 부사 (D) systemically(조직적으로)가 정답이다. 명사 (A), 형용사 (B)와 (C)는 동사를 꾸밀 수 없다.
해석 새로 임명된 회계부장은 이전 관리자보다 과제들에 더 조직적으로 접근한다.
어휘 appointed adj. 임명된 head of accounting 회계부장 approach v. 접근하다 challenge n. 과제, 도전 systemic adj. 조직의, 전체에 영향을 주는 systematic adj. 체계적인

11 | 형용사 자리 채우기

해설 빈칸 앞에 be동사(are)가 있으므로 be동사의 보어 자리에 올 수 있는 명사 (B)와 형용사 (C)가 정답의 후보이다. 빈칸 앞의 부사(highly)의 꾸밈을 받을 수 있는 것은 형용사이므로 형용사 (C) resistant(저항력 있는)가 정답이다. 명사 (B)는 부사의 꾸밈을 받을 수 없고, 동사 (A)와 부사 (D)는 보어 자리에 올 수 없다.
해석 농업 센터에 있는 과학자들은 흔한 식물 질병에 매우 저항력이 있는 농작물 품종들을 연구하고 있다.
어휘 agriculture n. 농업 crop n. 농작물, 수확량 variety n. 품종, 다양성 resist v. 저항하다, 참다 resistance n. 저항

12 | 부사 자리 채우기

해설 빈칸 앞의 동사구(should be handed in)를 꾸밀 수 있는 것은 부사이므로 부사 (D) directly(곧장, 직접적으로)가 정답이다. 형용사 또는 동사 (A), 동사 또는 과거분사 (B), 동사 (C)는 동사를 꾸밀 수 없다.
해석 영업직에 대한 입사 지원서는 Capita사의 인사 부서로 곧장 제출되어야 한다.
어휘 hand in 제출하다 directed adj. 지시 받은, 규제된

13 | 부사 자리 채우기

해설 빈칸 앞의 시간 표현(20 years)과 함께 쓰일 수 있는 부사가 와야 하므로 부사 (B), (C), (D)가 정답의 후보이다. '20년 전에 설립된 CyberPulse Dynamics사'라는 문맥이므로 (B) ago(전에)가 정답이다. 참고로, ago는 시간 바로 다음에 와서, 현재를 기준으로 그 시간 이전에 일어난 일을 나타낸다. (C) later는 '나중에', (D) yet은 '아직'이라는 의미로 어색한 문맥을 만든다. 형용사 (A)는 부사 자리에 올 수 없다.
해석 20년 전에 설립된 CyberPulse Dynamics사는 사이버보안 분야에서 전통적인 접근 방식에 계속해서 도전하고 있다.
어휘 establish v. 설립하다 continue v. 계속하다 challenge v. 도전하다 traditional adj. 전통적인 approach n. 접근 방식; v. 접근하다 cybersecurity n. 사이버보안 previous adj. 이전의

14 | 부사 자리 채우기

해설 형용사(positive)를 꾸밀 수 있는 것은 부사이므로 부사 (A) noticeably(눈에 띄게)가 정답이다. 동사 (B), 형용사 (C), 동명사 또는 현재분사 (D)는 형용사를 꾸밀 수 없다.
해석 새로운 응대 지침을 시행한 이래로, 고객 서비스에 대한 고객들의 피드백은 눈에 띄게 긍정적이었다.
어휘 regarding prep. ~에 대한 implementation n. 시행 response n. 응대 protocol n. 지침, 의례

15 | 빈도 부사 채우기

해설 '강당 내 공간이 거의 남아 있지 않았다'라는 의미가 되어야 하므로 (D) Hardly(거의 ~ 않다)가 정답이다. (A) Never(결코 ~ 않다), (B) Unlikely(~할 것 같지 않게), (C) Slightly(약간)를 쓸 경우 어색한 문맥이 된다.
해석 회의에 늦게 도착한 부동산 중개인들을 위한 강당 내 공간이 거의 남아 있지 않았다.
어휘 remain v. 남아 있다 auditorium n. 강당 conference n. 회의

16 | 형용사 자리 채우기

해설 빈칸은 be동사 are의 주격 보어 자리이므로 형용사 (A)와 명사 (C)가 정답의 후보이다. '제조 공정은 환경 지속 가능성 지침을 준수한다'라는 의미가 되어야 하므로 형용사 (A) compliant(준수하는)가 정답이다. 명사 (C)를 쓸 경우 주어와 동격이 되어 '제조 공정은 환경 지속 가능성 지침과 준수이다'라는 어색한 의미가 되므로 답이 될 수 없다. 부사 (B)와 동사 (D)는 주격 보어 자리에 올 수 없다. (D) complied를 과거분사로 본다 해도 자동사이므로 수동형으로 쓰일 수 없다.
해석 모든 Virgo Star사 공장들에서 사용되는 제조 공정은 환경 지속 가능성 지침을 준수한다.
어휘 employ v. 사용하다 sustainability n. 지속 가능성

17-20번은 다음 이메일에 관한 문제입니다.

수신: Hunter Leitch <hunterleitch@shag.com>
발신: Marvin Goodly <marvingoodly@shag.com>
날짜: 1월 20일
제목: 판매 보고서

작년 매출 보고서를 준비해주심에 감사드립니다. 전반적으로, 보고서는 꽤 면밀하고, 구성이 이해하기 쉽습니다. [17]특히, 도표들이 논리적이고 해석하기 쉽습니다.

하지만, 몇 가지 사소한 수정을 요청하고 싶습니다. [18]그것들이 너무 많은 시간이 걸리지 않기를 바랍니다. [19]첫째로, 어느 지역이 Armin 바닥 깔개 구매 수의 가장 많은 비율을 차지했는지에 대해 더 많은 세부 사항이 있어야 하는데, 그것은 우리가 현재 국제적으로 파는 유일한 상품이기 때문입니다. 우리는 우리의 해외 시장을 확장하는 것을 고려하고 있기 때문에, 이 정보가 도움이 될 것입니다. 또한, Dudley 깔개가 홍보되는 방식에서의 변경 사항에 대해 더 알고 싶습니다. [20]보고서는 새로운 전략이 판매된 수량에 커다란 영향을 끼쳤는지 명확히 나타내야 합니다. 질문이 있다면, 주저 말고 물어보십시오.

Marvin Goodly

overall adv. 전반적으로 thorough adj. 면밀한, 철저한
layout n. 구성, 배치, 기획 straightforward adj. 쉬운, 간단한
interpret v. 해석하다, 이해하다 minor adj. 사소한, 중요치 않은
modification n. 수정, 변경 account for (~의 비율을) 차지하다
area rug 바닥 깔개 presently adv. 현재
internationally adv. 국제적으로, 국제간에
market n. 시장; v. 홍보하다, 시장에 내놓다 significant adj. 커다란, 중요한
impact n. 영향, 충격

17 | 접속부사 채우기 주변 문맥 파악

해설 빈칸이 콤마와 함께 문장의 맨 앞에 온 접속부사 자리이므로, 앞 문장과 빈칸이 있는 문장의 의미 관계를 파악하여 정답을 선택한다. 앞 문장에서 보고서가 꽤 면밀하고 구성이 이해하기 쉽다고 했고, 빈칸이 있는 문장에서는 도표들이 논리적이고 해석하기 쉽다고 했으므로, 앞 문장에서 언급된 내용 중 특별한 일부 내용에 대해 언급할 때 사용되는 (C) In particular(특히)가 정답이다.

어휘 granted adv. 가령 ~이라 하더라도 either way 어느 쪽이든
in reality 사실은

18 | 알맞은 문장 고르기

해석 (A) 당신은 그 자리에 매우 추천받았습니다.
(B) 우리는 다수의 오타를 발견했습니다.
(C) 그것들이 너무 많은 시간이 걸리지 않기를 바랍니다.
(D) 제가 당신의 요청을 올바르게 이해했는지 알려주시길 바랍니다.

해설 앞 문장 'I would like to request a few minor modifications'에서 몇 가지 사소한 수정을 요청하고 싶다고 했으므로, 빈칸에는 수정과 관련된 내용이 들어가야 함을 알 수 있다. 따라서 (C)가 정답이다.

어휘 recommend v. 추천하다 typographical error 오타

19 | 형용사 자리 채우기

해설 빈칸 뒤의 명사(number)를 꾸밀 수 있는 것은 형용사이므로 형용사 (A), (B), (D)가 정답의 후보이다. 빈칸 앞에 최상급 표현과 함께 쓰이는 the가 있으므로 형용사의 최상급 (D) greatest가 정답이다. 원급 (A)와 비교급 (B)는 최상급 자리에 올 수 없고, 부사 (C)는 형용사 자리에 올 수 없다.

20 | 부사 자리 채우기

해설 빈칸 뒤의 동사(indicate)를 꾸미기 위해서는 부사가 와야 하므로 부사 (C) clearly(명확히)가 정답이다. 명사 (A)와 (D), 동사 또는 형용사 (B)는 동사를 꾸밀 수 없다.

어휘 clarity n. 명료성 clearance n. 제거, 정리

고난도 문제 완전 정복
• p.57

01	(C)	02	(B)	03	(B)	04	(B)	05	(D)
06	(A)	07	(B)	08	(A)	09	(D)	10	(C)
11	(B)	12	(C)						

01 | 부정 형용사 채우기

해설 빈칸 뒤에 단수 가산 명사(option)가 있으므로 단수 가산 명사 앞에 쓰이는 (C) neither(둘 중 어느 것도 ~ 아니다)가 정답이다. (A) several(여러 개의)은 복수 가산 명사 앞에 쓰이고, (B) most(대부분의)는 불가산 명사 또는 복수 가산 명사 앞에 쓰인다. (D) none(어떤 ~도 없다)은 'none of the + 명사' 형태로 쓰여야 한다.

해석 두 마케팅팀의 제안을 들은 후에, Mr. Kowalski는 둘 중 어떤 선택도 적합해 보이지 않는다고 결정했다.

어휘 proposal n. 제안, 제의 determine v. 결정하다, 알아내다
appropriate adj. 적합한, 적절한

02 | 형용사 자리 채우기

해설 빈칸 뒤의 명사(differences)를 꾸밀 수 있는 형용사 (B)와 (D), 형용사 역할을 하는 현재분사 (C)가 정답의 후보이다. '주목할 만한 차이점을 찾지 못했다'라는 문맥이므로 형용사 (B) observable(주목할 만한)이 정답이다. 형용사 (D)와 현재분사 (C)를 쓰면 '관찰력 있는/관찰하는 차이점'이라는 어색한 의미가 된다. 명사 (A) observation(관찰)은 differences(차이점)와 복합 명사를 이루지 못하므로 답이 될 수 없다.

해석 연구자들은 새 치료법에 대한 환자들의 반응에서 통계적으로 유의미한 주목할 만한 차이점을 찾지 못했다.

어휘 researcher n. 연구원 statistical adj. 통계적인 response n. 반응, 응답
treatment n. 치료법, 치료

03 | 부사 자리 채우기

해설 빈칸 앞의 동사(has been running)를 꾸밀 수 있는 것은 부사이므로 부사 (B)와 (C)가 정답의 후보이다. '생산 일정이 늦어져서'라는 의미가 되어야 하므로 (B) late(늦게)가 정답이다. (C)는 '생산 일정이 최근에 되어 가다'라는 어색한 문맥을 만든다. 명사 (A)와 형용사의 최상급 (D)는 동사를 꾸밀 수 없다.

해석 생산 일정이 늦어져서, 관리자는 다른 교대조를 추가하지 않을 수 없다.

어휘 production n. 생산 supervisor n. 관리자, 감독관
shift n. 교대조; v. 옮기다, 이동하다

04 | 형용사 자리 채우기

해설 빈칸 뒤의 명사(phase)를 꾸밀 수 있는 것은 형용사이므로 형용사 (B) exploratory(탐색적인)가 정답이다. 명사 (C) explorations(탐험들)는 phase(단계)와 복합 명사를 이루지 못하므로 답이 될 수 없다. 동사 (A)는 명사를 꾸밀 수 없다. 동사 또는 과거분사 (D)는 동사일 경우 명사를 꾸밀 수 없고, 과거분사일 경우 '사업 개발팀은 현재 탐색된 단계에 있다'라는 어색한 문맥을 만든다.

해석 사업 개발팀은 현재 해외 확장 프로젝트의 탐색적 단계에 있다.

어휘 phase n. 단계 overseas adj. 해외의; adv. 해외로
explore v. 탐험하다, 조사하다

05 | 형용사 자리 채우기

해설 빈칸 뒤의 명사(party)를 꾸밀 수 있는 것은 형용사이므로 형용사 (D) Either(어느 쪽 ~이라도)가 정답이다. 부사 (A), (B), (C)는 명사를 꾸밀 수 없다. (B) Still을 형용사로 볼 경우, '소송의 고요한 당사자'라는 어색한 문맥이 되고, (C) Inside를 전치사로 볼 경우, 주어 자리에 전치사구가 오기 때문에 답이 될 수 없다.

해석 소송의 어느 쪽 당사자라도 모든 절차적 규칙이 준수되는 한 재판 중에 추가 증거를 제출할 수 있다.

어휘 party n. 당사자 lawsuit n. 소송 additional adj. 추가적인
evidence n. 증거 trial n. 재판 procedural adj. 절차적인
observe v. 준수하다, 관찰하다

06 | 부사 어휘 고르기

해설 '이번 연도 후반에 제조 공장을 방문할 예정이다'라는 문맥이므로 (A) later(말에, 나중에)가 정답이다. (B) almost는 '거의', (C) immediately는 '즉시', (D) soon은 '곧'이라는 의미이다.

해석 투자자들은 결정을 내리기 전에 생산 능력을 평가하기 위해 이번 연도 후반에 제조 공장을 방문할 예정이다.

어휘 investor n. 투자자 manufacturing plant 제조 공장 assess v. 평가하다
capability n. 능력

07 | 강조 부사 채우기

해설 형용사 역할을 하는 수 표현(two)을 꾸밀 수 있는 것은 부사이므로 부사 (A)와 (B)가 정답의 후보이다. '단지 두 개의 작은 사무실'이라는 의미가 되어야 하므로 강조를 나타내는 부사 (B) only(단지, 오직)가 정답이다. 형용사, 부사 또는 접속사 (A) else는 부사로 쓰일 경우 '또 다른'이라는 의미로 이미 언급된 것에 덧붙여 쓰이며, 형용사로 쓰일 경우 '그 밖의'라는 의미로 부정대명사 또는 의문대명사를 꾸미고, 접속사로 쓰일 경우 '아니면, 그렇지 않으면'이라는 의미로 or와 함께 쓰인다. 전치사 (C) including은 '~을 포함하여'라는 의미이고, (D) beyond는 '~을 넘어'라는 의미이다.

해석 온라인 교육 스타트업 Forsante사는 현재로서는 산호세 대도시 지역에 단지 두 개의 작은 사무실만 가지고 있다.

어휘 as of now 현재로서는 metropolitan adj. 대도시의

08 | 부사 자리 채우기

해설 형용사(experienced)를 꾸밀 수 있는 것은 부사이므로 부사 (A)와 (B)가 정답의 후보이다. '매우 경험이 풍부한 엔지니어'라는 의미가 되어야 하므로 (A) highly(매우)가 정답이다. 부사 (B)를 쓸 경우, '높이 경험이 풍부한 엔지니어'라는 어색한 문맥이 된다. 형용사의 비교급 (C)와 형용사의 최상급 (D)는 부사 자리에 올 수 없다. (C)와 (D)를 각각 부사의 비교급, 최상급으로 본다 해도, 부사의 비교급 및 최상급은 형용사를 앞에서 꾸미지 못하고, 동사를 뒤에서 수식하기 때문에 답이 될 수 없다.

해석 Sterkis Tech사는 제품 개발팀을 이끌 매우 경험이 풍부한 엔지니어들을 지속적으로 찾고 있다.

어휘 constantly adv. 지속적으로 experienced adj. 경험이 풍부한
lead v. 이끌다

09 | 접속부사 채우기

해설 빈칸은 접속사 and와 함께 절(Our new platform ~ responsive)과 절 (users ~ interactions)을 연결하고 있으므로, 절과 절을 연결하는 접속부사인 모든 보기가 정답의 후보이다. '우리의 새로운 플랫폼은 믿을 수 없을 정도로 반응이 빠르고, 더 중요하게는, 사용자들이 원활한 상호작용을 경험했다.'라는 의미가 되어야 하므로 (D) more importantly(더 중요하게는)가 정답이다. (A) first of all은 '우선', (B) on the contrary는 '그와는 반대로', (C) as an alternative는 '대안으로서'라는 의미이다.

해석 우리의 새로운 플랫폼은 믿을 수 없을 정도로 반응이 빠르고, 더 중요하게는, 사용자들이 원활한 상호작용을 경험했다.

어휘 incredibly adv. 믿을 수 없을 정도로 responsive adj. 반응이 빠른, 대답의
seamless adj. 원활한, 아주 매끄러운 interaction n. 상호작용

10 | 형용사 자리 채우기

해설 빈칸 뒤의 명사(fee)를 꾸밀 수 있는 것은 형용사이므로 형용사 (B)와 (C), 형용사 역할을 하는 과거분사 (D)가 정답의 후보이다. '검진에 대해 적정한 진단 비용을 청구한다'라는 의미가 되어야 하므로 형용사 (C) diagnostic (진단의)이 정답이다. 형용사 (B)는 '진단할 수 있는 비용', 과거분사 (D)는 '진단된 비용'이라는 어색한 문맥을 만들기 때문에 답이 될 수 없다. 동사 (A)는 명사를 꾸밀 수 없다.

해석 Ostia 건강 센터는 건강 악화의 초기 징후를 감지하기 위한 검진에 대해 적정한 진단 비용을 청구한다.

어휘 affordable adj. 적정한, 감당할 수 있는 screening n. 검진, 심사
indicator n. 징후, 지표

11 | 빈도 부사 채우기

해설 '중요한 고객 프레젠테이션이 필요한 때를 제외하고는 먼 지역으로 거의 출장을 가지 않는다'라는 의미가 되어야 하므로 (B) seldom(거의 ~ 않는)이 정답이다. (A) little(적은), (C) far(멀리), (D) almost(거의)를 쓸 경우 어색한 문맥이 된다.

해석 영업 담당자들은 중요한 고객 프레젠테이션이 필요한 때를 제외하고는 먼 지역으로 거의 출장을 가지 않는다.

어휘 sales representative 영업 담당자 remote adj. 먼 critical adj. 중요한

12 | 형용사 자리 채우기

해설 빈칸 뒤의 명사(factors)를 꾸밀 수 있는 것은 형용사이므로 형용사 (B)와 형용사 역할을 하는 현재분사 (C)가 정답의 후보이다. '기후 변화에 기여하는 결정적인 요인들'이라는 의미가 되어야 하므로 (C) determining (결정적인)이 정답이다. (B)는 '결정할 수 있는 요인들'이라는 어색한 문맥을 만들기 때문에 답이 될 수 없다. 동사 (A)는 명사를 꾸밀 수 없다. 명사 (D) determination(결정)은 factors(요인들)와 복합 명사를 이루지 못하므로 답이 될 수 없다.

해석 Halston 협회의 과학자들은 기후 변화에 기여하는 결정적인 요인들을 30년이 넘도록 조사해 왔다.

어휘 investigate v. 조사하다 factor n. 요인 contribute v. 기여하다
decade n. 10년

DAY 03 동사

빈출 문제 집중 훈련
p.58

01 (A)	02 (B)	03 (D)	04 (D)	05 (B)
06 (C)	07 (D)	08 (C)	09 (D)	10 (A)
11 (C)	12 (A)	13 (B)	14 (B)	15 (C)
16 (B)	17 (C)	18 (C)	19 (C)	20 (D)

01 | 올바른 시제의 동사 채우기

해설 문장에 동사가 없으므로 모든 보기가 정답의 후보이다. 과거 시점을 나타내는 표현(last month)이 있으므로 과거 시제 (A) hired가 정답이다. 현재완료 시제 (B), 현재진행 시제 (C), 미래 시제 (D)는 과거를 나타내는 표현과 함께 쓰일 수 없다.

해석 Mr. Mendoza는 지난달에 그의 새집의 실내 장식을 맡을 디자이너를 고용했다.

어휘 handle v. 맡다, 다루다, 처리하다 decoration n. 장식

02 | 주어와 수일치하는 동사 채우기

해설 문장에 주어(A National Medical Association committee)만 있고 동사가 없으므로 동사 (A)와 (B)가 정답의 후보이다. 주어가 3인칭 단수이므로 동사 choose(선정하다)의 3인칭 단수형 (B) chooses가 정답이다. (A)는 1인칭이나 2인칭 주어 및 3인칭 복수 주어와 함께 써야 한다. 동명사 또는 현재분사 (C)와 과거분사 (D)는 동사 자리에 올 수 없다.

해석 9명의 임원들로 구성된 전국 의료 협회 위원회는 전문가 모임에서 그 단체를 대변하기 위해 매년 한 명의 회원을 선정한다.

어휘 association n. 협회 compose v. 구성하다
represent v. 대변하다, 대표하다 gathering n. 모임, 수집

03 | 태에 맞는 동사 채우기

해설 be동사(is) 뒤에 와서 각각 진행시제와 수동태를 만들 수 있는 현재분사 (A)와 과거분사 (D)가 정답의 후보이다. 주어(Bridgeport's annual craft fair)와 동사(hold)가 'Bridgeport의 연례 공예 박람회가 개최되다'라는 수동의 의미가 되어야 하므로 과거분사 (D) held가 정답이다.

해석 Bridgeport의 연례 공예 박람회는 Oak Bay 커뮤니티 센터의 대강당에서 개최된다.

어휘 annual adj. 연례의 craft n. 공예 auditorium n. 강당

04 | 조동사 다음에 동사원형 채우기

해설 조동사(should) 다음에는 동사원형이 와야 하므로 동사원형 (D) address(다루다)가 정답이다. 동명사 또는 현재분사 (A), 동사 또는 과거분사 (B), 3인칭 단수형 동사 (C)는 조동사 다음에 올 수 없다.

해석 시 정부는 높은 세금과 복잡한 규제와 같이 소기업 경영주들이 흔히 마주하는 문제들을 다뤄야 한다.

어휘 complex adj. 복잡한 regulation n. 규제

05 | 올바른 시제의 동사 채우기

해설 문장에 동사가 없으므로 동사 (A), (B), (C)가 정답의 후보이다. 미래를 나타내는 시간 표현(next Wednesday)이 있으므로 미래 시제 (B) will return이 정답이다. (A)는 1인칭이나 2인칭 주어 및 3인칭 복수 주어와 함께 써야 한다. 과거 시제 (C)는 미래를 나타내는 표현과 함께 쓰일 수 없다. 동명사 또는 현재분사 (D)는 동사 자리에 올 수 없다.

해석 Mr. Didier는 중요한 고객 미팅에 딱 맞춰서 다음 주 수요일에 런던으로의 출장에서 돌아올 것이다.

어휘 business trip 출장

06 | 태에 맞는 동사 채우기

해설 문장에 동사가 없으므로 동사 (A), (B), (C)가 정답의 후보이다. 주어(Mai-Thai Resort)와 동사(situate)가 'Mai-Thai 리조트는 ~에 위치해 있다'라는 수동의 의미가 되어야 하므로 수동태 동사 (C) is situated가 정답이다.

해석 푸켓의 Mai-Thai 리조트는 해변 바로 옆에 위치해 있고 공항에서 차로 단지 10분 거리이다.

어휘 right adv. 바로, 아주; adj. 옳은 drive n. 차로 가는 거리; v. 차를 몰다

07 | 올바른 시제의 동사 채우기

해설 이 문장은 동사(realized)의 목적어 역할을 하는 명사절의 명사절 접속사 that이 생략된 문장이다. 명사절에 주어(she)만 있고 동사가 없으므로 동사 (A), (C), (D)가 정답의 후보이다. 명사절(she ~ key information)에서 나타내는 사건, 즉 정보를 누락한 시점은 주절(she realized)에서 나타내는 사건, 즉 그녀가 알아차린 시점보다 먼저 일어난 일이다. 주절에 과거 시제 동사(realized)가 쓰였으므로 과거의 특정 시점 이전에 발생한 일을 표현할 수 있는 과거완료 시제 (D) had left가 정답이다. 3인칭 복수 동사 (A)는 복수 주어와 함께 써야 하고, 수동태 동사 (C) is left는 '그녀가 누락되다'라는 어색한 문맥이 된다. 동명사 또는 현재분사 (B)는 동사 자리에 올 수 없다.

해석 Ms. Khalil은 그녀의 마케팅 자료 분석에 최종 수정을 하는 동안, 몇몇 중요한 정보를 누락한 것을 알아차렸다.

어휘 revision n. 수정, 정정 analysis n. 분석 leave out 누락하다, 생략하다

08 | 태에 맞는 동사 채우기

해설 문장에 동사가 없으므로 동사인 모든 보기가 정답의 후보이다. 주어(All orders)와 동사(send)가 '모든 주문들이 보내지다'라는 수동의 의미가 되어야 하므로 수동태 동사 (C) are sent가 정답이다.

해석 Bergdorf 의류 회사의 온라인 상점을 통해 이루어진 모든 주문들은 구매자의 집 주소로 구매 이틀 이내에 보내진다.

어휘 purchase n. 구매, 구매품; v. 구매하다 address n. 주소, 연설

09 | 올바른 시제의 동사 채우기

해설 문장에 동사가 없으므로 동사 (A), (C), (D)가 정답의 후보이다. 미래를 나타내는 시간 표현(In the coming weeks)이 있으므로 특정 미래 시점에 진행되고 있을 일을 표현하는 미래진행 시제 (D) will be preparing이 정답이다. 3인칭 복수 동사 (A)는 복수 주어와 함께 써야 하고, 과거진행 시제 (C)는 미래 시간 표현과 함께 쓰일 수 없다. 동명사 또는 현재분사 (B)는 동사 자리에 올 수 없다.

해석 앞으로 몇 주 안에 회계팀은 이사회 회의를 위해 분기별 재무 보고서를 준비하고 있을 것이다.

어휘 quarterly adj. 분기별의 board meeting 이사회 회의

10 | 올바른 시제의 동사 채우기

해설 주절(Two ~ report)에 동사가 없으므로 동사 (A), (B), (C)가 정답의 후보이다. 조건을 나타내는 종속절(once ~ collected)의 현재완료 시제(has been collected)는 미래를 나타내므로, 보고서(a report) 업무는 조건이 충족되는 시점인 미래에 일어나는 일임을 알 수 있다. 따라서 미래 시제 (C) will submit이 정답이다. 현재완료 시제 (A)는 미래를 나타낼 수 없고, 수동태 동사 (B)는 빈칸 뒤에 목적어(a report)가 왔으므로 답이 될 수 없다. to 부정사 (D)는 동사 자리에 올 수 없다.

해석 모든 정보가 모이자마자 관리부서의 두 직원이 보고서를 제출할 것이다.

어휘 administrative adj. 관리의 report n. 보고서
once conj. ~하자마자; adv. 한 번 collect v. 모으다, 수집하다

11 | 태에 맞는 동사 채우기

해설 be동사(was) 뒤에 와서 각각 진행시제와 수동태를 만들 수 있는 현재분사 (A)와 과거분사 (C)가 정답의 후보이다. 주어(The building)와 동사(fund)가 '건축이 자금을 지원받다'라는 수동의 의미가 되어야 하므로 과거분사 (C) funded가 정답이다.

해석 Bendersville의 새로운 병원 건축은 연방 및 주 정부 보조금에 의해 전적으로 자금을 지원받았다.

어휘 completely adv. 전적으로, 완전히 federal adj. 연방의
state adj. 주(州)의 fund n. 자금; v. 자금을 지원하다

12 | 제안·요청·의무의 주절 뒤 that절에 동사원형 채우기

해설 that이 이끄는 절(employees ~ development)에 주어(employees)만 있고 동사가 없으므로 모든 보기가 정답의 후보이다. 제안·요청·의무의 주절을 뒤따르는 that절엔 동사원형이 와야 하는데, 주절에 요청을 나타내는 동사(requested)가 왔으므로 동사원형 (A) dedicate(할애하다, 바치다)가 정답이다.

해석 지점장은 직원들에게 전문성 개발을 위해 분기마다 적어도 두 시간씩 그들의 시간을 할애할 것을 요청했다.

어휘 branch n. 지점 at least 적어도 quarter n. 분기

13 | 동사 자리 채우기

해설 이 문장은 주어가 없는 명령문이므로, 명령문의 동사 자리에 올 수 있는 동사원형 (B) Brighten(밝히다)이 정답이다. 형용사 또는 부사 (A), 3인칭 단수 동사 (C), 동명사 또는 현재분사 (D)는 명령문의 동사 자리에 올 수 없다.

해석 Desmond 디자인사의 다채로운 패턴 벽지로 당신의 집 내부를 밝혀 보세요.

어휘 wallpaper n. 벽지

14 | 태에 맞는 동사 채우기

해설 문장에 동사가 없으므로 동사인 모든 보기가 정답의 후보이다. 주어(The season premiere)와 동사(enjoy)가 '시즌 첫 방영이 (시청자들에 의해) 즐겨지다'라는 수동의 의미가 되어야 하므로 수동태 동사 (B) was enjoyed가 정답이다.

해석 TV쇼 Tucker Grant의 시즌 첫 방영이 1,580만 명이라는 기록적인 시청자들에 의해 즐겨졌다.

어휘 premiere n. 첫 방영, 초연 record adj. 기록적인

15 | 올바른 시제의 동사 채우기

해설 Because가 이끄는 절(Wilson Construction ~ stadium)에 주어(Wilson Construction)만 있고 동사가 없으므로 동사 (B), (C), (D)가 정답의 후보이다. Because가 이끄는 절에서 나타내는 사건, 즉 Wilson

건설이 새 스포츠 경기장의 예산을 최종적으로 승인한 시점은 주절(it ~ design)에서 나타내는 사건, 즉 Wilson 건설이 도안을 수정할 수 없었던 것보다 먼저 일어난 일이다. 주절에 과거 시제 동사(could not modify)가 쓰였으므로 과거의 특정 시점 이전에 발생한 일을 표현할 수 있는 과거완료 시제 (C) had finalized가 정답이다.

해석 Wilson 건설사는 새 스포츠 경기장의 예산을 최종적으로 승인했기 때문에, 도안을 수정할 수 없었다.

어휘 budget n. 예산 stadium n. 경기장 modify v. 수정하다
finalize v. 최종적으로 승인하다, 마무리짓다

16 | 주어와 수일치하는 동사 채우기

해설 who로 시작되는 관계절(____ ~ event)에 동사가 없으므로 동사 (A)와 (B)가 정답의 후보이다. 선행사(All those)가 복수 명사이므로 동사 assist(돕다, 지원하다)의 과거형 (B) assisted가 정답이다. 3인칭 단수형 (A)는 단수 선행사와 함께 써야 한다. 동명사 또는 현재분사 (C)와 to 부정사 (D)는 동사 자리에 올 수 없다.

해석 지역 사회 센터의 기금 모금 행사에서 도운 모든 사람들이 증명서를 받을 것이다.

어휘 fundraising n. 기금 모금 certificate n. 증명서

17-20번은 다음 편지에 관한 문제입니다.

3월 15일
Anthony Christie
121번지 Washington가
잭슨, 미시시피 주 39211

Mr. Christie께,

지난번 만남에서 논의했듯이, 저희는 귀하를 선임 연구 과학자로 채용할 의향이 있습니다. ¹⁷귀하의 고용 조건을 알아보기 위해 동봉된 계약서를 검토해 주시기 바랍니다. 만일 귀하가 이 제안을 수락하기로 결정한다면, 저희는 4월 4일 월요일을 근무 시작 일자로 제안드립니다.

¹⁸최소한, 귀하의 직무는 다양한 화학적 응용에 관한 연구 수행을 포함할 것입니다. 다른 업무들은 필요가 발생할 경우에 맡겨질 수 있습니다. ¹⁹물론, 이것들은 귀하의 전문 지식 분야에 한정될 것입니다.

귀하의 초봉은 월 7천 달러가 될 것입니다. ²⁰다른 혜택들은 동봉된 계약서에 열거되어 있습니다. 이 모든 것들이 만족스러우시다면, 3월 25일 이전에 이 편지에 답신함으로써 귀하의 결정을 알려 주시길 부탁드립니다.

Jennifer Williams
Apex Chemicals사

enclose v. 동봉하다 conduct v. 수행하다 chemical adj. 화학적인
application n. 응용, 활용 task n. 업무, 과업, 과제 assign v. 맡기다, 부여하다
satisfactory adj. 만족스러운 inform v. 알리다

17 | 명사 어휘 고르기 주변 문맥 파악

해설 '____ 조건을 알아보기 위해 동봉된 계약서를 검토해 달라'는 문맥이므로 모든 보기가 정답의 후보이다. 빈칸이 있는 문장만으로 정답을 고를 수 없으므로 주변 문맥이나 전체 문맥을 파악한다. 앞 문장에서 '선임 연구 과학자로 채용할 의향이 있다(we are willing to hire you as a senior research scientist)'라고 했으므로 고용에 대해 이야기하고 있음을 알 수 있다. 따라서 (B) employment(고용, 일자리)가 정답이다. (A) assistance는 '도움', (C) settlement는 '합의', (D) membership은 '회원 자격'이라는 의미이다.

18 | 올바른 시제의 동사 채우기 주변 문맥 파악

해설 '귀하의 직무는 다양한 화학적 응용에 관한 연구 수행을 포함하다'라는 문맥인데, 이 경우 빈칸이 있는 문장만으로는 올바른 시제의 동사를 고를 수 없으므로 주변 문맥이나 전체 문맥을 파악하여 정답을 고른다. 앞 문장에서 '4월 4일 월요일을 근무 시작 일자로 제안한다(we propose a start date of Monday, April 4)'라고 했으므로, 직무가 시작되는 시점이 미래임을 알 수 있다. 따라서 미래 시제 (C) will include가 정답이다.

19 | 알맞은 문장 고르기

해석 (A) 귀하는 부서의 활동을 경영진에게 해명해야 할 것입니다.
(B) 만약을 대비해, 다른 직원에게 이 과제들을 넘겼습니다.
(C) 물론, 이것들은 귀하의 전문 지식 분야에 한정될 것입니다.
(D) 저희는 모두가 가끔의 훈련으로부터 이익을 얻을 수 있다고 믿습니다.

해설 앞 문장 'Other tasks may be assigned as the need arises.'에서 다른 업무들은 필요가 발생할 경우에 맡겨질 수 있다고 했으므로, 빈칸에는 다른 업무들과 관련된 내용이 들어가야 함을 알 수 있다. 따라서 (C)가 정답이다.

어휘 justify v. 해명하다, 정당화하다 assignment n. 과제, 임무
limit v. 한정하다, 제한하다 expertise n. 전문 지식
benefit v. 이익을 얻다; n. 혜택, 이익 occasional adj. 가끔의

20 | 태에 맞는 동사 채우기

해설 문장에 동사가 없으므로 모든 보기가 정답의 후보이다. 주어(Other benefits)와 동사(detail)가 '다른 혜택들은 열거되다'라는 수동의 의미가 되어야 하므로 수동태 동사 (D) are detailed가 정답이다.

고난도 문제 완전 정복 p.61

01 (C)	02 (D)	03 (D)	04 (D)	05 (C)
06 (C)	07 (A)	08 (B)	09 (B)	10 (C)
11 (C)	12 (B)			

01 | 태에 맞는 동사 채우기

해설 주절에 주어(Mr. Nussbaum)만 있고 동사가 없으므로 동사 (A), (C), (D)가 정답의 후보이다. Mr. Nussbaum이 계약(contract)에 동의했다는 능동의 의미이고, 계약에 동의한 시점은 그의 회사가 기술을 실현 가능하게 만든 후(after his company made ~ technology feasible)인 과거이므로 과거 시제 능동태 동사 (C) agreed가 정답이다.

해석 Mr. Nussbaum은 그의 회사가 3D 인쇄 기술을 실현 가능하게 만든 후에 Decker 엔지니어링사와의 3년 계약에 동의했다.

어휘 contract n. 계약, 약정 printing technology 인쇄 기술
feasible adj. 실현 가능한

02 | 가정법 과거 완료

해설 if절(if the company ~ more comprehensive testing)에 had p.p.(had conducted)가 쓰였고, '회사가 더 종합적인 검사를 실시했었다면'이라는 과거의 반대 상황을 가정하는 문장이므로 가정법 과거 완료 구문임을 알 수 있다. 따라서 주절(A number of ~ avoided)에는 이와 짝을 이루는 'would(could, might, should) have p.p.'가 와야 한다. 따라서 (D) could have been이 정답이다.

해석 만약 그 회사가 더 종합적인 검사를 실시했었다면, 그 소프트웨어에 관한 많은 시스템적 취약점들이 예방될 수 있었을 것이다.

어휘 a number of 많은 vulnerability n. 취약점 avoid v. 예방하다, 막다, 피하다
conduct v. 실시하다 comprehensive adj. 종합적인

03 | 태에 맞는 동사 채우기

해설 관계부사(where)가 이끄는 절(a painting ____)에 동사가 없으므로 동

사 (A), (C), (D)가 정답의 후보이다. 주어(a painting)와 동사(restore)가 '그림이 복원되다'라는 수동의 의미가 되어야 하므로 현재진행 수동태 (D) is being restored가 정답이다.

해석 박물관 직원들은 방문객들이 그림이 복원되고 있는 장소 안으로 돌아다니는 것을 막기 위해 구역을 차단했다.

어휘 block off 차단하다, 막다   wander v. 돌아다니다, 헤매다

04 | 태에 맞는 동사 채우기

해설 빈칸 앞에 be동사(are)가 있으므로 be동사 다음에 올 수 있는 현재분사 (A)와 과거분사 (D)가 정답의 후보이다. 주어(Consumers)와 동사(think)가 '소비자들은 영향을 받는다고 여겨지다'라는 수동의 의미가 되어야 하므로 과거분사 (D) thought가 정답이다.

해석 소비자들은 어떤 모델의 스마트폰을 구매할지 선택할 때 온라인 리뷰에 의해 상당히 영향을 받는다고 여겨진다.

어휘 consumer n. 소비자   significantly adv. 상당히, 크게
influence v. 영향을 주다

05 | 올바른 시제의 동사 채우기

해설 절(Ms. Rodriguez ~ regulations)과 절(then ~ directors)이 등위접속사 and로 연결된 문장이다. 등위접속사로 연결된 절에서 등위접속사 뒤에 중복된 단어가 생략되고 동사원형(report)이 왔으므로 조동사(will) 다음에 동사원형이 온 (C) will research가 정답이다. (A), (B), (D)는 등위접속사로 연결된 절의 동사원형 report와 함께 쓰일 수 없다.

해석 Ms. Rodriguez는 유럽 은행 규제에 대해 연구하고 나서 이사회에 그녀의 조사 결과를 보고할 것이다.

어휘 regulation n. 규제   finding n. 결과   board of directors 이사회
research v. 연구하다

06 | 태에 맞는 동사 채우기

해설 빈칸 앞에 be동사(been)가 있으므로 be동사 다음에 올 수 있는 현재분사 (C)와 과거분사 (D)가 정답의 후보이다. 주어(costs)와 동사(rise)가 '비용이 상승하다'라는 능동의 의미가 되어야 하므로 현재분사 (C) rising이 정답이다. 참고로, 동사 rise(상승하다, 오르다)는 자동사이고, 수동태로 쓰일 수 없으므로 be동사와 함께 수동태 동사를 만드는 과거분사 (D)는 답이 될 수 없음을 알아둔다.

해석 CyberDyne사는 비용이 꾸준히 상승해 왔기 때문에 인공지능 모델 개발을 위한 활동을 축소하도록 강요받았다.

어휘 force v. 강요하다   scale back 축소하다   effort n. 활동, 노력
artificial intelligence 인공지능   steadily adv. 꾸준히

07 | 제안·요청·의무의 주절 뒤 that절에 동사원형 채우기

해설 that이 이끄는 절(the team ~ delays)에 주어(the team)만 있고 동사가 없으므로 모든 보기가 정답의 후보이다. 제안·요청·의무의 주절을 뒤따르는 that절엔 동사원형이 와야 하는데, 주절에 제안을 나타내는 동사(recommended)가 왔으므로 동사원형 (A) revise(수정하다)가 정답이다.

해석 관리자는 잠재적인 지연을 수용하기 위해 팀이 프로젝트 일정을 수정할 것을 권했다.

어휘 recommend v. 권하다   timeline n. 일정   accommodate v. 수용하다
potential adj. 잠재적인   delay n. 지연

08 | 올바른 시제의 동사 채우기

해설 문장에 주어(not all parking tickets)만 있고 동사가 없으므로 동사 (A)와 (B)가 정답의 후보이다. '작년에 발행된 주차 위반 딱지가 아직 모두 납부되지는 않았다'라는 의미가 되어야 하므로, 과거에 시작된 일이 현재까지 계속되는 것을 나타내는 현재완료 시제를 만드는 (B) have been이 정답이다. 참고로, 부사 yet은 현재완료 시제(has/have p.p.)와 함께 자주 쓰임을 알아둔다. 과거진행 시제 (A)는 과거에 시작된 일이 현재까지 계속되는 것을 나타낼 수 없다. to 부정사 (C)와 (D)는 동사 자리에 올 수 없다.

해석 Harford 교통국의 기록에 따르면, 작년에 발행된 주차 위반 딱지가 아직 모두 납부되지는 않았다.

어휘 Transportation Department 교통국   parking ticket 주차 위반 딱지
issue v. 발행하다

09 | 주어와 수일치하는 동사 채우기

해설 that으로 시작되는 관계절에 동사가 없으므로 동사 (A)와 (B)가 정답의 후보이다. 빈칸 앞의 명사(a software application)를 선행사로 갖는 관계절이므로 동사 allow(가능하게 하다)의 3인칭 단수형 (B) allows가 정답이다. (A)는 1인칭이나 2인칭 주어 및 3인칭 복수 주어와 함께 쓰인다. to 부정사 (C)와 동명사 또는 현재분사 (D)는 동사 자리에 올 수 없다.

해석 Reese Technologies사는 금융 분석가들이 시장 변동을 정확하게 추적하는 것을 가능하게 하는 소프트웨어 애플리케이션을 개발했다.

어휘 financial analyst 금융 분석가   accurately adv. 정확하게
track v. 추적하다   fluctuation n. 변동

10 | 올바른 시제의 동사 채우기

해설 직무 요건 목록(the list of job requirements)이 인사 관리자(the human resources manager)에 의해 승인되는 것이므로 수동태 동사 (C)와 (D)가 정답의 후보이다. 시간 부사절(until ~ manager)에서는 현재 시제 또는 현재완료 시제가 미래 시제 또는 미래완료 시제를 대신하기 때문에 현재완료 시제 (C) has been approved가 정답이다. 미래 시제 (D)는 답이 될 수 없다. 능동태 동사 (A)와 (B)는 뒤에 목적어가 와야 하므로 답이 될 수 없다.

해석 Mr. Reynolds는 직무 요건 목록이 인사 관리자에 의해 승인될 때까지 해당 직위 광고를 연기해야 한다.

어휘 postpone v. 연기하다   advertise v. 광고하다   job requirement 직무 요건
approve v. 승인하다

11 | 주어와 수일치하는 동사 채우기

해설 문장에 주어(The remarkable generosity)만 있고 동사가 없으므로 동사 (A), (C), (D)가 정답의 후보이다. 주어(The remarkable generosity)가 단수이므로 단수 동사 has를 포함하는 (C) has enabled가 정답이다. 참고로, 주어와 동사 사이에 있는 수식어 거품(of donors)은 동사의 수 결정에 아무런 영향을 주지 않는다. 복수 동사 (A)와 (D)는 1인칭이나 2인칭 주어 및 3인칭 복수 주어와 함께 써야 한다. 동명사 또는 현재분사 (B)는 동사 자리에 올 수 없다.

해석 기부자들의 놀라운 관대함은 그 재단이 수백 명의 자격 있는 학생들에게 장학금을 제공할 수 있게 해주었다.

어휘 remarkable adj. 놀라운   generosity n. 관대함   deserving adj. 자격 있는
enable v. ~할 수 있게 하다

12 | 태에 맞는 동사 채우기

해설 빈칸은 to 뒤에 있으므로 to 부정사를 만드는 (A)와 (B)가 정답의 후보이다. 빈칸 뒤에 목적어(a cost-effective solution)가 있고, '해결책을 찾다'라는 능동의 의미가 되어야 하므로 능동태를 만드는 (B) have found가 정답이다. 3인칭 단수형 동사 (C)와 과거형 동사 또는 과거분사 (D)는 to 뒤에 와서 to 부정사를 만들 수 없다.

해석 IT 지원팀은 전체 시스템을 교체하지 않고도 비용 효율이 높은 해결책을 찾아서 기뻤다.

어휘 cost-effective adj. 비용 효율이 높은   solution n. 해결책
replace v. 교체하다   entire adj. 전체의

DAY 04 to 부정사, 동명사, 분사

빈출 문제 집중 훈련
p.62

01 (C)	02 (D)	03 (A)	04 (C)	05 (D)
06 (A)	07 (C)	08 (A)	09 (D)	10 (C)
11 (C)	12 (D)	13 (C)	14 (B)	15 (A)
16 (B)	17 (A)	18 (D)	19 (C)	20 (C)

01 | to 부정사 채우기

해설 동사(has decided)의 목적어로 쓰일 수 있는 명사 (A)와 to 부정사 (C)가 정답의 후보이다. 빈칸 뒤에도 목적어인 명사구(needed services and goods)가 있으므로 목적어를 취할 수 있는 to 부정사 (C) to contribute가 정답이다. 명사 (A)는 목적어를 취할 수 없으므로 답이 될 수 없다. 동사 또는 과거분사 (B)와 동사 (D)는 목적어 자리에 올 수 없다.

해석 홍수 피해자들을 돕기 위해 돈을 기부하는 대신에, Mercer 에너지사는 필요한 서비스와 물자를 기증하기로 결정했다.

어휘 instead of ~ 대신에 donate v. 기부하다, 기증하다 flood n. 홍수
victim n. 피해자 goods n. 물자, 물품 contribute v. 기증하다, 기여하다

02 | 동명사 채우기

해설 동사(suggested)의 목적어로 쓰일 수 있는 명사 (A)와 (C), 동명사 (D)가 정답의 후보이다. 'Chordolla Chips사 제품의 건강에 좋은 측면에 초점을 맞추는 것을 제안했다'라는 의미가 되어야 하므로 동사 focus(초점을 맞추다)의 동명사 (D) focusing이 정답이다. 명사 (A)나 (C)를 쓸 경우 'Chordolla Chips사 제품의 건강에 좋은 측면에 초점/초점들을 제안했다'라는 어색한 문맥이 된다. 동사 또는 과거분사 (B)는 목적어 자리에 올 수 없다.

해석 그 컨설턴트는 경쟁 브랜드와 차별화하기 위해 Chordolla Chips사 제품의 건강에 좋은 측면에 초점을 맞추는 것을 제안했다.

어휘 aspect n. 측면 differentiate v. 차별화하다, 구별하다
compete v. 경쟁하다 focus n. 초점, 중점; v. 초점을 맞추다, 집중하다

03 | 현재분사와 과거분사 구별하여 채우기

해설 이 문장은 주어(Mr. Baker), 동사(delivered), 목적어(an insightful presentation)를 갖춘 완전한 절이므로, Widely ___ ~ industry는 수식어 거품으로 보아야 한다. 보기 중 부사(Widely)의 꾸밈을 받으면서 수식어 거품을 이끌 수 있는 것은 과거분사 (A)와 현재분사 (B)이고, '선두적인 인물로 널리 알려진 Mr. Baker'라는 수동의 의미이므로 과거분사 (A) recognized(알려진)가 정답이다. 현재분사 (B)는 능동의 의미를 나타내므로 답이 될 수 없다. 동사 (C)는 수식어 거품을 이끌 수 없고, to 부정사 (D)는 부사와 함께 쓰일 경우 'to + 부사 + 동사원형'의 형태가 되어야 하므로 답이 될 수 없다.

해석 태양열 산업에서 선두적인 인물로 널리 알려진 Mr. Baker가 에너지 총회에서 통찰력 있는 발표를 했다.

어휘 leading adj. 선두적인, 주요한 figure n. 인물, 모습
solar industry 태양열 산업 insightful adj. 통찰력 있는
convention n. 총회, 회의

04 | to 부정사 채우기

해설 이 문장은 필수 성분(users have to ~ mobile app)을 갖춘 완전한 절이므로, ___ ~ CrossArts Media는 수식어 거품으로 보아야 한다. 이 수식어 거품은 동사가 없는 거품구이므로, 거품구를 이끌 수 있는 to 부정사구 (C)와 분사구 (D)가 정답의 후보이다. '무료 체험을 요청하기 위해, 모바일 앱을 다운로드하고 등록해야 한다'라는 의미가 되어야 하므로 목적을 나타내는 to 부정사 (C) To claim이 정답이다. (D) Claiming(요청하는 것)을 쓸 경우 '무료 체험을 요청하면서, 사용자들은 회사의 모바일 앱을 다운로드하고 등록해야 한다'라는 어색한 문맥을 만들기 때문에 답이 될 수 없다. 명사 또는 동사 (A)와 (B)는 거품구를 이끌 수 없다.

해석 CrossArts 미디어사의 무료 체험을 요청하기 위해, 사용자들은 회사의 모바일 앱을 다운로드하고 등록해야 한다.

어휘 trial n. 체험 register v. 등록하다 claim v. 요청하다, 주장하다; n. 주장

05 | 현재분사와 과거분사 구별하여 채우기

해설 빈칸 뒤의 명사구(documentary film division)를 꾸밀 수 있는 것은 형용사이므로 형용사 역할을 하는 현재분사 (A)와 과거분사 (D)가 정답의 후보이다. 꾸밈을 받는 명사구와 분사가 '창설된 다큐멘터리 영화 부서'라는 수동의 의미이므로 과거분사 (D) created(창설된)가 정답이다. 현재분사 (A) creating은 '창설하는 다큐멘터리 영화 부서'라는 의미로 어색한 문맥을 만들기 때문에 답이 될 수 없다. 동사 (B)와 (C)는 명사구를 꾸밀 수 없으므로 답이 될 수 없다.

해석 Wentworth TV 스튜디오는 최근에 창설된 다큐멘터리 영화 부서를 위한 콘텐츠 개발 일정을 준비하고 있다.

어휘 development n. 개발 create v. 창설하다, 만들다

06 | 동명사 채우기

해설 전치사(Since)의 목적어가 될 수 있는 동명사 (A)와 명사 (D)가 정답의 후보이다. 빈칸 뒤의 명사(Anil Kahn)를 목적어로 취할 수 있는 것은 동명사이므로 동사 replace(대신하다)의 동명사 (A) replacing이 정답이다. 명사 (D)는 연결어 없이 빈칸 뒤의 명사와 나란히 올 수 없다. 동사 또는 과거분사 (B)와 동사 (C)는 전치사의 목적어 자리에 올 수 없다. 과거분사 (B)가 명사 Anil Kahn을 꾸미는 것으로 본다 해도, since 뒤에는 과거의 시간이나 사건을 나타내는 표현이 와야 하므로 답이 될 수 없다.

해석 Electa사의 최고 경영자로서 Anil Kahn을 대신한 이후로, Ms. Harris는 조직에 대한 대규모 구조 조정 계획을 발표했다.

어휘 announce v. 발표하다 large-scale adj. 대규모의
restructure v. 구조 조정하다 initiative n. 계획

07 | 분사 자리 채우기

해설 빈칸 뒤의 명사(devices)를 꾸밀 수 있는 것은 형용사이므로 형용사 역할을 하는 현재분사 (C) measuring(측정하는)이 정답이다. 명사 또는 동사 (A)는 명사일 경우 devices(장치)와 복합 명사를 이룰 수 없고, 동사일 경우 명사를 꾸밀 수 없다. 동사 (B)는 명사를 꾸밀 수 없고, to 부정사 (D)는 명사를 앞에서 꾸밀 수 없다.

해석 다양한 고급 측정 장치를 사용함으로써, 기상학자는 일부 날씨 변화를 수일 전에 예측할 수 있다.

어휘 various adj. 다양한, 각양각색의 advanced adj. 고급의, 선진의
meteorologist n. 기상학자 predict v. 예측하다 ahead adv. 전에, 미리

08 | 원형 부정사 채우기

해설 동사 let(~하게 하다)은 5형식 동사로 목적어와 목적격 보어를 가지는데, 동사(let) 뒤에 목적어(the experts ~ Education)가 있으므로 빈칸은 목적격 보어 자리이다. let은 목적격 보어로 원형 부정사를 가지므로 원형 부정사 (A) design(설계하다)이 정답이다. 참고로, 이 문장은 주어가 생략된 명령문이다.

해석 Mentoria 직업 교육 회사의 전문가들이 귀사의 직원들을 위한 맞춤형 교육 프로그램을 설계하도록 하십시오.

어휘 expert n. 전문가 professional adj. 직업의, 전문적인
tailored adj. 맞춤형의 employee n. 직원

09 | to 부정사 채우기

해설 동사 seek(seeking)의 목적어 자리에 올 수 있는 to 부정사 (D) to foster가 정답이다. 동사 (A)와 (B), 동사 또는 과거분사 (C)는 동사의 목적어 자리에 올 수 없다. 참고로, seeking to foster workplace diversity는 앞에 나온 주어(HR departments)를 수식하는 분사구이다.

해석 직장 내 다양성을 촉진하고자 하는 인사 부서는 포용적인 채용 전략을 수립해야 한다.

어휘 seek v. ~하려고 하다 workplace n. 직장 diversity n. 다양성
inclusive adj. 포용적인 recruitment n. 채용 strategy n. 전략
foster v. 촉진하다, 육성하다

10 | 현재분사와 과거분사 구별하여 채우기

해설 2형식 동사 appear는 주격 보어를 가지는 동사이고, 빈칸이 동사(appears) 뒤에 왔으므로 주격 보어 자리에 올 수 있는 명사 (A), 형용사 역할을 하는 과거분사 (C)와 현재분사 (D)가 정답의 후보이다. '현대 사무실 환경이 상당히 덜 어수선해 보인다'라는 의미가 되어야 하므로 과거분사 (C) cluttered(어수선한)가 정답이다. 명사 (A)를 쓰면 주어와 동격이 되어 '현대 사무실 환경이 상당히 덜 어수선함처럼 보인다'라는 어색한 문맥이 되고, 현재분사 (D)를 쓰면 '현대 사무실 환경이 상당히 덜 어수선하게 하는 것으로 보인다'라는 어색한 문맥이 되므로 답이 될 수 없다. 동사 (B)는 주격 보어 자리에 올 수 없다.

해석 현대 사무실 환경은 전통적인 칸막이 배치보다 상당히 덜 어수선해 보인다.

어휘 significantly adv. 상당히 traditional adj. 전통적인
cubicle n. 칸막이, 작은 구획 arrangement n. 배치, 준비
clutter n. 어수선함; v. 어지르다

11 | to 부정사 채우기

해설 이 문장은 주어가 없는 명령문(Subscribe to ~ newsletter)이므로, ___ informed about the latest industry trends는 수식어 거품으로 보아야 한다. 이 수식어 거품은 동사가 없는 거품구이므로, 거품구를 이끌 수 있는 분사구 (B), to 부정사구 (C)와 (D)가 정답의 후보이다. '최신 업계 동향에 대해 계속 알고 있기 위해, 디지털 소식지를 구독하세요'라는 의미가 되어야 하므로 목적을 나타내는 to 부정사구 (C) to stay가 정답이다. (B) staying(계속 있는 것)을 쓸 경우 어색한 문맥을 만들기 때문에 답이 될 수 없다. 동사 stay(계속 있다, 머무르다)는 자동사로 수동태로 쓰일 수 없으므로 수동형 (D)는 답이 될 수 없다. 명사 또는 동사 (A)는 거품구를 이끌 수 없다.

해석 최신 업계 동향에 대해 계속 알고 있기 위해, 우리의 디지털 소식지를 구독하세요.

어휘 subscribe v. 구독하다 newsletter n. 소식지 inform v. 알리다
trend n. 동향, 추세

12 | 동명사와 명사 구별하여 채우기

해설 전치사(by)의 목적어가 될 수 있는 명사 (C)와 동명사 (D)가 정답의 후보이다. 빈칸 뒤의 명사(thermal energy)를 목적어로 취할 수 있는 것은 동명사이므로 동사 absorb(흡수하다)의 동명사 (D) absorbing이 정답이다. 명사 (C)는 목적어를 취할 수 없다. 동사 (A)와 동사 또는 과거분사 (B)는 전치사의 목적어 자리에 올 수 없다.

해석 혁신적인 단열재는 열에너지를 흡수함으로써 온도 안정성을 유지하는 데 도움을 준다.

어휘 innovative adj. 혁신적인 insulation n. 단열, 절연 maintain v. 유지하다
stability n. 안정성 thermal adj. 열의, 온도의

13 | 동명사와 명사 구별하여 채우기

해설 문장에서 동사(has been) 앞에 위치한 ___ the yearly marketing plan은 주어 자리이고, 주어 자리에 올 수 있는 명사 (A)와 (D), 동명사 (C)가 정답의 후보이다. 빈칸 뒤의 명사구(the yearly ~ plan)를 목적어로 취할 수 있는 것은 동명사이므로 동사 produce(제시하다)의 동명사 (C) Producing이 정답이다. 명사 (A)와 (D)는 목적어를 취할 수 없고, 동사 또는 과거분사 (B)는 주어 자리에 올 수 없다. 과거분사 (B)를 빈칸 뒤의 명사구(the yearly ~ plan)를 꾸미는 것으로 본다 해도, 이때 과거분사는 관사(the) 다음에 와야 하므로 답이 될 수 없다.

해석 연간 마케팅 계획을 제시하는 것은 마이애미에 있는 Keener 의류 회사 본사의 Ms. Hurley와 그녀의 팀의 책임이었다.

어휘 yearly adj. 연간의 responsibility n. 책임, 의무
produce v. 제시하다, 생산하다; n. 농산물 production n. 생산, 생산량

14 | 분사구문 채우기

해설 이 문장은 필수성분(Rachel ~ Tournament)을 갖춘 완전한 절이므로, ___ her skills with exceptional precision은 수식어 거품으로 보아야 한다. 이 수식어 거품은 동사가 없는 거품구이므로, 거품구를 이끌 수 있는 현재분사 (B)와 to 부정사 (C)가 정답의 후보이다. '뛰어난 정확도로 그녀의 기술을 보여주면서 경쟁했다'라는 의미가 되어야 하므로 현재분사 (B) displaying이 정답이다. (C)는 빈칸 앞의 콤마와 함께 쓸 수 없기 때문에 답이 될 수 없다. 명사 또는 동사 (A)와 동사 (D)는 수식어 거품을 이끌 수 없다.

해석 Rachel은 뛰어난 정확도로 그녀의 기술을 보여주면서 전문 코딩 토너먼트에서 경쟁했다.

어휘 compete v. 경쟁하다, 참가하다 exceptional adj. 뛰어난
precision n. 정확도, 정밀함

15 | to 부정사 채우기

해설 이 문장은 주어(TechCore Solutions), 동사(implemented), 목적어 (a comprehensive ~ strategy)를 모두 갖춘 완전한 절이므로, To improve efficiency and ___ simplified frameworks는 수식어 거품으로 보아야 한다. 이 수식어 거품은 동사가 없는 거품구이므로, to 부정사(To improve)가 이끌고 있다. 거품구는 등위접속사 and로 연결된 형태인데, and 뒤에 온 to 부정사의 to는 생략이 가능하므로 to introduce를 대신하는 (A) introduce가 정답이다. (B), (C), (D)는 to 부정사의 to 다음에 올 수 없다.

해석 효율성을 개선하고 간소화된 체계를 도입하기 위해, TechCore Solutions사는 포괄적인 작업 흐름 최적화 전략을 시행했다.

어휘 improve v. 개선하다 framework n. 체계, 체제 implement v. 시행하다
comprehensive adj. 포괄적인 workflow n. 작업 흐름
optimization n. 최적화

16 | 현재분사와 과거분사 구별하여 채우기

해설 빈칸 뒤의 명사(board)를 꾸밀 수 있는 것은 형용사이므로 형용사 역할을 하는 과거분사 (A)와 현재분사 (B)가 정답의 후보이다. 꾸밈을 받는 명사와 분사가 '관리하는 이사회'라는 능동의 의미이므로 현재분사 (B) governing(관리하는)이 정답이다. 과거분사 (A) governed(관리되는)를 쓰면 '관리되는 이사회'라는 어색한 문맥이 되므로 답이 될 수 없다. 동사 (C)와 (D)는 명사를 꾸밀 수 없으므로 답이 될 수 없다.

해석 NovaMed 의료 보험사의 관리 이사회는 미니애폴리스에 새 지점을 열기로 한 최고 경영자의 결정을 승인했다.

어휘 board n. 이사회 approve v. 승인하다 location n. 지점, 위치

17-20번은 다음 기사에 관한 문제입니다.

제안된 쓰레기 매립지에 대한 강한 반대

5월 15일—¹⁷와이오밍 주 알타 시민들은 시장이 인구가 밀집된 주거 지역 근처에 쓰레기 매립지를 건설하려는 계획을 밝혔을 때 격분했다. ¹⁸지난 수요일 시청 회의에서, 지역 사업주들과 주요 지역 인사들은 그 제안에 대한 그들의 강한 우려를 드러내기 위해 힘을 합쳤다.

작은 농장 운영자인 Jacob Gormand는 회의에서 발언할 기회를 가졌을 때 프로젝트에 대한 반대를 분명히 했다. ¹⁹"이런 쓰레기 매립지는 지역의 지하수 오염을 초래할 수 있으며, 이는 알타의 식수 공급에 독성 오염 물질이 유입되는 결과를 초래할 것이다"라고 그는 주장했다.

전문가들은 더 나아가 다른 부정적인 환경적 영향도 있을 수 있다고 경고한다. 이런 우려들에도 불구하고, 정부 관계자들은 건설 계획을 변경하지 않을 것이라고 명시했다. ²⁰현장 작업은 현재 6월 17일에 시작될 예정이다.

opposition n. 반대 landfill n. 쓰레기 매립지
outrage v. 격분하게 만들다; n. 격분, 격노 mayor n. 시장
reveal v. 밝히다, 드러내다, 폭로하다 residential adj. 주거의 town hall 시청
prominent adj. 주요한, 유명한 figure n. 인사, 인물, 수치
combine v. 합치다, 결합하다 force n. 힘, 체력
operator n. 운영자, 조작하는 사람 groundwater n. 지하수 toxic adj. 독성의
pollution n. 오염 물질 adverse adj. 부정적인 alter v. 변경하다, 바꾸다

17 | 현재분사와 과거분사 구별하여 채우기

해설 빈칸 뒤의 명사구(residential areas)를 꾸밀 수 있는 것은 형용사이므로 형용사 역할을 하는 과거분사 (A)와 현재분사 (C)가 정답의 후보이다. 꾸밈을 받는 명사구와 분사가 '인구가 밀집된 주거 지역'이라는 수동의 의미이므로 과거분사 (A) populated(인구가 밀집된, 사람이 채워진)가 정답이다. 현재분사 (C) populating(사람을 채우는)을 쓰면, '사람을 채우는 주거 지역'이라는 어색한 문맥이 되므로 답이 될 수 없다. 명사 (B) population(인구)은 residential areas(주거 지역)와 복합 명사를 이룰 수 없고, 동사 (D)는 명사구를 꾸밀 수 없다.

18 | to 부정사 채우기

해설 이 문장은 주어(local business owners and prominent community figures), 동사(combined), 목적어(forces)를 갖춘 완전한 절이므로, ____ ~ the proposal은 수식어 거품으로 보아야 한다. 이 수식어 거품은 동사가 없는 거품구이므로, 거품구를 이끌면서 '그들의 강한 우려를 드러내기 위해'라는 의미의 목적을 나타내는 to 부정사구 (D) to express가 정답이다. 동사 또는 형용사 (A), 명사 (C)는 거품구를 이끌 수 없다. 동사 또는 과거분사 (B) expressed를 명사를 수식하는 과거분사로 본다 해도, '표현된 힘을 합치다'라는 의미로 어색한 문맥을 만들기 때문에 답이 될 수 없다.

19 | 명사 어휘 고르기

해설 '이런 쓰레기 매립지는 지역의 지하수 ____을 초래할 수 있으며, 이는 알타의 식수 공급에 독성 오염 물질이 유입되는 결과를 초래할 것이다'라는 문맥이므로 (C) contamination(오염)이 정답이다. (A) evaporation은 '증발', (B) utilization은 '이용', (D) precipitation은 '강수, 침전'라는 의미이다.

20 | 알맞은 문장 고르기

해석 (A) 주민들은 곧 완공된 건물로 입주할 수 있을 것으로 예상한다.
(B) 승인 과정은 보통 3~6개월이 소요된다.
(C) 현장 작업은 현재 6월 17일에 시작될 예정이다.
(D) 긴급 우려사항은 시의 응급 서비스 부서에서 처리한다.

해설 앞 문장 'In spite of these concerns, government officials have indicated that they will not alter the construction plans.'에서 우려들에도 불구하고 정부 관계자들은 건설 계획을 변경하지 않을 것이라고 명시했다고 했으므로, 빈칸에는 건설 계획의 진행과 관련된 내용이 들어가야 함을 알 수 있다. 따라서 (C)가 정답이다.

어휘 resident n. 주민 structure n. 건물, 구조물 commence v. 시작되다
urgent adj. 긴급한 handle v. 처리하다

고난도 문제 완전 정복

01 (A)	02 (D)	03 (A)	04 (C)	05 (D)
06 (A)	07 (D)	08 (B)	09 (A)	10 (D)
11 (C)	12 (C)			

01 | 분사 자리 채우기

해설 빈칸 뒤의 명사구(trade disputes)를 꾸밀 수 있는 것은 형용사이므로 형용사 역할을 하는 현재분사 (A) intensifying(심화되는)이 정답이다. 명사 (B) intensity(강렬함)와 (D) intension(강화)은 trade disputes(무역 분쟁)와 복합 명사를 이룰 수 없고, 동사 (C)는 명사를 꾸밀 수 없다.

해석 심화되는 무역 분쟁으로 인해, 주요 수출업체들은 다음 분기에 상당한 수익의 감소를 보고할 것으로 예상된다.

어휘 dispute n. 분쟁 exporter n. 수출업체 revenue n. 수익 quarter n. 분기
intensify v. 심화되다, 강하게 하다

02 | to 부정사 채우기

해설 빈칸 앞의 명사(platform)를 꾸밀 수 있는 것은 형용사이므로 형용사 역할을 하는 현재분사 (A)와 to 부정사 (D)가 정답의 후보이다. '어느 플랫폼을 구현할지 고려하다'라는 의미가 되어야 하므로 to 부정사 (D) to implement가 정답이다. 현재분사 (A) implementing을 쓰면 '구현하는 어느 플랫폼을 고려하다'라는 어색한 문맥을 만들기 때문에 답이 될 수 없다. 참고로, 이 문장은 동사(considered) 뒤 목적어 자리에 '의문형용사(which) + 명사(platform) + to 부정사'의 형태가 쓰였음을 알아둔다.

해석 여러 소프트웨어 옵션을 분석한 후, IT 관리자는 회사의 네트워크에 어느 플랫폼을 구현할지 고려했다.

어휘 analyze v. 분석하다 implement v. 구현하다, 시행하다

03 | 동명사 채우기

해설 전치사(with)의 목적어가 될 수 있는 동명사 (A), 명사 (C)와 (D)가 정답의 후보이다. 빈칸 뒤의 명사구(complex data analysis)를 목적어로 취할 수 있는 것은 동명사이므로 동사 conduct(수행하다)의 동명사 (A) conducting이 정답이다. 명사 (C)와 (D)는 연결어 없이 빈칸 뒤의 명사구와 나란히 올 수 없다. 동사 또는 과거분사 (B)는 전치사의 목적어 자리에 올 수 없다. 참고로, (C)와 (D)는 동사로 쓰일 경우, 전치사의 목적어 자리에 올 수 없다.

해석 Dr. Akira Nakamura는 국제 프로젝트를 위한 복잡한 데이터 분석을 수행하는 임무를 맡게 될 것이다.

어휘 complex adj. 복잡한 international adj. 국제적인

04 | to 부정사의 in order to 채우기

해설 이 문장은 필수성분(manufacturers must ~ regulations)을 갖춘 완전한 절이므로, ____ avoid fines from the state government는 수식어 거품으로 보아야 한다. 빈칸 뒤의 동사(avoid)를 이끌면서 '주 정부로부터의 벌금을 피하기 위해'라는 의미로 목적을 나타내는 (C) In order to가 정답이다. 전치사 (A)와 (D)는 명사 앞에 와야 하고, 부사절 접속사 (B)는 주어와 동사가 있는 거품절을 이끈다.

해석 주 정부로부터의 벌금을 피하기 위해, 제조업체들은 모든 환경 규제를 준

수하도록 조치를 취해야 한다.

어휘 avoid v. 피하다 fine n. 벌금 compliance n. 준수, 이행
regulation n. 규제, 규정 as long as ~하는 한 owing to ~ 때문에

05 | 동명사 채우기

해설 prevent A from B의 전치사 from 다음에는 동명사가 와야 한다. 따라서 동사 accumulate(쌓이다, 축적되다)의 동명사 (D) accumulating이 정답이다. prevent A from -ing(A가 ~하는 것을 막다)를 관용구로 외워 둔다.

해설 Wintex Solutions사의 새로운 AirBlock 여과 시스템은 민감한 전자 부품에 먼지가 쌓이는 것을 방지한다.

어휘 filtration n. 여과 prevent v. 방지하다 sensitive adj. 민감한
component n. 부품

06 | 원형 부정사 채우기

해설 동사 help(돕다)는 5형식 동사로 목적어와 목적격 보어를 가지는데, 동사 (help) 뒤에 목적어(administrators)가 있으므로 빈칸은 목적격 보어 자리이다. help는 목적격 보어로 원형 부정사 또는 to 부정사를 가지므로 원형 부정사 (A) identify(찾다, 확인하다)가 정답이다.

해설 그 연구의 결과는 관리자들이 더 나은 교육 전략을 찾는 데 도움이 될 수 있다.

어휘 finding n. 결과, 발견 administrator n. 관리자 strategy n. 전략

07 | 동명사 채우기

해설 명사절 접속사 that이 이끄는 절의 ___ improperly prepared seafood는 주어이므로, 주어 자리에 올 수 있는 명사 (A)와 (B), 동명사 (D)가 정답의 후보이다. 빈칸 뒤의 명사구(improperly prepared seafood)를 목적어로 취할 수 있는 것은 동명사이므로 동사 consume (섭취하다)의 동명사 (D) consuming이 정답이다. 명사 (A)와 (B)는 연결어 없이 빈칸 뒤의 명사구와 나란히 올 수 없다. 동사 (C)는 주어 자리에 올 수 없다.

해설 공중 보건 지침은 부적절하게 준비된 해산물을 섭취하는 것이 심각한 질병으로 이어질 수 있다는 것을 대중에게 알리기 위해 만들어졌다.

어휘 guideline n. 지침 improperly adv. 부적절하게 seafood n. 해산물
lead to ~으로 이어지다 illness n. 질병 consume v. 섭취하다, 소비하다

08 | 분사 자리 채우기

해설 빈칸 뒤의 명사(approach)를 꾸밀 수 있는 것은 형용사이므로 형용사 역할을 하는 과거분사 (B) determined(결의가 굳은)가 정답이다. 명사 (A) determiner(결정하는 사람, 결정하는 것)와 (D) determination(투지, 결정)은 approach(접근)와 복합 명사를 이룰 수 없고, 부사 (C)는 명사를 꾸밀 수 없다.

해설 Dyson Tek사는 새로운 기술을 개발하려는 결의가 굳은 접근의 결과로 생명공학 분야의 선두 주자로 부상했다.

어휘 emerge v. 부상하다, 나타나다 bioengineering n. 생명공학
as a result of ~의 결과로

09 | 형용사 자리 채우기

해설 이 문장은 주어(Bowman's latest smartwatch), 동사(includes), 목적어(a number of innovative features)를 갖춘 완전한 절이므로, ___ ~ competitors는 수식어 거품으로 보아야 한다. 이 수식어 거품은 '(Bowman사의 최신 스마트워치가) 경쟁사들의 제품들과 다르게'라는 문맥으로 주어를 수식하는 역할을 한다. 따라서 형용사 (A) Different가 정답이다. 참고로, 이 수식어 거품구는 원래 앞에 Being이 있는 분사구문(Being different ~ competitors) 형태인데, 'Being + 형용사/과거분사'로 이루어진 분사구문에서 Being은 생략될 수 있기 때문에 빈칸은 형용사 자리임을 알 수 있다. 명사 (B), 부사 (C), 동사 (D)는 주어를 수식할 수 없다.

해설 경쟁사들의 제품들과 다르게, Bowman사의 최신 스마트워치는 다수의 혁신적인 기능들을 포함한다.

어휘 competitor n. 경쟁사, 경쟁자 innovative adj. 혁신적인
feature n. 기능, 특징 differentiate v. 구별하다

10 | 동명사 채우기

해설 전치사(of)의 목적어가 될 수 있는 명사 (B)와 동명사 (D)가 정답의 후보이다. 빈칸 뒤의 명사구(the artist's photography)를 목적어로 취할 수 있는 것은 동명사이므로 동사 appreciate(감상하다)의 동명사 (D) appreciating이 정답이다. 명사 (B)는 연결어 없이 빈칸 뒤의 명사구와 나란히 올 수 없다. 동사 (A)와 형용사 (C)는 명사 자리에 올 수 없다.

해설 Haeda 갤러리의 Inna Endo 전시회 방문객들은 그 예술가의 사진 작품을 감상하는 새로운 방법을 발견할 것이다.

어휘 exhibit n. 전시회 discover v. 발견하다
appreciative adj. 감상을 즐기는, 고마워하는

11 | to 부정사 채우기

해설 동사 encourage(encouraged)의 목적격 보어 자리에 올 수 있는 to 부정사 (C) to streamline이 정답이다. 동명사 또는 현재분사 (A), 동사 또는 과거분사 (B), 동사의 3인칭 단수형 (D)는 encourage의 목적격 보어 자리에 올 수 없다.

해설 프로젝트 관리자는 그녀의 팀원들에게 더 효과적인 의사소통을 위해 보고 방식을 간소화하라고 권고했다.

어휘 encourage v. 권고하다 method n. 방식, 방법 efficient adj. 효율적인
streamline v. 간소화하다

12 | 현재분사와 과거분사 구별하여 채우기

해설 빈칸 앞의 명사(brochure)를 꾸밀 수 있는 것은 형용사이므로 형용사 역할을 하는 과거분사 (B), 현재분사 (C), to 부정사 (D)가 정답의 후보이다. 빈칸 뒤에 목적어(all exhibitions)가 있고, "모든 전시와 위치를 나열하는 책자"라는 능동의 의미가 되어야 하므로 현재분사 (C)가 정답이다. 동사 (A)는 명사를 꾸밀 수 없다.

해설 박물관은 모든 전시와 건물 내 그것의 해당 위치를 나열하는 정보 책자를 제작했다.

어휘 informative adj. 정보의, 유익한 exhibition n. 전시
corresponding adj. 해당하는 list v. 나열하다

DAY 05 전치사, 접속사, 관계사

빈출 문제 집중 훈련   p.66

01 (B)	02 (C)	03 (B)	04 (D)	05 (A)
06 (D)	07 (C)	08 (C)	09 (D)	10 (D)
11 (A)	12 (A)	13 (B)	14 (B)	15 (C)
16 (D)	17 (A)	18 (D)	19 (D)	20 (A)

01 | 등위접속사 채우기

해설 빈칸은 동사구(earned higher profits)와 동사구(received poorer reviews)를 대등하게 연결하는 등위접속사 자리이므로 (B)와 (C)가 정답의 후보이다. '더 높은 수익을 올렸지만 더 나쁜 비평을 받았다'라는 의미가 되어야 하므로 (B) but(하지만)이 정답이다. (C) so는 '그래서'라는 의

미로 어색한 의미를 만들기 때문에 답이 될 수 없다. 접속사 (A)는 neither A nor B(A도 B도 아닌) 형태의 상관접속사로 자주 쓰이며, 부사 (D) still (아직)은 접속사 자리에 올 수 없다.

해석 그 영화 속편 *Eight Dragons*는 더 높은 수익을 올렸지만 이전 영화보다 더 나쁜 비평을 받았다.

어휘 sequel n. 속편 earn v. (이자·수익 등을) 올리다 profit n. 수익, 이익 review n. 비평

02 | 전치사 채우기

해설 '이번 해 초부터 10개 지점으로 확장되었다'라는 의미가 되어야 하므로 '~부터, ~ 이래로'라는 의미를 갖는 전치사 (C) since가 정답이다. 참고로, 전치사 since는 현재완료 시제(has/have p.p.)와 함께 자주 쓰임을 알아둔다. (A) by는 '(늦어도) ~까지는', (B) until은 '~(때)까지', (D) within은 '~ 이내에'라는 의미이다.

해석 오사카에 있는 Mr. Shimojo의 레스토랑 체인점은 이번 해 초부터 10개 지점으로 확장되었다.

어휘 expand v. 확장되다, 확장시키다 location n. 지점, 장소, 위치

03 | 등위접속사 채우기

해설 빈칸은 전치사구(to 112th Avenue)와 전치사구(to 97th Street)를 연결할 수 있는 접속사 자리이므로 등위접속사 (B) or(또는)가 정답이다. 전치사 (A) like(~처럼)와 (C) at(~에서)은 접속사 자리에 올 수 없다. (D) either는 or와 자주 함께 쓰여 상관접속사 either A or B(A 또는 B 중 하나)를 만든다.

해석 Edmonton사는 본사를 112번가나 97번가로 이전할 계획이었다.

어휘 relocate v. 이전하다 headquarters n. 본사

04 | 관계대명사 채우기

해설 이 문장은 주어(The district), 동사(has), 목적어(several ~ institutions)를 갖춘 완전한 절이므로, some ____ have yet to ~ curriculum은 수식어 거품으로 보아야 한다. 이 수식어 거품은 선행사(several ~ institutions)를 꾸며 주는 관계절로, 빈칸에 들어갈 관계대명사가 빈칸 앞의 some과 함께 쓰여 관계절 내의 주어 역할을 해야 하므로 명사 뒤에서 소유격처럼 쓰이는 (D) of which가 정답이다. (A) whose는 소유격 관계대명사이므로 뒤에 명사가 와야 한다. (B) which는 단독으로 관계절의 주어나 목적어 역할을 하고, (C) for that의 경우, 관계대명사 that은 전치사(for) 뒤에 올 수 없다.

해석 그 지역에는 여러 외국어 교육 기관이 있는데, 그들 중 일부는 아직 커리큘럼에 대한 공식 인증을 받지 못했다.

어휘 district n. 지역, 구역 several adj. 여러 개의, 몇몇의 yet adv. 아직, 여전히 obtain v. 받다, 얻다 official adj. 공식적인 accreditation n. 인증

05 | 전치사 채우기

해설 '컴퓨터 시스템의 성공적인 출시 후에 정규직으로 고용되었다'라는 의미가 되어야 하므로 '~ 후에, ~에 따라'의 의미를 갖는 전치사 (A) following이 정답이다. (C) according to(~에 따르면)도 해석상 그럴듯해 보이지만, 시간 순서 상 앞서는 것을 의미하는 following과 달리, 진술이나 기록 등에 따른다는 의미이므로 답이 될 수 없다. (B) under는 '~ 아래의', (D) on behalf of는 '~을 대표하여'라는 의미이다.

해석 그 컨설턴트는 그가 Allman 전자사에 상담해 주고 있던 컴퓨터 시스템의 성공적인 출시 후에 정규직으로 고용되었다.

어휘 hire v. 고용하다 full-time adv. 정규직으로 launch n. 출시, 착수

06 | 전치사 채우기

해설 '안전상의 이유로 인해 차량 내에 귀중품을 두지 말 것을 권고한다'라는 의미가 되어야 하므로 '~으로 인해'라는 의미를 갖는 전치사 (D) For가 정답이다. (A) Around는 '~ 주위에', (B) Upon은 '~ 위에, ~하자마자', (C) Since는 '~ 이래로'라는 의미이다.

해석 안전상의 이유로 인해, 주차장 관리자는 고객들에게 차량 내에 귀중품을 두지 말 것을 권고한다.

어휘 safety n. 안전 parking garage 주차장 urge v. 권고하다, 충고하다 valuable adj. 귀중한 vehicle n. 차량

07 | 부사절 접속사 채우기

해설 이 문장은 주어(The firm), 동사(will be), 보어(unable ~ loan)를 갖춘 완전한 절이므로, ____ it ~ in funding은 수식어 거품으로 보아야 한다. 이 수식어 거품은 동사(can secure)가 있는 거품절이므로, 부사절 접속사 (A)와 (C)가 정답의 후보이다. '자금 110만 달러를 확보하지 못하면 대출금을 상환하지 못할 것이다'라는 의미가 되어야 하므로 (C) unless(~하지 못하면)가 정답이다. (A) as if는 '마치 ~인 것처럼'이라는 의미이다. 부사 (B) furthermore(더욱이), (D) hence(그러므로)는 거품절을 이끌 수 없다.

해석 그 회사는 자금 110만 달러를 확보하지 못하면 대출금을 상환하지 못할 것이다.

어휘 repay v. 상환하다, 갚다 loan n. 대출금, 대출; v. (돈을) 빌려주다 secure v. 확보하다

08 | 전치사 채우기

해설 이 문장은 진짜주어(employment figures)와 동사(have ~ improved)가 있는 완전한 절이므로 ____ ~ problems는 수식어 거품으로 보아야 한다. 이 수식어 거품은 동사가 없는 거품구이므로, 전치사 (A), (B), (C)가 정답의 후보이다. '지역의 경제상 문제에도 불구하고 고용 수치가 꾸준히 개선되었다'라는 의미가 되어야 하므로 '~에도 불구하고'의 의미를 갖는 전치사 (C) Despite가 정답이다. (A) Including은 '~을 포함하여', (B) Except는 '~ 이외에'라는 의미이다. 부사절 접속사 (D) While(~하는 동안)은 수식어 거품구를 이끌 수 없다.

해석 지역의 경제상 문제에도 불구하고, 의료 서비스나 기술 같은 분야에서 고용 수치가 꾸준히 개선되었다.

어휘 economic adj. 경제상의, 경제의 healthcare n. 의료 서비스

09 | 부사절 접속사 채우기

해설 이 문장은 주어(the second one)와 동사(will be sent in)를 갖춘 완전한 절이므로, ____ the shop ~ delivery truck은 수식어 거품으로 보아야 한다. 이 수식어 거품은 동사(completes)가 있는 거품절이므로, 부사절 접속사 (D) As soon as(~하자마자)가 정답이다. 전치사 (A) Thanks to(~ 덕분에)는 거품절을 이끌 수 없고, to 부정사의 to처럼 쓰이는 (B) In order to(~하기 위해) 뒤에는 동사원형이 와야 한다. 상관접속사 (C) As well as(~에 더하여)는 단어와 단어, 구와 구, 절과 절 사이에 와서 둘을 대등하게 연결한다.

해석 그 자동차 정비공이 첫 번째 배달 트럭에 대한 수리를 마치자마자, 두 번째 트럭이 보내질 것이다.

어휘 mechanic n. 정비공 complete v. 마치다, 완료하다; adj. 완벽한 repair n. 수리; v. 수리하다

10 | 전치사 채우기

해설 '일정보다 늦게 운행되고 있다'라는 의미가 되어야 하므로 '늦게, 뒤떨어져'라는 의미를 갖는 전치사 (D) behind가 정답이다. (A) toward는 '~ 쪽으로', (C) beyond는 '~ 너머로'라는 의미이다. 부사 (B) ahead(미리, 앞으로)는 명사를 꾸밀 수 없다. 참고로, behind schedule(일정보다 늦게)을 관용구로 알아둔다.

해석 교통 직원은 승강장의 혼잡으로 인해 파란색 노선이 일정보다 늦게 운행

되고 있다고 알렸다.

어휘 transit n. 교통, 수송 overcrowding n. 혼잡, 초만원 platform n. 승강장

11 | 전치사 채우기

해설 이 문장은 주어(the international airport), 동사(canceled), 목적어(all inbound flights)를 갖춘 완전한 절이므로 ____ ~ equipment는 수식어 거품으로 보아야 한다. 이 수식어 거품은 동사가 없는 거품구이므로 거품구를 이끌 수 있는 전치사 (A)와 (C)가 정답의 후보이다. '결함이 있는 지상 교통 시설 때문에 모든 입국 항공편을 취소하였다'라는 의미가 되어야 하므로 '~ 때문에'라는 의미를 갖는 전치사 (A) Because of가 정답이다. (C) Apart from은 '~을 제외하고'라는 의미이다. 접속부사 (B) Subsequently(그 후에)와 (D) Therefore(그러므로)는 수식어 거품구를 이끌 수 없다.

해석 결함이 있는 지상 교통 시설 때문에, 국제 공항은 금요일에 모든 입국 항공편을 취소하였다.

어휘 defective adj. 결함이 있는, 불완전한 ground adj. 지상의; n. 땅, 지면, 근거
traffic n. 교통, 운행 equipment n. 시설, 장비, 용품
inbound adj. 입국의, 귀항하는

12 | 부사절 접속사 채우기

해설 이 문장은 주어(Sales), 동사(have been), 보어(slow)를 갖춘 완전한 절이므로 ____ ~ months는 수식어 거품으로 보아야 한다. 이 수식어 거품은 주어(it)와 동사(has been promoted)를 갖춘 완전한 절이므로 부사절 접속사 (A), (B), (C)가 정답의 후보이다. '비록 몇 달 동안 많이 홍보되었지만 그 냉동식품의 매출은 저조했다'라는 의미가 되어야 하므로 (A) even though(비록 ~이지만)가 정답이다. (B) so that은 '~할 수 있도록', (C) whereas는 '~한 반면에'라는 의미이다. 부사구 (D) until then (그때까지)은 수식어 거품절을 이끌 수 없다.

해석 비록 몇 달 동안 상점에서 많이 홍보되었지만 그 냉동식품의 매출은 저조했다.

어휘 sale n. 매출, 영업 slow adj. 저조한, 느린 promote v. 홍보하다, 판촉하다
heavily adv. 많이, 심하게

13 | 부사절 접속사 채우기

해설 빈칸은 절(Mystery ~ movie)과 절(it was ~ two months)을 연결할 수 있는 접속사 자리이므로 접속사 (B)와 등위접속사 (D)가 정답의 후보이다. '매우 인기 있는 영화여서 매진되었다'라는 의미가 되어야 하므로 빈칸 앞의 such와 짝을 이뤄 결과를 나타내는 'such ~ that …(매우 ~해서 …하다)'를 만드는 (B) that이 정답이다. 등위접속사 (D) yet은 '매우 인기 있는 영화이지만, 매진되었다'라는 어색한 문맥을 만들기 때문에 답이 될 수 없다. 부사 (A)와 형용사 또는 부사 (C)는 절과 절을 연결할 수 없다.

해석 Mystery at Dawn은 매우 인기 있는 영화여서 영화관에서 두 달간 주말마다 매진되었다.

어휘 popular adj. 인기 있는, 대중적인 sell out 매진시키다, 다 팔다

14 | 전치사 채우기

해설 '소프트웨어 문제를 고치는 것은 그 어느 누구의 능력 밖이었다'라는 의미가 되어야 하므로 '~ 밖의, ~을 넘어서'라는 의미를 갖는 전치사 (B) beyond가 정답이다. (A) except는 '~을 제외하고', (C) without은 '~ 없이'라는 의미이다. 형용사 또는 부사 (D) opposite(반대편의; 반대편에)은 정관사(the) 앞에 올 수 없다.

해석 소프트웨어 문제를 고치는 것은 부서 내의 그 어느 누구의 능력 밖이었기 때문에, 외부 기술 지원이 요청되었다.

어휘 fix v. 고치다, 고정시키다 external adj. 외부의 technical adj. 기술의

15 | 전치사 채우기

해설 '고객 불만을 조사하다'라는 의미가 되어야 하므로 빈칸 앞의 동사 look과 함께 쓰여 '~을 조사하다'라는 의미를 완성하는 (C) into가 정답이다. 'look into(~을 조사하다)'를 덩어리로 암기해 두도록 하자. (A) within은 '~ 이내에', (B) amid는 '~ 중에, ~으로 둘러싸여', (D) onto는 '~ 위로, ~ 쪽으로'라는 의미이다.

해석 마케팅팀은 회사의 웹사이트에 등록된 고객 불만을 조사할 것을 요청받았다.

어휘 complaint n. 불만, 불평 register v. 등록하다

16 | 전치사 채우기

해설 '유럽 도처에 수많은 서비스 가입자를 보유하다'라는 의미가 되어야 하므로 '~ 도처에'라는 의미를 갖는 전치사 (D) throughout이 정답이다. (A) along은 '~을 따라', (B) above는 '~ 위에', (C) without은 '~ 없이'라는 의미이다.

해석 Sempercom사는 이미 유럽 도처에 수많은 전화 및 인터넷 서비스 가입자를 보유하고 있고, 스트리밍 서비스로 사업을 확장하려고 계획 중이다.

어휘 numerous adj. 수많은 subscriber n. 구독자
branch out 사업을 확장하다, 활동을 다른 분야까지 넓히다

17-20번은 다음 광고에 관한 문제입니다.

> Cook Art사의 Home Pro로 프로처럼 요리하세요
>
> Cook Art사의 최신 Home Pro 스테인리스 조리 기구 세트는 명절 기간에 이상적인 선물입니다. [17]사랑하는 사람 또는 심지어 당신 자신을 위해서도 하나를 구매하세요. 이 세트에 포함된 냄비와 프라이팬은 사용자들에게 우수한 요리 경험을 제공하며, 전문 요리사 Eric Warner에 의해 디자인되었습니다.
>
> [18]Warner는, "저는 사용자가 집에서 레스토랑 품질의 음식을 만들 수 있게 하는 세트를 만들고자 노력했습니다. [19]모든 10개의 구성품이 고른 열의 분배를 위해 높은 등급의 강철로 만들어졌을 뿐만 아니라, 세척하기 쉽고, 식기 세척기를 사용할 수 있으며, 외관이 멋집니다."라고 말합니다.
>
> [20]다음 2주간, Home Pro 세트는 129.99달러의 할인된 가격으로 판매될 것이며, 이는 정상 가격에서 50달러나 할인된 믿을 수 없는 절약된 금액입니다! 이 할인을 이용하시려면, 오늘 www.cookart.com을 방문하세요.

cookware n. 조리 기구 ideal adj. 이상적인 superior adj. 우수한
pot n. 냄비 even adj. 고른 distribution n. 분배
incredible adj. 믿을 수 없는, 믿기 힘든

17 | 알맞은 문장 고르기

해석 (A) 사랑하는 사람 또는 심지어 당신 자신을 위해서도 하나를 구매하세요.
(B) 무료 샘플은 앞으로 2주 이내에 도착할 예정입니다.
(C) 30일 동안 무료로 사용해보고 언제든지 취소하세요.
(D) 상품권은 매장에서 결제 수단으로 사용될 수 있습니다.

해설 앞 문장 'Cook Art's all-new Home Pro stainless steel cookware set makes an ideal gift for the holiday season.'에서 Cook Art사의 최신 Home Pro 스테인리스 조리 기구 세트는 명절 기간에 이상적인 선물이라고 했으므로, 빈칸에는 선물과 관련된 내용이 들어가야 함을 알 수 있다. 따라서 (A)가 정답이다.

어휘 gift card 상품권

18 | 관계대명사 채우기

해설 이 문장은 주어(I), 동사(tried), 목적어(to create a set)를 갖춘 완전한 절이므로, ____ ~ home은 수식어 거품으로 보아야 한다. 이 수식어 거품

은 빈칸 앞의 명사(a set)를 선행사로 갖는 관계절이므로 관계대명사 (B)와 (D)가 정답의 후보이다. 관계절(___ ~ home) 내에 주어가 없고 선행사 a set가 사물이므로, 선행사의 종류와 관계없이 사용할 수 있는 주격 관계대명사 (D) that이 정답이다. (B) who는 선행사가 사람일 때 올 수 있다. (A) all은 접속사 없이 두 개의 절을 연결할 수 없고, (C) what은 선행사와 함께 쓰일 수 없으므로 답이 될 수 없다.

19 | 전치사 채우기

해설 '높은 등급의 강철로 만들어졌을 뿐만 아니라, 세척하기 쉽고'라는 의미가 되어야 하므로 '~ 뿐만 아니라'라는 의미를 갖는 전치사 (C) In addition to가 정답이다. (A) Regardless of는 '~에 상관없이', (B) As a result of는 '~의 결과로서', (D) With regard to는 '~에 관해서는'이라는 의미이다.

20 | 전치사 채우기

해설 '할인된 가격으로 판매되다'라는 의미가 되어야 하므로 빈칸 앞의 be동사 is, 빈칸 뒤의 명사 sale과 함께 쓰여 '판매되다'라는 의미를 완성하는 (A) on이 정답이다. 'be on sale(판매되다)'을 덩어리로 암기해 두도록 하자. (B) in은 '~ 안에', (C) onto는 '~ 위에', (D) within은 '~ 이내에'라는 의미이다.

고난도 문제 완전 정복 p.69

01	(D)	02	(C)	03	(A)	04	(D)	05	(C)
06	(A)	07	(C)	08	(C)	09	(A)	10	(B)
11	(B)	12	(A)						

01 | 전치사 채우기

해설 '매출과 수익을 경쟁사들의 것과 비교하여 평가하는 것'이라는 의미가 되어야 하므로 '~과 비교하여'라는 의미를 갖는 전치사 (D) against가 정답이다. (A) except는 '~을 제외하고', (B) throughout은 '~ 도처에, ~ 내내', (C) between은 '~ 사이에, ~ 중간에'라는 의미이다.

해석 회사의 매출과 수익을 경쟁사들의 것과 비교하여 평가하는 것은 그 회사가 얼마나 잘해냈는지를 보여준다.

어휘 measure v. 평가하다, 측정하다 revenue n. 수익
competitor n. 경쟁사, 경쟁자 perform v. 일을 해내다, 이행하다

02 | 전치사 채우기

해설 '직원들이 도착하기 전에 사무실을 깨끗하게 하다'라는 의미가 되어야 하므로 '~ 전에'라는 의미를 갖는 전치사 (C) before가 정답이다. (A) despite는 '~에도 불구하고', (B) from은 '~에서, ~부터', (D) within은 '~ 이내에'라는 의미이다.

해석 보수 관리 팀은 직원들이 도착하기 전에 사무실을 깨끗하게 하는 것을 확실히 하기 위해 오전 7시에 일을 시작한다.

어휘 maintenance n. 보수 관리, 유지 crew n. 팀, 승무원
ensure v. 확실하게 하다, 보장하다 arrive v. 도착하다

03 | 부사절 접속사 채우기

해설 이 문장은 주어(most participants), 동사(believed), 목적어(the ~ success)를 갖춘 완전한 절이므로 ___ weather conditions ~ the marathon은 수식어 거품으로 보아야 한다. 이 수식어 거품은 주어 (weather conditions), 동사(were), 보어(not optimal)를 갖춘 완전한 절이므로 부사절 접속사 (A), (D)와 복합관계부사 (C)가 정답의 후보이다. '비록 날씨 조건이 최적은 아니었지만, 행사가 대성공이었다고 생각했다'라는 문맥이 되어야 하므로 (A) Though(비록 ~이지만)가 정답이다. (C) However(아무리 ~하더라도)도 해석상 그럴듯해 보이지만, 'however + 형용사/부사 + 주어 + 동사'의 형태로 주로 쓰인다. (D) After는 '~ 후에'라는 의미이다. 의문사 또는 관계부사 (B)는 수식어 거품을 이끌 수 없다.

해석 비록 날씨 조건이 마라톤에 최적은 아니었지만, 대부분의 참가자들은 행사가 대성공이었다고 생각했다.

어휘 optimal adj. 최적인

04 | 전치사 채우기

해설 '진행 중인 협상에 관련된 질문은 다뤄지지 않을 것이다'라는 의미가 되어야 하므로 '~에 관련된'이라는 의미를 갖는 전치사 (D) pertaining to가 정답이다. (A) on account of는 '~ 때문에', (B) inside는 '~의 안에', (C) across는 '~을 가로질러'라는 의미이다.

해석 Price사와 진행 중인 회사의 협상에 관련된 질문은 목요일의 기자회견 중에 다뤄지지 않을 것이다.

어휘 ongoing adj. 진행 중인 address v. 다루다 press conference 기자회견

05 | 전치사 채우기

해설 'Dr. Sophia Sanchez가 원래 연설자를 대신하여 강연을 할 것이다'라는 의미가 되어야 하므로 '~을 대신하여'라는 의미를 갖는 전치사 (C) in place of가 정답이다. (A) in light of는 '~에 비추어, ~을 고려하여', (B) as of는 '~일자로, ~ 현재로', (D) except for는 '~을 제외하고'라는 의미이다.

해석 Dr. Sophia Sanchez가 원래 연설자를 대신하여 재생 가능 자원에 대한 오늘 오전 강연을 할 것이다.

어휘 renewable resource 재생 가능 자원 original adj. 원래의

06 | 명사절 접속사 채우기

해설 타동사(indicate)의 목적어 자리에 주어(it), 동사(is), 보어(necessary)가 있는 완전한 절이 왔으므로 빈칸에는 완전한 절을 이끄는 명사절 접속사가 와야 한다. 따라서 완전한 절 앞에 오는 명사절 접속사로 쓰이는 의문부사 (A) where가 정답이다. (B) what, (C) whose, (D) which도 명사절 접속사로 쓰일 수 있지만, 그 자체가 의문대명사로써 명사절의 주어나 목적어 역할을 하므로 뒤에 주어나 목적어가 없는 불완전한 절이 온다.

해석 책갈피들은 계약 당사자 각각이 그들의 서명을 써넣을 필요가 있는 곳을 가리킨다.

어휘 page marker 책갈피 indicate v. 가리키다, 나타내다
necessary adj. 필요한 party n. 당사자, 정당 agreement n. 계약, 합의
affix v. (서명을) 써넣다, 덧붙이다 signature n. 서명

07 | 전치사 채우기

해설 이 문장은 필수성분(many of the company's staff ~ much longer)을 갖춘 완전한 절이므로 ____ ~ facility는 수식어 거품으로 보아야 한다. 이 수식어 거품은 동사가 없는 거품구이므로, 거품구를 이끌 수 있는 전치사 (B)와 (C)가 정답의 후보이다. '도시의 고속 철도 시설이 없다면, 훨씬 더 오래 걸릴 것이다'라는 의미가 되어야 하므로 전치사 (C) But for (~이 없다면)가 정답이다. (B) With all은 '~에도 불구하고'라는 의미로 양보를 나타낸다. (A) Given that은 '~을 고려하면', (D) Whereas는 '반면에'라는 의미의 부사절 접속사로 거품구가 아닌 거품절을 이끈다.

해석 도시의 고속 철도 시설이 없다면, 그 회사 직원 다수는 회사로 통근하는 데 훨씬 더 오래 걸릴 것이다.

어휘 rail n. 철도, 난간 commute v. 통근하다

08 | 부사절 접속사 채우기

해설 이 문장은 주어(Ms. Gluck)와 동사(will be leaving)를 갖춘 완전한 절 이므로, ____ ~ replacement는 수식어 거품으로 보아야 한다. 이 수

식어 거품은 동사(does not find)가 있는 거품절이므로 부사절 접속사 (B), (C), (D)가 정답의 후보이다. '비록 경영진이 후임자를 찾지 못하더라도 회사를 떠나게 될 것이다'라는 의미가 되어야 하므로 (C) even if(비록 ~하더라도)가 정답이다. (B) as though는 '마치 ~처럼', (D) provided that은 '~을 고려할 때'라는 의미이다. 전치사 (A)는 거품절을 이끌 수 없다.

해석 비록 경영진이 후임자를 찾지 못하더라도 Ms. Gluck은 이달 말에 회사를 떠나게 될 것이다.

어휘 firm n. 회사 management n. 경영진 replacement n. 후임자

09 | 명사절 접속사 채우기

해설 전치사(in)의 목적어 역할을 하는 명사절(___ was formerly ~ manufacture steel)을 이끌면서, 그 자체가 명사절의 주어 역할을 할 수 있는 의문대명사 (C) what이 정답이다. 참고로, 이 문장에서 what은 '선행사 + 관계대명사'(the place + that) 대신 사용되었다는 것을 알아둔다. (A)와 (B)는 의문부사로서 명사절을 이끌기 때문에, 뒤에 완전한 절이 와야 한다. 관계대명사 (D)는 빈칸 앞에 선행사가 없기 때문에 답이 될 수 없다.

해석 예술가들은 이전에 철을 제조하는 데 사용되던 공업단지였던 곳에 전시 공간을 설립했다.

어휘 establish v. 설립하다, 수립하다 exhibit n. 전시, 전시품; v. 전시하다
formerly adv. 이전에 industrial park 공업단지
manufacture v. 제조하다, 생산하다 steel n. 철, 철강업

10 | 전치사 채우기

해설 '지하철 노선이 Ogden가 전 구간의 밑으로 지나간다'라는 의미가 되어야 하므로 '~ 밑으로'라는 의미를 갖는 전치사 (B) beneath가 정답이다. (A) toward는 '~을 향해', (C) after는 '~ 다음에', (D) behind는 '~ 뒤에'라는 의미이다.

해석 지하철 노선은 Ogden가 전 구간의 밑으로 지나가고, 거리를 따라 3개의 정거장이 위치해 있다.

어휘 run v. 지나가다, 이어지다 length n. 구간, 길이 stop n. 정거장, 정류장
locate v. 위치시키다, 두다

11 | 복합관계대명사 채우기

해설 동사(should report)의 주어 역할을 하는 절(___ ~ malfunction)의 맨 앞에 올 수 있는 것은 명사절 접속사이므로 복합관계대명사 (A)와 (B), 의문형용사 (D)가 정답의 후보이다. '장비 고장에 책임이 있는 누구든 간에'라는 의미가 되어야 하므로 복합관계대명사 (B) Whoever(누구든 간에)가 정답이다. 복합관계대명사 (A) Whatever(무엇이든 간에)는 사물을 지칭할 때 쓰이므로 답이 될 수 없다. 의문형용사 (D) Whose는 '누구의'라는 의미로 뒤에 명사가 와야 한다. 대명사 (C)는 절을 이끌 수 없다.

해석 장비 고장에 책임이 있는 누구든 간에 즉시 유지보수 부서에 보고해야 한다.

어휘 responsible adj. 책임이 있는 malfunction n. 고장
immediately adv. 즉시 maintenance department 유지보수 부서

12 | 상관접속사 채우기

해설 동사(will address)의 목적어인 명사구(current industry trends)와 명사구(future market projections ~ decade)를 대등하게 연결해 주는 등위접속사 또는 상관접속사가 필요하고 '현재 업계 동향뿐만 아니라 향후 10년에 대한 미래 시장 전망도 다루다'라는 의미가 되어야 하므로 상관접속사 (A) as well as(~뿐 아니라 -도)가 정답이다. 부사절 접속사 (B)와 접속부사 (C)는 명사구와 명사구를 대등하게 연결할 수 없다.

해석 그 사업 회의는 현재 업계 동향뿐만 아니라 향후 10년에 대한 미래 시장 전망도 다룰 것이다.

어휘 address v. 다루다 current adj. 현재의 projection n. 전망
decade n. 10년

DAY 06   어휘와 어구

빈출 문제 집중 훈련   p.70

01 (A)	02 (C)	03 (A)	04 (D)	05 (C)
06 (A)	07 (A)	08 (B)	09 (D)	10 (D)
11 (D)	12 (D)	13 (D)	14 (D)	15 (C)
16 (D)	17 (B)	18 (D)	19 (C)	20 (A)

01 | 형용사 어휘 고르기

해설 '물가가 일 년 내내 안정적으로 유지되면, 중앙은행은 금리를 조정할 명분이 없다'라는 문맥이므로 (A) stable(안정적인)이 정답이다. (B) credible은 '믿을 수 있는', (C) feasible은 '실현 가능한', (D) adaptable은 '적응할 수 있는'이라는 의미이다.

해석 물가가 일 년 내내 안정적으로 유지되면, 중앙은행은 금리를 조정할 명분이 없다고 생각한다.

어휘 provided that (만약) ~이라면 remain v. 유지되다, 유지하다
adjust v. 조정하다, 적응하다 interest rates 금리

02 | 동사 어휘 고르기

해설 '참여하고자 하는 지역 구성원들은 그들의 시간이나 기술을 바치도록 장려된다'라는 문맥이므로 (C) devote(바치다, 헌신하다)가 정답이다. (A) import는 '수입하다', (B) benefit은 '~에 유익하다', (D) delegate는 '위임하다'라는 의미이다.

해석 자원봉사 프로그램에 참여하고자 하는 지역 구성원들은 그들의 시간이나 기술을 바치도록 장려된다.

어휘 participate v. 참여하다

03 | 부사 어휘 고르기

해설 '연혁 초기에, Edelman's 슈퍼마켓은 단 한 개의 상점으로 시작했다'라는 문맥이므로 (A) Early(초기에, 처음에)가 정답이다. (B) Away는 '~에서 떨어져, 다른 데(로)', (C) Even은 '~도(조차), 훨씬', (D) Instead는 '대신에'라는 의미이다. 추가로, since가 '~ 이래로'라는 의미의 전치사/접속사, 또는 '~ 때문에'라는 의미의 접속사로 흔히 쓰이지만, 이 문장에서처럼 '그 이후, 그때 이래로'라는 의미의 부사로도 사용될 수 있음을 알아둔다.

해석 연혁 초기에, Edelman's 슈퍼마켓은 단 한 개의 상점으로 시작했지만, 그 이후 50개의 지점으로 확장해 왔다.

어휘 expand v. 확장하다 location n. 지점

04 | 짝을 이루는 표현

해설 빈칸 앞의 동사 gain(얻다)과 뒤의 전치사 to와 함께 '~에 접근하다'라는 의미의 어구 gain access to를 완성하는 명사 (D) access(접근)가 정답이다. (A) report는 '보도, 보고서', (B) perspective는 '관점', (C) confidence는 '자신감'이라는 의미이다.

해석 학생들은 자신들의 지정된 학번을 사용하여 대학교의 온라인 학술지 데이터베이스에 접근할 수 있다.

어휘 assign v. 지정하다, 맡기다, 배정하다

05 | 동사 어휘 고르기

해설 '음악 경연 대회의 우승자들이 관중들에게 발표되기 전에'라는 문맥이므로, 동사 announce(발표하다)의 과거분사형 (C) announced가 정답이다. (A)의 vote는 '투표하다', (B)의 monitor는 '추적 관찰하다, 감시하다', (D)의 enter는 '들어가다'라는 의미이다.

해석 음악 경연 대회의 우승자들이 관중들에게 발표되기 전에 심사위원들은 모여서 최종 결정을 내릴 것이다.

어휘 judge n. 심사위원, 판사 convene v. 모이다, 소집하다
competition n. 경연 대회, 경쟁 audience n. 관중, 청중

06 | 명사 어휘 고르기

해설 '그 기사가 게재될 수 있기 전에 상당한 수정이 필요하다'라는 문맥이므로 (A) revision(수정)이 정답이다. (B) notification은 '알림, 통지', (C) negotiation은 '협상', (D) correlation은 '상관관계'라는 의미이다.

해석 그 편집장은 Ms. Oakley의 기사를 검토했고 그 기사가 게재될 수 있기 전에 상당한 수정이 필요할 것이라고 말했다.

어휘 managing editor 편집장 review v. 검토하다, 복습하다 article n. 기사, 글
substantial adj. 상당한 publish v. (기사 등을) 게재하다, 출판하다

07 | 동사 어휘 고르기

해설 '대표할 사람을 세 사람까지만 지명하다'라는 문맥이므로 (A) nominate(지명하다, 추천하다)가 정답이다. (B) evaluate는 '평가하다', (C) commit는 '저지르다, 맡기다', (D) attach는 '~에 붙이다, (중요성을) 두다'라는 의미이다.

해석 주주들은 이사회에서 자신들을 대표할 사람을 세 사람까지만 지명하는 것이 허용된다.

어휘 shareholder n. 주주 represent v. 대표하다, 나타내다

08 | 형용사 어휘 고르기

해설 '수십억 달러의 가치가 있는 수익성 높은 계약들을 확보했다'라는 문맥이므로 (B) lucrative(수익성 높은)가 정답이다. (A) variable은 '가변적인', (C) moderate는 '보통의, 중간의', (D) knowledgeable은 '아는 것이 많은'이라는 의미이다.

해석 그 회사는 키르기스스탄, 인도, 그리고 남아프리카 공화국으로의 출장 이후에, 통틀어서 수십억 달러의 가치가 있는 수익성 높은 계약들을 확보했다.

어휘 secure v. 확보하다; adj. 안전한 contract n. 계약, 계약서
worth adj. ~의 가치가 있는

09 | 부사 어휘 고르기

해설 '최신형 Simtek 휴대폰은 보통 매장에서 약 400달러에 팔린다'라는 문맥이므로 (D) ordinarily(보통, 정상적으로)가 정답이다. (A) rarely는 '드물게, 좀처럼 ~하지 않는', (B) before는 '~ 전에', (C) almost는 '거의'라는 의미이다.

해석 최신형 Simtek 휴대폰은 보통 매장에서 약 400달러에 팔리지만 온라인에서는 단 325달러에 구매될 수 있다.

어휘 brand-new adj. 최신형의, 완전 새것인

10 | 동사 어휘 고르기

해설 '그녀가 달성하려고 세웠던 직장 생활의 모든 목표를 이뤘다'라는 문맥이므로 (D) accomplish(달성하다)가 정답이다. (A) believe는 '믿다, 생각하다', (B) determine은 '알아내다, 결정하다', (C) challenge는 '이의를 제기하다, 도전하다'라는 의미이다.

해석 40살이 되었을 때쯤, Ms. Henry는 젊은 언론학부 졸업생으로서 그녀가 달성하려고 세웠던 직장 생활의 모든 목표를 이뤘다.

어휘 achieve v. 이루다, 달성하다 career n. 직장 생활, 직업

11 | 명사 어휘 고르기

해설 '주가가 연초에 세웠던 예상치를 달성하는 데 실패한 후 떨어졌다'라는 문맥이므로, 명사 projection(예상치, 계획)의 복수형 (D) projections가 정답이다. (A)의 impression은 '인상', (B)의 outcome은 '결과, 결론', (C)의 conclusion은 '결론'이라는 의미이다.

해석 Sandona Retail사의 주가는 연초에 세웠던 예상치를 달성하는 데 실패한 후 떨어졌다.

어휘 drop v. 떨어지다 meet v. 달성하다, 충족시키다

12 | 동사 어휘 고르기

해설 '고객들이 장비를 쉽게 설치할 수 있도록, 컬러 사진을 넣은 사용자 설명서를 제공한다'라는 문맥이므로, 동사 illustrate(사진이나 삽화를 넣다)의 과거분사형 (A) illustrated가 정답이다. (B)의 subscribe는 '구독하다, 응모하다', (C)의 compliment는 '칭찬하다', (D)의 abbreviate는 '생략하다, 짧게 하다'라는 의미이다.

해석 고객들이 장비를 쉽게 설치할 수 있도록, Peninsula Networks사는 컬러 사진을 넣은 사용자 설명서를 제공한다.

어휘 customer n. 고객, 손님 install v. 설치하다 equipment n. 장비, 용품
provide v. 제공하다, 공급하다

13 | 명사 어휘 고르기

해설 '지역 사업가들에 의해 마련된 기부금과 함께, 정부 보조금은 보수 비용을 지불하는 데 도움이 되었다'라는 문맥이므로, 명사 contribution(기부금)의 복수형 (D) contributions가 정답이다. (A)의 admission은 '승인, 가입', (B)의 proposition은 '제의', (C)의 evaluation은 '평가'라는 의미이다.

해석 지역 사업가들에 의해 마련된 기부금과 함께, 정부 보조금은 병동의 보수 비용을 지불하는 데 도움이 되었다.

어휘 grant n. 보조금 renovation n. 보수, 수리

14 | 형용사 어휘 고르기

해설 '합의에 이르기 위한 수많은 시도에도 불구하고, 두 회사는 계속해서 의견을 달리한다'라는 문맥이므로 (B) numerous(수많은)가 정답이다. (A) successful은 '성공적인', (C) executive는 '경영의', (D) premature는 '시기상조의, 이른'이라는 의미이다.

해석 합의에 이르기 위한 수많은 시도에도 불구하고, 두 회사는 제시된 계약서에 있는 몇 가지 조건에 대해 계속해서 의견을 달리한다.

어휘 attempt n. 시도, 도전 differ v. 의견이 다르다, 동의하지 않다
condition n. 조건, 상태 propose v. 제시하다, 제안하다
contract n. 계약서, 계약

15 | 부사 어휘 고르기

해설 'Ms. Haryadi는 뛰어난 성과를 냈고 그 결과로 승진과 약간의 임금 인상을 받았다'라는 문맥이므로 (C) consequently(그 결과, 따라서)가 정답이다. (A) considerably는 '많이, 상당히', (B) receptively는 '수용성 있게, 잘 받아들여', (D) alternatively는 '그 대신에, 그렇지 않으면'이라는 의미이다.

해석 Ms. Haryadi는 개발 프로젝트에서 뛰어난 성과를 냈고 그 결과로 승진과 약간의 임금 인상을 받았다.

어휘 exceptional adj. 뛰어난, 이례적인 development n. 개발
promotion n. 승진, 진급 modest adj. 약간의, 보통의

16 | 부사 어휘 고르기

해설 '그럼에도 불구하고 그 건축물은 유감스럽게도 철거되었다'라는 문맥이므로 (D) anyway(그럼에도 불구하고, 그래도)가 정답이다. (A) apart(떨어져, 별개로)와 (B) enough(충분히)는 부사로 쓰이지만 절을 수식할 수 없다. (C) however(하지만, 그러나)는 문장 마지막에 접속부사로 오려면 앞에 콤마(,)가 와야 한다.

해석 수많은 주민들이 역사적인 건물을 보존하기 위해 탄원서에 서명했지만, 그럼에도 불구하고 그 건축물은 유감스럽게도 철거되었다.

어휘 resident n. 주민 petition n. 탄원서, 탄원 save v. 보존하다, 모으다 historic adj. 역사적인 unfortunately adv. 유감스럽게도, 불행히도 structure n. 건축물, 구조 demolish v. 철거하다

17-20번은 다음 편지에 관한 문제입니다.

주주 여러분께,

Gravura Development사가 Lydia Capital Ventures사의 투자를 받기 위해 모든 필요 요건들을 완료했다는 것을 알리게 되어 기쁩니다. ¹⁷이제 저희는 잠비아의 루사카에 있는 저희의 첫 번째 구리선 공장 건설을 진행할 수 있습니다. 아시다시피, 그 시설은 많은 동광 근처에 위치하게 될 것입니다. ¹⁸따라서, 저희는 몇몇 좋은 원자재 공급원을 갖게 될 것입니다. ¹⁹다음 몇 달 동안, 저는 그곳의 건설 공사 진척을 확인하러 직접 그 지역을 방문할 것입니다. 프로젝트에 대한 주기적인 최근 정보를 받으시려면, 저희 웹사이트 www.gravura.com에 가서 우편물 수신자 명단에 가입하십시오. ²⁰마지막으로, 저희가 이 설레는 새 사업에 착수하면서 지지해 주신 것에 대해 여러분 모두에게 다시 한 번 감사드립니다.

감사합니다,
Peter Merck
최고 경영자, Gravura Development사

announce v. 알리다, 발표하다 complete v. 완료하다, 완성하다
necessary adj. 필요한, 불가피한 requirement n. 요건, 필요조건
obtain v. 받다, 얻다 proceed v. 진행하다 construct v. 건설하다, 구성하다
copper n. 구리 multiple adj. 많은 copper mine 동광
coming adj. 다음의, 다가오는 personally adv. 직접, 개인적으로
check on ~을 확인하다, 조사하다 periodic adj. 주기적인
in closing 마지막으로, 끝으로 enterprise n. 사업, 기업

17 | 형용사 관련 어구 완성하기

해설 '이제 잠비아의 루사카에 있는 첫 번째 구리선 공장 건설을 진행할 수 있다'라는 문맥이므로 빈칸 앞의 be동사 are과 뒤의 to 부정사(to proceed)와 함께 '~할 수 있다'라는 의미의 어구 be able to를 만드는 형용사 (B) able이 정답이다. (A) easy는 '쉬운', (C) right은 '옳은', (D) useful은 '유용한'이라는 의미이다.

18 | 알맞은 문장 고르기

해석 (A) 그 지역은 놀라운 식물과 동물의 생태로 유명합니다.
(B) 구리는 실용적인 용도가 많기 때문에 수요가 많습니다.
(C) 투자하실 의향을 말씀해 주십시오.
(D) 따라서, 저희는 몇몇 좋은 원자재 공급원을 갖게 될 것입니다.

해설 앞 문장 'the facility will be located near multiple copper mines'에서 그 시설은 많은 동광 근처에 위치하게 될 것이라고 했으므로, 빈칸에는 동광과 관련된 내용이 들어가야 함을 알 수 있다. 따라서 (D)가 정답이다.

어휘 region n. 지역 incredible adj. 놀라운 demand n. 수요
practical adj. 실용적인 willingness n. 의향, 기꺼이 하는 마음
investment n. 투자 source n. 공급원 raw material 원자재

19 | 명사 어휘 고르기

해설 '다음 몇 달 동안 그곳의 건설 공사 진척을 확인하러 직접 그 지역을 방문할 것이다'라는 문맥이므로 (C) progress(진척)가 정답이다. (A) span은 '기간', (B) deposit은 '착수금, 보증금', (D) subsidy는 '보조금'이라는 의미이다.

20 | 동사 관련 어구 완성하기 전체 문맥 파악

해설 this exciting new enterprise(이 설레는 새 사업)를 목적어로 취하면서 전치사 on과 어구를 이루어 자연스러운 문맥을 만드는 (A)와 (D)가 정답의 후보이다. 빈칸이 있는 문장만으로 정답을 고를 수 없으므로 주변 문맥이나 전체 문맥을 파악한다. 지문 앞부분에서 '공장 건설을 진행할 수 있다(We are now ~ proceed with constructing ~ factory)'고 했으므로 새로운 사업을 시작하고 있음을 알 수 있다. 따라서 빈칸 뒤의 on과 함께 '~에 착수하다'라는 의미의 어구를 만드는 (A) embark(착수하다)가 정답이다. (D) reflect는 reflect on의 형태로 '~을 곰곰이 생각하다, 숙고하다'라는 의미인데, 이미 사업을 시작해서 진행하고 있는 이 문맥에는 맞지 않는다. (B) remain은 '남다, 계속 ~이다', (C) appear는 '나타나다, ~인 것처럼 보이다'라는 의미이다.

고난도 문제 완전 정복 p.73

01 (B)	02 (B)	03 (A)	04 (D)	05 (D)
06 (B)	07 (B)	08 (C)	09 (D)	10 (C)
11 (B)	12 (A)			

01 | 동사 어휘 고르기

해설 '축제에 참여하고 싶은 사람들은 티켓을 구매해야 한다'라는 문맥이므로 (B) attend(참여하다)가 정답이다. (A) engage(참여하다)와 (C) participate(참가하다)도 해석상 그럴듯해 보이지만, 자동사이므로 뒤에 목적어(the ~ Festival)가 올 수 없다. 참고로, engage와 participate는 전치사 in과 함께 각각 engage in(~에 참여하다)/participate in(~에 참가하다)의 형태로 쓰임을 알아둔다. (D) perform(공연하다)도 해석상 그럴듯해 보이지만 다음에 song(노래)과 같이 공연되는 것이 오거나 perform at the festival과 같은 형태로 쓰이므로 이 문장에는 적절하지 않다.

해석 이번 5월의 Aylesbury 봄 축제에 참여하고 싶은 사람들은 시청에서 티켓을 구매해야 한다.

어휘 purchase v. 구매하다 town hall 시청

02 | 명사 어휘 고르기

해설 '국내 통화가 그 가치를 빠르게 잃는 속도에 대해 우려한다'라는 문맥이므로 (B) rate(속도, 비율)가 정답이다. (A) point는 '시점, 의견', (C) time은 '시간', (D) account는 '계좌, 장부'라는 의미이다. 참고로, (A)와 (C)는 빈칸에 들어갈 명사를 꾸며 주는 관계절(at which ~ value)의 현재완료 시제(has lost)와 함께 썼을 때 '통화가 그 가치를 잃어 온 시점/시간'이라는 어색한 의미를 만들기 때문에 답이 될 수 없다.

해석 분석가들은 국내 통화가 그 가치를 빠르게 잃는 속도에 대해 우려하고 있다.

어휘 analyst n. 분석가 concerned adj. 우려하는, 걱정하는 currency n. 통화
rapidly adv. 빠르게, 급격히 value n. 가치

03 | 동사 관련 어구 완성하기

해설 'Randall 대학교는 교수진 관리자를 구하는 구인 공고를 게시했다'라는 문맥이므로 빈칸 뒤의 부사 out과 함께 '게시하다, 출판하다'라는 의미의 어구 put out을 만드는 동사 put(놓다)의 과거분사형 (A) put이 정답이

다. (B)의 reach는 '내밀다, 뻗다', (C)의 carry는 '나르다, 전달하다', (D)의 figure는 '계산하다'라는 의미이다. (B), (C), (D)도 부사 out과 함께 쓰일 수 있지만 문맥상 적절하지 않으므로 답이 될 수 없다.

해석 Randall 대학교는 새로 개설한 로봇 공학과를 위한 교수진 관리자를 구하는 구인 공고를 게시했다.

어휘 seek v. 구하다, 찾다 faculty n. 교수진 administrator n. 관리자, 행정인

04 | 형용사 어휘 고르기

해설 '부담이 많이 되는 일정 때문에 임시 직원을 고용하는 것을 계획하고 있다'라는 문맥이므로 (D) demanding(부담이 많이 되는, 힘든)이 정답이다. (A) standard는 '표준의, 보통의', (B) permanent는 '영구적인', (C) continual은 '거듭되는, 반복되는'이라는 의미이다.

해석 부담이 많이 되는 10월의 일정 때문에, 그 회사는 임시 직원을 고용하는 것을 계획하고 있다.

어휘 temporary adj. 임시의

05 | 부사 어휘 고르기

해설 '모든 프로젝트를 꼼꼼하게 계획하는 데 시간을 들인다'라는 문맥이므로 (D) meticulously(꼼꼼하게)가 정답이다. (A) comparatively는 '비교적', (B) symmetrically는 '대칭적으로', (C) equitably는 '공정하게'라는 의미이다.

해석 그 관리자는 항상 모든 프로젝트를 꼼꼼하게 계획하는 데 시간을 들이고, 이는 프로젝트의 정확한 실행을 보장한다.

어휘 plan v. 계획하다, 구상하다 ensure v. 보장하다, 반드시 ~하게 하다 precise adj. 정확한, 정밀한 implementation n. 실행, 이행

06 | 명사 어휘 고르기

해설 '도급업자는 잔해의 제거를 처리하기 위해 다른 회사를 고용했다'라는 문맥이므로 (B) removal(제거)이 정답이다. (A) shortage는 '부족', (C) sacrifice는 '희생', (D) renewal은 '재개, 갱신'이라는 의미이다.

해석 도급업자는 건물의 공사 현장으로부터 나오는 잔해의 제거를 처리하기 위해 다른 회사를 고용했다.

어휘 contractor n. 도급업자, 계약자 hire v. 고용하다 handle v. 처리하다 debris n. 잔해, 쓰레기 construction site 공사 현장

07 | 형용사 어휘 고르기

해설 '회사 정책에 대한 결정에 직원들을 참여시킴으로써 포용적인 업무 환경을 조성하다'라는 문맥이므로 (B) inclusive(포용적인)가 정답이다. (A) enriched는 '풍부한', (C) orderly는 '정돈된', (D) exotic은 '이국적인'이라는 의미이다.

해석 경영진은 회사 정책에 대한 결정에 직원들을 참여시킴으로써 포용적인 업무 환경을 조성하려고 노력한다.

어휘 involve v. 참여시키다

08 | 명사 어휘 고르기

해설 '보상 위원회의 입장은 Emblem사가 상여금을 수여하지 않아야 한다는 것이다'라는 문맥이므로 (C) position(입장)이 정답이다. (A) setting은 '환경, 배경', (B) capacity는 '용량, 능력', (D) admission은 '입장(료), 인정'이라는 의미이다.

해석 보상 위원회의 입장은 수익성이 향상되기 전까지 Emblem사가 상여금을 수여하지 않아야 한다는 것이다.

어휘 compensation n. 보상(금) committee n. 위원회 award v. 수여하다, 주다 bonus n. 상여금 profitability n. 수익성, 이윤율 improve v. 향상되다, 개선하다

09 | 부사 어휘 고르기

해설 '위원회는 철저히 검증된 연구 결과를 조사했다'라는 문맥이므로 (C) comprehensively(철저히, 완벽하게)가 정답이다. (A) assuredly는 '틀림없이', (B) inherently는 '타고나서, 본질적으로', (D) leniently는 '관대하게'라는 의미이다.

해석 위원회는 정책 수정을 승인하기 전에 철저히 검증된 연구 결과를 조사했다.

어휘 examine v. 조사하다 validate v. 검증하다, 입증하다 amendment n. 수정, 개정

10 | 형용사 관련 어구 완성하기

해설 '기존의 기계들과 호환되는 제품을 구매함으로써 장비 업그레이드 비용을 절감할 수 있다'라는 문맥이므로 빈칸 앞의 be동사 are과 뒤의 전치사 with와 함께 '~과 호환되다'라는 의미의 어구 be compatible with를 만드는 형용사 (C) compatible(호환되는)이 정답이다. (A) collective는 '집단의, 단체의', (B) cooperative는 '협력하는', (D) cordial은 '다정한'이라는 의미이다.

해석 Horizon 섬유사는 기존의 기계들과 호환되는 제품을 구매함으로써 장비 업그레이드 비용을 절감할 수 있다.

어휘 purchase v. 구매하다 existing adj. 기존의, 현존하는 machinery n. 기계(류) reduce v. 절감하다 expense n. 비용

11 | 동사 어휘 고르기

해설 '기술 혁신에 적응하기 위해 투자 전략을 점검하다'라는 문맥이므로 (B) overhaul(점검하다, 조사하다)이 정답이다. (A) deliver는 '전달하다', (C) embrace는 '수용하다', (D) prohibit은 '금지하다'라는 의미이다.

해석 업계 전문가들은 전통적인 은행들이 금융 기술 혁신에 적응하기 위해 투자 전략을 점검할 것을 권고한다.

어휘 traditional adj. 전통적인 adapt v. 적응하다 innovation n. 혁신

12 | 부사 어휘 고르기

해설 '원활하게 통합되어서 추가 환경 설정이 필요하지 않다'라는 문맥이므로 (A) seamlessly(원활하게, 균일하게)가 정답이다. (B) sporadically는 '산발적으로', (C) graciously는 '자애롭게, 우아하게', (D) durably는 '튼튼하게'라는 의미이다.

해석 새 소프트웨어 업데이트는 기존 시스템과 원활하게 통합되어서, 사용자로부터의 추가 환경 설정이 필요하지 않다.

어휘 integrate v. 통합되다 existing adj. 기존의 configuration n. 환경 설정, 배열

PART 7

DAY 07 이메일/편지, 메시지 대화문, 광고

빈출 문제 집중 훈련 p.76

01 (C)	02 (A)	03 (B)	04 (D)	05 (C)
06 (C)	07 (D)	08 (C)	09 (C)	10 (C)
11 (C)	12 (B)	13 (C)		

01-02번은 다음 이메일에 관한 문제입니다.

수신: Lenny Stewart <lstewart@bigmail.com>
발신: Michelle Andrews <m_andrews@tiletown.com>
날짜: 11월 14일

[01]저는 현재 휴가로 사무실을 떠나 있으며 12월 6일까지 돌아오지 않을 것입니다. 이 기간 동안, 저는 이메일 접속이 제한될 것이고 전화를 받을 수 없을 것입니다. 만일 즉각적인 조치가 필요한 시급한 요구사항이 있으시다면, [02]제 비서 Theodore Larson에게 555-2309로 연락해 주십시오. 그렇지 않다면, 12월 6일이나 그 이후에 답장을 기대해 주십시오. 감사합니다.

[02]Michelle Andrews
회계부서 담당자
Tile Town사

return v. 돌아오다, 돌려주다 limited adj. 제한된 urgent adj. 시급한, 긴급한
request n. 요구사항, 요구 require v. 필요하다, 요구하다
immediate adj. 즉각적인 contact v. 연락하다; n. 연락, 접촉
response n. 답장, 회신, 반응 account n. 회계, 계정, 계좌

01 | 목적 찾기 문제

해석 이메일의 목적은 무엇인가?
(A) 경영진에게 문제를 통지하기 위해
(B) 계정 접속 권한을 요청하기 위해
(C) 수신자에게 부재를 알리기 위해
(D) 고객의 연락처 정보를 제공하기 위해

해설 지문의 'I am currently away from the office on vacation and will not be returning until December 6. During this time, I will have limited access to my e-mail and will not be available to answer my phone.'에서 현재 휴가로 사무실을 떠나 있으며 12월 6일까지 돌아오지 않을 것이라고 한 후, 이 기간 동안 이메일 접속이 제한될 것이고 전화를 받을 수 없을 것이라고 했으므로 (C)가 정답이다.

어휘 recipient n. 수신자 absence n. 부재

Paraphrasing

away from the office 사무실을 떠나 있는 → an absence 부재

02 | 추론 문제

해석 Theodore Larson에 대해 암시되는 것은?
(A) Tile Town사의 직원이다.
(B) 12월 6일까지 휴가를 떠나 있다.
(C) Ms. Andrews의 상사이다.
(D) 기술부서 담당자이다.

해설 지문의 'please contact my assistant Theodore Larson at 555-2309'에서 자신의 비서 Theodore Larson에게 555-2309로 연락해 달라고 하였고, 'Michelle Andrews, Account representative, Tile Town'에서 Michelle Andrews가 Tile Town사의 회계부서 담당자라고 했으므로 Theodore Larson 또한 Tile Town사의 직원이라는 것을 추론할 수 있다. 따라서 (A)가 정답이다.

어휘 supervisor n. 상사, 관리자

03-05번은 다음 광고에 관한 문제입니다.

Web Space사가 귀하가 온라인에서 주목받는 데 도움을 드립니다!
120번지 Laramie가, 시카고, 일리노이 주 60644
555-9002 | | www.webspace.com

오늘날의 세상에서, [03]귀하의 사업이나 조직의 성공은 웹사이트의 내용, 품질, 그리고 디자인에 종종 달려 있습니다. ─ [1] ─. 웹사이트는 빠르게 로딩되어야 하고 스마트폰에서도 깔끔하고 알아보기 쉬운 레이아웃을 제공해야 합니다. ─ [2] ─. [05]만일 그것이 지나치게 기술적이고, 매력적이지 않고, 구식이고, 사용하기 어렵다면, 귀하의 고객은 다른 곳에 일을 가져갈지도 모릅니다. ─ [3] ─. Web Space사에 맡겨 주시면, 저희는 시각적으로 매력적이고, 모든 사용자들이 접근 가능하고, 둘러보기 쉬운 웹사이트를 제작하는 것을 도와드릴 수 있습니다.

[04-(C)]Web Space사는 20년간 다양한 집단에 서비스를 제공해 왔습니다. ─ [4] ─. 우리는 빠르게 발전하는 인터넷 세상과 함께 줄곧 성장해 왔으며 온라인상의 기능, 트렌드, 레이아웃을 최신으로 유지하고 있습니다. 현재, [04-(D)]우리는 웹사이트 디자인과 제작에 있어서 다음 서비스를 제공합니다:

- 내용 편집
- [04-(D)]일정표
- 검색 엔진 최적화
- [04-(D)]등록 양식
- [04-(D)]멀티미디어 콘텐츠
- 웹사이트 보안

www.webspace.com을 둘러봄으로써 저희가 기업과 단체를 위해 디자인한 다양한 멋진 사이트를 살펴볼 수 있습니다. info@webspace.com으로 이메일을 보내 저희에게 연락주세요.

organization n. 조직, 단체 depend on ~에 달려 있다, ~에 의존하다
content n. 내용 readable adj. 알아보기 쉬운, 재미있는
overly adv. 지나치게 technical adj. 기술적인, 전문의
unattractive adj. 매력적이지 않은, 보기 좋지 않은 outdated adj. 구식인
visually adv. 시각적으로, 눈에 보이게 appealing adj. 매력적인, 흥미로운
accessible adj. 접근 가능한, 이용하기 쉬운 navigate v. 둘러보다, 길을 찾다
up-to-date adj. 최신의 function n. 기능 creation n. 제작, 창조
editing n. 편집 optimization n. 최적화 browse v. 둘러보다, 훑어보다

03 | 주제 찾기 문제

해석 광고되고 있는 것은 무엇인가?
(A) 컴퓨터 장비 소매점
(B) 웹사이트 개발 회사
(C) 인터넷 조사업체
(D) 온라인 결제 서비스

해설 지문의 'the success of your business or organization often depends on the content, quality, and design of your Web site'에서 사업이나 조직의 성공은 웹사이트의 내용, 품질, 그리고 디자인에 종종 달려 있다고 한 후 Web Space사가 웹사이트 제작과 관련하여 제공하는 서비스를 제시하고 있으므로 (B)가 정답이다.

어휘 equipment n. 장비, 기기 retailer n. 소매점, 소매 상인 research n. 조사
payment n. 결제, 지불

04 | Not/True 문제

해석 Web Space사에 대해 언급된 것은?
(A) 고객 설문 조사를 진행하고 있다.
(B) 제품 다수를 온라인에서 판매한다.
(C) 10년간 사업에 종사해 왔다.
(D) 여러 가지의 온라인 콘텐츠를 창작할 수 있다.

해설 광고의 'we offer the following services in Web site design and creation'에서 웹사이트 디자인과 제작에 있어서 다음의 서비스를 제공한다고 한 후, 'Calendars', 'Registration forms', 'Multimedia content'에서 일정표, 등록 양식, 멀티미디어 콘텐츠 등의 다양한 온라인 콘텐츠 목록을 제시하였으므로 (D)가 정답이다. (A)와 (B)는 지문에 언급되지 않은 내용이다. 'Web Space has been serving various communities for two decades.'에서 Web Space사가 20년간 다양한 집단에 서비스를 제공해 왔다고 했으므로, (C)는 지문의 내용과 일치하지 않는다.

어휘 conduct v. 진행하다, 수행하다 an assortment of 여러 가지의

05 | 문장 위치 찾기 문제

해석 [1], [2], [3], [4]로 표시된 위치 중, 다음 문장이 들어갈 곳으로 가장 적절한 것은?

"귀하의 경쟁사들이 귀하를 앞서가게 하지 마십시오."

(A) [1]
(B) [2]
(C) [3]
(D) [4]

해설 주어진 문장은 경쟁사와 관련된 내용 주변에 나올 것임을 예상할 수 있다. [3]의 앞 문장인 'If it's overly technical, unattractive, outdated, and difficult to use, your customers may take their business elsewhere.'에서 만일 웹사이트가 지나치게 기술적이고, 매력적이지 않고, 구식이고, 사용하기 어렵다면, 고객이 다른 곳에 일을 가져갈지도 모른다고 했으므로, [3]에 주어진 문장이 들어가면 고객이 다른 회사로 일을 가져갈지도 모르는데, 경쟁사들이 앞서가게 하지 말라는 자연스러운 문맥이 된다는 것을 알 수 있다. 따라서 (C)가 정답이다.

어휘 competitor n. 경쟁사, 경쟁자 leave behind ~을 앞서다

06-09번은 다음 문자 메시지 대화문에 관한 문제입니다.

Hilda Jacobsen [오전 9시 37분]
Larry, 이번 주 당신의 일정은 어때요? 무슨 중요한 일 있나요?

Larry Boyd [오전 9시 39분]
그다지요. 06Hanifan사의 프로젝트를 작업하는 데 대부분의 시간을 쓸 계획이었는데, 서두를 필요 없어요. 그들은 앞으로 2주 동안은 그들의 사무실 인테리어를 위한 제 디자인을 필요로 하지 않아요.

Larry Boyd [오전 9시 40분]
제가 도와 드릴 일이 있을까요?

Hilda Jacobsen [오전 9시 42분]
07-(D)/08수요일에 Digitek사의 직원들 몇 명을 만나는 자리에 당신이 저와 함께할 시간이 되는지 궁금해요. 그들에게 로비 개조 아이디어를 홍보할 거예요. 07-(D)저는 정말로 그들의 회사를 고객으로 원해서, 만약 당신이 제 제안서의 장점으로 대화를 이끌어 가는 것을 도와줄 수 있다면 좋을 것 같아요.

Larry Boyd [오전 9시 42분]
알겠어요. 이 미팅이 몇 시에 있죠?

Hilda Jacobsen [오전 9시 43분]
오전 10시 30분에 있어요. 08/09여기서 제 차를 타고 갈 수 있어요. 끝나면 제가 당신에게 점심을 살게요.

Larry Boyd [오전 9시 44분]
그렇게 합시다. 08/09수요일에 뵐게요. 09우리는 사무실로 다시 돌아오는 것이죠, 그렇죠?

Hilda Jacobsen [오전 9시 45분]
09맞아요. 제가 프로젝트에 대한 더 많은 세부사항들을 바로 이메일로 보내드릴게요. 감사해요!

---

major adj. 중요한, 주요한 go on 일어나다, (일이) 되어가다
rush n. 서둘러야 하는 상황
pitch v. 홍보하다, (구입, 거래 등을 하도록) 설득하려 하다
renovation n. 개조, 수리, 혁신 direct v. ~을 이끌다; adj. 직접적인
proposal n. 제안(서), 제의 selling point 장점, 판매에 유리한 점

06 | 추론 문제

해석 Mr. Boyd에 대해 암시되는 것은?
(A) 고객 미팅의 일정을 변경해야 한다.
(B) 마감일 연장을 요청했다.
(C) 인테리어 계획안을 작업하고 있다.
(D) 새로운 프로젝트를 다시 맡게 될 것이다.

해설 지문의 'I was planning to spend most of my time working on the Hanifan project, but there's no rush. They don't need my designs for their office interior for another two weeks.'에서 Mr. Boyd가 Hanifan사의 프로젝트를 작업하는 데 대부분의 시간을 쓸 계획이었는데 서두를 필요가 없다고 한 후, Hanifan사가 앞으로 2주 동안은 그들의 사무실 인테리어를 위한 자신의 디자인을 필요로 하지 않는다고 한 것을 통해, Mr. Boyd가 인테리어 계획안을 작업하고 있음을 추론할 수 있다. 따라서 (C)가 정답이다.

어휘 extension n. (기간의) 연장, 확대 reassign v. 다시 맡기다, 새로 발령 내다

07 | Not/True 문제

해석 Ms. Jacobsen에 대해 사실인 것은?
(A) 사무실 인테리어 디자인의 세부 사항들을 마무리 지었다.
(B) Hanifan사의 대표와 만날 계획이다.
(C) 일정이 마지막 순간에 변경되었다.
(D) Digitek사를 새로운 고객으로 얻기를 바란다.

해설 지문의 'I was wondering if you were available to join me on Wednesday to meet with some representatives from Digitek.'에서 Ms. Jacobsen이 Mr. Boyd에게 수요일에 Digitek사의 직원들 몇 명을 만나는 자리에 함께할 시간이 되는지 물어본 후, 'I really want their company as a client'에서 정말로 그들의 회사를 고객으로 원한다고 했으므로 (D)가 정답이다. (A), (B), (C)는 지문에 언급되지 않은 내용이다.

어휘 acquire v. 얻다, 습득하다

08 | 의도 파악 문제

해석 오전 9시 44분에, Mr. Boyd가 "It's a deal"이라고 썼을 때 그가 의도한 것은?
(A) 사업 협상의 결과에 만족한다.
(B) 제안서의 성공 가능성에 자신감이 있다.
(C) 미팅에 그의 동료와 동행하는 것에 동의한다.
(D) 업무에 대한 도움을 받는 대가로 일을 할 의향이 있다.

해설 지문의 'I was wondering if you were available to join me on Wednesday to meet with some representatives from Digitek.'에서 Ms. Jacobsen이 수요일에 시내에서 Digitek사의 직원들 몇 명을 만나는 자리에 Mr. Boyd가 함께할 시간이 되는지 궁금하다고 했고, 'We can take my car from here. I'll buy you lunch when we're done.'에서 미팅에 자신의 차를 타고 갈 수 있고 끝나면 점심을 산다고 하자, Mr. Boyd가 'It's a deal'(그렇게 합시다)이라고 한 후, 'I'll see you on Wednesday.'에서 수요일에 보자고 한 것을 통해, Mr. Boyd는 미팅에 그의 동료와 동행하는 것에 동의함을 알 수 있다. 따라서 (C)가 정답이다.

어휘 outcome n. 결과, 성과 negotiation n. 협상, 협의
consent v. 동의하다, 허락하다 accompany v. 동행하다, 동반하다

09 | 육하원칙 문제

해석 Mr. Boyd는 수요일 점심 이후에 무엇을 할 것인가?
(A) 직원들과의 회의를 안내한다.
(B) 프로젝트 세부사항들을 이메일로 보낸다.
(C) 직장으로 돌아간다.
(D) 로비에 대한 수정사항을 제안한다.

해설 지문의 'We can take my car from here. I'll buy you lunch when we're done.'에서 Ms. Jacobsen이 미팅에 자신의 차를 타고 갈 수 있고, 끝나면 점심을 산다고 하자 'I'll see you on Wednesday. We'll be coming back to the office, right?'에서 Mr. Boyd가 수요일에 보자고 한 후 사무실로 다시 돌아오는 것이 맞는지 물었고, 'Yes.'에서 Ms. Jacobsen이 맞다고 했으므로, Mr. Boyd는 수요일 점심 이후에 직장으로 돌아갈 것임을 알 수 있다. 따라서 (C)가 정답이다.

어휘 direct v. 안내하다, 지시하다

Paraphrasing

| coming back to the office 사무실로 다시 돌아오다 → Return to ~ workplace 직장으로 돌아간다 |

10-13번은 다음 온라인 채팅 대화문에 관한 문제입니다.

Adriana Scorsese [오전 10시 10분]
5월 14일에 제가 두 분 모두에게 보냈던 이메일에서 언급했듯이, ¹⁰저의 부서가 다음 달에 지원자들을 찾기 시작할 거예요. 저는 당신 부서들 각각의 채용 요구사항을 확인하고 싶어요. ¹¹Kathy, 회계팀은 두 명의 새로운 직원이 필요한 것이죠, 그렇죠?

Kathy Chiu [오전 10시 14분]
¹¹사실, 저희가 마지막으로 이야기한 이후로 상황이 바뀌었습니다. Jack Wallace가 5월 31일에 우리를 떠나기로 한 결정을 저에게 알려줬어요. 이 문제와 관련해서는 나중에 다시 연락드려도 될까요?

Adriana Scorsese [오전 10시 14분]
알겠습니다. Charles, 당신은 어때요? 마케팅팀에 여전히 6명의 신입 사원들이 필요하나요?

Charles Jones [오전 10시 15분]
맞아요. 저희는 회사의 최신 제품 판매를 증가시키기 위해 몇 개의 캠페인을 계획하고 있기 때문에, 많은 직원이 필요할 거예요. 그리고 그들은 소셜 미디어 홍보에 경험이 있어야 해요. 아마도 이것은 구인광고에 명시될 수 있을 거예요.

Adriana Scorsese [오전 10시 18분]
제 비서인 Judith Harper가 광고 쓰는 것을 담당하고 있고, 그녀가 그 요구사항을 포함하도록 제가 확실히 할게요. ¹²5월 18일에 검토를 위해 여러분 각자에게 제가 광고를 보낼게요.

Kathy Chiu [오전 10시 19분]
¹²저는 그날 시카고의 세미나에 참석할 예정이에요. 5월 20일에 제 의견을 드려도 괜찮을까요?

Adriana Scorsese [오전 10시 19분]
문제없어요. 한 가지가 더 있어요. ¹³저는 여러분의 교육 계획을 미리 검토하고 싶어요. 저는 Kathy의 것은 이미 받았지만, Charles 당신의 것은 여전히 기다리고 있어요.

Charles Jones [오전 10시 21분]
죄송합니다. ¹³저는 그것을 금요일 오후에 당신에게 이메일로 보내드릴 수 있어요. 그때가 괜찮을까요?

Adriana Scorsese [오전 10시 22분]
완벽해요. 고마워요.

applicant n. 지원자 confirm v. 확인하다 requirement n. 요구사항 accounting team 회계팀 boost v. 증가시키다 promotion n. 홍보 specify v. 명시하다 in charge of ~을 담당하는 assistant n. 비서 make sure 확실히 하다, 확인하다 in advance 미리

10 | 추론 문제

해석 Ms. Scorsese는 어느 부서에서 일할 것 같은가?
(A) 회계

(B) 마케팅
(C) 인사
(D) 판매

해설 지문의 'my department will begin looking for applicants next month'에서 Ms. Scorsese가 본인의 부서가 다음 달에 지원자들을 찾기 시작할 것이라고 한 후, 'I'd like to confirm the hiring requirements for each of your departments.'에서 당신 부서들, 즉 회계팀과 마케팅팀의 채용 요구사항을 확인하고 싶다고 했으므로 Ms. Scorsese는 인사 부서에서 일하고 있음을 추론할 수 있다. 따라서 (C)가 정답이다.

11 | 의도 파악 문제

해석 오전 10시 14분에, Ms. Chiu가 "Regarding this issue, may I get back to you later?"라고 썼을 때 그녀가 의도한 것은?
(A) 다가오는 날짜에 바쁠 것이다.
(B) 그녀는 긴급한 이메일에 답장해야 한다.
(C) 그녀의 요구사항을 업데이트해야 한다.
(D) 그녀는 부서를 옮길 계획이다.

해설 지문의 'Kathy, the accounting team needs two new members, right?'에서 Ms. Scorsese가 Ms. Chiu에게 회계팀에 두 명의 새로운 직원이 필요한 것이 맞는지 묻자, Ms. Chiu가 'Actually, the situation has changed since we last spoke. Jack Wallace informed me of his decision to leave us on May 31.'에서 마지막으로 이야기한 이후로 상황이 바뀌었고, 사실 Jack Wallace가 5월 31일에 회사를 떠나겠다는 결정을 지난주에 알렸다고 한 후, 'Regarding this issue, may I get back to you later?'(이 문제와 관련해서는 나중에 다시 연락드려도 될까요?)라고 했으므로 두 명의 새로운 직원이 필요하다고 했던 그녀의 요구사항을 업데이트해야 함을 알 수 있다. 따라서 (C)가 정답이다.

어휘 upcoming adj. 다가오는 respond v. 답장하다 urgent adj. 긴급한 transfer v. 옮기다

12 | 육하원칙 문제

해석 Ms. Chiu는 어느 날짜에 사무실에 부재할 것인가?
(A) 5월 14일
(B) 5월 18일
(C) 5월 20일
(D) 5월 31일

해설 지문의 'I'll send the advertisements to each of you on May 18 to review.'에서 Ms. Scorsese가 5월 18일에 검토를 위해 광고를 보낼 것이라고 하자, 'I'm going to be attending a seminar in Chicago that day.'에서 Ms. Chiu가 그날 시카고의 세미나에 참석할 예정이라고 했으므로 (B)가 정답이다.

Paraphrasing

| attending a seminar 세미나에 참석하는 것 → be absent from the office 사무실에 부재하다 |

13 | 육하원칙 문제

해석 Mr. Jones는 그가 무엇을 할 것이라고 말하는가?
(A) 직원들을 위한 교육 세미나를 준비한다.
(B) 소셜 미디어 플랫폼의 게시물을 검토한다.
(C) 동료에게 몇 가지 정보를 제공한다.
(D) 회사 기록에서 몇 가지 정보를 갱신한다.

해설 지문의 'I'd like to review your training plans in advance. I've already received Kathy's, but I am still waiting for yours, Charles.'에서 Ms. Scorsese가 여러분의 교육 계획을 검토하고 싶으며 Charles, 즉 Mr. Jones의 것을 여전히 기다리고 있다고 하자, 'I can e-mail it to you on Friday afternoon.'에서 Mr. Jones가 금요일 오후에 Ms.

Scorsese에게 이메일로 그의 교육 계획을 보낼 수 있다고 했으므로 (C)가 정답이다.

어휘 organize v. 준비하다 colleague n. 동료

고난도 문제 완전 정복   p.80

01 (C)	02 (C)	03 (D)	04 (D)	05 (B)
06 (A)	07 (C)			

01-03번은 다음 이메일에 관한 문제입니다.

수신: Steven Joyce <sjoyce@fastmail.com>
발신: Fast Track 음반사 <information@fasttrackrecords.com>
날짜: 5월 20일
제목: 정보

Mr. Joyce께,

매년 5월의 세 번째 토요일에, 저희는 음반 상점의 독립적인 정신을 기리는 방식으로 Record Store Day를 기념합니다. 올해 ⁰¹Fast Track 음반사가 음악 기념 행사일을 위해 시의 다른 모든 주요 상점들과 다시 한번 제휴할 것입니다. 귀하는 Music Fans 클럽의 회원이므로, 저희는 그날에 계획된 볼거리를 귀하께 보내드립니다:

오전 11시 - 오후 12시	John Kher, Sarah Feinstein, Ernest Yates, 그리고 다른 ⁰²⁻⁽ᴰ⁾지역 음악 비평가들이 Gold Sounds 음반사에서 그들의 저작물 중 엄선된 것들을 읽을 것입니다.
오후 12시 - 오후 5시	⁰³⁻⁽ᴬ⁾Marshalltown 음반사가 모든 재즈와 블루스 음반에 특별 할인을 제공할 것입니다. 상점에 들르셔서, 가장 좋아하는 앨범을 50퍼센트까지 할인 받으세요.
오후 1시 - 오후 5시	Duke 음반사가 음반 케이스, 티셔츠, 그리고 다른 물품들을 포함한 다양한 상품에 대해 추첨식 판매를 개최할 것입니다.
오후 2시 30분 - 오후 3시 30분	⁰²⁻⁽ᴮ⁾지역 록 밴드 The Chimney Sweeps가 Desert Island 음반사에서 매장 내 콘서트 공연을 할 것입니다.
오후 4시 - 오후 5시	⁰²⁻⁽ᴬ⁾Gold Sounds 음반사가 음악을 주제로 하는 퀴즈 대회를 열 것입니다. 우승자들은 사인 음반과 포스터를 포함한 특별한 상품을 받을 것입니다.
⁰³⁻⁽ᴰ⁾오후 5시 - 오후 8시	파티가 Marshalltown 음반사에서 열릴 것입니다.

만약 행사와 활동에 대해 질문이 있으시면, Fast Track 음반사에 555-3009로 전화 주시거나 이 이메일에 답장해 주십시오. 추가적인 축제 행사에 대한 상세한 일정은 www.fasttrackrecords.com/recordstoreday에서 보실 수 있습니다.

---

independent adj. 독립적인, 독자적인 spirit n. 정신, 영혼
partner v. 제휴하다, 협력하다 celebration n. 기념 행사, 축하 행사
forward v. 보내다, 전달하다
highlight n. 볼거리, 가장 흥미 있는 부분; v. 강조하다 critic n. 비평가, 평론가
selection n. 엄선된 것, 선택 up to ~까지 stage v. 개최하다; n. 단계
raffle n. 추첨식 판매(물건값을 여럿이 치르고 제비로 당첨된 사람이 차지함); v. 추첨식 판매로 팔다 merchandise n. 상품, 물품 vinyl n. 음반
in-store adj. 매장 내의 theme n. ~을 주제로 다루다; n. 주제
trivia contest 퀴즈 대회 autograph v. ~에 사인하다; n. 서명
festivity n. 축제 행사

01 | 목적 찾기 문제

해석 이메일의 목적은 무엇인가?
(A) 음반 상점의 개점을 알리기 위해
(B) 여름 동안의 음악 관련 행사의 목록을 작성하기 위해
(C) 특별 기념 행사의 일정을 제공하기 위해
(D) 회원들이 지역 콘서트에 대해 알게 하기 위해

해설 이메일의 'Fast Track Records will once again be partnering with all the other major stores in the city for a day of music celebration'과 'As you are a member of our Music Fans Club, we are forwarding you the planned highlights of the day'에서 Fast Track 음반사가 음악 기념 행사일을 위해 시의 다른 모든 주요 상점들과 다시 한번 제휴할 것이라고 하고, Mr. Joyce가 Music Fans 클럽의 회원이므로, 그날에 계획된 볼거리를 보내준다고 한 후, 행사의 일정을 제공하고 있으므로 (C)가 정답이다.

어휘 grand opening 개점, 개장 list v. 목록을 작성하다, 나열하다; n. 목록, 명단

Paraphrasing
are forwarding 보내다 → provide 제공하다

02 | Not/True 문제

해설 Record Store Day에 계획된 활동으로 언급되지 않은 것은?
(A) 상점이 후원하는 대회
(B) 음악 공연
(C) 음악가의 연설
(D) 지역 비평가들의 낭독

해설 지문의 'Gold Sounds Records will be holding a music-themed trivia contest.'에서 Gold Sounds 음반사가 음악을 주제로 하는 퀴즈 대회를 열 것이라고 했으므로 (A)는 지문의 내용과 일치한다. 'Local rock band The Chimney Sweeps will be performing an in-store concert at Desert Island Records.'에서 지역 록 밴드 The Chimney Sweeps가 Desert Island 음반사에서 매장 내 콘서트 공연을 할 것이라고 했으므로 (B)는 지문의 내용과 일치한다. 'local music critics will be reading selections from their work at Gold Sounds Records'에서 지역 음악 비평가들이 Gold Sounds 음반사에서 그들의 저작물 중 엄선된 것들을 읽을 것이라고 했으므로 (D)는 지문의 내용과 일치한다. (C)는 지문에 언급되지 않은 내용이다. 따라서 (C)가 정답이다.

Paraphrasing
critics 비평가들 → reviewers 비평가들

03 | Not/True 문제

해석 Marshalltown 음반사에 대해 언급된 것은?
(A) 재즈와 블루스 음반을 전문적으로 다룬다.
(B) 시에 두 개의 지점이 있다.
(C) 다양한 상품들을 선물로 준다.
(D) 마지막 행사를 위한 장소가 될 것이다.

해설 지문의 '5 P.M. - 8 P.M., A party will be held at Marshalltown Records.'에서 오후 5시부터 오후 8시까지 파티가 Marshalltown 음반사에서 열릴 것이라고 했고 8시 이후에 계획된 일정이 없으므로 지문의 내용과 일치한다. 따라서 (D)가 정답이다. (B)와 (C)는 지문에 언급되지 않은 내용이다. (A)는 'Marshalltown Records will be offering a special discount on all jazz and blues records.'에서 Marshalltown 음반사가 모든 재즈와 블루스 음반에 특별 할인을 제공할 것이라고는 했지만 재즈와 블루스 음반을 전문적으로 다루는지는 언급되지 않았으므로 지문의 내용과 일치하지 않는다.

어휘 specialize in ~을 전문적으로 다루다 give away ~을 선물로 주다
a selection of 다양한 venue n. 장소, 행사장

04-07번은 다음 편지에 관한 문제입니다.

10월 15일

Jeremiah Nam
3049번지 Oak로
서니데일, 위스콘신 주 84774

Mr. Nam께,

뉴스에서 듣거나 읽으셨을 수도 있지만, ⁰⁴Sunny-Link 인터넷 서비스 회사는 SC Media라는 새로운 이름으로 Cranston Connect사와 합병할 것입니다. 고객을 섬기는 것에 대한 Sunny-Link사의 열정과 Cranston Connect사의 기술 역량을 결합함으로써, ⁰⁵SC Media사는 더 다양한 고속 광대역 상품을 경쟁력 있는 가격에 제공할 수 있을 것입니다. ⁰⁶이 새로운 가능성은 계획되고 있는 흥미진진한 새 상품을 저희 고객들이 접할 수 있게 할 것이기 때문에 저희는 들떠 있는데, 이 상품은 주문형 비디오 서비스, TV 시청권, 전화 요금 상품을 포함합니다.

안심하십시오, 기존의 또는 진행 중인 계약이 있는 고객들은 요금 변경 없이 중단되지 않는 서비스를 계속해서 즐길 것입니다. 청구서는 SC Media사라는 새로운 이름으로 처리될 것이며, 은행과 다른 금융 회사들은 이미 그 변화에 대해 통지를 받았습니다. 그러나, 온라인으로 납입금을 내는 고객들은 새로운 웹사이트인 www.scmedia.com에 등록해야 할 것입니다. 등록하고 나면, 귀하께서는 저희의 웹사이트로 돌아오는 링크가 포함된 확인 이메일을 받을 것입니다. 링크를 클릭한 후에, 귀하의 온라인 계정이 이용 가능하게 될 것이고, ⁰⁷온라인 결제 사이트에서의 신용카드 또는 계좌 입금을 통한 결제가 가능할 것입니다.

귀하의 지속적인 이용에 감사드립니다.

Miriam Steinberg
Miriam Steinberg
고객관리부 이사

merge v. 합병하다, 통합하다, 합치다 combine v. 결합하다, 합치다
capability n. 역량, 능력 a wide range of 다양한, 넓은 범위의
broadband n. 광대역 competitive adj. 경쟁력 있는
video-on-demand n. 주문형 비디오 서비스 ongoing adj. 진행 중인
uninterrupted adj. 중단되지 않는 fee n. 요금, 수수료 billing n. 청구서
notify v. 통지하다, 알리다 payment n. 납입금 register v. 등록하다
account n. 계정, 계좌, 장부 accessible adj. 이용 가능한, 접근 가능한
direct deposit 계좌 입금 patronage n. 이용, 애용, 후원

04 | 목적 찾기 문제

해석 편지는 왜 작성되었는가?
(A) 수수료 변경 관련 세부 사항을 제공하기 위해
(B) 새로운 인터넷 서비스를 알리기 위해
(C) 요금 납부를 요청하기 위해
(D) 고객에게 회사의 변화를 알리기 위해

해설 편지의 'Sunny-Link Internet Services will be merging with Cranston Connect under the name of SC Media'에서 Sunny-Link 인터넷 서비스 회사가 SC Media라는 새로운 이름으로 Cranston Connect사와 합병할 것이라고 한 후, 회사의 변화에 대해 설명하고 있으므로 (D)가 정답이다.

어휘 announce v. 알리다, 발표하다 solicit v. 요청하다, 간청하다
inform v. 알리다, 통지하다

05 | 추론 문제

해석 편지에 따르면, 고객들은 어떤 혜택을 얻을 것 같은가?
(A) 월 요금 인하
(B) 더 나은 상품 모음
(C) 새로운 상품의 시험 사용 제공
(D) 더 높은 수준의 고객 서비스

해설 지문의 'SC Media will be able to offer a wider range of high-speed broadband packages at competitive prices'에서 SC Media사는 더 다양한 고속 광대역 상품을 경쟁력 있는 가격에 제공할 수 있을 것이라고 했으므로 최근 합병의 결과로 고객들은 더 나은 상품 모음을 얻을 수 있음을 추론할 수 있다. 따라서 (B)가 정답이다.

어휘 reduction n. 인하, 감축 a selection of ~의 모음, 여러 가지의
trial offer 시험 사용 제공

06 | 동의어 찾기 문제

해석 1문단 다섯 번째 줄의 단어 "prospect"는 의미상 -와 가장 가깝다.
(A) 기회
(B) 예측
(C) 찾기
(D) 제안

해설 prospect를 포함하는 구절 'We are excited about this new prospect as it will also allow our customers to gain access to exciting new products being planned, including a streaming service for video-on-demand, TV subscriptions, and phone plans.'에서 prospect는 '가능성'이라는 뜻으로 사용되었다. 따라서 (A)가 정답이다.

07 | Not/True 문제

해석 SC Media사에 대해 명시되는 것은?
(A) 은행에 변화에 대해 알릴 것이다.
(B) 웹사이트를 업데이트하는 과정에 있다.
(C) 여러 가지 결제 수단을 받는다.
(D) 다른 회사에 의해 매입되었다.

해설 지문의 'you will be able to make payments by credit card or direct deposit from an online payment site'에서 온라인 결제 사이트에서의 신용카드 또는 계좌 입금을 통한 결제가 가능할 것이라고 했으므로 여러 가지 결제 수단을 받음을 추론할 수 있다. 따라서 (C)가 정답이다.

어휘 method n. 수단, 방법 purchase v. 매입하다, 구매하다; n. 매입, 구매

DAY 08 기사, 양식, 공고

빈출 문제 집중 훈련   p.82

01 (A)	02 (C)	03 (A)	04 (C)	05 (B)
06 (C)	07 (A)	08 (B)	09 (B)	10 (C)
11 (D)	12 (B)	13 (C)		

01-02번은 다음 브로슈어에 관한 문제입니다.

제주의 바다와 서핑 활동

한국에서 가장 큰 섬인 제주에 오신 것을 환영합니다. 제주는 젖는 것을 개의치 않는 모험심 있는 여행객들에게 많은 활동을 제공합니다! 여러분이 시도해 볼 수 있는 많은 활동 중 일부가 아래에 나열되어 있습니다.

· 제주시의 북쪽 항구부터 두 시간짜리 유람선 여행을 하시고 섬 주변의 고대 암반층에 감탄해 보십시오.
· 한림 마을 주변의 바다로 스쿠버다이빙을 가셔서 수백 종류의 다채로운 해양종을 만나보십시오.
· 섬 남쪽의 파도는 숙련된 서퍼들에게 최적이지만, ⁰¹⁻⁽ᴬ⁾초보자들은 서쪽의 더 잔잔한 물에 머무르셔야 합니다.

제주도 주변의 해양 활동을 탐험하면서 시간을 즐기시되, 혼자 물에

들어가는 것은 삼가십시오. 또한, ⁰²섬 주변의 절벽에서는 다이빙하지 마십시오. 물 표면 바로 밑에 매우 위험할 수 있는 바위가 있을 수 있습니다.

plenty of 많은 adventurous adj. 모험심 있는, 대담한 wet adj. 젖은, 축축한
marvel v. 감탄하다, 놀라다 ancient adj. 고대의, 오래된
formation n. 층, 형성 marine adj. 해양의 species n. 종
stick v. 머무르다, 고수하다 calm adj. 잔잔한, 고요한
explore v. 탐험하다, 조사하다 cliff n. 절벽, 낭떠러지 surface n. 표면, 외면

01 | Not/True 문제

해석 제주도에 대해 언급된 것은?
(A) 서쪽의 파도가 더 잔잔하다.
(B) 종종 강우량이 높다.
(C) 여행객을 위한 암벽 등반 시설들이 있다.
(D) 보통 여름에 가장 붐빈다.

해설 지문의 'beginners should stick to the calmer water in the west'에서 초보자들은 서쪽의 더 잔잔한 물에 머무르야 한다고 했으므로 서쪽의 파도가 더 잔잔함을 알 수 있다. 따라서 (A)가 정답이다. (B), (C), (D)는 지문에 언급되지 않은 내용이다.

어휘 rainfall n. 강우량, 강수량

Paraphrasing

the calmer water in the west 서쪽의 더 잔잔한 물 → It has calmer waves on the west side 서쪽의 파도가 더 잔잔하다

02 | 육하원칙 문제

해석 브로슈어에 따르면, 방문객들은 왜 절벽에서 뛰어내리는 것을 피해야 하는가?
(A) 절벽을 오르는 것은 매우 미끄럽다.
(B) 바다 생물이 다칠 수 있다.
(C) 물 속에 위험한 바위가 있다.
(D) 그 지역은 대중에게 개방되지 않는다.

해설 브로슈어의 'please do not dive from the cliffs around the island. There may be rocks just below the surface of the water which can be very dangerous.'에서 섬 주변의 절벽에서는 다이빙하지 말라고 한 후, 물 표면 바로 밑에 매우 위험할 수 있는 바위가 있을 수 있다고 하였다. 따라서 (C)가 정답이다.

어휘 slippery adj. 미끄러운 creature n. 생물 harm v. 다치게 하다, 해치다

Paraphrasing

do not dive from the cliffs 절벽에서 다이빙하지 않다 → avoid jumping from the cliffs 절벽에서 뛰어내리는 것을 피하다
below the surface of the water 물 표면 바로 밑에 → in the water 물 속에

03-05번은 다음 기사에 관한 문제입니다.

Chic Life 잡지

Marilyn DuBois의 봄 작별 인사

(12월 20일)—다음 달, 유명 디자이너 Marilyn DuBois는 그녀의 봄 컬렉션 쇼를 할 것인데, 이것이 그녀가 제작할 마지막 의류 라인이 될 것이다. ⁰³11월에 패션 업계는 Ms. DuBois가 내년 2월에 은퇴할 계획에 관해 예상치 못한 발표를 했을 때 충격을 받았다. 45세밖에 되지 않았음에도 불구하고, Ms. DuBois는 전 세계적으로 거의 200개의 부티크를 열며, 의류 디자인 업계에서 저명한 경력을 가졌다.

우리 잡지와의 독점 인터뷰에서, Ms. DuBois는 그녀의 은퇴에 관한 몇 가지 세부 사항을 우리에게 제공하였다. "저는 옷을 디자인하며 아주

멋진 경력을 가져 왔습니다."라고 그녀가 말했다. "하지만 ⁰⁴제가 획기적인 작품을 만들 것이라는 대중으로부터의 끊임없는 기대는 부담이 되었습니다." ⁰⁵Ms. DuBois는 더 나아가 그녀의 여동생 Janelle이 2월부터 DuBois사의 최고 경영자 자리를 맡을 것이라고 설명했다. "그녀는 시작하기를 열망하고 있으며, 저는 그 역할에 대해 전적으로 자신감을 가지고 있습니다."라고 Ms. DuBois는 말했다.

Ms. DuBois가 그녀의 경력에서 최고의 시점에 있어서, 패션 전문가들은 그녀가 자리를 떠나는 것을 보게 되어 슬퍼하고 있다. 동시에, ⁰⁵그들은 그녀의 여동생의 리더십 하에 미래가 DuBois사에 어떤 일을 가져올지 들떠서 기대하고 있다.

farewell n. 작별(인사) famed adj. 유명한 unexpected adj. 예상치 못한
announcement n. 발표 retire v. 은퇴하다 illustrious adj. 저명한
career n. 경력 apparel n. 의류 exclusive adj. 독점의
constant adj. 끊임없는 expectation n. 기대 innovative adj. 획기적인
take over 맡다, 인수하다 eager adj. 열망하는 professional n. 전문가
anticipate v. 기대하다, 고대하다

03 | 육하원칙 문제

해석 기사에 따르면, 내년에 무슨 일이 일어날 것인가?
(A) 의류 디자이너가 그녀의 경력을 끝마칠 것이다.
(B) 업계 행사에 대한 발표가 있을 것이다.
(C) 잡지용 사진 촬영이 있을 것이다.
(D) 패션쇼가 부티크에서 열릴 것이다.

해설 지문의 'The fashion world was shocked in November when Ms. DuBois made the unexpected announcement about her plans to retire next February.'에서 11월에 패션 업계는 Ms. DuBois가 내년 2월에 은퇴할 계획에 관해 예상치 못한 발표를 했을 때 충격을 받았다고 했으므로 (A)가 정답이다.

어휘 garment n. 의류 photo shoot 사진 촬영 take place 있다, 일어나다

Paraphrasing

retire 은퇴하다 → come to the end of ~ career 경력을 끝마치다

04 | 육하원칙 문제

해석 Marilyn DuBois의 걱정의 원인은 무엇이었는가?
(A) 그녀의 가게의 줄어든 판매량
(B) 그녀의 일에 대해 줄어드는 열정
(C) 창의적이어야 한다는 압박
(D) 대중 생각의 변화

해설 지문의 'the constant expectation from the public for me to create innovative work has been stressful'에서 자신, 즉 Marilyn DuBois가 획기적인 작품을 만들 것이라는 대중으로부터의 끊임없는 기대는 부담이 되었다고 했으므로 (C)가 정답이다.

어휘 decline v. 줄어들다, 감소하다 passion n. 열정 opinion n. 생각, 의견

Paraphrasing

create innovative work 획기적인 작품을 만들다 → creative 창의적인
stressful 부담이 되는 → Pressure 압박

05 | 추론 문제

해석 Janelle DuBois에 대해 추론될 수 있는 것은?
(A) 새로운 패션모델들을 고용할 계획이 있다.
(B) 최고 경영자로의 그녀의 승진이 좋은 반응을 얻었다.
(C) 대학에서 패션 디자인을 전공했다.
(D) 그녀의 디자인들은 그녀의 언니의 것들보다 더 많은 이목을 끌었다.

해설 지문의 'Ms. DuBois further explained that her sister Janelle will take over as CEO of DuBois Corporation beginning in February.'에서 Ms. DuBois는 그녀의 여동생 Janelle이 2월부터 DuBois사의 최고 경영자 자리를 맡을 것이라고 설명했다고 했고, 'they excitedly anticipate what the future might bring for DuBois Corporation under her sister's leadership'에서 그들, 즉 패션 전문가들이 그녀의 여동생의 리더십 하에 미래가 DuBois사에 어떤 일을 가져올지 들떠서 기대하고 있다고 했으므로 최고 경영자로의 Janelle DuBois의 승진이 좋은 반응을 얻었음을 추론할 수 있다. 따라서 (B)가 정답이다.

어휘 promotion n. 승진 attract v. 끌다 attention n. 이목

06-09번은 다음 웹페이지에 관한 문제입니다.

MyPost.com

홈 | 사업 | 제품과 서비스 | 소개 | 도움말 | 회원가입 | 로그인

현재 위치: MyPost > 도움말

MyPost는 무엇이며 어떤 식으로 운영됩니까?
MyPost는 해외에 사는 고객들을 위해 미국에 기반을 둔 배송 주소를 제공합니다. 06/07미국의 모든 온라인 소매업체들이 국제적으로 배송하지는 않을 것이기 때문에, MyPost는 귀하께서 주문한 물품을 일시적으로 보관하기 위해 미국에 위치한 저희의 물리적인 주소를 배송 전달 지점으로 이용하실 수 있도록 합니다. — [1] —. 그래서, 06다음에 미국 온라인 소매업체에서 쇼핑을 한다면, 귀하의 MyPost 주소를 배송 양식에 입력하시기만 하면 나머지는 저희가 처리하겠습니다. 08-(C)MyPost는 고급 추적 시스템을 이용하며 임시 보관과 물품 재포장과 같은 추가적인 서비스도 제공할 수 있습니다. 현재, 저희는 전 세계 64개 이상의 국가로 배송합니다.

MyPost에 어떻게 가입합니까?
MyPost를 이용하시려면, 여기를 클릭하여 온라인 계정을 등록하십시오. 09등록이나 가입 비용은 없습니다. — [2] —.

한 항목을 배송하는 데 얼마가 듭니까?
08-(B)비용은 귀하의 소포의 무게와 크기를 기준으로 합니다. 저희 홈페이지의 배송 계산기를 사용하여 언제든지 배송 비용을 추정하실 수 있습니다. — [3] —.

MyPost를 통해 보내지는 항목들에 무게와 크기 제한이 있습니까?
금액이 청구되는 최소 무게는 500그램입니다. 최대 소포 무게는 30킬로그램입니다. 최대 소포 크기는 3미터입니다(가로×세로).

배송을 받는 데에는 얼마나 걸립니까?
저희의 해외 창고로부터 귀하의 소포가 발송되면, 귀하께서 지정하신 주소로 배달되는 데까지 약 7~10일의 영업일이 걸릴 것으로 예상됩니다. — [4] —.

retailer n. 소매업체, 소매 internationally adv. 국제적으로
physical adj. 물리적인, 신체의 temporarily adv. 일시적으로, 임시로
rest n. 나머지, 휴식; v. 쉬다 advanced adj. 고급의, 선진적인
track v. 추적하다, 탐지하다 repacking n. 재포장
subscription n. 가입, 구독 dimension n. 크기, 치수 parcel n. 소포, 택배
estimate v. 추정하다, 예상하다 calculator n. 계산기
chargeable adj. (금액이) 청구되는, 부과되는 length n. 세로, 길이
width n. 가로, 폭 specify v. 지정하다, 명시하다

---

06 | 추론 문제

해석 MyPost의 서비스에 누가 관심이 있을 것 같은가?
(A) 해외로 이전하는 회사들
(B) 국내 배송이 필요한 사업체 소유주들
(C) 미국 웹사이트에서 물품을 주문하는 고객들
(D) 운송비를 줄이길 희망하는 고객들

해설 지문의 'Since not all online retailers in the US will ship internationally, MyPost allows you to use its physical address located in the US as a shipment transfer point to temporarily store ordered items.'에서 미국의 모든 온라인 소매업체들이 국제적으로 배송하지는 않을 것이기 때문에, MyPost는 주문한 물품을 일시적으로 보관하기 위해 미국에 위치한 물리적인 주소를 배송 전달 지점으로 이용할 수 있도록 한다고 했고, 'the next time you shop with an online US retailer, simply enter your MyPost address on the shipping form, and we will take care of the rest'에서 미국 온라인 소매업체에서 쇼핑을 한다면, MyPost 주소를 배송 양식에 입력하기만 하면 나머지는 자신들이 처리한다고 한 것을 통해, 미국 웹사이트에서 물품을 주문하는 고객들이 관심이 있을 것임을 추론할 수 있다. 따라서 (C)가 정답이다.

어휘 relocate v. 이전하다 domestic adj. 국내의

Paraphrasing

shop with an online US retailer 미국 온라인 소매업체에서 쇼핑하다
→ ordering items from US Web sites 미국 웹사이트에서 물품을 주문하는

07 | 추론 문제

해석 MyPost에 대해 암시되는 것은?
(A) 미국에 창고 시설이 있다.
(B) 트럭 수송 회사들과 특별 합의를 맺고 있다.
(C) 500그램 이하의 품목은 보험에 들지 않는다.
(D) 길이가 3미터가 넘는 소포에 대해 추가 비용을 부과한다.

해설 지문의 'MyPost allows you to use its physical address located in the US as a shipment transfer point to temporarily store ordered items'에서 MyPost가 고객이 주문한 물품을 일시적으로 보관하기 위해 미국에 위치한 물리적인 주소를 배송 전달 지점으로 이용할 수 있도록 한다고 했으므로, 주문한 물품을 일시적으로 보관하기 위한 창고가 미국에 있음을 추론할 수 있다. 따라서 (A)가 정답이다.

어휘 arrangement n. 합의, 준비 trucking n. 트럭 수송 insure v. 보험에 들다

08 | Not/True 문제

해석 서비스에 대해 언급된 것은?
(A) 다시 찾는 고객들은 할인이 된다.
(B) 무게와 크기에 따라 가격이 정해진다.
(C) 포장 용품의 판매를 포함한다.
(D) 다른 회사들보다 가격이 낮다.

해설 웹페이지의 'Cost is based on the weight and dimensions of your parcel.'에서 비용은 소포의 무게와 크기를 기준으로 한다고 했으므로 (B)가 정답이다. (A)와 (D)는 지문에 언급되지 않은 내용이다. 웹페이지의 'MyPost uses an advanced tracking system and can also provide additional services, such as temporary storage and item repacking.'에서 MyPost는 고급 추적 시스템을 이용하며 임시 보관과 물품 재포장과 같은 추가적인 서비스도 제공할 수 있다고 했으나, 포장용품의 판매를 제공한다는 것은 아니므로, (C)는 지문의 내용과 일치하지 않는다.

어휘 repeat customer 다시 찾는 고객 price v. 가격을 정하다; n. 가격, 값
supply n. 용품, 공급

Paraphrasing

Cost is based on the weight and dimensions 비용은 무게와 크기를 기준으로 한다 → are priced according to weight and size 무게와 크기에 따라 가격이 정해지다

09 | 문장 위치 찾기 문제

해석 [1], [2], [3], [4]로 표시된 위치 중, 다음 문장이 들어갈 곳으로 가장 적절한 것은?

"오직 필요한 서비스에 대해서만 지불하시기 바랍니다."

(A) [1]
(B) [2]
(C) [3]
(D) [4]

해설 주어진 문장은 서비스 비용과 관련된 내용 주변에 나올 것임을 예상할 수 있다. [2]의 앞 문장인 'There are no registration or subscription fees.'에서 등록이나 가입 비용은 없다고 했으므로, [2]에 주어진 문장이 들어가면 등록이나 가입 비용은 없으며, 오직 필요한 서비스에 대해서만 지불하라는 자연스러운 문맥이 된다는 것을 알 수 있다. 따라서 (B)가 정답이다.

10-13번은 다음 기사에 관한 문제입니다.

더 밝은 미래를 향해 건물을 짓다

(7월 17일)—10-(C)Jamane시에서 자라고 있는 어린 소년 Antonio에게 인생은 도전의 연속이다. 그러나, EduAid의 Fund-A-School 프로젝트 덕분에, 그는 교육을 받게 될 것이다. Antonio는 EduAid의 교육 지원 프로그램에 관여된 수백 명의 수혜자 중 한 명인데, 이 프로그램은 세계 곳곳의 소외된 지역에 학교 건물을 건설한다.

EduAid의 Fund-A-School 프로젝트는 주로 사업체들의 기부금으로부터 지원을 받는다. 12-(B)/(A)1,000달러에서 시작해서 그 이상의 기부금에 대한 대가로, 기업들은 교육에 대한 그들의 공헌을 입증하기 위해 EduAid의 로고를 그들의 상품에 사용할 수 있다. 추가로, 11그들은 납세 의무에서 그러한 기부 금액을 공제할 수 있다. 그러한 회사 중 하나인 12-(C)영국의 Goodman Industries사는 추후 12개월간 다섯 개의 학교를 지을 수 있는 충분한 자금을 기부하기로 약속했다.

학교를 짓는 것 외에도, 12-(D)EduAid는 특정 지역들의 주민들에게 합당한 임금을 제공함으로써 지역 경제를 이롭게 하기를 원한다. 이 지역의 주민들은 EduAid에 의해 공사 인부나 교사 자리를 제공받는다. 교사들은 지역의 요구와 관습에 대한 그들의 익숙함을 바탕으로 한 그들만의 교육 방식을 개발한다. 13그러나 그들은 또한 교사 교육을 감독하고 다른 행정 업무를 하는 자격을 갖춘 자원봉사자들로부터 전문적인 도움을 받는다.

재정적 기부나 자원봉사를 통해 EduAid의 후원자가 되는 것에 관심이 있는 개인이나 기업들은 추가적인 세부 사항을 위해 www.eduAid.org로 온라인 사이트를 방문할 수 있다.

recipient n. 수혜자, 수령인 underserved adj. 소외된
contribution n. 기부금, 기부 in exchange for ~에 대가로, ~와 교환하여
donation n. 기부금, 기부 upwards adv. ~ 이상, 위쪽으로
demonstrate v. 입증하다, 보여주다 commitment n. 공헌, 헌신
deduct v. 공제하다, 감하다 inhabitant n. 주민 fair adj. 합당한, 공평한
wage n. 임금, 급여 familiarity n. 익숙함, 친숙함 custom n. 관습, 풍습
administrative adj. 행정의

---

10 | Not/True 문제

해설 기사가 Antonio에 대해 언급하는 것은?
(A) EduAid의 시간제 자원봉사자이다.
(B) 최근 Jamane시로 이사했다.
(C) Fund-A-School 프로젝트로부터 도움을 받을 것이다.
(D) 식료품을 위한 일급을 받는다.

해설 지문의 'For Antonio, a young boy growing up in the city of Jamane, life is a series of challenges. But thanks to EduAid's Fund-A-School project, he will have access to an education.'에서 Jamane시에서 자라고 있는 어린 소년 Antonio에게 인생은 도전의 연속이지만, EduAid의 Fund-A-School 프로젝트 덕분에 그는 교육을 받게 될 것이라고 했으므로 (C)가 정답이다. (A), (B), (D)는 지문에 언급되지 않은 내용이다.

어휘 part-time adj. 시간제의 daily allowance 일급

11 | 동의어 찾기 문제

해설 2문단 네 번째 줄의 "obligations"는 의미상 -와 가장 가깝다.
(A) 약속
(B) 헌신
(C) 필요
(D) 책임

해설 obligations를 포함하는 구절 'they may deduct the amounts of such donations from their tax obligations'에서 obligations가 '의무'라는 뜻으로 사용되었다. 따라서 (D)가 정답이다.

12 | Not/True 문제

해설 Fund-A-School 프로젝트에 대해 언급되지 않은 것은?
(A) 큰 기부를 했다는 것을 증명하기 위해 회사들은 로고를 보여줄 수 있다.
(B) 여태껏 받은 가장 큰 액수는 1,000달러이다.
(C) 한 회사가 다섯 개의 학교를 더 짓도록 도울 것이다.
(D) 활동이 지역 경제 또한 이롭게 한다.

해설 (A)는 지문의 'In exchange for donations starting from $1,000 and proceeding upwards, companies can use EduAid's logo on their products to demonstrate their commitment to education.'에서 1,000달러에서 시작해서 그 이상의 기부금에 대한 대가로 기업들은 교육에 대한 그들의 공헌을 입증하기 위해 EduAid의 로고를 그들의 상품에 사용할 수 있다고 했으므로 지문의 내용과 일치한다. (C)는 'England's Goodman Industries, promised to donate enough money to construct five schools over the next 12 months'에서 영국의 Goodman Industries사가 추후 12개월간 다섯 개의 학교를 지을 수 있는 충분한 자금을 기부하기로 약속했다고 했으므로 지문의 내용과 일치한다. (D)는 'EduAid hopes to benefit local economies by providing the inhabitants of certain areas with fair wages'에서 EduAid는 특정 지역의 주민들에게 합당한 임금을 제공함으로써 지역 경제를 이롭게 하기를 원한다고 했으므로 지문의 내용과 일치한다. (B)는 지문에 언급되지 않은 내용이다. 따라서 (B)가 정답이다.

Paraphrasing

donate ~ to construct five schools 다섯 개의 학교를 짓기 위해 기부하다
→ helping ~ to build five more schoolhouses 다섯 개의 학교를 더 짓도록 돕다

demonstrate 입증하다 → prove 증명하다

13 | 육하원칙 문제

해설 기사에 따르면, 몇몇 자원봉사자들은 무엇을 하는가?
(A) 해외에서 자금을 모은다.
(B) 학교 건물을 짓는다.
(C) 행정 업무를 수행한다.
(D) 가장 가까운 도시로부터 공급물자를 실어 나른다.

해설 지문의 'But they also receive expert assistance from qualified volunteers who oversee teacher training and conduct other administrative work.'에서 그들은 또한 교사 교육을 감독하고 다른 행정 업무를 하는 자격을 갖춘 자원봉사자들로부터 전문적인 도움을 받는다고 했으므로 (C)가 정답이다.

어휘 raise v. 모으다 carry v. 실어 나르다, 들고 있다

Paraphrasing

conduct (업무를) 하다 → perform 수행하다

고난도 문제 완전 정복　　　　　　　p.86

01 (D)	02 (C)	03 (B)	04 (C)	05 (B)
06 (D)	07 (C)			

01-03번은 다음 공고에 관한 문제입니다.

Cultural Invasion

⁰¹⁻⁽ᴰ⁾작년 행사의 성공에 뒤이어, 싱가포르는 4월 20일 금요일부터 4월 22일 일요일까지 제2회 Cultural Invasion을 개최할 것입니다. 대중에게 공개되는 이 독특한 예술 기념 행사는 3일간의 문화 교류에 참여하도록 독창적인 재능을 가진 사람들을 전 세계로부터 끌어모읍니다. 특별 전시, 강연, 그리고 싱가포르 예술 박물관에 의해 기획되는 워크숍에 더하여, 이 행사는 다음을 포함할 것입니다:

- ⁰³⁻⁽ᴮ⁾두바이 출신 멀티미디어 전문가 Tima Khan이 그녀의 다채로운 영상들을 거대한 옥외 화면에 투사할 개막 파티. 이 행사는 무료이며 대중에게 공개됩니다.

- ⁰²/⁰³⁻⁽ᴮ⁾유명한 보석 디자이너 Palma Quinn과 싱가포르 출신의 Vicki Vong에 의해 공동 주최되는 ⁰³⁻⁽ᴬ⁾Marina Bay 공원에서의 ⁰³⁻⁽ᴮ⁾합작 예술 전시회. 이 행사는 무료이지만, ⁰³⁻⁽ᶜ⁾예약이 요구됩니다.

- ⁰³⁻⁽ᴮ⁾홍콩 행위 예술가 Xia Ben에 의해 해설될 ⁰³⁻⁽ᴬ⁾차이나타운의 Smith 가를 따라 있는 쌍방향 빛과 거울 설치 미술. 이 행사는 무료이고 대중에게 공개됩니다.

- ⁰³⁻⁽ᴮ⁾유명한 헝가리 거리 예술가 Koborlo의 디자인으로 장식될 ⁰³⁻⁽ᴬ⁾싱가포르 역사 지구의 가이드 안내 문화 여행. 관광은 한 사람당 20싱가포르 달러로 대중에게 제공되고, 아티스트와의 만남과 인사가 포함되어 있습니다. 단체로 Orchard로 버스 터미널에서 출발합니다.

더 많은 정보를 얻고 계획된 활동의 전체 예정표를 보시려면 www.culturalinvasion.sg를 방문하십시오. 근방 지도와 참여 업체에 의해 지원되는 음식 및 오락거리 옵션 할인 쿠폰을 다운로드 받으세요.

---

hold v. 개최하다, 갖고 있다, 들고 있다　unique adj. 독특한, 고유한
gather v. 끌어모으다, 수집하다　talent n. 재능을 가진 사람, 재능
exchange n. 교류, 교환　feature v. 특별히 포함하다, 특징으로 삼다
specialist n. 전문가, 전공자　project v. 투사하다, 계획하다, 기획하다
outdoor adj. 옥외의, 야외의　collaborative adj. 합작의
famed adj. 유명한, 저명한　interactive adj. 쌍방향의, 상호적인
narrate v. 해설하다, 이야기하다　performance artist 행위 예술가
district n. 지구, 구역　decorate v. 장식하다, 꾸미다　noted adj. 유명한
sponsor v. 지원하다, 후원하다　establishment n. 업체, 상회, 점포

01 | Not/True 문제

해석 Cultural Invasion에 대해 언급된 것은?
(A) 싱가포르의 관광을 촉진시키는 것을 목표로 한다.
(B) 보통 4월 중순에 개최된다.
(C) 싱가포르 예술 박물관에 의해 자금 지원을 받는다.
(D) 일 년 전에 한 번 열렸다.

해설 지문의 'Following the success of last year's event, the city of Singapore will be holding a second Cultural Invasion from Friday April 20 to Sunday April 22.'에서 작년 행사의 성공에 뒤이어 싱가포르는 4월 20일 금요일부터 4월 22일 일요일까지 제2회 Cultural Invasion을 개최할 것이라고 했으므로 (D)가 정답이다. (A), (B), (C)는 지문에 언급되지 않은 내용이다.

어휘 promote v. 촉진하다, 홍보하다

Paraphrasing

last year 작년 → the year before 일 년 전

02 | 육하원칙 문제

해석 포함된 행사 중 어떤 것이 두 사람에 의해서 주최될 것인가?
(A) 개막 파티
(B) 쌍방향 전시
(C) 공원 예술 전시회
(D) 문화 여행

해설 지문의 'A collaborative art fair co-hosted by famed jewelry designer Palma Quinn and Singapore's own Vicki Vong at the Marina Bay Public Gardens.'에서 유명한 보석 디자이너 Palma Quinn과 싱가포르 출신의 Vicki Vong에 의해 공동 주최되는 Marina Bay 공원에서의 합작 예술 전시회라고 했으므로 (C)가 정답이다.

어휘 excursion n. (짧은) 여행

03 | Not/True 문제

해석 계획된 활동에 대해 명시된 것은?
(A) 거의 한 지역에서 열린다.
(B) 모두 전문 예술가를 특징으로 할 것이다.
(C) 모두 사전 등록을 요구한다.
(D) 변경될 수도 있다.

해설 공고의 'Dubai-based multimedia specialist Tima Khan', 'famed jewelry designer Palma Quinn and Singapore's own Vicki Vong', 'Hong Kong performance artist Xia Ben', 'include a meet-and-greet with the artist'에서 모든 행사가 전문 예술가를 특징으로 한다는 것을 알 수 있으므로, (B)가 정답이다. (D)는 지문에 언급되지 않은 내용이다. 공고의 'Marina Bay Public Gardens', 'Smith Street in Chinatown', 'Singapore's historic districts'에서 세 행사의 장소가 서로 다른 곳임을 알 수 있으므로, (A)는 지문의 내용과 일치하지 않는다. 'A collaborative art fair ~ reservations are required'에서 합작 예술 전시회만 예약이 필요하다는 것을 알 수 있으므로, (C)는 지문의 내용과 일치하지 않는다.

어휘 be subject to ~할 수 있다, ~의 대상이다

04-07번은 다음 안내문에 관한 문제입니다.

Wyndham 스튜디오

Wyndham 스튜디오에서는, 미술이 가치 있는 투자 대상이라고 생각합니다. 그러나 어떤 투자든 마찬가지로, ⁰⁴그것의 가치가 보호되는 것을 확실히 하기 위해서 반드시 적절한 관리가 이루어져야 합니다. 앞으로 수년간 귀하께서 미술품 구매를 즐기실 수 있게 하기 위해, 저희는 다음의 도움이 되는 지침을 제공합니다.

- 그림을 다룰 때에는, 반드시 귀하의 손이 깨끗하도록 하고 작품의 표면을 직접적으로 만지는 것을 피하십시오. 항상 필수적인 것은 아니지만, 일회용 비닐장갑을 끼는 것은 좋은 생각입니다.

- 귀하의 미술품을 전시하려고 계획하신다면, 전문가에게 맡겨 액자에 끼우십시오. 부적절한 액자 작업은 작품의 품질을 상당히 낮출 수 있습니다. ⁰⁵⁻⁽ᴮ⁾저희와 함께 일하는 액자 작업자 명단을 위해 연락 주십시오.

- 귀하의 미술품으로 무엇을 하실 계획이든지, 항상 극도의 온도, 물로 인한 훼손, 그리고 햇빛으로부터 보호하십시오. 그것을 밝은 창가, 난로, 그리고 실내 환풍구로부터 멀리 떨어뜨려 놓으십시오. 강한 열을 방출하는 백열전구는 섬세한 미술품을 일그러뜨릴 수 있으므로 주의하십시오. ⁰⁶만일 귀하께서 습한 기후에서 거주하신다면, 제습기를 고려해 보십시오. 이것은 대기에서 수분을 제거하는 데 도움을 줍니다. 또한 온도가 조절되는 방에 미술품을 보관하실 수도 있습니다.

- 마지막이지만 역시 중요한 것으로, 귀하의 미술품을 공기 중의 오염 물질로부터 보호하십시오. 아무것도 덮여 있지 않은 작품은 특히 먼지에 ↻

민감하며 쌓인 입자들을 제거하기 위해 가볍게 솔질되어야만 합니다. 07어떤 종류의 화학 세제든 절대 사용하지 마십시오.

추가 정보를 위해서, 혹은 05-(C)저희 제품 카탈로그에서 앞서 언급된 물품 중 일부를 구입하시려면, www.wyndhamstudio.com으로 가십시오. 05-(A)/(D)어떤 미술 작품에든 500달러 이상 쓰시는 분은 저희 사이트에 나와 있는 제품들에 대해 25퍼센트 할인을 받을 자격이 있습니다.

fine art 미술(품) investment n. 투자 make sure 반드시 ~하다
surface n. 표면, 지면, 수면 disposable adj. 일회용의, 이용 가능한
frame v. 액자에 넣다 improper adj. 부적절한 substantially adv. 상당히
diminish v. 낮추다 air vent 환풍구 emit v. 방출하다, 내뿜다
distort v. 일그러뜨리다 delicate adj. 섬세한, 연약한 humid adj. 습한
dehumidifier n. 제습기 airborne adj. 공기 중의, 비행 중인
pollutant n. 오염 물질 susceptible to ~에 민감한 particle n. 입자, 미립자
chemical cleaner 화학 세제 aforementioned adj. 앞서 언급한, 진술한
eligible adj. 자격이 있는, 바람직한

04 | 주제 찾기 문제

해석 안내문은 주로 무엇에 대한 것인가?
(A) 미술품의 가치 평가하기
(B) 투자의 일환으로 미술품 구매하기
(C) 미술품 보관 및 유지하기
(D) 평판이 좋은 미술상 찾기

해설 지문의 'proper care must be taken to ensure that its value is protected. To help you enjoy your fine art purchase for many years to come, we offer the following helpful tips.'에서 미술의 가치가 보호되는 것을 확실히 하기 위해서 반드시 적절한 관리가 이루어져야 한다고 하고, 앞으로 수년간 미술품 구매를 즐길 수 있게 하기 위해 다음의 도움이 되는 지침을 제공한다고 했으므로 (C)가 정답이다.

어휘 appraise v. 평가하다, 살피다, 뜯어보다 preserve v. 보관하다, 보호하다
maintain v. 유지하다, 주장하다 reputable adj. 평판이 좋은
art dealer 미술상

Paraphrasing

proper care 적절한 관리 → Preserving and maintaining 보관 및 유지하기

05 | Not/True 문제

해석 Wyndham 스튜디오에 대해 명시되지 않은 것은?
(A) 예술 작품을 판매한다.
(B) 사내 액자 작업을 제공한다.
(C) 온라인 상점을 운영한다.
(D) 몇몇 구매에 대해 할인을 제공한다.

해설 (A)와 (D)는 지문의 'Those spending more than $500 on any artwork are eligible for a 25 percent discount on items listed on our site.'에서 어떤 미술 작품에든 500달러 이상을 쓰는 사람은 사이트에 나와 있는 제품들에 대해 25퍼센트 할인을 받을 자격이 있음을 알 수 있으므로 지문의 내용과 일치한다. 'to purchase some of the aforementioned items from our product catalog, go to www.wyndhamstudio.com'에서 제품 카탈로그에서 앞서 언급된 물품 중 일부를 구입하려면 www.wyndhamstudio.com으로 가라고 했으므로 (C)는 지문의 내용과 일치한다. (B)는 'Contact us for a list of framers that we work with.'에서 우리, 즉 Wyndham 스튜디오와 함께 일하는 액자 작업자 명단을 얻기 위해 연락하라고 했으므로 사내 액자 작업을 제공하지는 않는다는 것을 알 수 있다. 따라서 (B)가 정답이다.

어휘 in-house adj. 사내의, 조직 내부의

06 | 육하원칙 문제

해석 습한 환경에 대해서는 무엇이 권장되는가?
(A) 밀폐 용기에 미술품 보관하기
(B) 햇살이 내리쬐는 방에 미술품 전시하기
(C) 플라스틱 용기에 미술품 넣어 두기
(D) 습기를 줄이는 장치 사용하기

해설 지문의 'If you live in a humid climate, consider a dehumidifier.'에서 만일 습한 기후에서 거주한다면 제습기를 고려해 보라고 했으므로 (D)가 정답이다.

어휘 airtight adj. 밀폐의 container n. 용기, 그릇
display v. 전시하다, 보여주다; n. 전시, 진열 device n. 장치, 기구

Paraphrasing

dehumidifier 제습기 → a device that reduces moisture 습기를 줄이는 장치

07 | 육하원칙 문제

해석 미술품 소유자들은 미술품을 다룰 때 무엇을 피하라고 주의받는가?
(A) 비닐 장갑을 착용하는 것
(B) 미술품을 거는 것
(C) 세정액을 사용하는 것
(D) 특정한 천으로 덮는 것

해설 지문의 'Never use chemical cleaners of any kind.'에서 어떤 종류의 화학 세제도 사용하지 말라고 했으므로 (C)가 정답이다.

어휘 fabric n. 천, 직물 cleaning solution 세정액

Paraphrasing

chemical cleaners 화학 세제 → cleaning solutions 세정액

DAY 09 이중 지문

빈출 문제 집중 훈련   p.88

| 01 (C) | 02 (D) | 03 (C) | 04 (A) | 05 (D) |
| 06 (B) | 07 (C) | 08 (C) | 09 (D) | 10 (B) |

01-05번은 다음 송장과 이메일에 관한 문제입니다.

| 송장: MR-3848589 | Drapers Window Coverings사 |
| 날짜: 9월 1일 | (702) 555-4523, www.draperswindow.com |

고객	Marilyn Ravenwood	
01-(A)주소	01-(A)738번지 Grover가, 매디슨, 위스콘신 주 53532	
주문과 서비스 내역	04수량	비용
빨간 실크 커튼	1	488달러
04대나무 블라인드	041	238달러
01-(C)배송 및 설치 서비스		160달러
	소계	886달러
	세금	88달러
	지불해야 하는 금액	974달러

01-(D)현금, 은행 송금 또는 신용카드 지불이 가능합니다. 02지불은 송장 날짜로부터 일주일 내에 전액 이루어져야 합니다. 영수증은 명시된 주소로 발송될 것입니다. 송장에 대한 문의가 있으시면 scottforester@drapers.com으로 이메일을 보내주십시오.

installation n. 설치 payable adj. 지불해야 하는
transfer n. 송금, 이동; v. 옮기다 receipt n. 영수증, 수령

수신: Scott Forester <scottforester@drapers.com>
발신: Marilyn Ravenwood <mraven@tomail.com>
날짜: 9월 6일
제목: 송장 문의

Mr. Forester께,

당신의 직원이 어제 커튼과 블라인드를 배달해 주었고, 저는 그것들의 결과에 대해 매우 만족스럽습니다. 제품들은 거의 정확히 웹사이트에서 보였던 것처럼 보입니다. 게다가, 제공된 설치 서비스는 많은 시간과 고생을 덜어 주었습니다. 03-(B)저는 어제 은행 송금을 통하여 지불금을 보냈습니다. 그것을 받으시면 저에게 알려주시기 바라고, 03-(C)영수증은 위스콘신 주 53534 매디슨, 03-(A)Larch로 83번지에 있는 제 회사 Ferndale Interiors사로 보내 주시기 바랍니다. 송장에 명시되어 있는 주소는 제 고객의 것입니다.

또한, 04식당을 다시 꾸미려고 저를 고용한 또 다른 고객이 있습니다. 그의 작업을 위해, 그는 제가 Grover가를 위해 주문한 것과 같은 상품들을 원합니다. 04/03-(B)저는 정확히 같은 수의 커튼을 필요로 할 것이지만 블라인드는 두 배로 필요할 것입니다. 05얼마를 청구하실지 저에게 알려주실 수 있으신가요? 추가적인 세부 사항이 필요하시면 저에게 알려주십시오.

매우 감사합니다!

Marilyn Ravenwood

turn out (결과가) ~이 되다 exactly adv. 정확히 via prep. 통하여
redecorate v. 다시 꾸미다, 실내 장식을 새로 하다

01 | Not/True 문제

해석 Drapers Window Coverings사에 대해 명시된 것은?
(A) Grover가에 위치해 있다.
(B) 전국에 몇몇 매장이 있다.
(C) 배송 서비스를 제공한다.
(D) 신용카드 지불을 받지 않는다.

해설 송장의 'Delivery and installation services'에서 배송 및 설치 서비스를 제공한다는 것을 알 수 있으므로 (C)가 정답이다. (B)는 지문에 언급되지 않은 내용이다. 송장의 'ADDRESS', '738 Grover Avenue'에서 Grover가는 고객의 주소이지 Drapers Window Coverings사의 주소가 아니므로, (A)는 지문의 내용과 일치하지 않는다. 송장의 'Payments by cash, bank transfer, or credit card are accepted.'에서 현금, 은행 송금 또는 신용카드 지불이 가능하다고 했으므로 (D)는 지문의 내용과 일치하지 않는다.

02 | 육하원칙 문제

해석 송장에 따르면, 언제 전액 납부가 이루어져야만 하는가?
(A) 구매 시에
(B) 주문품 수령 시에
(C) 배송 후 48시간 이내에
(D) 송장 날짜로부터 7일 이내에

해설 송장의 'Payment must be made in full within one week of the invoice date.'에서 결제는 송장 날짜로부터 일주일 내에 전액 지불되어야 한다고 했으므로 (D)가 정답이다.

03 | Not/True 문제

해석 Ms. Ravenwood에 대해 언급된 것은?
(A) 매디슨의 Larch로에 거주한다.
(B) 그녀는 진행 중인 주문을 변경하고 싶어한다.
(C) 인테리어 장식 사업체를 운영한다.
(D) 잘못된 지불 금액을 보냈을 수 있다.

해설 이메일의 'send the receipt to my company at: Ferndale Interiors, 83 Larch Drive, Madison, WI 53534'에서 영수증은 위스콘신 주 53534 매디슨, Larch로 83번지에 있는 자신의 회사 Ferndale Interiors 사로 보내 달라고 했으므로 (C)가 정답이다. (D)는 지문에 언급되지 않은 내용이다. 이메일의 'my company at: Ferndale Interiors, 83 Larch Drive'에서 Larch로 83번지에 자신의 회사 Ferndale Interiors사가 있다고는 했지만, 본인이 거주하는지는 알 수 없으므로, (A)는 지문의 내용과 일치하지 않는다. 이메일의 'I sent you a payment via bank transfer yesterday.'에서 은행 송금을 통하여 지불금을 보냈다고 했으므로, (B)는 지문의 내용과 일치하지 않는다.

04 | 추론 문제 연계

해석 Ms. Ravenwood의 새로운 고객에 대해 사실일 것은?
(A) 블라인드 두 세트를 구매하고 싶어 한다.
(B) 여러 방들을 새로 장식하고 있다.
(C) Drapers사에서 이전에 쇼핑한 적이 있다.
(D) 새로운 집으로 이사할 것이다.

해설 Ms. Ravenwood가 작성한 이메일을 먼저 확인한다.
단서 1 이메일의 'I have another client that has hired me to redecorate his dining room. For his project, he would like the same items I ordered for Grover Avenue.'에서 식당을 다시 꾸미려고 Ms. Ravenwood를 고용한 또 다른 고객이 있으며, 그의 작업을 위해 그는 Ms. Ravenwood가 Grover가를 위해 주문한 것과 같은 상품들을 원한다는 것을 알 수 있고, 'I will need the exact same number of curtains but double that of the blinds.'에서 Ms. Ravenwood는 Grover가를 위해 주문한 것과 정확히 같은 수의 커튼을 필요로 할 것이지만 블라인드는 두 배로 필요할 것이라고 한 사실을 확인할 수 있다. 그런데 Ms. Ravenwood가 Grover가를 위해 주문한 상품의 수량이 제시되지 않았으므로, 송장에서 관련 내용을 확인한다.
단서 2 송장의 'Bamboo blinds', 'QUANTITY: 1'에서 Ms. Ravenwood가 대나무 블라인드를 한 세트 주문한 것을 확인할 수 있다. 두 단서를 종합할 때, 새로운 고객이 블라인드 두 세트에 관심이 있음을 추론할 수 있다. 따라서 (A)가 정답이다.

Paraphrasing

another client 또 다른 고객 → new client 새로운 고객

05 | 육하원칙 문제

해석 Mr. Forester는 무엇을 해 달라고 요청받았는가?
(A) 교환품을 발송한다.
(B) 다른 제품을 추천한다.
(C) 아파트를 방문한다.
(D) 비용 견적을 제공한다.

해설 이메일의 'Could you inform me how much you would charge?'에서 얼마를 청구할지 알려줄 수 있는지 물었으므로 (D)가 정답이다.

어휘 replacement n. 교환품, 대체물 cost estimate 비용 견적(서)

06-10번은 다음 이메일과 양식에 관한 문제입니다.

수신: Warren Dawson <w.dawson@wamail.com>
발신: Amber Sulaporn <amsula@redrubyresort.com>
날짜: 7월 24일
제목: 작은 요청

Mr. Dawson께,

귀하가 이곳 태국, 푸켓 섬에 있는 Red Ruby 리조트에서 7월 16일

부터 18일까지의 방문을 즐기셨기를 바랍니다. 귀하를 모실 수 있어 기뻤습니다.

⁰⁶서비스 수준을 높게 유지하기 위해, 저희는 손님들께 방문과 관련한 설문을 작성해 주실 것을 진심으로 요청 드립니다. 설문지는 저희 웹사이트에서 찾으실 수 있습니다. 그 양식을 작성하여 제출해 주신다면 감사하겠습니다.

설문지를 완료하시면, 향후 숙박 시 20퍼센트 할인을 받을 수 있는 쿠폰 번호를 제공받을 것입니다. ⁰⁷예약하실 때 간단히 번호를 넣으면, 해당 액수가 최종 청구서에서 공제될 것입니다.

¹⁰Amber Sulaporn
고객 관리 부서 관리자, Red Ruby 리조트

complete v. (서식을) 작성하다, 끝마치다; adj. 완벽한, 완전한
grateful adj. 감사하는, 고마워하는 **make a reservation** 예약하다

Red Ruby 리조트   고객 설문 양식

귀하의 의견에 감사드립니다. 귀하께서 제공하시는 응답은 저희가 시설과 서비스를 개선하도록 할 것입니다.

이름	Warren Dawson	나이	42
⁰⁸⁻⁽ᴬ⁾방문객 수	네 명	국적	미국

1. 어떻게 Red Ruby 리조트에 대해 알게 되었습니까?
   동료로부터 추천받았습니다.

2. 저희의 객실과 시설에 대해 어떻게 생각하셨습니까?
   시설이 깨끗했고, 수영장은 놀라웠으며, 해변으로의 접근성이 만족스러웠습니다. 그러나, ⁰⁸⁻⁽ᴰ⁾우리는 해변에 위치한 오두막 중 하나에서 머물렀는데, 그것이 구식이라고 느껴졌습니다. 실내 장식이 구식으로 보였고, 오래된 에어컨이 시끄러웠습니다.

3. 서비스와 식사 선택에 대해서는 어떻게 생각하셨습니까?
   ⁰⁸⁻⁽ᴮ⁾제 가족과 저는 모든 음식을 즐겼는데, 특히 뷔페식 아침 식사에 있는 현지 과일 모음을 즐겼습니다. 직원들은 친절했고 상냥했습니다.

4. Red Ruby 리조트에서 다시 머무르시겠습니까?
   네. ⁰⁹우리는 방문을 즐겼고, 특히 방문 이틀차의 짧은 섬 여행이 즐거웠습니다! 저는 가격도 합리적이라고 느꼈습니다.

5. Red Ruby 리조트의 월간 이메일 수신자 명단에 등록하시겠습니까?
   네.

¹⁰만일 한 달 이내에 소식지를 받지 못하시면, Amber Sulaporn에게 연락해 주십시오.

response n. 응답 **beachfront** adj. 해변에 위치한 **cottage** n. 오두막
outdated adj. 구식인 **décor** n. 실내 장식 **old-fashioned** adj. 구식인
assortment n. 모음, 모듬

---

06 | 육하원칙 문제

해석 Ms. Sulaporn은 Mr. Dawson에게 무엇을 하라고 요청하는가?
(A) 상품권을 보낸다.
(B) 의견을 제공한다.
(C) 대금을 지불한다.
(D) 여행 일자를 확정한다.

해설 이메일의 'To keep our level of service high, we kindly ask our guests to complete a survey concerning their visit. The questionnaire can be found on our Web site. We would be grateful if you could complete the form and submit it.'에서 서비스 수준을 높게 유지하기 위해 손님들에게 방문과 관련한 설문을 작성해 주기를 요청한다고 하고, 설문지는 웹사이트에서 찾을 수 있다고 한 후, 그 양식을 작성하여 제출해 달라고 했으므로 (B)가 정답이다.

Paraphrasing

a survey 설문 → a feedback form 의견 양식

07 | 동의어 찾기 문제

해석 이메일에서, 3문단 두 번째 줄의 단어 "deducted"는 의미상 -와 가장 가깝다.
(A) 분리되다
(B) 단축되다
(C) 공제되다
(D) 감소되다

해설 deducted를 포함한 구절 'Simply provide the number when making a reservation, and the amount will be deducted from your bill.'에서 deducted는 '공제되다'라는 뜻으로 사용되었다. 따라서 (C)가 정답이다.

08 | Not/True 문제

해석 Mr. Dawson에 대해 명시되지 않은 것은?
(A) 단체와 함께 여행했다.
(B) 식사 선택에 만족했다.
(C) 머무는 동안 객실을 바꿨다.
(D) 일부 시설이 개선되어야 한다고 생각한다.

해설 (A)는 양식의 'Number of Guests, Four'에서 방문객 수가 네 명이라고 했으므로 지문의 내용과 일치한다. (B)는 'My family and I enjoyed all the food'에서 가족과 자신이 모든 음식을 즐겼다고 했으므로 지문의 내용과 일치한다. (D)는 'we stayed in one of the beachfront cottages, and it felt outdated'에서 해변에 위치한 오두막 중 하나에서 머물렀는데, 그것이 구식이라고 느껴졌다고 했으므로 지문의 내용과 일치한다. (C)는 지문에 언급되지 않은 내용이다. 따라서 (C)가 정답이다.

Paraphrasing

enjoyed all the food 모든 음식을 즐겼다 → satisfied with the dining options 식사 선택에 만족했다

one of the beachfront cottages ~ felt outdated 해변에 위치한 오두막 중 하나는 구식이었다 → some facilities need to be updated 일부 시설이 개선되어야 한다

09 | 추론 문제

해석 Mr. Dawson이 Red Ruby 리조트에 대해 암시하는 것은?
(A) 단체를 위한 할인이 있다.
(B) 일부 직원들이 무뚝뚝했다.
(C) 지역 투어 가이드를 고용한다.
(D) 손님들에게 짧은 여행을 제공한다.

해설 양식의 'We enjoyed the visit, particularly the island excursions on the second day of our visit!'에서 방문을 즐겼고, 특히 방문 이틀차의 짧은 섬 여행이 즐거웠다고 한 것을 통해, Red Ruby 리조트가 손님들에게 짧은 여행을 제공함을 추론할 수 있다. 따라서 (D)가 정답이다.

어휘 **inattentive** adj. 무뚝뚝한, 부주의한

Paraphrasing

excursions (보통 단체로 하는) 짧은 여행 → short trips 짧은 여행

10 | 육하원칙 문제 연계

해석 소식지가 오지 않으면, 손님들은 무엇을 해야 하는가?
(A) 리조트 대표에게 전화한다.
(B) 고객 관리 부서 관리자에게 연락을 한다.

(C) 또 다른 구독 양식을 작성한다.
(D) 온라인 계정 정보를 확인한다.

해설 질문의 핵심 어구인 newsletter가 언급된 양식을 먼저 확인한다.

단서 1 양식의 'If you do not receive the newsletter within a month, contact Amber Sulaporn at amsula@redrubyresort.com.'에서 한 달 이내에 소식지를 받지 못하면 amsula@redrubyresort.com으로 Amber Sulaporn에게 연락하라고 하였다. 그런데 Amber Sulaporn이 누구인지 제시되지 않았으므로 이메일에서 관련 내용을 확인한다.

단서 2 이메일의 'Amber Sulaporn', 'Guest relations supervisor'에서 Amber Sulaporn이 고객 관리 부서 관리자라고 하였다.

두 단서를 종합할 때, 소식지가 오지 않으면 손님들은 고객 관리 부서 관리자에게 편지를 써야 함을 추론할 수 있다. 따라서 (B)가 정답이다.

어휘 representative n. 대표, 대리인 fill in (서식 등을) 작성하다, 채우다
subscription n. 구독, 구독료

고난도 문제 완전 정복   p.92

| 01 | (B) | 02 | (D) | 03 | (B) | 04 | (B) | 05 | (B) |

01-05번은 다음 광고와 이메일에 관한 문제입니다.

Crystalline 호텔
여러분의 다음 특별한 행사를 훨씬 더 특별하게 만드세요!

⁰¹결혼식이나 기념일 파티를 열든, 기업 행사를 개최하든, 칠레의 Crystalline 호텔은 산티아고, 콘셉시온, 발파라이소, 그리고 라 세레나의 4개 지점 중 하나에서 여러분을 위해 모든 준비를 기획할 수 있습니다! 그저 휴식을 취하시면서 저희가 모든 일을 처리하도록 맡겨 주십시오.

넓은 행사장은 250명까지의 단체를 수용할 수 있습니다. 그것들은 여러분의 요구에 맞게 장식될 수 있고, 꽃 장식 또한 가능합니다. 각각의 연회장은 최첨단 음향과 조명 시스템을 갖추고 있고, 프로젝터와 스크린도 이용하실 수 있도록 포함됩니다. ⁰²⁻⁽ᴰ⁾저희가 오락거리를 제공해드리지는 않지만, 제공하는 대행사 목록을 드릴 수 있습니다.

⁰²⁻⁽ᶜ⁾다양한 뷔페나 테이블 서비스 메뉴 중에서 모두의 취향에 맞는 요리를 선택하십시오. 저희 전문 요리사들은 유럽, 아시아, 미국 요리를 준비할 수 있고 특별한 식단 선호도가 있는 분들을 위해서도 요리할 수 있습니다.

그리고 사전 예약 할인의 기회를 이용하세요! ⁰⁵저희 내부 플로리스트에 의해 준비되는 무료 테이블 세팅을 받기 위해 최소 3개월 전에 예약하세요! Crystalline 호텔에서 여러분의 다음 행사를 예약하시려면 events@crystalline.com으로 저희에게 연락 주십시오!

⁰²⁻⁽ᴬ⁾스페인어, 영어, 포르투갈어로 서비스를 이용하실 수 있습니다. ⁰²⁻⁽ᴮ⁾호텔은 손님들을 위해 무료 대리 주차를 제공합니다.

orchestrate v. 기획하다 relax v. 휴식을 취하다, 쉬다
take care of 처리하다, 돌보다 spacious adj. 넓은, 널찍한
requirement n. 요구, 필요 floral arrangement 꽃 장식, 꽃꽂이
state-of-the-art adj. 최첨단의, 최신식의 suit v. ~에 맞추다, 편리하다
dietary adj. 식단의, 식이 요법의 preference n. 선호(도)
take advantage of ~을 이용하다 advance booking 사전 예약
in advance 사전에, 미리 앞서 complimentary adj. 무료의
in-house adj. (회사·조직) 내부의 valet parking 대리 주차

수신: Celia Perez <celiap@crystalline.com>
발신: Mindy Johnson <mjohnson@fastemail.com>
제목: ⁰⁵10월 22일 결혼식
⁰⁵날짜: 1월 2일

Ms. Perez께,

제 메시지에 답해 주시고 10월 22일에 있을 결혼식 피로연을 위한 빈 연회장이 있다는 것을 확인해 주셔서 매우 감사합니다. ⁰³⁻⁽ᴮ⁾저의 약혼자와 저는 당신의 호텔 웨딩 서비스에 대한 훌륭한 후기를 그의 친구로부터 들었는데, 그는 특히 장소의 우아함에 인상 깊었던 것처럼 보였습니다. 그래서, 저희는 그 날짜에 주류를 모두 갖춘 바와 손님 250명을 위한 저녁 뷔페와 함께 연회장을 예약하고 싶습니다.

또한, ⁰³⁻⁽ᶜ⁾/⁰⁴저는 원래 호주 출신이라서, 친척 20명 정도가 결혼식을 위해 비행기로 도착할 것이고, 그들 중 일부는 객실이 필요합니다. 10월 21일과 22일에 이용 가능한 방이 있는지 알려 주시겠습니까?

다시 한번, 귀하께서 저희의 피로연을 주관해 주실 것이라 매우 기쁩니다.

Mindy Johnson

confirm v. 확인하다 vacant adj. 빈 elegance n. 우아함
originally adv. 원래 relative n. 친척 fly in 비행기로 도착하다

01 | 추론 문제

해석 광고는 누구를 대상으로 하는가?
(A) 독특한 칠레 명소를 찾는 관광객들
(B) 특별한 행사를 계획하는 사람들
(C) 호텔 서비스에 대해 배우는 수습 직원들
(D) 회의 장소를 필요로 하는 출장 여행객들

해설 광고의 'Whether you are holding a wedding or anniversary party, or hosting a business event, Chile's Crystalline Hotel can orchestrate all the arrangements for you'에서 결혼식이나 기념일 파티를 열든, 기업 행사를 개최하든, 칠레의 Crystalline 호텔은 모든 준비를 기획할 수 있다고 했으므로 광고는 특별한 행사를 계획하는 사람들을 대상으로 함을 추론할 수 있다. 따라서 (B)가 정답이다.

어휘 seek v. 찾다 attraction n. 명소 venue n. 장소

02 | Not/True 문제

해석 Crystalline 호텔에 의해 제공되는 서비스가 아닌 것은?
(A) 다언어 지원
(B) 대리 주차
(C) 음식 공급
(D) 음악 연주

해설 광고의 'Although we do not provide entertainment'에서 오락거리를 제공하지 않는다고 했으므로 지문의 내용과 일치하지 않는다. 따라서 (D)가 정답이다. (A)는 'Service in Spanish, English, and Portuguese is available.'에서 스페인어, 영어, 포르투갈어로 서비스를 이용할 수 있다고 했으므로 제공되는 서비스가 맞다. (B)는 'The hotel offers free valet parking for guests.'에서 손님들을 위해 무료 대리 주차를 제공한다고 했으므로 제공되는 서비스가 맞다. (C)는 'Choose from a wide variety of buffet or table-service menus with dishes to suit every taste.'에서 다양한 뷔페나 테이블 서비스 메뉴 중에서 모두의 취향에 맞는 요리를 선택하라고 했으므로 제공되는 서비스가 맞다.

어휘 multilingual adj. 다언어의, 여러 언어를 사용하는

Paraphrasing

entertainment 오락거리 → Musical entertainment 음악 연주

03 | Not/True 문제

해석 Ms. Johnson이 그녀의 약혼자에 대해서 언급하는 것은?
(A) 호텔 후기를 작성했다.
(B) 호텔에서 결혼한 누군가를 안다.
(C) 해외에서 도착하는 친척들이 있다.

(D) 그의 손님들을 위해 방을 예약했다.

해설 이메일의 'My fiancé and I have heard excellent reviews about your hotel's wedding services from a friend of his, who seemed particularly impressed by the elegance of your location.'에서 약혼자와 Ms. Johnson이 호텔 웨딩 서비스에 대한 훌륭한 후기를 그의 친구로부터 들었는데, 그는 특히 장소의 우아함에 인상 깊었던 것처럼 보였다고 했으므로 (B)가 지문의 내용과 일치한다. 따라서 (B)가 정답이다. (A)와 (D)는 지문에 언급되지 않은 내용이다. (C)는 'as I am originally from Australia, I will have around 20 relatives flying in for the wedding'에서 Ms. Johnson이 호주 출신이라서, 친척 20명 정도가 결혼식을 위해 비행기로 도착할 것이라고 했으므로 지문의 내용과 일치하지 않는다.

04 | 육하원칙 문제

해석 Ms. Johnson은 무엇에 대해 문의하는가?
(A) 특별 메뉴의 이용 가능성
(B) 숙소의 빈 객실
(C) 서비스 비용
(D) 공항 교통편

해설 이메일의 'as I am originally from Australia, I will have around 20 relatives flying in for the wedding, and some of them will require rooms. Could you let me know if you have any available for October 21-22?'에서 Ms. Johnson이 원래 호주 출신이라서 친척 20명 정도가 결혼식을 위해 비행기로 도착할 것이고, 그들 중 일부는 객실이 필요할 것이라고 한 후, 10월 21일과 22일에 이용 가능한 방이 있는지 알려줄 수 있는지 묻고 있으므로 (B)가 정답이다.

어휘 availability n. 이용 가능성, 유효성

05 | 추론 문제 연계

해석 Ms. Johnson의 행사에 대해 결론지을 수 있는 것은?
(A) 호텔 수영장 옆에서 열릴 것이다.
(B) 꽃을 특별 제공받을 자격이 된다.
(C) 시청각 시스템을 필요로 할 것이다.
(D) 아직 확정되지 않았다.

해설 Ms. Johnson이 작성한 이메일을 먼저 확인한다.
단서 1 이메일의 'October 22 wedding'과 'DATE: January 2'에서 결혼식은 10월 22일이고, 예약을 하는 이메일은 1월 2일에 보냈으므로, 행사 9개월 전에 예약했다는 것을 확인할 수 있다.
단서 2 광고의 'Make a reservation at least three months in advance to receive complimentary table settings prepared by our in-house florist!'에서 내부 플로리스트에 의해 준비되는 무료 테이블 세팅을 받기 위해 최소 3개월 전에 예약하라고 하였다.
두 단서를 종합할 때, Ms. Johnson은 꽃을 특별 제공받을 자격이 된다는 것을 추론할 수 있다. 따라서 (B)가 정답이다.

DAY 10 삼중 지문

빈출 문제 집중 훈련
p.94

| 01 (C) | 02 (B) | 03 (A) | 04 (C) | 05 (C) |
| 06 (C) | 07 (C) | 08 (C) | 09 (D) | 10 (B) |

01-05번은 다음 기사, 이메일, 일정표에 관한 문제입니다.

Skyliner사가 범위를 넓히다

마이애미 (1월 2일)—Skyliner사는 올해 마이애미에서 출발하는 새로운 노선을 취항할 것이라고 발표했다. 다음 달부터, 그 항공사는 라스베이거스로 매일 직항 운행을 시작할 것이다. 추가적으로, 킹스턴, 나소, 포트오브스페인과 같은 카리브해 지역의 도시들로 주 2회 직항편들이 생길 것이다.

"우리는 이 도착지들을 추가함으로써 고객들에게 더 넓은 선택지들을 제공하게 되어 기쁩니다."라고 Jeff Prince 회장이 성명서에서 말했다. "6월 말까지, ⁰³Skyliner사는 주요 중심지와 본사 모두 있는 장소인 마이애미에서 30개의 다른 목적지로 비행할 것입니다. ⁰¹남미의 더 많은 도착지를 포함하기 위해 저희의 범위를 늘림에 따라 이 수는 증가할 것입니다."

Skyliner사는 몇 년간 낮은 요금으로의 자리매김과 강건한 고객 중심 지향 덕분에 최근 굳건히 성장했다. ⁰²이 회사의 확장은 또한 경쟁 항공사인 Midway사의 폐업 이후에 늘어나는 시장 수요를 만족시키는 데 일조했다.

새로운 노선의 세부 사항들은 차후 날짜에 회사 웹사이트에 발표될 것이다. 더 자세한 정보는 www.skylinerairlines.com을 방문하면 된다.

extend v. 넓히다, 연장하다 reach n. 범위, 구역 route n. 노선, 길
initiate v. 시작하다 nonstop adj. 직항의, 직행의
twice-weekly adj. 주 2회의 destination n. 도착지, 목적지
statement n. 성명서, 성명 augment v. 늘리다 robustly adv. 굳건히
position v. 자리매김하다 vigorous adj. 강건한, 격렬한
satisfy v. 만족시키다, 충족시키다 demand n. 수요; v. 요구하다
closure n. 폐업, 폐쇄 carrier n. 항공사

수신: Linda Ferry <l.ferry@skylinerairlines.com>
발신: Paul Adams <p.adams@skylinerairlines.com>
제목: 교육
날짜: 1월 19일
첨부 파일: 일정표

Linda,

저희는 Skyliner사의 최신 목적지들에서의 직원 교육을 위한 날짜를 임시로 정했습니다. ⁰⁵하지만, 도시들 중 한 곳으로의 취항을 연기하기로 결정하면서 사소한 변경 사항이 있었습니다. 이 지연된 취항에 대한 교육 일정은 추후에 발표될 예정입니다.

그래서 ⁰³2월 16일부터 20일까지, 당신은 본사에서 모든 새로운 직원들을 위한 일주일짜리 오리엔테이션을 담당하게 되었고, 그 이후에는 라스베이거스에서 현장 교육을 맡게 될 것입니다. ⁰⁴Ms. Warren은 남은 두 도시를 담당할 예정이지만 오리엔테이션도 도울 수 있다고 내비쳤습니다. 일정이 겹치는 것이 있다면 알려주시기 바랍니다. 일정이 확정되면, 출장 준비를 모두 처리하겠습니다.

Paul

tentatively adv. 임시로, 시험적으로 delay v. 연기하다; n. 연기
in charge of ~을 담당해서 headquarters n. 본사
on-site adj. 현장의, 현지의 conflict n. 겹치는 것, 상충, 충돌
finalize v. 확정하다, 마무리짓다 take care of 처리하다, ~을 맡다
arrangement n. 준비, 마련

Skyliner사 교육 일정표

날짜	행사
2월 16-20일 (마이애미)	새로운 도착지와 노선에서 일하는 모든 새로운 직원들을 위한 오리엔테이션 교육
2월 23-27일 (⁰⁵라스베이거스)	발권 직원과 행정 직원을 위한 교육
3월 1-5일 (⁰⁵킹스턴)	발권 직원과 행정 직원을 위한 교육
3월 8-12일 (⁰⁵포트오브스페인)	발권 직원과 행정 직원을 위한 교육

administrative adj. 행정의, 관리의

01 | 육하원칙 문제

해석 Skyliner사에 무슨 일이 있을 것으로 예상되는가?
(A) 가장 가까운 경쟁사들을 앞지를 것이다.
(B) 주요 중심지를 마이애미로 옮길 것이다.
(C) 남미 노선을 더 추가할 것이다.
(D) 온라인 탑승 수속 서비스 제공을 시작할 것이다.

해설 기사의 'This number will go up as we augment our reach to include more destinations in South America.'에서 남미의 더 많은 도착지를 포함하기 위해 범위를 늘림에 따라 이 수가 증가할 것이라고 했으므로 (C)가 정답이다.

어휘 overtake v. 앞지르다, 추월하다   competitor n. 경쟁사, 경쟁자
check-in n. (공항의) 탑승 수속, 탑승 수속대

02 | 추론 문제

해석 기사가 Skyliner사에 대해 암시하는 것은?
(A) 지난해 동안 요금을 인상했다.
(B) Midway사의 폐업으로부터 이익을 얻었다.
(C) 새로운 노선들에 할인을 제공할 것이다.
(D) 고객 설문을 진행했다.

해설 기사의 'Its expansion has also helped to satisfy rising market demand following the closure of competing carrier Midway.'에서 Skyliner사의 확장은 경쟁 항공사인 Midway사의 폐업 이후에 늘어나는 시장 수요를 만족시키는 데 일조했다고 한 것을 통해, Skyliner사가 Midway사의 폐업으로부터 이익을 얻었다는 것을 추론할 수 있다. 따라서 (B)가 정답이다.

어휘 raise v. 인상하다, 올리다   fare n. 요금

03 | 추론 문제 연계

해석 Ms. Ferry는 2월 18일에 무엇을 할 것 같은가?
(A) 마이애미에서 오리엔테이션을 감독한다.
(B) 항공사의 새로운 도착지에 간다.
(C) 킹스턴에서 Ms. Warren과 합류한다.
(D) 서비스 교육을 받는다.

해설 질문의 핵심 어구인 Ms. Ferry가 언급된 이메일을 먼저 확인한다.
단서 1 이메일의 'from February 16 to 20, we have you in charge of the one-week orientation for all new staff at our headquarters'에서 2월 16일부터 20일까지, Ms. Ferry는 본사에서 모든 새로운 직원들을 위한 일주일짜리 오리엔테이션을 담당하게 되었다고 하였다.
단서 2 기사의 'Skyliner will be flying to 30 different locations from Miami, the site of both its main hub and corporate headquarters'에서 Skyliner사는 주요 중심지와 본사 모두 있는 장소인 마이애미에서 30개의 다른 목적지로 비행할 것이라고 했으므로, Skyliner사의 본사는 마이애미에 있음을 확인할 수 있다.
두 단서를 종합할 때, 2월 18일에 Ms. Ferry는 마이애미에서 오리엔테이션 교육을 감독할 것임을 추론할 수 있다. 따라서 (A)가 정답이다.

어휘 oversee v. 감독하다, 감시하다

Paraphrasing

be in charge of ~ orientation 오리엔테이션을 담당하다 → Oversee an orientation 오리엔테이션을 감독하다

04 | 육하원칙 문제

해석 Ms. Warren은 무엇을 하기로 자원했는가?
(A) 더 상세한 교육 자료를 작성한다.
(B) 여행 준비를 처리한다.
(C) 직원들이 회사 운영에 익숙해지도록 돕는다.
(D) 동료에게 업데이트된 일정을 제공한다.

해설 이메일의 'Ms. Warren will handle the two remaining cities but has indicated that she can also assist with the orientation.'에서 Ms. Warren은 남은 두 도시를 담당할 예정이지만 오리엔테이션도 도울 수 있다고 내비쳤다고 했으므로 (C)가 정답이다.

05 | 육하원칙 문제 연계

해석 Skyliner사는 어떤 노선을 연기하기로 결정했는가?
(A) 포트오브스페인
(B) 라스베이거스
(C) 나소
(D) 킹스턴

해설 질문의 핵심 어구인 delay가 언급된 이메일을 먼저 확인한다.
단서 1 이메일의 'However, there has been one minor alteration in that we've decided to delay the launch of service to one of the cities. The training schedule for this delayed launch will be announced later.'에서 도시들 중 한 곳으로의 취항을 연기하기로 결정한 사소한 변경 사항이 있었고, 이 지연된 취항에 대한 교육 일정은 추후에 발표될 예정이라고 했다.
단서 2 일정표의 'Las Vegas', 'Kingston', 'Port of Spain'에서는 라스베이거스, 킹스턴, 포트오브스페인의 교육 일정을 확인할 수 있다.
두 단서를 종합할 때, 지연된 취항에 대한 교육 일정은 추후 발표될 예정이라 일정표에 포함되지 않았고, Skyliner사는 나소 노선을 연기하기로 결정했음을 추론할 수 있다. 따라서 (C)가 정답이다.

06-10번은 다음 웹페이지, 광고지, 이메일에 관한 문제입니다.

홈	소개	뉴스	연락처

Applewood Interiors사

Applewood Interiors사와 봄이 온 것을 기념하세요! [07]4월 1일부터 4월 15일까지 여러분의 거실, 주방, 식당, 사무실을 위한 저희의 제품을 둘러보시고 작년 재고 품목의 할인을 최대 50퍼센트까지 누리십시오. 이 혜택은 매장에서 구매된 상품에만 한정됩니다. [06]가장 가까운 Applewood Interiors사 지점에서 물건을 구매하세요. 문의나 지원을 위해서는, 555-8999로 전화하시거나 cs2@applewoodint.com으로 이메일을 보내주세요.

inventory n. 재고, 재고 목록   **location** n. 지점   **inquiry** n. 문의
assistance n. 지원

[07]Applewood Interiors사 봄 세일
4월 1일부터 15일까지

식당	침실
Paulina 체리나무 식탁, 8인용, 970달러	Komfort 킹사이즈 소나무 침대 프레임, 379달러
Richardson 호두나무 식탁, 6인용, 649달러	Clover 오크나무 침실용 탁자, 319달러
Onyx 오크나무 식탁, 6인용, 629달러	Ambassador 체리나무 옷장, 229달러
[09]Remington 체리나무 식탁, 8인용, 779달러	**사무실**
주방&옥외	Scrito 2단 서랍 책상, 399달러
Enthuse 소나무 부엌 조리대, 299달러	Buchtal 호두나무 책장, 278달러
Montaigne 오크나무 옥외 의자, 239달러	Doozie 서류 정리 캐비닛, 244달러

* [07]모든 가격은 50퍼센트 할인을 포함한 것입니다. 990달러 이상의

구매 시 무료 배송이 포함됩니다. 제품들은 제한된 3년짜리 보증서가 제공됩니다.

walnut n. 호두나무, 호두색 **pine** n. 소나무 **dresser** n. 옷장, 찬장
drawer n. 서랍, 장롱 **bookcase** n. 책장, 서가
filing n. 서류 정리, 서류 철하기 **inclusive** adj. 포함한 **warranty** n. 보증서

수신: 고객 서비스 <cs2@applewoodint.com>
발신: Ida Shermer <ida_shermer@mountainmail.com>
제목: 문의
날짜: 4월 2일

안녕하세요,

저는 최근 헤이스팅스에 새로운 집을 구입하였고, 집에 가구를 비치하고 있습니다. 식당에, ⁰⁹저는 체리나무로 만들어진 캐비닛과 뷔페 테이블을 가지고 있으며, 같은 자재로 만든 식탁을 원합니다. ⁰⁸빠듯한 예산 때문에, 저는 식탁에 900달러 이상 지불할 수 없습니다. 어떤 옵션들이 있는지 알려주시겠습니까?

저는 저의 새로운 집의 실내 장식에 어울리게 하기 위해 같은 자재의 옷장을 구매하는 것에도 관심이 있습니다.

¹⁰제 새 집으로 이 가구들이 늦어도 25일까지 도착할 수 있는지 가능성을 확인해 주신다면 감사하겠습니다.

감사합니다.
Ida Shermer

furnish v. 가구를 비치하다 **material** n. 자재, 재료, 물질
verify v. 확인하다, 입증하다 **feasibility** n. (실현) 가능성
furnishing n. 가구, 비품

06 | 추론 문제

해석 웹페이지에 따르면, Applewood Interiors사에 대해 암시되는 것은?
(A) 상점 기념일을 축하하고 있다.
(B) 자체 제품을 제조한다.
(C) 여러 지점에서 운영된다.
(D) 디자이너 제품을 출시할 것이다.

해설 지문의 'Shop now at your nearest Applewood Interiors location.'에서 가장 가까운 Applewood Interiors사 지점에서 물건을 구매하라고 했으므로, Applewood Interiors사가 여러 지점에서 운영됨을 추론할 수 있다. 따라서 (C)가 정답이다.

어휘 **manufacture** v. 제조하다 **operate** v. 운영하다

07 | Not/True 문제 연계

해석 광고지의 제품에 대해 명시된 것은?
(A) 온라인에서도 구매될 수 있다.
(B) 추가 할인이 제공된다.
(C) 오래된 상품들로 구성되어 있다.
(D) 무료 배송으로 제공된다.

해설 제품 정보가 담긴 광고지를 먼저 확인한다.
[단서 1] 광고지의 'Applewood Interiors Spring Sale'과 'April 1 to 15'에서 Applewood Interiors사의 봄 세일이 4월 1일부터 15일까지 진행된다고 하였고, 'All prices shown are inclusive of 50% discounts.'에서 모든 가격은 50퍼센트 할인을 포함한 것이라고 하였다.
[단서 2] 웹페이지의 'Browse our collection of products for your living room, kitchen, dining room, and office from April 1 to April 15 and enjoy discounts of up to 50 percent on items from last year's inventory.'에서 4월 1일부터 4월 15일까지 거실, 주방, 식당, 사무실을 위한 제품을 둘러보고 작년 재고 품목의 할인을 최대 50퍼센트까

지 누리라고 한 것을 확인할 수 있다.
두 단서를 종합할 때, 광고지의 제품들은 작년 재고 품목인 오래된 상품들로 구성되어 있음을 추론할 수 있다. 따라서 (C)가 정답이다.

어휘 **consist of** ~로 구성되다

Paraphrasing

items from last year's inventory 작년 재고 품목 → old merchandise 오래된 상품들

08 | 동의어 찾기 문제

해석 이메일에서, 1문단 세 번째 줄의 단어 "tight"는 의미상 -와 가장 가깝다.
(A) 비좁은
(B) 회수된
(C) 한정된
(D) 부착된

해설 tight를 포함한 구절 'Due to my tight budget, I cannot spend more than $900 on a dining table.'에서 tight는 '빠듯한'이라는 뜻으로 사용되었다. 따라서 (C)가 정답이다.

09 | 추론 문제 연계

해석 Applewood Interiors사는 Ms. Shermer에게 어떤 제품을 추천할 것 같은가?
(A) Onyx
(B) Paulina
(C) Richardson
(D) Remington

해설 Ms. Shermer가 작성한 이메일을 먼저 확인한다.
[단서 1] 이메일의 'I have a cabinet and buffet table made of cherry wood and would like a dining table made of the same material. Due to my tight budget, I cannot spend more than $900 on a dining table.'에서 Ms. Shermer는 체리나무로 만들어진 캐비닛과 뷔페 테이블을 가지고 있으며, 같은 자재로 만든 식탁을 원한다고 한 후, 빠듯한 예산 때문에 식탁에 900달러 이상은 지불할 수 없다고 했다.
[단서 2] 광고지의 'Remington cherry table, seats 8, $779'에서 Remington 체리나무 식탁이 900달러를 넘지 않는다는 것을 확인할 수 있다.
두 단서를 종합할 때, Applewood Interiors사는 Ms. Shermer에게 Remington 체리나무 식탁을 추천할 것임을 추론할 수 있다. 따라서 (D)가 정답이다.

10 | 추론 문제

해석 Ms. Shermer는 왜 이메일에서 월의 25일을 언급하는가?
(A) 그 기한까지 집 리모델링이 완료되도록 보장하기 위해
(B) 그 날짜까지 가구가 배송될 것을 확인하기 위해
(C) 그 날짜 이후에 도착하는 손님들을 맞이하기 위해
(D) 추가적인 구매를 위한 예산 계획을 마무리하기 위해

해설 이메일의 'I would be grateful if you could verify the feasibility of having these furnishings arrive at my new residence no later than the 25th.'에서 Ms. Shermer는 이 가구들이 늦어도 25일까지 도착할 수 있는지 가능성을 확인해 준다면 감사하겠다고 하였다. 따라서 (B)가 정답이다.

어휘 **accommodate** v. 맞이하다, 수용하다

고난도 문제 완전 정복					p.98
01 (D)	02 (C)	03 (B)	04 (C)	05 (D)	

01-05번은 다음 양식, 이메일, 영수증에 관한 문제입니다.

GEORGIAN 유람선 여행사
여행 일정표 및 예약 확인서

이름	Antonia Blaine	이메일	anblaine@itmail.com
여권 번호	PV948344	전화번호	(507) 555-4995
예약 번호	AB-4995	주소	1233번지 Minton가, 스포캔, 워싱턴 주 99485

지중해 유람선 패키지: 8월 3일-8월 12일

출발	8월 3일, 오전 10시 30분
도착	8월 12일, 오후 4시
여행자 수	2명
여행자 이름	Antonia Blaine, Rosalind Purefoy
선실	303
유형	고급 특실
⁰¹기항지	나폴리, 사르디니아, 바르셀로나, 마요르카

상단에 나열된 모든 정보가 정확한지 확인해 주시고, 오류가 있는 경우, reservations@georgiancruiselines.com으로 Georgian 유람선 여행사에 알려 주십시오. ⁰²출발 한 달 이내의 예약 취소는 환불이 불가능합니다. 다른 모든 변경 요청에는 승객당 150유로의 수수료가 부과될 것입니다.

itinerary n. 여행 일정표 reservation n. 예약 confirmation n. 확인서, 확인
Mediterranean adj. 지중해의 cabin n. 선실, 객실
executive suite 고급 특실
port of call 기항지, (여러 곳을 다니는 길에) 잠시 들르는 곳
nonrefundable adj. 환불이 불가능한

수신: <reservations@georgiancruiselines.com>
발신: Antonia Blaine <anblaine@itmail.com>
⁰²날짜: 6월 12일
제목: 예약 AB-4995

담당자께,

⁰²저는 귀사에 8월 3일부터 8월 12일까지 제 여동생과 저 자신을 위해 유람선 여행을 예약했습니다. 유감스럽게도, 저는 여동생의 예약을 취소해야 합니다. ⁰³그녀가 일하는 은행에 그 날짜 동안 예상치 못한 일이 생겼습니다. 하지만, 저는 예정된 대로 여전히 유람선 여행을 갈 것입니다.

⁰⁵저는 또한 더 좋은 전망의 선실을 요청하고 싶습니다. 저는 현재 3층에 있는 객실에 있지만, 8층 이상에 있고 싶습니다. ⁰⁴우리의 여행에 대해 신용카드로 지불했으니, 예약 변경에 따른 위약금을 지불하기 위해 그것을 쓸 수 있을까요? 귀하의 기록에 번호가 남아 있을 텐데, 확인이 필요하다면 555-4995로 저에게 연락하시면 됩니다. 보안상의 이유로, 제 카드 정보를 이메일을 통해 제공하고 싶지 않습니다.

Antonia Blaine

book v. 예약하다 unexpected adj. 예상치 못한, 뜻밖의 penalty fee 위약금
security n. 보안, 안전

Georgian 유람선 여행사
유람선 패키지 영수증

예약: AB-4995   여행 날짜: 8월 3일부터 12일까지
발행일: 8월 12일
승객 이름: Antonia Blaine
선실 유형: 특등 선실
⁰⁵갑판 층: 9층

세부 내역	가격
객실 요금 (무료 식사 포함)	450.00유로
식음료 (추가)	84.00유로
오락거리 (추가)	59.00유로
기타:	
사르디니아 패키지 여행	60.00유로
바르셀로나 패키지 여행	125.00유로
합계:	778.00유로

청구: Worldpass 신용카드
신용카드 상의 성명: Antonia Blaine

issue n. 발행; v. 발행하다 deck n. 갑판

---

01 | 육하원칙 문제

해석 양식에는 어떤 정보가 제공되어 있는가?
(A) 유람선 티켓 가격
(B) Ms. Purefoy의 연락처 세부 사항
(C) 인정되는 지불 방법
(D) 도착지 목록

해설 송장의 'Ports of Call'에서 기항지, 즉 유람선이 들르게 되는 지역들을 확인할 수 있으므로 (D)가 정답이다.

Paraphrasing

Ports of Call 기항지 → destinations 도착지

02 | 추론 문제 연계

해석 Ms. Blaine에 대해 암시되는 것은?
(A) 그녀의 여동생의 카드로 지불했다.
(B) 서류에 서명해야 했다.
(C) 환불을 받을 자격이 있었다.
(D) 자신의 예약을 취소했다.

해설 Ms. Blaine이 작성한 이메일을 먼저 확인한다.
[단서 1] 이메일의 'DATE June 12', 'I booked a cruise with your company for my sister and myself from August 3 through August 12. Unfortunately, I need to cancel the booking for my sister.'에서 Ms. Blaine이 6월 12일에 작성한 이메일에서 8월 3일부터 8월 12일까지 여동생과 자신을 위해 유람선을 예약했지만, 여동생의 예약을 취소해야 한다고 하였다.
[단서 2] 송장의 'Reservations canceled within one month of departure are nonrefundable.'에서 출발 한 달 이내의 예약 취소는 환불이 불가능하다고 하였다.
두 단서를 종합할 때, Ms. Blaine은 환불을 받을 자격이 있었음을 추론할 수 있다. 따라서 (C)가 정답이다.

03 | Not/True 문제

해석 Ms. Blaine의 여동생에 대해 언급된 것은?

(A) 유람선 예약에 과다 청구되었다.
(B) 금융 기관에 고용되어 있다.
(C) 출발 시간을 변경했다.
(D) 업무와 관련된 일의 일정을 변경할 것이다.

해설 이메일의 'She has an unexpected commitment at the bank where she works during those dates.'에서 여동생이 일하는 은행에 그 날짜 동안 예상치 못한 일이 생겼다고 하였다. 따라서 (B)가 정답이다.

어휘 overcharge v. 과다 청구하다 financial institution 금융 기관

Paraphrasing

| bank 은행 → financial institution 금융 기관 |

04 | 육하원칙 문제

해석 Ms. Blaine은 무엇에 대해 질문이 있는가?
(A) 어른들을 위한 선상 활동
(B) 그녀의 예정된 출발일
(C) 위약금 지불 방법
(D) 기술 지원 요청

해설 이메일의 'I paid for our trip by credit card, so would it be possible to use that to pay the penalty fee for the change to my booking?'에서 Ms. Blaine이 여행에 대해 신용카드로 지불했으니, 예약 변경에 따른 위약금을 지불하기 위해 그것을 쓸 수 있을지 물었다. 따라서 (C)가 정답이다.

어휘 onboard adj. 선상의, 기내의

05 | 추론 문제 연계

해석 Georgian 유람선 여행사에 대해 결론지을 수 있는 것은?
(A) 예약 정책을 변경했다.
(B) 장기 고객들에게 무료 패키지 여행을 제공한다.
(C) Ms. Blaine의 결제 세부 정보를 이메일로 요청했다.
(D) Ms. Blaine을 다른 객실로 옮겼다.

해설 Georgian 유람선 여행사가 발행한 영수증을 먼저 확인한다.

단서 1 영수증의 'Deck Level: 9'에서 Ms. Blaine이 9층 갑판에서 묵었음을 확인할 수 있다.

단서 2 이메일의 'I would also like to request a cabin with a better view. I am currently in a one on the third level, but I would prefer to be on the eighth level or higher.'에서 Ms. Blaine이 더 좋은 전망의 선실을 요청하고 싶다고 하고, 현재 3층에 있는 객실에 있지만 8층 이상에 있고 싶다고 했음을 확인할 수 있다.

두 단서를 종합할 때, Georgian 유람선 여행사가 Ms. Blaine을 다른 객실로 옮겨 주었음을 추론할 수 있다. 따라서 (D)가 정답이다.

실전모의고사 1

LISTENING TEST
p.102

1 (C)	2 (A)	3 (B)	4 (D)	5 (D)
6 (A)	7 (A)	8 (C)	9 (B)	10 (B)
11 (B)	12 (C)	13 (C)	14 (C)	15 (B)
16 (C)	17 (C)	18 (B)	19 (A)	20 (C)
21 (B)	22 (A)	23 (C)	24 (A)	25 (C)
26 (A)	27 (C)	28 (B)	29 (C)	30 (C)
31 (C)	32 (C)	33 (B)	34 (D)	35 (D)
36 (C)	37 (B)	38 (C)	39 (C)	40 (A)
41 (C)	42 (A)	43 (D)	44 (A)	45 (D)
46 (A)	47 (A)	48 (D)	49 (C)	50 (B)
51 (C)	52 (C)	53 (C)	54 (B)	55 (C)
56 (C)	57 (A)	58 (C)	59 (B)	60 (A)
61 (B)	62 (D)	63 (A)	64 (C)	65 (D)
66 (A)	67 (C)	68 (C)	69 (B)	70 (A)
71 (C)	72 (C)	73 (B)	74 (B)	75 (A)
76 (A)	77 (B)	78 (C)	79 (B)	80 (C)
81 (D)	82 (B)	83 (D)	84 (A)	85 (C)
86 (A)	87 (C)	88 (D)	89 (D)	90 (B)
91 (A)	92 (C)	93 (C)	94 (C)	95 (A)
96 (C)	97 (B)	98 (B)	99 (B)	100 (A)

READING TEST
p.114

101 (A)	102 (C)	103 (A)	104 (D)	105 (A)
106 (A)	107 (C)	108 (C)	109 (C)	110 (B)
111 (B)	112 (B)	113 (B)	114 (D)	115 (B)
116 (B)	117 (C)	118 (B)	119 (C)	120 (C)
121 (C)	122 (D)	123 (C)	124 (D)	125 (C)
126 (B)	127 (C)	128 (C)	129 (C)	130 (B)
131 (C)	132 (A)	133 (B)	134 (C)	135 (C)
136 (D)	137 (B)	138 (D)	139 (C)	140 (A)
141 (A)	142 (D)	143 (D)	144 (C)	145 (A)
146 (B)	147 (C)	148 (B)	149 (A)	150 (C)
151 (C)	152 (C)	153 (B)	154 (C)	155 (D)
156 (C)	157 (A)	158 (B)	159 (D)	160 (D)
161 (B)	162 (C)	163 (D)	164 (C)	165 (B)
166 (B)	167 (C)	168 (A)	169 (D)	170 (D)
171 (B)	172 (D)	173 (B)	174 (D)	175 (D)
176 (B)	177 (C)	178 (C)	179 (C)	180 (D)
181 (D)	182 (C)	183 (B)	184 (B)	185 (D)
186 (A)	187 (D)	188 (B)	189 (D)	190 (D)
191 (C)	192 (A)	193 (C)	194 (C)	195 (D)
196 (D)	197 (B)	198 (B)	199 (D)	200 (D)

PART 1

1 | 1인 사진 캐나다

(A) The woman is wiping down a counter.
(B) The woman is putting a plate in the sink.
(C) The woman is bending over a kitchen appliance.
(D) The woman is resting on a wooden chair.

counter n. 조리대, 계산대   bend over 몸을 ~위로 숙이다
appliance n. (가정용) 기기, 가전제품   rest v. 쉬다

해석 (A) 여자가 조리대를 닦고 있다.
　　 (B) 여자가 접시를 싱크대에 놓고 있다.
　　 (C) 여자가 주방 기기 위로 몸을 숙이고 있다.
　　 (D) 여자가 나무 의자에서 쉬고 있다.

해설 (A) [x] wiping down a counter(조리대를 닦고 있다)는 여자의 동작과 무관하므로 오답이다.
　　 (B) [x] putting a plate in the sink(접시를 싱크대에 놓고 있다)는 여자의 동작과 무관하므로 오답이다. The woman is putting a plate (여자가 접시를 놓고 있다)까지만 듣고 정답으로 선택하지 않도록 주의한다.
　　 (C) [o] 여자가 주방 기기 위로 몸을 숙이고 있는 모습을 가장 잘 묘사한 정답이다.
　　 (D) [x] resting on a wooden chair(나무 의자에서 쉬고 있다)는 여자의 동작과 무관하므로 오답이다. 사진에 있는 의자(chair)를 사용하여 혼동을 주었다.

2 | 2인 이상 사진 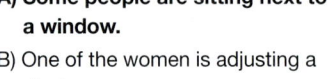 미국

(A) Some people are sitting next to a window.
(B) One of the women is adjusting a clock.
(C) Some people are browsing in a shop.
(D) One of the women is rearranging some tables.

adjust v. 조정하다, 맞추다   browse v. 둘러보다   rearrange v. 재배치하다

해석 (A) 몇몇 사람들이 창문 옆에 앉아 있다.
　　 (B) 여자들 중 한 명이 시계를 조정하고 있다.
　　 (C) 몇몇 사람들이 가게 안을 둘러보고 있다.
　　 (D) 여자들 중 한 명이 몇몇 테이블들을 재배치하고 있다.

해설 (A) [o] 창문 옆에 앉아 있는 사람들의 모습을 가장 잘 묘사한 정답이다.
　　 (B) [x] 사진에 시계를 조정하고 있는(adjusting a clock) 여자가 없으므로 오답이다. 사진에 있는 시계(clock)를 사용하여 혼동을 주었다.
　　 (C) [x] browsing in a shop(가게 안을 둘러보고 있다)은 사람들의 동작과 무관하므로 오답이다.
　　 (D) [x] rearranging some tables(몇몇 테이블들을 재배치하고 있다)는 여자의 동작과 무관하므로 오답이다. 사진에 있는 테이블들(tables)을 사용하여 혼동을 주었다.

3 | 1인 사진

호주

(A) He's pouring water into a pot.
(B) **Utensils have been hung from a rack.**
(C) He's cooking food on a stove.
(D) Some dishes have been stacked on a table.

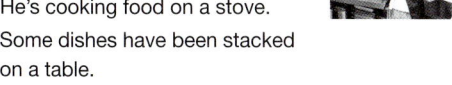

pour v. 붓다 utensil n. 도구, 기구 rack n. 고정대, 받침대
stove n. (요리용) 화로 stack v. 쌓다

해석 (A) 그는 냄비에 물을 붓고 있다.
(B) 도구들이 고정대에 매달려 있다.
(C) 그는 화로에 음식을 요리하고 있다.
(D) 몇몇 접시들이 테이블 위에 쌓여 있다.

해설 (A) [×] pouring water into a pot(냄비에 물을 붓고 있다)은 남자의 동작과 무관하므로 오답이다. 사진에 있는 물(water)을 사용하여 혼동을 주었다.
(B) [○] 도구들이 고정대에 매달려 있는 모습을 가장 잘 묘사한 정답이다.
(C) [×] 사진에 음식(food)이 없으므로 오답이다.
(D) [×] 사진에 접시들(dishes)은 보이지만, 테이블 위에 쌓여 있는(have been stacked on a table) 모습은 아니므로 오답이다.

4 | 2인 이상 사진

미국

(A) They're climbing some steps of a structure.
(B) They're posing for a picture by a tree.
(C) They're picking up branches on a road.
(D) **They're carrying backpacks on a trail.**

structure n. 건축물, 구조물 pick up 줍다 branch n. 나뭇가지
trail n. 등산로, 둘레길

해석 (A) 그들은 건축물의 몇몇 계단들을 오르고 있다.
(B) 그들은 사진을 찍기 위해 나무 옆에서 포즈를 취하고 있다.
(C) 그들은 길에서 나뭇가지들을 줍고 있다.
(D) 그들은 등산로에서 배낭을 메고 있다.

해설 (A) [×] 사진에 계단들(steps)이 없으므로 오답이다. They're climbing(그들이 오르고 있다)까지만 듣고 정답으로 선택하지 않도록 주의한다.
(B) [×] posing(포즈를 취하고 있다)은 사람들의 동작과 무관하므로 오답이다.
(C) [×] picking up(줍고 있다)은 사람들의 동작과 무관하므로 오답이다.
(D) [○] 두 사람이 등산로에서 배낭을 메고 있는 모습을 가장 잘 묘사한 정답이다.

5 | 1인 사진

영국

(A) The man is kneeling in a hallway.
(B) The man is making repairs to a window.
(C) A tool has been set down on a toolbox.
(D) **A helmet has been placed on the floor.**

kneel v. 무릎을 꿇다 hallway n. 복도 repair n. 수리; v. 수리하다
toolbox n. 공구 상자 helmet n. 안전모

해석 (A) 남자가 복도에 무릎을 꿇고 있다.
(B) 남자가 창문을 수리하고 있다.
(C) 도구가 공구 상자에 놓여있다.
(D) 안전모가 바닥에 놓여있다.

해설 (A) [×] kneeling(무릎을 꿇고 있다)은 남자의 동작과 무관하므로 오답이다.
(B) [×] making repairs to a window(창문을 수리하고 있다)는 남자의 동작과 무관하므로 오답이다. The man is making repairs(남자가 수리하고 있다)까지만 듣고 정답으로 선택하지 않도록 주의한다.
(C) [×] 사진에 공구 상자(toolbox)가 없으므로 오답이다. 사진에 있는 도구(tool)를 사용하여 혼동을 주었다.
(D) [○] 안전모가 바닥에 놓여있는 모습을 가장 잘 묘사한 정답이다.

6 | 야외 사진

호주

(A) **A sign is attached to a lamppost.**
(B) Lines are being painted on a road.
(C) A fence has been installed around a yard.
(D) Some cars are pulling into a driveway.

attach v. 붙이다, 첨부하다 lamppost n. 가로등 기둥 install v. 설치하다
yard n. 마당 pull into ~에 들어서다 driveway n. 진입로

해석 (A) 표지판이 가로등 기둥에 붙어 있다.
(B) 선들이 도로에 그려지고 있다.
(C) 울타리가 마당 주위에 설치되어 있다.
(D) 몇몇 차들이 진입로에 들어서고 있다.

해설 (A) [○] 표지판이 가로등 기둥에 붙어 있는 모습을 가장 잘 묘사한 정답이다.
(B) [×] 사진에서 선들(Lines)은 보이지만, 그려지고 있는(being painted) 모습은 아니므로 오답이다.
(C) [×] 사진에 마당(yard)이 없으므로 오답이다. A fence has been installed(울타리가 설치되어 있다)까지만 듣고 정답으로 선택하지 않도록 주의한다.
(D) [×] 사진에서 차들(cars)은 보이지만 진입로에 들어서고 있는(pulling into a driveway) 모습은 아니므로 오답이다.

PART 2

7 | Where 의문문

영국 → 미국

Where should we meet up after work?
(A) **Wait for me at Frye Street Station.**
(B) Both meetings went well.
(C) I work at a department store.

department store 백화점

해석 우리 일을 마치고 어디에서 만나야 할까요?
(A) Frye가 역에서 저를 기다려 주세요.
(B) 두 회의 모두 잘 됐어요.
(C) 저는 백화점에서 일해요.

해설 (A) [○] Frye가 역이라는 말로, 만나야 할 장소를 언급했으므로 정답이다.
(B) [×] meet - meetings의 유사 발음 어휘를 사용하여 혼동을 준 오답이다.
(C) [×] 질문의 work(일)를 '일하다'라는 의미의 동사로 반복 사용하여 혼동을 준 오답이다.

8 | 조동사 의문문
호주 → 미국

Do I need a receipt to return this item?
(A) No. I meant to buy some.
(B) I often shop there.
(C) That won't be necessary.

receipt n. 영수증   return v. 반품하다   mean to ~하려고 하다
necessary adj. 필요한

해석 이 물품을 반품하기 위해서 영수증이 필요한가요?
　　(A) 아니요. 저는 몇 개를 사려고 했어요.
　　(B) 저는 그곳에서 자주 쇼핑해요.
　　(C) 그것은 필요하지 않을 거예요.

해설 (A) [×] 질문의 receipt(영수증)와 관련 있는 buy(사다)를 사용하여 혼동을 준 오답이다. No까지만 듣고 정답으로 고르지 않도록 주의한다.
　　(B) [×] 질문의 receipt(영수증)와 관련 있는 shop(쇼핑하다)을 사용하여 혼동을 준 오답이다.
　　(C) [○] 그것은 필요하지 않을 거라는 말로, 반품을 위해 영수증이 필요하지 않음을 전달했으므로 정답이다.

9 | 평서문
호주 → 영국

We'll have your table ready shortly.
(A) It seats four to six people.
(B) I'm not in a hurry.
(C) The daily special sounds good.

shortly adv. 곧   in a hurry 바쁜

해석 당신의 테이블을 곧 준비해 드리겠습니다.
　　(A) 그것은 4~6인용이에요.
　　(B) 저는 바쁘지 않아요.
　　(C) 일일 특선이 좋을 것 같아요.

해설 (A) [×] 질문의 table(테이블)에서 연상할 수 있는 인원 수와 관련된 four to six people(4~6인)을 사용하여 혼동을 준 오답이다.
　　(B) [○] 바쁘지 않다는 말로, 테이블을 서둘러 준비할 필요가 없음을 간접적으로 전달했으므로 정답이다.
　　(C) [×] 질문의 table(테이블)에서 연상할 수 있는 식사와 관련된 daily special(일일 특선)을 사용하여 혼동을 준 오답이다.

10 | How 의문문
영국 → 호주

How can I make a payment for my streaming service?
(A) She's not able to pay it this afternoon.
(B) You can do that on our Web site.
(C) Yes. There are hundreds of shows.

make a payment 납부하다, 지불하다   show n. 방송

해석 제 스트리밍 서비스 대금을 어떻게 납부하면 되나요?
　　(A) 그녀는 오늘 오후에 그것을 납부할 수 없어요.
　　(B) 저희 웹사이트에서 하실 수 있습니다.
　　(C) 네. 수백 개의 방송들이 있어요.

해설 (A) [×] payment - pay의 유사 발음 어휘를 사용하여 혼동을 준 오답이다.
　　(B) [○] 웹사이트에서 할 수 있다는 말로, 스트리밍 서비스 대금을 납부하는 방법을 언급했으므로 정답이다.
　　(C) [×] 의문사 의문문에 Yes로 응답했으므로 오답이다. 질문의 streaming service(스트리밍 서비스)와 관련 있는 shows(방송들)를 사용하여 혼동을 주었다.

11 | 부정 의문문
미국 → 캐나다

Can't the deadline for the report be extended by a day?
(A) Around that time.
(B) The deadline is fixed.
(C) Last Monday.

deadline n. 마감 기한   extend v. 연장하다

해석 보고서 마감 기한이 하루 연장될 수 없나요?
　　(A) 그때쯤이요.
　　(B) 마감 기한은 정해져 있어요.
　　(C) 지난 월요일이요.

해설 (A) [×] 질문의 deadline(마감 기한)에서 연상할 수 있는 마감 시점과 관련된 time(때)을 사용하여 혼동을 준 오답이다.
　　(B) [○] 마감 기한은 정해져 있다는 말로, 보고서 마감 기한이 하루 연장될 수 없음을 간접적으로 전달했으므로 정답이다.
　　(C) [×] 질문의 deadline(마감 기한)에서 연상할 수 있는 마감 시점과 관련된 Last Monday(지난 월요일)를 사용하여 혼동을 준 오답이다.

12 | 평서문
영국 → 호주

The demonstration of our new product went extremely well this morning.
(A) The exposition continues throughout the week.
(B) A limited number of products are still available.
(C) The director seemed impressed.

exposition n. 박람회   available adj. 구할 수 있는, 이용 가능한
impressed adj. 인상 깊게 생각하는, 감명을 받은

해석 오늘 아침에 우리 신제품 시연이 매우 순조롭게 진행되었어요.
　　(A) 박람회는 일주일 내내 계속돼요.
　　(B) 한정된 수의 제품들을 아직 구할 수 있어요.
　　(C) 관리자가 인상 깊게 생각하는 것 같았어요.

해설 (A) [×] 질문의 new product(신제품)와 관련 있는 exposition(박람회)을 사용하여 혼동을 준 오답이다.
　　(B) [×] 질문의 product를 products로 반복 사용하여 혼동을 준 오답이다.
　　(C) [○] 관리자가 인상 깊게 생각하는 것 같았다는 말로 추가 의견을 전달했으므로 정답이다.

13 | Why 의문문
영국 → 캐나다

Why was our meeting delayed for over an hour?
(A) I'm glad you were able to attend.
(B) There's still time to postpone it.
(C) The conference room wasn't available.

attend v. 참석하다   postpone v. 연기하다, 미루다
conference room 회의실

해석 우리 회의는 왜 한 시간 넘게 연기되었나요?
　　(A) 당신이 참석할 수 있었다니 다행이네요.
　　(B) 아직 그것을 연기할 시간이 있어요.
　　(C) 회의실이 이용 가능하지 않았어요.

해설 (A) [×] 질문의 meeting(회의)에서 연상할 수 있는 행동과 관련된 attend(참석하다)를 사용하여 혼동을 준 오답이다.
　　(B) [×] delay(연기하다)와 같은 의미인 postpone을 사용하여 혼동을 준 오답이다.

(C) [o] 회의실이 이용 가능하지 않았다는 말로, 회의가 한 시간 넘게 연기된 이유를 언급했으므로 정답이다.

14 | Who 의문문
미국 → 호주

Who organized the seating arrangement?
(A) I can ask the manager.
(B) A seat near the entrance.
(C) No. I won't have time.

organize v. 준비하다   seating arrangement 좌석 배치   entrance n. 입구

해석 누가 좌석 배치를 준비했나요?
(A) 제가 관리자에게 물어볼 수 있어요.
(B) 입구 근처의 좌석이요.
(C) 아니요. 저는 시간이 없을 거예요.
해설 (A) [o] 관리자에게 물어볼 수 있다는 말로, 누가 좌석 배치를 준비했는지 모른다는 것을 간접적으로 전달했으므로 정답이다.
(B) [x] seating - seat의 유사 발음 어휘를 사용하여 혼동을 준 오답이다.
(C) [x] 의문사 의문문에 No로 응답했으므로 오답이다.

15 | 선택 의문문
미국 → 캐나다

Will you be presenting to the board today or tomorrow?
(A) We just shipped it today.
(B) This afternoon, if possible.
(C) My membership has expired.

present v. 발표하다   board n. 이사회   ship v. 보내다, 운송하다
expire v. 만료되다

해석 당신은 이사회에 오늘 발표할 것인가요 아니면 내일 발표할 것인가요?
(A) 우리는 오늘 막 그것을 보냈어요.
(B) 가능하다면 오늘 오후요.
(C) 제 회원권은 만료되었어요.
해설 (A) [x] 질문의 today를 반복 사용하여 혼동을 준 오답이다.
(B) [o] 가능하다면 오늘 오후라는 말로, 오늘을 선택했으므로 정답이다.
(C) [x] 이사회에 오늘 발표할 것인지 내일 발표할 것인지를 물었는데, 이와 관련이 없는 회원권이 만료되었다고 응답했으므로 오답이다.

16 | How 의문문
호주 → 영국

How can we improve the employee evaluations?
(A) How many people should we hire?
(B) Your proposal is very interesting.
(C) We should do them more often.

improve v. 개선하다   evaluation n. 평가   proposal n. 제안서

해석 우리가 직원 평가를 어떻게 개선할 수 있을까요?
(A) 우리가 얼마나 많은 사람들을 고용해야 하나요?
(B) 당신의 제안서는 매우 흥미로워요.
(C) 그것들을 더 자주 해야 해요.
해설 (A) [x] 질문의 employee(직원)에서 연상할 수 있는 행동과 관련된 hire(고용하다)를 사용하여 혼동을 준 오답이다.
(B) [x] 직원 평가를 어떻게 개선할 수 있을지를 물었는데, 이와 관련이 없는 제안서가 매우 흥미롭다고 응답했으므로 오답이다.
(C) [o] 그것들을 더 자주 해야 한다는 말로, 직원 평가를 개선할 수 있는 방법을 언급했으므로 정답이다.

17 | Where 의문문
캐나다 → 영국

Where are you likely to meet your client?
(A) Yes. I'd like to go soon.
(B) The meeting is at 9 A.M.
(C) Probably in San Alito.

likely adj. ~할 것 같은   probably adv. 아마

해석 당신의 고객을 어디에서 만날 것 같은가요?
(A) 네, 저는 곧 가려고 해요.
(B) 그 회의는 오전 9시에 있어요.
(C) 아마 San Alito에서요.
해설 (A) [x] 의문사 의문문에 Yes로 응답했으므로 오답이다. likely - like의 유사 발음 어휘를 사용하여 혼동을 주었다.
(B) [x] 고객을 어디에서 만날 것인지를 물었는데, 시간으로 응답했으므로 오답이다. 질문의 Where를 When으로 혼동하여 이를 정답으로 선택하지 않도록 주의한다.
(C) [o] 아마 San Alito에서라는 말로, 고객을 만날 장소를 언급했으므로 정답이다.

18 | 부가 의문문
미국 → 캐나다

You haven't approved the budget increase yet, have you?
(A) The stock price has increased.
(B) The director will make the final decision.
(C) Our fund-raiser was a great success.

approve v. 승인하다   budget n. 예산   increase n. 인상, 증가
stock price 주가   fund-raiser n. 모금 행사

해석 당신은 예산 인상을 아직 승인하지 않았죠, 그렇죠?
(A) 주가가 인상되었어요.
(B) 관리자가 최종 결정을 할 거예요.
(C) 저희 모금 행사는 대성공이었어요.
해설 (A) [x] 질문의 increase를 increased로 반복 사용하여 혼동을 준 오답이다.
(B) [o] 관리자가 최종 결정을 할 것이라는 말로, 자신이 예산 인상을 승인하지 않았음을 간접적으로 전달했으므로 정답이다.
(C) [x] 예산 인상을 아직 승인하지 않았는지를 물었는데, 이와 관련이 없는 모금 행사가 대성공이었다고 응답했으므로 오답이다.

19 | Be동사 의문문
호주 → 영국

Are you going to buy a new computer?
(A) My current one is just fine.
(B) I installed the software application.
(C) You can pay with a credit card.

current adj. 현재의, 지금의   install v. 설치하다

해석 당신은 새 컴퓨터를 살 것인가요?
(A) 제 현재 것이 딱 괜찮아요.
(B) 저는 그 소프트웨어 애플리케이션을 설치했어요.
(C) 신용카드로 지불하실 수 있어요.
해설 (A) [o] 현재 것이 딱 괜찮다는 말로, 새 컴퓨터를 사지 않을 것임을 간접적으로 전달했으므로 정답이다.
(B) [x] 질문의 computer(컴퓨터)와 관련 있는 software application (소프트웨어 애플리케이션)을 사용하여 혼동을 준 오답이다.
(C) [x] 질문의 buy(사다)와 관련 있는 pay(지불하다)를 사용하여 혼동을 준 오답이다.

20 | Who 의문문
캐나다 → 호주

Who came up with our company's new slogan?
(A) I will come down now.
(B) It was very effective.
(C) Has it been changed?

come up with 제안하다, 생각해 내다   slogan n. 표어
effective adj. 효과적인

해석 누가 우리 회사의 새로운 표어를 제안했나요?
(A) 제가 지금 내려갈게요.
(B) 그것은 매우 효과적이었어요.
(C) 그것이 변경되었나요?

해설 (A) [×] 질문의 came을 come으로 반복 사용하여 혼동을 준 오답이다.
(B) [×] 질문의 slogan(표어)을 나타낼 수 있는 It을 사용하여 혼동을 준 오답이다.
(C) [○] 그것이 변경되었냐고 되물어, 회사의 새로운 표어를 누가 제안했는지 모른다는 것을 간접적으로 전달했으므로 정답이다.

21 | 조동사 의문문
영국 → 캐나다

Did many people attend the product launch?
(A) It was released on March 15.
(B) The venue was packed.
(C) It includes many exciting features.

launch n. 출시   release v. 출시하다; n. 출시   venue n. 장소
packed adj. 사람으로 꽉 찬

해석 많은 사람들이 제품 출시에 참석했나요?
(A) 그것은 3월 15일에 출시되었어요.
(B) 그 장소는 사람으로 꽉 찼어요.
(C) 그것은 많은 흥미로운 기능을 포함해요.

해설 (A) [×] launch(출시)와 관련 있는 release(출시하다)를 사용하여 혼동을 준 오답이다.
(B) [○] 그 장소는 사람으로 꽉 찼다는 말로, 많은 사람들이 제품 출시에 참석했음을 간접적으로 전달했으므로 정답이다.
(C) [×] 질문의 product(제품)에서 연상할 수 있는 features(기능)를 사용하여 혼동을 준 오답이다.

22 | When 의문문
호주 → 미국

When would you like to arrange an appointment with Mr. Jones?
(A) I'll have to check with my assistant.
(B) That time will be convenient.
(C) Holston Community Center.

arrange an appointment 약속을 잡다   convenient adj. 편리한

해석 Mr. Jones와 언제 약속을 잡고 싶으신가요?
(A) 저의 비서와 확인을 해야 해요.
(B) 그 시간이 편리할 거예요.
(C) Holston 지역 문화 센터요.

해설 (A) [○] 비서와 확인을 해야 한다는 말로, 약속을 잡고 싶은 시기를 아직 정하지 않았다는 것을 간접적으로 전달했으므로 정답이다.
(B) [×] 질문의 appointment(약속)에서 연상할 수 있는 약속 시간과 관련된 time(시간)을 사용하여 혼동을 준 오답이다.
(C) [×] 언제 약속을 잡고 싶은지를 물었는데, 이와 관련이 없는 장소로 응답했으므로 오답이다. 질문의 When을 Where로 혼동하여 이를 정답으로 선택하지 않도록 주의한다.

23 | 조동사 의문문
캐나다 → 영국

Do you repair devices at this location?
(A) Our latest model is very popular.
(B) The store is open until 8 P.M.
(C) We only do sales.

repair v. 수리하다   device n. 기기   location n. 지점, 장소
latest adj. 최신의

해석 이 지점에서 기기들을 수리하나요?
(A) 저희의 최신 모델은 매우 인기 있어요.
(B) 그 가게는 오후 8시까지 열어요.
(C) 저희는 오직 판매만 해요.

해설 (A) [×] 질문의 devices(기기들)에서 연상할 수 있는 제품 모델과 관련된 model(모델)을 사용하여 혼동을 준 오답이다.
(B) [×] 질문의 location(지점)에서 연상할 수 있는 장소와 관련된 store(가게)를 사용하여 혼동을 준 오답이다.
(C) [○] 오직 판매만 한다는 말로, 이 지점에서 기기들을 수리하지 않음을 간접적으로 전달했으므로 정답이다.

24 | 요청 의문문
호주 → 캐나다

Can I renew my apartment lease for another year?
(A) The rent will go up slightly.
(B) A spare bedroom would be nice.
(C) No. We never got a receipt.

renew v. 갱신하다   lease n. 임대차 계약   rent n. 임대료   slightly adv. 약간
spare adj. 여분의   receipt n. 영수증

해석 제 아파트의 임대차 계약을 한 해 더 갱신할 수 있을까요?
(A) 임대료가 약간 오를 거예요.
(B) 여분 침실이 있으면 좋을 것 같아요.
(C) 아니요. 우리는 영수증을 받은 적이 없어요.

해설 (A) [○] 임대료가 약간 오를 것이라는 말로, 임대차 계약을 한 해 더 갱신할 수 있음을 간접적으로 전달했으므로 정답이다.
(B) [×] 질문의 apartment(아파트)와 관련 있는 bedroom(침실)을 사용하여 혼동을 준 오답이다.
(C) [×] 질문의 lease(임대차 계약)에서 연상할 수 있는 receipt(영수증)를 사용하여 혼동을 준 오답이다. No까지만 듣고 정답으로 고르지 않도록 주의한다.

25 | Which 의문문
영국 → 호주

Which event are we catering on Wednesday evening?
(A) Some people arrived late.
(B) We don't have anything booked.
(C) Several more plates are needed.

cater v. 음식을 공급하다   book v. 예약하다

해석 우리는 수요일 저녁에 어느 행사에 음식을 공급하나요?
(A) 몇몇 사람들이 늦게 도착했어요.
(B) 예약된 것이 아무것도 없어요.
(C) 몇 개의 접시들이 더 필요해요.

해설 (A) [×] 수요일 저녁에 어떤 행사에 음식을 공급하는지를 물었는데, 이와 관련이 없는 사람들이 늦게 도착했다는 말로 응답했으므로 오답이다.

(B) [o] 예약된 것이 아무것도 없다는 말로, 수요일 저녁에 아무 행사에도 음식을 공급하지 않음을 간접적으로 전달했으므로 정답이다.
(C) [×] catering(음식을 공급하다)에서 연상할 수 있는 식기와 관련된 plates(접시들)를 사용하여 혼동을 준 오답이다.

26 | Why 의문문
캐나다 → 영국

Why did Ken leave the delivery van outside the post office?
(A) The parking lot is completely full.
(B) The mail is delivered every day.
(C) He left it there at around noon.

leave v. 두다 delivery n. 배송 full adj. 가득 찬

해석 Ken은 왜 배송 밴을 우체국 밖에 두었나요?
(A) 주차장이 완전히 가득 찼어요.
(B) 우편은 매일 배송돼요.
(C) 그는 정오쯤에 그걸 그곳에 두었어요.
해설 (A) [o] 주차장이 완전히 가득 찼다는 말로, 배송 밴을 우체국 밖에 둔 이유를 간접적으로 전달했으므로 정답이다.
(B) [×] delivery - delivered의 유사 발음 어휘를 사용하여 혼동을 준 오답이다.
(C) [×] 질문의 delivery van(배송 밴)을 나타낼 수 있는 it을 사용하여 혼동을 준 오답이다.

27 | 평서문
미국 → 호주

An expert is coming in tomorrow to discuss stress management techniques.
(A) He had some very good advice to share.
(B) That was such an inspiring remark.
(C) I hope our employees find it helpful.

management n. 관리 technique n. 기법 advice n. 조언
inspiring adj. 영감을 주는 remark n. 말, 발언 find v. ~라고 생각하다

해석 내일 스트레스 관리 기법을 논의하기 위해 전문가가 와요.
(A) 그는 공유할만한 아주 좋은 몇몇 조언을 가지고 있었어요.
(B) 그것은 정말 영감을 주는 말이었어요.
(C) 우리 직원들이 그것을 유용하다고 생각하면 좋겠어요.
해설 (A) [×] 질문의 expert(전문가)를 나타낼 수 있는 He를 사용하여 혼동을 준 오답이다.
(B) [×] 내일 스트레스 관리 기법을 논의하기 위해 전문가가 온다고 말했는데, 이와 관련이 없는 그것은 영감을 주는 말이었다는 내용으로 응답했으므로 오답이다.
(C) [o] 직원들이 그것을 유용하다고 생각하면 좋겠다는 말로, 내일 스트레스 관리 기법을 논의하기 위해 전문가가 온다는 말에 추가 의견을 전달했으므로 정답이다.

28 | 부가 의문문
캐나다 → 미국

The EXS smartphone is going to be recalled, isn't it?
(A) Yes. We're all attending.
(B) That depends on the final inspection report.
(C) It has a very big screen.

recall v. 회수하다 inspection n. 검사

해석 EXS 스마트폰은 회수될 거예요, 그렇지 않나요?
(A) 네, 저희는 모두 참석해요.
(B) 그건 최종 검사 보고서에 달려 있어요.
(C) 그것은 매우 큰 화면을 가지고 있어요.
해설 (A) [×] 스마트폰이 회수될 것인지를 물었는데, 이와 관련이 없는 모두 참석한다는 내용으로 응답했으므로 오답이다. Yes까지만 듣고 정답으로 고르지 않도록 주의한다.
(B) [o] 최종 검사 보고서에 달려 있다는 말로, EXS 스마트폰이 회수되는지 모른다는 것을 간접적으로 전달했으므로 정답이다.
(C) [×] 질문의 smartphone(스마트폰)과 관련 있는 big screen(큰 화면)을 사용하여 혼동을 준 오답이다.

29 | What 의문문
캐나다 → 미국

What changes do you want in the brochure?
(A) I've read it already.
(B) There's a box full of them.
(C) It's not up to me.

brochure n. 소책자 be up to ~가 할 일이다, ~에 달려 있다

해석 당신은 소책자에서 어떤 변화를 원하시나요?
(A) 저는 그것을 이미 읽었어요.
(B) 그것들로 가득한 상자가 있어요.
(C) 제가 할 일이 아니에요.
해설 (A) [×] 질문의 brochure(소책자)와 관련 있는 read(읽었다)를 사용하여 혼동을 준 오답이다.
(B) [×] 소책자에서 어떤 변화를 원하는지를 물었는데, 이와 관련이 없는 그것들로 가득한 상자가 있다는 내용으로 응답했으므로 오답이다.
(C) [o] 자신이 할 일이 아니라는 말로, 소책자에서 어떤 변화를 원하는지 모른다는 것을 간접적으로 전달했으므로 정답이다.

30 | 평서문
미국 → 캐나다

Your insurance expires at the end of April.
(A) Check the expiration date.
(B) I didn't like the ending, either.
(C) Can I just extend it now?

insurance n. 보험 expire v. 만료되다 expiration date 유효 기간
extend v. 연장하다

해석 귀하의 보험이 4월 말에 만료됩니다.
(A) 유효 기간을 확인하세요.
(B) 저도 결말이 마음에 들지 않았어요.
(C) 그것을 그냥 지금 연장해도 되나요?
해설 (A) [×] expires - expiration의 유사 발음 어휘를 사용하여 혼동을 준 오답이다.
(B) [×] end - ending의 유사 발음 어휘를 사용하여 혼동을 준 오답이다.
(C) [o] 그것을 지금 연장해도 되냐고 되물어, 보험 만료에 대한 추가 정보를 요구한 정답이다.

31 | When 의문문
미국 → 영국

When was this package dropped off?
(A) You can drop me off at home.
(B) Shipping fees vary.
(C) I wasn't here when it arrived.

package n. 소포 drop off 배송하다, (차로) 내려주다 shipping fee 배송료
vary v. 서로 다르다

해석 이 소포는 언제 배송되었나요?
(A) 집에 내려 주시면 돼요.
(B) 배송료는 서로 달라요.
(C) 그것이 도착했을 때 저는 여기 없었어요.

해설 (A) [×] 질문의 dropped off를 drop off로 반복 사용하여 혼동을 준 오답이다.
(B) [×] 질문의 package(소포)와 관련 있는 shipping fees(배송료)를 사용하여 혼동을 준 오답이다.
(C) [○] 소포가 도착했을 때, 자신이 여기에 없었다는 말로, 소포가 언제 배송되었는지 모름을 간접적으로 전달했으므로 정답이다.

PART 3

[32-34] 영국 → 호주

Questions 32-34 refer to the following conversation.

W: Are you still working on that agreement for Harper Express? Let's go grab lunch. It's almost noon, and I heard there's a new food truck just down the block.
M: You can go without me. ³²I'm working on a legal document for another client I was assigned to. ³³The deadline's at 4 P.M. and I'm worried I won't have time to finish if I take a break for lunch.
W: Are you sure? It shouldn't take long. ³⁴We could get takeout and be back in less than 10 minutes.

agreement n. 계약서　legal adj. 법률의　deadline n. 마감 시간, 마감일
takeout n. 포장 음식

해석 32-34번은 다음 대화에 관한 문제입니다.
여: 아직 Harper Express사의 계약서를 작업 중이신가요? 점심 먹으러 가요. 정오가 다 되어 가고, 한 블록 아래에 새로운 푸드트럭이 있다고 들었어요.
남: 저 없이 가셔도 돼요. ³²저는 제가 배정받은 다른 고객을 위해 법률 문서를 작업하고 있어요. ³³마감 시간이 오후 4시인데 제가 점심 식사를 위해 휴식을 취하면 끝낼 시간이 없을까 봐 걱정이에요.
여: 정말요? 오래 안 걸릴 거예요. ³⁴포장 음식을 가지고 10분 이내로 돌아올 수 있어요.

32 | 화자 문제

해석 화자들은 어디에서 일하는 것 같은가?
(A) 식당에서
(B) 선적 회사에서
(C) 법률 사무소에서
(D) 소매점에서

해설 대화에서 신분 및 직업과 관련된 표현을 놓치지 않고 듣는다. 남자가 "I'm working on a legal document for another client I was assigned to."라며 자신이 배정받은 다른 고객을 위해 법률 문서를 작업하고 있다고 한 것을 통해 화자들이 법률 사무소에서 일함을 알 수 있다. 따라서 (C)가 정답이다.

어휘 shipping n. 선적　retail outlet 소매점

33 | 문제점 문제

해석 남자는 무슨 문제를 언급하는가?
(A) 몇몇 음식을 좋아하지 않는다.
(B) 마감 시간에 맞추지 못할지도 모른다.
(C) 업무를 받지 못했다.
(D) 고객 회의를 놓쳤다.

해설 남자의 말에서 부정적인 표현이 언급된 주변을 주의 깊게 듣는다. 남자가 "The deadline's at 4 P.M. and I'm worried I won't have time to finish if I take a break for lunch."라며 마감 시간이 오후 4시인데 자신이 점심 식사를 위해 휴식을 취하면 끝낼 시간이 없을까 봐 걱정이라고 하였다. 따라서 (B)가 정답이다.

어휘 meet a deadline 마감 시간에 맞추다　assignment n. 업무, 과제
client n. 고객

34 | 제안 문제

해석 여자는 무엇을 제안하는가?
(A) 마감 시간을 변경하기
(B) 예약하기
(C) 일을 집에 가져가기
(D) 음식을 가져오기

해설 여자의 말에서 제안과 관련된 표현이 언급된 주변을 주의 깊게 듣는다. 여자가 "We could get takeout"이라며 남자에게 포장 음식을 가져올 것을 제안하였다. 따라서 (D)가 정답이다.

어휘 make a reservation 예약하다

[35-37] 미국 → 캐나다

Questions 35-37 refer to the following conversation.

W: Alex, ³⁵I'm planning to attend the Global Business Summit on Wednesday. There will be many industry leaders giving presentations. Why don't you join me?
M: I have a client meeting at 1 P.M., but I'll be free after. ³⁶What time does it start, exactly?
W: The registration opens at 2 P.M., and the first keynote speaker begins at 3.
M: OK. I'll head over right after my meeting. That would be at around 2:30 P.M.
W: Great! ³⁷Just give me a call when you get there, so I can tell you where I am.

summit n. 수뇌 회담　registration n. 등록, 접수
keynote speaker 기조연설자　head over 가다, 향하다

해석 35-37번은 다음 대화에 관한 문제입니다.
여: Alex, ³⁵저는 수요일에 글로벌 비즈니스 수뇌 회담에 참석할 계획이에요. 많은 업계 지도자들이 발표를 할 거예요. 저와 함께하시는 게 어때요?
남: 저는 오후 1시에 고객 미팅이 있지만, 그 이후에는 한가할 거예요. ³⁶정확히 몇 시에 시작하나요?
여: 등록은 오후 2시에 시작하고 첫 번째 기조연설자는 3시에 시작해요.
남: 알겠어요. 미팅 직후에 갈게요. 오후 2시 30분쯤 될 거예요.
여: 좋아요! ³⁷제가 어디 있는지 알려드릴 수 있도록, 도착하면 전화 주세요.

35 | 다음에 할 일 문제

해석 수요일에 무슨 일이 일어날 것인가?
(A) 무역 박람회
(B) 회사 오찬
(C) 팀워크 행사
(D) 비즈니스 회의

해설 질문의 핵심 어구(Wednesday)가 언급된 주변을 주의 깊게 듣는다. 여자가 "I'm planning to attend the Global Business Summit on Wednesday. There will be many industry leaders giving presentations"라며 수요일에 글로벌 비즈니스 수뇌 회담에 참석할 계획이고, 많은 업계 지도자들이 발표를 할 것이라고 한 것을 통해 수요일에 비즈니스 회의가 있을 것임을 알 수 있다. 따라서 (D)가 정답이다.

어휘 trade fair 무역 박람회 luncheon n. 오찬

Paraphrasing

the Global Business Summit 글로벌 비즈니스 수뇌 회담 → A business conference 비즈니스 회의

36 | 특정 세부 사항 문제

해석 남자는 무엇을 알고 싶어 하는가?
(A) 장소가 어디에 위치해 있는지
(B) 다른 사람은 누가 참석할지
(C) 행사가 언제 시작할지
(D) 등록비가 얼마인지

해설 질문의 핵심 어구(man want to know)와 관련된 내용을 주의 깊게 듣는다. 남자가 여자에게 "What time does it start, exactly?"라며 정확히 몇 시에 시작하는지 물었다. 따라서 (C)가 정답이다.

어휘 venue n. 장소 attend v. 참석하다

37 | 이유 문제

해석 남자는 왜 여자에게 전화해야 하는가?
(A) 약속을 잡기 위해
(B) 위치를 알아내기 위해
(C) 일정을 확인하기 위해
(D) 태워주는 것을 요청하기 위해

해설 질문의 핵심 어구(give ~ a call)가 언급된 주변을 주의 깊게 듣는다. 여자가 "Just give me a call when you get there, so I can tell you where I am."이라며 자신이 어디 있는지 알려줄 수 있도록 도착하면 전화하라고 하였다. 따라서 (B)가 정답이다.

어휘 determine v. 알아내다 request v. 요청하다 ride n. 태우고 가기

[38-40]

영국 → 캐나다

Questions 38-40 refer to the following conversation.

W: Hey, Larry. ³⁸**How are things going here at the ticketing office? I just want to see if the new software we installed is working OK.**
M: ³⁹**Oh, it's been wonderful! It is easy to use and saves a lot of time.** I've been able to serve twice as many customers as usual this morning.
W: That's good news. I was hoping it would make your job easier. Do you think any other agents will need training on how to use it?
M: Yes. ⁴⁰**Two new employees are starting next week, so I'll have to provide them with detailed directions.**

ticketing n. 매표 install v. 설치하다 agent n. 직원, 관리자
direction n. 사용법

해석
38-40번은 다음 대화에 관한 문제입니다.
여: 안녕하세요, Larry. ³⁸이곳 매표소 일은 어떤가요? 우리가 설치한 새 소프트웨어가 잘 작동하고 있는지만 확인해 보고 싶어요.
남: ³⁹아, 아주 좋아요! 그것은 사용하기도 쉽고 시간을 많이 절약해 줘요. 저는 오늘 아침에 평소보다 두 배나 많은 고객들을 응대할 수 있었어요.
여: 그거 좋은 소식이네요. 그것이 당신의 작업을 더 수월하게 해 주길 바라고 있었어요. 다른 직원들이 그것을 어떻게 사용하는지에 대한 훈련이 필요할까요?
남: 네. ⁴⁰다음 주부터 신입 직원 두 명이 일을 시작해서, 제가 그들에게 상세한 사용법을 제공해 주어야 할 거예요.

38 | 목적 문제

해석 여자는 왜 사무실을 방문했는가?
(A) 입사 지원자들의 면접을 보기 위해
(B) 고객들을 응대하기 위해
(C) 프로그램을 확인하기 위해
(D) 일정에 대해 물어보기 위해

해설 여자가 사무실을 방문한 목적을 묻는 문제이므로, 대화의 초반을 반드시 듣는다. 여자가 "How are things going here at the ticketing office? I just want to see if the new software we installed is working OK."라며 이곳 매표소 일은 어떤지 물은 뒤, 설치한 새 소프트웨어가 잘 작동하고 있는지 확인해 보고 싶다고 했으므로, 여자가 사무실을 방문한 목적은 프로그램을 확인하기 위함임을 알 수 있다. 따라서 (C)가 정답이다.

어휘 candidate n. 지원자, 후보자 check on (이상이 없는지를) 확인하다

39 | 이유 문제

해석 남자는 왜 기뻐하는가?
(A) 이제 일자리가 났다.
(B) 요청이 승인되었다.
(C) 컴퓨터 프로그램이 잘 작동한다.
(D) 고객이 긍정적인 의견을 주었다.

해설 질문의 핵심 어구(pleased)와 관련된 내용을 주의 깊게 듣는다. 남자가 "Oh, it[new software]'s been wonderful! It is easy to use and saves a lot of time."이라며 새 소프트웨어가 아주 좋다고 한 후, 사용하기도 쉽고 시간을 많이 절약해 준다고 하였다. 따라서 (C)가 정답이다.

Paraphrasing

easy to use and saves ~ time 사용하기 쉽고 시간을 절약하다 → works well 잘 작동하다

40 | 다음에 할 일 문제

해석 남자는 다음 주에 무엇을 할 것 같은가?
(A) 몇몇 직원들을 교육한다.
(B) 부서를 옮긴다.
(C) 시스템을 업그레이드한다.
(D) 새로운 직무를 시작한다.

해설 남자의 말에서 질문의 핵심 어구(next week)가 언급된 주변을 주의 깊게 듣는다. 남자가 "Two new employees are starting next week, so I'll have to provide them with detailed directions."라며 다음 주부터 신입 직원 두 명이 일을 시작해서 자신이 그들에게 상세한 사용법을 제공해 주어야 할 것이라고 하였다. 따라서 (A)가 정답이다.

어휘 personnel n. 직원들 transfer v. 옮기다, 전송하다 position n. 직무, 직위

Paraphrasing

employees 직원들 → personnel 직원들

[41-43]

호주 → 영국

Questions 41-43 refer to the following conversation.

M: Ms. Ellison, ⁴¹is it possible for us to get new computer monitors for the office? The graphic designers say the quality of our current computer screens is rather poor. It's negatively impacting their work.

W: I've been planning to do that for some time. We couldn't afford to upgrade them in the past, but we should have enough funds now. ⁴²I'll ask the office manager to order new monitors for all the designers.

M: They will certainly appreciate it. ⁴³And if you're unsure about which models to get, I can ask the staff for their opinions on the matter.

current adj. 현재의, 지금의   impact v. 영향을 주다   fund n. 자금, 기금

해석
41-43번은 다음 대화에 관한 문제입니다.

남: Ms. Ellison, ⁴¹저희가 사무실에 둘 새 컴퓨터 모니터들을 구매하는 것이 가능할까요? 그래픽 디자이너들이 우리의 현재 컴퓨터 화면들의 품질이 다소 좋지 않다고 말해요. 그게 그들의 작업에 부정적인 영향을 주고 있어요.

여: 머지않아 그것을 할 계획이었어요. 우리가 과거에는 그것들을 업그레이드 할 여유가 없었지만, 이젠 충분한 자금이 있을 거예요. ⁴²사무장에게 모든 디자이너를 위해 새로운 모니터들을 주문하도록 요청할게요.

남: 그들은 틀림없이 그것을 고맙게 생각할 거예요. ⁴³그리고 어떤 모델을 사야 할지 잘 모르시겠다면, 제가 직원들에게 그 사안에 대한 그들의 의견을 물어볼 수 있어요.

41 | 주제 문제

해석 대화의 주제는 무엇인가?
(A) 견본 설계 계획
(B) 품질 관리 방법
(C) 장비 교체
(D) 소프트웨어 설치

해설 대화의 주제를 묻는 문제이므로, 대화의 초반을 반드시 듣는다. 남자가 "is it possible for us to get new computer monitors for the office?"라며 사무실에 둘 새 컴퓨터 모니터들을 구매하는 것이 가능할지를 물은 후, 컴퓨터 모니터 교체에 관한 내용으로 대화가 이어지고 있다. 따라서 (C)가 정답이다.

어휘 prototype n. 견본, 원형

42 | 특정 세부 사항 문제

해석 여자는 사무장에게 무엇을 하도록 요청할 것인가?
(A) 주문을 한다.
(B) 디자이너를 고용한다.
(C) 업무를 취소한다.
(D) 모델을 선택한다.

해설 질문의 핵심 어구(ask the office manager to do)와 관련된 내용을 주의 깊게 듣는다. 여자가 "I'll ask the office manager to order new monitors for all the designers."라며 사무장에게 모든 디자이너를 위해 새로운 모니터들을 주문하도록 요청하겠다고 하였다. 따라서 (A)가 정답이다.

어휘 assignment n. 업무

43 | 특정 세부 사항 문제

해석 남자는 무엇을 할 수 있다고 말하는가?
(A) 직원들의 불평을 처리한다.
(B) 제출 마감일을 연장한다.
(C) 프로젝트를 위한 기금을 요청한다.
(D) 직원의 선호 사항을 알아낸다.

해설 질문의 핵심 어구(man ~ can do)와 관련된 내용을 주의 깊게 듣는다. 남자가 "And if you're unsure about which models to get, I can ask the staff for their opinions on the matter."라며 어떤 모델을 사야 할지 잘 모르겠다면 직원들에게 그 사안에 대한 그들의 의견을 물어볼 수 있다고 하였다. 따라서 (D)가 정답이다.

어휘 deal with 처리하다   submission n. 제출   find out 알아내다

Paraphrasing

staff 직원들 → employee 직원

[44-46]

영국 → 호주

Questions 44-46 refer to the following conversation.

W: Hello. ⁴⁴I accidentally dropped my phone yesterday, and the screen broke. I was wondering if I could have it repaired for free.

M: OK. ⁴⁵Is it still under the one-year warranty?

W: Um . . . I bought it over two years ago.

M: In that case, it might be cheaper to replace the phone. We're offering a 15 percent discount on all phones this week, if you're interested. ⁴⁶Would you like to see our latest model?

W: ⁴⁶Sure. I'll take a look at it.

accidentally adv. 실수로   warranty n. 보증   replace v. 교체하다

해석
44-46번은 다음 대화에 관한 문제입니다.

여: 안녕하세요. ⁴⁴어제 제 휴대폰을 실수로 떨어뜨려서, 화면이 깨졌어요. 이것을 무료로 수리받을 수 있는지 궁금해요.

남: 네. ⁴⁵그것이 아직 1년 보증 기간 내에 있나요?

여: 음... 저는 이것을 2년 넘게 전에 샀어요.

남: 그렇다면, 휴대폰을 교체하시는 게 더 저렴할 수 있어요. 관심이 있으시다면, 저희는 이번 주에 모든 휴대폰에 15퍼센트 할인을 제공하고 있어요. ⁴⁶저희의 최신 모델을 보시겠어요?

여: ⁴⁶물론이죠. 그것을 한번 볼게요.

44 | 문제점 문제

해석 여자는 무슨 문제를 언급하는가?
(A) 기기가 손상되었다.
(B) 판촉 행사가 끝났다.
(C) 부품이 없어졌다.
(D) 쿠폰이 효력이 없다.

해설 여자의 말에서 부정적인 표현이 언급된 주변을 주의 깊게 듣는다. 여자가 "I accidentally dropped my phone yesterday, and the screen broke."라며 어제 휴대폰을 실수로 떨어뜨려서 화면이 깨졌다고 하였다. 따라서 (A)가 정답이다.

어휘 device n. 기기   promotion n. 판촉 행사   invalid adj. 효력이 없는

45 | 의도 파악 문제

해석 여자는 "저는 이것을 2년 넘게 전에 샀어요"라고 말할 때 무엇을 의도하는가?
(A) 모델이 이용 가능하지 않다.

(B) 수리가 되어야 한다.
(C) 제품이 오랜 시간 유지되었다.
(D) 보증이 만료되었다.

해설 질문의 인용어구(I bought it over two years ago)가 언급된 주변을 주의 깊게 듣는다. 남자가 "Is it[phone] still under the one-year warranty?"라며 휴대폰이 아직 1년 보증 기간 내에 있냐는 물음에 여자가 이것을 2년 넘게 전에 샀다고 한 것을 통해 보증이 만료되었음을 알 수 있다. 따라서 (D)가 정답이다.

어휘 repair n. 수리 last v. 유지되다, 견디다 guarantee n. 보증
expire v. 만료되다

46 | 특정 세부 사항 문제

해석 여자는 무엇을 하고 싶어 하는가?
(A) 제품을 살펴본다.
(B) 가격을 비교한다.
(C) 서비스에 등록한다.
(D) 다른 지점에 연락한다.

해설 질문의 핵심 어구(woman want to do)와 관련된 내용을 주의 깊게 듣는다. 남자가 "Would you like to see our latest model?"이라며 최신 모델을 보겠냐고 하자, 여자가 "Sure. I'll take a look at it."이라며 그것을 한번 보겠다고 하였다. 따라서 (A)가 정답이다.

어휘 compare v. 비교하다 sign up 등록하다 contact v. 연락하다

[47-49]

호주 → 미국

Questions 47-49 refer to the following conversation.

M: ⁴⁷There's a problem with our online banking system.
W: Yeah. ⁴⁷I heard that some of our customers can't access their transaction records. There must be something wrong with our database software.
M: Possibly. Can you let Robert Nolan from the IT team know about the issue?
W: I already did. He said that his team should have a solution to the problem by tomorrow morning.
M: OK. ⁴⁸Is Robert checking whether our new mobile application is affected as well? We need to make sure it is set to launch next Monday.
W: Oh, I'm not sure about that. ⁴⁹I'll call him back now and check.
M: ⁴⁹Give me an update on that as soon as possible, please.

transaction n. 거래 set adj. 준비가 된 launch v. 출시하다

해석
47-49번은 다음 대화에 관한 문제입니다.
남: ⁴⁷우리의 온라인 은행 거래 시스템에 문제가 있어요.
여: 네. ⁴⁷우리 고객들 중 일부가 그들의 거래 기록에 접근할 수 없다고 들었어요. 우리 데이터베이스 소프트웨어에 무슨 문제가 있는 것이 틀림없어요.
남: 어쩌면요. IT팀의 Robert Nolan에게 그 문제에 대해 알려주시겠어요?
여: 이미 했어요. 그의 팀이 내일 아침까지는 문제점에 대한 해결 방안이 있을 거라고 말했어요.
남: 알겠어요. ⁴⁸Robert가 우리의 새로운 모바일 애플리케이션이 영향을 받는지에 대해서도 확인하고 있나요? 우리는 확실히 그것이 다음 주 월요일에 출시될 준비가 되도록 해야 해요.
여: 아, 그것에 대해서는 잘 모르겠어요. ⁴⁹제가 지금 그에게 다시 전화해 확인할게요.

남: ⁴⁹제게 가능한 한 빨리 그것에 대한 최신 정보를 알려주세요.

47 | 화자 문제

해석 화자들은 어디에서 일하는 것 같은가?
(A) 금융 기관에서
(B) 휴대 전화 가게에서
(C) IT 컨설팅 회사에서
(D) 소프트웨어 회사에서

해설 대화에서 신분 및 직업과 관련된 표현을 놓치지 않고 듣는다. 남자가 "There's a problem with our online banking system."이라며 자신들의 온라인 은행 거래 시스템에 문제가 있다고 하자, 여자가 "I heard that some of our customers can't access their transaction records."라며 고객들 중 일부가 그들의 거래 기록에 접근할 수 없다고 들었다고 하였다. 따라서 (A)가 정답이다.

어휘 institution n. 기관

48 | 추론 문제

해석 모바일 애플리케이션에 관해 무엇이 암시되는가?
(A) Robert Nolan에 의해 설계되었다.
(B) 중요한 기능이 빠져 있다.
(C) 데이터베이스 문제에 영향을 받았다.
(D) 아직 대중에게 이용이 가능하지 않다.

해설 질문의 핵심 어구(mobile application)와 관련된 내용을 주의 깊게 듣는다. 남자가 "Is Robert checking whether our new mobile application is affected as well? We need to make sure it is set to launch next Monday."라며 Robert가 새로운 모바일 애플리케이션이 영향을 받는지에 대해서도 확인하고 있는지 물으며, 자신들은 확실히 그것이 다음 주 월요일에 출시될 준비가 되도록 해야 한다고 한 것을 통해 모바일 애플리케이션이 아직 대중에게 이용이 가능하지 않다는 것을 알 수 있다. 따라서 (D)가 정답이다.

어휘 feature n. 기능, 특징

49 | 요청 문제

해석 여자는 무엇을 하도록 요청받는가?
(A) 출시 파티에 참석한다.
(B) 휴대 전화번호로 전화한다.
(C) 상황에 대한 최신 정보를 제공한다.
(D) 인터넷 연결을 확인한다.

해설 남자의 말에서 요청과 관련된 표현이 포함된 문장을 주의 깊게 듣는다. 여자가 "I'll call him[Robert] back now and check."라며 Robert에게 다시 전화해서 확인할 것이라고 하였고, 남자가 "Give me an update on that[whether our new mobile application is affected] as soon as possible, please."라며 가능한 한 빨리 새로운 모바일 애플리케이션이 영향을 받는지에 대한 최신 정보를 알려달라고 하였다. 따라서 (C)가 정답이다.

어휘 attend v. 참석하다 status n. 상황

[50-52]

캐나다 → 영국

Questions 50-52 refer to the following conversation.

M: Hello. This is Joe Reynolds calling from radio station WRST. ⁵⁰/⁵¹Ms. Peters, we'd like to interview you at the station about your recently published novel, *Grains of Time*.
W: I'd love to. But . . . um . . . I'll be traveling for the next few weeks. ⁵¹I've been asked to do a book tour by my publisher.

M: I see. Would it be possible to interview you over the phone, instead?
W: Sure, but ⁵²I'll need to see a list of the questions you plan to ask. I'd prefer not to be surprised by anything unexpected.
M: ⁵²Oh, of course! I can e-mail them to you right now.

radio station 라디오 방송국 publish v. 출간하다 publisher n. 출판사
unexpected adj. 예기치 않은

해석
50-52번은 다음 대화에 관한 문제입니다.
남: 안녕하세요. 저는 WRST 라디오 방송국에서 전화 드리는 Joe Reynolds 입니다. ⁵⁰/⁵¹Ms. Peters, 당신의 최근에 출간된 소설인 Grains of Time에 대해 방송국에서 당신을 인터뷰하고 싶어요.
여: 그럼요. 하지만... 음... 저는 다음 몇 주 동안 여행을 갈 예정이에요. ⁵¹제 출판사에 의해 북투어를 요청받았거든요.
남: 그렇군요. 대신 전화로 인터뷰할 수 있을까요?
여: 물론이죠, 하지만 ⁵²물어보실 계획인 질문들의 목록을 봐야 해요. 저는 예기치 않은 어떤 것에 놀라고 싶지 않아요.
남: ⁵²아, 그럼요! 지금 바로 이메일로 보내드릴 수 있어요.

50 | 화자 문제

해석 여자는 누구인가?
(A) 라디오 사회자
(B) 작가
(C) 프로그램 프로듀서
(D) 기자

해설 대화에서 신분 및 직업과 관련된 표현을 놓치지 않고 듣는다. 남자가 여자에게 "Ms. Peters, we'd like to interview you at the station about your recently published novel, Grains of Time."이라고 한 말을 통해 여자가 작가임을 알 수 있다. 따라서 (B)가 정답이다.
어휘 host n. 사회자 show n. (라디오·TV의) 프로그램 journalist n. 기자

51 | 의도 파악 문제

해석 여자는 왜 "저는 다음 몇 주 동안 여행을 갈 예정이에요"라고 말하는가?
(A) 요청을 거절하기 위해
(B) 인터뷰 일정을 잡기 위해
(C) 설문조사 질문에 답하기 위해
(D) 논의 주제를 제안하기 위해

해설 질문의 인용어구(I'll be traveling for the next few weeks)가 언급된 주변을 주의 깊게 듣는다. 남자가 "Ms. Peters, we'd like to interview you at the station about your recently published novel, Grains of Time."이라며 Ms. Peters의 최근에 출간된 소설인 Grains of Time에 대해 방송국에서 그녀를 인터뷰하고 싶다고 하자, 여자가 "I've been asked to do a book tour by my publisher."라며 자신의 출판사에 의해 북투어를 요청받았다고 한 것을 통해 여자가 방송국에서의 인터뷰 요청을 거절하고 있음을 알 수 있다. 따라서 (A)가 정답이다.
어휘 schedule v. 일정을 잡다 survey n. 설문조사

52 | 다음에 할 일 문제

해석 남자는 다음에 무엇을 할 것 같은가?
(A) 인터뷰를 시작한다.
(B) 여행을 준비한다.
(C) 목록을 제공한다.
(D) 전화를 돌린다.

해설 대화의 마지막 부분을 주의 깊게 듣는다. 여자가 "I'll need to see a list of the questions you plan to ask"라며 남자가 물어볼 계획인 질문들의 목록을 봐야 한다고 하자, 남자가 "Oh, of course! I can e-mail them to you right now."라며 지금 바로 이메일로 보내줄 수 있다고 한 것을 통해 남자가 질문 목록을 제공할 것임을 알 수 있다. 따라서 (C)가 정답이다.
어휘 organize v. 준비하다, 조직하다 supply v. 제공하다
transfer a call 전화를 돌리다

[53-55]
캐나다 → 미국 → 영국
Questions 53-55 refer to the following conversation with three speakers.

M: Jasmine, ⁵³will you be available to teach another yoga class here at the studio next month? One of our scheduled instructors just backed out, so I'm looking for a replacement.
W1: Well, ⁵⁴I'm starting a new part-time job at an elementary school next week, so I'm not sure I'll have the time.
M: ⁵⁴Oh, congratulations! That's good news.
W1: Thank you. Why don't you ask Sheila? I think she is looking to pick up another class.
M: Is that right, Sheila? ⁵⁵Can you teach a class from 8 to 10 A.M.?
W2: I'd be happy to. Mine don't usually start until 2 P.M., so I've got the time.

scheduled adj. 예정된 back out (하기로 했던 일에서) 빠지다
replacement n. 대신할 사람 look to ~을 고려해 보다
pick up ~을 찾다, 회복되다

해석
53-55번은 다음 세 명의 대화에 관한 문제입니다.
남: Jasmine, ⁵³다음 달에 이곳 스튜디오에서 다른 요가 수업을 가르치실 수 있나요? 우리의 예정된 강사들 중 한 명이 막 빠졌기 때문에 대신할 사람을 찾고 있어요.
여1: 음, ⁵⁴다음 주에 초등학교에서 새로운 시간제 일자리를 시작할 예정이라서 시간이 있을지 모르겠어요.
남: ⁵⁴아, 축하해요! 그것 좋은 소식이네요.
여1: 감사해요. Sheila에게 물어보는 게 어때요? 그녀는 또 다른 수업을 찾는 것을 고려해 보고 있는 것 같아요.
남: 맞아요, Sheila? ⁵⁵오전 8시부터 10시까지 수업하실 수 있나요?
여2: 기꺼이요. 제 수업은 보통 오후 2시가 되어야 시작하니까 시간이 있어요.

53 | 주제 문제

해석 화자들은 주로 무엇에 대해 이야기하고 있는가?
(A) 사무실 수리
(B) 학생 등록
(C) 등록비
(D) 수업 가능 여부

해설 대화의 주제를 묻는 문제이므로, 대화의 초반을 반드시 듣는다. 남자가 "will you be available to teach another yoga class here at the studio next month?"라며 다음 달에 스튜디오에서 다른 요가 수업을 가르치실 수 있는지 물은 후, 수업 가능 여부에 대한 내용으로 대화가 이어지고 있다. 따라서 (D)가 정답이다.
어휘 enrollment n. 등록 registration fee 등록비

54 | 이유 문제

해석 남자는 왜 Jasmine을 축하하는가?
(A) 강좌를 마쳤다.
(B) 새로운 일을 찾았다.
(C) 직장에서 급여 인상을 받았다.
(D) 수업 시간을 늘렸다.

해설 질문의 핵심 어구(congratulate Jasmine)와 관련된 내용을 주의 깊게 듣는다. 여자1[Jasmine]이 "I'm starting a new part-time job at an elementary school next week, so I'm not sure I'll have the time"이라며 다음 주에 초등학교에서 새로운 시간제 일자리를 시작할 예정이라서 시간이 있을지 모르겠다고 하자, 남자가 "Oh, congratulations!"라며 축하한다고 하였다. 따라서 (B)가 정답이다.

어휘 employment n. 일, 직업 pay raise 급여 인상

55 | 특정 세부 사항 문제

해석 Sheila는 누구인 것 같은가?
(A) 사무실 관리자
(B) 판매원
(C) 요가 강사
(D) 축구 코치

해설 질문의 대상(Sheila)의 신분 및 직업과 관련된 표현을 놓치지 않고 듣는다. 남자가 "Can you teach a class from 8 to 10 A.M.?"이라며 오전 8시부터 10시까지 수업할 수 있는지 물은 것을 통해 요가 강사임을 알 수 있다. 따라서 (C)가 정답이다.

어휘 salesperson n. 판매원

[56-58]

호주 → 영국

Questions 56-58 refer to the following conversation.

> M: How's it going, Linda? ⁵⁶**Are you making any progress with your sketches for the fall clothing line?**
> W: Actually, ⁵⁶**I'd like to get your opinion on these designs I've been working on**.
> M: Well, ⁵⁷**I like that you chose orange and red for the line**. Is something bothering you about them?
> W: Our spring line featured similar patterns, so I don't think these new ones are distinct enough.
> M: Maybe we should get another opinion. ⁵⁸**We could show the creative director your sketches.**
> W: ⁵⁸**Sure**, that's a good idea.

progress n. 진전 bother v. 신경 쓰이게 하다 feature v. 특징으로 하다
distinct adj. 구별되는, 분명한

해석
56-58번은 다음 대화에 관한 문제입니다.

남: 일은 잘되고 있나요, Linda? ⁵⁶가을 의류 라인 스케치에 진전이 있나요?
여: 사실, ⁵⁶제가 작업하고 있는 이 디자인들에 대해 당신의 의견을 얻고 싶어요.
남: 음, ⁵⁷그 라인을 위해 주황색과 빨간색을 선택했다는 점이 좋아요. 그 디자인들에 대해 신경 쓰이는 것이 있나요?
여: 저희 봄 라인이 비슷한 패턴을 특징으로 했기 때문에 이 새로운 것들이 충분히 구별되는 것 같지 않아요.
남: 아마 다른 의견을 받아봐야 할 것 같아요. ⁵⁸크리에이티브 디렉터에게 당신의 스케치를 보여줄 수 있어요.
여: ⁵⁸물론이죠, 좋은 생각이에요.

56 | 화자 문제

해석 화자들은 어떤 산업에서 일하는 것 같은가?
(A) 마케팅
(B) 영화
(C) 패션 디자인
(D) 건설

해설 대화에서 신분 및 직업과 관련된 표현을 놓치지 않고 듣는다. 남자가 "Are you making any progress with your sketches for the fall clothing line?"이라며 가을 의류 라인 스케치에 진전이 있는지 묻자, 여자가 "I'd like to get your opinion on these designs I've been working on"이라며 자신이 작업하고 있는 디자인들에 대해 의견을 얻고 싶다고 말한 것을 통해, 화자들이 패션 디자인 분야에서 일함을 알 수 있다. 따라서 (C)가 정답이다.

57 | 특정 세부 사항 문제

해석 남자는 신제품 라인에 대해서 무엇을 좋아하는가?
(A) 색상
(B) 패턴
(C) 가격
(D) 착용감

해설 대화에서 질문의 핵심 어구(like about a new product line)가 언급된 주변을 주의 깊게 듣는다. 남자가 "I like that you chose orange and red for the line"이라며 여자가 그 라인을 위해 주황색과 빨간색을 선택했다는 점이 좋다고 하였다. 따라서 (A)가 정답이다.

58 | 다음에 할 일 문제

해석 화자들은 다음에 무엇을 할 것인가?
(A) 진열 제품을 옮긴다.
(B) 새로운 패턴들을 만든다.
(C) 몇몇 도안들을 보여준다.
(D) 판매 데이터를 분석한다.

해설 대화의 마지막 부분을 주의 깊게 듣는다. 남자가 "We could show the creative director your sketches."라며 크리에이티브 디렉터에게 당신의 스케치들을 보여줄 수 있다고 하자, 여자가 "Sure"라며 물론이라고 한 것을 통해, 화자들이 도안들을 보여줄 것임을 알 수 있다. 따라서 (C)가 정답이다.

어휘 display n. 진열 drawing n. 도안 analyze v. 분석하다

Paraphrasing

sketches 스케치들 → drawings 도안들

[59-61]

캐나다 → 영국 → 호주

Questions 59-61 refer to the following conversation with three speakers.

> M1: ⁵⁹**I've been reviewing recent artworks submitted to the gallery**, and I'm curious what you two think about this artist's paintings.
> W: I think they're quite nice. ⁵⁹**They'd make a great addition to next month's exhibition.**
> M2: I agree. We should put them near the entrance, as they're very eye-catching.
> M1: Great idea. But before we decide, ⁶⁰**one of us needs to discuss the exhibition terms with the artist in person**. She lives just outside Baltimore.
> W: ⁶⁰**I'm willing to do it.** ⁶¹**Do you think I could borrow your car, though?** Mine's in the repair shop.

M1: Sure thing. Let me call her to arrange a time.

artwork n. 작품 submit v. 제출하다 curious adj. 궁금한
quite adv. 꽤 exhibition n. 전시회, 전시 eye-catching adj. 눈길을 끄는
terms n. 조건 in person 직접 willing adj. 기꺼이 ~하는 arrange v. 정하다

해석
59-61번은 다음 세 명의 대화에 관한 문제입니다.
남1: 59저는 최근 갤러리에 제출된 작품들을 검토하고 있는데, 이 작가의 그림들에 대해 두 분이 어떻게 생각하시는지 궁금해요.
여: 꽤 괜찮은 것 같아요. 59다음 달 전시회에 좋은 보탬이 될 것 같아요.
남2: 동의해요. 그것들이 매우 눈길을 끌어서 입구 근처에 둬야겠어요.
남1: 좋은 생각이에요. 그런데 우리가 결정하기 전에, 60저희들 중 한 명이 직접 그 작가와 전시 조건을 논의해야 해요. 그녀는 볼티모어 바로 외곽에서 살고 있어요.
여: 60제가 기꺼이 할게요. 61하지만 제가 당신의 차를 빌릴 수 있을까요? 제 차는 정비소에 있어요.
남1: 물론이죠. 제가 시간을 정하기 위해 그녀에게 전화해 볼게요.

59 | 특정 세부 사항 문제

해석 화자들은 무슨 행사를 계획하는 것 같은가?
(A) 시설 견학
(B) 미술 전시회
(C) 미술관 이전
(D) 사진 촬영

해설 질문의 핵심 어구(planning)와 관련된 내용을 주의 깊게 듣는다. 남자1이 "I've been reviewing recent artworks submitted to the gallery"라며 최근 갤러리에 제출된 작품들을 검토하고 있다고 하자, 여자가 "They'd make a great addition to next month's exhibition."이라며 다음 달 전시회에 좋은 보탬이 될 것 같다고 하였다. 따라서 (B)가 정답이다.

어휘 relocation n. 이전 photo shoot 사진 촬영

60 | 특정 세부 사항 문제

해석 여자는 무엇을 하기로 동의하는가?
(A) 예술가를 만난다.
(B) 몇몇 제출작들을 불합격시킨다.
(C) 계약서 초안을 작성한다.
(D) 주소를 확인한다.

해설 질문의 핵심 어구(woman agree to do)와 관련된 내용을 주의 깊게 듣는다. 남자1이 "one of us needs to discuss the exhibition terms with the artist in person"이라며 자신들 중 한 명이 직접 그 작가와 전시 조건을 논의해야 한다고 하자, 여자가 "I'm willing to do it."이라며 자신이 기꺼이 하겠다고 한 것을 통해, 여자가 예술가를 만나기로 동의함을 알 수 있다. 따라서 (A)가 정답이다.

어휘 reject v. 불합격시키다, 거부하다 draft v. 초안을 작성하다
agreement n. 계약(서), 협약

61 | 요청 문제

해석 여자는 무엇을 요청하는가?
(A) 회의 장소
(B) 차량 이용
(C) 예술가의 이름
(D) 갤러리의 평면도

해설 여자의 말에서 요청과 관련된 표현이 포함된 문장을 주의 깊게 듣는다. 여자가 "Do you think I could borrow your car, though?"라며 차를 빌릴 수 있을지 물었다. 따라서 (B)가 정답이다.

어휘 floor plan 평면도

[62-64]

캐나다 → 미국

Questions 62-64 refer to the following conversation and movie list.

M: Miranda, we're still on for that film after work tonight, right? It's important for our review of the competitor's promotional approach.
W: Yes, definitely. 62I bought the tickets online this afternoon.
M: Good. I heard the movie includes some product placements they've been testing.
W: Exactly. That's what we need to analyze. We'll have to hurry, though. 63It's the first showing of the evening.
M: Yeah. And the Palace Theater is a little far from our office. 64Let's take my car. The buses will likely be crowded.

on adj. 예정된 definitely adv. 물론 placement n. 배치, 놓기
crowded adj. 붐비는

해석
62-64번은 다음 대화와 영화 목록에 관한 문제입니다.
남: Miranda, 우린 여전히 오늘 저녁에 일 끝나고 그 영화 보기로 예정된 거죠, 그렇죠? 이것은 경쟁사의 홍보 전략을 검토하는 데 중요해요.
여: 네, 물론이죠. 62제가 오늘 오후에 온라인으로 표를 샀어요.
남: 좋아요. 그 영화는 그들이 시험하고 있던 제품 배치를 포함하고 있다고 들었어요.
여: 맞아요, 우리가 분석해야 할 부분이 바로 그거예요. 그런데 서둘러야겠어요. 63그것은 저녁의 첫 상영이에요.
남: 네, 그리고 Palace 극장은 우리 사무실에서 조금 멀어요. 64제 차를 타고 가요. 버스가 붐빌 것 같아요.

영화	상영 시간
63Out of Town	오후 6시 30분
Tonight	오후 7시
With Peter	오후 7시 30분
When We Go	오후 8시

62 | 특정 세부 사항 문제

해석 여자는 오늘 오후에 무엇을 했는가?
(A) 극장을 방문했다.
(B) 기사를 읽었다.
(C) 음성 메시지를 들었다.
(D) 표 몇 장을 구매했다.

해설 질문의 핵심 어구(this afternoon)가 언급된 주변을 주의 깊게 듣는다. 여자가 "I bought the tickets online this afternoon."이라며 오늘 오후에 온라인으로 표를 샀다고 하였다. 따라서 (D)가 정답이다.

어휘 voice message 음성 메시지

63 | 시각 자료 문제

해석 시각 자료를 보아라. 화자들은 어떤 영화를 볼 것인가?
(A) *Out of Town*
(B) *Tonight*
(C) *With Peter*
(D) *When We Go*

해설 제시된 영화 목록의 정보를 확인한 후 질문의 핵심 어구(movie)와 관련된 내용을 주의 깊게 듣는다. 여자가 "It's the first showing of the evening."이라며 저녁의 첫 상영이라고 했고, 첫 상영은 *Out of Town*임을 영화 목록에서 알 수 있다. 따라서 (A)가 정답이다.

64 | 제안 문제

해석 남자는 무엇을 제안하는가?
(A) 버스를 타기
(B) 차로 가기
(C) 간식을 가져오기
(D) 예고편을 보기

해설 남자의 말에서 제안과 관련된 표현이 언급된 내용을 주의 깊게 듣는다. 남자가 여자에게 "Let's take my car."라며 자신의 차를 타고 가자고 하였다. 따라서 (B)가 정답이다.

어휘 snack n. 간식 trailer n. 예고편

[65-67]

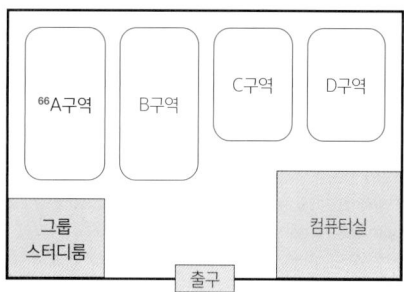

미국 → 호주

Questions 65-67 refer to the following conversation and floor plan.

W: Excuse me. This is my first time visiting Hillsdale Library. I'm looking for a book to read during my upcoming vacation. ⁶⁵**Can you recommend something?** I'm open to most genres.

M: Yes. Of course. A new book came out just last week called *Near the River*. It's getting excellent reviews. ⁶⁶**You'll find it on the shelves just across the Group Study Room over there.**

W: Great, I'll try that. Oh, one more thing. ⁶⁷**Does this library offer audiobooks?**

M: Yes. We do. ⁶⁷**You can find out more details about our selection by visiting our Web site.** There's a link on the main page.

upcoming adj. 다가오는 offer v. 제공하다 selection n. 선별된 것

해석
65-67번은 다음 대화와 평면도에 관한 문제입니다.

여: 실례합니다. 제가 이번에 처음 Hillsdale 도서관을 방문해서요. 저는 다가오는 방학 동안 읽을 책을 찾고 있어요. ⁶⁵무언가 추천해 주실 수 있나요? 저는 대부분의 장르에 열려 있어요.

남: 네. 물론이죠. 바로 지난주에 *Near the River*라는 새로운 책이 나왔어요. 좋은 평가들을 받고 있죠. ⁶⁶저쪽 그룹 스터디룸 바로 맞은편 선반에서 그것을 찾으실 수 있어요.

여: 좋아요, 그것을 읽어 볼게요. 아, 한 가지 더요. ⁶⁷이 도서관은 오디오북을 제공하나요?

남: 네. 제공합니다. ⁶⁷저희 웹사이트를 방문하시면 저희의 선별된 자료에 대한 세부 정보를 보실 수 있어요. 메인 페이지에 링크가 있습니다.

65 | 요청 문제

해석 여자는 남자에게 무엇을 하라고 요청하는가?
(A) 몇몇 품목들을 보류한다.
(B) 구독을 연장한다.
(C) 도서관 회원권을 갱신한다.
(D) 추천을 한다.

해설 여자의 말에서 요청과 관련된 표현이 포함된 문장을 주의 깊게 듣는다. 여자가 "Can you recommend something?"이라며 무언가 추천해 줄 수 있는지 물었다. 따라서 (D)가 정답이다.

어휘 put on hold ~을 보류하다 renew v. 연장하다, 갱신하다
subscription n. 구독

66 | 시각 자료 문제

해석 시각 자료를 보아라. 여자는 어떤 구역을 찾아볼 것인가?
(A) A구역
(B) B구역
(C) C구역
(D) D구역

해설 제시된 평면도의 정보를 확인한 후 질문의 핵심 어구(section ~ search)와 관련된 내용을 주의 깊게 듣는다. 남자가 "You'll find it[*Near the River*] on the shelves just across the Group Study Room over there."라며 그룹 스터디룸 바로 맞은편 선반에서 *Near the River*를 찾을 수 있다고 했다. 그룹 스터디룸 맞은편 선반은 A구역임을 평면도에서 알 수 있다. 따라서 (A)가 정답이다.

어휘 section n. 구역

67 | 특정 세부 사항 문제

해석 남자에 따르면, 웹사이트에서 무엇이 이용 가능한가?
(A) 회원들로부터의 후기
(B) 구매자들을 위한 쿠폰
(C) 오디오북에 대한 세부 사항
(D) 정책에 대한 정보

해설 질문의 핵심 어구(Web site)가 언급된 주변을 주의 깊게 듣는다. 여자가 "Does this library offer audiobooks?"라며 도서관이 오디오북을 제공하는지 묻자, 남자가 "You can find out more details about our selection by visiting our Web site."라며 웹사이트를 방문하면 소장 자료에 대한 세부 정보를 볼 수 있다고 하였다. 따라서 (C)가 정답이다.

[68-70]

미국 → 캐나다

Questions 68-70 refer to the following conversation and product list.

W: Preston, I heard you needed to talk to me?

M: Yeah. ⁶⁸**We've run out of one of our laptop models in the store—the 15-inch model.** Do we have any more units in the storage room?

W: Unfortunately, we don't have any more right now. ⁶⁹I checked on that yesterday while I was organizing some new merchandise.
M: I see. ⁷⁰I'll inform the sales team to let customers know we'll have a new shipment tomorrow morning.

run out of 떨어지다, ~을 바닥내다 laptop n. 노트북 컴퓨터
storage room 창고 unfortunately adv. 안타깝게도
organize v. 정리하다 merchandise n. 물품, 상품 shipment n. 배송품, 배송

해석
68-70번은 다음 대화와 제품 목록에 관한 문제입니다.

여: Preston, 저와 얘기가 필요하다고 들었는데요?
남: 네. ⁶⁸저희 노트북 컴퓨터 모델 중 하나인 15인치 모델이 매장에서 떨어졌어요. 창고에 몇 개가 더 없나요?
여: 안타깝게도, 지금 당장은 더 없어요. ⁶⁹어제 새 물품을 일부 정리하면서 그것을 확인했어요.
남: 그렇군요. ⁷⁰내일 아침에 새로운 배송품이 있을 것이라는 것을 고객들이 알 수 있도록 영업팀에 알릴게요.

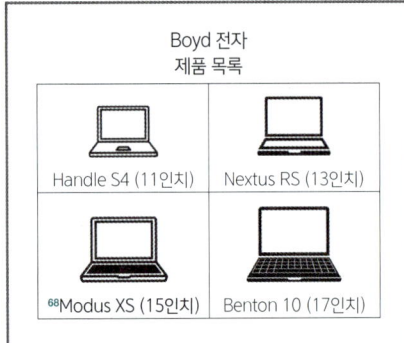

68 | 시각 자료 문제

해석 시각 자료를 보아라. 어떤 제품이 현재 재고가 없는가?
(A) Handle S4
(B) Nextus RS
(C) Modus XS
(D) Benton 10

해설 제시된 제품 목록의 정보를 확인한 후 질문의 핵심 어구(currently not in stock)와 관련된 내용을 주의 깊게 듣는다. 남자가 "We've run out of one of our laptop models in the store—the 15-inch model."이라며 노트북 컴퓨터 모델 중 하나인 15인치 모델이 매장에서 떨어졌다고 했고, 이 조건에 맞는 제품은 Modus XS임을 제품 목록에서 알 수 있다. 따라서 (C)가 정답이다.

어휘 currently adv. 현재

69 | 특정 세부 사항 문제

해석 여자는 최근에 무엇을 했는가?
(A) 물품을 배송했다.
(B) 재고품을 정리했다.
(C) 일정을 확인했다.
(D) 공급업체와 통화했다.

해설 질문의 핵심 어구(recently do)와 관련된 내용을 주의 깊게 듣는다. "I checked on that yesterday while I was organizing some new merchandise."라며 어제 새 물품을 일부 정리했다고 하였다. 따라서 (B)가 정답이다. 따라서 (B)가 정답이다.

어휘 inventory n. 재고(품)

70 | 언급 문제

해석 배송품에 관해 무엇이 언급되는가?
(A) 곧 배달될 것이다.
(B) 예상보다 더 작았다.
(C) 판매자에게 반환되어야 했다.
(D) 이틀 전에 발송되었다.

해설 남자의 말에서 질문의 핵심 어구(shipment)가 언급된 부분을 주의 깊게 듣는다. 남자가 "I'll inform the sales team to let customers know we'll have a new shipment tomorrow morning."이라며 내일 아침에 새로운 배송품이 있을 것이라는 것을 고객들이 알 수 있도록 영업팀에 알리겠다고 한 것을 통해, 배송품이 곧 배달될 것임을 알 수 있다. 따라서 (A)가 정답이다.

PART 4

[71-73] 영국

Questions 71-73 refer to the following telephone message.

Good morning. This message is for Gary Boris. ⁷¹I'm contacting you on behalf of Hart Federal Bank. Unfortunately, ⁷²your application for a home loan has been put on hold. This is because you filled out some of your personal information incorrectly on the application form. In order to resolve the issue, ⁷³you will need to visit our office at 382 Diller Avenue, complete a new application, and hand it in. If you have any questions, please call 555-0091.

on behalf of ~을 대표하여 application n. 신청 home loan 주택 자금 융자
put on hold 보류하다 incorrectly adv. 부정확하게 resolve v. 해결하다
hand in 제출하다

해석
71-73번은 다음 전화 메시지에 관한 문제입니다.

안녕하세요. 이 메시지는 Gary Boris를 위한 것입니다. ⁷¹Hart 연방 은행을 대표해서 연락 드립니다. 유감스럽게도, ⁷²귀하의 주택 자금 융자 신청이 보류되었습니다. 이는 귀하께서 신청서에 개인 정보 일부를 부정확하게 기재하셨기 때문입니다. 이 문제를 해결하시려면, ⁷³Diller가 382번지에 있는 저희 사무실을 방문하셔서, 새로운 신청서를 작성하신 후, 제출하셔야 할 것입니다. 문의 사항이 있으시면, 555-0091로 전화 주십시오.

71 | 화자 문제

해석 화자는 누구인 것 같은가?
(A) 은행 직원
(B) 여행사 직원
(C) 개인 회계사
(D) 프로젝트 관리자

해설 지문에서 신분 및 직업과 관련된 표현을 놓치지 않고 듣는다. "I'm contacting you on behalf of Hart Federal Bank."라며 Hart 연방 은행을 대표해서 연락 드린다고 한 것을 통해 화자가 은행 직원임을 알 수 있다. 따라서 (A)가 정답이다.

어휘 bank employee 은행 직원 travel agent 여행사 직원
accountant n. 회계사

72 | 특정 세부 사항 문제

해석 화자는 무슨 문제를 언급하는가?
(A) 신용카드가 만료되었다.
(B) 요금이 지불되지 않았다.
(C) 신청이 보류되었다.
(D) 계정에 접근할 수 없다.

해설 질문의 핵심 어구(problem)와 관련된 내용을 주의 깊게 듣는다. "your application for a home loan has been put on hold"라며 귀하의 주택 자금 융자 신청이 보류되었다고 하였다. 따라서 (C)가 정답이다.

어휘 bill n. 요금, 청구서 suspend v. 보류하다, 중지하다 account n. 계정
access v. 접근하다

Paraphrasing

has been put on hold 보류되었다 → was suspended 보류되었다

73 | 특정 세부 사항 문제

해석 화자는 청자가 무엇을 해야 한다고 말하는가?
(A) 프로그램에 지원한다.
(B) 문서를 제출한다.
(C) 사진들을 찍는다.
(D) 집주인에게 연락한다.

해설 질문의 핵심 어구(listener should do)와 관련된 내용이 언급된 주변을 주의 깊게 듣는다. "you will need to visit our office ~, complete a new application, and hand it in"이라며 사무실을 방문해서, 새로운 신청서를 작성한 후, 제출해야 한다고 하였다. 따라서 (B)가 정답이다.

Paraphrasing

complete a new application, and hand ~ in 새로운 신청서를 작성한 후 제출하다 → Submit a document 문서를 제출하다

[74-76]

Questions 74-76 refer to the following advertisement. 캐나다

Nothing is more frustrating than going on a trip and having to take public transportation with all your luggage. [74]**Make it easier for yourself by contacting On-call Rides! We offer prompt pickup, a smooth ride, and plenty of space for your bags.** [75]**All you have to do is sit back and enjoy your complimentary bottled water.** Plus, throughout the month of July, [76]**customers can get 10 percent off their fare by making a reservation through our mobile application.** That's a deal no one can beat, so try us today!

frustrating adj. 불만스러운 public transportation 대중교통
luggage n. 짐 prompt adj. 신속한 sit back 편안히 앉다
complimentary adj. 무료의 throughout prep. ~ 내내 fare n. 요금
deal n. 거래 beat v. 능가하다

해석
74-76번은 다음 광고에 관한 문제입니다.

여행을 가서 당신의 모든 짐을 가지고 대중교통을 타야 하는 것보다 더 불만스러운 것은 없습니다. [74]On-call Rides사에 연락하셔서 당신을 위해 그것을 더 쉽게 만드세요! 저희는 신속한 픽업, 편안한 승차감, 그리고 당신의 가방들을 위한 넉넉한 공간을 제공합니다. [75]당신은 편안히 앉아 무료 생수를 즐기시기만 하면 됩니다. 게다가, 7월 한 달 내내 [76]고객들은 저희 모바일 애플리케이션을 통해 예약을 함으로써 요금의 10퍼센트 할인을 받으실 수 있습니다. 누구도 능가할 수 없는 거래이니, 오늘 한번 시도해 보세요!

74 | 주제 문제

해석 무엇이 광고되고 있는가?
(A) 배송 회사
(B) 차량 제공 서비스
(C) 여행 가방 소매업자
(D) 자동차 제조업자

해설 광고의 주제를 묻는 문제이므로, 지문의 초반을 반드시 듣는다. "Make it easier for yourself by contacting On-call Rides! We offer prompt pickup, a smooth ride, and plenty of space for your bags."라며 On-call Rides사에 연락해서 모든 짐을 가지고 대중교통을 타야 하는 것을 더 쉽게 만들라고 한 후, 신속한 픽업, 편안한 승차감, 그리고 가방들을 위한 넉넉한 공간을 제공한다는 내용으로 이어지고 있다. 따라서 (B)가 정답이다.

어휘 retailer n. 소매업자 manufacturer n. 제조업자

75 | 특정 세부 사항 문제

해석 무엇이 무료로 제공되는가?
(A) 음료
(B) 여행용 파우치
(C) 하차 서비스
(D) 헤드폰

해설 질문의 핵심 어구(offered for free)와 관련된 내용을 주의 깊게 듣는다. "All you have to do is sit back and enjoy your complimentary bottled water."라며 편안히 앉아 무료 생수를 즐기기만 하면 된다고 하였다. 따라서 (A)가 정답이다.

Paraphrasing

bottled water 생수 → Drinks 음료

76 | 방법 문제

해석 화자에 따르면, 청자들은 어떻게 할인을 받을 수 있는가?
(A) 모바일 애플리케이션을 사용함으로써
(B) 할인 코드를 입력함으로써
(C) 온라인에서 의견을 줌으로써
(D) 소책자를 가져감으로써

해설 질문의 핵심 어구(receive a discount)와 관련된 내용을 주의 깊게 듣는다. "customers can get 10 percent off their fare by making a reservation through our mobile application"이라며 고객들은 모바일 애플리케이션을 통해 예약을 함으로써 요금의 10퍼센트 할인을 받을 수 있다고 했으므로 (A)가 정답이다.

어휘 promotional code 할인 코드

[77-79]

Questions 77-79 refer to the following excerpt from a meeting. 캐나다

As some of you may have heard, we recently partnered with the jewelry manufacturer, Lowell Inc. [77]**This means our shop will be the exclusive seller of the manufacturer's handmade wedding rings in Jacksonville.** We expect customers to begin asking about the pieces soon. Therefore, [78]**I've asked Mr. Foley from the marketing department to meet with us today.** [78/79]**He'll tell us all about the rings and let you know how to promote these products.** Most of you in the sales department are new, [79]**so please pay close attention**.

partner with ~와 협력하다　exclusive adj. 독점적인　seller n. 판매자
handmade adj. 수제의　sales department 영업부

해석
77-79번은 다음 회의 발췌에 관한 문제입니다.

여러분 중 몇몇은 들으셨겠지만, 우리는 최근에 보석 제조업체인 Lowell사와 협력하였습니다. ⁷⁷이는 우리 가게가 Jacksonville에서 그 제조업체의 수제 결혼반지의 독점적인 판매자가 된다는 것을 의미합니다. 우리는 곧 고객들이 그것들에 대해 문의하기 시작할 것으로 예상합니다. 따라서, ⁷⁸저는 마케팅부의 Mr. Foley에게 오늘 우리와 만날 것을 요청했습니다. ⁷⁸/⁷⁹그는 반지에 대한 모든 것을 우리에게 알려주고 여러분에게 이 제품들을 홍보하는 방법을 알려줄 것입니다. 영업부에 계신 여러분 중 대부분이 새로 오셨으니, ⁷⁹세심한 주의를 기울여 주시기 바랍니다.

77 | 청자 문제

해석 청자들은 어디에서 일하는 것 같은가?
(A) 서비스 센터에서
(B) 보석 가게에서
(C) 모델 업체에서
(D) 결혼식장에서

해설 지문에서 신분 및 직업과 관련된 표현을 놓치지 않고 듣는다. "This means our shop will be the exclusive seller of the manufacturer [Lowell Inc.]'s handmade wedding rings ~"라며 가게가 Lowell사의 수제 결혼반지의 독점적인 판매자가 된다는 것을 의미한다고 했으므로 청자들은 보석 가게에서 일하고 있음을 알 수 있다. 따라서 (B)가 정답이다.

어휘 jewelry n. 보석

78 | 다음에 할 일 문제

해석 Mr. Foley는 무엇을 할 것인가?
(A) 고객들과 만난다.
(B) 물품을 검사한다.
(C) 제품에 대해 논의한다.
(D) 온라인 주문을 처리한다.

해설 질문의 핵심 어구(Mr. Foley)가 언급된 주변을 주의 깊게 듣는다. "I've asked Mr. Foley ~ to meet with us today. He'll tell us all about the rings ~"라며 Mr. Foley에게 오늘 우리와 만날 것을 요청했고, 그는 반지에 대한 모든 것을 우리에게 알려줄 것이라고 하였다. 따라서 (C)가 정답이다.

어휘 inspect v. 검사하다　process v. 처리하다

79 | 의도 파악 문제

해석 화자는 왜 "영업부에 계신 여러분 중 대부분이 새로 오셨으니"라고 말하는가?
(A) 정책 변경의 목적을 설명하기 위해
(B) 회의의 중요성을 강조하기 위해
(C) 교육 일정을 다시 잡기 위해
(D) 개선점들을 제안하기 위해

해설 질문의 인용어구(Most of you in the sales department are new)가 언급된 주변을 주의 깊게 듣는다. "He'll ~ let you know how to promote these products."라며 그는 여러분에게 이 제품들을 홍보하는 방법을 알려줄 것이라고 하고, 영업부에 계신 여러분 중 대부분이 새로 오셨다고 한 후, "so please pay close attention"이라며 그러니 세심한 주의를 기울여 주시기 바란다고 하였으므로, 회의의 중요성을 강조하기 위함임을 알 수 있다. 따라서 (B)가 정답이다.

어휘 improvement n. 개선점

[80-82]
Questions 80-82 refer to the following announcement.

Attention, all Newton bus riders. ⁸⁰Several bus lines that travel along Horris Street and Parkway Boulevard will be rerouted next Saturday due to our city's annual Spring Parade. The bus lines affected are marked on signboards at each bus stop. ⁸¹We suggest you check our Web site for a map of the updated route information and the revised timetable. We're expecting heavy traffic that day, so whether you're driving or taking a bus, ⁸²please allow for extra travel time when planning any journeys. Thank you for your patience and understanding in this matter.

line n. 노선　reroute v. 경로를 변경하다　mark v. 표시하다
signboard n. 표시판, 간판　revise v. 수정하다　allow v. ~으로 잡아두다
matter n. 문제

해석
80-82번은 다음 공지에 관한 문제입니다.

Newton 버스 승객 여러분, 주목해 주십시오. 우리 시의 연례 Spring 퍼레이드로 인해 ⁸⁰Horris가와 Parkway로를 따라 운행하는 여러 버스 노선들이 다음 주 토요일에 경로가 변경될 예정입니다. 영향을 받는 버스 노선들은 각 버스 정류장의 표시판에 표시되어 있습니다. ⁸¹업데이트된 경로 정보와 수정된 시간표를 보시려면 저희 웹사이트를 확인하시는 것을 제안 드립니다. 당일 교통 혼잡이 예상되므로, 운전을 하시든 버스를 타시든, ⁸²여정을 계획하실 때 추가적인 이동 시간을 잡아두시기 바랍니다. 이 문제에 대한 여러분의 인내와 이해에 감사드립니다.

80 | 주제 문제

해석 공지는 주로 무엇에 대한 것인가?
(A) 월간 축제
(B) 개조된 버스 정류장
(C) 경로 변경
(D) 날씨 업데이트

해설 공지의 주제를 묻는 문제이므로, 지문의 초반을 반드시 듣는다. "Several bus lines that travel along Horris Street and Parkway Boulevard will be rerouted next Saturday"라며 Horris가와 Parkway로를 따라 운행하는 여러 버스 노선들이 다음 주 토요일에 경로가 변경될 예정이라고 한 후, 경로 변경에 대한 내용으로 이어지고 있다. 따라서 (C)가 정답이다.

어휘 remodel v. 개조하다

81 | 특정 세부 사항 문제

해석 청자들은 웹사이트에서 무엇을 찾을 수 있는가?
(A) 회사의 평가
(B) 참가 신청서
(C) 행사 시간표
(D) 수정된 일정표

해설 질문의 핵심 어구(find on a Web site)와 관련된 내용을 주의 깊게 듣는다. "We suggest you check our Web site for a map of the updated route information and the revised timetable."이라며 업데이트된 경로 정보와 수정된 시간표를 보려면 웹사이트를 확인하는 것을 제안한다고 하였다. 따라서 (D)가 정답이다.

어휘 sign-in sheet 참가 신청서

Paraphrasing

timetable 시간표 → schedule 일정표

82 | 제안 문제

해석 청자들은 무엇을 하도록 권장되는가?
(A) 자리를 미리 예약한다.
(B) 평소보다 더 많은 시간을 쓰기 위해 계획한다.
(C) 버스를 타는 대신 운전한다.
(D) 웹사이트에서 등록한다.

해설 지문 후반부에서 제안과 관련된 표현이 포함된 문장을 주의 깊게 듣는다. "please allow for extra travel time when planning any journeys"라며 여정을 계획할 때 추가적인 이동 시간을 잡아두기를 제안한다고 하였다. 따라서 (B)가 정답이다.

어휘 ahead of time 미리 register v. 등록하다

Paraphrasing

allow for extra travel time 추가적인 이동 시간을 잡아두다 → plan to spend more time 평소보다 더 많은 시간을 쓰기 위해 계획하다

[83-85]

미국

Questions 83-85 refer to the following talk.

Good afternoon. I'm Jenna, and **83I'll be your guide today at the South Bay Museum, which preserves the history of the city of South Bay**. This afternoon, you'll get a chance to see garments, artworks, and other artifacts, some of which date back nearly 600 years. Luckily for you, **84we have a very special exhibit this week that features pictures of the city taken over the last 120 years.** **85Though this attraction was busy yesterday, there are no group tours scheduled today.** Now, follow me, and we'll make our way to the first exhibit.

preserve v. 보존하다 garment n. 의류 artifact n. 유물
date back 역사가 ~이나 되다 founding n. 창립 nearly adv. 거의
luckily adv. 운 좋게도 attraction n. 볼거리, 명소 make one's way 가다

해석
83-85번은 다음 담화에 관한 문제입니다.

안녕하세요. 저는 Jenna이고, 83오늘 South Bay시의 역사를 보존하는 South Bay 박물관에서 여러분의 가이드가 될 것입니다. 오늘 오후에, 여러분은 의류, 미술품 그리고 다른 유물들을 보실 기회가 있을 것이고, 그중 일부는 역사가 거의 600년이나 됩니다. 여러분에게 운 좋게도, 84이번 주에는 지난 120년에 걸쳐 찍힌 도시의 사진들을 포함하는 매우 특별한 전시가 있습니다. 85어제는 이 볼거리가 붐볐지만, 오늘은 예정된 단체 관람이 없습니다. 이제, 저를 따라오시면, 첫 번째 전시로 가겠습니다.

83 | 장소 문제

해석 청자들은 어디에 있는가?
(A) 시청에
(B) 미술 박람회에
(C) 쇼핑몰에
(D) 역사 박물관에

해설 지문에서 장소와 관련된 표현을 놓치지 않고 듣는다. "I'll be your guide today at the South Bay Museum, which preserves the history of the city of South Bay"라며 오늘 South Bay시의 역사를 보존하는 South Bay 박물관에서 여러분의 가이드가 될 것이라고 한 것을 통해 담화가 이루어지고 있는 장소는 역사 박물관임을 알 수 있다. 따라서 (D)가 정답이다.

어휘 town hall 시청

84 | 특정 세부 사항 문제

해석 특별 전시에 무엇이 포함되는가?
(A) 사진
(B) 영화
(C) 유물
(D) 의류

해설 질문의 핵심 어구(special exhibit)가 언급된 주변을 주의 깊게 듣는다. "we have a very special exhibit this week that features pictures of the city ~"라며 이번 주에는 도시의 사진들을 포함하는 매우 특별한 전시가 있다고 하였다. 따라서 (A)가 정답이다.

85 | 의도 파악 문제

해석 화자는 "오늘은 예정된 단체 관람이 없습니다"라고 말할 때 무엇을 의도하는가?
(A) 인기 있는 볼거리의 표들은 매진되었다.
(B) 청자들은 전시에 참석하지 못할 것이다.
(C) 청자들은 인파에 대해 걱정할 필요가 없다.
(D) 건물이 예정보다 일찍 문을 닫을 예정이다.

해설 질문의 인용어구(there are no group tours scheduled today)가 언급된 주변을 주의 깊게 듣는다. "Though this attraction was busy yesterday"라며 어제는 이 볼거리가 붐볐지만 오늘은 예정된 단체 관람이 없다고 하였다. 따라서 (C)가 정답이다.

어휘 crowd n. 인파, 군중

[86-88]

미국

Questions 86-88 refer to the following telephone message.

Hello, my name is Rachel Johnston. **86/87I'm calling about an issue regarding my mail service.** I requested that my mail be held while I was on vacation. But now that the period has ended, **87my deliveries have not yet resumed.** I would like my mail to be delivered as usual. **88I've already asked about this on your Web site**, but I have not received a response. Please let me know what I can do to solve this problem.

regarding prep. ~에 대해 hold v. 보류하다 now that 이제 ~이므로
period n. 기간 resume v. 재개하다 response n. 답변

해석
86-88번은 다음 전화 메시지에 관한 문제입니다.

안녕하세요, 제 이름은 Rachel Johnston입니다. 86/87제 우편 서비스와 관련된 문제에 대해 전화드립니다. 저는 휴가 동안 제 우편이 보류되도록 요청했었습니다. 하지만 이제 그 기간이 끝났는데, 87배달이 아직 재개되지 않았습니다. 제 우편이 평소처럼 배달되었으면 좋겠습니다. 88저는 귀사의 웹사이트에서 이미 이에 대해 문의했지만, 답변을 받지 못했습니다. 이 문제를 해결하기 위해 제가 무엇을 할 수 있는지 알려 주세요.

86 | 청자 문제

해석 청자는 어디에서 일하는 것 같은가?
(A) 우체국에서
(B) 서점에서
(C) 호텔에서
(D) 수리 센터에서

해설 지문에서 신분 및 직업과 관련된 표현을 놓치지 않고 듣는다. "I'm calling about an issue regarding my mail service."라며 자신의 우편 서비스와 관련된 문제에 대해 전화드린다고 했으므로 청자는 우체국에서 일하고 있음을 알 수 있다. 따라서 (A)가 정답이다.

87 | 특정 세부 사항 문제

해석 화자는 무슨 문제를 언급하는가?
(A) 제품이 분실되었다.
(B) 물건이 손상되었다.
(C) 서비스가 다시 시작되지 않았다.
(D) 휴가 계획이 취소되었다.

해설 질문의 핵심 어구(problem ~ mention)와 관련된 내용을 주의 깊게 듣는다. "I'm calling about an issue regarding my mail service."라며 자신의 우편 서비스와 관련된 문제에 대해 전화드린다고 한 후, "my deliveries have not yet resumed"라며 배달이 아직 재개되지 않았다고 하였다. 따라서 (C)가 정답이다.

어휘 damage v. 손상을 주다

Paraphrasing

have not yet resumed 아직 재개되지 않았다 → has not restarted 다시 시작되지 않았다

88 | 특정 세부 사항 문제

해석 화자는 그녀가 무엇을 이미 했다고 말하는가?
(A) 영수증에 서명했다.
(B) 편지를 보냈다.
(C) 사무실을 방문했다.
(D) 온라인 문의를 했다.

해설 질문의 핵심 어구(speaker ~ already done)와 관련된 내용을 주의 깊게 듣는다. "I've already asked about this on your Web site"라며 웹사이트에서 이미 이에 대해 문의했다고 하였다. 따라서 (D)가 정답이다.

어휘 inquiry n. 문의

Paraphrasing

asked 문의했다 → made an ~ inquiry 문의를 했다

[89-91]

Questions 89-91 refer to the following announcement.   호주

> [89]I'd like to discuss one more thing about the TV show, *Saving Us All*, which we plan to premiere in March. It received positive reviews from the focus group on Tuesday. We did, however, receive some criticism for the song used at the beginning of the show. The producer and I agree with the criticism, so we're going to choose a new song. I've sent a few songs to your e-mails, and [90/91]I'd like you all to listen to them and let me know which you think is best. I'll be meeting the producer again next Tuesday.

premiere v. 개봉하다, 첫 방송을 하다
focus group 포커스 그룹(시장 조사 참가자들로 이뤄진 그룹) criticism n. 비판
producer n. 제작자

해석
89-91번은 다음 공지에 관한 문제입니다.
[89]3월에 개봉할 예정인 TV 프로그램 *Saving Us All*에 대해 한 가지를 더 논의하고 싶습니다. 그것은 화요일에 포커스 그룹에서 긍정적인 평가를 받았습니다. 하지만, 프로그램 초반에 사용된 곡에 대해서는 약간의 비판을 받았습니다. 제작자와 저는 그 비판에 동의해서, 새로운 노래를 선택할 것입니다. 여러분의 이메일로 몇 곡을 보냈으며, [90/91]그것들을 들어보시고 어떤 곡이 가장 좋다고 생각하시는지 알려주시기 바랍니다. 저는 다음 주 화요일에 제작자를 다시 만날 것입니다.

89 | 주제 문제

해석 공지는 주로 무엇에 대한 것인가?
(A) 상영 날짜
(B) 프로젝트의 기간
(C) 경영진으로부터의 조언
(D) 테스트 관객으로부터의 피드백

해설 공지의 주제를 묻는 문제이므로, 지문의 초반을 반드시 듣는다. "I'd like to discuss one more thing about the TV show ~. It received positive reviews from the focus group"이라며 TV 프로그램에 대해 한 가지를 더 논의하고 싶다고 하고, 그것은 포커스 그룹에서 긍정적인 평가를 받았다고 한 후, 프로그램 평가에 대한 내용으로 지문이 이어지고 있다. 따라서 (D)가 정답이다.

어휘 duration n. 기간

Paraphrasing

focus group 포커스 그룹 → test audience 테스트 관객

90 | 요청 문제

해석 청자들은 무엇을 하도록 요청받는가?
(A) 휴대폰을 무음으로 한다.
(B) 선호하는 것을 선택한다.
(C) 새로운 아이디어들을 개발한다.
(D) 한 집단의 사람들을 만난다.

해설 지문의 중후반에서 요청과 관련된 표현이 포함된 문장을 주의 깊게 듣는다. "I'd like you all to listen to them[a few songs] and let me know which you think is best"라며 그것들을 들어보고 어떤 곡이 가장 좋다고 생각하는지 알려주길 바란다고 하였다. 따라서 (B)가 정답이다.

어휘 select v. 선택하다 preference n. 선호하는 것, 선호(도)

Paraphrasing

which you think is best 가장 좋다고 생각하는지 → preference 선호하는 것

91 | 의도 파악 문제

해석 화자는 왜 "저는 다음 주 화요일에 제작자를 다시 만날 것입니다"라고 말하는가?
(A) 마감 기한을 나타내기 위해
(B) 일정을 변경하기 위해
(C) 오류를 정정하기 위해
(D) 항의를 하기 위해

해설 질문의 인용어구(I'll be meeting the producer again next Tuesday)가 언급된 주변을 주의 깊게 듣는다. "I'd like you all to listen to them[a few songs] and let me know which you think is best"라며 그것들을 들어보고 어떤 곡이 가장 좋다고 생각하는지 알려주길 바란다고 한 후, 다음 주 화요일에 제작자를 다시 만날 것이라고 하였으므로, 마감 기한을 나타내기 위함임을 알 수 있다. 따라서 (A)가 정답이다.

어휘 indicate v. 나타내다 complaint n. 항의, 불평

[92-94]

Questions 92-94 refer to the following introduction.   캐나다

> Everyone, I'd like to introduce Vikram Naresh. [92]Mr. Naresh has recently been promoted to assistant chief of the West Port Fire Department. As the assistant chief, [93]Mr. Naresh will be regularly stopping by your local stations to conduct safety inspections. He'll also be in charge

of purchasing new equipment and managing departmental resources. I know some of you have never met Mr. Naresh before, so [94]**join us for a small reception right after his speech**. Now please give a round of applause for Mr. Naresh.

promote v. 승진하다 assistant chief 부서장 fire department 소방서
regularly adv. 정기적으로 conduct v. 실시하다
safety inspection 안전 점검 resource n. 자원 reception n. 환영회
applause n. 박수

해석
92-94번은 다음 소개에 관한 문제입니다.
여러분, Vikram Naresh를 소개하겠습니다. [92]Mr. Naresh는 최근 West Port 소방서 부서장으로 승진했습니다. 부서장으로서, [93]Mr. Naresh는 안전 점검을 실시하기 위해 정기적으로 여러분의 지역 소방서에 들를 예정입니다. 그는 또한 새 장비 구입과 부서 자원 관리를 담당할 것입니다. 몇몇 분들이 Mr. Naresh를 한 번도 만나본 적이 없다는 것을 알고 있으니, [94]그의 연설이 끝난 직후에 있을 작은 환영회에 함께해 주세요. 이제 Mr. Naresh를 위해 박수 부탁드립니다.

92 | 언급 문제

해석 Mr. Naresh에 대해 무엇이 언급되는가?
(A) 새로운 부서로 전근했다.
(B) 최근 직장에서 은퇴했다.
(C) 더 많은 장비를 주문했다.
(D) 승진을 했다.

해설 질문의 핵심 어구(Mr. Naresh)와 관련된 내용을 주의 깊게 듣는다. "Mr. Naresh has recently been promoted to assistant chief of the West Port Fire Department."라며 Mr. Naresh는 최근 West Port 소방서 부서장으로 승진했다고 하였다. 따라서 (D)가 정답이다.

어휘 transfer v. 전근하다 retire v. 은퇴하다

Paraphrasing
has ~ been promoted 승진했다 → given a promotion 승진을 했다

93 | 이유 문제

해석 화자에 따르면, Mr. Naresh는 왜 지역 소방서들을 방문할 것인가?
(A) 정보를 제공하는 연설을 하기 위해
(B) 사무용품을 배송하기 위해
(C) 점검을 실시하기 위해
(D) 직원들을 교육하기 위해

해설 질문의 핵심 어구(visit local stations)와 관련된 내용을 주의 깊게 듣는다. "Mr. Naresh will be regularly stopping by your local stations to conduct safety inspections"라며 Mr. Naresh는 안전 점검을 실시하기 위해 정기적으로 지역 소방서에 들를 예정이라고 하였다. 따라서 (C)가 정답이다.

어휘 office supply 사무용품 carry out 실시하다 train v. 교육하다

Paraphrasing
conduct 실시하다 → carry out 실시하다

94 | 다음에 할 일 문제

해석 연설 후에 청자들은 무엇을 할 것인가?
(A) 시연을 본다.
(B) 행사에 등록한다.
(C) 설문을 작성한다.
(D) 모임에 참가한다.

해설 질문의 핵심 어구(after ~ speech)가 언급된 주변을 주의 깊게 듣는다. "join us for a small reception right after his speech"라며 그의 연설이 끝난 직후에 있을 작은 환영회에 함께해 달라고 한 것을 통해 청자들이 연설 후에 모임에 참가할 것임을 알 수 있다. 따라서 (D)가 정답이다.

어휘 demonstration n. 시연 fill out 작성하다 gathering n. 모임

Paraphrasing
reception 환영회 → gathering 모임

[95-97] 미국

Questions 95-97 refer to the following announcement and map.

[95]**Welcome to Devin Mall.** We are excited to inform you that [96]**Devin Mall's food fair will be held this weekend. It will take place in the parking lot across the street from our building.** Unfortunately, this means that customers won't be able to use that area for parking during the event. Instead, please park in one of the other nearby lots. Finally, [97]**don't forget to buy your admission passes to the fair at any kiosk in Devin Mall**. The cost is $10 per person and includes one meal and drink.

fair n. 박람회 take place 개최되다 across adv. 건너편에 lot n. 부지
admission pass 입장권

해석
95-97번은 다음 공지와 지도에 관한 문제입니다.
[95]Devin 쇼핑몰에 오신 것을 환영합니다. [96]Devin 쇼핑몰의 음식 박람회가 이번 주말에 열린다는 소식을 알려 드리게 되어 기쁩니다. [96]그것은 저희 건물에서 길 건너편 주차장에서 개최될 것입니다. 유감스럽게도, 이는 고객분들께서 행사 기간 동안에는 그 공간을 주차장으로 사용할 수 없을 것이라는 점을 의미합니다. 대신, 근처에 있는 다른 부지에 주차해 주세요. 마지막으로, [97]Devin 쇼핑몰에 있는 어느 키오스크에서든 박람회 입장권을 사는 것을 잊지 마세요. 비용은 1인당 10달러이며 식사 한 끼와 음료 1개가 포함되어 있습니다.

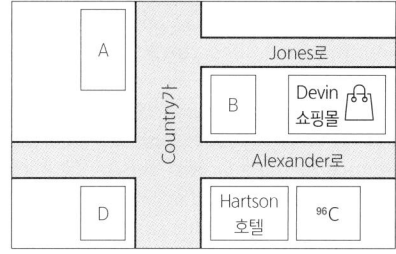

95 | 청자 문제

해석 청자들은 누구인 것 같은가?
(A) 쇼핑객
(B) 축제 기획자
(C) 뉴스 기자
(D) 판매 직원

해설 지문에서 신분 및 직업과 관련된 표현을 놓치지 않고 듣는다. "Welcome to Devin Mall."이라며 Devin 쇼핑몰에 오신 것을 환영한다고 한 것을 통해 청자들이 쇼핑객임을 알 수 있다. 따라서 (A)가 정답이다.

어휘 planner n. 기획자 personnel n. 직원

96 | 시각 자료 문제

해석 시각 자료를 보아라. 어떤 부지가 행사를 위해 사용될 것인가?
(A) 부지 A
(B) 부지 B
(C) 부지 C
(D) 부지 D

해설 지도의 정보를 확인한 후 질문의 핵심 어구(lot ~ used for an event)와 관련된 내용을 주의 깊게 듣는다. "Devin Mall's food fair will be held this weekend. It will take place in the parking lot across the street from our building."이라며 Devin 쇼핑몰의 음식 박람회가 이번 주말에 열리고, 그것은 Devin 쇼핑몰 건물의 길 건너편 주차장에서 개최될 것이라고 했으므로, 행사를 위해 사용될 부지가 C임을 지도에서 알 수 있다. 따라서 (C)가 정답이다.

97 | 특정 세부 사항 문제

해석 청자들은 무엇을 하라고 상기되는가?
(A) 대중교통을 이용한다.
(B) 표를 구매한다.
(C) 주차권을 보여준다.
(D) 새로운 메뉴 품목을 시도해 본다.

해설 질문의 핵심 어구(reminded to do)와 관련된 내용을 주의 깊게 듣는다. "don't forget to buy your admission passes to the fair at any kiosk in Devin Mall"이라며 Devin 쇼핑몰에 있는 어느 키오스크에서든 박람회 입장권을 사는 것을 잊지 말라고 하였으므로, 청자들이 표를 구매하라고 상기됨을 알 수 있다. 따라서 (B)가 정답이다.

어휘 remind v. 상기시키다

Paraphrasing

admission passes 입장권 → ticket 표

[98-100]

Questions 98-100 refer to the following talk and graph. 영국

> After reviewing last quarter's financial reports, ⁹⁸the CEO has asked every department to find ways to reduce its expenses. So we need to figure out how we can reduce costs in our marketing department. This is a top priority for now, so you should postpone any other projects that you're working on, if necessary. ⁹⁹There isn't much we can do about our largest operating expense, but I think we can reduce the next largest item by 20 percent. ¹⁰⁰I have prepared an overview of our department's monthly expenditures to help with this task. I'll hand it out to everyone in a minute.

quarter n. 분기 expense n. 비용 priority n. 우선 사항
postpone v. 미루다 overview n. 개요, 개관 expenditure n. 지출
hand out 나눠주다, 배부하다

해석
98-100번은 다음 담화와 그래프에 관한 문제입니다.

지난 분기의 재무 보고서를 검토한 후, ⁹⁸최고 경영자는 모든 부서에 비용을 절감할 방안들을 찾아달라고 요청했습니다. 그래서 우리는 마케팅 부서 내의 비용을 줄이는 방법을 생각해 내야 합니다. 현재로서는 이것이 우선 사항이므로, 필요하다면 여러분이 진행하고 있는 다른 프로젝트들을 미뤄야 할 것입니다. ⁹⁹우리의 가장 큰 운영 비용에 대해서는 할 수 있는 것이 많지 않지만, 그 다음으로 큰 항목을 20퍼센트까지 줄일 수 있을 것이라고 생각합니다. ¹⁰⁰이 업무에 대해 도움이 되도록 우리 부서의 월간 지출 개요를 준비했습니다. 제가 곧 모두에게 그것을 나눠드리겠습니다.

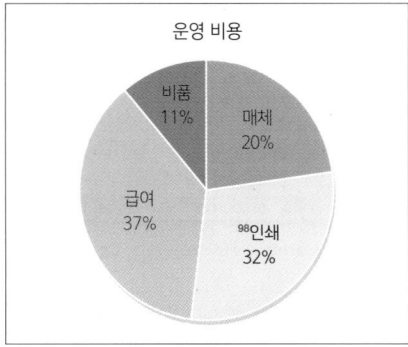

98 | 청자 문제

해석 청자들은 누구인 것 같은가?
(A) 재정 고문들
(B) 마케팅 전문가들
(C) 회계 직원들
(D) 회사 주주들

해설 지문에서 신분 및 직업과 관련된 표현을 놓치지 않고 듣는다. "the CEO has asked every department to find ways to reduce its expenses. So we need to figure out how we can reduce costs in our marketing department."라며 최고 경영자가 모든 부서에 비용을 절감할 방안들을 찾아달라고 요청했고, 자신들은 책임은 마케팅 부서 내의 비용을 줄이는 방법을 생각해 내야 한다고 한 것을 통해 청자들은 마케팅 부서의 직원들임을 알 수 있다. 따라서 (B)가 정답이다.

어휘 accounting n. 회계 shareholder n. 주주

99 | 시각 자료 문제

해석 시각 자료를 보시오. 어느 비용이 줄어들 것 같은가?
(A) 매체
(B) 인쇄
(C) 급여
(D) 비품

해설 제시된 그래프의 정보를 확인한 후 질문의 핵심 어구(expense ~ be reduced)와 관련된 내용을 주의 깊게 듣는다. "There isn't much we can do about our largest operating expense, but I think we can reduce the next largest item ~"이라며 가장 큰 운영 비용에 대해서는 할 수 있는 것이 많지 않지만, 그 다음으로 큰 항목을 줄일 수 있을 것이라고 생각한다고 했으므로, 두 번째로 큰 항목인 인쇄 비용이 줄어들 것임을 그래프에서 알 수 있다. 따라서 (B)가 정답이다.

100 | 다음에 할 일 문제

해석 다음에 무슨 일이 일어날 것인가?
(A) 보고서가 배부될 것이다.
(B) 발표가 진행될 것이다.
(C) 업무가 설명될 것이다.
(D) 결정이 발표될 것이다.

해설 지문의 마지막 부분을 주의 깊게 듣는다. "I have prepared an overview of our department's monthly expenditures ~. I'll hand it out to everyone in a minute."이라며 부서의 월간 지출 개요를 준비했으며 곧 모두에게 그것을 나눠주겠다고 한 것을 통해 보고서가 배부될 것임을 알 수 있다. 따라서 (A)가 정답이다.

Paraphrasing

overview 개요 → report 보고서

PART 5

101 | 등위접속사 채우기

해설 절(There ~ Hotel)과 절(several ~ Inn)을 연결할 수 있는 것은 접속사이므로 모든 보기가 정답의 후보이다. 'Starlight 호텔에는 빈 객실이 없지만, Pinehill 호텔에서는 여러 객실을 이용할 수 있다'라는 의미가 되어야 하므로 등위접속사 (A) but(하지만)이 정답이다. (B) as는 '~와 같이', (C) neither는 '또 ~하지 않다'라는 의미로, 모두 어색한 의미를 만들기 때문에 답이 될 수 없다. 참고로, 접속사 (D)는 부사 neither와 함께 상관접속사 neither A nor B(A도 B도 아닌)의 형태로 자주 쓰임을 알아둔다.

해석 Starlight 호텔에는 빈 객실이 없지만, Pinehill 호텔에서는 여러 객실을 이용할 수 있다.

어휘 vacancy n. 빈 객실, 텅 빔   available adj. 이용할 수 있는   inn n. (작은) 호텔

102 | 격에 맞는 인칭대명사 채우기

해설 명사구(marketing proposal) 앞에서 형용사처럼 쓰일 수 있는 인칭대명사는 소유격이므로 (C) his가 정답이다. 주격 인칭대명사 (A), 목적격 인칭대명사 (B), 재귀대명사 (D)는 명사구를 꾸밀 수 없다.

해석 프로젝트 관리자는 즉각적인 시행을 위해 어제 마케팅 제안서를 제출했다.

어휘 immediate adj. 즉각적인   implementation n. 시행

103 | 명사 자리 채우기

해설 동사(shows)의 목적어 자리에 오면서 형용사(significant)의 꾸밈을 받을 수 있는 것은 명사이므로 명사 역할을 할 수 있는 명사 (A)와 동명사 (D)가 정답의 후보이다. '에너지 사용에서의 상당한 감소를 보여준다'라는 의미가 되어야 하므로, 명사 (A) reduction(감소)이 정답이다. 동명사 (D) reducing(줄이기)를 쓰면 '에너지 사용에서의 상당한 줄이기를 보여준다'라는 어색한 의미를 만들기 때문에 답이 될 수 없다. 동사 또는 과거분사 (B), 동사 (C)는 명사 자리에 올 수 없다.

해석 Brinity 전자회사의 최신 냉장고는 그것의 이전 모델과 비교하여 에너지 사용에서의 상당한 감소를 보여준다.

어휘 latest adj. 최신의   significant adj. 상당한, 중요한   predecessor n. 이전 모델, 전임자   reduce v. 줄이다, 축소하다

104 | 부사 자리 채우기

해설 동사(must ~ handled)를 꾸밀 수 있는 것은 부사이므로 부사 (D) cautiously(조심스럽게)가 정답이다. 명사 또는 동사 (A)와 (C), 형용사 (B)는 동사를 꾸밀 수 없다. 참고로, handled를 복수 명사 (C) cautions(경고들)를 꾸미는 과거분사로 본다 해도, '소포들은 다루어진 경고들이 되어야 한다'라는 어색한 문맥이 된다.

해석 배달 중에, 부서지기 쉬운 물건들이 들어 있는 소포들은 조심스럽게 다루어져야 한다.

어휘 contain v. ~이 들어 있다, 포함하다   delicate adj. 부서지기 쉬운, 섬세한   handle v. 다루다, 처리하다   cautious adj. 조심스러운

105 | 현재분사와 과거분사 구별하여 채우기

해설 이 문장은 주어(Mr. Sawaya), 동사(asked), 목적어(all ~ managers), 목적격 보어(to cut expenses)를 갖춘 완전한 절이므로 ___ to ~ difficulties는 수식어 거품으로 보아야 한다. 보기 중 수식어 거품이 될 수 있는 것은 현재분사 (A)와 과거분사 (C)이고, 주절의 주어(Mr. Sawaya)와 분사가 'Mr. Sawaya가 회사의 재정적인 어려움을 암시하다'라는 의미의 능동 관계이므로 동사 point(암시하다, 가리키다)의 현재분사형 (A) pointing이 정답이다. 과거분사 (C) pointed를 쓸 경우 'Mr. Sawaya가 회사의 재정적인 어려움에 암시되다'라는 어색한 문맥이 된다. 명사 또는 동사 (B)와 (D)는 수식어 거품을 이끌 수 없다.

해석 Mr. Sawaya는 회사의 재정적인 어려움을 암시하면서 모든 부서장들에게 경비를 줄이도록 요청했다.

어휘 department manager 부서장   cut v. 줄이다, 단축하다   expense n. 경비   point v. 암시하다, 가리키다; n. 요점

106 | 주어와 수일치하는 동사 채우기

해설 문장에 동사가 없으므로 동사인 (A), (B), (D)가 정답의 후보이다. 주어(The service centers)가 복수이므로 복수 동사 (A) employ가 정답이다. 참고로, 주어(The service centers)와 동사 사이의 전치사구 of Terta Corporation은 수식어 거품구이므로 동사의 수 결정에 아무런 영향을 주지 않는다. 단수 동사 (B)와 (D)는 복수 주어의 동사 자리에 올 수 없다. 현재분사 또는 동명사 (C)는 동사 자리에 올 수 없다.

해석 Terta사의 서비스 센터들은 고객 불만을 추적하는 전문적인 소프트웨어를 이용한다.

어휘 specialized adj. 전문적인   track v. 추적하다   employ v. 이용하다, 고용하다   complaint n. 불만

107 | 동사 어휘 고르기

해설 '평균 임금이 더 낮은 지역으로 제조업을 옮김으로써 인건비를 줄이기를 기대한다'라는 문맥이므로 shift(옮기다, 이전하다)의 동명사형 (C) shifting이 정답이다. (A)의 invert는 '뒤집다', (B)의 substitute는 '대체하다', (D)의 transform은 '변형시키다'라는 의미이다.

해석 임원들은 평균 임금이 더 낮은 지역으로 제조업을 옮김으로써 인건비를 줄이기를 기대한다.

어휘 board member 임원, 이사   labor cost 인건비   manufacturing n. 제조업, 제조   region n. 지역, 지방   average adj. 평균의   wage n. 임금

108 | 부사 어휘 고르기

해설 '때때로 직원들은 교육 세미나에 참석한다'라는 문맥이므로 (C) Occasionally(때때로, 가끔)가 정답이다. (A) Potentially는 '잠재적으로', (B) Similarly는 '비슷하게', (D) Unanimously는 '만장일치로'라는 의미이다.

해석 때때로, Godsal 가전제품사의 직원들은 회사가 후원하는 시장의 신기술에 대한 교육 세미나에 참석한다.

어휘 attend v. 참석하다

109 | 사람명사와 사물/추상명사 구별하여 채우기

해설 형용사(one-year)의 꾸밈을 받을 수 있는 것은 명사이므로 명사 (B)와 (C)가 정답의 후보이다. 'Emerald 모바일사에 1년 가입을 신청하는 고객들'이라는 의미가 되어야 하므로 추상명사 (C) subscription(가입, 구독)이 정답이다. 사람명사 (B) subscriber를 쓰면 'Emerald 모바일사에 1년 구독자를 신청하는 고객들'이라는 어색한 문맥이 된다. 동사 (A)와 (D)는 형용사의 꾸밈을 받을 수 없다.

해석 Emerald 모바일사에 1년 가입을 신청하는 고객들은 한 달간의 무료 서비스를 받을 것이다.

110 | 부사 자리 채우기

해설 동사(push)를 꾸밀 수 있는 것은 부사이므로 부사 (B) Simply(간단히)가 정답이다. 형용사 (A), 형용사 simple(간단한)의 비교급 (C), 동사 (D)는 동사를 꾸밀 수 없다. 참고로, 첫 번째 절(___ push ~ disconnects)은 주어가 생략된 명령문임을 알아둔다.

해석 인터넷 접속이 끊어질 때마다 간단히 장치의 재설정 버튼을 누르면, 그 문

제는 즉시 고쳐질 것이다.
어휘 disconnect v. (접속이) 끊어지다, 끊다 immediately adv. 즉시
simplify v. 간단하게 하다

111 | to 부정사 채우기

해설 빈칸이 있는 절은 주어(you), 동사(can activate), 목적어(night mode)를 갖춘 완전한 절이므로, ___ the fan speed는 수식어 거품으로 보아야 한다. 이 수식어 거품은 동사가 없는 거품구이므로, 거품구를 이끌면서 '팬 속도를 낮추기 위해'라는 의미의 목적을 나타내는 to 부정사 (B) to lower가 정답이다. 동사 (A), 동사 또는 형용사 low(낮은)의 비교급 (C), 동사 또는 과거분사 (D)는 거품구를 이끌 수 없다. 참고로, 이 문장은 조건을 나타내는 부사절(If ~ sleep)과 주절(you ~ speed)이 있는 구조임을 알아둔다.

해석 공기 청정기 소음이 수면을 방해한다면, 팬 속도를 낮추기 위해 야간 모드를 활성화하실 수 있습니다.

어휘 air purifier 공기 청정기 disturb v. 방해하다 activate v. 활성화하다
lower v. 낮추다

112 | 형용사 자리 채우기

해설 빈칸은 be동사 be의 주격 보어 자리이므로 명사 (A)와 (D), 형용사 (B)가 정답의 후보이다. 부사(fully)의 꾸밈을 받고 있고, 보어가 주어(HynaCorp's ~ plant)의 상태를 설명하고 있으므로 형용사 (B) functional(가동되는)이 정답이다. 명사 (A)와 (D)를 쓸 경우 주어(HynaCorp's ~ plant)와 동격이 되어 각각 '공장이 완전히 기능/기능들일 것이다'라는 어색한 문맥이 된다. 참고로 (A)의 function은 동사일 때 '기능하다'라는 의미로 쓰임을 알아둔다. 부사 (C)는 보어 자리에 올 수 없다.

해석 HynaCorp사의 최신 화학 공장은 분기 말 무렵에 완전히 가동될 것이다.

어휘 plant n. 공장 fully adv. 완전히, 충분히 quarter n. 분기
functionally adv. 기능상, 함수적으로

113 | 형용사 어휘 고르기

해설 'Burnside 여행사의 고객은 선택적인 활동들을 고름으로써 쉽게 여행 패키지를 원하는 대로 구성할 수 있다'라는 문맥이므로 (B) optional(선택적인)이 정답이다. (A) admitted는 '인정된', (C) affluent는 '부유한, 돈이 많은', (D) reliable은 '신뢰할 수 있는'이라는 의미이다.

해석 Burnside 여행사의 고객은 선택적인 활동들을 고름으로써 쉽게 그들의 여행 패키지를 원하는 대로 구성할 수 있다.

어휘 customize v. 원하는 대로 구성하다, 주문제작하다

114 | 전치사 채우기

해설 'Harborview 아파트의 로비 안에 위치한 카페'라는 의미가 되어야 하므로 (D) in(~안에)이 정답이다. (A) among은 '~사이에', (B) at은 '~에서', (C) to는 '~로'라는 의미이다. 참고로, 전치사 at과 in 모두 장소를 나타낼 때 사용되지만, at은 특정 지점을 나타낼 때, in은 특정 공간을 나타낼 때 사용되는데, 로비는 아파트 안에 있는 특정 공간이므로 in이 쓰이는게 적절하다.

해석 Harborview 아파트의 로비 안에 위치한 카페는 모든 세입자들에게 할인을 제공한다.

어휘 condominium n. 아파트, 콘도 discount n. 할인; v. 할인하다
tenant n. 세입자, 임차인

115 | 동사 어휘 고르기

해설 '상당한 보조금을 지급하다'라는 문맥이므로 award(지급하다, 수여하다)의 과거형 (B) awarded가 정답이다. (D)의 donate(기부하다)도 해석상 그럴듯해 보이지만, donate는 사람명사가 아닌 기부하는 금액이나 물품을 목적어로 취하므로 답이 될 수 없다. (A)의 charge는 '청구하다', (C)의 access는 '접근하다'라는 의미이다.

해석 위원회가 Mr. Souko의 사업 제안서를 충분히 검토하자마자, 그것은 그에게 상당한 보조금을 지급했다.

어휘 committee n. 위원회 thoroughly adv. 충분히, 철저하게
review v. 검토하다 proposal n. 제안(서) considerable adj. 상당한
grant n. 보조금, 장려금

116 | 올바른 시제의 동사 채우기

해설 과거 시제와 함께 쓰이는 시간 표현(last month)이 있으므로 과거 시제 (B) moved가 정답이다. 현재 시제 (A), 현재완료 시제 (C), 미래 시제 (D)는 과거를 나타내는 시간 표현과 함께 쓰일 수 없다.

해석 지난달 초에 Hightower 은행의 웨스트코비나 지점이 El Monte로 옮겼다.

어휘 branch n. 지점

117 | 전치사 채우기

해설 '대부분의 기금을 기업 후원을 통해 받다'라는 의미가 되어야 하므로 (C) through(~을 통해)가 정답이다. (A) over도 '~을 통해'라는 의미를 가지지만, 전화, 라디오, TV, 컴퓨터 등의 방송 매체를 통하는 것을 의미하므로 답이 될 수 없다. (B) along은 '~을 따라', (D) across는 '~을 가로질러'라는 의미이다.

해석 Kerner 재단은 올해 대부분의 기금을 기업 후원을 통해 받을 것으로 예상한다.

어휘 expect v. 예상하다 receive v. 받다 funding n. 기금
corporate adj. 기업의 sponsorship n. 후원

118 | 수량 표현 채우기

해설 빈칸 뒤의 복수 가산 명사(vehicles)를 꾸밀 수 있는 것은 형용사이므로 수량 형용사 (B)와 (D)가 정답의 후보이다. 'Hamada사의 SUV가 Sunza사의 것보다 더 높은 안전 등급을 가지지만, 두 차량들 다 성능 면에서 높은 점수를 받았다'라는 의미가 되어야 하므로 (B) both(둘 다, 모두)가 정답이다. (D) several(몇몇의)을 쓸 경우, 'Hamada사의 SUV가 Sunza사의 것보다 더 높은 안전 등급을 가지지만, 몇몇 차량들은 성능 면에서 높은 점수를 받았다'라는 어색한 문맥이 된다. 등위접속사 (A)는 접속사(Although)로 이미 연결된 절을 연결할 수 없다. 한정사 (C)는 두 가지 대상 중 하나를 가리킬 때 사용되며 단수 명사와 쓰인다. 참고로, either or(또는)와 함께 상관접속사 either A or B(A 또는 B 중 하나)의 형태로 쓰일 수 있음을 알아둔다.

해석 비록 Hamada사의 SUV가 Sunza사의 것보다 더 높은 안전 등급을 가지지만, 두 차량들 다 성능 면에서 높은 점수를 받았다.

어휘 rating n. 등급, 순위 vehicle n. 차량, 차 performance n. 성능, 실적

119 | 형용사 어휘 고르기

해설 '환경을 보호하기 위해 일회용 플라스틱 용기 제작을 중단하다'라는 문맥이므로 형용사 (D) disposable(일회용의)이 정답이다. (A) capable은 '~을 할 수 있는', (B) decisive는 '결정적인, 중대한', (C) effective는 '효과적인'이라는 의미이다.

해석 Bolson Limited사는 환경을 보호하기 위해 일회용 플라스틱 용기 제작을 중단할 것이라고 발표했다.

어휘 announce v. 발표하다 container n. 용기, 그릇

120 | 형용사 자리 채우기

해설 빈칸 뒤의 명사(performance)를 꾸밀 수 있는 것은 형용사이므로 형용사 (C) notable(주목할 만한)이 정답이다. 현재분사 (A) noting은 '주목하는

성과'라는 어색한 의미를 만들고, 명사 (B) notability는 performance와 복합 명사를 이루지 못하므로 답이 될 수 없다. 부사 (D) notably는 명사를 꾸밀 수 없다.

해석 팀장으로서의 Mr. Kim의 주목할 만한 성과는 그가 Hartek 보험사에서 고위 관리직을 제안받는 것으로 이어졌다.

어휘 senior management 고위 관리직

121 | 동명사 채우기

해설 빈칸은 전치사(before)의 목적어 자리이므로 명사 (A)와 동명사 (C)가 정답의 후보이다. 빈칸 다음에 온 목적어(it)를 가질 수 있는 것은 동명사이므로 동사 upload(업로드하다)의 동명사형 (C) uploading이 정답이다. 명사 (A)는 목적어를 가질 수 없다. (A)는 동사로도 쓰이는데, 동사 (A), 동사 또는 과거분사 (B), to 부정사 (D)는 전치사의 목적어 자리에 올 수 없다.

해석 사실에 기반을 둔 오류가 있는 콘텐츠 발행을 방지하기 위해 웹사이트에 업로드하기 전에 기사를 확인하십시오.

어휘 check v. 확인하다　prevent v. 방지하다, 예방하다
publication n. 발행, 출간　factual adj. 사실에 기반을 둔

122 | 전치사 채우기

해설 이 문장은 주어(participants), 동사(will attend), 목적어(a ~ concert)를 갖춘 완전한 절이므로, ___ the charity auction은 수식어 거품으로 보아야 한다. 이 수식어 거품은 동사가 없는 거품구이므로 거품구를 이끌 수 있는 전치사 (A), (B), (D)가 정답의 후보이다. '자선 경매 후에 무료 콘서트에 참석할 것이다'라는 의미가 되어야 하므로 (D) Following(~ 후에)이 정답이다. (B) Upon(~의 직후에)도 해석상 그럴듯해 보이지만, '~의 직후에'라는 의미로 쓰이기 위해서는 동명사나 delivery(배달), arrival(도착) 등 동작을 나타내는 명사와 함께 쓰여야 한다. 참고로, upon이 '~일 때, ~에'라는 의미로 쓰이기 위해서는 시간 표현과 함께 쓰여야 하므로 upon the event가 아닌, upon the start of the event(행사가 시작할 때)와 같이 쓰여야 한다. (A) Toward는 '~ 쪽으로'라는 의미이다. 참고로, toward가 '~ 무렵에, (언제)쯤'이라는 의미로 쓰이기 위해서는 뒤에 시간(noon, evening 등) 및 시기(the end of this week 등)를 나타내는 표현이 와야 하므로 답이 될 수 없다. 접속사 (C) Whereas(~에 반해서, 반면)는 거품구를 이끌 수 없다.

해석 자선 경매 후에, 참가자들은 Brighton 홀에서 여러 지역 밴드들을 출연시키는 무료 콘서트에 참석할 것이다.

어휘 charity auction 자선 경매　feature v. 출연시키다

123 | 지시대명사 those 채우기

해설 주절(___ ~ do not)에 동사(do)만 있고, 주어가 없으므로 주어 자리에 올 수 있는 주격 인칭대명사 (A), 지시대명사 (C), 가짜주어로 쓰이는 (D)가 정답의 후보이다. 빈칸이 과거분사(offered)의 꾸밈을 받고 있고, 'Leisure 항공사에 의해 제공되는 것들은 그렇지 않다'라는 의미가 되어야 하므로 앞에 나온 복수 명사(airline miles)를 대신하는 지시대명사 (C) those(그것들)가 정답이다. 주격 인칭대명사 (A)는 수식어의 꾸밈을 받을 수 없고, (D)는 '~이 있다'를 나타내며 'there + 동사(be, remain, exist 등) + 진짜주어'의 형태로 쓰인다. 목적격 인칭대명사 (B)는 주어 자리에 올 수 없다.

해석 항공사 마일리지는 보통 일정 기간 후에 만료됨에도 불구하고, Leisure 항공사에 의해 제공되는 것들은 그렇지 않다.

어휘 expire v. 만료되다　offer v. 제공하다, 제안하다

124 | 명사 어휘 고르기

해설 '마감일들에 대해 내부 전산망에 있는 일정표를 참고할 수 있다'라는 문맥이므로 (D) timetable(일정표, 시간표)이 정답이다. (A) catalog는 '목록, 카탈로그', (B) category는 '범주', (C) formation은 '형성'이라는 의미이다.

해석 직원들은 다른 프로젝트 마감일들에 대해 내부 전산망에 있는 일정표를 참고할 수 있다.

어휘 refer to ~을 참고하다　intranet n. 내부 전산망

125 | 형용사 자리 채우기

해설 빈칸 앞에 정관사(The), 빈칸 뒤에 명사(growth)가 있으므로 명사를 꾸미는 형용사 (C) exceptional(이례적인)이 정답이다. 명사 (B)는 growth와 복합 명사를 이루지 못하므로 답이 될 수 없다. 전치사 또는 동사 (A)와 부사 (D)는 형용사 자리에 올 수 없다.

해석 소매업 부문에서의 이례적인 성장은 Coleman 백화점 체인의 현저히 높은 수익으로 이어졌다.

어휘 retail sector 소매업 부문　unusually adv. 현저히, 평소와 달리
except prep. ~을 제외하고; v. 제외하다　exception n. 예외, 이례

126 | 다른 명사를 수식하는 명사 채우기

해설 등위접속사 as well as로 연결되어 있는 명사구(pay raises)와 대등한 형태로 와야 하므로 빈칸 뒤 명사 package와 함께 복합 명사를 이룰 수 있는 명사 (B), (C)와 명사를 꾸밀 수 있는 분사 (A), (D) 모두 정답의 후보이다. '더 나은 복리 후생 제도뿐만 아니라 상당히 큰 급료 인상을 바라고 있었다'라는 의미가 되어야 하므로 명사 package(제도, 종합 정책)와 함께 '복리 후생 제도'라는 의미의 복합 명사 benefits package를 만드는 명사 (B) benefits(복리 후생)가 정답이다. 명사 (C) benefiter(수혜자)를 쓸 경우 '수혜자 제도'라는 어색한 의미를 만들기 때문에 답이 될 수 없다. 과거분사 (A)와 현재분사 (D)는 각각 '이득을 본 제도', '이득을 보는 제도'라는 어색한 의미를 만들기 때문에 답이 될 수 없다.

해석 Quartman사의 공장 직원들은 더 나은 복리 후생 제도뿐만 아니라 상당히 큰 급료 인상을 바라고 있었다.

어휘 sizable adj. 상당히 큰　pay raise 급료 인상

127 | 형용사 자리 채우기

해설 부정관사(a) 앞에 와서 명사(impression)를 꾸밀 수 있어야 하므로 형용사 (D) such(매우)가 정답이다. 참고로, such는 뒤에 온 that절과 연결되어 '매우 ~여서 -하다'는 의미를 가지고, 'such + (부정관사) + 형용사 + 명사'의 형태로 쓰인다. 부사 (A), (B), (C)는 부정관사(a) 앞에 와서 명사를 꾸밀 수 없다.

해석 영업직 지원자는 면접 동안 매우 긍정적인 인상을 주어서 그는 즉시 고용되었다.

어휘 candidate n. 지원자, 후보자　impression n. 인상, 감명
immediately adv. 즉시

128 | 동사 어휘 고르기

해설 '텔레비전 캠페인에 성공하지 못했고 제품들을 광고하기 위해 소셜 미디어로 방향을 돌렸다'라는 문맥이므로 (C) market(광고하다, 시장에 내놓다)이 정답이다. (A) generate는 '발생시키다, 만들어 내다', (B) exchange는 '교환하다', (D) contribute는 '기여하다'라는 의미이다.

해석 Venus 의류사는 그것의 텔레비전 캠페인에 성공하지 못했고 제품들을 광고하기 위해 소셜 미디어로 방향을 돌렸다.

어휘 unsuccessful adj. 성공하지 못한

129 | 형용사 자리 채우기

해설 관사(an) 뒤에 와서 명사(manner)를 꾸밀 수 있는 것은 형용사이므로 형용사 (C)와 형용사 역할을 하는 현재분사 (D)가 정답의 후보이다. '질서 정연한 방식으로 줄을 서다'라는 문맥이므로 형용사 (C) orderly(질서 정

연한, 정돈된)가 정답이다. 현재분사 (D)는 '고객들은 명령을 내리는/주문하는 방식으로 줄을 섰다'라는 어색한 문맥을 만든다. 명사 또는 동사 (A)와 (B)는 명사일 경우 빈칸 뒤의 명사(manner)와 복합 명사를 이루지 않고, 동사일 경우 형용사 자리에 올 수 없으므로 답이 될 수 없다.

해석 Beppo 컴퓨터사의 가장 신규 매장 개점에 참석한 수백 명의 고객들은 질서 정연한 방식으로 줄을 섰다.

어휘 line up 줄을 서다　manner n. 방식, 태도
order n. 명령, 순서; v. 명령하다, 주문하다

130 | to 부정사 채우기

해설 빈칸 앞에 to 부정사를 목적어로 취하는 동사 agree가 있으므로 to 부정사 (B) to volunteer가 정답이다. 명사 또는 동사 (A), 동명사 또는 현재분사 (C), 동사 (D)는 agree의 목적어 자리, 즉 to 부정사 자리에 올 수 없다.

해석 다음 주말 행사에서 자원 봉사하기로 동의한 모든 사람들을 위해 회의가 열릴 것이다.

어휘 volunteer v. 자원 봉사하다; n. 자원 봉사자

PART 6

131-134번은 다음 광고지에 관한 문제입니다.

Forge를 소개합니다

Lodz 공과 대학(LTI)이 Forge를 자랑스럽게 소개합니다. ¹³¹Forge는 창작자들의 공동체에 의해 운영되는 작업공간으로, 아마추어 발명가들이 그들의 프로젝트들을 개발할 수 있는 곳입니다. ¹³²당신의 관심사가 전자 기술에 있든 목공에 있든 혹은 금속세공에 있든, Forge는 당신의 창의적인 상상을 실현하도록 도와줄 수 있습니다. ¹³³그것은 3D 프린터, 레이저 절단기, 그리고 그 이상의 것들과 같은 다양한 장비에 대한 공동의 이용을 제공합니다. 모든 LTI 학생들은 대학 정상 운영 시간 동안 이 장비를 자유롭게 사용할 수 있습니다. 기계는 무료로 사용될 수 있고, 재료들은 필요 시 저렴한 가격에 제공됩니다. ¹³⁴저희는 당신이 필요할지도 모르는 무엇이든 주문하는 것을 도와줄 수도 있습니다. 더 많은 정보를 위해서는 Kaminski 건물에 들르거나, www.lodz.edu/forge를 방문하십시오.

proudly adv. 자랑스럽게　lie v. 있다, 위치해 있다　electronics n. 전자 기술
carpentry n. 목공(품)　metalworking n. 금속세공
realize v. (목표를) 실현하다, 알아차리다　vision n. 상상, 시력
a range of 다양한　laser cutter 레이저 절단기　equipment n. 장비
machinery n. 기계　material n. 재료, 물질　stop by ~에 (잠시) 들르다

131 | 명사 어휘 고르기 전체 문맥 파악

해설 'Forge는 창작자들의 공동체에 의해 운영되는 _____으로, 아마추어 발명가들이 그들의 프로젝트들을 개발할 수 있는 곳이다'라는 문맥이므로 모든 보기가 정답의 후보이다. 빈칸이 있는 문장만으로 정답을 고를 수 없으므로 주변 문맥이나 전체 문맥을 파악한다. 뒷부분에서 '그것은 3D 프린터, 레이저 절단기, 그리고 그 이상의 것들과 같은 다양한 장비에 대한 이용을 제공합니다(It offers ~ access to a range of equipment, such as 3D printers, laser cutters, and more).'라고 했고, '모든 LTI 학생들은 대학 정상 운영 시간 동안 이 장비를 자유롭게 사용할 수 있습니다(All LTI students are welcome to use the equipment ~ during regular university hours).'라고 했으므로, 빈칸에는 Forge가 창작자들의 공동체에 의해 운영되는 작업공간이라는 문맥이 되어야 한다. 따라서 (C) workspace(작업공간)이 정답이다. (A) group은 '집단', (B) course는 '과정, 강의', (D) conference는 '회의'라는 의미이다.

132 | 부사절 접속사 채우기 주변 문맥 파악

해설 이 문장은 주어(the Forge), 동사(can help), 목적어(you), 목적격 보어(realize ~ vision)를 갖춘 완전한 절이므로, _____ ~ metalworking은 수식어 거품으로 보아야 한다. 이 수식어 거품은 주어(your interest)와 동사(lies)를 갖춘 완전한 절이므로 부사절 접속사인 모든 보기가 정답의 후보이다. 빈칸이 있는 문장만으로 정답을 고를 수 없으므로 주변 문맥이나 전체 문맥을 파악한다. 뒤 문장에서 '그것은 3D 프린터, 레이저 절단기, 그리고 그 이상의 것들과 같은 다양한 장비에 대한 이용을 제공합니다(It offers ~ access to a range of equipment, such as 3D printers, laser cutters, and more).'라고 했으므로, '관심사가 전자 기술에 있든 목공에 있든 혹은 금속세공에 있든, Forge는 창의적인 상상을 실현하도록 도와줄 수 있다'는 것을 알 수 있다. 따라서 (A) Whether(~이든 ~이든)가 정답이다. (B) Unless는 '~하지 않는 한', (C) Although는 '비록 ~이긴 하지만', (D) Whereas는 '~에 반하여'라는 의미이다.

133 | 동사 어휘 고르기 전체 문맥 파악

해설 '다양한 장비에 대한 _____ 이용을 제공한다'라는 문맥이므로 (A), (B), (C)가 정답의 후보이다. 빈칸이 있는 문장만으로 정답을 고를 수 없으므로 주변 문맥이나 전체 문맥을 파악한다. 뒤 문장에서 '모든 LTI 학생들은 대학 정상 운영 시간 동안 이 장비를 자유롭게 사용할 수 있습니다(All LTI students are welcome to use the equipment on their own during regular university hours).'라고 했고, 뒷부분에서 '기계는 무료로 사용될 수 있고(Machinery may be used for free)'라고 했으므로, 빈칸에는 Forge는 다양한 장비에 대한 공동의 이용을 제공한다는 문맥이 되어야 한다. 따라서 share(공동으로 하다)의 과거분사 (B) shared가 정답이다. (A)의 pay는 '지불하다', (C)의 supervise는 '감독하다', (D)의 finish는 '끝나다'라는 의미이다.

134 | 알맞은 문장 고르기

해석 (A) 등록이 열리면 당신에게 알려드리겠습니다.
(B) 기부된 물품들은 사무실에 가져다 놓을 수 있습니다.
(C) 저희는 당신이 필요할지도 모르는 무엇이든 주문하는 것을 도와줄 수도 있습니다.
(D) 회원권 요금은 매달 미리 지불되어야 합니다.

해설 앞 문장 'Machinery may be used for free, and materials are provided at a low cost when required.'에서 기계는 무료로 사용될 수 있고, 재료들은 필요 시 저렴한 가격에 제공된다고 했으므로 빈칸에는 Forge가 제공하는 것과 관련된 내용이 들어가야 함을 알 수 있다. 따라서 (C)가 정답이다.

어휘 notify v. 알리다　enrollment n. 등록　drop off 가져다 놓다
in advance 미리, 사전에

135-138번은 다음 이메일에 관한 문제입니다.

수신: Joe Hamlin <joe.ham@homeready.com>
발신: Caroline Quigley <car.qui@homeready.com>
날짜: 8월 9일
제목: 판매 관리자

Mr. Hamlin께,

¹³⁵저는 우리의 판매 관리자들 중 한 명인 Deborah Watson이 8월 16일에 우리의 생산 시설을 방문할 것임을 당신께 알려드리기 위해 글을 씁니다. Ms. Watson은 우리 회사에 새로 들어왔습니다. ¹³⁶그러므로, 전체 공장을 둘러보고 어떻게 우리의 기기들이 만들어지는지 배우는 것이 그녀에게 중요합니다.

공장의 감독관으로서, 당신은 Ms. Watson을 안내하는 데 가장 자격이 있습니다. ¹³⁷우리가 우리의 제품을 생산하는 방식에 대해 그녀가

익숙해질 수 있도록 생산 시설 곳곳을 그녀와 동행해 주십시오. [138]조립 라인 구역에 특별한 주의를 기울여 주십시오. 또한, 그녀가 질문을 하고 우리의 직원들 중 일부와 이야기를 나누도록 장려해 주십시오.

Caroline Quigley 드림
지역 관리자, Home Ready 가전제품사

manufacturing facility 생산 시설 **entire** adj. 전체의
appliance n. (가정용) 기기, 기구 **qualified** adj. 자격이 있는
familiar adj. 익숙한 **encourage** v. 장려하다, 권장하다

135 | 동사 어휘 고르기 전체 문맥 파악

해설 'Deborah Watson이 8월 16일에 생산 시설을 ___할 것이다'라는 문맥이므로 모든 보기가 정답의 후보이다. 빈칸이 있는 문장만으로 정답을 고를 수 없으므로 주변 문맥이나 전체 문맥을 파악한다. 뒤 문장에서 'Ms. Watson은 우리 회사에 새로 들어왔습니다(Ms. Watson is new to our company).'라고 했고, 뒷부분에서 '전체 공장을 둘러보고 어떻게 우리의 기기들이 만들어지는지 배우는 것이 그녀에게 중요합니다(~ it is important for her to have a tour of the entire factory and learn how our appliances are made).'라고 했으므로, Ms. Watson이 생산 시설을 방문할 것임을 알 수 있다. 따라서 동사(will be)와 함께 미래진행형을 완성하는 visit(방문하다)의 현재분사 (C) visiting이 정답이다. (A)의 evaluate은 '평가하다', (B)의 leave는 '떠나다', (D)의 suspend는 '중단하다'라는 의미이다.

136 | 접속부사 채우기 주변 문맥 파악

해설 빈칸이 콤마와 함께 문장의 맨 앞에 온 접속부사 자리이므로, 앞 문장과 빈칸이 있는 문장의 의미 관계를 파악하여 정답을 선택한다. 앞 문장에서 Ms. Watson이 회사에 새로 들어왔다고 했고, 빈칸이 있는 문장에서는 전체 공장을 둘러보고 어떻게 기기들이 만들어지는지 배우는 것이 그녀에게 중요할 것이라고 했으므로, 빈칸에는 앞 내용의 상황에 대한 결과를 나타낼 때 사용되는 접속부사 (D) Accordingly(그러므로)가 정답이다.

어휘 **in contrast** 대조적으로 **unusually** adv. 평소와 달리, 특이하게

137 | 동사 어휘 고르기

해설 '그녀가 익숙해질 수 있도록 생산 시설 곳곳을 그녀와 동행해 달라'는 문맥이 되어야 하므로 (B) accompany(동행하다)가 정답이다. (D)의 demonstrate(설명하다)도 해석상 그럴듯해 보이지만 demonstrate A to B(B에게 A를 설명하다)의 형태로 쓰이므로 목적어로 사람이 아닌 무엇을 설명하려는지가 와야 한다. (A) promote는 '승진시키다, 홍보하다', (C) recruit은 '모집하다, 뽑다'라는 의미이다.

138 | 알맞은 문장 고르기

해설 (A) 그 방문 후에 만약 그녀가 고용되어야 한다고 생각한다면 저에게 알려 주십시오.
(B) 생산 전에 이 결함을 제거하는 것이 가능할지도 모릅니다.
(C) 당신의 모든 여행 경비는 8월까지 환급될 것입니다.
(D) 조립 라인 구역에 특별한 주의를 기울여 주십시오.

해설 앞 문장 'Please ~ so that she can become familiar with how we produce our merchandise.'에서 제품을 생산하는 방식에 대해 그녀가 익숙해질 수 있도록 해 달라고 했으므로, 빈칸에는 제품 생산 방식을 둘러보는 것과 관련된 내용이 들어가야 함을 알 수 있다. 따라서 (D)가 정답이다.

어휘 **hire** v. 고용하다 **eliminate** v. 제거하다 **defect** n. 결함
reimburse v. 환급하다, 배상하다 **attention** n. 주의, 주목

139-142번은 다음 기사에 관한 문제입니다.

Stelly의 신작이 매진되다

뉴올리언스 (4월 24일)—[139]지역 작가 Maria Stelly는 그녀의 소설 *Mystery Street*을 쓰기 위해 거의 10년이 걸렸다. [140]하지만 이 책이 월요일에 뉴올리언스 전역에 있는 17개 서점들에 마침내 배포되었을 때, 이틀 만에 매진되었다.

"비록 저의 첫 번째 출판물이 제법 성공하긴 했지만, 저는 *Mystery Street*의 인기에 놀랐으며, 저의 모든 팬들에게 감사드립니다."라고 Stelly가 말했다. 그녀는 획기적인 마케팅 전략이 그 책의 인기에 어느 정도 원인이 된다고 생각한다. [141]이것은 소셜 미디어에서 활발한 독자들을 겨냥하는 것을 포함한다. [142]Stelly의 새로운 책의 추가 부수들은 4월 30일에 구입할 수 있게 될 것이다.

local adj. 지역의 **decade** n. 10년 **novel** n. 소설 **sell out** 매진되다
publication n. 출판(물) **moderately** adv. 제법, 적절하게
popularity n. 인기 **innovative** adj. 획기적인, 혁신적인
partially adv. 어느 정도, 부분적으로 **responsible** adj. 원인이 되는, 책임이 있는
available adj. 구입할 수 있는

139 | to 부정사 채우기

해설 이 문장은 주어(Local writer Maria Stelly), 동사(took), 목적어(a decade)를 갖춘 완전한 절이므로, ___ ~ *Mystery Street*은 수식어 거품으로 보아야 한다. 이 수식어 거품은 동사가 없는 거품구이므로, 거품구를 이끌며 '쓰기 위해'라는 의미의 목적을 나타내는 to 부정사 (C) to write가 정답이다. 동사 (A)와 (B), 명사 (D)는 수식어 거품을 이끌 수 없다.

140 | 동사 어휘 고르기

해설 '뉴올리언스 전역에 있는 17개 서점들에 배포되었다'라는 문맥이므로 distribute(배포하다)의 과거분사 (A) distributed가 정답이다. (B)의 report는 '알리다', (C)의 connect는 '연결하다', (D)의 compare는 '비교하다'라는 의미이다.

141 | 알맞은 문장 고르기

해설 (A) 이것은 소셜 미디어에서 활발한 독자들을 겨냥하는 것을 포함했다.
(B) 뉴올리언스는 이전에 이 행사를 주최해본 적이 전혀 없다.
(C) Stelly는 고작 1년 전에 소설 쓰는 것을 시작했다.
(D) Stelly의 첫 번째 소설은 농장에서 자란 한 어린 소녀에 관한 것이었다.

해설 앞 문장 'She believes that an innovative marketing strategy is partially responsible for the book's popularity.'에서 그녀는 획기적인 마케팅 전략이 그 책의 인기에 어느 정도 원인이 된다고 생각한다고 했으므로, 빈칸에는 마케팅 전략과 관련된 내용이 들어가야 함을 알 수 있다. 따라서 (A)가 정답이다.

어휘 **involve** v. 포함하다, 수반하다 **target** v. 겨냥하다 **active** adj. 활발한
host v. 주최하다 **ceremony** n. 행사, 의식 **fiction** n. 소설

142 | 올바른 시제의 동사 채우기 전체 문맥 파악

해설 '새로운 책의 추가 부수들은 4월 30일에 구입할 수 있게 된다.'라는 문맥인데, 이 경우 빈칸이 있는 문장만으로는 올바른 시제의 동사를 고를 수 없으므로 주변 문맥이나 전체 문맥을 파악하여 정답을 고른다. 앞부분에서 '4월 24일(April 24)'이라고 했고, '하지만 이 책이 월요일에 마침내 발간되었을 때, 그것은 이틀 만에 매진되었다(But when the book was finally distributed on Monday, it sold out in just two days).'라고 했으므로, 4월 24일을 기준으로 보았을 때 책이 다시 입고되는 4월 30일은 미래임을 알 수 있다. 따라서 미래 시제 (D) will become이 정답이다.

143-146번은 다음 이메일에 관한 문제입니다.

수신: Rajesh Singh <rajesh.singh@indiaclothing.in>
발신: Faria Deveraj <f.deveraj@mumbai.gov.in>
날짜: 10월 12일
제목: 예정된 점검

Mr. Singh께,

10월 17일에 귀하의 의류 공장은 연례 정부 점검을 받게 될 것입니다. ¹⁴³이 연례 평가는 모든 노동법이 따라지고 있는지를 확인할 것입니다. ¹⁴⁴귀하의 공장은 이전의 평가를 큰 문제 없이 통과했으므로, 저희 검사관들은 이번에도 비슷한 정도의 준수를 확인하기를 기대합니다.

¹⁴⁵귀하는 검사관들이 살펴보기 원하는 공장의 어떠한 부분에라도 접근권을 제공하도록 법적으로 요구됩니다. 이와 관련하여 준수하지 않는 것은 벌금과 추가 조사를 야기할 수도 있습니다. 또한, 검사관들은 근무자들이 적절하게 보상을 받고 있는지 확인해야 합니다. ¹⁴⁶인사부는 관련 서류를 준비할 필요가 있을 것입니다.

이 사안에 대한 귀하의 배려에 감사드립니다.

Faria Deveraj 드림
점검팀장
뭄바이시 정부

inspection n. 점검, 검사   annual adj. 연례의   verify v. 확인하다, 입증하다
evaluation n. 평가   inspector n. 검사관, 조사관   compliance n. 준수, 이행
oblige v. 요구하다, 의무적으로 ~하게 하다   access n. 접근권; v. 접근하다
in this regard 이와 관련하여   result in 야기하다
fine n. 벌금; v. 벌금을 부과하다   further adj. 추가의, 더 이상의
investigation n. 조사, 수사   confirm v. 확인하다, 승인하다
compensate v. 보상하다, 보상금을 주다   attention n. 배려, 주의, 관심
matter n. 사안, 문제; v. 중요하다

143 | 명사 어휘 고르기 주변 문맥 파악

해설 '이 연례 ____는 모든 노동법이 따라지고 있는지를 확인할 것이다'라는 문맥이므로 (A)와 (D)가 정답의 후보이다. 빈칸이 있는 문장만으로 정답을 고를 수 없으므로 주변 문맥이나 전체 문맥을 파악한다. 앞 문장에서 '10월 17일에 귀하의 의류 공장은 연례 정부 점검을 받게 될 것입니다(On October 17, your clothing factory will undergo its yearly government inspection).'라고 했으므로 공장이 연례 정부 점검을 통해 평가를 받을 것임을 알 수 있다. 따라서 (D) assessment(평가, 조사)가 정답이다. (A) meeting은 '모임, 회의', (B) investment는 '투자', (C) summary는 '요약'이라는 의미이다.

144 | 형용사 어휘 고르기

해설 '귀하의 공장은 이전의 평가를 큰 문제 없이 통과했으므로 이번에도 비슷한 정도의 준수를 확인하기를 기대한다'라는 문맥이므로 (C) previous(이전의)가 정답이다. (A) decided는 '확실한, 결정적인', (B) forthcoming은 '곧 있을, 다가오는', (D) ultimate는 '궁극적인'이라는 의미이다.

145 | 부사 자리 채우기

해설 be동사(are)와 과거분사(obliged) 사이에 올 수 있는 것은 부사이므로 부사 (A) legally(법적으로)가 정답이다. 명사 (B), 형용사 (C)와 (D)는 be동사와 과거분사 사이에 올 수 없다.

어휘 legality n. 합법성, 정당함   legitimate adj. 정당한, 타당한

146 | 알맞은 문장 고르기

해설 (A) 귀하의 최근 지불금에 대한 영수증 사본이 우편으로 보내졌습니다.
(B) 인사부는 관련 서류를 준비할 필요가 있을 것입니다.
(C) 결과적으로, 그 회사는 그러한 어떤 벌금을 내는 것을 피하기를 원합니다.
(D) 저희는 회수되었던 특정 상품들에 대해 들을 의향이 있습니다.

해설 앞 문장 'Also, the inspectors need to confirm that workers are being properly compensated.'에서 검사관들은 근무자들이 적절하게 보상을 받고 있는지 확인해야 한다고 했으므로 빈칸에는 근무자들이 적절하게 보상을 받고 있는지 확인하는 것과 관련된 내용이 들어가야 함을 알 수 있다. 따라서 (B)가 정답이다.

어휘 receipt n. 영수증, 수령, 인수   relevant adj. 관련된, 적절한
document n. 서류, 문서   penalty n. 벌금, 형벌, 처벌
recall v. 회수하다, 기억해 내다

PART 7

147-148번은 다음 설명서에 관한 문제입니다.

Deena 정수기 관리 설명서

¹⁴⁷당신의 새로운 Deena 정수기가 수년간 지속되도록 보장하기 위해서, 다음의 간단한 관리 설명서를 반드시 따라주십시오:

• 필터를 설치하고 난 후, 필터를 사용할 수 있도록 준비하기 위해 아무 수도꼭지를 틀어서 최소 2분 동안 물이 그것을 통과하여 흐르도록 하십시오.

• ¹⁴⁸6개월마다 각 장치 내의 필터를 교체하십시오. 물에서 제거된 물질들의 축적은 막힘을 야기할 수 있습니다. 세제를 사용하는 것은 필터를 손상시키고 그것이 제대로 작동하는 것을 막을 것이므로 시도하지 마십시오.

water filtration system 정수기   maintenance n. 관리, 유지
ensure v. 보장하다, 확보하다   install v. 설치하다   faucet n. 수도꼭지
buildup n. 축적   substance n. 물질   blockage n. 막힘, (흐름을) 막는 것
attempt v. 시도하다   cleaning agent 세제, 세척제   prevent v. 막다
function v. 작동하다, 기능하다   properly adv. 제대로, 적절히

147 | 목적 찾기 문제

해석 설명서의 목적은 무엇인가?
(A) 적합한 모델을 선택하는 과정을 설명하기 위해
(B) 시스템의 이점들을 설명하기 위해
(C) 수리 절차에 대해 기술자들을 교육시키기 위해
(D) 제품 관리에 대한 지침을 제공하기 위해

해설 지문의 'To ensure your new Deena Water Filtration System lasts for years, be sure to follow these simple maintenance instructions'에서 당신의 새로운 Deena 정수기가 수년간 지속되도록 보장하기 위해서, 다음의 간단한 관리 설명서를 반드시 따르라고 했으므로 (D)가 정답이다.

어휘 suitable adj. 적합한   illustrate v. 설명하다   technician n. 기술자
procedure n. 절차, 과정

148 | 육하원칙 문제

해석 사용자들은 무엇을 정기적으로 해야 하는가?
(A) 점검 일정을 잡는다.
(B) 부품을 교체한다.
(C) 수질을 확인한다.
(D) 필터 세제를 바른다.

해설 지문의 'Change the filter in each device every six months.'에서 6개월마다 각 장치 내의 필터를 교체하라고 했으므로 (B)가 정답이다.

어휘 **inspection** n. 점검, 검사 **replace** v. 교체하다 **component** n. 부품, 요소 **apply** v. 바르다, 적용하다

Paraphrasing

> every six months 6개월마다 → on a regular basis 정기적으로
> Change the filter in ~ device 장치 내의 필터를 교체하다 → Replace a component 부품을 교체하다

149-150번은 다음 이메일에 관한 문제입니다.

> 발신: 관리팀 <admin@mtelecom.com>
> 수신: Vince Dantley <dantley_v@centercourt.com>
> 날짜: 3월 11일
> 제목: 당신의 Myer 통신사 코드
>
> Vince Dantley께,
>
> ¹⁴⁹당신은 현재 Myer 통신사의 무료 와이파이 서비스를 사용할 수 있게 되기까지 한 단계만이 남아 있습니다. 당신은 등록 페이지에서 다음의 코드를 입력하기만 하면 됩니다:
>
> g7z33xyu1g4
>
> 이것은 앞으로 24시간 이내로 행해져야 한다는 것에 유의하십시오. 그렇지 않으면, 당신은 등록 절차를 처음부터 시작해야 할 것이며 새로운 코드를 요청해야 할 것입니다. ¹⁵⁰⁻⁽ᴬ⁾성공적으로 등록하고 나면, 당신의 장치를 사용할 때마다 자동으로 로그인될 것입니다.
>
> ¹⁵⁰⁻⁽ᴮ⁾Myer 통신사의 와이파이 서비스는 중앙철도역, Burnett 공항, 그리고 Estuary 광장을 포함하여, 윌밍턴 주변에 있는 12개 이상의 장소에서 제공됩니다. ¹⁵⁰⁻⁽ᴰ⁾사용자들은 일주일에 20시간을 할당받습니다.
>
> Myer 통신사 드림

input v. 입력하다 **registration** n. 등록 **successfully** adv. 성공적으로 **automatically** adv. 자동으로 **dozen** n. 12개 **location** n. 장소 **plaza** n. 광장 **allot** v. 할당하다

149 | 추론 문제

해석 Mr. Dantley에 대해 추론될 수 있는 것은?
(A) 등록 절차를 완료하지 않았다.
(B) 코드를 기억할 수 없었다.
(C) 휴대폰 애플리케이션을 위해 돈을 지불했다.
(D) 최근에 윌밍턴으로 이사했다.

해설 지문의 'You[Mr. Dantley] are now just one step away from being able to use Myer Telecom's free Wi-Fi service. All you need to do is input the following code on the registration page'에서 Mr. Dantley는 현재 Myer 통신사의 무료 와이파이 서비스를 사용할 수 있게 되기까지 한 단계만이 남아 있으며, 등록 페이지에서 다음의 코드를 입력하기만 하면 된다고 했으므로 Mr. Dantley가 등록 절차를 완료하지 않았음을 추론할 수 있다. 따라서 (A)가 정답이다.

어휘 **relocate** v. 이사하다, 이동하다

150 | Not/True 문제

해석 Myer 통신사의 와이파이 서비스에 대해 명시되지 않은 것은?
(A) 등록된 사용자들에게는 자동으로 연결된다.
(B) 몇몇 교통 시설들에서 이용할 수 있다.
(C) 출시된 지 일 년이 채 되지 않는다.
(D) 제한된 시간 동안 사용될 수 있다.

해설 (A)는 지문의 'Once you have successfully registered, you will be logged in automatically every time you use your device.'에서 성공적으로 등록하고 나면, 당신의 장치를 사용할 때마다 자동으로 로그인

될 것이라고 했으므로 지문의 내용과 일치한다. (B)는 'Myer Telecom's Wi-Fi service is offered in over a dozen locations around Wilmington, including Central Rail Station, Burnett Airport, and Estuary Plaza.'에서 Myer 통신사의 와이파이 서비스는 중앙철도역, Burnett 공항, 그리고 Estuary 광장을 포함하여, 윌밍턴 주변에 있는 12개 이상의 장소에서 제공된다고 했으므로 지문의 내용과 일치한다. (D)는 'Users are allotted 20 hours per week.'에서 사용자들은 일주일에 20시간을 할당받는다고 했으므로 지문의 내용과 일치한다. (C)는 지문에 언급되지 않은 내용이다. 따라서 (C)가 정답이다.

어휘 **available** adj. 이용할 수 있는 **transportation** n. 교통 **facility** n. 시설 **launch** v. 출시하다 **limited** adj. 제한된

Paraphrasing

> Rail Station, ~ Airport 철도역, 공항 → transportation facilities 교통 시설들
> 20 hours per week 일주일에 20시간 → limited ~ time 제한된 시간

151-153번은 다음 기사에 관한 문제입니다.

> Faber Medical and Dental의 개조가 완료되다
>
> 6월 24일—¹⁵¹Wallberg Health Group사가 내일 Doeville에 있는 Faber Medical and Dental의 새롭게 개조된 3층을 다시 열 예정이다. 14개의 추가 검사실의 포함은 의료진들이 진찰에 더 많은 시간을 쓸 수 있도록 하는 동시에 환자 대기 시간을 줄이는 데 도움이 될 것으로 예상된다.
>
> Wallberg Health Group사 대표 Joan Bronson에 따르면, Faber Medical and Dental로의 방문은 작년에만 거의 22퍼센트가 증가했다. "¹⁵²Doeville의 거주자들은 점점 더 나이가 들고 있고, 이는 의사의 진찰을 받아야 하는 더 많은 환자들을 초래했습니다. 지금까지, Faber Medical and Dental은 이러한 환자들에게 그들이 마땅히 받아야 할 치료를 제공하기 위한 자원들이 부족했습니다."
>
> 증가하는 수요를 따라가기 위해, Faber Medical and Dental은 9명의 추가적인 공인된 간호사들과 2명의 의사들도 고용했다. ¹⁵³3층의 일부는 계속해서 행정실의 기능을 할 것이다. 그 층 전체를 이전에 사용했던 25명의 직원들은 그들의 업무들을 재개하기 위해 그곳으로 돌아갈 것이다. 약 140만 달러가 든 6개월짜리 개조 프로젝트가 시작되었을 때, 그들은 Wallberg Health Group사의 Sharaton 및 McCollough 지점들로 보내졌다.

renovation n. 개조, 보수 **reopen** v. 다시 열다, 재개하다 **examination room** 검사실 **consultation** n. 진찰, 상담 **representative** n. 대표, 직원 **result in** 초래하다, 야기하다 **lack** v. 부족하다 **resource** n. 자원 **attention** n. 치료, 보살핌 **deserve** v. 마땅히 받을 만하다 **keep up with** ~을 따라가다 **registered** adj. 공인된, 등록한 **administrative office** 행정실 **formerly** adv. 이전에 **occupy** v. 사용하다, 차지하다 **resume** v. 재개하다, 다시 시작하다 **duty** n. 업무, 의무 **location** n. 지점

151 | 목적 찾기 문제

해석 기사의 목적은 무엇인가?
(A) 병원의 경영진 변화를 알리기 위해
(B) 만날 수 있는 의료진의 부족에 대해 항의하기 위해
(C) 시설을 곧 이용할 수 있음을 알리기 위해
(D) 의사들을 고용하는 과정을 설명하기 위해

해설 지문의 'Wallberg Health Group will be reopening its newly renovated third floor at Faber Medical and Dental in Doeville tomorrow.'에서 Wallberg Health Group사가 내일 Doeville에 있는 Faber Medical and Dental의 새롭게 개조된 3층을 다시 열 예정이라고 했으므로 (C)가 정답이다.

어휘 announce v. 알리다, 발표하다 complain v. 항의하다, 불평하다
report v. 알리다, 보고하다 accessible adj. 이용할 수 있는

Paraphrasing

will be reopening ~ tomorrow 내일 다시 열 예정이다 → will soon be accessible 곧 이용할 수 있을 것이다

152 | 육하원칙 문제

해석 무엇이 Faber Medical and Dental의 수요가 증가하도록 했는가?
(A) 향상된 서비스들
(B) 병원의 폐업
(C) 노령화 인구
(D) 무료 진찰

해설 지문의 'The residents of Doeville are getting older, which has resulted in more patients needing to see a doctor.'에서 Doeville의 거주자들은 점점 더 나이가 들고 있고, 이는 의사의 진찰을 받아야 하는 더 많은 환자들을 초래했다고 했으므로 (C)가 정답이다.

어휘 improved adj. 향상된, 개선된 closure n. 폐업, 폐쇄
aging population 노령화 인구

Paraphrasing

The residents ~ are getting older 거주자들이 점점 더 나이가 들고 있다 → An aging population 노령화 인구

153 | 추론 문제

해석 행정 직원들에 대해 암시되는 것은?
(A) 그들의 새로운 직책들에 대한 교육을 받을 것이다.
(B) 임시로 다른 지점에 새로 발령을 받았다.
(C) 단기 휴가를 갈 것을 요청받았다.
(D) 새로 건설된 건물로 이동되었다.

해설 지문의 'Part of the third floor will continue to function as an administrative office. The 25 staff members that formerly occupied the entire floor will return there to resume their duties.'에서 3층의 일부는 계속해서 행정실의 기능을 할 것이고, 그 층 전체를 이전에 사용했던 25명의 직원들은 그들의 업무들을 재개하기 위해 그곳으로 돌아갈 것이라고 한 후, 'They were sent to Wallberg Health Group's Sharaton and McCollough locations when the six-month, nearly $1.4 million, renovation project began.'에서 약 140만 달러가 든 6개월짜리 개조 프로젝트가 시작되었을 때, 그들은 Wallberg Health Group사의 Sharaton 및 McCollough 지점들로 보내졌다고 했으므로 행정 직원들이 임시로 다른 지점에 새로 발령을 받았음을 추론할 수 있다. 따라서 (B)가 정답이다.

어휘 temporarily adv. 임시로, 일시적으로 reassign v. 새로 발령하다
short-term adj. 단기의 leave of absence 휴가

Paraphrasing

were sent to ~ locations 지점들로 보내졌다 → were ~ reassigned to other locations 다른 지점들에 새로 발령을 받았다

154-155번은 다음 문자 메시지 대화문에 관한 문제입니다.

Dan Hummel (오후 8시 19분)
저는 Natalia Manco의 유럽 순회공연에 관해 몇 가지 안 좋은 소식들을 접했어요. 154우리는 추가적인 공지 전까지 그녀의 남은 콘서트들을 연기해야 할 거예요.

Phoebe Fiscella (오후 8시 21분)
정말이에요? 우리는 이미 그 공연들의 많은 티켓들을 판매했어요.

Dan Hummel (오후 8시 24분)
저도 알지만, 154그녀가 매우 아파서, 금방 노래를 할 수 있을 가능성이 없어요. 제가 언론을 위한 성명서 작업을 시작할게요. 155우리는 또한 그녀가 공연하기로 예정되어 있는 공연장들에 이 상황에 대해 알려야 해요. 그것을 지금 당장 해줄 수 있나요?

Phoebe Fiscella (오후 8시 25분)
아마도요. 155그러나 지금은 꽤 늦었어요. 관리자들 중 일부가 이미 집으로 떠났다면, 내일 그들이 사무실에 돌아온 후에 그들에게 연락해야 할 것 같아요.

postpone v. 연기하다, 미루다 further adj. 추가적인, 더 이상의 ill adj. 아픈
chance n. 가능성, 기회 anytime soon 금방, 곧
statement n. 성명서, 진술서 media n. 언론, 매체 perform v. 공연하다

154 | 육하원칙 문제

해석 일부 순회공연은 왜 연기되었는가?
(A) 공연들이 좋은 평가를 받지 못했다.
(B) 공연자에게 일정 문제가 있다.
(C) 가수에게 건강 문제가 있다.
(D) 티켓들이 잘 팔리지 않았다.

해설 지문의 'We're going to have to postpone the rest of her[Natalia Manco's] concerts until further notice.'에서 추가적인 공지 전까지 Natalia Manco의 남은 콘서트들을 연기해야 할 것이라고 한 후, 'she is very ill, so there is no chance that she will be able to sing anytime soon'에서 그녀가 매우 아파서 금방 노래를 할 수 있을 가능성이 없다고 했으므로 (C)가 정답이다.

어휘 review n. 평가, 검토 conflict n. 문제, 충돌

Paraphrasing

ill 아픈 → has a health issue 건강 문제가 있다

155 | 의도 파악 문제

해석 오후 8시 25분에, Ms. Fiscella가 "Possibly"라고 썼을 때, 그녀가 의도한 것은?
(A) Ms. Manco의 콘서트들이 매진될 것인지 확신할 수 없다.
(B) 내일 언론사 대표와 만날 수도 있다.
(C) 아마 티켓을 구매했던 사람들에게 환불을 제공할 것이다.
(D) Mr. Hummel의 요청을 즉시 수행하지 못할 수도 있다.

해설 지문의 'We also need to let the halls where she[Natalia Manco] is scheduled to perform know about the situation. Could you do that right now?'에서 Mr. Hummel이 Natalia Manco가 공연하기로 예정되어 있는 공연장들에 이 상황에 대해 알려야 한다고 하고, 그것을 지금 당장 해줄 수 있냐고 묻자, Ms. Fiscella가 'Possibly'(아마도요)라고 한 후, 'But it's pretty late now. If some of the managers have left for home already, I'll have to contact them when they return to their offices tomorrow.'에서 그러나 지금은 꽤 늦었다며 관리자들 중 일부가 이미 집으로 떠났다면, 내일 그들이 사무실에 돌아온 후에 그들에게 연락해야 할 것 같다고 한 것을 통해, Ms. Fiscella가 Mr. Hummel의 요청을 즉시 수행하지 못할 수도 있다는 것을 알 수 있다. 따라서 (D)가 정답이다.

어휘 confirm v. 확신하다 sell out 매진되다 likely adv. 아마; adj. ~할 것 같은
refund n. 환불 fulfill v. 수행하다 immediately adv. 즉시

156-157번은 다음 공고에 관한 문제입니다.

Annenberg 카운티 지역사회 채용 박람회

6월 15일 화요일, 오후 1시에서 오후 5시까지
Annenberg 컨벤션 센터 2층 Seaview 대연회장에서

일자리가 필요하신가요?
다음을 포함하는 다양한 지역 회사들의 대표들을 만나보세요:

· Wender 호텔 서비스사
· Porter 의료 센터
· Gelec사
· Renew 제조회사
· Annenberg 운송회사
· Oarfield 기술회사

이 행사는 무료로 참석할 수 있지만, ¹⁵⁶참가자들은 www.annenbergcounty.com/events에서 사전에 등록해야 합니다. 등록 마감기한은 6월 5일입니다. 채용 박람회 당일에, 전문적으로 옷을 차려 입고, 나누어 줄 이력서와 자기소개서의 사본들을 가져오고, 현장 면접에 대비하십시오. ¹⁵⁷⁻⁽ᴬ⁾Annenberg 컨벤션 센터는 Gibbs역 6번 출구에서 도보 2분 거리에 있고, 주차는 시간당 10달러에 이용할 수 있습니다.

---

community n. 지역사회, 공동체 **various** adj. 다양한 **attend** v. 참석하다
register v. 등록하다 **in advance** 사전에 **professionally** adv. 전문적으로
résumé n. 이력서 **cover letter** 자기소개서 **hand out** 나누어 주다, 배포하다
on-the-spot adj. 현장의

---

156 | 육하원칙 문제

해석 채용 박람회에 참석하는 것에 관심 있는 사람들은 6월 5일까지 무엇을 해야 하는가?
(A) 온라인으로 지불한다.
(B) 등록 부스를 방문한다.
(C) 웹페이지에서 등록한다.
(D) 지원서를 작성한다.

해설 지문의 'participants must register in advance at www.annenbergcounty.com/events. The deadline for registration is June 5.'에서 참가자들은 웹사이트에서 사전에 등록해야 하며, 등록 마감기한은 6월 5일이라고 했으므로 (C)가 정답이다.

어휘 **make payment** 지불하다 **sign up** 등록하다
complete v. 작성하다, 완료하다 **application form** 지원서

Paraphrasing

deadline ~ is June 5 마감기한이 6월 5일이다 → must ~ do by June 5 6월 5일까지 해야 한다

register 등록하다 → Sign up 등록하다

157 | Not/True 문제

해석 Annenberg 컨벤션 센터에 대해 명시된 것은?
(A) 대중교통을 통해 접근할 수 있다.
(B) 얼마 안 되는 주차 공간들이 있다.
(C) 평일 아침에는 문을 닫는다.
(D) 유명한 호텔에 인접해 있다.

해설 지문의 'Annenberg Convention Center is a two-minute walk from Exit 6 of Gibbs Station'에서 Annenberg 컨벤션 센터는 Gibbs역 6번 출구에서 도보 2분 거리에 있다고 했으므로 (A)가 정답이다. (B), (C), (D)는 지문에 언급되지 않은 내용이다.

어휘 **accessible** adj. 접근할 수 있는 **public transportation** 대중교통
adjacent adj. 인접한, 가까운 **well-known** adj. 유명한, 잘 알려진

158-161번은 다음 온라인 채팅 대화문에 관한 문제입니다.

Neil Webb [오후 4시 20분]
안녕하세요, 여러분. ¹⁵⁸저는 우리 부서 팀장인 Mr. Tate를 오늘 아침에 만났고, ¹⁵⁹⁻⁽ᴮ⁾그는 제게 전국적인 슈퍼마켓 체인 Vatusi Foods사의 광고를 만들 팀을 조직해달라고 요청했어요. Elsa, 당신은 시간이 되나요?

Elsa Moss [오후 4시 23분]
도와드리고 싶지만, 저는 현재 Dresden 의류사 캠페인을 작업 중이에요. 저는 두 프로젝트 모두를 동시에 할 수 없을 거예요.

Neil Webb [오후 4시 23분]
제가 그것을 잊고 있었네요. Courtney, 당신이 그 캠페인의 팀장이죠. Elsa를 몇 주 동안 할애해 줄 수 있나요? ¹⁵⁹⁻⁽ᴰ⁾우리가 작년에 제작했던 Vatusi Foods사 광고를 그녀가 작업했어서, 이번 건에 그녀가 포함되어야 해요.

Courtney McGuire [오후 4시 24분]
만약 그것이 정말로 필수적이라면, 저는 그녀를 당신의 팀으로 이동시킬 수 있어요. 하지만 그것은 제 마감일을 맞추는 것을 어렵게 만들 거예요.

Neil Webb [오후 4시 25분]
¹⁶⁰제가 Mr. Tate에게 Elsa의 결손을 만회하기 위해 당신의 프로젝트에 두 명의 보조 마케팅 직원들을 배정해달라고 요청하는 것은 어떨까요?

Courtney McGuire [오후 4시 26분]
그러면 고맙겠어요. ¹⁶⁰그렇지 않으면, 저는 Dresden 의류사에 기간 연장을 요청해야 할 수도 있어요. Elsa, 당신은 이번 주 말부터 Vatusi Foods사 캠페인을 시작할 수 있어요.

Elsa Moss [오후 4시 27분]
알겠어요. Neil, ¹⁶¹당신은 팀이 이 프로젝트에 대해 논의하기 위해 언제 다 같이 모일 것인지 알고 있나요?

Neil Webb [오후 4시 30분]
¹⁶¹금요일 아침이요. 저희는 오전 10시에 2층 회의실에서 만날 거예요. 제가 당신에게 안건이 담긴 이메일을 보내줄게요.

---

organize v. 조직하다 **commercial** n. 광고 **chain** n. 체인(점)
help out 도와주다 **spare** v. 할애하다, 내어주다 **involve** v. 포함하다, 수반하다
absolutely adv. 정말로, 전적으로 **necessary** adj. 필수적인
transfer v. 이동시키다 **assign** v. 배정하다, 맡기다
make up for ~을 만회하다 **loss** n. 결손, 손실
extension n. (기간의) 연장, 확장 **get together** (다같이) 모이다
discuss v. 논의하다 **agenda** n. 안건

---

158 | 육하원칙 문제

해석 Mr. Tate는 오늘 아침에 무엇을 했는가?
(A) 새로운 팀원을 소개했다.
(B) 부하 직원에게 업무를 맡겼다.
(C) 부서장에게 이야기했다.
(D) 광고에 대한 의견을 제공했다.

해설 지문의 'I met with our department manager, Mr. Tate, this morning, and he asked me to organize a team to make a commercial for the national supermarket chain Vatusi Foods.'에서 자신이 부서 팀장인 Mr. Tate를 오늘 아침에 만났으며, 그가 자신에게 전국적인 슈퍼마켓 체인 Vatusi Foods사의 광고를 만들 팀을 조직해달라고 요청했다고 했으므로 (B)가 정답이다.

어휘 **subordinate** n. 부하 직원

159 | Not/True 문제

해석 Vatusi Foods사에 대해 명시된 것은?
(A) 최근에 추가적인 직원들을 고용했다.

(B) 지역 소유의 회사이다.
(C) 광고 아이디어를 싫어했다.
(D) 이전에 Ms. Moss와 일했었다.

해설 지문의 'She[Ms. Moss] worked on the Vatusi Foods advertisement we produced last year'에서 작년에 제작했던 Vatusi Foods사 광고를 Ms. Moss가 작업했다고 하였다. 따라서 (D)가 정답이다. (A)와 (C)는 지문에 언급되지 않은 내용이다. (B)는 'he[Mr. Tate] asked me to organize a team to make a commercial for the national supermarket chain Vatusi Foods'에서 Mr. Tate가 전국적인 슈퍼마켓 체인 Vatusi Foods사의 광고를 만들 팀을 조직해달라고 요청했다고 했으므로 지문의 내용과 일치하지 않는다.

어휘 dislike v. 싫어하다

160 | 의도 파악 문제

해설 오후 4시 26분에, Ms. McGuire가 "I'd appreciate that"이라고 썼을 때 그녀가 의도한 것 같은 것은?
(A) 직원이 새로 발령되면 안 된다고 생각한다.
(B) 프로젝트 마감일의 연장이 필요하다.
(C) 캠페인이 공개되면 안 된다고 생각한다.
(D) 몇몇 직원들이 그녀의 팀에 추가되길 원한다.

해설 지문의 'Why don't I ask Mr. Tate to assign two of the junior marketing staff to your project to make up for the loss of Elsa?'에서 Mr. Webb이 자신이 Mr. Tate에게 Elsa의 결원을 만회하기 위해 당신, 즉 Ms. McGuire의 프로젝트에 두 명의 보조 마케팅 직원들을 배정해달라고 요청하는 것은 어떨지 묻자, Ms. McGuire가 'I'd appreciate that'(그러면 고맙겠어요)이라고 한 후, 'Otherwise, I might have to ask Dresden Apparel for an extension.'에서 그렇지 않으면 자신이 Dresden 의류사에 기간 연장을 요청해야 할 수도 있다고 한 것을 통해, Ms. McGuire는 몇몇 직원들이 그녀의 팀에 추가되길 원한다는 것을 알 수 있다. 따라서 (D)가 정답이다.

어휘 release v. 공개하다, 발표하다

161 | 추론 문제

해설 Ms. Moss는 금요일에 무엇을 할 것 같은가?
(A) 몇몇 직원들의 성과를 평가한다.
(B) 새로운 팀의 팀원들과 회의에 참석한다.
(C) 회사의 이전 고객에게 이메일을 보낸다.
(D) Dresden 의류사에 대한 발표를 한다.

해설 지문의 'do you know when the team will get together to discuss this project?'에서 Ms. Moss가 Mr. Webb에게 그 팀, 즉 원래 있던 Dresden 의류사 프로젝트팀이 아닌 새롭게 합류하게 된 Vatusi Foods사 프로젝트팀이 이 프로젝트에 대해 논의하기 위해 언제 다같이 모일 것인지 알고 있는지 묻자, 'Friday morning.'에서 Mr. Webb이 금요일 아침이라고 답했으므로 Ms. Moss가 금요일 아침에 새로운 팀과 프로젝트에 대해 논의하는 회의에 참석할 것임을 추론할 수 있다. 따라서 (B)가 정답이다.

어휘 evaluate v. 평가하다   performance n. 성과, 수행
participate in ~에 참석하다, 참가하다   former adj. 이전의

162-164번은 다음 광고에 관한 문제입니다.

QUEENSBORO 피자

162-(A)저희는 하트포드의 모든 지역 주민들에게 무료로 배달해 드립니다!*
163-(D)지금부터 6월 30일까지, Queen's Combo를 할인된 가격인 19.99달러에 주문하실 수 있습니다. 다음의 품목 중 아무 세 가지를 고르세요:

162-(C)미디엄 치즈피자 1개
미트 소스 162-(B)스파게티 1개
구운 닭고기 162-(B)시저 샐러드 1개
버터 바른 162-(B)막대 빵 6개
매운 162-(B)닭 날개 10개

또한, 여름 내내, 162-(C)/164프리미엄 토핑이 있는 아무 라지 피자를 주문하고 라지 치즈 피자를 완전히 무료로 받으세요!

프리미엄 토핑은 다음을 포함합니다:
페타 치즈
햇볕에 말린 토마토
구운 피망

162-(D)저희의 새로운 스마트폰 애플리케이션을 이용하면 주문이 빠르고 쉽습니다! 애플리케이션을 다운로드하고 시작하기 위해 당신의 개인 정보와 결제 정보를 등록하세요. 당신의 첫 주문에 대해 20퍼센트 할인을 받기 위해 결제창에 홍보용 코드 4SUMR을 입력하세요.

*하트포드 시외 지역에 대해서는, 5달러의 배달 요금이 있습니다.

neighborhood n. 지역 주민, 이웃   grilled adj. 구운   breadstick n. 막대 빵
absolutely adv. 완전히   sun-dried adj. 햇볕에 말린   roasted adj. 구운
checkout n. 결제창, 계산   charge n. 요금

162 | Not/True 문제

해설 Queensboro 피자에 대해 사실이 아닌 것은?
(A) 모든 배달에 대해 요금을 청구한다.
(B) 피자 외에 다른 품목들도 제공한다.
(C) 최소 두 가지 크기의 피자를 만든다.
(D) 모바일 애플리케이션을 통해서 주문을 받는다.

해설 지문의 'spaghetti', 'Caesar salad', 'breadsticks', 'chicken wings'에서 스파게티, 시저 샐러드, 막대 빵, 닭 날개가 있다고 했으므로 (B)는 지문의 내용과 일치한다. 'medium cheese pizza'와 'buy any large pizza'에서 미디엄 치즈 피자를 언급하고, 아무 라지 피자를 주문하라고 했으므로 (C)는 지문의 내용과 일치한다. 'Ordering is quick and easy using our new smartphone application!'에서 새로운 스마트폰 애플리케이션을 이용하면 주문이 빠르고 쉽다고 했으므로 (D)는 지문의 내용과 일치한다. (A)는 'We deliver free to all neighborhoods in Hartford!'에서 자신들, 즉 Queensboro 피자가 하트포드의 모든 지역 주민들에게 무료로 배달해준다고 했으므로 지문의 내용과 일치하지 않는다. 따라서 (A)가 정답이다.

어휘 fee n. 요금   serve v. (음식을) 제공하다   besides prep. ~ 외에
at least 최소   through prep. ~을 통해서

163 | Not/True 문제

해설 Queen's Combo에 대해 명시된 것은?
(A) 무료 사이드 샐러드를 포함한다.
(B) 배달 주문에만 한정된다.
(C) 품목은 바뀔 수 있다.
(D) 가격은 제한된 기간 동안만 이용할 수 있다.

해설 지문의 'From now until June 30, you can order a Queen's Combo at a discounted price of $19.99'에서 지금부터 6월 30일까지, Queen's Combo를 할인된 가격인 19.99달러에 주문할 수 있다고 했으므로 (D)가 정답이다. (A), (B), (C)는 지문에 언급되지 않은 내용이다.

어휘 complimentary adj. 무료의

Paraphrasing

From now until ~ 지금부터 ~까지 → for a limited time 제한된 기간 동안

164 | 육하원칙 문제

해석 고객들은 어떻게 무료 피자를 받을 수 있는가?
(A) 결제하기 위해 신용카드를 사용함으로써
(B) 여름 경품 추첨에 참여함으로써
(C) 특별한 재료가 있는 품목을 주문함으로써
(D) 식당에서 상품권을 제시함으로써

해설 지문의 'buy any large pizza with premium toppings and receive a large cheese pizza absolutely free'에서 프리미엄 토핑이 있는 아무 라지 피자를 주문하고 라지 치즈 피자를 완전히 무료로 받으라고 했으므로 (C)가 정답이다.

어휘 enter v. 참여하다, 들어가다   prize draw 경품 추첨   voucher n. 상품권

Paraphrasing

pizza with premium toppings 프리미엄 토핑이 있는 피자 → item with special ingredients 특별한 재료가 있는 품목

165-167번은 다음 회람에 관한 문제입니다.

회람

수신: 전 직원
발신: Patricia Diaz, CEO, BestSnack사
날짜: 3월 18일
제목: 신나는 소식

¹⁶⁵저는 우리의 BestSnack 자판기가 다음 주 월요일부터 전국 1,000개의 테스트 장소에서 출시될 것임을 모두에게 알리게 되어 기쁩니다. 여러분 모두가 알다시피, BestSnack은 터치스크린 기술의 최신 발전을 갖춘 우리의 자판기입니다. — [1] —. 이것은 사용자들이 종류를 바탕으로 물품을 선택함으로써 그들의 영양의 필요에 따라 맞춤된 음료와 간식을 선택할 수 있게 합니다. 제로 칼로리, 저탄수화물, 그리고 무가당이라는 선택지들이 있습니다. — [2] —. ¹⁶⁶/¹⁶⁷마케팅팀은 현재 BestSnack에 관해 전국 언론 매체에 알리는 언론 보도자료를 제작하는 중입니다. — [3] —. 직원으로서, 여러분은 이 기계들에서 제품들을 시도함으로써 테스트 과정에 참여하도록 권장됩니다. — [4] —. 기계의 위치와 물품 가격에 대한 세부사항은 이번 주에 여러분에게 제공될 것입니다.

delighted adj. 기쁜   vending machine 자판기
launch v. 출시하다, 시작하다   nationwide adj. 전국의   beverage n. 음료
tailor v. 맞추다   nutritional adj. 영양의
low-carbohydrate adj. 저탄수화물의   sugar-free adj. 무가당의
press release 언론 보도자료   inform v. 알리다
news outlet 언론 매체, 방송국   participate in ~에 참여하다

165 | 목적 찾기 문제

해석 회람의 목적은 무엇인가?
(A) 회사 정책 변화를 알리기 위해
(B) 제품 시험 출시에 대한 계획을 설명하기 위해
(C) 회사 구내식당에 추가된 것을 알리기 위해
(D) 직원들에게 이용 가능한 새로운 혜택을 소개하기 위해

해설 지문의 'I'm delighted to announce to everyone that our BestSnack Vending Machine will be launched in 1,000 test locations nationwide starting next Monday.'에서 우리의 BestSnack 자판기가 다음 주 월요일부터 전국 1,000개의 테스트 장소에서 출시될 것임을 모두에게 알리게 되어 기쁘다고 했으므로 (B)가 정답이다.

어휘 policy n. 정책, 규정   trial n. 시험, 시용   addition n. 추가된 것, 부가물
benefit n. 혜택, 이득

166 | 육하원칙 문제

해석 Ms. Diaz는 마케팅 직원들이 무엇을 하고 있다고 말하는가?
(A) 사람들의 식습관에 대한 설문조사를 수행하기
(B) 언론사들을 위한 공식 성명서를 만들기
(C) 회사의 공급 업체들과의 회의를 준비하기
(D) 가까운 미래의 캠페인 행사를 계획하기

해설 지문의 'The marketing team is currently in the process of creating press releases informing national news outlets about the BestSnack.'에서 마케팅팀은 현재 BestSnack에 관해 전국 언론 매체에 알리는 언론 보도자료를 제작하는 중이라고 했으므로 (B)가 정답이다.

어휘 conduct v. 수행하다   statement n. 성명서, 진술서   arrange v. 준비하다
supplier n. 공급 업체

Paraphrasing

creating 제작하기 → Developing 만들기
press releases informing ~ news outlets 언론 매체에 알리는 언론 보도자료 → official statements for media companies 언론사들을 위한 공식 성명서

167 | 문장 위치 찾기 문제

해석 [1], [2], [3], [4]로 표시된 위치 중, 다음 문장이 들어갈 곳으로 가장 적절한 것은?

"우리는 웹사이트에도 공개 메시지를 게시할 것입니다."

(A) [1]
(B) [2]
(C) [3]
(D) [4]

해설 주어진 문장은 메시지와 관련된 내용 주변에 나올 것임을 예상할 수 있다. [3]의 앞 문장인 'The marketing team is currently in the process of creating press releases informing national news outlets about the BestSnack.'에서 마케팅팀이 현재 BestSnack에 관해 전국 언론 매체에 알리는 언론 보도자료를 제작하는 중이라고 했으므로 [3]에 주어진 문장이 들어가면 마케팅팀이 현재 언론 보도자료를 제작하고 있고 공개 메시지는 웹사이트에도 게시될 것이라는 자연스러운 문맥이 된다는 것을 알 수 있다. 따라서 (C)가 정답이다.

어휘 post v. 게시하다

168-171번은 다음 광고에 관한 문제입니다.

Freewater 라벤더 농장

특별한 경험을 찾고 있으신가요? Lewiston시 바로 외곽의 Corkscrew로 821번지에 있는 ¹⁶⁸Freewater 라벤더 농장에 방문하세요! 이 농장의 그림 같은 장소와 아름다운 환경은 이곳을 휴식을 취하기에 이상적인 공간으로 만듭니다.

저희의 향기로운 라벤더 들판 사이를 산책하고 ¹⁶⁹농장의 가장 질 좋은 라벤더로 모두 완벽하게 맛을 낸 ¹⁷⁰⁻⁽ᴬ⁾레모네이드, 차, 케이크, 그리고 쿠키와 같은 맛있는 수제 음식을 Freewater 카페에서 시식해 보세요. 비누, 로션, 오일을 포함한 라벤더 함유 제품들을 위해 ¹⁷⁰⁻⁽ᶜ⁾저희의 기념품점에 들르세요. 저희는 지역 장인들의 수공예품과 지역 농부들의 잼, 피클, 그리고 치즈도 취급합니다.

카페는 강과 산의 경관과 함께 앉을 수 있는 야외 공간을 특별히 포함합니다. Freewater 라벤더 농장에는 탁자와 벤치가 있는 ¹⁷⁰⁻⁽ᴮ⁾아름다운 야외 식사 공간이 있으며, 단체들이 소풍할 수 있는 구역 또한 있습니다.

그리고 당연히, 농장으로의 여행은 아름답고 향기로운 라벤더 꽃 구매 없이는 완벽하지 않을 것입니다! ¹⁷¹저희의 수확 부스에 잠깐 들러서

단 12달러에 말린 혹은 싱싱한 라벤더 한 다발을 사세요. 저희의 운영과 서비스들에 대한 추가적인 세부사항을 위해서는, 오늘 www.freewaterlavender.com을 방문하세요!

picturesque adj. 그림 같은, 생생한 surroundings n. 환경
ideal adj. 이상적인 stroll v. 산책하다 fragrant adj. 향기로운
sample v. 시식하다, 맛보다; n. 견본품 flavor v. 맛을 내다 carry v. 취급하다
handicraft n. 수공예품 artisan n. 장인 feature v. (특별히) 포함하다
naturally adv. 당연히, 자연히 drop by ~에 잠깐 들르다 harvest n. 수확
pick up ~을 사다, 얻다 bunch n. 다발

168 | 주제 찾기 문제

해석 광고는 주로 무엇에 대한 것인가?
(A) 농업 시설의 볼거리들
(B) 지역 농장의 새로운 제품들
(C) 자연식품의 건강상의 이점들
(D) 장인들을 위한 지역 공예 박람회

해설 지문의 'Visit the Freewater Lavender Farm'과 'The farm's picturesque location and beautiful surroundings make it the ideal place to relax.'에서 Freewater 라벤더 농장에 방문하라고 했고, 이 농장의 그림 같은 장소와 아름다운 환경은 이곳을 휴식을 취하기에 이상적인 공간으로 만든다고 한 후, 농장에 있는 카페, 기념품점, 수확 부스 등 여러 볼거리들을 소개하고 있으므로 (A)가 정답이다. (B)도 지문에서 농장의 여러 제품들을 소개하고 있어 답이 될 것 같지만, 새로운 제품인지는 알 수 없으므로 답이 될 수 없다.

어휘 attraction n. 볼거리, 명소 agricultural adj. 농업의 craft n. 공예, 기술

Paraphrasing

Lavender Farm 라벤더 농장 → agricultural facility 농업 시설

169 | 동의어 찾기 문제

해석 2문단 두 번째 줄의 단어 "finest"는 의미상 -와 가장 가깝다.
(A) 최고의
(B) 가장 부드러운
(C) 가장 많은
(D) 가장 큰

해설 finest를 포함한 구절 'all perfectly flavored with the farm's finest lavender'에서 finest는 '가장 질 좋은'이라는 뜻으로 사용되었다. 따라서 (A)가 정답이다.

170 | Not/True 문제

해석 Freewater 라벤더 농장의 특징이 아닌 것은?
(A) 수제 제품들을 제공하는 식사 시설
(B) 야외 식사를 하기 위한 공간
(C) 다양한 지역 상품들을 파는 가게
(D) 지역 예술가들의 작품을 포함하는 미술관

해설 지문의 'sample homemade delights such as lemonade, teas, cakes, and cookies ~ at the Freewater Café'에서 레모네이드, 차, 케이크, 그리고 쿠키와 같은 맛있는 수제 음식을 Freewater 카페에서 시식해 보라고 했으므로 (A)는 지문의 내용과 일치한다. 'a beautiful outdoor dining area'에서 아름다운 야외 식사 공간이 있다고 했으므로 (B)는 지문의 내용과 일치한다. 'Stop by our gift shop'과 'We also carry handicrafts from local artisans and jams, pickles, and cheeses from local farmers.'에서 기념품점에 들르라고 하며 지역 장인들의 수공예품과 지역 농부들의 잼, 피클, 그리고 치즈도 취급한다고 했으므로 (C)는 지문의 내용과 일치한다. (D)는 지문에 언급되지 않은 내용이다. 따라서 (D)가 정답이다.

어휘 dining establishment 식사 시설, 식당 serve v. 제공하다, 내다
meal n. 식사 a variety of 다양한

Paraphrasing

Café 카페 → dining establishment 식사 시설
outdoor dining area 야외 식사 공간 → area for having outdoor meals 야외 식사를 하기 위한 공간

171 | 육하원칙 문제

해석 방문객들은 농장의 부스에서 무엇을 할 수 있는가?
(A) 특별 행사를 주최하기 위해 등록한다.
(B) 몇몇 꽃들을 구매한다.
(C) 제품들의 견본품을 써 본다.
(D) 입장권을 구매한다.

해설 지문의 'Drop by our harvest booth and pick up a bunch of dried or fresh lavender for only $12.'에서 저희, 즉 농장의 수확 부스에 잠깐 들러서 단 12달러에 말린 혹은 싱싱한 라벤더 한 다발을 사라고 했으므로 (B)가 정답이다.

어휘 function n. 행사, 기능 admission ticket 입장권

Paraphrasing

pick up a bunch of ~ lavender 라벤더 한 다발을 사다 → Buy some flowers 몇몇 꽃들을 구매하다

172-175번은 다음 웹페이지에 관한 문제입니다.

https://www.clearyfoods.com
Cleary Foods

| 홈 | 상점 | 위치 | 보상 프로그램 | 소식 | 연락처 |

쇼핑객들께:

Cleary Foods는 단순히 높은 품질의 식료품이나 가정 필수품보다 제공할 것이 훨씬 더 많습니다.

1. 저희 신선육 구역의 정육점 주인들은 기꺼이 당신의 고기를 조각들로 잘라주고 지방을 제거해줍니다. ¹⁷²그들은 또한 당신을 위해 당신의 요리용 칼을 날카롭게 갈아줄 것입니다. — [1] —. ¹⁷²만약 그들이 주문을 받느라 바쁘다면, 그저 당신의 칼을 지정된 칼 두는 곳에 놓아두고 쇼핑을 다 끝낸 후에 그것들을 되찾아 가세요.

2. 날씨가 따뜻할 때, ¹⁷³⁻⁽ᴰ⁾저희 직원에게 집에 가는 길에 냉동 제품들이 녹지 않도록 그것들을 드라이아이스와 함께 포장해달라고 요청하는 것을 기억하세요. — [2] —. 또한, ¹⁷³⁻⁽ᴮ⁾만약 당신이 냉장 보관되지 않은 음료들을 구매한다면 저희의 완전 새로운 급속 음료 냉장 장치를 사용해보세요.

3. ¹⁷⁴⁻⁽ᴰ⁾저희는 저희 판매업체들이 제공하는 한, 가게에 없는 제품들을 특별 주문할 수 있습니다. 고객 서비스 데스크에서 신청서를 작성하시고 그것을 그곳에서 일하는 직원에게 주십시오. — [3] —.

당신의 다음 Cleary Foods 방문에서 이러한 서비스들을 반드시 이용해보세요. — [4] —. ¹⁷⁵참여하는 가게들의 전체 목록은 여기를 클릭하세요.

grocery n. 식료품 household n. 가정 necessity n. 필수품
butcher n. 정육점 주인 trim away 제거하다 sharpen v. 날카롭게 갈다
drop off 놓아두다 designated adj. 지정된 station n. 두는 곳, 장소
retrieve v. 되찾다 brand-new adj. 완전 새로운 rapid adj. 급속의, 빠른
chiller n. 냉장 장치 unrefrigerated adj. 냉장 보관되지 않은
stock v. (판매할 상품을 갖춰 두고) 있다; n. 재고품 vendor n. 판매업체
request form 신청서 complete adj. 전체의, 완전한

172 | 추론 문제

해석 Cleary Foods의 정육점 주인들에 대해 암시되는 것은?
(A) 기꺼이 특별한 양념들로 구입품에 풍미를 더한다.
(B) 고객들에게 고기 준비에 대한 조언들을 제공한다.
(C) 다양한 상품들에 대해 매일 할인을 제공한다.
(D) 서비스를 곧바로 행하지 못할 수도 있다.

해설 지문의 'They will also sharpen your cooking knives for you.'와 'If they are busy taking orders, just drop your knives off at the designated knife station and retrieve them when you're done shopping.'에서 그들, 즉 Cleary Foods의 정육점 주인들은 요리용 칼을 날카롭게 갈아줄 것이며, 만약 그들이 주문을 받느라 바쁘다면, 그저 칼을 지정된 칼 두는 곳에 놓아두고 쇼핑을 다 끝낸 후에 그것들을 되찾아가라고 했으므로, 정육점 주인들이 서비스를 곧바로 행하지 못할 수도 있음을 추론할 수 있다. 따라서 (D)가 정답이다.

어휘 glad adj. 기꺼이 ~하는, 기쁜 purchase n. 구입품, 구입; v. 구입하다
seasoning n. 양념 preparation n. 준비

173 | Not/True 문제

해석 Cleary Foods의 새로운 장비에 대해 언급된 것은?
(A) 계산대 통로 근처에 위치해 있다.
(B) 음료들을 빨리 차갑게 한다.
(C) 사용하려면 요금을 지불해야 한다.
(D) 장바구니를 위한 드라이아이스를 만든다.

해설 지문의 'try our brand-new rapid beverage chiller if you're purchasing unrefrigerated drinks'에서 만약 냉장 보관되지 않은 음료들을 구매한다면 우리, 즉 Cleary Foods의 완전 새로운 급속 음료 냉각 장치를 사용해보라고 했으므로 (B)가 정답이다. (A)와 (C)는 지문에 언급되지 않은 내용이다. 지문의 'remember to ask our staff to package frozen items with dry ice so they don't melt on the way home'에서 직원에게 집에 가는 길에 냉동 제품들이 녹지 않도록 그것들을 드라이아이스와 함께 포장해달라고 요청하는 것을 기억하라고는 했으나 새로운 장비가 드라이아이스를 만든다고는 하지 않았으므로, (D)는 지문의 내용과 일치하지 않는다.

어휘 aisle n. 통로 cool v. 차갑게 하다; adj. 서늘한 grocery bag 장바구니

Paraphrasing

try ~ rapid beverage chiller 급속 음료 냉각 장치를 사용하다 → cools beverages quickly 음료들을 빨리 차갑게 하다

174 | Not/True 문제

해석 특별 주문들에 대해 사실인 것은?
(A) 프로그램의 회원들만이 이용 가능하다.
(B) 고객들은 선불로 지불하도록 요구된다.
(C) 추가 요금을 내면 집 주소로 배달될 수도 있다.
(D) 신청서들은 고객 서비스 공간에 놓여있을 것이다.

해설 지문의 'We can place special orders for products that we do not have in stock, provided that our vendors offer them. Just fill out a request form at the customer service desk and give it to the employee working there.'에서 우리, 즉 Cleary Foods는 판매업체들이 제공하는 한, 가게에 없는 제품들을 특별 주문할 수 있다고 하고, 고객 서비스 데스크에서 신청서를 작성하고 그것을 그곳에서 일하는 직원에게 주라고 했으므로 (D)가 정답이다. (A), (B), (C)는 지문에 언급되지 않은 내용이다.

어휘 charge n. 요금 place v. 놓다, 두다

175 | 문장 위치 찾기 문제

해석 [1], [2], [3], [4]로 표시된 위치 중, 다음 문장이 들어갈 곳으로 가장 적절한 것은?

"그것들은 현재 전국의 선택된 지점들에서 이용할 수 있습니다."

(A) [1]
(B) [2]
(C) [3]
(D) [4]

해설 주어진 문장은 선택된 지점들과 관련된 내용 주변에 나올 것임을 예상할 수 있다. [4]의 뒤 문장인 'Click here for a complete list of participating stores.'에서 참여하는 가게들의 전체 목록은 링크를 클릭하라고 했으므로 [4]에 제시된 문장이 들어가면 그것들은 현재 전국의 선택된 지점들에서 이용 가능하며, 참여하는 가게들의 전체 목록은 링크를 클릭하라는 자연스러운 문맥이 된다는 것을 알 수 있다. 따라서 (D)가 정답이다.

어휘 currently adv. 현재, 지금 select adj. 선택된, 엄선된; v. 선택하다
location n. 지점

176-180번은 다음 광고와 이메일에 관한 문제입니다.

Littleton 도서관 주민 학습 시리즈에 참여하세요

[176]Littleton 도서관 주민 학습 시리즈가 많은 사람들의 요청으로 돌아왔습니다. 전문가와의 30분 상담을 예약하시고 사업 등록, 회계, 판매, 그리고 그 외 관련된 사안들에 대해 조언을 얻으십시오. 이 프로그램은 항상 인기 있었기 때문에 빨리 이것을 예약하십시오. Adamant Consulting사가 현재와 장래의 소규모 사업주들에게 예정된 시간 동안 도서관에서 도움을 제공할 것입니다. Adamant Consulting사는 기업가들을 위한 비즈니스 센터를 운영하고 있습니다. Adamant Consulting사에 관한 추가 세부사항들은 www.adamant.com에서 얻을 수 있습니다.

상담은 주민들에게 무료이며 오전 10시부터 오후 1시까지 아래 제시된 날짜들에 열릴 예정입니다. 예약을 신청하시려면, 555-7184로 도서관에 전화를 주시거나 info@littletonlib.net으로 이메일을 보내주십시오. 당신의 자리를 확정하기 위해서는 거주 증명서가 요구될 것입니다.

[179]상담 날짜들:
· 7월 18일 화요일
· 8월 2일 수요일
· 8월 17일 목요일
· [179]9월 2일 토요일
· 9월 12일 화요일

날짜들은 변경될 수 있다는 점을 유의해주십시오. [177]취소 또는 지연이 있을 경우에는, www.littletonlib.net에 공고문이 게시될 것입니다.

---

demand n. 요청 book v. 예약하다 consultation n. 상담
accounting n. 회계 assistance n. 도움 prospective adj. 장래의
scheduled adj. 예정된 entrepreneur n. 기업가
available adj. 얻을 수 있는 resident n. 주민 take place 열리다
register for 신청하다 appointment n. 예약
proof of residence 거주 증명서 confirm v. 확정하다
subject to ~될 수 있는 delay n. 지연

수신: Littleton 도서관 <info@littletonlib.net>
[178-(C)]발신: Mary Voss <m.voss@mtnmail.com>
제목: 문의
날짜: 7월 21일

담당자분께,

저는 친구로부터 당신의 도서관이 무료 사업 상담을 제공하고 있다는 것을 들었습니다. [178-(C)]저는 제 회사를 차리려고 계획 중이기 때문에,

이것은 저에게 안성맞춤일 것입니다. ¹⁸⁰저는 무료 상담을 위한 요건들을 충족시키지만, 몇몇 업무상 의무들 때문에 주중에는 불가능합니다. ¹⁷⁹주말에 참여할 수 있는 자리가 있나요? 만약 그렇다면, 저는 예약을 하고 싶습니다. 가능한 한 빨리 제게 알려주십시오. 감사합니다!

Mary Voss 드림

requirement n. 요건 complimentary adj. 무료의
unavailable adj. 불가한, (다른 사람과) 만날 수 없는 due to ~ 때문에
obligation n. 의무 slot n. 자리

176 | 추론 문제

해석 Littleton 도서관에 대해 암시되는 것은?
(A) 아침 10시에 문을 연다.
(B) 과거에 상담들을 주최하였다.
(C) 최근에 몇몇 비즈니스 강좌들을 도입하였다.
(D) 기업가들을 위한 센터가 있다.

해설 광고의 'The Littleton Library Community Learning Series is back ~. Book a 30-minute consultation with an expert ~.'에서 Littleton 도서관 주민 학습 시리즈가 돌아왔으며, 전문가와의 30분 상담을 예약하라고 했고, 'Be sure to book this soon, as this program has always been popular.'에서 이 프로그램은 항상 인기 있었기 때문에 빨리 이것을 예약하라고 했으므로 Littleton 도서관이 과거에 상담들을 주최하였음을 추론할 수 있다. 따라서 (B)가 정답이다.

어휘 host v. 주최하다, 열다 introduce v. 도입하다, 소개하다

177 | 육하원칙 문제

해석 광고에 따르면, 웹사이트에는 무엇이 게시될 것인가?
(A) 강좌 강사들의 소개
(B) 토론 주제에 관한 세부 사항
(C) 일정 변경에 대한 발표
(D) 장소로의 길 안내

해설 광고의 'In the event of cancellation or delay, a notice will be posted on www.littletonlib.net.'에서 취소 또는 지연이 있을 경우에는, 웹사이트에 공고문이 게시될 것이라고 했으므로 (C)가 정답이다.

어휘 profile n. 소개 instructor n. 강사 regarding prep. ~에 관한
directions n. 길 안내 venue n. 장소

Paraphrasing

cancellation or delay 취소 또는 지연 → schedule changes 일정 변경
a notice 공고문 → Announcements 발표

178 | Not/True 문제

해석 Ms. Voss에 대해 사실인 것은?
(A) 최근에 Littleton으로 이사했다.
(B) 그녀의 친구는 상담가이다.
(C) 사업을 시작하려고 생각한다.
(D) 그녀의 도서관 회원권이 만료되었다.

해설 이메일의 'I am planning to open my own company'에서 자신의 회사를 차리려고 계획 중이라고 했으므로 (C)가 지문의 내용과 일치한다. 따라서 (C)가 정답이다. (A), (B), (D)는 지문에 언급되지 않은 내용이다.

어휘 expire v. 만료되다

179 | 육하원칙 문제 연계

해석 Ms. Voss는 어느 날짜에 상담에 참석할 수 있는가?
(A) 8월 2일

(B) 8월 17일
(C) 9월 2일
(D) 9월 12일

해설 Ms. Voss가 작성한 이메일을 먼저 확인한다.

단서 1 이메일의 'Do you have any slots open on a weekend? If so, I'd like to make an appointment.'에서 Ms. Voss가 주말에 참여할 수 있는 자리들이 있는지 질문한 후, 만약 그렇다면, 예약을 하고 싶다고 했다. 그런데 상담 날짜가 제시되지 않았으므로 광고에서 관련 내용을 확인한다.

단서 2 광고의 'Consultation dates:', 'Saturday, September 2'에서는 9월 2일 토요일이 주말에 있는 유일한 상담 날짜라는 사실을 확인할 수 있다.

두 단서를 종합할 때, Ms. Voss는 주말인 9월 2일의 상담에 참석할 수 있음을 알 수 있다. 따라서 (C)가 정답이다.

어휘 attend v. 참석하다, 다니다

180 | 동의어 찾기 문제

해석 이메일에서, 1문단 두 번째 줄의 단어 "meet"은 의미상 -와 가장 가깝다.
(A) 맞닥뜨리다
(B) 가입하다
(C) 연락하다
(D) 충족시키다

해설 이메일의 meet을 포함한 구절 'I meet the requirement for a complimentary consultation ~.'에서 meet은 '충족시키다'라는 뜻으로 사용되었다. 따라서 (D)가 정답이다.

181-185번은 다음 보도 자료와 이메일에 관한 문제입니다.

2월 14일—¹⁸¹⁻⁽ᶜ⁾Larcorn 개발사는 포틀랜드 지역에 두 개의 새로운 주거 건물의 개장을 발표하게 되어 기쁩니다. City View 아파트는 올해 5월 10일에 완공될 것이고 200세대를 포함할 것입니다. ¹⁸²⁻⁽ᶜ⁾상업 지역에 있는 편리한 위치는 이것을 젊은 전문직 종사자들 사이에서 인기 있도록 만들 것이 확실합니다. ¹⁸³건물은 또한 주민들에 의해 비용 없이 이용될 수 있는 운동 센터와 오락 라운지 같은 생활 편의 시설을 포함할 것입니다. ¹⁸¹⁻⁽ᶜ⁾/¹⁸²⁻⁽ᴮ⁾Larcorn사는 Park로에 있는 Star 분양 아파트도 건설중인데, 이것은 20층의 건물에 100개의 호화로운 방과 여러 가지 고급 상점 및 식당을 포함할 것입니다. ¹⁸¹⁻⁽ᶜ⁾/¹⁸²⁻⁽ᴬ⁾이 프로젝트의 완공일은 7월 28일입니다. 두 건물 모두에 대한 더 많은 정보를 위해서는, www.larcorn.com을 방문하면 됩니다.

residential adj. 주거의, 거주의 property n. 건물, 부동산 unit n. 세대, 가구
business district 상업 지역 professional n. 전문직 종사자; adj. 전문적인
feature v. (특별히) 포함하다 amenity n. 생활 편의 시설 resident n. 주민
story n. (건물의) 층, 층수 an assortment of 여러 가지의
high-end adj. 고급의 completion date 완공일

수신: Sheila Bridges <s.bridges@mailranger.com>
발신: Victor Marino <v.marino@topspeedmovers.com>
날짜: 7월 22일
제목: 확인
첨부: 송장

Ms. Bridges께,

저는 그저 다음 주 일정을 확인하고자 했습니다. ¹⁸³저희 운송업자들은 8월 1일 오전 7시 30분에 당신의 현재 거주지에 도착할 것입니다. 저희는 당신의 소지품을 포장하고 그것들을 트럭에 싣는 데 대략 3시간이 걸릴 것으로 예상하는데, 이것은 저희가 City View 아파트에 오전 11시 30분까지 도착할 것을 의미합니다. ¹⁸⁴건물 관리자에게 그 시간에 저희가 세대에 접근하는 것을 승인하도록 상기시켜 주십시오.

저는 또한 당신이 7월 14일에 받은 송장에 오류가 있다는 것을 알려드리고 싶었습니다. 당신에게 882달러가 청구되었어야 했는데, 실수로 980달러가 청구되었습니다. [185]당신이 제시한 쿠폰은 10퍼센트의 가격 공제를 받을 자격이 있도록 하는데, 이것이 포함되지 않았습니다. 제가 정정한 송장을 이 이메일에 첨부했습니다. 저희의 실수가 야기했을 수 있는 모든 불편에 대해 사과드립니다.

Victor Marino 드림
부팀장, Topspeed Movers사

어휘 confirmation n. 확인 invoice n. 송장 residence n. 거주지, 주택
approximately adv. 대략, 거의 pack v. 포장하다 belonging n. 소지품
load v. 싣다; n. 짐, 화물 remind v. 상기시키다, 다시 한번 말하다
grant v. 승인하다, 허락하다 mistakenly adv. 실수로 deduction n. 공제
corrected adj. 정정된 inconvenience n. 불편

181 | Not/True 문제

해석 Larcorn 개발사에 대해 사실인 것은?
(A) 사무실 건물을 건설하는 경쟁 입찰에서 이겼다.
(B) 특정 날짜에 예정된 축하 행사가 있다.
(C) 같은 해에 두 개의 프로젝트를 완료할 계획이다.
(D) 구매자들이 볼 수 있는 모델 세대가 있다.

해설 보도 자료의 'Larcorn Development is pleased to announce the opening of two new residential properties in the Portland area. City View Apartments will be completed on May 10 of this year and will include 200 units.'에서 Larcorn 개발사는 포틀랜드 지역에 두 개의 새로운 주거 건물의 개장을 발표하게 되어 기쁘다고 하며, City View 아파트는 올해 5월 10일에 완공될 것이고 200세대를 포함할 것이라고 한 후, 'Larcorn is also constructing Star Condominiums on Park Drive', 'The completion date for this project is July 28.'에서 Larcorn사는 Park로에 있는 Star 분양 아파트도 건설중인데, 이 프로젝트의 완공일은 7월 28일이라고 했으므로 (C)가 정답이다. (A), (B), (D)는 지문에 언급되지 않은 내용이다.

어휘 competitive adj. 경쟁의 bid n. 입찰; v. 값을 부르다
celebration n. 축하 행사, 기념 행사 specific adj. 특정한, 구체적인

182 | Not/True 문제

해석 Star 분양 아파트에 대해 언급된 것은?
(A) 5월 10일에 완성될 것이다.
(B) 상업 공간들을 포함할 것이다.
(C) 상업 지역에 위치할 것이다.
(D) 도시공원을 내려다볼 것이다.

해설 보도 자료의 'Larcorn is also constructing Star Condominiums on Park Drive, which will include 100 luxury apartments and an assortment of high-end shops and restaurants in a 20-story building.'에서 Larcorn사는 또한 Park로에 있는 Star 분양 아파트도 건설할 예정인데, 20층의 건물에 100개의 호화로운 방과 여러 가지 고급 상점 및 식당을 포함할 것이라고 했으므로 (B)가 정답이다. (D)는 지문에 언급되지 않은 내용이다. 보도 자료의 'The completion date for this project is July 28.'에서 이 프로젝트, 즉 Star 분양 아파트의 개발 프로젝트의 완공일은 7월 28일이라고 했으므로, (A)는 지문의 내용과 일치하지 않는다. 'Its[City View Apartments'] convenient location in the business district'에서 상업 지역에 있는 편리한 위치는 City View 아파트의 위치를 나타내므로, (C)는 지문의 내용과 일치하지 않는다.

어휘 commercial adj. 상업의, 상업적인 overlook v. 내려다보다, 간과하다

Paraphrasing
shops and restaurants 상점 및 식당 → commercial spaces 상업 공간들

183 | 추론 문제 연계

해석 Ms. Bridges에 대해 암시되는 것은?
(A) 매달 관리비를 지불할 것이다.
(B) 체육관에 무료로 출입할 수 있을 것이다.
(C) 할인 쿠폰을 받을 것이다.
(D) 이삿짐 운송 회사의 사무실을 방문할 것이다.

해설 Ms. Bridges에게 발송된 이메일을 먼저 확인한다.
[단서 1] 이메일의 'Our movers will arrive at your current residence on August 1 at 7:30 A.M.'에서 운송업자들이 8월 1일 오전 7시 30분에 Ms. Bridges의 현재 거주지에 도착할 것이라고 하고, 'We estimate that it will take approximately three hours to pack your belongings and load them onto the truck, which means that we should arrive at City View Apartments by 11:30 A.M.'에서 Ms. Bridges의 소지품을 포장하고 그것들을 트럭에 싣는 데 대략 3시간이 걸릴 것으로 예상하는데, 이것은 운송업자들이 City View 아파트에 오전 11시 30분까지 도착할 것을 의미한다고 했다. City View 아파트가 언급된 보도 자료에서 추가적인 내용을 확인한다.
[단서 2] 보도 자료의 'The building will also feature amenities such as a fitness center and an entertainment lounge that can be used without charge by residents.'에서 건물, 즉 City View 아파트는 또한 주민들에 의해 비용 없이 이용될 수 있는 운동 센터와 오락 라운지 같은 생활 편의 시설을 포함할 것임을 확인할 수 있다.
두 단서를 종합할 때, Ms. Bridges는 체육관에 무료로 출입할 수 있을 것임을 추론할 수 있다. 따라서 (B)가 정답이다.

어휘 maintenance fee 관리비 have access to ~에 출입(접근)할 수 있다
moving company 이삿짐 운송 회사

Paraphrasing
fitness center 운동 센터 → gym 체육관
can be used without charge 비용 없이 이용될 수 있다 → have free access 무료로 출입할 수 있다

184 | 육하원칙 문제

해석 Ms. Bridges는 무엇을 하도록 요청되는가?
(A) 주문 수량을 확정한다.
(B) 건물 관리인에게 연락한다.
(C) 추가적인 지불금을 낸다.
(D) 이전의 이메일에 답한다.

해설 이메일의 'Please remind the building manager to grant us access to the unit at that time.'에서 이메일 수신자인 Ms. Bridges에게 건물 관리자에게 그 시간에 자신들, 즉 Topspeed Movers사가 세대에 접근하는 것을 승인하도록 상기시켜 달라고 했으므로 (B)가 정답이다.

어휘 reply to ~에 답하다 previous adj. 이전의

Paraphrasing
remind the building manager 건물 관리자에게 상기시키다 → Contact a building manager 건물 관리인에게 연락한다

185 | 육하원칙 문제

해석 Mr. Marino는 어떤 문제를 언급하는가?
(A) 청구서가 발송되지 않았다.
(B) 아파트에 접근할 수 없다.
(C) 예약은 변경될 수 없다.
(D) 할인이 적용되지 않았다.

해설 이메일의 'The coupon you presented qualifies you for a 10 percent price deduction, but this was not included.'에서 이메일

발신자인 Mr. Marino가 쿠폰은 당신, 즉 Ms. Bridges가 10퍼센트의 가격 공제를 받을 자격이 있도록 하는데, 이것이 포함되지 않았다고 했으므로 (D)가 정답이다.

어휘 **appointment** n. 예약, 약속 **discount** n. 할인

Paraphrasing

> price deduction ~ was not included 가격 공제가 포함되지 않았다 → A discount was not applied 할인이 적용되지 않았다

186-190번은 다음 두 이메일과 일정표에 관한 문제입니다.

수신: Maureen Chapman <maureen@lovetts.com>
발신: Rodney Tucker <rt77@exchanger.com>
날짜: 4월 10일
제목: 회신: 정규직 제안

Ms. Chapman께,

Lovett's 백화점에서의 정규직 근무를 제안해주신 것에 감사드립니다. 저는 제가 계산대 직원으로서 일을 잘하고 있다고 느끼며, 제 동료들과 함께 일하는 것을 즐겨왔습니다. 안타깝게도, 저는 그 제안을 거절해야 하는데, 제가 현재 소프트웨어 회사에 고용되어 있는 동안 학점을 얻게 해주는 저의 학교 컴퓨터학과의 여름 직무 프로그램에 고려되고 있기 때문입니다. ¹⁸⁶이 프로그램은 6월부터 8월까지 계속됩니다. 만약 제가 이 프로그램에 받아들여진다면, 저는 시간제 직무를 할 시간조차 없을 것입니다. ¹⁸⁹그렇지 않으면, 올해 12월에 제가 졸업할 때까지 저는 기꺼이 Lovett's 백화점에서 계속 일할 것입니다. 그 후에는, 저는 제 삼촌이 소유하고 있는 보험 회사에서 일할 계획입니다.

Rodney Tucker 드림

full-time adj. 정규직의 **position** n. 직무, 직책 **checkout** n. 계산대
colleague n. 동료 **turn down** ~을 거절하다 **course credit** 학점
admit v. 받아들이다, 허가하다 **part-time** adj. 시간제의 **insurance** n. 보험

전자제품 구역, Lovett's 백화점

¹⁸⁶6월 둘째 주의 평일 일정표

	6월 9일	6월 10일	6월 11일	6월 12일	¹⁸⁷6월 13일
오전	· Hazel Gates · Annie Montrose	· Dion Kirk · Hazel Gates	· Annie Montrose · Chico Benavidez	· Hazel Gates · Rodney Tucker	· Chico Benavidez · Rodney Tucker
점심 시간	· Annie Montrose	· Hazel Gates	· Chico Benavidez	· Rodney Tucker	· Dion Kirk
¹⁸⁷오후	· Rodney Tucker	· Chico Benavidez · Rodney Tucker	· Chico Benavidez · Rodney Tucker	· Chico Benavidez	¹⁸⁷· Annie Montrose ¹⁸⁷· Dion Kirk

¹⁸⁶/¹⁸⁸정규직 직원들: Chico Benavidez (35시간), Rodney Tucker (35시간)

¹⁸⁷시간제 직원들: Hazel Gates (12시간), Dion Kirk (11시간), Annie Montrose (15시간)

¹⁸⁸*한 달 내내 주말은 Chico Benavidez와 Rodney Tucker에 의해 담당됩니다.

electronics n. 전자제품

수신: 전 직원 <staff@lovetts.com>
발신: Maureen Chapman <maureen@lovetts.com>
¹⁸⁹날짜: 12월 3일
제목: 직원 사임

직원분들께,

¹⁸⁹저는 저희의 가장 소중한 직원들 중 한 명인 Rodney Tucker가 Lovett's 백화점을 떠날 것임을 모든 분들께 알리고자 합니다. Mr. Tucker는 저희 조직의 중요한 구성원이었습니다. 그는 시간제 직원으로 시작했고 이후 구역 관리자직으로 승진되었습니다. 그를 위해 송별회가 12월 5일 오후 8시에서 9시까지 직원실에서 열릴 것입니다. ¹⁹⁰Mr. Tucker가 지난 6개월 넘게 관리했던 가전제품 구역에서 일하고 있는 직원들은 확실히 참석하도록 요구됩니다. 저는 모든 분들을 그곳에서 만나길 바랍니다.

Maureen Chapman 드림
인사부장, Lovett's 백화점

resignation n. 사임, 사직 **valued** adj. 소중한, 높이 평가되는
promote v. 승진하다, 홍보하다 **farewell party** 송별회
appliance n. 가전제품 **obviously** adv. 확실히, 분명히

186 | 추론 문제 연계

해석 Mr. Tucker에 대해 암시되는 것은?
(A) 그가 원했던 여름 일자리를 얻지 못했다.
(B) 소매점을 위한 컴퓨터 프로그램을 설계했다.
(C) 주로 여름 휴가 동안 여행을 간다.
(D) 초과 근무 수당을 받을 기회를 받지 못했다.

해설 Mr. Tucker가 작성한 첫 번째 이메일을 먼저 확인한다.

[단서 1] 첫 번째 이메일의 'The program runs from June through August. If I'm admitted into the program, I will not even have time for a part-time position.'에서 프로그램, 즉 여름 직무 프로그램은 6월부터 8월까지 계속되며, 만약 자신이 그 프로그램에 받아들여진다면 시간제 직무를 할 시간조차 없을 것이라고 했다.

[단서 2] 일정표의 'Weekday Schedule for the second week of June'과 'Full-time staff: ~ Rodney Tucker (35 hours)'에서는 6월 둘째 주의 평일 일정표의 정규직 직원들 목록에 Mr. Tucker의 이름이 있음을 확인할 수 있다.

두 단서를 종합할 때, Mr. Tucker는 그가 원했던 여름 일자리를 얻지 못했음을 추론할 수 있다. 따라서 (A)가 정답이다.

어휘 **design** v. 설계하다, 디자인하다 **retail store** 소매점 **opportunity** n. 기회
overtime pay 초과 근무 수당

187 | 육하원칙 문제

해석 몇몇 시간제 근무 직원들은 언제 오후에 함께 일했는가?
(A) 6월 8일
(B) 6월 10일
(C) 6월 12일
(D) 6월 13일

해설 일정표의 'Part-time staff: ~ Dion Kirk ~, Annie Montrose'에서 Mr. Kirk와 Ms. Montrose가 시간제 직원들임을 알 수 있고 'June 13', 'Afternoon.', 'Annie Montrose', 'Dion Kirk'에서 Ms. Montrose와 Mr. Kirk가 6월 13일 오후에 함께 근무했음을 알 수 있으므로 (D)가 정답이다.

Paraphrasing

> Part-time staff 시간제 직원 → part-timer 시간제 근무 직원

188 | 추론 문제

해석 Lovett's 백화점에 대해 추론될 수 있는 것은?
(A) 지점들은 모두 동일한 운영 시간을 가진다.
(B) 시간제 직원들은 6월에 평일에만 일한다.

(C) 직원들을 위한 관리 교육 프로그램을 운영한다.
(D) 최근에서야 컴퓨터를 판매하기 시작했다.

해설 일정표의 'Full-time staff: Chico Benavidez (35 hours), Rodney Tucker (35 hours)', 'Weekends throughout the month[June] will be covered by Chico Benavidez and Rodney Tucker.'에서 주말은 정규직 직원들인 Mr. Benavidez와 Mr. Tucker에 의해 담당된다고 했으므로 시간제 직원들은 6월에 평일에만 일한다는 것을 추론할 수 있다. 따라서 (B)가 정답이다.

어휘 branch n. 지점 operation n. 운영, 작업

189 | 추론 문제 연계

해석 Mr. Tucker가 왜 Lovett's 백화점을 떠나는 것 같은가?
(A) 몇 가지 자격 요건을 충족시키는 데 실패했다.
(B) 그의 가족 사업을 확장할 계획이다.
(C) 다른 도시로 이사하는 것을 준비하고 있다.
(D) 친척의 회사에서 직책을 맡을 것이다.

해설 Mr. Tucker가 작성한 첫 번째 이메일을 먼저 확인한다.
단서 1 첫 번째 이메일의 '~ I would be happy to keep working for Lovett's Department Store until I graduate in December of this year. After that, I plan to work at the insurance firm my uncle owns.'에서 올해 12월에 자신이 졸업할 때까지 기꺼이 Lovett's 백화점에서 계속 일할 것이며, 그 후에 삼촌이 소유하고 있는 보험회사에서 일할 계획이라고 했다. 그런데 Mr. Tucker가 Lovett's 백화점을 떠난다는 내용이 제시되지 않았으므로 두 번째 이메일에서 관련 내용을 확인한다.
단서 2 두 번째 이메일의 'Date: December 3', 'I would like to inform everyone that Rodney Tucker, one of our most valued workers, will be leaving Lovett's Department Store.'에서 이메일이 작성된 날짜가 12월 3일이고, Mr. Tucker가 Lovett's 백화점을 떠날 것임을 알 수 있다.
두 단서를 종합할 때, Mr. Tucker가 친척의 회사에서 직책을 맡기 위해 Lovett's 백화점을 떠남을 추론할 수 있다. 따라서 (D)가 정답이다.

어휘 fail v. 실패하다 satisfy v. 충족시키다 requirement n. 자격 요건
expand v. 확장하다 relocate v. 이사하다 relative n. 친척

Paraphrasing

firm ~ uncle owns 삼촌이 소유하고 있는 회사 → relative's company 친척의 회사

190 | 육하원칙 문제

해석 두 번째 이메일에 따르면, 누가 송별회에 참석하도록 요구되었는가?
(A) 보상 프로그램의 회원들
(B) 단체의 기금 모금 행사의 기부자들
(C) 가전제품 구역의 공급 업체들
(D) 특정 구역에 배치된 직원들

해설 두 번째 이메일의 'Employees working in the Appliance Section, which Mr. Tucker has managed over the last six months, are obviously expected to attend.'에서 Rodney가 지난 6개월 넘게 관리했던 가전제품 구역에서 일하고 있는 직원들은 확실히 참석하도록 요구된다고 했으므로 (D)가 정답이다.

어휘 contributor n. 기부자, 기여자 fundraiser n. 기금 모금 행사, 기금 모금자
supplier n. 공급 업체, 공급 회사 station v. ~을 배치하다; n. 역, 정거장
certain adj. 특정한, 확실한

Paraphrasing

Employees working in the Appliances Section 가전제품 구역에서 일하고 있는 직원들 → Staff stationed in a certain area 특정 구역에 배치된 직원들

191-195번은 다음 평면도와 두 이메일에 관한 문제입니다.

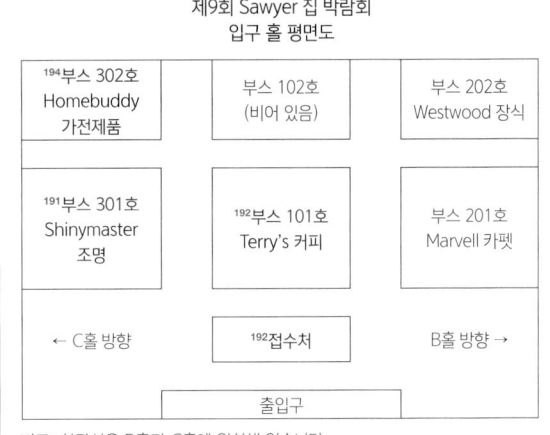

floor plan 평면도 vacant adj. 비어 있는 decor n. 장식
carpeting n. 카펫(류) entrance n. 출입구

수신: Carl Takata <c.takata@sawyerhome.org>
발신: Molly Manzotti <m.manzotti@sawyerhome.org>
날짜: 5월 26일
제목: 변경 사항

Carl,

저는 입구 홀의 부스 배정 변경 사항에 대한 몇 가지 요청을 받았습니다. 우선, 192/193-(A)우리는 우리의 주요 후원 업체인 Delta 은행을 접수처 뒤에 있는 부스에 배치해야 합니다. 이렇게 하여, 참가자들은 그들이 입구를 통과하여 들어올 때 그것을 즉시 볼 수 있을 것입니다. 192그곳에 지금 누가 배치되어 있는 현재 비어 있는 부스로 옮겨져야 할 것입니다.

또한, 193-(C)Westwood 장식은 그것의 가구 제품들을 위한 더 많은 공간이 필요하므로, 193-(B)우리는 그들을 Marvell사와 자리를 바꾸도록 할 것입니다. 저는 지금 다른 회의에 가는 길이지만, 후에 추가적인 변경 사항이 있으면 제가 당신께 알려드리겠습니다. 감사합니다!

Molly

assignment n. 배정, 배치 primary adj. 주요한 sponsor n. 후원 업체
immediately adv. 즉시, 즉각 empty adj. 비어 있는 switch v. 바꾸다

195수신: Carl Takata <c.takata@sawyerhome.org>
발신: Molly Manzotti <m.manzotti@sawyerhome.org>
날짜: 5월 26일
제목: 최신 정보

안녕하세요, Carl.

당신에게 더 일찍 연락하지 못해 정말 미안합니다. 저는 고객들과 가격 및 부스 배정에 대해 협상하느라 바빴고, 오늘 아침 이후로 추가적인 변경 사항이 생겼습니다. 194기획 위원회는 비슷한 제품들을 파는 회사들을 가능한 한 서로 가까이 위치시키고 싶어 합니다. 그것은 우리가 부스 302호의 사용자를 C홀로 이동시킬 것임을 의미합니다. 195저는 아직 부스 배정이 필요한 판매 회사들의 긴 목록을 가지고 있습니다. 내일 오전 9시쯤 그 장소에 잠시 들를 때 그것을 가져갈 것입니다. 제가 가는 길에 당신을 위해 가져갈 수 있는 것이 있다면 제게 알려주십시오. 또 뵙겠습니다!

Molly

negotiate v. 협상하다 additional adj. 추가적인
planning committee 기획 위원회 occupant n. 사용자, 거주자
vendor n. 판매 회사 stop by 잠시 들르다 venue n. 장소

191 | 추론 문제

해석 고객들은 어디에서 조명 기구들을 찾을 수 있겠는가?
(A) 부스 101호
(B) 부스 201호
(C) 부스 301호
(D) 부스 302호

해설 평면도의 'Booth 301 Shinymaster Lighting'에서 부스 301호에 배치된 판매업체가 Shinymaster 조명이라고 했으므로 고객들이 부스 301호에서 조명 기구를 찾을 수 있을 것임을 추론할 수 있다. 따라서 (C)가 정답이다.

어휘 light fixture 조명 기구

Paraphrasing
Lighting 조명 → light fixtures 조명 기구들

192 | 육하원칙 문제 연계

해석 Delta 은행은 누구의 부스를 대체하는가?
(A) Terry's 커피
(B) Marvell 카펫
(C) Westwood 장식
(D) Shinymaster 조명

해설 질문의 핵심 어구인 Delta 은행이 언급된 첫 번째 이메일을 먼저 확인한다.
단서 1 첫 번째 이메일의 'we need to place our primary sponsor, Delta Bank, in the booth behind the registration desk'에서 주요 후원 업체인 Delta 은행을 접수처 뒤에 있는 부스에 배치해야 한다고 한 후, 'Whoever we have there now will need to be moved to a booth that is currently empty.'에서 그곳에 지금 누가 배치되어 있든 현재 비어 있는 부스로 옮겨져야 할 것이라고 했다.
단서 2 평면도의 'Registration Desk', 'Booth 101 Terry's Coffee'에서 접수처 뒤에 위치한 부스 101호에 현재 Terry's 커피가 배치되어 있음을 확인할 수 있다.
두 단서를 종합할 때, Delta 은행은 Terry's 커피의 부스를 대체할 것임을 알 수 있다. 따라서 (A)가 정답이다.

어휘 replace v. 대체하다, 교체하다

193 | Not/True 문제

해석 Westwood 장식에 대해 명시된 것은?
(A) 주요 행사 후원 업체이다.
(B) 다른 홀로 이동될 것이다.
(C) 그것의 상품을 위한 더 많은 공간을 필요로 한다.
(D) Marvell 카펫 뒤의 부스를 요청했다.

해설 첫 번째 이메일의 'Westwood Decor needs more space for its furniture items'에서 Westwood 장식은 그것의 가구 제품들을 위한 더 많은 공간을 필요로 한다고 했으므로 (C)가 정답이다. (D)는 지문에 언급되지 않은 내용이다. (A)는 'our primary sponsor, Delta Bank'에서 주요 후원 업체인 Delta 은행이라고 했으므로 지문의 내용과 일치하지 않는다. (B)는 'we're going to have them switch places with Marvell'에서 그들, 즉 Westwood 장식을 Marvell사와 자리를 바꾸도록 할 것이라고 했으므로 지문의 내용과 일치하지 않는다.

어휘 merchandise n. 상품, 물품

Paraphrasing
furniture items 가구 제품들 → merchandise 상품

194 | 추론 문제 연계

해석 C홀에 대해 추론될 수 있는 것은?
(A) 낮은 가격의 부스들이 있다.
(B) 화장실이 하나도 없다.
(C) 모든 가전제품 판매업체들을 수용할 것이다.
(D) 더 많은 판매 회사들을 수용하기 위해 추가되었다.

해설 질문의 핵심 어구인 C홀이 언급된 두 번째 이메일을 먼저 확인한다.
단서 1 두 번째 이메일의 'The planning committee wants to keep companies that sell similar items located as close to each other as possible. That means we'll be moving the occupant of Booth 302 into Hall C.'에서 기획 위원회는 비슷한 제품들을 파는 회사들을 가능한 한 서로 가까이 위치시키고 싶어 한다고 한 후, 그것은 부스 302호의 사용자를 C홀로 이동시킬 것임을 의미한다고 했다. 그런데 부스 302호에 대해 제시되지 않았으므로 평면도에서 관련 내용을 확인한다.
단서 2 평면도의 'Booth 302 Homebuddy Appliances'에서 부스 302호에 배치된 판매업체가 Homebuddy 가전제품이라는 것을 확인할 수 있다.
두 단서를 종합할 때, C홀은 모든 가전제품 판매업체들을 수용할 것임을 추론할 수 있다. 따라서 (C)가 정답이다.

어휘 lower-priced adj. 낮은 가격의   accommodate v. 수용하다

195 | 육하원칙 문제

해석 Ms. Manzotti는 그녀가 Mr. Takata에게 무엇을 가져갈 것이라고 하는가?
(A) 평면도
(B) 주문한 음식
(C) 행사 달력
(D) 판매업체 목록

해설 두 번째 이메일의 'To: Carl Takata', 'I still have a long list of vendors in need of booth assignments. I'll bring it tomorrow when I stop by the venue at around 9 A.M.'에서 이메일 수신인 Mr. Takata에게 자신, 즉 Ms. Manzotti가 부스 배정이 필요한 판매 회사들의 긴 목록을 가지고 있고, 내일 오전 9시쯤 그 장소에 잠시 들를 때 그것을 가져갈 것이라고 했으므로 (D)가 정답이다.

196-200번은 다음 공고, 웹페이지, 이메일에 관한 문제입니다.

애리조나 의학 전문가 협회 (AMPA)
저희의 올해 봄 행사 일정표의 공개를 알리게 되어 기쁩니다.

4월 16일 – 새로운 회원 환영
196-(A)피닉스의 Desert 호텔에서 새로운 회원들을 위한 환영회가 196-(B)오후 4시부터 6시까지 열립니다. 196-(D)간식과 음료가 제공될 것입니다.

4월 19일 – 발표
197국내의 가장 인기 있는 의학 학술지, Modern Journal of Medicine 지가 피닉스의 AMPA 회의 센터에서 오후 6시부터 7시까지 특별한 발표를 주최할 예정입니다.

4월 23일 – 강연 및 책 사인회
AMPA는 존경받는 의학 저자이자 건강 관리 문제들에서 손꼽히는 전문가인 Dr. Katherine Bradley와 함께 오전 9시부터 11시까지 애리조나의 글렌데일에 있는 Book Stop 서점에서 강연 및 책 사인회 행사를 주최할 예정입니다.

5월 2일에서 4일까지 – 연례 회의
제 51회 AMPA 연례 회의가 올해 네바다의 라스베이거스에서 열릴 예정입니다.

모든 행사들은 오직 등록된 AMPA 회원들만을 위한 것입니다. 참여하시려면, www.ampa.org를 방문해주십시오.

professional n. 전문가; adj. 전문의   association n. 협회   release n. 공개
reception n. 환영회   journal n. 학술지   host v. 주최하다   lecture n. 강연
book-signing n. 책 사인회   esteemed adj. 존경받는, 호평받는
annual adj. 연례의   exclusively adv. 오직, 독점적으로
registered adj. 등록된

www.ampa.org
애리조나 의학 전문가 협회 (AMPA)

| 로그인 | 자료 | 행사 | **회원** | 연락 | 소개 |

¹⁹⁸등록하는 방법
1. 웹사이트에서 계정을 등록하고 회원 신청서를 작성하십시오.
2. ¹⁹⁸당신의 의사 면허증의 스캔된 복사본을 올리십시오.
3. 해당되는 곳에, 당신을 소개한 사람 또는 기관의 이름을 포함시키십시오.

혜택
- 다른 전문가들과 친해지십시오.
- 온라인 세미나를 통해 당신의 소양을 향상시키십시오.
- 전문 자료들에 접근하십시오.
- ¹⁹⁷모든 선도적인 의학 학술지들의 무료 구독권을 받으십시오.
- 새로운 소식! 유지비에 도움이 되기 위해, ¹⁹⁹/²⁰⁰저희는 최근에 저희 웹사이트에 배너 광고를 도입하였으며, 이에 대해 회원들은 할인을 받을 수 있습니다. ²⁰⁰더 많은 정보를 원하시면, 지원 팀에 연락해주십시오.

오늘 가입하기

sign up for 등록하다   account n. 계정   complete v. 작성하다
application form 신청서   medical license 의사 면허증
applicable adj. 해당되는   organization n. 기관   refer v. 소개하다, 가리키다
maintenance cost 유지비   administrator n. 관리자, 행정인

수신: Salvador Lopez <s.lopez@ampa.org>
발신: Amy Sharpe <a.sharpe@healthwide.com>
제목: 광고
날짜: 2월 18일

²⁰⁰Mr. Lopez께,

저는 Dr. Katherine Bradley의 신간 *New Age of Healing*을 출판하는 회사를 대표합니다. 4월에 AMPA의 행사에서 책의 출간을 기대하며, ²⁰⁰저희는 귀하의 웹사이트에 그 책을 광고하고 싶습니다. 이것과 관련하여, 저는 Dr. Bradley의 회원 혜택이 저희에게 적용될 수 있는지에 대해 궁금합니다. 만약 그렇다면, 저희는 그녀의 회원 번호를 귀하의 웹사이트에 있는 광고주들을 위한 신청서에 입력하고자 합니다. 되도록 빨리 저에게 알려주십시오.

Amy Sharpe 드림

마케팅 직원, Healthwide 출판사

represent v. 대표하다, 대변하다   in anticipation ~을 기대하며
in connection with ~와 관련하여   wonder v. 궁금하다, 궁금해하다
advertiser n. 광고주

196 | Not/True 문제

해설 새로 등록된 AMPA 회원을 맞이하는 행사에 대해 사실인 것은?
(A) 회의 센터에서 개최될 것이다.
(B) 저녁 6시에 시작될 것이다.
(C) 주최자의 연설을 특별히 포함할 것이다.
(D) 참석자들을 위한 다과를 포함할 것이다.

해설 공고의 'Snacks and beverages will be provided.'에서 간식과 음료가 제공될 것이라고 했으므로 (D)는 지문의 내용과 일치한다. 따라서 (D)가 정답이다. (C)는 지문에서 언급되지 않은 내용이다. (A)는 'Welcome reception for new members at the Desert Hotel in Phoenix'에서 피닉스의 Desert 호텔에서 새로운 회원들을 위한 환영회가 열린다고 했으므로 지문의 내용과 일치하지 않는다. (B)는 'from 4:00 to 6:00 P.M.'에서 오후 4시부터 6까지 열린다고 했으므로 지문의 내용과 일치하지 않는다.

어휘 take place 개최되다   feature v. 특별히 포함하다   refreshment n. 다과

Paraphrasing
Snacks and beverages 간식과 음료 → refreshments 다과

197 | 추론 문제 연계

해설 AMPA 회원들에 대해 암시되는 것은?
(A) 같은 기관에서 그들의 의료 수련 과정을 수료했다.
(B) *Modern Journal of Medicine*지를 무료로 구독할 수 있다.
(C) 그들의 도움을 자원하도록 권장된다.
(D) 국내의 가장 큰 전문가 협회를 구성한다.

해설 AMPA 회원 등록에 대한 웹페이지를 먼저 확인한다.
단서 1 웹페이지의 'Receive complimentary subscriptions to all leading medical journals.'에서 AMPA 회원들은 모든 선도적인 의학 학술지들의 무료 구독권을 받는다고 했다.
단서 2 공고의 'The country's most popular journal, *Modern Journal of Medicine*'에서 *Modern Journal of Medicine*지가 국내의 가장 인기 있는 의학 학술지라는 사실을 확인할 수 있다.
두 단서를 종합할 때, AMPA 회원들은 *Modern Journal of Medicine*지를 무료로 구독할 수 있음을 추론할 수 있다. 따라서 (B)가 정답이다.

어휘 institution n. 기관   volunteer v. 자원하다, 자원 봉사로 하다
form v. 구성하다

198 | 육하원칙 문제

해설 장래의 회원들은 무엇을 제공하도록 요청받는가?
(A) 연간 회비에 대한 지불
(B) 그들의 근무 장소에 대한 세부 사항
(C) 자격증의 전자 복사본
(D) 선호하는 연락 수단

해설 웹페이지의 'How to register', 'Upload a scanned copy of your medical license.'에서 등록하는 방법으로 의사 면허증의 스캔된 복사본을 올리라고 했으므로 (C)가 정답이다.

어휘 prospective adj. 장래의, 미래의   employment n. 근무, 고용
electronic adj. 전자의   certificate n. 자격증, 증명서   preference n. 선호

Paraphrasing
a scanned copy of ~ medical license 의사 면허증의 스캔된 복사본
→ electronic copy of a certificate 자격증의 전자 복사본

199 | 육하원칙 문제

해설 AMPA는 최근에 무엇을 했는가?
(A) 연례 행사의 날짜를 변경했다.
(B) 회원들의 회비를 인상했다.
(C) 협력 기관을 설립했다.
(D) 웹사이트에 광고를 추가했다.

해설 웹페이지의 'we have recently introduced banner advertising on our Web site'에서 자신들, 즉 AMPA가 최근에 자신들의 웹사이트에 배너 광고를 도입했다고 했으므로 (D)가 정답이다.

어휘 establish v. 설립하다   partner organization 협력 기관

Paraphrasing

introduced 도입했다 → Added 추가했다

200 | 추론 문제 연계

해석 Mr. Lopez는 누구일 것 같은가?
(A) 마케팅 컨설턴트
(B) 광고 연출가
(C) 이벤트 기획자
(D) 지원 관리자

해설 Mr. Lopez에게 발송된 이메일을 먼저 확인한다.
단서 1 이메일의 'Dear Mr. Lopez', 'we would like to advertise ~ on your Web site'에서 이메일 수신자인 Mr. Lopez에게 그의 웹사이트에 광고하고 싶다고 한 사실을 확인할 수 있다.
단서 2 웹페이지의 'we ~ introduced banner advertising on our Web site'와 'For more information, please contact the support team.'에서 AMPA가 최근 웹사이트에 배너 광고를 도입했고, 더 많은 정보를 원한다면 지원 팀에 연락하라고 했다.
두 단서를 종합할 때, Mr. Lopez는 지원 관리자임을 추론할 수 있다. 따라서 (D)가 정답이다.

어휘 commercial n. 광고   director n. 연출가, 감독

실전모의고사 2

LISTENING TEST
p.144

1 (C)	2 (D)	3 (C)	4 (C)	5 (C)
6 (D)	7 (C)	8 (B)	9 (A)	10 (C)
11 (B)	12 (C)	13 (A)	14 (B)	15 (C)
16 (A)	17 (B)	18 (A)	19 (A)	20 (C)
21 (B)	22 (A)	23 (A)	24 (B)	25 (C)
26 (A)	27 (A)	28 (B)	29 (A)	30 (B)
31 (C)	32 (C)	33 (A)	34 (A)	35 (B)
36 (C)	37 (A)	38 (C)	39 (A)	40 (D)
41 (A)	42 (B)	43 (B)	44 (D)	45 (C)
46 (A)	47 (C)	48 (D)	49 (C)	50 (B)
51 (B)	52 (C)	53 (B)	54 (A)	55 (C)
56 (A)	57 (C)	58 (C)	59 (A)	60 (C)
61 (C)	62 (B)	63 (D)	64 (C)	65 (D)
66 (C)	67 (B)	68 (C)	69 (B)	70 (A)
71 (B)	72 (C)	73 (D)	74 (A)	75 (C)
76 (A)	77 (C)	78 (D)	79 (C)	80 (A)
81 (B)	82 (C)	83 (D)	84 (A)	85 (B)
86 (B)	87 (B)	88 (C)	89 (D)	90 (A)
91 (B)	92 (B)	93 (A)	94 (C)	95 (D)
96 (C)	97 (B)	98 (D)	99 (D)	100 (B)

READING TEST
p.156

101 (C)	102 (C)	103 (B)	104 (D)	105 (D)
106 (C)	107 (B)	108 (B)	109 (D)	110 (C)
111 (C)	112 (D)	113 (C)	114 (D)	115 (A)
116 (D)	117 (D)	118 (D)	119 (A)	120 (C)
121 (B)	122 (D)	123 (C)	124 (C)	125 (A)
126 (A)	127 (C)	128 (B)	129 (A)	130 (C)
131 (A)	132 (C)	133 (D)	134 (B)	135 (C)
136 (B)	137 (D)	138 (D)	139 (B)	140 (C)
141 (C)	142 (C)	143 (A)	144 (C)	145 (D)
146 (C)	147 (B)	148 (C)	149 (D)	150 (B)
151 (D)	152 (C)	153 (A)	154 (B)	155 (B)
156 (C)	157 (A)	158 (B)	159 (C)	160 (A)
161 (D)	162 (C)	163 (D)	164 (D)	165 (A)
166 (C)	167 (D)	168 (A)	169 (D)	170 (A)
171 (A)	172 (B)	173 (B)	174 (C)	175 (D)
176 (C)	177 (C)	178 (C)	179 (A)	180 (A)
181 (D)	182 (B)	183 (C)	184 (D)	185 (D)
186 (C)	187 (D)	188 (B)	189 (A)	190 (D)
191 (C)	192 (D)	193 (C)	194 (B)	195 (D)
196 (D)	197 (C)	198 (D)	199 (B)	200 (C)

PART 1

1 | 1인 사진
캐나다

(A) She's opening a package in an office.
(B) She's printing out some documents.
(C) She's looking through a binder.
(D) She's replacing a book on a shelf.

package n. 소포 document n. 서류
look through 자세히 살펴보다 replace v. (제자리에) 돌려놓다, 교체하다

해석 (A) 그녀는 사무실에서 소포를 열고 있다.
(B) 그녀는 몇몇 서류를 출력하고 있다.
(C) 그녀는 바인더를 자세히 살펴보고 있다.
(D) 그녀는 선반에 책을 돌려놓고 있다.

해설 (A) [×] opening a package(소포를 열고 있다)는 여자의 동작과 무관하므로 오답이다.
(B) [×] printing out some documents(몇몇 서류를 출력하고 있다)는 여자의 동작과 무관하므로 오답이다. 사진에 있는 서류(documents)를 사용하여 혼동을 주었다.
(C) [○] 여자가 바인더를 자세히 살펴보고 있는 모습을 가장 잘 묘사한 정답이다.
(D) [×] replacing a book(책을 돌려놓고 있다)은 여자의 동작과 무관하므로 오답이다.

2 | 야외 사진
호주

(A) Some streetlamps are set up beside a curb.
(B) Some large bushes have been trimmed.
(C) A trash can is being emptied on a path.
(D) Benches are located along a walkway.

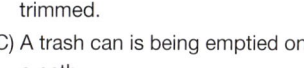

streetlamp n. 가로등 beside prep. ~ 옆에 curb n. (도로의) 연석
bush n. 덤불 trim v. 다듬다, 손질하다 empty v. 비우다; adj. 비어 있는
locate v. 위치하다 along prep. ~을 따라

해석 (A) 몇몇 가로등들이 연석 옆에 설치되어 있다.
(B) 몇몇 큰 덤불들이 다듬어져 있다.
(C) 쓰레기통이 길에서 비워지고 있다.
(D) 벤치들이 길을 따라 위치해 있다.

해설 (A) [×] 사진에 가로등들(streetlamps)이 없으므로 오답이다.
(B) [×] 사진에 덤불들(bushes)이 없으므로 오답이다.
(C) [×] 사진에서 쓰레기통(trash can)은 보이지만, 비워지고 있는(being emptied) 모습은 아니므로 오답이다.
(D) [○] 벤치들이 길을 따라 위치해 있는 모습을 가장 잘 묘사한 정답이다.

3 | 2인 이상 사진 호주

(A) Some furniture is arranged in rows.
(B) A man is paying for a purchase with a card.
(C) Some clothes are displayed on racks.
(D) A woman is trying on a jacket.

arrange v. 배치하다   purchase n. 구매; v. 구입하다   rack n. 선반, 받침대

해석 (A) 몇몇 가구가 줄지어 배치되어 있다.
     (B) 남자가 구매를 위해 카드로 지불하고 있다.
     (C) 몇몇 옷들이 선반 위에 진열되어 있다.
     (D) 여자가 재킷을 착용해 보고 있다.

해설 (A) [×] 사진에서 줄지어 배치되어 있는 가구(furniture)가 없으므로 오답이다.
     (B) [×] paying for a purchase(구매를 위해 지불하고 있다)는 남자의 동작과 무관하므로 오답이다.
     (C) [○] 옷들이 선반 위에 진열되어 있는 모습을 가장 잘 묘사한 정답이다.
     (D) [×] trying on a jacket(재킷을 착용해 보고 있다)은 여자의 동작과 무관하므로 오답이다.

4 | 2인 이상 사진 미국

(A) Some people are reading a sign above an entrance.
(B) Some people are entering a station through a gate.
(C) Some people are walking on a platform.
(D) Some people are boarding a train as a group.

sign n. 팻말, 신호   platform n. 승강장   board v. 타다

해석 (A) 몇몇 사람들이 출입구 위의 팻말을 읽고 있다.
     (B) 몇몇 사람들이 출입문을 지나 역으로 들어가고 있다.
     (C) 몇몇 사람들이 승강장에서 걷고 있다.
     (D) 몇몇 사람들이 단체로 기차에 타고 있다.

해설 (A) [×] reading a sign(팻말을 읽고 있다)은 사람들의 동작과 무관하므로 오답이다. 사진에 있는 sign(팻말)을 사용하여 혼동을 주었다.
     (B) [×] 사진에 역으로 들어가고 있는(entering a station) 사람들이 없으므로 오답이다.
     (C) [○] 몇몇 사람들이 승강장에서 걷고 있는 모습을 가장 잘 묘사한 정답이다.
     (D) [×] boarding a train(기차에 타고 있다)은 사람들의 동작과 무관하므로 오답이다. 사진에 있는 train(기차)을 사용하여 혼동을 주었다.

5 | 1인 사진 미국

(A) A glass is being filled with coffee from a pitcher.
(B) Books are piled on a countertop in an office.
(C) Magazines have been spread out on a table.
(D) A chair has been pushed against a wall.

pitcher n. 주전자   pile v. 쌓다   countertop n. 작업대, 조리대

해석 (A) 유리잔이 주전자의 커피로 채워지고 있다.
     (B) 책들이 사무실의 작업대 위에 쌓여 있다.
     (C) 잡지들이 테이블 위에 펼쳐져 있다.
     (D) 의자가 벽 쪽으로 밀려 있다.

해설 (A) [×] 사진에 유리잔(glass)은 보이지만, 커피로 채워지고 있는(being filled with coffee) 모습은 아니므로 오답이다.
     (B) [×] 사진에 책들(Books)은 보이지만, 작업대 위에 쌓여 있는(piled on a countertop) 모습은 아니므로 오답이다.
     (C) [○] 잡지들이 테이블 위에 펼쳐져 있는 모습을 가장 잘 묘사한 정답이다.
     (D) [×] 사진에 의자(chair)는 보이지만, 벽 쪽으로 밀려 있는(pushed against a wall) 모습은 아니므로 오답이다.

6 | 2인 이상 사진 영국

(A) Some workers are walking up a flight of stairs.
(B) One of the people is lifting a box onto a cart.
(C) One of the people is exiting a warehouse in a vehicle.
(D) Some items are leaning against a shelving unit.

flight of stairs 한 줄로 이어진 계단   lift v. 들어 올리다   exit v. 나가다, 떠나다
warehouse n. 창고   lean against ~에 기대다   shelving unit 선반

해석 (A) 몇몇 작업자들이 한 줄로 이어진 계단을 올라가고 있다.
     (B) 사람들 중 한 명이 상자를 카트 위로 들어 올리고 있다.
     (C) 사람들 중 한 명이 탈것을 타고 창고에서 나가고 있다.
     (D) 몇몇 물건들이 선반에 기대어 있다.

해설 (A) [×] 사진에 한 줄로 이어진 계단을 올라가고 있는(walking up a flight of stairs) 작업자가 없으므로 오답이다.
     (B) [×] 사진에 상자를 들어 올리고 있는(lifting a box) 사람이 없으므로 오답이다.
     (C) [×] 사진에 탈것을 타고 창고에서 나가고 있는(exiting a warehouse in a vehicle) 사람이 없으므로 오답이다.
     (D) [○] 몇몇 물건들이 선반에 기대어 있는 모습을 가장 잘 묘사한 정답이다.

PART 2

7 | How 의문문 영국 → 캐나다

How far is the grocery store from your apartment?
(A) I've been in the apartment for two months.
(B) The store closes at 7 P.M.
(C) The nearest one is a mile away.

grocery store 식료품점

해석 당신의 아파트에서 식료품점은 얼마나 먼가요?
     (A) 저는 이 아파트에 두 달 동안 있었어요.
     (B) 그 가게는 오후 7시에 닫아요.
     (C) 가장 가까운 것이 1마일 떨어진 곳에 있어요.

해설 (A) [×] 질문의 apartment를 반복 사용하여 혼동을 준 오답이다.
     (B) [×] 질문의 store를 반복 사용하여 혼동을 준 오답이다.
     (C) [○] 가장 가까운 것이 1마일 떨어진 곳에 있다는 말로, 식료품점까지의 거리를 언급했으므로 정답이다.

8 | Why 의문문
호주 → 영국

Why is the subway's Blue Line out of service?
(A) The green one, please.
(B) For maintenance work.
(C) Since last Wednesday.

out of service 이용 불가능한 maintenance n. 보수, 유지

해석 왜 지하철의 파란색 노선이 이용 불가능한가요?
(A) 녹색으로 부탁드려요.
(B) 보수 작업 때문에요.
(C) 지난 수요일부터요.

해설 (A) [x] 질문의 Blue(파란색)에서 연상할 수 있는 색상과 관련된 green (녹색)을 사용하여 혼동을 준 오답이다.
(B) [o] 보수 작업 때문이라는 말로, 이용 불가능한 이유를 언급했으므로 정답이다.
(C) [x] 왜 지하철의 파란색 노선이 이용 불가능한지 이유를 물었는데, 이와 관련이 없는 시점으로 응답했으므로 오답이다.

9 | 부가 의문문
미국 → 영국

Your computer is still under warranty, isn't it?
(A) That's correct.
(B) I called a repairperson.
(C) No. Under the television.

under warranty 보증 기간 내에 있는 repairperson n. 수리공

해석 당신의 컴퓨터는 아직 보증 기간 내에 있죠, 그렇지 않나요?
(A) 맞아요.
(B) 제가 수리공을 불렀어요.
(C) 아니요. 텔레비전 아래에요.

해설 (A) [o] 맞다는 말로, 컴퓨터가 아직 보증 기간 내에 있음을 전달했으므로 정답이다.
(B) [x] 질문의 under warranty(보증 기간 내에 있는)에서 연상할 수 있는 수리와 관련된 repairperson(수리공)을 사용하여 혼동을 준 오답이다.
(C) [x] 질문의 under를 반복 사용하여 혼동을 준 오답이다.

10 | What 의문문
캐나다 → 미국

What was the conference about?
(A) It was held in Mexico City.
(B) Yes. We want to go.
(C) Advertising methods.

conference n. 회의, 회담 advertising n. 광고 method n. 기법, 방식, 방법

해석 회의는 무엇에 관한 것이었나요?
(A) 그것은 멕시코 시티에서 개최됐어요.
(B) 네. 우리는 가고 싶어요.
(C) 광고 기법들이요.

해설 (A) [x] 회의가 무엇에 관한 것이었는지를 물었는데, 이와 관련이 없는 그것은 멕시코 시티에서 개최됐다는 내용으로 응답했으므로 오답이다. 질문의 conference(회의)를 나타낼 수 있는 It을 사용하여 혼동을 주었다.
(B) [x] 의문사 의문문에 Yes로 응답했으므로 오답이다. 질문의 conference(회의)에서 연상할 수 있는 동작과 관련된 go(가다)를 사용하여 혼동을 주었다.
(C) [o] 광고 기법들이라는 말로, 회의의 주제를 언급했으므로 정답이다.

11 | Be동사 의문문
캐나다 → 미국

Is the gym open this holiday weekend?
(A) One of the trainers.
(B) Only on Sunday.
(C) Spending time with my family.

holiday weekend 주말 연휴

해석 체육관은 이번 주말 연휴에 열려 있나요?
(A) 트레이너들 중 한 명이요.
(B) 일요일만요.
(C) 제 가족과 함께 시간을 보내는 것이요.

해설 (A) [x] 질문의 gym(체육관)과 관련 있는 trainers(트레이너들)를 사용하여 혼동을 준 오답이다.
(B) [o] 일요일만이라는 말로, 체육관이 주말 연휴 중 하루만 열려 있음을 전달했으므로 정답이다.
(C) [x] 체육관이 주말 연휴에 열려 있는지를 물었는데, 이와 관련이 없는 가족과 함께 시간을 보내는 것이라는 내용으로 응답했으므로 오답이다.

12 | Where 의문문
영국 → 호주

Where did you get your hair cut?
(A) It really suits you.
(B) Just take a little bit off.
(C) At the place on State Street.

suit v. 어울리다

해석 머리를 어디에서 잘랐나요?
(A) 그것이 당신에게 정말 잘 어울려요.
(B) 그냥 조금만 잘라 주세요.
(C) State가에 있는 곳에서요.

해설 (A) [x] 머리를 어디에서 잘랐는지를 물었는데, 이와 관련이 없는 당신에게 정말 잘 어울린다는 내용으로 응답했으므로 오답이다.
(B) [x] cut(자르다)과 같은 의미인 take off를 사용하여 혼동을 준 오답이다.
(C) [o] State가에 있는 곳에서라는 말로, 머리를 자른 장소를 언급했으므로 정답이다.

13 | 부가 의문문
미국 → 캐나다

You didn't have any issues during your business trip, did you?
(A) Everything went smoothly.
(B) No. They will leave tomorrow.
(C) That looks problematic.

business trip 출장 smoothly adv. 순조롭게

해석 당신은 출장 동안 어떤 문제도 없었죠, 그렇죠?
(A) 모든 것이 순조롭게 진행되었어요.
(B) 아니요. 그들은 내일 떠날 거예요.
(C) 그건 문제가 있어 보여요.

해설 (A) [o] 모든 것이 순조롭게 진행되었다는 말로, 출장 동안 어떤 문제도 없었음을 전달했으므로 정답이다.
(B) [x] 출장 동안 어떤 문제도 없었는지를 물었는데, 이와 관련이 없는 그들은 내일 떠날 것이라는 내용으로 응답했으므로 오답이다. No까지만 듣고 정답으로 고르지 않도록 주의한다.
(C) [x] 질문의 issues(문제)와 관련된 problematic(문제가 있는)을 사용하여 혼동을 준 오답이다.

14 | 부정 의문문
미국 → 캐나다

Can't we apply for a club membership online?
(A) What's the security code for the entrance?
(B) Yes, I'll show you how.
(C) Actually, there are many members.

apply for 신청하다, 지원하다 security n. 보안

해석 온라인으로 클럽 멤버십을 신청할 수 있지 않나요?
(A) 입구 보안 코드가 무엇인가요?
(B) 네, 제가 방법을 보여드릴게요.
(C) 사실, 많은 회원들이 있어요.

해설 (A) [×] 질문의 online(온라인)에서 연상할 수 있는 접속 방법과 관련된 security code(보안 코드)를 사용하여 혼동을 준 오답이다.
(B) [○] Yes로 온라인으로 클럽 멤버십을 신청할 수 있음을 전달한 후, 방법을 보여주겠다는 부연 설명을 했으므로 정답이다.
(C) [×] membership - members의 유사 발음 어휘를 사용하여 혼동을 준 오답이다.

15 | When 의문문
영국 → 호주

When is Faraj Sleiman's film going to be screened?
(A) It's a documentary.
(B) At more than a few theaters.
(C) The beginning of September.

screen v. 상영하다

해석 Faraj Sleiman의 영화는 언제 상영될 예정인가요?
(A) 다큐멘터리예요.
(B) 여러 극장에서요.
(C) 9월 초요.

해설 (A) [×] 질문의 film(영화)에서 연상할 수 있는 장르와 관련된 documentary(다큐멘터리)를 사용하여 혼동을 준 오답이다.
(B) [×] 질문의 film(영화)에서 연상할 수 있는 장소와 관련된 theaters(극장)를 사용하여 혼동을 준 오답이다.
(C) [○] 9월 초라는 말로, 영화가 상영될 시점을 언급했으므로 정답이다.

16 | 제안 의문문
미국 → 호주

Do you need help rearranging the display in the main window?
(A) If you have time.
(B) I see what they mean.
(C) No. Don't make dinner plans.

rearrange v. 재배치하다 display n. 진열, 전시 window n. (진열)창

해석 주 진열창의 진열을 재배치하는 데 도움이 필요하신가요?
(A) 시간이 있으시다면요.
(B) 그것들이 무슨 의미인지 알겠어요.
(C) 아니요. 저녁 계획을 짜지 마세요.

해설 (A) [○] 시간이 있으시다면 도움을 달라는 말로, 진열을 재배치하는 데 도움을 주겠다는 제안을 간접적으로 수락한 정답이다.
(B) [×] 진열을 재배치하는 데 도움이 필요한지 물었는데, 이와 관련이 없는 그것들이 무슨 의미인지 알겠다는 내용으로 응답했으므로 오답이다.
(C) [×] 진열을 재배치하는 데 도움이 필요한지 물었는데, 이와 관련이 없는 저녁 계획을 짜지 말라는 내용으로 응답했으므로 오답이다. No까지만 듣고 정답으로 고르지 않도록 주의한다.

17 | Who 의문문
캐나다 → 미국

Who organized our group tour of Vancouver?
(A) All participants must wear nametags.
(B) Wasn't it Camille?
(C) The city is very beautiful.

organize v. 준비하다, 정리하다 participant n. 참석자 nametag n. 이름표

해석 누가 우리의 밴쿠버 단체 여행을 준비했나요?
(A) 모든 참석자들은 이름표를 착용해야 해요.
(B) Camille 아니었나요?
(C) 그 도시는 매우 아름다워요.

해설 (A) [×] 질문의 group tour(단체 여행)와 관련 있는 participants(참석자들)를 사용하여 혼동을 준 오답이다.
(B) [○] Camille이 아니었는지를 되물어, Camille이 밴쿠버 단체 여행을 준비했을 것이라는 답변을 간접적으로 전달했으므로 정답이다.
(C) [×] 질문의 Vancouver(밴쿠버)를 나타낼 수 있는 The city를 사용하여 혼동을 준 오답이다.

18 | 평서문
영국 → 미국

An inspector will stop by our café on Sunday.
(A) Our employees should be informed.
(B) You'll probably like the espresso.
(C) The inspection was very thorough.

inspector n. 검사관 inform v. 알리다, 통보하다
thorough adj. 철저한, 빈틈없는

해석 검사관이 일요일에 우리 카페에 들를 거예요.
(A) 우리 직원들이 알아야 해요.
(B) 당신은 아마 에스프레소를 좋아할 거예요.
(C) 그 검사는 매우 철저했어요.

해설 (A) [○] 직원들이 알아야 한다는 말로, 검사관이 일요일에 카페에 들를 것이라는 말에 대한 의견을 제시했으므로 정답이다.
(B) [×] 질문의 café(카페)와 관련 있는 espresso(에스프레소)를 사용하여 혼동을 준 오답이다.
(C) [×] inspector - inspection의 유사 발음 어휘를 사용하여 혼동을 준 오답이다.

19 | When 의문문
호주 → 영국

When does Mr. Graves want to hold a press conference?
(A) By Friday at the latest.
(B) He announced a branch opening.
(C) It was an impressive speech.

press conference 기자회견 announce v. 발표하다 branch n. 지점
opening n. 개장 impressive adj. 인상적인

해석 Mr. Graves는 언제 기자회견을 열길 원하나요?
(A) 늦어도 금요일까지요.
(B) 그가 지점 개장을 발표했어요.
(C) 그것은 인상적인 연설이었어요.

해설 (A) [○] 늦어도 금요일까지라는 말로, 기자회견을 열길 원하는 시점을 언급했으므로 정답이다.
(B) [×] 질문의 press conference(기자회견)에서 연상할 수 있는 행동과 관련된 announced(발표했다)를 사용하여 혼동을 준 오답이다.
(C) [×] press - impressive의 유사 발음 어휘를 사용하여 혼동을 준 오답이다.

20 | Why 의문문
캐나다 → 미국

Why were these chairs moved?
(A) Next to the main entrance.
(B) Check the supply closet.
(C) Those workers might know.

supply closet 비품 보관함

해석 이 의자들은 왜 옮겨졌나요?
(A) 정문 옆이요.
(B) 비품 보관함을 확인하세요.
(C) 저 작업자들이 알 거예요.

해설 (A) [×] 의자들이 왜 옮겨졌는지 이유를 물었는데, 이와 관련 없는 위치로 응답했으므로 오답이다.
(B) [×] 의자들이 왜 옮겨졌는지 이유를 물었는데, 이와 관련 없는 비품 보관함을 확인하라는 내용으로 응답하였으므로 오답이다.
(C) [○] 저 작업자들이 알 것이라는 말로, 의자들이 옮겨진 이유를 모른다는 것을 간접적으로 전달했으므로 정답이다.

21 | 조동사 의문문
호주 → 영국

Can passengers get a refund for any flight?
(A) Baggage must be securely stored.
(B) Only for the canceled ones.
(C) Meals will be served after takeoff.

refund n. 환불   baggage n. 수하물   securely adv. 안전하게
store v. 보관하다   takeoff n. 이륙, 출발

해석 승객들이 어느 항공편이든 환불을 받을 수 있나요?
(A) 수하물은 안전하게 보관되어야 합니다.
(B) 취소된 것들에 대해서만요.
(C) 식사는 이륙 이후에 제공될 것입니다.

해설 (A) [×] 질문의 flight(항공편)과 관련 있는 Baggage(수하물)를 사용하여 혼동을 준 오답이다.
(B) [○] 취소된 것들에 대해서만이라는 말로, 승객들이 어느 항공편이든 환불을 받을 수 없음을 간접적으로 전달했으므로 정답이다.
(C) [×] 질문의 flight(항공편)과 관련 있는 takeoff(이륙)를 사용하여 혼동을 준 오답이다.

22 | When 의문문
캐나다 → 호주

When should we arrive at the stadium?
(A) The game starts at four.
(B) The tickets are for Section C, Row 15.
(C) It was an exciting finish.

stadium n. 경기장   finish n. 결승, 끝; v. 끝내다

해석 우리는 경기장에 언제 도착해야 하나요?
(A) 경기는 4시에 시작해요.
(B) C구역 15열 티켓들입니다.
(C) 흥미로운 결승이었어요.

해설 (A) [○] 경기는 4시에 시작한다는 말로, 4시 이전에 경기장에 도착하는 것이 좋겠다는 의견을 간접적으로 전달했으므로 정답이다.
(B) [×] 질문의 stadium(경기장)에서 연상할 수 있는 좌석 배치와 관련된 Section C, Row 15(C구역 15열)를 사용하여 혼동을 준 오답이다.
(C) [×] 질문의 stadium(경기장)에서 연상할 수 있는 경기와 관련된 finish(결승)를 사용하여 혼동을 준 오답이다.

23 | 조동사 의문문
영국 → 호주

Do you need to replace the battery in your car?
(A) No. It's working well.
(B) It was placed on your desk.
(C) I keep records of all repairs.

replace v. 교체하다   record n. 기록   repair n. 수리

해석 당신의 차 내부 배터리를 교체해야 하나요?
(A) 아니요. 그것은 잘 작동하고 있어요.
(B) 그것은 당신의 책상 위에 놓여 있었어요.
(C) 저는 모든 수리들의 기록을 보관해요.

해설 (A) [○] No로 교체가 필요하지 않음을 전달한 후, 그것, 즉 배터리가 잘 작동하고 있다는 말로 부연 설명을 했으므로 정답이다.
(B) [×] replace - placed의 유사 발음 어휘를 사용하여 혼동을 준 오답이다.
(C) [×] 질문의 replace(교체하다)와 관련 있는 repairs(수리들)를 사용하여 혼동을 준 오답이다.

24 | 선택 의문문
캐나다 → 영국

Where should we host the banquet, in Hall A or B?
(A) You should taste both drinks.
(B) Whichever one is bigger.
(C) Invitations can be sent out today.

host v. 주최하다   banquet n. 연회   whichever adj. 어느 쪽이든 ~한
invitation n. 초대(장)

해석 우리는 A홀과 B홀 중 어디에서 연회를 주최해야 할까요?
(A) 당신은 두 음료 모두 맛보셔야 해요.
(B) 어느 쪽이든 더 큰 곳이요.
(C) 초대장들은 오늘 발송될 수 있어요.

해설 (A) [×] 질문의 banquet(연회)에서 연상할 수 있는 음식과 관련된 drinks(음료)를 사용하여 혼동을 준 오답이다.
(B) [○] 어느 쪽이든 더 큰 곳이라는 말로, 연회를 주최할 장소를 간접적으로 선택했으므로 정답이다.
(C) [×] 질문의 banquet(연회)과 관련 있는 Invitations(초대장들)를 사용하여 혼동을 준 오답이다.

25 | Who 의문문
호주 → 미국

Who is giving directions to the volunteers?
(A) Thanks for the help.
(B) You can turn left at the corner.
(C) I was going to ask you that.

directions n. 지시, 명령

해석 누가 자원봉사자들에게 지시를 내리고 있나요?
(A) 도와주셔서 감사해요.
(B) 모퉁이에서 좌회전하시면 돼요.
(C) 당신에게 그것을 물어보려고 했어요.

해설 (A) [×] 누가 자원봉사자들에게 지시를 내리고 있는지를 물었는데, 이와 관련이 없는 도와주셔서 감사하다는 말로 응답했으므로 오답이다.
(B) [×] 질문의 directions(지시)를 '방향'이라는 의미의 명사로 이해할 경우 연상할 수 있는 방향과 관련된 turn left(좌회전하다)를 사용하여 혼동을 준 오답이다.
(C) [○] 당신에게 그것을 물어보려고 했다는 말로, 누가 자원봉사자들에

게 지시를 내리고 있는지를 모른다는 것을 간접적으로 전달했으
므로 정답이다.

26 | 부정 의문문
영국 → 호주

Weren't bonuses given to the top sales associates?
(A) Yes. Each got an extra $1,000.
(B) No, it's a brief presentation.
(C) Open a savings account.

bonus n. 상여금, 보너스   sales associate 영업 사원   brief adj. 간단한, 짧은
savings account 예금 계좌

해석 상위 영업 사원들에게 상여금이 주어지지 않았나요?
(A) 네. 각각 추가로 1,000달러를 받았어요.
(B) 아니요, 그건 간단한 발표예요.
(C) 예금 계좌를 개설하세요.

해설 (A) [o] Yes로 상여금이 주어졌음을 전달한 후, 각각 추가로 1,000달러를 받았다는 부연 설명을 했으므로 정답이다.
(B) [x] 질문의 sales(영업)에서 연상할 수 있는 업무와 관련된 presentation(발표)을 사용하여 혼동을 준 오답이다. No까지만 듣고 정답으로 고르지 않도록 주의한다.
(C) [x] 질문의 bonuses(상여금)에서 연상할 수 있는 돈과 관련된 savings account(예금 계좌)를 사용하여 혼동을 준 오답이다.

27 | 평서문
호주 → 캐나다

This is the fastest route to Ashbury Park.
(A) What about taking Oak Street?
(B) I parked it over there.
(C) I often visit parks on weekends.

route n. 길, 경로

해석 이것이 Ashbury 공원으로 가는 가장 빠른 길이에요.
(A) Oak가를 타는 것은 어때요?
(B) 저는 그것을 저기에 주차했어요.
(C) 저는 주말에 자주 공원을 방문해요.

해설 (A) [o] Oak가를 타는 것은 어떤지를 되물어, 다른 의견을 제시했으므로 정답이다.
(B) [x] Park - parked의 유사 발음 어휘를 사용하여 혼동을 준 오답이다.
(C) [x] 질문의 Park를 parks로 반복 사용하여 혼동을 준 오답이다.

28 | 선택 의문문
영국 → 호주

Are you saving these old folders or can I throw them away?
(A) No. They're not mine.
(B) I'm going to use them.
(C) I already looked in the trash.

throw away 버리다

해석 이 오래된 폴더들을 보관하고 계신가요, 아니면 제가 그것들을 버려도 되나요?
(A) 아니요. 그것들은 제 것이 아니에요.
(B) 제가 그것들을 사용할 거예요.
(C) 저는 이미 쓰레기를 살펴봤어요.

해설 (A) [x] 선택 의문문에 No로 응답했으므로 오답이다. 질문의 old folders(오래된 폴더들)를 나타낼 수 있는 They를 사용하여 혼동을 주었다.

(B) [o] 자신이 그것들을 사용할 것이라는 말로, 폴더들을 보관하고 있는 것을 간접적으로 선택했으므로 정답이다.
(C) [x] 질문의 throw away(버리다)와 관련 있는 trash(쓰레기)를 사용하여 혼동을 준 오답이다.

29 | How 의문문
미국 → 캐나다

How did you finish your assignment so quickly?
(A) I'll make an appointment now.
(B) Please finish that today.
(C) Ted offered to help.

assignment n. 업무   appointment n. 일정

해석 당신은 어떻게 그렇게 빨리 당신의 업무를 마쳤나요?
(A) 지금 일정을 잡을게요.
(B) 오늘 그것을 마쳐주세요.
(C) Ted가 도와주었어요.

해설 (A) [x] assignment - appointment의 유사 발음 어휘를 사용하여 혼동을 준 오답이다.
(B) [x] 질문의 finish를 반복 사용하여 혼동을 준 오답이다.
(C) [o] Ted가 도와주었다는 말로, 업무를 빨리 마친 방법을 언급했으므로 정답이다.

30 | 조동사 의문문
캐나다 → 미국

Can companies set up their booths at the front of the venue?
(A) The event is for the technology industry.
(B) A stage will be set up in that area.
(C) No. Companies can't change a quote.

set up 설치하다   venue n. 장소   industry n. 산업   quote n. 견적

해석 회사들은 그들의 부스를 장소 앞쪽에 설치할 수 있나요?
(A) 그 행사는 기술 산업에 관한 거예요.
(B) 무대가 그 구역에 설치될 거예요.
(C) 아니요. 회사들은 견적을 변경할 수 없어요.

해설 (A) [x] 질문의 booths(부스)에서 연상할 수 있는 event(행사)를 사용하여 혼동을 준 오답이다.
(B) [o] 무대가 그 구역, 즉 장소 앞쪽에 설치될 것이라는 말로, 부스를 장소 앞쪽에 설치할 수 없음을 간접적으로 전달했으므로 정답이다.
(C) [x] 질문의 companies를 반복 사용하여 혼동을 준 오답이다. No까지만 듣고 정답으로 고르지 않도록 주의한다.

31 | What 의문문
호주 → 영국

What city will the band be performing in next?
(A) Live performances can be a lot of fun.
(B) I used to be in a musical group, too.
(C) I need to check the tour schedule.

perform v. 공연하다

해석 그 밴드는 다음으로 어느 도시에서 공연할 예정인가요?
(A) 라이브 공연은 매우 재미있을 수 있어요.
(B) 저도 뮤지컬 단체에 있었던 적이 있어요.
(C) 투어 일정을 확인해 봐야 해요.

해설 (A) [x] performing - performances의 유사 발음 어휘를 사용하여 혼동을 준 오답이다.
(B) [x] 질문의 performing(공연하다)에서 연상할 수 있는 공연과 관련

된 musical(뮤지컬)을 사용하여 혼동을 준 오답이다.
(C) [○] 투어 일정을 확인해 봐야 한다는 말로, 밴드가 다음으로 어느 도시에서 공연할 예정인지 모름을 간접적으로 전달했으므로 정답이다.

PART 3

[32-34]
캐나다 → 영국
Questions 32-34 refer to the following conversation.

M: I'm not sure if you're aware, but ³²several diners have complained about our restaurant menu recently. They want more vegan choices.
W: Hmm . . . ³³Do you remember the vegan noodle dish we tried at the International Cuisine Fair last month? Maybe we can do something similar to that but with different toppings.
M: Great suggestion. We'd better talk to Mr. Riley. ³⁴As the owner, he'll have to approve the change.
W: He's on vacation, but ³⁴I'll e-mail him to share our thoughts.

diner n. 식사하는 손님 vegan n. 채식주의(자) cuisine n. 요리
topping n. 고명 approve v. 승인하다

해석
32-34번은 다음 대화에 관한 문제입니다.
남: 알고 계실지 모르겠지만, ³²식사하는 손님 몇 분이 최근 우리 식당 메뉴에 대해 불평해왔어요. 그들은 더 많은 채식주의 선택지를 원해요.
여: 흠... ³³지난달 국제 요리 박람회에서 시식했던 채식주의 면 요리를 기억하나요? 아마 우리가 그것과 비슷한 무언가를 다른 고명들로 할 수 있을 거예요.
남: 좋은 제안이네요. Mr. Riley에게 이야기하는 것이 좋겠어요. ³⁴주인으로서, 그가 변경 사항을 승인해야 할 거예요.
여: 그는 휴가 중이지만, ³⁴제가 그에게 우리의 생각을 공유하기 위해 이메일을 보낼게요.

32 | 특정 세부 사항 문제
해석 남자에 따르면, 손님들은 무엇에 대해 불평했는가?
(A) 공간의 크기
(B) 요리의 맛
(C) 메뉴 선택지
(D) 운영 시간
해설 질문의 핵심 어구(customers complain about)와 관련된 주변을 주의 깊게 듣는다. 남자가 "several diners have complained about our restaurant menu recently. They want more vegan choices."라며 식사하는 손님 몇 분이 최근 식당 메뉴에 대해 불평해왔고, 그들은 더 많은 채식주의 선택지를 원한다고 하였다. 따라서 (C)가 정답이다.
어휘 operating hours 운영 시간

Paraphrasing
choices 선택지 → options 선택지

33 | 특정 세부 사항 문제
해석 지난달에 무슨 일이 일어났는가?
(A) 산업 박람회

(B) 교육
(C) 영업 발표
(D) 요리 강좌
해설 질문의 핵심 어구(last month)가 언급된 주변을 주의 깊게 듣는다. 여자가 "Do you remember the vegan noodle dish we tried at the International Cuisine Fair last month?"라며 지난달 국제 요리 박람회에서 시식했던 채식주의 면 요리를 기억하는지 물었다. 따라서 (A)가 정답이다.
어휘 culinary adj. 요리의

Paraphrasing
International Cuisine Fair 국제 요리 박람회 → An industry fair 산업 박람회

34 | 특정 세부 사항 문제
해석 여자는 누구에게 이메일을 보낼 것인가?
(A) 주인
(B) 요리사
(C) 비평가
(D) 상담가
해설 질문의 핵심 어구(e-mail)가 언급된 주변을 주의 깊게 듣는다. 남자가 "As the owner, he'll have to approve the change."라며 주인으로서 그가 변경 사항을 승인해야 할 것이라고 하자, 여자가 "I'll e-mail him to share our thoughts"라며 그에게 자신들의 생각을 공유하기 위해 이메일을 보내겠다고 하였다. 따라서 (A)가 정답이다.
어휘 critic n. 비평가 consultant n. 상담가

[35-37]
미국 → 캐나다
Questions 35-37 refer to the following conversation.

W: Excuse me. ³⁵Does this city bus go to Fenton Street?
M: ³⁵Yes, it does.
W: Great. I'd like to put my bike on the rack at the front of the bus. Could you show me how to use it?
M: ³⁶I'm very sorry, but the rack is out of order right now. The locking mechanism is jammed, so bikes can't be securely fastened to it.
W: That's too bad. Well, ³⁷how much longer will it take for another bus to get here?
M: Buses stop at this corner every 15 minutes, so not very long. I suggest waiting for the next one. Sorry for the inconvenience.

rack n. 고정대 out of order 고장 난 jam v. 고장 나게 하다
fasten v. 고정시키다, 채우다, 매다

해석
35-37번은 다음 대화에 관한 문제입니다.
여: 실례합니다. ³⁵이 시내버스가 Fenton가로 가나요?
남: ³⁵네, 갑니다.
여: 좋아요. 저는 제 자전거를 버스 앞 쪽의 고정대에 놓고 싶어요. 이것을 어떻게 사용하는지 알려주시겠어요?
남: ³⁶정말 죄송합니다만, 고정대가 지금은 고장 났어요. 잠금장치가 고장 나서, 자전거가 거기에 안전하게 고정되지 못해요.
여: 유감이네요. 음, ³⁷다른 버스가 여기 오려면 얼마나 더 걸릴까요?
남: 버스들은 이 모퉁이에 15분마다 서니까, 아주 오래 걸리지는 않아요. 다음 것을 기다리는 것을 권해드려요. 불편을 드려 죄송합니다.

35 | 화자 문제

해석 남자는 누구인 것 같은가?
(A) 자전거 수리공
(B) 대중교통 운전사
(C) 시 공무원
(D) 버스 승객

해설 대화에서 신분 및 직업과 관련된 표현을 놓치지 않고 듣는다. 여자가 "Does this city bus go to Fenton Street?"라며 남자에게 이 시내버스가 Fenton가로 가는지 묻자, 남자가 "Yes, it does."라며 Fenton가로 간다고 답한 것을 통해 남자가 버스 운전사임을 알 수 있다. 따라서 (B)가 정답이다.

어휘 city official 시 공무원

Paraphrasing

city bus 시내버스 → public transport 대중교통

36 | 문제점 문제

해석 남자는 무슨 문제를 언급하는가?
(A) 엔진이 제대로 작동하지 않았다.
(B) 일부 설명이 확실하지 않다.
(C) 잠금장치를 채울 수 없다.
(D) 승객들을 위한 공간이 더는 없다.

해설 남자의 말에서 부정적인 표현이 언급된 주변을 주의 깊게 듣는다. 남자가 "I'm very sorry, but the rack is out of order right now. The locking mechanism is jammed, so bikes can't be securely fastened to it."이라며 정말 죄송하지만 고정대가 지금은 고장 났다고 한 후, 잠금장치가 고장 나서 자전거가 안전하게 고정되지 못한다고 하였다. 따라서 (C)가 정답이다.

어휘 malfunction v. 제대로 작동하지 않다

Paraphrasing

The locking mechanism is jammed 잠금장치가 고장 나다 → A lock cannot be fastened 잠금장치를 채울 수 없다

37 | 특정 세부 사항 문제

해석 여자는 무엇에 대해 문의하는가?
(A) 언제 다른 버스가 도착할지
(B) 서비스 비용이 얼마나 들지
(C) 승차가 왜 그렇게 오래 걸릴지
(D) 다른 누군가가 도와줄 수 있는지

해설 대화에서 여자의 말을 주의 깊게 듣는다. 여자가 남자에게 "how much longer will it take for another bus to get here?"라며 다른 버스가 여기 오려면 얼마나 더 걸릴지를 물었다. 따라서 (A)가 정답이다.

[38-40]

호주 → 미국

Questions 38-40 refer to the following conversation.

M: ³⁸Are you excited to be upgrading to a larger office, Cassie?

W: Definitely! It was hard keeping all my files organized at my old workspace, so I'm happy to have more room.

M: Good. While I'm here, do you need any help settling in?

W: Um . . . I think I'm doing OK. Although, ³⁹I could use a hand putting the furniture together. It might take me all day, otherwise.

M: It could take us both all day by the looks of it. But actually, ⁴⁰you can get someone from the maintenance department to help with that. I can give them a call for you.

definitely adv. 확실히   workspace n. 업무 공간   put together 조립하다
maintenance n. 유지보수   department n. 부서

해석
38-40번은 다음 대화에 관한 문제입니다.
남: ³⁸더 넓은 사무실로 업그레이드하게 되어 기쁘신가요, Cassie?
여: 확실히요! 제 예전 업무 공간에서는 모든 파일들을 체계적으로 보관하는 것이 힘들었어서, 더 많은 공간을 갖게 되어 기뻐요.
남: 좋아요. 제가 여기 있는 동안, 짐을 푸는 데 도움이 필요하신가요?
여: 음... 저는 잘하고 있는 것 같아요. 비록, ³⁹가구를 조립하는 데 도움을 받을 수 있을 것 같지만요. 그렇지 않으면 하루 종일 걸릴지도 몰라요.
남: 보기에는 우리 둘 다 하루 종일 걸릴 수도 있을 것 같네요. 하지만 사실 ⁴⁰유지보수 부서에서 도와줄 사람을 구할 수 있어요. 제가 대신 전화해 드릴 수 있어요.

38 | 주제 문제

해석 대화는 주로 무엇에 관한 것인가?
(A) 최근 주문
(B) 고객의 프로젝트
(C) 새로운 업무 공간
(D) 업무 할당

해설 대화의 주제를 묻는 문제이므로, 대화의 초반을 반드시 듣는다. 남자가 여자에게 "Are you excited to be upgrading to a larger office, Cassie?"라며 더 넓은 사무실로 업그레이드하게 되어 기쁜지 물은 후, 새로운 업무 공간에 대한 내용으로 대화가 이어지고 있다. 따라서 (C)가 정답이다.

어휘 assignment n. 할당

Paraphrasing

office 사무실 → workspace 업무 공간

39 | 이유 문제

해석 여자는 왜 도움이 필요한가?
(A) 작업이 많은 시간이 걸릴 수 있다.
(B) 공간이 청소되어야 한다.
(C) 몇몇 파일이 사라졌다.
(D) 마감일이 다가오고 있다.

해설 질문의 핵심 어구(woman need help)와 관련된 내용을 주의 깊게 듣는다. 여자가 "I could use a hand putting the furniture together. It might take me all day, otherwise."라며 가구를 조립하는 데 도움을 받을 수 있을 것 같다고 한 후, 그렇지 않으면 하루 종일 걸릴지도 모른다고 하였다. 따라서 (A)가 정답이다.

어휘 time-consuming adj. 많은 시간이 걸리는   missing adj. 사라진   approach v. 다가오다

40 | 제안 문제

해석 남자는 무엇을 해주겠다고 제안하는가?
(A) 고객에게 전화한다.
(B) 프로젝트를 인계받는다.
(C) 약속을 연기한다.
(D) 부서에 연락한다.

해설 남자의 말에서 여자를 위해 해 주겠다고 언급한 내용을 주의 깊게 듣는다. 남자가 "you can get someone from the maintenance department to help with that. I can give them a call for you."라며 유지보수 부서에서 도와줄 사람을 구할 수 있다고 한 후, 대신 전화해 줄 수 있다고 하였다. 따라서 (D)가 정답이다.

어휘 take over 인계받다 postpone v. 연기하다

Paraphrasing
give ~ a call 전화하다 → Contact 연락하다

[41-43]
🎧 캐나다 → 영국

Questions 41-43 refer to the following conversation.

M: Melanie, this is Paul from the accounting department. I noticed that you didn't submit that report I asked for last week.
W: Oh, yes. ⁴¹**I was on a business trip to China last week**, so I couldn't turn it in. ⁴²**Can I submit it before I leave the office today?**
M: ⁴²**Sorry, but I'd like to review it before this afternoon. Is there any way you can get it to me by noon at the latest?**
W: Sure. I can do that. ⁴³**I'm just on my way to a meeting with our department head.** I can send it to you in about an hour.

accounting n. 회계   notice v. 발견하다, 알아차리다   business trip 출장
turn in 제출하다

해설
41-43번은 다음 대화에 관한 문제입니다.

남: Melanie, 회계부의 Paul입니다. 당신이 제가 지난주에 요청한 보고서를 제출하지 않았다는 것을 발견했어요.
여: 아, 네. ⁴¹제가 지난주에 중국으로 출장을 가서 그것을 제출하지 못했어요. ⁴²오늘 사무실을 떠나기 전에 제출해도 될까요?
남: ⁴²죄송하지만, 저는 그것을 오늘 오후 이전에 검토하려고 해요. 늦어도 정오까지 제게 가져다 주실 수 있는 방법이 있을까요?
여: 그럼요. 그렇게 할 수 있어요. ⁴³저는 저희 부서 책임자와의 회의에 가고 있어요. 약 한 시간 내로 당신에게 보낼 수 있어요.

41 | 특정 세부 사항 문제

해설 여자는 지난주에 무엇을 했는가?
(A) 해외로 갔다.
(B) 보고서를 검토했다.
(C) 설문 조사를 실시했다.
(D) 지원서를 보냈다.

해설 질문의 핵심 어구(last week)가 언급된 주변을 주의 깊게 듣는다. 여자가 "I was on a business trip to China last week"이라며 지난주에 중국으로 출장을 갔다고 하였다. 따라서 (A)가 정답이다.

어휘 abroad adv. 해외로   conduct v. 실시하다, 수행하다

Paraphrasing
was on a business trip to China 중국으로 출장을 갔다 → traveled abroad 해외로 갔다

42 | 요청 문제

해설 남자는 무엇을 요청하는가?

(A) 마감일을 연장하기
(B) 업무를 우선시하기
(C) 이메일을 보내기
(D) 웹사이트를 업데이트하기

해설 남자의 말에서 요청과 관련된 표현이 포함된 문장을 주의 깊게 듣는다. 여자가 "Can I submit it before I leave the office today?"라며 오늘 사무실을 떠나기 전에 제출해도 될지 묻자, 남자가 "Sorry, but I'd like to review it before this afternoon. Is there any way you can get it to me by noon at the latest?"라며 죄송하지만 그것을 오늘 오후 이전에 검토하려고 한다고 한 후, 늦어도 정오까지 가져다 줄 수 있는 방법이 있을지 물었다. 따라서 (B)가 정답이다.

어휘 deadline n. 마감일   prioritize v. 우선시하다

43 | 다음에 할 일 문제

해설 여자는 다음에 무엇을 할 것 같은가?
(A) 사무 서식을 요청한다.
(B) 관리자와 만난다.
(C) 배달원에게 연락한다.
(D) 짧은 휴식을 취한다.

해설 대화의 마지막 부분을 주의 깊게 듣는다. 여자가 "I'm just on my way to a meeting with our department head."라며 부서 책임자와의 회의에 가고 있다고 하였다. 따라서 (B)가 정답이다.

어휘 office form 사무 서식

[44-46]
🎧 미국 → 호주

Questions 44-46 refer to the following conversation.

W: I have a favor to ask of you, Simon. As you know, ⁴⁴**we're going to hold a shareholders' meeting on March 12**, and I'd like to invite you to participate.
M: I'd be happy to. What do you need me to do?
W: ⁴⁶**I'm hoping someone who is familiar with our Canadian operation can discuss our factory configuration.** ⁴⁵**Our guests are particularly interested in the machinery that we installed earlier this month.** You were at the facility recently, weren't you?
M: I just got back last week. I was quite impressed with the setup.
W: Great. ⁴⁶**I'll set aside some time for your presentation, then.**

favor n. 부탁   shareholder n. 주주   operation n. 운영
configuration n. 배치   facility n. 시설   setup n. (기계 등의) 구성
set aside 확보하다

해설
44-46번은 다음 대화에 관한 문제입니다.

여: 부탁할 것이 있어요, Simon. 아시다시피, ⁴⁴우리는 3월 12일에 주주 회의를 여는데, 당신이 참석하도록 초대하고 싶어요.
남: 기꺼이 그렇게 할게요. 제가 무엇을 해야 하나요?
여: ⁴⁶저는 우리의 캐나다 공장 운영에 대해 잘 아는 사람이 우리 공장 배치에 대해 논의할 수 있으면 좋겠어요. ⁴⁵내빈들이 우리가 이번 달 초에 설치한 기계들에 특별히 관심이 있어요. 당신은 최근에 그 시설에 있었죠, 그렇지 않나요?
남: 지난주에 막 돌아왔어요. 저는 기계 구성에 꽤 감명을 받았어요.
여: 좋아요. ⁴⁶그러면, 약간의 시간을 당신의 발표를 위해 확보해 둘게요.

44 | 주제 문제

해석 화자들은 주로 무엇에 대해 이야기하고 있는가?
(A) 개점식
(B) 구직 면접
(C) 안전 점검
(D) 투자자 모임

해설 대화의 주제를 묻는 문제이므로, 대화의 초반을 반드시 듣는다. 여자가 "we're going to hold a shareholders' meeting on March 12"라며 우리는 3월 12일에 주주 회의를 연다고 한 후, 주주 회의에 대한 내용으로 대화가 이어지고 있다. 따라서 (D)가 정답이다.

어휘 grand opening 개점식 inspection n. 점검 investor n. 투자자
gathering n. 모임

Paraphrasing
shareholders' meeting 주주 회의 → investor gathering 투자자 모임

45 | 언급 문제

해석 공장에 대해 무엇이 언급되는가?
(A) 운영을 위한 준비가 거의 완료되었다.
(B) 더 많은 직원을 필요로 한다.
(C) 이전되어야 한다.
(D) 새로운 장비가 있다.

해설 질문의 핵심 어구(factory)와 관련된 내용을 주의 깊게 듣는다. 여자가 "Our guests are particularly interested in the machinery that we installed earlier this month."라며 내빈들이 우리가 이번 달 초에 설치한 기계들에 특별히 관심이 있다고 한 것을 통해, 공장에 새로운 장비가 있음을 알 수 있다. 따라서 (D)가 정답이다.

어휘 relocate v. 이전하다

46 | 의도 파악 문제

해석 여자는 "당신은 최근에 그 시설에 있었죠"라고 말할 때 무엇을 의도하는가?
(A) 남자가 행사에서 말하기를 원한다.
(B) 제조 공장을 조사할 계획이다.
(C) 남자가 작업 일정을 조정하는 것이 필요하다.
(D) 지연의 원인을 알아내길 바란다.

해설 질문의 인용어구(You were at the facility recently)가 언급된 주변을 주의 깊게 듣는다. 여자가 "I'm hoping someone who is familiar with our Canadian operation can discuss our factory configuration."이라며 자신들의 캐나다 공장 운영에 대해 잘 아는 사람이 공장 배치에 대해 논의할 수 있으면 좋겠다고 하고, "I'll set aside some time for your presentation, then."이라며 약간의 시간을 당신의 발표를 위해 확보해두겠다고 했으므로 남자가 행사에서 말하기를 원하고 있음을 알 수 있다. 따라서 (A)가 정답이다.

어휘 inspect v. 조사하다 adjust v. 조정하다 delay n. 지연

[47-49]
미국 → 영국 → 캐나다

Questions 47-49 refer to the following conversation with three speakers.

W1: ⁴⁷Thanks for visiting us, Ms. Willets. Before we head out, did you have any concerns about the properties we'll be seeing?

W2: Thank you, Amanda. Actually, I'd noticed that the house in Pinewood is near a major road. ⁴⁸Do you know if it gets a lot of noise from passing cars?

W1: Good question. I think my colleague Peter can answer that.

M: Yes. That area does get quite busy, particularly in the late afternoon. ⁴⁹I'd suggest we go there last, so you can experience it in person.

W2: That's a good idea. We can start with other listings first.

W1: Perfect. We'll start with the red-brick house and make our way from there.

head out 출발하다 concern n. 걱정, 우려 property n. 건물, 부동산
colleague n. 동료 particularly adv. 특히 in person 직접
listing n. 매물, 목록

해석
47-49번은 다음 세 명의 대화에 관한 문제입니다.

여1: ⁴⁷방문해주셔서 감사합니다, Ms. Willets. 출발하기 전에, 저희가 보게 될 건물들에 대해 걱정이 있으셨나요?
여2: 감사해요, Amanda. 사실 Pinewood에 있는 집이 큰 도로 근처에 있다는 걸 알게 됐어요. ⁴⁸지나가는 차로부터 소음이 많이 나는지 아시나요?
여1: 좋은 질문이네요. 제 동료 Peter가 대답할 수 있을 것 같아요.
남: 네. 그 지역은 특히 늦은 오후에 꽤 붐빕니다. 직접 체험하실 수 있도록 ⁴⁹마지막으로 그곳에 가보는 것을 제안드려요.
여2: 좋은 생각이에요. 저희는 다른 매물들부터 먼저 시작하면 돼요.
여1: 완벽해요. 저희는 빨간 벽돌 집으로 시작해서 그곳에서부터 이동할 거예요.

47 | 장소 문제

해석 대화는 어디에서 일어나고 있는가?
(A) 자동차 수리점에서
(B) 주차장에서
(C) 부동산 사무실에서
(D) 아파트 건물에서

해설 대화에서 장소와 관련된 표현을 놓치지 않고 듣는다. 여자1[Amanda]이 "Thanks for visiting us, Ms. Willets. Before we head out, did you have any concerns about the properties we'll be seeing?"이라며 Ms. Willets에게 방문해주셔서 감사하다고 한 후, 출발하기 전에 보게 될 건물들에 대해 걱정이 있었는지 물은 것을 통해, 화자들이 부동산 사무실에 있음을 알 수 있다. 따라서 (C)가 정답이다.

어휘 real estate 부동산

48 | 문제점 문제

해석 Ms. Willets는 무엇에 대해 걱정하는가?
(A) 거리에 주차장이 없다.
(B) 집이 공사 중이다.
(C) 지역에 접근하기 어렵다.
(D) 장소가 시끄러울 수 있다.

해설 여자2[Ms. Willets]의 말에서 부정적인 표현이 언급된 주변을 주의 깊게 듣는다. 여자2가 "Do you know if it gets a lot of noise from passing cars?"라며 지나가는 차들로부터 소음이 많이 나는지 아냐고 물었다. 따라서 (D)가 정답이다.

어휘 construction n. 공사 access v. 접근하다

49 | 제안 문제

해석 남자는 무엇을 제안하는가?
(A) 다른 길을 이용하기
(B) 매물에 대한 세부 사항들을 검토하기

(C) 건물로의 방문을 지연하기
(D) 문의를 직접 제출하기

해설 남자의 말에서 제안과 관련된 표현이 언급된 내용을 주의 깊게 듣는다. 남자가 "I'd suggest we go there[the house in Pinewood] last"라며 마지막으로 Pinewood에 있는 집에 가보는 것을 제안한다고 하였다. 따라서 (C)가 정답이다.

어휘 route n. 길 review v. 검토하다 submit v. 제출하다 inquiry n. 문의

[50-52]

영국 → 캐나다

Questions 50-52 refer to the following conversation.

W: Did you hear? ⁵⁰Management has agreed to modify our employee benefits. The human resources department just e-mailed all staff to provide the latest details about the decision.
M: No, uh . . . I didn't know. What are the terms of the agreement?
W: ⁵¹All Shop Center staff are going to receive a 7 percent raise and four additional vacation days per year. That's a big deal, since we only get 12 days as of now.
M: That's great news! By the way, are you coming to the department dinner?
W: I can't make it. ⁵²I have to finish the supply chain data assessment before the deadline.

modify v. 변경하다, 수정하다 latest adj. 최신의 terms n. 조건
raise n. 임금 인상 as of now 현재로서는 make it 참석하다
supply chain 공급망

해석
50-52번은 다음 대화에 관한 문제입니다.

여: 들으셨어요? ⁵⁰경영진이 우리 직원 혜택을 변경하기로 합의했어요. 인사부에서 방금 이 결정의 최신 세부 사항을 제공하기 위해 전 사원에게 이메일을 보냈어요.
남: 아니요, 어... 저는 몰랐어요. 합의 조건은 무엇인가요?
여: ⁵¹모든 Shop Center사의 직원들이 7퍼센트의 임금 인상과 연간 4일의 추가적인 휴가를 받을 거예요. 그건 상당한 일이죠, 현재로서는 우리가 12일 정도만 받고 있으니까요.
남: 그거 정말 좋은 소식이네요! 그런데, 혹시 부서 저녁 모임에 오나요?
여: 저는 참석 못 해요. ⁵²마감 기한 전에 공급망 데이터 평가를 끝내야 하거든요.

50 | 특정 세부 사항 문제

해석 무엇이 최근에 직원들에게 이메일로 보내졌는가?
(A) 설문지
(B) 혜택 최신 정보
(C) 교육 일정표
(D) 회의를 상기시키는 것

해설 질문의 핵심 어구(e-mailed to staff)와 관련된 내용을 주의 깊게 듣는다. 여자가 "Management has agreed to modify our employee benefits. The human resources department just e-mailed all staff to provide the latest details about the decision."이라며 경영진이 직원 혜택을 변경하기로 합의했고, 인사부에서 방금 이 결정의 최신 세부 사항을 제공하기 위해 전 사원에게 이메일을 보냈다고 한 것을 통해, 혜택 최신 정보가 이메일로 보내졌음을 알 수 있다. 따라서 (B)가 정답이다.

어휘 questionnaire n. 설문지

Paraphrasing

latest details 최신 세부 사항 → update 최신 정보

51 | 언급 문제

해석 직원들에 대해 무엇이 언급되는가?
(A) 합의서에 서명해야 한다.
(B) 더 많은 휴가를 받을 것이다.
(C) 설문조사를 완료해야 한다.
(D) 초과 근무를 해야 할 것이다.

해설 질문의 핵심 어구(employees)와 관련된 부분을 주의 깊게 듣는다. 여자가 "All Shop Center staff are going to receive a 7 percent raise and four additional vacation days per year."라며 모든 Shop Center사의 직원들이 7퍼센트의 임금 인상과 연간 4일의 추가적인 휴가를 받을 것이라고 한 것을 통해 직원들이 더 많은 휴가를 받을 것임을 알 수 있다. 따라서 (B)가 정답이다.

어휘 time off 휴가, 휴식 overtime adv. 초과 근무로

Paraphrasing

vacation days 휴가 → time off 휴가

52 | 특정 세부 사항 문제

해석 여자가 완료해야 하는 업무는 무엇인가?
(A) 예산 제안
(B) 인력 배치 일정
(C) 공급망 분석
(D) 설문조사 양식

해설 질문의 핵심 어구(need to complete)와 관련된 내용을 주의 깊게 듣는다. 여자가 "I have to finish the supply chain data assessment before the deadline."이라며 마감 기한 전에 공급망 데이터 평가를 끝내야 한다고 한 것을 통해, 여자가 완료해야 하는 업무는 공급망 분석임을 알 수 있다. 따라서 (C)가 정답이다.

어휘 staff v. 인력을 배치하다 analysis n. 분석

[53-55]

미국 → 캐나다 → 호주

Questions 53-55 refer to the following conversation with three speakers.

W: Hello, ⁵³I purchased a sofa here last week, but it turned out to be too bulky. ⁵³/⁵⁴I was hoping I could exchange it for a smaller one from your store.
M1: OK. Do you have the receipt for your purchase?
W: No. I must have thrown it out by mistake, unfortunately.
M1: We usually only exchange products with receipts. Um, Mr. Griggs, this customer wants to exchange a sofa without a receipt. She bought the item last week.
M2: ⁵⁵That's fine as long as the product isn't damaged. We can check the item number against our sales records, anyway.
W: ⁵⁵It's just like it was when I bought it.
M2: I see. If you follow me, I'll process your request.

bulky adj. 부피가 큰 receipt n. 영수증 damaged adj. 손상된
process v. 처리하다; n. 과정

해석
53-55번은 다음 세 명의 대화에 관한 문제입니다.

여: 안녕하세요, ⁵³제가 지난주에 여기에서 소파를 구매했는데, 그것이 너무

부피가 큰 것으로 드러났어요. ⁵³/⁵⁴저는 가게에서 더 작은 것으로 교환하고 싶었어요.

남1: 알겠습니다. 구매에 대한 영수증을 가지고 계신가요?
여: 아니요. 안타깝게도 제가 실수로 그것을 버린 것 같아요.
남1: 저희는 보통 영수증이 있는 제품들만 교환해드려요. 음, Mr. Griggs, 이 고객님께서 영수증 없이 소파를 교환하고 싶어 하시는데요. 지난주에 그 품목을 구매하셨어요.
남2: ⁵⁵그 제품이 손상되지만 않았다면 괜찮아요. 저희는 어차피 판매 기록을 통해 품목 번호를 확인할 수 있어요.
여: ⁵⁵그것은 처음 구매했을 때와 같아요.
남2: 그렇군요. 저를 따라오시면, 고객님의 요청을 처리해 드릴게요.

53 | 화자 문제

해석 남자들은 어떤 종류의 업체에서 일하는 것 같은가?
(A) 의류 가게
(B) 가구점
(C) 인테리어 디자인 회사
(D) 이사 업체

해설 대화에서 신분 및 직업과 관련된 표현을 놓치지 않고 듣는다. 여자가 "I purchased a sofa here last week, but it turned out to be too bulky. I was hoping I could exchange it for a smaller one from your store."라며 지난주에 여기에서 소파를 구매했는데 그것이 너무 부피가 큰 것으로 드러났다고 하고, 가게에서 더 작은 것으로 교환하고 싶었다고 한 후, 남자들이 여자의 교환을 처리하는 것에 대한 내용으로 대화가 이어지고 있다. 이를 통해, 남자들이 가구점에서 일한다는 것을 알 수 있다. 따라서 (B)가 정답이다.

54 | 특정 세부 사항 문제

해석 여자는 무엇을 하고 싶어 하는가?
(A) 교환을 한다.
(B) 몇몇 가격을 비교한다.
(C) 몇몇 물품을 시험해 본다.
(D) 할인 코드를 이용한다.

해설 질문의 핵심 어구(woman want to do)와 관련된 내용을 주의 깊게 듣는다. 여자가 "I was hoping I could exchange it for a smaller one from your store."라며 가게에서 더 작은 것으로 교환하고 싶었다고 하였다. 따라서 (A)가 정답이다.

어휘 test out 시험해 보다　merchandise n. 물품　utilize v. 이용하다

55 | 언급 문제

해석 여자의 제품에 대해 무엇이 언급되는가?
(A) 온라인으로 구매되었다.
(B) 곧 도착할 것이다.
(C) 손상되지 않았다.
(D) 사용할 수 없다.

해설 질문의 핵심 어구(woman's product)와 관련된 내용을 주의 깊게 듣는다. 남자2가 "That's fine as long as the product isn't damaged."라며 그 제품이 손상되지만 않았다면 괜찮다고 하자, 여자가 "It's just like it was when I bought it."이라며 그것은 처음 구매했을 때와 같다고 한 것을 통해, 여자의 제품이 손상되지 않았음을 알 수 있다. 따라서 (C)가 정답이다.

[56-58]

영국 → 미국

Questions 56-58 refer to the following conversation.

W1: Aiko, it's Maryam. ⁵⁶I'm just calling to discuss our business trip to New York City next week. There's something I'd like us to prepare for while we're there.
W2: What do you have in mind?
W1: ⁵⁷I just received word that our potential client, Global Solutions, wants us to deliver a product demonstration at their headquarters next Friday. This could be a major opportunity for our company. The presentation starts at 8 A.M.
W2: Actually, ⁵⁸I've already arranged a quarterly performance review with our regional sales managers that morning. Maybe I can reschedule it to the afternoon, though. Once we get off the phone, I'll contact the management team to see if that's possible.

have in mind 염두에 두다, (~에 관해) 생각하고 있다　potential adj. 잠재적인　demonstration n. 시연　headquarters n. 본사　opportunity n. 기회　quarterly adj. 분기별의　regional adj. 지역의　get off (전화를) 끊다

해석
56-58번은 다음 대화에 관한 문제입니다.
여1: Aiko, 저 Maryam이에요. ⁵⁶저는 단지 다음 주 우리의 뉴욕 출장에 관해 논의하기 위해 전화드려요. 우리가 거기 있는 동안 준비했으면 하는 것이 있어요.
여2: 무엇을 염두에 두고 계신가요?
여1: ⁵⁷방금 우리의 잠재 고객인 Global Solutions사가 다음 주 금요일에 우리가 그들의 본사에서 제품 시연을 해주길 원한다는 말을 들었어요. 이것은 우리 회사에 큰 기회가 될 수도 있어요. 발표는 오전 8시에 시작해요.
여2: 사실, ⁵⁸저는 그날 아침에 이미 지역 영업 관리자들과 분기 실적 평가 미팅을 잡아놨어요. 하지만 오후로 일정을 조정할 수 있을지도 몰라요. 전화를 끊고 나면 관리팀에 연락해서 가능한지 알아볼게요.

56 | 목적 문제

해석 전화의 목적은 무엇인가?
(A) 고객 미팅을 논의하기 위해
(B) 배송 상태를 문의하기 위해
(C) 마케팅 자료를 검토하기 위해
(D) 프로젝트 역할을 맡기기 위해

해설 전화의 목적을 묻는 문제이므로, 대화의 초반을 반드시 듣는다. 여자1[Maryam]이 "I'm just calling to discuss our business trip to New York City next week. There's something I'd like us to prepare for while we're there."라며 다음 주 우리의 뉴욕 출장에 관해 논의하기 위해 전화한다고 하고, 거기 있는 동안 준비했으면 하는 것이 있다고 한 후, 잠재 고객사의 본사에서의 제품 시연에 대한 내용으로 대화가 이어지고 있다. 따라서 (A)가 정답이다.

어휘 assign v. 맡기다

57 | 다음에 할 일 문제

해석 다음 주 금요일에 무엇이 일어날 것인가?
(A) 계약 협상
(B) 직원 교육
(C) 제품 발표
(D) 제휴 미팅

해설 질문의 핵심 어구(next Friday)가 언급된 주변을 주의 깊게 듣는다. 여자1[Maryam]이 "~ that our potential client, Global Solutions, wants us to deliver a product demonstration at their headquarters next Friday."라며 잠재 고객인 Global Solutions사가 다음 주 금요일에 자신들이 그들의 본사에서 제품 시연을 해주길 원한다고 하였다. 따라서 (C)가 정답이다.

어휘 partnership n. 제휴, 협력

58 | 다음에 할 일 문제

해설 Aiko는 무엇을 할 것이라고 말하는가?
(A) 다른 팀과 이야기한다.
(B) 기술 설명서를 준비한다.
(C) 재무 견적을 업데이트한다.
(D) 회사 웹사이트를 수정한다.

해설 대화의 마지막 부분을 주의 깊게 듣는다. 여자2[Aiko]가 "I've already arranged a quarterly performance review with our regional sales managers that morning. Maybe I can reschedule it to the afternoon, though. Once we get off the phone, I'll contact the management team to see if that's possible."이라며 그날 아침에 이미 지역 영업 관리자들과 분기 실적 평가 미팅을 잡아놨지만, 오후로 일정을 조정할 수 있을지도 모른다며, 전화를 끊고 나면 관리팀에 연락해서 가능한지 알아보겠다고 하였다. 따라서 (A)가 정답이다.

어휘 specification n. 설명서, 사양   projection n. 견적, 예측

Paraphrasing

contact 연락하다 → Speak with ~와 이야기하다

[59-61]

미국 → 호주

Questions 59-61 refer to the following conversation.

W: Did I tell you that Russell McCoy called me last Thursday?
M: No. ⁵⁹I wasn't in the office last week. I had to visit our Boston research facility to review the clinical trial results for our new diabetes medication. What did Mr. McCoy say?
W: Well, ⁶⁰it sounds like he's considering investing more money in our pharmaceutical company.
M: ⁶⁰That's a relief. We'll be expanding soon.
W: He's coming to our office on Wednesday to hash out the details. ⁶¹If you're available, I want you to join the meeting. Mr. McCoy would probably like to hear your thoughts on the development plan.

clinical trial 임상 시험   diabetes n. 당뇨병   medication n. 약(물)
invest v. 투자하다   pharmaceutical adj. 제약의, 약학의
expand v. 확장하다   hash out ~을 계속 논의하여 끝을 보다

해설
59-61번은 다음 대화에 관한 문제입니다.

여: 지난 목요일에 Russell McCoy가 제게 전화했었다고 말씀드렸나요?
남: 아니요. ⁵⁹저는 지난주에 사무실에 없었어요. 보스턴 연구 시설을 방문해서 우리의 신규 당뇨병 약에 대한 임상 시험 결과를 검토해야 했거든요. Mr. McCoy가 뭐라고 말했나요?
여: 음, ⁶⁰그가 우리 제약 회사에 더 많은 돈을 투자하는 것을 고려하고 있는 것 같아요.
남: ⁶⁰다행이네요. 우리는 곧 확장할 거잖아요.
여: 그는 세부 사항들을 계속 논의하여 끝을 보기 위해 수요일에 우리 회사에 올 거예요. ⁶¹만약 가능하다면, 저는 당신이 회의에 참석했으면 좋겠어요. Mr. McCoy는 아마 개발 계획에 대해 당신의 생각을 듣고 싶어 할 거예요.

59 | 이유 문제

해설 남자는 왜 지난주에 사무실을 벗어나 있었는가?
(A) 임상 시험 데이터를 검사했다.
(B) 실험실 장비를 점검했다.
(C) 병원을 방문했다.
(D) 회사 경영진과 만났다.

해설 질문의 핵심 어구(out of the office)와 관련된 내용을 주의 깊게 듣는다. 남자가 "I wasn't in the office last week. I had to visit our Boston research facility to review the clinical trial results for our new diabetes medication."이라며 자신은 지난주에 사무실에 없었는데, 보스턴 연구 시설을 방문해서 신규 당뇨병 약에 대한 임상 시험 결과를 검토해야 했기 때문이라고 하였다. 따라서 (A)가 정답이다.

어휘 laboratory n. 실험실   executive n. 경영진

Paraphrasing

review the clinical trial results 임상 시험 결과를 검토하다 → examined clinical trial data 임상 시험 데이터를 검사했다

60 | 의도 파악 문제

해설 남자는 왜 "우리는 곧 확장할 거잖아요"라고 말하는가?
(A) 직원이 승진할 것임을 나타내기 위해
(B) 법적 계약이 수정되어야 함을 설명하기 위해
(C) 몇몇 광고들이 제작되어야 함을 암시하기 위해
(D) 추가적인 자금이 필요할 수도 있음을 암시하기 위해

해설 질문의 인용어구(We'll be expanding soon)가 언급된 주변을 주의 깊게 듣는다. 여자가 "it sounds like he's considering investing more money in our pharmaceutical company"라며 그가 우리 제약 회사에 더 많은 돈을 투자하는 것을 고려하고 있는 것 같다고 하자, 남자가 "That's a relief."라며 다행이라고 한 후, 자신들이 곧 확장할 거라고 하였다. 따라서 (D)가 정답이다.

어휘 agreement n. 계약   fund n. 자금

61 | 요청 문제

해설 여자는 남자에게 무엇을 하라고 요청하는가?
(A) 발표를 한다.
(B) 예약 일정을 변경한다.
(C) 회의에 참여한다.
(D) 지점 관리자에게 이야기한다.

해설 여자의 말에서 요청과 관련된 표현이 포함된 문장을 주의 깊게 듣는다. 여자가 남자에게 "If you're available, I want you to join the meeting."이라며 만약 가능하다면 회의에 참석했으면 좋겠다고 하였다. 따라서 (C)가 정답이다.

어휘 reschedule v. 일정을 변경하다   take part in 참여하다

Paraphrasing

join the meeting 회의에 참석하다 → Take part in the meeting 회의에 참여하다

[62-64]

🎧 캐나다 → 미국

Questions 62-64 refer to the following conversation and manual.

M: ⁶²I didn't realize we were installing a new TV in the lobby. Were you finally able to get the manager's approval?

W: Yes. In fact, ⁶²Mr. Argyros chose this new one himself. I was able to convince him by showing how the old unit would turn on and off without warning.

M: I'm glad we won't have to deal with that anymore. Do you need my help?

W: Yes. ⁶³I've been going through the manual, but the instructions are confusing. ⁶⁴I can't figure out how to adjust the remote control so that it can be controlled through a smartphone or tablet device. Here's the booklet you can refer to.

convince v. 설득하다   remote control 리모컨   refer to 참고하다

해석
62-64번은 다음 대화와 설명서에 관한 문제입니다.

남: ⁶²로비에 새로운 텔레비전을 설치하는지 몰랐어요. 관리자의 승인을 드디어 받을 수 있었나요?

여: 네. 사실, ⁶²Mr. Argyros가 직접 이 새로운 것을 골랐어요. 기존 장치가 어떻게 예고도 없이 켜지고 꺼지는지 보여줌으로써 그를 설득할 수 있었어요.

남: 우리가 더 이상 그것을 처리하지 않아도 되어서 기쁘네요. 제 도움이 필요하신가요?

여: 네. ⁶³저는 설명서를 살펴보고 있었는데, 설명이 혼란스러워요. ⁶⁴스마트폰이나 태블릿 장치로 작동될 수 있도록 리모컨을 어떻게 조정해야 하는지 이해할 수가 없어요. 여기 참고할 수 있는 설명서가 있어요.

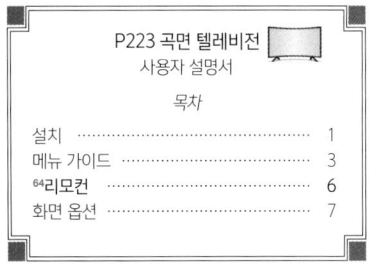

62 | 이유 문제

해석 관리자는 왜 텔레비전을 샀는가?
(A) 회의실이 개조되었다.
(B) 이전 기기가 제대로 작동하지 않고 있었다.
(C) 가게에서 판촉 행사를 하고 있었다.
(D) 제품이 긍정적인 평가를 받았다.

해설 질문의 핵심 어구(manager buy a television)와 관련된 내용을 주의 깊게 듣는다. 남자가 "I didn't realize we were installing a new TV in the lobby. Were you finally able to get the manager's approval?"이라며 로비에 새로운 텔레비전을 설치하는지 몰랐다고 하고, 관리자의 승인을 드디어 받을 수 있었는지 묻자, 여자가 "Mr. Argyros chose this new one himself. I was able to convince him by showing how the old unit would turn on and off without warning."이라며 Mr. Argyros가 직접 이 새로운 것을 골랐다고 하며, 기존 장치가 어떻게 예고도 없이 켜지고 꺼지는지 보여줌으로써 그를 설득할 수 있었다고 한 것을 통해, 이전 기기가 제대로 작동하지 않고 있어서 텔레비전을 샀음을 알 수 있다. 따라서 (B)가 정답이다.

어휘 renovate v. 개조하다   malfunction v. 제대로 작동하지 않다

Paraphrasing
turn on and off without warning 예고도 없이 켜지고 꺼지다
→ was malfunctioning 제대로 작동하지 않고 있었다

63 | 특정 세부 사항 문제

해석 여자는 자신이 이미 무엇을 했다고 말하는가?
(A) 몇몇 설정을 조정했다.
(B) 추가적인 스피커들을 설치했다.
(C) 포장재들을 재활용했다.
(D) 사용자 설명서를 읽었다.

해설 질문의 핵심 어구(woman ~ already did)와 관련된 내용을 주의 깊게 듣는다. 여자가 "I've been going through the manual"이라며 자신은 설명서를 살펴보고 있었다고 했다. 따라서 (D)가 정답이다.

어휘 adjust v. 조정하다, 조절하다   packaging material 포장재

64 | 시각 자료 문제

해석 시각 자료를 보아라. 남자는 어떤 페이지를 읽을 것 같은가?
(A) 1페이지
(B) 3페이지
(C) 6페이지
(D) 7페이지

해설 제시된 설명서의 정보를 확인한 후 질문의 핵심 어구(man ~ read)와 관련된 내용을 주의 깊게 듣는다. 여자가 남자에게 "I can't figure out how to adjust the remote control so that it can be controlled through a smartphone or tablet device."라며 스마트폰이나 태블릿 장치로 작동될 수 있도록 리모컨을 어떻게 조정해야 하는지 이해할 수가 없다고 했다. 리모컨과 관련된 내용은 6페이지임을 설명서에서 알 수 있다. 따라서 (C)가 정답이다.

[65-67]

🎧 영국 → 캐나다

Questions 65-67 refer to the following conversation and map.

W: Sunrise Dental Clinic. How can I help you?

M: ⁶⁵I was scheduled for a dental check-up an hour ago, but I completely forgot about it. My name is Noel Boyle.

W: Yes, Mr. Boyle. According to our records, you were supposed to see Dr. Akin. If you want to reschedule, Dr. Akin is available next Monday at 2 P.M.

M: That works for me. Thank you.

W: OK. I've scheduled you for then. However, ⁶⁶you should get here 15 minutes early to fill out a medical form.

M: No problem. Also, ⁶⁷where's the nearest parking lot to your clinic?

W: ⁶⁷Use the one near the intersection of Higgins Road and Roberts Avenue.

check-up n. 검진   record n. 기록   medical form 진료 양식
intersection n. 교차로, 교차 지점

해석
65-67번은 다음 대화와 지도에 관한 문제입니다.

여: Sunrise 치과입니다. 어떻게 도와드릴까요?

남: ⁶⁵한 시간 전에 치과 검진이 예약되어 있었는데, 제가 그것을 완전히 잊어버렸어요. 제 이름은 Noel Boyle이에요.

여: 네, Mr. Boyle. 저희 기록에 따르면, Dr. Akin과 만나기로 되어 있었습니다. 만약 일정을 변경하기를 원하신다면, Dr. Akin은 다음 주 월요일 오

후 2시에 시간이 있으세요.

남: 저는 좋아요. 감사합니다.

여: 알겠습니다. 그때로 예약해드렸어요. 하지만, ⁶⁶진료 양식을 작성하시기 위해 15분 일찍 여기에 도착하셔야 해요.

남: 문제없어요. 그리고, ⁶⁷병원에서 가장 가까운 주차장이 어디인가요?

여: ⁶⁷Higgins가와 Roberts가의 교차로 가까이에 있는 것을 이용하세요.

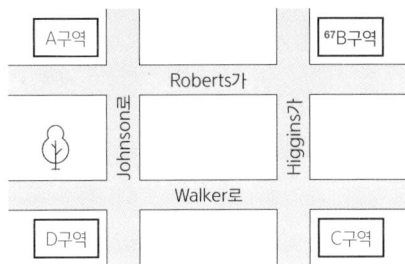

65 | 문제점 문제

해석 남자는 무슨 문제를 언급하는가?
(A) 잘못된 주소로 갔다.
(B) 교통편이 없다.
(C) 의사에게 불만족스럽다.
(D) 약속을 놓쳤다.

해설 남자의 말에서 부정적인 표현이 언급된 주변을 주의 깊게 듣는다. 남자가 "I was scheduled for a dental check-up an hour ago, but I completely forgot about it."이라며 한 시간 전에 치과 검진이 예약되어 있었는데, 그것을 완전히 잊어버렸다고 하였다. 따라서 (D)가 정답이다.

어휘 unhappy with ~에 불만족스럽다

Paraphrasing

a dental check-up 치과 검진 → appointment 약속

66 | 요청 문제

해석 여자는 남자에게 무엇을 하도록 요청하는가?
(A) 대중 교통을 탄다.
(B) 전화번호를 적는다.
(C) 일찍 도착한다.
(D) 의사에게 연락한다.

해설 여자의 말에서 요청과 관련된 표현이 포함된 문장을 주의 깊게 듣는다. 여자가 "you should get here 15 minutes early to fill out a medical form"이라며 진료 양식을 작성하기 위해 15분 일찍 도착해야 한다고 하였다. 따라서 (C)가 정답이다.

어휘 physician n. 의사

67 | 시각 자료 문제

해석 시각 자료를 보아라. 남자는 어디에 주차할 것 같은가?
(A) A구역
(B) B구역
(C) C구역
(D) D구역

해설 제시된 지도의 정보를 확인한 후 질문의 핵심 어구(man ~ park)와 관련된 내용을 주의 깊게 듣는다. 남자가 "where's the nearest parking lot to your clinic?"이라며 병원에서 가장 가까운 주차장이 어디인지 묻자, 여자가 "Use the one near the intersection of Higgins Road and Roberts Avenue."라며 Higgins가와 Roberts가의 교차로 가까이에 있는 것을 이용하라고 하였으므로, 남자가 B구역에 주차할 임을 지도에서 알 수 있다. 따라서 (B)가 정답이다.

[68-70]

호주 → 미국

Questions 68-70 refer to the following conversation and graph.

M: I just want to quickly check in. ⁶⁸How is your study going? I heard you've been analyzing the amount of rainfall at our company's farms in Iowa.

W: It's going well on the whole. However, there seems to be a minor issue with some of my data. ⁶⁹There was apparently a month with an average rainfall that's only half of August's amount. That seems very unusual, so I have to verify the information.

M: That does sound odd. You should definitely look into it . . . ⁷⁰Let's discuss your progress again later this week.

W: Sure. ⁷⁰When is a good time for you?

M: ⁷⁰Friday at 1 P.M. would be best.

rainfall n. 강우(량)   average adj. 평균의; n. 평균   verify v. 확인하다, 입증하다
odd adj. 이상한

해석
68-70번은 다음 대화와 그래프에 관한 문제입니다.

남: 저는 그저 빠르게 확인해 보고 싶어요. ⁶⁸당신의 연구는 어떻게 되어 가고 있나요? 당신이 아이오와에 있는 우리 회사 농장의 강우량을 분석하고 있다고 들었어요.

여: 전체적으로는 잘 되어 가고 있어요. 하지만, 제 자료의 일부에 작은 문제가 있는 것 같아요. ⁶⁹보아하니 평균 강우량이 8월 강우량의 고작 절반인 달이 있었어요. 그것은 매우 드문 것 같아서, 그 정보를 확인해야 해요.

남: 정말 이상하게 들리네요. 당신은 확실히 그것을 조사해야겠어요... ⁷⁰이번 주 후반에 당신의 진행 상황을 다시 논의해 봐요.

여: 좋아요. ⁷⁰시간은 언제가 괜찮으신가요?

남: ⁷⁰금요일 오후 1시가 가장 좋을 거예요.

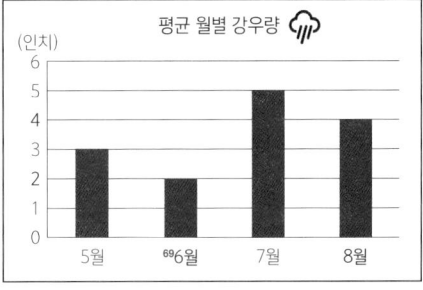

68 | 화자 문제

해석 여자는 누구인 것 같은가?
(A) 대학 교수
(B) 금융 상담가
(C) 기업 연구자
(D) 시장 분석가

해설 대화에서 신분 및 직업과 관련된 표현을 놓치지 않고 듣는다. 남자가 여자에게 "How is your study going? I heard you've been analyzing the amount of rainfall at our company's farms in Iowa."라며 여자의 연구는 어떻게 되어 가고 있는지 묻고, 여자가 아이오와에 있는 회사 농장의 강우량을 분석하고 있다고 들었다고 한 것을 통해, 여자가 기업 연구자임을 알 수 있다. 따라서 (C)가 정답이다.

어휘 consultant n. 상담가   corporate adj. 기업(의)   market n. 시장
analyst n. 분석가

69 | 시각 자료 문제

해석 시각 자료를 보아라. 여자가 걱정하는 것은 어떤 달인가?
(A) 5월
(B) 6월
(C) 7월
(D) 8월

해설 제시된 그래프의 정보를 확인한 후 질문의 핵심 어구(woman concerned about)와 관련된 내용을 주의 깊게 듣는다. 여자가 "There was apparently a month with an average rainfall that's only half of August's amount. That seems very unusual, so I have to verify the information."이라며 보아하니 평균 강우량이 8월 강우량의 고작 절반인 달이 있었다고 하고, 그것은 매우 드문 것 같아서 그 정보를 확인해야 한다고 하였으므로, 여자가 걱정하는 것은 6월임을 그래프에서 알 수 있다. 따라서 (B)가 정답이다.

70 | 특정 세부 사항 문제

해석 남자는 금요일에 무엇을 하고 싶어 하는가?
(A) 동료를 만난다.
(B) 보고서를 배포한다.
(C) 고객에게 이야기한다.
(D) 농장을 견학한다.

해설 질문의 핵심 어구(man ~ do on Friday)와 관련된 내용을 주의 깊게 듣는다. 남자가 "Let's discuss your progress again later this week."이라며 이번 주 후반에 여자의 진행 상황을 다시 논의하자고 한 후, 여자가 "When is a good time for you?"라며 시간은 언제가 괜찮은지 묻자 남자가 "Friday at 1 P.M. would be best."라며 금요일 오후 1시가 가장 좋을 것이라고 대답하였다. 따라서 (A)가 정답이다.

어휘 release v. 배포하다

PART 4

[71-73]
영국

Questions 71-73 refer to the following talk.

> Next on our tour, ⁷¹**we'll be walking through our plant's loading dock**. This is where the furniture is stored before it is sent to retail outlets around the world. While we walk around, I'll explain a bit about our merchandise. ⁷²**You'll get to see the new ElectraDesk, which is equipped with a wireless charging pad.** Now, as we make our way through the facility, ⁷³**please follow my lead and watch out for trucks**. OK. Let's keep moving.

loading dock 하적장, 짐 싣는 곳　store v. 보관하다　retail outlet 소매점
be equipped with ~을 갖추고 있다　wireless adj. 무선의
watch out 조심하다

해석
71-73번은 다음 담화에 관한 문제입니다.

우리 견학에서는 다음으로, ⁷¹우리 공장의 하적장을 통과해 걸어갈 것입니다. 이곳은 가구가 전 세계의 소매점으로 보내지기 전에 보관되는 곳이죠. 우리가 돌아다니는 동안, 제가 우리 제품에 대해 약간 설명해 드릴게요. ⁷²여러분은 새로운 ElectraDesk를 보게 될 것인데, 이것은 무선 충전 패드를 갖추고 있습니다. 이제, 우리가 시설 안으로 들어갈 테니, ⁷³제 안내를 따라오시고 트럭들을 조심해 주세요. 좋아요. 계속 이동합시다.

71 | 장소 문제

해석 청자들은 어디에 있는가?
(A) 도서관에
(B) 공장에
(C) 가구 상점에
(D) 자동차 판매 대리점에

해설 지문에서 장소와 관련된 표현을 놓치지 않고 듣는다. "we'll be walking through our plant's loading dock"이라며 우리 공장의 하적장을 통과해 걸어갈 것이라고 한 것을 통해 청자들이 공장에 있음을 알 수 있다. 따라서 (B)가 정답이다.

어휘 automobile dealership 자동차 판매 대리점

Paraphrasing
plant 공장 → factory 공장

72 | 언급 문제

해석 ElectraDesk에 대해 무엇이 언급되는가?
(A) 추가적인 조립을 필요로 한다.
(B) 현재 페인트칠되고 있다.
(C) 특별한 기능을 포함한다.
(D) 가장 잘 팔리는 품목이다.

해설 질문의 핵심 어구(ElectraDesk)가 언급된 주변을 주의 깊게 듣는다. "You'll get to see the new ElectraDesk, which is equipped with a wireless charging pad."라며 여러분은 새로운 ElectraDesk를 보게 될 것인데, 이것은 무선 충전 패드를 갖추고 있다고 하였다. 이를 통해, ElectraDesk가 특별한 기능을 포함하고 있음을 알 수 있다. 따라서 (C)가 정답이다.

어휘 further adj. 추가적인, 그 이상의　assembly n. 조립　currently adv. 현재

Paraphrasing
wireless charging pad 무선 충전 패드 → special feature 특별한 기능

73 | 요청 문제

해석 청자들은 무엇을 하도록 요청받는가?
(A) 안전 장비를 반납한다.
(B) 앞장 선다.
(C) 나중을 위해 질문을 모아 둔다.
(D) 차량을 조심한다.

해설 지문의 중후반에서 요청과 관련된 표현이 포함된 문장을 주의 깊게 듣는다. "please follow my lead and watch out for trucks"라며 자신의 안내를 따라오고 트럭들을 조심해 달라고 하였다. 따라서 (D)가 정답이다.

어휘 safety equipment 안전 장비　vehicle n. 차량

Paraphrasing
watch out for trucks 트럭들을 조심하다 → Be careful of vehicles 차량을 조심하다

[74-76]
미국

Questions 74-76 refer to the following telephone message.

> Hi, Sandy. ⁷⁴**I received the magazine article you sent me earlier today to edit.** Overall, I'm impressed. You've done a good job describing the strong leadership Rico Marcus has shown on the Grizzlies soccer team. However, ⁷⁵**I would like you to include some information regarding**

Mr. Marcus's childhood and charity work. ⁷⁶Let's meet tomorrow along with some other editorial employees to go over the draft in more detail. Ten in the morning should work.

overall adv. 전반적으로 impressed adj. 감명을 받은 describe v. 묘사하다
along with ~와 함께 editorial adj. 편집의 go over 검토하다
in detail 자세히

해석
74-76번은 다음 전화 메시지에 관한 문제입니다.
안녕하세요, Sandy. ⁷⁴오늘 일찍 당신이 편집을 위해 보내주신 잡지 기사를 받았습니다. 전반적으로, 저는 감명받았어요. 당신은 Rico Marcus가 Grizzlies 축구팀에서 보여준 강력한 리더십을 훌륭하게 묘사했습니다. 하지만, ⁷⁵저는 당신이 Mr. Marcus의 어린 시절과 자선 사업에 관련된 몇몇 정보를 포함해주었으면 좋겠어요. ⁷⁶초안을 좀 더 자세히 검토하기 위해 내일 다른 편집 직원들과 함께 만납시다. 오전 10시가 괜찮을 거예요.

74 | 화자 문제

해석 화자는 누구인 것 같은가?
(A) 잡지 편집자
(B) 스포츠 사진가
(C) 축구 선수
(D) 모금 행사 기획자

해설 지문에서 신분 및 직업과 관련된 표현을 놓치지 않고 듣는다. "I received the magazine article you sent me earlier today to edit."이라며 오늘 일찍 청자가 편집을 위해 보내준 잡지 기사를 받았다고 한 것을 통해 화자가 잡지 편집자임을 알 수 있다. 따라서 (A)가 정답이다.

어휘 fund-raiser n. 모금 행사

75 | 요청 문제

해석 화자는 청자에게 무엇을 하라고 요청하는가?
(A) 운동 선수를 인터뷰한다.
(B) 몇몇 사진을 추가한다.
(C) 문서를 수정한다.
(D) 자원 봉사를 한다.

해설 지문 중후반에서 요청과 관련된 표현이 포함된 문장을 주의 깊게 듣는다. "I would like you to include some information regarding Mr. Marcus's childhood and charity work."라며 Mr. Marcus의 어린 시절과 자선 사업에 관련된 몇몇 정보를 포함해주었으면 좋겠다고 하였다. 따라서 (C)가 정답이다.

어휘 revise v. 수정하다 volunteer work 자원 봉사

76 | 다음에 할 일 문제

해석 내일 아침에 무엇이 일어날 것 같은가?
(A) 직원 회의
(B) 자선 행사
(C) 스포츠 경기
(D) 제품 출시

해설 질문의 핵심 어구(tomorrow morning)와 관련된 내용을 주의 깊게 듣는다. "Let's meet tomorrow along with some other editorial employees to go over the draft in more detail. Ten in the morning should work."라며 초안을 좀 더 자세히 검토하기 위해 내일 다른 편집 직원들과 함께 만나자고 한 후, 오전 10시가 괜찮을 것이라고 한 것을 통해 내일 아침에 직원 회의가 있을 것임을 알 수 있다. 따라서 (A)가 정답이다.

어휘 competition n. 경기 launch n. 출시

Paraphrasing
meet ~ along with some ~ employees 직원들과 함께 만나다 → staff meeting 직원 회의

[77-79] 〔호주〕

Questions 77-79 refer to the following talk.

⁷⁷I'm pleased you've all joined us for Gainsville Middle School's information session about BookTalk. BookTalk is a new initiative designed to encourage students to read a wider range of both classic and contemporary books. ⁷⁸At first, we didn't know how many students would be interested. But as I look around, I can't see a single empty seat. In a few minutes, we're going to give a detailed overview of the program. But first, ⁷⁹we'll hear a brief speech from Carolyn Woods, the English department's head teacher, who came up with the idea for BookTalk. Please, let's give a round of applause for Ms. Woods.

information session 설명회 initiative n. 계획 encourage v. 장려하다
contemporary adj. 현대의 brief adj. 짧은 come up with ~을 제안하다
applause n. 박수

해석
77-79번은 다음 담화에 관한 문제입니다.
⁷⁷여러분 모두가 Gainsville 중학교의 BookTalk에 관한 설명회에 참석해 주셔서 기쁩니다. BookTalk은 학생들이 고전 도서와 현대 도서 모두를 폭넓게 읽도록 장려하기 위해 고안된 새로운 계획입니다. ⁷⁸처음에 저희는 얼마나 많은 학생들이 관심이 있을지 몰랐습니다. 하지만 제가 둘러보니, 빈자리를 하나도 볼 수 없네요. 몇 분 내에, 저희는 이 프로그램의 자세한 개요를 설명할 것입니다. 하지만 먼저, ⁷⁹BookTalk의 아이디어를 제안한 영어과 주임 교사인 Carolyn Woods의 짧은 연설을 들을 것입니다. Ms. Woods에게 박수를 보내주세요.

77 | 목적 문제

해석 담화의 목적은 무엇인가?
(A) 출판물을 판매하기 위해
(B) 운동을 장려하기 위해
(C) 프로그램을 소개하기 위해
(D) 상을 발표하기 위해

해설 담화의 목적을 묻는 문제이므로, 지문의 초반을 반드시 듣는다. "I'm pleased you've all joined us for Gainsville Middle School's information session about BookTalk."이라며 여러분 모두가 Gainsville 중학교의 BookTalk에 관한 설명회에 참석해 주셔서 기쁘다고 한 후, 프로그램에 대한 소개로 담화가 이어지고 있다. 따라서 (C)가 정답이다.

어휘 publication n. 출판(물)

78 | 의도 파악 문제

해석 화자는 "빈자리를 하나도 볼 수 없네요"라고 말할 때 무엇을 의도하는가?
(A) 청자들은 빨리 신청해야 한다.
(B) 청자들은 일어서야 한다.
(C) 발표가 곧 시작된다.
(D) 새로운 프로그램이 인기가 있다.

해설 질문의 인용어구(I can't see a single empty seat)가 언급된 주변을 주의 깊게 듣는다. "At first, we didn't know how many students would be interested."라며 처음에 얼마나 많은 학생들이 관심이 있을지 몰랐다고 한 후, 하지만 둘러보니 빈자리를 하나도 볼 수 없다고 하였

으므로, 새로운 프로그램이 인기가 있다는 것을 알 수 있다. 따라서 (D)가 정답이다.

79 | 특정 세부 사항 문제

해석 Carolyn Woods는 누구인가?
(A) 영화 제작자
(B) 교과서 출판인
(C) 학교 교사
(D) 행사 조직자

해설 질문의 핵심 어구(Carolyn Woods)가 언급된 주변을 주의 깊게 듣는다. "we'll hear a brief speech from Carolyn Woods, the English department's head teacher, who came up with the idea for BookTalk"이라며 BookTalk의 아이디어를 제안한 영어과 주임 교사인 Carolyn Woods의 짧은 연설을 들을 것이라고 하였다. 따라서 (C)가 정답이다.

어휘 organizer n. 조직자

[80-82]

🎧 캐나다

Questions 80-82 refer to the following advertisement.

Stop by Grand Decor over the next week to take advantage of our ongoing sale! ⁸⁰We have just opened our 10th store location, and we're holding a major promotion to celebrate. All of our beautiful carpets will be 15 percent off. Plus, ⁸¹purchases over $500 will include a stylish floor lamp at no extra charge! ⁸²Just visit our Web site to get the address of our nearest location. However, you'll want to act fast. Deals are only valid while supplies last.

take advantage of ~을 이용하다 ongoing adj. 진행 중인
charge n. 금액, 요금 valid adj. 유효한 supply n. 재고 last v. 남다

해석
80-82번은 다음 광고에 관한 문제입니다.

진행 중인 할인을 이용하기 위해 다음 주 동안 Grand Decor에 들르세요! ⁸⁰저희는 이제 막 열 번째 지점을 개점했고, 축하하기 위해 큰 판촉 행사를 열고 있습니다. 저희의 모든 아름다운 카펫이 15퍼센트 할인될 것입니다. 또한, ⁸¹500달러 이상의 구매는 추가 금액 없이 멋진 플로어 램프를 포함할 것입니다! ⁸²그저 저희의 웹사이트를 방문하셔서 가장 가까운 지점의 주소를 확인하세요. 하지만, 빨리 행동하셔야 할 것입니다. 할인은 오직 재고가 남아있을 동안만 유효합니다.

80 | 이유 문제

해석 기업은 왜 할인 행사를 열고 있는가?
(A) 개점을 기념하기 위해
(B) 휴일을 인정하기 위해
(C) 몇몇 고객들에게 감사하기 위해
(D) 몇몇 새로운 제품을 홍보하기 위해

해설 질문의 핵심 어구(holding a sale)와 관련된 내용을 주의 깊게 듣는다. "We have just opened our 10th store location, and we're holding a major promotion to celebrate."이라며 이제 막 열 번째 지점을 개점했고 축하하기 위해 큰 판촉 행사를 열고 있다고 하였다. 따라서 (A)가 정답이다.

어휘 mark v. 기념하다, 표시하다 recognize v. 인정하다

Paraphrasing
celebrate 축하하다 → mark 기념하다

81 | 특정 세부 사항 문제

해석 무엇이 몇몇 구매에 제공될 것인가?
(A) 바닥 깔개
(B) 조명 기구
(C) 청소 기기
(D) 의류용 액세서리

해설 질문의 핵심 어구(provided with ~ purchases)와 관련된 내용을 주의 깊게 듣는다. "purchases over $500 will include a stylish floor lamp at no extra charge"라며 500달러 이상의 구매는 추가 금액 없이 멋진 플로어 램프를 포함할 것이라고 하였다. 따라서 (B)가 정답이다.

어휘 rug n. 깔개, 양탄자

Paraphrasing
floor lamp 플로어 램프 → lighting fixture 조명 기구

82 | 특정 세부 사항 문제

해석 화자에 따르면, 청자들은 웹사이트에서 무엇을 찾을 수 있는가?
(A) 최신 가격
(B) 제품 사진
(C) 점포 주소
(D) 주문 양식

해설 질문의 핵심 어구(find on a Web site)와 관련된 내용을 주의 깊게 듣는다. "Just visit our Web site to get the address of our nearest location."이라며 그저 웹사이트를 방문하여 가장 가까운 지점의 주소를 확인하라고 하였다. 따라서 (C)가 정답이다.

어휘 store n. 점포, 가게

Paraphrasing
location 지점 → Store 점포

[83-85]

🎧 호주

Questions 83-85 refer to the following excerpt from a meeting.

Before we finish up, ⁸³I want to discuss the plan to update PaintPlus, our photo editing software. As many of you know, we have received numerous complaints from customers because of the confusing design of the user interface. ⁸⁴I've decided to put Keith Thompson in charge of the new version. He has managed similar issues for us in the past. ⁸⁵Keith will give a presentation at next week's meeting about his plan to address the program's usability. All right. That's it for now.

numerous adj. 많은 confusing adj. 혼란스러운 usability n. 사용성, 유용성

해석
83-85번은 다음 회의 발췌에 관한 문제입니다.

마무리하기 전에, ⁸³우리의 사진 편집 소프트웨어인 PaintPlus를 업데이트할 계획에 관해 논의하고 싶습니다. 많은 분들이 아시다시피, 저희는 혼란스러운 사용자 인터페이스 디자인으로 인해 고객들로부터 많은 항의를 받았습니다. ⁸⁴저는 Keith Thompson을 새로운 버전의 책임자로 임명하기로 결정했습니다. 그는 과거에 저희를 위해 비슷한 문제들을 관리했습니다. ⁸⁵Keith는 다음 주 회의에서 프로그램의 사용성을 개선할 그의 계획에 대해 발표를 할 것입니다. 좋아요. 지금은 그게 전부입니다.

83 | 주제 문제

해석 화자는 주로 무엇에 대해 이야기하고 있는가?

(A) 프로젝트 마감 기한
(B) 마케팅 기술
(C) 새로운 정책
(D) 소프트웨어 개발

해설 회의 발췌의 주제를 묻는 문제이므로, 지문의 초반을 반드시 듣는다. "I want to discuss the plan to update PaintPlus, our photo editing software"라며 사진 편집 소프트웨어인 PaintPlus를 업데이트할 계획에 관해 논의하고 싶다고 하였다. 따라서 (D)가 정답이다.

어휘 technique n. 기술   policy n. 정책

84 | 의도 파악 문제

해석 화자는 왜 "그는 과거에 저희를 위해 비슷한 문제들을 관리했습니다"라고 말하는가?
(A) 누군가의 적합성을 보여주기 위해
(B) 도움을 더 요청하기 위해
(C) 우려를 나타내기 위해
(D) 결정에 대해 불평하기 위해

해설 질문의 인용어구(He has managed similar issues for us in the past)가 언급된 주변을 주의 깊게 듣는다. "I've decided to put Keith Thompson in charge of the new version."이라며 Keith Thompson을 새로운 버전의 책임자로 임명하기로 결정했다고 한 후, 그가 과거에 자신들을 위해 비슷한 문제들을 관리했다고 하였으므로, 책임자가 된 사람의 적합성을 보여주기 위함임을 알 수 있다. 따라서 (A)가 정답이다.

어휘 suitability n. 적합성, 어울림   ask for help 도움을 요청하다

85 | 다음에 할 일 문제

해석 Keith Thompson은 다음 주에 무엇을 할 것인가?
(A) 고객을 만난다.
(B) 계획을 발표한다.
(C) 프로그램을 업그레이드한다.
(D) 디자이너를 고용한다.

해설 질문의 핵심 어구(next week)가 언급된 주변을 주의 깊게 듣는다. "Keith will give a presentation at next week's meeting about his plan to address the program's usability."라며 Keith는 다음 주 회의에서 프로그램의 사용성을 개선할 그의 계획에 대해 발표를 할 것이라고 하였다. 따라서 (B)가 정답이다.

어휘 present v. 발표하다

[86-88]

Questions 86-88 refer to the following news report.   캐나다

My name is Jack Ayers, and you're listening to EZTV's news report. ⁸⁶Elections will be held next Thursday, May 10, to decide who will be the new head of Bradenton's city council. ⁸⁷This vote comes at a crucial time, as the newly appointed city council head must make a proposal for future improvements to city infrastructure. These plans must include funding for the maintenance of Harraway Bridge and other aging structures. And ⁸⁸with the low budget, this task won't be easy. Remember to follow next week's election results by tuning in to our show.

election n. 선거   crucial adj. 결정적인, 중요한   appoint v. 임명하다
proposal n. 계획, 제안   maintenance n. 보수, 유지
aging adj. 낡아 가는, 나이든   task n. 작업, 업무

해석
86-88번은 다음 뉴스 보도에 관한 문제입니다.

저는 Jack Ayers이고, 여러분은 EZTV의 뉴스 보도를 듣고 계십니다. ⁸⁶Bradenton의 새로운 시의회 의장이 누가 될 것인지를 결정하기 위해 다음 주 목요일, 5월 10일에 선거가 치러질 것입니다. ⁸⁷이번 투표는 결정적인 시기에 다가왔는데요, 새롭게 임명된 시의회 의장은 미래의 도시 기반 시설 개선을 위한 계획을 제안해야 하기 때문입니다. 이 계획은 Harraway 다리와 다른 낡아 가는 건축물들의 보수를 위한 자금을 포함해야 합니다. 그리고 ⁸⁸적은 예산으로, 이 작업은 쉽지 않을 겁니다. 저희 쇼를 계속 들음으로써 다음 주의 선거 결과를 지켜보는 것을 기억해 주세요.

86 | 주제 문제

해석 보도는 주로 무엇에 관한 것인가?
(A) 건설 계획
(B) 다가오는 선거
(C) 도로 폐쇄
(D) 세금 인상

해설 뉴스 보도의 주제를 묻는 문제이므로, 지문의 초반을 반드시 듣는다. "Elections will be held next Thursday, May 10, to decide who will be the new head of Bradenton's city council."이라며 Bradenton의 새로운 시의회 의장이 누가 될 것인지를 결정하기 위해 다음 주 목요일인 5월 10일에 선거가 치러질 것이라고 한 후, 다가오는 선거에 관한 내용으로 보도가 이어지고 있다. 따라서 (B)가 정답이다.

어휘 closure n. 폐쇄

Paraphrasing
next Thursday 다음 주 목요일 → upcoming 다가오는

87 | 특정 세부 사항 문제

해석 화자에 따르면, 새로운 의회 의장은 무엇을 해야 하는가?
(A) 의원을 임명한다.
(B) 예산을 줄인다.
(C) 회의에 참석한다.
(D) 개발 계획을 수립한다.

해설 질문의 핵심 어구(new council head do)와 관련된 내용을 주의 깊게 듣는다. "This vote comes at a crucial time, as the newly appointed city council head must make a proposal for future improvements to city infrastructure."라며 이번 투표는 결정적인 시기에 다가왔는데, 새롭게 임명된 시의회 의장은 미래의 도시 기반 시설 개선을 위한 계획을 제안해야 하기 때문이라고 하였다. 따라서 (D)가 정답이다.

Paraphrasing
proposal for ~ improvements 개선을 위한 계획 → development plan 개발 계획

88 | 이유 문제

해석 화자는 왜 작업이 쉽지 않을 것이라고 말하는가?
(A) 대중의 반대가 있다.
(B) 훼손된 시설들이 있다.
(C) 자금이 제한되어 있다.
(D) 규정들이 너무 많다.

해설 질문의 핵심 어구(task ~ not be easy)와 관련된 내용을 주의 깊게 듣는다. "with the low budget, this task won't be easy"라며 적은 예산으로 이 작업은 쉽지 않을 것이라고 하였다. 따라서 (C)가 정답이다.

어휘 opposition n. 반대

Paraphrasing

low 적은 → limited 제한된

[89-91]   미국

Questions 89-91 refer to the following telephone message.

This is Rachel Foucault, owner of the Crest Apartment Building. ⁸⁹/⁹⁰I talked to you about repairing the wood floors in one of my units on April 19. Unfortunately, ⁹⁰I'm a bit worried about our arrangements. The new tenants contacted me yesterday, and they will move into the apartment sooner than I thought. I will probably be tied up with work later, but ⁹¹please call my office and my secretary can help you reschedule.

arrangement n. 계획, 준비   tenant n. 세입자   tied up 바쁜
secretary n. 비서   reschedule v. 일정을 변경하다

해석
89-91번은 다음 전화 메시지에 관한 문제입니다.
Crest 아파트 건물주인 Rachel Foucault입니다. ⁸⁹/⁹⁰저는 제 아파트 호실들 중 하나의 나무 바닥을 4월 19일에 수리하는 것에 관해 당신과 이야기했습니다. 안타깝게도, ⁹⁰저는 우리의 계획이 조금 걱정스럽습니다. 새로운 세입자들이 어제 제게 연락했는데, 그들은 제가 생각했던 것보다 더 일찍 아파트에 입주할 것입니다. 나중에는 아마 제가 업무로 바쁠 것이지만, ⁹¹사무실로 전화해 주시면 제 비서가 일정을 변경하는 것을 도와드릴 수 있을 것입니다.

89 | 청자 문제

해석 청자는 누구인 것 같은가?
(A) 트럭 운전사
(B) 여행사 직원
(C) 보안 요원
(D) 보수 작업자

해설 지문에서 신분 및 직업과 관련된 표현을 놓치지 않고 듣는다. "I talked to you about repairing the wood floors in one of my units on April 19."이라며 자신의 아파트 호실들 중 하나의 나무 바닥을 4월 19일에 수리하는 것에 관해 청자와 이야기했다고 한 말을 통해, 청자가 보수 작업자임을 알 수 있다. 따라서 (D)가 정답이다.

어휘 travel agent 여행사 직원   security guard 보안 요원

90 | 의도 파악 문제

해설 화자는 "그들은 제가 생각했던 것보다 더 일찍 아파트에 입주할 것입니다"라고 말할 때 무엇을 의도하는가?
(A) 계획이 변경되어야 한다.
(B) 업무가 일찍 완료되었다.
(C) 문제가 해결되었다.
(D) 배달이 연기되어야 한다.

해설 질문의 인용어구(they will move into the apartment sooner than I thought)가 언급된 주변을 주의 깊게 듣는다. "I talked to you about repairing the wood floors in one of my units on April 19."이라며 자신의 아파트 호실들 중 하나의 나무 바닥을 4월 19일에 수리하는 것에 관해 청자와 이야기했다고 한 후, "I'm a bit worried about our arrangements"라며 자신들의 계획이 조금 걱정스럽다며, 새로운 세입자들이 생각했던 것보다 더 일찍 아파트에 입주할 것이라고 하였으므로, 계획이 변경되어야 한다는 것임을 알 수 있다. 따라서 (A)가 정답이다.

어휘 postpone v. 연기하다

91 | 요청 문제

해석 화자는 청자에게 무엇을 하도록 요청하는가?
(A) 거주자에게 전화한다.
(B) 비서와 이야기한다.
(C) 몇몇 견본을 제공한다.
(D) 회의를 취소한다.

해설 지문에서 요청과 관련된 표현이 포함된 문장을 주의 깊게 듣는다. "please call my office and my secretary can help you reschedule"이라며 사무실로 전화해 주시면 비서가 일정을 변경하는 것을 도와드릴 수 있을 것이라고 하였다. 따라서 (B)가 정답이다.

어휘 resident n. 거주자   assistant n. 비서, 조수

Paraphrasing

secretary 비서 → assistant 비서

[92-94]   호주

Questions 92-94 refer to the following introduction.

Welcome, everyone. It's great to see you all again, and ⁹²I hope you've been practicing what we learned in last week's guitar lesson. This week's practice session is going to be different, as we have a special visitor to our class—Roman Brunelli, a professional musician. He'll be teaching you a simple Spanish piece. ⁹³If you haven't already grabbed the music sheets for today's class, they're stacked on the table beside the door. Now, let me introduce Mr. Brunelli to you. ⁹⁴He's going to demonstrate the piece for you right now.

professional adj. 전문의   piece n. 작품, 조각   music sheet 악보
stack v. 쌓다   demonstrate v. 보여주다

해석
92-94번은 다음 소개에 관한 문제입니다.
환영합니다, 여러분. 모두 다시 뵙게 되어 기쁘고, ⁹²지난주 기타 수업에서 우리가 배웠던 것들을 연습하고 계셨기를 바랍니다. 이번 주 연습 수업은 다를 예정인데, 전문 음악가인 Roman Brunelli가 우리 수업에 특별한 방문자로 오셨기 때문이죠. 그는 여러분에게 간단한 스페인 작품을 가르쳐 드릴 것입니다. ⁹³만약 오늘 수업을 위한 악보를 아직 가져오지 않으셨다면, 그것들은 문 옆의 탁자 위에 쌓여 있습니다. 이제, 여러분께 Mr. Brunelli를 소개해드리겠습니다. ⁹⁴그는 바로 지금 여러분을 위해 그 작품을 보여드릴 거예요.

92 | 장소 문제

해석 청자들은 어디에 있는 것 같은가?
(A) 미술관에
(B) 컨벤션 센터에
(C) 기타 상점에
(D) 음악 교육 기관에

해설 지문에서 장소와 관련된 표현을 놓치지 않고 듣는다. "I hope you've been practicing what we learned in last week's guitar lesson"이라며 지난주 기타 수업에서 배웠던 것들을 연습하고 계셨기를 바란다는 말을 통해 청자들이 음악 교육 기관에 있음을 알 수 있다. 따라서 (D)가 정답이다.

어휘 academy n. 교육 기관, 학원

93 | 특정 세부 사항 문제

해석 탁자에 무엇이 놓여 있는가?

(A) 악보
(B) 악기
(C) 사진 앨범
(D) 수업 일정

해설 질문의 핵심 어구(on the table)가 언급된 주변을 주의 깊게 듣는다. "If you haven't already grabbed the music sheets for today's class, they're stacked on the table beside the door."라며 만약 오늘 수업을 위한 악보를 아직 가져오지 않았다면, 그것들은 문 옆의 탁자 위에 쌓여 있다고 하였다. 따라서 (A)가 정답이다.

어휘 instrument n. 악기

94 | 다음에 할 일 문제

해석 청자들은 다음에 무엇을 할 것 같은가?
(A) 음악 작품에 대해 토론한다.
(B) 다과를 즐긴다.
(C) 연주를 본다.
(D) 그룹으로 모인다.

해설 지문의 마지막 부분을 주의 깊게 듣는다. "He's going to demonstrate the piece for you right now."라며 그가 바로 지금 여러분을 위해 그 작품을 보여드릴 것이라는 말을 통해 청자들이 연주를 볼 것임을 알 수 있다. 따라서 (C)가 정답이다.

어휘 refreshment n. 다과 gather v. 모이다

[95-97]

영국

Questions 95-97 refer to the following excerpt from a meeting and product list.

> Hi, everyone. ⁹⁵**I'd like to start with a brief observation of our clearance sale**, which is aimed at clearing out our stock of last year's smart watches. The event is supposed to end in two days, but we still have quite a few K33s and Z41s left. As of now, ⁹⁶**only the S64 is sold out**. So, ⁹⁷**if someone expresses an interest in that model, please encourage them to try one of the other options**.

observation n. 소견, 의견 clearance sale 재고 정리 할인
aimed at ~을 목표로 한, 겨냥한 clear out 소진하다, 정리하다 stock n. 재고

해설 95-97번은 다음 회의 발췌와 제품 목록에 관한 문제입니다.
안녕하세요, 여러분. 작년 스마트워치 재고를 소진하는 것을 목표로 하는 ⁹⁵재고 정리 할인에 관한 짧은 소견으로 시작하고 싶습니다. 이 행사는 이틀 안에 끝날 예정이지만, 우리는 여전히 K33과 Z41 모델이 꽤 여럿 남아 있습니다. 현재로서는, ⁹⁶S64만이 품절입니다. 그러니, ⁹⁷만약 누군가 그 모델에 관심을 표하면, 다른 선택지들 중 하나를 시도해 보도록 권장해 주세요.

95 | 주제 문제

해석 화자는 주로 무엇에 대해 이야기하고 있는가?
(A) 고객 불만
(B) 직원 일정
(C) 광고물
(D) 판매 행사

해설 회의 발췌의 주제를 묻는 문제이므로, 지문의 초반을 반드시 듣는다. "I'd like to start with a brief observation of our clearance sale"이라며 재고 정리 할인에 관한 짧은 소견으로 시작하고 싶다고 한 후, 판매 행사에 대한 내용으로 지문이 이어지고 있다. 따라서 (D)가 정답이다.

어휘 sales event 판매 행사

Paraphrasing

clearance sale 재고 정리 할인 → sales event 판매 행사

96 | 시각 자료 문제

해석 시각 자료를 보아라. 어떤 브랜드의 모델이 재고가 없는가?
(A) Knell
(B) Zenon
(C) Sonic
(D) Fringe

해설 제시된 제품 목록의 정보를 확인한 후 질문의 핵심 어구(out of stock)와 관련된 내용을 주의 깊게 듣는다. "only the S64 is sold out"이라며 S64만이 품절이라고 하였고, S64의 브랜드는 Sonic임을 제품 목록에서 확인할 수 있다. 따라서 (C)가 정답이다.

Paraphrasing

sold out 품절인 → out of stock 재고가 없는

97 | 제안 문제

해석 화자는 무엇을 하라고 제안하는가?
(A) 가격을 낮추기
(B) 쇼핑객들에게 재안내하기
(C) 제품 보증을 홍보하기
(D) 행사를 연장하기

해설 지문에서 제안과 관련된 표현이 포함된 문장을 주의 깊게 듣는다. "if someone expresses an interest in that model, please encourage them to try one of the other options"라며 만약 누군가가 그 모델에 관심을 표하면 다른 선택지들 중 하나를 시도해 보도록 권장해 달라고 하였다. 따라서 (B)가 정답이다.

어휘 warranty n. 제품 보증

Paraphrasing

encourage ~ to try one of the other options 다른 선택지들 중 하나를 시도해 보도록 권장하다 → Redirecting 재안내하기

[98-100]

영국

Questions 98-100 refer to the following telephone message and order form.

> Hi, Ken. It's Sally Griswald. I want to talk to you about something before I go to the meeting. ⁹⁸**You received an e-mail from me about the supplies we ordered to rearrange the displays in the main hall next week.** Well, I sent you the incorrect order form. Enough wall mounts, tables, and lights have been ordered. However,

⁹⁹**we need twice as many glass cases for the pottery displays**. It's not too late to modify the order, so please call and change it before the delivery is made. Oh, one other thing. ¹⁰⁰**I suggest you spring for express delivery to make sure the items arrive by Wednesday.**

supply n. 물품 rearrange v. 재배치하다 incorrect adj. 잘못된
wall mount 벽걸이 pottery n. 도자기 modify v. 수정하다
spring for ~의 값을 지불하다

해석
98-100번은 다음 전화 메시지와 주문 양식에 관한 문제입니다.

안녕하세요, Ken. Sally Griswald입니다. 제가 오늘 회의에 가기 전에 당신에게 이야기하고 싶은 것이 있어요. ⁹⁸당신은 다음 주에 메인 홀의 전시를 재배치하기 위해 우리가 주문한 물품에 관해 제가 보낸 메일을 받으셨을 거예요. 음, 제가 당신에게 잘못된 주문 양식을 보냈습니다. 벽걸이, 테이블 및 조명은 충분히 주문되었습니다. 하지만, ⁹⁹도자기 전시를 위해 유리 진열장이 2배 더 필요해요. 아직 주문을 수정하기에 너무 늦지 않았으니, 전화해서 배송이 진행되기 전에 그것을 수정해주세요. 아, 한 가지 더요. ¹⁰⁰물건들이 수요일까지 확실히 도착하도록 신속 배송의 값을 지불하시는 것을 제안드려요.

주문 양식	
품목	수량
벽걸이	12
테이블	5
조명	18
⁹⁹유리 진열장	7

98 | 다음에 할 일 문제

해석 다음 주에 무슨 일이 일어날 것 같은가?
(A) 갤러리가 특별 손님을 접대할 것이다.
(B) 사업 회의가 열릴 것이다.
(C) 예술가가 작품들을 전시할 것이다.
(D) 공간이 재편성될 것이다.

해설 질문의 핵심 어구(next week)가 언급된 주변을 주의 깊게 듣는다. "You received an e-mail from me about the supplies we ordered to rearrange the displays in the main hall next week."라며 다음 주에 메인 홀의 전시를 재배치하기 위해 주문한 물품에 관해 자신이 보낸 메일을 받으셨을 것이라고 하였다. 따라서 (D)가 정답이다.

어휘 host v. 접대하다 reorganize v. 재편성하다

Paraphrasing

rearrange 재배치하다 → be reorganized 재편성되다

99 | 시각 자료 문제

해석 시각 자료를 보아라. 어떤 숫자가 잘못되었는가?
(A) 12
(B) 5
(C) 18
(D) 7

해설 제시된 주문 양식의 정보를 확인한 후, 질문의 핵심 어구(number ~ incorrect)와 관련된 내용을 주의 깊게 듣는다. "we need twice as many glass cases for the pottery displays"라며 도자기 전시를 위해 유리 진열장이 2배 더 필요하다고 하였고, 유리 진열장의 수량이 7임을 주문 양식에서 알 수 있다. 따라서 (D)가 정답이다.

100 | 제안 문제

해석 화자는 무엇을 제안하는가?

(A) 전시 공간을 예약하기
(B) 속달 운송을 요청하기
(C) 이메일을 전달하기
(D) 물품을 교환하기

해설 지문의 중후반에서 제안과 관련된 표현이 포함된 문장을 주의 깊게 듣는다. "I suggest you spring for express delivery to make sure the items arrive by Wednesday."라며 물건들이 수요일까지 확실히 도착하도록 신속 배송의 값을 지불하는 것을 제안한다고 하였다. 따라서 (B)가 정답이다.

어휘 expedite v. 신속히 처리하다 forward v. 전달하다, 전송하다

Paraphrasing

express delivery 신속 배송 → expedited shipping 속달 운송

PART 5

101 | 부사 자리 채우기

해설 동사(have been working)를 꾸밀 수 있는 것은 부사이므로 부사 (C) tirelessly(지칠 줄 모르고)가 정답이다. 형용사 (A), 형용사의 비교급 (B), 명사 (D)는 동사를 꾸밀 수 없다.

해석 Vintron 연구소 직원들은 최종 제품이 반드시 완벽하도록 하기 위해 지칠 줄 모르고 일해 오고 있다.

어휘 tireless adj. 지칠 줄 모르는

102 | 전치사 채우기

해설 '주차장에 있는 기계는 모든 주요 신용카드뿐만 아니라 일부 모바일 결제 방식도 받는다'라는 의미가 되어야 하므로 전치사 (C) in(~에, ~ 안에)이 정답이다. (A) among은 '~ 중 하나, ~ 중 한 명', (B) to는 '~로, ~에게', (D) onto는 '~ 위에, ~ 위로'라는 의미이다.

해석 Nova 주차장에 있는 기계는 모든 주요 신용카드뿐만 아니라 일부 모바일 결제 방식도 받는다.

어휘 parking garage (실내) 주차장, 주차장 건물 accept v. 받다, 수락하다
form n. 방식, 형태

103 | 전치사 채우기

해설 '다음 15일 이내에 미지불된 요금이 지불된다면, 벌금을 적용하지 않을 것이다'라는 의미가 되어야 하므로 전치사 (B) within(~ 이내에)이 정답이다. (A) upon은 '~ 위에', (C) behind는 '~ 뒤에', (D) toward는 '~ 쪽으로'라는 의미이다. 참고로, 가정법 미래 문장에서 If가 생략되는 경우, 'Should + 주어 + 동사원형, 주어 + will(can, may, should) + 동사원형'의 형태를 만든다.

해석 다음 15일 이내에 미지불된 요금이 지불된다면, Hampton 전기는 벌금을 적용하지 않을 것이다.

어휘 outstanding adj. 미지불된, 아직 해결되지 않은 bill n. 요금, 고지서
apply v. 적용하다, 신청하다 penalty n. 벌금, 위약금

104 | 부정대명사 채우기

해설 동사(hire)의 목적어 자리이므로, 목적어 자리에 올 수 있는 대명사 (B), (C), (D)가 정답의 후보이다. '금융사는 Ms. Kovac의 업무를 처리할 누군가를 고용할 계획이다'라는 의미가 되어야 하므로 부정대명사 (D) someone(누군가)이 정답이다. (B) whom은 관계대명사일 경우 앞에 선행사가 나와야 하고, 의문대명사일 경우 의문문에서 쓰여야 한다. (C) anyone은 주로 부정문, 의문문, 조건문에 쓰이므로 답이 될 수 없다.

(A) other는 앞에 the가 없을 때 형용사로만 쓰이므로 목적어 자리에 올 수 없다.

해석 Western 금융사는 Ms. Kovac의 휴직 동안 그녀의 업무를 처리할 누군가를 고용할 계획이다.

어휘 handle v. 처리하다 duty n. 업무 leave of absence 휴직, 휴가

105 | 부사 어휘 고르기

해설 '실수로 삭제된 파일들을 복구하기 위해 고객 지원팀에 즉시 연락했다'라는 문맥이므로 (D) immediately(즉시)가 정답이다. (A) thoroughly는 '철저히', (B) enthusiastically는 '열광적으로', (C) nearly는 '거의'라는 의미이다.

해석 Mr. Walker는 실수로 삭제된 파일들을 복구하기 위해 Nevris 소프트웨어 사의 고객 지원팀에 즉시 연락했다.

어휘 contact v. 연락하다 support n. 지원; v. 지원하다 recover v. 복구하다
accidentally adv. 실수로

106 | 형용사 어휘 고르기

해설 '코치는 올해 그의 팀이 결승까지 진출할 것이라고 확신한다'라는 문맥이므로 (C) certain(확신하는)이 정답이다. (A) attentive는 '주의를 기울이는', (B) sharp는 '예리한', (D) diligent는 '근면한'이라는 의미이다.

해석 Agarwal 코치는 올해 그의 팀이 유소년 축구 리그 결승까지 진출할 것이라고 확신한다.

어휘 final n. 결승

107 | 명사 어휘 고르기

해설 '세탁기는 많은 유지보수를 필요로 하지 않고 20년 동안 작동해 왔다'라는 문맥이므로 (B) maintenance(유지보수)가 정답이다. (A) convenience는 '편의, 편리', (C) protection은 '보호', (D) resistance는 '저항, 반대'라는 의미이다.

해석 Sauber 가전제품사에 의해 생산된 이 세탁기는 많은 유지보수를 필요로 하지 않고 20년 동안 작동해 왔다.

어휘 function v. 작동하다, 기능하다

108 | 전치사 채우기

해설 이 문장은 필수성분(LightTrek's video-editing software ~ sell well)을 갖춘 완전한 절이므로 _____ ~ impressive features는 수식어 거품으로 보아야 한다. 이 수식어 거품은 동사가 없는 거품구이므로, 거품구를 이끌 수 있는 전치사 (B), (C), (D)가 정답의 후보이다. '여러 인상적인 특징들을 가지고 있음에도 불구하고 잘 팔리지 않았다'라는 의미가 되어야 하므로 전치사 (B) despite(~에도 불구하고)가 정답이다. (C) than은 '~보다', (D) since는 '~ 이후, ~ 이래로'라는 의미이다. 부사 또는 접속사 (A) yet(아직; 그런데도)은 수식어 거품구를 이끌 수 없다.

해석 LightTrek사의 영상 편집 소프트웨어는 여러 인상적인 특징들을 가지고 있음에도 불구하고 잘 팔리지 않았다.

어휘 video-editing n. 영상 편집 a number of 여러, 몇몇의
impressive adj. 인상적인, 멋진 feature n. 특징, 특색; v. 특별히 포함하다

109 | 명사 어휘 고르기

해설 '저작권이 있는 이미지를 사용하는 것에 대해 동의하지 않는다'라는 문맥이므로 (D) consent(동의)가 정답이다. (A) certification은 '증명, 증명서', (B) declaration은 '선언', (C) discipline은 '규율, 훈육'이라는 의미이다.

해석 Mara 미디어사는 다른 회사들이 자사의 저작권이 있는 이미지를 사용하는 것에 대해 절대 동의하지 않는 것을 정책으로 삼았다.

어휘 copyrighted adj. 저작권이 있는

110 | 동사 어휘 고르기

해설 '입사 지원서에 선호하는 사항을 명시해 주십시오'라는 문맥이므로 (C) state(명시하다, 알리다)가 정답이다. (A) recognize는 '알아보다', (B) initiate는 '착수시키다', (D) tolerate는 '용인하다, 참다'라는 의미이다.

해석 만약 당신이 Cooper 피트니스의 특정 지점에서 근무하는 것에 관심이 있으시면, 입사 지원서에 선호하는 사항을 명시해 주십시오.

어휘 particular adj. 특정한, 특수한 preference n. 선호
application form 지원서

111 | 동명사 채우기

해설 빈칸은 전치사(for)의 목적어 자리이므로 명사 (A)와 동명사 (C)가 정답의 후보이다. 빈칸 다음에 온 목적어(Stonefrost ~ department)를 가질 수 있는 것은 동명사이므로 동사 manage(관리하다)의 동명사 (C) managing이 정답이다. 동사 (B)와 동사 또는 과거분사 (D)는 명사 자리에 올 수 없다.

해석 Mr. Ebbets는 10년 넘게 Stonefrost Holdings사의 법무팀을 관리하는 것을 맡아왔다.

어휘 decade n. 10년

112 | 올바른 시제의 동사 채우기

해설 문장에 동사가 없으므로 동사 (A), (C), (D)가 정답의 후보이다. 미래를 나타내는 시간 표현(over the next few days)이 있으므로, 미래진행 시제 (D) will be using이 정답이다.

해석 Ms. Olsen은 사무실의 누수로 인해 앞으로 며칠 동안 임시 작업 공간을 사용할 예정이다.

어휘 temporary adj. 임시의 water leak 누수

113 | 현재분사와 과거분사 구별하여 채우기

해설 빈칸 뒤의 명사(land developers)를 꾸밀 수 있는 것은 형용사이므로 형용사 역할을 하는 과거분사 (A)와 현재분사 (C)가 정답의 후보이다. '선도적인 토지 개발 회사들'이라는 의미가 되어야 하므로 현재분사 (C) leading(선도적인)이 정답이다. 과거분사 (A) led는 '이끌어진 토지 개발 회사들'이라는 의미로 어색한 문맥을 만들기 때문에 답이 될 수 없다. 명사 또는 동사 (B)는 '선두, 우세'라는 의미의 명사일 경우 복합 명사의 첫 번째 단어인 leads는 단수형이어야 하므로 답이 될 수 없고, 동사일 경우 명사를 꾸밀 수 없다. 명사 (D)는 '선두, 지도자'라는 의미로서 빈칸 뒤의 land developers와 함께 복합 명사를 만드는 것으로 본다 해도, 복합 명사의 첫 번째 단어인 leaders는 단수형이어야 하므로 답이 될 수 없다.

해석 Green Valley 주택 사업을 성공적으로 완료한 후에, Goldfield Properties사는 아시아의 선도적인 토지 개발 회사들 중 하나가 되는 것을 목표로 한다.

어휘 complete v. 완료하다 aim v. 목표로 하다; n. 목적, 겨냥
land developer 토지 개발 회사 lead n. 선두, 우세; v. 선도하다, 이끌다

114 | 동사 어휘 고르기

해설 '뉴스 보도들은 Braxco 화학과 Haskill 산업이 다음 해에 합병을 고려하고 있다는 것을 시사한다'라는 문맥이므로 (D) indicate(시사하다)이 정답이다. (A) implement는 '시행하다', (B) respond는 '응답하다', (C) acquire는 '취득하다, 매입하다'라는 의미이다.

해석 여러 뉴스 보도들은 Braxco 화학과 Haskill 산업이 다음 해에 합병을 고려하고 있다는 것을 시사한다.

어휘 consider v. 고려하다 merger n. 합병

115 | 부정대명사 채우기

해설 주절(_____ ~ purchase)에 주어가 없으므로 주어 자리에 올 수 있는 부정

대명사인 모든 보기가 정답의 후보이다. '많은 사람들이 홍보 행사를 이용했다'라는 문맥이므로 (A) many(많은 사람들)가 정답이다. (B) either(둘 중 하나)는 두 가지 대상 중 하나를 의미하므로 답이 될 수 없다. (C) little(거의 없는 양)은 어색한 문맥을 만든다. (D) another(또 다른 하나)는 이미 언급한 것 이외의 또 다른 하나를 가리킬 때 사용되므로 이 문장의 문맥에는 적절하지 않다.

해석 Donald's Doughnuts의 기념 이벤트 기간 동안, 많은 사람들이 커피 구매 시 무료 샌드위치를 받는 홍보 행사를 이용했다.

어휘 anniversary adj. 기념의, 기념일의; n. 기념일
take advantage of ~을 이용하다   purchase n. 구매; v. 구매하다

116 | 형용사 자리 채우기

해설 be동사(are) 뒤의 보어 자리에 올 수 있는 것은 형용사이므로 형용사 역할을 하는 과거분사 (A)와 현재분사 (C), 형용사 (D)가 정답의 후보이다. '제품들이 더 저렴하다'라는 문맥이므로 형용사 (D) affordable(저렴한)이 정답이다. 과거분사 (A)와 현재분사 (C)를 쓸 경우 각각 'Red Pail Hardware사는 더욱 다양한 제품들을 보유하고 있지만, Jerry's Home Supplies사의 제품들이 더 제공된다/제공하고 있다'라는 어색한 문맥이 된다. 참고로, (C)가 동명사로 쓰인 경우 주어(the goods at ~ Supplies)와 동격이 되어 'Jerry's Home Supplies사의 제품들은 더 제공하는 것이다'라는 어색한 문맥이 되며 동사 afford(제공하다, ~할 여유가 되다)가 타동사이므로 뒤에 목적어가 와야 한다. 동사 (B)는 보어 자리에 올 수 없다.

해석 Red Pail Hardware사는 더욱 다양한 제품들을 보유하고 있지만, Jerry's Home Supplies사의 제품들이 더 저렴하다.

어휘 variety of 다양한

117 | to 부정사 채우기

해설 이 문장은 주어(Seaward Insurance's president), 동사(called), 목적어(a meeting)를 갖춘 완전한 절이므로, ____ ~ a replacement for Anita Wilson은 수식어 거품으로 보아야 한다. 이 수식어 거품은 동사가 없는 거품구이므로, 거품구를 이끌 수 있는 과거분사 (C)와 to 부정사 (D)가 정답의 후보이다. 'Anita Wilson의 후임자를 임명하기 위해 회의를 소집했다'라는 의미가 되어야 하므로 목적을 나타내는 to 부정사 (D) to appoint가 정답이다. 과거분사 (C) appointed를 쓰면 'Anita Wilson의 후임자로 임명된 회의를 소집했다'라는 어색한 의미를 만든다. 명사 (A)와 동사 (B)는 거품구를 이끌 수 없다.

해석 Seaward 보험사의 회장은 3개월 뒤에 사임하는 Anita Wilson의 후임자를 임명하기 위해 회의를 소집했다.

어휘 call a meeting 회의를 소집하다   resign v. 사임하다

118 | 형용사 자리 채우기

해설 2형식 동사 appear의 보어 자리에 올 수 있는 명사 (A), 형용사 (C)와 (D)가 정답의 후보이다. '그의 팀의 능력에 대해 자신감 있어 보였다'라는 의미로 보어가 주어(Mr. Hoffman)의 상태를 설명하고 있으므로 형용사 (D) confident(자신감 있는)가 정답이다. 명사 (A)는 보어로서 주어와 동격 관계가 되어 '그의 팀의 능력에 대해 자신감처럼 보였다'라는 어색한 문맥을 만든다. 형용사 (C)는 '그의 팀의 능력에 대해 비밀을 털어놓는 것처럼 보였다'라는 어색한 문맥을 만든다. 부사 (B)는 보어 자리에 올 수 없다.

해석 전략 회의 후에, Mr. Hoffman은 마감일을 지킬 수 있는 그의 팀의 능력에 대해 자신감 있어 보였다.

어휘 strategy n. 전략   appear v. (~처럼) 보이다
meet v. (기한 등을) 지키다, 만나다   confide v. 비밀을 털어놓다

119 | 전치사 채우기

해설 '각 직원은 그 또는 그녀의 직책에 관계없이 워크숍에 참가하도록 기대될 것이다'라는 의미가 되어야 하므로 전치사 (A) regardless of(~에 관계없이)가 정답이다. (B) other than은 '~외에', (C) such as는 '~과 같은', (D) except for는 '~을 제외하고'라는 의미이다.

해석 각 직원은 회사 내에서 그 또는 그녀의 직책에 관계없이 워크숍에 참가하도록 기대될 것이다.

어휘 expect v. 기대하다   participate in ~에 참가하다   position n. 직책, 직무

120 | 형용사 자리 채우기

해설 명사(information)를 꾸밀 수 있는 것은 형용사이므로 형용사 (C) contradictory(모순되는)가 정답이다. 명사 (A)와 (B)는 information과 복합 명사를 이루지 않고, 동사 (D)는 명사를 꾸밀 수 없으므로 답이 될 수 없다.

해석 Perkins 의료 보험사의 웹사이트는 직무 지원 과정에 관한 일부 모순되는 정보를 포함했다.

어휘 concerning prep. ~에 관한   contradiction n. 모순, 반박
contradict v. 모순되다, 반박하다

121 | 부사 어휘 고르기

해설 '항공사들은 비행기에서 그것들을 승객에게 미리 배포한다'라는 문맥이므로 (B) beforehand(미리)가 정답이다. (A) overhead는 '머리 위에', (C) indoors는 '실내에서', (D) elsewhere는 '다른 곳에서'라는 의미이다.

해석 세관 양식들은 도착하는 공항에서 얻을 수 있지만, 몇몇 항공사들은 비행기에서 그것들을 승객에게 미리 배포한다.

어휘 customs n. 세관, 관세   obtain v. 얻다   distribute v. 배포하다
passenger n. 승객

122 | 형용사 어휘 고르기

해설 'Mr. Turner의 독창적인 창작품들은 혁신적인 패션 디자이너라는 평판을 얻게 했다'라는 문맥이므로 (B) ingenious(독창적인, 기발한)가 정답이다. (A) cooperative는 '협력하는', (C) appreciative는 '고마워하는, 감탄하는', (D) conducive는 '~에 좋은'이라는 의미이다.

해석 Mr. Turner의 독창적인 창작품들은 그에게 혁신적인 패션 디자이너라는 평판을 얻게 했다.

어휘 creation n. 창작품, 창조   reputation n. 평판   innovative adj. 혁신적인

123 | 형용사 어휘 고르기

해설 '새로 채용된 직원에게 엄청난 도움이 될 것이다'라는 문맥이므로 (D) immense(엄청난)가 정답이다. (A) customary는 '습관적인, 관례적인', (B) extravagant는 '낭비하는', (C) intelligent는 '총명한, 똑똑한'이라는 의미이다.

해석 경험이 풍부한 직원과 2주 동안 파트너가 되는 것은 새로 채용된 직원에게 엄청난 도움이 될 것이다.

어휘 experienced adj. 경험이 풍부한   be of help to ~에게 도움이 되다

124 | 부사 자리 채우기

해설 동사(recovered)를 꾸밀 수 있는 것은 부사이므로 부사 (C) progressively(점차, 점진적으로)가 정답이다. 형용사 (A), 명사 또는 동사 (B), 명사 (D)는 동사를 꾸밀 수 없다.

해석 물리 치료 시간에 참석하고 자주 스트레칭을 함으로써, Ms. Lee는 그녀의 부상에서 점차 회복했다.

어휘 physical therapy 물리 치료   frequently adv. 자주, 흔히
recover v. 회복하다, 되찾다   injury n. 부상
progressive adj. 진보적인, 점진적인
progress n. 진전; v. 진전을 보이다, 진행하다   progression n. 진행, 진전

125 | 명사 어휘 고르기

해설 '명성 있는 달리기 대회의 예선을 통과함으로써 그녀의 운동 선수다운 잠재력을 보여주었다'라는 문맥이므로 (A) potential(잠재력, 가능성)이 정답이다. (C) property(속성, 특성)도 해석상 그럴듯해 보이지만 사물이나 물질 고유의 속성과 특성을 나타낼 때 사용하므로 이 문장에는 적절하지 않다. (B) authority는 '지휘권, 권한', (D) acquisition은 '습득, 매입'이라는 의미이다.

해석 Chloe Newman은 명성 있는 Valley River 달리기 대회의 예선을 통과함으로써 그녀의 운동 선수다운 잠재력을 보여주었다.

어휘 athletic adj. 운동 선수다운, 육상 경기의
qualify v. ~의 예선을 통과하다, 자격을 얻다 prestigious adj. 명성 있는, 일류의

126 | 부사 어휘 채우기

해설 '매우 수익성 높은 정부 계약에 만족했다'라는 문맥이므로 (A) extremely(매우, 극도로)가 정답이다. (B) heavily는 '무겁게, 심하게', (C) vividly는 '선명하게, 생생하게', (D) promptly는 '즉시'라는 의미이다.

해석 Wassco 엔지니어링사의 주주들은 회사가 확보한 매우 수익성 높은 정부 계약에 만족했다.

어휘 stockholder n. 주주 profitable adj. 수익성 높은 contract n. 계약
secure v. 확보하다, 획득하다

127 | 사람명사와 사물/추상명사 구별하여 채우기

해설 전치사(to)의 목적어 자리에 오면서 형용사(top)의 꾸밈을 받을 수 있는 것은 명사이므로 명사 (B)와 (C)가 정답의 후보이다. '고위 간부에게 지급되는 급여'라는 의미가 되어야 하므로 사람 명사 (C) executive(간부, 임원)가 정답이다. 추상명사 (B) execution(실행, 수행)을 쓸 경우 '고위 실행에 지급되는 급여'라는 어색한 문맥이 된다. 동사 (A)는 명사 자리에 올 수 없다. 동사 execute(실행하다, 수행하다)는 타동사이므로 동명사 또는 현재분사 (D) executing을 쓸 경우 전치사 없이 뒤에 목적어가 바로 나와야 한다.

해석 CK 물류 회사의 고위 간부에게 지급되는 급여는 업계에서 가장 높은 것 중 하나이다.

어휘 salary n. 급여, 월급 logistics n. 물류

128 | 전치사 채우기

해설 주절(Evertech ~ shelves)이 주어(Evertech ~ blender)와 동사(was removed)를 갖춘 완전한 절이므로, ___ ~ components는 수식어 거품으로 보아야 한다. 이 수식어 거품은 명사절 접속사(that)가 이끄는 절의 수식을 받는 명사(reports)만 있고 동사가 없는 거품구이므로, 거품구를 이끌 수 있는 전치사 (A)와 (B)가 정답의 후보이다. '보고 때문에'라는 의미가 되어야 하므로 전치사 (B) because of(~ 때문에)가 정답이다. (A) instead of는 '~ 대신에'라는 의미이다. 접속사 또는 부사 (C)와 접속사 또는 형용사 (D)는 거품구를 이끌 수 없다.

해석 Evertech사의 최신 믹서기는 결함이 있는 부품을 포함하고 있다는 보고 때문에 매장 선반에서 치워졌다.

어휘 blender n. 믹서기 remove v. 치우다, 제거하다 defective adj. 결함이 있는
component n. 부품, 요소

129 | 등위접속사 채우기

해설 절(A purchase ~ supervisor)과 절(it ~ approved)을 연결할 수 있는 것은 접속사이므로 등위접속사 (A)와 (C)가 정답의 후보이다. '구매 신청서는 관리자에 의해 서명되어야 하며, 그렇지 않으면 그것은 승인되지 않을 것이다'라는 의미가 되어야 하므로 등위접속사 (A) or(그렇지 않으면)가 정답이다. (C) and는 '그리고'라는 의미로, 어색한 의미를 만들기 때문에 답이 될 수 없다. 부사 (B) nevertheless(그럼에도 불구하고)와 (D) also(또한)는 접속사 자리에 올 수 없다.

해석 구매 신청서는 관리자에 의해 서명되어야 하며, 그렇지 않으면 그것은 승인되지 않을 것이다.

어휘 request n. 신청(서) supervisor n. 관리자 approve v. 승인하다

130 | 형용사 어휘 고르기

해설 '직원들은 수익 성장에 비례하는 연간 보너스를 받을 것이다'라는 문맥이므로 (D) proportional(비례하는)이 정답이다. (A) complimentary는 '무료의, 칭찬하는', (B) budgetary는 '예산의', (C) enough는 '충분한'이라는 의미이다.

해석 Lyon 방송국의 직원들은 수익 성장에 비례하는 연간 보너스를 받을 것이다.

어휘 revenue n. 수익 growth n. 성장

PART 6

131-134번은 다음 공지에 관한 문제입니다.

> 저희가 Landmark 공원을 보존할 수 있도록 도와주세요!
> 5월 15일 | 오전 10시에서 오후 4시
>
> Dothan시 청년 동맹의 연례 대청소 행사에 함께하세요. 활동들은 담과 오솔길을 씻어 내는 것뿐만 아니라 쓰레기를 줍는 것도 포함합니다. ¹³¹자원봉사자들에게 모든 작업을 위한 장비가 제공될 것입니다. 하지만, 공급품들이 부족할 수 있기 때문에, 저희는 여러분이 여러분 소유의 장비를 가지고 오는 것을 권장합니다.
>
> ¹³²참가자들은 그룹들로 나누어질 것이고 청소할 구체적인 구역들이 배정될 것입니다. 행사 당일 아침에 관리자가 여러분의 임무를 결정할 것입니다. ¹³³옷을 적절하게 입는 것을 명심하세요.
>
> 만약 여러분이 Dothan시 청년 동맹에 도움을 제공하는 것을 고려하고 있다면, 여러분의 기부금은 이번 행사와 향후 행사들에 사용될 것입니다. ¹³⁴저희는 여러분의 참여를 기다립니다. 여러분의 지원은 저희의 성공에 필수적입니다. www.dothanyouth.org에서 대청소 행사를 신청하세요.

preserve v. 보존하다, 지키다 **cleanup** n. 대청소 **litter** n. 쓰레기
footpath n. 오솔길 **supply** n. 공급품
limited adj. (시간이나 수가) 부족한, 한정된 **assign** v. 배정하다
specific adj. 구체적인 **aid** n. 도움, 지원 **contribution** n. 기부금, 공헌
register v. 신청하다, 등록하다

131 | 전치사 채우기

해설 빈칸은 명사(equipment)를 목적어로 취하는 전치사 자리이다. '자원봉사자들에게 모든 작업을 위한 장비가 제공될 것이다'라는 의미가 되어야 하므로 빈칸 앞의 동사 provide와 함께 provide A with B(A에게 B를 제공하다)의 수동형 A be provided with B의 형태를 완성하는 전치사 (A) with가 정답이다. (C) for와 (D) to도 provide와 쓰이기는 하지만 'provide (something) for/to (someone)'의 형태로 쓰이므로 for/to 다음에는 제공받은 대상인 사람이나 기관 등을 나타내는 표현이 와야 한다.

132 | 올바른 시제의 동사 채우기 전체 문맥 파악

해설 문장에 동사가 없고 '참가자들이 그룹들로 나누어지다'라는 수동의 의미가 되어야 하므로 수동태 (B), (C), (D)가 정답의 후보이다. 빈칸이 있는 문장만으로는 올바른 시제의 동사를 고를 수 없으므로 주변 문맥이나 전체 문맥을 파악하여 정답을 고른다. 앞부분에서 행사가 5월 15일에 있을 것이고 자원봉사자들에게 모든 작업을 위한 장비가 제공될 것이라고 했으므로 봉사활동이 아직 일어나지 않은 미래의 상황임을 알 수 있다. 따라서 미래 시제 수동태 (D) will be separated가 정답이다.

어휘 separate v. 나누다, 분리하다

133 | 부사 자리 채우기

해설 동사(dress)를 꾸밀 수 있는 것은 부사이므로 부사 (D) appropriately(적절하게)가 정답이다. 형용사 (A), 명사 (B), 형용사의 비교급 (C)는 동사를 꾸밀 수 없다.

어휘 appropriate adj. 적절한

134 | 알맞은 문장 고르기

해석 (A) 저희는 가을 대청소 날짜를 8월에 발표할 것입니다.
(B) 저희는 여러분의 참여를 기다립니다.
(C) 참석률이 예상했던 것보다 더 높았습니다.
(D) 공원은 개인적인 행사들을 위해 임대될 수 있습니다.

해설 앞 문장 'your contributions will be used for this and future events'에서 여러분의 기부금은 이번 행사와 향후 행사들에 사용될 것이라고 했고, 뒤 문장 'Your support is crucial to our success.'에서 여러분의 지원은 저희의 성공에 필수적이라고 했으므로 빈칸에는 지원과 관련된 내용이 들어가야 함을 알 수 있다. 따라서 (B)가 정답이다.

어휘 announce v. 발표하다 involvement n. 참여 attendance n. 참석률, 출석
anticipate v. 예상하다, 기대하다 rent v. 임대하다

135-138은 다음 이메일에 관한 문제입니다.

> 수신: Angela Thornberry <athornberry@fastmail.com>
> 발신: Vincent Nakamura <vnakamura@traxcomputers.com>
> 제목: 귀하의 노트북 컴퓨터
> 날짜: 6월 18일
>
> Ms. Thornberry께,
>
> 화면에 생긴 문제 때문에 6월 15일에 귀하께서 저희 상점에 맡기셨던 Trax 2700 노트북 컴퓨터에 대해 이메일을 씁니다. ¹³⁵검사를 위해 그것을 저희 기술자들에게 보낸 후, 저희는 그것에 결함이 있는 부품이 들어 있음을 발견했습니다. ¹³⁶현재, 귀하의 노트북 컴퓨터는 수리되고 있습니다. 요청하신 대로, 저희는 또한 기기에 다른 문제들이 있는지 확인하기 위해 철저히 검사하고 있습니다.
>
> 이 문제는 전적으로 저희 잘못으로 보이므로, 저희는 귀하께 저희 소매점에서 사용하실 수 있는 50달러짜리 상품권을 제공하고 싶습니다. ¹³⁷그 대신에, 저희 웹사이트에서 사용하실 수 있는 동일한 가격의 전자 쿠폰도 이용하실 수 있습니다. 귀하께서 어느 것을 선호하시는지 알려만 주십시오.
>
> ¹³⁸저희는 귀하께 3일 이내에 컴퓨터를 다시 보내드릴 것입니다. 만약 지연이 발생한다면, 고객 서비스로 전화해주십시오.
>
> Vincent Nakamura 드림
> 고객 만족 부서

examination n. 검사, 조사 contain v. 들어 있다, 포함하다
faulty adj. 결함이 있는, 잘못된 component n. 부품, 요소
thoroughly adv. 철저히, 완전히 device n. 기기, 장치
issue n. 문제, 사안 entirely adv. 전적으로, 완전히 voucher n. 상품권, 할인권
retail store 소매점

135 | 사람명사와 사물/추상명사 구별하여 채우기

해설 전치사(to)의 목적어 자리에서 빈칸 앞의 소유격 인칭대명사(our)의 꾸밈을 받을 수 있는 것은 명사이므로 명사 (A), (C), (D)가 정답의 후보이다. '검사를 위해 컴퓨터를 기술자들에게 보냈다'라는 의미가 되어야 하므로 사람명사 (C) technicians(기술자들)가 정답이다. 추상명사 (A) technicality(세부적인 내용, 전문적임)와 (D) technology(기술, 기계)를 쓰면 각각 '검사를 위해 컴퓨터를 세부적인 내용/기술에 보냈다'라는 어색한 문맥이 된다. 형용사 (B)는 명사 자리에 올 수 없다.

어휘 technical adj. 기술적인, 전문적인

136 | 동사 어휘 고르기 전체 문맥 파악

해설 '현재 노트북 컴퓨터는 ___ 되고 있다'라는 문맥이므로 모든 보기가 정답의 후보이다. 빈칸이 있는 문장만으로 정답을 고를 수 없으므로 주변 문맥이나 전체 문맥을 파악한다. 앞부분에서 화면에 생긴 문제 때문에 노트북 컴퓨터를 상점에 맡겼다고 했고, 뒤 문장에서 '기기에 다른 문제들이 있는지 확인하기 위해 검사도 하고 있다(we are also thoroughly testing the device to see if there are any other issues)'라고 했으므로 노트북 컴퓨터는 현재 수리되고 있음을 알 수 있다. 따라서 동사 repair(수리하다)의 과거분사 (B) repaired가 정답이다. (A)의 replace는 '대체하다', (C)의 ship은 '수송하다', (D)의 recall은 '회수하다, 상기하다'라는 의미이다.

137 | 접속부사 채우기 주변 문맥 파악

해설 빈칸이 콤마와 함께 문장의 맨 앞에 온 접속부사 자리이므로, 앞 문장과 빈칸이 있는 문장의 의미 관계를 파악하여 정답을 선택한다. 앞 문장에서 소매점에서 사용할 수 있는 50달러짜리 상품권을 제공하고 싶다고 했고, 빈칸이 있는 문장에서는 웹사이트에서 사용할 수 있는 동일한 가격의 전자 쿠폰도 이용할 수 있다고 했으므로, 앞에서 언급한 것 외의 다른 대안을 소개할 때 사용되는 (D) Alternatively(그 대신에, 그렇지 않으면)가 정답이다.

어휘 regrettably adv. 후회하여, 유감스럽게 subsequently adv. 그 후에, 나중에
approximately adv. 대략

138 | 알맞은 문장 고르기

해석 (A) 귀하께서 문의하셨던 모델은 더 이상 이곳에서 구할 수 없습니다.
(B) 저희는 귀하께 3일 이내에 컴퓨터를 다시 보내드릴 것입니다.
(C) 품질 보증서가 만료되었기 때문에 귀하는 보상을 받지 않습니다.
(D) 저희는 저희 서비스에 대해 많은 불만 사항들을 접수받고 있습니다.

해설 뒤 문장 'Please call customer service if there is a delay.'에서 만약 지연이 발생한다면, 고객 서비스로 전화해달라고 했으므로, 빈칸에는 지연이 될 수 있는 것에 대한 내용이 들어가야 함을 알 수 있다. 따라서 (B)가 정답이다.

어휘 inquire v. 문의하다 location n. 곳, 장소 cover v. 보상하다, 덮다
warranty n. 품질 보증서 expire v. 만료되다, 만기가 되다
a number of 많은, 다수의 complaint n. 불만 사항, 불평

139-142번은 다음 공고에 관한 문제입니다.

> 고객님들께,
>
> Banerjee Roof Tiles사가 컴퓨터 시스템을 업그레이드할 것입니다. 이것은 저희가 주문 의뢰를 관리하고, 이메일을 처리하고, 고객 지원을 제공하는 방식에 영향을 미칠 것으로 예상됩니다. 저희의 온라인 주문 시스템은 5월 20일과 5월 31일 사이에 사용할 수 없게 될 것입니다. ¹³⁹만약 여러분이 주문하고자 한다면, 영업시간 중에 저희에게 전화해 주십시오. 저희 직원들이 기꺼이 여러분을 도와드릴 것입니다. ¹⁴⁰모든 것이 순조롭게 진행된다면, 정상적인 운영이 6월 1일까지는 재개될 것입니다.
>
> ¹⁴¹5월의 마지막 주 동안, 저희는 또한 직원 교육에 집중할 예정인데, 그렇게 함으로써 직원들이 새로운 시스템에 익숙해질 것입니다. ¹⁴²따라서, 저희는 평상시의 서비스 및 지원을 제공할 수 없을 것입니다.
>
> 불편에 사과드리며, 여러분의 인내심에 감사드립니다.

submission n. 의뢰, 부탁 handle v. 처리하다 disable v. 사용할 수 없게 하다
assist v. 돕다, 도움이 되다 provided conj. ~라면
smoothly adv. 순조롭게, 부드럽게 normal adj. 정상적인, 보통의
resume v. 재개되다 consequently adv. 따라서 inconvenience n. 불편
patience n. 인내심, 참을성

139 | 알맞은 문장 고르기

해석 (A) 대체 경로들에 대한 안내는 저희 웹사이트에서 이용 가능합니다.
(B) 만약 여러분이 주문하고자 한다면, 영업시간 중에 저희에게 전화해 주십시오.
(C) 따라서, 이 문제의 지속 기간 동안 몇몇 제품들은 재고가 없을 수도 있습니다.
(D) 저희는 저희의 계약 조건들에 따라 반품을 받을 것입니다.

해설 앞 문장 'Our online ordering system will be disabled between May 20 and May 31.'에서 자신들의 온라인 주문 시스템이 5월 20일과 5월 31일 사이에 사용할 수 없게 될 것이라고 했고, 뒤 문장 'Our personnel will be glad to assist you.'에서 직원들이 기꺼이 여러분, 즉 고객들을 도와줄 것이라고 했으므로 빈칸에는 온라인 주문 외에 다른 방법으로 주문하는 것과 관련된 내용이 들어가야 함을 알 수 있다. 따라서 (B)가 정답이다.

어휘 alternative adj. 대체의, 대안의 in stock 재고가 있는
terms and conditions 계약 조건

140 | 올바른 시제의 동사 채우기

해설 Provided로 시작하는 종속절(Provided ~ smoothly)에 단수 주어(everything)만 있고 동사가 없으므로 동사 (A), (B), (D)가 정답의 후보이다. 주절(normal ~ June 1)에 미래를 나타내는 시간 표현(by June 1)이 있고, 운영이 6월 1일까지는 재개될 것이라는 의미가 되어야 하므로 Provided로 시작하는 종속절도 미래를 나타내야 한다. 조건의 부사절에서는 미래를 나타내기 위해 미래 시제 대신 현재 시제를 사용해야 하므로 현재 시제 (B) proceeds가 정답이다.

어휘 proceed v. 진행되다

141 | 접속부사 채우기

해설 이 문장은 주어(we)와 동사(will ~ focus)를 갖춘 완전한 절이므로, ___ ~ system은 수식어 거품으로 보아야 한다. 이 수식어 거품은 분사구문이므로, 분사구문을 이끌 수 있는 접속부사 (A)와 (C), 부사절 접속사 (B)가 정답의 후보이다. '직원 교육에 집중할 예정인데, 그렇게 함으로써 직원들이 새로운 시스템에 익숙해질 것이다'라는 의미가 되어야 하므로 (C) thereby(그렇게 함으로써)가 정답이다. (A) otherwise(그렇지 않으면)나 (B) in case(~에 대비하여)를 사용할 경우 어색한 문맥이 된다. 전치사 (D)는 분사구문을 이끌 수 없으며, 현재분사 familiarizing을 전치사의 목적어 자리에 온 동명사로 본다고 하더라도 '새로운 시스템에 직원들을 익숙하게 하는 것의 결과로서, 직원 교육에 집중할 예정이다'라는 어색한 의미를 만든다.

142 | 형용사 어휘 고르기 전체 문맥 파악

해설 '___ 서비스 및 지원을 제공할 수 없을 것이다'라는 문맥이므로 모든 보기가 정답의 후보이다. 빈칸이 있는 문장만으로 정답을 고를 수 없으므로 주변 문맥이나 전체 문맥을 파악한다. 앞부분에서 '컴퓨터 시스템 업그레이드는 주문 의뢰를 관리하고, 이메일을 처리하고, 고객 지원을 제공하는 방식에 영향을 미칠 것으로 예상된다(This[upgrading ~ computer system] is expected to affect how we manage order submissions, handle e-mails, and deliver customer support).'라고 했고, '정상적인 운영이 6월 1일까지는 재개될 것이다(normal operations should resume by June 1)'라고 했으므로, 평소와 같은 서비스 및 지원을 제공할 수 없을 것임을 알 수 있다. 따라서 (C) usual(평상시의, 보통의)이 정답이다. (A) public은 '공공의', (B) approved는 '인가된, 승인된', (D) selective는 '선택적인'이라는 의미이다.

143-146번은 다음 이메일에 관한 문제입니다.

수신: Alison Jackson <ajackson@champleather.com>
발신: Victoria Green <vgreen@champleather.com>
제목: 새로운 정책
날짜: 6월 15일

안녕하세요, Alison.

다음의 정보를 우리의 직원들과 공유해주십시오. ¹⁴³저는 회사의 모두가 우리의 새로운 정책에 대해 알고 있다는 것을 확실히 하고 싶습니다. 11월 1일부터 시행되어, 회사는 특정 집단의 직원들의 정기적인 건강검진을 요구할 것입니다. ¹⁴⁴위원회는 지난주에 이 정책을 승인했습니다. ¹⁴⁵구체적으로 말하자면, 이 정책은 화학 물질들을 다루는 근로자들과 같이, 직장에서 위험한 환경들에 노출되는 직원들에게 적용됩니다. 이 정책은 또한 업무의 안전한 수행에 그들의 건강이 중요한 직원들에게도 영향을 미칩니다. ¹⁴⁶특히, 우리의 배달 트럭 운전기사들은 그들이 대형 차량들을 운전하기에 적합한지를 확실히 하기 위해 건강검진을 받아야 합니다. 우리는 앞으로 며칠간 이것에 대해 더 자세히 논의할 것입니다.

Victoria Green 드림
Champ Leather사

aware adj. 알고 있는, 인지한 effective adj. ~부터 시행되는, 효과적인
periodic adj. 정기적인 specifically adv. 구체적으로 말하자면, 분명히
cover v. (규칙 등이) 적용되다 personnel n. 직원(들) hazardous adj. 위험한
condition n. 환경, 조건 handle v. 다루다 crucial adj. 중요한
undergo v. ~을 받다, 겪다 fit adj. 적합한; v. 맞다
operate v. (기계 등을) 운전하다, 조작하다

143 | 부정대명사 채우기

해설 동사구(make sure)의 목적어 자리에 온 명사절(___ ~ policy)에서 복수 동사(are)의 주어가 될 수 있는 부정대명사 (A)와 지시대명사 (D)가 정답의 후보이다. '회사의 모두가 알고 있다는 것을 확실히 하고 싶다'라는 의미가 되어야 하므로 부정대명사 (A) all(모두)이 정답이다. 참고로, (D) these는 '이들, 이것들'이라는 의미로 이미 앞에서 명시되었거나, 시간, 공간, 심리적으로 가까이에 있는 사람이나 사물을 가리킬 때 사용됨을 알아둔다. 목적격 인칭대명사 (B)는 주어 자리에 올 수 없다. 수량 형용사 (C)는 단수 가산명사 앞에 오거나 단수 동사와 함께 쓰인다.

144 | 알맞은 문장 고르기

해석 (A) 세부 제안서는 당신의 책상 위에 놓여 있습니다.
(B) 인건비 상승은 문제가 될 것으로 예상됩니다.
(C) 위원회는 지난주에 이 정책을 승인했습니다.
(D) 경영진은 일부 직원을 분류하는 방식을 변경했습니다.

해설 뒤 문장 'Specifically, the policy covers personnel'에서 구체적으로 말하자면 이 정책이 직원들에게 적용된다고 했으므로 빈칸에는 정책과 관련된 내용이 들어가야 함을 알 수 있다. 따라서 (C)가 정답이다.

어휘 proposal n. 제안서, 제의 cost of labor 인건비 challenge n. 문제, 도전
commission n. 위원회, 수수료 approve v. 승인하다
measure n. 정책, 조치 classify v. 분류하다

145 | 태에 맞는 동사 채우기

해설 주격 관계절(who ~ at work)에 동사가 없으므로 동사인 모든 보기가 정답의 후보이다. expose(노출시키다)는 타동사인데, 빈칸 뒤에 목적어가 없고, 주격 관계대명사(who)의 선행사(personnel)와 동사(expose)가 '직원들이 노출되다'라는 의미의 수동 관계이므로 수동태 (D) are exposed가 정답이다. 능동태 (A), (B), (C)는 답이 될 수 없다.

146 | 접속부사 채우기 주변 문맥 파악

해설 빈칸이 콤마와 함께 문장의 맨 앞에 온 접속부사 자리이므로, 앞 문장과 빈칸이 있는 문장의 의미 관계를 파악하여 정답을 선택한다. 앞 문장에서 '정책은 업무의 안전한 수행에 건강이 중요한 직원들에게도 영향을 미친다'고 했고, 빈칸이 있는 문장에서는 배달 트럭 운전기사들이 건강검진을 받아야 한다고 했으므로, 구체적인 사항을 추가할 때 사용되는 (C) In particular (특히)가 정답이다.

어휘 conversely adv. 정반대로 rather than 대신에, ~보다는
continuously adv. 계속해서

PART 7

147-148번은 다음 광고에 관한 문제입니다.

대여를 위한 공간

¹⁴⁷57번지 Buckwold로에 위치한, 최근에 개조된 이 상업 용지는 Renuville의 중심부에 있으며 많은 카페들과 가게들의 도보 거리 내에 있습니다. 또한, 그것은 Renfrew 공원으로부터 단 두 블록 떨어져 있습니다. 그것의 11층들 각각은 10,500제곱피트의 사무실 공간을 포함합니다. ¹⁴⁸큰 지하 주차장도 있습니다. 입주자들과 그들의 방문객들은 그들의 자동차를 그곳에 무료로 둘 수 있습니다. 건물의 모든 층들은 즉시 사용할 준비가 되어 있습니다. 더 많은 정보를 원하시거나 둘러보는 것을 요청하시려면 555-9982로 전화해 주십시오.

renovate v. 개조하다 commercial property 상업 용지
heart n. 중심부, 핵심 distance n. 거리 underground garage 지하 주차장
tenant n. 입주자 vehicle n. 자동차 at no charge 무료로
immediate adj. 즉시의 occupancy n. 사용, 이용 viewing n. 둘러보는 것

147 | 육하원칙 문제

해설 57번지 Buckwold로의 특징은 무엇인가?
(A) 주거 공간을 포함한다.
(B) 중심에 위치한다.
(C) 공원의 경치가 보인다.
(D) 가구가 비치된 사무실들을 포함한다.

해설 지문의 'Located at 57 Buckwold Drive, ~ commercial property is in the heart of Renuville'에서 57번지 Buckwold로에 위치한 상업 용지가 Renuville의 중심부에 있다고 했으므로 (B)가 정답이다.

어휘 feature n. 특징 contain v. 포함하다, 가지다 residential adj. 주거의
view n. 경치 furnished adj. 가구가 비치된

Paraphrasing

is in the heart 중심부에 있다 → is centrally located 중심에 위치한다

148 | 육하원칙 문제

해설 입주자들은 무엇을 할 수 있는가?
(A) 대형 사무실에 대해 할인을 받는다.
(B) 정기 청소 서비스를 요청한다.
(C) 주차 시설을 무료로 이용한다.
(D) 첫 임대료의 지불을 연기한다.

해설 지문의 'There is ~ underground garage. Tenants ~ may leave their vehicles there at no charge.'에서 지하 주차장이 있으며, 입주자들은 그들의 자동차를 그곳에 무료로 둘 수 있다고 했으므로 (C)가 정답이다.

어휘 obtain v. 받다, 얻다 regular adj. 정기적인 facility n. 시설
delay v. 연기하다 initial adj. 첫, 처음의

Paraphrasing

underground garage 지하 주차장 → parking facility 주차 시설
at no charge 무료로 → for free 무료로

149-150번은 다음 이메일에 관한 문제입니다.

수신: Robert Sutton <r_sutton@jagmail.com>
발신: Kimbel 백화점 고객 서비스 <customercare@kimbeldept.com>
제목: 귀하의 CP3 Console 선주문
날짜: 5월 3일

Mr. Sutton께,

¹⁴⁹지난 금요일, 귀하께서는 올해 10월에 Tensa Tech사에 의해 출시될 예정인 게임 시스템 CP3 Console을 주문하셨습니다. 유감스럽게도, ¹⁴⁹이 매우 기대되는 기기를 예약할 수 있는 옵션이 원래 그래야만 했던 것보다 훨씬 이전에 실수로 Kimbel 백화점의 웹사이트에서 이용할 수 있게 되었습니다. 결과적으로, 저희는 귀하의 주문을 취소해야 합니다. 저희는 이번 실수에 대해 정말 죄송하게 생각하며 ¹⁵⁰고객분들이 상품을 주문할 수 있게 되자마자 귀하께 알려드릴 것을 약속드립니다. 저희는 또한 귀하께서 이 상품에 대한 어떠한 최신 정보든 찾기 위해 저희의 상품 페이지를 정기적으로 방문하시길 권장합니다.

¹⁴⁹귀하께서 신용카드로 지불하셨다면, 환불은 24시간 이내에 처리될 것입니다. 상품권을 사용하여 지불하셨다면, 귀하의 돈이 환불되기 위해 5일까지 감안해주시기 바랍니다.

Kimbel 백화점 고객 서비스 드림

place an order 주문하다 due adj. ~할 예정인 reserve v. 예약하다
highly adv. 매우, 몹시 anticipated adj. 기대되는
mistakenly adv. 실수로, 잘못하여 available adj. 이용할 수 있는
notify v. 알리다 as soon as ~하자마자 regularly adv. 정기적으로
refund n. 환불; v. 환불하다

149 | 추론 문제

해설 Mr. Sutton에 대해 암시되는 것은?
(A) 결함이 있는 제품을 구매했다.
(B) 실수로 주문을 취소했다.
(C) 상품권으로 제품을 결제했다.
(D) 지난 금요일에 온라인으로 비용을 지불했다.

해설 지문의 'Last Friday, you placed an order for the CP3 Console, a gaming system ~'과 'the option to reserve this highly anticipated device was mistakenly made available on Kimbel Department Store's Web site ~'에서 귀하, 즉 Mr. Sutton이 지난 금요일에 게임 시스템 CP3 Console을 주문했으며, 기기를 예약할 수 있는 옵션이 실수로 Kimbel 백화점의 웹사이트에서 이용할 수 있게 되었다고 했고, 'If you paid by credit card, ~. If you paid using a gift card, ~.'에서 신용카드와 상품권으로 돈을 지불한 경우에 대한 환불 처리에 대해 설명하고 있으므로 Mr. Sutton이 지난 금요일에 온라인으로 비용을 지불했음을 추론할 수 있다. 따라서 (D)가 정답이다.

어휘 defective adj. 결함이 있는 submit a payment 비용을 지불하다

150 | 육하원칙 문제

해설 Kimbel 백화점은 언제 Mr. Sutton에게 다시 연락할 것인가?
(A) 환불 요청이 승인된 후에
(B) 기기가 구매 가능해질 때
(C) 상점 재고가 다시 채워진 후에
(D) 상품 출시 장소가 알려질 때

해설 지문의 'we will notify you as soon as customers are able to order the product'에서 고객들이 상품을 주문할 수 있게 되자마자 알려드리겠다고 했으므로 (B)가 정답이다.

어휘 request n. 요청; v. 요청하다 approve v. 승인하다 inventory n. 재고 restock v. 다시 채우다 reveal v. 알리다, 드러내다

Paraphrasing

able to order 주문할 수 있는 → available for purchase 구매 가능한

151-152번은 다음 기사에 관한 문제입니다.

도시 이야기   Hamilton Enquirer지
Hamilton 출신이 상을 받다
Troy Cheung 작성

1월 6일—¹⁵¹Vino Kiwi사의 최고 경영자 Gloria Wilson이 지난주 전국 비즈니스 포럼(NBF)으로부터 올해의 회사 상을 받았다. 뉴질랜드의 와인 고장에서의 여행 상품들을 제공하는 그녀의 회사는 관광업 부문에서 몇몇 경쟁사들을 이겼다.

매년, 다양한 ¹⁵²전문 기관들이 고려할 회사들을 후보로 추천한다. NBF는 그 다음에 각 분야에서 최고의 회사를 결정하기 위해 서비스 수준 및 고객 만족과 같은 다양한 기준들로 이 회사들을 평가한다. 이 과정에서 Vino Kiwi사는 5점 만점에 4.5점을 받았다.

의견을 말해달라는 요청을 받았을 때, Ms. Wilson은 "이것은 수년간의 노력을 입증해주는 대단한 영광입니다."라고 말했다. 그녀는 가족, 친구들, 그리고 동료들에게 그들의 지지에 대해 감사를 표현했으며, 대중들에게는 그녀의 서비스를 이용해볼 것을 권유했다. Vino Kiwi사에 관한 더 많은 정보는 www.vinokiwi.com에서 찾을 수 있다.

holiday package 여행 상품 competitor n. 경쟁자, 경쟁사
tourism n. 관광업 category n. 부문 a wide range of 다양한
professional adj. 전문적인 nominate v. (후보로) 추천하다, 지명하다
consideration n. 고려 evaluate v. 평가하다 firm n. 회사
criteria n. 기준 determine v. 결정하다 process n. 과정
comment v. 의견을 말하다, 논평하다 honor n. 영광 validate v. 입증하다
support n. 지지, 도움

151 | 주제 찾기 문제

해석 기사는 주로 무엇에 대한 것인가?
(A) 지역 산업에 대한 정부 규제들
(B) 사업 단체의 자선 기부금
(C) 단체의 회원 기준
(D) 사업체의 최근 성취

해설 지문의 'Vino Kiwi CEO ~ received the Company of the Year award ~ last week.'에서 Vino Kiwi사의 최고 경영자가 지난주 올해의 회사 상을 받았다고 한 후, 회사의 수상 내용에 대해 설명하고 있으므로 (D)가 정답이다.

어휘 regulation n. 규제 local adj. 지역의 charitable adj. 자선의
contribution n. 기부금, 기여 accomplishment n. 성취

152 | 육하원칙 문제

해석 기사에 따르면, 전국 비즈니스 포럼의 임무 중 하나는 무엇인가?
(A) 세계 시장에서 사업체들을 홍보하는 것
(B) 지역 회사들을 지원하는 자금을 관리하는 것
(C) 다른 기관들로부터의 추천을 평가하는 것
(D) 국가를 대표할 기업가들을 선정하는 것

해설 지문의 'professional organizations nominate companies for consideration. The NBF then evaluates these firms on diverse criteria ~ to determine the best company in each field.'에서 전문

기관들이 고려할 회사들을 후보로 추천하면, NBF는 그 다음에 각 분야에서 최고의 회사를 결정하기 위해 이 회사들을 평가한다고 했으므로 (C)가 정답이다.

어휘 promote v. 홍보하다 fund n. 자금 assess v. 평가하다
recommendation n. 추천 entrepreneur n. 기업가
represent v. 대표하다

Paraphrasing

evaluates 평가하다 → Assessing 평가하는 것

153-155번은 다음 회람에 관한 문제입니다.

회람

수신: 전 직원
발신: Curtis Henderson, 관리자
날짜: 8월 29일
제목: 주간 진행 보고서

¹⁵³직원들에 의해 제출되고 있는 주간 진행 보고서들이 일관성 없고 불완전할 뿐만 아니라, 많은 경우에 늦게 제출되기도 한다는 것을 알게 되었습니다. 이 보고서들은 Mayfield사에서 여러분의 발전을 평가하는 데 중요한 역할을 합니다. 그러므로, 그 내용과 보고서를 제출하는 방식은 여러분의 분기별 평가에 분명히 영향을 끼칠 것입니다.

여러분이 보고서를 제시간에 제출하는 것을 돕고 그 내용이 전 부서에 걸쳐 획일적이도록 확실히 하기 위해, ¹⁵⁴우리는 이번 주부터 여러분이 사용할 새로운 양식을 만들었습니다. 그 양식은 여러분의 상관들에 의해 배포될 것인데, 그들이 양식을 어떻게 작성하는지와 무슨 정보가 요구되는지를 알려 줄 것입니다. 이 지시 사항들은 정확하게 지켜져야 합니다. 만약 정보가 누락되었거나 불명확하면, 보고서는 수정을 위해 여러분에게 돌려보내질 것입니다.

¹⁵⁵여러분은 이 보고서를 매주 금요일 오후 5시 30분에 제출하도록 요구됩니다. 휴가 중이거나 병가 중인 사람들만 이 마감 기한을 엄수하지 않아도 됩니다. 제시간에 보고서를 제출하지 않는 것은 여러분의 평가에 반영될 것입니다. 이는 또한 궁극적으로 여러분이 승진되거나 급여 인상을 받을 가능성에 영향을 끼칠 것입니다. 저는 여러분이 제대로 작성된 주간 진행 보고서를 상관에게 제시간에 전달하는 데 전적으로 협조해 주시길 바랍니다.

감사합니다.

progress n. 진행, 발전 submit v. 제출하다
inconsistent adj. 일관성 없는, 모순된 incomplete adj. 불완전한, 미완성의
turn in 제출하다 occasion n. 경우, 때, 행사 assess v. 평가하다
hence adv. 그러므로, 이런 이유로 definitely adv. 분명히, 틀림없이
quarterly adj. 분기별의 evaluation n. 평가, 사정 ensure v. 확실히 하다
uniform adj. 획일적인, 균일한 distribute v. 배포하다, 분배하다
supervisor n. 상관, 감독관 reflect v. 반영하다, 영향을 미치다
ultimately adv. 궁극적으로 promote v. 승진시키다, 촉진하다
salary n. 급여, 임금 properly adv. 제대로, 적절히

153 | 육하원칙 문제

해석 Mr. Henderson은 어떤 문제를 언급하는가?
(A) 직원들이 요구 사항을 제대로 충족시키지 않고 있다.
(B) 재무 보고서가 완료되지 않았다.
(C) 직원들이 낮은 평가 점수를 받았다.
(D) 고객들이 작업의 품질에 대해 불평했다.

해설 지문의 'It has come to my attention that the weekly progress reports ~ are not only inconsistent and incomplete but are also turned in late on many occasions.'에서 주간 진행 보고서들이 일관성 없고 불완전할 뿐만 아니라 많은 경우에 늦게 제출된다고 했으므로 (A)가 정답이다.

어휘 fulfill v. 충족시키다, 이행하다   requirement n. 요구 사항, 필요조건

154 | 육하원칙 문제

해석 상사들은 이번 주에 무엇을 할 것인가?
(A) 직원의 승진 적합성을 평가한다.
(B) 보고의 새로운 방식을 설명한다.
(C) 휴가 신청 양식을 수거한다.
(D) 발표에 필요한 서류를 수정한다.

해설 지문의 'we have designed a new form ~. The form will be distributed to you by your supervisors, who will explain how to fill it in and what information is required.'에서 이번 주부터 사용할 새로운 양식을 만들었다고 하고, 그 양식은 상관들에 의해 배포될 것이고, 그들이 그것을 어떻게 작성하는지와 무슨 정보가 요구되는지를 알려 줄 것이라고 했으므로 (B)가 정답이다.

어휘 suitability n. 적합성

Paraphrasing

explain 설명하다 → Demonstrate 설명하다

155 | 추론 문제

해석 Mr. Henderson이 마감 기한을 어기는 것에 대해 암시하는 것은?
(A) 상관과 직원 관계에 영향을 끼칠 것이다.
(B) 오직 명시된 사유에만 용인된다.
(C) 부서장의 체면을 손상시킬 것이다.
(D) 해명이 뒷받침되어야만 한다.

해설 지문의 'You are expected to submit these reports every Friday at 5:30 P.M. Only those on vacation or on sick leave are not required to meet this deadline.'에서 매주 금요일 오후 5시 30분에 보고서를 제출하도록 요구되는데 휴가 중이거나 병가 중인 사람들만이 이 기한을 엄수하지 않아도 된다고 했으므로, 오직 명시된 사유에만 마감 기한을 어기는 것이 용인됨을 추론할 수 있다. 따라서 (B)가 정답이다.

어휘 acceptable adj. 용인되는   specify v. 명시하다
reflect poorly on ~의 체면을 손상시키다   support v. 뒷받침하다
explanation n. 해명, 설명

Paraphrasing

not ~ meet this deadline 이 마감 기한을 엄수하지 않다 → missing the deadline 마감 기한을 어기는 것

156-157번은 다음 문자 메시지 대화문에 관한 문제입니다.

Frank Danes (오전 10시 40분)
귀찮게 해서 죄송하지만, 제가 금요일에 일찍 퇴근할 수 있을지 궁금해서요. 제가 주말 동안 덴버에 갈 예정인데 오후 4시 비행기를 타고 싶어요. 점심 식사 후에 퇴근해도 될까요?

Maria Faubert (오전 10시 42분)
그때 사무실이 그렇게 바쁠 것 같진 않은데, 156완료되어야 하는 급한 일은 아무것도 없는 게 확실한가요?

Frank Danes (오전 10시 43분)
보류 중인 것은 아무것도 없어요.

Maria Faubert (오전 10시 45분)
그렇다면 괜찮을 거예요. 금요일 아침에 제게 상기만 시켜주세요.

Frank Danes (오전 10시 48분)
좋아요! 아, 157제가 이것에 대해 휴가 신청서를 작성해야 하지 않나요?

Maria Faubert (오전 10시 50분)
157아니요, 하루 종일이 아니라서요.

Frank Danes (오전 10시 51분)
이해했어요. 감사합니다.

bother v. 귀찮게 하다, 괴롭히다   wonder v. 궁금하다   get off 퇴근하다
urgent adj. 급한   pending adj. 보류 중인, 미결인   fill out 작성하다
request n. 신청(서)

156 | 의도 파악 문제

해석 오전 10시 43분에, Mr. Danes가 "Nothing is pending"이라고 썼을 때, 그가 의도한 것 같은 것은?
(A) 특별한 요청을 받지 않았다.
(B) 항공편을 구할 수 있는지 확실하지 않다.
(C) 즉각적인 처리가 필요한 업무가 없다.
(D) 프로젝트 마감일을 옮길 수 있었다.

해설 지문의 'are you sure nothing urgent needs to be done?'에서 Ms. Faubert가 완료되어야 하는 급한 일은 아무것도 없는 게 확실하냐고 묻자, Mr. Danes가 'Nothing is pending'(보류 중인 것은 아무것도 없어요)이라고 한 것을 통해 Mr. Danes는 즉각적인 처리가 필요한 업무가 없음을 알 수 있다. 따라서 (C)가 정답이다.

어휘 receive v. 받다   uncertain adj. 확실하지 않은   immediate adj. 즉각적인
attention n. 처리, 주의

157 | 추론 문제

해석 회사에 대해 암시되는 것은?
(A) 하루 종일의 부재에 대해서는 직원들에게 양식 작성을 요구한다.
(B) 보통 오후 4시에 끝난다.
(C) 매주 직원 교육 시간을 준비한다.
(D) 출장을 위해 여행 준비를 해준다.

해설 지문의 'don't I need to fill out a leave request form for this?'에서 Mr. Danes가 이것, 즉 금요일에 일찍 퇴근하는 것에 대해 휴가 신청서를 작성해야 하는 것이 아닌지 묻자, Ms. Faubert가 'No, because it isn't a full day.'에서 하루 종일이 아니라서 그럴 필요가 없다고 했으므로 하루 종일의 부재에 대해서는 직원들에게 양식 작성을 요구함을 추론할 수 있다. 따라서 (A)가 정답이다.

어휘 absence n. 부재, 결근   organize v. 준비하다   arrangement n. 준비
business trip 출장

158-160번은 다음 회람에 관한 문제입니다.

Peele, Knowles, and Associates사
수신: 비서진
발신: Marjorie Dodds, 사무실 관리자

저는 법률 사무소의 비서진에게 점심시간 관련 회사 규정이 업데이트되었음을 알려드리게 되어 기쁩니다. 지난주 우리의 회의 동안 여러분의 의견을 받은 후, 158경영진은 다음의 변경사항들을 이행하기로 결정했습니다:

점심시간은 금요일에 30분 연장되어, 오후 12시에서 오후 1시 30분까지 계속될 것입니다. 이 시간 동안, 사무실은 문을 닫을 것이므로, 여러분의 전화를 저희의 자동 응답 서비스로 반드시 변경해주십시오. 저희의 단골 고객들에게도 이 변경사항에 대해 꼭 알려주십시오. 159행정 직원들이 기계에 새로운 메시지를 녹음하는 것을 맡을 것입니다.

160-(A)/(C) 비서진은 이제 점심시간 동안 일을 하라는 상사로부터의 요청을 거부할 수 있습니다. 물론, 초과 근무를 한다면 여러분은 평상시 급료의 두 배를 받을 것입니다.

이러한 변경사항들에 관하여 질문이 있으신 분들은 저에게 바로 이야기하시거나 marjdodds@peeleknowlesassoc.com으로 제게 이메일을 보내주시면 됩니다.

```
secretarial staff 비서진   extend v. 연장하다   switch v. 변경하다
notify v. 알리다, 공지하다   administrative adj. 행정의   take care of ~을 맡다
record v. 녹음하다, 기록하다   turn down 거부하다, 거절하다
superior n. 상사   overtime n. 초과 근무
```

158 | 동의어 찾기 문제

해석 1문단 세 번째 줄의 단어 "implement"는 의미상 -와 가장 가깝다.
(A) 설명하다
(B) 이행하다
(C) 처리하다
(D) 돌보다

해설 implement를 포함한 구절 'management has decided to implement the following changes'에서 implement는 '이행하다'라는 뜻으로 사용되었다. 따라서 (B)가 정답이다.

159 | 추론 문제

해석 행정 직원은 무엇을 할 예정인 것 같은가?
(A) 직원들에 의해 사용되는 휴가의 개수를 관리한다.
(B) 규정에 대한 의견과 제안들을 모은다.
(C) 수신 전화를 위한 녹음 메시지를 만들어낸다.
(D) 휴식 시간 동안 접수처를 인계받는다.

해설 지문의 'The administrative staff will take care of recording a new message for the machine.'에서 행정 직원들이 기계에 새로운 메시지를 녹음하는 것을 맡을 것이라고 했으므로 행정 직원들이 수신 전화를 위한 녹음 메시지를 만들어낼 것임을 추론할 수 있다. 따라서 (C)가 정답이다.

어휘 monitor v. 관리하다   gather v. 모으다, 수집하다   comment n. 의견
incoming call 수신 전화

160 | Not/True 문제

해석 비서진에 대해 언급된 것은?
(A) 그들의 점심시간 동안 근무하는 것에 대해 추가 급여를 받을 것이다.
(B) 초과 근무를 하기 위해서 관리자들로부터 허가를 받아야 한다.
(C) 요청받는다면 점심시간 동안 근무해야 할 의무가 있다.
(D) 관리자에게 그들의 휴식 일정표를 이메일로 보내야 한다.

해설 회람의 'Secretarial staff may ~ turn down requests ~ to work through the lunch break. ~ if they do work overtime, they will receive double their usual pay.'에서 비서진은 점심시간 동안 일을 하라는 요청을 거부할 수 있고, 초과 근무를 한다면 평상시 급료의 두 배를 받을 것이라고 했으므로 (A)가 정답이다. (B)와 (D)는 지문에 언급되지 않은 내용이다. 회람의 'Secretarial staff may now turn down requests from superiors to work through the lunch break.'에서 비서진은 이제 점심시간 동안 일을 하라는 상사로부터의 요청을 거부할 수 있다고 했으므로, (C)는 지문의 내용과 일치하지 않는다.

어휘 extra adj. 추가의   permission n. 허가   supervisor n. 관리자
obligated to ~할 의무가 있는

Paraphrasing

double their usual pay 평상시 급료의 두 배 → extra pay 추가 급여

161-163번은 다음 기사에 관한 문제입니다.

당신이 사업체 협회에 가입해야 하는 이유
Jan de Vries 작성

사업체 협회에 가입하는 것은 사업주들에게 지명도, 인적 교류 기회, 그리고 교육과 같은 많은 혜택을 제공한다. 이러한 것들 및 다른 이점들은 당신의 사업이 성장하고 번창하기 위해 필요한 안성맞춤의 것일 수 있다. — [1] —.

예를 들어, ¹⁶²Martha Yancey가 그녀의 그래픽 디자인 회사를 10년 전에 처음 열었을 때, 지역 사회에서 그녀가 잘 알려져 있지 않았기 때문에 고객들을 찾는 것이 어려웠다. ¹⁶¹한 사업체 협회에 가입함으로써, 그녀는 자신을 잠재적인 고객들에게 소개하고 많은 고객 소개를 받을 수 있었다. — [2] —. "또한," 그녀는 말했다. "¹⁶¹저의 교류들은 저의 현재 전기 기사와 회계사처럼, 제게 필수적인 서비스를 제공해 줄 수 있는 다른 사업주들에게로 저를 이끌었어요."

마찬가지로, ¹⁶²Lucas Smitt이 사업을 시작했을 때, 그는 가구 수리에 대해서는 많은 것을 알고 있었지만, 사업체를 운영하는 것에 대해서는 거의 아무것도 알지 못했다. "사업체 협회의 회원 자격을 통해, 저는 무료 및 할인된 세미나, 워크숍, 그리고 온라인 수업들에 대한 이용 권한을 얻을 수 있었습니다. — [3] —. 이것들로부터, 저는 회사를 올바르게 운영하는 방법에 대해 배웠습니다." ¹⁶²이번 11월, Smitt Restoration은 그것의 성공적인 10주년을 기념할 예정이다.

물론, 언급된 것과 같은 혜택들이 항상 무료인 것은 아니다. ¹⁶³대부분의 협회들은 연간 회비를 청구하며, 공식적인 모임과 행사에 정기적인 참여를 바란다. — [4] —.

```
association n. 협회   business owner 사업주   visibility n. 지명도
networking n. 인적 교류   advantage n. 이점   thrive v. 번창하다
potential adj. 잠재적인   referral n. 소개, 추천   interaction n. 교류, 상호작용
essential adj. 필수적인   electrician n. 전기 기사   accountant n. 회계사
similarly adv. 마찬가지로   start out 사업을 시작하다   operate v. 운영하다
access n. 이용 권한; v. 접근하다   discounted adj. 할인된
properly adv. 올바르게   naturally adv. 물론, 자연스럽게
participation n. 참여   function n. 모임, 행사
```

161 | 추론 문제

해석 Ms. Yancey에 대해 암시되는 것은?
(A) 처음에 새로운 친구들을 만나기 위해 단체에 가입하였다.
(B) 그녀의 회사는 접근하기 어려운 위치에 있었다.
(C) 다른 회원으로부터 그녀의 상품 아이디어를 얻었다.
(D) 그녀의 회계사를 사업체 협회를 통해 만났다.

해설 지문의 'By joining a business association'에서 Ms. Yancey가 사업체 협회에 가입했다고 했고, 'my interactions led me to other business owners ~ like my current ~ accountant'에서 Ms. Yancey의 교류들, 즉 사업체 협회를 통한 교류들이 현재 그녀의 회계사와 같은 다른 사업주들에게 그녀를 이끌었다고 했으므로, Ms. Yancey는 그녀의 회계사를 사업체 협회를 통해 만났음을 추론할 수 있다. 따라서 (D)가 정답이다.

162 | 추론 문제

해석 Mr. Smitt에 대해 추론될 수 있는 것은?
(A) 그의 회사를 시작했을 때 아직 학교에 다니고 있었다.
(B) Ms. Yancey에 의해 사업체 협회에 소개되었다.
(C) Ms. Yancey와 거의 같은 시기에 회사를 열었다.
(D) 다른 젊은 사업가들에게 그들의 사업체를 운영하는 방법에 대해 가르친다.

해설 지문의 'Martha Yancey first opened her graphic design company a decade ago'에서 Ms. Yancey가 그녀의 그래픽 디자인 회사를 10년 전에 처음 열었다고 했고, 'when Lucas Smitt was starting out'과 'This November, Smitt Restoration will be celebrating its 10th successful year.'에서 Mr. Smitt이 설립한 Smitt Restoration은 이번 11월에 성공적인 10주년을 기념할 예정이라고 했으므로 Mr. Smitt과 Ms. Yancey는 10년 전 거의 같은 시기에 회사를 열었음을 추론할 수 있다. 따라서 (C)가 정답이다.

어휘 entrepreneur n. 사업가

163 | 문장 위치 찾기 문제

해석 [1], [2], [3], [4]로 표시된 위치 중, 다음 문장이 들어갈 곳으로 가장 적절한 것은?

"그러나, 이 비용은 대가로 제공되는 가치에 비해 적습니다."

(A) [1]
(B) [2]
(C) [3]
(D) [4]

해설 주어진 문장은 비용과 관련된 내용 주변에 나올 것임을 예상할 수 있다. [4]의 앞 문장인 'Most associations charge an annual membership fee'에서 대부분의 협회들은 연간 회비를 청구한다고 했으므로, [4]에 주어진 문장이 들어가면 대부분의 협회들이 연간 회비를 청구하지만, 이 비용은 대가로 제공되는 가치에 비해 적다는 자연스러운 문맥이 된다는 것을 알 수 있다. 따라서 (D)가 정답이다.

어휘 compared to ~에 비해, ~와 비교하여 in return 대가로, 보답으로

164-167번은 다음 온라인 채팅 대화문에 관한 문제입니다.

Travis Coleman [오후 12시]
¹⁶⁴James Vine이라는 이름의 누군가가 전화하여 호텔이 새로운 장비를 살 것인지 물었어요.

Sheila Leblanc [오후 12시 3분]
맞아요. ¹⁶⁴지난주에 제가 그와 대화를 나누었고 우리에게 카탈로그를 보내 달라고 그에게 요청했어요. Travis, 제가 그것을 안내데스크에 당신에게 맡겼어요.

Gabby Ross [오후 12시 4분]
가능하다면, 저는 이제 식사 공간이 확장되었기 때문에 그것을 위해 우리가 더 큰 뷔페 테이블을 구매해야 한다고 생각해요. 그건 그렇고, ¹⁶⁵다른 수리들은 어떻게 되어가고 있나요?

Sheila Leblanc [오후 12시 4분]
문제가 되고 있어요. ¹⁶⁵저희가 고용했던 계약자들이 수영장이 제때 준비되지 않을 것이라고 말해요. 호텔 문을 다시 여는 것을 2주 더 연기해야 할 수도 있어요.

Sheila Leblanc [오후 12시 4분]
뷔페 테이블에 관해서는, 저도 동의해요. 안내 책자에서 두 개를 표시해 놓았어요. Travis, Gabby를 위해 그것들을 찾아서 설명해줄 수 있나요?

Travis Coleman [오후 12시 7분]
그럼요. ¹⁶⁶첫 번째 것은 검은색이고 유리로 된 재채기 막이와 진열대 아래의 냉장 장치를 갖추고 있어요. 두 번째 것은 단풍나무 재목이고 음식 팬 위의 열 램프와 얼음을 담는 상자가 있어요. 어느 것을 선호하나요?

Gabby Ross [오후 12시 10분]
¹⁶⁶첫 번째 것이 더 좋아 보이네요. 단지 얼음으로만 음식을 시원하게 유지하기가 쉽지 않잖아요. 하지만 최종 결정을 내리기 전에 그것에 대해 생각할 시간이 좀 필요할 것 같아요.

Sheila Leblanc [오후 12시 11분]
알겠어요, 제게 알려주세요. ¹⁶⁷오늘 레크리에이션실을 마무리할 예정이라서, 만약 제가 필요하다면 저는 지하에 있을 거예요.

---

equipment n. 장비 renovation n. 수리, 보수 challenge n. 문제
contractor n. 계약자 delay v. 연기하다
bookmark v. (나중에 참조할 수 있도록) 표시를 해두다
sneeze guard 재채기 막이 (식품의 오염 방지를 위해 덮는 유리판)
counter n. 진열대 refrigeration n. 냉장 (장치) tray n. 상자, 쟁반

164 | 육하원칙 문제

해석 Mr. Coleman은 최근 누구와 이야기했는가?
(A) 호텔 관리자
(B) 행사 주최자
(C) 부동산 중개인
(D) 장비 판매원

해설 지문의 'Someone ~ called to ask whether the hotel will be purchasing any new equipment.'에서 Mr. Coleman이 누군가가 전화하여 호텔이 새로운 장비를 살 것인지 물었다고 했고, 'I talked to him last week and asked him to send us a catalog.'에서 Ms. Leblanc이 지난주에 그와 대화를 나누었고 자신들에게 카탈로그를 보내 달라고 그에게 요청했다고 했다. 따라서 (D)가 정답이다.

어휘 organizer n. 주최자 salesperson n. 판매원

165 | 의도 파악 문제

해석 오후 12시 4분에 Ms. Leblanc이 "They've been a challenge"라고 썼을 때 그녀가 의도한 것은?
(A) 리모델링 프로젝트의 진행이 느리다.
(B) 몇몇 제품 설명서가 이해하기 어렵다.
(C) 작업이 서비스 제공업체들에 의해 완료될 수 없다.
(D) 몇몇 가전제품들에 설명서가 딸려 있지 않았다.

해설 지문의 'how are the other renovations going?'에서 Ms. Ross가 다른 수리들은 어떻게 되어가고 있는지 묻자, Ms. Leblanc이 'They've been a challenge'(문제가 되고 있어요)라고 한 후, 'The contractors ~ say the pool won't be ready in time.'에서 계약자들이 수영장이 제때 준비되지 않을 것이라고 말했다고 한 것을 통해, 리모델링 프로젝트의 진행이 느리다는 것을 알 수 있다. 따라서 (A)가 정답이다.

어휘 progress n. 진행 description n. 설명(서) appliance n. 가전제품, 기구
come with ~이 딸려 있다 instruction n. 설명(서)

166 | 추론 문제

해석 뷔페 테이블의 어떤 특징이 Ms. Ross의 결정에 영향을 미칠 것 같은가?
(A) 달려 있는 발열체
(B) 견목 외부
(C) 내장된 냉장고
(D) 유리로 된 재채기 막이

해설 지문의 'The first one ~ has ~ under-the-counter refrigeration.'에서 Mr. Coleman이 첫 번째 것은 진열대 아래의 냉장 장치를 갖추고 있다고 하자, 'The first one sounds better. It's not easy to keep food cool just with ice.'에서 Ms. Ross가 첫 번째 것이 더 좋아 보이며, 단지 얼음으로만 음식을 시원하게 유지하기가 쉽지 않다고 했으므로 내장된 냉장고가 Ms. Ross의 결정에 영향을 미칠 것임을 추론할 수 있다. 따라서 (C)가 정답이다.

어휘 heating adj. 발열의 hardwood n. 견목 exterior n. 외부
built-in adj. 내장된

Paraphrasing

under-the-counter refrigeration 진열대 아래의 냉장 장치 → built-in refrigerators 내장된 냉장고

167 | 육하원칙 문제

해석 Ms. Leblanc은 곧 어디에 갈 예정인가?
(A) 수영장
(B) 안내 데스크
(C) 식사 공간
(D) 레크리에이션실

해설 지문의 'I'm finishing up the recreation room today, so I'll be down in the basement if you need me.'에서 Ms. Leblanc이 오늘 레크리에이션실을 마무리할 예정이라서 자신이 필요하다면 자신은 지하에 있을 것이라고 했으므로 (D)가 정답이다.

168-171번은 다음 이메일에 관한 문제입니다.

발신: Jean-Luc Caron <jlc@caronwrites.uk>
171-(A)수신: Olivia Wright <oliv@okaypubs.com>
제목: Diot 프로젝트
날짜: 6월 8일

Ms. Wright께,

제가 오늘 저의 은행 잔고를 확인하였을 때, Okay 출판사에 의해 10,770달러가 제 계좌로 송금되었음을 확인했습니다. 168저는 귀사의 때맞춘 지급에 감사드리지만, 제 계산에 따르면, 이 액수는 232.05달러가 부족합니다. 제가 The Thoughts of Anne Diot을 프랑스어에서 영어로 번역하는 계약에 서명하기 전에, 대금은 한 단어당 0.15달러로 합의되었습니다. 169게다가, 제 기록은 책의 본문이 총 71,800개의 단어가 되었음을 나타내며, 이는 제가 지불받았던 것에 해당하는 정확한 분량입니다. 귀하께서 알고 계시는지 잘 모르겠습니다만, 지난주에 170Mr. Stuart가 그가 새로 쓴 각주들을 제게 보냈는데, 이들 역시 번역이 필요했습니다. 1,547개의 단어로 구성된 이 각주들은, 제 보수가 계산되었을 때 고려되지 않던 것처럼 보입니다.

프로젝트의 총 단어 수를 재확인해주시길 바라며, 만약 정말 실수가 있었다면 제게 알려주십시오. 171-(A)귀사의 프로젝트들은 보통 내부의 직원들에 의해서만 처리된다고 알고 있으며, 어쩌면 이것이 지불에 대한 혼동으로 이어졌을 것입니다.

Jean-Luc Caron 드림

balance n. 잔고 transfer v. 송금하다 account n. 계좌
appreciate v. 감사하다 timely adj. 때맞춘 payment n. 지급
calculation n. 계산 sum n. 액수, 합계 short adj. 부족한, 불충분한
translate v. 번역하다 rate n. 대금, 비용 indicate v. 나타내다, 보여주다
total v. 총 ~이 되다; adj. 총, 전체의; n. 합계
footnote n. 각주(책 페이지 하단에 붙이는 주석) consist of ~으로 구성되다
double-check v. 재확인하다 indeed adv. 정말 handle v. 처리하다
in-house adj. 내부의 confusion n. 혼동

168 | 목적 찾기 문제

해석 Mr. Caron은 왜 이메일을 썼는가?
(A) 거래액 오류를 알려 주기 위해
(B) 몇몇 글쓰기 지시사항들을 명확하게 하기 위해
(C) 원고에 대해 수정들을 제안하기 위해
(D) 기한이 지난 업무를 끝까지 하기 위해

해설 지문의 'While I appreciate ~ timely payment, ~ this sum is short by $232.05.'에서 때맞춘 지급에 감사하지만, 액수가 232.05달러 부족하다고 했으므로 (A)가 정답이다.

어휘 point out 알려 주다, 지적하다 billing n. 거래액 clarify v. 명확하게 하다
instruction n. 지시(사항) correction n. 수정 manuscript n. 원고
follow up on ~을 끝까지 하다 overdue adj. 기한이 지난

Paraphrasing

sum is short 액수가 부족하다 → billing error 거래액 오류

169 | 동의어 찾기 문제

해설 1문단 여섯 번째 줄의 단어 "precise"는 의미상 -와 가장 가깝다.
(A) 엄격한
(B) 가까운
(C) 사실인
(D) 정확한

해설 precise를 포함한 구절 'Further, my records indicate that the main text of the book totaled 71,800 words, which was the precise amount for which I was paid.'에서 precise는 '정확한'이라는 뜻으로 사용되었다. 따라서 (D)가 정답이다.

170 | 추론 문제

해석 Mr. Stuart는 누구일 것 같은가?
(A) 작가
(B) 출판 관리자
(C) 문서 번역가
(D) 잡지 편집자

해설 지문의 'Mr. Stuart sent ~ his newly written footnotes'에서 Mr. Stuart가 그가 새로 쓴 각주들을 보냈다고 한 것을 통해 Mr. Stuart가 작가임을 알 수 있다. 따라서 (A)가 정답이다.

어휘 author n. 작가, 저자 publishing n. 출판(사업) translator n. 번역가

171 | Not/True 문제

해석 Ms. Wright에 대해 명시된 것은?
(A) 외부 계약자들과는 드물게 일을 한다.
(B) 현재 환율을 확인하지 않았다.
(C) 재무부의 관리자이다.
(D) 계약을 수정해야 할 것이다.

해설 지문의 'To: Olivia Wright'에서 이메일이 Ms. Wright에게 쓰였음을 확인할 수 있고 'your projects are usually only handled by in-house staff members'에서 귀사, 즉 Ms. Wright이 일하는 회사의 프로젝트들은 보통 내부의 직원들에 의해서만 처리된다고 했으므로 (A)는 지문의 내용과 일치한다. 따라서 (A)가 정답이다. (B), (C), (D)는 지문에 언급되지 않은 내용이다.

어휘 exchange rate 환율 director n. 관리자 revise v. 수정하다

Paraphrasing

projects are usually only handled by in-house staff members
프로젝트들은 보통 내부의 직원들에 의해서만 처리된다 → rarely works with outside contractors 외부 계약자들과 드물게 일을 하다

172-175번은 다음 양식에 관한 문제입니다.

OAKPORT COMPUTING사
직업 교육 프로그램

Oakport Computing사는 직업 교육 프로그램을 통해 직원들에게 그들의 기술과 지식을 향상시킬 수 있는 기회를 정기적으로 제공합니다. ─ [1] ─.

아래 강좌들의 목록은 전 직원들에 의해 완료된 온라인 설문조사를 바탕으로 합니다. 173표시된 곳을 제외하고, 각 강좌는 반나절 안에 완료될 수 있도록 계획되었습니다. 그러나, 172예산 제한 때문에, 저희는 한 번에 단 3개만 제공할 수 있습니다. ─ [2] ─. 첨부된 양식을 사용하여, 참석하는 것에 가장 관심 있는 3개의 강좌를 선택하시고 6월 3일까지 제출하여 주십시오. 172/174회사는 6월 6일에 모두의 선택을 바탕으로 최종 선정된 강좌들을 공개하고 강좌 날짜를 발표할 것입니다. ─ [3] ─.

172/174참석하는 것에 가장 관심 있는 3개의 강좌를 선택해 주십시오:

직원 이름: Kevin Montoya 날짜: 6월 1일
- 일반적인 직무 기술
  ___ 시간 관리
  ___ 발표 기술
  ___ 문제 해결*
  ✓ ¹⁷³팀과의 협업
- 전문적인 기술
  ___ 고급 프로그래밍*
  ✓ 빅 데이터 분석*
  ✓ 네트워크 보안*
  ___ 사용자 인터페이스 디자인

¹⁷³* 일일 강좌

어떤 강좌들이 제공될 것인지 알기 위해서는, 6월 6일에 www.oakport.com/training으로 가십시오. 등록하는 방법에 대한 정보도 있을 것입니다. ¹⁷⁵직원들은 참석하기 위해 그들의 관리자로부터 허가를 얻어 낼 책임이 있습니다. ─ [4] ─.

어휘 enhance v. 향상시키다 course n. 강좌 indicate v. 표시하다, 가리키다 restriction n. 제한 at a time 한 번에 present v. 공개하다, 보여주다 announce v. 발표하다 management n. 관리 advanced adj. 고급의 analysis n. 분석 responsible for ~할 책임이 있는 secure v. 얻어 내다, 확보하다 supervisor n. 관리자

172 | 목적 찾기 문제

해석 양식의 목적은 무엇인가?
(A) 자원봉사자들에게 활동에 참여할 것을 권하기 위해
(B) 선택 과목 목록을 줄이기 위해
(C) 한 강좌에 대한 의견을 수집하기 위해
(D) 신입 직원들을 위한 강좌를 알리기 위해

해설 지문의 'due to budget restrictions, we can only offer three at a time'에서 예산 제한 때문에 한 번에 단 3개, 즉 3개의 강좌만 제공할 수 있다고 한 후, 'The company will present a final selection of courses based on everyone's choices ~'에서 회사는 모두의 선택을 바탕으로 최종 선정된 강좌를 공개할 것이라 했고, 'Please choose the three courses that you are most interested in attending'에서 참석하는 것에 가장 관심 있는 3개의 강좌를 선택해 달라고 했으므로 (B)가 정답이다.

어휘 invite v. 권하다, 초대하다 option n. 선택 과목 feedback n. 의견

173 | 육하원칙 문제

해석 어떤 강좌가 반나절 안에 완료될 수 있는가?
(A) 문제 해결
(B) 팀과의 협업
(C) 고급 프로그래밍
(D) 네트워크 보안

해설 지문의 'Except where indicated, each course has been designed to be completed in half a day.'에서 표시된 곳을 제외하고, 각 강좌는 반나절 안에 완료될 수 있도록 계획되었다고 했고, 'Working with Teams', '* One-day course'에서 팀과의 협업 강좌에는 일일 강좌에 표시되는 *표시가 없으므로 (B)가 정답이다.

174 | 추론 문제

해석 Mr. Montoya에 대해 암시되는 것은?
(A) 그의 신청서를 늦게 제출했다.
(B) 그의 관리자는 요청을 승인하지 않을 것이다.
(C) 그가 선택한 모든 강좌들을 듣지 못할 수도 있다.
(D) 그의 주요 직무는 발표하는 것을 포함한다.

해설 지문의 'The company will present a final selection of courses based on everyone's choices ~'에서 회사는 모두의 선택을 바탕으로 최종 선정된 강좌를 공개할 것이라고 했고, 'Please choose the three courses that you are most interested in attending'에서 참석하는 것에 가장 관심 있는 3개의 강좌를 선택하라고 했으므로 Mr. Montoya는 그가 선택한 3개의 모든 강좌들을 듣지 못할 수도 있음을 추론할 수 있다. 따라서 (C)가 정답이다.

어휘 application form 신청서 approve v. 승인하다

175 | 문장 위치 찾기 문제

해석 [1], [2], [3], [4]로 표시된 위치 중, 다음 문장이 들어갈 곳으로 가장 적절한 것은?

"이것은 강좌들이 시작되기 최소 2주 전에 완료되어야 합니다."

(A) [1]
(B) [2]
(C) [3]
(D) [4]

해설 주어진 문장은 강좌들에 참석하기 전에 해야 하는 것과 관련된 내용이 나오는 부분에 들어가야 함을 알 수 있다. [4]의 앞 문장인 'Employees are responsible for securing permission from their supervisors to participate.'에서 직원들은 참석하기 위해 그들의 관리자로부터 허가를 얻어 낼 책임이 있다고 했으므로, [4]에 제시된 문장이 들어가면 직원들은 참석하기 위해 그들의 관리자로부터 허가를 얻어 낼 책임이 있으며, 이것은 강좌들이 시작되기 최소 2주 전에 완료되어야 한다는 자연스러운 문맥이 된다는 것을 알 수 있다. 따라서 (D)가 정답이다.

어휘 at least 최소한 prior to ~ 전에, 앞서

176-180번은 다음 공고와 회람에 관한 문제입니다.

자선 자동차 경매

¹⁷⁹제21회 연례 자선 자동차 경매가 6월 25일에 Metropolitan 공원에서 열릴 것입니다. ¹⁷⁶이 연례 활동은 몇몇 주요 자동차 제조업체로부터 후원을 받으며 주 전역의 아동 자선단체들을 위한 기금을 모읍니다.

공원은 오전 10시에 대중에게 개방될 것입니다. 경매는 오후 1시에 시작되며 오후 6시에 끝나고, 상업용 차량들을 포함하여, 자동차와 트럭들에 대한 좋은 거래들을 찾으실 수 있을 것입니다. 가족을 데려와 야외에서 재미있는 하루를 즐기세요. 경매에 더하여, 빈티지 자동차 전시, 음식 부스, 놀이 공간, 그리고 다양한 자동차 관련 제품들을 판매하는 노점상들이 있을 것입니다. 이 행사의 티켓은 1인당 5달러입니다.

문의가 있으시다면, 555-3403으로 전화주시고, ¹⁷⁷판매용 자동차들을 미리 보기 위해서는 www.charitycarauction.org를 방문하세요.

어휘 charity n. 자선, 자선 사업 sponsor v. 후원하다 major adj. 주요한 automobile n. 자동차 manufacturer n. 제조업체 raise v. 모으다 commercial adj. 상업용의 exhibit n. 전시(물) vendor n. 노점상, 행상인 inquiry n. 문의 preview n. 미리 보기, 시사회

회람

6월 15일
수신: 모든 Metropolitan 공원 직원들
발신: Joel Gage, 공원 서비스 책임자
제목: 행사 준비

¹⁷⁹제21회 연례 자선 자동차 경매의 준비로, 저는 모든 분들께 몇 가지를 상기시켜 드리고자 합니다. 행사 하루 전날, 우리는 경매 및 예정된 전시를 위한 차량들을 배달받을 것입니다. ¹⁷⁸⁻⁽ᶜ⁾빈티지 자동차들은 북쪽 출입구를 통해 안으로 들여질 반면 ¹⁷⁸⁻⁽ᴰ⁾판매용 자동차들은 우리의 안전한 주차장에 그대로 있을 것입니다.

행사 당일에, 남쪽 출입구는 보행자들에게 개방될 것이며, 동쪽 출입구는 공원 및 행사 직원들을 위해 따로 남겨두어 질 것이며, 서쪽 출입구는 구급 요원용으로 지정될 것입니다. ¹⁸⁰시의 경찰서로부터 교통 및 군중

관리에 대한 지원이 제공될 것입니다.

어떠한 질문이라도 있으시다면, 망설이지 말고 전화해 주시거나 공원 내 있는 제 사무실에 들러주십시오. ¹⁷⁹저는 회의에 참석하기 위해 시카고로 출장을 갈 예정이기 때문에 다음 주에는 저를 만날 수 없다는 것을 유의해 주십시오. 저는 배달일에 여러분 모두를 뵙겠습니다.

in preparation for ~의 준비로 secure adj. 안전한 pedestrian n. 보행자
reserve v. 따로 남겨두다, 예약하다 designate v. 지정하다
emergency personnel 구급요원 assistance n. 지원 traffic n. 교통, 차량
crowd n. 군중 hesitate v. 망설이다, 주저하다
unavailable adj. 만날 수 없는, 이용할 수 없는

176 | 주제 찾기 문제

해석 공고는 주로 무엇에 대한 것인가?
(A) 제품 출시
(B) 야외 콘서트
(C) 모금 활동
(D) 스포츠 행사

해설 공고의 'This yearly activity is sponsored by several major automobile manufacturers and raises money for children's charities around the state.'에서 이 연례 활동은 몇몇 주요 자동차 제조업체들로부터 후원을 받으며 주 전역의 아동 자선단체들을 위한 기금을 모은다고 했으므로 (C)가 정답이다.

어휘 launch n. 출시 fundraising n. 모금

Paraphrasing
activity ~ raises money for ~ charities 활동은 자선단체들을 위한 기금을 모은다 → A fundraising activity 모금 활동

177 | 육하원칙 문제

해석 독자들은 왜 웹사이트를 방문해야 하는가?
(A) 부스 예약을 하기 위해
(B) 향후 행사들을 위한 제안서들을 제출하기 위해
(C) 몇몇 판매 상품들을 미리 보기 위해
(D) 단체를 위한 티켓들을 구매하기 위해

해설 공고의 'visit www.charitycarauction.org to get a preview of the cars for sale'에서 판매용 자동차들을 미리 보기 위해서는 www.charitycarauction.org를 방문하라고 했으므로 (C)가 정답이다.

어휘 submit v. 제출하다 proposal n. 제안서 offering n. 판매 상품, 제공하는 것

Paraphrasing
get a preview of ~을 미리 보다 → see ~ in advance 미리 보다
cars for sale 판매용 자동차들 → offerings 판매 상품들

178 | Not/True 문제

해석 빈티지 자동차들에 대해 언급된 것은?
(A) 추첨에서 경품으로 제공될 것이다.
(B) 행사 마지막 날에 판매될 것이다.
(C) 북쪽 출입구를 통해 운송될 것이다.
(D) 안전한 주차장에 주차될 것이다.

해설 회람의 'the vintage ones will be brought inside through the north entrance'에서 빈티지 자동차들은 북쪽 출입구를 통해 안으로 들여질 것이라고 했으므로 (C)가 정답이다. (A)와 (B)는 지문에 언급되지 않은 내용이다. 회람의 'The cars for sale will stay in our secure parking lot'에서 판매용 자동차들은 우리의 안전한 주차장에 그대로 있을 것이라고 했으므로, (D)는 지문의 내용과 일치하지 않는다.

어휘 draw n. 추첨; v. 추첨하다

179 | 추론 문제 연계

해석 Mr. Gage에 대해 추론될 수 있는 것은?
(A) 6월 25일 전에 출장에서 돌아올 것이다.
(B) 구급 팀원들을 도와줄 자원봉사자들을 찾고 있다.
(C) 월말에 새로운 사무실로 이동할 것이다.
(D) 다음 주에 시카고에서 휴가를 보낼 계획을 하고 있다.

해설 질문의 핵심 어구인 Mr. Gage가 작성한 회람을 먼저 확인한다.

단서 1 회람의 'In preparation for the 21st Annual Charity Car Auction, I'd like to give everyone some reminders. One day before the event, we will be receiving deliveries of vehicles for the auction and the planned display.'에서 제21회 연례 자선 자동차 경매의 준비로, 몇 가지를 상기시켜 드리고자 한다고 하고, 행사 하루 전날 경매 및 예정된 전시를 위한 차량들을 배달받을 것이라고 한 후, 'Note that I will be unavailable next week as I will be traveling to Chicago to attend a conference. I will see all of you on the day of the deliveries.'에서 자신, 즉 Mr. Gage가 회의에 참석하기 위해 시카고로 출장을 갈 예정이기 때문에 다음 주에는 만날 수 없다는 것을 유의해 달라고 하고, 배달일에 모두를 뵙겠다고 하였다.

단서 2 공고의 'The 21st Annual Charity Car Auction will be held on June 25 at Metropolitan Park.'에서 제21회 연례 자선 자동차 경매가 6월 25일에 Metropolitan 공원에서 열린다고 하였다.

두 단서를 종합할 때, Mr. Gage는 6월 25일 전에 출장에서 돌아올 것임을 추론할 수 있다. 따라서 (A)가 정답이다.

어휘 seek v. 찾다, 구하다 assist v. 돕다 crew n. 팀원, 팀
take a vacation 휴가를 보내다

180 | 동의어 찾기 문제

해석 회람에서, 2문단 세 번째 줄의 단어 "management"는 의미상 -와 가장 가깝다.
(A) 관리
(B) 권한
(C) 경영진
(D) 운영

해설 management를 포함한 구절 'Assistance with traffic and crowd management will be provided by the city's police department.'에서 management는 '관리'라는 뜻으로 사용되었다. 따라서 (A)가 정답이다.

181-185번은 다음 웹페이지와 이메일에 관한 문제입니다.

Atlantic 장난감 및 게임 박람회

축하합니다! 귀하는 성공적으로 Atlantic 장난감 및 게임 박람회에 등록하셨습니다. 올해의 행사는 4월 4일 포르투갈의 풍살에 있는 Noguiera 컨벤션 홀에서 열립니다.

시간을 내어 귀하의 등록 세부사항을 주의 깊게 검토하여 주십시오.

등록자 이름:	Kenneth Fruman
이메일 주소:	kenfrum@burgudeco.com
등록 날짜:	1월 15일
입장 종류:	¹⁸²⁻⁽ᴬ⁾/⁽ᶜ⁾/⁽ᴰ⁾전체 입장권 * ¹⁸²⁻⁽ᴬ⁾/⁽ᶜ⁾/⁽ᴰ⁾60개의 부스들과 20개의 전시들을 포함하는 전시 홀, 초청 전문가들의 연설 세션들, 그리고 업계 내부자 모임들에 대한 입장을 포함함

¹⁸⁴티셔츠 사이즈: 대	* ¹⁸⁴행사 꾸러미에 포함될 선물
선택한 지불 방법: 은행 이체	* ¹⁸¹1월 23일 또는 그 이전에 대금이 지불되어야 함
지불될 금액: 35유로	* 확인 이메일은 대금 수령 후에 발송될 것임
은행 세부 정보	
은행 이름: Avantage 은행	
예금주: ATGF	
계좌 번호: 7334-8921-5960-66	

[수정하기] [홈으로 돌아가기]

successfully adv. 성공적으로 take place 열리다 carefully adv. 주의 깊게
review v. 검토하다 registrant n. 등록자 entry n. 입장
all-access pass 전체 입장권, 무제한 입장권 admittance n. 입장
display hall 전시 홀 exhibit n. 전시 insider n. 내부자 meet-up n. 모임
package n. 꾸러미, 소포 payment n. 지불, 대금 prior to ~이전에
confirmation n. 확인 receipt n. 수령, 영수증 account holder 예금주
account number 계좌 번호

수신: ¹⁸³⁻⁽ᶜ⁾Kenneth Fruman <kenfrum@burgudeco.com>
발신: Patricia Laroux <assistant@atgf.com>
제목: 등록
날짜: 1월 17일

Mr. Fruman께,

Atlantic 장난감 및 게임 박람회에 등록해주셔서 감사드립니다. ¹⁸³⁻⁽ᴬ⁾/⁽ᶜ⁾저희는 귀하의 은행 이체 대금 70유로를 수령하였으며 1월 20일에 귀하께 귀하의 행사 꾸러미를 발송할 것입니다. ¹⁸³⁻⁽ᶜ⁾꾸러미는 두 개의 전체 입장권을 포함할 것입니다. 유감스럽게도, ¹⁸⁴저희는 원래 광고되었던 선물 꾸러미가 다 소진되어 귀하께 보내드릴 수 없습니다. 따라서, 저희는 대신 귀하께 탁상 달력을 제공할 예정입니다.

만약 귀하께서 아직 숙소를 예약하지 않으셨다면, ¹⁸⁵⁻⁽ᴰ⁾Noguiera 컨벤션 홀 부근에 단 3개의 호텔들만 있기 때문에 가능한 한 빨리 예약하실 것을 권장합니다. 풍샬의 호텔들에 대한 정보를 위해서는 www.visitfunchal.com/placestostay를 확인하십시오.

Patricia Laroux 드림, 기획 보조

Atlantic 장난감 및 게임 박람회

bank transfer 은행 이체 run out 소진되다 consequently adv. 따라서
provide v. 제공하다 accommodation n. 숙소

181 | 목적 찾기 문제

해설 웹페이지의 목적은 무엇인가?
(A) 협회 회원들에게 행사에 대해 알리기 위해
(B) 부스 예약을 확정하기 위해
(C) 돈을 보내는 것에 대한 설명을 제공하기 위해
(D) 참가자를 워크숍에 등록시키기 위해

해설 웹페이지의 'payment must be submitted on or prior to January 23'에서 1월 23일 또는 그 이전에 대금이 지불되어야 한다고 한 후, 대금 지불과 관련된 세부 정보들을 설명하고 있으므로 (C)가 정답이다.

어휘 inform v. 알리다 association n. 협회 instruction n. 설명
participant n. 참가자

182 | Not/True 문제

해설 전체 입장권 소지자들이 이용 가능한 것으로 언급되지 않은 것은?
(A) 전문가들의 연설
(B) 제품 시연
(C) 전시 공간들
(D) 인적 교류 세션들

해설 (A), (C), (D)는 웹페이지의 'all-access pass', 'includes admittance to display hall ~, speaker sessions by guest experts, and industry insider meet-ups'에서 전체 입장권은 전시 홀, 초청 전문가들의 연설 세션들, 그리고 업계 내부자 모임들에 대한 입장을 포함한다고 했으므로 지문에 언급된 내용이다. (B)는 언급되지 않은 내용이다. 따라서 (B)가 정답이다.

어휘 demonstration n. 시연

Paraphrasing

speaker sessions by ~ experts 전문가들의 연설 세션들 → Talks by specialists 전문가들의 연설
display hall 전시 홀 → Display spaces 전시 공간들
insider meet-ups 내부자 모임들 → Networking sessions 인적 교류 세션들

183 | Not/True 문제

해설 Mr. Fruman에 대해 명시된 것은?
(A) 1월 17일에 행사 꾸러미가 발송되었다.
(B) 첨부된 영수증과 함께 확인 이메일을 받았다.
(C) 다른 사람을 위해서도 입장권을 구매했다.
(D) 전시 홀에 있는 전시 공간을 대여하고 있다.

해설 이메일의 'We have received your bank transfer payment of €70 ~. The package will include two all-access passes.'에서 은행 이체 대금 70유로를 수령하였으며, 꾸러미는 두 개의 전체 입장권을 포함할 것이라고 했으므로 (C)가 정답이다. 이메일의 '~ will mail your event package to you on January 20.'에서 1월 20일에 행사 꾸러미를 발송할 것이라고 했으므로, (A)는 지문의 내용과 일치하지 않는다. (B)와 (D)는 지문에 언급되지 않은 내용이다.

어휘 attached adj. 첨부된

184 | 추론 문제 연계

해설 Atlantic 장난감 및 게임 박람회에 대해 추론될 수 있는 것은?
(A) 올해 등록비를 인상했다.
(B) 매번 다른 나라에서 열린다.
(C) 1월 23일까지만 티켓 환불을 제공한다.
(D) 참석자들에게 제공할 티셔츠가 더 이상 없다.

해설 Atlantic 장난감 및 게임 박람회의 관계자 Patricia Laroux가 작성한 이메일을 먼저 확인한다.
[단서 1] 이메일의 'we cannot send you the package gift that was originally advertised as we have run out'에서 자신들, 즉 Atlantic 장난감 및 게임 박람회는 원래 광고되었던 선물 꾸러미가 다 소진되어 보내줄 수 없다고 했다. 그런데 선물 꾸러미가 무엇인지 제시되지 않았으므로 웹페이지에서 관련 내용을 확인한다.
[단서 2] 웹페이지의 'T-shirt', 'gift to be included in event package'에서는 티셔츠가 행사 꾸러미에 포함될 선물이라고 했다.
두 단서를 종합할 때, Atlantic 장난감 및 게임 박람회는 참석자들에게 제공할 티셔츠가 더 이상 없음을 추론할 수 있다. 따라서 (D)가 정답이다.

어휘 refund n. 환불 attendee n. 참석자

Paraphrasing

run out 소진되다 → no longer has 더 이상 없다

185 | Not/True 문제

해설 Noguiera 컨벤션 홀에 대해 언급된 것은?

(A) 도시의 공항에 인접해 있다.
(B) 과거에 박람회를 위한 장소였다.
(C) 동시에 두 개의 행사를 개최하고 있다.
(D) 숙박 시설들 가까이에 위치해 있다.

해설 이메일의 'there are ~ three hotels near the Noguiera Convention Hall'에서 Noguiera 컨벤션 홀 부근에 3개의 호텔들이 있다고 했으므로 (D)가 지문의 내용과 일치한다. 따라서 (D)가 정답이다. (A), (B), (C)는 지문에서 언급되지 않은 내용이다.

어휘 adjacent adj. 인접한 hold v. 개최하다
accommodation facility 숙박 시설

Paraphrasing

hotels 호텔들 → accommodation facilities 숙박 시설들
near 부근에 → close to 가까이에

186-190번은 다음 광고, 송장, 이메일에 관한 문제입니다.

Dyna Flooring사
재고 정리 할인

186이번 8월 내내, Dyna Flooring사는 새로운 재고품을 위한 공간을 만들기 위해 재고 정리 할인을 열 예정입니다. Disena, Molik, Maitland 와 같은 가장 인기 있는 브랜드들 및 더 많은 브랜드들의 제품들을 포함해 187-(C)집과 사무실에서 쓰이는 186다양한 상품에 대한 엄청난 혜택들을 누리세요.

✓ 모든 제품에 대한 전반적인 10퍼센트 할인
✓ 188다음 달에 가격이 오르는 상품에 대한 20퍼센트 할인
✓ 단종된 제품들의 대량 구매에 대한 30퍼센트 할인

할인은 온라인 및 중서부 지역 전역의 가게들에서 판매되는 상품들까지 포함합니다. 189가게에서 상품을 구매하는 고객들에게는 10퍼센트의 추가 특별 할인이 적용되고, Dyna 클럽 보상 프로그램 회원들은 20퍼센트 의 추가 할인을 받습니다.

187-(D)500달러 이상의 모든 주문은 무료 배송입니다!

더 많은 정보를 위해서는, www.dynaflooring.com으로 가시거나 당신의 가장 가까운 Dyna Flooring사 지점을 방문해주십시오.

clearance sale 재고 정리 할인 throughout prep. ~내내, 전역에
inventory n. 재고품, 물품 목록 a variety of 다양한 merchandise n. 상품
top-rated adj. 가장 인기 있는 general adj. 전반적인, 공통된
bulk adj. 대량의 discontinued adj. 단종된 extend v. 포함하다, 연장하다
additional adj. 추가의 delivery n. 배송

Dyna Flooring사
www.dynaflooring.com

구매자: Danielle Welch   거래 날짜: 8월 29일
회사: Westwood 회계 사무소   Dyna 클럽 회원입니까?: 네
지불 방법: Verifian 신용카드

제품 코드	상품	수량	가격
MKT1431Y	Molik 도자기 부엌 타일 (10퍼센트 할인)	24	388.80달러
CTJN9091G	Johnson 회색 카펫 타일 (10퍼센트 할인)	16	264.00달러
CTLS3816B	Laster 파란색 카펫 타일 (30퍼센트 할인)	58	740.95달러
FTIN643RW	188Intone 목재 마감 바닥 타일 (20퍼센트 할인)	12	787.20달러
	소계		2,180.95달러
	18910퍼센트 할인		(218.10달러)
	세금		130.86달러
	배송료		0.00달러
	총액		2,093.71달러

약관: 환불은 상점 포인트의 형태로만 지급됩니다. 구매한 상품들은 재고품이 있는 한 같거나 더 적은 가격의 상품으로 교환될 수 있습니다.

귀하의 거래에 감사드립니다!

refund n. 환불; v. 환불하다 exchange v. 교환하다 equal adj. 같은
value n. 가격, 가치 as long as ~하는 한 supply n. 재고품
less prep. ~를 뺀, 줄인 shipping n. 배송료

수신: 고객 서비스 <cs@dynaflooring.com>
발신: Danielle Welch <c.welch@westwoodaccts.com>
날짜: 9월 2일
제목: 최근 주문

관계자분께,

저는 최근 8월에 귀사의 할인 판매 동안 몇 가지 상품들을 구매하였습니다. 유감스럽게도, 상품들 중 하나가 저희의 새롭게 다시 디자인된 사무실 부엌에 적절하지 않은 색으로 드러나서, 저는 그것을 비슷한 제품으로 교환하기를 원합니다. 만약 알맞은 상품을 구할 수 없다면, 저는 대신 환불을 하고 싶습니다. 190저는 또한 Dyna 클럽 회원으로서 제가 20퍼센트의 추가 특별 할인을 받았어야 했다는 것을 알아차렸습니다. 이 추가 할인 금액을 제 계정에 적립해 주시거나 취해야 할 앞으로의 조치들에 대해 제게 알려주십시오. 감사합니다.

Danielle Welch 드림
구매 담당자
Westwood 회계 사무소

turn out ~임이 드러나다 suitable adj. 알맞은 notice v. 알아차리다, 인지하다
credit v. 적립하다, 입금하다

186 | 목적 찾기 문제

해석 광고의 목적은 무엇인가?
(A) 온라인 쇼핑 서비스의 개시를 홍보하기 위해
(B) 고객들이 멤버십 프로그램에 가입하도록 장려하기 위해
(C) 한 달 간의 비용 절감 기회를 소개하기 위해
(D) 새로운 소재로 만들어진 제품을 알리기 위해

해설 광고의 'Throughout this August, Dyna Flooring will be holding a clearance sale ~'에서 Dyna Flooring사가 8월 내내 재고 정리 할인을 열 예정이라고 했고, 'Enjoy great deals on a variety of merchandise'에서 다양한 상품들에 대한 엄청난 혜택들을 누리라고 한 후, 할인에 대해 설명하고 있으므로 (C)가 정답이다.

어휘 promote v. 홍보하다 launch n. 개시 cost-saving adj. 비용 절감의
material n. 소재

Paraphrasing

clearance sale 재고 정리 할인 → cost-saving opportunity 비용 절감 기회

187 | Not/True 문제

해석 Dyna Flooring사에 대해 언급된 것은?
(A) Disena 제품의 독점 유통업체이다.
(B) 여러 나라에 매장을 열었다.
(C) 사무실 사용에 적합한 물품만 취급한다.

(D) 조건을 충족하는 주문들에 무료 배송을 제공한다.

해설 광고의 'Free delivery on all orders of $500 or more!'에서 500달러 이상의 모든 주문은 무료 배송이라고 했으므로 (D)는 지문의 내용과 일치한다. 따라서 (D)가 정답이다. (A)와 (B)는 지문에 언급되지 않은 내용이다. 광고의 'Enjoy great deals on a variety of merchandise for home and office use'에서 집과 사무실에서 쓰이는 다양한 상품들에 대한 엄청난 혜택들을 누리라고 했으므로, (C)는 지문의 내용과 일치하지 않는다.

어휘 exclusive adj. 독점의, 배타적인   distributor n. 유통업체
carry v. (가게에서 품목을) 취급하다

Paraphrasing

Free delivery 무료 배송 → free shipping 무료 배송

188 | Not/True 문제 연계

해설 송장에서 명시된 것은?
(A) Ms. Welch는 할인 판매 마지막 날에 참석했다.
(B) 몇몇 상품들은 현재 품절되었다.
(C) Johnson 타일은 일정보다 빨리 배송되었다.
(D) Intone 타일들은 다음 달에 가격이 오를 것이다.

해설 송장을 먼저 확인한다.
단서 1 송장의 'Intone ~ tile (20% off)'에서 Intone 타일에 20퍼센트 할인이 적용된다는 사실을 확인할 수 있다.
단서 2 광고의 '20 percent off merchandise increasing in price next month'에서 다음 달에 가격이 오르는 상품에 20퍼센트 할인이 제공된다고 했다.
두 단서를 종합할 때, Intone 타일들은 다음 달에 가격이 오를 것임을 알 수 있다. 따라서 (D)가 정답이다.

어휘 attend v. 참석하다   out of stock 품절된

189 | 추론 문제 연계

해설 Ms. Welch에 대해 암시되는 것은?
(A) 그녀는 상품들을 직접 결제했다.
(B) 약 200달러의 상점 포인트를 받을 수도 있다.
(C) 사무실을 다시 디자인하는 것을 맡았다.
(D) 구매 대금을 지불하기 위해 보상 포인트를 사용했다.

해설 Ms. Welch가 받은 송장을 먼저 확인한다.
단서 1 송장의 'Less 10%'에서 Ms. Welch가 10퍼센트의 추가 할인을 받은 것을 확인할 수 있다. 그런데 추가 할인을 받는 조건이 제시되지 않았으므로 광고에서 관련 내용을 확인한다.
단서 2 광고의 'An additional special discount of 10 percent applies to customers who purchase items at a store'에서 가게에서 상품을 구매하는 고객들에게는 10퍼센트의 추가 특별 할인이 적용된다는 것을 알 수 있다.
두 단서를 종합할 때, Ms. Welch가 가게에서 상품들을 직접 결제하였음을 추론할 수 있다. 따라서 (A)가 정답이다.

어휘 in charge of ~을 맡은

190 | 육하원칙 문제

해설 Ms. Welch는 Dyna Flooring사가 무엇을 하기를 원하는가?
(A) 멤버십 프로그램에 그녀를 가입시킨다.
(B) 배송 비용을 환불해 준다.
(C) 그녀에게 설치 설명서를 보낸다.
(D) 추가 가격 인하를 적용한다.

해설 이메일의 'I also noticed that I should have received an additional special discount of 20 percent as a Dyna Club member. Please credit my account for this additional discount'에서 자신, 즉 Ms. Welch가 Dyna 클럽 회원으로서 20퍼센트의 추가 특별 할인을 받았어야 했다는 것을 알아차렸다고 하며 추가 할인 금액을 본인의 계정에 적립해 달라고 했으므로 (D)가 정답이다.

어휘 instruction n. 설명(서)

Paraphrasing

additional discount 추가 할인 → additional price reduction 추가 가격 인하

191-195번은 다음 안내문과 두 양식에 관한 문제입니다.

Elfman Home Cooling사
품질 보증 청구

Elfman사는 고객들의 요구를 충족시키는 것에 전념합니다. [192]저희가 판매하는 모든 장비는 6개월짜리 부품 및 수리 보증서가 딸려 있습니다. 만약 당신이 품질 보증 기간 동안 문제들을 경험한다면, 기술자가 당신의 자택 혹은 사업체를 방문하여 모든 필요한 수리들을 무료로 실행할 것입니다. 또한, [194]만약 구매 후 한 달 이내에 당신의 기기가 제대로 작동하지 않는다면, 저희는 그것을 저희의 비용으로 교체할 것입니다.

[191]품질 보증 청구를 제출하려면, www.elfmanequip.com/customers로 가십시오. 당신은 사용자 이름과 비밀번호를 입력하도록 요청될 것입니다. 그 후, 온라인 양식에 접속하기 위해 화면 하단의 '청구' 버튼을 클릭하십시오. 적시의 처리를 보장하기 위해, 청구서를 완벽하게 작성하십시오.

warranty n. 품질 보증(서)   claim n. 청구, 요청; v. 주장하다
be committed to ~에 전념하다   serve v. 충족시키다, 제공하다
come with ~이 딸려 있다   unit n. 기기, 장치
malfunction v. 제대로 작동하지 않다; n. 오작동   replace v. 교체하다
expense n. 비용   ensure v. 보장하다   timely adj. 적시의, 때맞춘
processing n. 처리   completely adv. 완벽하게

Elfman Home Cooling사 청구서

청구 번호: EC1081626
[193-(D)]날짜: 8월 3일
[192/193-(C)]고객 성함: Larry Regan
주소: 219번지 Duncan가, Forsyth, 조지아주 31029
전화번호: 555-4086
이메일: l.regan@pellstone.com
제품: Elfman사 중앙 에어컨
모델: AU-0951   일련번호: P118946QJ

문제 설명:
[193-(C)]그 기기는 그것이 작동되기 시작한 후 처음 30분 동안은 괜찮지만, 그 후 그것은 서서히 더 커지는 이상한 소음을 내기 시작합니다. 제 사무실의 직원들이 일하기가 매우 어렵습니다. [192/193-(D)]이것은 제가 기기를 약 7개월 전에 구매한 이후로 겪은 첫 번째 문제입니다.

progressively adv. 서서히, 점차적으로

Elfman Home Cooling사 청구서

청구 번호: EK0194114
날짜: 8월 15일
[194/195-(C)]고객 성함: Michelle Bowman
주소: 176번지 King대로, High Springs, 플로리다주 32643
전화번호: 555-7182
이메일: m.bowman@springmail.com
제품: Elfman사 환기 시스템
모델: PK-4317   [195-(D)]일련번호: T27386HX

문제 설명:
오늘 아침, 195-(C)저는 환기구에서 공기가 거의 나오지 않고 있었다는 것을 알아차렸습니다. 저는 어떤 막혀 있는 부분이 있는지 확인하기 위해 기기를 껐지만, 어떤 이상한 것도 보지 못했습니다. 194그것이 설치된 지 2주가 되지 않았다는 것을 고려했을 때, 이것은 용납할 수 없습니다.

어휘 ventilation n. 환기, 통풍 notice v. 알아차리다
blockage n. 막혀 있는 것, 막힘 out of the ordinary 이상한, 색다른
unacceptable adj. 용납할 수 없는, 받아들일 수 없는

191 | 육하원칙 문제

해석 고객들은 어떻게 품질 보증 청구를 제출할 수 있는가?
(A) 서비스 센터를 방문함으로써
(B) 서면 요청을 우편으로 보냄으로써
(C) 온라인 계정에 접속함으로써
(D) 모바일 애플리케이션을 설치함으로써

해설 안내문의 'To submit a warranty claim, go to www.elfmanequip. com/customers. You will be asked to enter your username and password.'에서 품질 보증 청구를 제출하려면, 웹사이트로 가서 사용자 이름과 비밀번호를 입력하라고 했으므로 (C)가 정답이다.

어휘 mail v. (우편으로) 보내다

192 | 추론 문제 연계

해석 Mr. Regan에 대해 암시되는 것은?
(A) 기술자가 방문하려면 며칠을 기다려야 할 것이다.
(B) 이메일로 회사 대표에게 연락했다.
(C) 에어컨에 대한 할인을 요구했다.
(D) 수리비를 지불해야 할 것이다.

해설 Mr. Regan이 작성한 첫 번째 양식을 먼저 확인한다.
단서 1 첫 번째 양식의 'Customer name: Larry Regan', 'This is the first problem ~ since I purchased the unit about seven months ago.'에서 고객인 Mr. Regan이 기기, 즉 에어컨을 약 7개월 전에 구매한 이후로 겪은 첫 번째 문제라고 했다. 그런데 품질 보증을 받는 조건이 제시되지 않았으므로 안내문에서 관련 내용을 확인한다.
단서 2 안내문의 'All equipment we sell comes with a six-month parts and labor warranty. If you experience problems during the warranty period, a technician will ~ perform all necessary repairs free of charge.'에서 Elfman Home Cooling사가 판매하는 모든 장비는 6개월짜리 부품 및 수리 보증서가 딸려 있으며 만약 고객이 품질 보증 기간 동안 문제들을 경험한다면, 기술자가 모든 필요한 수리들을 무료로 실행할 것이라고 했음을 확인할 수 있다.
두 단서를 종합할 때, Mr. Regan은 수리를 무료로 받지 못하기 때문에 수리비를 지불해야 할 것임을 추론할 수 있다. 따라서 (D)가 정답이다.

어휘 representative n. 대표

193 | Not/True 문제

해석 Mr. Regan에 의해 작성된 양식에서 언급된 것은?
(A) 가전제품의 최신 모델을 주문했다.
(B) 그의 사무실은 수리가 실행될 때까지 폐쇄될 것이다.
(C) 그의 기기가 처음 켜졌을 때는 제대로 작동한다.
(D) Elfman사의 제품을 8월 3일에 구매했다.

해설 첫 번째 양식의 'Customer name: Larry Regan', 'The unit is fine for the first 30 minutes after it starts'에서 작성자 Mr. Regan이 그 기기는 작동되기 시작한 후 처음 30분 동안은 괜찮다고 했으므로 (C)는 지문의 내용과 일치한다. 따라서 (C)가 정답이다. (A)와 (B)는 지문에 언급되지 않은 내용이다. (D)는 'Date: August 3', 'This is the first problem I have had since I purchased the unit about seven months ago.'에서 8월 3일에 작성된 청구서에 자신, 즉 Mr. Regan이 기기를 약 7개월 전에 구매한 이후로 겪은 첫 번째 문제라고 했으므로 지문의 내용과 일치하지 않는다.

어휘 latest adj. 최신의, 최근의 appliance n. 가전제품

Paraphrasing
unit is fine 기기는 괜찮다 → unit functions properly 기기가 제대로 작동하다
for the first 30 minutes after ~ starts 작동되기 시작한 후 처음 30분 동안 → when first turned on 처음 켜졌을 때

194 | 추론 문제 연계

해석 Ms. Bowman에 대해 추론될 수 있는 것은?
(A) 양식을 완벽하게 작성하지 못했다.
(B) 교체 제품을 받을 것이다.
(C) 몇몇 장비를 부정확하게 설치했다.
(D) 환기 시스템을 위한 추가 부품들을 주문했다.

해설 Ms. Bowman이 작성한 두 번째 양식을 먼저 확인한다.
단서 1 두 번째 양식의 'Customer name: Michelle Bowman', 'it was installed less than two weeks ago'에서 Ms. Bowman이 그것, 즉 환기 시스템이 설치된 지 2주가 되지 않았다고 했다. 그런데 2주가 되지 않은 제품에 대한 보증 내용이 제시되지 않았으므로 안내문에서 관련 내용을 확인한다.
단서 2 안내문의 'if your unit malfunctions within one month of purchase, we will replace it at our expense'에서 만약 구매 후 한 달 이내에 당신, 즉 고객의 기기가 제대로 작동하지 않는다면, 그것을 저희, 즉 Elfman Home Cooling사의 비용으로 교체할 것이라고 했다.
두 단서를 종합할 때, Ms. Bowman은 교체 제품을 받을 것임을 추론할 수 있다. 따라서 (B)가 정답이다.

어휘 replacement n. 교체 incorrectly adv. 부정확하게 extra adj. 추가의

195 | Not/True 문제

해석 Ms. Bowman에 의해 작성된 양식에서 명시된 것은?
(A) 기술자의 방문을 받았다.
(B) 회사 웹사이트에 등록하지 않았다.
(C) 문제의 원인을 알아내려고 노력했다.
(D) 장치의 일련번호를 모른다.

해설 두 번째 양식의 'Customer name: Michelle Bowman', 'I noticed that very little air was coming out of the vents. I turned the unit off to check for any blockages but did not see anything out of the ordinary.'에서 자신, 즉 Ms. Bowman은 환기구에서 공기가 거의 나오지 않고 있었다는 것을 알아차렸고 어떤 막혀 있는 부분이 있는지 확인하기 위해 기기를 껐지만, 어떤 이상한 것도 보지 못했다고 했으므로 (C)는 지문의 내용과 일치한다. 따라서 (C)가 정답이다. (A)와 (B)는 지문에 언급되지 않은 내용이다. (D)는 'Serial number: T27386HX'에서 Ms. Bowman이 일련번호를 작성한 것을 알 수 있으므로 지문의 내용과 일치하지 않는다.

어휘 determine v. 알아내다, 결정하다 cause n. 원인

Paraphrasing
check for any blockages 어떤 막혀 있는 부분이 있는지 확인하다 → tried to determine the cause of a problem 문제의 원인을 알아내려고 노력했다

196-200번은 다음 편지, 브로슈어, 안내문에 관한 문제입니다.

9월 20일

Arapali Express사
Nichi 건물, 랄마티
자발푸르, 마디야 프라데시 482002

담당자분께,

¹⁹⁶저는 Arapali Express사의 9월 7일 AE010 항공편 승객으로서 제 경험에 대해 말씀드리고 싶습니다. 전반적으로, 그것은 만족스러웠습니다. ¹⁹⁷저는 몇몇 다른 승객들보다 먼저 탑승할 수 있었던 것과 와이파이를 사용하는 데 비용이 많이 들지 않았던 것을 높이 평가합니다. 하지만, 저는 거의 즉시 저의 영상 모니터에 문제가 생겼고, 승무원의 도움에도 불구하고, 그것을 작동시키지 못했습니다. 다행히도, 비행이 그리 길지는 않았지만, 그랬다면 저는 매우 불만족스러웠을 것입니다. 저는 귀사가 향후에는 모든 기내 기기들이 제대로 작동하는지 확실하게 하는 조치를 취하시길 바랍니다.

Sandra Bulsara 드림

passenger n. 승객 satisfactory adj. 만족스러운 board v. 탑승하다
crew n. 승무원 assistance n. 도움 extremely adv. 매우
frustrated adj. 불만족스러운 take steps 조치를 취하다
ensure v. 확실하게 하다, 보장하다 on-board adj. 기내의, 선상의

Arapali Express사 객실 등급 및 편의시설

¹⁹⁸**퍼스트 클래스**
• 증가된 수하물 허용량
• 우선 체크인 및 탑승
• 무료 와이파이
• 무료 고급 간식과 음료가 있는 고급 식사 서비스
• 휴대용 장치가 있는 특대형 좌석 모니터
• ¹⁹⁸무료 고급 피부 관리 키트

비즈니스 클래스
• 증가된 수하물 허용량
• 우선 체크인 및 탑승
• 무료 와이파이
• 무료 고급 간식과 음료가 있는 예정된 식사 서비스
• 터치스크린을 사용할 수 있는 대형 좌석 모니터

¹⁹⁷/¹⁹⁹**프리미엄 이코노미 클래스 (국제선 전용)**
• 증가된 수하물 허용량
• ¹⁹⁷우선 탑승
• ¹⁹⁷유료 와이파이 이용
• 예정된 식사 서비스
• 일반 좌석 모니터

이코노미 클래스
• 유료 와이파이 이용
• 예정된 식사 서비스
• 일반 좌석 모니터

amenity n. 편의시설 baggage n. 수하물, 짐 allowance n. 허용량, 비용
priority n. 우선(권) complimentary adj. 무료의 gourmet adj. 고급의
extra-large adj. 특대형의 handheld adj. 휴대용의, 손에 쥘 수 있는
regular adj. 일반의, 보통의

Arapali Express사 기내 잡지

이달의 새로운 영화들:

영화를 보기 위해, 당신의 영상 모니터 전원을 켜고 화면을 조종하기 위해 이용 가능한 제어 장치를 사용하십시오. 헤드폰은 무료로 제공됩니다. 도움을 원하시면, 기내 승무원을 부르십시오.

¹⁹⁹노선	¹⁹⁹영화	장르	길이
¹⁹⁹인도 국내	¹⁹⁹Mr. Matchbox	다큐멘터리	83분
인도에서 아프리카로	Tabla in Heaven	드라마	112분
인도에서 동남아시아로	Boman Verma's Fantastic Adventures	코미디	98분
인도에서 중동으로	Bride from Nagpur	로맨스	121분
인도에서 유럽으로	Tiger that Roams the City	스릴러	105분

참고:
1. ²⁰⁰⁻⁽ᶜ⁾P360과 P380 항공기만 터치스크린과 휴대용 장치를 갖추고 있습니다.
2. P110과 P120을 제외한 모든 항공기에서 와이파이를 이용할 수 있습니다.

switch on 전원을 켜다 control n. 제어 장치, 통제
navigate v. 조종하다, 항해하다 free of charge 무료로 in-flight adj. 기내의

---

196 | 목적 찾기 문제

해석 편지는 왜 쓰였는가?
(A) 보상을 신청하기 위해
(B) 비행 일정을 변경하기 위해
(C) 규정 위반을 보고하기 위해
(D) 몇 가지 의견을 전달하기 위해

해설 편지의 'I wish to tell you about my experience as a passenger on Arapali Express Flight AE010 on September 7.'에서 Arapali Express사의 9월 7일 AE010 항공편 승객으로서 경험에 대해 말하고 싶다고 한 후 자신의 비행 경험에 대해 느낀 점을 말하고 있으므로 (D)가 정답이다.

어휘 compensation n. 보상 itinerary n. 일정(표) policy n. 규정, 정책
violation n. 위반, 방해 convey v. 전달하다

197 | 추론 문제 연계

해석 Ms. Bulsara는 어떤 등급에 앉았을 것 같은가?
(A) 퍼스트 클래스
(B) 비즈니스 클래스
(C) 프리미엄 이코노미 클래스
(D) 이코노미 클래스

해설 Ms. Bulsara가 작성한 편지를 먼저 확인한다.
[단서 1] 편지의 'I appreciated being able to board before some of the other passengers and that the Wi-Fi was not very costly to use.'에서 자신, 즉 Ms. Bulsara는 몇몇 다른 승객들보다 먼저 탑승할 수 있었던 것과 와이파이를 사용하는 데 비용이 많이 들지 않았던 것을 높이 평가한다고 했다. 그런데 좌석 등급이 제시되지 않았으므로 브로슈어에서 관련 내용을 확인한다.
[단서 2] 브로슈어의 'Premium Economy Class', 'Priority boarding', 'Paid Wi-Fi access'에서 프리미엄 이코노미 클래스가 우선 탑승 권한과 유료 와이파이 이용을 포함한다는 것을 확인할 수 있다.
두 단서를 종합할 때, Ms. Bulsara는 프리미엄 이코노미 클래스에 앉았

음을 추론할 수 있다. 따라서 (C)가 정답이다.

198 | 육하원칙 문제

해석 퍼스트 클래스의 승객들에게는 무엇이 독점적으로 이용 가능한가?
(A) 보너스 항공사 마일리지
(B) 더 큰 수하물 허용량
(C) 무료 와이파이
(D) 피부 관리 제품들

해설 브로슈어의 'First Class', 'Complimentary luxury skin-care kit'에서 퍼스트 클래스만 무료 고급 피부 관리 키트를 포함한다는 것을 확인할 수 있으므로 (D)가 정답이다.

어휘 exclusively adv. 독점적으로

Paraphrasing

skin-care kit 피부 관리 키트 → Skin-care products 피부 관리 제품들

199 | 추론 문제 연계

해석 영화 *Mr. Matchbox*에 대해 암시되는 것은?
(A) 모든 등급에서 무료로 제공되는 유일한 것이다.
(B) 프리미엄 이코노미 승객들은 볼 수 없다.
(C) 항공사의 선택물에 추가된 최신 영화이다.
(D) 터치스크린 모니터가 있는 항공기에서는 재생되지 않을 것이다.

해설 질문의 핵심 어구인 *Mr. Matchbox*가 언급된 안내문을 먼저 확인한다.
단서 1 안내문의 'Route: Within India', 'Movie: *Mr. Matchbox*'에서 노선이 인도 국내일 때 영화 *Mr. Matchbox*를 볼 수 있다고 했다.
단서 2 브로슈어의 'Premium Economy Class (international flights only)'에서는 프리미엄 이코노미 클래스는 국제선 전용임을 확인할 수 있다.
두 단서를 종합할 때, 영화 *Mr. Matchbox*는 프리미엄 이코노미 클래스 승객들은 볼 수 없음을 추론할 수 있다. 따라서 (B)가 정답이다. (C)도 안내문에서 이달의 새로운 영화들이라고 소개하고 있어 답이 될 것 같지만, 최신 영화인지는 알 수 없으므로 답이 될 수 없다.

어휘 view v. 보다, 생각하다   latest adj. 최신의, (가장) 최근의
selection n. 선택물, 선택

200 | Not/True 문제

해석 휴대용 영상 제어 장치에 대해 명시된 것은?
(A) 국제선에는 제공되지 않는다.
(B) 사전에 구체적으로 요청되어야 한다.
(C) 몇몇 항공기 모델들에는 설치되지 않았다.
(D) 사용하기 위해 약간의 추가 요금이 든다.

해설 안내문의 'Only P360 and P380 aircraft are equipped with touch screens and handheld devices.'에서 P360과 P380 항공기만 터치스크린과 휴대용 장치를 갖추고 있다고 했으므로 (C)가 정답이다. (A), (B), (D)는 지문에 언급되지 않은 내용이다.

어휘 specifically adv. 구체적으로   ahead of time 사전에

Paraphrasing

handheld devices 휴대용 장치 → handheld video controls 휴대용 영상 제어 장치

실전모의고사 3

LISTENING TEST   p.186

1 (B)	2 (A)	3 (A)	4 (C)	5 (D)
6 (D)	7 (A)	8 (C)	9 (C)	10 (B)
11 (A)	12 (C)	13 (B)	14 (A)	15 (B)
16 (A)	17 (A)	18 (B)	19 (B)	20 (C)
21 (C)	22 (B)	23 (A)	24 (C)	25 (A)
26 (C)	27 (B)	28 (A)	29 (A)	30 (B)
31 (C)	32 (C)	33 (A)	34 (B)	35 (D)
36 (C)	37 (D)	38 (B)	39 (A)	40 (C)
41 (C)	42 (C)	43 (A)	44 (B)	45 (B)
46 (D)	47 (C)	48 (D)	49 (A)	50 (D)
51 (B)	52 (D)	53 (D)	54 (C)	55 (D)
56 (C)	57 (B)	58 (D)	59 (A)	60 (D)
61 (C)	62 (D)	63 (A)	64 (C)	65 (A)
66 (C)	67 (C)	68 (A)	69 (C)	70 (C)
71 (B)	72 (C)	73 (A)	74 (D)	75 (C)
76 (B)	77 (C)	78 (D)	79 (B)	80 (A)
81 (D)	82 (D)	83 (D)	84 (B)	85 (C)
86 (C)	87 (A)	88 (B)	89 (D)	90 (D)
91 (A)	92 (D)	93 (D)	94 (C)	95 (B)
96 (C)	97 (A)	98 (A)	99 (D)	100 (B)

READING TEST   p.198

101 (B)	102 (C)	103 (A)	104 (A)	105 (C)
106 (C)	107 (B)	108 (B)	109 (D)	110 (C)
111 (C)	112 (B)	113 (C)	114 (B)	115 (C)
116 (C)	117 (C)	118 (C)	119 (D)	120 (D)
121 (C)	122 (C)	123 (C)	124 (C)	125 (C)
126 (C)	127 (D)	128 (A)	129 (C)	130 (B)
131 (C)	132 (C)	133 (D)	134 (C)	135 (C)
136 (D)	137 (D)	138 (D)	139 (D)	140 (C)
141 (B)	142 (A)	143 (D)	144 (A)	145 (B)
146 (C)	147 (A)	148 (D)	149 (D)	150 (D)
151 (B)	152 (B)	153 (B)	154 (C)	155 (C)
156 (B)	157 (A)	158 (D)	159 (C)	160 (D)
161 (D)	162 (D)	163 (D)	164 (A)	165 (B)
166 (D)	167 (B)	168 (C)	169 (D)	170 (B)
171 (C)	172 (D)	173 (B)	174 (C)	175 (C)
176 (B)	177 (C)	178 (C)	179 (D)	180 (D)
181 (C)	182 (A)	183 (B)	184 (B)	185 (B)
186 (D)	187 (A)	188 (B)	189 (B)	190 (C)
191 (B)	192 (D)	193 (D)	194 (B)	195 (D)
196 (B)	197 (C)	198 (B)	199 (A)	200 (B)

PART 1

1 | 1인 사진   호주

(A) He's lifting a vase off the floor.
(B) He's shaping a piece of pottery.
(C) He's setting bowls onto a shelf.
(D) He's wiping off his hands.

vase n. 꽃병   pottery n. 도자기   shelf n. 선반   wipe off 닦다

해석 (A) 그는 바닥에서 꽃병을 들어 올리고 있다.
(B) 그는 도자기 한 점을 빚고 있다.
(C) 그는 그릇들을 선반에 놓고 있다.
(D) 그는 손을 닦고 있다.

해설 (A) [x] lifting(들어 올리고 있다)은 남자의 동작과 무관하므로 오답이다.
(B) [o] 남자가 도자기 한 점을 빚고 있는 모습을 가장 잘 묘사한 정답이다.
(C) [x] setting(놓고 있다)은 남자의 동작과 무관하므로 오답이다. 사진에 있는 그릇들(bowls)과 선반(shelf)을 사용하여 혼동을 주었다.
(D) [x] wiping off his hands(손을 닦고 있다)는 남자의 동작과 무관하므로 오답이다.

2 | 2인 이상 사진   영국

(A) They're preparing a meal.
(B) They're rinsing some plates in a sink.
(C) They're serving food to some guests.
(D) They're standing across a table.

rinse v. 헹구다, 씻어내다   serve v. (음식을) 내다, 제공하다
across prep. 맞은 편에서, 가로질러

해석 (A) 그들은 식사를 준비하고 있다.
(B) 그들은 싱크대에서 접시들을 헹구고 있다.
(C) 그들은 손님들에게 음식을 내고 있다.
(D) 그들은 테이블 맞은 편에 서 있다.

해설 (A) [o] 두 사람이 식사를 준비하고 있는 모습을 가장 잘 묘사한 정답이다.
(B) [x] rinsing(헹구고 있다)은 사람들의 동작과 무관하고, 사진에 접시들(plates)도 없으므로 오답이다.
(C) [x] serving food(음식을 내고 있다)는 사람들의 동작과 무관하고, 사진에 손님들(guests)도 없으므로 오답이다.
(D) [x] 사진에 테이블(table)이 없으므로 오답이다. They're standing(그들은 서 있다)까지만 듣고 정답으로 고르지 않도록 주의한다.

3 | 2인 이상 사진 🎧 영국

(A) Some people are working on a lift.
(B) Workers are climbing a ladder to a roof.
(C) Some windows are being shut from inside.
(D) Materials are being transported via carts.

lift n. 리프트(수하물 및 사람을 들어 올려주는 장비)   ladder n. 사다리
material n. 자재, 재료   transport v. 운반하다, 이동하다
via prep. ~으로, 을 통하여

해석 (A) 몇몇 사람들이 리프트 위에서 일하고 있다.
(B) 작업자들이 지붕을 향해 사다리를 오르고 있다.
(C) 창문들이 내부에서 닫히고 있다.
(D) 자재들이 카트로 운반되고 있다.

해설 (A) [○] 몇몇 사람들이 리프트 위에서 일하고 있는 모습을 가장 잘 묘사한 정답이다.
(B) [×] climbing(오르고 있다)은 작업자들의 동작과 무관하고, 사진에 사다리(ladder)도 없으므로 오답이다.
(C) [×] 사진에서 창문들(windows)은 보이지만, 닫히고 있는(being shut) 모습은 아니므로 오답이다.
(D) [×] 사진에 카트(carts)가 없으므로 오답이다.

4 | 1인 사진 🎧 캐나다

(A) The man is fishing from a pier.
(B) The man is swimming across a lake.
(C) The man is facing the water.
(D) The man is strolling along the shore.

pier n. 부두   stroll v. 산책하다   shore n. 물가

해석 (A) 남자가 부두에서 낚시하고 있다.
(B) 남자가 호수를 가로질러 수영하고 있다.
(C) 남자가 물을 마주 보고 있다.
(D) 남자가 물가를 따라 산책하고 있다.

해설 (A) [×] 사진에 부두(pier)가 없으므로 오답이다. The man is fishing(남자가 낚시하고 있다)까지만 듣고 정답으로 고르지 않도록 주의한다.
(B) [×] swimming(수영하고 있다)은 남자의 동작과 무관하므로 오답이다.
(C) [○] 남자가 물을 마주 보고 있는 모습을 가장 잘 묘사한 정답이다.
(D) [×] strolling(산책하고 있다)은 남자의 동작과 무관하므로 오답이다.

5 | 2인 이상 사진 🎧 호주

(A) Workers are fixing the wing of an aircraft.
(B) An aircraft is being landed on a runway.
(C) A worker is walking into a storage area.
(D) Suitcases are being handled by a worker.

aircraft n. 항공기   land v. 착륙하다   runway n. 활주로
storage area 저장소   handle v. 다루다

해석 (A) 작업자들이 항공기 날개를 수리하고 있다.
(B) 항공기가 활주로에 착륙되고 있다.
(C) 작업자가 저장소 안으로 걸어 들어가고 있다.
(D) 여행 가방들이 작업자에 의해 다뤄지고 있다.

해설 (A) [×] 사진에 항공기 날개를 수리하고 있는(fixing the wing of an aircraft) 작업자들이 없으므로 오답이다.
(B) [×] 사진에서 항공기(aircraft)는 보이지만, 착륙되고 있는(being landed) 모습은 아니므로 오답이다.
(C) [×] walking into a storage area(저장소 안으로 걸어 들어가고 있다)는 작업자의 동작과 무관하므로 오답이다.
(D) [○] 여행 가방들이 작업자에 의해 다뤄지고 있는 모습을 가장 잘 묘사한 정답이다.

6 | 실내 사진 🎧 미국

(A) A sofa has been covered with a blanket.
(B) Chairs have been arranged on a patio.
(C) A glass door leads to an outdoor pool.
(D) A picture is mounted on the wall.

arrange v. 정리하다, 배열하다   patio n. 안마당
mount v. 고정시키다, 올려놓다

해석 (A) 소파가 담요로 덮여 있다.
(B) 의자들이 안마당에 정리되어 있다.
(C) 유리문이 야외 수영장으로 통한다.
(D) 그림이 벽에 고정되어 있다.

해설 (A) [×] 사진에 담요(blanket)가 없으므로 오답이다. 사진에 있는 소파(sofa)를 사용하여 혼동을 주었다.
(B) [×] 사진의 안마당에 의자들(Chairs)이 없으므로 오답이다.
(C) [×] 사진에 야외 수영장(outdoor pool)이 없으므로 오답이다. A glass door leads to(유리문이 ~으로 통한다)까지만 듣고 정답으로 고르지 않도록 주의한다.
(D) [○] 그림이 벽에 고정되어 있는 모습을 가장 잘 묘사한 정답이다.

PART 2

7 | Who 의문문 🎧 영국 → 호주

Who prepared these documents?
(A) The new intern.
(B) Some customer surveys.
(C) He's ready now.

survey n. 설문 조사

해석 누가 이 문서들을 준비했나요?
(A) 신입 인턴이요.
(B) 고객 설문 조사요.
(C) 그는 이제 준비됐어요.

해설 (A) [○] 신입 인턴이라는 말로, 문서들을 준비한 사람을 언급했으므로 정답이다.
(B) [×] 질문의 documents(문서들)와 관련 있는 surveys(설문 조사)를 사용하여 혼동을 준 오답이다.
(C) [×] 누가 문서들을 준비했는지를 물었는데, 이와 관련이 없는 그는 이제 준비됐다는 내용으로 응답했으므로 오답이다. 질문의

prepared(준비했다)에서 연상할 수 있는 상태인 ready(준비된)를 사용하여 혼동을 주었다.

8 | Why 의문문
캐나다 → 영국

Why is the company hiring more employees?
(A) I'll accompany you.
(B) The personnel department.
(C) There are many upcoming projects.

employee n. 직원   accompany v. 함께 가다, 동반하다
upcoming adj. 다가오는

해석 회사는 왜 직원들을 더 고용하고 있나요?
(A) 제가 당신과 함께 갈게요.
(B) 인사부요.
(C) 다가오는 프로젝트들이 많아요.

해설 (A) [x] 회사가 왜 직원들을 더 고용하고 있는지를 물었는데, 이와 관련이 없는 자신이 함께 가겠다는 내용으로 응답했으므로 오답이다. company - accompany의 유사 발음 어휘를 사용하여 혼동을 주었다.
(B) [x] 질문의 hiring(고용하고 있다)과 관련 있는 personnel department(인사부)를 사용하여 혼동을 준 오답이다.
(C) [o] 다가오는 프로젝트들이 많다는 말로, 직원들을 더 고용하고 있는 이유를 언급했으므로 정답이다.

9 | When 의문문
호주 → 영국

When do I need to return the car?
(A) Leave the keys on the table.
(B) Park anywhere you like.
(C) By noon at the latest.

at the latest 늦어도

해석 제가 언제 차를 반납해야 하나요?
(A) 열쇠를 테이블 위에 두세요.
(B) 당신이 원하는 아무 곳에 주차하세요.
(C) 늦어도 정오까지요.

해설 (A) [x] 질문의 car(차)에서 연상할 수 있는 물건과 관련된 keys(열쇠)를 사용하여 혼동을 준 오답이다.
(B) [x] 언제 차를 반납해야 하는지 시점을 물었는데, 이와 관련이 없는 주차 장소에 대한 내용으로 응답했으므로 오답이다. 질문의 When을 Where로 혼동하여 이를 정답으로 선택하지 않도록 주의한다.
(C) [o] 늦어도 정오까지라는 말로, 차를 반납해야 하는 시점을 언급했으므로 정답이다.

10 | 제공 의문문
캐나다 → 미국

Do you want me to look over our budget figures?
(A) Over 100 attendees.
(B) Thanks, that would help a lot.
(C) To the accounting division.

budget figure 예산액   attendee n. 참석자   accounting n. 회계

해석 제가 우리의 예산액을 검토할까요?
(A) 백 명 이상의 참석자요.
(B) 고마워요, 그건 큰 도움이 될 거예요.
(C) 회계 부서로요.

해설 (A) [x] 질문의 over를 반복 사용하고, figures(액수)에서 연상할 수 있는 숫자와 관련된 100(백)을 사용하여 혼동을 준 오답이다.
(B) [o] Thanks로 제공을 수락한 후, 큰 도움이 될 거라고 부연 설명을 했으므로 정답이다.
(C) [x] 질문의 budget figures(예산액)와 관련 있는 accounting division(회계 부서)을 사용하여 혼동을 준 오답이다.

11 | Who 의문문
호주 → 영국

Who will be in charge of organizing the safety drill?
(A) Either Angela or Matthew.
(B) It's for our security.
(C) Actually, it's still too large.

be in charge of ~을 담당하다   drill n. 훈련

해석 누가 안전 훈련 준비를 담당할 건가요?
(A) Angela 아니면 Matthew요.
(B) 그것은 우리의 보안을 위한 거예요.
(C) 사실은, 그것이 여전히 너무 커요.

해설 (A) [o] Angela 아니면 Matthew라는 말로, 안전 훈련 준비를 담당할 사람을 언급했으므로 정답이다.
(B) [x] 질문의 safety(안전)에서 연상할 수 있는 security(보안)를 사용하여 혼동을 준 오답이다.
(C) [x] 누가 안전 훈련 준비를 담당할 것인지를 물었는데, 이와 관련이 없는 그것이 여전히 너무 크다는 내용으로 응답했으므로 오답이다. 질문의 safety drill(안전 훈련)을 나타낼 수 있는 it을 사용하여 혼동을 주었다.

12 | 조동사 의문문
캐나다 → 호주

Do you know how to use this new copier?
(A) It didn't cost much.
(B) When we return from the meeting.
(C) Sure, let me show you how.

cost v. 비용이 들다

해석 이 새 복사기를 사용하는 방법을 아시나요?
(A) 그것은 비용이 많이 들지 않았어요.
(B) 우리가 회의에서 돌아올 때요.
(C) 물론이죠, 어떻게 하는 건지 제가 보여드릴게요.

해설 (A) [x] 질문의 new copier(새 복사기)에서 연상할 수 있는 가격과 관련된 didn't cost much(비용이 많이 들지 않았다)를 사용하여 혼동을 준 오답이다.
(B) [x] 새 복사기를 사용하는 방법을 아는지를 물었는데, 이와 관련이 없는 회의에서 돌아올 때라는 내용으로 응답했으므로 오답이다.
(C) [o] Sure로 새 복사기를 사용하는 방법을 알고 있음을 전달한 후, 어떻게 하는 건지 보여주겠다는 부연 설명을 했으므로 정답이다.

13 | 부가 의문문
미국 → 캐나다

Putting this bookcase together was fairly easy, wasn't it?
(A) It wasn't there when I looked.
(B) Yes, it only took 10 minutes.
(C) My personal collection of novels.

put ~ together ~을 조립하다   fairly adv. 꽤, 상당히
collection n. 소장품, 수집물

해석 이 책꽂이를 조립하는 것은 꽤 쉬웠어요, 그렇지 않나요?

(A) 제가 봤을 때는 거기에 없었어요.
(B) 네, 10분밖에 안 걸렸어요.
(C) 제 개인적인 소설 소장품이에요.

해설 (A) [×] 책꽂이를 조립하는 것이 쉬웠는지를 물었는데, 이와 관련이 없는 자신이 봤을 때는 거기에 없었다는 내용으로 응답했으므로 오답이다. It wasn't까지만 듣고 정답으로 고르지 않도록 주의한다.
(B) [○] Yes로 의견에 동의한 후, 10분밖에 안 걸렸다는 부연 설명을 했으므로 정답이다.
(C) [×] 질문의 bookcase(책꽂이)와 관련 있는 novels(소설)를 사용하여 혼동을 준 오답이다.

14 | 요청 의문문   호주 → 미국

Would you be able to mail this parcel today?
(A) I'll take care of it now.
(B) I checked my mail last night.
(C) Sorry, I'll make a new one.

mail v. 부치다, 보내다; n. 우편물 parcel n. 소포

해설 오늘 이 소포를 부칠 수 있나요?
(A) 제가 지금 처리할게요.
(B) 제가 어젯밤에 제 우편물을 확인했어요.
(C) 죄송해요, 제가 새로운 것을 만들어 드릴게요.

해설 (A) [○] 자신이 지금 처리하겠다는 말로, 요청을 수락한 정답이다.
(B) [×] 질문의 mail(부치다)을 '우편물'이라는 의미의 명사로 반복 사용하여 혼동을 준 오답이다.
(C) [×] 오늘 이 소포를 부칠 수 있는지를 물었는데, 이와 관련이 없는 새로운 것을 만들어 드리겠다고 응답했으므로 오답이다. Sorry까지만 듣고 정답으로 고르지 않도록 주의한다.

15 | How 의문문   미국 → 캐나다

How did you do on your exams last semester?
(A) For biology and history.
(B) I did well. Thanks for asking.
(C) It lasted longer than I thought.

last adj. 지난; v. 지속되다 semester n. 학기 biology n. 생물학

해설 당신은 지난 학기에 시험을 어떻게 봤나요?
(A) 생물학과 역사학이요.
(B) 잘 봤어요. 물어봐 주셔서 감사합니다.
(C) 제가 생각했던 것보다 오래 지속됐어요.

해설 (A) [×] 질문의 semester(학기)에서 연상할 수 있는 수업 과목과 관련된 biology and history(생물학과 역사학)를 사용하여 혼동을 준 오답이다.
(B) [○] I did well로 지난 학기에 시험을 잘 봤음을 전달한 후, 물어봐 준 것에 대한 감사를 전달했으므로 정답이다.
(C) [×] 질문의 last(지난)를 '지속되다'라는 의미의 동사로 반복 사용하여 혼동을 준 오답이다.

16 | Be동사 의문문   캐나다 → 미국

Are travel expenses covered by our firm?
(A) As long as receipts are submitted.
(B) We're a manufacturing company.
(C) That's quite expensive.

expense n. 비용 cover v. 충당하다 firm n. 회사

해설 출장 비용이 우리 회사에 의해 충당되나요?
(A) 영수증이 제출되기만 한다면요.
(B) 우린 제조 회사예요.
(C) 그건 꽤 비싸네요.

해설 (A) [○] 영수증이 제출되기만 한다면이라는 말로, 출장 비용이 회사에 의해 충당됨을 간접적으로 전달했으므로 정답이다.
(B) [×] 질문의 firm(회사)과 같은 의미인 company를 사용하여 혼동을 준 오답이다.
(C) [×] 출장 비용이 회사에 의해 충당되는지를 물었는데, 이와 관련이 없는 그건 꽤 비싸다는 내용으로 응답했으므로 오답이다. expenses - expensive의 유사 발음 어휘를 사용하여 혼동을 주었다.

17 | 평서문   영국 → 미국

Our first prototype was delivered this morning.
(A) How does it look?
(B) Some test results.
(C) Yes, I can watch over them.

prototype n. 견본, 시제품 deliver v. 배달하다, 배송하다
watch over ~을 지키다

해설 오늘 아침에 우리의 첫 견본이 배달되었어요.
(A) 어떻게 생겼나요?
(B) 몇몇 테스트 결과들이요.
(C) 네, 제가 그것들을 지킬 수 있어요.

해설 (A) [○] 어떻게 생겼는지를 되물어, 배달된 견본에 대한 추가 정보를 요구한 정답이다.
(B) [×] 질문의 prototype(견본)에서 연상할 수 있는 test(테스트)를 사용하여 혼동을 준 오답이다.
(C) [×] 오늘 아침에 첫 견본이 배달되었다고 했는데, 이와 관련이 없는 자신이 그것들을 지킬 수 있다는 내용으로 응답했으므로 오답이다.

18 | 부가 의문문   미국 → 캐나다

The gym should replace these cycling machines, shouldn't it?
(A) I would rather walk there instead.
(B) They don't seem that old to me.
(C) Those are the membership rates.

replace v. 교체하다, 바꾸다 rather adv. 오히려, 차라리 rate n. 요금

해설 체육관이 이 사이클링 기기들을 교체해야 해요, 그렇지 않나요?
(A) 저는 대신에 그곳에 걸어가는 것이 오히려 낫겠어요.
(B) 제가 보기에 그것들은 그렇게 낡아 보이지 않아요.
(C) 그것들은 회원제 요금이에요.

해설 (A) [×] 질문의 cycling(사이클링)에서 연상할 수 있는 운동과 관련된 walk(걷다)를 사용하여 혼동을 준 오답이다. 질문의 gym(체육관)을 나타낼 수 있는 there를 사용하여 혼동을 주었다.
(B) [○] 자신이 보기에 그것들은 그렇게 낡아 보이지 않는다는 말로, 체육관이 사이클링 기기들을 교체하지 않아도 됨을 간접적으로 전달했으므로 정답이다.
(C) [×] 질문의 gym(체육관)과 관련 있는 membership(회원제)을 사용하여 혼동을 준 오답이다. 질문의 cycling machines(사이클링 기기들)를 나타낼 수 있는 Those를 사용하여 혼동을 주었다.

19 | 부정 의문문
영국 → 캐나다

Isn't there supposed to be a thunderstorm later today?
(A) Yes, it should be in the drawer.
(B) I'll check the weather app on my phone.
(C) Put your umbrella over there.

be supposed to ~라고 한다, ~하기로 되어 있다   thunderstorm n. 뇌우
drawer n. 서랍

해석 오늘 늦게 뇌우가 있을 거라고 하지 않나요?
(A) 네, 그것은 서랍 안에 있을 거예요.
(B) 제 핸드폰의 날씨 앱을 확인해 볼게요.
(C) 당신의 우산을 저쪽에 두세요.

해설 (A) [x] 오늘 늦게 뇌우가 있을 거라고 하지 않는지를 물었는데, 그것은 서랍 안에 있을 거라며 관련이 없는 내용으로 응답했으므로 오답이다. 질문의 thunderstorm(뇌우)을 나타낼 수 있는 it을 사용하여 혼동을 주었다. Yes까지만 듣고 정답으로 고르지 않도록 주의한다.
(B) [o] 핸드폰의 날씨 앱을 확인해 보겠다는 말로, 뇌우가 있을 것인지 모른다는 것을 간접적으로 전달했으므로 정답이다.
(C) [x] 질문의 thunderstorm(뇌우)과 관련 있는 umbrella(우산)를 사용하여 혼동을 준 오답이다.

20 | 요청 의문문
영국 → 호주

Could you put these shirts on hangers?
(A) No, the space is very modern.
(B) I bought some new clothes.
(C) Let me finish the dishes first.

hanger n. 옷걸이   modern adj. 현대적인

해석 이 셔츠들을 옷걸이에 걸어 줄 수 있나요?
(A) 아니요, 그 공간은 매우 현대적이에요.
(B) 저는 새 옷을 몇 벌 샀어요.
(C) 설거지를 먼저 끝낼게요.

해설 (A) [x] 셔츠들을 옷걸이에 걸어 줄 수 있는지를 물었는데, 그 공간은 매우 현대적이라며 관련이 없는 내용으로 응답했으므로 오답이다. No까지만 듣고 정답으로 고르지 않도록 주의한다.
(B) [x] 질문의 shirts(셔츠들)와 관련 있는 clothes(옷)를 사용하여 혼동을 준 오답이다.
(C) [o] 설거지를 먼저 끝내겠다는 말로, 셔츠들을 옷걸이에 걸어 줄 수 있냐는 요청을 간접적으로 거절했으므로 정답이다.

21 | Where 의문문
영국 → 캐나다

Where are the laundry soaps in this store?
(A) During the selection process.
(B) At a special discount price.
(C) I think they've run out.

laundry n. 세탁   run out 다 떨어지다

해석 이 가게에 세탁 비누는 어디에 있나요?
(A) 선정 과정 동안에요.
(B) 특별 할인 가격에요.
(C) 제 생각엔 그것들이 다 떨어진 것 같아요.

해설 (A) [x] 가게에 세탁 비누는 어디에 있는지를 물었는데, 선정 과정 동안이라며 관련이 없는 내용으로 응답했으므로 오답이다.
(B) [x] 질문의 store(가게)와 관련 있는 discount price(할인 가격)를 사용하여 혼동을 준 오답이다.
(C) [o] 그것들이 다 떨어진 것 같다는 말로, 가게에 세탁 비누가 없음을 간접적으로 전달했으므로 정답이다.

22 | 조동사 의문문
미국 → 캐나다

Have you met our new board president?
(A) No, it wasn't on the bulletin board.
(B) We were introduced this morning.
(C) These are only for employees.

board n. 이사회, 위원회   bulletin board 게시판
introduce v. 인사시키다, 소개하다

해석 당신은 우리의 새 이사장을 만났나요?
(A) 아니요, 그것은 게시판에 있지 않았어요.
(B) 우리는 오늘 아침에 인사했어요.
(C) 이것들은 직원들만을 위한 거예요.

해설 (A) [x] 질문의 board를 반복 사용하여 혼동을 준 오답이다. No까지만 듣고 정답으로 고르지 않도록 주의한다.
(B) [o] 오늘 아침에 인사했다는 말로, 새 이사장을 만났음을 간접적으로 전달했으므로 정답이다.
(C) [x] 새 이사장을 만났는지를 물었는데, 이와 관련이 없는 이것들은 직원들만을 위한 것이라는 내용으로 응답했으므로 오답이다.

23 | Which 의문문
호주 → 영국

Which store did you pick up that jacket at?
(A) A boutique beside Taylor Apparel.
(B) I usually do my shopping on weekends.
(C) Please pick me up at 3 P.M.

boutique n. 부티크, 양품점

해석 당신은 어느 상점에서 그 재킷을 구했나요?
(A) Taylor Apparel 옆에 있는 부티크요.
(B) 저는 주로 주말에 쇼핑을 해요.
(C) 저를 오후 3시에 태우러 와주세요.

해설 (A) [o] Taylor Apparel 옆에 있는 부티크라는 말로, 재킷을 구한 상점을 언급했으므로 정답이다.
(B) [x] 질문의 store(상점)와 관련 있는 shopping(쇼핑)을 사용하여 혼동을 준 오답이다.
(C) [x] 어느 상점에서 그 재킷을 구했는지를 물었는데, 이와 관련이 없는 오후 3시에 태우러 와달라는 내용으로 응답했으므로 오답이다. 질문의 pick up(구하다, 사다)을 '태우러 가다'라는 의미로 반복 사용하여 혼동을 주었다.

24 | Why 의문문
미국 → 호주

Why do you plan to leave so early?
(A) At 5 o'clock, precisely.
(B) Yes, as soon as possible.
(C) My tennis club has a match today.

precisely adv. 정확하게

해석 당신은 왜 이렇게 일찍 출발할 계획인가요?
(A) 정확하게 5시에요.
(B) 네, 가능한 한 빨리요.
(C) 제 테니스 클럽이 오늘 경기가 있어요.

해설 (A) [x] 왜 이렇게 일찍 출발할 계획인지 이유를 물었는데, 이와 관련이

없는 시간으로 응답했으므로 오답이다.
(B) [×] 의문사 의문문에 Yes로 응답했으므로 오답이다. 질문의 early(일찍)와 관련 있는 soon(빨리)을 사용하여 혼동을 주었다.
(C) [o] 자신의 테니스 클럽이 오늘 경기가 있다는 말로, 일찍 출발하려고 계획하는 이유를 언급했으므로 정답이다.

25 | 선택 의문문 　　　영국 → 캐나다

Shall we meet the investors at the construction site or in our office?
(A) They want to tour the location.
(B) His office is the door on your left.
(C) I'll have the contractor come as well.

investor n. 투자자 construction n. 공사, 건설 location n. 부지, 용지
contractor n. 계약자

해석 투자자들을 공사 현장에서 만날까요, 아니면 우리 사무실에서 만날까요?
(A) 그들은 그 부지를 견학하고 싶어 해요.
(B) 그의 사무실은 당신의 왼쪽 방이에요.
(C) 제가 계약자도 오게 할게요.

해설 (A) [o] 그들이 그 부지를 견학하고 싶어 한다는 말로, 공사 현장에서 만날 것을 간접적으로 선택했으므로 정답이다.
(B) [×] 투자자들을 공사 현장에서 만날지 아니면 사무실에서 만날지를 물었는데, 이와 관련이 없는 그의 사무실은 상대방의 왼쪽 방이라는 내용으로 응답했으므로 오답이다. 질문의 office를 반복 사용하여 혼동을 주었다.
(C) [×] 질문의 investors(투자자들)와 관련 있는 contractor(계약자)를 사용하여 혼동을 준 오답이다.

26 | Where 의문문 　　　캐나다 → 영국

Where would you like me to leave this shipment of posters?
(A) They're for this weekend's event.
(B) We paid extra for rush delivery.
(C) Right here at reception is fine.

shipment n. 배송물, 배송 extra n. 추가 요금; adj. 추가의
reception n. 접수처

해석 제가 이 포스터 배송물을 어디에 두기 원하세요?
(A) 그것들은 이번 주말 행사용이에요.
(B) 저희는 긴급 배달을 위한 추가 요금을 냈어요.
(C) 바로 여기 접수처에 두시면 괜찮아요.

해설 (A) [×] 질문의 posters(포스터)에서 연상할 수 있는 event(행사)를 사용하여 혼동을 준 오답이다.
(B) [×] 포스터 배송물을 어디에 둘지를 물었는데, 이와 관련이 없는 긴급 배달을 위한 추가 요금을 냈다고 응답했으므로 오답이다.
(C) [o] 바로 여기 접수처에 두면 괜찮다는 말로, 포스터 배송물을 둘 장소를 언급했으므로 정답이다.

27 | 제공 의문문 　　　호주 → 미국

Would you like a hand contacting our donors?
(A) At the previous fundraiser.
(B) Patrick is helping me.
(C) The contract was completed.

hand n. 도움 contact v. 연락하다 donor n. 기부자, 기증자
fundraiser n. 모금 행사

해석 우리의 기부자들에게 연락하는 것에 도움을 드릴까요?
(A) 지난번 모금 행사에서요.
(B) Patrick이 저를 돕고 있어요.
(C) 그 계약은 완료되었어요.

해설 (A) [×] 질문의 donors(기부자들)와 관련 있는 fundraiser(모금 행사)를 사용하여 혼동을 준 오답이다.
(B) [o] Patrick이 자신을 돕고 있다는 말로, 도움을 간접적으로 거절했으므로 정답이다.
(C) [×] 기부자들에게 연락하는 것에 도움을 줄지를 물었는데, 이와 관련이 없는 계약이 완료되었다는 내용으로 응답했으므로 오답이다. contacting - contract의 유사 발음 어휘를 사용하여 혼동을 주었다.

28 | 평서문 　　　영국 → 캐나다

These pamphlets need to be put into envelopes.
(A) I'll get some from the supply room.
(B) They came from a stationery store.
(C) They're full of good information.

pamphlet n. 소책자, 팸플릿 envelope n. 봉투 supply room 비품실
stationery store 문구점

해석 이 소책자들은 봉투에 넣어져야 해요.
(A) 제가 비품실에서 몇 개 가져올게요.
(B) 그것들은 문구점에서 왔어요.
(C) 그것들은 좋은 정보가 가득해요.

해설 (A) [o] 비품실에서 몇 개 가져오겠다는 말로, 소책자들을 넣을 봉투를 가져오겠다고 제안했으므로 정답이다.
(B) [×] 질문의 envelopes(봉투)에서 연상할 수 있는 구매 장소와 관련된 stationery store(문구점)를 사용하여 혼동을 준 오답이다. 질문의 envelopes(봉투)를 나타낼 수 있는 They를 사용하여 혼동을 주었다.
(C) [×] 질문의 pamphlets(소책자들)에서 연상할 수 있는 good information(좋은 정보)을 사용하여 혼동을 준 오답이다. 질문의 pamphlets(소책자들)를 나타낼 수 있는 They를 사용하여 혼동을 주었다.

29 | How 의문문 　　　미국 → 호주

How will the company celebrate its 25th anniversary?
(A) Several options are being considered.
(B) We celebrated it together.
(C) I have worked here for 20 years.

celebrate v. 기념하다 several adj. 여러 consider v. 고려하다

해석 회사는 25주년을 어떻게 기념할 것인가요?
(A) 여러 선택지들이 고려되고 있어요.
(B) 우리는 함께 기념했어요.
(C) 저는 이곳에서 20년 동안 일했어요.

해설 (A) [o] 여러 선택지들이 고려되고 있다는 말로, 25주년을 어떻게 기념할지 아직 모른다는 것을 간접적으로 전달했으므로 정답이다.
(B) [×] 질문의 celebrate을 celebrated로 반복 사용하여 혼동을 준 오답이다.
(C) [×] 질문의 company(회사)와 관련 있는 worked(일했다)를 사용하여 혼동을 준 오답이다.

30 | Be동사 의문문 　　　미국 → 영국

Are you interested in advanced golf lessons?
(A) We're holding more orientation sessions.

(B) I'm not sure I'm ready for that yet.
(C) I played golf with him, too.

advanced adj. 고급의, 상급의   hold v. 열다, 주최하다

해석 당신은 고급 골프 수업에 관심이 있나요?
(A) 우리는 더 많은 오리엔테이션 수업을 열 거예요.
(B) 제가 아직 그것에 준비되었는지 잘 모르겠어요.
(C) 저도 그와 골프를 했었어요.

해설 (A) [×] 질문의 lessons(수업)와 같은 의미인 sessions를 사용하여 혼동을 준 오답이다.
(B) [○] 아직 그것에 준비되었는지 잘 모르겠다는 말로, 고급 골프 수업에 관심이 없음을 간접적으로 전달했으므로 정답이다.
(C) [×] 질문의 golf를 반복 사용하여 혼동을 준 오답이다.

31 | 평서문 호주 → 미국

The color of this carpet sample seems far too bright.
(A) After we spread them around the room.
(B) Some rugs for our main reception area.
(C) Would you like to see another selection?

spread v. 펼치다, 펴다   rug n. 깔개, 양탄자

해석 이 카펫 샘플의 색깔은 너무 밝은 것 같아요.
(A) 우리가 그것들을 방에 펼친 후에요.
(B) 우리의 가장 큰 응접실에 둘 깔개들 몇 개요.
(C) 다른 선택지들을 보시겠어요?

해설 (A) [×] 카펫 샘플의 색깔이 너무 밝은 것 같다고 했는데, 이와 관련이 없는 그것들을 방에 펼친 후라는 말로 응답했으므로 오답이다. 질문의 carpet(카펫)에서 연상할 수 있는 행동과 관련된 spread(펼치다)를 사용하여 혼동을 주었다.
(B) [×] 질문의 carpet(카펫)과 관련 있는 rugs(깔개들)를 사용하여 혼동을 준 오답이다.
(C) [○] 다른 선택지들을 보시겠는지를 되물어, 문제점에 대한 해결책을 제시했으므로 정답이다.

PART 3

[32-34] 캐나다 → 영국

Questions 32-34 refer to the following conversation.

M: ³²**Welcome to the Excel Corporate Charity Event.** ³³**If you tell me your full name and the company you work for, I can let you know which seat you have been assigned to.**
W: My name is Prema Khan, and I'm representing my investment firm, Mumbai International. But before I find my seat, is there a place where I can hang my coat? I'd rather not keep it with me all night.
M: ³⁴**First, let me lead you to your table.** Then, I would be happy to check your coat for you.

assign v. 배정하다, 맡기다   represent v. 대표하다   investment n. 투자
check v. (임시로) 보관하다

해석
32-34번은 다음 대화에 관한 문제입니다.

남: ³²Excel사의 자선 행사에 오신 것을 환영합니다. ³³저에게 성함과 일하시는 회사를 알려 주시면, 배정된 좌석을 안내해 드릴 수 있습니다.
여: 제 이름은 Prema Khan이고, 투자 회사인 Mumbai International사를 대표하고 있습니다. 그런데 좌석을 찾기 전에, 제 코트를 걸 수 있는 곳이 있나요? 이걸 저녁 내내 갖고 있고 싶지 않아서요.
남: ³⁴우선, 테이블로 안내해 드리겠습니다. 그다음에, 기꺼이 당신의 코트를 보관해 드리겠습니다.

32 | 특정 세부 사항 문제

해석 무슨 행사가 열리고 있는가?
(A) 사업 세미나
(B) 시상식
(C) 자선 기금 모금 행사
(D) 주주 회의

해설 질문의 핵심 어구(event)와 관련된 주변을 주의 깊게 듣는다. 남자가 "Welcome to the Excel Corporate Charity Event."라며 Excel사의 자선 행사에 온 것을 환영한다고 하였다. 따라서 (C)가 정답이다.

어휘 shareholder n. 주주

Paraphrasing
Charity Event 자선 행사 → charity fund-raiser 자선 기금 모금 행사

33 | 요청 문제

해석 남자는 무엇을 요청하는가?
(A) 회사 이름
(B) 직장 주소
(C) 좌석 번호
(D) 확인 코드

해설 남자의 말에서 요청과 관련된 표현이 포함된 문장을 주의 깊게 듣는다. 남자가 "If you tell me your full name and the company you work for, I can let you know which seat you have been assigned to."라며 여자의 이름과 일하는 회사를 알려 주면 배정된 좌석을 안내해 줄 수 있다고 하였다. 따라서 (A)가 정답이다.

어휘 confirmation n. 확인, 확증

34 | 다음에 할 일 문제

해석 남자는 다음에 무엇을 할 것 같은가?
(A) 음료를 꺼낸다.
(B) 손님을 안내한다.
(C) 명단을 확인한다.
(D) 안건을 설명한다.

해설 대화의 마지막 부분을 주의 깊게 듣는다. 남자가 "First, let me lead you to your table."이라며 우선 테이블로 안내해 주겠다고 하였다. 따라서 (B)가 정답이다.

어휘 bring out 꺼내다, 끌어내다   escort v. 안내하다, 인도하다
agenda n. 안건, 의제

Paraphrasing
lead 안내하다 → Escort 안내하다

[35-37] 미국 → 캐나다 → 호주

Questions 35-37 refer to the following conversation with three speakers.

W: Hey, Mike and Floyd. ³⁵**Did you guys see the memo from human resources about changes to the travel expense policy?**

M1: Yes. The company's increasing the amount that employees can be reimbursed to $5,000 per trip.
W: Don't you think that's high? ³⁶**On my last business trip, I didn't spend more than $1,600 for all my expenses.**
M1: Sure . . . but ³⁷**you and the other technology staff don't have to travel for as long as we do**.
M2: Exactly. ³⁷**We also have to rent presentation equipment for sales events and take clients out to secure new projects.**
W: I suppose you're right. I didn't think of it that way.

travel expense 출장비   reimburse v. 상환하다, 배상하다
secure v. 확보하다

해석
35-37번은 다음 세 명의 대화에 관한 문제입니다.
여: 안녕하세요, Mike와 Floyd. ³⁵출장비 방침의 변화에 관해 인사 부서에서 보낸 회람을 봤나요?
남1: 네. 회사가 직원들이 상환받을 수 있는 금액을 출장당 5,000달러로 인상할 거래요.
여: 그게 높다고 생각하지 않나요? ³⁶지난 출장에서 저는 제 모든 경비에 1,600달러 이상을 쓰지 않았어요.
남1: 그렇죠... 하지만 ³⁷당신과 다른 기술부 직원들은 저희만큼 길게 출장을 갈 필요가 없잖아요.
남2: 바로 그거예요. ³⁷저희는 영업 행사들을 위해 발표 장비도 빌려야 하고 새로운 프로젝트들을 확보하기 위해 고객들도 대접해야 해요.
여: 당신 말이 맞는 것 같네요. 제가 그렇게 생각하지 못했어요.

35 | 주제 문제

해석 화자들은 주로 무엇에 관해 이야기하고 있는가?
(A) 고객 계약서
(B) 프로젝트 마감 기한
(C) 항공편 예약
(D) 회사 규정

해설 대화의 주제를 묻는 문제이므로, 대화의 초반을 반드시 듣는다. 여자가 "Did you guys see the memo from human resources about changes to the travel expense policy?"라며 출장비 방침의 변화에 관해 인사 부서에서 보낸 회람을 봤는지 물은 후, 변경되는 회사 규정에 관한 내용으로 대화가 이어지고 있다. 따라서 (D)가 정답이다.

어휘 deadline n. 마감 기한   regulation n. 규정

36 | 언급 문제

해석 여자는 그녀의 지난 출장에 관해 무엇을 말하는가?
(A) 매우 길지는 않았다.
(B) 전체 팀을 포함했다.
(C) 비용이 많이 들지 않았다.
(D) 완전히 상환되지 않았다.

해설 여자의 말에서 질문의 핵심 어구(her last business trip)와 관련된 내용을 주의 깊게 듣는다. 여자가 "On my last business trip, I didn't spend more than $1,600 for all my expenses."라며 지난 출장에서 그녀의 모든 경비에 1,600달러 이상을 쓰지 않았다고 하였다. 따라서 (C)가 정답이다.

37 | 화자 문제

해석 남자들은 어느 부서에서 일하는 것 같은가?

(A) 인사
(B) 회계
(C) 기술
(D) 영업

해설 대화에서 신분 및 직업과 관련된 표현을 놓치지 않고 듣는다. 남자 1이 "you and the other technology staff don't have to travel for as long as we do"라며 여자와 다른 기술부 직원들은 남자1과 남자2만큼 길게 출장을 갈 필요가 없다고 하자, 남자2가 "We also have to rent presentation equipment for sales events and take clients out to secure new projects."라며 자신들은 영업 행사들을 위해 발표 장비도 빌려야 하고 새로운 프로젝트들을 확보하기 위해 고객들도 대접해야 한다고 한 것을 통해 남자들이 일하는 부서가 영업 부서임을 알 수 있다. 따라서 (D)가 정답이다.

[38-40]
영국 → 호주

Questions 38-40 refer to the following conversation.

W: Hello, Mr. Lowell. My name is Margot Collins, and ³⁸**I'm calling from *The Norwood Chronicle*.** ³⁸/³⁹**Our paper is planning a series of articles on local entrepreneurs, and I'd like to interview you.** Would you be open to that?
M: Sure, but ³⁹**I want to know more about the series before committing**.
W: The articles will focus on how Portland residents came to own their companies. Since you're one of the city's most prominent businesspeople, our readers would be interested in learning about you.
M: In that case, ⁴⁰**I'd be happy to be interviewed. How's Tuesday?**

entrepreneur n. 사업가   commit v. 약속하다   resident n. 주민
prominent adj. 저명한, 중요한

해석
38-40번은 다음 대화에 관한 문제입니다.
여: 안녕하세요, Mr. Lowell. 제 이름은 Margot Collins이고, ³⁸*The Norwood Chronicle*지에서 전화드립니다. ³⁸/³⁹저희 신문사에서 지역 사업가들에 대한 기사 시리즈를 계획 중인데, 당신을 인터뷰하고 싶어요. 그것을 하실 의향이 있으신가요?
남: 물론이죠, 하지만 ³⁹저는 약속하기 전에 그 시리즈에 대해 더 알고 싶어요.
여: 기사는 포틀랜드의 주민들이 어떻게 그들의 회사를 소유하게 되었는지에 초점을 맞출 거예요. 당신이 이 도시의 가장 저명한 기업인들 중 한 명이기 때문에, 우리의 독자들이 당신에 대해 알게 되는 것에 관심이 있을 거예요.
남: 그렇다면, ⁴⁰기꺼이 인터뷰를 할게요. 화요일은 어떠세요?

38 | 화자 문제

해석 여자는 어디에서 일하는 것 같은가?
(A) 홍보 회사에서
(B) 신문사에서
(C) 경영 회사에서
(D) 관공서에서

해설 대화에서 신분 및 직업과 관련된 표현을 놓치지 않고 듣는다. 여자가 "I'm calling from *The Norwood Chronicle*. Our paper is planning a series of articles on local entrepreneurs, and I'd like to interview you."라며 *The Norwood Chronicle*지에서 전화했다고 한 후, 자신들의 신문사에서 지역 사업가들에 대한 기사 시리즈를 계획 중인데 남자를 인터뷰하고 싶다고 한 것을 통해 여자가 신문사에서 일한다는 것을 알 수

39 | 특정 세부 사항 문제

해석 남자는 무엇에 대해 더 알고 싶어 하는가?
(A) 곧 나올 기사들
(B) 잠재적인 독자 수
(C) 특별 구독 할인
(D) 조기 등록 기간

해설 질문의 핵심 어구(want to learn more about)와 관련된 내용을 주의 깊게 듣는다. 여자가 "Our paper is planning a series of articles on local entrepreneurs, and I'd like to interview you."라며 자신들의 신문사에서 지역 사업가들에 대한 기사 시리즈를 계획 중인데 남자를 인터뷰하고 싶다고 하자, 남자가 "I want to know more about the series before committing"이라며 약속하기 전에 그 시리즈에 대해 더 알고 싶다고 하였다. 따라서 (A)가 정답이다.

어휘 upcoming adj. 곧 나올   readership n. 독자 수   enrollment n. 등록, 입학

40 | 다음에 할 일 문제

해석 화요일에 무슨 일이 일어날 것 같은가?
(A) 몇몇 기자들이 만날 것이다.
(B) 주민들이 행사를 위해 모일 것이다.
(C) 인터뷰가 진행될 것이다.
(D) 기사가 공개될 것이다.

해설 질문의 핵심 어구(Tuesday)가 언급된 주변을 주의 깊게 듣는다. 남자가 "I'd be happy to be interviewed. How's Tuesday?"라며 기꺼이 인터뷰를 하겠다고 하고, 화요일은 어떤지 물었다. 따라서 (C)가 정답이다.

어휘 journalist n. 기자   story n. 기사, 이야기

[41-43]

미국 → 캐나다

Questions 41-43 refer to the following conversation.

W: Hey, I need to talk to you about tomorrow. I know I offered to drive us to the conference venue in the morning, but I don't think I can. **⁴¹For some reason, my car won't start. I need to have it towed to a repair center.**
M: That's OK. **⁴²Rachel will have room in her van, so I'm sure we can ride with her instead.**
W: Great. **⁴³Do you think she can also pick me up at home?** Since I won't have a vehicle, it will be hard for me to go anywhere.
M: I don't think she'll mind.

tow v. 견인하다, 끌다   room n. 자리, 공간   pick up ~를 태우러 가다

해석
41-43번은 다음 대화에 관한 문제입니다.
여: 안녕하세요, 내일에 대해 이야기할 게 있어요. 아침에 제 차로 콘퍼런스 장소까지 가자고 제안한 건 알지만, 그럴 수 없을 것 같아요. ⁴¹무슨 이유인지 제 차가 시동이 걸리지 않아요. 그것을 수리 센터로 견인시켜야 해요.
남: 괜찮아요. ⁴²Rachel의 승합차에 자리가 있을 테니, 대신 우리가 그녀와 함께 타면 될 거예요.
여: 잘됐네요. ⁴³그녀가 저를 태우러 집으로 와줄 수도 있을 것 같나요? 제가 차가 없을 테니, 어디든 가기가 어려울 거예요.
남: 그녀는 기꺼이 해줄 것 같아요.

41 | 문제점 문제

해석 여자는 무슨 문제를 언급하는가?
(A) 계획들에 대해 잊었다.
(B) 행사에 갈 수 없다.
(C) 그녀의 차가 수리되어야 한다.
(D) 그녀의 콘퍼런스 자료가 분실되었다.

해설 여자의 말에서 부정적인 표현이 언급된 주변을 주의 깊게 듣는다. 여자가 "For some reason, my car won't start. I need to have it towed to a repair center."라며 무슨 이유인지 차가 시동이 걸리지 않는다고 한 후, 차를 수리 센터로 견인시켜야 한다고 하였다. 따라서 (C)가 정답이다.

42 | 제안 문제

해석 남자는 무엇을 제안하는가?
(A) 일부 부품을 교체하는 것
(B) 대중교통을 이용하는 것
(C) 다른 사람과 함께 차를 타는 것
(D) 고객에게 연락하는 것

해설 남자의 말에서 제안과 관련된 표현이 언급된 내용을 주의 깊게 듣는다. 남자가 "Rachel will have room in her van, so I'm sure we can ride with her instead."라며 Rachel의 승합차에 자리가 있을 테니 대신 그녀와 함께 타면 될 것이라고 제안하였다. 따라서 (C)가 정답이다.

어휘 component n. 부품, 요소

43 | 특정 세부 사항 문제

해석 여자는 무엇에 관해 문의하는가?
(A) 그녀를 태우러 올 수 있는지
(B) 그녀가 일정을 바꿔야 하는지
(C) 장소가 얼마나 멀리 있는지
(D) 동료가 어디에 가고 싶어 하는지

해설 대화에서 여자의 말을 주의 깊게 듣는다. 여자가 "Do you think she[Rachel] can also pick me up at home?"이라며 Rachel이 자신을 태우러 집으로 와줄 수도 있을 것 같은지를 묻고 있다. 따라서 (A)가 정답이다.

[44-46]

호주 → 미국

Questions 44-46 refer to the following conversation.

M: I'm glad I caught you, Beth. **⁴⁴Our company is designing Fieldstone Financial's new office building. ⁴⁵I'm meeting with one of their representatives next week to talk about the project timetable**, and I'd like you to join me.
W: OK. I heard about the new contract, but I didn't know I'd be involved. I assume you're running the project?
M: Jenna Adams is leading the team. I'm only involved in the early stages.
W: This is going to be her first time in a management role, isn't it?
M: **⁴⁶Yes. But she's worked on similar projects in the past, so I'm confident that she'll do well.**

catch v. 때마침 만나다, 발견하다   representative n. 대표   timetable n. 일정   management n. 관리

해석
44-46번은 다음 대화에 관한 문제입니다.
남: 때마침 당신을 만나서 기쁘네요, Beth. ⁴⁴우리 회사는 Fieldstone

Financial사의 새로운 사무실 건물을 설계하고 있어요. ⁴⁵저는 다음 주에 프로젝트 일정에 관해 논의하기 위해 그 회사의 대표들 중 한 명과 만날 것인데, 당신이 저와 함께했으면 해요.

여: 좋아요. 새로운 계약에 관해서는 들었는데, 저도 참여하게 될지는 몰랐어요. 당신이 이 프로젝트를 진행할 것이죠?

남: Jenna Adams가 팀장이 될 거예요. 저는 초기 단계에만 관여해요.

여: 이번이 그녀가 처음으로 관리직을 맡는 거네요, 그렇지 않나요?

남: ⁴⁶네. 하지만 그녀가 과거에 비슷한 프로젝트들을 해 봐서 잘할 거라고 확신해요.

44 | 화자 문제

해석 화자들은 어디에서 일하는 것 같은가?
(A) 채용 업체에서
(B) 건축 회사에서
(C) 금융 기관에서
(D) 법률 사무소에서

해설 대화에서 신분 및 직업과 관련된 표현을 놓치지 않고 듣는다. 남자가 "Our company is designing Fieldstone Financial's new office building."이라며 자신들의 회사가 Fieldstone Financial사의 새로운 사무실 건물을 설계하고 있다고 한 것을 통해 화자들이 건축 회사에서 일한다는 것을 알 수 있다. 따라서 (B)가 정답이다.

어휘 architectural adj. 건축의

45 | 다음에 할 일 문제

해석 다음 주 회의 동안 무슨 일이 일어날 것인가?
(A) 계약이 마무리될 것이다.
(B) 일정이 논의될 것이다.
(C) 시범이 보여질 것이다.
(D) 디자인이 공개될 것이다.

해설 질문의 핵심 어구(the meeting next week)와 관련된 내용을 주의 깊게 듣는다. "I'm meeting with one of their representatives next week to talk about the project timetable"이라며 다음 주에 프로젝트 일정에 관해 논의하기 위해 그 회사의 대표들 중 한 명과 만날 것이라고 하였다. 따라서 (B)가 정답이다.

어휘 finalize v. 마무리하다 demonstration n. 시범

46 | 의도 파악 문제

해석 여자는 왜 "이번이 그녀가 처음으로 관리직을 맡는 거네요"라고 말하는가?
(A) 프로젝트의 중요성을 강조하기 위해
(B) 동료가 승진했다는 것을 나타내기 위해
(C) 남자가 계획을 지원하도록 장려하기 위해
(D) 개인의 능력에 대한 의구심을 표하기 위해

해설 질문의 인용어구(This is going to be her first time in a management role)가 언급된 주변을 주의 깊게 듣는다. 여자가 이번이 그녀[Jenna Adams]가 처음으로 관리직을 맡는 것이 아닌지 묻자, 남자가 "Yes. But she's worked on similar projects in the past, so I'm confident that she'll do well."이라며 Jenna Adams가 처음으로 관리직을 맡게 되었지만, 그녀가 과거에 비슷한 프로젝트들을 해 봐서 잘할 거라고 확신한다고 한 말을 통해 여자의 말이 개인의 능력에 대한 의구심을 표하기 위한 의도임을 알 수 있다. 따라서 (D)가 정답이다.

어휘 initiative n. 계획 doubt n. 의구심

[47-49]

영국 → 캐나다 → 호주

Questions 47-49 refer to the following conversation with three speakers.

W: ⁴⁷For the next stage of this focus group meeting, I want to ask both of you about the instruction manual for our desktop computer. What are your impressions?

M1: Personally, I think it could be improved.

W: Can you elaborate on that?

M1: Well ... ⁴⁸the part about modifying interior components is vague.

M2: Yeah, and I couldn't find directions on how to use the orange cable that's provided.

W: OK. I'll make a note of those points.

M2: ⁴⁹It'd also be useful if the manual had more graphics.

M1: ⁴⁹Right—to illustrate the various set-up steps.

focus group 포커스 그룹(테스트할 상품에 대해서 토의하는 소비자 그룹)
impression n. 생각, 인상 elaborate v. 자세히 설명하다
modify v. 변경하다, 바꾸다 component n. 부품 vague adj. 모호한
make a note of ~을 적어 두다, 써 놓다 illustrate v. 설명하다
set-up n. 설치

해석
47-49번은 다음 세 명의 대화에 관한 문제입니다.

여: ⁴⁷이 포커스 그룹 모임의 다음 단계로, 두 분께 저희의 데스크톱 컴퓨터의 사용 설명서에 관해 여쭤보고 싶습니다. 여러분들의 생각은 어떠신가요?

남1: 개인적으로, 저는 그것이 개선될 수 있다고 생각해요.

여: 그것에 대해 자세히 설명해 주시겠습니까?

남1: 음... ⁴⁸내부 부품들을 변경하는 것에 관한 부분이 모호해요.

남2: 네, 그리고 제공되는 주황색 케이블을 사용하는 방법에 대한 설명도 찾을 수가 없었어요.

여: 알겠습니다. 제가 그 의견들을 적어 두겠습니다.

남2: ⁴⁹또한 설명서에 더 많은 삽화가 있으면 유용할 거예요.

남1: ⁴⁹맞아요, 다양한 설치 단계들을 설명하기 위해서요.

47 | 화자 문제

해석 남자들은 누구인 것 같은가?
(A) 수리 전문가들
(B) 영업 사원들
(C) 조사 참여자들
(D) 학회 참석자들

해설 대화에서 신분 및 직업과 관련된 표현을 놓치지 않고 듣는다. 여자가 "For the next stage of this focus group meeting, I want to ask both of you about the instruction manual for our desktop computer."라며 포커스 그룹 모임의 다음 단계로 남자들에게 데스크톱 컴퓨터의 사용 설명서에 관해 물어보고 싶다고 한 것을 통해 남자들이 포커스 그룹 모임에 참석한 조사 참여자들임을 알 수 있다. 따라서 (C)가 정답이다.

48 | 언급 문제

해석 컴퓨터 설명서에 관해 무엇이 언급되는가?
(A) 최근에 업데이트되었다.
(B) 작은 서체 크기를 사용한다.
(C) 다수의 언어들로 인쇄되어 있다.
(D) 특정 부분에서 명확성이 부족하다.

해설 질문의 핵심 어구(computer manual)와 관련된 내용을 주의 깊게 듣

는다. 남자1이 "the part about modifying interior components is vague"라며 내부 부품들을 변경하는 것에 관한 부분이 모호하다고 하였다. 따라서 (D)가 정답이다.

어휘 **multiple** adj. 다수의 **clarity** n. 명확성

Paraphrasing

vague 모호한 → lacks clarity 명확성이 부족하다

49 | 제안 문제

해설 남자들은 무엇을 제안하는가?
(A) 더 많은 그림들을 사용하기
(B) 사본을 출력하기
(C) 안내서를 짧게 하기
(D) 도입부를 추가하기

해설 남자들의 말에서 제안과 관련된 표현이 언급된 내용을 주의 깊게 듣는다. 남자2가 "It'd also be useful if the manual had more graphics."라며 설명서에 더 많은 삽화가 있으면 유용할 것이라고 하자, 남자1이 "Right"이라며 동의하였다. 따라서 (A)가 정답이다.

[50-52]

호주 → 미국

Questions 50-52 refer to the following conversation.

M: ⁵⁰**Thanks for choosing Prim Hair. I hope you found our services satisfactory.** Is there anything else I can help you with?

W: Actually, ⁵¹**I'm interested in some of your merchandise. Your stylist recommended trying Nature's Touch shampoo. Could you add a bottle of that to my bill?**

M: Certainly. ⁵²**We also have a promotion on that brand this week, so everything from that line is available for 10 percent off its normal retail price.**

W: Great. Then please add a bottle of conditioner as well.

satisfactory adj. 만족스러운 **merchandise** n. 상품, 제품 **stylist** n. 미용사 **promotion** n. 판촉 행사, 홍보 **retail price** 소매가

해석

50-52번은 다음 대화에 관한 문제입니다.

남: ⁵⁰Prim Hair를 선택해 주셔서 감사합니다. 저희 서비스가 만족스러우셨기를 바랍니다. 도움이 더 필요한 것이 있으신가요?

여: 사실 ⁵¹저는 이곳의 몇몇 상품에 관심이 있습니다. 미용사가 Nature's Touch 샴푸를 사용해보라고 추천했어요. 제 계산서에 그 상품 한 병을 추가해 주실 수 있나요?

남: 물론이죠. ⁵²저희는 이번 주에 그 브랜드에 대해 판촉 행사도 하고 있어서 그 라인의 모든 제품은 정상 소매가에서 10퍼센트 할인된 가격에 구매 가능합니다.

여: 잘됐네요. 그러면 컨디셔너 한 병도 추가해 주세요.

50 | 장소 문제

해설 화자들은 어디에 있는 것 같은가?
(A) 의류 가게에
(B) 소매 판매점에
(C) 백화점에
(D) 미용실에

해설 대화에서 장소와 관련된 표현을 놓치지 않고 듣는다. 남자가 "Thanks for choosing Prim Hair. I hope you found our services satisfactory."

라며 Prim Hair를 선택해 주셔서 감사하다고 한 후, 서비스가 만족스러우셨기를 바란다고 하였다. 이를 통해 미용실에서 대화가 이루어지고 있음을 알 수 있다. 따라서 (D)가 정답이다.

어휘 **boutique** n. 가게, 상점 **department store** 백화점 **beauty salon** 미용실

51 | 특정 세부 사항 문제

해설 여자는 무엇을 하고 싶어 하는가?
(A) 머리를 자른다.
(B) 물건을 구매한다.
(C) 약속을 정한다.
(D) 관리자와 이야기한다.

해설 질문의 핵심 어구(want to do)와 관련된 내용을 주의 깊게 듣는다. 여자가 "I'm interested in some of your merchandise. Your stylist recommended trying Nature's Touch shampoo. Could you add a bottle of that to my bill?"이라며 이곳의 몇몇 상품에 관심이 있고, 미용사가 Nature's Touch 샴푸를 사용해보라고 추천했다고 한 후, 계산서에 그 상품 한 병을 추가해 줄 수 있는지 물었다. 따라서 (B)가 정답이다.

어휘 **arrange** v. 정하다, 준비하다

Paraphrasing

add ~ to ~ bill 계산서에 추가하다 → Make a purchase 물건을 구매하다

52 | 언급 문제

해설 남자는 Nature's Touch 브랜드에 관해 무엇을 말하는가?
(A) 몇몇 미용사들에 의해 사용된다.
(B) 유기농 원료들로 만들어졌다.
(C) 완전히 매진되었다.
(D) 주말까지 할인 중이다.

해설 질문의 핵심 어구(Nature's Touch brand)와 관련된 내용을 주의 깊게 듣는다. 남자가 "We also have a promotion on that brand[Nature's Touch] this week, so everything from that line is available for 10 percent off its normal retail price."라며 이번 주에 Nature's Touch에 대해 판촉 행사도 하고 있어서 그 라인의 모든 제품은 정상 소매가에서 10퍼센트 할인된 가격에 구매 가능하다고 하였다. 따라서 (D)가 정답이다.

어휘 **organic** adj. 유기농의 **ingredient** n. 원료, 재료 **sold out** 매진된

[53-55]

영국 → 호주

Questions 53-55 refer to the following conversation.

W: ⁵³**I went through our sales reports yesterday** and I'm a little concerned. ⁵⁴**Revenues have declined at many of the stores we operate.**

M: I know. Apparently, our main competitor now offers an online service. ⁵⁵**Customers can order their cosmetics through the company's Web site and have them delivered the same day.** In contrast, our customers have to visit our shops in person.

W: That's not good. We need to turn things around.

M: Well, the solution seems obvious . . . We should develop a similar service.

W: Yes. I'm going to put together a presentation for the CEO.

go through ~을 검토하다 **in person** 직접 **obvious** adj. 명백한 **put together** 준비하다, 조립하다

해석
53-55번은 다음 대화에 관한 문제입니다.

여: ⁵³우리의 판매 보고서를 어제 검토했는데 저는 조금 걱정이 되네요. ⁵⁴우리가 운영하는 다수의 가게에서 수익이 하락했어요.
남: 그러니까요. 듣자하니, 우리의 주요 경쟁 업체가 이제 온라인 서비스를 제공한대요. ⁵⁵고객들은 그 회사의 웹사이트에서 그들의 화장품을 주문하고 당일에 배송되도록 할 수 있어요. 그에 반해서, 우리 고객들은 가게를 직접 방문해야 해요.
여: 그거 안 좋네요. 우리는 상황을 반전시켜야 해요.
남: 음, 해결책은 명백한 것 같아요... 우리는 비슷한 서비스를 개발해야 해요.
여: 네. 제가 최고 경영자를 위한 발표를 준비할게요.

53 | 특정 세부 사항 문제

해석 여자는 최근에 무엇을 했는가?
(A) 발표를 했다.
(B) 매장을 방문했다.
(C) 팀에 합류했다.
(D) 서류를 검토했다.

해설 질문의 핵심 어구(recently do)와 관련된 내용을 주의 깊게 듣는다. 여자가 "I went through our sales reports yesterday"라며 판매 보고서를 어제 검토했다고 하였다. 따라서 (D)가 정답이다.

Paraphrasing
went through ~ reports 보고서를 검토했다 → Reviewed a document 서류를 검토했다

54 | 문제점 문제

해석 여자는 무슨 문제를 언급하는가?
(A) 재무 보고서가 부정확했다.
(B) 새로운 서비스가 출시하지 못했다.
(C) 회사의 매출이 감소했다.
(D) 경쟁사가 더 큰 할인을 제공한다.

해설 여자의 말에서 부정적인 표현이 언급된 주변을 주의 깊게 듣는다. 여자가 "Revenues have declined at many of the stores we operate."이라며 자신들이 운영하는 다수의 가게에서 수익이 하락했다고 하였다. 따라서 (C)가 정답이다.

55 | 의도 파악 문제

해석 남자는 왜 "우리 고객들은 가게를 직접 방문해야 해요"라고 말하는가?
(A) 과정을 설명하기 위해
(B) 제안을 거절하기 위해
(C) 결정을 확인하기 위해
(D) 문제를 나타내기 위해

해설 질문의 인용어구(our customers have to visit our shops in person)가 언급된 주변을 주의 깊게 듣는다. 남자가 "Customers can order their cosmetics through the company[our main competitor]'s Web site and have them delivered the same day."라며 고객들은 주요 경쟁 업체의 웹사이트에서 그들의 화장품을 주문하고 당일에 배송되도록 할 수 있다고 한 것을 통해 문제를 나타내기 위함임을 알 수 있다. 따라서 (D)가 정답이다.

[56-58] 캐나다 → 미국
Questions 56-58 refer to the following conversation.

M: ⁵⁶Do you have plans for Friday evening, Brenda? I was hoping to go to a photo exhibit at the Mendez Gallery with other members of the department. Would you like to come?
W: Well, ⁵⁷I was planning to finalize a budget report, but I just heard that the deadline has been postponed until next week. So, I'd be happy to go with you to the exhibit instead.
M: Wonderful! I'm sure you'll like the landscape pictures at the gallery. By the way, ⁵⁸we're thinking of having dinner at a café in the area first. You're more than welcome to join us.

finalize v. 마무리하다 postpone v. 연기하다 landscape n. 풍경

해석
56-58번은 다음 대화에 관한 문제입니다.

남: ⁵⁶금요일 저녁에 계획이 있나요, Brenda? 저는 부서의 다른 팀원들과 Mendez 미술관의 사진전에 갈 생각 중이었어요. 오실래요?
여: 음, ⁵⁷저는 예산 보고서를 마무리할 예정이었지만, 방금 전에 마감일이 다음 주까지 연기되었다는 소식을 들었어요. 그래서, 대신 당신과 함께 전시회에 가면 좋을 것 같아요.
남: 좋아요! 당신은 분명히 미술관의 풍경 사진들을 좋아할 거예요. 그런데, ⁵⁸저희는 근처 카페에서 저녁을 먼저 먹으려고 생각 중이에요. 얼마든지 합류하셔도 돼요.

56 | 특정 세부 사항 문제

해석 남자는 금요일 저녁에 무엇을 할 계획인가?
(A) 무역 박람회에 들른다.
(B) 사진 촬영 수업에 참석한다.
(C) 전시회에 간다.
(D) 워크숍에 참가한다.

해설 질문의 핵심 어구(Friday evening)가 언급된 주변을 주의 깊게 듣는다. 남자가 "Do you have plans for Friday evening, Brenda? I was hoping to go to a photo exhibit at the Mendez Gallery with other members of the department."라며 금요일 저녁에 계획이 있는지 물은 후, 자신은 부서의 다른 팀원들과 Mendez 미술관의 사진전에 갈 생각 중이었다고 하였다. 따라서 (C)가 정답이다.

어휘 stop by 들르다 trade n. 무역

57 | 언급 문제

해석 여자는 예산 보고서에 대해 무엇을 말하는가?
(A) 재정적 오류가 포함되어 있다.
(B) 마감일이 연장되었다.
(C) 추가 데이터가 필요하다.
(D) 이미 제출되었다.

해설 여자의 말에서 질문의 핵심 어구(budget report)가 언급된 주변을 주의 깊게 듣는다. 여자가 "I was planning to finalize a budget report, but I just heard that the deadline has been postponed until next week."이라며 예산 보고서를 마무리할 예정이었는데 마감일이 다음 주까지 연기되었다는 소식을 들었다고 하였다. 따라서 (B)가 정답이다.

어휘 extend v. 연장하다

58 | 제안 문제

해석 남자는 무엇을 제안하는가?
(A) 박물관을 답사하기
(B) 친척을 만난기
(C) 동료에게 연락하기
(D) 식사를 하기

해설 남자의 말에서 제안과 관련된 표현이 언급된 내용을 주의 깊게 듣는다. 남자가 "we're thinking of having dinner at a café in the area first. You're more than welcome to join us."라며 근처 카페에서 저녁을 먼저 먹을 생각 중이니 얼마든지 합류해도 된다고 하였다. 따라서 (D)가 정답이다.

어휘 explore v. 답사하다, 탐험하다

Paraphrasing

having dinner 저녁을 먹기 → Having a meal 식사를 하기

[59-61]

캐나다 → 영국

Questions 59-61 refer to the following conversation.

M: Hello. ⁵⁹This is Joshua Curtis from the Ridley Institute. We were supposed to receive a piece of specialty laboratory equipment from your company last week, but it wasn't delivered.

W: Oh, I apologize for that. Your item was most likely included in a recent shipment that was delayed due to bad weather. Now that conditions have improved, your order should be on its way.

M: ⁶⁰We urgently need it for an important research project. ⁶¹Can you tell me when it should be arriving?

W: Expect it in three to five days.

institute n. 연구소, 협회 specialty n. 전문, 특제품 urgently adv. 급히

해설
59-61번은 다음 대화에 관한 문제입니다.
남: 안녕하세요. ⁵⁹저는 Ridley 연구소의 Joshua Curtis입니다. 저희는 지난주에 당신의 회사로부터 전문 실험 장비를 하나 받기로 되어 있었는데, 그것이 배송되지 않았어요.
여: 아, 그것에 대해 사과드립니다. 귀하의 물품은 아마도 날씨가 좋지 않아서 지연된 최근의 선적에 포함되었을 것입니다. 이제 상황이 나아졌으니, 귀하의 주문품은 배송 중일 겁니다.
남: ⁶⁰저희는 중요한 연구 프로젝트에 그것이 급히 필요해요. ⁶¹그것이 언제 도착할지 말씀해주실 수 있나요?
여: 3일에서 5일 정도를 예상해주세요.

59 | 화자 문제

해설 남자는 어디에서 일하는 것 같은가?
(A) 연구소에서
(B) 운송 회사에서
(C) 전자 제품 소매점에서
(D) 창고에서

해설 대화에서 신분 및 직업과 관련된 표현을 놓치지 않고 듣는다. 남자가 "This is Joshua Curtis from the Ridley Institute. We were supposed to receive a piece of specialty laboratory equipment from your company last week"이라며 자신이 Ridley 연구소의 Joshua Curtis라고 하고, 지난주에 여자의 회사로부터 전문 실험 장비를 하나 받기로 되어 있었다고 말한 것을 통해 남자가 일하는 장소가 연구소임을 알 수 있다. 따라서 (A)가 정답이다.

어휘 laboratory n. 연구소, 실험실 warehouse n. 창고

Paraphrasing

Institute 연구소 → laboratory 연구소

60 | 이유 문제

해설 남자는 왜 물품을 빨리 받기를 원하는가?
(A) 그것의 정확성을 실험해야 한다.
(B) 제품 분석을 수행할 것이다.
(C) 고장 난 기계를 교체해야 한다.
(D) 곧 있을 업무를 위해 그것이 필요하다.

해설 질문의 핵심 어구(get an item soon)와 관련된 내용을 주의 깊게 듣는다. 남자가 "We urgently need it for an important research project."라며 중요한 연구 프로젝트에 그것이 급히 필요하다고 하였다. 따라서 (D)가 정답이다.

어휘 accuracy n. 정확성, 정밀도 analysis n. 분석
upcoming adj. 곧 있을, 다가오는

Paraphrasing

need it for ~ project 프로젝트에 필요하다 → requires it for ~ work 업무를 위해 필요하다

61 | 특정 세부 사항 문제

해설 남자는 무엇에 관해 묻는가?
(A) 몇몇 장비들의 설치
(B) 프로젝트의 마감 기한
(C) 배송 날짜
(D) 연구의 진행 상황

해설 대화에서 남자의 말을 주의 깊게 듣는다. 남자가 "Can you tell me when it[order] should be arriving?"이라며 주문품이 언제 도착할지 말해줄 수 있는지 묻고 있다. 따라서 (C)가 정답이다.

어휘 installation n. 설치

[62-64]

미국 → 호주

Questions 62-64 refer to the following conversation and map.

W: ⁶²I heard the CEO of Lorcam Industries is visiting us this afternoon. Apparently, she's considering placing a large order.

M: ⁶²I know. Our director wants me to organize a dinner for her and the management team.

W: Have you found somewhere suitable yet?

M: Yes, ⁶³the Belleview Bistro on the corner of Johnson Street and Elm Avenue. I'm stopping by this afternoon to pay the deposit for a private room.

W: Do you know if the Lorcam Industries CEO is visiting alone? You might want to confirm exactly how many people are coming to dinner.

M: ⁶⁴I already spoke with her secretary before lunch, actually.

apparently adv. 듣자하니 organize v. 준비하다, 계획하다
suitable adj. 적절한, 알맞은 stop by 들르다 deposit n. 예약금, 보증금
secretary n. 비서

해설
62-64번은 다음 대화와 지도에 관한 문제입니다.
여: ⁶²저는 Lorcam Industries사의 최고 경영자가 오늘 오후에 우리를 방문할 것이라고 들었어요. 듣자하니, 그녀가 대량 주문하는 것을 고려하고 있나 봐요.
남: ⁶²알아요. 우리 관리자는 제가 그녀와 경영팀을 위한 저녁 식사를 준비하기를 원해요.
여: 적절한 장소를 찾았나요?

남: 네, ⁶³Johnson가와 Elm가의 모퉁이에 있는 Belleview Bistro요. 저는 전용 룸을 위한 예약금을 지불하기 위해 오늘 오후에 그곳에 들를 거예요.
여: Lorcam Industries사의 최고 경영자가 혼자 방문할 것인지 알고 있나요? 저녁 식사에 정확히 몇 명이 오는지 확인하는 것이 좋을 것 같아요.
남: ⁶⁴사실 점심 전에 이미 그녀의 비서와 이야기했어요.

공원		⁶³A 건물	B 건물
Johnson가			
C 건물	지하철역	Elm가	우체국	D 건물

62 | 이유 문제

해석 저녁 식사는 왜 열리게 될 것인가?
(A) 관리자의 승진을 발표하기 위해
(B) 회사의 창립을 기념하기 위해
(C) 지점 개점을 축하하기 위해
(D) 잠재적인 고객을 맞이하기 위해

해설 질문의 핵심 어구(dinner)와 관련된 내용을 주의 깊게 듣는다. 여자가 "I heard the CEO of Lorcam Industries is visiting us this afternoon. Apparently, she's considering placing a large order."라며 Lorcam Industries사의 최고 경영자가 오늘 오후에 자신들을 방문할 것이라고 들었다고 하고, 그녀가 대량 주문하는 것을 고려하고 있는 것 같다고 하자, 남자가 "I know. Our director wants me to organize a dinner for her and the management team."이라며 자신들의 관리자는 자신이 그녀와 경영팀을 위한 저녁 식사를 준비하기를 원한다고 하였다. 따라서 (D)가 정답이다.

어휘 promotion n. 승진 commemorate v. 기념하다, 기리다
founding n. 창립, 설립 potential adj. 잠재적인

63 | 시각 자료 문제

해석 시각 자료를 보아라. 남자는 오후에 어떤 건물에 방문할 것인가?
(A) A 건물
(B) B 건물
(C) C 건물
(D) D 건물

해설 제시된 지도의 정보를 확인한 후 질문의 핵심 어구(visit in the afternoon)와 관련된 내용을 주의 깊게 듣는다. 남자가 "the Belleview Bistro on the corner of Johnson Street and Elm Avenue. I'm stopping by this afternoon to pay the deposit for a private room."이라며 Johnson가와 Elm가의 모퉁이에 있는 Belleview Bistro라며 전용 룸을 위한 예약금을 지불하기 위해 오늘 오후에 그곳에 들를 것이라고 하였으므로 남자가 오후에 방문할 건물은 Johnson가와 Elm가의 모퉁이에 위치한 A 건물임을 지도에서 알 수 있다. 따라서 (A)가 정답이다.

64 | 특정 세부 사항 문제

해석 남자는 오늘 아침에 무엇을 했는가?
(A) 관리자와 만났다.
(B) 방문하는 최고 경영자를 맞이했다.
(C) 예약금을 지불했다.
(D) 비서와 얘기했다.

해설 질문의 핵심 어구(this morning)와 관련된 내용을 주의 깊게 듣는다. 남자가 "I already spoke with her secretary before lunch, actually."라며 사실 점심 전에 이미 그녀의 비서와 이야기했다고 하였다. 따라서 (D)가 정답이다.

어휘 greet v. 맞이하다, ~에게 인사하다 deposit n. 예약금
assistant n. 비서, 조수

Paraphrasing
spoke with ~ secretary 비서와 이야기했다 → Spoke with an assistant 비서와 얘기했다

[65-67]

캐나다 → 영국

Questions 65-67 refer to the following conversation and list.

M: ⁶⁵Sorry, ma'am. I know you've been sitting here for a few minutes, but I had to finish up at another table before serving you.
W: That's OK. I know what I want—the olive and artichoke pasta, please.
M: Excellent choice. ⁶⁶And for your side dish? The lemon kale salad is wonderful.
W: That may be too light. ⁶⁶I'll go with the third choice on the menu, please. Also . . . ⁶⁷do you have chamomile tea?
M: ⁶⁷Let me ask the kitchen when I put in your order. I'll let you know shortly.

finish up 마무리하다
artichoke n. 아티초크(국화과 식물. 엉겅퀴 꽃같이 생긴 꽃봉오리의 속대를 식용함)
shortly adv. 즉시, 바로

해석
65-67번은 다음 대화와 목록에 관한 문제입니다.

M: ⁶⁵죄송합니다, 손님. 손님께서 몇 분 동안 이곳에 앉아계셨던 것을 알지만, 손님을 응대하기 전에 다른 테이블을 마무리해야 했어요.
W: 괜찮아요. 저는 제가 원하는 것이 무엇인지 알아요. 올리브와 아티초크 파스타를 주세요.
M: 탁월한 선택이시네요. ⁶⁶그리고 곁들임 요리로는요? 레몬 케일 샐러드가 훌륭합니다.
W: 너무 가벼울 수도 있을 것 같아요. ⁶⁶저는 메뉴에 있는 세 번째 선택지로 할게요. 그리고... ⁶⁷캐모마일 차가 있나요?
M: ⁶⁷손님의 주문을 넣을 때 제가 주방에 물어볼게요. 즉시 알려드리겠습니다.

Stonewall 카페

곁들임 요리 선택지

하우스 샐러드
레몬 케일 샐러드
⁶⁶구운 감자
프라이팬에 구운 초록 강낭콩

65 | 이유 문제

해석 남자는 왜 여자에게 사과하는가?
(A) 시기적절한 서비스를 제공하지 않았다.
(B) 사소한 실수를 했다.
(C) 주 요리를 더 이상 이용할 수 없다.
(D) 대기 줄이 예상보다 길었다.

해설 질문의 핵심 어구(apologize to the woman)와 관련된 내용을 주의 깊게 듣는다. 남자가 "Sorry, ma'am. I know you've been sitting here for a few minutes, but I had to finish up at another table before serving you."라며 죄송하다고 한 후, 여자가 몇 분 동안 앉아있던 것을 알지만 여자를 응대하기 전에 다른 테이블을 마무리해야 했다고 하였다. 따라서 (A)가 정답이다.

어휘 timely adj. 시기적절한 minor adj. 사소한 entrée n. 주 요리
available adj. 이용 가능한

66 | 시각 자료 문제

해석 시각 자료를 보아라. 여자는 어떤 곁들임 요리를 선택하는가?
(A) 하우스 샐러드
(B) 레몬 케일 샐러드
(C) 구운 감자
(D) 프라이팬에 구운 초록 강낭콩

해설 제시된 목록의 정보를 확인한 뒤 질문의 핵심 어구(side dish)가 언급된 주변을 주의 깊게 듣는다. 남자가 "And for your side dish?"라며 그리고 곁들임 요리로는 무엇을 할지 묻자, 여자가 "I'll go with the third choice on the menu, please."라며 메뉴에 있는 세 번째 선택지로 하겠다고 하였으므로, 여자가 선택하는 곁들임 요리는 구운 감자임을 목록에서 알 수 있다. 따라서 (C)가 정답이다.

어휘 select v. 선택하다, 고르다

67 | 제안 문제

해석 남자는 무엇을 해주겠다고 제안하는가?
(A) 기존의 주문을 수정한다.
(B) 다른 메뉴를 가져온다.
(C) 식당 관리자와 이야기한다.
(D) 음료에 관해 문의한다.

해설 남자의 말에서 제안과 관련된 표현이 언급된 내용을 주의 깊게 듣는다. 여자가 "do you have chamomile tea?"라며 캐모마일 차가 있는지 묻자, 남자가 "Let me ask the kitchen when I put in your order."라며 여자의 주문을 넣을 때 주방에 물어보겠다고 하였다. 따라서 (D)가 정답이다.

어휘 modify v. 수정하다 existing adj. 기존의 bring v. 가져오다
inquire v. 문의하다, 묻다 beverage n. 음료

[68-70]

호주 → 미국

Questions 68-70 refer to the following conversation and schedule.

M: ⁶⁸Did you hear that we're taking a business trip to Denver soon?
W: ⁶⁸Yeah. I found out an hour ago that we've been selected to present our firm's strategic plan to shareholders.
M: That's right. We've got a lot to prepare. But I'm looking forward to seeing Denver. I've always wanted to go. Plus, ⁶⁹I was informed all of our costs will be covered.
W: Oh, that reminds me . . . We should book our flight. ⁷⁰What time do you want to leave on June 6?
M: I have a big meeting that morning, so ⁷⁰let's take the earliest afternoon flight.

strategic adj. 전략의 shareholder n. 주주 cover v. 충당하다, 보상하다
earliest adj. 가장 빠른

해석
68-70번은 다음 대화와 일정표에 관한 문제입니다.

남: ⁶⁸우리가 곧 덴버로 출장을 가게 될 거라는 소식을 들었어요?
여: ⁶⁸네. 저는 한 시간 전에 우리가 회사의 전략 계획을 주주들에게 발표하도록 선정되었다는 것을 알게 되었어요.
남: 맞아요. 우리는 준비해야 할 것이 많아요. 하지만 저는 덴버에 방문하는 것이 기대돼요. 항상 가보고 싶었거든요. 게다가, ⁶⁹우리의 모든 경비가 충당될 거라고 통지받았어요.
여: 아, 그러고 보니 생각나네요... 우리의 항공편을 예약해야 해요. ⁷⁰6월 6일에 몇 시에 떠나고 싶으세요?
남: 저는 그날 아침에 중요한 회의가 있어서, ⁷⁰가장 빠른 오후 항공편을 타도록 해요.

SkyJet 항공	
댈러스, 텍사스주 → 덴버, 콜로라도주 6월 6일	
시간	항공편
오전 8시	247
오전 10시 30분	451
⁷⁰오후 1시 15분	663
오후 3시 45분	819

68 | 이유 문제

해석 화자들은 왜 덴버로 가는가?
(A) 발표를 하기 위해
(B) 캠페인을 시작하기 위해
(C) 새로운 지역의 지사를 홍보하기 위해
(D) 투자 기회를 고려하기 위해

해설 질문의 핵심 어구(Denver)가 언급된 주변을 주의 깊게 듣는다. 남자가 "Did you hear that we're taking a business trip to Denver soon?"이라며 자신들이 곧 덴버로 출장을 가게 될 거라는 소식을 들었는지 묻자, 여자가 "Yeah. I found out an hour ago that we've been selected to present our firm's strategic plan to shareholders."라며 그렇다고 한 후, 한 시간 전에 자신들이 회사의 전략 계획을 주주들에게 발표하도록 선정되었다는 것을 알게 되었다고 하였다. 따라서 (A)가 정답이다.

어휘 launch v. 시작하다 investment n. 투자

Paraphrasing

present 발표하다 → give a presentation 발표를 하다

69 | 특정 세부 사항 문제

해석 남자는 무엇에 대해 통지받았는가?
(A) 수상 후보 지명
(B) 고객과의 회의
(C) 프로젝트 마감 기한
(D) 환급 계획

해설 질문의 핵심 어구(was ~ informed)가 언급된 주변을 주의 깊게 듣는다. 남자가 "I was informed all of our costs will be covered"라며 자신들의 모든 경비가 충당될 거라고 통지받았다고 하였다. 따라서 (D)가 정답이다.

어휘 nomination n. 지명 reimbursement n. 환급, 상환

70 | 시각 자료 문제

해석 시각 자료를 보아라. 화자들은 어떤 항공편을 탈 것 같은가?
(A) 247 항공편
(B) 451 항공편
(C) 663 항공편
(D) 819 항공편

해설 제시된 일정표의 정보를 확인한 후 질문의 핵심 어구(flight)가 언급된 주변을 주의 깊게 듣는다. 여자가 "What time do you want to leave on June 6?"라며 6월 6일에 몇 시에 떠나고 싶은지 묻자, 남자가 "let's take the earliest afternoon flight"이라며 가장 빠른 오후 항공편을 타자고 하였고 오후 중 가장 빠른 항공편은 663 항공편임을 일정표에서 알 수 있다. 따라서 (C)가 정답이다.

PART 4

[71-73]

미국

Questions 71-73 refer to the following telephone message.

Hello. This is Jamie Foster from Phoenix Merchandising calling for Ms. Helen Rohan. [71]**I need to inform you that the specific model of VelociClean vacuum cleaner that you ordered is out of stock.** However, we do have a comparable alternative called the Weyden Platinum. [72]**Because of its design, it can be moved around any indoor space without difficulty.** And since we were unable to fulfill your original request, we will offer you a discount if you purchase the Weyden product. [73]**If you're interested, you should visit our shop, and I'll show the vacuum to you.**

inform v. 알리다 specific adj. 특정한 out of stock 재고가 없는
comparable adj. 비슷한 alternative n. 대체, 대안 fulfill v. 충족시키다

해석
71-73번은 다음 전화 메시지에 관한 문제입니다.

안녕하세요. Ms. Helen Rohan께 전화드리는 Phoenix Merchandising사의 Jamie Foster입니다. [71]귀하께서 주문하신 VelociClean 진공청소기 특정 모델의 재고가 없음을 알려드리고자 합니다. 하지만, 저희는 Weyden Platinum이라는 비슷한 대체제가 있습니다. [72]디자인 덕분에, 그것은 실내 공간 어디에서나 어려움 없이 움직일 수 있습니다. 그리고 저희가 귀하의 본래 요구 사항을 충족시키지 못했기 때문에, 귀하께서 이 Weyden 제품을 구매하시면 할인을 제공해 드리겠습니다. [73]관심 있으실 경우, 저희 가게를 방문해 주시면 제가 그 청소기를 고객님께 보여드리겠습니다.

71 | 목적 문제

해석 화자는 왜 전화하고 있는가?
(A) 환불을 요청하기 위해
(B) 문제를 알리기 위해
(C) 주문을 확인하기 위해
(D) 회의의 일정을 변경하기 위해

해설 전화 메시지의 목적을 묻는 문제이므로, 지문의 초반을 반드시 듣는다. "I need to inform you that the specific model of VelociClean vacuum cleaner that you ordered is out of stock."이라며 청자가 주문한 VelociClean 진공청소기 특정 모델의 재고가 없음을 알리고자 한다고 하였다. 따라서 (B)가 정답이다.

어휘 refund n. 환불 issue n. 문제 reschedule v. 일정을 변경하다

Paraphrasing
inform 알리다 → report 알리다

72 | 특정 세부 사항 문제

해석 화자에 따르면, Weyden Platinum의 이점은 무엇인가?
(A) 강력한 모터를 가지고 있다.
(B) 여러 개의 설정을 가지고 있다.
(C) 움직이기가 쉽다.
(D) 다양한 크기로 이용 가능하다.

해설 질문의 핵심 어구(Weyden Platinum)와 관련된 내용을 주의 깊게 듣는다. "Because of its design, it[Weyden Platinum] can be moved around any indoor space without difficulty."라며 디자인 덕분에 Weyden Platinum은 실내 공간 어디에서나 어려움 없이 움직일 수 있다

고 하였다. 따라서 (C)가 정답이다.

어휘 benefit n. 이점, 이익 multiple adj. 여러 개의, 다수의

73 | 제안 문제

해석 화자는 무엇을 제안하는가?
(A) 직접 기기를 보는 것
(B) 기간이 연장된 보증서를 받는 것
(C) 대회에 참가하는 것
(D) 물품을 가게로 돌려주는 것

해설 지문의 중후반에서 제안과 관련된 표현이 포함된 문장을 주의 깊게 듣는다. "If you're interested, you should visit our shop, and I'll show the vacuum to you."라며 관심이 있을 경우 가게를 방문하면 자신이 그 청소기를 보여주겠다고 제안하였다. 따라서 (A)가 정답이다.

어휘 device n. 기기, 장치 in person 직접, 몸소 warranty n. 보증(서)

[74-76]

영국

Questions 74-76 refer to the following talk.

Today marks an important development for both Hanaway Industries and Glarris Technologies. [74]**We have officially combined our companies to form Hanaway and Glarris Incorporated.** In the process, [75]**we have become the largest information technology firm in Europe.** This will surely be a benefit to our customers and the industry as a whole. However, we still have to improve efficiency. To that end, [76]**our primary focus over the next two months will be to establish clear lines of communication between our different departments.**

efficiency n. 효율성 primary adj. 주된 establish v. 확립하다

해석
74-76번은 다음 담화에 관한 문제입니다.

오늘은 Hanaway Industries사와 Glarris Technologies사 모두에게 중요한 발전을 기념하는 날입니다. [74]우리는 공식적으로 우리의 회사들을 합병하여 Hanaway and Glarris사를 만들었습니다. 그 과정에서, [75]우리는 유럽에서 가장 큰 정보 기술 회사가 되었습니다. 이는 틀림없이 우리의 고객들과 산업 전체에 이익이 될 것입니다. 하지만, 우리는 여전히 효율성을 향상시켜야 합니다. 그 목적을 달성하기 위해서, [76]다음 두 달 동안 우리의 주된 초점은 우리의 다른 부서들 간의 분명한 의사소통을 확립하는 것이 될 것입니다.

74 | 주제 문제

해석 화자는 주로 무엇에 관해 이야기하고 있는가?
(A) 기자 회견
(B) 제품 출시
(C) 잠재적인 계약
(D) 회사 합병

해설 담화의 주제를 묻는 문제이므로, 지문의 초반을 반드시 듣는다. "We have officially combined our companies to form Hanaway and Glarris Incorporated."라며 공식적으로 회사들을 합병하여 Hanaway and Glarris사를 만들었다고 한 후, 회사 합병에 대한 내용으로 이어지고 있다. 따라서 (D)가 정답이다.

어휘 news conference 기자 회견 launch n. 출시 merger n. 합병

75 | 언급 문제

해석 화자는 Hanaway and Glarris사에 관해 무엇을 언급하는가?
(A) 소비자 제품을 개발하고 있다.

(B) 컨설팅 서비스를 제공한다.
(C) 유럽에서 영업한다.
(D) 본사를 이전하고 있다.

해설 질문의 핵심 어구(Hanaway and Glarris Incorporated)와 관련된 내용을 주의 깊게 듣는다. "we[Hanaway and Glarris Incorporated] have become the largest information technology firm in Europe"이라며 Hanaway and Glarris사가 유럽에서 가장 큰 정보 기술 회사가 되었다고 하였다. 따라서 (C)가 정답이다.

어휘 operate v. 영업하다, 가동하다

76 | 다음에 할 일 문제

해설 화자에 따르면, 다음 두 달 동안 무슨 일이 일어날 것인가?
(A) 직원들이 전근 가게 될 것이다.
(B) 의사소통이 향상될 것이다.
(C) 소비자 설문조사가 실시될 것이다.
(D) 홍보 자료들이 준비될 것이다.

해설 질문의 핵심 어구(next two months)가 언급된 주변을 주의 깊게 듣는다. "our primary focus over the next two months will be to establish clear lines of communication between our different departments"라며 다음 두 달 동안 주된 초점은 다른 부서들 간의 분명한 의사소통을 확립하는 것이 될 것이라고 하였다. 따라서 (B)가 정답이다.

어휘 transfer v. 전근 가다

[77-79]

Questions 77-79 refer to the following advertisement.   호주

⁷⁷**Are you interested in giving your workout a boost? Then try Power Source, the brand-new enhanced drink from Pure Athletics.** ⁷⁸**Power Source is infused with various essential vitamins that will give you the extra energy you require during your favorite physical activity.** And if you fill out a short survey on our Web site, you will receive a free bottle of our newest Power Source flavor, Berry Mix. ⁷⁹**But this offer is only good until supplies run out.** This won't last for long!

workout n. 운동 boost n. 활력 infuse v. 가득 채우다 good adj. 유효한
supply n. 재고 run out 다 떨어지다 last v. 지속하다

해석
77-79번은 다음 광고에 관한 문제입니다.

⁷⁷당신의 운동에 활력을 불어넣는 데 관심이 있으신가요? 그렇다면 Pure Athletics사의 새로운 강화 음료, Power Source를 마셔보세요. ⁷⁸Power Source는 여러분이 가장 좋아하는 신체 활동을 하는 동안 필요한 여분의 활기를 제공해 줄 다양한 필수 비타민으로 가득 차 있습니다. 그리고 저희 웹사이트에서 간단한 설문조사를 기입하시면 Power Source의 최신 맛인 Berry Mix 한 병을 무료로 받으실 것입니다. ⁷⁹하지만 이 제공은 재고가 다 떨어질 때까지만 유효합니다. 이것은 오래 지속되지 않을 것입니다!

77 | 주제 문제

해설 어떤 종류의 상품이 광고되고 있는가?
(A) 에너지바
(B) 아침용 시리얼
(C) 스포츠 음료
(D) 건강 지표 추적기

해설 광고의 주제를 묻는 문제이므로, 지문의 초반을 반드시 듣는다. "Are you interested in giving your workout a boost? Then try Power Source, the brand-new enhanced drink from Pure Athletics."라며 운동에 활력을 불어넣는 데 관심이 있는지 물은 후, Pure Athletics사의 새로운 강화 음료인 Power Source를 마셔보라고 하였다. 따라서 (C)가 정답이다.

78 | 언급 문제

해설 화자는 Power Source에 관해 무엇을 언급하는가?
(A) 유명 인사에 의해 추천되었다.
(B) 운동선수들에 의해 개발되었다.
(C) 긍정적인 평가를 받아왔다.
(D) 여러 종류의 비타민을 함유한다.

해설 질문의 핵심 어구(Power Source)가 언급된 주변을 주의 깊게 듣는다. "Power Source is infused with various essential vitamins that will give you the extra energy you require during your favorite physical activity."라며 Power Source는 가장 좋아하는 신체 활동을 하는 동안 필요한 여분의 활기를 제공해 줄 다양한 필수 비타민으로 가득 차 있다고 하였다. 따라서 (D)가 정답이다.

어휘 athlete n. 운동선수

Paraphrasing
is infused with ~로 가득 차 있다 → includes 함유하다

79 | 의도 파악 문제

해설 화자는 "이것은 오래 지속되지 않을 것입니다"라고 말할 때 무엇을 의도하는가?
(A) 상품은 구할 수 없다.
(B) 판촉 행사는 인기가 많을 것으로 예상된다.
(C) 새로운 제품군이 출시될 것이다.
(D) 할인이 곧 끝날 것이다.

해설 질문의 인용어구(This won't last for long)가 언급된 주변을 주의 깊게 듣는다. "But this offer is only good until supplies run out."이라며 이 제공은 재고가 다 떨어질 때까지만 유효하다고 했으므로 판촉 행사가 인기가 많을 것으로 예상됨을 알 수 있다. 따라서 (B)가 정답이다.

어휘 product line 제품군 expire v. 끝나다, 만료되다

[80-82]

Questions 80-82 refer to the following broadcast.   캐나다

This is Nikolai West reporting live for *WRRE Eyewitness News*. ⁸⁰**The annual Cherry Festival is underway here at Wellington Park**, so come on down. There's something for everyone. Kids will enjoy the exciting rides and games, while ⁸¹**parents will appreciate the musical and cultural shows**. There are also booths serving delicious foods. ⁸²**The festival's final show will start at 8 P.M. with a concert by the Mississippi Mounds.** I'll be joined by the event organizer after a short commercial break, so stay tuned.

ride n. 놀이기구 appreciate v. 감상하다, 음미하다

해석
80-82번은 다음 방송에 관한 문제입니다.

저는 *WRRE Eyewitness* 뉴스를 생방송으로 전해드리는 Nikolai West입니다. ⁸⁰연례 벚나무 축제가 이곳 Wellington 공원에서 진행되고 있으니, 이곳으로 오십시오. 모두를 위한 것이 있습니다. 아이들은 신나는 놀이기구와 게임을 즐길 것이고, ⁸¹부모들은 음악과 문화 공연을 감상할 것입니다. 맛있는 음식을 제공하는 부스들도 있습니다. ⁸²축제의 마지막 공연은 오후 8시에 Mississippi

Mounds의 콘서트로 시작됩니다. 짧은 광고 후에 행사 기획자와 함께할 것이니, 채널을 고정해 주시기 바랍니다.

80 | 주제 문제

해석 방송은 주로 무엇에 관한 것인가?
(A) 지역 기념행사
(B) 운동 경기
(C) 새로운 공원 명소
(D) 시립 음악 기관

해설 방송의 주제를 묻는 문제이므로, 지문의 초반을 반드시 듣는다. "The annual Cherry Festival is underway here at Wellington Park"라며 연례 벚나무 축제가 Wellington 공원에서 진행되고 있다고 한 후, 지역 기념행사에 대한 내용으로 이어지고 있다. 따라서 (A)가 정답이다.

어휘 attraction n. 명소

Paraphrasing
annual ~ Festival 연례 축제 → A local celebration 지역 기념행사

81 | 특정 세부 사항 문제

해석 화자는 부모들이 무엇을 즐길 것이라고 말하는가?
(A) 경품
(B) 공연
(C) 놀이기구
(D) 대회

해설 질문의 핵심 어구(parents will enjoy)와 관련된 내용을 주의 깊게 듣는다. "parents will appreciate the musical and cultural shows"라며 부모들은 음악과 문화 공연을 감상할 것이라고 하였다. 따라서 (B)가 정답이다.

어휘 prize n. 경품, 상품 contest n. 대회, 경연

Paraphrasing
the musical and cultural shows 음악과 문화 공연 → performances 공연

82 | 다음에 할 일 문제

해석 오후 8시에 무슨 일이 일어날 것인가?
(A) 축제 광고가 방영될 것이다.
(B) 공무원이 인터뷰를 할 것이다.
(C) 음식 부스가 설치될 것이다.
(D) 음악 행사가 열릴 것이다.

해설 질문의 핵심 어구(8 P.M.)가 언급된 주변을 주의 깊게 듣는다. "The festival's final show will start at 8 P.M. with a concert by the Mississippi Mounds."라며 축제의 마지막 공연은 오후 8시에 Mississippi Mounds의 콘서트로 시작된다고 하였다. 따라서 (D)가 정답이다.

어휘 air v. 방영되다, 방송되다

Paraphrasing
concert 콘서트 → musical event 음악 행사

[83-85]
Questions 83-85 refer to the following instructions. 미국

Hello, everyone. It's a pleasure to have you all here at The Culinary House. Today, you will be learning how to make homemade pizza. ⁸³**This will be the first of three dishes that you're going to make.** ⁸⁴**I've printed the recipes you will need and put them on the counters.** But before you start cooking this meal, you all need to break up into pairs. ⁸⁵**Since there aren't enough utensils for each student, everyone will have to find someone else to work with.**

counter n. 조리대 break up into ~로 나누다 utensil n. 주방용품

해석
83-85번은 다음 설명에 관한 문제입니다.
여러분, 안녕하세요. 이곳 The Culinary House에서 여러분 모두를 만나게 되어 반갑습니다. 오늘, 여러분은 집에서 만든 피자를 만드는 방법을 배울 것입니다. ⁸³이것은 여러분이 만들 세 개의 음식 중에 첫 번째가 될 것입니다. ⁸⁴제가 여러분이 필요로 할 조리법을 출력하여 조리대에 올려 두었습니다. 그러나, 이 음식을 요리하는 것을 시작하기 전에, 모두 두 명씩 짝을 지어 나누어지셔야 합니다. ⁸⁵각 학생을 위한 충분한 주방용품이 없기 때문에, 여러분은 함께 작업할 다른 사람을 찾아야 할 것입니다.

83 | 특정 세부 사항 문제

해석 화자는 청자들이 무엇을 할 것이라고 말하는가?
(A) 전문 요리사를 지켜본다.
(B) 전채 요리들을 시식한다.
(C) 앞치마를 두른다.
(D) 여러 개의 음식을 요리한다.

해설 질문의 핵심 어구(listeners will do)와 관련된 내용을 주의 깊게 듣는다. "This will be the first of three dishes that you're going to make." 라며 이것이 청자들이 만들 세 개의 음식 중에 첫 번째가 될 것이라고 하였다. 따라서 (D)가 정답이다.

어휘 observe v. 지켜보다, 관찰하다 sample v. 시식하다, 맛보다
apron n. 앞치마

84 | 특정 세부 사항 문제

해석 화자는 청자들을 위해 조리대에 무엇을 놓았는가?
(A) 등록 양식
(B) 조리법 인쇄물
(C) 제빵용 재료
(D) 주방용품

해설 질문의 핵심 어구(on the counters)가 언급된 주변을 주의 깊게 듣는다. "I've printed the recipes you will need and put them on the counters."라며 청자들이 필요로 할 조리법을 출력하여 조리대에 올려 두었다고 하였다. 따라서 (B)가 정답이다.

어휘 ingredient n. (요리의) 재료

Paraphrasing
printed the recipes 조리법을 출력했다 → Recipe printouts 조리법 인쇄물

85 | 이유 문제

해석 청자들은 왜 파트너가 필요한가?
(A) 팀워크 활동을 할 것이다.
(B) 아이디어를 브레인스토밍 해야 한다.
(C) 요리 도구가 한정되어 있다.
(D) 재료가 부족하다.

해설 질문의 핵심 어구(partner)와 관련된 내용을 주의 깊게 듣는다. "Since there aren't enough utensils for each student, everyone will have to find someone else to work with."라며 각 학생을 위한 충분한 주방용품이 없기 때문에 청자들은 함께 작업할 다른 사람을 찾아야 할 것이라고 하였다. 따라서 (C)가 정답이다.

어휘 implement n. 도구 shortage n. 부족

Paraphrasing

there aren't enough utensils 충분한 주방용품이 없다 → There are limited cooking implements 요리 도구가 한정되어 있다

[86-88]   ♫ 영국

Questions 86-88 refer to the following telephone message.

Hello, Zack. This is Allison Peng from Creative Prime Agency. I contacted the Electric Space gallery about displaying your work. ⁸⁶The curator expressed great interest in the paintings you created and said she'd be delighted to exhibit them there in October. ⁸⁷I know you use oversized canvasses for your work, and Electric Space has tall ceilings and a large back entrance. So ⁸⁸please let me know whether you would like to take advantage of this opportunity.

exhibit v. 전시하다 oversized adj. 대형의 entrance n. 문
take advantage of ~을 이용하다

해석
86-88번은 다음 전화 메시지에 관한 문제입니다.

안녕하세요, Zack. 저는 Creative Prime 대행사의 Allison Peng입니다. 당신의 작품을 전시하는 것과 관련하여 Electric Space 미술관에 연락을 했습니다. ⁸⁶큐레이터가 당신이 창작한 회화 작품들에 큰 관심을 보였고 그 작품들을 10월에 그곳에서 전시하게 된다면 아주 기쁠 것이라고 말했습니다. ⁸⁷저는 당신이 작품에 대형 캔버스를 사용하는 것을 알고 있으며, Electric Space에는 높은 천장과 큰 후문이 있습니다. 그러니, ⁸⁸이 기회를 이용하고 싶은지 제게 알려 주세요.

86 | 청자 문제

해석 청자는 누구인 것 같은가?
(A) 큐레이터
(B) 부동산 중개인
(C) 화가
(D) 미술관 관리자

해설 지문에서 신분 및 직업과 관련된 표현을 놓치지 않고 듣는다. "The curator expressed great interest in the paintings you created and said she'd be delighted to exhibit them there in October."라며 큐레이터가 청자가 창작한 회화 작품들에 큰 관심을 보였고 그 작품들을 10월에 그곳에서 전시하게 된다면 아주 기쁠 것이라고 했다고 한 것을 통해 청자가 화가임을 알 수 있다. 따라서 (C)가 정답이다.

87 | 의도 파악 문제

해석 화자는 "Electric Space에는 높은 천장과 큰 후문이 있습니다"라고 말할 때 무엇을 의도하는가?
(A) 잠재적인 장소가 이상적이다.
(B) 건물이 최근에 개조되었다.
(C) 위치가 정확하게 광고되었다.
(D) 임대 시설의 가격이 적절하게 매겨졌다.

해설 질문의 인용어구(Electric Space has tall ceilings and a large back entrance)가 언급된 주변을 주의 깊게 듣는다. "I know you use oversized canvasses for your work"라며 자신은 청자가 작품에 대형 캔버스를 사용하는 것을 알고 있다고 한 것을 통해 화자가 언급하는 잠재적인 장소가 이상적임을 알 수 있다. 따라서 (A)가 정답이다.

어휘 venue n. 장소 ideal adj. 이상적인 renovate v. 개조하다
fairly adv. 적절하게 price v. 가격을 매기다

88 | 특정 세부 사항 문제

해석 화자는 청자에게 무엇을 하라고 지시하는가?
(A) 임대 계약서의 조건을 살펴본다.
(B) 자신에게 결정을 알려준다.
(C) 미술관에 직접 들른다.
(D) 작품 포트폴리오를 제출한다.

해설 질문의 핵심 어구(instruct)와 관련된 내용을 주의 깊게 듣는다. "please let me know whether you would like to take advantage of this opportunity"라며 이 기회를 이용하고 싶은지 자신에게 알려달라고 하였다. 따라서 (B)가 정답이다.

어휘 lease n. 임대 계약서

Paraphrasing

let ~ know 알리다 → Inform 알리다

[89-91]   ♫ 캐나다

Questions 89-91 refer to the following announcement.

May I have your attention, please? ⁸⁹An inspector from the Federal Department of Safety will be visiting our plant next Friday, so I just want to remind you of a few things. First, you must ensure that our safety equipment is in good condition. Also, ⁹⁰there will be a short meeting at 3 o'clock this afternoon for all department managers. Since the conference room has been reserved already, we'll gather in my office. ⁹¹At that time, we will go over the entire schedule of events for the day the inspector visits our facility. OK, that's all for now.

inspector n. 조사관, 조사자 federal adj. 연방의
ensure v. 반드시 ~하게 하다, 보장하다 go over 검토하다

해석
89-91번은 다음 공지에 관한 문제입니다.

모두 주목해 주시겠습니까? ⁸⁹다음 주 금요일에 연방 안전부의 조사관이 우리 공장을 방문할 것이므로, 저는 여러분에게 그저 몇 가지 사항을 상기시켜 드리고 싶습니다. 먼저, 여러분은 반드시 우리의 안전 장비가 좋은 상태에 있도록 해야 합니다. 또한, ⁹⁰오늘 오후 3시에 모든 부서장들을 대상으로 한 짧은 회의가 있을 것입니다. 회의실이 이미 예약되어 있으므로, 우리는 제 사무실에서 모일 것입니다. ⁹¹그때, 우리는 조사관이 우리 시설을 방문하는 날의 전체 일정을 검토할 것입니다. 좋습니다, 지금은 이게 전부입니다.

89 | 특정 세부 사항 문제

해석 화자는 누가 방문할 것이라고 말하는가?
(A) 연구 시설의 책임자
(B) 보험 중개인
(C) 대기업의 임원
(D) 정부 조사관

해설 질문의 핵심 어구(coming to visit)와 관련된 내용을 주의 깊게 듣는다. "An inspector from the Federal Department of Safety will be visiting our plant next Friday"라며 다음 주 금요일에 연방 안전부의 조사관이 공장을 방문할 것이라고 하였다. 따라서 (D)가 정답이다.

어휘 head n. 책임자, 우두머리 insurance n. 보험

90 | 특정 세부 사항 문제

해석 회의는 어디에서 열릴 것인가?
(A) 중앙 로비에서
(B) 휴게실에서

(C) 회의실에서
(D) 사무실에서

해설 질문의 핵심 어구(meeting)가 언급된 주변을 주의 깊게 듣는다. "there will be a short meeting at 3 o'clock this afternoon for all department managers. Since the conference room has been reserved already, we'll gather in my office."라며 오후 3시에 모든 부서장들을 대상으로 한 짧은 회의가 있을 것이라고 하고, 회의실이 이미 예약되어 있으므로 자신의 사무실에서 모일 것이라고 하였다. 따라서 (D)가 정답이다.

91 | 특정 세부 사항 문제

해설 화자에 따르면, 회의 중에 무슨 내용이 논의될 것인가?
(A) 곧 있을 방문의 세부 사항들
(B) 안전 장비의 업그레이드
(C) 회사 직원들을 위한 새로운 임무들
(D) 공장의 변경된 목표

해설 질문의 핵심 어구(discussed)와 관련된 내용을 주의 깊게 듣는다. "At that time[meeting], we will go over the entire schedule of events for the day the inspector visits our facility."라며 회의 때 조사관이 시설을 방문하는 날의 전체 일정을 검토할 것이라고 하였다. 따라서 (A)가 정답이다.

어휘 personnel n. 직원들   revise v. 변경하다, 개정하다

Paraphrasing
go over 검토하다 → be discussed 논의되다

[92-94]

Questions 92-94 refer to the following news report. [영국]

This is Claudia Jordan reporting for CBIZ. ⁹²**The search engine provider Connexion held a press conference to announce that it had acquired MapPro.** The acquisition of the satellite mapping company will enable Connexion to include updated maps in its search results. This isn't significant by itself. ⁹³Most major search engines already allow their users to access this type of information. ⁹³/⁹⁴But according to Connexion's president Briana Clinton, the company has several other planned uses for MapPro's technology. We now welcome her to talk more about the acquisition and what it means for the company.

press conference 기자 회견   acquisition n. 인수   satellite n. 위성   significant adj. 중요한, 의미 있는   access v. 접근하다

해석
92-94번은 다음 뉴스 보도에 관한 문제입니다.
CBIZ에서 보도 드리는 Claudia Jordan입니다. ⁹²검색 엔진 제공 업체인 Connexion사가 MapPro사를 인수했음을 알리기 위해 기자 회견을 열었습니다. 그 위성 지도 회사의 인수는 Connexion사가 검색 결과에 최신 지도들을 포함하는 것을 가능하게 할 것입니다. 이것은 그것 자체로 중요하지는 않습니다. ⁹³대부분의 주요 검색 엔진 업체들은 이미 그들의 사용자들이 이런 종류의 정보에 접근할 수 있도록 합니다. ⁹³/⁹⁴그러나 Connexion사의 회장인 Briana Clinton에 의하면 회사는 MapPro사의 기술에 대한 여러 다른 이용 계획을 가지고 있다고 합니다. 이제 이 인수와 이것이 회사에 어떤 의미인지에 관해 더 이야기하기 위해 그녀를 모시겠습니다.

92 | 주제 문제

해설 뉴스 보도의 주제는 무엇인가?

(A) 소셜 미디어 서비스
(B) 새로운 소프트웨어 프로그램
(C) 기술 최신화
(D) 기업 인수

해설 뉴스 보도의 주제를 묻는 문제이므로, 지문의 초반을 반드시 듣는다. "The search engine provider Connexion held a press conference to announce that it had acquired MapPro."라며 검색 엔진 제공 업체인 Connexion사가 MapPro사를 인수했음을 알리기 위해 기자 회견을 열었다고 한 후, 기업 인수에 대한 내용으로 지문이 이어지고 있다. 따라서 (D)가 정답이다.

93 | 의도 파악 문제

해설 화자는 "이것은 그것 자체로 중요하지는 않습니다"라고 말할 때 무엇을 의도하는가?
(A) 검색 엔진이 제대로 기능하지 않는다.
(B) 장비 하나가 사소한 업데이트를 받았다.
(C) 서비스가 일부 사용자들에게 인기가 없다.
(D) 발전이 다른 이점들을 포함할 수 있다.

해설 질문의 인용어구(This isn't significant by itself)가 언급된 주변을 주의 깊게 듣는다. "Most major search engines already allow their users to access this type of information."이라며 대부분의 주요 검색 엔진 업체들은 이미 그들의 사용자들이 이런 종류의 정보에 접근할 수 있도록 한다고 한 후, "But according to Connexion's president Briana Clinton, the company has several other planned uses for MapPro's technology."라며 Connexion사의 회장인 Briana Clinton에 의하면 회사는 MapPro사의 기술에 대한 여러 다른 이용 계획을 가지고 있다고 했으므로, 발전이 다른 이점들을 포함할 수 있음을 알 수 있다. 따라서 (D)가 정답이다.

어휘 function v. 기능하다   minor adj. 사소한

94 | 특정 세부 사항 문제

해설 Briana Clinton은 누구인가?
(A) 투자 담당자
(B) 소프트웨어 개발자
(C) 회사 간부
(D) 미디어 관계자

해설 질문의 대상(Briana Clinton)의 신분 및 직업과 관련된 표현을 놓치지 않고 듣는다. "But according to Connexion's president Briana Clinton, the company has several other planned uses for MapPro's technology."라며 Connexion사의 회장인 Briana Clinton에 의하면 회사는 MapPro사의 기술에 대한 여러 다른 이용 계획을 가지고 있다고 하였다. 따라서 (C)가 정답이다.

어휘 investment n. 투자

[95-97]

Questions 95-97 refer to the following telephone message and invoice. [호주]

Hello, Mr. Meade. This is Matthew from Larkville Interiors. ⁹⁵**I want to let you know that we can put up the wallpaper in your new office on March 29 rather than April 3.** You wanted us to start as soon as possible, so ⁹⁶**I assume this plan is acceptable, but . . . um, please call me back to confirm.** One more thing. I double-checked the measurements of your office, and ⁹⁷**it will actually take 11 rolls of wallpaper to cover the walls. I'll update the original invoice and send a copy this afternoon.**

assume v. 생각하다, 추정하다   measurement n. 치수   invoice n. 송장

해석
95-97번은 다음 전화 메시지와 송장에 관한 문제입니다.

안녕하세요, Mr. Meade. 저는 Larkville 인테리어사의 Matthew입니다. ⁹⁵4월 3일이 아닌 3월 29일에 고객님의 새로운 사무실에 벽지를 바를 수 있음을 알려드리고자 합니다. 고객님께서는 저희가 가능한 한 빨리 시작하기를 원하시기 때문에, ⁹⁶이 계획이 받아들여질 것으로 생각합니다만... 음, 제게 다시 전화주셔서 확인해 주시기 바랍니다. 한 가지 더 있습니다. 제가 고객님의 사무실 치수를 다시 확인해 보았는데, ⁹⁷벽을 덮는 데에 실제로는 11롤의 벽지가 필요할 것입니다. 제가 기존의 송장을 업데이트하고 오늘 오후에 사본을 보내드리겠습니다.

Larkville 인테리어사 송장		
항목	수량	가격
⁹⁷벽지	10	380달러
접착제	11	175달러
롤러	2	50달러
근로	5	200달러
	합계:	805달러

95 | 목적 문제

해석 화자는 왜 전화하고 있는가?
(A) 프로젝트의 상황을 확인하기 위해
(B) 일정 변경을 제안하기 위해
(C) 사무실 위치를 확인하기 위해
(D) 약속을 취소하기 위해

해설 전화 메시지의 목적을 묻는 문제이므로, 지문의 초반을 반드시 듣는다. "I want to let you know that we can put up the wallpaper in your new office on March 29 rather than April 3."라며 4월 3일이 아닌 3월 29일에 청자의 새로운 사무실에 벽지를 바를 수 있음을 알려 주고자 한다고 하였으므로, 일정 변경을 제안하기 위해 전화했음을 알 수 있다. 따라서 (B)가 정답이다.

어휘 status n. 상황, 상태 confirm v. 확인하다

96 | 요청 문제

해석 화자는 청자에게 무엇을 하라고 요청하는가?
(A) 자신의 비서에게 연락한다.
(B) 대금을 지불한다.
(C) 계획을 승인한다.
(D) 물품들을 주문한다.

해설 지문에서 요청과 관련된 표현이 포함된 문장을 주의 깊게 듣는다. "I assume this plan is acceptable, but . . . um, please call me back to confirm"이라며 계획이 받아들여질 것으로 생각하지만 자신에게 다시 전화해서 확인해 달라고 요청하였다. 따라서 (C)가 정답이다.

97 | 시각 자료 문제

해석 시각 자료를 보아라. 송장의 어느 수량이 업데이트되어야 하는가?
(A) 10
(B) 11
(C) 2
(D) 5

해설 제시된 송장의 정보를 확인한 뒤 질문의 핵심어구(quantity ~ be updated)와 관련된 내용을 주의 깊게 듣는다. "it will actually take 11 rolls of wallpaper to cover the walls. I'll update the original invoice and send a copy this afternoon."이라며 벽을 덮는 데에 실제로는 11롤의 벽지가 필요할 것이라고 한 후, 자신이 기존의 송장을 업데이트하고 오후에 사본을 보내줄 것이라고 하였으므로, 10으로 기록된 벽지의 수량이 업데이트되어야 함을 송장에서 알 수 있다. 따라서 (A)가 정답이다.

어휘 quantity n. 수량

[98-100]

Questions 98-100 refer to the following announcement and floor plan.

Everyone, ⁹⁸I want to remind you that one of our technical personnel will be installing some scanners in the office tomorrow morning. Be careful when you enter through the front door, as the technician will be working near that area. Also, Printer 101 will be disabled while the work is being done. Instead, ⁹⁹please use Printer 102, which is located next to the conference room. The installation should only last for about one hour, so it won't be a major disruption to your work. Oh, one more thing . . . ¹⁰⁰I e-mailed everyone information on how to use the new scanners. Please go through it carefully.

remind v. 상기시키다 install v. 설치하다
disable v. (기계 등을 일시적으로) 사용 불가능하게 하다
disruption n. 방해, 혼란

해석
98-100번은 다음 공지와 평면도에 관한 문제입니다.

여러분, ⁹⁸내일 아침에 우리 기술 직원 중 한 명이 사무실에 스캐너 몇 대를 설치할 것임을 여러분에게 상기시켜드리고 싶습니다. 기술자가 정문 근처 구역에서 작업하고 있을 것이므로, 정문을 통해 들어오실 때 주의해 주세요. 또한, 작업이 진행되는 동안 101 프린터는 사용 불가능할 것입니다. 대신, ⁹⁹회의실 옆에 위치해 있는 102 프린터를 사용해 주세요. 설치는 오직 한 시간 정도만 지속될 것이므로, 여러분의 업무에 큰 방해가 되지는 않을 것입니다. 아, 한 가지 더요... ¹⁰⁰제가 새로운 스캐너를 사용하는 방법에 대한 정보를 모두에게 이메일로 보내드렸습니다. 그것을 주의 깊게 읽어 주세요.

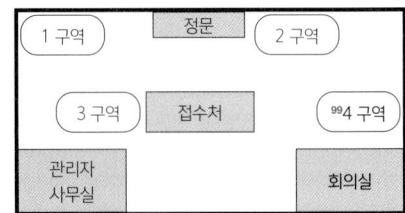

98 | 다음에 할 일 문제

해석 화자에 따르면, 내일 무슨 일이 일어날 것인가?
(A) 몇몇 기기가 설치될 것이다.
(B) 책상이 치워질 것이다.
(C) 손님 목록이 인쇄될 것이다.
(D) 몇몇 기기가 시연될 것이다.

해설 질문의 핵심 어구(tomorrow)가 언급된 주변을 주의 깊게 듣는다. "I want to remind you that one of our technical personnel will be installing some scanners in the office tomorrow morning"이라며 내일 아침에 기술 직원 중 한 명이 사무실에 스캐너 몇 대를 설치할 것임을 상기시켜주고 싶다고 하였다. 따라서 (A)가 정답이다.

어휘 remove v. 치우다, 제거하다 device n. 기기

99 | 시각 자료 문제

해석 시각 자료를 보아라. 102 프린터는 어디에 놓여 있는가?
(A) 1 구역
(B) 2 구역

(C) 3 구역
(D) 4 구역

해설 제시된 평면도의 정보를 확인한 후 질문의 핵심 어구(Printer 102)가 언급된 주변을 주의 깊게 듣는다. "please use Printer 102, which is located next to the conference room"이라며 회의실 옆에 위치해 있는 102 프린터를 사용해 달라고 하였으므로, 102 프린터가 회의실 옆 4 구역에 놓여 있음을 평면도에서 알 수 있다. 따라서 (D)가 정답이다.

100 | 제안 문제

해설 화자는 청자들에게 무엇을 하라고 제안하는가?
(A) 기술자에게 연락한다.
(B) 설명을 참고한다.
(C) 접수처를 방문한다.
(D) 이메일을 보낸다.

해설 지문에서 제안과 관련된 표현이 포함된 문장을 주의 깊게 듣는다. "I e-mailed everyone information on how to use the new scanners. Please go through it carefully."라며 새로운 스캐너를 사용하는 방법에 대한 정보를 모두에게 이메일로 보냈다고 한 후, 그것을 주의 깊게 읽어 달라고 하였다. 따라서 (B)가 정답이다.

어휘 refer to ~을 참고하다 instruction n. 설명

Paraphrasing

information on how to use ~ scanners 스캐너를 사용하는 방법에 대한 정보 → instructions 설명

PART 5

101 | 재귀대명사 채우기

해설 동사(helped)의 목적어 자리에 올 수 있는 재귀대명사 (B), 소유대명사 (C), 목적격 인칭대명사 (D)가 정답의 후보이다. '무료 간식과 음료를 마음껏 먹다'라는 의미가 되어야 하므로 동사 help와 함께 쓰여 '~을 마음껏 먹다'라는 의미의 어구 help oneself to를 만드는 재귀대명사 (B) herself가 정답이다. 소유대명사 (C) hers와 목적격 인칭대명사 (D) her도 동사 helped와 함께 쓰일 수 있지만, 각각 '그녀의 것을 도왔다', '그녀를 도왔다'라는 의미로 어색한 문맥이 되므로 답이 될 수 없다. 주격 인칭대명사 (A)는 목적어 자리에 올 수 없다.

해석 Emily는 매장 개업식 행사에서 무료 간식과 음료를 마음껏 먹었다.

어휘 complimentary adj. 무료의 beverage n. 음료 grand opening 개업식

102 | 동사 자리 채우기

해설 이 문장은 주어가 없는 명령문이므로, 명령문의 동사 자리에 올 수 있는 동사원형 (C) Respond(답장을 보내다, 반응하다)가 정답이다. 명사 (A), 동명사 또는 현재분사 (B), 3인칭 단수형 동사 (D)는 명령문의 동사 자리에 올 수 없다.

해석 Mr. Yates의 이메일에 가능한 한 빨리 답장을 보내고, 명확하지 않은 부분이 있으면 질문을 하십시오.

어휘 unclear adj. 명확하지 않은, 막연한

103 | 부사절 접속사 채우기

해설 이 문장은 주어(its construction)와 동사(should begin)를 갖춘 완전한 절이므로, ___ ~ community center는 수식어 거품으로 보아야 한다. 이 수식어 거품은 동사(has voted)가 있는 거품절이므로, 거품절을 이끌 수 있는 부사절 접속사 (A), (B), (C)가 정답의 후보이다. '시의회가 새로운 시민 문화 회관에 자금을 대는 것에 찬성 투표를 했으므로, 그것의 공사가 조만간 시작될 것이다'라는 의미가 되어야 하므로 이유를 나타내는 부사절 접속사 (A) Now that(~이므로, ~이기 때문에)이 정답이다. (B) If only(~하기만 했더라면)를 쓸 경우 가정법 구문이 되어 현재나 과거의 반대 상황을 가정하며 뒤에 과거 시제 또는 과거완료 시제가 와야 하므로 현재완료 시제와 함께 쓰일 수 없다. (C) Rather than(~보다는)은 어색한 문맥을 만든다. 전치사 (D) In spite of(~에도 불구하고)는 거품절을 이끌 수 없다.

해석 시의회가 새로운 시민 문화 회관에 자금을 대는 것에 찬성 투표를 했으므로, 그것의 공사가 조만간 시작될 것이다.

어휘 vote in favor of ~에 찬성 투표를 하다 construction n. 공사, 건설

104 | 동사 자리 채우기

해설 빈칸 앞의 to와 함께 사용되어 to 부정사를 만드는 동사원형 (A) protect(보호하다)가 정답이다. 명사 (B), 형용사 (C), 동명사 또는 현재분사 (D)는 to 부정사를 만들 수 없다.

해석 야생 동물 보호구는 주의 멸종 위기에 처한 종을 보호하기 위해 플로리다 자연 위원회에 의해 만들어졌다.

어휘 wildlife n. 야생 동물 preserve n. 보호구; v. 보존하다
commission n. 위원회, 수수료; v. 의뢰하다
endangered adj. 멸종 위기에 처한, 위험에 처한 species n. 종

105 | 부사 자리 채우기

해설 빈칸 뒤의 형용사(late)를 수식할 수 있는 것은 부사이므로 부사 (A), (B), (C)가 정답의 후보이다. '일상적으로 늦는 직원들에 대한 문제에 대처하다'라는 문맥이므로 (C) routinely(일상적으로)가 정답이다. (A) adequately는 '적절히, 충분히', (B) formerly는 '이전에, 예전에'라는 의미이다. 참고로, 부사 formerly는 이전에 일어난 과거의 일을 나타낼 때 사용되므로 현재 시제와 함께 쓰일 수 없고, 주로 과거 시제 또는 과거완료 시제 등과 함께 쓰임을 알아둔다. 형용사 (D)는 형용사를 수식할 수 없다.

해석 Delvium 자동차사의 새로운 정책은 직장에 일상적으로 늦는 직원들에 대한 문제에 대처하는 것을 목표로 한다.

어휘 aim to ~하는 것을 목표로 하다 address v. (일·문제 등에) 대처하다, 다루다

106 | 올바른 시제의 동사 채우기

해설 첫 번째 절(The Lexington Building's ~ days)에 동사가 없으므로 동사 (B)와 (C)가 정답의 후보이다. 미래 시간 표현(in the next couple of days)이 있으므로 미래를 나타낼 수 있는 현재진행 시제 (C) is arriving이 정답이다. 현재완료 시제 (B)는 미래 시간 표현과 함께 쓰일 수 없다. to 부정사 (A)와 명사 (D)는 동사 자리에 올 수 없다. 참고로, 현재진행 시제(be + -ing)는 예정된 일이나 곧 일어나려고 하는 일을 표현하여 미래를 나타낼 수 있음을 알아둔다.

해석 Lexington 건물의 새로운 세입자가 앞으로 며칠 내에 도착할 것이므로, 집주인은 모든 것이 준비되도록 하고 있다.

어휘 tenant n. 세입자, 거주자; v. 임차해서 살다

107 | 부사 자리 채우기

해설 동사(was decorated)를 꾸밀 수 있는 것은 부사이므로 부사 (B) attractively(보기 좋게, 매력적으로)가 정답이다. 형용사 (A), 명사 (C), 동명사 또는 현재분사 (D)는 동사를 꾸밀 수 없다.

해석 연회장은 6월 11일의 Langhorne 재단의 모금 경축 행사를 위해 보기 좋게 꾸며졌다.

어휘 banquet hall 연회장 fundraising n. 모금, 모금 활동 gala n. 경축 행사

108 | 형용사 자리 채우기

해설 빈칸 뒤의 명사(role)를 꾸밀 수 있는 것은 형용사이므로 형용사 (B) active(적극적인, 활동적인)가 정답이다. 동사 (A)는 명사를 꾸밀 수 없고, 명사 (C) action(행동, 동작)과 (D) activity(활동, 활기)는 role(역할)과 복합 명사를 이루지 못한다.

해석 Whitby시 의회는 주민들이 지역 사회에서 적극적인 역할을 할 수 있는 방안을 명시하는 소책자를 최근에 준비했다.

어휘 brochure n. 소책자   specify v. 명시하다   role n. 역할, 임무   community n. 지역 사회

109 | 동사 어휘 고르기

해설 '새로운 사무실 정책들에 익숙해지다'라는 문맥이므로 (D) familiarize(익숙하게 하다)가 정답이다. (A) relieve는 '완화하다', (B) converse는 '대화를 나누다', (C) arrange는 '정리하다, 배열하다'라는 의미이다.

해석 업데이트된 직원 설명서를 참고함으로써 새로운 사무실 정책들에 익숙해지시기 바랍니다.

어휘 policy n. 정책   consult v. 참고하다, 상담하다   manual n. 설명서

110 | 전치사 채우기

해설 '광고팀은 사업 기획 세션에 맞춰 캠페인 제안서를 완성해야 한다는 압박을 받고 있다'라는 의미가 되어야 하므로 빈칸 뒤의 명사 pressure와 함께 '압박을 받는, 압박감을 느끼는'이라는 의미의 어구 under pressure를 만드는 전치사 (C) under가 정답이다. (A) within은 '~ 이내에', (B) through는 '~을 통해서', (D) among은 '~ 사이에'라는 의미이다.

해석 광고팀은 사업 기획 세션에 맞춰 캠페인 제안서를 완성해야 한다는 압박을 받고 있다.

어휘 pressure n. 압박, 압력   complete v. 완성하다, 완료하다   proposal n. 제안서   in time ~에 맞춰, 이윽고

111 | 부사 어휘 고르기

해설 'BelTrax사는 지속적으로 최고의 시장 조사 제공 기관 중 하나로 평가되어 왔다'라는 문맥이므로 부사 (C) consistently(지속적으로)가 정답이다. (A) conveniently는 '편리하게', (B) temporarily는 '일시적으로', (D) wishfully는 '갈망하여'라는 의미이다.

해석 BelTrax사는 7년 전 설립 이래로 지속적으로 최고의 시장 조사 제공 기관 중 하나로 평가되어 왔다.

어휘 rank as ~로 평가되다   provider n. 제공 기관, 공급자   marketing research 시장 조사   foundation n. 설립, 기초

112 | 올바른 시제의 동사 채우기

해설 that절(that ~ machinery)에 동사가 없으므로 동사 (A), (B), (C)가 정답의 후보이다. 증축 건물이 지어진다면 추가적인 공간을 제공할 것이라는 가정이나 예측을 나타내므로 조건부 상황을 나타내는 (B) would provide가 정답이다. 미래완료 시제 (A)는 미래 특정 시점 이전에 발생한 동작이 미래의 그 시점에 완료될 것임을 나타내므로 답이 될 수 없다. 과거완료 시제 (C)는 과거 시점보다 더 과거에 일어난 일을 나타내므로 답이 될 수 없다. to 부정사 (D)는 동사 자리에 올 수 없다.

해석 Mansfield Chemical사는 새로 구매한 기계를 위한 추가적인 공간을 제공할 증축 건물을 짓는 것을 고려하고 있다.

어휘 extension n. 증축 건물, 확대   additional adj. 추가적인   newly adv. 새로, 최근에   machinery n. 기계(류)

113 | 형용사 어휘 고르기

해설 '몇 가지 사소한 불만 사항 외에, 바이러스 퇴치 프로그램에 대한 의견은 대체로 긍정적이었다'라는 문맥이므로 형용사 (C) minor(사소한, 중요하지 않은)가 정답이다. (A) defensive는 '방어적인, 수비의', (B) current는 '현재의', (D) complex는 '복잡한'이라는 의미이다.

해석 쉽게 해결된 몇 가지 사소한 불만 사항 외에, ShieldX사의 바이러스 퇴치 프로그램에 대한 의견은 대체로 긍정적이었다.

어휘 antivirus adj. 바이러스 퇴치용인   generally adv. 대체로

114 | 지시대명사 those 채우기

해설 문장에 동사(will be required)만 있고 주어가 없으므로 주어 역할을 할 수 있는 부정대명사 (A), 지시대명사 (B)와 (C)가 정답의 후보이다. 빈칸 뒤의 관계절(who ~ time)의 동사(return)가 복수형이고 '차량을 반납하는 사람들'이라는 의미가 되어야 하므로 복수를 나타내는 지시대명사 (B) Those(~하는 사람들)가 정답이다. (A) Everybody는 '모두', (C) This는 '이것'이라는 의미로 단수 취급되므로 답이 될 수 없다. (D) Which는 관계대명사일 경우 앞에 선행사가 나와야 하고, 의문형용사일 경우 뒤에 명사가 나와야 한다.

해석 지정된 시간 이후에 차량을 Speedy 자동차 대여점으로 반납하는 사람들은 45달러의 연체료를 지불해야 할 것이다.

어휘 return v. 반납하다   vehicle n. 차량   designated adj. 지정된   late fee 연체료, 지체료

115 | 수량 표현 채우기

해설 빈칸 뒤의 단수 가산 명사(seat)를 꾸밀 수 있는 수량 표현 (C) every(모든)가 정답이다. 명사 (A) plenty(많음, 풍부함)는 전치사 of와 함께 plenty of(많은)의 형태로 쓰여 뒤에 복수 가산 명사 또는 불가산 명사가 오므로 답이 될 수 없다. (B) all(모든)은 복수 가산 명사를 꾸미고, (D) most(대부분의)는 가산 명사를 꾸미는 경우 복수 가산 명사를 꾸며야 하므로 답이 될 수 없다.

해석 기조 연설자가 무대에 오르기로 예정된 약 15분 전에 강당의 모든 좌석이 가득 찼다.

어휘 keynote speaker 기조 연설자   auditorium n. 강당

116 | 형용사 자리 채우기

해설 빈칸 뒤의 명사(ways)를 꾸밀 수 있는 것은 형용사이므로 형용사 (C)와 형용사 역할을 하는 과거분사 (D)가 정답의 후보이다. '새로운 고객들을 끌어 모으기 위한 독창적인 방법들을 개발했다'라는 의미가 되어야 하므로 형용사 (C) inventive(독창적인)가 정답이다. 과거분사 (D)는 '발명된 방법들을 개발했다'라는 어색한 문맥이 되므로 답이 될 수 없다. 동사 (A)는 명사를 꾸밀 수 없다. 명사 (B) invention(발명)은 ways(방법들)와 복합 명사를 이루지 못한다.

해석 Limerick Books사는 새로운 고객들을 끌어 모으기 위한 독창적인 방법들을 개발함으로써 경쟁력을 유지하고 있다.

어휘 competitive adj. 경쟁력 있는   attract v. 끌어 모으다

117 | 명사 어휘 고르기

해설 '몇몇 직원들에게 연설의 요점을 다루는 개요를 제공했다'라는 문맥이므로 (C) overview(개요, 개관)가 정답이다. (A) objection은 '반대, 이의', (B) expansion은 '확대, 확장', (D) experience는 '경험, 경력'이라는 의미이다.

해석 Ms. Waddill은 부서의 몇몇 직원들에게 최고 경영자의 연설의 요점을 다루는 개요를 제공했다.

어휘 department n. 부서   cover v. 다루다, 포함시키다   key point 요점   speech n. 연설, 말하는 능력

118 | 전치사 채우기

해설 '안전 교육 덕분에 작업 현장에서 일어나는 사고의 수를 상당히 줄였다'라는 의미가 되어야 하므로 '~의 덕분에'의 의미를 갖는 전치사 (C) Owing to가 정답이다. (A) Prior to는 '~에 앞서', (B) On behalf of는 '~을 대신하여', (D) According to는 '~에 따르면'이라는 의미이다.

해석 광범위한 안전 교육 덕분에, Desmond 건설사는 작업 현장에서 일어나는 사고의 수를 상당히 줄였다.

어휘 extensive adj. 광범위한 significantly adv. 상당히 reduce v. 줄이다

119 | 사람명사와 사물/추상명사 구별하여 채우기

해설 동사(increased) 앞에 주어가 없으므로 주어 자리에 올 수 있는 명사 (B), (C), (D)가 정답의 후보이다. '축제의 참가자 수는 거의 30퍼센트 증가했다'라는 의미가 되어야 하므로 추상명사 (D) Attendance(참가자 수, 참석)가 정답이다. 사람명사 (B) Attendee(참석자)와 (C) Attendant(참석자, 안내원)는 가산 명사이므로 복수형으로 쓰이거나 관사와 함께 쓰여야 하므로 답이 될 수 없다. 동사 (A)는 주어 자리에 올 수 없다.

해석 올해 Latipa 영화 축제의 참가자 수는 거의 30퍼센트 증가했지만, 주최 측은 여전히 손실을 입었다.

어휘 nearly adv. 거의 organizer n. 주최 측

120 | 전치사 채우기

해설 이 문장은 주어(the popular Marigold Hotel)와 동사(is ~ booked)를 갖춘 완전한 절이므로, ____ the large number of rooms in the facility는 수식어 거품으로 보아야 한다. 이 수식어 거품은 동사가 없는 거품구이므로, 거품구를 이끌 수 있는 전치사 (C)와 (D)가 정답의 후보이다. '시설 내의 많은 방에도 불구하고 항상 완전히 예약된다'라는 의미가 되어야 하므로 양보를 나타내는 전치사 (D) notwithstanding(~에도 불구하고)이 정답이다. (C) aside from은 '~을 제외하고'라는 의미이다. 부사 (A) thereby(그렇게 함으로써)는 수식어 거품을 이끌 수 없다. 부사절 접속사 (B) even though(~임에도 불구하고)는 동사가 있는 거품절을 이끈다.

해석 여름 동안, 시설 내의 많은 방에도 불구하고 인기 있는 Marigold 호텔은 항상 완전히 예약된다.

어휘 fully adv. 완전히, 충분히 book v. 예약하다, 기록하다 facility n. 시설, 기관

121 | 명사 자리 채우기

해설 빈칸 앞의 형용사(official)의 꾸밈을 받을 수 있는 것은 명사이므로 명사 (A)와 (C)가 정답의 후보이다. 빈칸 앞의 부정관사(an)와 함께 쓰일 수 있는 것은 단수 명사이므로 단수 명사 (A) permit(허가, 허가증)이 정답이다. 복수 명사 (C)는 부정관사 다음에 올 수 없다. 형용사 (B)와 부사 (D)는 형용사의 꾸밈을 받을 수 없다.

해석 Madison 음악 콘서트의 관리자들은 행사를 개최하기 위해 시 정부로부터 공식 허가를 받았다.

어휘 administrator n. 관리자 official adj. 공식의, 공식적인 permissive adj. 허용하는, 묵인하는 permissively adv. 허용되어, 관대하게

122 | 부사 어휘 고르기

해설 '작은 구역은 오로지 반려동물과 그 주인들을 위해 확보되어 있다'라는 문맥이므로 부사 (D) exclusively(오로지, 오직 ~뿐)가 정답이다. (A) relatively는 '비교적', (B) intensely는 '강렬하게, 격렬하게', (C) immeasurably는 '헤아릴 수 없이, 대단히'라는 의미이다.

해석 Glegg 공원의 작은 구역은 오로지 반려동물과 그 주인들을 위해 확보되어 있다.

어휘 set aside 확보하다, 따로 떼어 두다

123 | 형용사 자리 채우기

해설 빈칸 뒤의 명사(place)를 꾸밀 수 있는 형용사 (A), (C), (D)가 정답의 후보이다. 비교급과 함께 쓰이는 표현 than(~보다)이 사용되었고, '기숙사보다 더 조용한 공부할 장소'라는 의미가 되어야 하므로 형용사 quiet(조용한)의 비교급 (C) quieter가 정답이다. 원급 (A)와 최상급 (D)는 비교급 표현과 함께 쓰일 수 없다. 부사 (B)는 형용사 자리에 올 수 없다.

해석 Coast 대학의 도서관은 기숙사보다 더 조용한 공부할 장소를 찾는 학생들을 위해 늦게까지 열려 있다.

어휘 dormitory n. 기숙사

124 | 동사 어휘 고르기

해설 '효과적인 영업 전략에 대해 연설을 하다'라는 문맥이므로 '연설을 하다'라는 의미의 동사 어구 deliver a talk를 만드는 동사 (A) deliver ((연설이나 강연 등을) 하다)가 정답이다. (B) register는 '등록하다', (C) showcase는 '전시하다, 소개하다', (D) imply는 '암시하다'라는 의미이다.

해석 Hartwell Industries사의 설립자인 Ms. Nissim은 글로벌 상공회의에서 효과적인 영업 전략에 대해 연설을 할 것이다.

어휘 founder n. 설립자, 창시자 strategy n. 전략, 계획

125 | 형용사 자리 채우기

해설 빈칸 뒤의 명사(discussion)를 꾸며줄 수 있는 것은 형용사이므로 형용사 (C) further(추가의)가 정답이다. 부사 (A)와 (B), 부사 또는 전치사 (D)는 명사를 꾸밀 수 없다.

해석 추가 논의가 필요한 항목들은 다음 주 월요일 회의 안건에 추가될 예정이다.

어휘 agenda n. 안건

126 | 동사 어휘 고르기

해설 '공급업체들과 협상할 때, Mr. Sinclair는 주로 지불 조건과 배송 시간에 집중한다'라는 문맥이므로 동사 negotiate(협상하다)의 현재분사형 (C) negotiating이 정답이다. (A)의 adopt(채택하다)도 해석상 그럴듯해 보이지만, 타동사이므로 전치사 with와 함께 쓰일 수 없다. (B)의 appear는 '나타나다', (D)의 finish는 '끝내다, 마치다'라는 의미이다.

해석 공급업체들과 협상할 때, Mr. Sinclair는 주로 지불 조건과 배송 시간에 집중한다.

어휘 primarily adv. 주로 payment terms 지불 조건

127 | 명사 어휘 고르기

해설 '매우 뛰어난 공연으로 광범위한 인정을 받았다'라는 문맥이므로 (D) recognition(인정, 인식)이 정답이다. (A) criticism은 '비판, 비평', (B) persuasion은 '설득', (C) deliberation은 '숙고, 신중함'이라는 의미이다.

해석 테너 Michael Amato는 프랑크푸르트 오페라에서 그의 매우 뛰어난 공연으로 광범위한 인정을 받았다.

어휘 widespread adj. 광범위한, 널리 퍼진 superb adj. 매우 뛰어난, 최고의

128 | 전치사 채우기

해설 이 문장은 주어(Nicholson Media), 동사(owns), 목적어(several magazines and newspapers)를 갖춘 완전한 절이므로, ____ ~ state는 수식어 거품으로 보아야 한다. 이 수식어 거품은 동사가 없는 거품구이므로, 거품구를 이끌 수 있는 전치사 (A), (C), (D)가 정답의 후보이다. '텔레비전 방송국을 소유한 것 외에도 여러 잡지사와 신문사를 소유하고 있다'라는 의미가 되어야 하므로 '~ 외에도'의 의미를 갖는 전치

사 (A) Besides가 정답이다. (C) Among은 '~ 사이에', (D) Along은 '~을 따라'라는 의미이다. 부사 (B) Rather(꽤, 약간)는 수식어 거품구를 이끌 수 없다.

해석 주 전역에 텔레비전 방송국을 소유한 것 외에도, Nicholson 미디어사는 여러 잡지사와 신문사를 소유하고 있다.

어휘 station n. 방송국, 정류장 own v. 소유하다; adj. 고유한

129 | 형용사 자리 채우기

해설 빈칸 뒤의 명사(financial services firms)를 꾸며줄 수 있는 것은 형용사이므로 형용사 역할을 하는 과거분사 (C)와 형용사 (D)가 정답의 후보이다. '국제적으로 가장 높이 평가되는 금융 서비스 회사의 대표들'이라는 의미가 되어야 하므로 과거분사 (C) respected(높이 평가되는, 훌륭한)가 정답이다. 형용사 (D)는 '각각의 금융 서비스 회사'라는 어색한 문맥을 만들기 때문에 답이 될 수 없다. 부사 (A)와 동사 (B)는 명사를 꾸밀 수 없다. (B)는 명사로도 쓰이는데, 명사 (B) respect(존경)는 financial services firms(금융 서비스 회사)와 복합 명사를 이룰 수 없다.

해석 국제적으로 가장 높이 평가되는 금융 서비스 회사의 대표들은 다음 주의 정상 회담에서 연설할 것이다.

어휘 representative n. 대표 internationally adv. 국제적으로
summit n. 정상 회담, (산의) 정상

130 | 부사 어휘 고르기

해설 '5월 1일까지 무료로 다운로드될 수 있지만 그 후에는 19.99달러일 것이다'라는 의미가 되어야 하므로 부사 (B) thereafter(그 후에)가 정답이다. (A) since도 '그 이후에'라는 의미로 쓰이지만, 과거와 현재 사이의 시점을 나타내며 미래 시제와 같이 쓰일 수 없다. (C) consequently는 '그 결과, 따라서', (D) now는 '현재'라는 의미이다.

해석 TNP Tech사의 소프트웨어는 5월 1일까지 무료로 다운로드될 수 있지만 그 후에는 19.99달러일 것이다.

어휘 for free 무료로, 공짜로

PART 6

131-134번은 다음 공고에 관한 문제입니다.

모든 세입자들은 주목해주십시오

¹³¹Wimberley Group사는 청구 시스템을 전자로 전환할 것입니다. 2월 1일부로, 현금과 개인 수표는 더 이상 받아들여지지 않을 것입니다. ¹³²이는 모든 세입자들이 임대료를 온라인으로 내야 함을 의미합니다.

모든 세입자는 www.wimberleygroup.com에서 사용자 프로필을 만들어야 합니다. ¹³³로그인을 한 후에, 여러분은 지불금을 납부할 수 있을 것입니다. 여러분은 미납된 청구서를 선택한 다음에 화면 아래쪽의 "지불"을 클릭함으로써 이것을 하실 수 있습니다. ¹³⁴버튼을 누르자마자, 여러분이 지정하는 금액이 등록된 신용카드 또는 은행 계좌에서 공제될 것입니다. 만약 자동 납부로 처리하기를 원하시면, "매달 지불"이라고 적힌 버튼을 클릭해주십시오.

질문이 있으시면, help@wimberleygroup.com으로 저희에게 이메일을 보내주십시오. 여러분의 협조에 감사드립니다.

no longer 더 이상 ~아닌 accept v. 받아들이다, 수락하다
tenant n. 세입자; v. 임차해서 살다 unpaid adj. 미납의, 지불되지 않은
bill n. 청구서, 계산서 hit v. (기계 등을 작동시키기 위해 버튼 등을) 누르다
designate v. 지정하다 deduct v. 공제하다 arrange v. 처리하다, 마련하다
automatic adj. 자동의 label v. (표 같은 것에 필요한 정보를) 적다
cooperation n. 협조, 협력

131 | 동사 어휘 고르기

해설 '청구 시스템을 전자로 전환할 것이다'라는 문맥이므로 동사 convert(전환하다, 변경하다)의 현재분사형 (C) converting이 정답이다. (A)의 induce는 '설득하다', (B)의 fluctuate는 '변동하다, 오르내리다', (D)의 recover는 '회복하다, 복구하다'라는 의미이다.

132 | 알맞은 문장 고르기

해설 (A) 세입자들은 시스템이 사용하기 쉽다는 것을 알게 되었습니다.
(B) 이는 모든 세입자들이 임대료를 온라인으로 내야 함을 의미합니다.
(C) 새로운 시스템의 사용은 전적으로 선택적일 것입니다.
(D) 특정 Wimberley Group사의 입주자들만 영향을 받을 것입니다.

해설 앞 문장 'Effective February 1, cash and personal checks will no longer be accepted.'에서 2월 1일부로 현금과 개인 수표는 더 이상 받아들여지지 않을 것이라고 했으므로, 빈칸에는 지불 방식과 관련된 내용이 들어가야 함을 알 수 있다. 따라서 (B)가 정답이다.

어휘 rent n. 임대료 completely adv. 전적으로 optional adj. 선택적인
certain adj. 특정한, 확실한 occupant n. 입주자, 사용자
affect v. ~에 영향을 끼치다, 작용하다

133 | 동사 어휘 고르기 전체 문맥 파악

해설 '로그인을 한 후에 지불금을 ___할 수 있다'라는 문맥이므로 모든 보기가 정답의 후보이다. 빈칸이 있는 문장만으로 정답을 고를 수 없으므로 주변 문맥이나 전체 문맥을 파악한다. 뒤 문장에서 '미납된 청구서를 선택한 다음에 화면 아래쪽의 "지불"을 클릭함으로써 이것을 할 수 있다(You can do this by selecting the unpaid bill and then clicking "Pay" at the bottom of the screen.)'고 했고, '지정하는 금액이 등록된 신용카드 또는 은행 계좌에서 공제될 것이다(~ the amount you designate will be deducted from your registered credit card or bank account)'라고 했으므로, 로그인 후에 지불금을 납부할 수 있을 것임을 알 수 있다. 따라서 '지불금을 납부하다, 내다'라는 의미의 어구 make a payment를 만드는 (D) make(만들다)가 정답이다. (A) afford는 '여유가 되다', (B) receive는 '받다', (C) demand는 '요구하다'라는 의미이다.

134 | 부사절 접속사 채우기

해설 이 문장은 주어(the amount)와 동사(will be deducted)를 갖춘 완전한 절이므로, ___ you hit the button은 수식어 거품으로 보아야 한다. 이 수식어 거품은 동사(hit)가 있는 거품절이므로, 거품절을 이끌 수 있는 부사절 접속사 (A), (C), (D)가 정답의 후보이다. '버튼을 누르자마자 지정하는 금액이 등록된 신용카드 또는 은행 계좌에서 공제될 것이다'라는 의미가 되어야 하므로, '~ 하자마자'라는 의미의 부사절 접속사 (D) As soon as가 정답이다. (A) Even if와 (C) Although는 '비록 ~이지만'이라는 의미이다. 전치사 (B) During(~ 동안)은 거품절을 이끌 수 없다.

135-138번은 다음 회람에 관한 문제입니다.

수신: Brentwood사의 전 직원
발신: Dale Rosen, 인사부 부장
날짜: 2월 26일
제목: 휴대폰 사용

지난 한 달 동안, 몇몇 부서장들은 직장에서의 휴대폰 사용에 관한 걱정을 표했습니다. ¹³⁵특히, 교육 세션의 생산성이 상당히 감소하였습니다. ¹³⁶따라서, Brentwood사는 새로운 규정을 시작하기로 결정했습니다. 이제부터 직원들의 휴대폰은 세션 동안 꺼져 있어야 합니다. ¹³⁷이것은 방해 요소들을 막기 위한 것입니다. 직원들이 논의되고 있는 주제에 더 잘 집중할 수 있게 되는 것이 저희의 바람입니다. ¹³⁸우리는 이 회사 규정에 한 가지 예외를 허용할 것입니다. 만약 긴급한 전화나 메시지가 예상된다면, 관리자에게 미리 알려주시고, 당신은 휴대폰을 무음 모드로 켜둘 수 있습니다.

concern n. 걱정, 관심 in particular 특히, 특별히 decrease v. 감소하다
significantly adv. 상당히 launch v. 시작하다, 개시하다 policy n. 규정, 정책
prevent v. 막다, 예방하다 concentrate v. 집중하다 urgent adj. 긴급한
supervisor n. 관리자 silent mode 무음 모드

135 | 명사 어휘 고르기 전체 문맥 파악

해설 '교육 세션의 _____이 상당히 감소했다'라는 문맥이므로 모든 보기가 정답의 후보이다. 빈칸이 있는 문장만으로 정답을 고를 수 없으므로 주변 문맥이나 전체 문맥을 파악한다. 앞 문장에서 '지난 한 달 동안, 몇몇 부서장들은 직장에서의 휴대폰 사용에 관한 걱정을 표현했다(Over the past month, several department managers have expressed concerns about the use of mobile phones in the workplace).'라고 했고, 뒷부분에서 '직원들의 휴대폰은 세션 동안 꺼져 있어야 한다(employees' mobile phones must be turned off during a session)'라고 한 후, '직원들이 논의되고 있는 주제에 더 잘 집중할 수 있게 되는 것이 바람직하다(It is our hope that staff will be able to better concentrate on the topics being discussed).'라고 했으므로 휴대폰 사용이 교육 세션의 생산성을 떨어뜨렸음을 알 수 있다. 따라서 (C) productivity(생산성)가 정답이다. (A) duration은 '지속, 기간', (B) attendance는 '출석', (D) number는 '개수, 수'라는 의미이다.

136 | 올바른 시제의 동사 채우기 주변 문맥 파악

해설 'Brentwood사가 새로운 규정을 시작하기로 결정하다'라는 문맥인데, 이 경우 빈칸이 있는 문장만으로는 올바른 시제의 동사를 고를 수 없으므로 주변 문맥이나 전체 문맥을 파악하여 정답을 고른다. 뒤 문장에서 '이제부터 직원들의 휴대폰은 세션 동안 꺼져 있어야 한다(From now on, employees' mobile phones must be turned off during a session).'라고 했으므로, 새로운 규정을 시작하기로 결정한 과거에 발생한 일이 현재까지 영향을 미치고 있음을 알 수 있다. 따라서 현재완료 시제 (D) has decided가 정답이다.

137 | 명사 어휘 고르기 주변 문맥 파악

해설 '이것은 _____을 막기 위한 것이다'라는 문맥이므로 (A), (B), (D)가 정답의 후보이다. 빈칸이 있는 문장만으로 정답을 고를 수 없으므로 주변 문맥이나 전체 문맥을 파악한다. 뒤 문장에서 '직원들이 논의되고 있는 주제에 더 잘 집중할 수 있게 되는 것이 바람직하다(It is our hope that staff will be able to better concentrate on the topics being discussed).'라고 했으므로 방해를 막기 위해 새로운 규정을 시작함을 알 수 있다. 따라서 명사 interruption(방해 요소)의 복수형 (D) interruptions가 정답이다. (A)의 error는 '오류', (B)의 charge는 '요금', (C)의 regulation은 '규정'이라는 의미이다.

138 | 알맞은 문장 고르기

해석 (A) 개인용 기기들은 회사에 의해 제공될 것입니다.
(B) 당신은 필요에 따라 휴대폰을 통해 인터넷에 접속할 수 있습니다.
(C) 시청각 시스템은 사전에 예약되어야 합니다.
(D) 우리는 이 회사 규정에 한 가지 예외를 허용할 것입니다.

해설 뒤 문장 'If an urgent call or message is expected, please notify your supervisor beforehand, and you may keep your phone on in silent mode.'에서 만약 긴급한 전화나 메시지가 예상된다면, 관리자에게 미리 알리고 휴대폰을 무음 모드로 켜둘 수 있다고 했으므로, 빈칸에는 휴대폰을 켤 수 있는 예외 사항과 관련된 내용이 들어가야 함을 알 수 있다. 따라서 (D)가 정답이다.

어휘 audiovisual adj. 시청각의 reserve v. 예약하다 in advance 사전에
exception n. 예외

139-142번은 다음 공고에 관한 문제입니다.

전 직원을 위한 공고

우리 매장이 위치해 있는 쇼핑몰은 12월 24일부터 26일까지 문을 닫을 것입니다. [139]하지만, 여러분 중 일부는 연휴 이후의 세일을 준비하기 위해 12월 24일에 출근할 것입니다. 평소 아침에 쇼핑몰의 문을 여는 경비원은 이 기간 동안에 근무하지 않을 것입니다. [140]그러므로 건물에 들어가기 위해서는 보안 코드가 요구될 것입니다. Daniel Monahan이 가장 선임 직원이므로, 저는 그에게 그것을 알려줄 것이며, 그가 모두를 안으로 들어오게 할 것입니다.

[141]여러분이 정확히 오전 10시에 입구에서 Daniel을 만나는 것이 중요합니다. [142]문을 열기 위해 그가 왔다 갔다 하게 해서 시간을 낭비하는 것을 원치 않으므로, 배려하셔서 시간을 엄수하여 도착해 주시기 바랍니다.

이해해 주셔서 감사드립니다.

Alison Culpepper 드림
매장 관리인

set up 준비하다, 설립하다 guard n. 경비원; v. 지키다 off duty 근무 중이 아닌
senior adj. 선임의, 고위의; n. 연장자 vital adj. 중요한, 필수의
entrance n. 입구, 입장 back and forth 왔다 갔다, 앞뒤로
considerate adj. 배려하는, 사려 깊은

139 | 접속부사 채우기 주변 문맥 파악

해설 빈칸이 콤마와 함께 문장의 맨 앞에 온 접속부사 자리이므로, 앞 문장과 빈칸이 있는 문장의 의미 관계를 파악하여 정답을 선택한다. 앞 문장에서 쇼핑몰이 12월 24일부터 26일까지 문을 닫을 것이라고 했고, 빈칸이 있는 문장에서는 직원들 중 일부는 12월 24일에 출근할 것이라고 했으므로, 앞 문장과 반대되는 내용을 나타낼 때 사용되는 (D) However(하지만)가 정답이다.

어휘 besides adv. 게다가 otherwise adv. 그렇지 않으면
accordingly adv. 그에 따라서

140 | 알맞은 문장 고르기

해석 (A) 고객의 문의에 반드시 적시에 답변하는 것은 우리의 우선순위입니다.
(B) 여러분은 쇼핑몰에 들어가기 위해 직원 출입 허가증을 사용할 수 있습니다.
(C) 그러므로 건물에 들어가기 위해서는 보안 코드가 요구될 것입니다.
(D) 여러분은 그의 부재로 인해 끝나지 않은 업무를 처리해야 할 것입니다.

해설 뒤 문장 'Daniel Monahan is the most senior staff member, so I will give it to him, and he will let everyone inside.'에서 Daniel Monahan이 가장 선임 직원이므로 그에게 그것을 알려줄 것이며, 그가 모두를 안으로 들어오게 할 것이라고 했으므로, 빈칸에는 모두를 안으로 들어오게 하는 것과 관련된 내용이 들어가야 함을 알 수 있다. 따라서 (C)가 정답이다.

어휘 make sure 반드시 ~하다, 확실히 ~하게 하다 inquiry n. 문의, 질문
in a timely manner 적시에, 제 시간에 priority n. 우선 순위
pass n. 출입 허가증; v. 통과하다 handle v. 처리하다, 다루다
absence n. 부재, 결석

141 | 제안·요청·의무의 주절을 뒤따르는 that절에 동사원형 채우기

해설 주절에 의무를 나타내는 형용사(vital)가 올 경우, 종속절에 동사원형이 와야 하므로 동사원형 (B) meet(만나다)이 정답이다. 현재진행 시제 동사 (A), 과거완료 시제 동사 (C), 과거 시제 동사 또는 과거분사 (D)는 동사원형 자리에 올 수 없다.

142 | 부사 어휘 고르기

해설 '문을 열기 위해 그가 왔다 갔다 하게 해서 시간을 낭비하는 것을 원치 않으므로, 배려해서 시간을 엄수하여 도착해 주기를 바란다'라는 문맥이므로, (A) punctually(시간을 엄수하여)가 정답이다. (B) regularly는 '규칙적으로', (C) politely는 '정중하게', (D) impressively는 '인상 깊게'라는 의미이다.

143-146번은 다음 편지에 관한 문제입니다.

> Eric Frears
> 6633번지 7번가
> 새크라멘토, 캘리포니아주 95673
>
> Mr. Frears께,
>
> 샤스타 레이크에 있는 The Aldrich를 고려해주셔서 감사합니다. ¹⁴³높은 삶의 질을 제공하는 것이 항상 저희의 우선 사항이었던 것을 고려하면, 저희가 수백 명의 만족한 주민들을 보유하고 있는 것은 놀랍지 않습니다.
>
> ¹⁴⁴저희 주택 지구의 구성원으로서, 귀하는 24시간 계속되는 의료 서비스와 요리 및 청소에 대한 지원을 이용할 수 있을 것입니다. 또한, 빈번한 모임들과 지역 행사들에서 자원봉사 기회들이 있습니다. ¹⁴⁵저희는 매일을 가능한 한 만족스럽게 만들기를 바랍니다.
>
> 방문해서 주위를 둘러보고, 샤스타 레이크에 있는 The Aldrich에서의 은퇴 생활을 경험해보세요. ¹⁴⁶저희는 귀하께서 이곳을 집이라고 부를 가치가 있음을 알게 되리라 확신합니다. 귀하를 맞이하기를 기다리겠습니다!
>
> Mona Sorenstein 드림
> 전무 이사
> The Aldrich 노인 주택 지구

quality n. 질 around-the-clock adj. 24시간 계속되는
assistance n. 지원, 원조 frequent adj. 빈번한 get-together n. 모임
opportunity n. 기회 retirement n. 은퇴

143 | 부사절 접속사 채우기

해설 이 문장은 주어(it), 동사(is), 보어(no surprise)를 갖춘 완전한 절이므로, ___ ~ priority는 수식어 거품으로 보아야 한다. 이 수식어 거품은 동사(has been)가 있는 거품절이므로, 거품절을 이끌 수 있는 부사절 접속사인 (A), (C), (D)가 정답의 후보이다. '높은 삶의 질을 제공하는 것이 항상 우리의 우선 사항이었던 것을 고려하면 우리가 수백 명의 만족한 주민들을 보유하고 있는 것은 놀랍지 않다'라는 의미가 되어야 하므로, '~을 고려하면'이라는 의미의 부사절 접속사 (D) Given that이 정답이다. (A) Whether는 '~이든 아니든', (C) Although는 '비록 ~이지만'이라는 의미이다. 부사 (B) Especially(특히)는 거품절을 이끌 수 없다.

144 | 명사 자리 채우기

해설 타동사(have)의 목적어 역할을 할 수 있는 것은 명사이므로 명사 (A)와 명사 역할을 하는 동명사 (C)가 정답의 후보이다. '의료 서비스와 요리 및 청소에 대한 지원을 이용할 수 있을 것이다'라는 의미가 되어야 하므로 빈칸 앞의 동사 have와 빈칸 뒤의 전치사 to와 함께 '~을 이용할 수 있다'라는 의미의 어구 have access to를 만드는 명사 (A) access(이용, 접근)가 정답이다. 동명사 (C)는 '이용하는 것을 가지다'라는 문장을 만드는 것으로 본다 해도, access가 타동사이므로 빈칸 뒤에 목적어가 와야 한다. 동사 또는 과거분사 (B)와 형용사 (D)는 명사 자리에 올 수 없다.

145 | 형용사 어휘 고르기 전체 문맥 파악

해설 '매일을 가능한 한 ___ 만들기를 바란다'라는 문맥이므로 모든 보기가 정답의 후보이다. 빈칸이 있는 문장만으로 정답을 고를 수 없으므로 주변 문맥이나 전체 문맥을 파악한다. 앞부분에서 '24시간 계속되는 의료 서비스와 요리 및 청소에 대한 지원을 이용할 수 있다(you will have ~ around-the-clock medical care and assistance with cooking and cleaning)'라고 했고, '빈번한 모임들과 지역 행사들에서 자원봉사 기회들이 있다(There are also frequent get-togethers and volunteering opportunities at local events).'라고 했으므로, The Aldrich가 매일을 가능한 한 만족스럽게 만들기를 바란다는 문맥임을 알 수 있다. 따라서 (B) fulfilling(만족스러운)이 정답이다. (A) obvious는 '명백한', (C) influential은 '영향력 있는', (D) fortunate은 '운 좋은'이라는 의미이다.

146 | 알맞은 문장 고르기

해석 (A) 저희의 성수기가 시작되기 전에 전화하세요.
(B) 저희는 이곳의 저희 직원들을 가족처럼 대우합니다.
(C) 저희는 귀하께서 이곳을 집이라고 부를 가치가 있음을 알게 되리라 확신합니다.
(D) 귀하께서 요청하신 대로 방이 준비되어 있습니다.

해설 앞 문장 'Come for a visit, take a look around, and experience retirement living in The Aldrich at Shasta Lake.'에서 방문해서 주위를 둘러보고, 샤스타 레이크에 있는 The Aldrich에서의 은퇴 생활을 경험해보라고 했으므로 빈칸에는 귀하, 즉 잠재적 고객이 The Aldrich를 방문한 후에 어떻게 느끼게 될지와 관련된 내용이 들어가야 함을 알 수 있다. 따라서 (C)가 정답이다.

어휘 peak season 성수기 treat v. 대우하다, 대하다
confident adj. 확신하는, 자신감이 있는 worthy adj. ~할 가치가 있는, 적합한

PART 7

147-148번은 다음 광고에 관한 문제입니다.

> 구인 자리
>
> ¹⁴⁷⁻⁽ᴬ⁾Fentonville 지역 계획 위원회는 회의록을 작성하고 기록을 정리할 사무원을 구하고 있습니다. ¹⁴⁸새로 고용되는 사무원은 오직 월요일과 수요일에 오전 9시부터 오후 5시까지 업무를 수행하면 될 것입니다. 이상적인 지원자는 탁월한 타자 실력을 갖추고, 세부 사항에 세심한 주의를 기울이며, 독립적으로 일하는 것이 편안한 사람일 것입니다. 사무직 경험이 선호되지만 필수는 아닙니다. 보수는 시간당 25달러입니다. 이력서는 3월 4일까지 recruitment@fentonville.gov로 이메일로 보내져야 합니다.

zoning n. (도시 계획의) 지역제 office clerk 사무원 file v. 정리하다; n. 서류철
record n. 기록; v. 기록하다 duty n. 업무, 직무 candidate n. 지원자
independently adv. 독립적으로 clerical adj. 사무직의

147 | 육하원칙 문제

해석 광고에는 무슨 정보가 포함되어 있는가?
(A) 직무
(B) 초과 근무 수당
(C) 시작 날짜
(D) 보험 혜택

해설 지문의 'The Fentonville Board of Planning and Zoning is seeking an office clerk to take meeting notes and file records.'에서 Fentonville 지역 계획 위원회는 회의록을 작성하고 기록을 정리할 사무원을 구하고 있다고 하였다. 따라서 (A)가 정답이다.

148 | 추론 문제

해석 직무에 대해 추론될 수 있는 것은?
(A) 강도 높은 팀 워크를 포함한다.

(B) 기록 관리 경험이 필요하다.
(C) 많은 출장을 포함한다.
(D) 시간제 근무이다.

해설 지문의 'The newly hired clerk will only have to perform their duties from 9:00 A.M. to 5:00 P.M. on Mondays and Wednesdays.'에서 새로 고용되는 사무원은 오직 월요일과 수요일에 오전 9시부터 오후 5시까지 업무를 수행하면 될 것이라고 했으므로 직무가 시간제 근무임을 추론할 수 있다. 따라서 (D)가 정답이다.

어휘 intensive adj. 강도 높은, 집중적인 part-time adj. 시간제의

149-150번은 다음 티켓에 관한 문제입니다.

WALLACE 운송: 티켓

이것을 출력하십시오

149-(D)승객: William Singer
전화번호: 555-3201
149-(D)집 주소: 21번지 West 74번가, 뉴욕시, 뉴욕주 10023

티켓 번호: 41249101ABKOA
등급: 일반
요금: 52달러
출발 날짜: 8월 11일
여행 일정:

149-(A)출발: 뉴욕시	오전 5시 10분
150-(B)도착: 피츠버그	오후 12시 12분
출발: 피츠버그	오후 1시 20분
149-(C)도착: 콜럼버스	오후 4시 50분
149-(C)출발: 콜럼버스	오후 5시 30분
149-(A)도착: 시카고	오후 10시 5분

당신의 버스는 오전 5시 10분에 뉴욕시의 Park가 버스 터미널을 출발할 것입니다. 탑승하실 때 기사에게 제시할 티켓이 준비되도록 하십시오. 150-(C)승객들은 차내에 두 개의 짐을 가지고 타는 것이 허용됩니다. 150-(A)출발을 놓친 승객들에게는 환불이 제공되지 않을 것입니다. 티켓을 취소하시려면, 555-8843으로 전화 주십시오.

passenger n. 승객, 탑승객 class n. 등급, 종류 fare n. 요금, 통행료
itinerary n. 여행 일정, 여정 coach terminal 버스 터미널
permit v. 허용하다, 허가하다 luggage n. 짐, 수하물 on board 차내에, 탑승한

149 | Not/True 문제

해설 Mr. Singer에 대해 명시된 것은?
(A) 왕복표를 구매했다.
(B) 할인 요금을 청구받았다.
(C) 콜럼버스에서 하룻밤을 묵을 계획이다.
(D) 뉴욕시의 거주민이다.

해설 지문의 'PASSENGER: William Singer'와 'HOME ADDRESS: 21 West 74th St., New York, NY 10023'에서 승객 William Singer의 집 주소가 뉴욕시로 되어 있으므로 (D)는 지문의 내용과 일치한다. 따라서 (D)가 정답이다. (B)는 지문에 언급되지 않은 내용이다. (A)는 'Depart: New York City'와 'Arrive: Chicago'에서 출발이 뉴욕시이고 마지막 도착이 시카고인 편도 티켓임을 알 수 있으므로 지문의 내용과 일치하지 않는다. (C)는 'Arrive: Columbus, 4:50 P.M.'과 'Depart: Columbus, 5:30 P.M.'에서 콜럼버스에 오후 4시 50분에 도착해서 오후 5시 30분에 출발한다고 했으므로 지문의 내용과 일치하지 않는다.

어휘 return ticket 왕복표 charge v. (요금·값을) 청구하다; n. 요금, 기소
stay the night 하룻밤 묵다 resident n. 거주민, 주민

150 | Not/True 문제

해설 티켓에 포함되지 않은 정보는?
(A) 회사의 환불 정책
(B) 피츠버그 도착 시각
(C) 수하물 허용량
(D) 버스 터미널의 운영 시간

해설 (A)는 'No refunds will be provided to passengers who miss their departure.'에서 출발을 놓친 승객들에게는 환불이 제공되지 않을 것이라고 했으므로 지문의 내용과 일치한다. (B)는 'Arrive: Pittsburgh, 12:12 P.M.'에서 피츠버그 도착은 오후 12시 12분이라고 했으므로 지문의 내용과 일치한다. (C)는 'Passengers are permitted to bring two pieces of luggage on board.'에서 승객들은 차내에 두 개의 짐을 가지고 타는 것이 허용된다고 했으므로 지문의 내용과 일치한다. (D)는 지문에 언급되지 않은 내용이다. 따라서 (D)가 정답이다.

어휘 policy n. 정책, 방침 baggage n. 수하물, 짐 allowance n. 허용량, 용돈
operating hours 운영 시간, 영업시간

Paraphrasing

luggage 짐 → baggage 수하물

151-152번은 다음 편지에 관한 문제입니다.

8월 12일

Nisa Miskin
Inman 제약회사
92450번지 164번 주간 고속도로
보이시, 아이다호주 83714

Ms. Miskin께,

151저는 Well Time 보험사의 직원이고, 저희가 귀사에 제공할 수 있는 것에 대해 논의하기 위해 귀하와 만나는 데 매우 관심이 있습니다. 저희의 직원 보험 패키지는 많은 사업체와 기관들에 인기가 있습니다.

Well Time 보험사는 종합 검진, 정신 건강, 치아, 생명, 그리고 그 이상의 모든 종류의 보험이 필요한 것을 다루는 다양한 패키지를 제공합니다. 인기 있는 패키지는 Health Plus와 필요한 모든 것이 갖춰진 Choice Care를 포함합니다. 152귀하께서는 Health Plus 패키지를 귀사의 필요를 충족하기 위해 맞추실 수 있습니다. 장애와 육아 휴가는 Choice Care 패키지에 포함되어 있습니다.

귀하께서 약속을 잡기 원하실지 알아보기 위해 다음 2주 이내로 귀하의 사무실에 연락을 드리겠습니다. 더 일찍 저와 이야기하고 싶으시면, 555-4433으로 전화 주십시오.

Lucas Moreland 드림
Well Time 보험사 고객 서비스

pharmaceutical n. 제약; adj. 제약의 representative n. 직원, 대리인
insurance n. 보험, 보험료 medical n. 종합 검진; adj. 의료의
customize v. 맞추다, 특별한 주문에 따라 만들다 disability n. 장애
parental leave 육아 휴가 appointment n. 약속, 임명, 지명

151 | 목적 찾기 문제

해설 편지의 목적은 무엇인가?
(A) 직원 교육 프로그램을 소개하기 위해
(B) 비즈니스 미팅을 제안하기 위해
(C) 세미나에 초대하기 위해
(D) 다양한 보험 패키지를 비교하기 위해

해설 지문의 'I am a representative of Well Time Insurance, and we would be very interested in meeting with you to discuss what we can offer your firm.'에서 자신이 Well Time 보험사의 직원이고 편지 수신자의 회사에 제공할 수 있는 것에 대해 논의하기 위해 상대방을 만나는 데 매우 관심이 있다고 한 후, Well Time 보험사가 제공하는 보험 패키지들에 대해 설명하고 있으므로 (B)가 정답이다.

어휘 extend an invitation 초대하다 compare v. 비교하다, 필적하다

152 | 육하원칙 문제

해석 Health Plus 패키지의 이점은 무엇인가?
(A) 모든 종류의 보험을 포함한다.
(B) 요구사항을 충족하도록 조정될 수 있다.
(C) 가장 가격이 적당한 요금제이다.
(D) 새로 부모가 된 사람들을 위한 장기 휴가를 포함한다.

해설 지문의 'You can customize the Health Plus package to suit your organization's needs.'에서 Health Plus 패키지를 회사의 필요를 충족하기 위해 맞출 수 있다고 했으므로 (B)가 정답이다.

어휘 adjust v. 조정하다 requirement n. 요구사항, 요구
affordable adj. (가격이) 적당한 cover v. 포함하다
extended leave 장기 휴가

Paraphrasing
customize ~ to suit ~ needs 필요를 충족하기 위해 맞추다 → be adjusted to meet requirements 요구사항을 충족하도록 조정되다

153-154번은 다음 문자 메시지 대화문에 관한 문제입니다.

David Lee	오전 11시 5분

안녕하세요, Ms. Jones. ¹⁵³Brentwood 타워의 방을 보러 가기 위해 제가 오전 11시에 당신을 만나기로 되어 있었다는 것을 알지만, 조금 전에 자동차 사고가 났어요.

Beth Jones	오전 11시 7분

정말 안타깝네요. 당신이 다치지 않았기를 바라요.

David Lee	오전 11시 10분

저는 괜찮은데 제 차는 수리가 좀 필요할 것 같아요. 견인차가 그것을 치우러 오는 중이에요. 모든 게 해결되고 나면, 택시를 탈게요. 1시간 정도 후에 그곳에 도착할 거예요.

Beth Jones	오전 11시 11분

안타깝게도, 저는 정오에 다른 고객을 만나야 해요. ¹⁵⁴대신 내일 오전 10시에 아파트를 보여드려도 될까요?

David Lee	오전 11시 13분

완벽해요. ¹⁵⁴협조해 주셔서 감사해요.

be supposed to ~하기로 되어 있다 injured adj. 다친, 부상을 입은
tow truck 견인차 deal with ~을 해결하다
accommodate v. 협조하다, 수용하다

153 | 육하원칙 문제

해석 Mr. Lee는 왜 약속에 가지 못했는가?
(A) 혼잡한 길을 선택했다.
(B) 교통사고에 연루되었다.
(C) 잘못된 아파트로 갔다.
(D) 오전에 다른 부동산 업자를 만났다.

해설 지문의 'I know I was supposed to meet you at 11:00 A.M. to view the Brentwood Tower unit, but I got into a car accident a short while ago.'에서 Mr. Lee가 Brentwood 타워의 방을 보러 가기 위해 오전 11시에 Ms. Jones를 만나기로 되어 있었지만 조금 전에 자동차 사고가 났다고 했으므로 (B)가 정답이다.

어휘 route n. 길 congest v. 혼잡하게 하다 realtor n. 부동산 업자

154 | 의도 파악 문제

해석 오전 11시 13분에, Mr. Lee가 "That would be perfect"라고 썼을 때, 그가 의도한 것은?
(A) 위치에 익숙하다.
(B) 아파트에 만족한다.
(C) 다음 날 시간이 된다.
(D) 정오에 만날 준비가 되어 있다.

해설 지문의 'Could I show you the apartment tomorrow at 10 A.M. instead?'에서 Beth Jones가 대신 내일 오전 10시에 아파트를 보여줘도 될지 묻자, Mr. Lee가 'That would be perfect'(완벽해요)라고 한 후, 'Thanks for accommodating me.'에서 협조해 줘서 감사하다고 한 것을 통해, Mr. Lee가 다음 날 시간이 된다는 것을 알 수 있다. 따라서 (C)가 정답이다.

어휘 location n. 위치, 장소 following day 다음 날 noon n. 정오

155-157번은 다음 이메일에 관한 문제입니다.

수신: Peter Leopold <peterleopold@netmail.com>
발신: Susan Wright <susanw@greatwebwork.com>
제목: 사과
날짜: 8월 15일

Mr. Leopold께,

자사의 서비스에 만족하지 못하셨다는 점에 대해 죄송하며 귀하에서 겪으셨을 모든 불편을 유감스럽게 생각합니다. ¹⁵⁵귀사의 웹사이트에 대한 저희 디자인 작업이 왜 귀하의 기대에 미치지 못했다고 느끼셨는지 시간을 내어 알려 주셔서 감사합니다. 귀하의 의견은 유용하고 타당합니다. 귀하의 고객들은 필요한 정보를 찾는 데 어려움을 겪지 않아야 하며, 일부 페이지에 맞지 않는 이미지가 사용되었다는 사실은 전적으로 용납할 수 없습니다.

¹⁵⁶첫 회의에서 분명 잘못된 의사소통이 일부 있었을 것이라고 생각하며, 문제들을 의논하여 귀하를 위한 몇 가지 만족스러운 해결책을 내놓을 수 있기를 바랍니다.

¹⁵⁷귀하는 과거에 저희의 작업에 만족을 표했고 저희는 귀하를 위해 완성한 모든 프로젝트에서 일반적으로 일정 수준의 품질을 유지해 왔다고 생각합니다. 귀하는 소중한 고객이며, 귀하의 최근 경험이 미래에 우리의 업무 관계에 있어서 부정적인 영향을 끼치지 않기를 바랍니다.

곧 연락 주시기를 바랍니다.

Susan Wright
Great Web Work사

regret v. 유감스럽게 생각하다, 후회하다 inconvenience n. 불편, 애로
appreciate v. 감사하다, 높이 평가하다
take time to do ~을 하기 위해 시간을 내다
communicate v. (생각·느낌 등을) 알리다, 대화하다
meet an expectation 기대에 미치다 feedback n. 의견, 반응
constructive adj. 유용한, 건설적인 fair adj. 타당한, 공평한
struggle v. 어려움을 겪다, 애쓰다 incorrect adj. 맞지 않는, 부정확한
unacceptable adj. 용납할 수 없는, 받아들일 수 없는
initial adj. 처음의, 초기의 solution n. 해결책, 정답
generally adv. 일반적으로, 보통 maintain v. 유지하다, 지지하다
valued adj. 소중한 negatively adv. 부정적으로, 소극적으로

155 | 육하원칙 문제

해석 Ms. Wright에 따르면, Mr. Leopold는 최근에 무엇을 했는가?
(A) 기업 웹사이트를 디자인했다.
(B) 디자이너를 추천했다.

(C) 몇 가지 의견을 제공했다.
(D) 양식을 작성했다.

해설 지문의 'I appreciate that you took the time to communicate why you felt our design work on your Web site did not meet your expectations. Your feedback was constructive and fair.'에서 Mr. Leopold에게 웹사이트에 대한 디자인 작업이 왜 기대에 미치지 못했다고 느꼈는지 시간을 내어 알려줘서 감사하다고 했고, 의견이 유용하고 타당했다고 했으므로 (C)가 정답이다.

어휘 recommend v. 추천하다 fill out 작성하다

Paraphrasing

communicate why ~ felt 왜 ~이라고 느꼈는지 전달하다 → Provided some feedback 몇 가지 의견을 제공했다

156 | 추론 문제

해설 Ms. Wright에 따르면, 무엇이 몇몇 문제를 일으킨 것 같은가?
(A) 발표 일정이 불편하게 변경되었다.
(B) 중요한 팀원들이 회의에 불참했다.
(C) 몇몇 요구사항이 잘못 이해되었다.
(D) Mr. Leopold는 그의 필요 사항을 설명할 시간이 부족했다.

해설 지문의 'I believe that there must have been some miscommunication during our initial meeting and I would like to discuss the problems and come up with some acceptable solutions for you.'에서 첫 회의에서 분명 잘못된 의사소통이 일부 있었을 것이라고 생각하며 문제들을 의논하여 몇 가지 만족스러운 해결책을 내놓을 수 있기를 바란다고 했으므로 몇몇 요구사항이 잘못 이해되었음을 추론할 수 있다. 따라서 (C)가 정답이다.

어휘 inconveniently adv. 불편하게 reschedule v. 일정을 변경하다
absent adj. 불참한, 결석한 insufficient adj. 부족한, 불충분한

Paraphrasing

miscommunication 잘못된 의사소통 → Some requests were interpreted incorrectly 몇몇 요구사항이 잘못 이해되었다

157 | 추론 문제

해설 Ms. Wright에 대해 암시되는 것은?
(A) 이전에 Mr. Leopold와 함께 일했다.
(B) 부분적인 환불에 동의했다.
(C) 몇몇 지적에 동의하지 않는다.
(D) 서비스 계약을 해지했다.

해설 지문의 'You have expressed satisfaction with our work in the past, and I feel that we've generally maintained a certain level of quality in all the projects we have completed for you.'에서 Mr. Leopold가 과거에 Ms. Wright의 회사의 작업에 만족을 표했고, Ms. Wright의 회사가 완성한 모든 프로젝트에서 일반적으로 일정 수준의 품질을 유지해 왔다고 생각한다고 했으므로 Mr. Leopold와 Ms. Wright가 이전에 함께 일한 적이 있음을 추론할 수 있다. 따라서 (A)가 정답이다.

어휘 partial adj. 부분적인 refund n. 환불; v. 환불하다
disagree v. 동의하지 않다, 일치하지 않다 comment n. 지적, 비평

Paraphrasing

in the past 과거에 → before 이전에

158-161번은 다음 공고에 관한 문제입니다.

Eagle Canyon 도시공원

158지난 한 달 동안 공원의 녹지에서 신고된 미국너구리의 목격이 급격하게 증가했습니다. 공원 경비원들은 공원 방문객들이 고의로든 우연히든 남기고 간 음식 찌꺼기에 의해 동물들이 모여든다고 추측합니다. ㅡ [1] ㅡ. 시의 공중 보건부는 그것들이 질병의 매개체가 될 수 있고 방문객과 그들의 반려동물에게 위험을 끼칠 수 있으므로 미국너구리들이 공원의 삼림 지역을 떠나도록 조장하기를 원치 않습니다. ㅡ [2] ㅡ. 이를 염두에 두고:

· 공원에 어떠한 쓰레기도 남기지 말아 주십시오. 떠나실 때 가지고 가시거나, 159-(C)공원 도처에 위치한 뚜껑이 있는 쓰레기통에 두십시오.
· 미국너구리를 보신다면, 그들은 날카로운 발톱을 지닌 야생동물이며 겁을 먹으면 위험해질 수 있으므로 다가가거나 음식을 주지 마십시오.

ㅡ [3] ㅡ. 이 동물들을 유인할 수 있는 공원 내 쓰레기를 없애기 위해 6월 27일 토요일에 자발적 공원 청소를 할 것입니다. 161참여를 원하시는 분들은 등록하기 위해 공원의 정문 근처에 있는 방문객 센터에 알리셔야 합니다. ㅡ [4] ㅡ. 160모든 참여자들에게는 보호용 장갑과 조끼, 물, 그리고 간단한 점심이 제공될 것입니다.

sighting n. 목격, 발견 raccoon n. 미국너구리 open space 녹지, 빈터
park ranger 공원 경비원 suspect v. 추측하다, 의심하다
creature n. 동물, 생물 food scraps 음식 찌꺼기 on purpose 고의로
accidentally adv. 우연히, 잘못하여 carrier n. 매개체, 운반인
pose a risk 위험을 끼치다 garbage n. 쓰레기
throughout prep. 도처에, 내내 approach v. 다가가다, 접근하다
claw n. 발톱; v. 할퀴다 frightened adj. 겁먹은, 무서워하는
eliminate v. 없애다 refuse n. 쓰레기 cleanup n. 청소, 정화
take part 참여하다, 참가하다 report v. 알리다, 발표하다; n. 보도
register v. 등록하다, 기재하다 participant n. 참여자, 참가자
protective adj. 보호용의, 보호하는

158 | 목적 찾기 문제

해설 공고는 왜 쓰였는가?
(A) 공청회를 공표하기 위해
(B) 야생 동물 공원의 개장을 알리기 위해
(C) 방문객 센터로 가는 길을 알려주기 위해
(D) 방문객들에게 문제를 의식하게 하기 위해

해설 지문의 'Over the past month, there has been a sharp increase in reported sightings of raccoons in the open spaces of the park.'에서 지난 한 달 동안 공원의 녹지에서 신고된 미국너구리의 목격이 급격하게 증가했다고 한 후, 미국너구리 문제와 관련된 주의 사항을 설명하고 있으므로 (D)가 정답이다.

어휘 declare v. 공표하다, 선언하다 public meeting 공청회
opening n. 개장, 빈자리, 공터 alert v. 의식하게 하다, 알리다, 경고하다

159 | Not/True 문제

해설 Eagle Canyon 도시공원에 대해 언급된 것은?
(A) 보건부의 검사를 받았다.
(B) 토요일에는 유지보수를 위해 문을 닫는다.
(C) 쓰레기통이 몇 개 설치되어 있다.
(D) 곧 더 많은 피크닉 구역이 포함될 예정이다.

해설 지문의 'place it in the closed garbage bins that are located throughout the park'에서 쓰레기를 공원 도처에 위치한 뚜껑이 있는 쓰레기통에 두라고 했으므로 (C)가 정답이다. (A), (B), (D)는 지문에 언급되지 않은 내용이다.

어휘 inspect v. 검사하다 maintenance n. 유지보수
trash receptacle 쓰레기통

160 | 육하원칙 문제

해석 자원봉사자들은 무엇을 받을 것인가?
(A) 공원 지도
(B) 동물들에게 나눠줄 약간의 음식
(C) 수료증
(D) 몇몇 보호용 장비

해설 지문의 'All participants will be provided with protective gloves and vests, water, and a light lunch.'에서 모든 참여자들에게는 보호용 장갑과 조끼, 물, 그리고 간단한 점심이 제공될 것이라고 했으므로 (D)가 정답이다.

어휘 distribute v. 나누어 주다, 분배하다 certificate n. 수료증, 자격증
gear n. 장비

Paraphrasing

protective gloves and vests 보호용 장갑과 조끼 → protective gear 보호용 장비

161 | 문장 위치 찾기 문제

해석 [1], [2], [3], [4]로 표시된 위치 중, 다음 문장이 들어갈 곳으로 가장 적절한 것은?

"이 행사에 최소 15명이 참가하기를 바랍니다."

(A) [1]
(B) [2]
(C) [3]
(D) [4]

해설 주어진 문장은 행사에 참가하는 것과 관련된 내용 주변에 나와야 함을 예상할 수 있다. [4]의 앞 문장인 'Anyone interested in taking part should report to the visitor center near the park's main entrance to register.'에서 참여를 원하는 사람들은 등록하기 위해 공원의 정문 근처에 있는 방문객 센터에 알려야 한다고 했으므로, [4]에 주어진 문장이 들어가면 참여를 원하는 사람들은 등록하기 위해 공원의 정문 근처에 있는 방문객 센터에 알려야 하는데, 이 행사에 최소 15명이 참가하기를 바란다는 자연스러운 문맥이 된다는 것을 알 수 있다. 따라서 (D)가 정답이다.

어휘 sign up 참가하다, ~에 등록하다

162-165번은 다음 온라인 채팅 대화문에 관한 문제입니다.

Ana Muller 오후 4시 55분
¹⁶²제 관리자가 방금 회사가 새로운 상여금 제도를 도입할 거라고 말해주었어요. 정말 기대되네요.

Dennis Judd 오후 4시 57분
저도 같은 내용을 들었어요. ¹⁶²평가에서 4.5점 이상을 받는 직원들은 상여금을 받을 자격을 얻을 거예요. 그것은 그들의 총연봉의 10퍼센트에 상당하는 액수일 거예요.

Ana Muller 오후 4시 58분
맞아요. 상여금은 평가가 완료되고 한 달 후에 주어질 거예요.

Carrie Novak 오후 4시 59분
이 제도가 언제 시행될까요?

Dennis Judd 오후 5시
제 생각에는, 약 한 달 후 정도예요. 이번 주 후반에 공식 발표가 있을 거예요.

Carrie Novak 오후 5시 2분
하지만 ¹⁶³제 연례 평가는 세 달 전 제가 계약을 연장했을 즈음에 있었어요. 제가 받기 전에 다른 직원들이 상여금을 받게 되는 것은 공정하지 않아 보이는데요.

Carrie Novak 오후 5시 3분
어쩌면 이 문제에 대한 회의 자리를 마련해야 할 것 같아요.

Ana Muller 오후 5시 4분
저라면 정보를 더 얻을 때까지 기다리겠어요. ¹⁶⁴회사가 몇몇 직원들을 불리한 입장에 처하게 하는 방식으로 이 제도를 시작할 것 같지는 않아요.

Carrie Novak 오후 5시 6분
당신의 말이 맞을 수도 있겠네요. 그래도, 우리가 조만간 좀 더 많은 세부 내용을 얻으면 좋겠어요.

Dennis Judd 오후 5시 8분
¹⁶⁵⁻⁽ᴮ⁾다음 주에 발표가 나면 아마 인사팀에서 모두에게 최신 직원 안내서를 제공해 줄 거예요. 듣자 하니, 그들이 지금 그것을 작업하고 있어요.

introduce v. 도입하다 evaluation n. 평가 qualify for ~할 자격을 얻다
equivalent n. 상당하는 것; adj. 상당하는, 동등한 award v. 주다, 수여하다
take effect 시행되다, 실시되다 extend v. 연장하다 roll out 시작하다
at a disadvantage 불리한 입장에 있는 likely adv. 아마; adj. ~할 것 같은

162 | 육하원칙 문제

해석 회사는 무엇을 할 계획인가?
(A) 직원들에게 장려금을 지급한다.
(B) 전 직원의 연봉을 인상한다.
(C) 몇몇 평가 기준을 변경한다.
(D) 관리직 채용 공고를 낸다.

해설 지문의 'My manager just told me that our company will be introducing a new bonus system.'에서 관리자가 방금 회사가 새로운 상여금 제도를 도입할 것이라고 말해주었다고 했고, 'Employees who receive a score of 4.5 or higher on their evaluations will qualify for a bonus.'에서 평가에서 4.5점 이상을 받는 직원들은 상여금을 받을 자격을 얻을 것이라고 했으므로 (A)가 정답이다.

어휘 incentive n. 장려금 criteria n. 기준
advertise a position 채용 공고를 내다

Paraphrasing

bonus 상여금 → incentives 장려금

163 | 육하원칙 문제

해석 Ms. Novak은 무엇을 걱정하는가?
(A) 프로젝트 일정이 업데이트되지 않았다.
(B) 관리자가 그녀의 작업에 대해 불만을 나타냈다.
(C) 장려금이 몇몇 직원들에게 분배되지 않았다.
(D) 인사 고과가 이미 끝났다.

해설 지문의 'I had my annual evaluation three months ago, around the time I extended my contract'에서 자신, 즉 Ms. Novak의 연례 평가가 세 달 전 계약을 연장했을 즈음에 있었다고 했으므로 (D)가 정답이다.

164 | 의도 파악 문제

해석 오후 5시 6분에, Ms. Novak이 "Maybe you're right"이라고 썼을 때 그녀가 의도한 것은?
(A) 정책이 공정하게 시행될 것 같다.
(B) 요청이 아마 승인되지 않을 것이다.
(C) 기회가 없을 수도 있다.
(D) 곧 회의가 준비될 수 있다.

해설 지문의 'I don't think the company will roll out the system in a way that puts some employees at a disadvantage.'에서 Ana Muller가 회사가 몇몇 직원들을 불리한 입장에 처하게 하는 방식으로 제도를 시작할 것 같지 않다고 하자, Ms. Novak이 'Maybe you're right'(당신의 말이 맞을 수도 있겠네요)라고 한 것을 통해, Ms. Novak이 회사의 정책이 공정하게 시행될 것 같다고 생각함을 알 수 있다. 따라서 (A)가 정답이다.

어휘 implement v. 시행하다 fairly adv. 공정하게 approve v. 승인하다

165 | Not/True 문제

해설 인사팀에 대해 언급된 것은?
(A) 여러 직원들을 재배치하기로 결정했다.
(B) 지침들을 수정하는 과정 중에 있다.
(C) 다음 주에 설명회를 개최할 것이다.
(D) 혜택에 관해 직원들의 의견을 요구했다.

해설 지문의 'The human resources team will likely provide everyone with an updated employee manual when the announcement is made next week. Apparently, they are working on it now.'에서 다음 주에 발표가 나면 아마 인사팀에서 모두에게 최신 직원 안내서를 제공해 줄 것이라고 하고, 그들이 지금 그것을 작업하고 있다고 했으므로 (B)가 정답이다. (A), (C), (D)는 지문에 언급되지 않은 내용이다.

어휘 reassign v. 재배치하다, 새로 발령내다 revise v. 수정하다, 개정하다
benefit n. 혜택

166-168번은 다음 안내문에 관한 문제입니다.

Hanlan's Coffee사—윤리적 구매 정책

Hanlan's사에서는, 저희 고객들이 전 세계에서 가장 질 좋은 커피만을 마시고 싶어 한다는 것을 알고 있습니다. 또한 저희는 그들이 그 커피를 재배하는 사람들이 확실히 공정하게 대우받았으면 한다는 점도 알고 있습니다. 많은 커피 제조사들이 열악한 근무 조건을 만들어 내고 직원들에게 낮은 임금을 제공하는데, 이것은 Hanlan's사가 지지하는 관행이 아닙니다. — [1] —.

일반 시장에서 재고품을 구매하는 커피 회사들은 그것이 어디로부터 오는지 절대 정확히 알지 못합니다. 그러나 Hanlan's사에서는, 다른 접근 방법을 택합니다. 166-(D)저희는 과테말라, 에티오피아, 그리고 베트남의 농장과 독점 계약을 맺고 있습니다. — [2] —. 이 때문에, 저희는 누가 커피를 생산하는지와 그것이 재배되는 환경을 정확하게 알고 있습니다. 168저희는 저희 농부들의 모든 노고에 감사하고 그들이 만족할 만한 근무 조건을 갖는 것을 보장합니다. 하지만 저희의 헌신은 거기서 끝이 아닙니다. — [3] —. Hanlan's사는 그들에게 감사를 표하는 저희의 방법으로 현재 시장 가격 이상으로 추가적인 10퍼센트를 지불합니다.

게다가, 167이 지역사회에 더 많이 돌려주기 위해, 저희는 Hanlan's 개발 재단을 설립했습니다. 매년 이 기관을 통해, 저희는 총 기업 수익의 5퍼센트를 저희의 커피가 재배되는 주변 마을에 학교를 짓고 개선하는 데 사용합니다. 167주목표는 저희 모든 농부들의 자녀들이 반드시 완전한 교육을 받을 기회를 갖고 그들의 꿈을 좇도록 하는 것입니다. — [4] —.

Hanlan's사의 개발 프로젝트, 커피 제조사, 그리고 저희 목표를 지지하기 위해 귀하께서 하실 수 있는 것에 관해 www.hanlancoffee.com/foundation에서 더 알아보십시오.

---

treat v. 대우하다, 다루다 fairly adv. 공정하게, 꽤 practice n. 관행, 실행
stock n. 재고품, 저장 open market 일반 시장, 자유 시장
approach n. 접근 방법; v. 다가가다 exclusive adj. 독점적인, 배타적인
ensure v. 보장하다, 확보하다 acceptable adj. 만족할 만한, 수락할 수 있는
market price 시장 가격 cause n. 목표, 대의

166 | Not/True 문제

해설 Hanlan's Coffee사의 파트너 농장들에 대해 명시된 것은?
(A) 일반 시장에 제품을 판매한다.
(B) 지역 정부의 보조금을 받는다.
(C) 많은 다양한 작물을 재배한다.
(D) 몇몇 국가에 위치하고 있다.

해설 지문의 'We have exclusive contracts with farms in Guatemala, Ethiopia, and Vietnam.'에서 저희, 즉 Hanlan's Coffee사는 과테말라, 에티오피아, 그리고 베트남의 농장과 독점 계약을 맺고 있다고 했으므로 (D)가 정답이다. (A), (B), (C)는 지문에 언급되지 않은 내용이다.

어휘 subsidize v. 보조금을 주다 a number of 많은 crop n. 작물, 농작물
situate v. 위치시키다

167 | 육하원칙 문제

해설 Hanlan's 개발 재단은 주로 누구에게 도움이 되는가?
(A) 국제 농업 연구원들
(B) 커피 농부의 자녀들
(C) 해외에서 근무하는 직원들
(D) 커피 재배자 협회의 회원들

해설 지문의 'to give even more back to these communities, we have started the Hanlan's Development Foundation'과 'The main goal is to make certain that all our farmers' children have the opportunity to receive a full education and pursue their dreams.'에서 이 지역사회, 즉 커피 농장이 있는 지역에 더 많이 돌려주기 위해 Hanlan's 개발 재단을 설립했고, 주목표는 모든 농부들의 자녀들이 반드시 완전한 교육을 받을 기회를 갖고 그들의 꿈을 좇도록 하는 것이라고 했으므로 (B)가 정답이다.

어휘 benefit v. ~에게 도움이 되다, 이롭다 association n. 협회, 연계

168 | 문장 위치 찾기 문제

해설 [1], [2], [3], [4]로 표시된 위치 중, 다음 문장이 들어갈 곳으로 가장 적절한 것은?

"저희는 또한 그들이 그들의 노력에 대한 적절한 보상을 받을 수 있도록 합니다."

(A) [1]
(B) [2]
(C) [3]
(D) [4]

해설 주어진 문장은 Hanlan's Coffee사의 대우와 관련된 내용 주변에 나올 것임을 예상할 수 있다. [3]의 앞 문장인 'We appreciate all the hard work of our farmers and ensure that they have acceptable working conditions. But our commitment doesn't end there.'에서 Hanlan's Coffee사는 농부들의 모든 노고에 감사하고 그들이 만족할 만한 근무 조건을 갖는 것을 보장한다고 하고, Hanlan's Coffee사의 헌신이 거기서 끝이 아니라고 했으므로, [3]에 제시된 문장이 들어가면 그 외에도 농부들이 그들의 노력에 대한 적절한 보상을 받을 수 있도록 한다는 자연스러운 문맥이 된다는 것을 알 수 있다. 따라서 (C)가 정답이다.

어휘 adequate adj. 적절한, 충분한 compensation n. 보상 effort n. 노력

169-171번은 다음 기사에 관한 문제입니다.

Ping사의 사장이 올해의 과학 기술 여성으로 영예를 받다

Carmen Morris 작성

170-(C)소프트웨어 회사 Ping사의 최고 경영자인 Rebecca Curtis는 *Gadget Lover*지에 의해 기술계에서 가장 성공적인 여성으로 지명되었다. 169-(B)/170-(A)5년 전에 회사를 넘겨받아 번창하는 다중 플랫폼 회사로

전환한 Ms. Curtis는 12월 2일에 *Gadget Lover*지 연례 회의에서 연설을 하기 위해 초대를 수락했다.

최고 경영자로서의 Ms. Curtis의 업적은 널리 칭송되고 있다. 그녀가 이전의 최고 경영자인 Mark Spalding의 후임자가 되었을 때, ¹⁶⁹⁻⁽ᴰ⁾Ping사는 주로 문서 작성 소프트웨어로 알려져 있었다. 새로운 문서 작성 제품들의 유입으로 인해, Ping사의 소프트웨어는 한때 그랬던 만큼이 잘 팔리지는 않았다. ¹⁷⁰⁻⁽ᴰ⁾Ms. Curtis는 사진 편집과 스프레드시트 프로그램을 포함한 다양한 종류의 고품질 소프트웨어를 개발함으로써 상황을 빠르게 반전시켰다. 이제 Ping이라는 이름은 그것의 신뢰할 수 있는 최첨단 기술로 유명하다.

향후 몇 년 내에, Ms. Curtis는 Ping사가 고객들을 위해 멤버십 제도를 만들 것이라고 말한다. ¹⁷¹가입하는 사람들은 새로운 Ping사 제품들을 할인된 가격으로 다운로드할 수 있을 것이다. Ms. Curtis는 회사가 웹사이트도 다시 만들 계획이라고 말한다. 이러한 모든 계획들을 앞두고, Ping사는 더 성장할 것으로 기대된다. 대부분의 전문가들은 Ms. Curtis가 회사의 성공에 주된 이유가 되어 왔다는 것에 동의한다.

name v. 지명하다, 명명하다 take over 넘겨받다, 인수하다
transform v. 전환하다, 변형시키다 thriving adj. 번창하는
enterprise n. 회사, 기업 replace v. ~의 후임자가 되다, 대신하다
word processing 문서 작성 influx n. 유입, 도래
reverse v. 반전시키다, 역전시키다 notable adj. 유명한, 중요한
cutting-edge adj. 최첨단의 dependable adj. 신뢰할 수 있는
plan n. 제도, 계획 sign up 가입하다, 등록하다 rate n. 가격, 비율
primary adj. 주된, 주요한

169 | Not/True 문제

해석 Ping사에 대해 언급된 것은?
(A) 최근에 새로운 프로그래머들을 고용했다.
(B) 5년 전에 설립되었다.
(C) 정기적으로 기술 행사를 후원한다.
(D) 특정 소프트웨어 종류와 관련지어 생각되었다.

해설 지문의 'Ping was mainly known for its word processing software'에서 Ping사는 주로 문서 작성 소프트웨어로 알려져 있었다고 했으므로 (D)가 정답이다. (A)와 (C)는 지문에 언급되지 않은 내용이다. 지문의 'Ms. Curtis, who took over the company five years ago'에서 Ms. Curtis가 5년 전에 회사를 넘겨받았다고 했으므로, (B)는 지문의 내용과 일치하지 않는다.

어휘 found v. 설립하다, 세우다 associate v. 관련지어 생각하다, 연관 짓다

170 | Not/True 문제

해석 Rebecca Curtis에 대해 언급되지 않은 것은?
(A) 회의에서 연설을 하는 것에 동의했다.
(B) Ping사의 첫 번째 여성 최고 경영자였다.
(C) 잡지에 의해 인정받았다.
(D) Ping사가 제품 라인을 확장하는 것을 도왔다.

해설 (A)는 'Ms. Curtis, who took over the company five years ago and transformed it into a thriving multi-platform enterprise, has accepted an invitation to deliver a speech at the *Gadget Lover* annual conference on December 2.'에서 5년 전에 회사를 넘겨받아 번창하는 다중 플랫폼 회사로 전환한 Ms. Curtis는 12월 2일에 *Gadget Lover*지 연례 회의에서 연설을 하기 위해 초대를 수락했다고 했으므로 지문의 내용과 일치한다. (C)는 'Rebecca Curtis, CEO of software company Ping, has been named the most successful woman in the tech world by *Gadget Lover* magazine.'에서 소프트웨어 회사 Ping사의 최고 경영자인 Rebecca Curtis는 *Gadget Lover*지에 의해 기술계에서 가장 성공적인 여성으로 지명되었다고 했으므로 지문의 내용과 일치한다. (D)는 'Ms. Curtis quickly reversed that situation by developing a wide range of high-quality software including photo editing and spreadsheet programs.'에서 Ms. Curtis가 사진 편집과 스프레드시트 프로그램을 포함한 다양한 종류의 고품질 소프트웨어를 개발함으로써 상황을 빠르게 반전시켰다고 했으므로 지문의 내용과 일치한다. (B)는 지문에 언급되지 않은 내용이다. 따라서 (B)가 정답이다.

어휘 recognize v. 인정하다, 인식하다 expand v. 확장하다

Paraphrasing

deliver ~ speech 연설을 하다 → speak 연설을 하다

has been named the most successful woman 가장 성공적인 여성으로 지명되었다 → was recognized 인정받았다

developing a wide range of high-quality software 다양한 종류의 고품질 소프트웨어를 개발하다 → expand its product line 제품 라인을 확장하다

171 | 육하원칙 문제

해석 기사에 따르면, Ping사는 무엇을 할 것으로 예상되는가?
(A) 새로운 하드웨어 제품을 개발할 것이다.
(B) 웹사이트를 영구히 폐쇄할 것이다.
(C) 저렴한 가격에 프로그램들을 제공할 것이다.
(D) 다른 회사와 합병할 것이다.

해설 지문의 'Those who sign up will be able to download new Ping products at a reduced rate.'에서 가입하는 사람들은 새로운 Ping사 제품들을 할인된 가격으로 다운로드할 수 있을 것이라고 했으므로 (C)가 정답이다.

어휘 close down 폐쇄하다, 종료하다 permanently adv. 영구히, 상시
merge v. 합병하다

Paraphrasing

reduced rate 할인된 가격 → lower prices 저렴한 가격

172-175번은 다음 보고서에 관한 문제입니다.

도시 동향 보고서—발렌시아

¹⁷²스페인의 동쪽 해안에 있는 종종 낮게 평가되던 이 도시를 사람들이 발견하기 시작하면서 발렌시아의 관광객 수가 3년 연속으로 증가하고 있다. 조사 기간 초기에, 이 도시는 1년에 단 백만 명 이하의 관광객들을 맞이했으나, 최근의 수치는 140만 명 이상으로 뛰어올랐다.

이러한 변화를 설명할 수 있는 많은 요인들이 있다. ¹⁷³⁻⁽ᴬ⁾새로운 Sanchez 이베리아 반도 예술 박물관과 근처의 회의 시설이 작년에 개장한 이후로 큰 인기를 끄는 것으로 드러났다. 또한, ¹⁷³⁻⁽ᴰ⁾/¹⁷⁴⁻⁽ᶜ⁾발렌시아에서 마드리드와 바르셀로나로의 철도편 개선은 이동 시간을 현저하게 줄여주었다. 연내에 완공될 주요 공항의 확장과 함께, 상황은 발렌시아에 더 좋아질 것으로 기대된다.

게다가, ¹⁷³⁻⁽ᶜ⁾2년 전 시 정부의 국제 광고 캠페인 개시도 도움이 되는 것으로 드러났다. 이 도시는 텔레비전, 출판물, 소셜 미디어 광고에 관광 목적지로 광고되었다. 캠페인에 대한 반응은 계속해서 긍정적이다.

마지막으로, 관광객들과 비즈니스 방문객들을 위한 목적지로 칭찬될 뿐만 아니라, 발렌시아는 살기 좋은 장소로 점점 더 알려지고 있다. ¹⁷⁴⁻⁽ᴬ⁾/¹⁷⁵자문 회사인 Apollo and Company사는 최근 유럽 소도시의 삶의 질을 평가하는 보고서에서 이 도시를 3위로 선정했다. ¹⁷⁵그들은 높은 순위의 이유로 멋진 해안가 장소, 낮은 집값, 그리고 현대적 공공 기반 시설을 들었다.

tourism n. 관광객, 관광 사업 running adj. 연속의, 계속되는
underrate v. 낮게 평가하다 figure n. 수치, 인물; v. 계산하다
account for 설명하다, 밝히다 draw n. 인기를 끄는 것; v. 끌어당기다
rail service 철도편 significantly adv. 현저하게, 상당히

expansion n. 확장, 팽창 due adj. ~하기로 되어 있는
before the end of the year 연내에
launch n. 개시, 출시; v. 시작하다, 출시하다 beneficial adj. 도움이 되는, 유익한
market n. 광고하다, 내놓다; n. 시장, 소비자 수 destination n. 목적지, 목표
reaction n. 반응, 반작용 increasingly adv. 점점 더
consultancy n. 자문 회사 measure v. 평가하다, 측정하다
cite v. (이유·예를) 들다, 인용하다 waterfront n. 해안가
infrastructure n. 공공 기반 시설

172 | 주제 찾기 문제

해석 보고서는 주로 무엇에 대한 것인가?
(A) 도시를 살기에 더 적합하도록 만드는 캠페인
(B) 국제 회의 시설의 개선
(C) 정부의 건축 법규 변화
(D) 도시 관광 산업의 발전

해설 지문의 'Tourism numbers in Valencia have been increasing for three years running as people are beginning to discover this often-underrated city on the eastern coast of Spain.'에서 스페인의 동쪽 해안에 있는 종종 낮게 평가되던 도시를 사람들이 발견하기 시작하면서 발렌시아의 관광객 수가 3년 연속으로 증가하고 있다고 한 후, 관광객의 수가 늘어난 요인에 대해 설명하고 있으므로 (D)가 정답이다.

어휘 livable adj. 살기에 적합한 code n. 법규, 암호, 부호

173 | Not/True 문제

해석 수치 증가의 이유로 언급되지 않은 것은?
(A) 새로운 박물관 시설
(B) 갱신된 조세 정책
(C) 마케팅 캠페인
(D) 개선된 운송 체계

해설 지문의 'The new Sanchez Museum of Iberian Art and its nearby conference facilities have proven to be a big draw since opening last year.'에서 새로운 Sanchez 이베리아 반도 예술 박물관과 근처의 회의 시설이 작년에 개장한 이후로 큰 인기를 끄는 것으로 드러났다고 했으므로 (A)는 지문의 내용과 일치한다. 'the city government's launch of an international advertising campaign two years ago has also proved beneficial'에서 2년 전 시 정부의 국제 광고 캠페인 개시도 도움이 되는 것으로 드러났다고 했으므로 (C)는 지문의 내용과 일치한다. 'upgrades to rail services from Valencia to Madrid and Barcelona have reduced travel time significantly'에서 발렌시아에서 마드리드와 바르셀로나로의 철도편 개선은 이동 시간을 현저하게 줄여주었다고 했으므로 (D)는 지문의 내용과 일치한다. (B)는 지문에 언급되지 않은 내용이다. 따라서 (B)가 정답이다.

어휘 transportation n. 운송

Paraphrasing

advertising campaign 광고 캠페인 → marketing campaign 마케팅 캠페인
upgrades to rail services 철도편 개선 → improved transportation system 개선된 운송 체계

174 | Not/True 문제

해석 마드리드에 대해 명시된 것은?
(A) 자문 회사에 의해 높은 삶의 질을 가진 곳으로 선정되었다.
(B) 3년간 바르셀로나에 비해 관광객들에게 덜 유명했다.
(C) 발렌시아로의 철도 연결이 강화되었다.
(D) 시 의회가 마케팅 전략을 개발할 회사를 고용했다.

해설 지문의 'upgrades to rail services from Valencia to Madrid and Barcelona have reduced travel time significantly'에서 발렌시아에서 마드리드와 바르셀로나로의 철도편 개선은 이동 시간을 현저하게 줄여주었다고 하였다. 따라서 (C)가 정답이다. (B)와 (D)는 지문에 언급되지 않은 내용이다. 지문의 'The consultancy Apollo and Company recently put the city in third place in a report measuring the quality of life in small European cities.'에서 자문 회사인 Apollo and Company사는 최근 유럽 소도시의 삶의 질을 평가하는 보고서에서 이 도시, 즉 발렌시아를 3위로 선정했다고 했으나 마드리드에 대해서는 언급되지 않았으므로, (A)는 지문의 내용과 일치하지 않는다.

어휘 enhance v. 강화하다 strategy n. 전략, 계획

175 | 육하원칙 문제

해석 유럽 소도시들 중 발렌시아가 3위를 차지한 이유는 무엇인가?
(A) 비즈니스 여행객들에게 유명하다.
(B) 최근에 해안가를 새롭게 했다.
(C) 거주민들에게 적당한 가격의 집을 제공한다.
(D) 많은 국제 행사를 주최한다.

해설 지문의 'The consultancy Apollo and Company recently put the city[Valencia] in third place in a report measuring the quality of life in small European cities.'에서 자문 회사인 Apollo and Company사는 최근 유럽 소도시의 삶의 질을 평가하는 보고서에서 발렌시아를 3위로 선정했다고 한 후, 'They cited its lovely waterfront location, low housing costs, and modern infrastructure as reasons for its high ranking.'에서 그들은 높은 순위의 이유로 멋진 해안가 장소, 낮은 집값, 그리고 현대적 공공 기반 시설을 들었다고 했으므로 (C)가 정답이다.

어휘 rank v. 차지하다, 평가하다; n. 등급, 계급
affordable adj. 적당한 가격의, 가격이 알맞은

Paraphrasing

low housing costs 낮은 집값 → affordable homes 적당한 가격의 집

176-180번은 다음 편지와 이메일에 관한 문제입니다.

Maxfield Financial Group사

5월 10일

Bethany Aldridge
18번지 Juniper로
웨스트포트, 코네티컷주 06880

Ms. Aldridge께,

176이 편지는 종이를 쓰지 않는 명세서를 신청한 귀하의 요청에 대한 답신입니다. 귀하의 명세서는 이제 매달 25일에 이메일로 발송될 것입니다. 177-(C)이러한 명세서는 또한 편하실 때에 온라인 계정에서 이용하실 수 있고, 인쇄하실 수 있습니다. 177-(D)그것들은 종이 명세서에 포함된 것과 동일한 모든 정보를 포함할 것입니다. 귀하의 계좌 세부 정보를 보호하기 위해, 종이를 쓰지 않는 명세서를 다운로드하고 저장하는 데 사용하는 장치가 안전한지를 확실히 하십시오.

178만약 종이를 쓰지 않는 명세서뿐만 아니라 종이 명세서를 원래의 주소로 우편으로 받고 싶으시다면, 귀하의 계정에 로그인해서 "배달 선호도" 아래의 "내 명세서 우편으로 발송하기" 박스에 체크하십시오.

180Maxfield Financial Group사는 종이 명세서를 받는 것을 선택한 고객들에게 24달러의 연회비를 부과한다는 것을 명심하십시오.

고객 서비스 드림
Maxfield Financial Group사

paperless adj. 종이를 쓰지 않는 statement n. 명세서, 성명서
accessible adj. 이용(접근) 가능한 ensure v. 확실하게 하다, 반드시 ~하게 하다
device n. 장치 secure adj. 안전한, 확실한 primary adj. 원래의, 주요한
keep in mind 명심하다, 유념하다

수신: Bethany Aldridge <bethanyal22@totalmail.net>
발신: 고객 서비스 <cs@maxfieldfin.com>
날짜: 5월 25일
제목: 귀하의 5월 명세서
첨부 파일: 5월_명세서

Ms. Aldridge께,

첨부된 귀하의 Maxfield Financial Group사의 5월 전자 계좌 명세서를 확인하십시오. [179]이것이 귀하께 발송된 첫 번째 전자 명세서이므로, 주의 깊게 살펴보시고 질문이나 문제가 있으시면 저희 서비스 센터로 연락 주십시오. [180]저희는 귀하의 납입금을 받았으며, 귀하의 명세서 출력본은 우편으로 다음 5일에서 7일 내에 도착할 것입니다.

귀하께서 월별 명세서를 받는 것을 확실하게 하기 위해, 반드시 최신 이메일과 우편 주소가 저희 파일에 기록되어 있도록 하십시오. 만약 그것들을 바꾸실 계획이시라면, 간단히 저희 웹사이트의 "개인 정보" 섹션에서 업데이트하십시오.

고객 서비스 드림
Maxfield Financial Group사

electronic adj. 전자의, 컴퓨터의 payment n. 납입금
hard copy 출력본, 종이로 인쇄한 것 make sure 반드시 ~하다
current adj. 최신의, 현재의 postal address 우편 주소

176 | 목적 찾기 문제

해석 편지의 목적은 무엇인가?
(A) 비밀번호 변경 방법을 설명하기 위해
(B) 고객에게 변경 사항을 알리기 위해
(C) 요금 납부를 요청하기 위해
(D) 정책에 대한 문의에 답변하기 위해

해설 편지의 'This letter is in response to your request to sign up for paperless statements. Your statements will now be sent via e-mail on the 25th of each month.'에서 이 편지는 종이를 쓰지 않는 명세서를 신청한 요청에 대한 답신이라고 하고, 명세서는 이제 매달 25일에 이메일로 발송될 것이라고 한 후, 종이를 쓰지 않는 명세서로의 신청과 관련된 사항에 대해 알리고 있으므로 (B)가 정답이다.

어휘 charge n. 요금 inquiry n. 문의

177 | Not/True 문제

해석 편지에서 종이를 쓰지 않는 명세서에 대해 언급된 것은?
(A) 수령인에 의해 조세 용도로 보관되어야 한다.
(B) 열기 위해서 지정된 비밀번호를 요구한다.
(C) 온라인 계정에서 이용할 수 있다.
(D) 우편으로 발송되는 종이 서류보다 더 많은 세부 사항을 포함한다.

해설 편지의 'These statements will also be accessible from your online account, and you will be able to print them at your convenience.'에서 이러한 명세서, 즉 종이를 쓰지 않는 명세서는 편한 때에 온라인 계정에서 이용하고 인쇄할 수 있다고 했으므로 (C)가 정답이다. (A)와 (B)는 지문에 언급되지 않은 내용이다. (D)는 'They will contain all of the same information that is included in your paper statements.'에서 그것들, 즉 종이를 쓰지 않는 명세서는 종이 명세서에 포함된 것과 동일한 모든 정보를 포함할 것이라고 했으므로 지문의 내용과 일치하지 않는다.

어휘 retain v. 보관하다, 유지하다 recipient n. 수령인, 수취인
assign v. 지정하다, 할당하다 document n. 서류, 문서

Paraphrasing
be accessible 이용할 수 있다 → can be accessed 이용할 수 있다

178 | 육하원칙 문제

해석 편지에 따르면, 명세서의 인쇄본은 어떻게 요청될 수 있는가?
(A) 서비스 센터에 이메일을 보냄으로써
(B) 회계부서에 전화를 함으로써
(C) 온라인에서 옵션을 선택함으로써
(D) 신청서를 보냄으로써

해설 편지의 'If you would like a paper statement mailed to your primary address in addition to the paperless one, log on to your account and check the "Mail My Statement" box under "Delivery Preferences."'에서 만약 종이를 쓰지 않는 명세서뿐만 아니라 종이 명세서를 원래의 주소로 우편으로 받고 싶다면, 계정에 로그인해서 "배달 선호도" 아래의 "내 명세서 우편으로 발송하기" 박스에 체크하라고 했으므로 (C)가 정답이다.

179 | 육하원칙 문제

해석 Ms. Aldridge는 왜 디지털 명세서를 살펴볼 것을 요청받았는가?
(A) 중요한 통지를 포함하고 있다.
(B) 부정확한 연락처를 포함하고 있다.
(C) 서비스에 대한 추가 요금 일부를 보여준다.
(D) 그녀가 받은 첫 번째 것이다.

해설 이메일의 'As this is the first electronic statement that has been sent to you, please review it carefully'에서 이것은 귀하, 즉 Ms. Aldridge에게 발송된 첫 번째 전자 명세서이므로 주의 깊게 살펴보라고 했으므로 (D)가 정답이다.

어휘 incorrect adj. 부정확한, 틀린 additional adj. 추가의

180 | 추론 문제 연계

해석 Ms. Aldridge에 대해 추론될 수 있는 것은?
(A) 금융 제공 기관에 주소 변경을 통지했다.
(B) 7일 이내에 납입금 전액을 내야 한다.
(C) 월별 명세서에서 발견된 오류를 알렸다.
(D) Maxfield Financial Group사에 연간 요금을 지불했다.

해설 Ms. Aldridge에게 보내진 이메일을 먼저 확인한다.
단서 1 이메일의 'We have received your payment, and the hard copy of your statement will arrive via mail within the next five to seven days.'에서 저희, 즉 Maxfield Financial Group사는 상대방, 즉 Ms. Aldridge의 납입금을 받았고 명세서 출력본은 우편으로 다음 5일에서 7일 내에 도착할 것이라고 했다. 그런데 Ms. Aldridge가 어떤 납입금을 지불했는지 제시되지 않았으므로 편지에서 관련 내용을 확인한다.
단서 2 편지의 'Keep in mind that Maxfield Financial Group does charge an annual fee of $24 to clients who choose to receive paper statements.'에서 Maxfield Financial Group사는 종이 명세서를 받는 것을 선택한 고객들에게 24달러의 연회비를 부과한다는 것을 알 수 있다.
두 단서를 종합할 때, Ms. Aldridge는 우편으로 종이 명세서를 받는 것을 신청했고 이를 위해 연간 요금을 지불했다는 것을 추론할 수 있다. 따라서 (D)가 정답이다.

Paraphrasing
an annual fee 연회비 → a yearly charge 연간 요금

181-185번은 다음 초대장과 온라인 게시물에 관한 문제입니다.

특별 행사 초대장

[182-(A)]Pakori가 Luton에 세 번째 지점을 열 것이고, [181]귀하는 이곳이 공식적으로 영업을 시작하기 전에 저희가 제공하는 제품과 서비스에 대해 알아볼 수 있도록 초대되었습니다!

언제
4월 6일 일요일, 오후 12시

어디서
A209 상점, Ayleswood 쇼핑몰
1452번지 Crestwood가

무엇을
이것은 엄선된 예술가, 블로거, 그리고 언론 대표자를 위한 독점적인 행사입니다. ¹⁸¹Pakori의 사업 관행, 서비스, 그리고 상품에 대한 이야기를 포함할 것입니다. 다과와 선물이 제공될 것입니다.

¹⁸⁴4월 1일 전에 555-9922로 저희에게 전화 주셔서 귀하의 참석을 확정해주시기 바랍니다. 그렇지 않을 경우, 귀하의 성함은 저희의 참석자 명단에서 삭제될 것입니다.

Pakori는 특별한 수공예품을 판매하는 고급 장신구 가게입니다. 더 많은 정보를 위해서는, www.pakori.com을 방문해 주십시오.

exclusive adj. 독점적인 select adj. 엄선된 representative n. 대표(자)
refreshment n. 다과 confirm v. 확정하다, 확인하다 attendance n. 참석
one-of-a-kind adj. 특별한, 독특한 handmade adj. 수공예의, 수제의

---

www.blogaboutit.com/juliescharms
Julie's Charms—고급 장신구 블로그

Ayleswood 쇼핑몰의 Pakori—게시됨: 4월 9일

Ayleswood 쇼핑몰의 새로운 Pakori 상점은 화려한 결혼반지 컬렉션을 자랑합니다. 관리자인 Arlene Pitts에 따르면, 이것들은 이 지점의 특별 상품입니다. ¹⁸³6개월 전에 런던의 Pakori 본점에 대해 블로그를 썼기 때문에, ¹⁸⁴저는 새 상점이 공식적으로 열리기 직전에 그곳의 특별 관람에 참석해달라고 요청받았습니다. 그것은 여러분이 기대하는 모든 것으로, 고급스럽고, 넓고, 조명도 밝습니다. ¹⁸⁴다른 손님들과 저는 Ms. Pitts가 Pakori가 어떻게 운영되는지에 대해 설명하는 것을 들으며 선물 가방에 들어 있던 수공예 장식품에 감탄했습니다. 저는 이미 이들의 친환경적인 관행과 품질에 대한 전념에 대해서 어느 정도 잘 알고 있었지만, ¹⁸⁵Pakori가 마다가스카르의 광산과 제휴했다는 것을 알게 되어 매우 감명받았습니다. 그들의 보석이 어디에서 오는지에 대해 모를 수도 있는 다른 장신구 제조업체들과 달리, Pakori는 그 과정에 직접적으로 관여합니다.

자세히 읽기 >

¹⁸³**저에 관해**
¹⁸³저는 Julie's Charms의 블로거 Julie Mendel입니다. 장신구에 대한 제 열정을 공유하기 위해 저는 이 블로그를 10년 전 시작했습니다. 저는 Luton의 한 장신구 부티크에서 6년간의 경험을 지닌 공인 보석감정사이고 다른 출판물들에 정기적으로 기고합니다.

boast v. 자랑하다 gorgeous adj. 화려한, 아주 멋진 specialty n. 특별 상품
flagship store 본점 shortly before 직전에 spacious adj. 넓은
charm n. 장식 mine n. 광산 gem n. 보석 certified adj. 공인된
gemologist n. 보석감정사 contribute v. 기고하다

---

181 | 주제 찾기 문제

해설 초대장은 무엇을 위한 것인가?
(A) 예술 워크숍
(B) 제품 출시 파티
(C) 설명회
(D) 미술 전시

해설 초대장의 'you are invited to learn about the goods and services we offer before it officially opens for business'에서 이곳, 즉 Pakori가 Luton에 여는 세 번째 지점이 공식적으로 영업을 시작하기 전에 제공하는 제품과 서비스에 대해 알아볼 수 있도록 초대되었다고 했고, 'It will include a discussion of Pakori's business practices, services, and products.'에서 Pakori의 사업 관행, 서비스, 그리고 상품에 대한 이야기를 포함할 것이라고 했으므로 (C)가 정답이다.

어휘 launch n. 출시

182 | Not/True 문제

해설 Pakori에 관해 언급된 것은?
(A) 하나보다 많은 지점이 있다.
(B) 많은 인기 브랜드 제품들을 판매한다.
(C) Luton시에 본사를 두고 있다.
(D) 고객들을 위해 주문 제작 상품을 만든다.

해설 초대장의 'Pakori is opening its third store in Luton'에서 Pakori가 Luton에 세 번째 지점을 열 것이라고 했으므로 (A)가 정답이다. (B), (C), (D)는 지문에 언급되지 않은 내용이다.

Paraphrasing
is opening ~ third store 세 번째 지점을 열 것이다 → has more than one location 하나보다 많은 지점이 있다

183 | 육하원칙 문제

해설 Ms. Mendel은 왜 행사에 초대되었는가?
(A) 결혼반지를 구입했다.
(B) 온라인에 상점에 대한 글을 썼다.
(C) 가맹점 영업권을 구매하는 데 관심을 표현했다.
(D) Luton에서 기자로 일한다.

해설 온라인 게시물의 'ABOUT ME', 'I'm Julie Mendel, the blogger behind Julie's Charms.'에서 온라인 게시물의 작성자가 Ms. Mendel임을 알 수 있고, 'Having blogged about Pakori's flagship store in London six months ago, I was asked to attend a special viewing of the new store shortly before it officially opened.'에서 6개월 전에 런던의 Pakori 본점에 대해 블로그를 썼기 때문에 새 상점이 공식적으로 열리기 직전에 특별 관람에 참석해달라고 요청받았다고 했으므로 (B)가 정답이다.

Paraphrasing
blogged 블로그를 썼다 → wrote ~ online 온라인에 글을 썼다

184 | 추론 문제 연계

해설 Ms. Mendel에 대해 암시되는 것은?
(A) 4월 1일 이전에 Pakori에 연락했다.
(B) 자신의 보석 가게를 소유하고 있다.
(C) 행사에 손님을 데려갔다.
(D) 친환경적인 사업에 대해서만 글을 쓴다.

해설 Ms. Mendel이 작성한 온라인 게시물을 먼저 확인한다.

단서 1 온라인 게시물의 'I was asked to attend a special viewing of the new store shortly before it officially opened'에서 자신, 즉 Ms. Mendel은 새 상점이 공식적으로 열리기 직전에 특별 관람에 참석해달라고 요청받았다고 한 후, 'The other guests and I admired the handcrafted charms in our gift bags as we listened to Ms. Pitts describe how Pakori operates.'에서 다른 손님들, 즉 특별 관람에 참여한 손님들과 자신이 Ms. Pitts가 Pakori가 어떻게 운영되는지에 대해 설명하는 것을 들으며 선물 가방에 들어 있던 수공예 장식품에 감탄했다고 했으므로 Ms. Mendel이 특별 관람에 참석했다는 사실을 알 수 있다. 그런데 특별 관람 참석과 관련한 세부 정보가 제시되지 않았으므로 초대장에서 관련 내용을 확인한다.

단서 2 초대장의 'Please confirm your attendance by calling us at

555-9922 before April 1. Otherwise, your name will be removed from our guest list.'에서 4월 1일 전에 Pakori에 전화하여 참석을 확정해달라고 한 후, 그렇지 않을 경우 이름이 참석자 명단에서 삭제될 것이라고 했다.

두 단서를 종합할 때, Ms. Mendel은 4월 1일 이전에 Pakori에 연락했음을 추론할 수 있다. 따라서 (A)가 정답이다.

185 | 육하원칙 문제

해석 온라인 게시물에 따르면, Pakori는 왜 다른 보석 가게들과 구별되는가?
(A) 마다가스카르에 상점을 열었다.
(B) 원자재 공급업체와 제휴되어 있다.
(C) 희귀한 보석만을 사용하여 장신구를 제작한다.
(D) 결혼반지에 주로 집중한다.

해설 온라인 게시물의 'I was really impressed to learn that Pakori has partnered with a mine in Madagascar'에서 Pakori가 마다가스카르의 광산과 제휴했다는 것을 알게 되어 매우 감명받았다고 했고, 'Unlike other jewelry makers who may not be aware of where their gems come from, Pakori is directly involved in the process.'에서 보석이 어디에서 오는지에 대해 모를 수도 있는 다른 장신구 제조업체들과 달리, Pakori는 그 과정에 직접적으로 관여한다고 했으므로 (B)가 정답이다.

어휘 **stand out** 구별되다, 두드러지다 **affiliate with** ~와 제휴하다
rare adj. 희귀한 **primarily** adv. 주로

186-190번은 다음 기사, 웹페이지, 이메일에 관한 문제입니다.

Gunton시 의회가 Blandfolk Superstore사 제안을 고려할 예정

[186]5월 2일의 Gunton시 의회 회의에서, 의원들은 도시 근처에 지점을 짓는 것에 대한 Blandfolk Superstore사 대표들의 발표를 들었다. [188]그 거대 소매업체는 시 경계 바로 안쪽 Medford가에 소매점을 건설하는 것을 제안했다. 하지만, 선택된 부지는 아직 상업 시설용으로 허가되지 않아서, Blandfolk사는 그 부지가 구분 변경되도록 요청했다. [187]Gunton시 시장 Claire O'Rourke는 의회가 이번 달에 그 제안에 대해 논의할 것이라고 대표들에게 말했다. Blandfolk사 대변인은 회사에서 제안이 통과되기를 바라고 있다고 말하며, 이 개발이 최대 190명의 지역 주민에게 일자리를 제공할 것임을 강조했다.

council n. 의회, 위원회 **representative** n. 대표, 대리인
branch n. 지점, 나뭇가지; v. 갈라지다 **locally** adv. 근처에, 근방에
erect v. 건설하다, 세우다 **authorize** v. 허가하다, 권한을 부여하다
rezone v. 구분 변경하다, 재구분하다 **proposition** n. 제의, 건의
emphasize v. 강조하다 **resident** n. 주민, 거주자

---

*Gunton Herald*지
www.guntonherald.com

홈 | 뉴스 | 스포츠 | 비즈니스 | 연예 | 생활 | 사설 | 연락하기

독자의 논평

*Ronald Pinero*가 5월 7일에 게시:

[187]저는 5월 3일 자 신문에 실린 Blandfolk Superstore사의 건설 제안에 대한 기사에 관해 글을 씁니다. Gunton시의 오랜 사업체 소유주로서, 저는 걱정이 됩니다. [190]저는 시내에서 의류 상점 Ballas Closet을 운영합니다. 대기업 소매업체들은 개업한 곳의 많은 소규모 상점들을 폐업하게 만들었습니다. 제 상점과 같은 많은 사업체들이 가격과, 더 나아가, 제품의 품질을 크게 낮추지 않고는 경쟁을 할 수 있을지 잘 모르겠습니다. 현재, Gunton시는 매우 활기차고 다양한 도시이고, [187]저는 시장님과 의회 의원님들이 도시를 이 상태로 유지하기 위해 그 제안을 거절해 주시기를 바랍니다.

comment n. 논평, 언급 **in regard to** ~에 관해

---

concern v. 걱정하다; n. 관심, 우려 **out of business** 폐업한
compete v. 경쟁하다, 겨루다 **by extension** 더 나아가
vibrant adj. 활기찬, 진동하는 **reject** v. 거절하다, 거부하다

수신: Ronald Pinero <rpinero@dailymaily.com>
발신: Adeline Morris <amorris@guntoncoc.org>
날짜: 5월 8일
제목: Gunton시 상공회의소의 요청

Mr. Pinero께,

저는 *Gunton Herald*지 웹사이트에서 귀하의 논평을 우연히 발견했습니다. 귀하의 우려는 Gunton시 상공회의소 위원회가 논의해오던 것이고, [190]저희는 귀하의 상점과 같은 시내의 상점들을 보호하기 위해 무언가가 행해져야 한다는 것에 동의합니다. [189]6월 3일에, 시 의회는 저희 중 일부가 참석할 공청회를 열 것입니다. 귀하께서 그 행사에 저희와 함께하신다면 도움이 될 것입니다. 귀하께서는 논평에서 언급하셨던 우려에 대해 설명하는 짧은 연설을 하실 수 있습니다. 참석하기를 원하신다면 제게 알려 주십시오.

[189]Adeline Morris 드림
사무관, Gunton시 상공회의소

come across ~을 우연히 발견하다 **board** n. 위원회, 이사회
protect v. 보호하다, 지키다

186 | 주제 찾기 문제

해석 기사는 주로 무엇에 대한 것인가?
(A) 시장의 최근 제안
(B) 회사의 구분 변경을 위한 요청
(C) 도시의 번화한 시내 경관
(D) 실업률을 감소시키기 위한 위원회의 노력

해설 기사의 'At a Gunton City Council meeting on May 2, members listened to a presentation by representatives of Blandfolk Superstore about building a branch locally.'에서 5월 2일의 Gunton시 의회 회의에서 의원들은 근처에 지점을 짓는 것에 대한 Blandfolk Superstore사 대표들의 발표를 들었다고 한 후, Blandfolk Superstore사의 지점 건설을 위한 구분 변경 요청에 대한 내용을 전달하고 있으므로 (B)가 정답이다.

어휘 **thriving** adj. 번화한, 번성하는 **scene** n. 경관, 상황
unemployment n. 실업률, 실업

Paraphrasing

building a branch 지점을 짓는 것 → build a store 상점을 짓다

187 | 육하원칙 문제 연계

해석 Mr. Pinero는 Ms. O'Rourke가 무엇을 하기를 원하는가?
(A) Blandfolk Superstore사의 제의를 거절한다.
(B) Ballas Closet의 경영진과 만난다.
(C) 건설을 허용하기 위해 부지 일부를 구분 변경한다.
(D) 개인 사업체 소유주들을 위한 자금을 보류한다.

해설 Mr. Pinero가 작성한 논평이 있는 웹페이지를 먼저 확인한다.

단서 1 웹페이지의 'I am writing in regard to an article printed in your newspaper's May 3 edition about the construction proposal from Blandfolk Superstore.'와 'I hope the mayor and council members will reject the proposal in order to keep it that way'에서 자신, 즉 Mr. Pinero가 5월 3일 자 신문에 실린 Blandfolk Superstore사의 건설 제안에 대한 기사에 관해 글을 쓴다고 하고, 시장과 의회 의원들이 도시를 이 상태로 유지하기 위해 그 제안을 거절해 주

기를 바란다고 했다. 그런데 시장에 대해 제시되지 않았으므로 기사에서 관련 내용을 확인한다.

단서 2 기사의 'Gunton mayor Claire O'Rourke told representatives that the council would discuss the proposition this month.'에서 Gunton시 시장 Claire O'Rourke는 의회가 이번 달에 그 제의에 대해 논의할 것이라고 대표들에게 말했다고 하였다.

두 단서를 종합할 때, Mr. Pinero는 시장인 Ms. O'Rourke가 Blandfolk Superstore사의 제의를 거절하기를 원한다는 점을 알 수 있다. 따라서 (A)가 정답이다.

어휘 turn down ~을 거절(거부)하다 executive n. 경영진, 대표
defer v. 보류하다, 연기하다

Paraphrasing

reject the proposal 제안을 거절하다 → Turn down a proposition 제의를 거절하다

188 | 동의어 찾기 문제

해석 기사에서, 1문단 네 번째 줄의 단어 "limits"는 의미상 -와 가장 가깝다.
(A) 규제
(B) 경계
(C) 수준
(D) 장애물

해설 기사의 limits를 포함하는 구절 'The retail giant proposed erecting an outlet just within city limits on Medford Avenue.'에서 limits가 '경계, 한계선'이라는 뜻으로 사용되었다. 따라서 (B)가 정답이다.

189 | 육하원칙 문제

해석 6월 3일에 무엇이 일어날 것인가?
(A) Gunton시 의회 사람들이 계획에 대해 투표할 것이다.
(B) 상공회의소의 몇몇 직원들이 공청회에 참석할 것이다.
(C) 대규모의 거대 소매점 건설이 진행될 것이다.
(D) Ms. Morris가 기자회견에서 우려를 표명할 것이다.

해설 이메일의 'On June 3, the city council will be holding a public meeting that some of us will be attending.'과 'Adeline Morris, Secretary, Gunton Chamber of Commerce'에서 6월 3일에 시 의회는 우리 중 일부, 즉 이메일의 발신자인 Gunton시 상공회의소의 사무관 Adeline Morris를 포함한 상공회의소 직원 중 일부가 참석할 공청회를 열 것이라고 했으므로 (B)가 정답이다.

어휘 underway adj. 진행 중인 voice v. 표명하다, 나타내다; n. 목소리, 음성
press conference 기자회견

Paraphrasing

public meeting 공청회 → public hearing 공청회

190 | 추론 문제 연계

해석 Ms. Morris에 대해 암시되는 것은?
(A) 시 의회의 이전을 책임지고 있다.
(B) 물품을 할인 가격에 파는 상점을 운영한다.
(C) Ballas Closet이 지원되어야 한다고 생각한다.
(D) Gunton시 의회의 지지를 받는 청원서에 서명했다.

해설 Ms. Morris가 작성한 이메일을 먼저 확인한다.

단서 1 이메일의 'we agree that something must be done to protect stores in the downtown area, like yours'에서 우리, 즉 Ms. Morris와 상공회의소 직원들은 이메일 수신자의 상점, 즉 Mr. Pinero의 상점과 같은 시내의 상점들을 보호하기 위해 무언가가 행해져야만 한다는 것에 동의한다고 했다. 그런데 Mr. Pinero의 상점이 무엇인지 제시되지 않았으므로 Mr. Pinero가 작성한 논평이 있는 웹페이지에서 관련 내용을 확인한다.

단서 2 웹페이지의 'I manage Ballas Closet, a clothing store in the downtown area.'에서 자신, 즉 Mr. Pinero는 시내에서 의류 상점 Ballas Closet을 운영한다는 사실을 확인할 수 있다.

두 단서를 종합할 때, Ms. Morris는 Ballas Closet이 지원되어야 한다고 생각함을 추론할 수 있다. 따라서 (C)가 정답이다.

어휘 in charge of ~을 책임지고, ~을 담당하여 relocation n. 이전, 재배치
bargain price 할인 가격 petition n. 청원서; v. 청원하다

Paraphrasing

protect 보호하다 → be supported 지원되다

191-195번은 다음 송장, 이메일, 소식지에 관한 문제입니다.

송장   날짜: 10월 4일

발신: Oresund Graphics and Design사
49번지 Rozenstraat가, 아른헴, 네덜란드

수신: 191-(D)Kaiser Investment Services사
1번지 Kornmarkt가, 4층, 프랑크푸르트, 독일

서비스	요금
연례 주주 보고서의 디자인, 레이아웃, 사진 촬영	745유로
*Kaiser*사와 투자하기 책자의 디자인과 레이아웃	545유로
191-(B)약관 소책자의 디자인과 레이아웃	300유로
총 요금	1,590유로

지불은 15일 이내에 이루어져야 합니다. 192추가적인 수정 요청은 서류마다 100유로의 추가 요금을 발생시킬 것입니다. 빠른 인쇄를 위해서는 250유로를 추가하십시오. 191-(A)저희는 더 이상 수표를 받지 않는다는 점에 유의하십시오.

invoice n. 송장, 청구서 charge n. 요금, 고발; v. 요금을 청구하다
shareholder n. 주주 terms and conditions 약관, 조건 booklet n. 소책자
due adj. 지불 기일이 된 incur v. 발생시키다, 초래하다
surcharge n. 추가 요금; v. 추가 요금을 부과하다 no longer 더 이상 ~이 아닌

수신: Alexander Svensson <alex.svensson@oresund.nl>
발신: Christine Kaufmann <ckaufmann@kaiserinvestment.de>
날짜: 10월 7일
제목: 출판물에 대한 변경 사항

Mr. Svensson께,

저희는 어제 교정쇄와 함께 귀사의 송장을 받았습니다. 귀하의 훌륭한 작업에 감사드립니다. 저는 최종안을 상무 이사님께 보여드렸고, 전반적으로 그는 만족하셨습니다. 하지만, 192그는 앞표지에 사용된 사진을 변경할 것을 요청했습니다. 그는 그것이 저희가 얻고자 하는 분위기를 전달하지 못했다고 생각합니다. 저희는 사진 작가에게 새로운 사진을 찍어달라고 의뢰하였고, 귀하께 그것을 금요일까지 보내드리겠습니다. 안타깝게도, 19511월에 계획한 캠페인 개시 행사를 위해 책자가 늦지 않게 배송되어야 하므로 저희의 원래 마감일을 미룰 수는 없습니다.

193저희의 요청이 문제를 야기한다면, 즉시 제게 알려주십시오. 귀하께서는 555-2309, 내선 42번으로 제게 전화로 연락하실 수 있습니다. 감사합니다!

Christine Kaufmann 드림
출판 관리자

Kaiser Investment Services사

along with ~과 함께 proof n. 교정쇄, 증거, 증명서 draft n. 초안, 원고
managing director 상무 이사 convey v. 전달하다, 운반하다
go for 얻고자 하다 commission v. 의뢰하다; n. 위원회 due date 마감일
in time 늦지 않게 present v. 야기하다, 주다 extension n. 내선, 확대

Kaiser Investment Services사 소식지

최고 경영자의 연말 메시지

연말이 가까워짐에 따라, 이 기회를 빌려 모두의 헌신과 노고에 대해 감사 드리고 싶습니다. 다시 한번 ¹⁹⁴Kaiser Investment Services사는 분석가들의 예상을 능가하였고 고객과 주주들을 위해 상당한 수익을 만들어 냈습니다. 그뿐 아니라, 우리는 독일의 금융 서비스 회사에 관한 고객 만족 조사에서 계속해서 1위를 하고 있습니다. 이러한 성공을 되새기면서, 계속해서 낙관적으로 앞날을 생각합시다. ¹⁹⁵이번 12월호 소식지에서, 진행 중인 우리의 북미로의 확장에 대해 더 알아보시고 몇몇 잠재 고객들이 많이 참석한 지난달 미국에서의 마케팅 캠페인 개시 행사의 사진을 확인하십시오. 여러분 모두를 연례 휴일 파티에서 뵙겠습니다!

Matthias Furst 드림

newsletter n. 소식지, 회보 year-end adj. 연말의; n. 연말
commitment n. 헌신, 약속 expectation n. 예상, 기대
substantial adj. 상당한, 많은, 튼튼한 profit n. 수익, 이윤
look forward 앞날을 생각하다 optimism n. 낙관(론) issue n. 호, 문제
ongoing adj. 진행 중인 expansion n. 확장, 확대
potential adj. 잠재적인, 가능성이 있는

191 | Not/True 문제

해석 Oresund Graphics and Design사에 대해 사실인 것은?
(A) 우편을 통해 보내진 수표를 지불금으로 받는다.
(B) 소책자를 위한 사진을 찍지 않았다.
(C) 자체 회계부서가 있다.
(D) 건물의 4층에 있다.

해설 송장의 'Design and Layout of Terms and Conditions Booklet'에서 약관 소책자의 디자인과 레이아웃만을 작업했다고 했으므로 (B)가 지문의 내용과 일치한다. (C)는 지문에 언급되지 않은 내용이다. (A)는 'Please note that we no longer accept checks.'에서 우리, 즉 Oresund Graphics and Design사는 더 이상 수표를 받지 않는다는 점에 유의하라고 했으므로 지문의 내용과 일치하지 않는다. (D)는 'Kaiser Investment Services', '1 Kornmarkt, Floor 4, Frankfurt, Germany'에서 Kaiser Investment Services사의 주소가 1번지 Kornmarkt가, 4층, 프랑크푸르트, 독일이라고 했으므로 지문의 내용과 일치하지 않는다.

어휘 finance department 회계부서

192 | 추론 문제 연계

해석 Kaiser Investment Services사에 대해 암시되는 것은?
(A) 전임 사진작가의 고용을 계획하고 있다.
(B) 약속된 모든 서류를 받지 못했다.
(C) 송장의 비용을 늦게 지불한 것에 대한 요금이 청구될 수도 있다.
(D) 수정을 위해 100유로의 요금을 지불해야 할 것이다.

해설 Kaiser Investment Services사의 Christine Kaufmann이 작성한 이메일을 먼저 확인한다.
단서 1 이메일의 'he[our managing director] has requested that we change the photograph used on the front cover'에서 상무 이사가 앞표지에 사용된 사진을 변경하도록 요청했다고 했다. 그런데 앞표지의 사진을 변경할 경우 무엇을 해야 하는지 제시되지 않았으므로 송장에서 관련 내용을 확인한다.
단서 2 송장의 'Requests for additional changes will incur a €100 surcharge per document.'에서 추가적인 수정 요청은 서류마다 100유로의 추가 요금을 발생시킬 것이라는 사실을 확인할 수 있다.
두 단서를 종합할 때, Kaiser Investment Services사는 수정을 위해 100유로의 요금을 지불해야 할 것임을 추론할 수 있다. 따라서 (D)가 정답이다.

어휘 fee n. 요금, 수수료

Paraphrasing

surcharge 추가 요금 → fee 요금
changes 수정 → revision 수정

193 | 육하원칙 문제

해석 Ms. Kaufmann은 왜 연락을 받을 것인가?
(A) 약속을 확정하기 위해
(B) 마감 기한 연장을 요청하기 위해
(C) 결제 세부 정보를 확인하기 위해
(D) 우려 사항을 해결하기 위해

해설 이메일의 'If our request presents a problem, please let me know right away. You can reach me by phone at 555-2309, extension #42.'에서 요청이 문제를 야기한다면, 즉시 알려달라고 한 후, 555-2309, 내선 42번 전화로 연락할 수 있다고 했다. 따라서 (D)가 정답이다.

어휘 appointment n. 약속 extension n. 연장 verify v. 확인하다

194 | 목적 찾기 문제

해석 소식지의 목적은 무엇인가?
(A) 회사의 최고 직원들을 표창하기 위해
(B) 회사의 성취를 제시하기 위해
(C) 판매의 결과를 발표하기 위해
(D) 최근의 회사 합병을 보고하기 위해

해설 소식지의 'Kaiser Investment Services has outperformed analysts' expectations and generated substantial profits for its clients and shareholders. Not only that, but we also continue to top customer satisfaction surveys on financial services companies in Germany.'에서 Kaiser Investment Services사는 분석가들의 예상을 능가하였고 고객과 주주들을 위해 상당한 수익을 만들어 냈을 뿐 아니라, 독일의 금융 서비스 회사에 관한 고객 만족 조사에서 계속해서 1위를 하고 있다고 했으므로 (B)가 정답이다.

어휘 recognize v. 표창하다, 인정하다 present v. 제시하다
achievement n. 성취, 업적

195 | 추론 문제 연계

해석 Kaiser Investment Services사는 최근에 무엇을 했을 것 같은가?
(A) 직원들을 위해 은퇴 기념 파티를 열었다.
(B) 직원들 사이에서 설문 조사를 했다.
(C) 독일에서 신제품 시리즈를 출시했다.
(D) 잠재적인 미국 고객들에게 책자를 배부했다.

해설 Kaiser Investment Services사의 소식지를 먼저 확인한다.
단서 1 소식지의 'In this December issue of the newsletter, ~ see photos from last month's launch of our marketing campaign in the United States, which was well attended by several potential clients.'에서 이번 12월호 소식지에서, 몇몇 잠재 고객들이 많이 참석한 지난달 미국에서의 마케팅 캠페인 개시 행사의 사진을 확인하라고 했다. 그런데 11월 마케팅 캠페인 개시 행사에 대해 제시되지 않았으므로 이메일에서 관련 내용을 확인한다.
단서 2 이메일의 'we cannot move our original due date as the brochures have to be shipped in time for a campaign launch

event we have planned for November'에서 11월에 계획한 캠페인 개시 행사를 위해 책자가 늦지 않게 배송되어야 하므로 원래 마감일을 미룰 수는 없다고 했다.

두 단서를 종합할 때, Kaiser Investment Services사는 최근에 잠재적인 미국 고객들에게 책자를 배부했음을 추론할 수 있다. 따라서 (D)가 정답이다.

어휘 conduct v. 하다, 수행하다   distribute v. 배부하다, 나누어 주다

196-200번은 다음 이메일, 일정표, 양식에 관한 문제입니다.

수신: 엘패소 디지털 아트 센터 <questions@elpasodigital.com>
발신: Raymond Hardy <rayhardy@goodmail.com>
날짜: 4월 30일
제목: 강좌

담당자분께:

이곳 엘패소의 아마추어 사진 동호회 회장으로서, 196귀하의 단체에서 이번 여름 사진 촬영 강좌에 단체 할인을 제공할 것이라는 사실을 듣고 매우 기뻤습니다. 199저희 중 네 명이 풍경 사진 촬영 강좌를 듣는 것에 관심이 있습니다. 197나머지 세 명의 회원들은 결혼사진 촬영에 대한 강좌에 등록할 계획입니다. 196제게 좀 더 많은 정보를 보내주실 수 있나요?

이 강좌들이 열릴 장소와 수강료에 대한 세부 정보를 포함해 주시면, 제가 그 정보를 전달하겠습니다.

Raymond Hardy 드림
회장
Homestead 사진 동호회

landscape n. 풍경, 풍경화   register v. 등록하다, 기재하다
take place 열리다, 개최되다

엘패소 디지털 아트 센터 - 다가오는 일일 강좌, 5월 8일-12일

날짜	5월 8일 (월)	5월 9일 (화)	5월 10일 (수)	5월 11일 (목)	197 5월 12일 (금)
시간	오후 7시 30분	오후 8시	오후 8시	오후 8시 30분	오후 7시
강좌	전문가용 사진 소프트웨어	당신의 사진 마케팅 하기	패션 사진 촬영	풍경 사진 촬영	197결혼사진 촬영
강사	Lindsay Arias	Carrie Felix	Ben Greenwood	Sue Adler	Finley Kolwalski
수강료	50달러	48달러	52달러	54달러	47달러

upcoming adj. 다가오는, 곧 있을   instructor n. 강사, 교사

엘패소 디지털 아트 센터 - 강좌 신청서

다음의 세부 사항을 기재해 주십시오:

199이름	Raymond Hardy	주소	2094번지 Firebird로, 엘패소, 텍사스주 79901
전화	555-3004	이메일	rayhardy@goodmail.com

전문 사진 촬영 경험이 있습니까?	예 □ 아니요 ■
199강좌	풍경 사진 촬영
지불 방법	현금

199엘패소 디지털 아트 센터는 영화, 사진, 그리고 그래픽 디자인에 대한 사람들의 지식을 증진하기 위해 설립된 비영리 기관입니다. 200센터는 어떠한 카메라나 부속품도 제공하지 않으므로, 참가자들이 자신의 것을

준비해야 함을 알아두십시오. 199세 명 이상의 단체로 등록하는 분들은 각각 30달러의 특별 단체 요금을 납부하시면 됩니다. 저희는 납부금 수령 24시간 이내에 등록을 확정해 드릴 것입니다. 수업료는 환불되지 않으며 강좌 시작 일주일 전까지 납부되어야 합니다.

registration form 신청서   payment n. 지불, 납입
nonprofit adj. 비영리적인   sign up 등록하다   confirm v. 확정하다, 확인하다
nonrefundable adj. 환불되지 않는   prior to ~ 전에, 앞서

196 | 목적 찾기 문제

해석 이메일의 목적은 무엇인가?
(A) 사진 동호회에 사람을 모집하기 위해
(B) 몇몇 강좌에 대한 정보를 요청하기 위해
(C) 다가오는 대회에 등록하기 위해
(D) 최근의 강연에 대한 의견을 주기 위해

해설 이메일의 'I was very excited to hear that your organization will be offering a group discount on photography classes this summer'에서 귀하의 단체, 즉 엘패소 디지털 아트 센터에서 이번 여름 사진 촬영 강좌에 단체 할인을 제공할 것이라는 사실을 듣고 매우 기뻤다고 한 후, 'Could you send me some more information?'에서 좀 더 많은 정보를 보내줄 수 있는지 요청하고 있으므로 (B)가 정답이다.

어휘 recruit v. 모집하다, 채용하다   lecture n. 강연, 강의

Paraphrasing

classes 강좌 → courses 강좌

197 | Not/True 문제 연계

해석 Homestead 사진 동호회에 대해 사실인 것은?
(A) 모든 회원들은 전문 사진작가로 일한다.
(B) 대부분의 회원들은 이전에 수업을 들은 적이 있다.
(C) 몇몇 회원들은 금요일에 열리는 수업을 듣고 싶어 한다.
(D) 몇몇 회원들은 세 개 이상의 강좌에 등록하기를 원한다.

해설 Homestead 사진 동호회의 회장 Raymond Hardy가 작성한 이메일을 먼저 확인한다.
단서 1 이메일의 'Three other members plan to register for the one on wedding photography.'에서 나머지 세 명의 회원들은 결혼사진 촬영에 대한 강좌에 등록할 계획이라고 했다. 그런데 결혼사진 촬영 강좌에 대해 제시되지 않았으므로 일정표에서 관련 내용을 확인한다.
단서 2 일정표의 'May 12 (Fri)', 'Wedding Photography'에서 결혼사진 촬영 수업이 5월 12일 금요일에 진행됨을 알 수 있다.
두 단서를 종합할 때, 몇몇 회원들이 금요일에 열리는 수업을 듣고 싶어 함을 알 수 있다. 따라서 (C)가 정답이다.

198 | 동의어 찾기 문제

해석 양식에서, 1문단 첫 번째 줄의 단어 "established"는 의미상 -와 가장 가깝다.
(A) 지지되다
(B) 설립되다
(C) 입증되다
(D) 결정되다

해설 양식의 established를 포함하는 구절 'The El Paso Center for the Digital Arts is a nonprofit organization established to advance people's knowledge of film, photography, and graphic design.'에서 established는 '설립되다'라는 뜻으로 사용되었다. 따라서 (B)가 정답이다.

199 | 추론 문제 연계

해석 Mr. Hardy는 강좌를 위해 얼마를 내야 할 것 같은가?
(A) 30달러
(B) 47달러
(C) 52달러
(D) 54달러

해설 Mr. Hardy가 작성한 양식을 먼저 확인한다.

단서 1 양식의 'Name, Raymond Hardy', 'Course, Landscape Photography'에서 Raymond Hardy가 풍경 사진 촬영 강좌를 등록하고 있고, 'Those who sign up as a group of three or more will receive a special group rate of $30 each.'에서 세 명 이상의 단체로 등록하는 사람들은 각각 30달러의 특별 단체 요금을 납부하면 된다는 것을 알 수 있다. 그런데 Raymond Hardy가 세 명 이상의 단체로 등록하는지 제시되지 않았으므로 이메일에서 관련 내용을 확인한다.

단서 2 이메일의 'Four of us are interested in taking the landscape photography class.'에서 저희, 즉 Homestead 사진 동호회 회원 중 네 명이 풍경 사진 촬영 강좌를 듣는 것에 관심이 있다고 한 것을 통해, Raymond Hardy를 포함한 네 명의 회원이 풍경 사진 촬영 강좌를 들을 것이라는 사실을 알 수 있다.

두 단서를 종합할 때, Mr. Hardy는 30달러를 내야 할 것임을 추론할 수 있다. 따라서 (A)가 정답이다.

200 | 육하원칙 문제

해석 Mr. Hardy는 무엇을 하도록 요구될 것인가?
(A) 강좌 시작 전에 강사와 이야기를 나눈다.
(B) 자신의 사진 촬영 장비를 가져온다.
(C) 신분증을 제시한다.
(D) 이전의 경험에 대한 증명서를 제출한다.

해설 양식의 'Please note that the center does not provide any cameras or accessories, so participants must supply their own.'에서 센터는 어떠한 카메라나 부속품도 제공하지 않으므로 참석자들이 자신의 것을 준비해야 함을 알아두라고 했으므로 (B)가 정답이다.

어휘 **identification** n. 신분증, 신원 확인 **submit** v. 제출하다
proof n. 증명서, 증거물

Paraphrasing

cameras or accessories 카메라나 부속품 → **photography equipment** 사진 촬영 장비

| MEMO |

| MEMO |

해커스인강 HackersIngang.com
본 교재 인강 · 무료 교재 MP3 · 단어암기장 · 고득점 핵심 노트(교재 내 QR 수록) · 토익 기출 VOCA(부록)

해커스토익 Hackers.co.kr
온라인 실전모의고사 · 매월 적중예상 특강 · 실시간 토익시험 정답확인/해설강의 ·
매일 실전 LC/RC 문제 · 정기토익 기출단어 · 토익 단어시험지 자동생성기

327만이 선택한 외국어학원
1위 해커스어학원

토익 단기졸업 달성을 위한 해커스 약점관리 프로그램

자신의 약점을 정확히 파악하고 집중적으로 보완하는 것이야말로
토익 단기졸업의 필수코스입니다.

토익종합반 수강생 0원

취약점 분석표 제공

STEP 01
약점체크 모의고사 응시

*비매품

최신 토익 출제경향을 반영한
약점체크 모의고사 응시

STEP 02
토익 취약점 분석표 확인

파트별 취약점 분석표를 통해
객관적인 실력 파악

STEP 03
개인별 맞춤 보완문제 증정

최대 180제 제공

*PDF

영역별 취약 부분에 대한
보완문제로 취약점 극복

[327만] 해커스어학원 누적 수강생 수(중복 수강 포함/2003~2024.01 기준)
[1위] 한국표준협회, 프리미엄 브랜드 지수(KS-PBI) 종합외국어학원 부문 1위(2019~2021)

지금 바로 신청하고
토익 취약점 완벽 극복 ▶

해커스잡·해커스공기업 누적 수강건수 700만 선택
취업교육 1위 해커스

합격생들이 소개하는 **단기합격 비법**

삼성 그룹 최종 합격!
오*은 합격생

정말 큰 도움 받았습니다!
삼성 취업 3단계 중 많은 취준생이 좌절하는 GSAT에서 해커스 덕분에 합격할 수 있었다고 생각합니다.

국민건강보험공단 최종 합격!
신*규 합격생

모든 과정에서 선생님들이 최고라고 느꼈습니다!
취업 준비를 하면서 모르는 것이 생겨 답답할 때마다, 강의를 찾아보며 그 부분을 해결할 수 있어 너무 든든했기 때문에 모든 선생님께 감사드리고 싶습니다.

해커스 대기업/공기업 대표 교재

GSAT 베스트셀러
279주 1위

7년간 베스트셀러
1위 326회

[279주 베스트셀러 1위] YES24 수험서 자격증 베스트셀러 삼성 GSAT 분야 1위(2014년 4월 3주부터, 1판부터 20판까지 주별 베스트 1위 통산)
[326회] YES24/알라딘/반디앤루니스 취업/상식/적성 분야, 공사 공단 NCS 분야, 공사 공단 수험서 분야, 대기업/공기업/면접 분야 베스트셀러 1위 횟수 합계 (2016.02~2023.10/1~14판 통산 주별 베스트/주간 베스트/주간집계 기준)
[취업교육 1위] 주간동아 2024 한국고객만족도 교육(온·오프라인 취업) 1위
[700만] 해커스 온/오프라인 취업강의(특강) 누적신청건수(중복수강/무료 강의 포함/2015.06~2024.11.28)

대기업　**공기업**

최종합격자가 수강한 강의는? 지금 확인하기!

해커스잡　**ejob.Hackers.com**

시험 당일! 토익 시험일 실검 1위 해커스토익!

14만 토익커가 해커스토익으로 몰리는 이유는?

1. 시험 종료 직후 공개!
토익 정답 실시간 확인 서비스

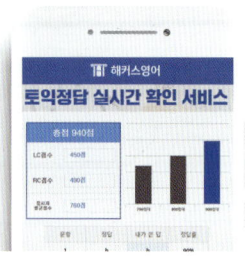

· 정답/응시자 평균점수 즉시 공개
· 빅데이터 기반 가채점+성적 분석
· 개인별 취약 유형 약점보완문제 무료

2. 실시간 시험 후기 확인!
해커스토익 자유게시판

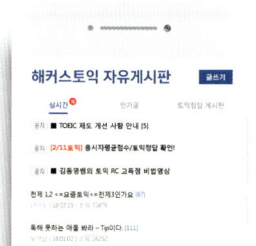

· 토익시험 난이도 & 논란문제 종결
· 생생한 시험후기 공유
· 고득점 비법/무료 자료 공유

3. 오늘 시험에서는요!
스타강사의 해커스토익 총평강의

· 스타강사의 파트별 총평강의
· 토익시험 정답 & 난이도 분석
· 취약 파트별 전략 공개

4. 토익에 대한 모든 정보가 모여있는 곳!
토익 전문 커뮤니티 해커스토익

· 토익 고득점 수기, 비법자료 및 스타강사 비법강의 100% 무료!
· 전국 토익 고사장 스피커/시설/평점 공개
· 물토익 VS 불토익 시험당일 난이도 투표부터 나에게 맞는 공부법 추천까지!

[실검 1위] N사 실시간 급상승 검색어 20대 1위(2018.10.14, 13:00 기준)
[14만] 해커스토익(Hackers.co.kr) 일일 방문자 수(2021.02.07, PC+모바일/중복 방문자 포함)

시험당일, 토익 정답을 바로 확인하고 싶다면 해커스토익 검색

 해커스토익 바로가기▶
 토익정답 확인하고 혜택 몽땅 받기▶